Baseball State by State

Baseball State by State

*Major and Negro League Players,
Ballparks, Museums and Historical Sites*

CHRIS JENSEN
Foreword by Peter Golenbock

McFarland & Company, Inc., Publishers
Jefferson, North Carolina, and London

LLibrary of Congress Cataloguing-in-Publication Data

Jensen, Chris, 1963–
Baseball state by state : major and Negro league players, ballparks, museums and historical sites / Chris Jensen ; foreword by Peter Golenbock.
        p.   cm.
Includes bibliographical references and index.

ISBN 978-0-7864-6895-9
softcover : acid free paper ∞

1. Baseball — United States — History.
2. Negro leagues — History.
3. Baseball players — United States — History.
4. Baseball Museums — United States.
5. Baseball fields — United States.   I. Title.
GV863.A1J45 2012   796.357 — dc23   2012024869

British Library cataloguing data are available

© 2012 Chris Jensen. All rights reserved

No part of this book may be reproduced or transmitted in any form or by any means, electronic or mechanical, including photocopying or recording, or by any information storage and retrieval system, without permission in writing from the publisher.

Cover image © 2012 Shutterstock

Manufactured in the United States of America

*McFarland & Company, Inc., Publishers
Box 611, Jefferson, North Carolina 28640
www.mcfarlandpub.com*

To Abby and Brandon, who lovingly tolerate
their father's obsession with baseball research.
You guys represent the only two times
I've hit it out of the park.

Contents

Acknowledgments viii
Foreword by Peter Golenbock 1
Preface 3

Alabama 7
Alaska 15
Arizona 18
Arkansas 21
California 27
Colorado 44
Connecticut 47
Delaware 52
District of Columbia 55
Florida 58
Georgia 66
Hawaii 73
Idaho 75
Illinois 78
Indiana 88
Iowa 100
Kansas 105

Kentucky 111
Louisiana 119
Maine 126
Maryland 129
Massachusetts 137
Michigan 147
Minnesota 155
Mississippi 161
Missouri 167
Montana 177
Nebraska 179
Nevada 184
New Hampshire 186
New Jersey 190
New Mexico 197
New York 201
North Carolina 216

North Dakota 223
Ohio 225
Oklahoma 238
Oregon 246
Pennsylvania 249
Rhode Island 265
South Carolina 269
South Dakota 277
Tennessee 280
Texas 285
Utah 296
Vermont 299
Virginia 302
Washington 308
West Virginia 313
Wisconsin 317
Wyoming 324

Appendix 1: Canada 327
Appendix 2: The 100 Greatest Players of All Time 333
Source Notes 335
Bibliography 349
Index 353

Acknowledgments

A book of this magnitude does not come together without a lot of help. I was fortunate to find a bunch of baseball experts who were willing to lend a hand, whether it meant reviewing all-time lists for a state or two, suggesting a nickname or a neat place, passing along an unusual fact or making sure my honorable mention lists kept expanding. Their contributions strengthened the final product and their positive feedback gave me confidence I was on the right track.

Many of the contributors were fellow SABR (Society for American Baseball Research) members such as Pete Cava, Dan O'Brien and Mike McCormick of my local Oscar Charleston Chapter; plus Joel Rippel, Tom Busch, Travis and Jason Christopherson, Jon Dunkle, Tom Simon, Dave Eskenazi, Len Levin, Harry Lee, David Matchett, Eric Sallee, Joseph Pisano, Dave Fallen, Charles Faber, Jim Price, Norman Klein, Lyle Spatz, Adam Hyman and David Trombley. I apologize if I left any out.

Gabriel Schechter deserves special recognition for wading through the entire text. Gabriel is a walking encyclopedia of baseball knowledge and a skilled editor, and he wasn't shy about offering his opinions and forcing me to defend my selections. His feedback helped me improve the content immeasurably and saved me from making a few silly mistakes.

I am indebted to Mike Lynch for helping me get my start in baseball writing through his terrific site, Seamheads.com. Mike also put aside his own projects to read through nearly half the book, and he passed along some useful bits of information. Fellow Seamheads writers who contributed include Bob Lazzari, Dave Stalker, Daniel Shoptaw, Joe Williams, Brad Berreman, Jim Elfers and Matthew Tarini.

Sean Forman cannot be praised enough for developing the amazing Baseball-Reference.com site, which was an indispensable resource for stats and biographical information on major league players, managers and teams.

Timing is everything, and Gary Ashwill (with major help from Scott Simkus, Daniel Hirsh, Kevin Johnson and others) unveiled the Seamheads.com Negro Leagues Database powered by The Baseball Gauge just as this project was nearing conclusion. The ambitious site is the first step toward providing a comprehensive statistical encyclopedia for Negro Leagues players. The biographical information on Negro Leaguers was particularly helpful, and Gary helped me clear up some confusion about Bill Foster's birthplace as well as took the time to answer other questions.

Jim Gates, Tim Wiles and Freddy Berowski were exceedingly helpful at the National Baseball Hall of Fame Library in Cooperstown, and I also appreciate the help of Pat Kelly and John Horne in the Hall's photo archives department. Additional assistance came from Scott Campbell of the Canadian Baseball Hall of Fame and Museum; Julie Ridgway and Sharri Hobbs of the Ty Cobb Museum; Duane Rieder of the Clemente Museum; Bruce Hellerstein and Kathy Johnsmiller of B's Ballpark Museum; Steve Johnson of the Bottomley-Ruffing-Schalk Baseball Museum; Dave Kaplan of the Yogi Berra Museum; and Arlene Marcley of the Shoeless Joe Jackson Museum. Thanks to Eric and Wendy Pastore of Digitalballparks.com and Brian Merzbach of BallparkReviews.com for sharing some of their wonderful pictures of historic ballparks combined with good historical overviews — what terrific resources!

And a special thank you to Peter Golenbock for graciously agreeing to contribute the foreword.

Finally, I would be remiss if I didn't express gratitude to the many dedicated researchers and historians who have painstakingly researched and chronicled the lives and careers of African American players before baseball was integrated. James Riley, John Holway, Lawrence Hogan, Larry Lester, Dick Clark, Gary Ashwill, Robert Peterson, Phil Dixon, Neil Lanctot, Kyle McNary, Geri Strecker and many others keep pushing the ball up the hill, allowing writers such as myself to benefit from their hard labor. Their good work continues, as we all collectively seek to bring proper recognition where it's due.

Foreword by Peter Golenbock

Chris Jensen, who fancied himself a baseball fan, one morning opened up *The Indianapolis Star* and noticed an article listing the best current major league baseball players from the state of Indiana.

After seeing Craig Counsell, who is a second baseman and shortstop, listed at first base, Chris figured he could build a better Indiana all-star team than that. He started doing research, and although he discovered that the list of current players in the *Star* was pretty much right on, he began looking for old-timers from the state. He immersed himself in their stories, and pretty soon Chris set off on a mission to research *every* Indiana major leaguer.

When he was done, he asked himself "What about players from Illinois?" And then Michigan, and then Ohio, and before he knew it he was embarked on a five-year project to complete all-time rosters of major league ballplayers from each of the 50 states (plus the District of Columbia and Canada).

The research became an obsession that began to take over his life. He was the editor of a trade magazine, and after working all day on the magazine, he'd burn the midnight oil researching his book. He'd try to sleep, but his head would be filled with names and places and statistics and arcane information that both fascinated him and kept him awake. He'd toss and turn, hounded by Ty Cobb and Heinie Manush and Moonlight Graham, and after sleeping fitfully, he'd drag himself out of bed the next morning and go back to work at the magazine.

Frustrated, Chris quit his job and started his own publishing company, hoping he would have more time to feed his baseball jones. With more time, the project sprouted wings. The more he worked on the book, the more interesting angles he discovered. In researching players he kept saying to himself, "I'm finding there are a lot of funny names," and so he decided to incorporate some of those funny names into the book. After coming across "Poosh 'Em Up" Tony Lazzeri and "Puddin' Head" Jones, he decided he wanted to delineate all the great baseball nicknames. Chris has listed over 1,600 of them. In his travels he frequently visited baseball places of interest, and before long he decided that they should be in the book as well. More than 200 are listed on a state-by-state basis. Labor of love is putting it mildly.

"I had considered myself a knowledgeable baseball fan, but not an expert or a historian," Chris said. "But in these five years I've learned so much about this game." His knowledge is contained in these pages. He has researched baseball in the nineteenth century and mined the libraries and books about the Negro Leagues, an exercise in frustration because the statistics and history of Negro League baseball are so sketchy. He knew how good Satchel Paige and Josh Gibson were, but many of the Negro Leagues players were just names. How good were they really? How do they stack up against the major leaguers? He didn't always know, but he tried to find out.

Chris grew up in Morris and Delhi, New York, two towns not far from Cooperstown, the home of the National Baseball Hall of Fame and Museum. He only went to the museum a couple of times as a kid, but it was enough to fuel his love for the game. A die-hard New York Yankees fan, as a kid he studied the backs of baseball cards and embraced the game from afar.

After graduating from Potsdam College in upstate New York, he moved to Indiana to attend graduate school at Ball State University. After graduation he remained in Indiana and it was there that he read that first list of Indiana greats that led him to his current obsession.

One of his first decisions was to place every player in the state of his *birth*, which was not necessarily the state where the player grew up and became known. Carlton Fisk, for example, was born in Vermont, not New Hampshire, where he gained his fame. Fisk, in fact, is the most prominent major leaguer ever to hail from the state of Vermont. Manny Ramirez grew up and played high school ball in New

York City. But he was born in the Dominican Republic and so is not listed here.

One of Chris's discoveries from his research is that certain states are rich with star players, and others are not. Florida, Texas, New York and California, for example, are overflowing with names of baseball's greats.

California boasts a Hall of Fame–quality team in Gary Carter, Eddie Murray, Jeff Kent, Darrell Evans, Joe Cronin, Joe DiMaggio, Ted Williams, Barry Bonds, Tom Seaver, Randy Johnson and Trevor Hoffman. It also boasts some of the great nicknames in baseball history including Dick "Dr. Strangeglove" Stuart, Frank "Toys in the Attic" Bertaina, Al "The Mad Hungarian" Hrabosky, and perhaps the greatest nickname of them all, "The Yankee Clipper," Joe DiMaggio. One of the most unusual names of players from California is Mark Rzepczynski, an active pitcher who not surprisingly ended up with "Scrabble" for a nickname.

Chris has sprinkled fun facts into each of the states. One of his California facts surprised me: The great pitcher from the Dodgers, Don Drysdale, was a high school teammate of Robert Redford, the star of *The Natural* and so many other movies. He also includes notable achievements such as the fact a pitcher, Lefty Grove, drove in the first run in an All-Star Game. Contrast the California aggregation with the players hailing from Vermont. Fisk is by far the best known, backed up at catcher by Birdie Tebbetts, who played and then managed in the big leagues. The rest of the infield: Pat Putnam at first, Amby McConnell at second, Ralph LaPointe at short and Larry Gardner at third. In the outfield are Fred Mann, Chris Duffy and Frank Olin. Who? I knew the name Larry Gardner. He was a Red Sox player early in the twentieth century, and in fact Chris noted that Gardner drove in the winning run in the 1912 World Series with a sacrifice fly against New York Giants great Christy Mathewson.

Perhaps the only state with less-known players is Alaska. Now there's a list of nobodies, with the exception of pitcher Curt Schilling, a possible Hall of Famer in the future. Schilling became a high school star in Phoenix, Arizona, but he was, in fact, born in Alaska.

I live in Florida, and so I checked to see who came from Florida. My co-author Johnny Damon wasn't listed, although he starred in high school in Orlando. Why not? He was actually born in Kansas. But Dwight Gooden and three Hall of Fame–caliber outfielders were among those listed: Gary Sheffield, Tim Raines and Andre Dawson. Chris also shared interesting tidbits about Andy Abad and Elisha "Bitsy" Mott. Look them up.

I am always fascinated by those with compulsions, because the results often are so interesting. Chris Jensen's obsession with baseball history has produced this quirky book that is not only interesting but fun. There's a surprise on every page. Who knew, for instance, that the player the diminutive Eddie Gaedel batted for was Missouri's Frank Saucier, or that for his career Saucier batted 1-for-14? Maybe batting a "little person" for Saucier wasn't such a bad idea after all. Or that Pennsylvania's Ernie Padgett, playing in only his fourth game, made an unassisted triple play on October 6, 1923? I love this stuff.

Peter Golenbock is one of the nation's best-known sports authors. Some of his baseball books include *The Bronx Zoo*; *Balls* (with Graig Nettles); *BUMS: An Oral History of the Brooklyn Dodgers*; *George: The Poor Little Rich Boy Who Built the Yankee Empire*; *The Forever Boys*; *Wrigleyville: A Magical History of the Chicago Cubs*; *Dynasty: The New York Yankees 1949–1964*; *Idiot* (with Johnny Damon) and *Wild, High and Tight: The Life and Death of Billy Martin*.

Preface

I've always found all-time player lists interesting, whether they be all-time players by decade, team, greatness or quirky name combinations. Of course, I cannot resist seeing if I can come up with a better list, which is how I stumbled onto this book project.

An all-time team of current major league players from Indiana (where I live) didn't seem nearly as interesting as an all-time team of players from the state. That opens up a lot more possibilities, including the ability to replace Craig Counsell at first base — where the *Indianapolis Star* had him on their list of the state's active players — with a legitimate star such as Don Mattingly or Gil Hodges. Choosing between Mattingly and Hodges was just the first of many difficult choices I would have to make, once I decided to expand my quest to other states.

I spent a year or so creating and playing around with my all-time lists of players by state, but I kept facing the same nagging feeling. It bothered me that Indiana's all-time outfield boasted three Hall of Fame outfielders, but not the best one from the state — Oscar Charleston. It's easy to say that Charleston belongs in the Indiana outfield and that Josh Gibson is the best catcher from Georgia, but what about all the other Negro Leagues players? Now my fun little research project started to feel more like a worthwhile book project, even if it meant there was a lot more research to be done.

It didn't take long to determine that no one has ever compiled a list of all-time players by state, including Negro Leaguers. As I researched the players by state, I kept coming across fascinating information that could not be left out. There were unusual names, funny nicknames, little-known facts, historic ballparks, obscure museums, but also lots of unknown players who did something noteworthy and no one seemed to note it. We note them in *Baseball State by State*.

So here is the full scope of what the book encompasses: a section devoted to each state (plus the District of Columbia and an appendix for Canada) listing all-time teams by players' state of birth. It covers major leaguers and Negro Leaguers (denoted by italics) and includes a top selection by position followed by a listing of honorable mention players for that position in ranked order. The player's birthplace can be found in parentheses. The idea was not to judge who had the most talent or the most dominant stretch of a few short years, but to evaluate who had the greatest career by the time the players hung up their spikes.

In addition, each state includes:

A fairly comprehensive listing of player nicknames — more than 1,600. These are grouped by player last name for easier reference and include major leaguers and Negro Leaguers. For added fun, I list the most unusual player names for each state.

All-time major league stats leaders in nine categories: games, hits, average, runs batted in, home runs, stolen bases, pitching wins, strikeouts and saves.

Future stars, either minor league prospects or those who have reached the majors recently. In some cases I list college players with promise.

All-time best player, whether a position player or pitcher. Just one per state.

Historic baseball places to see — more than 200 are covered, including the usual ones (Hall of Fame in Cooperstown, Fenway Park) and places you might not know about, like B's Ballpark Museum. The listings cover museums, classic ballparks, gravesites, notable minor league parks, statues and more. "Historic" is a loose definition, since I couldn't resist including new ballparks and other places that are worth seeing.

Notable achievements — noteworthy firsts and records you might not know. That means George Kell's record for fewest strikeouts by a batting champion is listed but Joe DiMaggio's 56-game hitting streak is not.

Each state begins with a brief section that provides an overview of the state's baseball history such as the first pro team, origins of black baseball in the state or use as a spring training site. In some states, I weave together a narrative related to the teams, players and places from a specific city. In other states I cover the origins of nicknames or lead off with some of the interesting stories behind obscure players like Heinie Stafford, Bert Shepard, Boots Poffenberger, Guy Hecker and Harry O'Neill.

Finally, each state describes the career accomplishments of the players selected to the all-time state team, including some (but not all) of the honorable mention players. I explain why one player was picked over another and share any interesting tidbits I might have dug up.

That's a lot of ground to cover, but the result is, as Peter Golenbock points out, a surprise on every page. There is something for everyone, whether you are a hardcore expert and baseball researcher or a casual fan. Let this book be the starting point for further discussion about where the all-time greats really stack up. Instead of arguing about whether Greg Maddux or Nolan Ryan is the best right-handed starter from Texas, widen the scope to include Smokey Joe Williams, Hilton Smith and Rube Foster. Just because baseball was segregated for so long does not mean we should evaluate its all-time great players in the same manner.

Through the years many articles have put forward all-time teams of players by state, and they typically include players who were born there, players who grew up there and players who became famous there. That's easy to do when you're only concerned with compiling the best list for that state, but it's a slippery slope to follow across the board. For a book of this scope it was not feasible to research the age a player moved to a particular state or how many years of his life he lived there, so I followed a simple guideline: players were placed in the state in which they were born, if it's known. That means Carlton Fisk belongs to Vermont and not New Hampshire. Regrettably, it also means Negro Leaguers like Jap Payne and Stringbean Williams were left out, because researchers have not been able to verify their birthplace with certainty. Perhaps someday books such as this one will be able to include them.

Many a baseball writer has been frustrated by the lack of statistical information available on Negro Leagues players, since box scores don't exist for every game and many of the teams spent more time barnstorming than playing league games. In addition, the sources that are out there don't match up, which means we know Babe Ruth hit 714 home runs but we don't know with certainty how many Josh Gibson hit.

That makes it especially hard to rank major leaguers and Negro Leaguers together. Not only are you comparing apples to oranges, you can quantify the apples but not all the oranges. The recent unveiling of the Seamheads.com Negro Leagues Database, powered by the Baseball Gauge, is a much-needed step in the right direction. Gary Ashwill (with support from Mike Lynch and help from many others) has developed and posted a database that contains batting, fielding and pitching statistics for the first three years of the Negro National League (1920–22), the top-notch independent black teams from 1916 to 1922, as well as the Cuban leagues, with more years and players to come. It offers hope that someday in the near future we'll be able to use statistical analysis from one comprehensive source to more properly evaluate the Negro Leagues players. I used that database where I could for this book — it was particularly useful helping me nail down birthplaces for some players.

So what method was used to come up with my all-time team lists? Baseball-Reference, the authoritative source for major league player birthplaces and statistics, allowed me to sort players by state. Once I knew there were 2,014 players from California who have played in the major leagues, I could start determining the best catchers, best first basemen, and so forth. Next I looked at the top 100 rankings by position in Bill James' *Historical Baseball Abstract*, which utilizes Career Win Shares. James separately included a short list of top Negro Leaguers by position. I agreed with most but not all of his selections (Illinois catcher being one area where I disagreed), plus I had to take into account the players whose careers had advanced in the decade since James' book came out.

With that legwork behind me, it was time to really dive into the numbers and the achievements of the major leaguers so I could make a case for my top selections. How did a player rank among his peers in career statistics? I did not rely heavily on advanced sabermetric analysis, but did look some at Career Win Shares and Wins Above Replacement (WAR) from The Baseball Gauge@Seamheads.com. I especially noted adjusted ERA (shortened in the book as ERA+) for pitchers and adjusted OPS (shortened in the book as OPS+) for batters, since those are adjusted for park and league context. I looked at career totals for Runs from Fielding (the number of runs better or worse than average the player was for all fielding) to see how good they were in the field. I made note of the number of All-Star selections and Gold Glove Awards, as well as how they ranked in MVP and Cy Young voting (obviously not possible for older players). Finally, I looked to see how often their teams made the postseason and how they did individually in the postseason.

Preface

Statistics tell a big part of the story, but I needed to do more digging. I am a member of the Society for American Baseball Research, and SABR has some great tools available for researchers. The society's books *Deadball Stars of the American League* and *Deadball Stars of the National League* were especially useful in helping me understand the key players from that era, while SABR's Biography Project profiles were a valuable resource for background information. In addition I used more than 180 books in the course of my research, including many biographies and as many state-specific books as I could find, such as *The Rise of Milwaukee Baseball* and *Baseball in the Carolinas*. I spent three days looking through books, documents and files at the National Baseball Hall of Fame's A. Bartlett Giamatti Research Center in Cooperstown and wish I could have spent three months.

I had my all-time teams of major leaguers completed before I started slotting in Negro Leaguers. Since I couldn't directly compare Negro Leaguers to major leaguers by crunching numbers, I instead relied on a preponderance of statistical and anecdotal evidence from historians such as John Holway, James Riley, Lawrence Hogan, Robert Peterson, Larry Lester, Kyle McNary and others. Holway's *Complete Book of Baseball's Negro Leagues* and *Blackball Stars* and Riley's *Biographical Encyclopedia of the Negro Baseball Leagues* were relied on heavily, as was the Hall of Fame–sanctioned study detailed in Hogan's *Shades of Glory*. I made note of how many East-West All-Star games a player appeared in, what their peers had to say about them and how they performed in exhibitions against white players. I read through all the player biographical forms filled out by Negro Leagues players and on file in Cooperstown, which contained some interesting information. The Seamheads.com Negro Leagues Database filled in more blanks.

About 2,250 major leaguers made the cut for the various all-time teams, which represents about 14 percent of the 15,584 who have played in the majors through the 2011 season (according to Baseball-Reference). In addition, I include 281 Negro League players, so they represent about 11 percent of all players listed. The all-time teams were much more inclusive for states with fewer players such as Hawaii and New Mexico. In fact, I found spots for all the major league players from Alaska, North Dakota and Wyoming. As a rule of thumb, I listed players whose careers were long enough and accomplished enough to make them worthy. They were starters for the majority of their careers and they made meaningful contributions to their teams, either making All-Star teams or ranking among league leaders in hitting, fielding or pitching categories. I went back and forth, expanding my lists and then cutting them down, repeating this cycle a few times until I was finally comfortable with the selections.

As for the nicknames, I jotted them down every time I came across them in my research. I didn't look at books on nicknames, such as Phil Blazovich's *Having Fun with Baseball Nicknames*, until late in the process, because I wanted to do my own legwork. I discovered I had a pretty comprehensive list, but there are still more out there. One of the hardest parts for me was deciding the best nickname for each state. How can one choose between Dick "Dr. Strangeglove" Stuart and Frank "Toys in the Attic" Bertaina?

Here are some other ground rules I followed for the book:

Only players who played the majority of their career in the Negro Leagues are highlighted in italics. So Satchel Paige is listed as a Negro Leaguer but Hank Aaron and Willie Mays are not.

Players ineligible for the Hall of Fame such as Pete Rose, Shoeless Joe Jackson and Happy Felsch are included, as are nineteenth-century players.

With a few exceptions — the less densely populated states such as Montana, Nevada, and Alaska, for instance — players were put at the position they played the most in the majors. I resisted the temptation to field the nine best players by moving a guy to a position he barely played.

It was sometimes difficult to determine whether a player was primarily a left fielder or right fielder, and in several states it was difficult just filling out the outfield. As a result, I took the MLB All-Star Game approach, selecting the three best outfielders per state without regard to specific position. I did sort the honorable mention outfielders in California by position as a means of breaking up a big group.

Not every state has a Trevor Hoffman or a Billy Wagner, who were closers throughout their career, so I went with the best relief pitcher and not necessarily the best closer.

I did my best to list the honorable mention players in order of demonstrated greatness, but that was sometimes difficult for the lesser-known players from the Negro Leaguers. Was Joe Hewitt more like Ozzie Smith or Fred Stanley? Was Dave Hoskins a better pitcher than Rufus Lewis? In some cases, I learned enough about the Negro Leaguers to know they deserved to be ranked but not enough to know whether they were the sixth-best shortstop or the seventh-best shortstop from the state. These evaluations will be easier in the future as the Seamheads Negro Leagues database evolves.

I did not include saves figures for players from before 1969, when the save became an official statistic, although Baseball-Reference includes those stats. How can you count something that didn't exist in 1920 or 1950? (Our officially recognized metrics both reflect and, sometimes, change the way we see the game; in ways subtle or not, they can also change the way we play the game, which in turn changes the values of our metric.) That's one of the few instances where I didn't follow Baseball-Reference.com, which was the primary source for statistics, recognition (All-Star appearances, Gold Gloves, etc.), career rankings and biographical information.

Some of the all-time team selections proved particularly difficult. I went back and forth deciding between Mule Suttles and Willie McCovey for all-time first baseman from Alabama. Mike Piazza or Roy Campanella for Pennsylvania catcher? Joe Morgan or Rogers Hornsby for Texas second baseman? Cy Young or Roger Clemens for right-handed starter from Ohio? I guess you can't go wrong selecting any of those players, but I'd like to think most experts would call it the same way I did. See if you agree with my selections or have fun compiling your own all-time teams.

This book is a starting point for further discussion as to how the Negro Leagues players through history compare to the peers they were prevented from competing against in the majors. It's also a mini-history about the players, places, teams and pioneers that have captivated generations of baseball fans. From the dusty sandlots of gritty Alabama mill towns and the boiling hot springs of Arkansas to the green cathedrals of cities big and small, America truly is a baseball nation of remarkable spirit. Pick a state to explore and begin the journey.

ALABAMA

*Names in **bold** represent Major League selections by position, followed by honorable mentions. Negro Leagues players are in **bold italics**, followed by honorable mentions in italics. City of birth is in parentheses.*

Catcher — *Ted Radcliffe* (Mobile). Also: Spud Davis (Birmingham); Luke Sewell (Titus); *Larry Brown* (Pratt City); Charlie Moore (Birmingham); Bruce Benedict (Birmingham); *Henry Robinson* (Birmingham)

First Base — *Mule Suttles* (Blocton). Also: Willie McCovey (Mobile); Lee May (Birmingham); Rudy York (Ragland); *Showboat Thomas* (Mobile); Don Mincher (Huntsville); *Jim West* (Mobile); *Piper Davis* (Piper); Hal Morris (Fort Rucker)

Second Base — *George Scales* (Talladega). Also: Frank Bolling (Mobile); Ted Sizemore (Gadsden); Fresco Thompson (Centreville); *Jack Marshall* (Montgomery); *Tommy Sampson* (Calhoun); *John Henry Russell* (Dolcito); *Fred Bankhead* (Empire)

Third Base — *Alex Radcliffe* (Mobile). Also: *Newt Joseph* (Montgomery); *Parnell Woods* (Birmingham); Jim Davenport (Siluria); *Bobbie Robinson* (Whistler); Jim Tabor (New Hope); *Felton Snow* (Oxford)

Shortstop — Ozzie Smith (Mobile). Also: Joe Sewell (Titus); *Sam Bankhead* (Empire); *Artie Wilson* (Springville)

Outfield — Willie Mays (Westfield)

Outfield — Hank Aaron (Mobile)

Outfield — Billy Williams (Whistler). Also: *Monte Irvin* (Columbia); Heinie Manush (Tuscumbia); George Foster (Tuscaloosa); Amos Otis (Mobile); Willie Wilson (Montgomery); *Jerry Benjamin* (Montgomery); Riggs Stephenson (Akron); Terry Moore (Vernon); Juan Pierre (Mobile); Bill Bruton (Panola); Lou Finney (Buffalo); Cleon Jones (Plateau); Bo Jackson (Bessemer); Tommie Agee (Magnolia); Alex Rios (Coffee)

Designated Hitter — Andre Thornton (Tuskegee). Also: Oscar Gamble (Ramer)

Right Handed Starter — Satchel Paige (Mobile). Also: Don Sutton (Clio); Early Wynn (Hartford); *Dan Bankhead* (Empire); Virgil Trucks (Birmingham); *Dizzy Dismukes* (Birmingham); Doyle Alexander (Cordova); Frank Lary (Northport); Rip Sewell (Decatur); Guy Morton (Vernon); *Harry Salmon* (Warrior); *Terris McDuffie* (Mobile); *Franklin Sykes* (Decature); Jake Peavy (Mobile); *Willie Powell* (Eutaw)

Left Handed Starter — Jimmy Key (Huntsville). Also: Bob Veale (Birmingham); *Sam Streeter* (New Market); *Lefty McKinnis* (Union)

Relief Pitcher — Clay Carroll (Clanton). Also: Jeff Brantley (Florence); Al Worthington (Birmingham); Dick Coffman (Veto); Dave Veres (Montgomery)

Manager — Gabby Street (Huntsville). Also: Luke Sewell (Titus); Lum Harris (New Castle); *Dizzy Dismukes* (Birmingham); *Ted Radcliffe* (Mobile); *Felton Snow* (Oxford)

The Names

Best Nickname: Willie "The Say Hey Kid" Mays

Other Nicknames: "Hammerin Hank" Aaron; "Poison" Ivy Andrews; Otha "L'il Catch" Bailey; "Downtown" Ollie Brown; Jeremy "The Badger" Brown; Larry "Iron Man" Brown; Ernest "Spoon" Carter; George "Slick" Coffman; Lorenzo "Piper" Davis; Virgil "Spud" Davis; William "Dizzy" Dismukes; Hersh "Buster" Freeman; Kyle "Skinny" Graham; Rusty "The Red Baron" Greer; Alonzo "Candy" Harris; Clarence "Shovel" Hodge; Monte "Mr. Murder" Irvin; Vincent "Bo" Jackson; Walter "Newt" Joseph; Lorenzo "Rimp" Lanier; Frank "Taters" Lary; Henry "Heinie" Manush; Guido "Southern" Martini; Guy "Alabama Blossom" Morton Sr.; Guy "Moose" Morton, Jr.; Andre "Thunder" Thornton; Lee "Boomer from Birmingham" May; Willie "Stretch" McCovey; Terris "Speed" and "The Great" McDuffie; Lamar "Skeeter" Newsome; Leroy "Satchel" Paige; Ed "Dixie" Parsons; Willie "Piggy" Powell; Wellington "Wimpy" Quinn; Ted "Double Duty" Radcliffe; James "Sap" Randall; James "Dusty" Rhodes; David "Houdini" Robertson; Henry "Sloe" Robinson; Carvel "Bama" Rowell; John Henry "Pistol" Russell; Harry "Beans" Salmon; Tommy "Toots" Sampson; George "Tubby" Scales; Ozzie "The Wizard of Oz" Smith; Felton "Mammy" and "Beautiful" Snow; Charles "Gabby" and "Old Sarge" Street; George "Mule" Suttles; Don "Black & Decker" Sutton; Franklin "Doc" Sykes; Danny "Sundown Kid" Thomas; Dave "Showboat" Thomas; Lafayette "Fresco" Thompson; Andre "Thunder" Thornton; Virgil "Fire" Trucks; Paul "Pee-Wee" Wanninger;

Charles "Two Sides" Wesley; "Shifty Jim" West; "Sweet Swingin' Billy" Williams; Early "Gus" Wynn

Most Unusual Name: Drungo Hazewood; Guido Martini

All-Time Leaders

Games: Hank Aaron, 3298
Hits: Hank Aaron, 3771
Batting Average: Riggs Stephenson, .336
Home Runs: Hank Aaron, 755
RBI: Hank Aaron, 2297
Stolen Bases: Willie Wilson, 668
Wins: Don Sutton, 324
Strikeouts: Don Sutton, 3574
Saves: Jeff Brantley, 172
Future Stars: Desmond Jennings (Birmingham); Kasey Kiker (Phenix City); Adam Warren (Birmingham)
Best Player: Willie Mays

Historic Baseball Places

Rickwood Field in Birmingham — America's oldest ballpark marked its 100th anniversary in 2010. The Friends of Rickwood hold the annual Rickwood Classic to raise money for the park's upkeep, with players wearing period uniforms. Plans are moving forward for the Negro and Southern Leagues Hall of Fame, an educational museum that will be located adjacent to Rickwood Field. It will showcase memorabilia from the Center for Negro League Baseball Research.

Hank Aaron Childhood Home and Museum in Mobile — The slugger's boyhood home was relocated to Hank Aaron Stadium in his hometown of Mobile, opening as a museum that pays tribute to his formative years and the legacy he built over a legendary career.

Alabama Sports Hall of Fame in Birmingham — Current list of inductees includes more than 50 baseball greats such as Willie Mays, Hank Aaron, Ozzie Smith, Monte Irvin, Willie McCovey, Mule Suttles, Don Sutton, Satchel Paige and Billy Williams.

Montgomery Riverwalk Stadium in Montgomery — Home of the Montgomery Biscuits, which opened in 2004, was built directly into an historic train station.

Notable Achievements

Tommie Agee was the first player to win Gold Glove Awards in both leagues. He won the award in the AL in 1966 and in the NL in 1970.

Early Wynn led the AL in strikeouts in consecutive seasons while pitching for different teams — the Cleveland Indians in 1957 and the Chicago White Sox in 1958.

Cleon Jones made the last putout in Game 5 as the Miracle Mets won the 1969 World Series championship.

Virgil Trucks is one of only five pitchers to pitch two no-hitters in the same season, joining Nolan Ryan, Allie Reynolds, Johnny Vander Meer and Roy Halladay.

Dan Bankhead (Empire) became the first African

Rickwood Field in Birmingham dates to 1910, making it the oldest professional baseball park in the United States. It has played host to some of baseball's greatest players, including Babe Ruth and Dizzy Dean (courtesy BallparkReviews.com).

American pitcher in the major leagues when he pitched for the Brooklyn Dodgers on August 26, 1947. He also homered in his first at-bat.

Oscar Gamble got the last hit at Connie Mack Stadium on October 1, 1970.

Bill Bruton (Panola) hit the first home run at Milwaukee County Stadium on Opening Day in 1953. It was the rookie's only home run that season in 613 at-bats. Bruton is also one of only three players since 1900 to hit two bases loaded triples in the same game, a feat he accomplished on August 2, 1959.

Pete Milne (Mobile) hit just one home run in his career, but it was an inside-the-park grand slam in 1949 that knocked in what proved to be the winning runs in the game.

Juan Pierre became the second player (after Ron LeFlore) to lead both leagues in stolen bases. He led the NL in 2001 and 2003 and the AL in 2010.

Hank Aaron and Eddie Mathews combined to hit the most home runs of any teammate tandem — 863.

Hank Aaron and **Tommie Aaron** (Mobile) combined to hit the most career home runs of any pair of brothers — 768.

Baseball Came Alive in Mobile and Birmingham

The narrative of baseball's origins centers on distant fields in New York and New Jersey, mythical tales of an army officer inspired to innovate in Cooperstown and other hard to pinpoint half-truths. But it seems baseball really came alive in the sandlot fields of Mobile and the unheralded mill towns around Birmingham, where determined boys of African American heritage spent countless hours forgetting their hardscrabble lives while refining skills that would later amaze and entertain generations of American baseball fans.

If you are looking for the roots of our national pastime, then it requires a journey to past and present Alabama, where the pain and struggle to overcome adversity parallels the remarkable rise of great teams and transcendent players. Alabama's vibrant baseball history is a testament to the triumph of the spirit, and the ghosts of baseball's past spring to life when one digs into the stories of the state's legendary players.

It could be argued that no state has produced more iconic superstars and more historic achievements than Alabama. Not only can the state boast one of the greatest collections of African American players from the Negro Leagues and major leagues, but the All-Time-Alabama team compares favorably to that of any other state. Powerful sluggers, flame-throwing hurlers, lightning-fast speed merchants, spectacular fielders — Alabama has it all.

Many of these great players showcased their talents at historic Rickwood Field in Birmingham, which remains a cultural beacon even as it embarks on its second century of use. It was modeled after Forbes Field in Pittsburgh, but its legacy has proved to be more enduring. Not only did it host the Birmingham Barons in the Southern League from 1910 to 1987, for many years it was also the home of the Birmingham Black Barons in the Negro Leagues and even played host to college football games featuring Alabama and Auburn. From the outfield signs that harken back to the 1920s, to the imposing 75-year-old light towers that made Rickwood Field one of the first parks to present night baseball, seeing the ballpark is like stepping back in time.

Ty Cobb, Christy Mathewson, Stan Musial, Babe Ruth, Honus Wagner and Dizzy Dean are among the Hall of Famers who played exhibition games on the historic field. Hall of Famers Burleigh Grimes and Rube Marquard pitched for the Birmingham Barons at Rickwood. Hank Aaron and the Milwaukee Braves played an exhibition game at Rickwood against Jackie Robinson and the Dodgers on April 2, 1954. Reggie Jackson later played for the Birmingham A's at Rickwood in 1967.

Willie Mays, who was born in Tuscaloosa but grew up in some of the mill towns scattered around Birmingham, first demonstrated his other-worldly talents as a 17-year-old playing for the Black Barons. He viewed baseball as his best chance to escape the tough mining and mill jobs that defined the city, and he'd learned the game watching his father, Cat, play in Birmingham's competitive Industrial League.

Another legendary player who performed at Rickwood was Mobile native Leroy "Satchel" Paige, who picked up his memorable nickname from his job carrying satchels for passengers at rail stations. Satchel entertained like a rock star several decades before Elvis Presley made rock 'n' roll a household phrase, and he used his wiry body and unorthodox high-kicking style to whip fastballs past overmatched batters. Although he attracted a lot of notoriety for his time with the Kansas City Monarchs, Paige won more Negro Leagues games with the Black Barons.

Satchel was a pioneer who was as responsible as Jackie Robinson for paving the way for African American players to play in the major leagues. In sold-out exhibition games against barnstorming white stars such as Bob Feller and Charlie Gehringer, Paige demonstrated that ballplayers of color could more than hold their own when matched up against some of baseball's greatest white players.

Paige honed his pitching skills playing on the sandlot fields of Mobile, which has proved to be a hotbed of great baseball. Only New York City is home to more Hall of Fame players than Mobile, which boasts five native sons as enshrinees: Satchel Paige, Hank Aaron, Willie McCovey, Ozzie Smith and Billy Williams. Williams was known as "Sweet Swingin' Billy from Whistler," which was an unincorporated area of Mobile.

Hank Aaron Stadium opened in 1997 as the new home of the Mobile BayBears and the slugger's baseball roots are now on display there. The modest home in the Toulminville neighborhood where Aaron grew up, which his father, Herbert, built from scrap wood in 1942, has been relocated to Hank Aaron Stadium, fixed up and turned into a museum. Seven rooms are filled with artifacts and memorabilia that highlight Aaron's struggles to persevere in the Jim Crow South while serving as a celebration of his ability to rise above and achieve greatness.

Willie Mays, Ozzie Smith, Rickey Henderson, Bob Feller, Reggie Jackson and Commissioner Bud Selig joined Aaron when the Hank Aaron Childhood Home & Museum officially opened in April 2010. "Every athlete who plays the game today and in the future should look at Hank Aaron," said Commissioner Selig, a longtime friend of Aaron dating back to his days on the Milwaukee Braves.

Other top-notch Negro Leagues players from Mobile include Ted "Double Duty" Radcliffe and his brother Alex, Dave "Showboat" Thomas, "Shifty Jim" West and Terris McDuffie. Double Duty Radcliffe, who grew up five blocks from Satchel in Mobile and played sandlot ball with him, also played against the fathers of Aaron, Williams, McCovey and Cito Gaston as a boy.

In 1971 Satchel became the first player inducted into the Hall of Fame based mostly on his feats in the Negro Leagues, but a number of great Alabama-born players built legacies that were all or largely defined by their performance in the Negro Leagues. In fact, seven of the 12 positions on the All-Time Alabama team are filled by players who spent some or all of their careers in the Negro Leagues.

All-Time Alabama Selections

Let's move on to the selections for Team Alabama. At catcher, the best candidate is "Double Duty" Radcliffe, who is considered one of the five best catchers in Negro Leagues history. A convincing argument can be made for his selection to the Hall of Fame. It was estimated that Radcliffe hit more than 400 home runs during his long career while also picking up over 400 wins as a pitcher (counting barnstorming games). No major leaguer has ever regularly played catcher and pitcher, but Double Duty sometimes did it in the same game (hence the nickname). He would start off a doubleheader by catching the first game and then pitch a complete game in the nightcap. He was a three-time Negro Leagues All-Star at both positions.

Double Duty's professional career was so long—36 years—that he played against Honus Wagner and Willie Mays. He lived until the age of 103 and while alive wasn't shy about touting his achievements. "Satchel Paige was the greatest pitcher in baseball history and Josh Gibson was the greatest hitter in baseball history and I'm the only man in the history of baseball to hit a homer off Satchel and strike out Josh," he liked to point out.

Spud Davis would have to be considered for his skill with the bat, not his lumbering and unrefined ability behind the plate. He hit only 77 home runs during his 16-season career but managed to surpass .300 10 times, including a career-high .349 in 1933 when he finished second in the National League in batting.

Luke Sewell deserves mention, but his outstanding defensive abilities as a catcher cannot mask his deficiencies with the bat. He ended his career with a .259 batting average and just 20 homers.

Negro Leaguer Larry Brown, who played in seven East-West All-Star games, was a similar player whose hitting deficiencies masked his excellence as a receiver. "Larry Brown was one of the best," noted Nat Rogers, who played with and against Brown throughout the 1930s and 1940s. "He never pulled off his mask to catch foul balls and in all of his years I saw him drop one," Rogers added.

One of the toughest positions to decide in any state is the All-Time-Alabama first baseman, where a strong case can be made for both Willie McCovey and Mule Suttles. Conventional wisdom would dictate the selection of McCovey, especially since "Stretch" would have ended up with far more than 521 home runs if he had managed to stay healthy. His career got a late start, because Orlando Cepeda was entrenched at the position for the Giants when he was ready to break into the majors. Still, McCovey was named Rookie of the Year in 1959 despite playing only 52 games that year. He led the league in homers three times and won the NL MVP Award in 1969.

McCovey became the first player to slug at least 30 home runs in a season and have more intentional walks than home runs. He hit 39 homers and had 40 intentional walks in 1970. When he retired his home run total was the most ever by a left-handed batter in National League history, although he has since been passed by Barry Bonds.

Suttles was a prodigious slugger who stood out on some of the best Negro Leagues teams ever, with every teammate seemingly able to recall a different tape-measure shot. He hit three home runs in one inning against the Memphis Red Sox in 1929, causing his opponent to leave the field the next time he came up. Eyewitnesses swear Suttles hit a ball 600 feet in Havana's Tropical Park, and he crushed a walk-off home run to win the 1935 East-West All-Star Game. Charlie Biot, a teammate on the Newark Eagles, said in Lawrence Hogan's *Shades of Glory*, "I never saw a man hit a ball that far with such a beautiful swing."

Baseball-Reference lists Suttles as the all-time home run leader in the Negro Leagues with 237. His 27 homers in 1926 are tied with Willie Wells for the single-season high and that year he also averaged a record .498. He appeared in five East-West All-Star games.

But was Suttles a better player than McCovey? Bill James thinks so—he ranks Suttles #43 and McCovey #69 in his Top 100 list. However, he also lists Suttles as an outfielder, while the Hall of Fame lists him as a first baseman. Derek Gentile's book, *Baseball's Best 1,000*, gives Suttles a slight edge with a #74 ranking compared to #78 for McCovey.

Neither was a good baserunner, but Suttles was a free swinger who struck out more frequently. McCovey was not a good fielder in the outfield, but he picked up his nickname for his ability to stretch out and save errant throws at first. McCovey was injury-prone and only exceeded 500 at-bats four times in 22 seasons due to injuries and led his team to the playoffs just twice — losing in the World Series in 1962 and losing in the NLCS in 1971. Suttles, on the other hand, played for 26 years and led his teams to four championships. Although not very graceful in the field, he batted .341 in games against white players and the Hall of Fame credits him with a .327 lifetime average. Suttles gets the nod by the narrowest of margins.

McCovey and Suttles are not the only talented first basemen from Alabama. Lee May hit more than 25 home runs on eight occasions, but he was not the threat McCovey was with the bat and was unskilled with the glove. Rudy York was named to seven All-Star teams but made his managers cringe with his unrefined fielding ability. He set major league records as a rookie with 18 home runs and 49 RBI in the month of August 1937, and he is one of many players who could have benefited if the designated hitter spot was available in his day.

Dave "Showboat" Thomas was a slick-fielding, nimble first baseman who liked to put on a show for fans. As the *Denver Post* described his play, "The 'Showboat' danced around the bag and scooped throws as though he were doing it to music." The Mobile native is generally regarded as one of the greatest fielders at the position in Negro Leagues history. Thomas was also a clutch hitter who delivered many a big hit during a career that lasted from 1928 to 1946.

Second base is manned by Negro League star George Scales, a powerful line-drive hitter who was stocky (hence the nickname "Tubby") and a little ornery. Scales typically hit in the middle of the order during a 25-year career that lasted from 1921–46. He played a number of years with the New York Lincoln Giants, then found himself hitting behind Josh Gibson on the Homestead Grays' powerhouse 1931 team. The next season he assumed the role of player-manager for the New York Black Yankees, and he would manage off and on for the rest of his career.

Scales edges out Frank Bolling, who had a strong arm and some pop in his bat, with 106 homers during his 12-year career. Bolling was a two-time All-Star who compiled 1,415 hits but a weak .313 OBP. He led NL second basemen in fielding percentage three times and won a Gold Glove in 1958.

Another notable second baseman is Ted Sizemore, who was named NL Rookie of the Year in 1969 with the Dodgers. He batted .306 his second year but then got traded to the Cardinals for Dick Allen. Sizemore didn't possess much speed or power, but he was a steady fielder and dependable player for 12 seasons.

Alex Radcliffe, Double Duty's brother, joins his brother in the starting lineup for Team Alabama at third base. He was a good all-around player who appeared in 11 East-West All-Star games in the Negro Leagues and is the all-time leader in All-Star game hits. Radcliffe was not known for his hustle but was an accomplished batter with good power whose teams (primarily the Chicago American Giants) were perennial contenders for the pennant. He swung a massive 40 oz. bat and was generally considered the greatest third baseman in the history of the Negro American League, even though his feats were often overshadowed by the accomplishments of his brother.

Radcliffe beats out another Negro Leaguer, Newt Joseph, who didn't look like much of a ballplayer because he was short and stocky. However, Joseph proved to be a valuable contributor at third base for the Kansas City Monarchs from 1922–35. He hit .334 to help the Monarchs win the second of three consecutive pennants in 1924.

Ozzie Smith is considered by many to be the greatest defensive shortstop to ever play the game, winning 13 Gold Glove awards for his ability to make the acrobatic and the routine play. Smith simply did things that even the most venerable observers said they had never seen done before and never expected to see done again — until Ozzie next took the field. And that's not even counting the many times he did a back-flip to get the fans excited.

When he was six, Ozzie moved with his family from Mobile to the rugged inner-city of Los Angeles. He was drafted by the Padres in the fourth round in 1977, playing his first four seasons for the Padres before being traded to St. Louis for Garry Templeton.

Smith led NL shortstops in fielding percentage eight times and is the all-time leader in assists by a shortstop with 8,375, leading the league eight times in that category. Smith set the record for double plays but was later passed by Omar Vizquel, and he remains the NL all-time leader in games by a shortstop. He was elected to the Hall of Fame in 2002.

The Wizard of Oz was a threat on the bases, stealing 580 bases to go with 2,460 hits. His career highlights were not all on defense, as he hit the game-winning home run in the bottom of the ninth inning of Game 5 of the 1985 National League Championship Series to beat the Dodgers.

It is tempting to move Joe Sewell, Luke's brother, over to the top spot at third base, but he played twice as many games at shortstop. His batting statistics certainly outshine those of Smith. Sewell, who received MVP votes in seven seasons, collected 2,226 hits, scored 1,141 runs and batted .312 with a .391 OBP. He didn't even get in a full year in the minors before being called up by the Indians in 1920 at the age of 21. Sewell was needed to replace Ray Chapman at shortstop, after Chapman tragically died from a beaning. Sewell batted .329 in 22 games, playing a key role as the Indians went on to win the World Series that year.

Sewell was the toughest person to strike out in the history of the game, fanning only 114 times in 7,132 career at-bats. By comparison, Mark Reynolds struck out almost twice as many times — 223 to be exact — just in the 2009 season. In 1925, Sewell struck out only four times all season despite having 608 at-bats. It's been said that Sewell was so efficient with his swings that he used the same bat throughout his 14-year career.

Two Negro Leagues shortstops are also worth mentioning: Sam Bankhead and Artie Wilson. Bankhead was a supremely gifted defender whether he was playing shortstop, second base or the outfield. He played in seven East-West All-Star Games at five different positions. A 1952 Pittsburgh Courier poll selected Bankhead as the first-team utility player on the all-time Negro Leagues All-Star team. Blessed with quick feet, soft hands and a strong arm, Bankhead was also an accomplished hitter with good speed. One of five brothers to play in the Negro Leagues, he stood out for his competitive fire. Unfortunately, Bankhead's life ended tragically as he was shot and killed in 1976.

Wilson started his career with the Birmingham Black Barons, making the All-Star team in four of his five seasons and leading the league with a .402 average in 1948. That marks the last time any player in the majors or Negro Leagues has batted over .400. That year he also took a 17-year-old outfielder named Willie Mays under his wing. Wilson was considered the best shortstop in the Negro Leagues in his day, and his contract was sold to the Oakland Oaks of the Pacific Coast League in 1949. Although Wilson led the PCL in batting and stolen bases his first season, he found himself stuck in the minors for most of his playing career. He got to play 19 games for the New York Giants at the age of 30 in 1951, but was sent back to the minors to make room on the roster for a budding superstar — his former teammate Mays. Wilson would go on to record 1,609 hits with a .312 average in 10 minor league seasons.

Mays and Aaron are no-brainer selections for the outfield — they collected more than 7,000 hits and 1,400 home runs combined between them. Where it gets interesting is trying to decide who should be called the best player in Alabama history. According to Bill James' Win Shares system, Mays was deserving of winning the National League MVP award in as many as seven years but only won the award twice.

Baseball had never seen a player like Mays with his combination of breath-taking speed, prodigious power and eye-catching defense, and it hasn't seen one since. Not only could Willie do it all on the field, he made it look easy. He was a marvel to behold in center field, boasting an awe-inspiring combination of grace, speed, instincts and strong arm. Most baseball fans have seen a replay of him catching Vic Wertz's deep fly ball in the 1954 World Series — known famously as "The Catch" — but Mays made catches like that regularly along with his trademark basket catches. He remains the all-time leader in outfield putouts with 7,095.

Mays led the league in stolen bases four straight seasons while averaging 33 home runs in those years. Not only was Willie the first player to collect 50 homers and 20 steals in a season, he also was the first member of the 3,000 hit–500 home run club. Despite going hitless in his first 12 major league at-bats in 1951, he never lost his confidence and went on to win the NL Rookie of the Year Award. "I think I was the best baseball player I ever saw," he famously said.

Willie played three years for the Birmingham Barons in the Negro Leagues and lost nearly two full seasons to military service, yet he still made 24 All-Star teams in 20 seasons. He led the league in home runs four times and ranks ninth in most games played with 2,992. Mays didn't bat over .300 his last eight seasons yet still ended up with a .302 average for his career.

In his terrific biography of Mays (*Willie Mays: The Life, The Legend*), James Hirsch points out that Mays is the only player in baseball history to hit a home run in every inning from one to 16. That's an amazing feat that is unlikely to be matched.

In 1951, four years after Jackie Robinson broke the color barrier, Aaron was signed to his first professional contract by the Indianapolis Clowns in the Negro Leagues. He led them to the Negro League championship and then had his contract picked up by the Boston Braves. After tearing up the minors in two stops, Aaron debuted for the Braves in 1954, batting .280 with 13 home runs. The next time he hit fewer than 20 home runs in a season was 1975, and by then Aaron had already passed Babe Ruth as the all-time leader in home runs.

Although Aaron could not match Mays for spectacular plays, he combined greatness with unsurpassed consistency and durability. Hammerin' Hank never hit more than 47 home runs in a season, but he had eight seasons with at least 40 homers and posted 20 straight seasons with at least 20 homers. He remains the all-time leader in RBI with 2,297, extra-base hits with 1,477 and in total bases with 6,856 while ranking third in hits with 3,771. His appearance in 25 All-Star Games edges Mays by one for the most ever.

No hitting coach would ever advise a young player to mimic Aaron's bizarre cross-handed batting technique, but you certainly can't argue with his results. He was not a big, imposing player — at 6-feet tall and 180 pounds — but his wrists were immensely powerful and quick. As Joe Adcock put it, "Trying to sneak a pitch past Hank Aaron is like trying to sneak the sunrise past a rooster."

His best season was 1957, when he won his only MVP Award (he finished third in MVP voting six times). He led the NL with 44 homers, 132 RBI and 118 runs that season while finishing fourth with a .322 average. Aaron would also win his only championship that year, leading the way with a .393 average and three home runs in the Series as the Braves knocked off the Yankees.

Aaron set the all-time home run record with remarkable dignity, suffering in silence despite an unfathomable amount of hate directed his way. Engulfed by fans as he made his way around the bases after hitting home run number 715 off Al Downing, Aaron resisted the attempts of teammates to place him on their shoulders. Instead, he sought out the embrace of his parents, the two people who knew most what he had endured to climb that mountain. "I never knew that my mother could hug so tight," Aaron joked after the game, relieved that the chase of a lifetime was finally over. It was not just the culmination of a personal crusade but a historic achievement for an entire race, showing a fractured nation that African Americans were not only capable of a great feats on the ball field but were also worth admiring for their character.

It would have been understandable if Aaron had been bitter and disillusioned to see the most important record in baseball — the all-time home run record — get broken in a tainted manner by Barry Bonds in 2007. Yet he continued to display great class and graciousness in congratulating his unworthy successor. "My hope today, as it was on that April evening in 1974, is that the achievement of this record will inspire others to chase their own dreams," Aaron said in his videotaped message that was played on the scoreboard in AT&T Park on the night Bonds broke his record.

Aaron was a legendary player and one of the most important sports figures of the twentieth century, but Mays was the better all-around player. Aaron won three Gold Glove awards, while Mays won 12 consecutive Gold Gloves. Mays was a little faster and a more daring baserunner, but Aaron scores points for maintaining his greatness a little longer. He hit .301 with 40 home runs at age 39, while Mays' highest average in his last eight seasons was .291. Aaron suffers in comparison because he did things without flair, while Mays could seemingly look good hitting into a double play.

Mays is the all-time leader in extra-inning home runs with 22 (six more than runner-up Babe Ruth), as though he had the singular ability to decide which inning he would defeat you. He made the impossible — scoring from first on a single — seem not only possible, but probable. Mays was once described this way: "deep down we know we'll never again see the game embodied so well, so completely, in one man." Mays takes the honor as Alabama's All-Time Best Player.

The third outfield spot is a tougher choice, as a case could be made for Monte Irvin and Heinie Manush in addition to the conventional choice of Hall of Famer Billy Williams. In the end it was hard to bypass Williams, who was like Aaron in that he was a durable and consistent player who put up above-average statistics year after year.

Williams was a great team player who could be counted on for 25–30 homers, 100 RBI and a .300 average. In addition to becoming the first Cubs player to win Rookie of the Year, he was named to six All-Star teams and played in 1,117 consecutive games. In 1970, he led the NL in hits, runs and total bases and finished second in homers, RBI and the MVP voting (losing out to Johnny Bench). Two years later, he had an even better year, winning the batting title with a .333 average and leading the league in slugging, OPS, OPS+ and total bases while clubbing 37 homers. He again lost the MVP Award to Bench, although it was a closer vote.

Williams, who ended up with 426 career home runs, was given the nickname "Sweet Swingin' Billy" while in the minors. "My coaches commented that I had a good approach and good balance at the plate. They even asked me if I knew what was coming from the pitcher. I'd hear guys say, 'There's the sweet swinger.' The press picked up on it after that," Williams said.

Monte Irvin made only one All-Star team during his eight-year major league career (which didn't begin until he was 30), but he showed what he could do by batting .458 in a losing effort against the Yankees in the 1951 World Series. Also that year Irvin became the first African American player to lead the league in RBI. He was elected to the Hall of Fame in 1973 despite playing only 764 games in the major leagues. If he had played his whole career in the major leagues, Irvin's numbers would probably look very similar to those posted by Williams.

Irvin joined the Newark Eagles as a promising but unseasoned 19-year-old in 1938. The next year he hit .365 to finish fourth in the Negro National League and his apprenticeship was over. He bumped his average up to .383 in 1940, good for second in the league, and then tied for the home run lead the next season. Irvin would miss three years while serving in the army, but he returned to hit three big homers to lead Newark to the 1946 Negro World Series title. Said Roy Campanella, "Monte was the best all-around player I have ever seen. As great as he was in 1951, he was twice that good 10 years earlier in the Negro Leagues." Irvin was also honored as MVP of the Mexican League after batting .397 in 1942. He ended up being named to five All-Star teams in the Negro Leagues.

Manush, who is also in the Hall of Fame, was a lefty who sprayed line drives all over the park. He led the American League with a .378 average, 241 hits and 47 doubles in 1926, when he finished a close second to Mickey Cochrane for the MVP Award. Two years later he batted .378 again but lost the batting race to Goose Goslin by one point. He ended up with a lifetime average of .330 with 2,524 hits. Manush led the league in hits and doubles twice and posted four seasons with over 200 hits. Heinie would certainly make the all-ornery team, but he didn't offer much speed, power or defense and he batted .111 in his only World Series appearance in 1933.

Neither Williams nor Irvin ever had a year like George Foster did in his MVP season of 1977, when the Tuscaloosa native led the league with 52 homers, 149 RBI and 124 runs while batting .320 (fourth-best). He again led the NL in homers and RBI the next season and retired with 348 home runs. Foster was essentially a one-dimensional slugger who didn't do much else to help his team win.

Amos Otis was a spectacular center fielder for the Royals who could occasionally beat you with his bat. He won three Gold Gloves for his stellar outfield play and also stole 341 bases. Another Royal with tremendous talent was Willie Wilson, who collected 668 stolen bases, led the league in triples five times and won a batting championship in 1982. He shares the record with Pete Rose for most hits in a season by a switch-hitter with 230. Still, chicks (and fans) dig the long ball, and Willie only hit 41 dingers in his 19-year career.

The player most similar to Wilson at various ages is

Juan Pierre, another Mobile native. Pierre is a singles-hitting speed demon whose weak arm makes him a liability in the outfield. Through the 2011 season he had posted four years with at least 200 hits and batted over .300 five times. He had led the league in steals three times and recorded eight straight seasons with more than 40 stolen bases.

Several other outfielders deserve mention. Bo Jackson was one of the greatest athletes of the twentieth century, and he has the distinction of being the first person to make All-Star teams in two professional sports. We are still waiting for the home run he hit in the 1989 All-Star game to re-enter the atmosphere. Bo hit 32 homers and drove in 105 runs that season for the Royals while also striking out a league-high 172 times. He ended up with 141 home runs in eight seasons. Unfortunately, we never got to see what he could do with a 20-year baseball career.

Although Carlos May didn't make the final cut for the All-Time-Alabama team, the outfielder from Birmingham deserves recognition for being the only player to have his birthday shown on the back of his uniform. May, whose birthday is May 17, wore uniform #17 for most of his White Sox career.

Another outfielder from Alabama, Ike Boone, is the all-time leader for minor league batting average at .370. He ended up with 2,521 hits over 14 minor league seasons, hitting .407 with an eye-popping 323 hits in 1929. Boone batted .321 in the majors, but managed just 372 hits over eight seasons, held back by a weak glove and lack of speed.

Andre Thornton is the most deserving selection for designated hitter. Thornton appeared in 738 games as a DH, nine more than he appeared at first base during his career. The two-time All-Star won a Silver Slugger Award as a DH in 1984 and finished his career with 252 home runs.

Alabama is also the birthplace of the incomparable Oscar Gamble, who was discovered on the sandlots of Birmingham by Buck O'Neil, who was a scout for the Cubs at the time. Not only did he have power (200 home runs over a 17-year career) and a cool name, Gamble possessed the most impressive Afro ever displayed on the diamond. The Yankees acquired the outfielder from the Indians in 1975 for Pat Dobson and a hair pick to be named later. Although an outfielder by trade, Gamble is an honorable mention selection at DH.

The All-Time Alabama Team is top-heavy with quality right-handed starters. Although Hall of Famers Don Sutton and Early Wynn are worthy choices, Satchel Paige was a better pitcher ... by far. In fact, people who should know such things (such as Joe DiMaggio) say Satchel was the greatest pitcher of all-time. Even the boastful Dizzy Dean said Satchel was the best pitcher he ever saw.

Satchel was a flamethrower with great control, who seemed to make up pitches on the spot. Paige once struck out Rogers Hornsby five times in one game, and his control was so impeccable he would show off by throwing strike after strike using chewing gum wrappers or matchbook covers for home plate. Baseball historians estimate his career wins total to be approximately 600 if exhibitions are counted, which would top Cy Young for tops all-time.

According to research by Negro Leagues historian John Holway, Satchel went 160–91 in Negro Leagues action alone, which is akin to Sandy Koufax's career numbers. He went 56–7 in nine years of action in the California Winter League, and was nearly unbeatable pitching for the Bismarck Churchills in North Dakota in 1933 and 1935, posting a 35–2 record.

Paige didn't make his major league debut until 1948 when he was at least 42, which made him the oldest rookie in major league history. His work in the majors was largely done in relief and although his record was 28–31 he remained effective. Satchel was the ultimate entertainer who knew how to put on a show, and the fans seldom went home disappointed. The stands were never filled because people wanted to see Don Sutton pitching that day, so this is one team the great Satchel cannot be kept off.

Sutton is third on the career list with 756 games started, seventh in strikeouts with 3,574 and is tied with Nolan Ryan for fourteenth all-time in victories with 324. The four-time All-Star wasn't blessed with overpowering stuff, but he was durable and skilled at doctoring the ball (which is where he picked up the nickname "Black & Decker"). Sutton came close to throwing a no-hitter on five occasions, but each time had to settle for a one-hitter.

One mark against him is that he only won 20 games once during a 23-year career, making him the only 300-game winner with that distinction. Sutton did have shutout streaks of 36 and $30\frac{2}{3}$ innings during the 1972 season, and he won more games than any other pitcher in Dodgers history.

Wynn won the Cy Young Award in 1959 at the age of 39, but only won 29 more games the rest of his career—just enough to end up with 300. However, he won 20 games five times and was a master at brushing batters off the plate. He was part of Cleveland's Big Four—along with Bob Feller, Bob Lemon and Mike Garcia—a quartet that combined for 443 wins between 1949 and 1955. Wynn led the league in wins and strikeouts twice, ERA and WHIP once, games started five times and innings pitched three times.

Several other starting pitchers deserve mention. Virgil Trucks won 177 games and made two All-Star teams. Rip Sewell—a cousin of Joe and Luke—was a four-time All-Star who finished his career with a record of 143–97. And an active pitcher from Mobile, Jake Peavy, won the NL Triple Crown for pitchers while receiving the Cy Young Award in 2007.

Sam Bankhead's brother, Dan, was a flame-throwing righty in the Negro Leagues for the Birmingham Black Barons and Memphis Red Sox. He was also a threat with the bat, boasting good power. Signed by the Brooklyn Dodgers in 1947, Bankhead became the first African American pitcher in the majors when he debuted on August 26 against the Pirates. His pitching debut wasn't a success but he hit a home run in his first at-bat, becoming the first National League pitcher to accomplish that feat. His only full season in the majors was 1950, when he posted a 9–4 record in 41 appearances. Bankhead continued to play in the minors and in Canada and Mexico up until the age of 46, gradually spending more time at first base as he got older.

You will find only one Morton on the All-Time Alabama team, but two members of the family were born in Alabama and saw the highs and lows of professional baseball. Guy Morton Sr., nicknamed "Alabama Blossom," set a record by losing the first 13 games of his career in 1914. He rebounded to win his final decision that season, finishing with a respectable 3.02 ERA. Morton would go 16–15 with a 2.14 ERA the next year while allowing just 7.1 H/9 IP, and he retired with 98 wins over 11 seasons. It's good enough to make the honorable mention list as a right-handed starter. His son, Guy Morton, Jr., nicknamed "Moose," struck out in his only career at-bat with the Red Sox in 1954. If given 12 more at-bats, we'd like to think he would not have struck out every time.

The top lefty starter is the dependable Jimmy Key, a four-time All-Star who was Cy Young runner-up twice (in 1987 and 1994). He won 186 games with a winning percentage of .614. Key was a key player in helping the Blue Jays win the 1992 World Series. He won Game 4 by holding the Braves to five hits and one run and he came back three days later to enter Game 6 in the 10th inning, getting four outs and the Series-clinching win. Key also won the Series-clinching Game 6 of the 1996 World Series for the Yankees, again holding the Braves to five hits and one run.

The only other notable lefty is Bob Veale, who was a workhorse for the Pirates in the 1960s. Veale led the NL with 250 strikeouts in 1964 and finished second with 276 K's in 1965. The two-time All-Star won 120 career games over 13 seasons, playing on the Pirates 1971 championship team.

For relief pitcher, only two worthy candidates emerge once it's decided that Satchel Paige is to be considered as a starting pitcher. A case could be made for both Clay Carroll and Jeff Brantley. Brantley had the edge in lifetime saves — 172 to 143 — but Carroll had a better ERA and appeared in two All-Star games compared to one for Brantley. In fact, Carroll was named Fireman of the Year in 1972, when he set the single-season saves record with 37. He was also clutch in the playoffs, posting a lifetime ERA of 1.39 in 22 postseason appearances. Brantley has the edge in strikeouts per 9 innings (7.6 to 4.5) and batting average against (.237 to .254), but Carroll gets the nod because he made a bigger impact on the teams he pitched for than Brantley.

At manager, Gabby Street is the only Alabama native to win a World Series, skippering the underdog St. Louis Cardinals to a championship in 1931 over Connie Mack's A's. He led the team to first-place finishes his first two seasons at the helm but was replaced before the end of the 1933 season, so he was not around when the 1934 Cardinals team forged a new identity as the Gashouse Gang. Luke Sewell is the only other manager from Alabama to win a pennant, but he had an overall losing record as a manager. Lum Harris guided the Atlanta Braves to a division title in 1969, but they lost to the Mets in the Championship Series.

Double Duty Radcliffe served as player-manager with the Cincinnati Tigers in 1937, the Memphis Red Sox in 1938 and the Chicago American Giants in 1943. However, he had more success organizing traveling all-star teams with Satchel Paige and he also attracted attention by signing several white players to play for the Chicago American Giants, an experiment that didn't pan out.

ALASKA

*Names in **bold** represent Major League selections by position, followed by honorable mentions. City of birth is in parentheses.*

Catcher — Tom Sullivan (Nome)
First Base — Josh Phelps (Anchorage)
Second Base — Steve Staggs (Anchorage)
Third Base — Randy Kutcher (Anchorage)
Shortstop — Randy Kutcher (Anchorage)
Outfield — Randy Kutcher (Anchorage)
Outfield — Scott Loucks (Anchorage)
Outfield — Aaron Cunningham (Anchorage)
Designated Hitter — Josh Phelps (Anchorage)
Right Handed Starter — Curt Schilling (Anchorage)
Left Handed Starter — Dave Williams (Anchorage)
Relief Pitcher — Shawn Chacon (Anchorage). Also: Daniel Schlereth (Anchorage); Chad Bentz (Seward)
Manager — None

The Names

Best Nickname: Curt "Schill" Schilling
Most Unusual Name: Shawn Chacon

All-Time Leaders

Games: Curt Schilling, 569
Hits: Josh Phelps, 380
Batting Average: Josh Phelps, .273
Home Runs: Josh Phelps, 64
RBI: Josh Phelps, 244
Stolen Bases: Randy Kutcher, 13
Wins: Curt Schilling, 216
Strikeouts: Curt Schilling, 3116

Saves: Shawn Chacon, 36
Future Star: Chris Aure (North Pole)
Best Player: Curt Schilling

Historic Baseball Places

Growden Memorial Park in Fairbanks — This old-time stadium features a handful of seats that were salvaged from Sick's Stadium in Seattle and is home to the Alaska Goldpanners of Fairbanks. Barry Bonds played for the Goldpanners in 1983 and was known back then for his extremely normal-sized head.

Mulcahy Stadium in Anchorage — Home of the Anchorage Bucs and Anchorage Glacier Pilots in the Alaska Baseball League dates back to 1964. Randy Johnson and Jacoby Ellsbury once played for the Anchorage Glacier Pilots, while Jeff Kent and Jered Weaver are among the alumni of the Anchorage Bucs.

Notable Achievements

Curt Schilling holds the major league record for consecutive starts without allowing an unearned run, at 69 games.

Josh Phelps was named the Southern League MVP in 2001.

A Summer Tradition Takes Root in an Unlikely Spot

The Alaska Goldpanners baseball club marks the summer solstice by playing through the night (no lights necessary) with the annual Midnight Sun Baseball Game — an Alaskan tradition for more than a century. What baseball fan wouldn't want to watch baseball all night long? Tom Seaver and Dave Winfield are among the players who have taken part in the tradition, which typically attracts a capacity crowd.

Summer baseball in Alaska first got its start with the formation of the Fairbanks Goldpanners in 1960. Two years later the team was battling for the championship at the National Baseball Congress in Wichita, and a great summer tradition was off and running.

The 1968 Goldpanners team featured Bob Boone, Dan Pastorini and Dave Kingman. Boone, who batted .405 that season, went on to set the record for most games caught in the majors. Pastorini was an outfielder who batted .311 for the Goldpanners, but he decided to concentrate on football and three years later was the third pick of the NFL Draft. Kingman pitched in 11 games for the team and walked 37 batters in 27 innings, demonstrating that he was better off concentrating on batting.

Satchel Paige once pitched in Alaska, at Mulcahy Stadium in Anchorage in 1965, according to Lew Freedman's *Diamonds in the Rough*. He was not exactly in his prime anymore, but he demonstrated that he still knew how to put on a show during the four-game exhibition series.

Still, there is no getting around the fact that there are some inherent challenges to playing baseball in Alaska. There are only 26 schools in the state that even play the sport, so it's not surprising that just 11 players from Alaska have ever made it to the major leagues. Chad Bentz is the only one we could definitely determine graduated from high school in Alaska, while two other players' high schools could not be verified.

Alaska's most famous player, Curt Schilling, attended high school in Phoenix and is a member of the Arizona Sports Hall of Fame. Shawn Chacon and Daniel Schlereth attended in Colorado, while Dave Williams played his high school ball in Delaware. Scott Loucks actually went to high school in Hawaii and we discovered other players graduated from Washington, Idaho and California.

If you want to learn more about what it's like to play baseball in Alaska, check out "Touching the Game Alaska," an excellent film about the Alaska Baseball League.

All-Time Alaska Selections

Since five of Alaska's 11 players are pitchers it was necessary to stretch positions a little to field the All-Time Alaska team. Kudos to Tom Sullivan of Nome for appearing in one game at the age of 18 and even getting to the plate once. He was Alaska's first major league player in 1925. He didn't get a hit but at least he provides the All-Time Alaska Team with a legitimate catcher. If he gets tired then Randy Kutcher could fill in — he also played one game at catcher.

Josh Phelps, who played for six major league teams between 2004 and 2008, was originally drafted as a catcher but mainly has played first base. His best position is probably designated hitter. He wears the crown from Alaska as the all-time leader in home runs, hits and just about every other batting category.

Kutcher was mainly an outfielder in the big leagues, but for this team he's pressed into duty on the left side of the infield — the whole left side. He played 25 games at third base and 14 games at shortstop and that's good enough for Team Alaska. Steve Staggs, who played for the Toronto Blue Jays in their inaugural season of 1977, saw some action at third and short but the bulk of his brief career came at second base.

Kutcher not only has to hold down the left side of the infield, his range needs to extend to the outfield, too, at least until Alaska can grow some more major league prospects. After collecting 102 hits with a .228 average in five seasons, Kutcher's major league career seemed to be over in 1990. However, when the 1994 baseball strike carried over into spring training the next year, Kutcher came back as a replacement player for the Yankees.

Active player Aaron Cunningham is the second outfielder. He made brief appearances for the A's in 2008 and 2009 and then batted .288 for the Padres in 2010 followed by a .178 average in 2011. Filling out the outfield is Loucks, who led the nation in stolen bases as a college player at Southeastern Oklahoma State in 1977 but did not get refills on the cup of coffee he had in the big leagues.

There is only one star player from Alaska — Curt Schilling. He is the first native Alaskan to pitch in the major leagues, although few fans seem aware of his birthplace. Drafted in the second round of the 1986 MLB Draft by the Red Sox, Schilling played 16 years for four teams before being traded back to the Red Sox in late 2003. The hard-throwing righty threw a wicked split-finger fastball, was mentally tough and had impeccable control.

He proved himself one of the best postseason pitchers in baseball history, with a record of 11–2 and sparkling 2.23 ERA in the postseason. His .846 winning percentage in the postseason is the best ever by a pitcher with a minimum of 10 decisions. He was named NLCS MVP for the Phillies in 1993 and World Series co–MVP (with Randy Johnson) for the Diamondbacks in 2001. He set the tone for that Series by scoffing about the Yankees' invincibility with the following memorable line: "Mystique and aura? Those are dancers at a nightclub."

Everyone remembers Schilling's gritty performance for the Red Sox in the 2004 playoffs when he tore the tendon sheath in his right ankle. He vanquished the hated Yankees in Game 6 of the ALCS, pitching through pain and with blood seeping through his sock to help the Sox complete an improbable comeback from a 3–0 Series deficit. Not finished, he beat the Cardinals in Game 2 of the World Series that year without surrendering an earned run to help the Red Sox break the Curse and end an 86-year championship drought.

The six-time All-Star finished second in Cy Young Award voting three times in four years and was a three-time 20-game winner. He led the league in complete games four times; wins, innings pitched, WHIP and strikeouts twice; and won-loss percentage once. He won just about every non-playing award you can win including the Lou Gehrig Memorial Award, National League Babe Ruth Award, Branch Rickey Award, Hutch Award and Roberto Clemente Award.

Perhaps Schilling's most impressive feat was ending his career with more than 3,000 strikeouts (3,116 to be exact) and less than 1,000 walks — only three other pitchers have done that. And he ended up far short of 1,000 with only 711 walks issued. His 4.383 SO/BB ratio is second-best in baseball history behind nineteenth century pitcher Tommy Bond and he ranks fifteenth on the all-time strikeouts list. Schilling said, "Earlier in my career, the two guys I wanted to emulate were Clemens and Maddux. I wanted Clemens' power with Maddux's control. I never quite got to either one of them, but I felt like I was kind of a mishmash of the two in some cases."

In 2002, he completed the rare feat of having more starts (35) than walks (33), striking out 316 batters in the process. His SO/BB ratio of 9.58 that year ranks fifth in baseball history and is the third-best mark since 1900. He hit the rare mark again in 2006 with 31 games started and only 28 walks.

An outspoken critic of steroids use both during and after his playing career, Schilling first becomes eligible for election to the Hall of Fame in 2013, the same year as accused steroids users Barry Bonds, Roger Clemens and Sammy Sosa. With only 216 career wins he may have a hard time getting into Cooperstown, but at least his bloody sock has a home there.

Dave Williams offers the team a serviceable left-handed pitcher. He won 10 games for the Pirates in 2005 and produced a 22–31 career record. Williams pitched in Japan in 2008 and last saw action in the minors for the Nationals in 2009.

Shawn Chacon had an up-and-down career, intermingling bouts of wildness with bouts of churlishness. An All-Star as a starter in 2003, he recorded 35 saves as a closer the next year despite a 1–9 record and 7.11 ERA. He had as many walks as strikeouts that year — 52. Traded to the Yankees midway through the 2005 season, Chacon helped the team reach the postseason by going 7–3 with a 2.85 ERA down the stretch. However, after getting into a physical altercation with Astros General Manager Ed Wade in June 2008, Chacon was cut loose and his major league career is most likely over. He posted a 6.29 ERA pitching for the A's Triple-A affiliate in 2009 and then finished out the year playing independent ball.

Chacon had only one productive season as a reliever, but he is more qualified for the All-Time relief pitcher spot than Chad Bentz, who does have an uplifting personal story. Bentz is only the second person to play in the major leagues after being born without one of his hands (following the lead of Jim Abbott). It's hard enough to make it to the majors when you are born in Alaska — Bentz grew up in Juneau — but his perseverance in following the trail blazed by Abbott shows he is worthy of gaining honorable mention status. Bentz appeared in 40 games in 2004 and 2005 for the Expos and Marlins, going 0–3 with a 7.58 ERA.

The Tigers are hoping that Anchorage native Daniel Schlereth harnesses his potential and turns into a bullpen star. He has averaged 8.9 SO/9IP over his first three seasons.

Chris Aure was born in that hotbed of baseball action — North Pole, Alaska — and he was drafted in the fifteenth round of the 2008 amateur draft by the Pirates. However, Aure, who bats, throws and ice fishes with his left hand, was released in 2010 after two minor league seasons.

ARIZONA

*Names in **bold** represent Major League selections by position, followed by honorable mentions. Negro Leagues players are in italics. City of birth is in parentheses.*

Catcher — Tom Pagnozzi (Tucson). Also: Ron Hassey (Tucson)
First Base — Shea Hillenbrand (Mesa). Also: *Willie Bobo* (Phoenix)
Second Base — Ian Kinsler (Tucson). Also: Rex Hudler (Tempe)
Third Base — Jack Howell (Tucson)
Shortstop — Solly Hemus (Phoenix). Also: J.J. Hardy (Tucson)
Outfield — Billy Hatcher (Williams)
Outfield — Andre Ethier (Phoenix)
Outfield — Hank Leiber (Phoenix). Also: Chris Duncan (Tucson); Lou Novikoff (Glendale)
Right Handed Starter — John Denny (Prescott). Also: *Ford Smith* (Phoenix); Gary Gentry (Phoenix); Gil Heredia (Nogales); Phil Ortega (Gilbert)
Left Handed Starter — Alex Kellner (Tucson). Also: Dallas Braden (Phoenix)
Relief Pitcher — Bobby Howry (Phoenix). Also: Jeremy Accardo (Phoenix); Lerrin LaGrow (Phoenix); Jeremy Affeldt (Phoenix)
Manager — Solly Hemus (Phoenix)

The Names

Best Nickname: Lou "The Mad Russian" Novikoff
Other Nicknames: Earl "Hap" Collard; Lee "Flame" Delhi; Chris "Big Dipper" Duncan; Solomon "Solly" Hemus; Filomeno "Kemo" Ortega; John Ford "Geronimo" Smith
Most Unusual Name: Marshall Boze; Willie Bobo

All-Time Leader

Games: Billy Hatcher, 1233
Hits: Billy Hatcher, 1146
Batting Average: Andre Ethier, .291 (still active)
Home Runs: Ian Kinsler, 124 (still active)
RBI: Hank Leiber, 518
Stolen Bases: Billy Hatcher, 218
Wins: John Denny, 123
Strikeouts: John Denny, 1146
Saves: Bobby Howry, 66
Future Stars: Lou Marson (Scottsdale); Brad Mills (Tucson); Jaff Decker (Peoria)
Best Player: Ian Kinsler

Historic Baseball Places

Warren Ballpark in Bisbee — Dates back to 1909, which gives it some claim as the oldest ballpark despite the fact that the grandstand was replaced in 1930.
Salt River Fields at Talking Stick in Scottsdale — Baseball's newest spring training facility opened in 2011 as the Cactus League home of the Diamondbacks and Rockies.
Hi Corbett Field in Tucson — First the Indians and then the Rockies held spring training here from 1947 to 2010. Willie Mays, Ted Williams, Mickey Mantle and Bob Feller are among the greats who played games at the stadium, which was built in 1937.
Phoenix Municipal Stadium in Phoenix — Spring training home of the A's since 1982, it features an accordion-style roof and is billed as the first air-conditioned ballpark. Willie Mays hit the park's first home run during a spring training game in 1964.
Tempe Diablo Stadium in Tempe — Spring training home of the Angels opened in 1968. After the Seattle Pilots completed their second spring training at Tempe Diablo in 1970, they immediately moved the franchise to Milwaukee before the regular season started.
Camelback Ranch in Phoenix — It took a lot to get the Dodgers to leave Dodgertown in Vero Beach, Fla., but you can see why with this gorgeous ballpark, which is shared with the White Sox. A huge man-made lake separates the two teams' facilities.
Goodyear Ballpark in Goodyear — Opened in 2009 as the spring training home of the Reds and Indians, the stadium is part of a $108 million baseball complex. The stunning entryway to the park includes a 60-foot-six-inch Ziz statue, which looks like a stretched out and deflated banana baseball and is named for a giant bird in Jewish mythology. This makes sense when you realize the Ziz is supposed to have a wingspan large enough to block out the sun, which comes in handy in the desert.
Hohokam Park in Mesa — Opened in 1997 as the spring training home of the Cubs. If you're a passionate Cubs fan what can be better than grabbing a Chicago-style dog and an Old Style beer and hanging out with other Cubbies?
Chase Field in Phoenix — Home of the Diamondbacks opened as Bank One Ballpark in 1998. It's the first park to have a retractable roof and a natural-grass field. One neat retro feature is the dirt strip between the pitcher's mound and home plate.

Notable Achievements

Billy Hatcher set a World Series record with seven consecutive hits in 1990 with the Reds.
Ian Kinsler made history with Willie Harris of the Nationals on June 22, 2008 — it was the first time two players both hit a home run on their birthday in the same game.

Salt River Fields at Talking Stick in Scottsdale opened in 2011 as the dual Cactus League home of the Diamondbacks and Rockies. The fan-friendly design incorporates fan observation areas and a soaring roof to provide shade (courtesy Digitalballparks.com).

Ron Hassey is the only player to catch two perfect games in the major leagues. He caught Len Barker's perfect game in 1981 and Dennis Martinez's perfect game in 1991.

John Denny is one of only two pitchers to win the Cy Young Award without ever being named to an All-Star team. The other is Pete Vukovich.

Dallas Braden, who lost his mother to cancer while in high school, pitched a perfect game on Mother's Day in 2010.

Doug Mirabelli, from 2001–2006, became the first player to hit six or more home runs in six consecutive seasons of less than 200 at-bats.

Flaming Out in the Desert

Here is a riddle for you. How does a pitcher pick up a nickname like "Flame" when he only appears in one major league game, giving up seven hits and six runs in three innings? I've got to give props to Lee "Flame" Delhi, and not just because I'm from a small town in New York named Delhi.

Actually, Flame Delhi got that nickname because of his red hair, not his blazing fastball (or the fact his career flamed out). He also has a SABR chapter named after him in Arizona, due to the fact that he was the first Arizona native to appear in a major league game back in 1912. It is even documented that Flame Delhi was part of the inspiration for Ring Lardner's character of Jack Keefe in his "You Know Me Al" stories. Those Delhi boys have it going on.

On the subject of interesting players in Arizona history, doesn't it stand to reason that a baseball player with the name of Phoenix, who coincidentally was born in Phoenix, was destined to be a great player? Unfortunately, that is not the case with the less than immortal Steve Phoenix, who appeared in just three games with the A's in 1994 and 1995 and retired (to Phoenix?) with an ERA of 13.50. His is a strange case, to say the least. I mean, even if there are some players named Tucson or Sedona, I bet they weren't born there. Take Al Alburquerque — he was born in the Dominican Republic, which is a little baffling.

The folks in Alabama think they have the country's oldest ballpark, but Arizona might have them beat. Warren Ballpark officially opened in Bisbee in 1909 — a year ahead of Rickwood Field in Birmingham and three years before Arizona even became a state. The original wooden grandstand was replaced with concrete and steel in 1930, which is the date some ballpark historians want to use for the stadium's age.

Bisbee, which was once the largest town west of the Mississippi, has a colorful history as a mining town. The ballpark's history includes being the scene for a post–World Series exhibition game by the White Sox and Giants in 1913. In 1917, it was used as a jail for striking miners — those who refused to return to work were then shipped out in boxcars in what was known as the Bisbee Deportation. Hal Chase, Chick Gandil and Buck Weaver played in Warren Ballpark in the 1920s after being banished from baseball.

Of course one cannot discuss Arizona baseball without mentioning the historic role played by the Cactus League. Professional baseball teams have been journeying to Arizona for spring training for roughly a century, although at first it was just minor league teams playing exhibitions. The first major league spring training game in Arizona was held between the Tigers and Pirates in 1929.

Then in 1946, the Cleveland Indians and New York Giants became the first major league teams to move their spring training camps out to Arizona. The Indians held camp at venerable Hi Corbett Field in Tucson, while the Giants played at Phoenix Municipal Stadium. The Yankees joined the party for one year in 1951, giving fans a chance to see Joe DiMaggio and Mickey Mantle in their only year in pinstripes together.

The Cubs became the third major league team to permanently move spring training to Arizona in 1952, and the Orioles' arrival in 1954 gave rise to the official designation of "Cactus League." Teams continued to trickle in over the years, leading to an eight-team league, while competition among cities in Arizona and Florida led to an explosion of new and remodeled ballparks. By 2003, 12 teams were holding spring training in Arizona as the state was increasingly successful in convincing teams to move their camps from Florida.

The newest ballparks are Camelback Ranch in Phoenix and Goodyear Ballpark in Goodyear (opened in 2009), followed by the Salt River Fields at Talking Stick complex in Scottsdale, which opened in 2011. The Cactus League now comprises 15 teams playing in 10 stadiums, and they are located much closer together than the teams playing in the Grapefruit League in Florida. This makes it a lot easier for fans to come to Arizona and take in a bunch of games without driving all over the place.

"Play Ball! The Cactus League Experience" exhibit at the Arizona Museum for Youth in Mesa highlights the 100-year history of spring training in Arizona with historical film clips, interactive displays and vintage memorabilia.

Who can forget the time Randy Johnson accidentally killed a bird with a pitch during a spring training game at Kino Veterans Memorial Stadium on March 24, 2001? Said catcher Rod Barajas afterwards: "I'm sitting there waiting for it, and I'm expecting to catch the thing, and all you see is an explosion. It's crazy. There (are) still feathers down there."

All-Time Arizona Selections

At catcher, we gave strong consideration to Ron Hassey, who played in three World Series with the A's and compiled a stellar .323 postseason batting average. However, he never exceeded 390 at-bats in a season and was a below-average receiver. By comparison, Tom Pagnozzi made the All-Star team in 1992 and earned three Gold Glove awards for his defense, so he gets the selection. Perhaps someone can explain how Pagnozzi won the Gold Glove in 1994 even though he only appeared in 70 games that year. Evidently it's the same way Rafael Palmeiro won the AL Gold Glove in 1999 for being the best-fielding designated hitter.

First base goes to Shea Hillenbrand, even though he appeared in slightly more games at third base during his career. He did play more games at first than third for Toronto in 2005 when he was named to the All-Star team — his other All-Star nod came as a third baseman in 2002. Hillenbrand ended his career in 2007 with 1,014 hits, 108 home runs and a .284 average.

Willie Bobo gets the honorable mention nod at first base for his stellar eight years in the Negro Leagues. Bobo starred for the St. Louis Stars and Nashville Elite Giants from 1924–30 and was also a fixture in the California Winter League, averaging .310 in that high-caliber league. His premature death in 1931 came under unusual circumstances — he drank too much moonshine while on a bender with teammates in Tijuana, Mexico.

After six seasons, Ian Kinsler has demonstrated he is one of the top second basemen in baseball. He won two state titles playing at Canyon del Oro High School in Tucson. Drafted twice by his home-state Diamondbacks, Kinsler instead chose to play baseball at Arizona State. He transferred to the University of Missouri after Dustin Pedroia beat him out as the starting shortstop. Kinsler debuted with the Rangers in 2006 and is already Arizona's all-time home run leader. He had his first 30–30 season in 2009 and then did it again in 2011 after slugging 32 homers and stealing 30 bases. Although injuries curtailed his production in 2010, he rebounded to bat .444 with three home runs in the ALDS against the Rays.

Kinsler made baseball history on April 15, 2009, when he went 6-for-6 and hit for the cycle against the Orioles in a nine-inning game. It was the first time that had been accomplished in the majors since Farmer Weaver did it 119 years earlier. Kinsler's big day included two doubles, two singles, a home run and a triple, with five runs scored.

Moving on to third base, our selection is Jack Howell, who was confounded by left-handed pitchers throughout his career. His .179 lifetime average versus lefties caused his stint as a starting third baseman to be a short one. He topped out with 23 homers and 63 RBI in 1987, then later had more success playing in Japan.

The fiery Solly Hemus is Team Arizona's shortstop, as well as the manager. He led the National League in runs scored once and hit by pitch three times, and ended his career with an excellent .390 on-base percentage. Cardinals fans who were used to seeing Marty Marion play shortstop were not impressed when Hemus replaced him as starter in 1951, but Solly was a very productive player.

Hemus posted roughly a .500 winning percentage in his nearly three years as a player-manager, with his best finish being third. He managed to get ejected from eight games during his first year as St. Louis skipper, as he adopted a confrontational approach to players, opponents and umpires.

At the beginning of his career J.J. Hardy was often compared to Robin Yount — pretty heady stuff. Since getting off to a torrid start in the first half of 2007 — and making the All-Star team that year — he struggled to match that production and even found himself sent down to the minors in 2009. Hardy is a high-character guy who plays hard, so it was not surprising to see him bounce back with a strong year for the Orioles in 2011, smacking 30 home runs. He has good range, a strong throwing arm and has above-average power for a shortstop.

The outfield is led by the Dodgers star Andre Ethier, who is developing a reputation for clutch hitting. The Phoenix native compiled six walk-off hits (four of them homers) during the 2009 regular season to keep the Dodgers atop the division. He finished sixth in voting for the MVP Award in 2009 after hitting 31 homers with 106 RBI, but he has struggled to remain consistently productive. Ethier made the NL All-Star team in 2010 and 2011.

Billy Hatcher mans another outfield spot, and he was a real corker, literally. He served a 10-game suspension in 1987 for having a corked bat, which is probably why he broke out with a career-high total of 11 homers that year. Hatcher did hit a memorable home run for the Astros in the bottom of the fourteenth inning of Game 6 of the 1986 National League Championship Series. He also set a record for a four-game World Series for the Reds with a batting average of .750 in 1990.

Hank Leiber's first full season (1935) was outstanding — .331 average with 22 homers, 107 RBI and 203 hits. He even finished ahead of teammate Mel Ott in the MVP voting that year. Known for crowding the plate, Leiber had the misfortune to get hit in the head by pitches twice. Although he would go on to make three All-Star teams as an outfielder, his career never lived up to its initial promise.

The ace of the pitching staff is not hard to determine, since there is only one Arizona native who has won the Cy Young Award. Righty John Denny went 19–6 with a 2.37 ERA in 1983, which is the only year in his 13-year career he won more than 14 games. Coming off a 6–13 season in 1982, Denny won the Comeback Player of the Year in addition to the Cy Young Award in 1983. He was essentially a back-of-the-rotation starter who had one good year — heck, he didn't even make the All-Star team in 1983.

The top southpaw is Alex Kellner, who won 20 games as a rookie in 1949 and then never won more than 12 games the rest of his career. He walked nearly as many batters as he struck out in his career and finished with a losing record.

Our relief pitcher is Bobby Howry, who saved 28 games for the White Sox in 1999 and has relieved in 731 games during his 12-year career. He edges out Lerrin LaGrow, who saved 54 games in his career — mostly in a two-year period — but also spent two years as a starter for the Tigers. Another notable reliever is Jeremy Accardo, who posted 30 of his 38 career saves for the Blue Jays in 2007.

ARKANSAS

*Names in **bold** represent Major League selections by position, followed by honorable mentions. Negro Leagues players are in italics. City of birth is in parentheses.*

Catcher — **Sherm Lollar (Durham)**. Also: Earl Smith (Sheridan); Glenn Myatt (Argenta); Walter Schmidt (London)
First Base — **Tommy McCraw (Malvern)**. Also: *Goose Tatum* (El Dorado)
Second Base — **Aaron Ward (Booneville)**. Also: *Marshall Riddle* (Warren)
Third Base — **Brooks Robinson (Little Rock)**. Also: George Kell (Swifton); Randy Jackson (Little Rock); *Henry Spearman* (Arkadelphia)
Shortstop — **Arky Vaughan (Clifty)**. Also: Travis Jackson (Waldo); Don Kessinger (Forrest City)
Outfield — **Lou Brock (El Dorado)**
Outfield — **Willie Davis (Mineral Springs)**
Outfield — **Torii Hunter (Pine Bluff)**. Also: Rick Monday (Batesville); Kevin McReynolds (Little Rock); Wally Moon (Bay); Taylor Douthit (Little Rock); *Jelly Gardner* (Russellville); Lloyd Moseby (Portland); Alex Johnson (Helena); Floyd Robinson (Prescott); *Clyde Spearman* (Arkadelphia)
Designated Hitter — **Pat Burrell (Eureka Springs)**
Right Handed Starter — **Dizzy Dean (Lucas)**. Also: Lon Warneke (Mount Ida); Johnny Sain (Havana); *Booker McDaniels* (Blackwell); *Andy Porter* (Little Rock); A.J. Burnett (North Little Rock); Paul Dean (Lucas)
Left Handed Starter — **Preacher Roe (Ash Flat)**. Also: Cliff Lee (Benton); *Verdell Mathis* (Crawfordsville)
Relief Pitcher — **Ellis Kinder (Atkins)**. Also: Ryan Franklin (Fort Smith)
Manager — **Bobby Winkles (Tuckerman)**. Also: Don Kessinger (Forrest City)

The Names

Best Nickname: Lon "The Arkansas Hummingbird" Warneke
Other Nicknames: Grady "Butcher Boy" Adkins; Gene "Arkansas Traveler" Bearden; "Jittery Joe" Berry; "Pat the Bat" Burrell; Otis "Scat" Davis; Willie "3-Dog"

Davis; Henry "Pea Ridge" Day; Jay "Dizzy" Dean; Paul "Daffy" Dean; Raphael "Choo" Freeman; Floyd "Jelly" Gardner; Torii "Spider Man" Hunter; Travis "Stonewall" Jackson; Smead "Guinea" and "Smudge" Jolley; Everett "Skeeter" Kell; Ellis "Old Folks" Kinder; Lloyd "Shaker" Moseby; Andy "Pullman" Porter; Merle "Fancy Dan" Porter; Ray "Rabbit" Powell; Marshall "Jit" Riddle; Brooks "The Human Vacuum Cleaner" Robinson; Elwin "Preacher" Roe; Charles "Boss" Schmidt; Enoch "Ginger" Shinault; Hal "Cura" Smith; Earl "Oil" Smith; Clyde "Big Splo" Spearman; Henry "Little Splo" Spearman; Reece "Goose" Tatum; Joseph "Arky" Vaughan; David "Mutt" Williams; Edwin "Dib" Williams; Hank "Hooks" Wyse

Most Unusual Name: Smead Jolley, Brent Dlugach; Enoch Shinault

All-Time Leaders

Games: Brooks Robinson, 2896
Hits: Lou Brock, 3023
Batting Average: Arky Vaughan, .318
Home Runs: Brooks Robinson, 268
RBI: Brooks Robinson, 1357
Stolen Bases: Lou Brock, 938
Wins: Lon Warneke, 192
Strikeouts: A.J. Burnett, 1791 (still active)
Saves: Ryan Franklin, 84 (still active)
Future Star: Travis Wood (Little Rock)
Best Player: Arky Vaughan

Historic Baseball Places

Dickey-Stephens Park in North Little Rock — It was honored as Ballpark of the Year by baseballparks.com when it opened in 2007 as a replacement to Ray Winder Field. The stadium's name is a tribute to Bill Dickey (who grew up in Arkansas) and his brother Skeeter Dickey (who was born in Arkansas and also played in the majors), as well as members of Stephens family, who owned an investment firm where both Dickeys worked after baseball.

Arvest Ballpark in Springdale — Took the Ballpark of the Year designation from Dickey-Stephens when it opened in 2008. This conservation-oriented park features a gorgeous light limestone that gives the exterior a look that is different from all the other parks being built.

Notable Achievements

Sherm Lollar won the first Gold Glove for catchers in 1957.
Rick Monday was the top pick in the first-ever MLB draft in 1965.
George Kell holds the record for fewest strikeouts by a batting champion with 13 in 1949.
Gene Stephens (Gravette) became the only player in the twentieth century to have three hits in one inning when he accomplished that feat in the seventh inning on June 18, 1953.
Kevin McReynolds holds the record for most stolen bases in a season without getting caught — 21 in 1988.
Orville Armbrust (Beirne) recorded his only big-league win in Babe Ruth's last game as a Yankee on September 30, 1934. It would be Armbrust's third and last appearance in the majors.
Lou Brock was the fourth and last player to hit the ball out in center field at the Polo Grounds, which was 483 feet from home. He did it on June 18, 1962, one day after Hank Aaron became the third player to do it.
Arky Vaughan's .385 average in 1935 is the second-highest by a shortstop in the twentieth century after Luke Appling's .388 in 1936.
Sammy and Solly Drake (Little Rock) were the first African American brothers to play in the major leagues in the twentieth century.

Spring Training Tradition Catches on at Hot Springs

Catcher Emmett Rogers became the first Arkansas-born player to reach the majors when he played for the Toledo Maumees of the American Association on April 19, 1890. He would be the only player from the state to appear in a nineteenth-century game.

Arkansas' enduring baseball tradition dates back to the formation of the Little Rock Travelers in 1895. Native son Travis Jackson is one of several Hall of Famers who played at one point for the team, which won exhibition games in 1937 against the Yankees and Lou Gehrig and the Indians and Bob Feller. Hall of Famer Bill Dickey played for the team in 1925, which is why the team's new stadium is named Dickey-Stephens Park. The team became so engrained in the culture of the state that it changed its name to the Arkansas Travelers in 1957. These days, special visitors to the state are given proclamations honoring them as "Arkansas Travelers."

Sadly, baseball fans can no longer experience Ray Winder Field in Little Rock, a classic old-time ballpark that dated back to 1932. The Arkansas Travelers played their last game there in 2006 and the decision was eventually made to convert the space to a parking lot. Known as "The Fenway of the Minors," Ray Winder Field once showcased stars such as Babe Ruth, Lou Gehrig and Jackie Robinson in exhibition games.

Arkansas does have another important tie to major league baseball — it was the site of one of the earliest spring training camps in 1886. Chicago White Stockings manager Cap Anson brought his team to Hot Springs as a way of sweating the toxins out of his hard-partying players' bodies. In his book, *Boiling Out at the Springs*, Don Duren points out that it was actually owner Al Spalding's idea, since he thought his team drank too much, and that Anson just happened to go agree with the plan. The White Stockings went 90–34 and won the pennant that season, so the plan worked.

Other teams started coming to Hot Springs starting with the Pirates in 1901, long before teams began flocking to Florida en masse. While manager of the Cleveland Naps, Nap Lajoie started the tradition of having pitchers and catchers report early. He would have his battery mates come 15 days early to Hot Springs to detox and then they would rejoin their teammates at spring training elsewhere.

Eight major league teams have held spring training in Hot Springs: Pirates (1901–13, 1920–23); Reds (1910–11); Cubs (1909–10); Brooklyn Robins (1910–12, 1917–18); St. Louis Browns (1911); Phillies (1912); Tigers (1908) and Red Sox (1909–10, 1912–18, 1920–23). Little Rock was the spring training home of the Red Sox in 1907 and 1908 and the St. Louis Cardinals in 1909–10. In other cases, veteran players made their way to Hot Springs to get into shape by soaking in the hot waters for a bit before joining their teams in other locales for formal spring training.

In 1892, Buck Ewing had tried everything to rehab his injured throwing arm and nothing seemed to work. After soaking in the hot baths at Hot Springs for a few days he tested his arm and discovered he was pain-free.

Plans are under way in Hot Springs to install a series of wooden markers around town to commemorate the site of Whittington Park, where much of the spring training action took place, as well as to recognize the many well-known players who made appearances there such as Babe Ruth, Ty Cobb, Tris Speaker and Rogers Hornsby. Ruth spent as much time playing golf and attending races as playing baseball, while Cy Young came to view Hot Springs as his second home.

Only two natives of Hot Springs have made it to the majors: Emmett Rogers (1890) and Jack McMahan (1956) each played only one season. Little Rock has sent 20 players to the big leagues including Hall of Famer Brooks Robinson, Randy Jackson, Taylor Douthit and Kevin McReynolds. Brooks learned the finer points of fielding at Lamar Porter Field, which was built as a Works Progress Administration project and opened in 1937. It is on the National Register of Historic Places.

A handful of obscure players from Arkansas deserve mention for their cup-of-coffee careers. Otis "Scat" Davis, a native of Charleston, only played in one game and it was as a pinch-runner. He scored a run for the Brooklyn Dodgers on April 22, 1946. That's a little better than Leroy Reames of Pine Bluff, who struck out in his only major league at-bat for the Phillies in 1969. Then there's Little Rock's Joe Brown, who debuted for the White Sox on May 17, 1927, pitching to three batters. Two got hits, the other walked and all three ended up scoring. Brown would never appear in another major league game, but he resides in the special category of players whose ERA is "infinity."

Terry Felton sure knew the agony of defeat. He posted an 0–3 record for the Twins in 1980 sandwiched around two seasons with no decisions, but then came the career-ending finale. He went 0–13 in 1982, leaving him with a career record of 0–16. Felton holds the dubious records of most losses without a win in a career

The Boston Red Sox, shown in 1912, are one of many teams that traveled to Hot Springs for formal and informal spring training in the early part of the century (Library of Congress, Prints & Photographs Division, LC-DIG-ggbain-11551).

and most consecutive losses to start a career. The righty also did not post a winning record over the course of eight years in the minors. On the positive side, the Texarkana native managed to appear in 39 other games in the majors without suffering a loss and only surrendered 123 hits in 138 career innings.

Felton's agony still does not compare to that of Charles "Boss" Schmidt. The Tigers catcher became the only player to make the last out in two World Series — and he did it in consecutive years. Schmidt, whose brother Walter also caught in the big leagues, popped up to shortstop to end the 1907 World Series and grounded out to end the 1908 World Series. He probably had mixed emotions about the Tigers returning to the World Series in 1909, but luck was on his side this time. Schmidt was in the on-deck circle when Tom Jones made the final out as the Tigers lost their third straight Series.

All-Time Arkansas Selections

A number of great players were born in Arkansas, including six who made it into the Hall of Fame. In fact, two Hall of Fame players did not make the All-Time Arkansas Team because they were edged out by other Hall of Famers.

At catcher, we have Sherm Lollar, who won three Gold Gloves in the 1950s and led the league in fielding five times. He didn't hit much for average but rarely struck out and had some pop in his bat (155 career home runs). Playing the bulk of his career in spacious Comiskey Field undoubtedly impacted his power numbers. Once Lollar established himself with the White Sox (after starting his career behind Jim Hegan with the Indians and Yogi Berra with the Yankees) he went on to be named to seven All-Star teams, and in 1959 he was instrumental in helping the White Sox win their first pennant since the Black Sox scandal 40 years earlier. He finished his career in 1963 with the highest career fielding percentage (.992) for a catcher.

Earl "Oil" Smith is a worthy backup, particularly since he platooned for much of his 12-year career. The most games he caught in one season was 98, but he batted over .300 five times and finished with a career average of .303. He also made it to five World Series with three different teams — New York Giants, Pittsburgh and St. Louis — winning three championships. Other Arkansas-born catchers of note are Hal Smith (two-time All-Star) and Glenn Myatt, who played 16 seasons and batted .342 for the Indians in 1924.

First base is a weak position for Arkansas, and it was tempting to move Wally Moon there, even though he played only 136 games at first in his career. Tommy McCraw had an undistinguished career playing for four teams over 13 seasons. His career highs were 11 home runs and 48 RBI and his lifetime average was .246, which is pretty weak for what is supposed to be a power position. He did hit three home runs in a game in 1967. Despite his mediocre hitting statistics, McCraw would go on to spend more than 20 years in the majors as a hitting coach.

Another less appealing option at first base is Reece "Goose" Tatum, who achieved greater fame with the Harlem Globetrotters. Goose carried over his clowning around to the diamond, entertaining fans before and during games, but he used his lanky 6-foot-6 frame to good advantage at first. Tatum started his career with the Birmingham Black Barons in 1941 and fittingly played for the Indianapolis Clowns from 1946–49, making the East-West All-Star Game in 1947. The Goose was much better at basketball than baseball, so McCraw holds onto the first base spot.

At second base, Aaron Ward was a key contributor for the Yankees from 1917 through 1926. He batted .306 as they won the pennant in 1921 and hit .417 with 10 hits to help the Yankees defeat the Giants for the World Series title in 1923. Ward led AL second basemen in fielding percentage in 1923. He retired with 966 hits and a .268 average.

Few states can match the quality of the third basemen from Arkansas. George Kell and Brooks Robinson have a lot of interesting parallels in their careers, in addition to both being born in Arkansas. Both were named to the All-Star team as a third baseman from the Orioles. Both were named to the Hall of Fame in 1983. Kell even spent the last season of his career (1957) mentoring Robinson on how to play third base for the Orioles. And Kell's lifetime fielding percentage as a third baseman (.969) is not far behind Robinson's (.971).

Robinson has a big edge in Gold Gloves — 16 to 0 — because the award didn't exist until Kell's last season. Brooks was AL MVP in 1964 and was named to 15 consecutive All-Star teams compared to 10 total for Kell. Brooks hit 268 home runs playing in a pitcher's park compared to just 78 homers by Kell. And Robinson ended his career with 2,848 hits, 794 more than Kell. While Brooks played his whole career with the Orioles, Kell played for five teams. Not only does Robinson hold nearly every lifetime fielding record for third basemen — most games (2,870), most putouts (2,697), most assists (6,205), most chances (8,902) and most double plays (618) — he is the leader by a wide margin in most categories.

Robinson played in four World Series, winning two and being named MVP of the 1970 Series as much for the fielding exhibition he put on as his nine hits and two homers. He robbed Johnny Bench of three hits in the Series, causing the great catcher to comment, "I hope we can come back and play the Orioles next year. I also hope Brooks Robinson has retired by then."

Kell led A.L. third basemen in fielding percentage seven times, in double plays six times, in assists four times and putouts twice. He was not nicknamed "The Human Vacuum Cleaner" like Robinson, but the man could field. He worked hard to be good at all facets of the game, leading Red Rolfe to describe Kell this way: "He's a seven-day-a-week player."

Kell wasn't a slugger, but he finished with a .306 lifetime average — 39 points higher than Brooks. In 1949, Kell whiffed just 13 times on the way to preventing Ted Williams from winning the Triple Crown, edging him out .3429 to .3427 to become the first third baseman to win a batting championship in either league since 1912. He ended up batting over .300 nine times, eight consecutive. It's not Kell's fault he played for some crappy teams and never made it to the postseason.

One play in 1948 seemed to define Kell. Joe DiMaggio hit a hard shot right at Kell that took a bad hop and smacked him right in the face, breaking his jaw. Unfazed, he picked up the ball and threw out DiMaggio at first.

It is not far-fetched to say that the best third baseman in the American League for four consecutive decades came from Arkansas — Kell in the 1940s and 1950s and Robinson in the 1960s and 1970s. And let's not forget Little Rock native Randy Jackson, who made the N.L. All-Star team playing third base for the Cubs in 1954 and 1955.

Shortstop is another strong position, with three worthy candidates: Joseph "Arky" Vaughan, Travis Jackson and Don Kessinger. Vaughan earns bonus points for Team Arkansas because his nickname was a reference to his state of birth. Bill James ranks him as the second-best shortstop of all time — behind only Honus Wagner. A nine-time All-Star, Vaughan became the starting shortstop for the Pirates at the age of 20 and benefited from being tutored by Wagner, who was a Pirates coach. Wagner was the Pirates shortstop from 1900–17 and Vaughan from 1932–41, so the team's shortstop spot was in great hands for the better part of three decades.

Vaughan was a gifted hitter who batted over .300 his first 10 seasons and won the NL batting crown in 1935 with a .385 average — he was only 23. He wasn't blessed with blazing speed yet hit 10 or more triples eight times and led the league in that category three times.

Vaughan left the game at the age of 31 and sat out three years of his prime because he loathed Dodgers manager Leo Durocher. He returned to spend two final years as a part-time player for the Dodgers before retiring for good in 1948. Despite his stellar record, Vaughan never received much Hall support from the baseball writers. He was eventually voted in by the Veterans Committee in 1985, 37 years after his career ended and 33 years after he drowned in a boating accident at the age of 40.

For an interesting comparison, let's check out Derek Jeter's stats through 2007 and then compare to Vaughan's career stats, which gives both of them 12 seasons as a regular.

	G	R	H	2b	3b	HR	RBI	AVE	SLG
Vaughan	1817	1173	2103	356	128	96	926	.318	.453
Jeter	1835	1379	2356	386	54	195	933	.317	.462

It's a shame there is not room in the lineup for Jackson, because Hall of Famers don't grow on trees. Jackson had great range and a strong arm at short and he was also an accomplished batter, ending up with a lifetime .291 average. Sportswriter Red Smith called him the greatest shortstop to ever play in New York.

"Stonewall" Jackson batted over .300 six times and led the NL in fielding percentage twice. Jackson played on four Giants teams that made it to the World Series, although he batted just .149 in 67 lifetime at-bats in the Series. He was elected to the Hall of Fame in 1982, five years before he died.

Kessinger was a great fielder and a mediocre hitter. He made six All-Star teams and earned two Gold Gloves, but ended up with a .252 lifetime average. Many Cubs fans blame his late-season slump for the team's collapse in 1969. Maybe he started drinking goat milk or something. Give the guy a break — any team expecting Don Kessinger's bat to lead them to a championship is asking for disappointment.

On to the outfield, where Hall of Famer Lou Brock and his 938 stolen bases and 3,023 hits are a lock. Although not known for his power, Brock became the first player to hit 20 homers and steal 50 bases in 1967. He was perhaps the first player to religiously study film of opposing pitchers so he could learn how to steal against their moves. A six-time All-Star, Brock owned the career record for stolen bases until Rickey Henderson shattered that mark. He stole 50 or mores bases in 12 straight seasons.

Brock was on top of his game when it counted, as he holds the World Series record for highest batting average (.391) for players with at least 65 plate appearances. Brock was also the first player to bat in a regular season major league game in Canada, which happened on April 14, 1969 in Montreal.

The second outfield spot is in good hands with Torii Hunter, a four-time All-Star. He won nine consecutive Gold Gloves (2001–2009) and his acrobatic catches in center field have been a staple on ESPN highlight shows, which is how he earned the nickname "Spider Man." Blessed with good speed and power in addition to his defensive prowess, Hunter has always been a high-character leader on his teams. He passed the 1,000 RBI mark in 2011 and ended the year with 281 career home runs.

Actually, there may be an even better defensive center fielder from Arkansas — Willie Davis. He had the unenviable task of following Duke Snider in center field for the Dodgers, facing extra scrutiny because he was a local star signed out of Roosevelt High. Davis was an outstanding fielder who won three Gold Gloves and played on two All-Star teams, but his career numbers don't accurately reflect his prodigious talent. He hit 182 homers, which is the result of playing most of his career in a pitcher's park rather than a lack of power. He never drove in 100 runs and only scored over 100 runs once. However, Davis was one of the fastest players of his era, stealing 398 bases and leading the NL in triples twice. His nickname, "3-Dog," reflected both his uniform number and the fact he hit a lot of triples. When he retired in 1979 only two players had played more games in center field than his 2,237.

Davis is the Dodgers' franchise leader in hits, runs and triples, but a lasting memory for many Dodgers fans is when he committed three errors in one inning in Game 2 of the 1966 World Series. It would prove to be Sandy Koufax's last game in the majors.

Davis edged out Wally Moon, who hit 142 homers, batted .289 and was named to two All-Star teams. He was voted Rookie of the Year for the Cardinals in 1954, despite earning the ire of fans who were upset Country Slaughter was traded to make room for him in the lineup. Still, Moon was an above-average outfielder who won a Gold Glove in 1960 and was a key player on the Dodgers' 1959 championship team.

Rick Monday deserves consideration not only for hitting 241 home runs and making two All-Star teams, but also for one of the greatest saves in baseball history when he rescued the U.S. flag from two war protesters who were getting ready to burn it in the outfield during a game in 1976. What a great moment in baseball history, all thanks to the fast actions of this former Marine reserve.

Jelly Gardner was a Negro Leagues star, serving as a leadoff sparkplug for Rube Foster's Chicago American Giants in the 1920s. Blessed with blazing speed and superb defensive ability, Gardner played on teams that won four pennants and one Black World Series.

Other notable outfielders include Alex Johnson, who won a batting crown in 1970, Taylor Douthit, a defensive whiz who set an AL record for center fielders with 547 putouts in 1928, and Smead Jolley, one of the worst-fielding outfielders in history. Jolley led various minor leagues in batting six times and homers twice, but his major league career was brief because he was a butcher in the field. He committed 44 errors in 413 games in the outfield. Too bad there was no designated hitter during his career (1920s and '30s), because anyone who accumulates 3,043 hits and 336 homers with a .367 average in the minors clearly knows how to hit. Jolley collected an amazing 309 hits with a .404 average playing for the San Francisco Seals in 1928, then followed up with 314 hits the next season.

The DH spot goes to Pat Burrell, a terrible fielder who had appeared in just 159 games at DH through 2011 because he had largely played in the National League. Burrell, who won World Series rings with the Phillies in 2008 and Giants in 2010, entered the 2012 season with 292 homers.

Few pitchers have dominated like Dizzy Dean did from 1933 through 1936. He won 102 games in that four-year stretch, winning the MVP award in 1934 and finishing second the next two years. His 30–7 record in 1934 marks the last time a National League pitcher has won 30 games. Dizzy struck out 17 batters in a game in 1933, which was a record at the time, and he led the NL in strikeouts four straight seasons. Not only did the right-hander start 34 games with 28 complete games in 1936, he also finished 17 games out of the bullpen.

Pitching with an injured toe in 1937 caused Dizzy to blow out his arm, and he was never the same pitcher again. Still, despite his relatively short career he was elected to the Hall of Fame in 1953. His induction speech contained this self-deprecating line: "The Good Lord was good to me. He gave me a strong body, a good right arm and a weak mind."

Dizzy was an entertainer as much as an athlete, and his folksy mannerisms and constant quips made him a fan favorite. Stories are still being told about him, some of them even true. Such as the time he asked a batter, "Son, what kind of pitch would you like to miss?"

As teammate Pepper Martin described him, "When ol' Diz was out there pitching it was more than just another ball game. It was a regular three-ring circus and everybody was wide awake and enjoying being alive."

Dizzy's younger brother, Paul "Daffy" Dean, didn't have the oversized personality of his brother, nor was he his equal as a pitcher. Paul, who hated being called "Daffy," had a promising start to his career in 1934, pitching a no-hitter and winning 19 games as the "Gashouse Gang" Cardinals won the World Series that year. The two Dean brothers combined for 49 victories during the regular season and all four wins in the World Series. Daffy won 19 games again the next year before injuries derailed his promising career. "I ain't no Dizzy," he once confessed. "But no one else is neither."

Lonnie Warneke's career ran concurrent to Dizzy Dean's in the National League, and "The Arkansas Hummingbird" managed to win 42 more games than Dean. Warneke outpitched Dizzy in 1932, arguably did so again in 1933 and was not far behind in 1934 and 1935. The five-time All-Star was one of the best fielding pitchers of his generation, committing only eight errors in his career. He didn't have Dean's talent for self-promotion, but he was close to his equal as a pitcher.

Johnny Sain teamed up with Warren Spahn to give the Boston Braves the major's best one-two punch from 1946–51. In 1948, the duo went 8–0 over a 12-day stretch toward the end of the season, leading the Braves to the pennant and immortalizing them with the line "Spahn and Sain and two days of rain." Spahn finished second to Stan Musial for NL MVP in 1948. He won 20 games four times and finished his career with 139 victories, a 3.49 ERA and 140 complete games. He later enjoyed success as a relief pitcher for the Yankees, leading the American League with 39 games finished in 1954.

The lefty starter for the All-Time Arkansas Team is Preacher Roe, who was called "a great pitcher, a great competitor" by teammate Jackie Robinson. Preacher went 22–3 for the 1951 Dodgers and was a five-time All-Star who pitched in three World Series. He shut out the Yankees in the 1949 World Series, accounting for the only game the Dodgers won that Series. Preacher once said, "I've got three pitches: my change, my change off my change, and my change off my change off my change." Of course later in his career, he admitted his out pitch was a spitball. Roe finished with a 127–84 record and 116 ERA+.

Preacher narrowly edges out Cliff Lee, whose pitching has been transformed since he was shipped to the minors for a stretch in 2007. He returned and has been pitching brilliantly since, starting with his Cy Young season of 2008 when he went 22–3 and led the league with a 2.54 ERA for an Indians team that finished .500. Bounced from the Indians to the Phillies to the Mariners to the Rangers and then back to the Phillies in a span of 17 months, Lee helped pitch the Phillies and Rangers to consecutive World Series. After dominating the Yankees in the 2010 ALCS with a 13-strikeout performance, Lee had an astounding postseason record of 7–0 with a 1.26 ERA. That's the rarified air occupied by Sandy Koufax, Bob Gibson and Curt Schilling. His performance slipped in the 2010 World Series against the Giants, but Lee has proved himself as a big-game pitcher.

Lee has turned into a strike-throwing machine since turning around his career. In his short stint with the Mariners in 2010, Lee recorded an amazing SO/BB ratio of 14.83 — 89 strikeouts with just six walks. He ended up with a 10.28 SO/BB rate for the year, which is the second best all-time behind Bret Saberhagen's 11.00 in the strike-shortened 1994 season. He ended up with 10 more starts than walks for the year, then followed up with a lights-out year for the Phillies in 2011 with six shutouts and a career-high 238 strikeouts.

Another notable lefty is Verdell Mathis, one of the premier left-handed pitchers in the Negro Leagues in the 1940s while hurling for the Memphis Red Sox. Mathis, who was slight of build but fearless on the mound, had a deceptive pick-off move and excellent control. He and Satchel Paige are the only pitchers to win two East-West All-Star games.

The Arkansas bullpen is led by Ellis Kinder, who was nearly 32 when he made his debut for the St. Louis Browns in 1946. He appeared in 362 games in relief between 1946 and 1957, leading the AL in games finished three times. He won 23 games for the Red Sox in 1949, leading the AL in shutouts and winning percentage while starting 30 games and coming out of the bullpen 13 times. His 69 appearances in 1953 were an American League record at the time.

Ryan Franklin, who was mediocre as a starter for the Mariners early in his career and then found himself suspended for steroids in 2005, reinvented himself as a reliever in 2007. He collected 17 saves for the Cardinals in 2008 and then blossomed into an All-Star in 2009 on the way to posting 38 saves. He followed up with 27 more the next season before enduring an ugly season in 2011 that led to his release from the Cardinals. His 84 career saves through 2011 are the most in Arkansas history.

For manager, it's possible to select someone who won three World Series ... but Bobby Winkles won those in college. He led Arizona State to national titles in 1965, 1967 and 1969, coaching future big leaguers such as Reggie Jackson, Rick Monday and Sal Bando. Winkles managed one full season and three partial seasons for the Angels and A's, winning just 44 percent of his games. The only other Arkansas native who managed in the major leagues is Don Kessinger, who went 46–60 as a player-manager for the White Sox in 1979.

CALIFORNIA

*Names in **bold** represent Major League selections by position, followed by honorable mentions. City of birth is in parentheses.*

Catcher — Gary Carter (Culver City). Also: Ernie Lombardi (Oakland); Bob Boone (SD); Jason Kendall (SD); Del Crandall (Ontario); Earl Battey (LA); Harry Danning (LA); Gus Triandos (SF); Mike Liberthal (Glendale); Don Slaught (Long Beach); Alan Ashby (Long Beach); Joe Ferguson (SF); Brian Harper (LA); Chief Meyers (Riverside)

First Base — Eddie Murray (LA). Also: Mark McGwire (Pomona); Keith Hernandez (SF); Frank Chance (Fresno); Jason Giambi (West Covina); Dolph Camilli (SF); Bob Watson (LA); George Kelly (SF); Cecil Fielder (LA); Derrek Lee (Sacramento); Hal Chase (Los Gatos); Bill Buckner (Vallejo); Gus Suhr (SF); Jim Gentile (SF); J.T. Snow (Long Beach); Jason Thompson (Hollywood); Alvin Davis (Riverside); Gregg Jefferies (Burlingame); Adrian Gonzalez (SD); Prince Fielder (Ontario)

Second Base — Jeff Kent (Bellflower). Also: Joe Gordon (LA); Bobby Doerr (LA); Tony Lazzeri (SF); Chase Utley (Pasadena); Gil McDougald (SF); Steve Sax (Sacramento); Bret Boone (El Cajon); Jerry Priddy (LA); Mark Loretta (Santa Monica); Adam Kennedy (Riverside); Dustin Pedroia (Woodland)

Third Base — Darrell Evans (Pasadena). Also: Stan Hack (Sacramento); Graig Nettles (SD); Bob Elliott (SF); Robin Ventura (Santa Maria); Matt Williams (Bishop); Troy Glaus (Tarzana); Ken Caminiti (Hanford); Tim Wallach (Huntington Park); Terry Pendleton (LA); Doug DeCinces (Burbank); Carney Lansford (San Jose); Eric Chavez (LA); Todd Zeile (Van Nuys); Bob Bailey (Long Beach); Jeff Cirillo (Pasadena); Willie Kamm (SF); Hubie Brooks (LA); Ray Boone (SD); Ken McMullen (Oxnard)

Shortstop — Joe Cronin (SF). Also: Alan Trammell (Garden Grove); Nomar Garciaparra (Whittier); Jim Fregosi (SF); Jimmy Rollins (Oakland); Michael Young (Covina); Eddie Joost (SF); Larry Bowa (Sacramento); Roy Smalley (LA); Frankie Crosetti (SF); Rick Burleson (Lynwood); Chris Speier (Alameda); Lyn Lary (Armona); Bud Harrelson (Niles); Red Kress (Columbia); Royce Clayton (Burbank)

Outfield — Ted Williams (SD)
Outfield — Joe DiMaggio (Martinez)
Outfield — Barry Bonds (Riverside)
Also (Left Field): Roy White (LA); Augie Galan (Berkeley); Garret Anderson (LA); Chick Hafey (Berkeley);

Gary Matthews, Sr. (San Fernando); Dusty Baker (Riverside); Lefty O'Doul (SF); Kevin Mitchell (SD); Joe Rudi (Modesto); Bob Meusel (San Jose); Duffy Lewis (SF); Irish Meusel (Oakland); Ryan Klesko (Westminster)

Also (Center Field): Duke Snider (LA); Jim Edmonds (Fullerton); Brett Butler (LA); Dom DiMaggio (SF); Eric Davis (LA); Willie McGee (SF); Lenny Dykstra (Santa Ana); Ray Lankford (LA); Bill Lange (SF); Sam Chapman (Tiburon)

Also (Right Field): Tony Gwynn (LA); Harry Heilmann (SF); Bobby Bonds (Riverside); Dwight Evans (Santa Monica); Gavvy Cravath (Escondido); Harry Hooper (Bell Station); Darryl Strawberry (LA); Brian Giles (El Cajon); Jermaine Dye (Oakland); George Hendrick (LA); Jackie Jensen (SF); Tim Salmon (Long Beach); Jeff Burroughs (Long Beach); Jeromy Burnitz (Westminster); Claudell Washington (LA); Frank Demaree (Winters)

Designated Hitter — Brian Downing (LA). Also: Mike Sweeney (Orange); Greg Vaughn (Sacramento); Deron Johnson (SD)

Right Handed Starter — Tom Seaver (Fresno). Also: Don Drysdale (Van Nuys); Bob Lemon (San Bernardino); Dave Stieb (Santa Ana); Kevin Appier (Lancaster); Mike Garcia (San Gabriel); Jim Maloney (Fresno); Ray Kremer (Oakland); Dave Stewart (Oakland); Jim Lonborg (Santa Maria); Larry Dierker (Hollywood); Dock Ellis (LA); Darryl Kile (Garden Grove); Jack McDowell (Van Nuys); Bob Forsch (Sacramento); Mike Scott (Santa Monica); Gary Nolan (Herlong); Orval Overall (Farmersville); Tiny Bonham (Ione); Monte Pearson (Oakland); Tom Candiotti (Walnut Creek)

Left Handed Starter — Randy Johnson (Walnut Creek). Also: Lefty Gomez (Rodeo); David Wells (Torrance); CC Sabathia (Vallejo); Mark Langston (SD); Larry French (Visalia); Dutch Ruether (Alameda); Mike McCormick (Pasadena); Scott McGregor (Inglewood); Bill Lee (Burbank)

Relief Pitcher — Trevor Hoffman (Bellflower). Also: Dennis Eckersley (Oakland); Dan Quisenberry (Santa Monica); John Wetteland (San Mateo); Troy Percival (Fontana); Jesse Orosco (Santa Barbara), Doug Jones (Covina); Tug McGraw (Martinez); Dave Righetti (San Jose); Todd Worrell (Arcadia); Rod Beck (Burbank); Rick Aguilera (San Gabriel); Robb Nen (San Pedro); Al Hrabosky (Oakland); Dave Smith (Richmond); Brad Lidge (Sacramento); Eddie Guardado (Stockton); Brian Fuentes (Merced); Mitch Williams (Santa Ana); Bobby Jenks (Mission Hills); Jim Brewer (Merced)

Manager — Frank Chance (Fresno). Also: Billy Martin (Berkeley); Dusty Baker (Riverside); Joe Cronin (SF); Jim Fregosi (SF); Bill Rigney (Alameda)

The Names

Best Nickname: Frank "Toys in the Attic" Bertaina
Other Nicknames: Gary "Hard Rock" Allenson; Mack "Shooty" Babbit; Bob "Beetle" Bailey; Johnnie "Dusty" Baker; Clyde "Jersey" Beck; Carroll "Footsie" Belardi; Ewell "The Whip" Blackwell; Frank "Ping" Bodie; Ray "Ike" Boone; Stanley "Frenchy" Bordagaray; Larry "Gnat" Bowa; Ryan "The Hebrew Hammer" Braun; William "California" Brown; Rick "Rooster" Burleson; Eric "Captain America," "Pigpen," "Crash Test Dummy" and "Flipper" Byrnes; George "Ug" Caster; Bill "Cuffs" Caudill; Frank "The Peerless Leader" Chance; "Prince Hal" Chase; Walter "Cuckoo" and "Seacap" Christensen; "Coaster Joe" Connolly; "Cactus Gavvy" Cravath; Covelli "Coco" Crisp; Clay "Dimples" Dalrymple; Harry "The Horse" Danning; Joseph "Oats" Demaestri; Joe "The Yankee Clipper" and Joltin' Joe" DiMaggio; Brian "The Incredible Hulk" Downing; Lenny "Nails" Dykstra; Bob "Mr. Team" Elliott; Darrell "Howdy Doody" Evans; Dwight "Dewey" Evans; Froilan "Nanny" Fernandez; Cecil "Big Daddy" Fielder; Tim "Crazy Horse" Foli; Frank "The Great Gabbo" Gabler; "Dirty Al" Gallagher; Mike "Big Bear" Garcia; Nomar "The Whittier Whip" Garciaparra; "Diamond Jim" Gentile; Joe "Flash" Gordon; Vernon "Lefty" and "Goofy" Gomez; "Everyday Eddie" Guardado; "Smiling Stan" Hack; Charles "Chick" Hafey; Charley "Sea Lion" Hall; Cole "Hollywood" Hamels; Nelson "Chicken" Hawks; Harry "Slug" Heilmann; Steve "Tennis Ball Head" and "Orbit" Hovley; Al "The Mad Hungarian" Hrabosky; Howard "Hondo" Johnson; Randy "The Big Unit" Johnson; John "Spider" Jorgensen; George "High Pockets" Kelly; Eddie "Scrap Iron" Kenna; Ray "Wiz" Kremer; Mike "Buffy" LaCoss; Bill "Little Eva" Lange; "Broadway" Lyn Lary; Attilio "Cookie" Lavagetto; "Poosh 'Em Up" Tony Lazzeri; Bill "Spaceman" Lee; Ernie "Schnozz" Lombardi; Harry "Peanuts" Lowrey; Billy "The Kid" Martin; Gary "Sarge" Matthews; William "Buckshot" May; John "Windy" McCall; Frank "Tug" McGraw; Mark "Big Mac" McGwire; Lloyd "Citation" Merriman; Kevin "Boogie Bear" and "World" Mitchell; Fenton "Muscles" Mole; Nyjer "Tony Plush" Morgan; Don "The Sphinx" and "Ears" Mossi; Leslie "Little Nemo" Munns; Graig "Puff" Nettles; Frank "Dink" O'Brien; Lowell "Lulu" Palmer; Monte "Hoot" Pearson; Dustin "Laser Show" Pedroia; "Sailor" Bill Posedel; Bill "The Cricket" Rigney; Leon "Bip" Roberts; Marc "Scrabble" Rzepczynski; "Kingfish" Tim Salmon; Ralph "Blackie" Schwamb; "Tom Terrific" Seaver; Dick "Mortimer Snerd" Selma; Don "Sluggo" Slaught; Edwin "The Duke of Flatbush" Snider; Dave "Smoke" Stewart; Dick "Dr. Strangeglove" Stuart; Ron "Little General" Theobald; Dick "Dirt" Tidrow; Jim "Abba Dabba" Tobin; Bernard "Frenchy" Uhalt; Lee "Captain Midnight" Walls; Bob "Bull" Watson; David "Boomer" Wells; Matt "Carson Crusher" Williams; Mitch "Wild Thing" Williams; Ted "The Splendid Splinter," "Teddy Ballgame" and "Thumper" Williams; Dontrelle "D Train" Willis; George "Icehouse" Wilson; Elwood "Kettle" Wirts; Al "A-1" Wright; Frank "Noodles" Zupo

Most Unusual Name: Marc Rzepczynski; Biff Pocoroba; Garth Iorg; Orval Overall

All-Time Leaders

Games: Eddie Murray, 3026
Hits: Eddie Murray, 3255
Batting Average: Lefty O'Doul, .349
Home Runs: Barry Bonds, 762
RBI: Barry Bonds, 1996
Stolen Bases: Brett Butler, 558
Wins: Tom Seaver, 311
Strikeouts: Randy Johnson, 4875
Saves: Trevor Hoffman, 601
Future Stars: Stephen Strasburg (SD); Mike Stanton (Sherman Oaks); James Darnell (Danville); Gerrit Cole (Newport Beach)
Best Player: Joe DiMaggio

Historic Baseball Places

Joe DiMaggio gravesite in Colma — The Yankee Clipper's grave marker in Holy Cross Cemetery says it all: "Grace, Dignity and Elegance Personified." And no, Marilyn Monroe is not buried beside him.

Lefty O'Doul's Restaurant in San Francisco — O'Doul opened his famous restaurant and bar in 1958, foreseeing that patrons would want to rub elbows with sports stars.

Dodger Stadium in Los Angeles — Fenway and Wrigley are ancient, but Dodger Stadium is now the third-oldest major league stadium. Outside the stadium are murals of former Dodgers greats and perhaps the surrounding Elysian hills should have the ballpark viewed as the West Coast version of the historic Elysian Fields.

AT&T Park in San Francisco — Barry Bonds is no longer launching rocket shots into McCovey Cove, but you can still see the McCovey statue beside the water. A statue and tribute to the Say Hey Kid stands by the entrance to the stadium in Willie Mays Plaza, and statues of Marichal and Cepeda are also on display.

San Diego Hall of Champions Sports Museum in San Diego — Located in the Federal Building in Balboa Park, the museum outlines the history of baseball in the area. It highlights the accomplishments of Padres stars such as Tony Gwynn, Dave Winfield, Goose Gossage, Rollie Fingers and Graig Nettles as well as native sons who went on to fame such as the Boone family, Ted Williams and Don Larsen.

Petco Park in San Diego — New park of the Padres opened in 2004 next to the historic Gaslamp Quarter and is where home runs go to die. Features a statue of "Mr. Padre," Tony Gwynn.

Sports Museum of Los Angeles — The country's most amazing sports museum did not stay open to the public for long and can now be viewed only by private appointment. Gary Cypres' extensive collection includes the uniform Babe Ruth wore while barnstorming through Japan in 1934, some of the earliest leather gloves, an original cornice stone from old Yankee Stadium, nineteenth century Allen & Ginter advertising posters and an exact-replica model of the original Polo Grounds.

McCovey's Restaurant in Walnut Creek — Designed to mimic the look of AT&T Park on the outside, it features "infield" and "outfield" tables dedicated to some of Willie's favorite athletes and an impressive collection of memorabilia.

Rancho Cucamonga Epicenter in Rancho Cucamonga — It's hard to beat the stunning view of Mount San Antonio beyond the field in this tiered stadium, which has been used to film many movies and commercials due to its proximity to Hollywood.

Blair Field in Long Beach — The Cubs held spring training here in 1966, but the ballpark has largely been used for independent league baseball. A plaque honors Hall of Famer Bob Lemon, who played high school ball at Recreation Park, a wooden ballpark that preceded Blair Field in the same location.

Notable Achievements

Tony Lazzeri became the first major leaguer to hit two grand slams in the same game when he connected off Herman Fink and George Turbeville on May 24, 1936.

Gil McDougald was the first rookie to hit a grand slam in the World Series when he did it on October 9, 1951.

Kevin Kouzmanoff (Newport Beach) and **Daniel Nava** (Redwood City) are the only players to hit a grand slam on the first pitch they faced in the majors. Kouzmanoff did it on September 2, 2006 against Texas, while Nava did it on June 12, 2010 against the Phillies.

Jesse Orosco is the only relief pitcher to win three games in one playoff series, which he accomplished for the Mets in the 1986 NLCS against the Astros.

Lefty Gomez drove in the first run in an All-Star Game when he singled in Jimmy Dykes in the second inning of the 1933 All-Star Game.

Charlie "Red" Barrett (Santa Barbara) holds the known record for fewest pitches in a nine-inning complete game. He needed just 58 pitches to complete a two-hit shutout (with no walks) for the Boston Braves on August 10, 1944.

John Sipin (Watsonville) hit triples in his first two major league at-bats in 1969 ... and never hit another one the rest of his career.

Todd Zeile was the first player to homer for 11 different teams, a feat since matched by Matt Stairs. Zeile played for 11 different teams between 1995 and 2004, tying a mark for position players that is now held by Stairs.

Mike Morgan (Tulare) played in four different decades and set the record by pitching for 12 different teams. Morgan's .431 career winning percentage is the lowest of any pitcher having at least 400 starts.

Ricky Nolasco (Corona) struck out nine consecutive batters on Sept. 29, 2009. Tom Seaver holds the NL record with 10 while the AL record is eight.

On April 5, 2010, **Ian Stewart** (Long Beach) became the first major leaguer to hit a home run in his first at-bat in his team's season opener on his birthday.

Jimmy Qualls (Exeter) only had 31 career hits, but one broke up Tom Seaver's perfect game on July 9, 1969. Qualls singled with one out in the ninth inning for the Cubs, the only base runner Seaver allowed in the game.

Bob Watson was the first player to hit for the cycle in the American and National Leagues. He did it while playing for Houston on June 24, 1977, and with Boston on September 15, 1979. John Olerud later matched the feat.

Mike Witt (Fullerton) is the only pitcher to throw a no-hitter on the last day of the regular season — he pitched a perfect game on September 30, 1984.

California Leads the Way in Prospecting

Frontier prospectors discovered "there's gold in them thar hills," but today's prospectors are more interested in mining for five-tool baseball players. Baseball's Gold Rush has been ongoing in the Golden State for several decades, as the state has produced more major league players than any other state (2,014 through the 2011 season, about 650 more than runner-up Pennsylvania).

Baseball's roots in California predate the arrival of the Giants in San Francisco and the Dodgers in Los Angeles in 1958, although those moves did create a seismic shift in major league baseball's power structure and fan base. No longer did the center of the baseball universe begin and end in New York City.

Alexander Cartwright journeyed out to California in search of gold in 1849 — one year before California became the 31st state — bringing with him a passion for the new sport he helped organize in New York, if his journals are to be believed. Cartwright found illness and not gold in the Golden State, so he moved on to Hawaii and spread the gospel of baseball in that tropical paradise. It's a wonder that tales of Cartwright's pioneering efforts cannot be traced to each of the 50 states along with credit for developing the designated hitter rule and Fantasy Baseball.

One of baseball's enduring legacies can be traced back to the state. Ernest Thayer's famous poem "Casey at the Bat" was first published by William Randolph Hearst in his newspaper, *The San Francisco Examiner*, in June 1888. The California city of Stockton claims to be the inspiration for Mudville (since that used to be the town's name for a short time), as does a town in Massachusetts, but Thayer denied the poem was based on any specific location.

Baseball was growing in popularity at the dawn of the twentieth century, but major league baseball was largely confined to the Northeast and industrial Midwest. The Pacific Coast League (PCL), founded in 1903, quickly established itself as one of the top regional leagues in the country and helped popularize the game on the West Coast. Since California's mild weather meant baseball could be played nearly year-round, the PCL teams routinely played 170–180 games a year including a record 230 games played by the San Francisco Seals in 1905. In the first half of the twentieth century, the best baseball in the West was being played in the Pacific Coast League.

Joe DiMaggio hit .340 with 259 hits in 187 games for the Seals in 1933 and then did even better in 1935 — 270 hits in 172 games and a .398 average. DiMaggio and his brothers Dom and Vince learned to play the game at North Beach Playground in the Italian district of San Francisco, despite their father's belief they should follow in his footsteps as a fisherman.

Ted Williams, the last player to bat .400 in a season, refined his hitting stroke while growing up in the North Park neighborhood of San Diego. After starring at Hoover High School in San Diego, Williams was able to play his first two years of professional ball for the San Diego Padres in the Pacific Coast League in 1936 — his manager was Frank Shellenback, who is the PCL's all-time leader in pitching wins with 295.

Jackie Robinson was born in Georgia, but he grew up in Pasadena and attended Pasadena City College before lettering in four sports at UCLA. Baseball was actually his worst sport — he batted .097 during his one season on the team at UCLA. Branch Rickey was more impressed with Robinson's background growing up in an integrated school system than in his ability as a baseball player, which is why he brought Jackie to the majors before more experienced African American players like Roy Campanella and Don Newcombe.

Joe Morgan and Frank Robinson were Texans by birth but both future Hall of Famers played their high school ball in Oakland. Willie Stargell was a native Oklahoman who played his ball in Alameda, just outside Oakland. Bert Blyleven was born in the Netherlands and spent four years in Canada, but he spent the rest of his youth in California, which is where he learned to play baseball.

Walter "The Big Train" Johnson was born in Kansas, but moved with his family to Orange County when he was 14. In high school he spent as much time in the oil fields of Olinda as he did the baseball diamond, although he managed to strike out 27 batters in a game pitching for Fullerton High School.

Another star at Fullerton High School was Willard Hershberger, who had battled depression after his father committed suicide in 1928. Hershberger, a career backup who was uncomfortable being thrust into the spotlight after the Reds' starting catcher, Ernie Lombardi, went down with an injury in 1940, slashed his throat in his room at the team hotel. The 30-year-old remains the only player to commit suicide during the season.

A player of historical note is John "Chief" Meyers, who was born in Riverside as a member of the Cahuilla tribe of Indians. Meyers was one of the best offensive

John "Chief" Meyers, a member of the Cahuilla tribe of Indians, was one of the best-hitting catchers of the Deadball Era. His success was instrumental in helping popularize the game on Indian reservations in Southern California (Library of Congress, Prints & Photographs Division, LC-DIG-ggbain-22979).

catchers of the Deadball Era, batting .291 lifetime with a 117 OPS+. He spent seven seasons catching Christy Mathewson on John McGraw's Giants, batting over .300 each year from 1911–13 as the Giants won the pennant all three seasons. Meyers finished third in the Chalmers Award (MVP) voting in 1912 after batting .358 (2nd in the NL) and leading the league with a .441 OBP. He also finished third in the league in batting in 1911 with a .332 average. Meyers' rise to baseball prominence helped popularize the game on Indian reservations throughout Southern California.

Meyers' teammate on those Giants teams, Ventura native Fred Snodgrass, gained notoriety for dropping a fly ball in the 10th inning of the last game of the 1912 Series — it became known as "Snodgrass's Muff." Snodgrass finished fourth in the league in batting in 1910 and third in stolen bases in 1911–12, yet he joins players such as Fred Merkle in being remembered for one negative play. Ironically, the Giants had gone ahead in the top of the 10th in the 1912 Series when Merkle singled in a runner from second.

Only 36 players from California started their careers in the nineteenth century, but 203 players from the state were active during the 2011 season. That gives us plenty of options for coming up with an All-California All-Star team comprised of active players.

C — **Rod Barajas**, Matt Treanor, Gerald Laird
First Base — **Adrian Gonzalez**, Prince Fielder, Derrek Lee, Mark Trumbo, Jason Giambi, Adam LaRoche
Second Base — **Dustin Pedroia**, Chase Utley, Aaron Hill, Skip Schumacher, Adam Kennedy, Freddy Sanchez
Third Base — **Evan Longoria**, Ty Wigginton, Casey McGehee, Kevin Kouzmanoff, Eric Chavez
SS — **Troy Tulowitzki**, Jimmy Rollins, Jack Wilson
OF — **Ryan Braun, Adam Jones, Carlos Quentin,** Mike Stanton, Brennan Boesch, Nyjer Morgan, Coco Crisp, Jonny Gomes, Ben Francisco, Mark Kotsay
DH — **Michael Young**
LHP — **C.C. Sabathia**, Cole Hamels, C.J. Wilson, Ted Lilly, Randy Wolf
RHP — **Jered Weaver**, Dan Haren, Ian Kennedy, James Shields, Matt Garza, Trevor Cahill, Phil Hughes, Jon Garland, Stephen Strasburg, Colby Lewis, Kyle Lohse, Brandon McCarthy, Vance Worley, Ricky Nolasco, Aaron Harang
RP — **Heath Bell**, Brad Lidge, Ryan Madson, Brian Fuentes, Brandon League, Bobby Jenks
Mgr — **Dusty Baker**, Ron Roenicke, Bob Melvin, Bud Black, Ned Yost, Brad Mills

Playing the Naming Game

Looking at the full roster of names, there is a Gross, a Klutts and a Hack, but also a Ferrari and a Pate. San Francisco native Alan Mitchell Edward George Patrick Henry Gallagher is tied with Bruno Betzel (or as his mother used to yell at him, Christian Frederick Albert John Henry David Betzel) for the most names in baseball history. Either Gallagher's parents couldn't agree on a middle name or they wanted to make it difficult for him to fill out official forms. The third baseman was known as "Dirty Al" during his uneventful four-year career.

The nicknames range from the demented — The Mad Hungarian, Dr. Strangeglove, Cuckoo and Wild Thing — to the super heroes: Captain America, Flash Gordon and The Incredible Hulk. Eric Byrnes leads the state in nicknames, since in addition to Captain America he is also known as Flipper, Crash Test Dummy and Pigpen. Ted Williams also had four nicknames: Splendid Splinter, Teddy Ballgame, Thumper and The Kid.

Animals and creatures of nature are well-represented by the nicknames of California-born players, with enough to start up a zoo. The infield would consist of Nelson "Chicken" Hawks at first, Bill "The Cricket" Rigney at second, Frankie "Crow" Crosetti moving to third and Rick "Rooster" Burleson at short. Tim "Kingfish" Salmon, Bob "Beetle" Bailey and John "Spider" Jorgensen are available to man the outfield, while Mike "Big Bear" Garcia and Charley "Sea Lion" Hall are the pitchers. At catcher we have Harry "The Horse" Danning. Not a bad lineup.

Two players share the nickname "Frenchy": Bernard Uhalt and Stanley Bordagaray. Uhalt played only one season in the majors, collecting 40 hits for the White Sox in 1934, but the outfielder spent 22 seasons in the minors. With his exaggerated crouch at the plate, Frenchy Uhalt recorded 3,123 hits with a .299 average and was inducted into the Pacific Coast League Hall of Fame.

Bordagaray picked up the Frenchy moniker because his last name sounded French — it's not. However, he later managed the Trois-Rivières Royals (in French-speaking Quebec) to the Canadian-American League championship in 1946. On the Royals team that year were two African American players — John Wright and Roy Partlow. Wright had been signed by the Dodgers at the same time as Jackie Robinson and both he and Partlow roomed briefly with Jackie on the Montreal Royals before being sent down to the Can-Am League. Frenchy Bordagaray spent six seasons with the Brooklyn Dodgers, batting .315 in 1936. "He's either the greatest rotten third baseman in baseball or the rottenest great third baseman. But he's never in between," commented a frustrated Branch Rickey.

Oakland native Jim "Abba Dabba" Tobin was a fair pitcher who won 105 games and pitched two no-hitters in 1944 (one lasted just five innings). He also is the only pitcher to smack three consecutive home runs in a game, which he did on May 3, 1942, while playing for Casey Stengel's Boston Braves. In fact, he's the only pitcher to hit three home runs in a game during the twentieth century. Although Tobin got the complete game win that day, he went on to lead the league with 21 losses that season. He was used often as a pinch hitter, ending up with 17 career home runs.

Ralph Schwamb picked up the nickname "Blackie" during his youth, because he identified with the bad guys and liked to dress all in black. He grew up to be a bad guy in real life, drinking heavily and graduating from petty theft to armed robbery. He was working as a mob enforcer when his baseball talents were discovered. A meteoric rise to the majors in 1948 was followed by an even quicker fall from grace. Blackie self-destructed with an 8.53 ERA in 12 appearances, his pitching talent overshadowed by drinking and volatile outbursts. Things got worse from there, as he was sentenced to life in prison for beating a man to death in 1949. Away from the distractions of civilian life, Blackie gained notoriety as the unhittable pitching star of the San Quentin prison team, even pitching a no-hitter while facing a team primarily comprised of major league players.

San Francisco native Walter Christensen was a Californian original. He liked to do somersaults in the outfield *before* making catches and on occasion could be found reading the newspaper while in the field. Not surprisingly, he was nicknamed "Cuckoo" and his major league career lasted just two seasons despite leading the National League with a .426 OBP his rookie year of 1926.

All-Time California Selections

The All-Time California team selections start at catcher, with two Hall of Famers among the options: Gary Carter and Ernie Lombardi. Both were great hitters, with Carter demonstrating greater power and Lombardi hitting for a higher average. Carter was named to 11 All-Star teams and won three Gold Gloves and three Silver Sluggers, establishing himself as the best catcher in the National League after Johnny Bench retired. He hit two homers in the 1981 All-Star Game and homered again in the 1984 All-Star Game, being named game MVP both times. Carter also slugged two homers in Game 4 of the 1986 World Series to help the Mets beat the Red Sox.

Lombardi earned seven All-Star selections and one MVP award to go with two batting titles. He caught Johnny Vander Meer's back-to-back no-hitters in 1938. The Oakland native, who was called "Schnozz" due to his large nose, would receive serious consideration for slowest player in baseball history. It's a wonder he found a way to leg out nine triples in 1932. He did possess a powerful arm, throwing out 44 percent of base stealers for his career but also leading the league in passed balls nine times. Lombardi batted over .300 10 times on the way to a lifetime average of .306, finishing in the top 10 in batting average seven times. In his MVP season with the Reds in 1938 he hit 19 homers, drove in 95 runs and won the batting crown with a .342 average while throwing out a league-best 52 percent of base stealers.

Carter, nicknamed "The Kid," caught 2,056 games — fourth all-time and 512 more than Lombardi — and had 10 seasons with at least 500 at-bats, a threshold Lombardi never reached. Carter's 324 career home runs are tied with Lance Parrish for fifth place among catchers — Lombardi hit a respectable 190. Carter's superior defense combined with his big advantage over Lombardi in Wins Above Replacement (66–39) and Career Win Shares (344–213) prove to be the deciding factors.

When San Diego native Bob Boone retired in 1990 he held the major league record for most games caught with 2,225. Pudge Fisk hung around long enough to pass him by one game in 1993 and now Pudge Rodriquez holds the record. Boone didn't offer much with the bat — he averaged .254 with a career OPS+ of 82 — but he was smart and skilled behind the plate. A seven-time Gold Glove winner, he led the league in assists six times and putouts and caught stealing percentage three times each. Boone followed his father Ray into the majors and when his son Bret made it to the majors in 1992 it marked the first time three generations of a family had played in the majors. A second son, Aaron, debuted in 1997.

Few would describe Jason Kendall as a great catcher, but he continues to climb the all-time rankings in select categories. He ranks right behind Boone and Carter in games caught with 2,025 and ranks second in putouts with 13,019 and fifth in times hit by a pitch with 254. Kendall is a second-generation major league catcher whose father, Fred, caught 795 games over a 12-year career. He has demonstrated great durability, catching at least 118 games in 14 of his 15 seasons through 2010 (he missed the 2011 season due to injury).

A three-time All-Star, Kendall is a contact hitter who has demonstrated a knack for getting on base and stealing bases. His 189 career stolen bases are the second most by a catcher (behind Roger Bresnahan) since the new rules were established in 1898. From 1998 to 2000 he batted over .300, had an OBP over .400 and stole at least 20 bases each season. In 2009 he became the eighth catcher to reach 2,000 hits — he had 2,195 through the 2010 season.

Overshadowed by his more famous teammates on the Milwaukee Braves in the 1950s — Aaron, Mathews and Spahn — Del Crandall was a team captain who stood out for his intelligence, power and defensive skills. He hit 151 home runs between 1953 and 1960 and received MVP votes in seven seasons while making eight All-Star teams and winning four Gold Gloves. He led NL catchers in assists six times and fielding percentage four times, throwing out 46 percent of base stealers for his career. Crandall later spent six years managing the Brewers and Mariners but never finished higher than fifth place. A native of Ontario, Calif., Crandall attended Fullerton High School, the same school as Walter Johnson and Willard Hershberger.

Another notable catcher is Gus Triandos, a slow-footed slugger who is tied for the best stolen base percentage in baseball history — he was one for one in stolen base attempts over his 13-year career. Triandos tied Yogi Berra's American League record for homers by a catcher when he belted 30 in 1958 — he ended up with 167 for his career. He was also part of a 17-player trade between the Yankees and the Orioles in late 1954 that delivered righties Don Larsen and Bob Turley to the Bronx Bombers but gave the Birds a starting catcher who would make three All-Star teams.

It was initially tough deciding between Eddie Murray and Mark McGwire for the all-time first base position, at least until McGwire confessed to using steroids. Now it looks highly unlikely that "Big Mac" will join "Steady Eddie" in the Hall of Fame. Murray is in select company as one of only four players to collect 500 home runs and 3,000 hits, along with Aaron, Mays and Rafael Palmeiro. He ended up with 504 homers (25th all-time), 3,255 hits (twelfth) and 1,917 RBI (ninth). Murray ranks first in games and assists by a first baseman. As his nickname suggests, Murray was more steady than spectacular, but he was a very good player for a long time. The Orioles slugger recorded at least 16 homers, 70 RBI and 110 hits in each of his first 20 seasons, posting 16 seasons with 20 or more home runs.

After being named AL Rookie of the Year in 1977 Murray went on to place in the top six of the AL MVP voting every season from 1980–85, with another fifth place finish with the Dodgers in 1990. That year he led the majors in batting (.330), yet didn't even win the NL batting crown because Willie McGee got traded to the AL late in the season and had already qualified for the NL title. The only time Murray led the league in homers and RBI was in the strike-shortened 1981 season. He and Carter were elected to the Hall of Fame together in 2003. "Eddie Murray's bronze bust in Cooperstown will chatter only slightly less than the man himself. The first line of text on the monument should read: He spoke rarely and carried a mighty bat," said Associated Press sportswriter David Ginsburg.

Fans will always have their memories of "Big Mac" and Sammy Sosa and the summer of 1998, even if they don't know what to make of McGwire's career accomplishments. After all, he was a one-dimensional player whose singular skill was hitting home runs and we will never know how many of those were PED-aided. He didn't run well, didn't field well (especially in 1998), didn't hit doubles or triples and struck out a lot. He and others cheated, and now baseball fans everywhere feel cheated.

When Gaylord Perry continually found ingenious ways to load up the baseball with foreign substances, well, that just seemed to be sneaky, clever and a forgivable sin. Maybe if Perry had been challenging Cy Young's record for career wins there would have been more of an outcry over his "cheating," but the reality is that Hall of Fame voters didn't have a problem voting Perry the Cheater into Cooperstown in his third year on the ballot. It's increasingly apparent that McGwire will never be elected to the Hall of Fame unless a cheater's wing is established.

At the time, McGwire's epic home-run battles with Sosa dwarfed Roger Maris' duel with Mickey Mantle and Hank Aaron's chasing of Babe Ruth's career mark, largely because the media glare had become much brighter. Even people who didn't normally follow baseball wanted to know whether "Big Mac" had homered each day. After hitting his final homer of the season, he declared, "I'm in awe of myself" and no one took it as bragging. McGwire made baseball relevant again, wiping away the stain of the 1994–95 labor strife. Character and integrity are supposed to count in the voting process, but that seems to be a selective proposition.

Maybe we shouldn't be here to talk about the past, but McGwire set a rookie record with 49 home runs in 1987 while looking downright slender. He is one of a handful of players to hit two game-ending grand slams — the record is three. Between 1996 and 1999 he hit 245 home runs, which is the most ever hit in a four-year period. He was the first player to hit 50 homers in three straight seasons. In that magical year of 1998, McGwire set an NL record with 162 walks, a mark that has since been obliterated by Barry Bonds. McGwire's slash line that year was an unbelievable .470/.752/1.222, yet Sosa was named MVP in a landslide with a slash line of .377/.647/1.024.

Keith Hernandez was decidedly not a home run hitter — he hit only 162 in 17 seasons — but he might be the best-fielding first baseman in baseball history. He won 11 straight Gold Gloves after it looked like Steve Garvey was going to own the award in the National League. "Mex" led NL first basemen in assists five times and putouts four times. He had great range and was incredibly agile, saving many an errant throw while also possessing a strong and accurate arm. His presence at first base deterred many teams from even attempting a bunt. He had his moments with the bat, including many a clutch hit. One of the biggest was his two-run single with the bases loaded in Game 7 of the 1986 World Series, helping erase an early 3–0 deficit and send the Mets on to victory over the Red Sox.

Everyone was singing along to "We Are Family" in 1979 in honor of Willie Stargell's champion Pirates, but Hernandez managed to tie Pops for the MVP Award. He only hit 11 home runs that year, but he led the league with 116 runs, 48 doubles and a .344 average while collecting 210 hits and 105 RBI. With 2,182 career hits, .296 lifetime average, .384 OBP and 128 OPS+ in addition to his brilliance as a fielder, it would seem a strong case can be made for Hernandez's election to the Hall. Appearing in the final episode of *Seinfeld* evidently doesn't carry much weight with voters but getting caught up in a drug scandal does, and Hernandez dropped off the ballot after failing to get more than five percent of the vote in his ninth year.

Frank Chance led the NL with 67 stolen bases in 1903, a .450 OBP in 1905 and 103 runs and 57 steals in 1906. His 403 career stolen bases are the most ever for a first baseman. His career marks of .394 OBP and 135 OPS+ reflect his real value on the offensive side, making up for the paltry 20 home runs he accumulated during the Deadball Era. His numbers are hurt by the fact he sat out a lot of games after suffering beanings — he was hit by a pitch five times during a doubleheader on May 30, 1904 — and he was nearly deaf by the end of his career. The famous infield of Tinker to Evers to Chance was immortalized for good when all were elected to the Hall of Fame in 1946, but Chance may be the only one who deserved the honor.

It's hard to believe the Phillies sold Dolph Camilli to the Dodgers for $45,000 before the 1938 season after the lefty first baseman had just produced three stellar seasons for the bottom-dwelling team. Camilli batted .339 and led the league with a .446 OBP in 1937, which was in the middle of an eight-year stretch in which he averaged 26 homers and 99 RBI. He finished in the top four in homers and the top 10 in RBI each of those seasons between 1935 and 1942. Brooklyn was happy to have him, as he turned into the National League's MVP in their pennant-winning season of 1941. That year Camilli finished first with 34 homers and 120 RBI and recorded a .407 OBP and .962 OPS. He had a son, Doug Camilli, who played nine years in the majors and caught one of Sandy Koufax's no-hitters; and a brother, Frankie Campbell, who was killed during a boxing match against Max Baer.

George "High Pockets" Kelly was an accomplished fielder at first base despite being less than nimble on his feet, and he wielded a capable bat to help the Giants win four straight pennants in the early 1920s. He led the league in homers once and RBI twice and batted over .300 seven times as the Lively Ball Era was taking off. However, Kelly produced only two seasons with an OPS+ over 120 and ended up with a 109 OPS+ for his career. That is decidedly not the record of a Hall of Famer, but Kelly's plaque can be found on the wall beside Cobb, Ruth and the other immortals in Cooperstown. He was accused during a bribery scandal that erupted regarding the 1924 World Series but was later exonerated.

Many trees have been killed in an effort to make sense of Hal Chase's life in baseball, so there is no need to rehash his sordid history. "Prince Hal" managed to stay in the majors for another decade after first being accused of chicanery in 1910, which is perhaps his most impressive accomplishment. He was a brilliant fielder who had the ability to be an all-time great but instead is left with a legacy as perhaps the most crooked, immoral and disruptive player in baseball history. Here is Chase's mea culpa on his deathbed: "I am an outcast and I haven't a good name. I'm the loser just like all the gamblers are. I lived to make great plays. What did I gain? Nothing. Everything was lost because I raised hell after hours. I was a wise guy, a know-it-all, I guess."

Moving on to second base, we find four players who are close in overall ability: Joe Gordon, Bobby Doerr, Tony Lazzeri and Jeff Kent. The first three are in the Hall of Fame and Kent should join them when he becomes eligible in 2014. All of them demonstrated superior power for the position while Gordon and Doerr also excelled on defense.

Kent ranks up there with Rogers Hornsby as the best RBI man to ever play the position and it's quickly apparent that he should be the top choice. As the chart below illustrates, Kent has a significant advantage over the other three in many of the hitting categories.

	R	H	2b	HR	RBI	AVE	OBP	SLG	OPS	OPS+
Kent	1320	2461	560	377	1518	.290	.356	.500	.855	123
Gordon	914	1530	264	253	975	.268	.357	.466	.822	120
Doerr	1094	2042	381	223	1247	.288	.362	.461	.823	115
Lazzeri	986	1840	334	178	1191	.292	.380	.467	.846	120

Kent's 351 home runs as a second baseman are the most of all-time and Hornsby and Nap Lajoie are the only second sackers to top his RBI total. He knocked in over 100 runs eight times in a nine-year period — he had 93 RBI the other year. The five-time All-Star drove in more runs than Mickey Mantle and hit more home runs than Joe DiMaggio. Kent's .500 slugging percentage blows away Hall of Famers Charlie Gehringer (.480), Ryne Sandberg (.452) and Joe Morgan (.427) and is topped only by Hornsby and active player Chase Utley. Kent beat out teammate Barry Bonds to win the 2000 NL MVP Award after hitting .334 with 33 homers and 125 RBI.

Bouncing around from the Blue Jays to the Mets to the Indians, he finally emerged as a star with the Giants in 1997, serving as a fearsome one-two punch with Bonds. He hit three homers for the Giants in the 2002 World Series and belted three more in the 2004 NLCS for the Astros including a game-winning blast in the ninth inning of Game 5.

Gordon was a reserved and humble gentleman, but he was as fine an all-around second baseman as has ever played the game. He was a master at making the double-play pivot and led the league in assists four times and in double plays three times. His career lasted only 11 seasons due to missing two years to the war, but he made the AL All-Star team nine straight seasons and earned MVP votes eight times. Although Ted Williams produced a Triple Crown season in 1942, "Flash" Gordon beat out the "Splendid Splinter" for the AL MVP Award with his more modest figures of .322 average, 18 homers and 103 RBI. He recorded four seasons with at least 100 RBI and set career highs with 32 homers and 124 RBI with Cleveland in 1948. Gordon led his teams to six World Series, winning five rings.

Doerr holds a mark of unusual distinction: most career games at second base without playing another position (1,852). Some might give the honor to Lou Whittaker, since he played 2,308 games at second and his only other position was 32 games at designated hitter. Overshadowed on the Red Sox by Williams, Doerr was a steady and indispensable contributor who could beat you with his glove or bat. He was a contemporary of Gordon, matching him with nine All-Star selections and MVP votes in eight seasons. He recorded double-digit totals in home runs 12 straight years and posted six seasons with over 100 RBI. Doerr was still playing at a high level when forced to retire at age 33 due to back problems.

The most similar player to Doerr is Lazzeri, the San Francisco native who won five championships with the Yankees. He first attracted attention by blasting 60 homers and driving in 222 runs in 1925 for the Salt Lake City Bees in the PCL. Lazzeri knocked in 114 runs in his rookie year, 1926, but then earned the wrath of Yankee fans by getting struck out by Pete Alexander with the bases loaded in the seventh inning of Game 7 of the World Series to help the Cardinals hang on to a lead they wouldn't lose. That doesn't seem like such an unpardonable sin considering Babe Ruth was thrown out trying to steal second to end the game. However, Lazzeri's untimely strikeout is even mentioned on Alexander's Hall of Fame plaque, which seems a little rude. The ironic thing is that both Lazzeri and Alexander suffered from epilepsy.

Lazzeri was one of four players on the 1927 Murderers' Row squad with 100 RBI. He finished fourth in the AL with a .354 average in 1929 and recorded seven seasons with at least 100 RBI. Lazzeri, who picked up the nickname "Poosh 'em up Tony" from an Italian restaurant owner in Salt Lake City, was brought in by the Yankees to appeal to New York's Italian-American community. He quickly turned into baseball's first Italian-American star and his quiet demeanor helped change the prevailing stereotypes of immigrant Italians as loud and brash.

With Lazzeri helping pave the way, it's now possible to name an all-Italian team of players from California. At catcher is Lombardi; Camilli and Jason Giambi at first; Lazzeri and Billy Martin at second; Ken Caminiti and Robin Ventura at third; Frankie Crosetti and Jim Fregosi at short; an all-DiMaggio outfield with Joe, Dom and Vince; Pete Incaviglia at DH; starting pitcher Tom Candiotti; relief pitcher Dave Righetti; and Martin and Fregosi as manager.

Continuing on with other notable second basemen we come to Gil McDougald, who spent 10 years as the Yankees' jack-of-all-trades in the infield and then retired at age 32 because he didn't want to play for the expansion California Angels. He played 599 games at second, 508 at third and 284 at short, providing Gold Glove caliber defense wherever he was asked to play. He led AL second basemen in fielding in 1954 and 1955 and then led AL shortstops in fielding in 1956. A five-time All-Star, McDougald helped the Bronx Bombers win eight pennants and five World Series titles. Although 1951 was also Mickey Mantle's rookie season, it was McDougald who won the Rookie of the Year Award after batting .306 and outhomering "The Mick" 14–13.

According to Bill James, seven of the top 25 third basemen in baseball history hail from California, yet none of them have been elected to the Hall of Fame. The state's best bet is for Evan Longoria to stay healthy and keep producing, since he has so far demonstrated the ability to become an all-time great. As for the others, let's take a closer look at Stan Hack, Darrell Evans, Graig Nettles, Bob Elliott, Robin Ventura, Matt Williams and Ken Caminiti.

Evans recorded a weak .248 lifetime average but posted a .361 OBP due to 1,605 career walks (twelfth best). He led the NL in walks two straight years and recorded eight seasons with at least 90 walks. Evans belted 414 career home runs, more than Duke Snider, Al Kaline, Johnny Bench or Tony Perez. His 1,354 RBI trail only Brett, Schmidt, Mathews and Robinson (by three) among Hall of Fame third basemen. Nicknamed "Howdy Doody," Evans was an above-average fielder who led the league in putouts four times and assists three times. He was forced to spend eight years of his prime playing in pitcher-friendly Candlestick Park, averaging just 17 homers a season there. His neutralized batting stats (adjusted for park and league context) show him with 453 homers, 1,471 RBI, 1,771 walks and a more respectable .263 average — the type of numbers that were might have gained him entry to Cooperstown. Bill James calls Evans the most underrated player in baseball history and ranks him in the number 10 position, one spot behind Hack. We believe Evans' sustained excellence in drawing walks, slugging and fielding are enough to earn him the selection as California's all-time best third baseman.

Hack was an accomplished base stealer, leading the league twice and finishing with 165 career steals. He only struck out 466 times, nearly 1,000 fewer than Evans. He scored over 100 runs seven times and led the NL in hits twice. His .301 average and .394 OBP are way above the others, as is his Gray Ink score of 125. Hack was also skilled with the glove, leading the league in fielding percentage three times, putouts five times and assists twice. He has to be considered the best third baseman in the National League from the mid–1930s to the mid–1940s. What hurts him are his power numbers — 57 home runs, 642 RBI and .397 slugging. "Smiling Stan" played on four pennant winners with the Cubs, batting .471 in the 1938 World Series but falling short each time.

Nettles, who produced 390 home runs over a 22-year career, was a spectacular fielder who was finally able to win two Gold Gloves in the American League once Brooks Robinson retired. Mike Schmidt and Eddie Mathews are the only third basemen in the Hall who can top his home run total. The six-time All-Star ranks second (behind Brooks) in games played at third with 2,412. His 2,225 career hits are two more than Evans and only nine behind Schmidt. Nettles led AL third basemen in assists four times, putouts twice and fielding percentage once. He played in five World Series, winning back-to-back titles with the Yankees in 1977–78. His .248 average (same as Evans) and .329 OBP undoubtedly hurt his Hall candidacy.

Elliott was the best third baseman in the National League throughout the decade of the 1940s. He was named MVP with the Boston Braves in 1947 after posting 22 homers with 113 RBI, .317 average and .410 OBP. Elliott averaged 6.3 homers per season in eight years with the Pirates and 20.2 homers per season in five years with the Braves, winding up with 170 for his career. Nicknamed "Mr. Team," he led the NL with 131 walks in 1948 and recorded six seasons with at least 100 RBI. Elliott tops the other California contenders in doubles (382), OPS (.815) and OPS+ (124). He was merely adequate in the field, also playing 537 games in the outfield.

Ventura was a slick-fielding slugger whose most memorable career highlight was getting pummeled by 46-year-old Nolan Ryan after foolishly charging the mound in 1993. Ventura hit 294 home runs with a career-high 34 in 1996 and made two All-Star teams. He was Nettles' equal in the field and earned six Gold Gloves while leading the AL in putouts and assists three times each. His 18 grand slams are tied with Willie McCovey for fifth place all-time and he is the only one in the top 25 with fewer than 300 career home runs. On September 4, 1995, he became the eighth player to hit two grand slams in a game and he is also the only player to hit a grand slam in both games of a doubleheader, which he accomplished on May 20, 1999.

Williams looked like he might challenge Roger Maris' home run record in 1994 until the baseball strike ended his chance. He finished with a league-high 43 homers in 112 games that year; Maris had 41 homers after 112 games in 1961. Williams had trouble staying healthy during his career, but he managed to make five All-Star teams and win four Gold Gloves and four Silver Slugger Awards while blasting 378 home runs. He later admitted using human growth hormone and was one of the players linked to steroids in the Mitchell Report.

Joining Williams in the steroids Hall of Shame (and in the Mitchell Report) is Caminiti, who became the first baseball player to confess to steroid use in an interview with *Sports Illustrated* in 2002. Not only that, he admitted he was taking steroids during his MVP season of 1996. Caminiti battled substance abuse during and after his career and died at the age of 41 of a drug-induced heart attack. His story certainly serves as a cautionary tale for the many other players who used performance-enhancing drugs while baseball officials had their heads buried in the sand on the issue. Caminiti's 239 career home runs, MVP Award and three All-Star selections can now be viewed as an irrelevant fraud.

When deciding on a shortstop for Team California it doesn't help that the players most similar to Joe Cronin are Barry Larkin and Alan Trammell. Cronin was elected to the Hall of Fame in 1956, Larkin should get elected soon and Trammell, well, it looks like his excellence is going to remain unrecognized. For our purposes, we had to decide if Trammell was good enough to beat out Cronin.

Both played 20 seasons and both played in only one World Series, although Trammell emerged with a championship in 1984 after batting .450 in the World Series against the Padres. Cronin was named to seven All-Star teams while Trammell was selected to six. Cronin scored 1,233 runs, exactly two more than Trammell, who holds a slight edge in home runs, 185–170. Trammell mostly batted second in the order, while Cronin predominantly batted in the clean-up spot and so had more opportunities to drive in runs. Trammell was the better fielder and holds a distinct advantage in career fielding percentage. In fact, Trammell's .977 career mark is just a tick behind Ozzie Smith career fielding percentage of .978 and it blows away Cronin's .952 mark. However, Cronin did lead AL shortstops in putouts and assists three times and fielding percentage twice, while Trammell never led in any of those categories despite winning four Gold Gloves. Cronin has a decisive edge in the Black Ink and Gray Ink tests and the final deciding factor was Cronin's edge in Career Win Shares: 332–313.

Trammell was MVP runner-up in 1987 but had only two other top 10 finishes in the MVP voting. Cronin had five top 10 finishes but it was his 1933 season that stands out. That year the 26-year-old Cronin was named player-manager of the Washington Senators, guiding a team that featured five position players and four key pitchers over the age of 30. Cronin batted .309 with 118 RBI and a league-high 45 doubles while guiding the team to 99 wins and the pennant. Along the way he started for the American League in the first All-Star Game and finished second in the MVP race. He spent one more year as player-manager of the Senators before serving the next 11 years as player-manager of the Red Sox. When he finally stopped playing and devoted his full-time attention to managing, he won another pennant with the Red Sox in 1946.

Cronin's career stats are all the more impressive when you consider that he was able to concentrate fully on his playing duties in only four seasons as a regular. He spent the last 13 years of his career juggling the dual responsibilities of playing and managing, which is something today's players cannot comprehend. Cronin's 1,071 wins as Red Sox manager remain the team record, but he was unable to do much with a lineup featuring Ted Williams, Jimmie Foxx and Bobby Doerr. He later moved into the Red Sox front office but had no more luck turning the team into a winner. His tenure as president of the American League from 1959–73 was marked by clumsy bungling of franchise moves and expansion.

Another California-born shortstop, Nomar Garciaparra, appeared a lock for Cooperstown after his first six full seasons with the Red Sox. Nomar averaged .326 with 110 runs, 198 hits, 45 doubles, 28 homers and 108 RBI in that period, was named Rookie of the Year, won two batting titles and earned five All-Star selections and MVP runner-up. He shared the spotlight with Derek Jeter and Alex Rodriquez as a shortstop triumvirate for the ages. A virtual hitting machine, Nomar reached 2,000 total bases faster than any player in baseball history and even hit three home runs on his twenty-ninth birthday in 2002. Then the wheels came off his career. Jettisoned to the Cubs in the middle of the 2004 season, Garciaparra saw his production slowed by injuries and ineffectiveness and he turned into a part-time utility player as his career wound down to an unsatisfying end. His lifetime marks of .313 average, .521 slugging and 124 OPS+ are nice, but his career production (229 homers, 936 RBI, 1,747 hits) fell short of what was expected of him.

Jim Fregosi was a six-time All-Star shortstop for the Angels when the Mets got the bright idea he was just what they needed to spark a third-place team. So in December 1971 they shipped a package of four middling players to California in exchange for Fregosi. One of the players they gave up was a wild righty who had a 29–38 record with 6.1 BB/9—Nolan Ryan, who would go on to win 295 more games and become baseball's all-time strikeout king. As for Fregosi, his days as a regular (let alone as an All-Star) were over and he batted .233 in 146 games for the Mets before being dumped on the Rangers in the middle of the 1973 season. The San Francisco native compiled a .265 average with 1,726 hits and 151 home runs and won 1,028 games managing four different teams over 15 years. His highlight as a manager came in 1993, when he guided the Phillies to 97 wins and the National League pennant.

Some outstanding fielding shortstops have come from California. Larry Bowa won two Gold Gloves and led the NL in fielding percentage six times. His .980 career fielding percentage ranks eighth in baseball history—ahead of Ozzie Smith—and five of the players above him were still active in 2011 so they could fall in the rankings. One of those active players is Oakland native Jimmy Rollins, who ranked third with a .983 career fielding percentage through the 2011 season. Rollins has earned three Gold Gloves for his stellar glove work (through 2010) but he has also used his speed to lead the league in triples four times and runs and steals once. In his MVP season of 2007 he became just the fourth player to record at least 20 doubles, 20 triples, 20 homers and 20 stolen bases—he ended up with 38 doubles, 20 triples, 30 homers and 41 stolen bases while leading the NL with 139 runs. His brilliant all-around play as leadoff hitter helped the Phillies make the playoffs four straight seasons.

The All-Time California outfield is filled by three giants of the game: Ted Williams, Joe DiMaggio and Barry Bonds. All were iconic players whose skills dwarfed those of their peers. Williams was baseball's greatest and most natural hitter, while DiMaggio was elegance and grace personified. Bonds took surly to another level while rewriting baseball's record books with an unmatched combination of power and speed. His ownership of the single-season and career home run records is widely viewed as an outrageous fraud over allegations of steroids use.

The Yankee Clipper led a glamorous life that most Americans could only dream about, between playing center field for the New York Yankees and being married to Marilyn Monroe. On Joe DiMaggio Day at Yankee Stadium in 1949, Joltin' Joe made the following memorable comment, which for decades has been featured on a sign overhead the tunnel leading to the field: "I'd like to thank the Good Lord for making me a Yankee." Derek Jeter taps the sign for good luck or for reverence every time he heads out to the field.

DiMaggio led his team to an incredible 10 pennants and nine World Series titles in his 13-year career. His 56-game hitting streak in 1941 has not been seriously challenged since, and he also holds the official minor league record with a 61-game hitting streak in 1933. That hit streak was broken up by Ed Walsh, Jr., son of the Hall of Famer.

It's hard to believe DiMaggio didn't get elected to the Hall of Fame until his third ballot, but that was typical back in those days. "There was never a day when I was as good as Joe DiMaggio at his best. Joe was the best, the very best I ever saw," an overly modest Stan Musial once said.

Williams spent the first half of his brilliant career being overshadowed by the Yankees and DiMaggio, and he spent the second half of his career being overshadowed by the Yankees and Mickey Mantle. He was brash and cantankerous and spent his career with a chip on his shoulder, but boy could he ever wallop the ball. In 19 terrific seasons Williams made it to one World Series, batting .200 in a losing effort. He led the AL in OBP 12 times and remains the all-time leader at .482 while ranking second in slugging (.634), OPS (1.116) and OPS+ (190).

In 1941 the "Splendid Splinter" nearly won the Triple Crown and became the last player to bat .400. He also led the league in eight other hitting categories, compiling 147 walks with only 27 strikeouts and finishing first with 135 runs and a ridiculous OBP of .553. His 234 OPS+ is the fourth-highest in the twentieth century behind three Ruth seasons. However, DiMaggio rode his 56-game hit streak to the MVP Award that year. Teddy Ballgame had to settle for second place despite outslugging DiMaggio by 105 points and posting an OPS+ 50 points higher. Williams' best hit streak that year was 23 games, but he showed his consistency with a .405 batting average before the All-Star break and .406 average after the break.

Bobby Shantz described the frustration of trying to get the "Splendid Splinter" out. "Did they tell me how to pitch to (Ted) Williams? Sure they did. It was great advice, very encouraging. They said he had no weakness, won't swing at a bad ball, has the best eyes in the business, and can kill you with one swing. He won't hit anything bad, but don't give him anything good," Shantz recalled.

Williams became the oldest player to win a batting title when he batted .388 at age 39 in 1957. That record didn't last long, since he won his fifth and last batting crown in 1958. If Williams had not missed three full seasons and most of two others due to war service, he would be ranked even higher on the all-time lists. Looking at his production in the years before and after his service time, a conservative estimate is that he might have produced 150 more home runs, which would give him 671 and move him ahead of Willie Mays for fourth all-time. The estimated addition of 500 RBI, 550 runs and 700 walks would convert those career figures to 2,329, 2,300 and 2,721 respectively and make him the all-time leader in those categories. An extra 825 hits would put him at 3,479 and move him up from 70th place to just behind Tris Speaker in sixth place.

DiMaggio also missed three years due to war service, which means he also would have padded his stats and added to his nine World Series rings and 10 pennants. In fact, the Yankees won the World Series in the first year he was away, 1943. Joltin' Joe's nine championships were the decisive factor in selecting him as California's All-Time Best Player over Williams. Williams was the better hitter if not the best hitter of all-time, but DiMaggio did more to help his teams win with his exceptional fielding and base running ability. He hit in the clutch and did whatever was necessary to help his team win, while Williams was more concerned with his own stats and did not shine in his one World Series appearance. After all, it was DiMaggio who was voted "The Greatest Living Baseball Player" by sportswriters in 1969. Williams agreed, calling his rival the greatest he ever saw and the most graceful.

No one can match Bonds' seven Most Valuable Player trophies, although that award was mostly not available to players like Babe Ruth, Ty Cobb and Honus Wagner. It's hard to get a handle on how outlandish some of Bonds' numbers are, but it almost seems like he was a super-human cartoon figure playing against kids in a sandlot game. He accumulated 688 intentional walks in his career — Hank Aaron is runner-up with 293. He drew 120 intentional walks in 2004 and holds down spots two and three with 68 and 61 IBB — Willie McCovey is next at 45. It's hard to fathom anyone matching his 232 walks in 2004, but Bonds again holds spots two and three with the Babe coming in fourth with 170. He recorded the three highest OPS+ marks with 268 (in 2002), 263 and 259. In 2001 Bonds posted the only OBP over .600 in baseball history when he recorded a .609 mark.

His power transformation has been well-documented, but Bonds also won eight Gold Gloves for his defense. He ranks sixth all-time in defensive WAR at 20.4, ahead of his godfather, Willie Mays, and among left fielders is ranked number one in games and putouts and second in assists. The third element of his game was speed, and he produced nine seasons with at least 30 steals and ranks 33rd with 514 career stolen bases. Not only is he the only member of the 700 (homer)-500 (stolen base) club, he's the only member of the 400-400 club for that matter. "I've seen a lot of good things from him, and I've seen him rub a lot of people the wrong way. But he played every day for me and he busted his tail. What else can you ask of a player?" says former manager Jim Leyland.

What drives baseball fans nuts, beyond the disdain for cheating, is that Bonds was so supremely talented that he didn't need to take performance-enhancing drugs. If he had stayed clean, then he probably would have ended up with 3,000 hits (since he wouldn't have been intentionally walked 249 times in three seasons), still had over 500 steals and perhaps 600 homers. What's wrong with being the only member of the 600-500 club? Instead, baseball fans got to watch the game's most cherished record get broken in a joyless pursuit of glory. Bonds was an all-time great player and an all-time great jerk, and his place in baseball history will always be listed with a great big invisible asterisk.

Moving on from the immortals to the mortals, we listed the honorable mention outfielders by position (left, center, right) simply as a way to better organize an otherwise unwieldy list — California is the only state where this is done. Other notable left fielders include Roy White, Augie Galan, Garret Anderson, Chick Hafey and Lefty O'Doul. White was a steady, well-rounded player whose career was winding down just as the Yankees started to win again in the mid-1970s. He didn't produce eye-popping stats but did a little bit of everything with 160 homers and 233 stolen bases. White led AL left fielders in fielding percentage four times and putouts three times. He paced the league in walks in 1972 and runs in 1976. His one weakness was a weak throwing arm. As researcher Gabriel Schechter points out, "Roy White lollipopped his throws from left field so badly that umpires were tempted to call the infield fly rule."

Galan was a speedy switch-hitter who excelled at drawing walks and getting on base. He posted an OBP over .400 each of his last seven seasons, ending up with a career mark of .390. In his first full season, 1935, he led the league with 22 stolen bases and 133 runs while compiling 203 hits and 41 doubles. He managed to bat 646 times without grounding into a single double play, which remains a major league record.

One of his best years was 1944, by which time he was batting exclusively left-handed. That season Galan led the league with 101 walks and finished second in doubles (43), third in OBP (.426), sixth in average (.318), OPS (.922) OPS+ (161) and triples (9) and seventh in runs with 96. He was fourth in runs created, yet finished 29th in MVP voting. The NL MVP that year was Marty Marion, he of the .267 average, .324 OBP and 90 OPS+. Even Reds shortstop Eddie Miller, who batted .209 and slugged .289 with a 60 OPS+, ranked higher in the 1944 MVP voting than Galan.

Marion was exceptional in the field, leading NL shortstops in fielding percentage for a Cardinals team that won 105 regular-season games and won the World Series. Galan, on the other hand, toiled for a Brooklyn Dodgers team that finished seventh. Anderson had a career similar to Bill Buckner (not counting the goat incident), compiling numbers over a long period of time but fitting no one's definition of a great player. He posted four straight seasons with over 100 RBI and led the AL with 56 doubles in 2002 but managed to surpass 2,500 career hits with little fanfare. He finished in the top 10 of the MVP race just once and ended the 2010 season with a career OPS+ of 102. Still, Anderson recorded more hits than Joe Morgan or Jim Rice. His 1,365 RBI are more than Johnny Mize, Duke Snider or Roberto Clemente. His 522 doubles are only one behind Willie Mays and more than Babe Ruth. Anderson was undoubtedly hurt by playing on the West Coast, where he attracted little attention as a second-tier star.

When healthy, Hafey sprayed hits all around the field. He batted at least .329 for six straight seasons and recorded three straight years with at least 25 homers and 100 RBI. He won a batting crown with a .349 average in 1931 and led the league by slugging .590 in 1927. However, Hafey battled sinus and headache problems, shoulder injuries and poor eyesight, which meant he exceeded 500 at-bats just four times in 13 seasons. His .317 lifetime average and 133 career OPS+ are excellent, but Hafey was able to generate only 1,466 hits. Although that would seem to fall far short of Hall of Fame standards, Hafey was elected to the Hall by the Veterans Committee in 1971.

It took a while for O'Doul to flame out as a pitcher, so he didn't start making his reputation as a batter until the age of 31. He batted .319 for the Giants in 1928 and then had the good fortune to be traded to the Phillies, where he feasted on pitching in the bandbox that was Baker Bowl. In 1929 O'Doul banged out a National League record 254 hits and led the league with a .398 average and .465 OBP while generating 32 homers and 122 RBI with only 19 strikeouts in 638 at bats. He batted .383 the next year and then won a second batting crown with Brooklyn in 1932. That year he also wore a glove to protect his injured hand while batting, which is the earliest recorded use of a batting glove. After ending his big league career in 1934 with a .349 lifetime average, O'Doul moved on to serve a long time as manager and part-time player for the San Francisco Seals in the Pacific Coast League, taking a young Joe DiMaggio under his wing. O'Doul was a noted ambassador for the sport, bringing traveling all-star teams to Japan dozens of times to help popularize the game there.

Three other center fielders deserve mention beyond the DiMaggio brothers: Duke Snider, Jim Edmonds and Brett Butler. Snider had the misfortune to be the third center fielder playing in New York when Mickey Mantle and Willie Mays ruled the city, but he was an all-time great in his own right and is the greatest left-handed slugger in Dodgers history. He made his major league debut for the Dodgers on April 17, 1947, but people were still paying more attention to the fact Jackie Robinson broke the color barrier in the previous game two days before.

Snider hit more home runs (326) and drove in more runs (1,031) than any other player in the 1950s. He belted 40 homers in five consecutive seasons and led the league in runs three straight years. "The Duke of Flatbush" led the Dodgers to six pennants and two championships, hitting four home runs in both the 1952 and 1955 World Series. His production declined noticeably after the team moved from the friendly confines of Ebbets Field to the cavernous LA Memorial Coliseum. "When they tore down Ebbets Field, they tore down a little piece of me," he said after the Dodgers made the move out to LA. Also known as "The Silver Fox," Snider retired with 407 home runs and was elected to the Hall of Fame in 1980.

Among the players most similar to Edmonds are Snider, Ellis Burks, Andruw Jones, Dale Murphy and Fred Lynn — pretty good company. Edmonds was among the game's top center fielders when healthy. An eight-time Gold Glover with great range and a strong arm, Edmonds hit at least 25 homers every season he had at least 400 at bats, which was 10 times. Through the 2010 season he had produced 1,949 hits, 1,199 RBI and 393 home runs with an outstanding OPS+ of 132. He had also struck out 1,729 times.

Butler got thrown out stealing a lot — he was only successful on 68 percent of his stolen base attempts — but he generated 14 straight seasons with at least 20 steals and retired with 558 stolen bases (24th all-time). He was good at drawing walks, hitting triples (led the league four times) and scoring runs. Butler ended up with 2,375 hits and 1,359 runs scored but had a higher OBP (.377) than slugging percentage (.376). Even though his career was winding down when he discovered he had cancer in 1996, Butler recovered and returned before the season was over, batting .283 with 15 stolen bases at age 40 in 1997.

Joe DiMaggio's brothers Dom and Vince were also center fielders but not in his class. Nicknamed "The Little Professor" because he looked studious with his glasses, Dom was a seven-time All-Star who spent his entire 11-year career with the Red Sox. He was an excellent fielder and led the league in runs twice and triples and steals once. He scored over 100 runs six times and finished with 1,680 hits and a .298 average. The only category Vince led in was strikeouts — six times!

Five distinguished right fielders need to be recognized: Tony Gwynn, Harry Heilmann, Bobby Bonds, Dwight Evans and Gavvy Cravath. Gwynn is tied with Honus Wagner for most National League batting titles with eight. He batted .289 in a short stint in 1982 and never again batted below .300 in 19 additional seasons. Gwynn was a hitting machine who led the league in hits seven times, five times with hit totals over 200 and only struck out 434 times in 9,288 at-bats. Anyone who saw Gwynn late in his career would have trouble believing he stole 56 bases in 1987 and had 319 steals for his career. "Mr. Padre" earned 15 All-Star nods, five

Gold Gloves and seven Silver Sluggers. His .338 average ranks nineteenth all-time and his 3,143 hits rank eighteenth.

Nicknamed "Slug," Heilmann won four batting titles with the Tigers and became one of only 13 players to bat over .400 in the twentieth century when he batted .403 in 1923. He came close the other three years with averages of .393, .394 and .398. Once the Deadball Era ended, he batted over .300 in 12 straight seasons and finished with a career average of .342, just ahead of Pete Browning for twelfth on the all-time list. Although he teamed up with Ty Cobb in the Detroit outfield for many years, Heilmann never reached the postseason.

Barry's father, Bobby, displayed a breath-taking combination of power and speed in the 1970s. He produced seven seasons with 40 stolen bases and six seasons with at least 30 home runs. In 1973 he missed becoming the first member of the 40-40 club when he fell one homer short. Not surprisingly, Barry and Bobby Bonds top the list of father-son combinations for career home runs (1,094) and stolen bases (975) and they remain the only two members of the 300 (homer)-400 (stolen base) club.

Evans remains one of the most underrated players in baseball history. "Dewey" was a better overall player than teammate Jim Rice, but dropped off the Hall of Fame ballot after three years. Evans was a steady contributor who was an expert at handling Fenway Park's difficult right field and possessed a cannon for an arm. He was never viewed as a slugger, yet he hit 385 home runs and drove in 1,384 runs. Selected to three All-Star teams, he earned eight Gold Gloves.

"Cactus Gavvy" Cravath led the NL in home runs six times in seven years as the Deadball Era was drawing to a close. As a right-handed slugger, he was able to successfully hit the ball the other way to take advantage of right field at the Baker Bowl. He just missed a Triple Crown in 1913 after finishing second with a .341 average but leading with 19 homers and a then-record 128 RBI and also finishing first in hits, slugging, OPS, OPS+ and total bases that year. He didn't reach the majors until the age of 27 and didn't stick until 31, as he was busy compiling 1,644 hits in the minors. Cravath's 24 homers in 1915 exceeded or equaled the collective output of 12 of the 15 other teams. He led the league in outfield assists three times with totals of 26, 34 and 28. Cravath's career OPS+ of 151 ranks 30th.

Brian Downing really had three careers. From 1974-80 he was a light-hitting catcher batting at the bottom of the order. Then from 1981-86 he transformed into a muscular outfielder with modest power who batted in the middle of the order and picked up the nickname "The Incredible Hulk." In his final incarnation he closed out his career as a full-time designated hitter from 1987-92, demonstrating an improved ability to draw walks and get on base while batting primarily in the leadoff position. Needless to say, there haven't been a lot of slow 40-year-old designated hitters batting leadoff, but Downing made it work. His only All-Star selection came in 1979 when he produced his lone .300 season at .326. Downing's 20-season career produced 2,099 hits and 275 home runs. He ended up playing 824 games at DH, 777 in the outfield and 675 at catcher.

Another noteworthy DH is Mike Sweeney, who produced some outstanding years as a first baseman for the Royals. A five-time All-Star with a .297 lifetime average, Sweeney played 607 games at DH and 588 at first base.

Selecting the All-Time California right-handed starter was not difficult, since Tom Seaver is arguably the greatest righty of the modern era. With his right knee scraping the dirt as he churned his powerful legs toward the plate, "Tom Terrific" was a master on the mound for 20 seasons. The most popular pitcher in New York Mets' history won 311 games and ranks sixth in career strikeouts with 3,640. His 61 shutouts are tied with Nolan Ryan for seventh on the all-time list — Warren Spahn is the only pitcher ahead of him who pitched in the second half of the twentieth century. Seaver posted at least 200 strikeouts in nine straight seasons.

The Fresno native won three National League Cy Young Awards, but one of his best seasons was 1971, when he finished runner-up to Ferguson Jenkins. Jenkins won 24 games that year to Seaver's 20, and back then voters had the tendency to hand out the hardware to the guy with the most wins. That year "Tom Terrific" led the league with a microscopic 1.76 ERA, roughly half the league average of 3.47; Jenkins' ERA was 2.77. Seaver also led in strikeouts with 289, while Jenkins led the league in hits and home runs allowed. Seaver's 194 ERA+ that year blows away Jenkins' mark of 142. The voters got things right in 1973 when Seaver won the Cy Young with a 19-10 record while Ron Bryant of the Giants went 24-12. Bryant recorded a 3.53 ERA (close to the league average of 3.66), while Seaver led the NL with a 2.08 ERA.

Seaver was certainly worthy of his first Cy Young Award in 1969, when he won his last 10 starts to lead the underdog Miracle Mets to their first championship. He led the league with 25 wins that year and finished fourth with a 2.21 ERA.

When Seaver tied a major league record by striking out 19 Padres on April 22, 1970, he had to do it the hard way — by fanning the final 10 batters. The Padres lineup was beyond bewildered that day as 11 batters were caught looking at the third strike. Seaver understood the science and the art of pitching like few others. "My job isn't to strike guys out, it's to get them out, sometimes by striking them out," he said. His excellence was rewarded when he was elected to the Hall of Fame in 1992 with 98.8 percent of the vote, which remains the highest percentage in the Hall's history.

No pitcher was better at knocking batters on their butts than Don Drysdale, who was big (6-foot-6) and ruthless. He hit 154 batters in 518 career games, leading the league five times in that category to ensure batters never felt comfortable against him. By comparison, Nolan Ryan hit 158 batters in 807 games. Drysdale won 209 games for the Dodgers over 14 seasons, forming a dynamic duo with Sandy Koufax.

The Van Nuys native, who was a high school teammate of Robert Redford at Van Nuys High School in Los Angeles, led the NL in strikeouts three times and innings pitched twice while winning 20 games twice. He won the NL Cy Young Award in 1962 after pacing the NL with 25 wins and 232 strikeouts. Drysdale set a major league record by tossing 58 consecutive scoreless innings in 1968, a mark topped 20 years later by Orel Hershiser. He was forced to retire at age 33 due to a rotator cuff injury that couldn't be repaired back then, but he had impressed enough to get elected to the Hall of Fame in 1984.

Drysdale was an excellent hitter who clubbed 29 home runs and twice hit seven homers in a season, which tied Don Newcombe's NL record for a pitcher. He was the only player who batted over .300 (minimum 15 at bats) on the Dodgers' 1965 championship team — he batted exactly .300 and his seven home runs that year were only five behind the club leader.

Another excellent-hitting pitcher who joins Drysdale in the Hall of Fame is Bob Lemon, a native of San Bernardino. Lemon started out as a third baseman before switching to pitcher, and he was frequently used as a pinch-hitter. His lifetime average of .232 included 37 home runs, one behind Wes Ferrell for most all-time by a pitcher. When Bob Feller pitched his second no-hitter in 1946 against the Yankees, rookie Lemon was the center fielder. Lemon would go on to join Feller along with Early Wynn and San Gabriel native Mike Garcia as Cleveland's "Big Four" pitchers during the 1950s. Lemon, who spent his entire 13-year career with Cleveland, won 20 games seven times and made seven straight All-Star teams.

One other California righty who deserves mention is Dave Stieb, who relied on a devastating slider to serve as the ace of the Blue Jays throughout the 1980s. A seven-time All-Star who wound up with 176 career victories, Stieb won the AL ERA crown in 1985. On September 2, 1990, Stieb pitched what remains the only no-hitter in the history of the Blue Jays franchise. He had previously lost three no-hitters (including a perfect game) with two outs in the ninth inning.

Lefties from California have practically owned the Cy Young Award, or at least it seems that way. Mike McCormick won the 1967 Cy Young Award after winning 22 games for the Giants in 1967. Randy Jones completed a dramatic turnaround from a 22-loss season in 1974 to win the Cy Young Award two years later. Jones led the league in victories, complete games, innings and WHIP while winning 22 games for the fifth-place Padres in 1976. Another Padre, Mark Davis, won the 1989 Cy Young Award after leading the NL with 44 saves. CC Sabathia won the AL Cy Young Award in 2007 after going 19–7 for the Indians, and his 157 wins were the most in baseball for the period of 2001–2010. Rubber-armed David "Boomer" Wells finished third in the Cy Young voting in two different seasons on the way to winning 239 games during a controversial 21-year career.

Then we come to Randy Johnson, one of the greatest lefties of all-time — he ranks fifth among southpaws with 303 wins. The "Big Unit" won the Cy Young Award with the Mariners in 1995 and then won the award four straight years with the Diamondbacks from 1999 to 2002. In addition, he finished runner-up three other times and in third place once. Johnson was one of the most intimidating pitchers to ever grace the mound, as John Kruk can attest from his laughably futile attempt to bat against him in the 1993 All-Star Game. Johnson threw the first pitch 15 feet over his head and then watched Kruk wave feebly at the next three pitches.

The Big Unit threw a fastball that approached 100 mph, but his best pitch was a wicked slider that proved unhittable coming from his 6-foot-10 frame. He is the second-tallest player ever behind 6-foot-11 Jon Rauch. Johnson led the league in strikeouts and SO/9 nine times, ERA and winning percentage four times and complete games four times. He ranks first in baseball history with a 10.6 SO/9 ratio and his 4,875 strikeouts are a record for southpaws and trail only Nolan Ryan on the all-time list. The crowning achievement of Johnson's career had to be pitching seven innings to beat the Yankees in Game 6 of the 2001 World Series and then emerging from the bullpen a day later to get four outs and the win in Game 7.

That leaves a pretty fair southpaw in the honorable mention category: Hall of Famer Lefty Gomez. He won the pitching Triple Crown in 1934 and 1937 — the first year he led the league in 10 pitching categories and the second year he led in eight categories. The seven-time All-Star only won 189 games in his career, but Gomez produced 10 very good seasons with the Yankees and helped the team win five World Series by going 6–0 with a 2.86 ERA in Series action. Not known for his bat, he drove in what proved to be the winning run in the final game of the 1937 World Series. Nicknamed "Goofy" for his on-field and off-field antics, Gomez once quipped as his career was winding down, "I'm throwing twice as hard but the ball is getting there half as fast."

A final lefty worth noting is San Diego native Mark Langston, who earned seven Gold Gloves for his terrific fielding. Langston was a workhorse who pitched over 200 innings in 10 different seasons, won 179 games and made four All-Star teams. However, he is most remembered as the pitcher the Expos acquired when they shipped promising but wild southpaw Randy Johnson to the Mariners in 1989.

Three of baseball's greatest relievers were born in California. Trevor Hoffman is the all-time saves leader and Dennis Eckersley is enshrined in the Hall of Fame, while Dan Quisenberry had a shorter but brilliant career that should not be overlooked. Ultimately, we decided Hoffman's production over 18 years was more impressive than Eckersley's decade of dominance.

Hoffman never struck fear in batters like Goose Gossage — despite the playing of AC/DC's "Hells Bells" as his entrance song — but he managed to get the job done year after year. His pitches rarely exceeded 90 mph as he relied on a deceptive change-up to lock down the ninth inning. In addition to retiring as the all-time leader in saves with 601 and in games finished with 856 (since passed by Mariano Rivera in both categories), Hoffman's 902 appearances with the Padres are the most ever by a pitcher with one team. He was a great teammate and an even better person, winner of the Hutch, Lou Gehrig and Branch Rickey Awards.

Hoffman recorded at least 30 saves every season between 1995 and 2009, apart from 2003 when he pitched just 9 innings due to injury. He led the NL with 53 saves in 1998 and with 46 saves in 2006, emerging as Cy Young Award runner-up both years. Hoffman recorded seven seasons with a SO/9 ratio of at least 10.0 and averaged 9.2 SO/9 for his career. It's hard to imagine that Bruce Sutter and Rollie Fingers can get into Cooperstown and Hoffman can't, so he should start working on his acceptance speech.

Eckersley had a fascinating career, or two careers actually. He had sporadic success in his 12 seasons as a starter, winning 20 games once and making two All-Star teams. The flamboyant hurler pitched a no-hitter with the Indians in 1977 as part of a hitless streak that reached 22⅔ innings. A year later he suffered the indignity of having his wife ditch him for teammate and best friend Rick Manning.

Moved to the bullpen after being traded to the A's in 1987, "Eck" was tackling a bigger change off the field by checking into rehab and finally getting sober. Transformed in every way possible, Eck saved 390 games over the next 12 seasons, which ranks sixth all-time. A's Manager Tony LaRussa changed how relief pitchers are used by relying on Eck to go no more than one inning. Eckersley responded by winning the Cy Young and MVP Awards after saving 51 games in 1992. In 207 innings between 1989 and 1991, he only walked 12 batters unintentionally. His 0.61 ERA in 1990 doesn't tell the whole story. Eckersley allowed only five earned runs and four walks all season and actually had more saves than base runners allowed. Eck struggled some in the postseason including a memorable home run he served up to Kirk Gibson to end Game 1 of the 1988 World Series. He was elected to the Hall of Fame in 2004.

Quisenberry led the AL in saves each season between 1982 and 1985, finishing second or third in Cy Young voting each year. The submariner also led in saves in 1980 and his 45 saves in 1983 established a new major league record. His adjusted ERA of 147 is tied with Walter Johnson and Hoyt Wilhelm for fifth all-time and trails only Mariano Rivera among relief pitchers. "Quiz" was neither dominant nor overpowering — he averaged 9.2H/9 and 3.3 SO/9 for his career — but no relief pitcher was more effective in the early 1980s. After earning the AL Fireman of the Year Award in 1982, Quisenberry was quoted saying, "I want to thank all the pitchers who couldn't go nine innings, and Manager Dick Howser, who wouldn't let them." Tragically, Quiz died of a brain tumor at age 45 in 1998.

Another California reliever, Dave Righetti, also made a successful conversion from starter to closer. He was named AL Rookie of the Year in 1981 and then no-hit the Red Sox on the Fourth of July in 1983. The next year he was moved to the bullpen and broke Quisenberry's year-old record by compiling 46 saves. "Rags" ended his career with 252 saves.

Troy Percival had a dominant nine-year stretch with the Angels, relying on heat in the high 90s to average 34.7 saves between 1996 and 2004 and make four All-Star teams. He burst onto the scene in 1994 by striking out 94 batters in 74 innings while allowing only 37 hits. The Fontana native was even better the next year with 100 strikeouts in 74 innings while surrendering only 38 hits. Percival's 358 career saves rank eighth. John Wetteland had a similar nine-year stretch in which he averaged 36.5 saves between 1992 and 2000. He led the AL with 43 saves in 1996 while combining with set-up man Mariano Rivera as a devastating one-two punch that delivered a World Series title to the Yankees. Wetteland finished with 330 saves.

The ageless Jesse Orosco carved out a long career as a lefty specialist, finding work for 24 seasons and retiring in 2003 as the all-time leader in games pitched with 1,252. Those appearances totaled only 1,295 innings as he made just four starts. He held lefty batters to a .209 average over a career that lasted four decades — 1979 to 2003. Orosco spent a handful of seasons closing games for the Mets, with a high of 31 saves in 1984 and a career total of 144 saves. Covina native Doug Jones, who attended high school and college in Indiana, compiled 303 saves for seven teams and made five All-Star teams.

Tug McGraw played a major role in helping three teams win pennants. The screwball pitcher went 9–3 with a 2.24 ERA and 12 saves as the Miracle Mets of '69 won 100 games and the franchise's first World Series (he didn't appear in that Series). The brash reliever was more vocal in 1973 as his "You gotta believe" mantra became the team's rallying cry. McGraw saved 25 games that year, 11 in the last month of the season, punctuating each win by slapping his glove against his thigh and letting out a scream. Tug won a game and saved a game in that Series but the Mets fell to the A's in seven games. His last bit of magic came with the Phillies in 1980, when he came off the disabled list in July and saved 13 games while allowing only three earned runs the rest of the season. Four more saves came in the playoffs as the Phillies won the championship. When asked what he intended to do with his new contract in 1975, McGraw said, "Ninety percent I'll spend on good times, women and Irish whiskey. The other 10 percent I'll probably waste." McGraw, whose son is country star Tim McGraw, suffered the same fate as Quisenberry, dying of a brain tumor in 2004.

In deciding on the manager for the All-Time California team it was necessary to weigh the good vs. the bad with Billy Martin. His teams were invariably winners and they were never dull. Martin possessed a brilliant baseball mind, but the Berkeley native could never overcome the psychological demons that tortured him and affected his judgment. He brought energy and passion but also dysfunction and drama. Although it made sense every time George Steinbrenner fired Billy for his antics, it was beyond puzzling why The Boss kept rehiring him. A sixth return engagement to skipper the Yankees was in the works when Martin died in a car crash on Christmas Day 1989.

Martin was a protégé of Casey Stengel, who taught him to manage by instinct rather than by numbers. Many of his players firmly believed if they could keep the game close Billy would find a way for them to win it in the eighth or ninth inning. Not too many managers instill such confidence in their players. Billy was a complex person filled with contradictions. He was a combative, irresponsible, paranoid scoundrel with a drinking problem who could also be charming and loyal, a tough guy with a warm heart. Martin once admitted, "The day I become a good loser, I'm quitting baseball ... I always had a temper. I think it's nothing to be ashamed of. If you know how to use it, it can help."

No manager in baseball history has ever been better at transforming bad teams into good. Billy inherited a Twins team that had stumbled to seventh place in 1968 and guided them to 97 wins and a first-place finish in 1969. He took over a Tigers team that had finished fourth in 1970 and delivered 91 wins and a second-place finish his first year and a division title the second year. The 1973 Rangers were a mess under Whitey Herzog, staggering to a 47–91 start before Martin was brought in with 23 games left. It was too late to save that season, but he delivered 84 wins and a second-place showing in 1974. Replacing Bill Virdon as manager of the Yankees two-thirds through the 1975 season, he guided his former team to its first pennant in 12 years in 1976 and a World Series title in 1977. The Boss kept bringing him back because he knew Billy would always provide a spark. The problem was that the spark would inevitably fizzle due in large part to Martin's unstable personality.

Martin's .553 winning percentage is better than that of Hall of Fame managers Sparky Anderson, Leo Durocher, Herzog, Ned Hanlon, Tommy Lasorda, Bill McKechnie, Dick Williams, Wilbert Robinson and Casey Stengel. It is nearly equal to that of revered Yankees skipper Miller Huggins, who won at a .555 clip. Martin's 1,253 wins are more than Hall of Famer Billy Southworth.

What Billy loved more than anything was being a Yankee, both as a player and as a manager, and when the pinstripes were taken away from him it crushed his spirit, even though it was his confrontational actions that caused each breakup. It seems altogether fitting that Billy is buried in the same cemetery as the greatest Yankee ever, Babe Ruth — Gate of Heaven Cemetery in Hawthorne, N.Y. — where Billy's epitaph aptly summarizes his life: "I may not have been the greatest Yankee to put on the uniform, but I was the proudest."

Frank Chance was a born leader — hence the nickname "The Peerless Leader" — who took over as player-manager of the Cubs at the age of 28 and guided them to four pennants, two World Series and the best five-year stretch in baseball history. The Cubs won a record 116 games under his inspired direction in 1906, followed by seasons with 107, 99, 104 and 104 victories — a remarkable .693 winning percentage.

Chance was a smart, hard-nosed, competitive player and those traits characterized his managerial style as well. Although his Cubs teams were stacked with talent, he also excelled at getting the most out of that talent. His teammates on the Cubs voted him in as manager in 1905 when Frank Selee was forced to step down due to illness, and Chance went 55–33 down the stretch for a third-place finish.

It is true that when Chance skippered the 1906 Cubs to 116 wins there were only eight teams in the National League and four of them were terrible. However, he pushed the right buttons before falling short to their cross-town rivals the White Sox in the World Series that year. When the Cubs broke through with back-to-back titles in 1907 and 1908, it looked like a dynasty was in the making. Chance had no way of knowing the Cubs would still be without another title more than one hundred years later, but then again he was increasingly distracted by his own health issues as his tenure with the Cubs went on.

Just as Martin had clashed with the Boss, Chance grew frustrated with Cubs owner Charles Murphy's penurious ways. He was cut loose by Murphy as a manager and player after the 1912 season, despite the fact he had won at least 90 games in every full season he managed the Cubs.

Inheriting a Yankees squad that had finished in last place the year before, Chance guided the 1913 Yankees to a 57–94 record and seventh place. They weren't much better in 1914 before Chance was replaced by Roger Peckinpaugh. Given a third opportunity to manage with the Red Sox in 1923, Chance limped home to a last-place finish with a 61–91 record. He ended up with a .593 overall winning percentage including a .664 mark guiding the Cubs. Chance is a better choice than Martin, because he inspired his teams to greater heights without causing day-to-day drama.

Another manager who received consideration is Dusty Baker, whose teams have generally been in the pennant race each year. Baker had produced 1,484 wins against 1,367 losses in 18 years of managing the Giants, Cubs and Reds through 2011. His teams have won four division titles and finished second six times, but he has only produced one pennant and no championships. Baker has been named NL Manager of the Year three times: 1993, 1997 and 2000. He had the Cubs within a game of the World Series in 2003 and can always be found with the ubiquitous toothpick in his mouth.

Baker was a fine outfielder who never quite lived up to his billing. He played 19 years in the majors, compiling 1,981 hits and earning two All-Star selections and one Gold Glove. Baker was in the on-deck circle when Hank Aaron broke Babe Ruth's career home run record in 1973.

Bill Rigney's managerial record of 1,239–1,321 doesn't overwhelm and he only had one division title and no pennants to show for his 18 years of managing. However, not even Billy Martin could have outperformed the expectations like Rigney did with the 1962 Los Angeles Angels. The second-year expansion team was filled with enough misfits, castoffs and rascals to give any manager a headache, yet Rigney still had them in first place late in the summer. His top starter was colorful bon vivant Bo Belinsky, who led the AL in walks and would be a thorn in Rigney's side until he finally convinced owner Gene Autry to trade him after the 1964 season. Out of the bullpen was the always wild Ryne Duren, who allowed 57 walks in 71 innings. Rigney, who was nicknamed "Cricket" for the way he chirped at players, continued to pull all the right strings, but the Angels faded down the stretch to finish in third place with an 86–76 record. Rigney's masterful job did not go unnoticed as he was named AL Manager of the Year. He replaced Martin as manager of the Twins in 1970, winning his only division title that year.

COLORADO

Names in **bold** *represent Major League selections by position, followed by honorable mentions. City of birth is in parentheses.*

C — John Stearns (Denver). Also: Mark Johnson (Wheat Ridge)
First Base — Buddy Gremp (Denver)
Second Base — George Myatt (Denver). Also: Bert Niehoff (Louisville); Chuck Cottier (Delta)
Third Base — Roy Hartzell (Golden). Also: Chase Headley (Fountain)
SS — Ike Davis (Pueblo). Also: Dud Lee (Denver)
OF — Johnny Lindell (Greeley)
OF — Jimmy Welsh (Denver)
OF — Johnny Frederick (Denver). Also: Buster Adams (Trinidad); James Mouton (Denver); Larry Harlow (Colorado Springs)
Right Handed Starter — Roy Halladay (Denver). Also: Scott Elarton (Lamar); Brian Lawrence (Fort Collins)
Left Handed Starter — Gene Packard (Colorado Springs)
Relief Pitcher — Goose Gossage (Colorado Springs). Also: Dave LaRoche (Colorado Springs); Tippy Martinez (La Junta); David Aardsma (Denver)
Manager — Chuck Cottier (Delta). Also: Tom Runnells (Greeley)

The Names

Best Nickname: Rich "Goose" Gossage
Other Nicknames: Elvin "Buster" Adams; Grant "Moose" Bowler; Lewis "Buddy" Gremp; Roy "Doc" Halladay; "Salida Tom" Hughes; Albert "Cowboy" Jones; Ernest "Dud" Lee; Felix "Tippy" Martinez; George "Foghorn" or "Mercury" Myatt; Johnnie "Durango Kid" Seale; John "Bad Dude" Stearns
Most Unusual Name: David Aardsma

All-Time Leaders

Games: Roy Hartzell, 1290
Hits: Roy Hartzell, 1146
Batting Average: Johnny Frederick, .308
Home Runs: Johnny Frederick, 85
RBI: Johnny Lindell, 404
Stolen Bases: Roy Hartzell, 182
Wins: Roy Halladay, 188 (still active)
Strikeouts: Roy Halladay, 1934 (still active)
Saves: Goose Gossage, 310
Future Stars: Mark Melancon (Wheat Ridge)
Best Player: Goose Gossage

Historic Baseball Places

B's Ballpark Museum in Denver — Bruce Hellerstein's collection of baseball artifacts was featured in Stephen Wong's *Smithsonian Baseball* book as one of the finest private collections in the world. Now it's all on display in a museum across the street from Coors Field. Hellerstein has authentic seats from each of the 14 "classic" ballparks and something related to every major league team such as a complete panel from the Green Monster at Fenway Park with a visible imprint of a ball and the "NY" drainage cover that Mickey Mantle tripped over during the 1951 World Series, which permanently damaged his leg.
Coors Field in Denver — Opened as the home of the Rockies in 1995. Fans along first base and right field have a great view of Rocky Mountains. It was known as a launching pad for home runs until the team started storing baseballs in a humidor to counterbalance the effects of the high altitude. You can check out the 108 glazed tiles that depict the "Evolution of the Ball" near the front entrance.

Notable Achievements

Johnny Frederick set a record by pinch-hitting six home runs in a season for the Dodgers in 1932. Dave Hansen and Craig Wilson now hold the record with seven.
Bert Niehoff (Louisville) led the National League with 42 doubles in 1916.

This Ebbets Field turnstile, which dates to the ballpark's opening in 1913, is one of many historic artifacts on display at B's Ballpark Museum in Denver (courtesy B's Ballpark Museum).

Tippy Martinez once picked off three base runners in the same inning — all at first base — while pitching against the Blue Jays on August 24, 1983.

Roy Halladay had more starts (33) than walks (30) for the third time in 2010 (following 2003 and 2005). He just missed the mark in 2009 and 2011 (32 starts and 35 walks both years).

Reaching New Heights in the Rocky Mountains

When the pioneers were lugging their wagons westward across the mountains they evidently were hauling pots, pans ... and baseball bats. Settlers from the East helped transport the great game of baseball to the Rocky Mountain region during the Civil War era, with the game flourishing in the bustling frontier towns scattered around the Colorado Territory.

Colorado has only had a major league team since 1993, but early references to baseball in Denver appear as far back as 1862. The first organized pro team in Colorado was called the Denvers. The semi-pro team played their games at Ford Ball Park beginning around 1885, according to an article by Tom Noel in *Above the Fruited Plain: Baseball in the Rocky Mountain West*. The action shifted to River Front Park when it opened in 1887, although the ballpark along the banks of the South Platte River was more likely to be hosting rodeos and horse races. The Chicago White Stockings came to town and played an exhibition against the locals at River Front Park.

Even the smallest Colorado towns fielded a team of nine. Semi-pro teams like the Pueblo Soapweeds and Trinidad Vampires flourished alongside teams from rowdy mining towns such as Bonanza, Alma, Fairplay, Durango, Greeley and Grand Junction. Mark Rucker's article "Ghost Town Nines" points out that the Leadville Blues sent four players to the majors in the 1880s: Alex Voss, Lou Meyers, Edward Flynn and Warren Fitzgerald.

The Rocky Mountain League of the National Semi-Pro Baseball Congress was known as the Hispanic League because it was a showcase for the talents of Mexican immigrants who worked in the sugar beet fields. Teams were located in Ault, Ft. Collins, Gilchrist, Gill, Greeley and Longmont, with the Greeley Grays emerging as a powerhouse. The Grays, who were founded in 1925, soon fielded teams integrated with African American and white players.

The *Denver Post* staged a semi-pro tournament for many years (it was sometimes referred to as the "Little World Series") that was notable for allowing black teams, providing a great showcase for black players to compete against whites. Drawn by the big prize money, Satchel Paige helped pitch the House of David to the 1934 championship over his former and future team the Kansas City Monarchs. Pete Alexander pitched in the tournament at the age of 50, eight years after he ended his major league career.

Marv Throneberry won three home run crowns while playing for the Denver Bears in the old American Association, and Barry Larkin, Tim Raines and Joe Tinker are among the stars who once played for the minor league team. Billy Martin even managed part of the 1968 season in Denver, where the high altitude probably caused him to get winded when he was kicking dirt on umpires.

Denver is home to one of the hidden gems of baseball — B's Ballpark Museum. Bruce Hellerstein is a CPA who in his spare time started a tribute to classic ballparks as a museum in his basement. He amassed such an astounding collection of baseball artifacts that he soon outgrew the basement.

This must-see museum is now located in a standalone space across the street from Coors Field. Among the gems of Hellerstein's priceless collection are the light fixtures from the marble rotunda entrance to Ebbets Field; arched window, cornerstone and turnstile from Forbes Field; a turnstile from old Yankee Stadium; a complete usher's uniform from Crosley Field; an Ebbets Field usher's cap; stanchion aisle seats from the Polo Grounds; and a piece of Babe Ruth's bat and home flannel Yankee jersey. "It's been a labor of love that brings me a lot of joy," says Hellerstein, who served on a committee that consulted on the design of Coors Field. "I'm just glad that all these baseball treasures have been preserved for future generations of baseball fans to enjoy."

All-Time Colorado Selections

A total of 85 players born in Colorado have played in the major leagues, with just one Hall of Famer ... and a recent inductee at that — Goose Gossage. The pickings were slim at several positions, but the All-Time Colorado team has several standouts.

At catcher, John Stearns had the tough luck of being a good player on a series of bad teams — the New York Mets from 1975 to 1984. Still, the advantage of such fate is that you've got a better chance to make it to the All-Star Game, which is perhaps how Stearns ended up being named to four teams. For a catcher, he achieved the impressive feat of generating twice as many stolen bases as homers in his career (91–46). Let's see Bengie Molina try and do that. Stearns was also drafted by the NFL's Buffalo Bills as a defensive back.

The options at first base include Buddy Ryan (who played one game there), John Stenhouse (who played 30 games there and batted .190 lifetime), Johnny Lindell (an outfielder who played only 16 games at first), Chase Headley (who played one inning there in 2009) or my winner by default: Buddy Gremp. Buddy played 86 games at first for the Boston Braves in the 1940s, ending his playing career with a .223 average and three home runs. I'm pretty sure he never expected to make any all-time lists of baseball players.

George Myatt gets the nod at second base. Nicknamed "Mercury" for his speed on the bases, he finished second in the American League with 30 stolen bases in 1945 and batted .283 over seven seasons with the Senators and Giants. His accomplishments edge out Bert Niehoff, who led the National League in doubles in 1916 but also managed to get just one hit in 16 at-bats during the 1915 World Series.

Third base is manned by Roy Hartzell, even though he played slightly more games in the outfield. Hartzell only hit 12 home runs in his career, but he made himself valuable by bouncing between different positions. He set a record for most RBI in a game when he drove in eight runs in 1911, a record that lasted for 22 years. Highly touted as a prospect, Chase Headley took over as the Padres' starting third baseman in 2010 and still has the potential to blossom into a star.

Another weak position was shortstop. Ike Davis had one half-decent year in 1925, with 135 hits and 105 runs scored, and then he called it a career. That's still better than Dud Lee, who appears to have been aptly named. The Dudster appeared in only 253 games and batted .223. He also played under the names Ernest Dudley, Ernest Dudley Lee and Dud Dudley. I'm guessing he kept changing his name either to keep the baseball groupies at bay or perhaps to confuse the manager into putting him in the lineup.

Turning to the outfield, Johnny Frederick was predominantly a center fielder who had over 200 hits and scored more than 100 runs his first two seasons, batting .328 and .334. He also set a rookie record by legging out a league-high 52 doubles. Frederick wound up with a .308 lifetime average and is also the all-time Colorado leader in home runs with 85.

The second outfield spot goes to Johnny Lindell from Greeley, who started out as a pitcher but played mainly in the outfield in the majors. He was an All-Star for the Yankees in his first full season —1943 — and then batted .300 with 103 RBI the next year. He led the league in triples both years, but had unspectacular numbers the rest of his career. After his batting career bottomed out, a successful stint pitching in the minors led to one final chance as a pitcher in 1953. The knuckleballer walked 139 in 199 innings and ended his pitching career with eight wins and 18 losses.

Denver native Jimmy Welsh rounds out the outfield. He hit .312 as a rookie in 1925 and then had the misfortune to be traded two years later with Shanty Hogan for Rogers Hornsby. The next year Hornsby hit .387 for the Giants to win the batting title while Welsh only played three more years.

Another outfielder of note is Buster Adams, who finished eighteenth in the AL balloting for MVP in 1945 and drove in more than 100 runs twice.

The ace of the pitching staff is easy to select when you have a Cy Young Award winner among the candidates. Roy "Doc" Halladay is a eight-time All-Star who won the Cy Young Award after going 22–7 with 204 strikeouts in 2003, then became the fifth player to win the Cy Young Award in both leagues after winning the award with the Phillies in 2010.

Considered by some to be the top pitcher in the game today, Halladay ranks among such luminaries as Sandy Koufax, Christy Mathewson and Roger Clemens in career winning percentage — twelfth all-time at .671. Halladay is a master at keeping batters off-balance with a mixture of sinkers, cutters and changeups. He never throws a ball over the middle of the plate, but instead paints the corners with precision.

Halladay is a perfectionist who almost pitched a perfect game in his second career start in 1998. An error in the field ended the perfect game and he lost the no-hitter and the shutout when he surrendered a home run with two outs in the ninth. Not a bad way to get your first career victory and a precursor to the sustained excellence to come.

Perfection finally arrived on May 29, 2010, when Halladay pitched a perfect game against the Florida Marlins, becoming the twentieth pitcher to set down all 27 batters in order. For an encore, Halladay went out and pitched just the second no-hitter in postseason history in his very first playoff start for the Phillies in 2010.

Another righty, Mike Oquist, deserves mention for a dubious achievement. On August 3, 1998, he surrendered 16 hits, four homers and 14 earned runs in five innings of pitching. Oquist ended his seven-year career with a 25–31 record bouncing between the rotation and the bullpen.

Team Colorado's lefty starter is Gene Packard, who won 20 games twice for the old Kansas City Packers in the Federal League. He went 85–69 in his career with a 3.01 ERA. Although mainly a starter, Packard also pitched 98 games out of the bullpen. He managed to surrender 12 runs in a game in 1918 without taking the loss, an achievement that happens about once a century.

Few relief pitchers have ever intimidated batters like the sinister-looking Goose Gossage, with his bushy Fu Manchu mustache and high-octane fastball. Yankees teammate Rudy May once described the fear Gossage induced in batters this way: "Hitters always have that fear that one pitch might get away from him and they'll wind up D.O.A. with a tag on their toe."

The Goose became Colorado's first inductee into the Hall of Fame in 2008, a long overdue accomplishment for someone who helped redefine the role of relief pitchers. Goose saved 310 games during his 22-year career and 52 involved getting seven outs or more — an unheard of feat with today's bullpens filled with one inning or one batter specialists. Gossage was elected to nine All-Star teams and led the league in saves three times. He even finished third in the balloting for the MVP Award in 1980, when he registered 33 saves for the Yankees. Trivia buffs might know that it was Gossage who surrendered George Brett's infamous "pine tar" home run in 1983.

Goose played an integral role in helping the Bronx Bombers win the 1978 World Series, giving up just 87 hits while pitching 134 relief innings during the regular season and then pitching six scoreless innings against the Dodgers in the Series. If you take out the 1976 season, when Manager Paul Richards had the bright idea of converting him to a starter, Gossage pitched 409 innings of relief over the 1975, '77 and '78 seasons, allowing only 264 hits and striking out 403 batters. By the time Halladay is done with his career he may have surpassed Gossage as Colorado's All-Time Best Player, but for now the "Goose" has the honor.

Three other relievers deserve mention. Dave LaRoche, who appeared in 632 games in relief, saved 126 games and was named to two All-Star teams during a 14-year career. Tippy Martinez pitched 544 games in relief and registered 115 saves. He won two World Series championships with the Orioles and made one All-Star team. Finally, Denver native David Aardsma came out of obscurity to save 38 games for the Mariners in 2009. When Aardsma debuted in 2004, he was literally replacing an icon — Hank Aaron. Aardsma is now the first player listed alphabetically in baseball's biographical player list.

Chuck Cottier is the manager, even though he never got the Mariners to finish higher than fifth in one full and two partial seasons of managing. He managed and won more games than anyone else from Colorado. Also under consideration was Greeley native Tom Runnells, who compiled a 68–81 record over parts of two seasons with Montreal.

CONNECTICUT

*Names in **bold** represent Major League selections by position, followed by honorable mentions. Negro Leagues players are in italics. City of birth is in parentheses.*

C — **Brad Ausmus (New Haven)**. Also: Brook Fordyce (New London); Jim Keenan (New Haven)
First Base — **Roger Connor (Waterbury)**. Also: Mo Vaughn (Norwalk); Candy LaChance (Putnam); Walt Dropo (Moosup)
Second Base — **Dick McAuliffe (Hartford)**. Also: Tim Teufel (Greenwich); Billy Gardner (Waterford)
Third Base — **Pete Castiglione (Greenwich)**. Also: Jim Donnelly (New Haven)
SS — **Tommy Corcoran (New Haven)**. Also: Jack Barry (Meriden); Hod Ford (New Haven); Larry Kopf (Bristol)
OF — **Jim O'Rourke (East Bridgeport)**.
OF — **Jimmy Piersall (Waterbury)**
OF — **Johnny Moore (Waterville)**. Also: Jay Johnstone (Manchester); Ned Hanlon (Montville); *Charles Earle* (Meriden); Matty McIntyre (Stonington); Mike Dorgan (Middletown); Danny Hoffman (Canton)
Designated Hitter — **John Ellis (New London)**
Right Handed Starter — **Bill Hutchinson (New Haven)**. Also: Red Donahue (Waterbury); Charles Nagy (Bridgeport); Fred Goldsmith (New Haven); Joey Jay (Middletown); *Johnny Taylor* (Hartford); Steve Blass (Canaan); Carl Pavano (New Britain)
Left Handed Starter — **Fred Klobedanz (Waterbury)**
Relief Pitcher — **Rob Dibble (Bridgeport)**. Also: Ricky Bottalico (New Britain); Bill Dawley (Norwich); Pete Appleton (Terryville)
Manager — **Ned Hanlon (Montville)**. Also: Bobby Valentine (Stamford)

The Names

Best Nickname: Spec "The Naugatuck Nugget" Shea
Other Nicknames: Ed "Scrap Iron" Beecher; Tommy "Corky" Corcoran; George "Kiddo" Davis; Francis "Red" Donahue; Walt "Moose" Dropo; Walter "Monk" Dubiel; Jim "Troy Terrier" Egan; Horace "Hod" Ford; Mauro "Goose" Gozzo; William "Wild Bill" Hutchinson; Jay "Moon Man" Johnstone; "Jumping Jack" Jones; Fred "Duke" Klobedanz; George "Candy" LaChance; Arthur "Hi" Ladd; Jim "Grasshopper" Lillie; Dick "Muggsy" McAuliffe; Frank "Beauty" McGowan; Frederick "Tricky"

Nichols; Michael "Fancy" O'Neil; James "Queenie" O'Rourke; "Orator" Jim O'Rourke; John "Pretzel" Pezzullo; Jimmy "The Waterbury Wizard" Piersall; Cecil "Squiz" Pillion; James "General" Stafford; "Schoolboy Johnny" Taylor; Mo "Hit Dog" Vaughn; George "Pinky" Woods

Most Unusual Name: Augie Swentor; Mauro Gozzo; Billy Lush

All-Time Leaders

Games: Tommy Corcoran, 2200
Hits: Jim O'Rourke, 2643
Batting Average: Roger Connor, .316
Home Runs: Mo Vaughn, 328
RBI: Roger Connor, 1302
Stolen Bases: Tommy Corcoran, 387
Wins: Bill Hutchinson, 182
Strikeouts: Charles Nagy, 1242
Saves: Ricky Bottalico, 116
Future Stars: A.J. Pollock (Hebron); Jesse Hahn (Norwich); George Springer (New Britain)
Best Player: Roger Connor

Historic Baseball Places

James O'Rourke Statue at the Ballpark at Harbor Yard in Bridgeport — Unveiled in 2010 to honor the first player from Connecticut inducted into the Hall of Fame.

Jackie Robinson Park of Fame in Stamford — Life-size statue of Robinson commemorates the fact he spent the last 17 years of his life living in Stamford.

Yale Field in New Haven — Babe Ruth made one of his last public appearances in 1948 when he showed up at Yale Field to present a copy of his autobiography to a Yale captain and first baseman named George H.W. Bush. Baseball has been played continuously on this site since 1885 and the current park was constructed in 1927.

Muzzy Field in Bristol — The cozy ballpark staged its first game in 1913, and it was rebuilt in 1939 after being largely destroyed by a fire. Babe Ruth reportedly hit the stadium's first home run when he planted a ball in the Pequabuck River while playing an exhibition game with the Red Sox in 1919, and Hall of Famers Max Carey, Kiki Cuyler and Pie Traynor came to Muzzy Field while with the Pirates in 1926. Jim Rice, Fred Lynn and Wade Boggs all starred at Muzzy Field while playing for the Bristol Red Sox in the 1970s, but the old ballpark is now home to amateur baseball.

Bobby V's Sports Gallery Café in Stamford — Every square inch of wall space is filled with sports memorabilia, much of it related to Bobby Valentine's career as a player and manager in the majors and in Japan.

Notable Achievements

Jim O'Rourke was credited with the first hit in the National League when he singled on April 22, 1876.

Walt Dropo tied a record with 12 consecutive hits in July 1952. He capped the streak off by batting 7-for-7 in a doubleheader. The only other person to accomplish the feat, Pinky Higgins in 1938, walked two times during his streak.

Steve Blass led the National League in winning percentage at .750 in 1968.

Roger Connor was the first player to hit a grand slam in the majors when he did it on September 10, 1881.

Fred Goldsmith was the first pitcher to hit two doubles in one inning when he did it on September 6, 1883. Only three other pitchers have done it: Hank Borowy in 1946, Ted Lyons in 1935 and Joe Wood in 1913.

A Colorful Cast of Connecticut Characters

A total of 186 players born in Connecticut have gone on to play in the major leagues, starting with Jim Carleton back in 1871. The state has produced more than its fair share of flakes, characters and strange cases, considering it's the birthplace of Jimmy Piersall, Jay Johnstone, Steve Blass, Steve Dalkowski and the unfortunately named Billy Lush.

Lush had a largely uneventful career, collecting 429 hits in seven seasons around the turn of the century. However, the Bridgeport native made history on September 23, 1903, when he hit three triples in one game. Only 38 players have accomplished the feat since 1900. Lush also had a hand in discovering future Hall of Famer Eddie Collins.

Righty pitcher Blass, who was born in Canaan and went to Housatonic High School in Falls Village, produced some nice highlights before his career took an unfortunate turn. "Steve Blass Disease" is now used to refer to players who lose the ability to accurately throw the baseball. Blass went from a 19-game winner and Cy Young Award runner-up in 1972 to being out of baseball two years later. In 1973 he demonstrated an acute inability to throw strikes, going 3-9 with a 9.95 ERA and walking 84 batters in 88⅔ innings. He also hit 12 batters and threw nine wild pitches. Blass was even worse toiling in the minors the next season, walking 103 in 61 innings, and he would be released during spring training in 1975.

As his career took a nosedive Blass looked nothing like the pitcher who led the NL in winning percentage in 1968 or in shutouts in 1971 or who pitched two complete-game wins in the 1971 Series for the champion Pirates. It was Blass who stood triumphantly on the mound after recording the final out in Game 7 before jumping into the arms of catcher Manny Sanguillen to celebrate. So what caused his inexplicable wildness? It wasn't related to injury or mechanical problems, which means he suffered from some kind of a mental block that snowballed on him. Maybe he was still shook up over his teammate Roberto Clemente's tragic death in the offseason. At least he walked away from the game with the memory of what it felt like to be a World Champion.

Blass, to his credit, was less worked up about the way

his career ended than others. "I'm not bitter about this. I've had the greatest moments a person could ever want," he said in an interview with Roger Angell, recounted in *Five Seasons*. "Nobody's ever enjoyed winning a big-league game more than I have."

At least Blass exhibited good control for most of his career, unlike New Britain native Dalkowski. "Dalko" is in the conversation as the fastest pitcher of all-time, as it's been speculated that he threw as hard as 110 mph. A stronger case could be made that he was the wildest pitcher in baseball history. Believed to be the inspiration for the character Nuke LaLoosh in *Bull Durham*, Dalkowski spent nine years toiling in the minors and never made it to the majors primarily because he walked 1,354 batters in 995 innings and there was a real fear he would kill someone.

He once threw a pitch that tore off part of a batter's ear and launched several pitches that crashed straight through the backstop. In 1960 he struck out 262 batters in 170 innings, which gave him an impressive 13.81 K/9IP ratio (the major league record is 13.40 by Randy Johnson). Unfortunately, he also walked 262 batters that year. His final minor league tally was 12.62 SO/9IP, which obliterates the major league mark currently held by "The Big Unit" at 10.6 SO/9IP.

Nicknamed "White Lightning," Dalkowski's erratic performance was exacerbated by his chronic battle with alcoholism. He once struck out 24 batters in a game but lost due to 18 walks and six wild pitches. Ted Williams, after facing him in spring training, said, "Fastest ever. I never want to face him again." Dalkowski still holds the Connecticut high school record with 24 strikeouts in a game.

Piersall's much publicized battle with mental illness and bipolar disorder was detailed in his autobiography, "Fear Strikes Out," which was later turned into a movie. His career was filled with episodes of erratic behavior. Like the time he ran the bases backwards after hitting a home run. Or the time he squirted an umpire with a water pistol. Then there were the fights with teammates and opponents, as well as his habit of bowing after making a catch in the outfield. He may have frustrated managers, teammates and opponents, but fans loved the colorful free-spirit. In a second book, "The Truth Hurts," Piersall sums up his appeal by writing: "Probably the best thing that happened to me was going nuts. Nobody knew who I was until that happened."

Johnstone led the league in practical jokes each year, whether it was nailing teammates' cleats to the floor or climbing into the stands in full uniform to get a hot dog. He has written several humorous books if you want to know more about his many pranks such as the time he put on the uniform of a groundskeeper and swept the infield during a game or impersonated Tommy Lasorda while visiting the pitcher on the mound.

There was nothing fancy about Fancy O'Neil — he went 0-for-3 in his career. As for Tricky Nichols, with a career record of 28–73 the righty pitcher clearly wasn't tricky enough.

Not all of Connecticut's players had a screw loose.

Roger Connor and Jim O'Rourke had distinguished careers that ended with their induction into the Hall of Fame as players, and they are joined by manager Ned Hanlon and executives Morgan Bulkeley and George Weiss.

Bulkeley got his start in baseball as founder of the Hartford Dark Blues, and he went on to become the first president of the National League in 1876 and later the governor of Connecticut and a U.S. Senator. New Haven native George Weiss is in the Hall of Fame for his work in the Yankees front office. His keen eye for talent, while running the farm team from 1932–1947 and as general manager from 1947–1960, helped lead the team to 19 pennants and 15 World Series titles.

Another Connecticut native, Louis Wadsworth, has gained new standing recently as one of the early pioneers of the game. John Thorn, Major League Baseball's official historian, credits Wadsworth with being the first to introduce the concept of nine players on a side and nine innings to a game while playing for first the Knickerbockers and then the Gothams in the 1850s. Little definitive information exists about Wadsworth's real contributions to the game.

"Yankee Doodle" is the official state song of Connecticut, but you won't find any famous Yankees players who hail from the state. Yankees legend Lou Gehrig did get his start in professional baseball playing for the Hartford Senators in the Eastern League in 1921. It was the only team he played for other than the Yankees.

These days Connecticut is home to just as many fans of the Red Sox as of the Yankees. Another Boston team, the Boston Braves, held spring training in Wallingford, Conn., in 1943 and 1944, as teams stayed close to home during the War.

Spec Shea was nicknamed "The Naugatuck Nugget" in honor of his birthplace. Shea attracted attention by winning 14 games for the Yankees as a rookie in 1947 while leading the AL in winning percentage and allowing just 127 hits in 178⅔ innings. For an encore that year, he won Games 1 and 5 in the World Series as the Yankees won the championship. Shea later taught Robert Redford how to throw like an old-time pitcher for *The Natural*.

All-Time Connecticut Selections

Moving on to the team selections, we have Brad Ausmus at catcher. Although he never produced much with the bat, his masterful way of handling pitchers and strong throwing arm helped him stay in the league for 18 seasons. You would expect him to be a heady player since he graduated from Dartmouth. Ausmus made the All-Star team in 1999 and won three Gold Gloves. Only Ivan Rodriguez and Jason Kendall have recorded more putouts at the position and Ausmus is tied with Mike Matheny for the third-best lifetime fielding percentage (.9943) for catchers who have caught more than 8,000 innings. In his book *The Baseball Talmud*, Howard Megdal names Ausmus the third-best Jewish catcher in baseball history.

First base is in the capable hands of Hall of Famer Connor, who held the all-time home run record before Babe Ruth with a grand total of 138. He once hit three homers in a game, which was almost beyond belief in his day, and became the first player to hit an over-the-wall home run at the Polo Grounds. He was a large (6-2, 210 pounds) and imposing man at the plate and on the bases, stealing as many as 43 bases in a season and finishing his career with 233 triples (25 in just 99 games for St. Louis in 1894). Connor's .371 average led the league in 1885 and he batted over .300 11 times. The lefty was a pretty good fielder, too, leading the league in fielding percentage four times.

Leading the list of honorable mention first basemen is Mo Vaughn, who was nicknamed "Hit Dog" for his slugging prowess. Vaughn averaged 34 home runs between 1993 and 2002, leading the AL in RBI with 126 RBI in 1995 when he was named MVP. He had an even better season the next year, setting career highs with 118 runs, 207 hits, 44 homers, 143 RBI and a 1.003 OPS. A three-time All-Star, Vaughn retired with 328 homers, most in Connecticut history.

At second base we have Dick McAuliffe, who managed to finish seventh in the MVP balloting in 1968 during the Tigers championship season despite batting .249. All he did that season was lead the league in runs scored and tie a major league record by not hitting into a single double play despite 570 at-bats. McAuliffe made three consecutive All-Star teams (1965–67), although the first two were as a shortstop. He ended up playing 971 games as a second baseman and 666 as a shortstop.

For a middle infielder McAuliffe had some pop in his bat, using an unconventional batting stance and swing to smack 197 career homers. Although his career average is just .249, McAuliffe is ranked #22 all-time among second basemen by Bill James, who writes, "He was as odd in the field as he was at the plate."

Odd or not, McAuliffe was more accomplished than Waterford native Billy Gardner. Gardner led the American League in doubles and plate appearances in 1957, but was only a regular for five of his 10 seasons. His lifetime average was .237 in 1,034 games, although he did win a World Series with the Yankees in 1961.

Third base is manned by Pete Castiglione, who had an undistinguished career with the Pirates and Cardinals. He played in 545 games from 1947 to 1954 and batted .255. He edges out Jim Donnelly, who collected 552 career hits with a .229 average while playing at the end of the nineteenth century.

A strong case can be made for two players at shortstop. Tommy Corcoran started playing barehanded in 1890 but eventually switched to using a glove. "Corky" compiled 2,256 hits including 155 triples and stole 387 bases. As Bill James points out, Corcoran is the only player to score more than 1,000 runs and have a career on-base percentage below .300 (he ended up at .289). He also set a record that still stands by recording 14 assists in a nine-inning game in 1903.

Corcoran's longevity gives him the nod over Jack Barry, who was an exceptionally steady fielder. And his teams always seemed to win, as evidenced by the fact that teams he played on finished first or second eight out of his 11 seasons. Barry teamed up with Eddie Collins, Stuffy McInnis and Frank Baker to form one of the greatest infields ever, helping Connie Mack win three World Series for the A's. Traded to the Red Sox in 1915, Barry helped them win the World Series that year. He got more clutch hits than his .243 average would indicate. After his playing career ended, Barry became the baseball coach at Holy Cross, leading them to victory in the College World Series in 1952 and setting a college record for winning percentage (.806).

Another shortstop of note is Hod Ford, who formed a great double-play combination with Hughie Critz on the Cincinnati Reds in the late 1920s. The New Haven native collected 1,296 hits during a 15-year career, batting .263.

The outfield is highlighted by "Orator" Jim O'Rourke, who was the Julio Franco of his era. He started playing in 1872, before the National League was even formed, and made a final appearance at the age of 54 in 1904 — going 1-for-4 to become the oldest person to get a hit. O'Rourke led the NL in batting in 1884 with a .350 average and he batted over .300 11 times in the majors, winding up his career at .311. His 2,643 hits included just 62 homers, although he led the league in home runs in 1880 with a grand total of six. O'Rourke even pitched in six games in addition to playing some at catcher, first base, third base and shortstop. He was elected to the Hall of Fame in 1945.

While O'Rourke was known for his gentlemanly behavior, he has to share the outfield with one of the most eccentric characters to ever play the game. Piersall was just 20 years old when he made it to the majors and he went on to play 17 seasons with many highs and lows. He made two All-Star teams and won two Gold Gloves for his play in center field — Billy Martin called him the best defensive center fielder he ever saw.

For the third outfield spot it's necessary to focus on which of three players — Johnny Moore, Ned Hanlon or Jay Johnstone — made more of an impact over the course of their careers. Hanlon was never a standout and Johnstone was largely a platoon and bench player, while Moore packed nice production into his career considering he didn't become a regular until the age of 30.

Moore batted over .300 five times, ending his career with a .307 mark. His best year was 1935, when he hit .323 with 19 homers and 93 RBI, finishing fifteenth in the MVP voting that year. Moore played half as many seasons as Johnstone but holds the advantage in average, OBP, slugging, OPS and OPS+. Johnstone only had one season with more than 450 at-bats, while Moore had four such seasons and batted .263, .330, .323 and .328 in them. Johnstone played for nine teams over 20 seasons and never took himself too seriously. He batted 7-for-9 in a losing effort for the Phillies against the Big Red Machine in the 1976 NLCS and later won World Series titles with the Yankees and Dodgers.

As for Hanlon, he made the Hall of Fame as a manager and not an outfielder. In a playing career that lasted from 1880-92, he finished with 1,317 hits and a .260 average and is credited with 329 stolen bases under the rules of the day. Other than hits, his career batting and slugging stats are greatly overshadowed by Moore and Johnstone.

Our staff ace is righty Bill Hutchinson from New Haven, who pitched in nine seasons between 1884 and 1897. Out of his 346 career starts, 321 were complete games. He led the National League in victories three straight years, winning 112 games over that stretch and finishing 182-163 for his career. Hutchison pitched an amazing 622 innings during the 1892 season, or 477 more innings than Pavano ended up pitching for the Yankees during his four-year contract.

Red Donahue was a contemporary who won 20 games three times. He finished his career with a record of 165-175, but he dug himself an early hole. Few pitchers would still be around after the year Donahue had for the St. Louis Browns in 1897. He went 10-35 with a 6.13 ERA and gave up 484 hits in 348 innings while striking out just 64 batters. The Browns gave up twice as many runs as they scored that year and ended up 29-102 and in twelfth place.

Charles Nagy was a dependable starter during his 14-year career, mainly with the Indians. Known for having a strong curveball and excellent control, he won 129 games and was named to three All-Star teams. The Bridgeport native pitched for Team USA in the 1988 Baseball World Cup, not allowing any runs in 15⅔ innings, and he also won a gold medal in the Olympics that year.

Fred Goldsmith was one of the first pitching stars in the National League. The righty went 112-68 with a 2.73 ERA, winning over 20 games four times. Goldsmith went to his grave believing he invented the curveball and when he died, he was found on his bed clutching an article about an exhibition he put on for people to prove that he could make a ball curve.

Joey Jay, fell one victory shy of 100 for his career as well as one strikeout shy of 1,000. Jay won 20 games twice and was named to the All-Star team in 1961 for the Reds, finishing fifth in the MVP race that year. He won the only game the Reds captured during the World Series that year against the Maris-led Yankees. Jay was a switch-hitter as a batter, a rarity for a major league pitcher.

Quality left-handed starters from Connecticut have evidently been in short supply through the years, but we finally unearthed Fred Klobedanz. "Duke," as he was known, went 26-7 in 1897 and finished his brief career with a winning percentage of .679.

One of the original "Nasty Boys," Rob Dibble, is our closer. Although his career was shortened to seven seasons due to injury, Dibble was one of the hardest throwers in baseball history. With a fastball that approached 100 mph, he was an intimidator on the mound. Named to two All-Star teams, Dibble only saved 89 games in his career but wound up with 645 strikeouts in 477 innings. He is one of about 40 pitchers in history to strike out the side on nine pitches. He averaged 13.5 K/9 in 1991 and did even better the next year with 14.0 K/9.

Dibble was a more dominant reliever than Rickey Bottalico, who saved 116 games for six different teams, appearing in 562 games in relief. Bottalico made the All-Star team for the Phillies in 1996, saving 34 games that year.

Turning to manager, Hanlon won 1,313 games against 1,164 losses and his teams were known for their aggressive base running and bunting. Hanlon won three consecutive pennants with the Baltimore Orioles from 1894-1896 and then followed that up by winning pennants with Brooklyn in 1899 and 1900. He was elected to the Hall of Fame in 1996.

Another accomplished manager from Connecticut

Ned Hanlon was a nineteenth-century outfielder who played 13 years in the majors, serving as player-manager his last four seasons. His managerial style relied on aggressive bunting and base running, and he led his teams to five pennants in seven seasons. Hanlon was elected to the Hall of Fame in 1996 as a manager (Library of Congress, Prints & Photographs Division, LC-DIG-bbc-0188f).

is Stamford native Bobby Valentine, who has been more successful as a skipper than he ever was as a shortstop. During 15 years of managing the Rangers and Mets, Valentine came in second four times but never finished first. His 2000 Mets team did make it to the World Series, where they lost to the Yankees in five games. Valentine did lead the Chiba Lotte Marines to the Japan Series championship in 2005. Valentine is the son-in-law of Ralph Branca, the famed Brooklyn Dodgers pitcher who surrendered Bobby Thomson's "Shot Heard 'Round the World" in 1951.

DELAWARE

*Names in **bold** represent Major League selections by position, followed by honorable mentions. Negro Leagues players are in **bold italics**, followed by honorable mentions in italics. City of birth is in parentheses.*

Catcher — Chris Widger (Wilmington)
First Base — John Mabry (Wilmington)
Second Base — Delino DeShields (Seaford). Also: Spook Jacobs (Cheswold)
Third Base — Hans Lobert (Wilmington)
Shortstop — Will Holland (Georgetown)
Outfield — *Ed Stone* **(Black Cat)**
Outfield — Dave May (New Castle)
Outfield — Randy Bush (Dover)
Designated Hitter — Kevin Mench (Wilmington)
Right Handed Starter — Sadie McMahon (Wilmington). Also: *Webster McDonald* (Wilmington); Bert Cunningham (Wilmington)
Left Handed Starter — Chris Short (Milford). Also: *Sy Simmons* (Middleton)
Relief Pitcher — Huck Betts (Millsboro). Also: Renie Martin (Dover)
Manager — Dallas Green (Newport)

The Names

Best Nickname: Webster "56 Varieties" McDonald
Other Nicknames: Walter "Huck" Betts; Bill "Skip" Crouch; Delino "Bop" DeShields; Robert "Spook" Jacobs; Frank "Flip" Lafferty; John "Hans" Lobert; John "Sadie" McMahon; Kevin "Shrek" Mench; Ed "Ace" Stone; John "Happy" and "Peach Stone Jack" Townsend
Most Unusual Name: Ken Szotkiewicz

All-Time Leaders

Games: Delino DeShields, 1615
Hits: Delino DeShields, 1548
Batting Average: Hans Lobert, .274
Home Runs: John Mabry, Dave May, Randy Bush — tied at 96
RBI: Delino Deshields, 561
Stolen Bases: Delino Deshields, 463
Wins: Sadie McMahon, 173
Strikeouts: Chris Short, 1629
Saves: Renie Martin, 12
Future Stars: Derrik Gibson (Seaford); Robert Bryson (Newark); Brett Oberholtzer (New Castle); Paul Goldschmidt (Wilmington)
Best Player: Sadie McMahon

Historic Baseball Places

Delaware Sports Museum and Hall of Fame in Wilmington — The highlight of the museum is Judy Johnson's "Talking Exhibit," which tells the Hall of Famer's story from Delaware to Cooperstown.
Frawley Stadium and Judy Johnson Field in Wilmington — The park, originally called Legends Stadium when it opened in 1993, is where the Wilmington Blue Rocks play.

Notable Achievements

Dallas Green managed the Philadelphia Phillies to the franchise's first championship in 1980, as they won the series over the Royals.
Bill Hawke (Elsmere) is the only Delaware-born pitcher to throw a no-hitter. His no-hitter on August 16, 1893 also represented the first thrown in the majors with the pitching distance at 60-feet, 6-inches.
On April 7, 1896, **Pete Cassidy** (Wilmington) became the first professional baseball player to be x-rayed when he had a bone splinter removed from his wrist.
Bill Crouch (Kiamensi) pitched a complete game in his only major league appearance on July 12, 1910.
Spook Jacobs posted four hits in his major league debut on April 13, 1954, tying the AL record with six other players.
Negro Leagues star **Sy Simmons** lived longer than anyone else who has ever played professional baseball. Simmons, who was born the same year as Babe Ruth (1895), died in 2006 at the age of 111.
John Mabry is the only Delaware-born player to hit for the cycle, which he did while playing for the Cardinals on May 18, 1996.

Delaware's Month in the Big Leagues

If you want to win a bar bet, ask whether the state of Delaware has ever been home to a major league baseball team. The surprising answer is ... yes! It was a short-lived run, but as Yogi Berra would say, "You can look it up."

The National League, which had been organized in 1876, found itself eight years later facing competition from a new professional league — the Union Association. While the fledgling Union Association season was getting underway, the Wilmington Quicksteps were running roughshod over their fellow Eastern League teams. They would end their short season 50–12.

When the Philadelphia Keystones disbanded with one month left in the Union Association season, league founder Henry Lucas turned to the Wilmington team as a replacement. The Quicksteps won their first game, but things went downhill quickly as key players such as Oyster Burns and Tony Cusick started jumping ship to play on other teams for more money. The team would go 2–16 before disbanding — an inglorious end to Delaware's brief moment on the big stage.

Wilmington-born George Fisher actually played on that Quicksteps team in 1884, making him the only Delaware native to play for a major league team in Delaware. Fisher batted .069 in 29 at-bats. Fred "Sure Shot" Dunlap hit the only major league home run hit in Delaware when he connected off John Murphy on September 10, 1884, while playing for the St. Louis Maroons against the host Wilmington Quicksteps.

A total of 50 players born in Delaware have played in the major leagues, including Happy Townsend, who is one of the few major league players to be born in a town with the same name as his last name. Townsend, who won only 35 games against 82 losses during his career, played for the 1904 Washington Nationals, arguably one of the worst teams in baseball history. The Nationals' record was 38–113 that year and they finished 55½ games out of first place by being bad in all facets of the game. They were last in the league in batting, fielding and pitching. Townsend led the league in losses (with a record of 5–26) and wild pitches and was second in walks and earned runs, while teammate Case Patten picked up the slack by leading the league in hits allowed and earned runs.

If you can suffer through that kind of season and still be called Happy, then you should win some sort of award. My guess is that his managers that year — Malachi Kittridge and Patsy Donovan — were more Grumpy than Happy. Poor Malachi didn't get another managerial chance after flaming out with a 1–16 record that year.

Frank "Flip" Lafferty earns recognition as Delaware's first major league player, making his debut for the Philadelphia Athletics in 1876. He pitched one game for the A's that year, allowing no earned runs and five hits in a complete game loss, leaving him with a lifetime ERA of 0.00. The next year he appeared in four games in center field for the Louisville Grays, ending his career with just one hit in 20 at-bats for a lifetime average of .050.

Hall of Famer Vic Willis is sometimes listed as being born in Delaware — particularly since his nickname is Delaware Peach — but he was actually born in Maryland, moving soon after with his family to Delaware.

The Hall of Fame does feature one Delaware native. Wilmington's Bill McGowan is one of only nine umpires enshrined in Cooperstown. McGowan was the Cal Ripken of umpires, as he umpired for 2,541 consecutive games.

All-Time Delaware Selections

Let's get to the All-Time Delaware team selections. Wilmington native Chris Widger earns the nod at catcher. Widger only registered 435 hits during his 10-season career, with 55 home runs, but he won a World Series ring with the White Sox in 2005 and is the best of a thin group. He was the nominal starter for the Expos in 1998 and 1999 but otherwise was a backup.

Charlie Marshall is Delaware's version of "Moonlight" Graham. Marshall came in as a defensive replacement at catcher for one game in 1941, didn't get to bat and never again appeared in a major league game. Marshall had a long career in the minors and was considered an excellent defensive catcher.

John Mabry earns the selection at first base, although he played slightly more games in the outfield. It was a shame no team picked up Mabry after he was released by the Rockies in 2007, since he remains tied with Dave May and Randy Bush for the most home runs by a Delaware native with 96. And if Team Delaware's pitching staff needs reinforcement he can pitch in a pinch — he made two appearances as a pitcher. The other thing noteworthy about Mabry is the fact that he preferred not to wear batting gloves. Some people are scared of clowns, others shy away from batting gloves — go figure.

Future star Paul Goldschmidt of Wilmington rose quickly through the minor leagues for the Diamondbacks. He hit .334 in rookie ball in 2009 and then belted 35 homers with 108 RBI in 2010, leading him to be named MVP of the California League. After clubbing 30 homers in 103 games in Double-A ball in 2011, he was called up by the Diamondbacks and made his major league debut on August 1, 2011.

One of the standouts of the team is second baseman Delino DeShields. "Bop" had a pretty good career, but he will always be remembered as the guy the Expos traded away in 1993 for Pedro Martinez. He ended his career with 463 stolen bases with a high of 56. After finishing second for NL Rookie of the Year in 1990, his average dropped 51 points the next season while leading the league in strikeouts. A three-sport star at Seaford High School, DeShields was named Delaware Athlete of the Decade in 1989.

Another second baseman of note is Spook Jacobs, who might have had a decent career but found himself stuck in the minors by the Brooklyn Dodgers for eight seasons. Spook, who got his nickname due to his speed on the bases, compiled 1,927 hits and 148 stolen bases over 11 minor league seasons, batting .299.

The third baseman is another speedster, Hans Lobert, who actually spent very little of his life in Delaware. He batted over .300 four times and stole 316 bases during his 14-year career. He was once timed running the bases in 13.8 seconds, or about the time it takes Bengie Molina to get out of the batter's box. In 1913 he beat Olympian Jim Thorpe in a footrace and two years later Lobert accepting the challenge of racing around the bases against a horse, narrowly losing. If Bill Veeck had been around, he probably would have signed the horse.

Lobert's career started in 1903 with the Pirates, where star Honus Wagner noted they shared the same given name (John or Johannus), heritage (German) and facial features (big nose), so he started calling him "Hans Number Two," reports Jonathan Dunkle in *Deadball Stars of the National League.* Lobert only hit 32 home runs during his career playing in the Deadball Era, and the first 13 were all inside-the-park homers. He led NL third basemen in fielding percentage once and putouts twice. His brother, Frank, appeared in 11 games in the Federal League.

Named manager of the Phillies at the age of 60 in 1942, Lobert decided the team would do better if it was called the Phils. "We've been at the bottom of the standing so long the syllable seems to imply we're lying dormant," he told *The Sporting News.* After finishing last with a 42–109 record, Lobert was out as manager after one year and the team went back to being called the Phillies.

Shortstop is a bit of a dead spot. Ken Szotkiewicz played 44 games for the Tigers in 1970 and batted a frigid .107 while Ed Cihocki played 28 games in 1933 and batted .143. Will Holland emerged as the slugger of the group, batting .189 in 1889 with 27 hits playing in 39 games at short for the Baltimore Orioles. He wins the prize, qualifying as perhaps the least accomplished of any all-time state's player.

In the outfield we find two players with remarkably similar career statistics. Dave May and Randy Bush both ended their 12-year playing careers with 96 home runs and batting averages of .251. May had 13 more RBI, while Bush recorded four more walks and four more strikeouts. However, May is one of only two Delaware natives to play in the All-Star Game. He had a fantastic season for the Brewers in 1973, leading the AL in total bases while batting .303 with 25 homers and 93 RBI.

The third outfielder is Ed "Ace" Stone, a Negro Leagues star who could do it all, but his best skill was a throwing arm that rivaled any in baseball history. Stone got his start playing for the semipro Wilmington Hornets. Stone played in three East-West All-Star Games and was a formidable batter on some of the top Negro Leagues teams including the Newark Eagles, the Kansas City Monarchs and the Pittsburgh Crawfords. In 1946 he was selected to play with Jackie Robinson's All-Stars, a barnstorming team that competed against an all-star team of white players put together by Bob Feller.

While Bush and May are tied with Mabry for the all-time home run lead for a Delaware native, our designated hitter, Kevin Mench, could theoretically still pass them. "Shrek" needs only eight more dingers to take the lead. Mench was the 1998 Collegiate Player of

Hans Lobert was a speedster from Wilmington, Delaware, who was one of the top third basemen of the Deadball Era. He stole more than 30 bases seven times in an eight-year stretch and retired with 316 stolen bases. He was once timed running the bases in 13.8 seconds and later raced around the bases against a horse, narrowly losing (Library of Congress, Prints & Photographs Division, LC-DIG-ggbain-12001).

the Year at the University of Delaware, leading the NCAA in home runs that year with 33. He hit a home run in seven consecutive games during the 2006 season, a record for a right-handed batter. Mench spent 2009 playing in Japan and appeared in 27 games for the Nationals in 2010.

Our left-handed starter is Chris Short, who is the only other Delaware native to be an All-Star. He was named to two All-Star teams (in 1964 and 1967), but not in the year in which he won 20 games (1966). Best known as one of the aces on the Phillies team that choked on a six-game advantage with 10 games to play in 1964, Short finished with a career mark of 135–132. Managers now know you shouldn't go with a two-man rotation down the stretch. Although predominantly a starter during his career, Short is the all-time Delaware leader in relief appearances in addition to being a close second in games started.

A half-century before Short was retiring batters, another Delaware lefty was making a name for himself.

Silas "Sy" Simmons, who started playing before the Negro Leagues were even officially organized, played for the Homestead Grays and New York Lincoln Giants in a career that spanned 1912–1929. Simmons, who also played a lot in the outfield, relied on a powerful fastball and a dazzling curve.

The right-handed starter is Sadie McMahon, who pitched at the end of the nineteenth century. McMahon won 20 or more games four times, pitched 279 complete games and ended up 173–127 with a 3.51 ERA. McMahon was a starter on the 1896 Baltimore Orioles team that won the National League pennant with a 90–39 record. Managed by Ned Hanlon, the Orioles' regular lineup featured future Hall of Famers Willie Keeler, Hughie Jennings and Joe Kelley and outscored opponents 995–662.

Here's the case for McMahon as Delaware's All-Time Best Player: He was one of the best (and definitely the hardest worked) pitchers in the American Association over that league's last two seasons. In 1890 and 1891 McMahon won 71 games (of the 121 he pitched in), started 115 games and threw over 1,000 innings. Only four other pitchers threw 500 innings combined during those two seasons. McMahon threw that many each of those seasons. No other Delaware players were ever that clearly important to their team's success.

Although he never pitched in an East-West All-Star game, Webster McDonald was a solid pitcher over a 20-year career in the Negro Leagues. Nicknamed "Submarine" for his underhanded throwing motion and also "56 Varieties" for his wide assortment of pitches, McDonald threw three no-hitters one season.

Bert Cunningham, set a major league record in 1890 by throwing five wild pitches in one inning, a record since tied by Rick Ankiel in 2000. Cunningham won 142 games over a 12-season career, winning 28 games for Louisville in 1898 and 22 for Baltimore in 1888.

Another starter from Delaware whose career got off to a promising start is Ian Snell, who was the Pirates minor league pitcher of the year in 2003 and then pitched a no-hitter in the minors in 2005. Snell won 14 games for the Pirates in 2006 before stumbling the next few seasons. Sent down to the minors early in 2009, he set a Victory Field record with 17 strikeouts while pitching for the Indianapolis Indians. Traded to the Mariners in July 2009, Snell finished the season strong by going 5–2 down the stretch but that was the last success he would enjoy.

Huck Betts gave up a lot of hits (10.4 per 9 innings) and posted nearly as many walks (321) as strikeouts (323), but his Career Win Shares total of 77.4 far outpaces the other relievers from Delaware. Betts won 61 games and registered a 3.93 ERA over 307 games (182 in relief). Also considered was Renie Martin, who posted 12 saves in 122 relief appearances between 1979 and 1984.

Another relief pitcher from Delaware, Dallas Green, didn't have an illustrious pitching career but he is certainly qualified to skipper Team Delaware. Green managed the Phillies to the 1980 World Series title, beating the Royals in six games. He later managed the Yankees and Mets and ended up with 454 career wins as a manager. During his tenure in the Cubs front office he was responsible for securing city approval to install lights at Wrigley Field.

DISTRICT OF COLUMBIA

*Names in **bold** represent Major League selections by position, followed by honorable mentions. Negro Leagues players are in **bold italics**, followed by honorable mentions in italics. City of birth is in parentheses.*

Catcher—Pop Snyder Also: Tom Kinslow; *Arthur Thomas*; Vic Correll
First Base—Lu Blue
Second Base—Bump Wills Also: Joe Gerhardt
Third Base—Don Money Also: Art Devlin
Shortstop—Maury Wills Also: *Jelly Jackson*; Sadie Houck; Sonny Jackson
Outfield—Milt Thompson
Outfield—Algie McBride
Outfield—Bubba Morton Also: Denny Sothern; Earl Clark
Designated Hitter—Curtis Pride
Left Handed Starter—*Jesse Winters* Also: Doc White
Right Handed Starter—Clay Kirby Also: *Ping Gardner*; Billy Taylor; *Scrip Lee*
Relief Pitcher—Johnny Klippstein Also: Brendan Donnelly; Johnny Welch; Frank Funk
Manager—Pop Snyder Also: Joe Gerhardt

The Names

Best Nickname: Joe "The Barnum of the Bushes" Engel
Other Nicknames: Kenneth "Ping" Gardner; Sargent "Sadie" Houck; Norman "Jelly" Jackson; Roland "Sonny" Jackson; Holsey "Scrip" Lee; Wycliffe "Bubba" Morton; Charles "Pop" Snyder; Fred "Bubby" Talbot; "Bolicky Bill" Taylor; Guy "Doc" White; Elliott "Bump" Wills; Maury "Mousey" Mills; Jesse "Nip" Winters
Most Unusual Name: Franklin Funk

All-Time Leaders

Games: Maury Wills, 1942
Hits: Maury Wills, 2134
Batting Average: Algie McBride, .292

Home Runs: Don Money, 176
RBI: Don Money, 729
Stolen Bases: Maury Wills, 586
Wins: Doc White, 189
Strikeouts: Doc White, 1384
Saves: Brendan Donnelly, 6
Future Star: Mike Sheridan
Best Player: Maury Wills

Historic Baseball Places

Nationals Park— When the Nationals new ballpark opened in 2008 it was the first stadium to be green certified. The Washington Hall of Stars display at Nationals Park, which can be found hanging above the center field plaza, highlights players such as Josh Gibson (who played many games for the Homestead Grays at Griffith Stadium in DC), as well as Walter Johnson and Bucky Harris (who played for the old Senators).

National Museum of American History— The impressive Lou Newman Collection of Baseball Memorabilia is stored here in the archives and available to researchers. It contains team programs dating back to 1895, baseball sheet music, old advertising with baseball images, old postcards of baseball parks, teams and players and much more.

Smithsonian Institute— The National Portrait Gallery has a permanent exhibit of Champions that features more than 50 baseball figures such as Pedro Martinez.

Notable Achievements

Maury Wills was the first player to bat for the Montreal Expos, when he served as the leadoff hitter for the expansion team's first game on April 8, 1969.

Bump Wills was one of the players involved the only time back-to-back, inside-the-park home runs have been hit in a major league game. Wills was followed by teammate Toby Harrah on August 27, 1977.

Don Money hit the first home run in Veterans Stadium in Philadelphia on April 10, 1971.

Maury Wills set a record for most games played in a season with 165 in 1962.

Doc White pitched five consecutive shutouts in 1904, with his 45-inning scoreless streak setting a record that lasted 64 years.

Playing the Changing Name Game

It's not hard to imagine confusion taking place in the nation's capitol, but politicians cannot be blamed for the historical mess regarding the names of the Washington ball clubs.

Baseball in our nation's capitol dates back to 1871, when the Olympic Base Ball Club began play in the National Association. The team was also known as the Washington Olympics, the Washingtons, the Nationals, the Blue Legs and the Blue Stockings, before the league disbanded in 1875. You can see where a team might get an identity crisis, but the confusion was just beginning.

When the short-lived Union Association started up in 1884 it included a team called the Washington Nationals, but occasionally referred to as the Unions or the Washingtons. The same year another team called the Washington Nationals was competing in the American Association along with a Washington-based team nicknamed the Statesmen, which moved to Richmond during the season. None of these teams lasted past the season.

The city was not without a baseball team for long. The Washington Nationals entered the National League in 1886. *The Evening Post* preferred calling the team the Statesmen, while other papers took to calling them the Senators. The team folded after the 1889 season, dashing the hopes of their bewildered fans. Washington was again without a team for 1890, but got back in the game with the Washington Senators in the American Association for the 1891 season. Keeping to form, Nationals was used interchangeably as the nickname.

The Washington franchise switched over to the National League for the 1892 season, with the Senators emerging as the preferred name. That team was the victim of contraction after the 1899 season.

The Washington Senators that were a founding member of the American League in 1901 were a completely different franchise that had moved from Kansas City, although the tradition of losing continued. As researcher Norman Macht points, the team's owners tried to settle the name confusion in 1905 by polling fans for their preference. They didn't get a consensus, so the local papers continued to call the team the Nationals or Nats while everyone else referred to them as the Senators. When the franchise moved to Minneapolis to become the Twins, a new team called the Senators took over in D.C. and lasted 11 seasons until moving to Texas to become the Rangers. Major League Baseball returned baseball to Washington by converting the Expos franchise into the Nationals in 2005.

All-Time D.C. Selections

Watching losing teams year after year probably didn't do much to inspire the local youth to pursue the game. However, one great player did emerge. Maury Wills is the most notable player to come out of the D.C. area among the nearly 100 who have reached the major leagues.

Wills helped restore the stolen base to prominence when he pilfered a record 102 in 1962—more than any other team posted that year. When Wills got on base, he gave pitchers a lot to worry about. He led the National League in stolen bases his first six full seasons and finished with a career total of 586. He won three World Series rings with the Dodgers.

Wills not only made five All-Star teams and earned two Gold Gloves for his defense at shortstop, he was named the National League MVP over Willie Mays in 1962. That year the switch-hitting Wills led the league with 10 triples, recorded 208 hits and scored 130 runs in addition to his record for stolen bases.

What hurt his career totals more than anything was the fact he got a late start — he spent over eight years in the minors and didn't make his debut until the age of 26. He stole 52 bases in 1968, a year in which he turned 36. Wills would have stolen even more bases if he walked more often — his career high for walks was 59. Amazingly, he didn't even try switch-hitting until he was well into his minor league career.

Thankfully we don't have to make Wills the manager of the D.C. team, because he was horribly overmatched in that role. A strong case can be made that he was the worst manager in major league history. Rob Neyer's book of baseball blunders and Steve Rudman, in an article in the *Seattle Post-Intelligencer*, both detailed Wills' many managerial goofs. For example, he once made out a lineup that had two third basemen and no center fielder, while another time he went out to the mound to change pitchers and discovered no one had been warming up. Wait, there's much more. Wills left in the middle of a spring training game because he had a flight to catch, and he once waived a player before a game but used him in the game anyway. You can't make up this stuff.

A better choice for manager is Pop Snyder, who led Cincinnati to a first-place finish in the American Association in 1882 and won at a .572 clip over four seasons of managing. Snyder is also our catcher, although he had a lifetime average of .235 and a career high of two home runs. At least he hung around to play 18 seasons, some as a player-manager. He was a fine receiver, leading the league in fielding percentage, putouts and assists three times.

Lu Blue was a top-notch first baseman who was adept with the bat and glove. The switch hitter scored more than 100 runs six times and ended his career with a terrific .402 OBP because he knew how to work pitchers for a walk.

At second base is Maury's son, Bump. He could do everything his father could do, just not nearly as well. He had less speed than his dad but more power. After five good seasons in Texas and one with the Cubs, Bump went on to play in Japan. He still holds the Rangers team record for stolen bases in a season with 52.

Steady Don Money is our third baseman. The four-time All-Star started off as a shortstop but quickly found a comfort level at the hot corner after being moved to make room for Larry Bowa at shortstop on the Phillies. A great fielder, he later had the misfortune of playing third base in the American League the same time as Brooks Robinson, so he never won a Gold Glove for his fielding prowess even though he set a major league record with 86 consecutive errorless games. In 1974 he played 157 games at third while committing only five errors, setting an American League record for fewest errors that still stands. By comparison, Brooks was charged with 18 errors that year on the way to his fifteenth straight Gold Glove.

Money barely edges Art Devlin, who led the New York Giants to the 1905 World Series title, leading the league with 59 stolen bases that year. He batted .269 for his career with 1,185 hits and OPS+ of 110.

It was tempting to place Sonny Jackson in the outfield, but he played three times as many games at short. The diminutive Jackson stole 49 bases in 1966 — the year he was runner-up for Rookie of the Year — but managed to slug just seven homers in his 12-season career.

Headlining the outfield is Milt Thompson, who bounced around the National League collecting 1,028 hits during a vagabond career but was mainly known for his spectacular catches in the outfield. Thompson drove in five runs during a 1993 World Series game for the Phillies, who ended up losing that year to Toronto. Turn-of-the-century player Algie McBride ends up with the second outfield spot — he batted .292 over five seasons and was considered an above-average fielder. Our third outfielder is Bubba Morton, who had an unremarkable seven-season career as a bench player in the 1960s.

Curtis Pride, who ended up playing 11 seasons in the major leagues despite being born deaf, finds a spot on the team as designated hitter. Pride played 11 seasons for six different teams in the majors and was still playing in an independent league in 2008 at age 40, giving him 22 years in professional baseball. Pride's best year was 1996 when he batted .300 with 10 homers and 80 hits for the Tigers.

It was tough choosing the all-time lefty for D.C., since a strong case can be made for both Doc White and Jesse "Nip" Winters. Ultimately, Winters was judged to be more dominant during his career. Winters struggled with alcoholism but still was one of the best lefties in the Negro Leagues. Winters, who possessed a wicked curveball but had control problems, pitched no-hitters in 1922 and 1924 and won three games for the Hilldale Daisies during the first Negro World Series in 1925. His combined record in was 32–6 in 1923 followed by a 27–4 mark in 1924, and he led the Daisies to three consecutive pennants in the Eastern Colored League.

White won 189 games for the Phillies and White Sox, including 27 games while forming a formidable trio with Ed Walsh and Frank Smith for the 1907 Sox. He finished his career with a 2.39 ERA (tied for twenty-fifth all-time) and 1.12 WHIP.

Southpaw Joe Engel had an unremarkable career as a pitcher for the Washington Senators/Nationals, rooming with Walter Johnson as a rookie but winning just 17 games in seven seasons. He had served as a batboy and mascot for the team in his youth, hanging around the ballpark and developing a knack for pranks. Working later as a scout for the Senators he had a hand in discovering Goose Goslin and Joe Cronin. However, he made a lasting mark on the game once he took over as president of the Chattanooga Lookouts just as the Great Depression hit.

Over the next 34 years Engel entertained fans with a never-ending series of wacky promotions to gain the nickname "The Barnum of the Bushes." He brought in a 17-year-old girl, Jackie Mitchell, to pitch to (and strike out) Babe Ruth and Lou Gehrig. He raffled off a house, held a wild elephant hunt and once traded away a player for a turkey, although some called it an even trade.

Our right-handed starter, Clay Kirby, got off to an inauspicious start. Pitching for the last-place Padres he led the NL in losses in 1969 with 20 against just seven wins. He rebounded to have an outstanding season for the Padres in 1971, winning 15 games with a 2.83 ERA and allowing just 213 hits in 267 innings. Kirby won 10 games for the Reds in 1975 as they won the World Series that year.

Another righty considered was "Bollicky Bill" Taylor, who went a combined 43–16 in 1884 pitching for the St. Louis Maroons in the Union Association and the Philadelphia A's in the American Association. He won just seven other games in his career. Ping Gardner used a submarine style to success over 15 years in the Negro Leagues.

Holsey "Scrip" Lee was a leading pitcher in the Negro Leagues from 1922–34. Relying on a sidearm delivery and an endless assortment of pitches to keep batters off balance, Lee went 24–8 for the Hilldale Daisies in 1923, leading the team to the Eastern Colored League championship in 1925. He also had a number of successful years with the Baltimore Black Sox.

The top relief pitcher is Johnny Klippstein, who appeared in 550 games in relief from 1950 to 1967. He spent the first half of his career bouncing between starting and relieving, before finally switching more or less full time to the pen in 1958. His father-in-law, Dutch Leonard, was a more accomplished pitcher, but Klippstein was a valuable contributor in relief who ended up winning 101 games and finishing 276.

FLORIDA

*Names in **bold** represent Major League selections by position, followed by honorable mentions. Negro Leagues players are in **bold italics**, followed by honorable mentions in italics. City of birth is in parentheses.*

Catcher — Al Lopez (Tampa). Also: Charles Johnson (Fort Pierce); Mike Stanley (Fort Lauderdale); Mike Heath (Tampa); Brian Schneider (Jacksonville)

First Base — Fred McGriff (Tampa). Also: Steve Garvey (Tampa); Boog Powell (Lakeland); Tino Martinez (Tampa); Bill White (Lakewood); *Buck O'Neil* (Carrabelle); Glenn Davis (Jacksonville)

Second Base — Davey Johnson (Orlando). Also: Robby Thompson (West Palm Beach); *Ray Neil* (Apopka); Jody Reed (Tampa); Jimmy Bloodworth (Tallahassee)

Third Base — Chipper Jones (DeLand). Also: Larry Parrish (Winter Haven); Howard Johnson (Clearwater); Dean Palmer (Tallahassee); Dave Magadan (Tampa); Jim Presley (Pensacola); Ed Charles (Daytona Beach); *Harold Hair* (Jacksonville)

Shortstop — *Pop Lloyd* (Palatka). Also: Jay Bell (Eglin Air Force Base); *Dick Lundy* (Jacksonville); David Eckstein (Sanford); Scott Fletcher (Fort Walton Beach); Alex Gonzalez (Miami)

Outfield — Tim Raines (Sanford)

Outfield — Andre Dawson (Miami)

Outfield — Gary Sheffield (Tampa). Also: Luis Gonzalez (Tampa); Dante Bichette (West Palm Beach); *Vic Harris* (Pensacola); Lou Piniella (Tampa); Mickey Rivers (Miami); Vince Coleman (Jacksonville); J.D. Drew (Tallahassee); Derek Bell (Tampa); Carl Everett (Tampa)

Designated Hitter — Hal McRae (Avon Park)

Left Handed Starter — Steve Carlton (Miami). Also: Mike Hampton (Brooksville); *Jimmy Hill* (Plant City)

Right Handed Starter — Dwight Gooden (Tampa). Also: Tim Wakefield (Melbourne); Rick Rhoden (Boynton Beach); Mudcat Grant (Lacoochee); Jack Billingham (Orlando); *Ted Trent* (Jacksonville); Alex Fernandez (Miami Beach)

Relief Pitcher — Tom Gordon (Sebring). Also: Bobby Thigpen (Tallahassee); Jay Howell (Miami); Scot Shields (Fort Lauderdale); Gene Nelson (Tampa); Doug Corbett (Sarasota); Rob Murphy (Miami)

Manager — Tony LaRussa (Tampa). Also: Al Lopez (Tampa); Lou Piniella (Tampa); *Vic Harris* (Pensacola); *Pop Lloyd* (Palatka); Davey Johnson (Orlando)

The Names

Best Nickname: Bronson "Saturn Nuts" Arroyo

Other nicknames: Don "The Weasel" Bessent; Ulysses "Buster" Brown; Steve "Lefty" Carlton; Ed "The Glider" Charles; Clarence "Choo Choo" Coleman; Vincent "Van Go" Coleman; "Jurassic Carl" Everett; Albert "Cool Papa" Frazier; Dwight "Dr. K" Gooden; Tom "Flash" Gordon; Jim "Mudcat" Grant; Harold "Buster" Hair; "Vicious Vic" Harris; Leo "Preacher" Henry; Jimmy "Squab" Hill; Howard "HoJo" Johnson; Larry "Chipper" Jones; John Henry "Pop" Lloyd; "King Richard" Lundy; Fred "Crime Dog" McGriff; Elisha "Bitsy" Mott; Raymond "Smoky" Owens; "Sweet Lou" Piniella; John "Boog" Powell; Tim "Rock" Raines; John "Bubbles" and "Pepper" Reese; "Mick the Quick" Rivers; Deion "Prime Time" Sanders; Ted "Big Florida" and Highpockets

Trent; Henry "Flash" Turner; Tim "Melbourne Medicine Man" Wakefield; "Hard Hittin'" Mark Whitten

Most Unusual Name: Jarrod Saltalamacchia; Boof Bonser; Anders Gar Finnvold

All-Time Leaders

Games: Andre Dawson, 2627
Hits: Andre Dawson, 2774
Batting Average: Lance Richbourg, .308
Home Runs: Gary Sheffield, 509
RBI: Gary Sheffield, 1676
Stolen Bases: Tim Raines, 808
Wins: Steve Carlton, 329
Strikeouts: Steve Carlton, 4136
Saves: Bobby Thigpen, 201
Future Stars: Eric Hosmer (Cooper City); Matt Moore (Fort Walton Beach); Dee Gordon (Windermere); Karsten Whitson (Chipley); A.J. Cole (Winter Springs); Ian Desmond (Sarasota); Nick Franklin (Longwood); Chris Sale (Lakeland); Anthony Rizzo (Fort Lauderdale)
Best Player: Pop Lloyd

Historic Baseball Places

The Ted Williams Museum and Hitters Hall of Fame at Tropicana Field in St. Petersburg — Not only can you see exhibits that highlight the Splendid Splinter's career (including a bronze statue of him at the main entrance), you will also find displays dedicated to all-time greats such as Willie Mays, Mickey Mantle, Roger Maris and Joe DiMaggio.

The Elliott Museum in Stuart — The museum was torn down in June 2011 and the new Elliott Museum under construction will be nearly twice the size. When reopened it will feature an impressive collection of baseball artifacts dating back to the nineteenth century including a baseball signed by the 1932 world champion Yankees, Shoeless Joe Jackson's bat and baseball cards signed by the famous double-play combination of Tinker, Evers and Chance.

Jackie Robinson Ballpark in Daytona Beach — Baseball has been played at the site since 1914 and the stadium, now home to the Daytona Cubs, is listed on the National Register of Historic Places due to the fact that it's where Robinson made his first pro appearance in 1946.

George Steinbrenner gravesite in Trinity — Folks continue to pay their respects to the Boss, who was laid to rest in a mausoleum at Trinity Memorial Gardens.

Baseball Boulevard in St. Petersburg — Recounts the history of spring training baseball through a series of sidewalk plaques designed to look like a home plate. The plaques begin at Progress Energy Park/Al Lang Field (named after Florida's Sunshine Ambassador to Major League Baseball) and end 10 blocks later at Tropicana Field.

Joker Marchant Stadium in Lakeland — This stadium

Jackie Robinson made history when he played his first professional baseball game at City Island Park in Daytona Beach, Florida, on March 17, 1946. Robinson was participating in his first spring training since his historic signing with the Dodgers, and Daytona Beach was the first city to allow him to play after other Florida cities refused. The stadium is now known as Jackie Robinson Ballpark (courtesy BallparkReviews.com).

The Detroit Tigers have been holding spring training in Lakeland, Florida, since 1934, and their home since 1966 has been Joker Marchant Stadium. A Mediterranean-style façade was added as part of an extensive renovation in 2003 but the original grandstand remains (courtesy BallparkReviews.com).

opened in 1966 as the new Tigertown, but Lakeland has been the spring training home of the Tigers since 1934, which is the longest tenure between a team and a spring training host. Catch a game from the Al Kaline Suite and marvel at the old-fashioned appeal of this venerable ballpark.

Bright House Field in Clearwater — Phillies' spring training park opened in 2004. By the west entrance is a sculpture titled *The Ace*, which was designed to represent 90 years of Phillies history.

George M. Steinbrenner Field in Tampa — Spring training home of the Yankees now features a life-size bronze statue of The Boss by the entrance that is identical to the one at Yankee Stadium. The 16 Yankees that have had their numbers retired are honored with a plaque in the Monument Park.

Tinker Field in Orlando — Stadium is named after Hall of Famer Joe Tinker, who spent his retirement years in the area. Opened in 1963, it was the longtime spring training home of the Twins until 1990, and baseball has been played there since 1914. Professional baseball has been absent since 2000, but the ballpark is unlikely to be torn down since it's on the National Register of Historic Places.

McKechnie Field in Bradenton — Opened as the spring training home of the Cardinals in 1923, it has been host to the Pirates since 1969. It is named for Hall of Fame Manager Bill McKechnie, who was a longtime resident of Bradenton. This classic stadium, which features a charming Spanish Mission-style exterior, didn't install lights until 2008. Babe Ruth and Ted Williams are among the greats who played on the field.

Hammond Stadium in Fort Myers — The park, which opened in 1991, hosts the Twins for spring training. The visually appealing exterior was designed to look like Churchill Downs.

JetBlue Park in Fort Myers — Scheduled to open in 2012 as the spring training home of the Red Sox. The design is meant to mesh modern-style architecture with quaint features of Fenway Park in Boston, including the Green Monster in left field.

Notable Achievements

Jarrod Saltalamacchia (West Palm Beach) has the longest surname in MLB history.

Andre Dawson became the first player to be intentionally walked five times in a game in 1990.

Lenny Harris (Miami) holds the record for most career pinch hits with 212.

Davey Johnson became the first player to hit two game-winning grand slams as a pinch hitter in the same season when he connected on April 30 and then had a walk-off slam against the Dodgers on June 3, 1978. Twenty-seven days later, Mike Ivie tied his feat.

Rick Rhoden became the first pitcher to start a game at designated hitter when he did it on June 11, 1988.

Dave Eiland (Dade City) is the only player to give up a home run to the first batter he faced (Paul Molitor) and also hit a home run in his first at-bat, which happened while playing for the Padres in 1992.

Chipper Jones holds the record for most career home runs by a switch hitter in the National League.

Jim "Mudcat" Grant was the first African American to lead the American League in wins. He won 21 games for the Twins in 1965.

Casey Kotchman (St. Petersburg) set a major league record for consecutive errorless games at first base with 274 between 2008 and 2010.

When **Casey Coleman** (Fort Myers) debuted with the Cubs in 2010 he represented the third generation of his family to play in the majors, joining his father and grandfather, both named Joe Coleman. The Boone, Bell and Hairston families are the only other three-generation families.

Grapefruit League Tradition Shapes Florida Baseball History

One of the most popular annual rites of spring — watching big leaguers shake off the rust in spring training camps — is synonymous with Florida. Spring training in the Sunshine State can be traced back to a four-day camp held by the Washington Statesmen in Jacksonville in 1888, more than a century before major league teams came to Tampa/St. Petersburg and Miami.

Connie Mack's Philadelphia Athletics created a buzz when they rolled into Jacksonville to hold the first official spring training in Florida in 1903. The A's eccentric hurler Rube Waddell was a big attraction when he showed up, but he was just as likely to be found wrestling alligators or leading parades through downtown. Rube even suited up for the local Rollins College baseball team that winter.

The Reds came to Jacksonville in 1905, followed by the Boston Beaneaters in 1906 and Brooklyn Superbas in 1907. The Cubs arrived in Tampa in 1913, holding workouts at Plant Field and playing three games against a team of Cuban stars. The Indians held spring training in Pensacola that year.

Joining the Cubs the next year were the St. Louis Browns in St. Petersburg, the St. Louis Cardinals in St. Augustine and the Philadelphia Athletics in Jacksonville. The Grapefruit League tradition has held pretty steady since then. Florida dominated spring training action for many years, but the state has seen a number of teams leave for Arizona over the past two decades as that state has been more aggressive in getting new stadiums built to entice teams. Fifteen teams still play Grapefruit games in 13 Florida cities, with the Tigers boasting the longest tenure dating back to 1934 in Lakeland.

In the early years, spring training was a series of informal workouts with barnstorming games thrown in to recoup costs. Back then players didn't train year-round, so they really needed some time to get in game shape. By 1910 spring training was an accepted tradition among clubs and over the years teams gradually realized the benefits of turning their spring training camps into a tourist attraction.

Baseball history was made during spring training in 1946, when Jackie Robinson became the first African American to break the color barrier in professional baseball while playing for the Montreal Royals in Daytona Beach against the Brooklyn Dodgers. Other Florida cities had refused to allow Jackie to play there. The ballpark is now named after Robinson and a statue of Jackie can be found outside the park along with plaques that commemorate his achievement. Spring training facilities in Florida were not integrated until the mid–1960s.

Black baseball was big in Jacksonville around the turn of the century, with the Red Caps playing at Durkee/Red Cap Field. Jacksonville native Dick Lundy got his start at age 17 with the Jacksonville Duval Giants and after leaving baseball he worked as a redcap at the Jacksonville Terminal Station.

Jacksonville was one of the cities that wouldn't let Jackie Robinson play there with the Royals. Instead, it would be Hank Aaron on the 1953 Jacksonville Braves who would integrate the city for baseball (along with teammate Felix Mantilla). It helped that Aaron batted .362 that season on the way to being named the South Atlantic League MVP.

Buck O'Neil, the legendary ambassador of the Negro Leagues, was born in Carrabelle but grew up in Sarasota, where he could watch the New York Giants play spring training games at Payne Park. Today, you can find the Buck O'Neil Baseball Complex at Twin Lakes Park in Sarasota, where the Orioles minor leaguers hold spring training.

Fort Myers native Esix Snead played 18 games for the Mets in 2002 and 2004. Luckily he was an outfielder and not a shortstop. Fort Myers' most famous ballplayer is Deion Sanders, who played nine full or partial seasons in the majors between 1989 and 2001, when he wasn't moonlighting as a football player. Neion Deon led the NL with 14 triples in just 303 at-bats with the Braves in 1992 and later stole 56 bases for the Reds in 1997. When he ended his flirtation with baseball he had accumulated 186 stolen bases, 558 hits and a respectable .263 average.

Two of the best Florida nicknames belong to players with the last name of Coleman. Vince "Van Go" Coleman picked up his moniker due to his speed on the bases and not his skill with the paint brush. He led the National League in stolen bases his first six seasons, surpassing 100 steals the first three and retiring with 752 stolen bases. Clarence "Choo Choo" Coleman started his career with the Indianapolis Clowns in the Negro Leagues, but the 5-foot-9, 165-pound catcher was a perfect fit for the expansion New York Mets, who were the clowns of the National League in their early years. Choo Choo claimed to not know where his nickname came from, but he sure didn't hit like a locomotive. He batted .197 playing three seasons for the Mets and one for the Phillies.

Sometimes you're a-good and sometimes you're a-bad — in the case of Andy Abad, well, he was well-named. Abad managed to get 21 at-bats for three teams between 2001 and 2006 and he collected just two singles, which works out to a batting average and slugging percentage of .095. At least he was a-good in the minors, recording 1,485 hits and 157 homers with a .288 average across 15 minor-league seasons.

Elisha "Bitsy" Mott didn't attract much attention during his one-year career. He was the semi-regular shortstop for the Philadelphia Phillies in 1945 and ended up playing 14 years in the minors. What's interesting is that his sister married Colonel Tom Parker in 1935, 20 years before the Army deserter with a shady past discovered Elvis Presley. After his playing career ended, Mott spent time working as a personal security guard for Elvis and even got to appear in several Elvis movies, according to the HistoricBaseball.com site. Now there's a man who probably had some interesting tales to tell.

All-Time Florida Selections

The All-Time Florida Team features a Hall of Famer at catcher, although Al Lopez was elected to the Hall as a manager. His batting statistics were pedestrian, but Lopez was an excellent defensive catcher with a strong arm who led the National League in fielding percentage and assists three times. Selected to two All-Star teams, he debuted at the age of 20 and continued playing until he was nearly 40. He passed Gabby Hartnett for most career games caught, a record that held up for 42 years.

Florida natives have played a key role on the three American League teams that have won the most regular season games ever. The 1954 Cleveland Indians were managed by Lopez, a Tampa native and the first-ever Hispanic manager in the majors, and they set an American League record with 111 victories. That was topped by the 1998 Yankees, who won 114 games and were led in homers and RBI by Tino Martinez, who was also born in Tampa. In the twilight of his career, Florida native Tim Raines was a sparkplug for the Yanks that year.

Three years later, the Mariners won 116 games under the mercurial managing of Tampa-born Lou Piniella. They were knocked out of the playoffs by the Yankees, who were again led in homers and RBI that year by Tino Martinez. That great Yankee team was defeated in the World Series by the Arizona Diamondbacks, when Luis Gonzalez (another Tampa native) squibbed a soft hit to center off Mariano Rivera in the bottom of the ninth inning of Game 7 to score Jay Bell (who was born on Eglin Air Force base in Florida) with the winning run.

The Florida connection has foiled the Yankees in other ways through the years. In a 16-year period between 1949 and 1964, Lopez's teams were the only ones to knock the Yankees out of the World Series. In addition to the '54 Indians, the '59 White Sox managed by Lopez also won the pennant. His teams finished second to the Yankees the other years from 1951 to 1959. However, Lopez's 1954 Indians team still holds the league record for the best winning percentage at .721.

Getting back to catcher, heading the honorable mention list is Charles Johnson, who won four straight Gold Gloves and made two All-Star teams. He hit .357 in the 1997 World Series to help the Marlins win their first championship, but his best season was 2000. He set career highs with 31 homers, 91 RBI and a .304 average in a season that was split between the Orioles and the White Sox. He never batted above .259 in any of his other 11 seasons.

You could name at least a half-dozen worthy candidates to man the All-Time Florida team at first base. We went with the Crime Dog—Fred McGriff, who ironically happens to be Charles Johnson's cousin. McGriff was Mr. Consistent; you could count on him for 35 homers and 100 RBI every year. He fell just short of 500 home runs for his career—finishing up at 493, which is the same career total of another first baseman who wasn't too bad—guy named Gehrig. There are 13 first basemen in the Hall of Fame who have fewer homers than McGriff, who led the league twice in that category. More importantly, he was clutch in the postseason, batting .303 with 10 home runs. The five-time All-Star finished in the top 10 in the MVP balloting six times, a mark of a great player. Although he should be a strong candidate for the Hall of Fame, it looks like he will have a tough road ahead to get elected.

Forced into the unenviable task of replacing Yankee icon Don Mattingly in the lineup for the 1996 season, Tino Martinez helped lead the team to four World Series wins in his first five years with the team. He appeared to be channeling the ghost of Lou Gehrig in 1997, when he finished second in the MVP race after hitting 44 homers and driving in 141 runs. Tino was a gamer who wound up his career with 339 home runs.

Although he started out as a left fielder, Boog Powell literally grew into a first baseman. He won an MVP award in 1970 and was named to four All-Star teams—twice as many as Martinez—but their stats are remarkably similar. In fact, they ended up with the same number of career home runs while Martinez had a slight edge in batting average and hits. Powell was a feared slugger in the Orioles lineup as they won championships in 1966 and 1970.

Bill White was named to five All-Star teams and earned seven Gold Gloves for his work at first. The left-handed batter was equal parts steady and spectacular, especially in 1963 when he had 200 hits, scored 106 runs and batted .304 for the Cardinals. After an 18-year stint as a Yankee broadcaster, White went on to serve as National League president from 1989 to 1994, becoming the first African American executive for Major League Baseball.

If ever a player seemed headed to the Hall of Fame, it was Steve Garvey. He hit for power and average, drove in runs, made 10 All-Star teams, won four Gold Gloves and set a National League record by playing in 1,207 consecutive games. Garvey had more than 200 hits six times, which is quite a feat for a first baseman. He won the NL MVP Award in 1974 and finished second in 1978. He hit four homers in the 1978 NLCS against the Phillies and batted .338 in 55 lifetime playoff games. A statistical analysis of his defense reveals that Garvey's work at first was less than stellar, despite his reputation. However, he was a selfish, robotic player whose personal reputation took a big hit when his ex-wife blew the whistle on his sexual indiscretions. He received 41 percent of the votes for the Hall of Fame when first eligible in 1993 but dropped off the ballot after failing to get elected in 15 years.

McGriff, Powell, Martinez, White and Garvey were all great players, but none of them made as big an impact on the game as Buck O'Neil, who was the most eloquent spokesman of the Negro Leagues and its greatest ambassador. O'Neil was a good but not great first baseman, a steady and productive player who appeared in four East-West All-Star games and won a batting crown with a .353 average in 1946. He played almost his entire career with the Kansas City Monarchs, where he was a teammate of Satchel Paige. O'Neil spent his last eight years with the Monarchs as player-manager, guiding the team to two league titles. His career average was .300.

After his playing career ended Buck became a scout for the Cubs, signing Lou Brock for the team. In 1952 he made history by becoming the first African American coach in the major leagues when he joined the Cubs coaching staff. His contributions to baseball were just beginning. After the major leagues integrated it was O'Neil who emerged front and center as an eloquent spokesman to make sure the feats of his Negro Leagues comrades lived on in history. He was an instrumental force in the creation of the Negro Leagues Baseball Museum in Kansas City, serving as honorary board chairman up until his death in 2006. A bronze statue of O'Neil greets each visitor to the museum in Kansas City, just as one does in Cooperstown.

Unfortunately, Hall of Fame voters never quite knew how to properly evaluate Buck's candidacy and he fell short again in 2006, the year the Hall elected a special class of 17 Negro Leagues players and executives. O'Neil's playing accomplishments may not have been good enough to earn him entry into Cooperstown, but his overall contributions to the game made him a true legend. Ironically, O'Neil spent nearly two decades as a member of the Hall's Veterans Committee, helping ensure six Negro Leagues players gained induction.

That final voting slight had to break O'Neil's heart, but he expressed no bitterness over it. He passed away a few months after appearing in Cooperstown to watch the special class of 2006 get inducted without him. The great storyteller had finally run out of stories to tell, kids to mentor, strangers to embrace and laughs to share. He was truly an American original. Buck was posthumously granted the Presidential Medal of Freedom and the Hall of Fame named a Lifetime Achievement Award after him in 2008.

Strong arguments can be made for two players at second base. Davey Johnson and Robby Thompson posted remarkably similar career statistics, but Johnson has a slight edge in hits, homers, batting average and OBP, plus he made four All-Star teams and earned three Gold Gloves — compared to two All-Star selections and one Gold Glove for Thompson. They are almost dead even in Career Win Shares — 169 for Johnson and 164 for Thompson.

Johnson only had one exceptional year batting, 1973, but he tied Rogers Hornsby's record that year by hitting 42 homers as a second baseman. That achievement overshadows Thompson's best year, 1993, when he batted .312 with 19 homers. After that, Thompson saw his career cut short by a shoulder injury. Johnson and Thompson were pretty equal as hitters and fielders, but Johnson played a key role on Orioles teams that won three straight pennants (four overall) and two championships. Johnson's home run mark combined with his postseason record proves to be the final deciding factors to earn him the selection.

Ray Neil was among the best second basemen to play in the Negro Leagues. Few could make the double play better than the quick, sure-handed Neil, who was also a skilled batsman. He led the Negro American League with a .397 average in 1953 at the age of 33.

At third base, Chipper Jones is one of the best switch hitters to ever play the game. Growing up in the "fern capital of the world"— Pierson, Fla.— Chipper honed his baseball skills to become the top overall pick in the 1990 amateur draft. The Braves sure got that pick right. If he can keep his career batting average over .300, Chipper will be the only switch hitter with an average over .300 in addition to 400 homers. His career line of .306/.402/.533 puts him in rarified air with Ruth, Williams, Gehrig and a handful of others and ahead of such all-time greats as Mays and Aaron, whose on-base percentage fell short of .400.

With 18 home runs in 2009, Jones fell just short of breaking a record he shared with Eddie Mathews — most consecutive seasons to start a career with at least 20 home runs. The two Braves greats both did it for 14 seasons. Chipper probably should have been named to more All-Star teams than he has (seven), considering he has received MVP votes after 12 seasons. Jones won a batting title in 2008 at age 36 and he will definitely see his plaque enshrined in Cooperstown one day.

Also worth mentioning at third base are Larry Parrish and Howard Johnson. Parrish made two All-Star teams and slugged 256 homers over 15 seasons. Johnson spent nine of his 14 years manning the hot corner for the New York Mets, leading the NL in homers and RBI in 1991 while finishing fifth in voting for the MVP Award. A two-time All-Star, he retired with 228 homers.

John Henry "Pop" Lloyd is considered the greatest shortstop in the history of the Negro Leagues, and he just might have been the best shortstop of any league. Babe Ruth expressed the opinion that Lloyd was the greatest baseball player of all-time, regardless of color, according to James Riley's *Biographical Encyclopedia of the Negro Baseball Leagues*. That type of testimonial helps earn Lloyd bragging rights as Florida's All-Time Best Player.

Lloyd got started on the sandlots of Jacksonville and his career lasted from 1906 to 1932, when he was 48 years old. He considered himself a free agent every year available to the highest bidder, so he jumped from team to team, a dozen in all. His presence in the lineup and at short immediately made his new team an instant contender. Lloyd won championships with Sol White's Philadelphia Giants, the New York Lincoln Giants, Chicago American Giants, and as player-manager of the Hilldale Daisies.

Often called "the black Honus Wagner," Lloyd blended line-drive power and speed with excellent glove work and great range. Lloyd is credited with a lifetime average of .343 playing largely during black baseball's Deadball Era, according to the Hall of Fame, and averaged 321 against major league competition. He collected 14 hits in 15 at-bats during one hot stretch.

Dick Lundy belongs in the same conversation, as he was the premiere Negro Leagues shortstop in the 1920s. Lundy was a deceptively powerful switch hitter with excellent speed and base-running instincts. He was an even better fielder than Pop Lloyd and finished with a .306 average in Negro Leagues action. Peers such as Chance Cummings, Ted Page and Yank Deas all expressed the opinion that Lundy was the greatest shortstop.

Also receiving honorable mention status was Jay Bell, a smart player who did all the little things well, establishing a reputation as one of the best overall shortstops of the 1990s. In 1993 Bell became the first shortstop not named Ozzie Smith to win the NL Gold Glove and he was named to two All-Star teams.

Just three outfielders from Florida merit Hall of Fame consideration, so Andre Dawson, Gary Sheffield and Tim Raines are the logical choices for the All-Time Florida Team. It is unfortunate that Dawson had to wait so long to be enshrined in Cooperstown. The list of players who have accumulated more than 400 home runs and 300 stolen bases is exceptionally brief: Barry Bonds, Willie Mays, Alex Rodriquez and Andre Dawson.

"The Hawk" was clearly one of the best all-around players of his time, especially when he was in his prime with the Expos. In addition to winning the 1987 MVP Award (becoming the first player on a last-place team to win) and Rookie of the Year in 1977, Dawson was named to eight All-Star teams and earned eight Gold Gloves. "No player in baseball history worked harder, suffered more or did it better than Andre Dawson," said teammate Ryne Sandberg during his 2005 Hall of Fame induction speech. "He's the best I've ever seen."

Sheffield's numbers may be tainted somewhat by documented steroids usage, but he was one of the most feared sluggers in baseball for the better part of two decades. He swung at every pitch with ferocious intensity and always seemed to be mad about some perceived slight. The nine-time All-Star kept climbing the ranks of the all-time home run leaders and now ranks 24th with 509 after not catching on with a team after the 2009 season.

Sheffield compiled eight seasons with more than 100 RBI and retired with 1,676 for his career, which ranks 25th. He ended up with a .393 OBP, .514 slugging percentage and .907 OPS. Early in his career Sheffield committed the unpardonable sin of intentionally making errors in the field to get himself traded out of Milwaukee. That revelation combined with his admitted steroid use greatly reduces the likelihood he will get elected to the Hall of Fame.

Raines was one of the finest leadoff hitters and base stealers in baseball history. He is number five all-time in stolen bases with 808 and his 84.6 percent success rate on steals is astounding. "Rock" Raines was named to seven straight All-Star teams with the Expos and he was also a vital cog on the Yankees' 1996 and 1998 championship teams.

Sports Illustrated writer Joe Posnanski makes a compelling argument for Raines to be elected to the Hall of Fame, noting that he has 390 Career Win Shares, which puts him ahead of dozens of players who are already enshrined in Cooperstown, including Roberto Clemente, Rod Carew, Wade Boggs, Johnny Bench, Ernie Banks and Duke Snider, among others. The player he's compared to most often, Hall of Famer Lou Brock, is credited with 349 Career Win Shares.

Raines is one of only 10 players to reach base 3,500 times, compile 3,500 total bases and steal 500 bases since 1901, joining a list that includes Cobb, Henderson, Brock and Morgan. By any measure of greatness, Raines meets the standard.

Looking to the bench now, Luis Gonzalez is one of those players whose numbers catch people by surprise. Unable to catch on with a team in 2009, he ended his 19-year career with 354 home runs, 2,591 hits and four All-Star selections. He had one great season sandwiched around four good seasons, all starting at the age of 32. He pounded 57 home runs in 2001 (blasting 35 before the All-Star break) and only hit more than 30 one other time — 31 in 2000. He also led the NL in hits in 1999 on the way to batting .336.

Other notable Florida outfielders include Lou Piniella, Mickey Rivers, Dante Bichette and Vic Harris. "Sweet Lou" Piniella was named Rookie of the Year with the Kansas City Royals in 1969 and proved himself a valuable contributor to Yankees teams that won four pennants and two World Series during his tenure. Piniella was a lifetime .291 hitter, but he never developed much power — his career high was 12 home runs. Rivers was a speedy leadoff hitter who led the AL with 70 stolen bases in 1975 and then joined Piniella in the Yankees outfield for their run of three straight pennants from 1976–78. Rivers finished third in the 1976 MVP race after batting .312 with 43 steals. "Mick the Quick" was famous for his malapropisms such as "Me and George and Billy are two of a kind" and "Pitching is 80 percent of the game and the other half is hitting and fielding."

Bichette put up some big numbers with the Colorado Rockies, but a lot of that production can be attributed to the Coors Field factor. He finished second in the MVP voting in 1995 after batting .340 and leading the NL with 40 homers, 128 RBI and 197 hits. The four-time All-Star ended his career with 274 homers and a .299 average. Harris was a long-time star in the Negro Leagues, spending 23 years with the Homestead Grays and playing in six East-West All-Star Games. A skilled left-handed batter and aggressive base runner, he was not to be messed with on or off the field—hence the nickname "Vicious Vic." As player-manager Harris led the Grays to nine straight pennants and two Black World Series titles.

Team Florida's designated hitter is Hal McRae, who was one of the first players whose primary position was DH. An outfielder by trade, he was mainly a DH the last 12 years of his 19-year career. McRae was a .290 career hitter who led the league in doubles twice and compiled a league-best 133 RBI in 1982—41 more than his next-best total.

Any pitcher nicknamed "Lefty" is a logical choice for best left-handed starter, and Steve Carlton certainly has the credentials. In addition to winning the Cy Young Award four times, Carlton ranks fourth all-time in strikeouts and his 329 victories rank 11th (with little chance anyone else will pass him in his lifetime). He is second on the all-time list in wins and strikeouts for lefties. His greatest achievement, though, might be winning 27 games for a Phillies team that won only 59 times in 1972. Carlton won the pitcher's Triple Crown that year, as he also led the league with 310 strikeouts and a 1.97 ERA. He came back and led the NL with 20 losses the next season, part of the frustrating circumstances he faced playing for bad teams.

Carlton, who was elected to the Hall of Fame in 1994, posted at least 150 strikeouts in 18 straight years, leading the league five times. He also recorded 16 straight seasons with double-figure totals in complete games, ending his career with 254 complete games. He ranks ninth in innings pitched, sixth in games started and fourteenth in shutouts. Said Richie Ashburn, "Lefty was a craftsman, an artist. He was a perfectionist. He painted a ballgame. Stroke, stroke, stroke, and when he got through (pitching a game) it was a masterpiece."

Another accomplished southpaw is Mike Hampton, who had to overcome injuries and the high expectations that came with signing an eight-year, $121 million contract with the Rockies in 2001. Hampton was runner-up for the Cy Young Award in 1999 after going 22–4 with a 2.90 ERA for the Astros. His two-year stint in Colorado was a disaster, as he went 21–28 with a bloated 5.75 ERA. He later had some success with the Braves but also missed the last two months of the 2005 season and all of the next two seasons with injuries. Hampton never struggled with the bat, clubbing seven home runs in 2001 on the way to winning five straight Silver Slugger Awards. He retired in 2011 after winning 148 games.

Dwight Gooden is the most talented pitcher to ever come from Florida—blessed with a powerful fastball and the game's best curveball—but he got sidetracked on the way to Cooperstown. At 19, he became the youngest-ever All-Star and at 20, the youngest Cy Young Award winner. His 276 strikeouts in 1984 were a rookie record and he set another record that year with most strikeouts across three starts with 43. Gooden was almost unhittable on the way to earning the pitching Triple Crown in 1985, leading the NL with 24 wins, 268 strikeouts and a 1.53 ERA. That last figure is the second-lowest in the Live Ball Era (behind Bob Gibson's 1.12 ERA in 1968).

It was evidently too much success at too young an age. After being named to four All-Star teams his first five seasons, Gooden's performance slipped as he gave in to the temptation of drugs and alcohol. While he ended up winning 192 games with a .634 winning percentage, "Doc" never lived up to his enormous potential.

Gooden, whose nephew is Sheffield, was one of the many players given a second chance by George Steinbrenner. He responded by pitching a no-hitter for the Yankees in 1996. It was one final moment of greatness from the once-in-a-generation talent.

Tim Wakefield was still pitching at the age of 44 in 2011 and the knuckleballer was able to reach 200 career victories. In 2009 he became the oldest first-time All-Star ever at the age of 42. After spending his first two seasons with the Pirates, Wakefield pitched for the Red Sox for 17 years.

Rick Rhoden was another pretty good hitter for a pitcher, winning three straight Silver Sluggers. He even started a game at DH for the Yankees in 1988. The right-handed Rhoden was named to two All-Star teams a decade apart and ended up with 151 career wins over 16 seasons.

Ted Trent was the star pitcher of the St. Louis Stars pennant-winning teams in the late 1920s, appearing in four straight East-West All-Star games in the Negro Leagues. He mowed down the competition in 1928 with a 21–2 record.

If Zach Greinke continues pitching like he did during his Cy Young season in 2009 and in 2011 as opposed to his performance in 2010, then he has a chance to someday surpass Gooden as Florida's best right-handed starter. Greinke's teammates scored a total of 13 runs in the eight games he lost in 2009, so his record should have been much better than 16–8 to go with 242 strikeouts and a league-leading 2.16 ERA. He seemed distracted throughout 2010, seeing his production drop to 10–14 with a 4.17 ERA, and then he forced a trade to Milwaukee in the off-season. Greinke went 16–6 to help the Brewers win their division in 2011.

For the best relief pitcher it was hard to overlook the body of work produced by Tom "Flash" Gordon, who had a longer and more impressive career than Bobby Thigpen. Gordon made the All-Star team as a set-up man in between two All-Star appearances as a closer. Gordon posted 158 saves over 21 seasons with a career-high 46 for the Red Sox in 1998. He was lights out in the eighth inning for the Yankees in 2004 and 2005, making 159 appearances and striking out 165 batters while allowing just 115 hits in 170 innings.

Thigpen set a major league record with 57 saves in 1990 (later broken by Francisco Rodriguez in 2008).

Thigpen ended his career with 201 saves, making him the all-time leader in White Sox history and among Florida-born pitchers.

Another notable reliever is Jay Howell, who saved 155 games over 15 seasons. He posted a career-high 29 saves in 1985 with the A's and made three All-Star teams.

Although Al Lopez is one of the all-time greats as a manager, he is still not in the same league as Tony LaRussa, who is second all-time in games managed and third in wins. LaRussa is one of only two managers to win the World Series in each league, leading the A's to three consecutive Series (winning in 1989) and guiding the Cardinals to championships in 2006 and 2011. He is known as a deep thinker and a brilliant if unconventional strategist.

A four-time Manager of the Year, he has won 12 division titles and six pennants (through the 2011 season). His 2011 Cardinals squad overcame a 10½-game deficit to win the wildcard and then upset the heavily favored Phillies in the NLDS before taking the World Series, four games to three, against the Rangers. LaRussa wasn't much of a player, finishing with a .199 batting average over parts of six seasons, but one day he will be enshrined in Cooperstown for his managerial feats.

Piniella relied on a fiery temper to win 1,835 games over 23 seasons, winning his only pennant and World Series in 1990 with the Reds. He won six division titles—three with the Mariners, two with the Cubs and one with the Reds. Vic Harris was a successful manager in the Negro Leagues who guided the Homestead Grays to nine consecutive pennants (1937–45) as well as two Black World Series championships in 1943 and 1944.

GEORGIA

*Names in **bold** represent Major League selections by position, followed by honorable mentions. Negro Leagues players are in **bold italics**, followed by honorable mentions in italics. City of birth is in parentheses.*

Catcher—*Josh Gibson* (Buena Vista). Also: *Quincy Trouppe* (Dublin); Brian McCann (Athens); *Joe Greene* (Stone Mountain); *Bill Perkins* (Unknown); *Pop Watkins* (Augusta); Ivey Wingo (Gainesville); Jody Davis (Gainesville); Michael Barrett (Atlanta); *Bill Cash* (Round Oak)

First Base—Johnny Mize (Demorest). Also: Bill Terry (Atlanta); Wally Joyner (Atlanta); *Red Moore* (Atlanta); *Tank Carr* (Atlanta); Ron Fairly (Macon); John Milner (Atlanta); *Lem Hawkins* (Macon)

Second Base—Jackie Robinson (Cairo). Also: Tony Phillips (Atlanta)

Third Base—Ray Knight (Albany). Also: *Perry Hall* (Obidgeville); Chone Figgins (Leary); Russell Branyan (Warner Robins)

Shortstop—Cecil Travis (Riverdale). Also: *Dobie Moore* (Atlanta); *Pee Wee Butts* (Sparta); Bucky Dent (Savannah); Adam Everett (Austell); Stephen Drew (Hahira)

Outfield—Ty Cobb (Narrows)
Outfield—Moises Alou (Atlanta)
Outfield—Dixie Walker (Villa Rica). Also: Marquis Grissom (Atlanta); Wally Moses (Uvalda); *Rap Dixon* (Kingston); Mike Cameron (LaGrange); Rondell White (Milledgeville); *Eddie Dwight* (Dalton); Harry Simpson (Atlanta)

Designated Hitter—Frank Thomas (Columbus). Also: Ron Blomberg (Atlanta)

Right Handed Starter—Kevin Brown (Milledgeville). Also: Spud Chandler (Commerce); *Dick Redding* (Atlanta); Tim Hudson (Columbus); *Bill Byrd* (Canton); Jim Bagby (Barnett); *Max Manning* (Rome); Whit Wyatt (Kensington); Jim Hearn (Atlanta); *Chin Evans* (Atlanta); Phil Douglas (Cedartown); Phil Cockrell (Augusta); Connie Johnson (Stone Mountain); Erskine Mayer (Atlanta); Tully Sparks (Etna)

Left Handed Starter—Kenny Rogers (Savannah). Also: Nap Rucker (Crabapple); Sherry Smith (Monticello); *Roy Welmaker* (Atlanta); *Pud Flournoy* (Monticello)

Relief Pitcher—Todd Jones (Marietta). Also: Jonathan Broxton (Augusta); Hugh Casey (Atlanta); Rick Camp (Trion); Matt Capps (Douglasville); John Rocker (Statesboro);

Manager—Bill Terry (Atlanta). Also: George Stallings (Augusta); *Quincy Trouppe* (Dublin); Jerry Manuel (Hahira); Ty Cobb (Narrows); *Pop Watkins* (Augusta)

The Names

Best Nickname: John "Blue Moon" Odom

Other Nicknames: Karl "Rebel" Adams; James "Sarge" Bagby; Bob "Jumbo" Barrett; Cecil "Slewfoot" Butler; Tom "Pee Wee" Butts; Bill "Daddy" Byrd; Sammy "Babe Ruth's Legs" Byrd; Merritt "Sugar" Cain; George "Tank" Carr; Hugh "Fireman" Casey; Bill "Ready" Cash; Ty "The Georgia Peach" Cobb; Lawrence "Crash" Davis; Russell "Bucky" Dent; Walter "Steel Arm" Dickey; "Shufflin' Phil" Douglas; Eddie "Flash" Dwight; Felix "Chin" Evans; Willis "Pud" Flournoy; Charles "Greek" George; Joe "Pig" and "Pea" Greene; Marquis "Grip" Grissom; Arthur "Rats" Henderson; Alva "Bobo" Holloman; Clarence "Half Pint" Israel; "Mack the Knife" Jones; Todd "Rollercoaster" Jones; Max "Dr. Cyclops" Manning; Pryor "Humpty" McElveen; John "The Hammer" Milner; Johnny "The Big Cat" Mize; Walter "Dobie" and

"The Black Cat" Moore; James "Red" Moore; Wally "Peepsight" Moses; Lawrence "Bobo" Osborne; "Cannonball Dick" Redding; Kenny "The Gambler" Rogers; Johnny "Crabapple Comet" Rucker; Harry "Suitcase" Simpson; Elisha "Camp" Skinner; "Memphis Bill" Terry; Frank "The Big Hurt" Thomas; Quincy "Big Train" and "El Roro" Trouppe; Fred "Dixie" and "The People's Cherce" Walker; Roy "Snook" Welmaker; David "Speed" and "Hammerman" Whatley

Most Unusual Name: Burke Badenhop; Euthumn Napier

All-Time Leaders

Games: Ty Cobb, 3035
Hits: Ty Cobb, 4189
Batting Average: Ty Cobb, .366
Home Runs: Johnny Mize, 359
RBI: Ty Cobb, 1937
Stolen Bases: Ty Cobb, 892
Wins: Kenny Rogers, 219
Strikeouts: Kevin Brown, 2397
Saves: Todd Jones, 319
Future Stars: Tyler Flowers (Roswell); Andrew Smith (Roswell); Lorenzo Cain (Valdosta); Charles Blackmon (Suwanee)
Best Player: Ty Cobb

Historic Baseball Places

Ty Cobb Museum in Royston — Opened in 1998 as a tribute to "The Georgia Peach," this museum in Cobb's hometown showcases the Cobb Collection of photographs, artwork and memorabilia. It's an engaging roadmap to lead fans on a journey to learn how Cobb became one of the most celebrated and controversial athletes of the twentieth century. Highlights of his career are engraved on bats. Don't miss the video tribute, which includes rare footage of Cobb in action.

Richard B. Russell Library for Political Research and Study at the University of Georgia — Senator Russell's impressive childhood baseball card collection can be found here. There are about 1,100 tobacco cards dating from 1911–1913, representing one of the largest private collections of tobacco cards anywhere.

Turner Field in Atlanta — A big number 715 and 100-foot picture mural of Hammerin' Hank's record-breaking home run command attention in the Fan Plaza. Ivan Allen, Jr., Braves Museum & Hall of Fame showcases more than 600 Braves artifacts and photographs that outline Braves history from Boston to Milwaukee to Atlanta. The bronze statue of Hank Aaron shown hitting his 715th home run was sculpted by the son of Negro Leagues outfielder Eddie Dwight.

Johnny Mize Baseball Museum in Demorest — The athletic center at Piedmont College is named after Mize and it features space devoted to a museum that

The Ty Cobb Museum in Royston, Georgia, features film, video, books and artifacts that highlight the Hall of Famer's credentials as the "Century's Greatest Hitter" (courtesy Ty Cobb Museum).

highlights the accomplishments of the "Big Cat" and displays memorabilia from his career.

Luther Williams Field in Macon — Baseball Commissioner Kenesaw Mountain Landis was on hand to throw out the first pitch in 1929, and not much has changed with the ballpark since then. Pete Rose, Tony Perez and Chipper Jones are among those who played on the field.

Notable Achievements

Ron Fairly became the first player to play for both Canadian franchises. He played for the Expos from 1969–1974 and for the Blue Jays in 1977.

Pitcher **Chris Hammond** (Atlanta) smashed a pinch-hit grand slam for the Marlins in 1993.

Johnny Mize became the first player to hit 50 home runs with fewer than 50 strikeouts. He hit 51 home runs in 1947 with just 42 strikeouts.

Ron Blomberg became the first designated hitter in baseball history when he walked in his first at-bat for the Yankees on April 6, 1973.

Jeremy Hermida (Marietta) is one of only four players to hit a grand slam in their first major league at-bat, and he's the only one to do it as a pinch hitter.

Cecil Travis is one of only two players to get five hits in their first game. He collected five hits on May 16, 1933, matching Fred Clarke for best debut.

Sammy Byrd (Bremen) was nicknamed "Babe Ruth's Legs" because he was often called on to pinch run for the Babe late in games.

Mike Ivie (Atlanta) became the second player to hit two pinch-hit grand slams in the same season when he connected on May 28 and June 30 in 1978, trailing Davey Johnson by 27 days in accomplishing the feat. Ivie hit four pinch-hit homers that season, one a walkoff.

Jim Bagby of the Cleveland Indians hit the first home run by an American League pitcher during a World Series game when he connected during Game 5 of the 1920 World Series.

Peach State Lays Claim to Three Legends of the Game

Georgia has produced three of the greatest players in baseball history, who were all legendary for different reasons. Ty Cobb is one of the most accomplished, and also most controversial, figures to ever play the game, while Josh Gibson is frequently called the greatest Negro Leagues slugger. Then there is Cairo native Jackie Robinson, who made history for breaking the color barrier in the major leagues.

Actually, it was another Georgia-born player who really broke the color barrier. William Edward White, a native of Milner, is now believed to be the first African American player to appear in a major league game. White was used as an injury replacement at first base for the Providence Grays on June 21, 1879 — 68 years before Robinson — going 1-for-4. It would be his only appearance in the majors and no one paid any attention to it at the time, primarily because the biracial White was light-skinned and passing himself off as white.

That does not diminish the accomplishment of Robinson, who was under the microscope like no player before or since. Robinson was selected as the first Rookie of the Year in the National League and won MVP in his third season. He nearly carried the Dodgers to the pennant in 1951 by hitting a game-winning homer in the fourteenth inning of the last regular season game, but they ended up losing the pennant on Bobby Thomson's "shot heard round the world." He would later win a Series title with the Dodgers in 1955, losing five other times to the Yankees.

One of the most exciting plays to see in baseball was Robinson caught in a rundown. Said teammate Carl Erskine, "Jackie was so quick, so elusive that even seasoned major league players looked like inept amateurs trying to catch him. Then, most often, Jackie would find a way to weave and dodge all tags and arrive safely on the base." Robinson rarely struck out and he drove pitchers to distraction when he reached third base — he stole home 19 times during his career (Cobb is credited with 35).

Robinson made six All-Star teams in his 10 seasons and was elected to the Baseball Hall of Fame in 1962 and the Georgia Sports Hall of Fame in 1968. "The way I figured it, I was even with baseball and baseball with me. The game had done much for me, and I had done much for it," he wrote in his autobiography, *I Never Had it Made*.

There was only one Georgia Peach — Ty Cobb. Cobb, who won a record 12 batting titles and still holds the mark for highest career batting average at .366, is generally regarded as the fiercest competitor in baseball history. He batted over .400 three times, won the Triple Crown in 1909 and retired as the career leader in runs scored, hits, games played, at-bats and stolen bases. He still holds the record for most hits in one month with 68 in July 1912, which is not likely to be broken anytime soon since teams today play fewer games each month.

Cobb proved that a competitive will to win can take a man far. His mean streak and dirty play were legendary, but that's not what defined him as a man or a player. Cobb simply approached the game as a take-no-prisoners battle that required him to vanquish and humiliate his opponents.

He developed an unconventional batting grip — with his hands apart — and worked himself into a frenzy while in the on-deck circle. By the time he stepped up to the plate, he literally wanted to kill the pitcher. He wanted his opponents to think he was both dirty and crazy, because he thought that gave him an edge. As the record shows, it did.

Tris Speaker said Cobb was greater than Babe Ruth. "Babe could knock your brains out, but Cobb would drive you crazy," he said. Added Rogers Hornsby, "Cobb was the greatest ball player of all time and will never be equaled."

So was Cobb the greatest player ever? Many people have expressed that sentiment through the years. When the voting for the first Hall of Fame class was conducted in 1936, Cobb received the most votes (222), seven more than Babe Ruth and Honus Wagner. When *The Sporting News* polled 102 former players and managers in 1942 and asked them who the best player was in baseball history, Cobb got 60 votes followed by Wagner with 17 and Ruth with 11. There was little doubt he deserved our vote as the All-Time Best Player from Georgia and he holds down one of the outfield spots.

Josh Gibson was known as the "black Babe Ruth," which pretty much ends any debate about who is the best catcher from Georgia. Sorry six-time All-Star Brian McCann, unless you can end your career being unofficially credited with hitting "almost 800 home runs," like Gibson is on his Hall of Fame plaque. He is officially credited with 115 home runs and a .359 average in the Negro Leagues, according to a study sanctioned by the Hall of Fame, and he batted .424 against major league competition.

A number of baseball historians call Gibson the greatest catcher ever, some say he was the greatest Negro Leagues player, while there are even those who believe he may be the best right-handed hitter of all-time. *The*

Sporting News' 1999 ranking of the 100 Greatest Baseball Players ranks Gibson eighteenth, while Bill James ranks him the ninth-best player in baseball history.

Gibson's blasts routinely went more than 500 feet including a ball he crushed an estimated 580 feet during an exhibition in Yankee Stadium. "He would have hit more if all the parks had been fenced in like the majors," said Cool Papa Bell. "Sometimes the outfielders got back 500 feet and Gibson would still hit the ball over their heads."

Gibson's team, the Homestead Grays, won nine straight Negro National League pennants with him as catcher, and he never played on a losing team. Sadly, he died of a stroke at the age of 35, just three months before Robinson broke the color barrier.

In addition to Cobb, Gibson and Robinson, Georgia is home to another one of the most famous baseball players ever — of course we are talking about Crash Davis. He was born in Canon, Ga., but actually grew up in Gastonia, N.C. Davis picked up the nickname "Crash" as a youth after colliding with another player in the outfield. He served in the same ROTC unit with Bobby Kennedy at Harvard and compiled 102 hits with a .230 average across three unremarkable seasons for the Philadelphia Athletics.

Crash Davis later came out of retirement to play seven seasons in the minor leagues, including a year with the Durham Bulls. Then four decades later he achieved unexpected fame when the producers of the movie *Bull Durham* asked permission to use his name for a character. Unlike the character in the movie, the real Crash Davis was a second baseman, not a catcher.

It's too bad that Atlanta native Burke Badenhop was a pitcher, because if he were an infielder he had a perfect excuse for why the ball got past him — sorry Skip, it was just a Badenhop. And for those who thought the Red Baron was a mortal enemy of Snoopy or a famous German fighter pilot in World War I, you should know he was actually a left fielder from Clarksville ... and he spelled it Barron. The Gary Cooper who appeared in 21 games for the Braves but only had two at-bats was a pinch-runner from Savannah and had no relation to the movie star.

Thomaston native Bobo Holloman appeared to be headed to a brilliant career after throwing a no-hitter in his first major-league start, on May 6, 1953, becoming the only pitcher to accomplish the feat in the modern era. He also drove in three runs with the only two hits of his career. It would be the only complete game of Holloman's career and he was out of baseball by the end of that season.

More than 20 major league clubs held spring training workouts in Georgia cities between 1871 and 1953, according to research published by William F. Ross III in SABR's *Baseball in the Peach State*. Atlanta was not the most popular locale, as Augusta, Savannah and Macon were more popular destinations. In some cases teams just set up a base in Georgia to stage exhibitions in the South. Ross notes that Ned Hanlon's Baltimore Orioles became the first team to undergo a grueling eight-week training camp while in Macon in 1894, a practice that was eventually copied by other clubs. In the early part of the twentieth century as many as five to six clubs were coming each spring to Georgia.

Atlanta has sent 64 players to the major leagues including Hall of Famer Bill Terry, Moises Alou, Wally Joyner, Marquis Grissom and Tony Phillips. Some of the city's best talent was kept out of the majors due to segregation, so players such as Red Moore, Tank Carr, Dobie Moore, Dick Redding, Chin Evans and Roy Welmaker only became stars on the Negro Leagues stage.

Moore and Evans both played on the Atlanta Black Crackers team that won the second half pennant in 1938, their only year in the Negro American League. The Black Crackers had formed in 1919, playing at Ponce De Leon Park when the white Crackers team was not in town. The club often struggled financially and on the field, but it managed to stick around until 1952. The Black Crackers won the Negro Southern League title in 1945 by winning both halves behind the slugging of Lomax "Fence Bustin'" Davis.

The Atlanta Crackers became known as the "Yankees of the Minors" because they generally fielded a top team. They first began play in the Southern Association in 1895, continuing until 1965 when the Braves brought major league baseball to town. Luke Appling played his only minor league season with the Crackers, batting .326 in 1930. Villa Rica native Dixie Walker returned to Georgia after his playing career ended, accepting the chance to manage the Crackers in 1950. He got 32 homers from 18-year-old Eddie Mathews and coaxed 10 wins out of 36-year-old hurler Hugh Casey as the Crackers won 92 games and the Southern Association pennant.

Legendary broadcaster Ernie Harwell was an Atlanta native who grew up rooting for the Crackers and even served as their batboy. He started his broadcasting career doing the radio calls for Crackers games beginning in 1943 until Harwell was traded to the Brooklyn Dodgers for catcher Cliff Dapper in 1949. That is believed to be the only time a broadcaster has been traded for a player.

All-Time Georgia Selections

We've already got a head start on Team Georgia by detailing the accomplishments of Gibson, Robinson and Cobb. A case could be made that another Negro Leagues catcher from Georgia, Quincy Trouppe, should join Gibson in the Hall. Trouppe played for 23 seasons and was an All-Star in 17 of those years in one league or another. A switch-hitter with some power, Trouppe posted a .311 average in Negro Leagues action, appearing in five East-West All-Star games. He was a great defensive catcher with a strong arm, and he hung around long enough to make it to the majors, playing six games with the Indians in 1952 at the age of 40.

Trouppe would not have made it to the majors without the trail-blazing done by Robinson, who belongs in the Hall of Fame for his talent and competitive spirit and not just for breaking the color barrier. Imagine his statistics if he had not been forced to start his major league career so late — at the age of 28.

Three of the greatest first basemen happen to hail from Georgia: Frank Thomas, Johnny Mize and Bill Terry. Mize's final numbers are hurt by the fact that he missed three prime years to serve his country during World War II. "The Big Cat" was a 10-time All-Star who relied on quickness to excel as a fielder. His stats in 1947 and 1948 were remarkable — a combined 91 home runs (leading the league both years) and 263 RBI yet only 79 strikeouts.

Mize also led the National League in slugging percentage and OPS three consecutive seasons and hit three homers in a game six times. Here is another interesting stat: he led the NL with 16 triples in 1938 but didn't steal any bases that year. The next year he had 14 triples, again with no stolen bases. Mize also had the good fortune to be traded to the Yankees in 1949 so he could wind down his career by winning five straight World Series titles.

Here is Mize's philosophy about hitting: "The pitcher has to throw the ball in the strike zone sooner or later and the rules allow the hitter to hit only one fair ball each time he bats, so why not hit the pitch you want to hit and not the one he wants you to hit?"

Bill James calls Terry "one of the more over-rated players in baseball history," but he did wind up with a .341 career average, which is the fifteenth-best in baseball history and he is in the select club of hitters who have batted .400 in a season. Terry didn't hit a lot of homers in his career — just 154 total — but he knew how to hit for average. He batted over .320 for nine consecutive seasons.

One could argue that Frank Thomas deserves to be ahead of Mize at first, but it makes the most sense to pencil him in at designated hitter, where he played 1,311 games. Thomas established himself as one of the greatest players of the 1990s, but fielding was not his forte. Surprisingly, the Big Hurt never led the league in home runs or RBI but did win a batting crown.

The two-time MVP, who has to be considered the greatest White Sox player ever, batted over .300 in 10 of his first 11 seasons. He had over 100 walks, 100 runs and 100 RBI in each of his first eight full seasons. He finished in the top four of MVP voting six times.

His former manager, Ozzie Guillen, had this to say about Thomas: "As far as the Sox, with all due respect to (Luis) Aparicio and Nellie Fox, to me Frank was not only the best right-handed hitter I've ever seen, but the best all-around hitter. He was amazing."

Thomas didn't play much in the field after 1997, which may be part of the reason why he stopped being named to the All-Star team, but 521 home runs (ranked eighteenth), 1,667 walks (ranked ninth) and a lifetime average of .301 aren't too shabby. In fact, only six other players have retired with more than 500 homers and a .300 average: Aaron, Ruth, Mays, Foxx, Ott and Williams — pretty select company. He should be joining Mize and Terry in the Hall of Fame in 2014.

Perhaps Thomas' most notable achievement was his willingness to speak with Senator George Mitchell when he was investigating baseball's steroids culture — the only active player to cooperate with the investigation. Hall voters may struggle deciding what to do about tainted sluggers like McGwire, Sosa and Palmeiro, but it should not take them long to figure out the Big Hurt earned his place in Cooperstown legitimately.

Negro Leaguer Red Moore also deserves mention at first base. When James Riley profiled Moore for SABR's *The National Pastime*, he recounted the oft-repeated description of his play: "He could pick it." Moore had few peers as a fielder at first base and often entertained fans before games by catching balls behind his back. Moore, who played primarily for the Atlanta Black Crackers, made three All-Star teams and was part of the Newark Eagles' "Million Dollar Infield" in 1937 with Dick Seay, Ray Dandridge and Willie Wells. He was one of the first players to wear a glove for batting, three decades before Ken Harrelson is credited with starting the trend in the majors. Moore was inducted into the Atlanta Sports Hall of Fame in 2006.

Tony Phillips played every position on the field except catcher during his career, so he would make an excellent utility player for the All-Georgia team. Phillips was a valuable role player who was excellent at drawing walks. He wound up his 18-year career with 2,023 hits, 160 home runs and 1,300 runs scored, winning a World Series with the A's in 1989. Phillips played 777 games at second base, 786 in the outfield and saw a lot of action at third and short as well.

Ray Knight was a steady player at third base. Few remember he is the Mets player who scored the winning run when Mookie Wilson's grounder got past Bill Buckner in Game 6 of the World Series. Perhaps more folks remember his homer put the Mets ahead for good in Game 7 and he wound up being named MVP of that Series. He was named to two All-Star teams. Earning honorable mention status at third base is Perry Hall, a dangerous hitter whose Negro Leagues career lasted from 1921–45.

Cecil Travis is the All-Time-Georgia shortstop. The farm boy from Riverdale appeared headed to a Hall of Fame career until the war interrupted. The sweet-swinging lefty lost almost four years during his prime and was never the same player, some say due to the frostbite he contracted on his left foot. He had been at the top of his game before the war, as his 1941 season with the Senators is one for the ages. Travis ended that year with 218 hits and 101 RBI despite hitting only seven homers and his .359 average topped Joe DiMaggio, he of the 56-game hitting streak that year. Travis' .314 career average is the best-ever for an American League shortstop now that Derek Jeter has dropped below him.

Dobie Moore was a supremely talented shortstop with the Kansas City Monarchs who had his career cut short at the age of 31 after getting shot by his girlfriend. Casey Stengel touted Moore as one of the best shortstops who ever lived, while Babe Herman called him the best black player ever. Moore batted .386, .366 and .352 for the years 1922–24, sparking the Monarchs to three league crowns in his seven seasons with the team. He finished with a lifetime average of .346.

Pee Wee Butts was one of the top shortstops in the Negro Leagues while playing for the Baltimore Elite Giants in the 1940s, making six East-West All-Star game appearances. He was the steady starting shortstop for the Black Crackers' 1938 pennant winners. Butts was slick in the field and capable with the bat, averaging a league-high .391 in 1940. "I'd compare Butts with Reese or Rizzuto or anyone," said Roy Campanella. "Butts could do everything."

Speaking of clutch home runs, few can compare to the one hit by Bucky Dent, he of the infamous middle name courtesy of Sox fans. Yankee and Red Sox fans remember where they were when his unforgettable shot cleared the Green Monster in 1978. Although Dent was a three-time All-Star, he was a lifetime .247 hitter who only hit a total of 40 home runs in his career. It's ironic that some of the biggest home runs in baseball history have been hit by non-sluggers like Dent, Bill Mazeroski and Aaron Boone.

Cobb is joined in the Georgia outfield by six-time All-Star Moises Alou, who posted a lifetime average of .303 along with 332 home runs in a career plagued by injuries. He finished second in the NL batting race in 2000 with a .355 average and batted over .300 eight times. You would never know Alou did not start playing organized baseball until he was in college, because he quickly evolved into one of the best natural hitters in the game. Apparently peeing in your hands before games really works.

The third outfielder, Dixie Walker, was Robinson's teammate on the Dodgers and an outspoken critic of integration at first. He was soon won over by Robinson's talent and character. Named to his first All-Star team at the age of 33, Walker was named to five straight All-Star teams with the Brooklyn Dodgers, whose fans loved him so much they called him the "Peoples Cherce." He led the NL in batting in 1944 and incredibly led the league in RBI with 124 in 1945 despite hitting only eight home runs all season. Walker's 1946 season was even better, as he finished second in hits and RBI and third in average on the way to being the MVP runner-up (to Stan Musial). He later managed the Atlanta Crackers, guiding them to the Southern Association pennant in 1950.

Walker ended up edging out Marquis Grissom, a multi-talented threat who could beat you with his bat, glove and feet. In addition to stealing 429 bases, he hit 227 home runs and won four straight Gold Gloves with the Expos and Braves. For a speedy player, Grissom had a subpar career on-base percentage of .318, because he didn't walk much and generally batted in the .260 to .270 range. But Grissom came up big in the postseason, winding up with a 15-game hitting streak across three World Series and was also MVP of the 1997 ALCS while with the Indians.

Herbert "Rap" Dixon was an accomplished batter who was more of a line-drive hitter than a slugger. The right fielder did blast three home runs in the first game played between two black teams in Yankee Stadium in 1930. Dixon played from 1922–37 and finished his career with a .315 average in league play, including .382 and .369 averages for the Baltimore Black Sox in 1928–29.

Other outfielders of note who hailed from Georgia include Wally Moses and Mike Cameron. Cameron is one of 12 players to hit four homers in one game (he did it in 2002 while with Seattle). A lifetime .249 batter who strikes out a lot — ranking eigth all-time with 1,901 whiffs through 2011— Cameron was terrific defensively during his prime, winning three Gold Gloves as a center fielder. He also excelled at the underappreciated skill of going from first to third on a base hit. Cameron still has an outside chance to finish his career with more than 300 homers and 300 stolen bases, since he was at 278 homers and 297 stolen bases after a disappointing 2011 season. Moses was a two-time All-Star who drew a lot of walks but didn't hit many homers. The one exception was 1937 when he blasted 25 home runs; he never hit more than nine in any other season.

Two starting pitchers from Georgia posted similar career stats but had completely different pitching styles. Our left-handed starter is Kenny Rogers, who has an edge over our right-handed starter, Kevin Brown, in victories — 219 to 211 — although Brown was more dominant during his prime. Rogers didn't win 20 in a season, while Brown did once. Brown has the edge in All-Star selections, six to four. Brown, who relied on a devastating sinking fastball to go with a plus-slider, also led the league in ERA twice and finished runner-up for the Cy Young Award in 1996. Rogers, who pitched a perfect game in 1994, won five Gold Glove Awards and had one of the best pickoff moves in baseball history. Brown nearly matched Rogers in perfection, but ended up with one hit batter while throwing a no-hitter in 1997.

Then there are the negative factors to consider. Brown was implicated in the Mitchell Report for steroids use, while Rogers was suspended for 13 games for shoving two cameramen in 2005. Brown has the ignominious honor of becoming baseball's first $100 million man when he signed a seven-year/$105 million contract with the Dodgers in 1998. You have to give Rogers credit for fashioning a stellar career, considering he toiled for seven years in the minors and spent his first three years in the majors as a reliever. The left-hander was 29 when he switched to starting for the Rangers.

It is hard to know how much of Brown's accomplishments came while on steroids, so we gave strong consideration to Spud Chandler. Chandler also didn't get his chance until he was 29 years old and missed most of two seasons due to war service. He pitched 11 seasons for the Yankees, winning 20 games twice and finishing with a career ERA of 2.84. His lifetime winning percentage of .717 trails only nineteenth-century pitcher Al Spalding on the all-time list. The four-time All-Star won three World Series with the Bronx Bombers during the 1940s. The highlight of his career was being named the American League Most Valuable Player in 1943 after going 20–4 with a league-leading (and Yankees team record) ERA of 1.64. However, it is hard to overlook Brown's 243 Career Win Shares, which about doubles Chandler's figure of 125.

"Cannonball Dick" Redding was probably more talented than either Chandler or Brown, and his feats in black baseball become more legendary as the years pass. He combined with Smokey Joe Williams to make the Lincoln Giants virtually unbeatable from 1912–1914. In 1915 he won 20 straight games, while he is credited with a 14–3 mark and 0.70 ERA in 1917. Relying on a sneaky no-windup delivery to go with a baffling "hesitation pitch," Redding threw somewhere between 12 and 30 no-hitters during his career, depending on whether you count barnstorming exhibitions. Teammate Frank Forbes compared Redding to Walter Johnson with the way he blew the ball by batters.

Crafty Bill Byrd appeared in seven East-West All-Star games and compiled a record of 101–71 in Negro Leagues action, according to the Hall of Fame's research. He was reliable and durable, and his deep repertoire of pitches included an effective spitball. Byrd helped the Baltimore Elite Giants win the pennant in his last season, 1949, going 12–3 at the age of 42.

Connie Johnson, Max Manning, Phil Cockrell and Chin Evans are other right-handed starters who made their mark in the Negro Leagues. Johnson got to pitch five seasons in the majors after playing in the Negro Leagues from 1940–52. He pitched for the Atlanta Black Crackers and joined a fearsome rotation on the Kansas City Monarchs with Satchel Paige and Hilton Smith. Johnson was a shell of his former self when he joined the White Sox in 1953, but he did win 14 games for the Orioles and finish third in the league with 177 strikeouts in 1957.

Manning picked up the nickname "Dr. Cyclops" due to the thick glasses he wore, a trait he worked to his advantage by feigning wildness. He was a star pitcher on the Newark Eagles' 1946 Negro National League championship team. Cockrell, who is credited with tossing four no-hitters, relied on a blazing fastball and spitball while pitching for Hilldale from 1918–32. He was shot to death in 1951 while leaving a bar in a case of mistaken identity. Evans was a tall, lanky curveball specialist who was the ace for the Atlanta Black Crackers' 1938 championship team and spent nine years with the Memphis Red Sox.

Active player Tim Hudson has been a superb pitcher when healthy, posting a .655 winning percentage through 2010 with an ERA+ of 128. He won 20 games and finished runner-up for the Cy Young Award in his second season, 2000.

Shufflin' Phil Douglas went out with a bang, leading the league in ERA and ERA+ in 1922 before being banned from baseball for life. Douglas was mad at Giants manager John McGraw and had fallen off the wagon when he sent a letter to Cardinals player Les Mann offering to throw away the pennant for the Giants. There are some who believe Douglas had a hand in throwing the 1918 World Series for the Cubs — he did throw a ball away in Game 4 that allowed the go-ahead run to score. Douglas ended up with a career record of 94–93 with a 2.80 ERA and ERA+ of 111.

Tom Cheney didn't do enough to earn honorable mention status since his career record was 19–29, but he produced one magical game. Pitching for the Washington Senators on September 12, 1962, he struck out a record 21 batters while hurling a 16-inning complete game. He ended up throwing 228 pitches in the game.

One of the top lefties of the Deadball Era was Nap Rucker, who was better than his .500 record (134–134) suggested but spent his entire 10-year career with the downtrodden Brooklyn Superbas/Robins. Rucker's 2.42 ERA ranks 30th and he hurled 38 shutouts and posted an ERA+ of 119. His best season was 1910 when he led the league with 39 starts, 27 complete games, six shutouts and 320 innings. He pitched a no-hitter in 1908 and tied a record with 16 strikeouts in a game the next year. When he started to lose steam off his fastball late in his career Rucker adapted by becoming one of the first to throw a knuckleball.

Team Georgia's closer is Marietta native Todd Jones, who finally retired after the 2008 season. He appeared in 981 games in relief (with just one start) over 16 seasons, collecting 319 saves despite not being blessed with overpowering stuff. He was more effective during his career as a middle reliever, as he had a tendency to give up a lot of hits, walks and runs. Jones led the AL with 42 saves in 2000, the year he made his only All-Star team and won the AL Rolaids Relief Award.

Jonathan Broxton turned in a dominating performance as the closer for the Dodgers in 2009, posting 36 saves with an eye-popping 13.5 SO/9IP after recording 114 strikeouts in 76 innings while allowing only 44 hits. His production slipped in 2010 and he endured an injury-plaqued and ineffective season in 2011.

Hugh Casey spent seven of his nine seasons with the Brooklyn Dodgers, leading the NL in saves in 1942 and 1947. Nicknamed "Fireman," he was on the mound when catcher Mickey Owen suffered a passed ball on a third strike to the Yankees' Tommy Henrich with two outs in the ninth inning in Game 4 of the 1941 World Series. Casey ended up surrendering four runs as the Dodgers lost the game and the Series. He had a chance to redeem himself in 1947 when the Dodgers squared off against the Yankees again in the Series. Casey appeared in six games and won twice with a 0.87 ERA in a losing effort. Casey struggled with an addiction to alcohol and ended up committing suicide at age 37 in 1951.

Two Georgia natives have won World Series as managers: Bill Terry and George Stallings. Stallings, who started off as a player-manager, managed from 1897 to 1920, leading the Boston Braves to the title in 1914. That was his only trip to playoffs and he finished just below a .500 winning percentage for his managerial career.

Stallings had been removed as manager of the New York Highlanders in 1910 in favor of Hal Chase after it was discovered that Stallings had planted the team's trainer beyond the center field fence at Hilltop Park with a pair of binoculars. The trainer would steal the catcher's signs and then relay them to Highlander batters. When Ban Johnson learned of Stallings' tactics, he demanded that Stallings be removed as manager. It was ironic that Chase replaced him as skipper, since Stallings had been one of the first to raise suspicions that Chase was throwing games.

Terry managed the NY Giants for 10 seasons, the first four as player-manager, and finished with a winning percentage of .555. He won the World Series in 1933 (his second season managing) and later added two more pennants. Considering he had the tough task of following in the footsteps of John McGraw, Terry gets bonus points that earn him the selection as manager of the All-Time Georgia Team.

HAWAII

*Names in **bold** represent Major League selections by position, followed by honorable mentions. City of birth is in parentheses.*

Catcher — Kurt Suzuki (**Wailuku**). Also: Dane Sardinha (Honolulu); Tony Rego (Wailuku)
First Base — John Matias (**Honolulu**). Also: Kila Ka'aihue (Kailua); Joe DeSa (Honolulu)
Second Base — Lenn Sakata (Honolulu)
Third Base — Mike Huff (Honolulu)
Shortstop — Keith Luuloa (Honolulu)
Outfield — Benny Agbayani (Honolulu)
Outfield — Shane Victorino (Wailuku)
Outfield — Mike Lum (Honolulu)
Designated Hitter — Joey Meyer (Honolulu)
Left Handed Starter — Sid Fernandez (Honolulu). Also: Steve Cooke (Lihue)
Right Handed Starter — Ron Darling (Honolulu). Also: Milt Wilcox (Honolulu); Jerome Williams (Honolulu)
Relief Pitcher — Charlie Hough (Honolulu). Also: Brian Fisher (Honolulu); Doug Capilla (Honolulu); Scott Feldman (Kailua); Carlos Diaz (Kaneohe)
Manager-Prince Oana (Waipahu)

The Names

Best Nickname: Shane "The Flyin' Hawaiian" Victorino
Other Nicknames: Benny "Hawaiian Punch" Agbayani; Charles "El Sid" Fernandez; Henry "Prince" Oana; "Honolulu Johnnie" Williams
Most Unusual Name: Micah Kila Ka'aihue

All-Time Leaders

Games: Mike Lum, 1517
Hits: Shane Victorino, 908 (still active)
Batting Average: Shane Victorino, .279 (still active)
Home Runs: Mike Lum, 90
RBI: Mike Lum, 431
Stolen Bases: Shane Victorino, 162 (still active)
Wins: Charlie Hough, 216
Strikeouts: Charlie Hough, 2362
Saves: Charlie Hough, 61
Best Player: Sid Fernandez
Future Star: Kolten Wong (Hilo)

Historic Baseball Places

The Hilo Walk of Fame in Hilo — Babe Ruth planted a banyan tree here in 1933 while on the island to play exhibition games, and it is marked with a wooden plaque.
Hans L'Orange Park in Waipahu — Built in 1923, it is currently used by Hawaii Pacific University's baseball team. The West Oahu CaneFires and North Shore Honu played Hawaii Winter Baseball League games there until 2008.
Les Marakami Stadium in Honolulu — Known as Rainbow Stadium when it opened in 1984, the ballpark now hosts the independent Hawaii Island Movers and the University of Hawaii teams. Hawaii Winter Baseball teams played there from 2006–2008. The stadium features sunken dugouts and a view of the Waikiki skyscrapers and Diamond Head volcanic core beyond the outfield.
Grand Ichiro "Iron" Maehara Stadium in Wailuku — Built in 1973 with a capacity of 1,500, it was the home field of the Maui Sting Rays in the Hawaii Winter Baseball League from 1993–97. An independent team now plays there. A neat tradition takes place in the first game of a home stand when Hawaiian girls come out and place leis on each of the visiting players to welcome them. If you sit on the first base side you can see mountains in front of you and the ocean to your right.

Notable Achievements

Johnnie Williams (Honolulu) was the first Hawaii-born player to appear in the major leagues, pitching in four games for the Tigers in 1914, 45 years before Hawaii became a state.
Mike Lum is the only player to ever pinch-hit for Hank Aaron, which he did on May 21, 1969. Lum also led the National League with 17 pinch-hits in 1979.
Ron Darling once hit home runs in consecutive starts in 1989.
Charlie Hough is the only player to make at least 400 starts and 400 relief appearances.

Making History Hawaiian Style

Seemingly all of Hawaii was watching as Shane Victorino of Wailuku helped lead the Phillies to the World Series championship in 2008. Victorino blasted a grand slam off CC Sabathia in Game 2 of the 2008 NLDS and then for an encore he hit a game-tying two-run dinger in Game 4 of the NLCS. Hawaii had a new sports hero.

Victorino, known as the "Flyin' Hawaiian," made the first of two All-Star teams in 2009, leading the NL with 13 triples while scoring over 100 runs for the second straight year. In 2010 he earned his third straight Gold Glove, while he led the NL with 16 triples to spark the Phillies in 2011. His .279 average through the 2011 season is the all-time best by a Hawaiian player and he is also the major league's active and career leader in fielding percentage for an outfielder due to the fact that he's only committed eight errors.

The so-called "Father of Modern Baseball," Alexander Cartwright, reportedly played a pivotal role in getting baseball to flourish in Hawaii. Cartwright, who spent the last 44 years of his life in Hawaii, is credited with laying out Hawaii's first baseball diamond in Makiki around 1852 and then devoted much time to introducing the game across Hawaii. Historian John Thorn makes the case that many of Cartwright's pioneering baseball accomplishments were fabricated by his son.

If you make it to Honolulu you can visit Cartwright gravesite at Oahu Cemetery. Also in Honolulu is Aloha Stadium, which hosted the Cardinals and Padres in a three-game exhibition series in 1997. It replaced the old wooden Honolulu Stadium in Moiliili, which was built in 1926 and played host to Babe Ruth and Joe DiMaggio before being torn down in 1976. All that's left is a plaque detailing some of the history.

Honolulu is the birthplace of 24 of 36 Hawaii natives who have made it to the majors. Stars such as Sid Fernandez and Ron Darling, long-time players Charlie Hough, Milt Wilcox and Mike Lum and one-year dreamers like John Matias and Keith Luuloa all came from Honolulu.

Some of Hawaii's best native players actually attended high school on the mainland. Ron Darling played his high school ball in Massachusetts, Charlie Hough in Florida, Milt Wilcox in Oklahoma and Brian Fisher in Colorado.

Wally Yonamine never made it to the majors, but the Maui native was a true baseball pioneer. After a brief career as a halfback and defensive back with the San Francisco 49ers, he switched to baseball. With encouragement from Lefty O'Doul, the son of Japanese immigrants became the first American to play professional baseball in Japan after World War II ended.

Four years after Jackie Robinson broke the color barrier in baseball and stood tall in the face of vicious racism, Yonamine found himself enduring a similar experience in a country still raw with emotion and hatred toward the United States. He persevered and eventually won over fans with his hard-nosed play, helping pave the way for future American players to migrate to Japan. Yonamine was selected to seven All-Star teams, won three batting titles, and was named Central League MVP in 1957. When his playing career ended he managed the Chunichi Dragons for six seasons and in 1994 became the first American elected to the Japanese Baseball Hall of Fame.

Hawaii Winter Baseball, which was founded in 1993, featured players under contract with teams or leagues affiliated with Major League Baseball or the Korean and Japanese professional leagues. In addition, Lee Anne Ketchum and Julie Croteau had been members of the Colorado Silver Bullets, a professional women's baseball team managed by Phil Niekro. They became the first female players to play under the major league system when they appeared in games for the Maui Stingrays in 1994.

Ichiro Suzuki played for the Hilo Stars in 1993, right before he became a hitting sensation in Japan. The 20-year-old gained notoriety for blasting a reported 500-foot home run at Vidinha Stadium. One of Suzuki's teammates on the Stars was Bobby Bonds, Jr., Barry's brother, who played 11 years in the minors but never made it to the big leagues. Other current MLB players who played in the Hawaii Winter Baseball League include Joba Chamberlain (West Oahu CaneFire, 2006), Todd Helton (Maui Stingrays, 1995), Jason Giambi (Kaui Emeralds, 1993) and Derrek Lee (Maui Stingrays, 1993).

Hawaii's players have been a part of some memorable moments in baseball history. It's hard to forget Benny Agbayani throwing the ball in the stands during a game while playing for the Mets in 2000, only to realize there weren't three outs. And what was going through the mind of the poor kid who had caught the lucky ball and then saw Agbayani come over and snatch the ball back so he could try and get the third out?

Mets fans are more likely to remember him for his extra-innings home run that year off the Giants in Game 3 of the NLDS. Agbayani, who comes from Filipino and Samoan descent, went on to play in Japan beginning in 2004, helping Bobby Valentine's team win the Asia championship in 2005.

All-Time Hawaii Selections

Knuckleballer Charlie Hough won 216 games over a 25-year career, making him Hawaii's all-time leader in victories. Since he pitched nearly half his games in relief and accumulated 61 saves, he gets selected as Hawaii's all-time relief pitcher. There are not apt to be too many closers who throw the knuckleball, because most managers cannot handle the stress of worrying about passed balls.

Hough was not dominant or spectacular and was never an All-Star, but he was steady for a long time. He is the only pitcher to play a complete decade with two separate teams — the Dodgers throughout the 1970s and the Rangers throughout the 1980s. An interesting footnote to history is that Hough surrendered one of the three home runs Reggie Jackson hit in Game 6 of the 1977 World Series. He also owns the most wins by a pitcher with a .500 career record.

Hough had a long career and won a lot of games, but Sid Fernandez is Hawaii's greatest pitcher and All-Time Best Player. "El Sid" was a two-time All-Star who gave up just 5.7 hits per 9 innings in 1985. Not only that, Fernandez gave up just 6.85 hits per nine innings during his career, which trails only Sandy Koufax and Nolan Ryan in baseball history. Fernandez wore uniform number 50 in honor of Hawaii being named the 50th state. The left-handed starter helped lead the 1986 Mets to the World Series, winning 16 games that year.

His right-handed teammate on that team, Ron Darling, had an even better season for the Mets. He went 15–6 in 1986 with a 2.81 ERA (just a tick better than Dwight Gooden). The previous season Darling earned the distinction of becoming the first native Hawaiian to be named to the All-Star team. He cobbled together a pretty good career, winning 136 games against just 116 losses, with a 3.86 ERA. Not bad for a Yale guy.

Milt Wilcox came within one out of a perfect game in 1983 and won 17 games for the Tigers' 1984 championship team. He was a dependable if non-descript pitcher who finished his career with 119 wins, winning between 11 and 13 games every season from 1978 to 1983.

Oakland A's catcher Kurt Suzuki, Hawaii's all-time catcher, was the star as his college team, Cal State Fullerton, captured the 2004 College World Series. He has already been part of history during his short MLB career. On July 17, 2007, he caught Shane Komine in a game, marking the first time the battery-mates were both from Hawaii.

The Sardinha brothers could be called Hawaii's first family of baseball. Dane has played sparingly in six seasons since being called up to the Reds in 2003, while younger brother Bronson, who was with the Yankees in 2007, has hit over 100 home runs in 10 minor league seasons. Bronson holds the unofficial title of longest middle name in major league history — Kiheimahanaomauiakeo — which is 17 more letters than hits he recorded in the majors. A third Sardinha brother, Duke, was a minor league infielder in the Rockies system for seven years.

Another player of note is first baseman John Matias, who played 12 seasons in the minors, hitting .286 with 110 homers. He appeared in 58 games for the White Sox in 1970 and did not impress enough to stick around. Matias went on to play six summers in the Mexican League, where he added pitching to his repertoire, ending his professional career playing for the Hawaii Islanders in 1980. His nephew, Joe DeSa, made brief appearances mainly as a first baseman for the Cardinals in 1980 and White Sox in 1985.

Second baseman Lenn Sakata played 11 seasons as a valuable reserve in the majors, compiling 296 hits but batting just .230. He won a World Series in 1983 with the Orioles. To fill out the All-Time Hawaii infield it was necessary to include Mike Huff, who was primarily an outfielder, as well as Keith Luuloa, who only played in six career games (four at short).

Prince Oana was a great player in the minors, compiling 2,292 hits, 261 home runs and a .304 average during 23 seasons, plus a record of 80–54 with 3.22 ERA after converting to pitcher. But he never got much of an opportunity in the majors, playing four games in the outfield in 1934 and 13 games as a pitcher in 1943 and 1945. Oana later managed four seasons in the minors, which gives him the best qualification to be the All-Time Hawaii manager.

Hawaii has also produced a pretty good hitting instructor in Mike Lum, the long-time hitting coordinator for the White Sox. Lum played on the Big Red Machine's 1976 championship team. The Honolulu native was actually of Chinese-American heritage, making him one of the first Asian players in the majors. He compiled 877 hits over 15 seasons.

IDAHO

*Names in **bold** represent Major League selections by position, followed by honorable mentions. City of birth is in parentheses.*

Catcher — Bill Salkeld (Pocatello). Also: Skipper Roberts (Wardner)
First Base — Harmon Killebrew (Payette). Also: Kent Hadley (Pocatello)
Second Base — Hal Luby (Blackfoot)
Third Base — Vance Law (Boise)
Shortstop — Pep Goodwin (Pocatello)
Outfield — Chris Latham (Coeur d'Alene)
Outfield — Bob Martyn (Weiser)
Outfield — Joe Mather (Sand Point)
Right Handed Starter — Larry Jackson (Nampa). Also: Vern Law (Meridian); Jason Schmidt (Lewiston); Ken Schrom (Grangeville)
Left Handed Starter — Ken Dayley (Jerome)
Relief Pitcher — Matt Lindstrom (Rexburg). Also: Mike Garman (Caldwell); Frank Reberger (Caldwell)
Manager — Hal Luby (Blackfoot)

The Names

Best Nickname: Vance "Long Arm of the" Law
Other Nicknames: Claire "Pep" Goodwin; Harmon

"Killer" Killebrew; Vern "Deacon" and "Preacher" Law; Frank "Crane" Reberger; Clarence "Skipper" Roberts
Most Unusual Name: Carl Spongberg

All-Time Leaders

Games: Harmon Killebrew, 2435
Hits: Harmon Killebrew, 2086
Batting Average: Bill Salkeld, .273
Home Runs: Harmon Killebrew, 573
RBI: Harmon Killebrew, 1584
Stolen Bases: Vance Law, 34
Wins: Larry Jackson, 194
Strikeouts: Jason Schmidt, 1758
Saves: Matt Lindstrom, 45 (still active)
Future Star: Nick Hagadone (Sandpoint)
Best Player: Harmon Killebrew

Historic Baseball Place

Melaleuca Field in Idaho Falls — Built in 2006, the ballpark plays host to the Idaho Falls Chukars in the Pioneer League. If you were wondering why they named the team after the national bird of Pakistan, you should know the chukar is also a mountain partridge found in the Idaho foothills. Sure glad they didn't name the team after the national bird of Hungary, which is the Great Bustard.

Notable Achievements

Vance Law holds the American League record for the longest errorless game by a third baseman. He played all 25 innings for the White Sox in the longest game in AL history against the Milwaukee Brewers on May 8–9, 1984.

Harmon Killebrew set a record in 1964 for fewest doubles (11) in a season by a player hitting at least 40 home runs — he hit 49 homers.

Small Idaho Town Produces One of Baseball's Greatest Sluggers

Harmon Killebrew, who was born in Payette and starred in three sports at Payette High School, developed into one of the greatest sluggers in baseball history. Killebrew claimed his slugging power can be traced back to his Idaho roots. "When I was 14, and for the next four years, I was lifting and hauling 10-gallon milk cans full of milk," he said in an interview with the *Washington Post* in 1984. "That will put muscles on you even if you're not trying."

He made his major league debut for the Washington Senators at age 17 in 1954 ... as a pinch runner. Although no speed demon, he was not yet the lumbering slugger. Ironically, it took a Senator to get him on the Senators. Idaho Senator Herman Welker had convinced Senators owner Clark Griffith to scout Killebrew, and farm director Ossie Bluege came out and witnessed him blast a monster home run.

Killebrew would languish on the bench for his five years, an unwitting victim of the "bonus baby" rule that prevented teams from hoarding the best young players in the minors. Once given a regular opportunity, he quickly showed what he was capable of doing, blasting 42 home runs in 1959 to lead the AL for the first of six times. "Killebrew can knock the ball out of any park — including Yellowstone," exclaimed Orioles manager Paul Richards.

Although he never hit much for average, "Killer" developed more patience at the plate as his career progressed, leading the league in walks four times. Pitchers feared his power, so he was often pitched around, drawing 160 intentional walks during his career.

His best season was 1969, when he led the Twins to their first AL West division title and won the MVP Award. That year he led the league with 49 homers, 140 RBI, 145 walks and a .427 OBP. His most incredible stat that season was eight stolen bases, which is one more than the slugger had accumulated in his 15 previous seasons combined.

Killebrew posted nine seasons with over 100 RBI and eight seasons with over 40 home runs. Although he played 969 games at first base, the Twins also shuffled him back and forth between the outfield and third base, and he was never adept in the field.

Known for his tape-measure shots, he hit some of the longest home runs ever recorded in Metropolitan Stadium in Minnesota. When he retired in 1975 the 11-time All-Star's 573 home runs ranked as the fifth best all-time and the most ever for a right-handed batter in the American League (he's since been passed by Alex Rodriquez). His career mark of hitting a home run every 14.2 at-bats currently places Killebrew eighth all-time.

Killebrew was not a large man — at 5-11 and 210 lbs., he was the prototypical size for a pre-steroids era slugger. The gentle giant, who was inducted into the Hall of Fame in 1984, was unquestionably Idaho's greatest player ever.

The baseball community mourned its loss when Killebrew died of cancer on May 17, 2011. Twins teammate Bert Blyleven said, "Harmon was a great man, on and off the field. He was a bigger Hall of Famer off the field. Everyone that Harmon ever came in contact with has a story about what a class man he was."

All-Time Idaho Selections

A total of 27 players born in Idaho have played in the major leagues, which makes it a little hard to fill out a respectable team. There is a Hall of Fame slugger at first base and a handful of good starting pitchers, but the rest of the team could be described as fill-in players.

Catcher Bill Salkeld showed promise as a rookie catcher with the Pirates in 1945, even capturing six points in the MVP race that year after hitting .311 with 15 home runs. But he never blossomed into a full-time catcher and was out of baseball by 1950.

Another Idaho catcher, Skipper Roberts, achieved some fame through the years, but not for his baseball play. Roberts died in 1963 and the next year Mattel introduced a doll named Skipper Roberts who was Barbie's little sister. For a baseball player, it's probably better to have a candy bar named after you like Reggie Jackson than to share a name with a doll. Roberts played in just 82 games over two seasons (1913–1914) and gets honorable mention at catcher.

Second baseman Hal Luby compiled more than 3,000 hits in his professional baseball career — 3,258 to be exact. Unfortunately, only 89 of them came in the major leagues (82 of them in 1944). The rest came during a minor league career that extended from 1931 to 1956. Luby stole a lot of bases in the minors and once played 866 consecutive games, but he barely had a cup of coffee in the big leagues. Luby went on to manage for 12 seasons in the minors (earning four playoff berths) and later served as president of the Northwest League. Since no one from Idaho has managed in the major leagues, Luby also gets selected as the manager of Team Idaho.

Vance Law followed in the big-league footsteps of his father, Vern, carving out a career as a versatile player. His mother and five siblings also have names beginning with "V." He played every position except catcher during his 11 seasons, even compiling a 3.38 ERA in seven pitching appearances, but was primarily a third baseman. Law made the 1988 All-Star team, finishing eighth in the league with a .293 average that year.

Shortstop Pep Goodwin's only experience came during two years in the Federal League. He batted .235 with 142 hits playing for the Kansas City Packers in 1914–15.

The All-Time Idaho outfield is not an accomplished bunch. Bob Martyn posted 94 hits in 1957–58 and Chris Latham had 43 hits in five seasons while Joe Mather is still active. Eight of Mather's 32 hits during his rookie year, 2008, were homers. He saw limited action for the Braves in 2011.

Mather had a memorable day on April 17, 2010, which turned into a marathon 20-inning game between the Cardinals and Mets. Mather entered the game as a pinch hitter in the 10th inning, later played in center field and third base and then was forced into duty as a pitcher in the nineteenth inning with the game still scoreless. He gave up one run that inning but the Cardinals tied the score in the bottom of the nineteenth. Mather came back out and pitched the twentieth inning, taking the loss after surrendering what proved to be the decisive run in the 2–1 game.

Vern Law has a Cy Young Award to his credit, but Nampa's Larry Jackson had a more impressive career as a right-handed starter. Jackson finished runner-up to Dean Chance in the 1964 Cy Young Award race, but that was before the award was given out to the top pitcher in each league — Chance pitched for the Angels in the American League. Jackson led the National League with 24 wins that year despite playing for the eighth-place Cubs.

Jackson, who later served four terms in the Idaho legislature, was a picture of consistency, winning at least 13 games each of his last 12 seasons. Named to four All-Star teams, Jackson finished with 194 wins and a 3.40 ERA. His ERA+ of 113 outpaces Law's 102 ERA+.

Law spent his entire 16-year career pitching for the Pirates, winning a World Series in 1960 when Bill Mazeroski hit a dramatic series-clinching home run in Game 7. Law was the staff ace that year, winning the Cy Young Award after going 20–9 with a 3.08 ERA and leading the National League in complete games with 18. Although he ended up winning 162 games, 1960 was the only year he was an All-Star. Nicknamed "Deacon" or "Preacher," Law posted nine seasons with double-digit wins and finished in the top 10 in shutouts six times and top 10 in ERA four times. His 2.15 ERA in 1965 ranked third in the NL and he was named NL Comeback Player of the Year that season.

Lewiston native Jason Schmidt played his high school baseball in Washington, where he was Gatorade Player of the Year. He made three All-Star teams and finished second in the NL Cy Young Award voting in 2003 after leading the league in winning percentage, ERA, ERA+ and WHIP. The next year he came in fourth in the Cy Young Award race after posting an 18–7 record. Schmidt ranks as Idaho's all-time leader in strikeouts with 1,758. He also tied Christy Mathewson for the Giants record with 16 strikeouts in a game in 2006. He finished his career with a 130–96 record over 14 seasons.

The top relief pitcher could be considered a toss-up among Mike Garman, Ken Dayley and Matt Lindstrom, but Dayley's 33 starts made him the only choice as Team Idaho's lefty starter. Dayley excelled on the big stage in two postseason stints for the Cardinals in 1985 and 1987. In 16 playoff appearances, Dayley registered one win and five saves while allowing only one earned run in over 20 innings pitched.

Garman registered 42 career saves and had three seasons of double-digit saves. He contributed four innings of scoreless relief in the 1977 World Series for the Dodgers. Hard-throwing Rexburg native Lindstrom passed Garman as Idaho's all-time saves leader in 2010, which was the deciding factor. He saved 15 games for the Marlins in 2009 and then posted 23 saves for the Astros in 2010. Lindstrom worked in a set-up role for Colorado in 2011, and in just five seasons he has already passed Garman in number of appearances.

ILLINOIS

*Names in **bold** represent Major League selections by position, followed by honorable mentions. Negro Leagues players are in italics. City of birth is in parentheses.*

Catcher — Ray Schalk (Harvel). Also: Jim Sundberg (Galesburg); Tom Haller (Lockport); Bob O'Farrell (Waukegan); Phil Masi (Chicago); Dan Wilson (Barrington); Joe Girardi (Peoria); Darrin Fletcher (Elmhurst); Ray Fosse (Marion)

First Base — Jim Bottomley (Oglesby). Also: Ted Kluszewski (Argo); Phil Cavarretta (Chicago); Moose Skowron (Chicago); Wally Pipp (Chicago); Earl Sheely (Bushnell); Charlie Comiskey (Chicago)

Second Base — Larry Doyle (Caseyville). Also: Red Schoendienst (Germantown); Marty McManus (Chicago); George Cutshaw (Wilmington); Frankie Gustine (Hoopeston); Germany Schaefer (Chicago); Ski Melillo (Chicago)

Third Base — Gary Gaetti (Centralia). Also: Fred Lindstrom (Chicago); Doug Rader (Chicago); Ossie Bluege (Chicago); Kevin Seitzer (Springfield); Milt Stock (Chicago); *Pat Patterson* (Chicago); Eddie Foster (Chicago); George Pinkney (Orange Prairie); Andy High (Ava); Ken Oberkfell (Highland)

Shortstop — Robin Yount (Danville). Also: Lou Boudreau (Harvey); Herman Long (Chicago); Dick Bartell (Chicago); Art Fletcher (Collinsville); Billy Rogell (Springfield); *Bill Riggins* (Colp); Dick Schofield, Jr. (Springfield)

Outfield — Rickey Henderson (Chicago)

Outfield — Kirby Puckett (Chicago)

Outfield — Wally Berger (Chicago). Also: Fred Lynn (Chicago); Shawn Green (Des Plaines); Greg Luzinski (Chicago); Mike Donlin (Peoria); *Jimmie Lyons* (Chicago); Lonnie Smith (Chicago); Cliff Floyd (Chicago); *Sam Jethroe* (East St. Louis); Hank Bauer (East St. Louis); Baby Doll Jacobson (Cable); Jesse Barfield (Joliet); Johnny Mostil (Chicago); Mike Kreevich (Mount Olive); Bruce Campbell (Chicago); Harry Rice (Ware Station); Jack Smith (Chicago)

Designated Hitter — Jim Thome (Peoria). Also: Greg Luzinski (Chicago); Brian Daubach (Belleville)

Right Handed Starter — Robin Roberts (Springfield). Also: Joe McGinnity (Rock Island); Red Ruffing (Granville); Al Spalding (Byron); Brett Saberhagen (Chicago Heights); Jack Powell (Bloomington); Dutch Leonard (Birmingham); Rick Reuschel (Quincy); Jeff Pfeffer (Seymour); Denny McLain (Chicago); Harry Staley (Jacksonville); Bob Turley (Troy); Cy Falkenberg (Chicago)

Left Handed Starter — Lefty Leifield (Trenton). Also: Charlie Leibrandt (Chicago); Larry Gura (Joliet); Mark Mulder (South Holland); Fritz Peterson (Chicago); Kirk Rueter (Hoyleton); Jeff Fassero (Springfield); Fritz Ostermueller (Quincy); Bill Walker (East St. Louis); Jim O'Toole (Chicago)

Relief Pitcher — Jason Isringhausen (Brighton). Also: John Wyatt (Chicago); Mike Myers (Arlington Heights); Dan Kolb (Sterling); Scott Garrelts (Urbana); Matt Herges (Champaign); Ron Mahay (Crestwood); Ed Farmer (Evergreen Park); Don Stanhouse (DuQuoin); Terry Fox (Chicago); Jason Frasor (Chicago)

Manager — Whitey Herzog (New Athens). Also: Charlie Comiskey (Chicago); Red Schoendienst (Germantown); Lou Boudreau (Harvey); Chuck Dressen (Decatur); Hank Bauer (East St. Louis)

The Names

Best Nickname: Joe "Wagon Tongue" Adams

Other Nicknames: Orie "Old Folks" Arntzen; Abraham "Sweetbread" Bailey; "Rowdy Richard" and "Shortwave" Bartell; Walter "Boom-Boom" Beck; "Sunny Jim" Bottomley; Lou "Old Shufflefoot" Boudreau; Thomas "The Gray Flamingo" Brennan; Larry "Possum" Burright; "Fidgety Phil" Collins; John "Jocko" Conlan; Brian "Belleville Basher" Daubach; Johnny "Ugly" Dickshot; Albert "Cozy" Dolan; "Turkey Mike" Donlin; "Laughing Larry" Doyle; Erv "Four Sack" Dusak; Paul "Li'L Abner" Erickson; Ray "Marion Mule" Fosse; Gary "The Rat" Gaetti; Roy "Snipe" Hansen; John "Egyptian" Healy; Henry "Hunkey" Hines; James "Jay Bird" Hook; William "Baby Doll" Jacobson; Sam "The Jet" Jethroe; Louis "Spitball" Johnson; Herman "The Flying Dutchman" Long; Greg "The Bull" Luzinski; Joe "Iron Man" McGinnity; Oscar "Spinach" Melillo; Russ "The Mad Monk" Meyer; Ward "Grump" or "Windy" Miller; Johnny "Bananas" Mostil; Hank "Peep" O'Day; "Voiceless Tim" O'Rourke; Donn "The Pope" Pall; Francis "Salty" Parker; Marty "Bulldog" Pattin; Ted "Porky" Pawelek; George "Filbert" Pearce; Doug "The Red Rooster" Rader; Arthur "Bugs" Raymond; Rick "Big Daddy" Reuschel; Kirk "Woody" Rueter; Jack "Gulfport" Ryan; Gene "Half-Pint" Rye; Germany "Liberty" Schaefer; Ray "Cracker" Schalk; Frederick "Crazy" Schmit; Albert "Red" Schoendienst; Lewis "Jumbo" Schoeneck; Howie "Hawk" Shanks; Lou "The Nervous Greek" Skizas; Bill "Moose" Skowron; Lonnie "Skates" Smith; Lee "Stinger" Stange; Don "Full Pack" Stanhouse; Arnold "Jigger" Statz; Allyn "Fish Hook" Stout; Clarence "Steamboat" Struss; Chester "Pinch" Thomas; "Tarzan" Joe Wallis; Jayson "Werewolf" Werth

Most Unusual Name: Tony Suck; Eli Grba; Emil Yde; Johnny Dickshot; Sigmund Gryska

All-Time Leaders

Games: Rickey Henderson, 3081
Hits: Robin Yount, 3142
Batting Average: Mike Donlin, .333
Home Runs: Jim Thome, 604 (still active)
RBI: Jim Thome, 1674 (still active)
Stolen Bases: Rickey Henderson, 1406
Wins: Robin Roberts, 286
Strikeouts: Robin Roberts, 2357
Saves: Jason Isringhausen, 300 (still active)
Future Stars: Christian Friedrich (Evanston); Casey Crosby (Maple Park); Jason Kipnis (Northbrook)
Best Player: Rickey Henderson

Historic Baseball Places

Wrigley Field in Chicago—The second-oldest major league ballpark is famous for its ivy vines on the outfield walls, hand-operated scoreboard and day baseball. When the ballpark first opened in 1914 it was home to the Chicago Whales of the old Federal League. It was renamed Wrigley Field in 1926.

Bottomley-Ruffing-Schalk Baseball Museum in Nokomis—Honors the baseball achievements of about 100 people from central Illinois, with special emphasis on the three namesake Hall of Famers.

U.S. Cellular Field in Chicago—White Sox Legends Sculpture Plaza (sections 100 and 164) features sculptures such as Nellie Fox flipping the ball to his double-play partner Luis Aparicio as well as statues of Minnie Miñoso, Carlton Fisk, Billy Pierce and Charles Comiskey.

Negro Leagues Grave Marker Project in Alsip—Unmarked for years, the gravesites of a number of Negro Leagues players are finally marked with proper tombstones, thanks to the efforts of Dr. Jeremy Krock. The first three headstones were installed for Jimmie Crutchfield, John Wesley Donaldson and Candy Jim Taylor at Burr Oak Cemetery in Alsip in 2004. More than 20 have been installed to date, but there are still many more unmarked graves of Negro Leagues players.

Bob Groom Monument in Belleville—Memorial is located at Whitey Herzog Legion Field to honor Belleville native Groom, who pitched a no-hitter on May 6, 1917. It is part of an organized effort to honor Deadball Era players.

Notable Achievements

Fred Lindstrom was the youngest player to appear in a World Series. He was 18 years, 10 months and 13 days old when he played in the 1924 World Series for the New York Giants.

Joe McGinnity is the only player to pitch two complete

The Bottomley-Ruffing-Schalk Baseball Museum in tiny Nokomis, Illinois, pays tribute to three of central Illinois' greatest players: Hall of Famers Jim Bottomley, Red Ruffing and Ray Schalk. Schalk, who once held the record for most games caught and still holds the record for double plays by a catcher, is considered one of baseball's greatest defensive catchers (courtesy Bottomley-Ruffing-Schalk Baseball Museum).

games in one day ... three times in a career. He accomplished this feat all in the same month — August 1903.

Lonnie Smith has appeared in the World Series with the most teams — four. He played with the Phillies in 1980, the Cardinals in 1982, the Royals in 1985 and the Braves in 1991 and 1992.

Rickey Henderson has broken up the most no-hitters with home runs — 81 times he hit a leadoff home run.

Lou Boudreau became the first player with five extra-base hits in one game when he did it on July 14, 1946.

Gary Gaetti set a record by starting two triple plays in one game on July 17, 1990.

Denny McLain was the first pitcher to strike out the first seven batters in a game. He did it on June 15, 1965.

Fred Lynn belted the first grand slam ever hit in an All-Star game in 1983.

Rick Reuschel is one of only two pitchers to surrender home runs to Hank Aaron and Barry Bonds. He surrendered homers to Aaron on June 16, 1973, and July 7, 1974, and to Bonds on May 27, 1990.

Charley O'Leary (Chicago) became the oldest player to score a run in major league history when he singled and scored a run for the St. Louis Browns in 1934 at age 58.

Jay Hook (Waukegan) was the first pitcher to win a game for the New York Mets. After the expansion Mets had lost their first nine games of the 1962 season, Hook got a complete game win on April 23.

Milt Stock is the only player to get four hits in four straight games, which he accomplished in 1925.

Chicago Remains Home to Baseball's National Treasure

Chicago took its first stab at professional baseball in 1870 and a year later the fledgling team had seen nearly all its assets destroyed by fire. The city bounced back, and the Chicago White Stockings not only were founding members of the National League in 1876, they won the first pennant behind budding star Cap Anson. They would finish first five times in the 1880s.

Renamed the Cubs in 1903, the franchise played in four World Series between 1906 and 1910, winning consecutive championships in 1907–08. It was perhaps the most dominant stretch of play by any team in baseball history, as the Cubs averaged 106 wins and won at a .692 clip. The long-suffering fans of the Cubs are still waiting for the next championship.

Venerable Wrigley Field was named Weedhman Park when it opened as the home of the Chicago Whales of the Federal League in 1914. It became the home of the Cubs in 1916 and was renamed Wrigley Field in 1926. It retains its place as the most famous and revered baseball stadium in the world, a true national treasure and cultural icon. Even fans of other teams cannot wait to experience the ballpark's quaint atmosphere.

The surrounding area of Wrigleyville serves as the gathering spot for long-suffering Cubs fans, who have watched their team's championship drought stretch into a second century. Outside the historic stadium you can pose for pictures beside statues of Harry Caray, Billy Williams, Ron Santo and Ernie Banks. The Santo statue, which was unveiled in August 2011, depicts the popular ex-Cubs player getting ready to make a throw from third base.

After taking in a Cubs game, wander over to The Cubby Bear on the corner of Clark and Addison for a cold one or Murphy's Bleachers on North Sheffield, which also features rooftop seats with a view of the action. You can even take a few swings in the batting cages at Sluggers World Class Sports Bar and Grill.

On the South Side of Chicago, the White Sox won the first American League pennant in 1901 and then won the World Series in 1906 by beating the Cubs. After winning another title in 1917, the team gained notoriety for the Black Sox Scandal of 1919, with eight players eventually kicked out of the game for conspiring to fix the Series. That ugly incident seemed to cast a spell over the team, which suffered through a long dryspell before finally winning another championship in 2005.

A total of 1,015 players from Illinois have appeared in the majors, about one-third from Chicago. Among the Chicago-born players are Hall of Famers Kirby Puckett, Rickey Henderson and Fred Lindstrom. Another Chicago native, Charlie Comiskey, collected 1,529 hits over 13 seasons but is in the Hall as an executive. Comiskey helped found the American League and won four pennants during his 31 years of ownership with the White Sox. The ballpark that bore his name was the home of the White Sox from 1910–90.

Two Chicago-born players hold the unmatched standard for endurance, as Leon Cadore and Joe Oeschger each went the distance during a 26-inning game on May 1, 1920, which also happens to be the longest game ever played. Oeschger had pitched a 20-inning complete game the previous year that also ended in a tie, so he's the king of exerting yourself for nothing.

Chicago native Tony Suck was aptly named — he batted .151 and slugged .161 during his brief career from 1883–84. He was even worse in the field, committing 32 errors in 32 games at catcher, 16 errors in 15 games at short and five errors in 13 games in the outfield. He managed to play one errorless game at third, but only because no balls were hit to him. Here's the kicker: he legally changed his last name to Suck. His given name was Charles Anthony Zuck. Keep in mind that "Suck" did not have a negative connotation back then, but we're guessing his direct descendants are not thrilled with his name choice.

Illinois Leads Way with Wacky Names and Eccentric Players

Illinois is home to ballplayers with some fascinating names. There are tough guys nicknamed Bull, Moose,

Bulldog and Werewolf, as well as softies like Baby Doll and Sweetbread. Then you have players with not so tough names like Chick, Jody, Patsy, Shawn, Polly and Robin. One can also vote for Robert, John and Ted Kennedy, all Illinois-born players.

We have a Johnny Walker, accompanied by five Illinois-born players with the nickname "Red." Three unrelated John Sullivans hail from Chicago and there are 10 players whose last name begins with "Z." We also find a catcher named Al Unser, a second baseman named Don Johnson and a pitcher named Phil Collins, as well as a Mad Monk, a Pope and a Deacon.

More than 1,000 major league players have been born in Illinois including two Moxies, two Paddys and a Chappie, Hobie, Cozy, Jocko and Hunkey. There is a Dummy, Rube, Malarkey and Savage, not to mention Crazy Schmit. Crazy is a more apt moniker for Schmit's managers, who kept pitching him despite terrible results. Schmit recorded a 7-36 lifetime record with 5.45 ERA, 1.796 WHIP and twice as many walks as strikeouts, which is why he ended up pitching for five teams in five seasons.

Waukegan native Johnny Dickshot not only had an unfortunate name, he was the self-proclaimed "ugliest man in baseball" and went by the nickname "Ugly."

Either he was trying to deflect attention from his last name or he had self-esteem issues, but at least he batted .276 for his career. Egyptian Healy, on the other hand, picked up his nickname from his birthplace — Cairo.

Homer Hiller Henry Hillebrand, who attended Princeton, unfortunately did not live up to his name as a slugger. The Freeport native started out as a first baseman and played a little catcher and outfield beginning in 1905 for the Pirates, who were not impressed with his hitting ability. He hit .237 in 26 games in the field before switching to pitcher, where he produced a respectable 8-4 record with a 2.51 ERA. Homer ended up hitting zero home runs.

Illinois has produced enough oddball players to fill a freak show: Joe Charboneau, who used to open beer bottles with his eyelids; Fritz Peterson, who swapped wives with teammate Mike Kekich; and Eddie Gaedel, the shortest player in the history of the game thanks to a promotional stunt by owner Bill Veeck. Don Stanhouse was called "Stan the Man Unusual" for the quirky stunts he pulled, such as his primal scream during warm-ups or the stuffed gorilla he kept atop his locker. Or how about Doug Rader, who once sat on top of a birthday cake in the clubhouse and who used to lie down on his back in the clubhouse shower and hold upside-down seal races with teammates. Rader explained away his eccentricity by saying, "I like people and things to be off-center."

Germany Schaefer was another goofball who once got ejected for walking up to home plate wearing a raincoat during a downpour. He liked to use the hidden-ball trick and even managed to steal first base on at least one occasion. Schaefer stole second trying to draw a throw that would allow the runner on third to score the go-ahead run, but the catcher didn't fall for it. So "The Prince," as he was called, raced back to first so he could try again. When White Sox manager Hugh Duffy came out to complain, Schaefer took off for second again and this time managed to draw a throw, although the relay got the runner at the plate. The ensuing argument established that it's perfectly acceptable, if not recommended, to steal first. However, Schaefer's antics also led directly to a rule change stipulating that the bases be run in consecutive order.

Schaefer teamed up with Charley O'Leary to develop a successful vaudeville act that served as the inspiration for the musical "Take Me Out to the Ballgame" with Gene Kelly. That leads to the curious case of Turkey Mike Donlin, a boozing carouser who derailed his Hall of Fame chances when he married a Hollywood actress and left baseball

Chicago native Germany Schaefer was one of the wackiest players in baseball history. This photograph shows him trying out the other side of the camera before a game in 1911. Whether it was wearing a fake mustache to the plate or using his bat as a fake gun to shoot at the pitcher while rounding the bases after a home run, Schaefer was willing to do anything to entertain the crowd (Library of Congress, Prints & Photographs Division, LC-DIG-ggbain-09131).

in the prime of his career to pursue acting and vaudeville.

Illinois is also home to a war hero named Roy Gleason, who is the only major leaguer to be drafted and sent to the front lines in the Vietnam War. Gleason played eight games with the Los Angeles Dodgers in 1963, mainly as a pinch runner. He got a double in his only at-bat, so he ended up with a perfect 1.000 average, 1.000 OBP and 2.000 slugging percentage. Although Gleason was ineligible for postseason play, he received a World Series ring after the Dodgers won the championship that year. During his 21-month tour of duty in Vietnam, he was wounded in combat and evacuated by helicopter after a skirmish that killed most of his platoon — along the way he lost his World Series ring. He was awarded a Purple Heart and later received a replacement for his Series ring during a touching onfield ceremony at Dodger Stadium.

Two players with the last name of Dolan were nicknamed Cozy. The Cozy Dolan from Massachusetts had a nice nine-year career as an outfielder and pitcher before dying at age 34 of typhoid fever. The Cozy Dolan from Illinois was a bit player for seven seasons and then got a coaching job with the New York Giants. He received a lifetime ban from baseball in 1924 after asking Giants player Jimmy O'Connell to offer $500 to a Phillies player to throw a game.

After batting .091 (2-for-22) for the Yankees in 1919, 24-year-old George Halas wisely decided to turn to football, so the Yankees grabbed Babe Ruth from Boston to take his place.

How about a toast for Jigger Statz, who collected nearly as many hits in professional baseball as Ty Cobb. Unfortunately, 3,356 of his 4,093 hits came during 18 seasons spent with the Los Angeles Angels in the Pacific Coast League. Statz batted over. 300 12 times and recorded 200 hits nine straight years in the minors, finishing with 1,996 runs and a .315 average. He produced when given a chance in the majors, batting .319 with 209 hits and 110 runs scored for the Cubs in 1923. If you total his hits in the majors and minors, then Statz ranks fourth in career hits as a professional, just two behind Hank Aaron.

All-Time Illinois Selections

A total of 11 players from Illinois have been elected to the Hall of Fame, but only six of them earned the top spot for their position on the All-Time Illinois team. Three of them were beaten out by other Hall of Famers, which leaves two players who were overshadowed by a supposed lesser player (Fred Lindstrom and Red Schoendienst). Six of the executives/pioneers who have been elected to the Hall — Al Spalding, Bill Veeck, Charlie Comiskey, Warren Giles, Ed Barrow and Will Harridge — hailed from Illinois, which is more than any other state.

With that background behind us, let's get to the team selections. Ray Schalk may have been elected to the Hall of Fame, but that doesn't necessarily mean he was the best catcher from the state. According to Bill James, that would be Tom Haller, whom he ranks as the #26 catcher of all-time followed by Jim Sundberg at #32 and Schalk at #35.

Sundberg was a three-time All-Star who won six Gold Gloves for his stellar defense over 16 seasons behind the plate. He ranks eighth with 1,927 games caught and is seventh in fielding percentage (.993). He wasn't much of a hitter, with a .248 average and modest power, but was a little better than Schalk. He outhomered him 95–11 (largely because Schalk played in the Deadball Era) and has the edge in most hitting categories.

At 5-foot-9 (if that) and 165 pounds, Schalk would be considered too small to catch today. However, his diminutive size did not keep him from becoming one of the all-time greats at handling pitchers. "As a manager of young pitchers, Schalk stands head and shoulders above the others of all time," wrote John Sheridan in *The Sporting News* in 1923.

Schalk caught three no-hitters during his 18-year career and ranks first among catchers in double plays with 226 and second in assists with 1,811. He led AL catchers in putouts nine times and in fielding percentage five times. He was one of the first catchers to regularly run down the line to back up plays and even made putouts at second base on occasion. Schalk committed more than twice as many errors as Sundberg in 200 fewer games, but that's because he was forced to catch spitball pitchers and defend more bunts and sacrifices. Schalk had good speed for a catcher and stole 177 bases, including 30 in 1916 that stood as the record for catchers for 66 years. He helped lead the White Sox to the 1917 World Series and was one of the clean players on the 1919 team. The Veterans Committee elected Schalk to the Hall of Fame in 1955.

Haller was the best hitter of the three, although he only produced a .257 lifetime average. He slugged 134 homers, including 27 for the Giants in 1966, and had a career OPS+ of 113. Named to three All-Star teams, Haller caught only 1,199 games and was average defensively.

Sundberg threw out 41 percent of runners, but Schalk was even better at 49 percent. Sundberg's best finish in the MVP Award balloting was fifteenth, while Schalk came in third in 1922 and sixth in 1914. In the final judgment, Schalk's innovative command of the diamond and expert handling of pitchers overshadows Sundberg's defensive prowess and Haller's hitting.

Another good catcher from Illinois was Bob O'Farrell, who hung around for 21 years and caught 1,338 games. He was named National League MVP in 1926 after batting .293 for the World Champion Cardinals. He caught 146 games in the regular season that year, one of only three times he caught more than 100 games. The other two years — 1922 and 1923 — he batted .324 and .319. When a foul tip fractured his skull in 1924, O'Farrell was replaced in the lineup by Gabby Hartnett, who proved so good that O'Farrell was traded to the Cardinals. He was the catcher who threw out Babe Ruth to end the 1926 Series, the only time a World Series has ended on a base runner caught stealing. Ruth probably wasn't aware that O'Farrell had a strong arm and had thrown out 50 percent of base stealers that season (48 percent for his career).

Ray Fosse and Gene Lamont have something in common. The Illinois natives are two of the seven catchers taken ahead of Johnny Bench in the 1965 Amateur Draft. Fosse was drafted seventh overall by the Indians while Lamont went number 13 to the Tigers. Bench lasted until the 36th pick in the second round. At least Fosse ended up having a decent career, earning two All-Star selections and two Gold Gloves and rebounding from a home plate collision with Pete Rose in the 1970 All-Star Game. Lamont batted .233 with just 37 hits in the majors while four of the other catchers taken ahead of Bench never made it out of the minors.

A case could be made for Peoria's Jim Thome as the first baseman, but appearing in 778 games as a designated hitter makes him the logical choice as DH. So our first baseman is Jim Bottomley, who banged out 2,313 hits while averaging .310 over 16 seasons. He gained notoriety for knocking in a record 12 runs on September 16, 1924, with two homers, a double and three singles, and went 6-for-6 again in a game in 1931. Nicknamed "Sunny Jim" for his upbeat personality, Bottomley earned MVP honors in 1928 after becoming the first player to collect 20 triples, 30 homers and 40 doubles — he led the league with 20 triples, 31 homers and 136 RBI while batting .325 and scoring 123 runs. In 1925 he averaged .367 and led the NL with 227 hits and 44 doubles.

Bottomley drove in at least 100 runs six straight years and the only time he didn't bat over .300 in his first 10 seasons he averaged .299. A key contributor to four pennant-winning teams with the Cardinals, he batted .345 with 10 hits to lead the team to the 1926 World Series title over the Yankees. He was elected to the Hall of Fame in 1974.

Ted Kluszewski was a slugging first baseman who was able to belt mammoth home runs while hitting for a high average and without striking out much. He had more homers than strikeouts four straight years, including 1954 when he led the league with 49 homers and 141 RBI while batting .326 and striking out only 35 times. The next year he led the NL in hits while also slugging 47 homers. A .298 lifetime hitter, "Big Klu" ended up with 279 career homers.

Another noteworthy first baseman is Phil Cavarretta, who debuted with the Cubs at the age of 18 in 1934 and ended up making three All-Star teams, turning into a fan favorite as the original "Mr. Cub." He fell just short of 2,000 hits (1,977) and averaged .293 over a 22-season career spent entirely in Chicago (20 with the Cubs and two with the White Sox). Cavarretta is the only major league player who was active during Babe Ruth's last year (1935) and Hank Aaron's first year (1954).

He earned NL MVP honors in 1945 despite hitting just six homers from a traditional power position, leading the Cubs to their last World Series appearance. Cavarretta drove in 97 runs that year and led the league with a .355 average and .449 OBP. He hit .423 in the 1945 Series but it wasn't enough to lead the Cubbies to the championship. The Cubs won two other pennants during his tenure — Cavarretta batted .462 during the 1938 Series and .125 during the '35 Series.

Also worth mentioning is Bill "Moose" Skowron, who made six All-Star teams and hit 211 homers in 14 seasons. Skowron won seven pennants and four championships playing with the Yankees from 1954–62 and won a fifth ring with the Dodgers in 1963. Another Yankee first baseman, Chicago native Wally Pipp, is best known as the player Lou Gehrig replaced in the lineup when he started his consecutive games streak in 1925. Pipp was already on the back side of his career, and he went on to play three seasons with the Reds, ending with 1,941 career hits.

Red Schoendienst was a pretty good second baseman, but Larry Doyle was just a tad better. Doyle's numbers are a little misleading since he played his entire career in the Deadball Era, but he was a significantly better batsman. Despite playing 450 fewer games than Red, Doyle compiled more RBI and walks and has a big edge in triples, stolen bases and OPS+. Doyle won the Chalmers Award as NL MVP in 1912 for the pennant-winning Giants after batting .330 with 90 RBI and 36 stolen bases. "Laughing Larry" came in third in the MVP voting in 1911 after batting .310 and leading the league with 25 triples. Then in 1915 he led the NL in batting (.320), hits (189) and doubles (40).

Doyle earned the respect of his fiercely competitive manager, John McGraw, serving as the Giants captain for a number of years. McGraw had paid a record sum of $4,500 to sign Doyle away from the minors, and he stuck with him when he struggled early in his career. That faith was rewarded, as Doyle turned into a star who boasted power and speed. He averaged 36 steals from 1909–13, also finishing in the top six in home runs four of those five seasons.

The switch-hitting Schoendienst was no slouch with the bat, averaging .289 over 19 seasons and collecting 2,449 hits while typically batting in the leadoff or second spot. He batted over .300 seven times and led the league in hits, stolen bases and doubles one time each. His best year was 1953, when he finished second in batting at .342, scored 107 runs and had career highs in homers (15) and RBI (79). He hit a home run in the fourteenth inning to win the 1950 All-Star Game. But the respected captain of the Cardinals made his mark on defense, on two occasions setting the National League record for most chances without an error. Blessed with soft hands and good range, he led NL second basemen in fielding percentage seven times and in assists and putouts three times each.

Red, who roomed on the road with Stan Musial for 11 years, was a 10-time All-Star who won two World Series titles. He played with the Cardinals for 15 seasons and managed them for 14 years, winning over 1,000 games and guiding the Cards to a World Series title in 1967 and a second pennant in 1968. He was elected to the Hall of Fame in 1989.

Another notable second baseman is Marty McManus, who played nearly as many games at third base. He batted over .300 four times and led the AL in stolen bases and doubles one time each. He ended up with 1,926 hits and matched Schoendienst with a .289 average (Doyle was one point better at .290).

The All-Time Illinois team ends up with another Hall of Famer on the bench at third base. Gary Gaetti was a slick-fielding slugger who is only outpaced by Fred Lindstrom in batting average. He batted just .255 lifetime compared to .311 for Lindstrom. However, Gaetti has a big edge in hits (2,280 to 1,747) and home runs (360 to 103) and was a superior fielder with four Gold Gloves.

Gaetti, who was a cornerstone of the Twins infield throughout the 1980s, had eight years with over 20 homers and led AL third basemen in putouts and assists four times and in fielding percentage three times. He was named ALCS MVP in 1987 after hitting two home runs and he added a third homer to help the Twins win the World Series that year. In a strange footnote to history, Gaetti is the only player who was a teammate of Mark McGwire and Sammy Sosa during their record-setting home run year of 1998 — Gaetti was traded from the Cardinals to the Cubs during the season.

Lindstrom was NL MVP runner-up for the Giants in 1928 after batting .358 with 107 RBI and leading the league with 231 hits. In 1930 he averaged .379 and drove in 106 runs with a career-high 22 homers. He batted over .300 seven years and finished with an OPS+ of 110. He earned the wrath of Giants fans in his rookie year, 1924, by watching two ground balls bounce over his head in the eighth and ninth innings of Game 7 of the World Series to cost the Giants the championship. In five years on the Hall of Fame ballot Lindstrom failed to get 5 percent of the vote, yet he was voted in by the Veteran's Committee in 1976. He was a fine player who had a nice career, but he falls far short of anyone's standard of a Hall of Famer.

Lindstrom's son, Chuck, has tied records that will never be broken — highest lifetime batting average and highest on-base percentage. Chuck Lindstrom was a catcher who played for the White Sox in one game in 1958. He hit a triple and walked in his only trips to the plate, ending his career with an enviable slash line of 1.000/1.000/3.000/4.000. He didn't commit an error either, so his fielding percentage is a perfect 1.000.

Doug Rader earned five straight Gold Gloves and would make anyone's all-flake team. He gained notoriety for sitting on top of a birthday cake in the clubhouse. Other noteworthy third basemen include Kevin Seitzer who batted .323 with 207 hits as a rookie; Ossie Bluege, who spent his entire 18-year career with the Washington Senators and was one of the first third basemen to guard the line in the late innings; and Milt Stock, who batted over .300 four straight years, collected at least 200 hits twice and is the only player to get four hits in four straight games.

At shortstop, it's hard to turn away Lou Boudreau, who was a fantastic all-around player very deserving of his election to the Hall of Fame. But Robin Yount produced 1,363 more base hits and 183 more home runs than Boudreau during his first-ballot Hall of Fame career and he won twice as many MVP awards. It's tempting to move Yount to center field, since he played 1,150 games there, but he did play more games at short.

Yount was destined for stardom ever since he debuted for the Brewers at age 18 in 1974. His first MVP season, 1982, was a sight to behold as he carried the Brewers on his back all the way to the AL pennant. He finished second in batting (.331) and runs (129), led the league in hits (210), doubles (46), slugging (.578), OPS (.957), OPS+ (166), total bases (367) and finished third in triples (12). Although the Brewers fell to the Cardinals in the Series, Yount batted .414.

He moved to the outfield at age 29 and had nine more good years, winning his second MVP in 1989 after batting .318 with 21 homers and 103 RBI. His 1,731 hits in the 1980s are more than any other player. Yount, who was still a productive player when he retired at 38, went over the 250 mark in homers and stolen bases and ranks seventh in at-bats, third in sacrifice flies, fourteenth in games played and seventeenth in hits and doubles.

Just as Yount took over the town of Milwaukee, Boudreau did the same in Cleveland 40 years earlier after taking over as player-manager at the age of 24 in 1942. It's safe to say we'll never see another 24-year-old player-manager, let alone a manager of that age. It took Lou a few years to get the team clicking, and he had an adversarial relationship with Veeck the owner, but he led the Indians to their second and so far, last, World Series championship in 1948.

All Boudreau did that year was finish second in batting (.355) and OBP (.453), slug .534, drive in 104 runs, collect 199 hits, score 116 runs and walk 98 times while only striking out nine times all season. He even caught in one game when the Indians found themselves short-handed behind the plate. With the Indians tied with the Red Sox at the end of the regular season, a one-game playoff became necessary. Boudreau took matters into his own hands by clubbing two homers and two singles as the Indians won 8–3 to win the pennant. He hit four doubles during the World Series as the Tribe won the championship. Boudreau's herculean effort that year did not go unnoticed as he beat out Joe DiMaggio and Ted Williams for the AL MVP Award.

"Handsome Lou" also won a batting crown in 1944 and led the league in doubles three times, but he earned his reputation as a fielder extraordinaire. He led AL shortstops in fielding percentage 10 straight years — every year of the 1940s — and set an American League record (since broken) for most double plays. A seven-time All-Star, the sure-handed Boudreau had a knack for moving into the right position. It was his innovative thinking that devised "The Williams Shift," in which the shortstop moves to the right side of the diamond and leaves the third baseman alone to defend the left side of the infield against a left-handed pull hitter.

Boudreau had this to say after being elected to the

Hall of Fame in his twelfth year of eligibility in 1970: "I'm really humbled by this because I never considered myself a super-star like Williams, DiMaggio or Aaron."

Two other shortstops from Illinois, Herman Long and Dick Bartell, both recorded more than 2,000 hits in their careers. Long was a nineteenth century player who led the league with 149 runs scored in 1893 and stole 593 bases in his career. He also committed more than 1,000 errors at shortstop. Bartell was an unpopular, mouthy player who moved around to five teams in 18 seasons, batting over .300 six times and making three All-Star teams. He led NL shortstops in Range Factor/Game seven times in the 1930s.

The All-Time Illinois team is fortunate to have the best leadoff hitter in baseball history, as well as the best base stealer. No one stole more bases or scored more runs than Rickey Henderson, who was still a dangerous threat and menace to pitchers after 25 years. He led the league in stolen bases 12 times, runs five times and walks four times. He ranks fourth all-time in games played (3,081) and was named AL MVP in 1990. Henderson had good power, too, with 297 career home runs. His 490.4 power-speed number is surpassed only by Barry Bonds.

Crouching down in the batter's box waiting to uncoil at the right pitch, Henderson was difficult to pitch to, although that pales in comparison to the havoc he caused once he reached base. His manager on the Oakland A's, Tony LaRussa, described him this way: "For the period of time that I've been around, I think the most dangerous player is Rickey."

Rickey was an original, a self-centered but supremely confident player who was famous for referring to himself in the third person. Before every game he played, Henderson would stand naked in front of a full-length locker room mirror and spend several minutes telling himself "Ricky's the best." Just think about how many teammates on eight different teams witnessed that act over 25 seasons.

Rickey once missed three games because he fell asleep on an ice pack and got frostbite. When he broke Ty Cobb's record for career runs scored by hitting a home run, Henderson punctuated the moment by sliding into home plate. If there was any doubt Rickey was the best, he reminded you. After breaking Lou Brock's career record for stolen bases, Rickey said, "Lou Brock was a great base stealer but today I am the greatest." Not sure how Brock felt about that comment, since he was standing next to Rickey at the time.

With 1,406 stolen bases, Rickey ended up surpassing Brock's total by 49 percent. To show how dominant that is, someone would have to hit 1,135 home runs to outdistance Barry Bonds' home run record to the same degree.

Flanking Rickey in center field is Kirby Puckett, whose career and life ended too soon. The most popular player in Minnesota Twins history, Puckett was at his best when the lights were bright, whether it was leaping the fence to rob a home run or belting a clutch hit in the postseason. He led the underdog Twins to World Series titles in 1987 and 1991, batting .357 in the first one and hitting two home runs in the second. The key blast was his walk-off 11th-inning homer off Braves pitcher Charlie Leibrandt in Game 6 of the 1991 Series that turned the momentum in the Twins' favor. The sight of Kirby pumping his fist while jogging around the bases is an indelible image of his ability to rise to the occasion as well as his passion for the game. Earlier in the same game Puckett had tripled in a run and climbed the wall to rob Ron Gant of an extra-base hit.

Braves pitcher John Smoltz paid him the ultimate compliment, saying, "In 1991 in playing against him in the World Series, if we had to lose and if one person basically was the reason, you never want to lose but you didn't mind it being (to) Kirby Puckett. When he made the catch and when he hit the home run, you could tell the whole thing had turned. His name just seemed to be synonymous with being a superstar."

After hitting no home runs in his rookie year, Kirby blasted 31 two years later, but he was not really a home run hitter. He was an all-around talent who led the AL in hits four times, each time exceeding 200 hits. A six-time Gold Glove winner for his spectacular play in center, Puckett's .318 lifetime average came after batting over .300 eight times. He won the batting crown after averaging .339 in 1989, made 10 All-Star teams and finished in the top seven in MVP voting seven times.

It shocked the baseball world when Puckett was forced to retire at age 35 after losing vision in one eye due to glaucoma. His number 34 was retired by the Twins in 1997, and he was inducted into the Hall of Fame in 2001, his first year of eligibility. Tragically, he was the second youngest member of the Hall of Fame to die (behind Lou Gehrig) when he succumbed to a stroke in 2006 at the age of 45.

The third outfielder is Wally Berger, who was sufficiently brilliant in his first seven years with the Boston Braves to overcome the fact he struggled with injuries later on and was done at age 34. Strong consideration was given to Fred Lynn, who also was hampered by injuries but ending up playing six more years than Berger and so understandably has the edge in counting stats. Berger's lifetime average of .300 trumps Lynn's .283 and Berger's 137 OPS+ places him in the number 87 spot all-time; Lynn is tied for 169th with a 129 OPS+.

In 1930 Berger set a rookie home run record with 38 homers while also knocking in 119 and batting .310. He also led the league with 34 homers and 130 RBI in 1935 and batted over .300 his first four seasons. He made four All-Star teams and retired with 242 homers.

Lynn was a smooth, graceful center fielder with five-tool talent who drew comparisons to Joe DiMaggio when he burst onto the scene and batted .419 as a September call-up in 1974. All he did his rookie year was lead the league in runs, doubles, slugging, OPS and OPS+, finish second with a .331 average and third with 105 RBI, lead the Red Sox to the pennant while making the All-Star team and earn the Gold Glove, Rookie of the Year and MVP awards. He was the first player to win the latter two awards in the same year, a feat later matched by Ichiro Suzuki. Lynn seemed destined for Cooperstown, especially matched with fearsome slugger Jim Rice in the Red Sox lineup.

Although Lynn had other good seasons and made nine straight All-Star teams, he only had one more great season: 1979 when he hit 39 homers, knocked in 122 runs and led the league with a .333/.423/.637/1.059 slash line. Injuries curtailed his productivity, but Lynn also struggled to live up to the initial hype. He was named ALCS MVP in 1982 after batting .611 for the Angels in a losing effort. He hit 306 career homers, won four Gold Gloves and went over 1,000 runs and 1,000 RBI for his career. His 129 career OPS+ is better than a number of Hall of Fame outfielders including Rice, Puckett, Henderson, Goose Goslin, Willie Keeler and Kiki Cuyler.

Other notable outfielders from Illinois include Shawn Green, Turkey Mike Donlin, Hank Bauer and Negro Leaguers Jimmie Lyons and Sam Jethroe. Green hit 328 career homers and had three seasons with over 40 homers. His most noteworthy feat came on May 23, 2002, when he went 6-for-6 with four homers, a single and a double. He set a record with 19 total bases and it's the last time a National League player has gotten six hits in a game. The flamboyant Donlin averaged .333 for his career, which is the highest by an Illinois player, and he ranks 44th all-time with an OPS+ of 144. He finished in the top three in average five times and batted over .300 in all but one season (discounting a brief stint in 1914). Bauer played on nine pennant winners with the Yankees in a 10-year stretch, earning seven World Series rings and hitting four homers in the 1958 Series.

Lyons has been called one of the fastest players in baseball history. The lefty-swinging leadoff hitter was nearly impossible to throw out on the bases and his aggressive style of play proved a weapon for Rube Foster's Giants in the early 1920s. Bill James ranks him as the fifth-best center fielder in the Negro Leagues and the best overall player in 1920. That year Lyons batted .379 with eight homers and 21 stolen bases in 59 games tracked by the Seamheads.com Negro Leagues Database powered by The Baseball Gauge.

Jethroe was a speedy outfielder who batted .341 over seven Negro League seasons, batting .353 in 1944 and .393 in 1945 to lead the league both years. He was judged by James as the best overall player in the Negro Leagues in 1945. Signed by the Brooklyn Dodgers in 1948 and traded to the Braves, he became the oldest Rookie of the Year in 1950 at the age of 32. He led the NL with 35 stolen bases and scored 100 runs that year. His stats were almost exactly the same the next year, but he ended up playing only three seasons in the majors.

With 604 home runs (eighth on the all-time list) and 1,674 RBI after the 2011 season, our DH, Thome, is the all-time Illinois leader in those categories. He's Paul Bunyan at the plate, swinging for the fences as hard as he can and connecting regularly with monstrous shots. Entering the 2012 season he trailed Reggie Jackson by 110 strikeouts for the most in baseball history, but he has also walked 1,725 times. His slash line of .277/.403/.556 shows he's not a one-trick pony. A five-time All-Star who has been a full-time DH since 2006, Thome has compiled nine seasons with at least 100 walks and 100 RBI.

Thome posted nine straight years with 30 or more homers, sat out much of 2005 with injuries and then was traded to the White Sox, where he proceeded to hit 42, 35 and 34 homers. Regularly acknowledged as one of the nicest guys in baseball and seemingly free of any suspicion over steroids, the lefty slugger should have little trouble getting into Cooperstown.

Thome, who has been making a positive impression on baseball fans his entire career, explains his outlook this way: "My dad told me when I went into high school, 'It's not what you do when you walk in the door that matters. It's what you do when you walk out.' That's when you've made a lasting impression."

Greg Luzinski, who slugged 307 homers in a career that lasted from 1970–84, fell just short as an outfielder and as DH for Team Illinois. Forced to display his lack of grace in the outfield while playing 11 years for the Phillies—the quintessential "Bull" in a china shop—Luzinski found a home at DH after being picked up by the White Sox in 1981. He recorded 30 homers, 100 RBI and a .300 average four times each. A four-time All-Star, he was MVP runner-up with the Phillies in 1975 and 1977 and posted a career OPS+ of 130.

There are three Hall of Fame right-handed pitchers from Illinois, but Robin Roberts is the best choice for the top spot. His career record of 286–245 is not indicative of how dominant he was from 1950–55 for the Phillies but more a result of playing on bad teams for much of his career. He was a workhorse who led the league in quite a few pitching categories during those six big years, winning 20 games each year (including at least 23 in four straight) and averaging 27 complete games.

Roberts' best year was 1952, when he went 28–7 with a 2.57 ERA and was MVP runner-up after finishing first in wins, complete games, innings, BB/9IP and SO/BB. Roberts was a deceptively hard thrower who posted double-figure win totals in 16 of 19 seasons. Until passed by Jamie Moyer in 2010, Roberts held the record for most home runs allowed with 505. "I had a high fastball, and I either overpowered them or they overpowered me," he said. A seven-time All-Star, he was elected to the Hall of Fame in 1976.

Another outstanding righty is Joe "Iron Man" McGinnity, who went 246–142 with a 2.66 ERA and 314 complete games pitching around the turn of the century. What's amazing about his numbers is that he was 28 years old when he debuted in the majors. McGinnity won 28 games his first two seasons and ended up with eight seasons with 20 or more wins (twice going over 30). His best season was 1904 with the New York Giants when he went 35–8 and led the NL in wins, win percentage (.814), ERA (1.61), shutouts

(9), saves (5), innings (408), ERA+ (170) and WHIP (0.963). McGinnity pitched until he was 54, winning 216 more games in the minors.

McGinnity frequently used an underhand or sidearm pitching motion to preserve his arm, which proved effective for him. Although his nickname seems to stem from the fact that he was a workhorse on the mound, it actually has its origins in his former work at an iron foundry. McGinnity was a controversial figure who was in the center of some big-time brawls with the Giants. He followed his manager, John McGraw, from Baltimore to the Giants as part of some back-room dealings that were common back in those days.

Another Hall of Fame righty is Red Ruffing, who won 273 games and pitched 335 complete games over 22 seasons. Ruffing really had two careers: a mediocre six-plus years with the Red Sox that produced a 39–96 record, and a superb 231–124 mark over 15 years with the powerhouse Yankee teams of the 1930s and early '40s. He never won more than 10 games for the Sox but posted 11 seasons with at least 15 wins for the Yankees including four straight 20-win seasons.

Ruffing went 7–2 with a 2.63 ERA in the postseason, being part of eight pennant winners and seven world championship teams. He was one of the best-hitting pitchers of all-time, batting over .300 eight times and finishing with a lifetime average of .269 with 36 homers and 273 RBI. If you want to know more about Ruffing's career, visit the Bottomley-Ruffing-Schalk Baseball Museum in Nokomis, which highlights the three Hall of Famers' careers.

Al Spalding is in the Hall of Fame for his role as a sporting goods and team executive, but he was also the most dominant pitcher of the 1870s. He led the league in wins each of his six full seasons, with win totals of 19, 38, 41, 52, 54 and 47. He finished with a record of 252–65 and his .795 career winning percentage ranks number one all-time.

Brett Saberhagen was a two-time Cy Young Award winner who was named to three All-Star teams, but not in the years he won the Cy Young. He won his first Cy Young Award in 1985, after going 20–6 for the Royals. The second one came in his best season, 1989, when he went 23–6 and led the AL in wins, winning percentage, ERA, complete games, innings, ERA+ and WHIP. Saberhagen battled arm troubles later in his career and retired with a 167–117 record.

It's impossible to overlook Denny McLain, the last pitcher to win 30 games in a season but whose life off the field has been a train wreck. He was cocky and self-centered and in constant need of living on the edge and being in the spotlight. McLain won back-to-back Cy Young Awards for the Tigers in 1968–69, going 31–6 with a 1.96 ERA the first year while leading the league in wins, won-lost percentage, games started, complete games, innings and SO/BB. He was also named MVP in that "Year of the Pitcher" for the world champion Tigers. He won Game 6 of the Series on two days of rest, but lost two other games to the Cardinals' ace, Bob Gibson. The next year he went 24–9 and pitched 325 innings in 41 starts, sharing the Cy Young Award with the Orioles' Mike Cuellar.

McLain, who used to drink a case of Pepsi a day during his playing days, missed a significant portion of the 1970 season due to a series of suspensions by the league and the team for gambling and then in 1971 he lost 22 games to punctuate his fall from grace. He was out of baseball by 29 and his shady off-field dealings finally caught up with him when he was charged in 1984 with racketeering, embezzlement and distributing cocaine. Although that conviction was overturned by the courts, McLain later went back to prison for six years after being convicted of embezzlement, mail fraud and conspiracy. Despite a lifetime of misdeeds, McLain insists his only regret is that he forced his daughter, Kristin, to move back home and she was killed by a drunk driver in 1992.

Rounding out the list of notable righties we have Dutch Leonard, a four-time All-Star who recorded 191 victories and won 20 games for Washington in 1939. He was able to pitch until the age of 44 by relying on a knuckleball. Rick "Big Daddy" Reuschel won 214 games and earned three All-Star selections and two Gold Gloves. Jack Powell was one of the best pitchers of the Deadball Era, winning 245 games and pitching 4,389 innings in 16 years. He also lost 254 games, but that was more a reflection of the fact he played on bad St. Louis Browns teams. Powell recorded a lifetime ERA of 2.97 and won 20 games four times. In 1900 he won a game despite surrendering seven runs in the first inning.

It was difficult to select a left-handed starter for the All-Time Illinois team, as there were a number of journeyman pitchers but few standouts. We ended up going with the player whose name indicated he was a good southpaw — Lefty Leifield. He won 18 games with a 1.87 ERA in his first full season, 1906, and then won 20 games with a 2.33 ERA in 1907. He won at least 15 games six straight seasons and finished with a 124–97 record and 2.47 ERA.

Larry Gura posted a nearly identical career record of 126–97, but with a 3.76 ERA. He won 18 games for the Royals in 1980 and finished fifth with a 2.95 ERA. Another Royals lefty, Charlie Leibrandt, won 140 games over 14 seasons, posting double-figure win totals eight times. His best season was 1985, when Leibrandt went 17–9 with a 2.69 ERA (second in AL) for the Royals, helping the team win the World Series while finishing fifth in Cy Young Award voting.

When healthy, lefty Mark Mulder was a dominant hurler. He won 21 games with the A's in 2001, placing second in voting for the Cy Young Award. He won 19 games the next year and led the AL in shutouts and complete games twice during his five years with Oakland. Mulder's career winning percentage of .632 is outstanding.

Another lefty, Fritz Peterson, was an All-Star with the Yankees in 1970 after going 20–11 with a 2.90 ERA. He led the AL in BB/9IP five straight seasons and in WHIP and SO/BB two times each. He was not the same pitcher after the wife-swapping story hit the national media in 1973, and he was out of the majors by the middle of the 1976 season.

Few people are aware that the best-fielding pitcher in baseball history is an Illinois native. Greg Maddux may have won 18 Gold Gloves, but Hoyleton's own Kirk Rueter is statistically the best-fielding pitcher in history, as documented by John Knox in *The Baseball Research Journal*. Rueter, who never won a Gold Glove, committed just seven errors in 13 seasons and ended his career with a .988 fielding percentage. By comparison, Maddux committed 53 errors and had a career fielding percentage of .970. With 54 double plays in 1,918 innings, Rueter started a double play every 35.5 innings. Maddux, on the other hand, tallied 98 double plays in 5,008 innings, or one every 51.1 innings.

The best relief pitcher is Jason Isringhausen, who has accumulated 300 saves and made two All-Star teams through 2011. He recorded 30 or more saves seven times in eight seasons and led the NL with 47 saves while tying a Cardinals record in 2004.

Also deserving mention in the bullpen are John Wyatt, Mike Myers and Dan Kolb. Wyatt led the league with 81 appearances in 1964 but also set a record by becoming the first relief pitcher to give up more than 20 homers in a season — he surrendered 23. Amazingly, Wyatt made his only All-Star team that year. Myers was a lefty specialist with a submarine style who appeared in just 541 innings across 883 games (all in relief) for nine teams. With 83 and 88 appearances, he led the AL in 1996 and 1997. Kolb was an All-Star with the Brewers in 2004 after recording 39 saves.

Forty-three managers were born in Illinois and four have won 1,000 or more games: Whitey Herzog (1,281), Lou Boudreau (1,162), Red Schoendienst (1,041) and Chuck Dressen (1,008). Eight of them are in the Hall of Fame, but only one of them as a manager — Herzog.

Whitey's managing career didn't get off to a good star after being hired by the Rangers in 1973. When asked his first impressions of his new team, Herzog bluntly responded, "To be honest about it, this is the worst excuse for a big-league club I ever saw." Forced to deal with a meddling owner, Bob Short, who insisted his manager pitch 18-year-old phenom David Clyde to increase fan interest and attendance, Herzog was replaced by Billy Martin in September after going 47–91.

Herzog would rebound to win six division titles, three pennants and one World Series over his 18-year managerial career. He led the Royals to three straight division titles, winning 102 games in 1977 but getting knocked out of the playoffs each year by the Yankees. Hired by the Cardinals in 1980, he added the dual role of general manager and helped build the team that won the championship in 1982. Among the players he acquired were future Hall of Famers Bruce Sutter and Ozzie Smith. He also liked speedy switch-hitters like Willie McGee, who could cover ground and take advantage of the artificial turf at Busch Stadium. The "White Rat" was inducted into the Hall of Fame in 2010.

Dressen managed five teams over 16 seasons but only found success during a three-year stretch skippering the Brooklyn Dodgers in the early 1950s, the team immortalized in Roger Kahn's classic book *The Boys of Summer*. He led the Dodgers to 97 wins and a tie for first place in 1951 before making the fateful decision to have Ralph Branca pitch to Bobby Thomson in the third and decisive game of the playoffs. Thomson's "Shot Heard 'Round the World" sent the Dodgers home empty-handed that year, but Dressen rebounded to deliver back-to-back pennants the next two seasons. The '53 squad won 105 regular-season games but lost the Series 4–2 to the Yankees. Emboldened by the team's success, Dressen's wife, Ruth, wrote a letter to Walter O'Malley demanding a three-year contract for her husband. O'Malley responded by replacing Dressen with Walter Alston, emphasizing the Dodgers' policy to only offer one-year contracts.

Dressen's next chance to manage was with the downtrodden Washington Senators, which produced a .354 winning percentage in 329 games. Taking over the Milwaukee Braves with Hank Aaron, Eddie Mathews and a still productive Warren Spahn in 1960, he led them to a second-place finish but didn't last the next season before getting replaced.

INDIANA

*Names in **bold** represent Major League selections by position, followed by honorable mentions. Negro Leagues players are in **bold italics**, followed by honorable mentions in italics. City of birth is in parentheses.*

Catcher — Bubbles Hargrave (New Haven). Also: Milt May (Gary); Dick Dietz (Crawfordsville); Bill Rariden (Bedford); Lou Criger (Elkhart); Butch Henline (Fort Wayne); Pinky Hargrave (New Haven)

First Base — Don Mattingly (Evansville). Also: Gil Hodges (Princeton); Bill Everitt (Fort Wayne); *George Crowe* (Whiteland)

Second Base — Billy Herman (New Albany). Also: *Frank Warfield* (Indianapolis); Craig Counsell (South Bend); Jamey Carroll (Evansville); Rollie Zeider (Auburn)

Third Base — Scott Rolen (Evansville). Also: Jeff King (Marion); Pinky May (Laconia)

Shortstop — Donie Bush (Indianapolis). Also: Dickie

Thon (South Bend); Everett Scott (Bluffton); Tommy Thevenow (Madison); Clint Barmes (Vincennes); *Will Owens* (Indianapolis)

Outfield—*Oscar Charleston* **(Indianapolis)**
Outfield—**Max Carey (Terre Haute)**
Outfield—**Edd Roush (Oakland City).** Also: Sam Rice (Morocco); Kenny Lofton (East Chicago); Sam Thompson (Danville); Chuck Klein (Indianapolis); Cy Williams (Wadena); *Ted Strong* (South Bend); Chick Stahl (Avilla); *Lester Lockett* (Princeton); Pete Fox (Evansville); Phil Bradley (Bloomington); Chad Curtis (Marion)

Designated Hitter—**Ron Kittle (Gary).** Also: Adam Lind (Muncie)

Right Handed Starter—**Mordecai "Three Finger" Brown (Nyesville).** Also: Amos Rusie (Mooresville); Babe Adams (Tipton); Nig Cuppy (Logansport); Dizzy Trout (Sandcut); Freddie Fitzsimmons (Mishawaka); Bob Friend (Lafayette); *Bill Holland* (Indianapolis); Andy Benes (Evansville); Carl Erskine (Anderson); Hooks Dauss (Indianapolis); Don Larsen (Michigan City)

Left Handed Starter—**Tommy John (Terre Haute).** Also: Art Nehf (Terre Haute); Paul Splittorf (Evansville); Toad Ramsey (Indianapolis)

Relief Pitcher—**Dan Plesac (Gary).** Also: Ron Reed (LaPorte); LaTroy Hawkins (Gary); Doc Crandall (Wadena); Jeff Parrett (Indianapolis); Tim Stoddard (East Chicago); Billy McCool (Batesville)

Manager—**Gil Hodges (Princeton).** Also: *Oscar Charleston* (Indianapolis); *Frank Warfield* (Indianapolis); Donie Bush (Indianapolis); Eric Wedge (Fort Wayne)

The Names

Best Nickname: Amos "The Hoosier Thunderbolt" Rusie

Other Nicknames: Vic "The Hoosier Schoolmaster" Aldridge; Bob "Hammond Hummer" Anderson; Ernie "Junie" Andres; Bruce "Squeaky" Barmes; Ollie "Polish Falcon" Bejma; Joe "Blitzen" and "Butcher Boy" Benz; Claude "Admiral" Berry; Emil "Hillbilly" Bildilli; Elmer "Shook" Brown; Mordecai "Three Finger" Brown; Dave "Chopper" Campbell; Max "Scoops" Carey; Oscar "The Hoosier Comet" and "The Black Ruth" Charleston; "Big George" Crowe; Carl "Oisk" Erskine; "Fat Freddie" Fitzsimmons; Bob "Warrior" Friend; George "Hooks or Hookey" Dauss; Gene "Suds" Fodge; Eugene "Bubbles" Hargrave; William "Pinky" Hargrave; Gil "Miracle Worker" Hodges; Hal "Grump" Irelan; Chuck "The Hoosier Hammerer" Klein; Don "Gooney Bird" Larsen; Don "Donnie Baseball" Mattingly; Merrill "Pinky" May; Bill "Bonehead" Pierce; "Rifle Jim" Middleton; Roscoe "Rubberlegs" Miller; Will "Gabie" Owens; Charles "Tex" Pruiett; Thomas "Toad" Ramsey; "Bedford Bill" Rariden; Sam "Man o' War" Rice; Everett "Deacon" Scott; Rodney "Cool Breeze" Scott; "Kickapoo Ed" Summers; Arlas "Foxy" Taylor; "Big Sam" Thompson; Paul "Dizzy" Trout; William "Peek-a-Boo" Veach; Frank "The Weasel" Warfield; "Jumping Johnny" Wilson; Rollie "Bunions" Zeider

Most Unusual Name: Emil Bildilli

All-Time Leaders

Games: Max Carey, 2476
Hits: Sam Rice, 2987
Batting Average: Sam Thompson, .331
Home Runs: Gil Hodges, 370
RBI: Sam Thompson, 1305
Stolen Bases: Max Carey, 738
Wins: Tommy John, 288
Strikeouts: Tommy John, 2245
Saves: Dan Plesac, 158
Future Stars: Jarrod Parker (Ossian); Drew Storen (Brownsburg); Conrad Gregor (Carmel)
Best Player: Oscar Charleston

Historic Baseball Places

Bosse Field in Evansville—Many of the game scenes for *A League of Their Own* were filmed at Bosse Field in 1991. Built in 1915, it is the third-oldest ballpark used regularly for professional baseball (behind Fenway Park and Wrigley Field). Hall of Famers Chuck Klein, Hank Greenberg and Warren Spahn all played in the minors at Bosse Field.

Indiana Baseball Hall of Fame in Jasper—Located on the campus of Vincennes University, the Hall nearly doubled in size in 2007. You will find Carl Erskine's Dodgers jersey, old-time jerseys and gloves dating back to the early 1900s and special exhibits on Don Mattingly and Scott Rolen.

Baseball exhibit at Vigo County Historical Society in Terre Haute—Chronicles the history of professional baseball in the Wabash Valley, such as the time the Cubs and Tigers met for a rematch shortly after they competed in the 1908 World Series. See artifacts from hometown great Tommy John as well as Hall of Famers Mordecai "Three Finger" Brown and Max Carey.

Carl Erskine statue in Anderson—Honoring his community service initiatives as much as his baseball achievements, the statue is located in front of the Carl D. Erskine Rehabilitation & Sports Medicine Center.

Victory Field in Indianapolis—Home of the Indianapolis Indians, the retro ballpark features a great view of the downtown skyline. Victory Field has been recognized as "Best Minor League Ballpark in America" several times since opening in 1996.

League Stadium in Huntingburg—This historic park dates back to 1894, although the field and grandstand were extensively renovated in 1991 to look like an old-time ballpark for the filming of "A League of Their Own."

Parkview Field in Fort Wayne—Special plaques and

Built in 1915, Bosse Field in Evansville, Indiana, is the third-oldest ballpark used regularly for professional baseball. Many of the game scenes for *A League of Their Own* were filmed at Bosse Field in 1991. Hall of Famers Chuck Klein and Hank Greenberg played for the Evansville Hubs at Bosse Field, while Warren Spahn won 19 games pitching for the Evansville Bees in 1941 (courtesy BallparkReviews.com).

signage point out the history of baseball in the city, such as the fact that the first professional baseball game was played in 1871 by the Fort Wayne Kekiongas.

Notable Achievements

Butch Metzger (Lafayette) set a record with 77 appearances as a rookie in 1976, when he was named Rookie of the Year. He also tied a record by winning his first 12 decisions.

Sam Rice is the only Hoosier to hit a home run off Babe Ruth. He did it on June 25, 1919, one of only 10 home runs surrendered by the Babe.

Don Mattingly hit a record six grand slams in 1987 and then never hit another one during his career. Travis Hafner later tied his mark in 2006.

Toad Ramsey is sometimes credited as the first pitcher to throw a knuckleball, although some say it was more of a knuckle-curve. He did post the second-highest strikeout total in MLB history — 499 in 1886 — but lost the strikeout crown that year to Matt Kilroy, who whiffed 513 batters.

Scott Sheldon (Hammond) is one of four players who

have played all nine positions in one game. He did it for the Texas Rangers on September 6, 2000.

On July 10, 1936, **Chuck Klein** became the first National League player in the twentieth century to hit four home runs in a game.

Phillies second baseman **Eric Bruntlett** (Lafayette) executed the fifteenth unassisted triple play in MLB history on August 23, 2009 and it was just the second game-ending one.

Billy Herman collected at least five hits in a game on six different occasions.

Rollie Zeider (Auburn) is one of two players to play for all three major league franchises in Chicago: the Cubs, the White Sox and the Chicago Whales in the Federal League.

Negro Leagues' Greatest All-Around Player Was Indy Native

Many people say Oscar Charleston was not only the greatest all-around Negro Leagues player, but that he was better than any white player. He combined Ruth's slugging ability and Cobb's aggressive and fiery base running with Tris Speaker's ability to play shallow and still chase down any ball hit over his head. In fact, Charleston's description as the "black Ty Cobb" and the "black Ruth" did not do justice to his talent.

An Indianapolis native who ran away and joined the army at age 15, Charleston would return to his hometown to play with the Indianapolis ABCs, leading them to a championship in 1916. He played seven seasons for the ABCs and later played on some of the greatest Negro Leagues teams ever such as the Homestead Grays and Pittsburgh Crawfords. When the Crawfords moved to Indianapolis for the 1940 season Charleston found himself back in his old stomping grounds as his career was winding down.

Charleston batted .437 with 91 RBI, a league-leading 32 steals and .517 OBP for the St. Louis Stars in 1921, followed by a .375 average with 19 homers and 100 RBI for the ABCs the next season, according to the Seamheads.com Negro Leagues Database. The Hall of Fame officially credits him with a lifetime average of .346 and he was among the league leaders in home runs and stolen bases nearly every season.

Ted Page and Buck O'Neil both said Charleston was better than Willie Mays, while Dizzy Dean, who barnstormed against him a few times, noted Charleston didn't seem to have a weakness. Ben Taylor called him the greatest outfielder who ever lived.

Reportedly strong enough to rip the cover off a baseball with his bare hands, Charleston was intense and volatile with a vicious competitive streak, willing and able to do whatever was necessary to win a game. That was evident during a game in 1915 when the 18-year-old rookie Charleston raced in from center field and punched out the umpire at second base after a disputed call. A near-riot ensued and Charleston and teammate Bingo DeMoss were arrested for assault, dodging the charges by fleeing to Cuba and getting an early start on Winter League ball.

"He hit so hard, he'd knock gloves off you. He was a stronger hitter than Josh Gibson," recalls Newt Allen, in John Holway's *Blackball Stars*. Bill James ranks Charleston as the fourth-best player of all-time behind Ruth, Wagner and Mays.

Charleston, who was elected to the Baseball Hall of Fame in 1976, stands alone for his extraordinary talent in all facets of the game, earning him the honor as Indiana's All-Time Best Player. His early years with the ABCs coincided with the team's heyday under manager C.I. Taylor. Charleston was joined in a powerful lineup by Taylor's three brothers—first baseman Ben Taylor, third baseman Candy Jim Taylor and pitcher Steel Arm Johnny Taylor—along with outfielder George Shively, ace hurler Dizzy Dismukes and second baseman DeMoss.

Oscar Charleston rose from the sandlots of Indianapolis to become what many consider the greatest player in the history of the Negro Leagues. The barrel-chested Indianapolis native starred for his hometown team, the Indianapolis ABCs, during three stints between 1915 and 1923 and later played on two of the greatest Negro teams ever: the 1931 Homestead Grays and the 1935 Pittsburgh Crawfords (National Baseball Hall of Fame Library, Cooperstown, New York).

The ABCs, who had moved from West Baden, Ind., would later become a founding member of the Negro National League (NNL) in 1920. Indianapolis played host to the first NNL game at West Washington Park on May 2, 1920, with Charleston in the lineup in center field. Today, a historical marker notes the significance of the former ballpark's location at the current site of the Indianapolis Zoo.

Indianapolis was home to another ground-breaking team in the Negro Leagues. Fresh off a decade of barnstorming largely as an entertainment act, the Indianapolis Clowns came to town on a part-time basis in 1943 and for good in 1946. The Clowns showed they could play sound baseball when necessary, winning the Eastern Division title in 1950. With 18-year-old shortstop Henry Aaron leading the way, the Clowns won the Negro American League championship in 1952. The next year the Clowns became the first team to have a female player—second baseman Toni Stone, who batted .243 in 50 games. In 1954 they featured two female players: Peanut Johnson and Connie Morgan.

Pro baseball in Indianapolis dates back to 1877 with the Indianapolis Blues, who went on to compete in the National League the next year. That stint in the majors lasted just one season, but by 1884 the Indianapolis Hoosiers were back in the American Association, which was considered a major league then. The Hoosiers finished last in the 13-team league with a 29–78 record as Larry McKeon lost 41 games.

The Hoosiers rejoined the National League in 1887, playing games at Seventh Street Park during a three-year return engagement. Their last year in the NL, 1889, saw the debut of future Hall of Famer Amos Rusie. The 18-year-old from Mooresville won 12 games as a rookie. The Hoosiers were part of the American League in 1900, one year before it became a major league. Indianapolis got one final crack at being a big-league city as the Hoosiers competed in the short-lived Federal League in 1913.

Speaking of Hoosiers, four Indiana-born players were given nicknames that incorporated "Hoosier." Charleston was called the "Hoosier Comet," Rusie was known as the "Hoosier Thunderbolt," Vic Aldridge was the "Hoosier Schoolmaster" and Chuck Klein went by the moniker "Hoosier Hammerer."

Indiana's capital city has seen Negro Leagues and big-league teams come and go, but the one constant has been the minor league Indianapolis Indians. The Indians were an original member of the American Association in 1902 and the franchise, which has won 22 pennants, is still around as a Triple-A affiliate of the Pirates. Harmon Killebrew, Randy Johnson, Nap Lajoie and Gabby Hartnett are among the stars who have played in the minors for the Indians.

Beginning in 1931 the Indians played their games at Perry Stadium, which was later renamed Victory Field. In 1967 the ballpark's name was changed to Bush Stadium in honor of Owen "Donie" Bush, an Indianapolis native and big-league shortstop who would become known as "Mr. Baseball" around Indiana. Bush played

Owen "Donie" Bush was the shortstop and leadoff batter for the Tigers during much of the Ty Cobb era. He led the league in walks five times, stole 406 bases and ranks fifth all-time with 337 sacrifice hits. His long association with the Indianapolis Indians franchise in his hometown as player, manager, co-owner and general manager led the team to rename its stadium in his honor (Library of Congress, Prints & Photographs Division, LC-DIG-ggbain-10670).

for the Indians in 1908 and then returned as player-manager in 1924. After bouncing back and forth between managing in the majors and minors he returned to his hometown as co-owner of the Indians in 1941, later serving another stint as manager and also as general manager and president until retiring in 1969. Historic Bush Stadium, with its ivy growing on the outfield walls, was used to film scenes from the movie *Eight Men Out* in 1987.

Before catching an Indians game at Victory Field, take a short detour to the nearby IUPUI campus, where the National Art Museum of Sport is located. In the courtyard of the University Place Hotel you will find a statue of Casey Stengel. Created by artist Rhoda Sherbell, the art bronze statue is 43 inches tall and depicts the "Ol Perfessor" in a Mets uniform.

Dana native Bert Shepard is the only player to appear in a major league game with an artificial leg. (Texan Monty Stratton, who lost his leg after a hunting accident in 1938, successfully pitched with a wooden leg in the minors but never made it back to the majors). Shepard lost his leg as a pilot in World War II and taught himself to pitch with an artificial leg while in a German POW camp.

Shepard made his debut with the Washington Senators on August 4, 1945. Tom McBride of the Red Sox had already tied a record with six RBI in the fourth inning when Shepard entered the game with the bases loaded. He struck out George Metkovich to end the threat and proceeded to pitch the final 5⅓ innings while allowing only three hits and one run. It was the beginning and end of his major league career, but Shepard was viewed as an inspiration to other wounded veterans. Later in the season he was awarded the Distinguished Flying Cross in an on-field presentation at Griffith Stadium.

The small city of Kokomo produced two brothers who made it to the majors. Pat Underwood had to pitch against his older brother, Tom, when he made his major league debut for the Indians on May 31, 1979. Pat won the game against the Blue Jays 1–0, but Tom ended up with 86 career wins compared to 13 for his brother.

Charlie Brown was not only a famous character in the Peanuts comic strip, he was also a lefty hurler from Bluffton. The real Charlie Brown had no more luck on the baseball diamond than his cartoon namesake, pitching in four games with a 7.77 ERA for the Cleveland Spiders in 1897. It would be his only action in the majors. One of his teammates on the Spiders was Cy Young, who would record 510 more career wins than Brown.

Harley Hisner, a farm boy from Maples, packed a lot of excitement into his brief stint in the big leagues. The righty debuted in the last game of the 1951 season, getting the start for the Boston Red Sox against the defending champion New York Yankees. Hisner ended up striking out Mickey Mantle twice and surrendering the last hit of Joe DiMaggio's career. Hisner took the loss and would never again appear in the majors, content with his own little piece of history.

One might not think of Indiana as a hotbed of spring training activity, but eight major league teams have held spring training in seven different Indiana cities. The St. Louis Browns and batting champion Jesse Burkett were first to partake in Hoosier hospitality, appearing in French Lick in 1902, followed by the Cardinals in nearby West Baden in 1911. A number of teams held spring training in Indiana during the war years (1943–45) including the Pirates in Muncie, the Reds in Bloomington, the Indians in Lafayette, the Tigers in Evansville, the Cubs in French Lick and the White Sox in French Lick and Terre Haute.

All-Time Indiana Selections

A total of 356 players born in Indiana had played in the major leagues through 2011 including 24 active players. Twenty-five Hoosiers have been named to at least one All-Star Game, including players with names like Dizzy, Dickie, Pinky, Oris and Oral. Nine Indiana-born players have been inducted into the Hall of Fame.

At catcher we had a choice between a Bubbles or a Pinky, and Bubbles was definitely the best Hargrave boy. Bubbles Hargrave became the first catcher to win a batting title when he led the National League with a .353 average in 1926. He finished sixth in MVP voting that year and would string together six straight seasons batting over .300. A lifetime .310 hitter, Hargrave did not stick in the majors for good until 1921, when he was nearly 29 years old. He batted .307 in 12 minor league seasons, spending three seasons in Terre Haute.

By comparison, Pinky Hargrave collected just 445 hits playing 10 seasons for four teams, averaging .278. He hit 10 homers in 1928 and .330 in 1929 as a part-time player for the Tigers. Pinky did accomplish something his brother didn't — he won a World Series ring with the Washington Senators in 1924 (although he didn't make any postseason appearances).

Other notable catchers include Lou Criger, who was Cy Young's preferred catcher and caught his perfect game in 1904; Milt May, who played 15 years and collected 971 career hits; and Dick Dietz, who was an All-Star with the Giants in 1970 after hitting 22 homers, driving in 107 runs and posting a .300/.426/.515 line.

Indiana is the birthplace of two outstanding first basemen, Don Mattingly and Gil Hodges, who were both among the most admired and beloved players of their generation. Mattingly picked up the nickname "Donnie Baseball" because he seemed to embody everything that was good and right about being a baseball player. Unfortunately, only one can be selected as the All-Time Indiana first baseman. Here is a look at how their stats line up:

	G	H	2b	HR	RBI	AVE	OBP	SLG	OPS	OPS+	SO
Mattingly	1785	2153	442	222	1099	.307	.358	.471	.830	127	444
Hodges	2071	1921	295	370	1274	.273	.359	.487	.846	120	1137

Hodges has the edge in games played, RBI, slugging, OPS and a big edge in homers, while Mattingly has a better OPS+ and a big advantage in doubles, average and strikeouts. Hodges was named to eight All-Star teams, Mattingly to six. They both led the league in fielding percentage four times and came in second three times. Mattingly won nine Gold Gloves to three for Hodges, but both were excellent fielders.

Hodges has a slight edge in Win Shares (264–255), a function of his longer career, but Mattingly has a decisive advantage in the Black-Ink Test (23–2), which examines how many times a player led the league in various categories. Hodges was a better home run hitter, but Mattingly was the better overall hitter. Bill James ranks Mattingly as the #12 first baseman of all-time and has Hodges at #30.

Mattingly had to fight off teammate Dave Winfield to win the 1984 batting title at .343, a year in which he also led the league in hits, doubles and OPS+. The next year he almost carried the Yankees on his back to the playoffs, batting .324 with career highs in homers and RBI. In 1986 he went down to the wire competing against Wade Boggs for the batting title, falling short with a .352 average but leading the AL in hits (238), doubles (53), slugging (.573) and OPS (.967). In 1987 he tied Dale Long's record by homering in eight straight games. Another amazing stat about Mattingly is that he never struck out more than 43 times in a season.

Hodges played on seven pennant winners with the Dodgers, winning two World Series titles, but went hitless (0–21) in the 1952 Series. That seemed to be an anomaly, as Hodges otherwise batted .318 in Series action and drove in the only runs in the Dodgers' 2–0 victory in Game 7 of the 1955 Series. The Princeton native ended up with 370 home runs, which was a National League record for right-handed batters at the time, and his 1,001 RBI in the 1950s was the most of any player for that decade.

Ultimately, the selection comes down to how the players stacked up against their peers. Hodges' highest placing in the MVP balloting is seventh, while Mattingly was AL Most Valuable Player and Major League Player of the Year in 1985. Donnie Baseball also finished fifth in MVP in 1984 and second in 1986, as he was widely considered one of the best, if not the best, players in baseball for the years 1984–87. Back then there seemed little doubt Mattingly was headed to the Hall of Fame until a bad back derailed him, curtailing his production his last six years and causing him to retire at 34, a year short of winning a World Series ring with Derek Jeter and crew.

Shortly after retiring, Mattingly confessed, "I wasn't the same player, powerwise. But you know what? That was OK, because you just make adjustments. I wasn't the same player; I was still the best player I could be."

Although Mattingly had a winning, positive attitude, he had the misfortune to play for the Yankees during their longest dry spell. His monster production from 1984–87 didn't result in any playoff berths. In fact, Mattingly's only trip to the postseason came in his last year, 1995—he batted .417 in a losing cause in the ALDS. He was later honored with a plaque in Monument Park at Yankee Stadium, which reads: "A Humble Man of Grace and Dignity. A Captain Who Led by Example. Proud of the Pinstripes Tradition and Dedicated to the Pursuit of Excellence. A Yankee Forever."

Hodges, on the other hand, was never in the conversation as the best player in baseball. He never led the league in any meaningful hitting categories but did have five straight seasons with at least 30 homers and seven straight seasons with over 100 RBI. As Roy Campanella once put it, "Gil Hodges is a Hall of Fame man."

Forced to end his career with the hapless expansion Mets in 1962–63, Hodges quickly moved into managing albeit with the equally bad Washington Senators. His teams showed improvement all five years but could only get as high as sixth place, leading to a new opportunity skippering those lovable losers the Mets.

Hodges was the right man at the right time to take the Mets to the promised land, as the Miracle Mets shocked the baseball world by winning 100 games and the NL pennant in 1969, followed by a 4–1 World Series victory over the Orioles. Two third-place finishes followed and then Hodges' life was cut short, the victim of a massive heart attack in spring training just shy of his 48th birthday.

Although he keeps falling short of the Hall of Fame and he loses out to Mattingly for the All-Time Indiana first base position, Hodges' skillful skippering of the Miracle Mets of '69 is enough to justify his selection as the manager for Team Indiana. Hodges is one of 14 Indiana natives to manage in the major leagues and not a single one has a career winning percentage over .500. John Kerins tops the list at .500 with 12 wins and 12 losses.

Not too many people outside Indiana have heard of George Crowe and that's a shame, because "Big George" was a pioneering legend whose accomplishments stack up against anyone. Crowe, a native of tiny Whiteland who died in January 2011, possessed Hall of Fame talent in two sports, but the color of his skin denied him full opportunity to showcase that ability.

In 1939 Crowe became the first Mr. Basketball selected in Indiana, which was no small feat in a state that was not exactly a hotbed of enlightened integration. His coach at Franklin High School, Fuzzy Vandivier, called Crowe, "The best money player I have ever seen."

He was the first African American player from Indiana to appear in a major league game when he debuted with the Boston Braves in 1952. Crowe's teammates on the Cardinals such as Curt Flood and Bill White credit him with paving the way for integration during spring training in St. Petersburg during the period of 1959–61.

Crowe was a teammate of Jackie Robinson ... in basketball. The two played together on the integrated Los Angeles Red Devils in the winter of 1946–47, a few months after Robinson had spent his first season in the minors and shortly before Jackie broke baseball's color barrier in the majors. Crowe's seven years in professional basketball included a stint with the New York Rens, the first all-black professional basketball team to have a black owner. When the forerunner to the NBA was created, the Rens were denied entry so Crowe turned to baseball.

The New York Black Yankees signed Crowe as a pitcher and first baseman and the 27-year-old Crowe responded by batting over .300 in 1948 and making the East-West All-Star Game. The Boston Braves signed him the next season, but Crowe stayed buried in the minors for three years despite demonstrating he could hit for power and average.

When he was finally called up to the majors he was used primarily in a pinch hitting and backup role until catching his first break in 1957. When the Reds' starting first baseman, Ted Kluszewski went down with an injury, Crowe filled in by clubbing 31 homers and driving in 92 runs. Despite leading the Reds in homers and RBI that year, Crowe was overlooked in a ballot-stuffing campaign that saw the Reds' other regulars voted in as All-Star starters.

The next year Crowe was selected to his first and only NL All-Star team at the age of 37. He spent the game on the bench because All-Star Manager Fred Haney decided to play Stan Musial the whole way at first. If it bothered "Big George," he kept those thoughts to himself.

When he retired in 1961 after nine seasons in the majors, Crowe had produced modest numbers with 81 homers, 467 hits and a .270 average. However, he did hold the record for most career pinch-hit homers with 14, a mark later topped by Jerry Lynch. Crowe was inducted into the Indiana Basketball Hall of Fame in 1976 and the Indiana Baseball Hall of Fame in 2004, his status as a legend preserved for posterity.

At second base, the All-Time Indiana team features Hall of Famer Billy Herman, a 10-time All-Star from New Albany who batted .304 lifetime. A durable and dependable sparkplug who played at least 150 games eight times, Herman was the prototypical number two hitter who could bunt, execute the hit-and-run and hit behind the runner as the situation warranted. His career got off to a memorable start when he knocked himself unconscious while fouling off a pitch in his major league debut in 1931, but he bounced back to hit .327 that year. Herman batted .314 with 206 hits and 102 runs in his first full season in 1932, and he was just getting started.

In 1935 he led the league with 227 hits, 57 doubles and 24 sacrifice hits while batting .341, finishing fourth in MVP balloting. The next year he got five hits on opening day against Dizzy Dean and went on to average .334 with 211 hits, finishing third in the MVP race. Herman was an outstanding fielder who led NL second basemen in putouts seven times, fielding percentage twice and double plays and assists three times. He still holds the National League record for putouts by a second baseman with 466 in 1933. "I always thought it was my glove that got me into the Hall of Fame," Herman told baseball writer Rich Westcott.

After spending 11 years with the Cubs, losing in three World Series along the way, Herman was traded to the Dodgers early in the 1941 season. He batted .291 to lead the Dodgers to their first pennant in 21 years, but they lost to the Yankees in the Series. He retired in 1947 after recording 2,345 hits over 15 seasons, gaining induction to the Hall of Fame in 1975. Herman had a brief and unsuccessful stint as player-manager of the Pirates in 1947 and didn't fare well in a later shot managing the Red Sox from 1964–66.

Earning honorable mention at second is Frank Warfield, who was serving as player-manager in the Negro Leagues when he died of a heart attack at the age of 37. Not only was Warfield a gifted defensive player with a strong arm and outstanding range, he could do all the things Herman could do with the bat. A speedy leadoff hitter with a fierce competitive streak, Warfield picked up the unflattering nickname "The Weasel" from his teammates.

Joining the Hilldale Daisies in 1923, Warfield batted .339 with 67 stolen bases and then took over as player-manager the next season. He guided the team to two straight pennants, vanquishing the Kansas City Monarchs for the championship in 1925. He would later manage the Baltimore Black Sox to the American Negro League pennant in 1929, teaming up that year with Dick Lundy, Oliver Marcelle and Jud Wilson to form the first so-called "million dollar infield." Playing in the Cuban Winter League later that year, Warfield got into a scrap with Marcelle while shooting craps. Marcelle slugged Warfield in the mouth, so he retaliated by biting off Marcelle's nose. The incident prematurely ended the career of Marcelle, widely hailed as one of the greatest third basemen in Negro Leagues history.

Craig Counsell could fill a valuable role as a utility player. He has spent significant time at second, third and short during a career that started in 1995 and was still going in 2011. During the 2011 season, Counsell set a single-season record by going hitless in 45 at-bats, ending the year with an OPS+ of 39. He is an above-average fielder who has demonstrated the ability to hit in the clutch. He was the 2001 NLCS MVP after batting .381 for the Diamondbacks, who went on to win the World Series that year. Counsell also won a championship with the Marlins in 1997, batting .429 in that NLCS.

Another active player, Scott Rolen, earns the selection at third base with his all-around ability to hit for power and average, run the bases and field. If he can stay healthy for a couple more years, no sure thing, he should receive strong consideration for election to the Hall of Fame. Rolen was named Rookie of the Year in 1997 with the Phillies and is a seven-time All-Star with eight Gold Gloves.

Rolen has produced 10 years with at least 20 homers and five seasons with more than 100 RBI. His Runs from Fielding score is +148, meaning he has been that many runs better than the average third baseman during his career. Although not blessed with good speed, Rolen's hard-nosed, competitive playing style is admired by teammates.

His best season was 2004 with the Cardinals, when he hit 34 homers, drove in 124 runs and produced a line of .314/.409/.598 with a 1.007 OPS. He led NL third basemen in assists and finished fourth in the MVP race that year. A lifetime .282 batter, the Evansville native had 308 home runs and 1,248 RBI at the end of the 2011 season.

Two other third basemen deserve mention. Pinky May, father of Milt May, only played five seasons but made the NL All-Star team for the Phillies in 1940 after batting .293. He joined the Navy for the end of World War II and went on to a long career as a minor league manager, winning 1,658 games in 27 years. Jeff King played 11 seasons for the Pirates and Royals at first and third base, finishing with 154 home runs. He hit 30 homers with 111 RBI for Pittsburgh in 1996 and then followed up with 28 homers and 112 RBI for the Royals the next year, leading the majors in fielding percentage for a first baseman both years. King played 586 games at third and 488 games at first.

The shortstop for Team Indiana is Owen "Donie" Bush, who played mainly during the Deadball Era for the Tigers. Bush didn't have a lot of pop in his bat, but he knew how to draw walks and move runners along. He led the league in walks five of his first six full seasons and led the AL with 52 sacrifice hits in 1909, the fourth-highest total in American League history. Bush's 337 sacrifice hits rank fifth in major league history. He scored 126 runs with just 130 hits in 1911 and later led the league with 112 runs scored in 1917. His 406 stolen bases included a career-high 53 in 1909, when he also scored 114 runs with a .380 OBP to lead the Tigers to their only pennant in his 14 years with the team.

A wisp of a man at 5-foot-6 and 140 pounds, Bush's intangible contributions as a leadoff hitter did not go unnoticed. He finished third in MVP voting in 1914 despite batting .252 with no home runs and 32 RBI while committing 58 errors at short for a Tigers team that finished fourth. His 425 putouts at short in 1914 remain tied with Hughie Jennings for the most ever.

Bush had several stints as a major league manager, beginning as player-manager of the Washington Senators in 1923. He skippered the Pittsburgh Pirates to the NL pennant in 1927 but got swept in the World Series by the powerhouse Yankees amid controversy over his benching of star Kiki Cuyler.

Other notable shortstops from Indiana include Dickie Thon, Everett Scott and Tommy Thevenow. Thon was just starting to establish himself as one of the top shortstops in the majors — hitting 20 homers and stealing 34 bases while earning a Silver Slugger in 1983 — when he was beaned in the eye by Mike Torrez in early 1984. He missed the rest of the season and was never the same player again, although he bounced back to have a 15-year career.

Scott, who won four World Series with the Red Sox and Yankees, was an outstanding fielder who led AL shortstops in fielding percentage seven straight years (1916–22). Scott played in 1,307 consecutive games between 1916 and 1925, which was the record before he was passed by Lou Gehrig. Thevenow finished fourth in MVP balloting in 1926 but also has the distinction of going the most at-bats (3,347) in between home runs. He hit two home runs during the 1926 season and then blasted one in the ninth inning of Game 2 of the 1926 World Series — he never hit another home run in a career that lasted until 1938.

Indiana has excelled at producing outstanding outfielders, which made the selection process difficult after penciling in Charleston for one spot. Six outfielders in the Hall of Fame were born in Indiana — Charleston, Sam Rice, Edd Roush, Chuck Klein, Max Carey and Sam Thompson — more than any other state except California.

Carey, Roush and Rice were contemporaries who played about half their careers during the Deadball Era and half during the Lively Ball Era. If you take a look at the 15-year period during which they all were active (1915–29) and compare Runs Above Replacement (RAR), you find that each player comes out on top six seasons (including ties). We ultimately settled on Carey, because he could beat you with his bat, his legs or his glove; and Roush, due to his string of 11 straight seasons over .300. Carey also outpaces his fellow Hoosier outfielders in Wins Above Replacement (67) and Career Win Shares (361).

Roush swung a massive 48-ounce bat, heavier than anyone in the majors, but he had no trouble making contact, striking out just 260 times in 18 seasons. The lefty swinger averaged .323 for his career, leading the National League with a .341 mark in 1917 and .321 in 1919 and finishing in the top five in batting five other times. He had 11 seasons with at least 10 triples. Pete Alexander called Roush the trickiest batter he ever faced, while Casey Stengel named him the second-best center fielder he had seen behind Willie Mays, according to Mitchell Stinson's biography of the Oakland City native.

After short stints with the Indianapolis Hoosiers and Newark Peppers in the Federal League, Roush was picked up by the New York Giants and later traded along with Christy Mathewson and Bill McKechnie to the Reds for Buck Herzog and Red Killefer. He spent

Oakland City native Edd Roush struck out only 260 times in his 18-year Hall of Fame career despite swinging a massive 48-ounce bat that he expertly wielded to place line drives in the gap. He was also an excellent defensive center fielder, but he saved his best defense for his annual salary disputes with owners (Library of Congress, Prints & Photographs Division, LC-DIG-ggbain-36159).

the next 11 years with the Reds, playing on the team that defeated the White Sox in the 1919 World Series tainted by a bribery scandal. Roush was elected to the Hall of Fame in 1962, along with his former teammate and long-time friend, McKechnie. He was the last remaining player from the Federal League when he died in 1988 at the age of 94.

Carey was one of the pre-eminent base stealers, swiping 738 bases (ninth all-time) and leading the National League in steals a record 10 times. His career high was 63 in 1916 and he is credited with 33 steals of home, surpassed only by Ty Cobb's 54. His 51 steals in 53 attempts in 1922 will be pretty hard to beat. Playing most of his career with the Pirates, Carey led the league in walks and triples twice and runs once. He also saved a lot of runs with his glove, leading NL outfielders in putouts nine times and assists four times — ranking seventh all-time with 339 assists (just a few spots ahead of fellow Hoosiers Thompson and Rice) and fourth all-time in putouts with 6,363.

Although he batted only .285 lifetime, the switch-hitting Carey picked it up a notch in 1925, batting a career-high .343 to lead the Pirates to the pennant. He averaged .458 in the World Series against the Senators, banging out three doubles and a single against Walter Johnson in Game 7 to help the Pirates claim the championship. Bill James ranks Carey as the #23 center fielder, eight spots behind Roush. Carey was elected to the Hall of Fame by the Veteran's Committee in 1961.

It's hard to imagine any player enduring more tragedy in his life than Edgar "Sam" Rice. In April 1912, while Rice was away playing minor league ball, a tornado ripped through the family farm in Illinois and killed his wife, two children, mother and two sisters. His father, Charles, managed to survive initially, but he too passed away a week later. In an instant, the 22-year-old Rice had lost six family members and was alone in the world except for one adult sister. Somehow he found a way to deal with his grief, enlisting in the Navy for a two-year tour of duty before resuming his baseball career in 1914.

Except for his last season, Rice played his whole career with the Washington Senators, falling just shy of 3,000 hits with 2,987. He batted over .300 in 15 of his 20 seasons with a lifetime average of .331 and collected at least 200 hits six times. Rice only hit 34 home runs, but 21 of them were inside the park. However, he was not just a singles hitter, as he was adept at driving balls into the alleys of Griffith Stadium, accumulating 10 straight seasons with 30 doubles and 10 triples.

His 351 career stolen bases included a league-leading 63 in 1920. Blessed with remarkable bat control, Rice struck out only 275 times in 9,269 at-bats. He played his first full season as a regular in 1917 at the age of 27 and was still productive at age 44 when he batted .293, the lowest average of his career. Rice, who collected 207 hits and scored a career-high 121 runs in 1930 at age 40, remains the only player over 40 to get 200 hits in a season. Ty Cobb and Pete Rose were both 38 when they had their final 200-hit seasons.

Rice was involved in a memorable play during Game 3 of the 1925 World Series when he tumbled into the stands in pursuit of a fly ball hit by Pirates catcher Earl Smith. After Rice emerged from the stands with the ball in his hands, the umpires ruled it a catch. Despite the protests of the Pirates, it stayed an out and the Senators won the game 4–3. Rice would go on to bat .364 for the Series, which was won by the Pirates in seven games. He left a sealed letter, opened after his death in 1974, that stated, "At no time did I lose possession of the ball."

"Big Sam" Thompson was a nineteenth century slugger who finished among the league leaders in home runs nearly every season. At 6-foot-2 and 200-plus pounds and sporting a large handlebar mustache, Thompson was an intimidating sight to pitchers, especially when the mound was still at 50 feet. At the time he hit his last home run in 1898, Thompson's career total of 126 home runs trailed only Roger Connor's 138. Starting his career with the Detroit Wolverines, Thompson led the National League in 1887 in slugging (.565), triples (23), RBI (166), average (.372) and hits (203) — in the process becoming the first NL batter to exceed 200 hits.

In 1894 he was one of four outfielders for the Philadelphia Phillies who batted over .400. Thompson batted .415 that year, while Ed Delahanty (.404), Billy Hamilton (.403) and reserve Tuck Turner (.418) also hit the mark. Thompson posted eight seasons with more than 100 RBI and had a lifetime average of .331. He was elected to the Hall of Fame in 1974.

After starring at Southport High School on the southside of Indianapolis, Chuck Klein quickly went from semipro ball to minor league teams in Evansville and finally Fort Wayne, where he attracted the attention of the Phillies. He debuted with the team on July 30, 1928 and was an instant success, hitting .360 the rest of the way.

Klein was just getting started. He had a five-year stretch of play from 1929–33 that stacks up against anyone. He hit between .337 and .386 those years and won a Triple Crown in 1933 with 28 homers, 120 RBI and .368 average. During those five seasons he averaged 36 home runs, 138 RBI, 46 doubles and 131 runs scored, leading the NL in homers and total bases four times; and runs and slugging three times. He even finished first with 20 steals in 1932, earning MVP honors that season and MVP runner-up in 1931 and 1933. His 135 games with a hit in 1930 are tied with four other players for the most ever.

Unfortunately, Klein never approached those numbers over the last 11 years of his career, as he was just an average player away from Philly's hitter-friendly Baker Bowl. He batted .192 with just 90 hits in his last five seasons and also saw his production curtailed by Phillies owner William Baker, who installed a 60-foot wall in right field to keep Klein's stats down as an aid in contract negotiations. His final stats are still good — 300 home runs, 1,201 RBI and a .320 average — but are more indicative of a borderline Hall of Famer than an all-time great. The friendly confines of right field at the

Baker Bowl, just 280 feet from home, also helped Klein set a modern-day record of 44 outfield assists in 1930, a mark that may never be matched.

Kenny Lofton probably won't make it into the Hall, but he had a terrific, underrated career along the lines of Tim Raines. The speedy leadoff hitter led the league in steals his first five seasons, with a high of 75 in 1996. He retired with 622 stolen bases, which ranks fifteenth on the all-time list, and is one of only 10 players to accumulate 2,400 hits and 600 steals. He played 10 seasons with the Cleveland Indians during three different stints, but never spent more than one season for the other 10 franchises he played with.

A lifetime .299 hitter, Lofton was named to six straight All-Star teams and also earned four Gold Gloves for his excellent play in center. His best season was probably 1994, when he led the AL with 160 hits and 60 stolen bases, was second in runs, fourth in batting at .349 and finished fourth in MVP voting. He had outstanding range and took advantage of his strong arm to lead the AL in outfield assists four times. Lofton batted over .300 eight times and had six seasons with more than 100 runs.

Cy Williams' final numbers are hurt by the fact his career bridged the Deadball and Lively Ball Eras, but the speedy center fielder was one of the best home run hitters of his time. Williams, who played football at Notre Dame with Knute Rockne, was the first National League player to reach 200 home runs, ending up with 251 (141 were hit at the Baker Bowl). He ended up with 13 inside-the-park homers and 11 pinch-hit homers, which were records at the time. He led the league in homers four times, showing the difference in the two eras by placing first with 12 dingers in 1916 and leading with 41 homers in 1923. Williams finished in the top three in home runs 11 times in 19 seasons and batted over .300 six times in a seven-year stretch.

Negro Leaguer Ted Strong played in seven East-West All-Star Games at three positions, eventually settling in at right field. The 6-foot-6, switch-hitting Strong got his start with the Indianapolis Athletics, batting .348 in 1937, and later spent a decade with the Kansas City Monarchs. Blessed with a strong throwing arm and good speed, he led the Negro American League in homers and RBI in 1946. In the off-season Strong played basketball with the Harlem Globetrotters.

Two Hoosiers have the credentials to be the All-Time designated hitter, but Ron Kittle has longevity over Adam Lind. The free-spirited Kittle was working as an iron worker in a steel plant when he saw the Dodgers were having a tryout in 1977. He put on a slugging show for them and signed a contract, but it would be six years before he broke through for good. Kittle appeared in 351 games at DH, just two shy of his total in the outfield. An All-Star and Rookie of the Year in 1983 after hitting 35 homers (third in AL) and driving in 100 runs for the division-winning White Sox, Kittle hit 176 home runs but finished with more career strikeouts than hits. He was popular with White Sox fans not just because of his prodigious blasts but because he grew up in nearby Gary. Lind hit .305 with 35 homers and 114 RBI as the primary DH for the Blue Jays in 2009 and had 106 career homers through 2011.

The Hoosier state has also produced a long line of accomplished right-handed starters, with six native righties winning at least 190 games. The All-Time Indiana right-handed starter also has one of the best nicknames. Mordecai "Three Finger" Brown lost part of two fingers during a childhood farming accident, which not only didn't deter him from pitching it helped his pitches take an unpredictable path to the plate. Brown emerged as one of the best pitchers of the Deadball Era, winning 239 games against just 130 losses while posting a splendid 2.06 ERA (sixth-best in history).

Rival Christy Mathewson, who was once beaten nine straight times by Three Finger, said, "Brown is my idea of the almost perfect pitcher.... It will usually be found at the end of a season, that he has taken part in more key games than any other pitcher in baseball."

Three Finger posted six straight 20-win seasons for the Cubs from 1906–1911, helping the team become a powerhouse that won four pennants and two World Series titles in five years. In 1906 he won 26 games and led the league with nine shutouts, 0.934 WHIP and a 1.04 ERA, the third-lowest mark in baseball history. He was just getting started, as he won 29 games in 1908, led the league with 27 wins and 32 complete games while posting a 1.31 ERA in 1909 and then won 25 games with six shutouts in 1910. His 55 shutouts rank fourteenth all-time.

Brown also finished 138 games over the course of his career, as he was routinely called on whenever his team needed key outs. Cubs teammate Orval Overall said, "When it comes to smoothing over internal troubles and patching up trouble spots on a ball club, Brown is a thirty-three degree diplomat."

Joining Three Finger in the Hall of Fame is Amos Rusie, who was known as "The Hoosier Thunderbolt" for his lightning-fast pitches. Rusie threw so hard he was one of the main reasons why the mound was moved from 50 feet to its current distance of 60-feet, six inches in 1893. Rusie started slow in his first season with the Indianapolis Hoosiers, 1889, but then averaged 29 wins over his next eight seasons with the New York Giants (sitting out the 1896 season in a contract dispute).

Rusie led the National League in strikeouts five times with a high of 341 in 1890, which was no small feat considering fouls didn't count as strikes then. However, he also led the league with five straight seasons of over 200 walks including a record 289 in 1890. After winning 20 games in 1898, Rusie sat out the next two seasons in another contract dispute and was then traded to the Reds for Christy Mathewson. Rusie pitched three winless games for the Reds and then retired, while Mathewson went on to record 373 wins for the Giants. Reds owner John T. Brush was not bothered by what turned out to be one of the worst trades in baseball history, as he knew he was about to gain controlling interest in the Giants.

Three Finger Brown and Rusie stand in a class by

themselves, but the Hoosier state has produced a number of other accomplished right-handed starters. With 194 career victories Babe Adams is often called the greatest pitcher in Pirates history. Known for his excellent control, Adams pitched a 21-inning complete game with no walks on July 17, 1914, losing the marathon outing 3–1 to Rube Marquard. As a rookie he pitched three complete game wins to lead the Pirates to the 1909 World Series, turning him into a mini-celebrity. Adams was forced to flee his home and hole up in a hotel to escape the affections of 436 women who were hoping to kiss him.

Nig Cuppy formed a tough one-two punch with Cy Young on the Cleveland Spiders in the 1890s. Cuppy won 20 or more games four times, collecting 162 career wins. Dizzy Trout was a two-time All-Star who led the league with 20 wins and five shutouts in 1943. The next year he won 27 games while leading the AL in ERA (2.12), complete games (33), shutouts (7), innings pitched (352) and ERA+ (168). He pitched a five-hitter to win Game 4 of the 1945 World Series for the champion Tigers and retired with 170 wins in 15 seasons.

Freddie Fitzsimmons went 217–146, posting 12 double-figure seasons in wins. He led the league in winning percentage twice and shutouts once. Bob Friend was a three-time All-Star whose best season was 1958 with the Pirates, when he won a league-high 22 games and finished third in Cy Young voting. Although Friend won 197 games, he also lost 230 games while leading the league in losses twice. After getting called up late in the 1912 season Hooks Dauss went on to become a steady contributor for the next 14 seasons, posting double-figure win totals every year. His 222 victories included three years with 20 or more wins but an adjusted ERA of just 102. Dauss surrendered the last hit of Shoeless Joe Jackson's major league career on September 27, 1920.

Carl Erskine was an indispensable member of the Dodgers "Boys of Summer" teams in the 1950s, pitching two no-hitters and posting a .610 winning percentage with 122 victories including a league-high 20 in 1953. He set a World Series record with 14 strikeouts in Game 3 that year, but the Dodgers fell to the Yankees for the third time in five years. An All-Star in 1954, "Oisk" helped the Dodgers finally break through to win the World Series in 1955.

Erskine's greatest accomplishments have come off the diamond, as he has been a tireless supporter of numerous causes. In 2010 he was honored with the Sachem Award, Indiana's highest honor, which is given "in recognition of a lifetime of excellence and virtue that has brought credit and honor to Indiana." Tommy Lasorda said, "Carl Erskine is class personified. Not only was he a great pitcher, he is a great person, which is why you live your life."

One final noteworthy righty is Don Larsen, who pitched the most remarkable game in baseball history but otherwise had a rather unremarkable career. The Michigan City native showed such promise with the bat (averaging .284 with three home runs in 1953) that his first team, the Browns, almost converted him into an outfielder, which would've derailed his date with destiny. Larsen would average .242 for his career with 14 home runs and 12 pinch-hits.

Larsen's pitching career got off to a rocky start. He went 3–21 for the Orioles during their first year in Baltimore, 1954, which led him to be included as part of a 17-player trade with the Yankees over the winter. Pitching for a better team led to better results, as Larsen went 9–2 for the Yankees in 1955 and then won a career-high 11 games in 1956 bouncing between the rotation and the bullpen.

Before his Game 5 heroics in the 1956 Series, Larsen lasted just 1⅔ innings in Game 2, surrendering four walks and four unearned runs as the Yankees fell behind 2–0 to the Dodgers. Not only is his Game 5 masterpiece the only perfect game in postseason history, there had not been another no-hitter pitched in the playoffs until Roy Halladay threw one in his first playoff start in 2010. Larsen claims he never gets tired talking about the game, and why should he?

The best left-handed starter from Indiana is Terre Haute native Tommy John. He may never get into the Hall of Fame despite accumulating 288 wins over 26 seasons, but perhaps his arm can be voted in. It was John's ground-breaking ligament replacement surgery in 1975 that has paved the way for many pitchers to continue careers that otherwise would have ended.

Called up to the Indians at the end of the 1963 season at the age of 20, John led the AL in shutouts in 1966 and 1967 and then made his first All-Star team with the White Sox in 1968 after posting a 1.98 ERA. Coming back from his surgery to win 10 games in 1976, John deservedly won the Comeback Player of the Year award. He then finished second in the 1977 Cy Young Award voting after going 20–7 with a 2.78 ERA. Signing with the Yankees as a free agent in 1979, he won 21 games his first year in the Bronx and was again the Cy Young Award runner-up, following that up with 22 wins and a league-leading six shutouts the next season.

His 46 shutouts rank 26th on the all-time list, but John's overall record seems to fall just short of Hall worthiness. While he should be applauded for winning 164 games after his surgery, John exhibited longevity more than greatness.

Lefty Paul Splittorff won 166 games and pitched three one-hitters while spending his entire 15-year career with the Kansas City Royals. Another southpaw worth mentioning is Art Nehf, a Terre Haute native who won 184 games pitching from 1915–1929. He won 20 games two years in a row for the New York Giants and played on five pennant winners, winning the final game of both the 1921 and 1922 World Series. Nehf pitched 20 scoreless innings in a duel with Pittsburgh on August 1, 1918, but ended up surrendering two runs in the 21st inning to lose 2–0.

The bullpen is led by Dan Plesac, who collected 158 saves over an 18-year career for six teams. The lefty reliever made the AL All-Star team three straight years for the Brewers, posting 23, 30 and 33 saves in the years 1987–89. Plesac posted an excellent K/9IP ratio of 8.7 with years such as 2001, when he struck out 68 batters in 45 innings at the age of 39. He remains sixth all-time in games pitched with 1,064.

Long before Deion Sanders, Ron Reed was a two-sport player. He played two seasons in the NBA with the Detroit Pistons (1965–67) — in between he made his major league debut with the Atlanta Braves. Reed went on to pitch 19 years in the majors, spending the first half of his career as a starter. The Phillies traded for him in 1976 and discovered he could be a reliable weapon out of the bullpen. Reed would go on to post 103 saves and help the Phillies make six playoff appearances in his eight seasons with the team.

Tim Stoddard is another dual-sport star who is the only person to win a World Series title and an NCAA championship in basketball. The 6-foot-7 Stoddard was a starter for Jim Valvano on North Carolina State's 1974 NCAA title team and later won Game 4 of the 1979 World Series while pitching for the Orioles, who went on to win the championship. He saved 26 games for the Orioles in 1980 and ended his career with 76 saves.

Doc Crandall led the NL in games finished five straight years (1909–13) and placed second in saves three times while pitching for the New York Giants, becoming one of the first pitchers to be used mainly out of the bullpen. Author Damon Runyon described him this way, "Crandall is the Giants' ambulance corps. He is first aid to the injured. He is the physician of the pitching emergency, and they sometimes call him old Doctor Crandall." He also played a lot in the field at second base and pinch hit, carving out a productive career as a jack-of-all-trades. Crandall would go on to pitch until the age of 42 in the minors, going 249–163 in 16 minor league seasons.

IOWA

Names in **bold** *represent Major League selections by position, followed by honorable mentions. City of birth is in parentheses.*

Catcher — Hank Severeid (Story City). Also: John Wathan (Cedar Rapids); Patsy Gharrity (Parnell)
First Base — Cap Anson (Marshalltown). Also: Hal Trosky (Norway); Cal McVey (Montrose)
Second Base — Dick Green (Sioux City). Also: Bobby Knoop (Sioux City); Gene Baker (Davenport); Johnny Rawlings (Bloomfield)
Third Base — Casey Blake (Des Moines). Also: Lee Handley (Clarion)
Shortstop — Dave Bancroft (Sioux City). Also: Denis Menke (Bancroft)
Outfield — Fred Clarke (Winterset)
Outfield — Bing Miller (Vinton)
Outfield — George Stone (Lost Nation). Also: Ken Henderson (Carroll); Ducky Holmes (Des Moines); Cliff Carroll (Clay Grove)
Designated Hitter — Jeff Larish (Iowa City)
Right Handed Starter — Bob Feller (Van Meter). Also: Red Faber (Cascade); Dazzy Vance (Orient); Jack Coombs (Le Grand); Mike Boddicker (Cedar Rapids); Stan Bahnsen (Council Bluffs); Jon Lieber (Council Bluffs)
Left Handed Starter — Earl Whitehill (Cedar Rapids). Also: Jake Weimer (Ottumwa)
Relief Pitcher — Bob Locker (George). Also: Joe Hoerner (Dubuque); Eddie Watt (Lamoni); Mace Brown (North English); Joel Hanrahan (Des Moines)
Manager — Fred Clarke (Winterset). Also: Cap Anson (Marshalltown); Gene Baker (Davenport)

The Names

Best Nickname: Don "The Bad Boy of the Diamond" Black

Other Nicknames: Adrian "Cap" Anson; Loren "Bee Bee" Babe; Gene "Bongo" Baker; Dave "Beauty" Bancroft; Charles "Buster" Brown; Fred "Cap" Clarke; Verne "Stinger" Clemons; Leonard "King" Cole; "Colby Jack" Coombs; Urban "Red" Faber; "Rapid" Robert Feller; George "Showboat" Fisher; Lee "Jeep" Handley; Robert "Ziggy" Hasbrook; Bill "Chick" and "Wizard" Hoffer; James "Ducky" Holmes; Alfred "Roxie" Lawson; Bob "Moose" Lee; Emil "Dutch" Levsen; Jim "Moms" McAndrew; Walter "Judge" McCredie; Fred "Chicken" Stanley; Billy "The Evangelist" Sunday; Les "Toots" Tietje; Clarence "Dazzy" Vance; Wilbur "Biggs" Wehde; "Tornado Jake" Weimer; Clarence "Yam" Yaryan
Most Unusual Name: Verle Tiefenthaler; Julius Willigrod; Cyril Slapnicka

All-Time Leaders

Games: Cap Anson, 2523
Hits: Cap Anson, 3418
Batting Average: Cal McVey, .346
Home Runs: Hal Trosky, 228
RBI: Cap Anson, 2076
Stolen Bases: Fred Clarke, 738
Wins: Bob Feller, 266
Strikeouts: Bob Feller, 2581
Saves: Eddie Watt, 57
Future Stars: Jeremy Hellickson (Des Moines); Dean McArdle (Sioux City)
Best Player: Bob Feller

Historic Baseball Places

Bob Feller Museum in Van Meter — Career highlights from Iowa's greatest player are showcased in this special museum, which has been open in his hometown since 1995. Exhibits feature his uniforms and trophies along with newspaper articles, photos and memorabilia from his Hall of Fame career. Also on display is the bat Babe Ruth was leaning on during his retirement celebration at Yankee Stadium in 1948 — the bat belonged to Feller.

Field of Dreams in Dyersville — Step on the field made famous in the Academy Award nominee for best picture: *Field of Dreams*.

Notable Achievements

Leonard "King" Cole (Toledo) surrendered Babe Ruth's first hit — a double on October 2, 1914.

Fred Clarke holds the record for most hits in a debut game (nine innings). He had five hits in five at-bats on June 30, 1894.

Cap Anson was the all-time leader in doubles with 582 when he retired in 1897. He now stands in eighteenth place.

Bing Miller was the first player to hit two doubles in one inning, which he did on April 29, 1929.

Cal McVey had a 30-game hitting streak during the 1876 season, becoming the first player to hit that mark. He only played in 63 games that season and pitched in 11 of them.

Hal Trosky set a record in 1934, since matched by Tony Oliva, for the most total bases by an American League rookie with 374.

Jon Lieber ranks 11th on the all-time list with a strikeout/walk ratio of 3.68.

John Wathan holds the record for most stolen bases in a season by a catcher with 36, set in 1982.

Emil "Dutch" Levsen (Wyoming) is the last pitcher to start and win both games of a doubleheader. Pitching for the Indians on August 28, 1926, he pitched a complete game to beat the Red Sox 6–1 in the opener and then won the nightcap 5–1 by hurling another four-hit complete game. The two games took a combined three hours and nine minutes to play.

Iowa Home to Iconic Fireballer and Charismatic Preacher

When it comes to baseball, Iowa is best known as the site for one of the greatest baseball movies ever made. *Field of Dreams* was filmed in Dyersville, Iowa, and people continue to demonstrate that if you build it, they will come. As many as 65,000 curious fans flock there each year to see where Kevin Costner filmed the baseball classic at the century-old Lansing family farm. Untold thousands of fathers have played toss-and-catch with their sons on the historic field, which is still ringed by corn fields and the ghosts of baseball's past.

No one from Dyersville has actually made it to the majors, but 16 have come from Des Moines including active players Joel Hanrahan, Jerry Hairston and Casey Blake, 143-game winner Kevin Tapani and nineteenth-century player Ducky Holmes.

Bob Feller was viewed as something of a living and breathing national treasure, right up until he passed away at age 92 at the end of 2010. Not only was he one of the fastest, most accomplished pitchers in baseball history, he was a decorated war hero who seemed to represent everything that is great about America. That greatness is on display everyday at the Bob Feller Museum in the Hall of Famer's hometown of Van Meter.

Iowa was the birthplace of one of the most important

Billy Sunday was a nineteenth-century player with blazing speed who didn't enjoy much success on the diamond, fashioning a .248 average over eight seasons. However, he sure made a name for himself after undergoing a religious conversion and quitting baseball. Sunday devoted himself to evangelism, preaching before ever-growing crowds as he turned into one of the country's most well-known and influential evangelists (Library of Congress, Prints & Photographs Division, LC-DIG-bbc-0155f).

and influential pioneers in the Negro Leagues — J.L. Wilkinson. His Kansas City Monarchs won a record 17 pennants and two Colored World Series. The Algona native founded the multi-ethnic All-Nations team in Des Moines in 1912, which barnstormed around the Midwest while featuring players of all races as well as a woman. When the Negro National League was formed in 1920, "Wilkie" was the only white owner. In 1930 he came up with a portable light system to hold the first night baseball game, beating Major League Baseball by five years. He was instrumental in keeping black baseball going during the Depression and signed Jackie Robinson to his first professional contract with the Monarchs in 1945.

Iowa was also home to a real original — Billy Sunday, who was shipped to an orphanage as a young child after his father died. While playing for a town team in Iowa, Sunday demonstrated incredible speed that attracted the attention of Cap Anson, manager of the Chicago White Stockings. He tried out for Anson and ended up joining the team in 1883 without spending any time in the minors, struggling at first with the bat. When Arlie Latham — billed as the fastest player in baseball — challenged him to a footrace, Sunday smoked him. To further illustrate his point, he became the first player to be timed running the bases in 14 seconds. He was credited with 71 stolen bases in 1888 and 84 in 1890, but he proved more adept at bunting than batting.

Sunday had a religious conversion in 1886, which caused him to leave baseball at age 28. He earned the nicknames "Evangelist" and "Preacher" for his fiery proselytizing, which was in stark contrast to the general uncouthness of ballplayers in those days. Pretty soon, everyone knew who Billy Sunday was, as he kept up an exhaustive schedule of tent revivals to become the most popular evangelist of his day. One of his memorable lines was: "I know there is a devil for two reasons: first, the Bible declares it; and second, I have done business with him."

Iowa briefly fielded a team in the major leagues, for those who consider the National Association (NA) one of the major leagues — Major League Baseball and the Hall of Fame do not. However, the National Association of Professional Base Ball Players (NA) was the first pro baseball league and represented the highest caliber of play during its run from 1871–75. The Keokuk Westerns had a short and unsuccessful stint in the National Association, going 1–12 in 1875. When some of the NA teams broke off to form the National League the next year, Keokuk was not invited to join the party.

Jack Saltzgraver was born in Croton, not far from Keokuk, and he got his baseball start playing for the Keokuk Cherry Blossoms and in the minors with Ottumwa. He made it to the major leagues with the New York Yankees in 1932, beginning a six-year stretch as a utility player for the Bronx Bombers. He was the starting third baseman on the 1934 club, which featured Babe Ruth, Lou Gehrig and six other future Hall of Famers. Saltzgraver won World Series rings with the Yankees in 1936 and 1937, although he didn't appear in either Series. He wound up playing 19 seasons in the minors, where he compiled 2,194 hits and a .304 average.

Iowa proved pretty good at producing Hall of Fame-caliber players in the first half of the twentieth century, but the last one to play in the majors was Feller in 1956. Six Iowa natives have been inducted into the Hall in Cooperstown: pitchers Feller, Dazzy Vance and Red Faber, shortstop Dave Bancroft, first baseman Cap Anson and outfielder Fred Clarke. Forty-one players from Iowa have played in the major leagues since 1990, but only three — Mike Boddicker, Jon Lieber and Joel Hanrahan — have made the All-Star team.

All-Time Iowa Selections

For catcher, the All-Time Iowa team features one of the most durable and hard-nosed receivers in baseball history. Hank Severeid's professional baseball career started in 1908 at the age of 17 and lasted 29 years until 1937. He spent 15 of those years catching 1,225 games in the majors, mainly for the St. Louis Browns, then finished his career catching 10 more years in the minors until age 46. Severeid batted over .300 five straight seasons with a high of .361 in 1925 playing part time for the Browns and then the Washington Senators, helping the latter to the pennant. His best season statistically was 1922 when he batted .321 with 78 RBI, although he finished sixth in voting for the MVP Award in 1924 after batting .308. He lacked power, hitting just 17 home runs among his 1,245 hits, but retired with a .289 average. Severeid is credited with throwing out 42 percent of base stealers during his career, never dipping below 30 percent.

Holding down first base is baseball's first superstar — Marshalltown native Cap Anson. He was one of the most important figures in nineteenth-century baseball, playing 27 years and becoming the first player to reach 3,000 hits. He led the league in RBI eight times and batted over .300 24 times, retiring with a .334 mark. His 2,075 RBI would rank third and his 3,435 hits would rank sixth all-time if his five seasons in the National Association were included, but Major League Baseball does not count those stats in official records. According to Fangraphs.com, Anson has the highest WAR (Wins Above Replacement) of any nineteenth-century player.

When Anson agreed to jump from the Philadelphia Athletics of the National Association to Chicago in 1876 it helped bring about the formation of the National League. He was a fixture with the White Stockings (later renamed the Colts) over the next 22 years, serving as player-manager for 19 of those years beginning in 1879. Among the innovations he is credited with are using more than one pitcher in a game and using the hit-and-run to aggressively attack the other team. He was also one of the first managers to adopt a formal spring training camp to ensure his players were ready for the season.

Known as a stern taskmaster with a hair-trigger temper, Anson was rude and crude but also brilliant and innovative. But for someone who did so much to advance the game, Anson was also an admitted racist whose refusal to play teams with black players did much to prevent integration of the game. He was elected to the Hall of Fame in 1939.

Also earning honorable mention status at first base is Hal Trosky, who was an absolute beast with the bat at the beginning of his career. At the age of 21 in 1934, the rookie from tiny Norway batted .330 with 35 homers and 142 RBI. In 1936, he blasted 42 homers, drove in a league-best 162 runs, batted .343 and slugged .644. The first six seasons of Trosky's career compare favorably with those of Lou Gehrig, Jimmie Foxx and Johnny Mize, his contemporaries. However, he could not overcome the debilitating effects of migraine headaches, retired for the first time at age 29 and was out of the game for good by 33.

Another first baseman, Cal McVey, would have the fifth-best batting average all-time if he had more career plate appearances. The nineteenth-century player, who played many positions including pitcher and catcher, batted .346 playing during a period when the seasons lasted between 30 and 82 games.

Dick Green is the best of a group of good field-no hit second basemen. Green batted just .240 over his 12-season career but was an outstanding fielder. He almost single-handedly helped the A's win the 1974 World Series with his sparkling play in the field. One of the reasons he didn't win any Gold Gloves is that fellow Sioux City native Bobby Knoop won three from 1966–68. Knoop had a similar career average, .236, but struck out more often and was a weaker overall hitter. Knoop did make one All-Star team in 1966, leading the league in triples and hitting 17 homers and driving in 72 runs that year.

Gene Baker also deserves recognition at second base. He was a promising shortstop in the Negro Leagues who finally made it to the majors in 1953 as a 29-year-old rookie after being buried in the minors for four years. As luck would have it, Ernie Banks replaced him at short for the Kansas City Monarchs in the Negro Leagues and would later do it again with the Cubs, this time on a permanent basis. Baker moved to second base and had three good years, even making the All-Star team in 1955. Baker and Banks formed the first all-black double-play duo in major league history and were nicknamed "Bingo and Bongo" for their hitting ability. Baker was traded to the Pirates during the 1957 season for Dale Long and his career wound down after that. Baker was a pretty adept fielder who could handle the bat and offered modest power.

Another noteworthy second baseman is Gene Rawlings, who won World Series championships with John McGraw's Giants in 1921 and 1922 and with the Pirates in 1925, although he only played in the first Series and batted .333.

Casey Blake edges out Lee Handley for the third base position. Blake didn't become a regular until he was 30 years old, but he has been able to accumulate 1,186 hits and 167 homers in his career to date. Blake played for Team USA in the 1994 World Cup competition and has played for five teams in his 13-year career.

Handley played mainly for the Pirates from 1936–47, collecting 902 hits with a .269 average. Nicknamed "Jeep," Handley didn't have much power (hitting only 15 homers) but made good contact, striking out just 204 times in his career. He tied for the league lead with 17 stolen bases in 1939 despite missing a third of the season after being beaned. It's been reported that Handley was the first major league opponent to offer a welcoming comment to Jackie Robinson after he broke the color barrier in 1947.

Filling out the infield is Hall of Fame shortstop Bancroft, who earned two World Series rings playing with Rawlings on the 1921 and 1922 Giants. Those were also his best seasons with the bat, as he hit .318 with 193 hits in 1921 and followed that up with 209 hits and a .321 average the next season. Bancroft was a smooth-fielding, switch-hitting leadoff hitter who just made it to 2,000 hits in his career (finishing with 2,004). In 1922 he set a record for shortstops with 984 total chances and also led National League shortstops in putouts four times. His manager on the Giants, John McGraw, often referred to him as "the best shortstop in baseball," but that didn't stop McGraw from trading Bancroft to the Boston Braves to free up the shortstop position for Travis Jackson.

Another shortstop of note is Denis Menke, who coincidentally hailed from Bancroft, Iowa. Menke made two All-Star teams with the Astros and tied a record by participating in five double plays at short on May 4, 1969. He owns another more dubious mark — highest OBP for a batter who batted below .200 for a season (minimum 100 games) — accomplished in 1973 after Menke batted .191 with 69 walks in just 322 plate appearances. That works out to a respectable .369 OBP.

Anchoring the outfield is Hall of Famer Fred Clarke, who is also Team Iowa's manager. Clarke spent most of his 19-year career as a player-manager, accumulating 2,678 hits and 1,602 wins (sixteenth all-time). He never won a batting title but the line-drive hitter finished in the top 10 seven times, retiring with a .312 average. His career best was .390 in 1897, when he collected 205 hits and stole 59 bases. Often overlooked as a star since he played virtually his entire career with Honus Wagner, Clarke guided the Pirates to four pennants and the 1909 World Series championship. Tough on the field and in the dugout, he posted just two losing seasons during his 16-year stint as Pirates manager — his last two in 1914–15 — and finished with a .576 winning percentage. Anson may have been a more innovative manager who made more of an impact on the game, but Clarke won 306 more games and is more deserving of the selection as manager for Team Iowa.

Bing Miller was a right fielder who debuted with the Washington Senators in 1921 and hung around long enough to post 1,934 hits in 1,820 games. Miller, who excelled at hitting curveballs, batted over .300 nine times, with a high of .342 in 1924. He batted .331 and had a 28-game hitting streak for the Philadelphia A's in 1929, but he really made his mark in the postseason. Miller was the hero of the World Series that year, smacking the ball off the Shibe Park wall to drive in Al Simmons with the winning run as the A's overcame a 2–0 deficit in the bottom of the ninth inning of the Series finale against the Cubs. It was the first time a team had overcome a multiple-run deficit in the bottom of the ninth inning of a World Series clincher.

The third outfielder is George Stone, who batted .301 but essentially had a six-year career because he didn't stick in the majors until age 28. Stone led the AL with 187 hits his rookie year with the St. Louis Browns in 1905 and followed that up by winning the batting title with a .358 average the next year while also leading the league in OBP, slugging and OPS.

There should be little debate about Iowa's All-Time Best Player—Bob Feller, the all-American boy next door who learned to play the game on a crude baseball field developed by his father on the family's farm in Iowa—a real-life Field of Dreams. He had a fastball that took your breath away, whether you were a fan in the stands watching or a batter at the plate trying to hit it. Feller was reportedly clocked throwing a ball at 107.9 MPH, which would be the fastest pitch ever recorded and justification for his nickname: "Rapid Robert."

Despite missing three full seasons of his prime due to World War II, he still won 266 games, 104 more than he lost. He won 20 games six times and led the league in strikeouts seven times, wins six times, shutouts four times, complete games three times and ERA once. He threw three no-hitters and 12 one-hitters An eight-time All-Star who was the youngest player in the league when he joined the Indians at 17, he had been a member of the Hall of Fame for 48 years—more than half his life—when he passed away in December 2010.

Ted Williams said Feller was the fastest and best pitcher he ever saw during his career, a sentiment echoed by many of his contemporaries. Johnny Pesky said, "God, he was a great pitcher. He struck me out too many times. He threw 100 mph and he had a great curveball. Bob Feller, by far, was the best pitcher of our time."

Feller began cultivating a friendship and business relationship with Satchel Paige as early as 1936 that a decade later would lead to an ambitious barnstorming tour featuring Negro Leagues players playing against major league stars. Bob Feller's All-Stars took on Satchel Paige's Negro All-Stars just as Jackie Robinson was getting ready to play for the Dodgers, giving African American players the chance to show they could compete on the same level as their white counterparts.

Noted Monte Irvin, "Bob Feller did as much for integration of baseball as Happy Chandler, Jackie Robinson, and Branch Rickey by playing so many exhibition games with African American players immediately after World War II." For his part, Feller said his greatest baseball achievement was serving as the first president of the Major League Baseball Players Association in the 1950s, the forerunner to today's powerful players union.

Perhaps Feller's most impressive accomplishment was enlisting in the Navy despite having a draft exemption. Coming off a season in which he won 25 games and led the league in 10 pitching categories, Feller became the first major leaguer to enlist after Pearl Harbor, joined eventually by more than 30 other future Hall of Famers such as Ted Williams and Hank Greenberg. Feller even volunteered for combat duty and was assigned to the USS *Alabama* as chief of a crew of anti-aircraft gunners, who were the ship personnel most exposed to enemy fire. He would earn five campaign ribbons and eight battle stars for his combat efforts.

Although proud of his war service, which is also prominently featured in the museum that bears his name in his hometown of Van Meter, Feller viewed himself as a survivor and not a war hero. "The heroes didn't come back," he told John Sickles, who authored *Bob Feller, Ace of the Greatest Generation.*

With Feller's spot on the team secure, two other Hall of Fame righties are forced to take a back seat: Red Faber and Dazzy Vance. Faber was the next-to-last legal spitballer (after Burleigh Grimes), winning 20 games four times on the way to 254 career wins. His most impressive season was 1921, when he won 25 games and led the league in ERA while pitching for a White Sox team that finished in seventh place. He would spend his entire career toiling for the increasingly uncompetitive Sox, whose only taste of the postseason during his tenure led to a 1917 World Series title. Faber was the hero of that Series, winning three games including two on just one days' rest. He pitched until the age of 45, gaining entry into the Hall of Fame 31 years later in 1964.

Vance was named National League MVP in 1924 after winning the pitching Triple Crown by leading the league with 28 wins, 262 strikeouts and a 2.16 ERA. As his career was winding down he finally won a World Series with the Cardinals in 1934. A three-time 20-game winner, Vance relied on a powerful fastball to lead the NL in strikeouts every season between 1922 and 1928, but he was only able to fashion a 197–140 career record because he didn't win his first major league game until the age of 31. Chronic arm troubles kept him toiling for 10 years in the minors at the start of his career, which generated 133 additional wins to push his professional victory total over 300. Once he put his arm troubles behind him, Vance dominated National League batters until he was well into his 40s.

Iowa's lefty starters are less accomplished than its strong group of righties. Earl Whitehill and Jake Weimer are the only southpaws of note. Whitehill actually has more wins than Hall of Famer Vance, but he also has 45 more losses and an ERA nearly a run per game higher. Whitehill went 218–185 pitching from 1923 to 1939, starting his career pitching under Ty Cobb on the Tigers. He only won 20 games once but did post double-figure wins in 13 straight seasons. Whitehill walked more batters than he struck out for his career.

Weimer was more dominant but in a career much

shorter. He won 20 games in three of his first four seasons, finishing with a 97–69 record playing just seven seasons. His sparkling 2.23 ERA ranks fourteenth in baseball history (minimum 1,000 innings). And unlike Whitehill, "Tornado Jake" knew how to miss bats — he averaged 7.5 hits per 9 innings. It's hard to overlook the fact Whitehill won 121 more games than Weimer in a career that was more than twice as long, so he earns the spot.

Three relief pitchers produced similar career statistics: Bob Hoerner, Bob Locker and Eddie Watt. All three pitched in the majors from the mid–1960s until the mid–'70s, which means they recorded official saves for only part of their careers. Counting only those saves posted after 1969 (when the save was officially adopted), Watt emerged as the all-time leader in saves with 57 compared to 54 for Hoerner and 51 for Locker. Locker has the edge in ERA at 2.75 (compared to 2.91 for Watt and 2.99 for Hoerner), as well as ERA+ at 123 (compared to 121 for Hoerner and 117 for Watt). He also appeared in the most games out of the bullpen with 576 — compared to 493 for Hoerner and 398 for Watt — which tipped the scales in his favor.

Locker led the American League with 77 appearances in 1967, recording a 2.09 ERA for the White Sox. He appeared in 60 or more games five times and was the losing pitcher in Game 4 of the 1972 ALCS. His 57–39 record gave him a career winning percentage of .594. An interesting footnote is the fact that Hoerner had an 8–2 record in 1968 and all eight wins came in extra innings (as did one of the losses).

Hoerner is the only one to make an All-Star team — he was a National League All-Star in 1970 with the Phillies — which is an impressive feat when you consider he almost didn't make it to the majors. He collapsed unconscious during a minor league game in 1958 and nearly died due to what was later diagnosed as a heart-related ailment. He continued to experience periodic blackouts on the mound until changing his motion to become a sidearm pitcher, which evidently placed less strain on his weak heart muscles.

Misfortune seemed to follow Hoerner around. In the midst of celebrating the Cardinals 1967 World Series championship, he suffered a severed tendon in his pitching hand while opening a champagne bottle. His career came to an ignominious end in 1977 when he threw a pitch that hit Frank Taveras of the Pirates, who charged the mound only to be punched by Hoerner. Hoerner was ejected from the game and released at the end of the season without appearing in another game. He would later die at age 59 in 1996 in a tragic farm accident.

Watt won four pennants and two World Series championships with the Orioles, although he didn't make the postseason roster in his rookie year of 1966. He came in fourth in the AL with 16 saves in 1969 and finished 240 games in his 10-year career, averaging 7.2 H/9IP.

KANSAS

*Names in **bold** represent Major League selections by position, followed by honorable mentions. Negro Leagues players are in **bold italics**, followed by honorable mentions in italics. City of birth is in parentheses.*

Catcher—**Darren Daulton (Arkansas City)**. Also: *T.J. Young* (Wichita); Ray Mueller (Pittsburg); Bob Swift (Salina)

First Base—**Tony Clark (Newton)**. Also: *George Giles* (Junction City)

Second Base—***Bingo DeMoss* (Topeka)**. Also: George Grantham (Galena); Don Gutteridge (Pittsburg); Cotton Tierney (Kansas City)

Third Base—**Bob Horner (Junction City)**. Also: Enos Cabell (Fort Riley)

Shortstop—**Joe Tinker (Muscotah)**. Also: Bill Russell (Pittsburg); Daryl Spencer (Wichita); Pat Meares (Salina)

Outfield—**Johnny Damon (Fort Riley)**

Outfield—**Duff Cooley (Leavenworth)**

Outfield—***Oscar Johnson* (Atchison)**. Also: *Dink Mothell* (Topeka); Mitch Webster (Larned); Don Lock (Wichita); Beals Becker (El Dorado)

Designated Hitter—**David Segui (Kansas City)**

Right Handed Starter—**Walter Johnson (Humboldt)**. Also: Claude Hendrix (Olathe); *Chet Brewer* (Leavenworth); Mike Torrez (Topeka); Larry Cheney (Belleville); Dummy Taylor (Oskaloosa); Elden Auker (Norcatur); *Frank Wickware* (Coffeyville); Steve Renko (Kansas City)

Left Handed Starter—**Rudy May (Coffeyville)**. Also: Ray Sadecki (Kansas City); Ross Grimsley (Topeka); Ed Siever (Goddard)

Relief Pitcher—**Paul Lindblad (Chanute)**. Also: Neil Allen (Kansas City); Kyle Farnsworth (Wichita); Tom Sturdivant (Gordon); Brad Ziegler (Pratt)

Manager—**Ralph Houk (Lawrence)**. Also: Gene Mauch (Salina)

The Names

Best Nickname: Walter "The Big Train" Johnson
Other Nicknames: Eldon "Submarine" Auker; Charles "Curly" Brown; Johnny "Trolleyline" Butler; Duff "Sir Richard" Cooley; Johnny "Caveman" Damon; Darren "Dutch" Daulton; "Slow Joe" Doyle; Charles "Victory" Faust; George "Boots" Grantham; Elon

"Chief" Hogsett; Ralph "Major" Houk; Oscar "Heavy" Johnson; Rod "The Mole" Kanehl; Carroll "Dink" Mothell; Ray "Iron Man" Mueller; Elmer "Spitball" Stricklett; Tom "Smoke" Sturdivant; Luther "Dummy" Taylor; Fay "Scow" Thomas; Keith "Kite" Thomas; James "Cotton" Tierney; Lon "Old Sleep" Ury; Art "Six O'Clock" Weaver; Frank "Rawhide," "Smokey" and "The Red Ant" Wickware; T.J. "Shack Pappy" Young; George "Zip" Zabel

Most Unusual Name: Urbane Pickering

All-Time Leaders

Games: Johnny Damon, 2426 (still active)
Hits: Johnny Damon, 2723 (still active)
Batting Average: George Grantham, .302
Home Runs: Tony Clark, 251
RBI: Johnny Damon, 1120 (still active)
Stolen Bases: Johnny Damon, 404 (still active)
Wins: Walter Johnson, 417
Strikeouts: Walter Johnson, 3509
Saves: Neil Allen, 75
Future Stars: Aaron Crow (Topeka); Derek Norris (Goddard); Bubba Starling (Gardner)
Best Player: Walter Johnson

Historic Baseball Places

Lawrence-Dumont Stadium and National Baseball Congress/Hall of Fame in Wichita — Built in 1934, it is home to the Wichita Wingnuts independent team and also hosts the annual National Baseball Congress World Series for semi-pro teams. The museum features artifacts from the history of the tournament, which has seen hundreds of players go on to the majors.

Charles Faust Memorial in Marion — Monument at Marion Baseball Complex honors Marion native Faust, who tried to convince Giants manager John McGraw he was destined to pitch them to a championship in 1911. McGraw let him stick around as a good-luck mascot and the team won 40 of 53 games down the stretch to win the pennant. Faust was allowed to make two token appearances at the end of the season, allowing one run in two innings. He returned to the team as mascot for part of the 1912 season, helping the Giants get off to a 54–11 start. Faust died three years later in an insane asylum.

Notable Achievements

Johnny Damon had three hits for the Red Sox in the first inning on June 27, 2003, marking the first time that had been done in 50 years and only the fifth time in history.

Walter Johnson is the only player to hit .400 and win 20 games in the same season, when he batted .433 and went 20–7 in 1925.

Rod Kanehl (Wichita) hit the first grand slam in Mets history on July 6, 1962.

Zip Zabel (Wetmore) holds the record for the longest relief stint. He pitched the last $18\frac{1}{3}$ innings to beat the Dodgers during a 19-inning game on June 17, 1915.

Brad Ziegler set a record for most consecutive scoreless innings to start a career with 39 in 2008.

Elmer Stricklett (Glasco) is often credited as the first pitcher to throw a spitball.

Slow Joe Doyle (Clay Center) was the first pitcher in the twentieth century to throw shutouts in his first two starts.

The Big Train Started Rolling in Kansas

Town teams were cropping up all over Kansas as early as the 1860s, as baseball grew in popularity across the plains. Then in 1882, the first Kansas-born player — Walt Kinzie of Burlington — appeared in a major league game at shortstop for the Detroit Wolverines.

Five years later, a star was born in Kansas who would grow to legendary status. Walter Johnson was a simple, humble Kansas farm boy at heart, who just happened to be blessed with an amazing ability to throw a baseball with unsurpassed ease and speed. Although he never played an organized game of baseball in Kansas — he moved with his family to California at the age of 14 — Johnson certainly honed his throwing motion on the sandlot fields of Humboldt.

Since radar guns didn't exist when Johnson pitched it's impossible to know if the "Big Train" really is the fastest pitcher who ever lived. The batters who had to face him can certainly offer a consensus opinion. Recalls Ty Cobb, "The first time I faced him, I watched him take that easy windup — and then something went past me that made me flinch. I hardly saw the pitch, but I heard it. The thing just hissed with danger. Every one of us knew we'd met the most powerful arm ever turned loose in a ballpark."

Ring Lardner once wrote about Johnson: "He's got a gun concealed on his person. They can't tell me he throws them balls with his arm."

Total Baseball ranks Johnson as the fifth-best player (and top pitcher) in baseball history, according to its Total Player Rating. Bill James places Johnson as the eighth-best player overall and first pitcher, ahead of Lefty Grove. Johnson was one of five players elected to the Hall of Fame with the first class in 1936.

Johnson set many pitching records that will probably never be broken. He holds records for most seasons leading league in strikeouts (12), most consecutive seasons leading the league in strikeouts (eight) and amazingly, most innings pitched in a season with no home runs allowed ($369\frac{2}{3}$).

Johnson certainly helped himself out by being a superb batter, hitting 24 home runs and a record 41 triples over his career. Johnson, who was also called "Sir Walter" and "Barney," won 20 or more games in 10 straight seasons, and he probably would have approached 500 career wins if he had played for a more competitive

Walter Johnson was the fastest pitcher of his era, a fireballer supreme who held the career strikeout record for 55 years. By the time he hung up his cleats in 1927, the farm boy from Humboldt, Kansas, held virtually every major pitching record. Among the major league records held by Johnson that will probably never be broken: most shutouts (110), most shutouts won 1–0 (38), most innings pitched in a season with no home runs allowed (369⅔) and most triples hit by a pitcher (41) (Library of Congress, Prints & Photographs Division, LC-DIG-hec-02661).

franchise. He had the misfortune to spend his entire career playing for the inept Washington Senators, who posted losing records in 11 of his 21 seasons, winning only two pennants during his tenure. Fittingly, it was Johnson who pitched four innings of shutout relief to win Game 7 of the 1924 World Series for the Senators.

He led the league in shutouts seven times and ERA five times, winning the MVP Award in 1913 and again in 1924. Johnson pitched shutouts in three consecutive games against the New York Highlanders over a four-day period—September 4, 5 and 7 in 1907—on the way to posting five complete-game wins in nine days. Clark Griffith, the owner of the Senators, called Johnson the greatest ballplayer he ever saw.

All-Time Kansas Selections

Let's move on to the All-Time Kansas selections. Our first-string catcher is Darren Daulton. "Dutch" was a blue-collar leader on and off the field for the Phillies, as well as a skilled batter. In 1992 he became just the fourth catcher to lead the National League in RBI while hitting a career-high 27 home runs and placing fourth in slugging and OPS. Daulton would make the first of three All-Star teams that year, win the Silver Slugger Award and finish sixth in voting for the MVP Award.

The 1993 season was even better from a team standpoint, as Daulton helped lead the Phillies to the NL pennant by hitting 24 home runs and knocking in 105 runs. They would lose the World Series to the Blue Jays, and Dalton would struggle with injuries after that. He hung up his spikes after winning the Series as a backup player for the Florida Marlins in 1997.

Daulton, who has been inducted into the Kansas Sports Hall of Fame and Kansas Baseball Hall of Fame, was ranked as the 25th-best catcher of all-time by Bill James, who noted he grounded into double plays at a lower rate than any catcher in history.

T.J. Young was an outstanding catcher in the Negro Leagues from 1925–41 (although he did not play some of those years). He and Frank Duncan comprised a formidable pair of backstops on the Kansas City Monarchs during the powerhouse team's barnstorming years. Records show the lefty slugger batting .307 in his Negro Leagues career.

Another Kansas catcher who deserves mention is Ray Mueller, who was known as "Iron Man" for his durability. Mueller caught 233 straight games for the Reds between 1943 and 1946, with the exception of time missed due to his war service in 1945. In 1944 he became the first NL player to catch all of his team's games since the schedule moved to 154 games. Mueller batted .286 that season with 159 hits and placed seventh in the MVP race while being selected to the All-Star team.

Our first baseman is switch-hitting slugger Tony Clark. His career got off to a promising start with 27 home runs in just 376 at-bats with the Tigers in 1996, leading to a third-place finish in voting for the Rookie of the Year Award. Clark hit more than 30 home runs the next three seasons and made the All-Star team in 2001, but then spent the last half of his career as a platoon/backup player due to his propensity to strike out. Clark provided a surprise spark by hitting 30 home runs in only 349 at-bats with the Diamondbacks in 2005. Released by the D-backs during the 2009 season, he finished his career with 251 home runs.

Earning honorable mention status at first base is George Giles, a lefty-swinging star of the Negro Leagues from 1925–39. Giles, who was sometimes called the "Black Bill Terry," was a rangy, agile fielder at first and a line-drive hitter with modest power. Negro Leagues historian John Holway credits him with a .309 average in Negro Leagues competition and .302 overall. "I never could understand this racial thing. It was kind of disgusting. When we were barnstorming, the white teams would stay in a hotel, and we'd be changing clothes in a farmer's barn," Giles said in an interview with Holway late in his life. "We slept in hotels where they had chinches and bedbugs. We'd leave the light on at night so the cockroaches wouldn't come out. So you had to love the game."

Our second baseman is Bingo DeMoss, who is widely considered the greatest second basemen in black baseball during his prime (his playing career lasted from 1910–30). He combined spectacular fielding ability with blazing speed and excellent bat control. DeMoss was probably the best bunter in black baseball, writes John Holway in *Blackball Stars*. DeMoss' aggressive playing style helped C.I. Taylor's Indianapolis ABCs win the 1916 championship and Rube Foster's Chicago American Giants capture three straight Negro National League pennants. DeMoss' all-around talent gives him the edge over the defensively challenged George Grantham. Grantham might best be called an accidental second baseman (he had to play somewhere in the field), but he stood out for his batting achievements. His nickname, "Boots," explains a lot about his awful fielding ability. Grantham managed to commit 314 errors over 13 seasons, including a league-high 55 in 1923. A career .302 hitter, the lefty-swinging Grantham batted over .300 eight straight years and finished with a .392 OBP. His career OPS+ of 122 matches that of Hall of Famers Ernie Banks and Paul Molitor.

Don Gutteridge also earns honorable mention at second base, although he also played quite a few games at third. Gutteridge earned MVP votes three straight years (1942–44) for the St. Louis Browns and finished in the top six in triples four times.

Third baseman Bob Horner was born in Junction City, Kansas, although he grew up and played high school baseball in Arizona. He was named MVP of the 1977 College World Series and once held the NCAA career home run record with 58. Horner is one of the few players who skipped the minor leagues and went straight to the majors. The top pick in the 1978 amateur draft showed he was ready by hitting 23 home runs for the Braves and winning the Rookie of the Year Award. Horner improved to .314 with 33 homers and 98 RBI the next year, then hit 35 home runs in 1980.

Horner made his only All-Star team in 1982 on the way to hitting 32 home runs, but was increasingly slowed by injuries. On July 6, 1986, Horner became just the 11th player to hit four home runs in one game. That year he also set a major league record by not hitting a grand slam until his 211th homer. He retired in 1988 after 10 seasons and 218 home runs.

Honorable mention at third base goes to Enos Cabell, who collected 1,647 hits over 15 seasons, batting .277 and stealing 238 bases for the Astros and four other teams. He appeared in 888 games at third and 655 more at first.

Another noteworthy third baseman is Fred McMullin, who was one of the eight White Sox players banned for life for conspiring to fix the 1919 World Series. McMullin was the oddest and least publicized member of this notorious group, as he was a bit player who barely played in the Series. He batted 1-for-2 in his two appearances. McMullin kept quiet about the affair afterwards and never asked for reinstatement to the league.

The All-Time Kansas team can turn to a Hall of Famer to man the shortstop position. Joe Tinker helped the Cubs win a lot of games between 1906 and 1910, but he probably doesn't belong in the Hall of Fame. Some people just get lucky, which is the best way to explain it. Tinker to Evers to Chance was a catchy line in a famous poem, and that notoriety seemed to sway the Old Timers Committee when it voted all three into the Hall in 1946.

The 1906 Cubs won 116 games with only 36 losses, and although Tinker was a key contributor he batted .233 with 45 errors that year. The next season the Cubs won 107 games and emerged victorious in the World Series, but Tinker batted .221 with just 89 hits and 39 errors.

Tinker had his good qualities — he was adept at the hit-and-run, wasn't afraid to hit in the clutch and stole a lot of bases (336) — but his lifetime average was a mediocre .262, tied for fifth-worst among Hall of Famers. Tinker's .308 OBP and 96 OPS+ illustrate that he was a below-average batsman. Despite his high error totals — they weren't that high for that time period — Tinker's defense was pretty good. He led NL shortstops in fielding percentage four times and assists and putouts twice.

One of many players to be embroiled in a contract dispute, Tinker was the first star to jump to the upstart Federal League in 1914. He spent two seasons as player-manager and led the Chicago franchise to a close-fought pennant. He returned to the Cubs as player-manager in 1916 but was essentially finished as a player and only able to coax a fifth-place showing for the team.

Another shortstop from Kansas produced very similar statistics to Tinker, with significantly less fanfare. Bill Russell averaged .263 with a .310 OBP over 18 seasons, all with the Dodgers. He finished with 1,926 hits and made three All-Star teams. Tinker and Russell were probably equal with the bat, but Tinker gets the edge with fielding and base stealing.

The All-Kansas outfield has some star power. Johnny Damon is not exactly thought of as a prototypical Kansas boy, and he really isn't. Born on the army base at Fort Riley, he soon moved with his family to Orlando, where he rose to become Florida Player of the Year coming out of high school. His teammate at Dr. Phillips High School was A.J. Pierzynski.

Largely overlooked while playing six seasons with the Royals, he led the American League in runs and stolen bases while batting .327 with 214 hits in 2000. After one subpar year with the A's, he signed with the Red Sox as a free agent and started gaining recognition for being one of the best leadoff hitters in the game.

Damon led the AL in triples and made his first All-

Star team in 2002, then set a career high with 20 home runs two years later. He was a major catalyst for the Red Sox in 2004 as they won their first World Series since 1918. He was selected to the All-Star team again in 2005 after hitting .316 with 197 hits. Moving on to join the Yankees as a free agent in 2006, Damon continued to demonstrate his durability, consistency and clutch-hitting ability, scoring over 100 runs for the ninth straight year and hitting a career high 24 home runs to help the Yanks win their 27th title in 2009. One of the highlights was Damon's heads-up play in Game 4 of the 2009 World Series when he swiped two bases on the same play. He is the only player to hit walk-off home runs for five different teams.

Popular with fans and beloved by teammates, Damon credits his success to hard work and determination. "It's never about your talent. Everybody in the minor leagues has talent," he wrote in his book, *Idiot*. "You've got to work harder than the next guy, and you have to want it more than the next guy."

If Damon can stay healthy and continue playing well for several more years his numbers will make him a viable candidate for the Hall of Fame, particularly if he makes it to 3,000 hits. He has played at least 140 games in 16 straight years, scored over 100 runs 10 times and accumulated 231 home runs, 404 stolen bases and 2,723 hits through the 2011 season. Working against him is the fact that he has only made two All-Star teams and his best showing in the MVP voting is thirteenth place.

Joining Damon in the All-Kansas outfield is Duff Cooley, who was nicknamed "Sir Richard." He batted .342 with 194 hits his third season, 1895, and hit over .300 five times. Primarily a left and center fielder, Cooley played all positions except pitcher during his career and compiled 1,579 hits and 224 stolen bases in 13 seasons.

The third outfielder is Oscar Johnson, whose large girth led to the nickname "Heavy." Johnson, who starred for 12 years in the Negro Leagues, reportedly hit 60 home runs in 1924 (including barnstorming exhibitions) while powering the Kansas City Monarchs to the championship. Negro leagues historian James Riley credits Johnson with a .337 career average.

Filling the role of super utility player is Dink Mothell. The Topeka native played in the Negro Leagues mainly with the Kansas City Monarchs from 1920–34, spending time at every position including pitcher and manager. He played the most in the outfield and at first and second base.

Joe Wilhoit of Hiawatha holds the record for professional baseball with a 69-game hitting streak in 1919 while playing for the Wichita Jobbers in the independent Western League. That year he batted .422 with 222 hits, which happens to be 21 more hits than he recorded in four big-league seasons.

Although primarily a first baseman, David Sequi gets selected as designated hitter for Team Kansas. He made 204 appearances at DH, with 1,412 hits and a respectable .291 average for his career. He is one of the few players to admit to using performance-enhancing drugs (specifically human growth hormone), but it's unclear how much it furthered his career. "I played more years where I didn't take anything than years where I did take something," Segui was quoted as saying. "I never denied it or pretended to be an angel."

Our left-handed starter is Rudy May, who relied on a strong curveball to carve out a long career. He won 152 games over 16 seasons, leading the American League with a 2.46 ERA in 1980 and allowing just 7.9 hits per 9 innings for his career. Ray Sadecki, another notable lefty, accumulated 135 wins over 18 seasons, winning 20 games for the Cardinals in 1964. He had a strange season in 1968, leading the league with 18 losses despite pitching six shutouts, striking out 206 and posting a 2.91 ERA.

Ross Grimsley would deserve strong consideration for the all-strange team. The lefty hurler was known to consult witches in between starts and had a superstitious aversion to showering, which did not endear him to teammates. Grimsely went 20–11 with a 3.05 ERA for the Expos in 1978, making the All-Star team that year, and finished with 124 career wins. He was not a strikeout artist, averaging just 3.3 SO/9IP.

Although they can't compare to the "Big Train" a number of other right-handed starters from Kansas deserve mention. Claude Hendrix won 20 games three times on the way to 144 career victories, posting a splendid 2.65 ERA and 1.189 WHIP. Chet Brewer is credited with a 90–64 record and 2.89 ERA over a Negro Leagues career that spanned 1925–49. He relied on a devastating "drop ball" among a wide assortment of pitches. His best achievement was fashioning a 31-inning scoreless streak during the 1929 season while leading the Kansas City Monarchs to the Negro National League pennant — he was 17–3 that season.

Mike Torrez compiled 185 wins by stringing together 10 seasons with double-figure wins, highlighted by a 20–9 mark for the Orioles in 1975. He won two games for the Yankees in the 1977 World Series, but is remembered by Red Sox fans as the pitcher who gave up the home run to Bucky Dent in the one-game playoff that decided the 1978 division title. Elden Auker, who won 130 games, is credited as the first pitcher to deploy the submarine style of pitching.

Frank Wickware was known as the "Black Walter Johnson" as his career in the Negro Leagues took off. In fact, Wickware beat Johnson in two out of three exhibition match-ups in 1913–14. The hard-throwing righty wins the prize for most nicknames, as he was also called Rawhide, Smokey, The Red Ant, Smiley and Big Red. He got his start in 1910 with the Leland Giants, the legendary team that went 123–6. The 22-year-old Wickware went 18–1 that year to emerge as the ace of the powerhouse team.

Journeyman righty Steve Renko, who won 134 games over 15 seasons, played with Gale Sayers as quarterback on the University of Kansas football team and was drafted by the Oakland Raiders in 1966.

Luther "Dummy" Taylor became the second deaf-mute to play in the big leagues (after Dummy Hoy) when he debuted for the New York Giants in 1900. Taylor's use of sign language on the field helped popularize the use of hand signals in the infield. He is also the central character in Darryl Brock's acclaimed 2000 novel, *Havana Heat*.

David Clyde was a can't-miss prospect who was born in Kansas City, Kansas. As a high school senior in Houston, the lefty went 18–0 and gave up only three earned runs while striking out 328 in 148 innings. His unlimited potential was the talk of baseball, and the Rangers didn't hesitate to select Clyde with the top pick in the 1973 amateur draft. The 18-year-old phenom with the blazing fastball was going to be the next Nolan Ryan or better yet, the next Sandy Koufax, who was Clyde's idol.

Unfortunately, the boneheaded greed of Rangers Owner Bob Short got in the way of Clyde's development and he was rushed to the majors without spending any time in the minors. The Rangers needed him to sell tickets, and fans were in a frenzy of excitement to see the sensational kid pitch. Clyde won his first start before a sold-out Arlington Stadium, striking out the side in the first after walking the first two batters. Said Clyde after the game, "I'm not kidding when I say I would've signed for popcorn to play professional baseball. I love this life. I've already had so many thrills."

Unfortunately, Clyde's early success fueled even greater expectations and tempered any suggestions he should be sent down for seasoning. He struggled through his rookie year with a 4–8 record and 5.01 ERA, and was suffering from arm problems by 1975. After an extended stint in the minors and more time on the disabled list, Clyde was out of baseball for good in 1981, finishing his career with an 18–33 record and lots of unanswered questions. We will never know how good he could have been with proper development, but his is a cautionary tale that gets repeated every time a new phenom comes along.

Clyde, for his part, refuses to point fingers at others for his failure to live up to the hype. "It's a very sobering experience. One day you think you have the world by the short ones, and then you turn around and don't know what the hell to do," he says, adding that he's thankful he got to live his dream.

If you need someone to buy a round of drinks, Clarence Beers is your guy. The El Dorado righty was probably drowning his sorrows after surrendering four runs (one earned) in two-thirds of an inning during his major league debut on May 2, 1948. He would never pitch again in the majors, retiring with a 13.50 ERA, but he did win 145 games in the minors.

The all-time best reliever for Kansas came down to two pitchers: Paul Lindblad and Neil Allen. Allen is the state's all-time saves leader with 75 compared to 64 for Lindblad, who has a big edge in relief appearances, 623 to 375. Lindblad also has more wins, fewer losses, a lower ERA, lower WHIP and a better ERA+ (104 to 98), so he gets the selection.

Kyle Farnsworth is another notable Kansas reliever who has made 750 relief appearances over 13 seasons, but his career highlights seem to be bench-clearing brawls and blown saves. He nearly doubled his saves total with 25 saves for the Rays in 2011. Who said glasses make a person look studious and nerdy? An ESPN Magazine poll in 2009 declared Farnsworth "the baddest man in baseball," and opponents have long known to steer clear of the 6-foot-6 hurler during a bench-clearing brawl. "I think I've been in the game long enough, everybody knows my reputation as it is," he said. "So it's not like I have to go out there and flip someone on their back every now and then. But I'll do it if I think it needs to be done."

There was never a doubt that Ralph Houk would make a good leader. After all, he served under General George Patton in World II, landing at Omaha Beach in Normandy and fighting in the Battle of the Bulge. He earned the Purple Heart, Bronze Star and Silver Star for his actions in combat. His nickname, "Major," came from his army rank.

"One day in the middle of the battle I sent Ralph out in a jeep to do some scouting of enemy troops," said Caesar Fiore, his commanding officer. "After being out two nights we listed him as 'missing in action.' When he turned up he had a three-day growth of beard and hand grenades hanging all over him. He was back of the enemy lines the entire time. I know he must have enjoyed himself. He had a hole in one side of his helmet, and a hole in the other where the bullet left."

Picked to succeed the popular Casey Stengel as manager of the Yankees in 1961, Houk made managing look easy at first, winning three pennants and two World Series in his first three seasons. His first Yankees squad won 109 games as Roger Maris held off teammate Mickey Mantle and made history by hitting a record 61 home runs. The Bronx Bombers beat the Reds in five games for the Series title that season and then prevailed the next year over the Giants.

Houk would manage 17 more seasons for the Yankees, Tigers and Red Sox without again making the postseason. He wound up with a 1,619–1,531 record as a manager and also served as GM of the Yankees. Here's his advice on how to win the pennant: "Get 30 games over .500 and you can break even the rest of the way."

Gene Mauch hung around as a manager in the big leagues for 26 seasons with four different teams, despite never winning a pennant. In fact, his teams only finished first two times: in his 23rd and 25th years of managing. His reliance on "small ball" fundamentals such as bunting and hit-and-run plays led to 1,902 victories but even more losses — 2,037.

Despite his brilliance as a strategist, Mauch's managerial record was marred by crushing setbacks. His 1982 Angels team lost the ALCS after winning the first two games of the series. Then in 1986 he had the Angels up 3–1 on the Red Sox with a 5–2 lead in the ninth inning ... and managed to lose the game and the series. The defining moment of his career as a manager came in 1964, when he relied on a two-man pitching rotation down the stretch as the Phillies lost 10 straight games to blow a 6½ game lead with 12 games to play.

Here's what Mauch had to say about his hard luck: "Losing streaks are funny. If you lose at the beginning, you got off to a bad start. If you lose in the middle of the season, you're in a slump. If you lose at the end, you're choking."

KENTUCKY

Names in **bold** *represent Major League selections by position, followed by honorable mentions. Negro Leagues players are in* ***bold italics****, followed by honorable mentions in italics. City of birth is in parentheses.*

Catcher — *Pops Coleman* (Louisville). Also: John Grim (Lebanon); Earl Grace (Barlow); Phil Roof (Paducah)

First Base — Dan McGann (Shelbyville). Also: Don Hurst (Maysville); Todd Benzinger (Dayton)

Second Base — *Sammy Hughes* (Louisville). Also: Fred Pfeffer (Louisville); Dan Uggla (Louisville); Bill Sweeney (Covington); Hub Collins (Louisville); Denny Doyle (Glasgow); Eddie Moore (Barlow); *Rainey Bibbs* (Henderson)

Third Base — *John Beckwith* (Louisville). Also: Travis Fryman (Lexington); Lee Tannehill (Dayton); Mark Reynolds (Pikeville) Barry McCormick (Maysville)

Shortstop — Pee Wee Reese (Ekron). Also: Ray Chapman (Beaver Dam); *Dick Wallace* (Owensboro)

Outfield — Earle Combs (Pebworth)

Outfield — Bobby Veach (St. Charles)

Outfield — Pete Browning (Louisville). Also: Gus Bell (Louisville); Mike Greenwell (Louisville); Stan Spence (S. Portsmouth); Jimmy Wolf (Louisville); *Clint Thomas* (Greenup); *Charlie Blackwell* (Brandenburg); *George Shively* (Lebanon); *Ted Page* (Glasgow); George Harper (Arlington); Joe Sommer (Covington)

Designated Hitter — Jay Buhner (Louisville)

Right Handed Starter — Jim Bunning (Southgate). Also: Carl Mays (Liberty); Gus Weyhing (Louisville); Paul Derringer (Springfield); *Harry Buckner* (Hopkinsville); Brandon Webb (Ashland); Howie Camnitz (Covington); Johnny Morrison (Pellville); Red Ehret (Louisville); *Joseph Strong* (Jackson)

Left Handed Starter — Jesse Tannehill (Dayton). Also: *Pat Dougherty* (Summershade); Don Gullett (Lynn); Woodie Fryman (Ewing); *Jim Jeffries* (Louisville); Ferdie Schupp (Louisville)

Relief Pitcher — Jon Rauch (Louisville). Also: Joe Heving (Covington); Dave Tomlin (Maysville); Don Robinson (Ashland); Steve Hamilton (Columbia); Scott Downs (Louisville); Trever Miller (Louisville)

Manager — Eddie Haas (Paducah). Also: *John Beckwith* (Louisville)

The Names

Best Nickname: "Jughandle Johnny" Morrison
Other Nicknames: Christopher "Burley" Bayer; Stanley "Rabbit" Benton; Todd "Mercedes" Benzinger; Junius "Rainey" Bibbs; Pete "The Gladiator" Browning; Harry "Green River" Buckner; Jay "Bone" Buhner; Jim "The Lizard" Bunning; Hercules "Poster Boy" Burnett; Paul "Frasier" Byrd; Howie "Kentucky Rosebud" Camnitz; John "Monk" Cline; Clarence "Pops" and "Captain Cola" Coleman; Earle "The Kentucky Colonel" Combs; Paul "Duke" Derringer; Mike "Gator" Greenwell; Irv "Major" Hach; Millard "Dixie" Howell; "Sweet Lou" Johnson; Johnny "Footsie" Marcum; Carl "Sub" Mays; Edward "Boots" McClain; Fred "Dandelion" Pfeffer; Maryland "Dykes" Potter; Robert "Squire" Potter; Phil "Donkey" Reccius; Harold "Pee Wee" Reese; Don "Caveman" Robinson; George "Rabbit" Shively; Joseph "Baby Face" Strong; Jesse "Powder" Tannehill; Clint "Hawk" Thomas; Gus "Cannonball" Weyhing; Jimmy "Chicken" Wolf

Most Unusual Name: Earl Bumpus; Hercules Burnett; George Burpo

All-Time Leaders

Games: Pee Wee Reese, 2166
Hits: Pee Wee Reese, 2170
Batting Average: Pete Browning, .341
Home Runs: Jay Buhner, 310
RBI: Bobby Veach, 1166
Stolen Bases: Fred Pfeffer, 382
Wins: Gus Weyhing, 264
Strikeouts: Jim Bunning, 2855
Saves: Jon Rauch, 58 (active)
Future Stars: Shawn Kelley (Louisville); Ben Revere (Lexington); Zach Cox (Louisville)
Best Player: Pee Wee Reese

Historic Baseball Places

Louisville Slugger Museum in Louisville — You can hold Mickey Mantle's bat, see what a 90 mph fastball looks like up close and take swings in the batting cage with Derek Jeter's bat. Out front is the world's tallest bat and the factory tour is a nice behind-the-scenes look at how bats get made.

Louisville Slugger Field in Louisville — Check out the Hall of Fame in the outer concourse, which was built

Standing sentry in front of the Louisville Slugger Museum is an exact-scale replica of Babe Ruth's 34-inch Louisville Slugger, billed as the world's biggest bat at 120 feet tall (photograph by the author).

over a century ago as a train warehouse. The Hall of Fame features memorabilia and championship banners from Louisville baseball history. In front of the stadium you will find a statue of Pee Wee Reese, who started his professional career playing two seasons for the Louisville Colonels.

Pee Wee Reese gravesite at Resthaven Memorial Park in Louisville — His tombstone reads: "His leadership helped win 7 Dodgers pennants. He eased the acceptance of baseball's first black player in to the major leagues."

Riverside/Tradewater Park in Dawson Springs — First built in the early 1900s, it was the spring training home of the Pittsburgh Pirates from 1914–1916 and the Reds and Red Sox reportedly played exhibition games there in the 1920s. The all-wood structure was destroyed by a flood in 1935. The park was rebuilt in 1999 to its original design — the first time that's ever been done, according to Eric and Wendy Pastore of Digital-ballparks.com — and the roof, the seats and the dugouts are made entirely of wood.

Notable Achievements

Dan McGann is one of only two players to drive in more runs in a World Series than the other team scored. He drove in four runs for the New York Giants in the 1905 Series, one more than the Philadelphia Athletics scored in the five games (they were shut out four times). The other player is Frank Robinson with the Baltimore Orioles in 1966.

Gus Weyhing was the first pitcher to win 100 games in two different leagues. He won 119 games in the National League and 115 in the American Association, plus 30 more in the Players League.

Fred Pfeffer and Chicago White Stockings teammates Tom Burns and Ned Williamson all collected three hits in one inning on September 6, 1883.

Dan Uggla is the only second baseman to hit 30 or more home runs in five consecutive seasons — no other second baseman has done it more than two years in a row.

Scott Stratton (Campbellsburg) won 15 consecutive games in 1890 to help the Louisville Colonels win the pennant that year.

Mike Greenwell set a record on September 2, 1996, by driving in all nine runs for the Red Sox in a 9–8 win over Seattle. He hit a two-run homer in the fifth, a grand slam in the seventh, a two-run double in the eighth, then drove in the winning run in the 10th inning with a single. Later that month he played in the final game of his career.

Jim Bunning recorded 1,000 strikeouts, 100 wins and a no-hitter in both the American and National Leagues.

Carving Out Sluggers in Louisville

As legend goes, Bud Hillerich, whose father owned a wood-turning shop in Louisville, was in the stands watching the Louisville Colonels play in 1884 when he saw his hero, Pete Browning, break a bat. He offered to make a custom bat for Browning, which is how the first Louisville Slugger came to be created.

It's a nice story, even if the facts seem to point to a slightly different reality. However, there's no disputing the fact that more than a century later Louisville-based

Hillerich & Bradsby is still churning out wood baseball bats for players of all abilities. The history lives on at the Louisville Slugger Museum, where you can take a tour and see bats being made for today's stars.

Louisville has an even earlier claim to baseball fame. In July 1865, a team from Louisville took on a team from Nashville in the first baseball game played under standard rules west of the Alleghenies.

There's more. Louisville was one of the founding teams of the National League in 1876. The Louisville Grays lasted just two seasons before four of its players were caught up in a scandal for fixing games to gamblers, 43 years before the Black Sox Scandal shook baseball to its core. Star pitcher Jim Devlin, team captain Bill Craver, outfielder George Hall and third baseman Al Nichols were all banned from baseball for life for their actions to throw the pennant race at the end of the 1877 season. It wasn't hard for the gamblers to identify one key player to go after — Devlin pitched all 559 innings the team played in that season.

The Grays didn't last long, but a few years later Kentucky was again the home to professional baseball with a team called the Louisville Eclipse, who played their games in Eclipse Park. Beginning in 1882, the team (which changed its name to the Colonels in 1885) was part of the American Association, which was considered a major league competitor to the National League. The team's best player was none other than local boy Pete Browning, who had developed into a hitting sensation. Louisville brothers Phil and John Reccius played together on the Louisville Colonels in 1882–83 and were believed to be twins for the longest time.

The Colonels played progressively worse each season until hitting rock-bottom in 1889, a year in which they lost 26 straight games on the way to finishing 27–111–2. Browning batted just .256, Louisville native Red Ehret and John Ewing combined to lose 59 games and the team went through four managers that season (including Louisville's Chicken Wolf), setting a mark for futility topped only by the 1899 Cleveland Spiders, who went 20–134.

In the midst of all that losing, some solidarity did materialize. Irritated by the heavy-handed fines handed down by captain Dude Esterbrook and owner Mordecai Davidson, six of the players decided they had enough and boycotted games for two days — it was the first player strike in major league history.

Louisville rebounded to improve its win total by 61 games the next year to win the pennant — it would be the last year Louisville fielded a winning team in the majors. After the American Association folded the Colonels switched over to the National League in 1892, and the team finished near the bottom of the standings the next eight years.

As the 1899 season was drawing to a close owner Barney Dreyfuss caught wind that the team was about to be eliminated, so he made a secret deal to purchase half-ownership of the Pirates. He then traded 12 of his best players on the Colonels (including future Hall of Famers Honus Wagner, Rube Waddell and Fred Clarke) to the Pirates for four players, who were all reassigned to Pittsburgh when the Louisville franchise folded shortly after. In other words, Dreyfuss traded 12 players to himself for nothing, which has to be the most one-sided deal in the history of professional sports.

Louisville came close to getting major league baseball back. Charlie Finley, owner of the Kansas City A's, signed an agreement in January 1964 to move the team to Louisville, but his fellow owners voted against the deal.

If you venture to Louisville, take the Walk of Fame along Main Street outside the Louisville Slugger Museum. You will find a bronze caste replica of the bat used by each of the 50 players inducted into the Louisville Slugger Hall of Fame, along with a bronze home plate that outlines their career achievements.

A total of 75 Louisville natives have made it to the majors including Negro Leaguers Pops Coleman, Sammy Hughes and Beckwith; nineteenth-century stars Pete Browning, Fred Pfeffer and Jimmy Wolf; and active players Dan Uggla, Jon Rauch, Scott Downs and Trever Miller. Every time fans hear the crack of a bat, they can thank the folks in Louisville.

Leaving Their Mark on History

It is impossible to ignore the significance of Kentucky's ties to a tragic moment in baseball history — Carl Mays throwing a pitch that hit and killed Ray Chapman on August 16, 1920.

Both were born in small Kentucky towns: Mays in Liberty and Chapman in Beaver Dam. Both were stars — Mays would win 26 games for the pennant-winning Yankees that season, while Chapman was batting .303 for the Indians. Two players on a collision course with history, partly because the league had told umpires to keep balls in play no matter how dirty, scuffed or brown they became. And of course, it was long before batting helmets were used.

Ducking down over the plate in his normal stance, Chapman probably never saw the brownish ball coming at him. He certainly didn't move as Mays, looking to brush him off the inside of the plate, instead hit him square on the head, with the ball bouncing so far it was fielded and thrown to first as though batted. A dazed and bloodied Chapman was helped to his feet, escorted to the clubhouse and rushed to the hospital, where he died the next morning, before his pregnant wife could arrive and see him.

For his part, Mays was unapologetic and unaffected by the incident, although he was widely condemned around the league. In Mike Sowell's book, *The Pitch That Killed*, he was quoted saying, "I intend to keep on and work as well as I can to provide a home and comfortable future for my family. This is what I shall try to do, for that is my lookout. What people may wish to think about me or say about me is their lookout."

Ironically, Mays had been traded to the Yankees in 1919 after he staged a mini-strike and left the Red Sox

Ray Chapman was a budding star shortstop for the Cleveland Indians when he suffered a fatal beaning from Carl Mays during a game on August 16, 1920. He died the next day in the hospital at the age of 29, and he remains the only major league player to die as a result of an on-field injury. Chapman's tragic death spurred baseball to ban the spitball and pass a rule that a clean ball should be used throughout games (Library of Congress, Prints & Photographs Division, LC-DIG-ggbain-31142).

for several weeks during the season. Seems he was upset after getting hit in the head by a ball thrown by catcher Wally Schang, who was trying to throw out a base runner.

As a result of Chapman's death, baseball reversed course and made a greater attempt to keep clean balls in play. However, it would be 51 years before batting helmets were made mandatory.

Another storyline needs to be detailed concerning Kentucky's role in baseball history. Two Kentucky natives played key roles in the integration of baseball: Happy Chandler and Pee Wee Reese.

Chandler served the state as senator and governor before replacing Kenesaw Mountain Landis as baseball commissioner in 1945. When owners took a vote in 1946 on whether to integrate, they voted 15–1 against allowing blacks to play. Chandler sided with the one baseball team in favor of integration — the Dodgers represented by President and General Manager Branch Rickey. It would be stretching things to say Chandler was supportive of the bold move, but rather he declined to stop Rickey and the Dodgers from signing Robinson.

As the years went on and proved he was on the right side of history, Chandler tended to take more credit for baseball's integration than he deserved. "I thought someday I'd have to meet my maker and He'd say, 'What did you do with those black boys?'" Chandler was quoted in the *Louisville Courier-Journal* in 1976.

Reese, on the other hand, proved to be a courageous champion of integration, since he lived up to his duties as captain by being the first player on the Dodgers to openly embrace Robinson as a worthy teammate. With a hostile crowd in Cincinnati heckling Robinson viciously during his first roadtrip in 1947, Reese walked over to Robinson on the field and put his arm around him in a show of solidarity.

Reese viewed his actions more as support for a teammate who proved he belonged in the majors than a statement on race relations, but the message of tolerance was delivered to his teammates, opponents and fans around the country. After all, if a white man from Louisville could embrace a black man in his time of need, why couldn't everyone else? Reese would increasingly befriend Robinson as time went on, and the two became one of the best double-play combinations in baseball history.

"Thinking about the things that happened, I don't know any other ballplayer who could have done what he did," Reese said. "To be able to hit with everybody yelling at him. He had to block all that out, block out everything but this ball that is coming in at a hundred miles an hour. To do what he did has got to be the most tremendous thing I've ever seen in sports."

Finally, Harry Clay Pulliam's story should be retold. Pulliam, who was born in Scottsburg, served as the president of the National League from 1903–09, which was a time in which the established league was finally learning to get along with the upstart American League. It was Pulliam who upheld umpire Hank O'Day's controversial decision in 1908 to deny the Giants the winning run when Fred Merkle stopped short of second base, with the Cubs going on to win the replayed game, the pennant and the World Series. The decision evidently weighed so heavily on Pulliam's mind that he shot himself in the head, dead at age 40. For the first time, players all across baseball wore armbands in his memory.

All-Time Kentucky Selections

Moving on to the rest of the All-Time Kentucky team, let's start at catcher. Pops Coleman was a well-rounded catcher who played in the Negro Leagues into his 50s. Starting in 1897, Coleman hung around until 1930, playing many years for the Indianapolis ABCs and later the Union Giants. An excellent receiver, he took command on the field and devoted considerable time to mentoring young catchers such as Ted "Double

Duty" Radcliffe. Teammates appreciated his fatherly approach, which is where he earned the nickname "Pops."

Other catchers of note include nineteenth-century player John Grim, who batted .267 over 11 seasons with a high of .299 in 1894; Phil Roof, who hung around for 15 years as a journeyman; and Earl Grace, who led NL catchers in fielding percentage in 1932, his only season as a full-time starter.

Dan McGann, a Shelbyville native who played from 1896–1908, gets the selection at first base. McGann batted over .300 four times, finished in the top 10 in homers four times and led the league in getting hit by pitch six times. He gained notoriety by jumping from the Orioles of the American League to the Giants of the National League in the middle of the 1902 season, becoming an important cog for Giants manager John McGraw. He retired with 1,482 hits and a .284 average, winning a World Series title with the Giants in 1905. McGann played two seasons in the minors before committing suicide in 1910.

Don Hurst's career as a first baseman got off to a promising start, but he faded fast. He batted .304 with 31 homers and 125 RBI in 1929, batted over .300 the next two years and then had his best year in 1932: 196 hits, 24 homers, league-leading 143 RBI and a .339 average. He would finish seventh in the MVP race that season but two years later he was forced to prolong his career by playing in the minors.

At second base, another nineteenth-century player, Fred Pfeffer, is edged out by Negro Leagues star Sammy Hughes. Hughes was a curious omission when the Hall of Fame held a special election for Negro Leagues and pre–Negro Leagues players in 2006. But then, the only Negro Leagues second baseman in the Hall is Frank Grant, who Bill James ranks as the sixth-best in Negro Leagues history — James has Hughes at number four and compares him to Barry Larkin and Ryne Sandberg.

Hughes was arguably the best second baseman in the Negro National League during the 1930s and early 1940s, appearing in six East-West All-Star games. He was a well-rounded player but especially good on defense. He started his career with his hometown Louisville White Caps in 1930 and later shined in the California Winter League, batting .384 with 17 home runs over seven seasons. Hughes is credited with a .297 lifetime average and a .353 mark against major leaguers.

Pfeffer, who was nicknamed "Dandelion," played four of his 16 seasons for Louisville in the National League, posting his only .300 season with the Colonels in 1894. He was second in the league with 25 homers and 101 RBI in 1884. An excellent defensive player with above-average range, Pfeffer led the NL in assists eight straight years and compiled 1,680 career hits. The infield fly rule came about in 1895, largely because Pfeffer liked to drop soft liners so he could turn a double play. He is also credited with another fielding innovation: coming in on the throw from the catcher and firing back home to prevent the front end of a double steal (when runners are on first and third), a play now taught in Little League.

The safe choice at third base would be Travis Fryman, but it's too hard to overlook the talent of Negro Leaguer John Beckwith. Beckwith could slug with anyone, although it was as likely to be a teammate he was slugging as the ball. He was as much a terror off the field as on, and his immoral lifestyle coupled with a severe drinking problem greatly curtailed his ability to maximize his on-field performance. He didn't make much of an effort at fielding, and he had a tendency to get in fistfights with teammates at the slightest affront. Then there was the time he got arrested for viciously beating up an umpire.

Strictly a pull hitter who was unfazed by the defensive shifts implemented to defeat him, Beckwith hit for average and power better than any third baseman who ever played in the Negro Leagues. He was the first player to hit a ball out of Redland Field in Cincinnati and he posted a lifetime average of .349. He batted .371 in 1921 and .358 in 1922. A special committee commissioned in 2006 to elect the last batch of Negro Leaguers to the Hall of Fame was undoubtedly swayed by character issues when it excluded Beckwith, but at least he is not overlooked on the All-Time Kentucky team.

Fryman, who also played 339 games at short, was a five-time All-Star. He won a Gold Glove with the Indians in 2000, when he had his best overall year with a .321 average, a .392 OBP and .516 slugging percentage along with 22 homers and 106 RBI. Fryman was a steady but not spectacular player during his 13-year career with the Tigers and Indians.

Another third baseman worth noting is Mark Reynolds, who set a batting record for most strikeouts in a season with 223 in 2009 but also hit 44 homers that year. He led the league in strikeouts for the third straight year in 2010 with another dubious distinction — his strikeout total (211) was higher than his batting average (.198). His 196 strikeouts led the American League in 2011, and combined with his 31 errors to offset his 37 home runs.

Tremendous is a good word to describe Pee Wee Reese's play at short, justifying his selection as Kentucky's All-Time Best Player. Reese, who picked up the nickname "Pee Wee" in reference to his skill at shooting pee wee marbles, spent his entire 16-year career with the Dodgers, the first 15 in Brooklyn.

When Reese made it to the majors in 1940, he was joining a Dodgers team that had not won a pennant since 1920. Quickly showing leadership, and taking the shortstop position from manager Leo Durocher, Reese led the team to a second-place finish his first year and a pennant the next. It was the first of seven pennants during his tenure with the team.

It was Pee Wee's strong leadership that kept the team from being discouraged after the disappointment of losing five World Series to the rival Yankees between 1941 and 1953, finally breaking through with a championship in 1955. As teammate Don Newcombe pointed out, "He loved the Dodgers, he always respected the Dodgers and the people who owned the Dodgers."

Reese was an exceptional fielder with quick feet and good range, leading the NL in putouts four seasons and in fielding percentage once. He was also an excellent base runner, leading the league with 30 steals in 1952 and compiling 232 career steals. His lifetime average was a respectable .269, with a career high of .309 in 1954, and only five shortstops in the Hall of Fame have hit more than his 126 home runs. On the 1947 pennant-winning team, Reese tied Jackie Robinson for the team lead with 12 home runs. A 10-time All-Star, Pee Wee finished in the top 10 in MVP voting eight times. His number 1 uniform number has been retired by the Dodgers. He was elected to the Hall of Fame in 1984.

If it weren't for Reese, Chapman would have made a pretty good selection for All-Time Kentucky shortstop. An outstanding fielder with excellent range, Chapman was third in the AL with 52 stolen bases while batting .302 in 1917 and then led the league in runs and walks the next season. He wound up with 1,053 hits and 238 stolen bases. Despite the fact he only played nine seasons, Chapman still ranks sixth on the all-time list for sacrifice hits. He set a record with 67 sacrifice hits in 1917.

The All-Time Kentucky outfield features three players who finished playing more than 75 years ago: Pete Browning, Earle Combs and Bobby Veach. Browning, who was known as "The Gladiator," was one of the pre-eminent hitters in the American Association, where he spent his first eight seasons playing with Louisville. He led the league by batting .378 in 1882 and .362 in 1885, then hit a career-high .402 in 1887. Switching to the Players League in 1890, Browning led that league with a .373 average and then spent his last four seasons playing for five different teams in the National League.

Browning finished in the top three in batting average nine of his 13 seasons, and his .341 lifetime average ranks thirteenth all-time. He was a bumbling incompetent in the outfield and also refused to slide on the base paths, but no one ever doubted his ability to hit. It was said that he owned as many as 700 bats and that each had a name that was somehow related to the Bible.

Bothered by a medical condition that caused him to go deaf in his youth and deal with chronic head pain, Browning dropped out of school at an early age and turned to booze. It's not likely he played many games without at least some alcohol in his system, which makes his accomplishments that much more impressive. Of course there was the time a hungover Browning literally fell asleep while taking his lead off second base and found himself picked off. After his playing career ended he was committed to an insane asylum, without cause it appears. SABR's committee on nineteenth-century players has named Browning the "Most Overlooked nineteenth Century Legend" and is trying to get him into Cooperstown.

Combs was the table-setting leadoff batter for the powerhouse Yankees squads of the late 1920s and early 1930s. Using his excellent speed and keen eye, Combs got on base at a .397 clip for his career and scored over 100 runs in eight straight years. He was a key part of the Murderers' Row, the 1927 Yankees team that outscored opponents by 376 runs on the way to winning 110 games and sweeping the Pirates in the World Series. That year, Combs batted .356, scored 137 runs and led the league with 231 hits and 23 triples. He won three titles with the Yankees, batting .350 in World Series action.

Nicknamed "The Kentucky Colonel," Combs finished in the top 10 in triples eight seasons, leading the league three times. His lifetime average of .325 ranks 44th all-time while his 154 triples rank 48th. He patrolled a lot of ground out in center field, leading the league in putouts twice, but had a weak arm. His career ended prematurely after two outfield collisions: the first in 1934 fractured his skull and knocked him unconscious, while the second in 1935 broke his collarbone. He was inducted into the Hall of Fame in 1970.

Veach spent most of his career with the Tigers, forming an all-time-great outfield first with Ty Cobb and Sam Crawford and then later with Cobb and Harry Heilmann. He was an excellent run producer, driving in 100 or more runs in six seasons and leading the league in RBI three times, largely because he had those great players batting in front of him.

The lefty-swinging Veach batted over .300 in 10 of his 14 seasons, finishing with a .310 lifetime average. He hit a career-high .355 in 1919, good for second-best in the AL, and also led the league in hits, doubles and triples while coming in third with a .519 slugging percentage that year. He compiled twice as many career stolen bases as Combs (195–98), collected nearly twice as many RBI (1166–632) and also had more hits, doubles and homers (despite playing largely in the Deadball Era). Yet Combs got into the Hall while Veach received less than 1 percent of the vote and dropped off the ballot after one year.

Veach had the good fortune to be picked up on waivers by the Washington Senators for the stretch drive in 1925—his last season in the majors—and the Senators went on to win the pennant that year. It was Veach's only appearance in the postseason—he batted 0-for-1 and the Senators lost to the Pirates. Earlier in the season, during a brief stint with the Yankees, Veach became one of the few players to pinch-hit for Babe Ruth.

Browning's childhood friend, Chicken Wolf, joined him in the Louisville outfield from 1882–89. Wolf would remain two extra seasons, making him the only player to play all 10 years of the American Association's existence. Not surprisingly, he holds the American Association record for most games, hits, doubles and triples. Wolf batted .290 for his career, leading the league with 197 hits and a .363 average in 1890. He received honorable mention for the All-Kentucky team.

Two other outfielders from Louisville deserve mention: Gus Bell and Mike Greenwell. Bell was a four-time All-Star for the Reds who hit 206 career home runs. His best season was 1953, when he hit .300 with 30 homers and 105 RBI. Greenwell, nicknamed "Gator," spent his entire 12-year career with the Red Sox, batting

.303 lifetime with 130 homers. Greenwell finished second in the MVP race in 1988 after posting a .325/.416/.531 line with 22 homers and 119 RBI.

Clint Thomas, Charlie Blackwell, George Shively and Ted Page all starred in the Negro Leagues. The speedy Page was a combative and aggressive line-drive hitter who batted .335 lifetime. Thomas picked up the nickname "Hawk" for his sharp batting eye and ball-hawking ability in center field. He hit .407 in 1924 and averaged around .330 during a career that lasted from 1920–38.

Blackwell teamed up with Oscar Charleston to form a dynamic outfield duo for the St. Louis Giants in 1921. Blackwell hit .409 with 12 homers, 88 RBI and 25 steals for the first-place Giants, according to the Seamheads.com Negro Leagues Database, while Charleston batted .437 and led the league with 32 steals. Shively was a lightning quick leadoff hitter who was the catalyst for the powerhouse 1916 Indianapolis ABCs, batting .333 with .394 OBP.

Jay Buhner makes the All-Time team as designated hitter, although he was a full-time outfielder throughout his career. He rated a memorable mention on *Seinfeld*, when George Steinbrenner is asked why he traded Buhner from the Yankees. Buhner was a productive slugger for the Mariners, belting over 40 homers three straight years and retiring with 310 home runs. His 307 homers as a Mariner are third-best in team history, just two behind Edgar Martinez.

Nicknamed "Bone," Buhner strutted up to the plate with his shaved head and goatee, as George Thorogood's "Bad to the Bone" played. Buhner won a Gold Glove in 1996 mainly for his strong arm, because he did not have good range. Buhner didn't hit for average and struck out a lot, but he drew walks and had a high slugging percentage. He was inducted into the Mariners Hall of Fame in 2004.

An impressive number of right-handed starters hail from Kentucky, so let's take a closer look at six pitchers. Jim Bunning, who is the only one in the Hall of Fame, posted a somewhat pedestrian 224–184 record with a 3.27 ERA and ERA+ of 114. It has been frequently pointed out that his numbers fall short of Hall of Fame worthiness. However, Bill James ranks him as the 30th-best pitcher in history and points out that Bunning actually pitched a lot better than his stats would indicate.

Bunning was a seven-time All-Star who won 20 games just once but won 19 games four times. He posted six seasons of 200-plus strikeouts, leading the league three times. Although he ranks seventeenth today, Bunning was number two in strikeouts when he retired. By any definition, he was a reliable workhorse and a true ace. He was one of the top pitchers in baseball from 1957–67, first in the American League for the Tigers and then later with the Phillies in the National League. This dominance is evidenced by the following number of top 10 finishes in various categories: ERA (7), wins (9), WHIP (9), K/BB (13), K/9IP (11), innings (10), games started (11), complete games (9), shutouts (7), won-loss pct. (4) and ERA+ (7). He finished in the top five in strikeouts 11 times in his 17 seasons.

Bunning is one of two Kentucky pitchers to throw a perfect game: he tossed his on June 21, 1964 (Father's Day), while Len Barker matched the feat on May 15, 1981. Bunning later served in the Kentucky State Senate, the U.S. House of Representatives and the U.S. Senate.

It took a while for his Hall support to build, but Bunning saw his vote totals climb six straight years until he just missed in his twelfth year on the ballot, falling four votes short with 74.2 percent of the vote. Hall candidates generally make it the next year when they come that close, but Bunning's support went in the other direction as he finished out his eligibility with 63, 57 and 63 percent. Five years later, in 1996, he was voted in by the Veterans Committee. There is no doubt Bunning was a dominant pitcher, making him a worthy selection as Kentucky's All-Time right-handed starter.

The year after the beaning incident Mays produced his best numbers, leading the league in wins with 27, won-loss percentage, games, saves and innings pitched. Mays won 20 games five times and finished with an excellent .623 winning percentage, but he dropped off the Hall ballot after one year, as his many accomplishments in baseball were overshadowed by one pitch. He told baseball writer Frederick Lieb, "I won over two hundred big league games, but no one remembers that. When they think of me, I'm the guy who killed Chapman with a fastball."

Gus Weyhing averaged 424 innings pitched in his first seven seasons, which is how he picked up the nickname "Rubber-Winged Gus." He won at least 20 games in each of those seasons, accumulating exactly 200 wins by the age of 27. He would win just 64 games over the remaining seven seasons of his career, retiring with 264 victories. The most amazing fact about Weyhing is that he pitched for 11 different teams in four different leagues over his 14-year career — only Mike Morgan and Ron Villone have pitched for more franchises.

Paul Derringer won 223 games but also lost 212, with a 3.46 ERA, pitching for the Cardinals, Reds and Cubs from 1931–45. He went 18–8 as a rookie for the Cards in 1931, leading the league in winning percentage and winning a World Series that year. His best season was 1939 with the Reds, when he went 25–7 with a 2.93 ERA, again led the NL in winning percentage and walked just 35 batters in 301 innings. He posted an outstanding 1.9 BB/9IP mark for his career. A four-time 20-game winner, Derringer was selected to six All-Star games.

Harry Buckner was one of the best pitchers in black baseball in the early part of the twentieth century. He teamed up as a dynamic duo with Dan McClellan on the Brooklyn Royal Giants' 1910 pennant winners and was the ace for the New York Lincoln Giants (1911–12) and Chicago Giants (1914–18). The multi-talented Buckner often caught and played the outfield or shortstop when not pitching.

Ashland native Brandon Webb won the Cy Young

Award in 2006 and then was runner-up the next two seasons, but was injured and only pitched in one game the next three years. Webb has led the league in wins, games started, shutouts and ERA+ twice and in complete games and innings pitched once. He won only 16 games during his Cy Young Award-winning season and didn't win the award in 2008, when he won a career-high 22 games.

Red Ehret was a nineteenth-century player whose career record was 139–167 with a 4.02 ERA. However, if you look at his neutralized pitching stats (adjusting for park and league context) he winds up with a 264–121 record with 2.72 ERA. Unfortunately, they don't vote on neutralized stats for Cooperstown, but it does demonstrate that he was a much better pitcher than his stats might indicate.

"Jughandle Johnny" Morrison of Owensboro, who also had a brother play in the majors, picked up his nickname for his sweeping curveball. Morrison won 25 games for the Pirates in 1923 on the way to 103 career victories and led the NL in shutouts twice.

Perhaps you didn't know that Ted Turner pitched in the majors and hailed from Lawrenceburg. Kentucky's Ted Turner was neither mouthy nor rich, and not especially accomplished as a pitcher either. The righty appeared in one game with the Cubs in 1920 and wound up with a 13.50 career ERA.

The All-Time Kentucky left-handed starter is Jesse Tannehill, a control artist who baffled hitters with a tantalizing curveball. In 1904 Tannehill pitched the third no-hitter in American League history, and he went on to post a 197–117 record with a 2.80 ERA. He won 20 games six times and led the AL with a 2.18 ERA in 1901. An excellent hitter, Tannehill played 87 games in the outfield and made 57 appearances as a pinch-hitter, batting .255 for his career.

Pat Dougherty was sometimes called the "Black Marquard," a sign of respect for the southpaw's skill as a pitcher. Dougherty was the ace of some top-notch teams in the Negro Leagues, going 13–0 for the Leland Giants in 1910.

Don Gullett was a valuable pitcher for the Cincinnati Reds in the 1970s, although he was overlooked for the All-Star team. He won 15 or more games four times in five years and led the NL in winning percentage twice. Forced to retire after 10 seasons due to arm trouble, Gullett's .686 career winning percentage ranks seventh-best in baseball history. He recorded a 3.11 ERA and allowed just 7.8 H/9IP. He played on five pennant winners and won back-to-back championships first with the Reds in 1976 and then with the Yankees in 1977.

Another lefty, Woodie Fryman, was a contemporary of Gullett who hung around for 18 years pitching for six different teams. Fryman won 141 games and made two All-Star teams. Jim Jeffries went 21–11 for the 1922 Indianapolis ABCs, according to the Seamheads.com Negro Leagues Database powered by The Baseball Gauge.

Special recognition should go to lefty Ferdie Schupp, who has a legitimate claim to having produced the season with the lowest ERA in baseball history. Pitching for the New York Giants in 1916, Schupp was untouchable all season, allowing just 79 hits in 140 innings and generating a microscopic 0.90 ERA. Schupp was recognized as the single-season ERA leader that year and his 0.90 mark was officially listed as the lowest ERA for many years. When baseball later changed the qualifications for the ERA title to one inning pitched for each game that a team plays in a season, it also decided to go back and change the single-season leaders based on these new rules. So if you check the record book and see Dutch Leonard's 0.96 ERA from 1914 listed as the modern era leader (or 0.86 for Tim Keefe dating to 1880), just know that Ferdie Schupp belongs on the list.

Kentucky's best relief pitcher is active pitcher Jon Rauch, who at 6-foot-11 is the tallest player in major league history. He is already Kentucky's all-time leader in saves with 58 after collecting 21 for the Twins in 2010 and 11 for the Blue Jays in 2011. He appeared in 85 games for the Nationals in 2006 and followed up with a league-leading 88 appearances the next season.

Joe Heving was a valuable righty out of the bullpen for the Indians and Red Sox in the late 1930s and early '40s. He relieved in 390 games and posted a 76–48 record — a .613 winning percentage. Heving had his best year at the age of 43 in 1944, going 8–3 with a 1.93 ERA and leading the AL with 63 appearances.

Don Robinson, nicknamed "Caveman," serves as a cautionary tale for how to handle young pitchers. After pitching 228 innings as a 21-year-old rookie with the Pirates, Robinson suffered a steady stream of elbow and shoulder surgeries that curtailed his production. He shifted to the bullpen, where he saved 57 games, which is the second-most in Kentucky history. Robinson was a terrific hitter, winning three Silver Sluggers and hitting 13 career home runs.

Scott Downs and Trever Miller are current players who have been effective in set-up roles, while Steve Hamilton was a valuable lefty specialist from 1961–72. Before he started his baseball career Hamilton played two seasons in the NBA with the Minneapolis Lakers, who lost in the NBA Finals both years. The 6-foot-6 forward-center played with Hall of Famers Elgin Baylor and Vern Mikkelsen.

Picking a manager for the All-Time Kentucky team was not easy. Eddie Haas didn't have much of a major league track record — he was 50–71 managing the Braves for part of 1985 — but he did manage 14 seasons in the minors. Haas' main claim to fame was having two cousins play in the majors (Phil and Gene Roof) plus a brother and six cousins who played in the minors.

Haas may have a weak managerial record, but he did not have the character issues of Beckwith, who served off and on as a player-manager for various teams in the Negro Leagues. Since Beckwith was unreliable and ornery and jumped teams a lot, it's hard to build a case for him as an all-time-best manager. He was player-manager of the Baltimore Black Sox when he punched out an umpire and later quit on the team during the season after a contract dispute.

LOUISIANA

Names in **bold** *represent Major League selections by position, followed by honorable mentions. Negro Leagues players are in* ***bold italics****, followed by honorable mentions in italics. City of birth is in parentheses.*

Catcher — **Bill Dickey (Bastrop)**. Also: *Doc Wiley* (Vernon); *Pepper Bassett* (Baton Rouge); Clint Courtney (Hall Summit)

First Base — **Will Clark (New Orleans)**. Also: Joe Adcock (Coushatta); Zeke Bonura (New Orleans); Bob Oliver (Shreveport); *Eldridge Mayweather* (Shreveport)

Second Base — **Odell Hale (Hosston)**. Also: Connie Ryan (New Orleans); *Barney Serrell* (Natchez); Lou Chiozza (Tallulah)

Third Base — ***Ollie Marcelle* (Thibodaux)**. Also: *Dave Malarcher* (Whitehall); Herb Souell (West Monroe)

Shortstop — **Wayne Causey (Ruston)**. Also: John Peters (New Orleans); Ryan Theriot (Baton Rouge); *Bobby Williams* (New Orleans); George Strickland (New Orleans); *Saul Davis* (Bayou)

Outfield — **Mel Ott (Gretna)**

Outfield — **Reggie Smith (Shreveport)**

Outfield — ***Willard Brown* (Shreveport)**. Also: Albert Belle (Shreveport); Tommy Harper (Oak Grove); Vernon Wells (Shreveport); Ralph Garr (Monroe); *Lloyd Davenport* (New Orleans); Darryl Hamilton (Baton Rouge); Rebel Oakes (Arizona)

Designated Hitter — **Rusty Staub (New Orleans)**

Left Handed Starter — **Andy Pettitte (Baton Rouge)**. Also: Ron Guidry (Lafayette); Vida Blue (Mansfield); Chuck Finley (Monroe); Mel Parnell (New Orleans); Howie Pollet (New Orleans); *Frank Thompson* (Maryville); *Jonas Gaines* (New Roads)

Right Handed Starter — **Ted Lyons (Lake Charles)**. Also: *Peanuts Davis* (New Orleans); Bill Lee (Plaquemine); J.R. Richard (Vienna); Ben Sheets (Baton Rouge); Don Wilson (Monroe); *Gene Bremer* (New Orleans); *Johnny Wright* (New Orleans); Shane Reynolds (Bastrop)

Relief Pitcher — **Lee Smith (Shreveport)**. Also: Jonathan Papelbon (Baton Rouge); B.J. Ryan (Bossier City); Norm Charlton (Fort Polk); Eddie Fisher (Shreveport); Cecil Upshaw (Spearsville); Scott Williamson (Fort Polk)

Manager — ***Dave Malarcher* (Whitehall)**. Also: Eddie Dyer (Morgan City); Mel Ott (Gretna)

The Names

Best Nickname: Ron "Louisiana Lightning" Guidry

Other Nicknames: Lloyd "Pepper" and "Rocking Chair Catcher" Bassett; Albert "Mr. Freeze" Belle; Zeke "Banana Nose" Bonura; Willard "Home Run" Brown; Ralph "Putsy" Caballero; Norm "The Sheriff" Charlton; Will "The Thrill" Clark; Clint "Scrap Iron" and "Toy Bulldog" Courtney; John "Fats" Dantonio; Lloyd "Ducky" Davenport; Edward "Peanuts" Davis; Harry "Stinky" Davis; Saul "Rareback" Davis; Al "Broadway" Flair; Ralph "Roadrunner" Garr; Harold "Tookie" Gilbert; Odell "Bad News" Hale; Ralph "Bruz" Hamner; Bill "Duckbreast" Handy; "Sunday Teddy" Lyons; Oliver "Ghost" Marcelle; Eldridge "Chili" Mayweather; Ennis "Rebel" Oakes; Mel "Master Melvin" Ott; Mel "Dusty" Parnell; Lee "Bee Bee" Richard; Rusty "Le Grand Orange" Staub; Frank "Groundhog" Thompson; John "Mule" Watson; Wabishaw "Doc" Wiley; Gerald "Ice" Williams; Johnny "Nature Boy" Williams; John "Needle Nose" Wright

Most Unusual Name: Harley Boss

All-Time Leaders

Games: Rusty Staub, 2951
Hits: Mel Ott, 2876
Batting Average: Bill Dickey, .313
Home Runs: Mel Ott, 511
RBI: Mel Ott, 1860
Stolen Bases: Tommy Harper, 408
Wins: Ted Lyons, 260
Strikeouts: Chuck Finley, 2610
Saves: Lee Smith, 478
Future Stars: Wade LeBlanc (Lake Charles); Mike Mahtook (Lafayette)
Best Player: Mel Ott
Historic Baseball Place to See:
Zephyr Field in New Orleans — Home to the New Orleans Zephyrs since it opened in 1997, the ballpark was used to film scenes in the movies "Mr. 3000" and "Failure to Launch."

Notable Achievements

Mel Ott holds the record for the most games played before his 30th birthday — 1,739, according to BR Bullpen. He is also the only player to score six runs in a game twice, which he did on August 4, 1934 and April 30, 1944.

Rusty Staub became just the second player to hit a home run as a teenager and as a 40-year-old, following Ty Cobb. Gary Sheffield joined the club in 2009 as did Ken Griffey, Jr., with his first home run in 2010.

Ralph Garr still holds the record for most hits before the All-Star Game with 149 in 1974.

Ron Guidry became the first American League left-hander to strike out 18 batters in a nine-inning game when he did it on June 17, 1978.

Matt Alexander (Shreveport) holds the record for most times appearing as a pinch-runner (271) as well as stolen bases (91) and runs (89) as a pinch-runner.

Andy Pettitte started the last game played at the old Yankee Stadium on September 21, 2008.

Earl Wilson (Ponchatoula) became the first pitcher to throw a no-hitter and homer in the same game, which he accomplished on June 26, 1962. His 35 career home runs are three behind Wes Ferrell for most all-time by a pitcher.

J.R. Richard ranks fourth all-time in hits per nine innings at 6.87.

Spring Training Gets Its Start in New Orleans

Organized baseball in New Orleans dates back to 1859, when amateur teams began playing on the grounds of the Delachaise Estate near present day Louisiana Avenue, according to the Schott-Pelican Chapter of SABR. The Lone Star Base Ball Club was also organized that year. A number of baseball clubs were organized during the 1860s, highlighted by the founding of the Louisiana Base Ball Association in New Orleans in 1867.

The first spring training reportedly took place in New Orleans in 1870 when Chicago and Cincinnati both held camps to get ready for the new season. The Boston Beaneaters held spring workouts in New Orleans in 1884 and a steady stream of major league teams followed. The Indians started coming to New Orleans in 1902 and also held spring training in the Crescent City from 1916-20 and 1928-39. The Reds, White Sox, Cubs, Red Sox, Giants, Yankees and Dodgers were other teams that came to New Orleans for spring training. Other Louisiana cities such as Baton Rouge, Shreveport, Alexandria and Monroe were also the site of MLB spring training camps at various times.

Imagine if spring training was still being held in New Orleans, with Mardi Gras thrown into the mix. We would be calling it the Bourbon League instead of the Grapefruit League, and Nick Swisher would be too busy throwing beads into the crowd to catch fly balls in right field.

New Orleans native John Peters became the first Louisiana-born player in the major leagues when he debuted for the Chicago White Stockings on May 23, 1874. Two years later he batted .351 for the White Stockings as they won the inaugural pennant in the National League. Peters would play 11 years and finish with a .278 average. By the turn of the century, 14 Louisiana natives had appeared in the majors, with 13 coming from New Orleans.

The Crescent City League formed in New Orleans in 1880, as the city's love of baseball was in full bloom. Sportsman's Park opened in 1886, which would be the home of the New Orleans Pelicans when they formed the next year. The New Orleans Pelicans hung around until 1959, playing at Heinemann Park (later renamed Pelican Stadium) beginning in 1915. Shoeless Joe Jackson played for the team in 1910, as did future Hall of Famers Dazzy Vance, Bob Lemon and Joe Sewell later on.

The Pelicans would win two Southern League titles and nine Southern Association pennants during their history. Pelicans player Abner Powell is credited with being the first to use a tarp to cover the infield in 1887, and while serving as manager and part-owner in 1899 he came up with the concept of a "rain check" to appease fans when games were rained out.

New Orleans has sent 69 players to the major leagues, headlined by Will Clark, Rusty Staub, Connie Ryan and Zeke Bonura. Bonura starred at Loyola University in New Orleans and for the Pelicans from 1929–31 before making it to the majors for good.

The New York Yankees are shown during spring training in New Orleans in the early 1920s. Babe Ruth is in the middle of the second row (Library of Congress, Prints & Photographs Division, LC-USZ62-103767).

Jesuit High School in New Orleans has been good at churning out future major league players, since that's where Clark, Staub and Ryan attended. Ryan and future major leaguers Charlie Gilbert and John "Fats" Dantonio led Jesuit to the 1936 state title. Gilbert's father, Larry, had also attended Jesuit and he played two years for the Boston Braves and served as the Pelicans' manager from 1923–38. He had another son, Tookie Gilbert, who led Jesuit to the 1946 state title and went on to play two seasons for the New York Giants. Staub led Jesuit to the 1961 state championship, while Clark led the storied high school to the 1980 state title. Another Jesuit graduate, Ralph "Putsy" Caballero, became one of the youngest players in major league history when he debuted with the Phillies at age 16 in 1944.

Negro Leagues stars from New Orleans include Bobby Williams, Ducky Davenport, Peanuts Davis and Gene Bremer. The New Orleans Black Pelicans began play in the Southern Negro League in 1920 and the city also fielded the New Orleans Stars briefly and the New Orleans Eagles in the Negro American League.

After a brief period without minor league ball in the city, the New Orleans Zephyrs started up as a Triple-A affiliate in 1993. Zephyr Field, known as the "Shrine on Airline" for its location on Airline Drive, opened in 1997.

All-Time Louisiana Selections

Louisiana has produced four Hall of Fame players — Mel Ott, Ted Lyons, Willard Brown and Bill Dickey — not to mention a number of borderline candidates. Negro Leagues players are well-represented on the All-Louisiana team as they hold down two starting spots, with 14 more receiving honorable mention status.

Catcher is an easy choice, with Bill Dickey generally considered the best catcher in the American League for the decade of the 1930s. He ranks 10th all-time among catchers in Career Win Shares with 314, just a tick behind Joe Torre and Ted Simmons. Dickey was a key component of the Yankees juggernaut that won eight World Series between 1928 and 1943 (although he didn't play in the 1928 Series). He is tied for the third-most Series rings behind Yogi Berra and Joe DiMaggio. He was elected to the Hall of Fame in 1954.

Dickey batted over .300 11 times, finishing with a .313 average that is third-highest in history by a catcher (behind Joe Mauer and Mickey Cochrane). An 11-time All-Star, he hit 202 home runs and had an excellent OBP of .382 — the eighth-best mark by a catcher. His .362 average in 1936 was the highest posted by a catcher until Joe Mauer came along and batted .365 in 2009 (Mike Piazza also matched the .362 in 1997). Dickey caught 100 or more games in 13 straight seasons, establishing a reputation as an excellent handler of pitchers. Carl Reynolds learned what happened when you bowled into him at the plate — Dickey broke his jaw with a punch, which earned him a 30-day suspension.

Two Negro Leagues catchers deserve mention: Wabishaw "Doc" Wiley and Pepper Bassett. Wiley was originally believed to be from Oklahoma with some Indian blood in him, but Negro Leagues researcher Gary Ashwill was able to document how Wiley reinvented himself through the years. Wiley's World War I draft card shows him as an "African" being born in Vernon, La., but he claimed to be from Oklahoma in the 1930 Census while his World War II draft card shows him as an Oklahoman of Indian heritage. Ashwill believes Vernon to be the most likely birthplace for Wiley, which means he's backing up Dickey rather than Johnny Bench. Wiley was a key player for the New York Lincoln Giants for a dozen years, batting .398 in 1913 and following that up with a .418 average the next year. The Seamheads.com Negro Leagues Database powered by The Baseball Gauge shows Wiley with .413 and .336 averages in 1916–17.

Bassett, a Baton Rouge native, appeared in seven East-West All-Star games. Some years he was a backup and he usually hit toward the bottom of the order, but he had some productive years with the bat. Bassett started off as Josh Gibson's replacement on the Pittsburgh Crawfords in 1937 and played with Willie Mays while with the Birmingham Black Barons from 1944–52. He gained notoriety by occasionally catching a game while sitting in a rocking chair, which entertained fans but doesn't help further the notion that the Negro Leagues players were on a professional par with their white counterparts.

At first base, Will "The Thrill" Clark put together a career that deserved serious consideration for election to the Hall of Fame. However, he inexplicably received only 4.4 percent of the votes in his first year of eligibility, 2006, and dropped off the ballot. When sabermetricians crunch the numbers to determine whether a player belongs in the Hall, they generally come out in Clark's favor.

With 331 Career Win Shares (CWS) Clark ranks thirteenth among first basemen, ahead of seven Hall of Famers. He was a fierce competitor who batted over .300 10 times, retiring with a .303 average. A six-time All-Star, he led the league in RBI, runs, walks, slugging and total bases one season each. Although he wasn't a slugger, he had power, clubbing 284 home runs with a high of 35 in 1987. Clark was also an excellent fielder, leading NL first basemen in 1991, but won just one Gold Glove because he was always overshadowed by players such as Keith Hernandez, Mark Grace and Don Mattingly. He was widely admired for having one of the sweetest swings in baseball.

Clark, who was the second overall pick in the 1985 amateur draft, seemed destined for stardom after connecting for a home run in his first at-bat against Nolan Ryan in 1986. He was named MVP of the 1989 NLCS for the Giants after batting .650 against the Cubs.

Joe Adcock was a great two-way player who gets honorable mention at first. He retired with the third-best fielding percentage in history for a first baseman, .994, although he was known more for his slugging. Adcock blasted 336 home runs over 17 seasons and drove in 1,122 runs, making one All-Star team. Teaming up with Hank Aaron and Eddie Mathews, he won a World Series with the Milwaukee Braves in 1957. Adcock was the first player to accumulate 18 total bases in one game. Against the Brooklyn Dodgers on July 7, 1954, he hit four home runs and a double. Shawn Green surpassed his feat with 19 total bases in 2002.

Odell Hale emerged as the best candidate at second base. Nicknamed "Bad News," Hale played nearly as many games at third during his career. He took over as the starting second baseman for the Indians in 1934, batting .302 with 101 RBI. The next season he started at third but with nearly the same results — a .304 average with 101 RBI. Hale combined with Earl Averill and Hal Trosky in 1936 to form a powerful trio, but the Indians still finished third. Hale batted .316 that season with 196 hits, 126 runs and 50 doubles (third-best in league).

Another second baseman from Louisiana, Connie Ryan, played 12 seasons but batted just .248. His best year was 1944 when he batted .295 for the Boston Braves and made his only All-Star team.

The third base position came down to two highly regarded Negro Leagues players: Ollie Marcelle and Dave Malarcher. Nicknamed "Ghost," Marcelle was a marvelous defensive player at the hot corner. Think Brooks Robinson with significantly more quickness and a slightly stronger arm. "He made some of the greatest stops you've ever seen," said Scrip Lee, who played with Marcelle on three championship teams. In a poll conducted by the *Pittsburgh Courier* in 1952 Marcelle was voted the first-team third baseman on the All-Time Negro Leagues All-Star Team, ahead of Hall of Famer Judy Johnson. In fact, when the two played together in Cuba Johnson always switched to second base to make way for the superior defender.

A fiery competitor, Marcelle once hit Oscar Charleston on the head with a bat during a game, and he had frequent run-ins with opponents, umpires and teammates. He was a Cuban League batting champion and was credited with a .293 Negro Leagues average by a Hall of Fame study.

"Gentleman Dave" Malarcher was not in Marcelle's class as a fielder but was certainly less temperamental. The switch-hitting Marcelle was a pretty good all-around player with great speed and bat control, playing from 1916 to 1934, primarily with the Chicago American Giants. He helped spark the American Giants to league championships in the first three seasons of the Negro National League, although his batting was up and down. Malarcher went on to become a successful player-manager, guiding the American Giants to titles in 1926, 1927 and 1933, losing in the playoffs two other seasons.

Wayne Causey emerged as the top selection at shortstop. Causey played from 1955 to 1968, batting .252. He played 307 games at second and 268 games at third in addition to 406 games at short. Causey's best seasons were 1963 and 1964 when he batted .280 and .281, earning MVP votes both years. Also considered was George Strickland, who played on the 1954 Indians team that set a record with 111 wins. Strickland was known for his defense at short, leading the AL in double plays in 1953 and in fielding in 1955. He shares the record for most double plays by a shortstop in a game with five, a feat he accomplished in 1952.

Louisiana has produced some great outfielders. In addition to Hall of Famers Ott and Brown, three other Louisiana-born outfielders put up numbers comparable to outfielders who are enshrined in Cooperstown: Rusty Staub, Reggie Smith and Albert Belle.

Ott was only 16 years old when he showed up for a tryout with Giants manager John McGraw in 1926. It didn't take him long to impress. As McGraw remarked later to a sportswriter, "That kid is remarkable. He's got the most natural swing I've seen in years. This lad is going to be one of the greatest left-handed hitters the National League has seen."

McGraw's statement certainly proved to be prophetic. Ott was starting in the outfield by 1928 and the next year he had about as good a season as a 20-year-old player has ever had — 42 home runs, 151 RBI, .328 average and .449 OBP. New York had a new star to cheer. Ott became adept at taking advantage of the short right-field porch at the Polo Grounds, and he still holds the record for most home runs in one ballpark with 323.

He led the National League in homers and walks six times, OBP four times, runs twice and RBI once. He went on to hit 511 home runs over his 22-season career with the Giants, which was the National League record at the time. Ott was named to 11 consecutive All-Star teams but never won the MVP because his teams often fell short of the playoffs. He played in three World Series, batting .389 as the Giants won the title in 1933. Ott's 528 Career Win Shares ranks third among right fielders and 10th all-time.

Ott was inducted into the Hall of Fame in 1951. Seven years later, the much-beloved and admired Giants star died tragically at the age of 49 from injuries suffered in a car accident. Teammate Fred Lindstrom remembered him this way: "My first impression of Mel was that he couldn't make the grade on account of his heavy, fat legs. But through constant play his legs tapered and he became, I think, about the greatest ballplayer we've ever seen."

Brown was one of the most feared sluggers in the Negro Leagues, combining with Josh Gibson to lead the Kansas City Monarchs to six pennants between 1937 and 1946. Nicknamed "Home Run" for his slugging feats, Brown reportedly once hit a home run on a pitch that bounced. The gifted but somewhat lazy player swung for the fences on every at-bat, following the lead of Bullet Joe Rogan by wielding a massive 40-ounce bat. He batted .351 over a career that lasted from 1935–58, making eight East-West All-Star appearances for the Monarchs. Brown also won three batting and home run titles and two Triple Crowns playing in the Puerto Rican Winter League, where he was known as "Ese Hombre" (That Man).

Shortly after Jackie Robinson paved the way for

African American players by breaking the color barrier, Brown was signed by Bill Veeck, owner of the St. Louis Browns. He was rushed to the majors, where he had trouble adjusting to the hostile environment as much as the level of play. Brown was released after batting just .179 in 21 games, although he managed to get noticed with one historic play. He hit an inside-the-park home run on August 13, 1947, off Hal Newhouser to become the first African American to homer in an American League game. He would not return to the majors, although he did play five more successful seasons in the minors.

Determining the third outfielder went hand in hand with deciding who ended up as designated hitter, with three players entering into the discussion: Smith, Staub and Belle. Staub had the inside track at designated hitter because he played the most games there, 477 compared to 222 for Belle. Statistical rankings of outfielders always show Smith and Staub fairly close together for their career batting production, but Smith was a much better fielder and overall player so he is a logical choice for the outfield spot. Belle was an intimidating slugger who was also a first-class jerk, so it's nice to run out of starting spots for him.

Smith was vastly underrated during and after his 17-year career. The switch-hitter produced 2,020 hits and 314 home runs with a .287 average, retiring with a .366 OBP and 137 OPS+. In 1971 he finished seventeenth in MVP voting despite placing first in total bases, extra-base hits and doubles; second in runs created; third in RBI and fourth in homers and hits. The seven-time All-Star won one Gold Glove and was runner-up for Rookie of the Year in 1967. He was an above-average fielder with a terrific throwing arm. He played in four World Series, hitting three home runs as part of a losing effort in 1977 but winning with the Dodgers in 1981.

With 326 Career Win Shares, Smith falls just below Staub, who accumulated 354 Career Win Shares—good for fourteenth place among all right fielders. Interestingly, Staub and Smith were almost polar opposites on union issues. Smith was one of the most outspoken critics of Marvin Miller's efforts to forge a strong players' union in the 1970s, while Staub was a stridently pro-union activist and constant irritant to management.

After one year in the minors, Staub made his debut for the Houston Colt 45's a week after his nineteenth birthday in 1963. He stuck around for 23 seasons and retired after playing in 2,951 games, which at the time was seventh-best in baseball history. He now ranks twelfth in that category. In Montreal, he quickly became a crowd favorite and was called "Le Grande Orange" in reference to his hair color. In the late '60s he became one of the first players to wear two batting gloves, a practice now followed by most major leaguers.

Staub was a productive hitter long enough to collect 2,716 hits, which places him 59th on the all-time list entering the 2012 season. Here are some of the Hall of Fame outfielders who have fewer career hits than Staub: Ted Williams, Willie Stargell, Joe DiMaggio, Mickey Mantle, Reggie Jackson, Richie Ashburn, Billy Williams, Max Carey, Harry Heilmann and Joe Medwick. We could go on for a bit because there are 44 of them. It is easier to list all the eligible outfielders not in the Hall of Fame who have more hits than Staub, because there are only three: Harold Baines, Vada Pinson and Al Oliver.

Here is another interesting stat about Staub—he is the only player to get more than 500 hits with four different teams: Houston, Montreal, Detroit and the Mets. Roberto Alomar is the only player even close—he fell just short with 497 hits with San Diego and 496 with Baltimore while going over 500 with Cleveland and Toronto.

Staub batted over .300 five times, led the league in doubles once and was named to six All-Star teams. One of his best seasons came in 1978, when he set a career high with 121 RBI (second in the AL), hit 24 homers and finished fifth in balloting for the MVP Award. Only 42 players in baseball history have gotten on base more often than Staub, who surprisingly ranks ahead of such players as Hornsby, Raines, Gwynn, Lajoie, Brock and Alomar in that category.

Toward the end of his career Staub turned into a valuable weapon as a pinch-hitter for the Mets. Seventy-four of his 99 career pinch-hits came in his last five seasons with the Mets. In 1983 he tied two National League records with eight consecutive pinch-hits and 25 pinch-hit RBI for the season.

It's safe to say Albert Belle has some anger management issues. The only all-time team he will make is the all-time surly team. Forced to retire at 34 due to a degenerative hip condition, Belle still managed to slug 381 home runs in essentially 10 seasons. After driving in 95 runs his rookie season, he knocked in at least 100 in each of his last nine seasons with a high of 152. He led the league in RBI three times; in homers, doubles and runs once; in total bases three times and slugging twice. His career OPS+ is 143, which beats Reggie Jackson, Harmon Killebrew, Eddie Mathews and Mike Piazza, to name a few. A five-time Silver Slugger selection, he finished in the top three of the MVP voting three times and made five All-Star teams. He homered in his last at-bat in 2000, and baseball is better without him around.

Looking at the top-winning pitchers from Louisiana, six of the top eight are lefties. Three rose to the top when deciding on the best lefty from the state: Yankees greats Ron Guidry and Andy Pettitte, along with former phenom Vida Blue.

Called up by the A's at the end of the 1970 season, all Blue did was pitch a one-hit shutout and a no-hitter. He was only 21 and just getting started. The next year he had one of the best seasons by a lefty in baseball history. He lost the season opener for the A's on April 5 and then didn't lose again until May 28, by which time he had 10 wins. Blue was 17–3 going into the All-Star game, which he won for the American League. He ended up 24–8 and led the league with a 1.84 ERA, eight shutouts and 0.95 WHIP, while finishing second with 301 strikeouts. He allowed just 209 hits in 312 innings, an eye-popping average of 6 hits per 9 innings. His other-worldly season was rewarded with the Cy Young and MVP awards.

After a season like that, Blue felt compelled to write a book about his life. Here's how he explained the secret to pitching success in his book *Vida: His Own Story:* "It's easy, man. I just take the ball and throw. Hard! It's a God-given talent. No one can teach it to you. They either hit it or they don't. They haven't been hitting it, that's all. No sweat!"

Pitching seemed simple to him at the time, but Blue would not enjoy quite as much success the rest of his career, partly because he battled drug addiction. Although he did win 20 games two more times and make five more All-Star teams, his next highest strikeout total for a season was 189. His career record ended up 209-161 with a 3.27 ERA — pretty good numbers, but definitely not the next Sandy Koufax.

Despite his early success with the A's, Blue found himself a pawn in owner Charlie Finley's mad shell game. Finley tried to sell Blue to the Yankees as part of a fire sale in 1976, but Commissioner Bowie Kuhn voided the deal. So Charlie O. turned around and tried to sell Blue to the Reds in 1977, but Kuhn again blocked the deal. Finley finally came up with a deal Kuhn could sign off on when he shipped Blue to the Giants in 1978 for seven players, none of whom had an impact with the A's.

Guidry wasn't big in stature — standing about 5-foot-11 and weighing 165 pounds — but he could bring the heat, which is where he got the nickname "Louisiana Lightning." He spent his entire 14-year career with the Yankees.

Blue's 1971 season was pretty spectacular, but Guidry might have had an even better year in 1978. Furthermore, Guidry's .893 winning percentage is the fourth-highest ever recorded by a starting pitcher in one season (behind Johnny Allen, Greg Maddux and Randy Johnson).

Guidry was never really viewed as a strikeout pitcher until June 17, 1978, the day he blew away 18 Angels to set a team record for strikeouts that still stands. Guidry would go on to win the Cy Young Award in 1978, but he finished second in the MVP race to Jim Rice despite the fact the Yankees won the division by beating the Red Sox in a one-game playoff. He was the undisputed staff ace who helped the Yankees win their second straight World Series title that year, winning two games in the playoffs while only giving up two runs.

Teammate Willie Randolph had this to say about Guidry: "I've always said Ron Guidry, pound for pound, was the fiercest competitor I ever played with. Nobody wanted to give him a chance when he first came up. Too skinny, too small, they all thought. They couldn't see what he had in his heart. He had a big one and a lot of determination."

Guidry came back and won the ERA crown again in 1979, although his ERA was more than a run higher. He would win at least 20 games in two more seasons: 1983 (when he also led in complete games) and 1985. He made four All-Star teams and used his cat-like reflexes to win five Gold Gloves.

It's not hard to conjure up an image of Andy Pettitte on the mound, cap tucked down tight to all but cover up his intense eyes, a fierce scowl radiating from his baby face. You knew he was dialed in, especially if a playoff game hung in the balance. He is one of the greatest postseason pitchers in baseball history, as evidenced by his record 19 postseason victories. He never dominated like Bob Gibson in the playoffs, but he always found a way to reach down deep and muster whatever strength he had to put his team in position to win. The best example of that was Game 5 of the 1996 World Series, when a 24-year-old Pettitte shut out the Braves on five hits for 8⅓ innings while outdueling John Smoltz for a 1-0 win.

Of course, it sure helps to have the best closer ever to finish what you start. Pettitte pitched zero complete games in the postseason, which highlights the indispensable role played by Mariano Rivera. Still, Pettitte won more games between 2000 and 2009 than anyone else in the major leagues — 148. In addition to possessing one of the best pickoff moves ever, he's also the only pitcher in baseball history to pitch 16 seasons without posting a losing record, a streak that remained intact when he decided to retire before the 2011 season.

If Pettitte had not run off to Houston for three seasons he would have passed Whitey Ford for most pitching wins as a Yankee — 236. Pettitte compiled 240 career wins with 203 of them coming with the Yankees. His best season came in 1996, when he led the league with 21 wins and finished second in the Cy Young Award voting. The only other year he won 20 games was 2003, his last season with the Yanks before jumping to the Astros as a free agent. Pettitte was named to three All-Star teams but never produced dominant numbers, allowing more than one hit per inning for his career and posting a 3.88 ERA.

The Yankees 2009 rotation was supposed to be anchored by high-priced free-agent acquisitions CC Sabathia and A.J. Burnett, but it was Pettitte who went 4-0 in the postseason, winning the clinching game in all three series. He will be linked forever with teammates Jeter, Posada and Rivera, the "Core Four" who won five championship rings as teammates. Pettitte probably did not hang around long enough to generate the career stats necessary to get elected to the Hall of Fame, particularly since he admitted taking human growth hormone on several occasions to speed his recovery from injury. However, his postseason accomplishments alone make him worthy of strong consideration, and it's enough to earn him the spot on the All-Time Louisiana team.

"I feel like if you're a Hall of Famer the game shouldn't be so difficult," Pettitte said in an interview with the *New York Daily News.* "I look at Derek and Mo, those guys are Hall of Famers and it's a joke how easy they make the game look. It's cool to hear it, but I'd just like to be remembered as a guy who took the ball no matter what."

Two other notable Louisiana-born lefties were Chuck Finley and Mel Parnell. Finley was a five-time All-Star who won 200 games and finished second in ERA twice. However, his career high was 18 wins and he was never a dominant starter. Parnell went 25–7 for the Red Sox in 1949 and won 21 games in 1953. He won only 123 games but had a .621 winning percentage.

Selecting the All-Time Louisiana lefty ultimately came down to consistency and postseason success. Finley never won 20 games, posted five seasons with a losing record and collected just one postseason win. Blue had three years with a losing record, four more with a .500 mark and also recorded only one postseason win. Guidry had five losing seasons and won five postseason games with two World Series titles. By comparison, Pettitte appeared in eight World Series, winning five championship rings. Not only does he hold the record for playoff victories, he is also the all-time leader in postseason starts and innings pitched. Sounds like a winner to us.

For right-handed starter, Team Louisiana can tap Hall of Famer Lyons, who was born in Lake Charles and made it to the majors in 1923 without a stop first in the minors. With a 260–230 record Lyons has one of the lowest winning percentages of any pitcher in the Hall, mainly because he spent his entire career with a White Sox franchise that failed to reach the postseason during his 21-year tenure. He won 20 games three times and led the league in wins, complete games, shutouts and innings twice. Near the end of his career, he mainly pitched on Sundays to draw crowds, leading to his nickname "Sunday Teddy." Spot starting seemed to agree with the aging pitcher, as he led the league with a 2.10 ERA at the age of 41 in 1942.

A closer examination of his pitching statistics reveals Lyons to be a borderline Hall of Famer. He gave up 9.7 hits per 9 innings yet struck out only 2.3 batters per 9 innings, as he relied on his guile more than dominant stuff. He posted just three seasons with a sub-3.00 ERA, leading to a high career ERA of 3.67, which is the second-highest in the Hall. His ERA+ of 118 places him 150th on the career rankings, although that equals Bert Blyleven and Tom Glavine and ranks ahead of Gaylord Perry, Steve Carlton and Phil Niekro. Joe McCarthy said if Lyons had pitched for the Yankees he would have won over 400 games.

Another excellent righty starter was Edward "Peanuts" Davis, who combined a blazing fastball with a baffling assortment of knuckleballs to dominate Negro Leagues batters during the 1940s. Davis, who put as much effort into entertaining fans as striking out batters, once outpitched the great Satchel Paige three times in a span of weeks. In 1946 he reportedly pitched all 20 innings of a marathon game against Gentry Jessup and the Chicago American Giants that ended in a 3–3 tie.

J. R. Richard was on his way to baseball glory when the cruel hands of fate intervened. With his 6-foot-8 frame towering over batters, the right-handed Richard seemingly overpowered batters before he even released his wicked fastball. Richard won 20 games in 1976 but was hurt by a league-high 151 walks. His strikeout totals kept going up — NL highs of 303 in 1978 and 313 in 1979 — while his walk totals were going down. He had finally harnessed his control, the only thing holding him back from superstardom, when he was stricken by a stroke after appearing in his first All-Star game in 1980. He would never pitch again in the majors.

Another Astros righty marked by tragedy was Don Wilson, who pitched a no-hitter as a rookie in 1967, tied a record with 18 strikeouts in 1969 and then added a second no-hitter on May 1, 1969, a day after Jim Maloney had no-hit the Astros. Wilson came close to a third no-hitter in September 1974, but he was pulled from the game after pitching eight no-hit innings. Four months later the 29-year-old Wilson was found dead in his garage after suffering carbon monoxide poisoning. His five-year-old son also perished from the incident, which was ruled an accident despite the fact Wilson's wife was unable to explain how she suffered a fractured jaw.

Lee Smith operated like a deadly assassin in the bullpen over his 18-year career, becoming one of the first relievers to master the one-inning shutdown in the ninth inning. A huge, intimidating presence on the mound, the 6-foot-5 Smith moved around a lot, playing for eight different teams, with his longest tenure being eight years with the Cubs. Relying on an overpowering fastball, he struck out nearly one batter per inning over his career. When he retired in 1997 he held the all-time record for saves with 478 and his 47 saves in 1991 set a National League record. Smith led the league in saves four times, converting 82 percent of his career chances for saves. He was named to seven All-Star teams (for four different teams) and won the Rolaids Relief Award three times.

Hall of Fame voters have so far been unimpressed with his career, perhaps because Smith pitched just 1,289 career innings, had a 71–92 record and was shelled in his only two postseason series. His vote totals in his first nine years of eligibility have ranged from 36 percent to a high of 47 percent in 2010. Smith has significantly more saves than any of the five relievers in the Hall, and he still has six more years of eligibility to sway voters.

Other notable relievers from Louisiana include Jonathan Papelbon, B.J. Ryan, Norm Charlton and Eddie Fisher. Papelbon has averaged 37 saves and 10.8 K/9IP during his six seasons as the Red Sox closer, making four All-Star teams. Ryan posted three seasons with over 30 saves and made two All-Star teams before arm injuries derailed his career. He is the second known pitcher to win a game without throwing a pitch. On May 1, 2003, Ryan entered the game in the bottom of the seventh inning and immediately picked off the runner on first for the final out of the inning. The Orioles went on to take the lead and hold on, with Ryan receiving an unusual win.

Charlton was one of the "Nasty Boys" in the Reds bullpen with Rob Dibble and Randy Myers. He won

12 games starting and relieving for the Reds in 1990, then allowed only one earned run in four appearances during the NLCS to help the team advance to and win and World Series. Charlton took over as Reds closer in 1992, saving 26 games and making his only All-Star team. He retired with 97 career saves in 568 relief appearances. Fisher, a Shreveport native, finished fourth in the AL MVP voting in 1965 after saving 24 games and leading the league in games and WHIP. He went 15–7 with a 2.40 ERA that year, allowing just 118 hits in 165 innings for the White Sox.

The best choice for manager is Negro Leagues star Dave Malarcher, who replaced the legendary Rube Foster as manager of the Chicago American Giants in 1926. Malarcher quickly demonstrated that he had picked up the finer points of baseball strategy from Foster as well as from his first manager, C.I. Taylor. He led the American Giants to World Series championships in his first two seasons and then captured the second-half title in 1928. Malarcher would win Negro Southern League titles with the American Giants in 1932 and 1933. Alex Radcliffe called him the best manager he ever saw, citing his intelligence and understanding.

Eddie Dyer was hired to skipper the St. Louis Cardinals for the 1946 season. With the war over and three of his players jumping to the Mexican League, Dyer had his hands full trying to mold a champion out of a thrown-together roster. He was named Manager of the Year after guiding the Cards to a World Series championship his first year at the helm, besting the Red Sox in Ted Williams' only Series appearance. Dyer would finish in second place with the Cards the next three seasons and then was dismissed after a disappointing fifth place finish in 1950. Dyer finished above .500 every season, ending with a 446–325 career mark.

Ott spent his last six seasons as player-manager for the Giants, which proved to be the wrong role for a reserved gentleman. A third-place finish his first year, 1942, was the best he could muster and he was let go during the 1948 season after winning just 47 percent of his games.

MAINE

*Names in **bold** represent Major League selections by position, followed by honorable mentions. City of birth is in parentheses.*

Catcher — **Bill Carrigan (Lewiston)**. Also: Clyde Sukeforth (Washington)
First Base — **Del Bissonette (Winthrop)**. Also: Sid Farrar (Paris Hill)
Second Base — **Tom Downey (Lewiston)**
Third Base — **Harry Lord (Porter)**
Shortstop — **Freddy Parent (Biddeford)**. Also: Candy Nelson (Portland); George Magoon (St. Albans)
Outfield — **George Gore (Saccarappa)**
Outfield — **Chet Chadbourne (Parkman)**
Outfield — **Billy Maloney (Lewiston)**. Also: Rip Cannell (South Bridgton); Louis Sockalexis (Indian Island)
Right Handed Starter — **Bill Swift (Portland)**. Also: Carl Willey (Cherryfield)
Left Handed Starter — **Kid Madden (Portland)**. Also: Irv Young (Columbia Falls)
Relief Pitcher — **Bob Stanley (Portland)**. Also: Pete Ladd (Portland); Bert Roberge (Lewiston); Don Brennan (Augusta)
Manager — **Bill Carrigan (Lewiston)**

The Names

Best Nickname: George "Piano Legs" Gore
Other Nicknames: Frank "Ham" Allen; Roland "Cuke" Barrows; Clarence "Climax" Blethen; Virgin "Rip" Cannell; Bill "Rough" Carrigan; Chet "Pop" Chadbourne; George "Chummy" Gray; Frederick "Happy" Iott; Raymond "Lanky" Jordan; Michael "Kid" Madden; George "Topsy" Magoon; Willard "Grasshopper" Mains; Bill "Dasher" Murray; John "Candy" Nelson; Freddy "The Flying Frenchman" Parent; Irv "Stubby" Ray; Louis "Chief" Sockalexis; Bob "Stanley Steamer"; Edward "Live Oak" Taylor; Ledell "Cannonball" Titcomb; Walter "Pop" Williams; George "Squanto" Wilson; Irv "Cy the Second" Young
Most Unusual Name: Wirt Virgin Cannell; Ledell Titcomb

All-Time Leaders

Games: Freddy Parent, 1327
Hits: George Gore, 1612
Batting Average: Del Bissonette, .305
Home Runs: Del Bissonette, 66
RBI: George Gore, 618
Stolen Bases: Harry Lord, 206
Wins: Bob Stanley, 115
Strikeouts: Bill Swift, 767
Saves: Bob Stanley, 132
Future Star: Mark Rogers (Brunswick)
Best Player: George Gore

Historic Baseball Place

Hadlock Field in Portland — Opened in 1994 as the home of the Portland Sea Dogs, a Red Sox affiliate of the Eastern League. The Maine Monster in left field is a replica of Fenway Park's Green Monster.

Notable Achievements

Bob Stanley is the only Maine-born player to play in the All-Star Game, representing the Red Sox in 1979 and 1983.

Freddy Parent was involved in six no-hitters between 1904 and 1910 and would have been in seven had he not broken one up and gotten his team's only hit.

George Gore holds the record for most stolen bases in a game. He had seven stolen bases on June 25, 1881, a mark later matched by Billy Hamilton in 1894.

Maine Natives Carve Out Role in Baseball History

Maine has only sent 75 players to the major leagues, beginning with Candy Nelson in 1872, but several have played a prominent role in baseball history.

Charlie Waitt, who was born in Hallowell, was one of the first players to wear a glove when he used a flesh-colored, unpadded glove in 1875.

Clyde Sukeforth was the manager of the Brooklyn Dodgers when Jackie Robinson played his first game in 1947. He was a fill-in manager for the suspended Leo Durocher and finished his managerial career undefeated at 2–0.

Louis "Chief" Sockalexis was the first full-blooded Native American to appear in the majors when he debuted for the Cleveland Spiders in 1897. Blessed with an unmatched combination of speed, slugging ability and powerful arm, Sockalexis found himself both cheered and jeered for his feats on the field. However, he was unable to control a drinking problem and soon drank himself out of the league, finishing with a .313 lifetime average in 94 games.

Maine first fielded a professional team with a Portland-based team in the Eastern New England League in 1884. Portland maintained a club in the New England League, off and on, until 1949, under names such as Phenoms, Blue Sox, Duffs, Eskimos, Mariners, Gulls and Pilots.

That was it for minor league baseball in Portland until Hadlock Field was opened in 1994, with the Portland Sea Dogs starting play in the Double-A Eastern League. Adrian Gonzalez, Kevin Youkilis, Hanley Ramirez, Jon Lester and Jacoby Ellsbury are among the players who have played their home games at Hadlock.

Some of Maine's best players through the years share Portland as their birthplace including Bob Stanley, Bill Swift and Kid Madden. Two Portland-born players were active in 2011: Charlie Furbush and Tim Stauffer. Furbush was a standout at South Portland High School and then at St. Joseph's College of Maine, followed by a strong stint in the Cape Cod League. He made his major league debut for the Tigers on May 23, 2011, and then found himself traded to the Mariners two months later.

Professional baseball has entertained fans in other Maine cities through the years such as Auburn, Augusta, Bangor, Belfast, Biddeford, Calais, Lewiston, Pine Tree, Rockland and Waterville. The Bangor Millionaires fielded teams from 1894–97, long before there were any baseball-playing millionaires.

The Augusta Millionaires were a semipro team that began play in the early 1920s. Future major leaguers such as Harry Agganis, Sukeforth and Augusta native Don Brennan got their start with the Millionaires, who attracted big crowds to Capitol Park.

If one takes a closer look at the members of the All-Time Maine Team, a pattern emerges — most played during or before the Deadball Era. In fact, Ron Tingley is the only Maine-born player in the last half-century to collect more than 100 career hits — he had 110 hits with a .195 average when his career ended in 1995. He didn't make the cut.

All-Time Maine Selections

When you consider the 75 Maine-born players for their career accomplishments, just a few jump out at you. One is George Gore, who was nicknamed "Piano Legs" due to his large calves. Not only did he become the first player to exceed 100 walks in a season when he got 102 free passes in 1886, Gore did it in a 124-game season. Keep in mind that a walk back then required seven balls, not four, so he obviously had a good eye and patience at the plate. The center fielder led the league in walks three times, with ever-increasing totals of 29, 61 and 102.

Tons of statistical oddities can be found from play in the 1880s. For example, Gore scored 150 runs one season but didn't lead the league that year. However, he did lead the league with run totals of 86 and 99. He also led the league in slugging percentage and OPS in 1880 despite hitting just two homers and two triples. Gore is also one of only three players to have more runs scored (1,327) than games played (1,310) during his career.

The Saccarappa native got his professional start with Fall River in the New England League in 1877. He got the attention of major league teams with a standout season the next year with the New Bedford Whalers, eventually signing with the Chicago White Stockings.

Gore batted over .300 eight times, finishing his 14-season career with a .301 average. His .360 average led the league in 1880 — the league average was .245 — and he finished in the top seven in on-base percentage 10 times. In 1885 he became the first player to record five extra-base hits in a game.

Gore maintained an active social life, marked by heaving drinking, which occasionally interfered with his ability to perform on the field. Still, he contributed enough to help lead his team to seven league championships and four World Series. The Series was viewed as an exhibition back in those days, which is why his 1885 Chicago White Stockings team played to a 3–3–1 Series tie with the St. Louis Browns. Or perhaps they were playing under the Bud Selig rules of engagement and just ran out of pitchers.

Since he is Maine's all-time leader in runs, doubles,

triples, hits, at-bats and RBI, Gore is a logical choice as the state's best player ever. He is joined in the outfield by Billy Maloney, who collected 585 hits playing for five teams between 1901 and 1908. Maloney tied Art Devlin for the league lead with 59 stolen bases in 1905.

The third Maine outfielder is Chet Chadbourne, who accumulated 3,561 hits during his professional baseball career. It should be pointed out that 3,216 of them came from 20 minor league seasons, including seven seasons of more than 200 hits. Most of Chadbourne's 345 major league hits came while playing for the Kansas City Packers during the two seasons of the Federal League (1914–1915).

Maine's all-time catcher is Bill Carrigan, who played on three World Series champions with the Red Sox. He finished eighth in batting in 1909 with a career-high .296 average and led AL catchers in fielding percentage twice and putouts once. The scrappy Carrigan, who was nicknamed "Rough" for his tenacious style of play behind the plate, spent his entire 10-year career with the Red Sox, finishing with 506 hits. He caught three no-hitters — Joe Wood in 1911 and Rube Foster and Dutch Leonard in 1916 — and was Babe Ruth's battery mate when he made his pitching debut on July 11, 1914.

Carrigan also gets the nod as the All-Time-Maine manager, because the last two Sox titles came while he was player-manager. It took 91 years for the next Red Sox manager to win two championships — Terry Francona. The Lewiston native was inducted into the Boston Red Sox Hall of Fame in 2004.

In retrospect, Carrigan probably regretted walking away from the team after the 1916 title. He had just won two consecutive World Series, he had Babe Ruth on his team (who he used solely as a pitcher) and yet Carrigan retired from playing and managing at age 32. When he returned to the team 11 years later, he didn't have Babe Ruth on his team and he watched the Red Sox finish last three straight years while Ruth's Yankees were dominating the league. Ironically, Ruth would call him the best manager he ever had.

Earning honorable mention at catcher is Cyde Sukeforth, who batted .264 over 10 seasons but was never a full-time starter. He batted .354 in 237 at-bats in 1929, but his average went down sharply as his at-bats went up the next two years. "Sukey's" major league career seemed to end in 1934, although he hung around to play in the minors through 1939. However, he returned during the war to play in 18 games for the Dodgers in 1945.

Our first baseman is Del Bissonette, a lefty batter with a .305 average in a career cut short by injury and illness. He hit .320 with 25 homers and 106 RBI as a 28-year-old rookie. In fact, he demonstrated enough batting prowess that less than one month into his big-league career Giants manager John McGraw showed him the ultimate respect — he walked him with the bases loaded in the ninth inning. Two years later Bissonette batted .336 with 16 homers and 113 RBI, but 1931 would be his last season in the majors as a regular

player. He would play the next six years in the minors, eventually assuming a player-manager role until making a final pinch-hit appearance in 1949.

A case could also be made for Sid Farrar at first, as he collected 905 hits over eight seasons. However, Farrar was never a standout player like Bissonette was his first few seasons, and his career average was a pedestrian .253 with an OPS+ of 90.

At second base we had to choose between two players with nearly identical records: Tom Downey and George Magoon. Both played more games at short than second and both had just one season where they were a regular at second. Downey edged Magoon in games at second (184 vs. 182), career hits (520 vs. 439) and average (.240 vs. .239). Downey played 129 games at second base in 1914, batting .218, and he gets the final nod.

Third base is in the capable hands of Harry Lord, who was Carrigan's teammate on the Red Sox for several seasons. He batted .320 with 180 hits (including 18 triples) and 103 runs for the White Sox in 1911, but later jumped to Buffalo in the Federal League after a salary dispute with owner Charlie Comiskey. Lord was a player-manager for that team, but found himself blacklisted from the majors after the renegade league folded. He wound up with 1,026 hits in the big leagues and a .277 average.

Lord's 206 stolen bases are officially the most in Maine history, but Gore's stolen base total is undoubtedly higher. Stolen bases were not tracked until 1886, so Gore's 170 official steals came from just seven of his 14 seasons. Keep in mind that the modern steal rules were not adopted until 1898, so quite a few of Gore's steals probably resulted from him advancing a base on a hit.

Our shortstop, Freddy Parent, played from 1899–1911 and was a real sparkplug for some fine Red Sox teams. An excellent fielder with outstanding range and a skilled base runner, Parent held his own at the plate, batting .262 with 1,306 hits over 12 seasons. He batted .306 with 158 hits during his rookie campaign and followed that up with a .304 average in 1903 for a Red Sox team that would win the first official World Series. Parent did his part by scoring eight runs in the Series to help the Sox defeat the Pirates. A series of beanings later in his career seemed to greatly impact his effectiveness as a batter and made him an early proponent of batting helmets.

Portland native Candy Nelson had a 13-year career in the nineteenth century, playing all positions but mainly shortstop. He led the American Association in walks in 1884–85 and finished with 833 career hits playing for nine teams in three leagues.

Big things were expected of Bill Swift of Portland, who was drafted by the Mariners with the second overall pick in the first round of the 1984 amateur draft. He went on to play for the U.S. Olympic team that year and made it to the big leagues the next season after just seven minor league games. His first four seasons produced mixed results before a more defined role out of the bullpen led to two breakout years. Then he got traded to the Giants and really blossomed.

Swift led the National League with a 2.08 ERA as a spot starter for the Giants in 1992. The next year he was even better as a full-time starter, going 21–8 with a 2.82 ERA and 157 strikeouts, which was good enough for second place in the Cy Young Award voting. Swift's high strikeout total in 1993 is clearly an anomaly, as he posted a weak ratio of 4.3 strikeouts per 9 innings over his career. In fact, his next highest strikeout total out of 13 seasons was 77. His final five seasons were subpar, but a career mark of 94–78 with a 3.95 ERA is certainly respectable.

Another righty, Carl Willey of Cherryfield, led the league with four shutouts as a rookie for the Milwaukee Braves in 1958. He never lived up to his initial promise, finishing with a 38–58 career record.

Kid Madden, another nineteenth-century player, is the best choice for lefty starter. He won just 54 games over five seasons but did win 21 games with three shutouts his rookie season. Madden was a decent batter who appeared in 13 games in the field.

A case could be made for Bob Stanley as Maine's all-time best player, but he will have to settle for being selected as the top reliever. A two-time All-Star, first as a starter and then as a reliever, Stanley won 115 games and recorded 132 saves over a 13-season career, all with the Red Sox. He finished seventh in the Cy Young Award voting after going 15–2 with a 2.60 ERA in 1978, followed by 16 wins and an All-Star berth the next year. His other All-Star nod came in 1983, when he posted 33 saves in 145 relief innings.

Stanley was a dependable pitcher for the Red Sox — he still tops the club in appearances with 637 and is now second in saves behind Jonathan Papelbon. However, many Red Sox fans cannot forget it was his wild pitch in the 10th inning of Game Six of the 1986 World Series that let the Mets tie the score. On the other hand, some Sox fans remain annoyed at catcher Rich Gedman for his futile effort to stop a pitch that was not especially errant. Stanley did his job when he induced Mookie Wilson to hit a slow roller to first base for what should have been the final out of the inning, and we all know what happened next. Buckner booted the ball and the Mets went on to win the game and the Series.

Another notable reliever, Peter Ladd of Portland, collected 25 of his 39 career saves in 1983. His other career highlight was getting the final out in the 1982 AL Championship Series while pitching for the Milwaukee Brewers.

MARYLAND

*Names in **bold** represent Major League selections by position, followed by honorable mentions. Negro Leagues players are in italics. City of birth is in parentheses.*

Catcher — Babe Phelps (Odenton). Also: Bill Schroeder (Baltimore); *Joe Lewis* (Sparrows Point)

First Base — Jimmie Foxx (Sudlersville). Also: Mark Teixeira (Annapolis); Dave Foutz (Carroll County); Bob Robertson (Frostburg); Gordy Coleman (Rockville)

Second Base — Cupid Childs (Calvert Co.). Also: Buck Herzog (Baltimore); Billy Ripken (Havre de Grace); Bobby Young (Granite); Ray Morgan (Baltimore)

Third Base — Frank Baker (Trappe). Also: *Judy Johnson* (Snow Hill); Bill Werber (Berwyn); *Maurice Watkins* (Towson)

Shortstop — Cal Ripken, Jr. (Havre de Grace). Also: Bill Keister (Baltimore); *Scrappy Brown* (Baltimore)

Outfield — Babe Ruth (Baltimore)

Outfield — Al Kaline (Baltimore)

Outfield — Charlie Keller (Middletown). Also: Bill Nicholson (Chestertown); Brady Anderson (Silver Spring); *Blainey Hall* (Baltimore); Brian Jordan (Baltimore); *Bob Harvey* (St. Michaels); Dick Porter (Princess Anne); Bill Lamar (Rockville)

Designated Hitter — Harold Baines (Easton).

Right Handed Starter — Vic Willis (Cecil County). Also: Eddie Rommel (Baltimore); Bobby Mathews (Baltimore); Dave Foutz (Carroll County); Jack Taylor (Sandy Hill); Tommy Thomas (Baltimore); Moose Haas (Baltimore)

Left Handed Starter — Lefty Grove (Lonaconing). Also: Babe Ruth (Baltimore); Denny Neagle (Annapolis); Steve Barber (Takoma Park); Geoff Zahn (Baltimore); *John Stanley* (Kings County); *Slim Jones* (Baltimore)

Relief Pitcher — Steve Farr (LaPlata). Also: Jeff Nelson (Baltimore); Ray Moore (Meadows); Allen Russell (Baltimore)

Manager — Cal Ermer (Baltimore). Also: Dave Foutz (Carroll County); Ray Miller (Tacoma Park); Johnny Neun (Baltimore)

The Names

Best Nickname: Bill "Wagon Tongue" Keister

Other Nicknames: Frank "Home Run" Baker; Desmond "Desperate" Beatty; Elmore "Scrappy" Brown; Richard "Stub" Brown; Joe "Jazzbow" Buskey; Clarence "Cupid" Childs; Lewis "Buttercup" Dickerson; Uriah "Bloody Jake" Evans; "Fat Jack" Fisher; Frank "Monkey" Foreman; Dave "Scissors" Foutz; Jimmie "Double X" and "The Beast" Foxx; Robert "Lefty" Grove; James "Blainey" Hall; Stuart "Slim" Jones; Clarence "Slats" Jordan; Charlie "King Kong"

Keller; "Good Time Bill" Lamar; Joe "Sleepy" Lewis; Phil "Mr. Laffs" Linz; Raymond "Farmer" Moore; Bill "Swish" Nicholson; Babe "Blimp" Phelps; Cletus "Boots" Poffenberger; Dick "Twitches" and "Wiggles" Porter; Cal "Iron Man" Ripken; Allen "Rubberarm" Russell; George "Babe," "The Sultan of Swat" and "The Bambino" Ruth; Samuel "Skyrocket" Smith; John "Neck" Stanley; Archie "Lumbago" Stimmel; Ron "Rocky" Swoboda; "Brewery Jack" Taylor; Maurice "Skeeter" Watkins; Charles "Spider" Wilhelm

Most Unusual Name: Harry Colliflower; Hanson Horsey; Cletus Poffenberger; Dorsey Riddlemoser; Carlton Molesworth; Russell Awkard

All-Time Leaders

Games: Cal Ripken, 3001
Hits: Cal Ripken, 3184
Batting Average: Babe Ruth, .342
Home Runs: Babe Ruth, 714
RBI: Babe Ruth, 2217
Stolen Bases: Buck Herzog, 320
Wins: Lefty Grove, 300
Strikeouts: Lefty Grove, 2266
Saves: Steve Farr, 132
Future Star: Brett Cecil (Dunkirk)
Best Player: Babe Ruth

Historic Baseball Places

Babe Ruth Birthplace & Museum in Baltimore — In addition to exhibits featuring the Ruthian baseball accomplishments of America's first great sports star, the museum also shows the softer side of the Babe as a father, husband and friend. You can even see the bedroom where Ruth was born.

Ripken Stadium in Aberdeen — Opened as a Class-A affiliate of the Orioles in 2002 and still sells out every game. The adjacent Cal Sr.'s Yard is a miniature replica of Camden Yards.

Oriole Park at Camden Yards/Sports Legends Museum in Baltimore — Check out exhibits on Babe Ruth, the Negro Leagues legacy with the Baltimore Elite Giants, minor league baseball in Maryland, the Orioles Hall of Fame and the history of the Orioles franchise. Watch the Babe's famous home run in Game 3 of the 1932 World Series in The Called Shot Theatre, see artifacts from his tour in Japan with the All American All Stars and relive the accomplishments of such Orioles stars as Cal Ripken, Jr., Eddie Murray and Brooks Robinson.

Jimmie Foxx statue in Sudlersville — The hometown of Double X unveiled a life-size bronze statue of the slugger in 1997.

New Cathedral Cemetery in Baltimore—Contains the gravesites for Baltimore Oriole greats John McGraw, Ned Hanlon, Wilbert Robinson and Joe Kelley as well as pitchers Eddie Rommel and Bobby Mathews.

Municipal Stadium in Hagerstown — One of the oldest minor league ballparks still in existence, dating back to 1930. Willie Mays played his first minor league game with the Trenton Giants at Municipal Stadium in 1950, going 0-for-3 while enduring racial taunts. Bryce Harper made his pro debut with the Hagerstown Suns in 2011.

Notable Achievements

Bill Holbert (Baltimore) has the most career at-bats without hitting a home run with 2,335.

Brady Anderson holds the record for most consecutive games with a leadoff home run with four.

Al Kaline was the first player to be inducted into the Hall of Fame who had served as a designated hitter.

Syd Cohen (Baltimore) was the last man to strike out Babe Ruth while he was with the Yankees and was also the last pitcher Ruth homered off in the American League.

Harold Baines has appeared in more games as designated hitter than anyone else—1,644.

Babe Ruth's 60 home runs in 1927 accounted for 14 percent of all homers hit in the American League that year.

Bobby Mathews was the first pitcher in major league history, if the National Association is considered a major league. Mathews got the win pitching for the Fort Wayne Kekiongas on May 4, 1871, against the Cleveland Forest Citys.

Bob Robertson hit three home runs in Game 2 of the 1971 National League Championship Series.

Justin Maxwell (Olney) hit grand slam home runs the first two times he batted with the bases loaded. The first on Sept. 11, 2007, represented his first major league hit and the second, on Sept. 20, 2009, was a walk-off grand slam to help the Nationals break a streak of 150 consecutive losses when trailing after the eighth inning.

Mark Teixeira became the sixth player to reach 1,000 RBI in his first nine seasons when he passed the mark in 2011.

Baltimore Gives Birth to Ruthless Playing Style and Ruthian Feats

To describe baseball in Baltimore in the formative decade of the 1890s it's appropriate to borrow a phrase from Dickens — it was the best of times, it was the worst of times. Some of the game's greatest players and managers were not only competing at a high level and reinventing the way the game was played strategically, but they were also doing it in a ruthless, underhanded and dirty way. Everything was fair game, from tripping base runners and intentionally spiking opposing fielders to screaming profanities at the umpires. Pitching, hitting, fielding and running were joined by a fifth skill: thuggery.

The ringleaders of the shenanigans were Ned Hanlon's Orioles squad, led by the feisty John McGraw, Willie Keeler and Hughie Jennings. McGraw and

Keeler refined the hit-and-run play and the Baltimore Chop, which involved hitting downward on the ball to chop it in front of the plate, where it would bounce up high and allow the runner to reach first. While playing third base, McGraw used to grab runners by their belt to keep them from tagging up and he'd cut across the diamond going from first to third if he caught the ump looking the other way. When he wasn't cussing out umpires and teammates he was starting fist fights with opposing players or hollering at fans.

McGraw once said, "Sportsmanship and easygoing methods are all right, but it is the prospect of a hot fight that brings out the crowds."

See if you can follow along. The Baltimore Orioles were contracted from the National League in 1899, joined the American League in 1901 and then moved two years later to New York to become first the Highlanders and then (starting in 1913) the Yankees. So people who hate the Yankees should also hate the Orioles, since they spawned the Evil Empire. The current Orioles franchise started as the Milwaukee Brewers in 1901, then moved the next year to St. Louis and changed its name to the Browns. In 1954 the team moved to Baltimore and changed to the current name of Orioles. Got that?

While teams were moving in and out of Baltimore, one constant was the ability of Maryland to produce some of the greatest players to ever play the game. Generally acknowledged as the greatest player of all time, George Herman Ruth — the Bambino, the Sultan of Swat, the one and only Babe — was born above a tavern in a rough-and-tumble neighborhood of Baltimore known as Pigtown. At the age of seven, the incorrigible Ruth was dropped off at St. Mary's Industrial School for Boys, where he finally had some semblance of order in his life and where he learned to throw and hit like no one before or since.

Ruth was once quoted saying, "I swing big, with everything I've got. I hit big or miss big. I like to live as big as I can." Actually, he usually connected when he swung; he never struck out more than 93 times in a season and walked 732 times more than he struck out for his career. That's how he was able to produce a .474 career OBP, which trails only the Splendid Splinter.

Another all-time great right fielder who hailed from Baltimore was Al Kaline, whose personality and playing style were the complete opposite of the bombastic, larger-than-life Ruth. Kaline was a "bonus baby" who went straight from Baltimore's Southern High School to the major leagues at the age of 18, carving out a Hall of Fame career through sustained excellence as Detroit's "Mr. Perfection."

While white stars such as Ruth and Eddie Rommel were making a name for themselves in the majors, African American players found themselves on the outside looking in. Hopes and aspirations were first formed on the sandlot fields of Prince George's County.

Maryland is also the home state of Cletus "Boots" Poffenberger, who was an all-time great character. The Williamsport-born righty pitched in 57 games from 1937 to 1939, compiling a 16–12 record. During his rookie season, Boots came out of the bullpen on June 11 to allow just one run in 6⅔ innings to defeat Lefty Grove for his first win. A month later he pitched a five-hitter on July 11 to outduel Bob Feller 3–2. The Yankees' Frank Crosetti got him to fall for the hidden ball trick a few days later, but that was just a rookie mistake.

Boots would go on to fashion a 10–5 record that year, leading Tigers fans to believe he could be a key part of the rotation. Boots, however, was more interested in securing and consuming his next case of beer and having a good time. When he showed up at all, he was typically drunk or hung over, which caused the Tigers to hire a private investigator to tail him. The Tigers quickly dropped him, and he had more fines and suspensions than wins in his short time with the Dodgers. Boots refused to report to the Dodgers' minor league team in Montreal because he didn't think the night life there was very promising, so he didn't pitch anywhere the rest of 1939. He was doing well with the Nashville Vols — winning 26 games in 1940 — until the game in 1941 when a somewhat inebriated Poffenberger decided to chuck the baseball at the umpire for calling too many balls on him.

Poffenberger was truly an original, in action and in name. Maryland has produced some other memorable names such as Hanson Horsey, Dorsey Riddlemoser and Carlton Molesworth. It's a safe bet they all got teased a bit in their youth. At least Molesworth could go back to his high school reunion and brag that he made it to the majors as a pitcher, although he probably left out the fact that he went 0–2 with a 14.63 ERA. That's better than Riddlemoser, whose one-game career produced an ERA of 18.00 with a 4.50 WHIP, while Horsey's one major league appearance resulted in a 22.50 ERA. If you want your son to grow up to be a Hall of Fame player, don't name him Cletus, Dorsey or Hanson, especially if you have a funky last name.

Molesworth may not have done much as a major league pitcher, but he went on to a distinguished career as an outfielder and player-manager with the Birmingham Barons. He managed the Barons from 1908–22, serving as player-manager for many of those seasons and winning pennants in 1912 and 1914. Burleigh Grimes and Pie Traynor played for him on the Barons and he was in the dugout when historic Rickwood Field first opened in Birmingham in 1910. Molesworth, who accumulated 1,712 hits over 14 minor league seasons with a .298 average, is a member of the Birmingham Barons Hall of Fame.

Maryland is also the birthplace of Frank Morrissey of Baltimore, who is believed to be tied with several others as the shortest pitcher in MLB history at 5-foot-4. Nicknamed "Deacon," he went 1–3 in six appearances in 1901–02.

All-Time Maryland Selections

Let's get to the selections for the All-Time Maryland team. For catcher, we have Babe Phelps, a lefty swinger who made three All-Star teams for his bat more than his defense. Phelps batted .367 for the Brooklyn Dodgers in 1936, which was second-best in the NL that year and set a record as the highest average for a catcher. Phelps had an irrational fear of flying and used to stay up all night listening to his heart to make sure it didn't stop beating, notes Floyd Conner in *Baseball's Most Wanted*. Nicknamed "Blimp" because of his stocky build, Phelps retired in 1942 with a lifetime average of .310.

Foxx gives the All-Maryland team a stud at first, as the pride of tiny Sudlersville was a muscular, intimidating slugger in a league filled with 150-pound infielders. As Lefty Gomez once described Foxx, "He has muscles in his hair." If Babe Ruth was in a league of his own with his prodigious slugging, then Foxx resided the next level down with only Lou Gehrig to keep him company.

If Foxx had come along 10 or 15 years earlier and played during the Deadball Era, then it would have been like watching a movie with the sound off — you get the general idea, but it's not the same experience. Luckily for baseball fans, they got to see "Double X" mashing the ball like a man possessed from 1929–1941. His slugging feats included hitting the first ball over the second-tier seats in left field at Comiskey Park, one that clanged into the third deck of left field and busted up a seat at the old Yankee Stadium and another that sailed over the double-decked stands of Shibe Park and bounced off the roof of a house across the street.

Starting off as a catcher, the versatile Foxx was also tried at third before he settled into a position at first base with Connie Mack's A's. He won the Triple Crown and MVP Award in 1933 after hitting .356 with 48 homers and 163 RBI. Believe it or not, his numbers were all down from the previous season when he also was voted MVP. In 1932, he led the AL with 58 homers (third-best at the time) and 169 RBI but finished second with a .364 average. That season he scored 151 runs and produced 438 total bases, which remains the fifth-best total.

He would win a third MVP in 1938 after finishing first with a .349 average and 175 RBI (fourth-best of all time), coming in second with 50 homers while also leading the league in OBP, slugging, OPS and OPS+. He is tied with the Babe and four other players for most walk-off homers with 12. "Next to Joe DiMaggio, Foxx was the greatest player I ever saw," commented Ted Williams, who also rated Foxx the most productive right-handed hitter.

Admired throughout baseball for his even temperament as well as his slugging ability, Foxx drove in at least 100 runs in 13 straight seasons, hitting 30 or more homers in the first 12 of those years — a mark passed by Alex Rodriquez. Foxx was the second player to reach 500 career home runs, trailing only the Babe. He hit over .300 14 times (including partial seasons), leading the league twice and averaging .325 lifetime. He finished in the top three in OBP and home runs nine times, top three in slugging and OPS eight times and top three in RBI six times. He still ranks fifth in slugging (.609), sixth in OPS (1.038) and eighth in RBI (1,922).

Playing in three straight World Series with Connie Mack's Philadelphia A's (1929–31), Foxx won two titles and batted .344 with four homers in Series action. When he retired in 1945 his 534 home runs were the most by a right-handed batter in baseball history. He was elected to the Hall of Fame in 1951.

Another Maryland first baseman who is building a case for Cooperstown is Mark Teixeira. In his first nine seasons he had already amassed 314 homers and 1017 RBI, earning two All-Star game selections and three Silver Sluggers. The switch-hitting Teixeira has exceeded 30 homers and 100 RBI in every season except his rookie year and had a career OPS+ of 132 through the 2011 season. An outstanding and agile fielder who immediately improved the Yankees infield defense when he signed in 2009, Teixeira has won four Gold Gloves and was MVP runner-up in 2009.

Dave Foutz was certainly not the equal of Babe Ruth as a batter, but the nineteenth-century two-way player produced some pretty good numbers on the mound. Nicknamed "Scissors" due to his rail-thin build, Foutz was unique in that he pitched and played the field his whole career, appearing in 596 games at first, 320 in the outfield and 251 as a pitcher. In 1886 Foutz appeared in 59 games and pitched 504 innings, going 41–16 with a 2.11 ERA and 11 shutouts. That year he also played 34 games in the outfield and 11 at first, batting .280 with 59 RBI. He finished with 1,253 career hits with a .276 average, but really shone as a pitcher, winding up 147–66 with a 2.84 ERA and OPS+ of 124.

Foutz earned honorable mention in three spots: first base, right-handed starter and manager. He produced a winning record in three of the four seasons he managed the Brooklyn Grooms. His final mark was 264–257, with two fifth-place finishes.

Honors at second base go to Cupid Childs, who exhibited consistent ability to get on base and score runs playing in the 1890s. His .416 career OBP ranks 24th. A career .306 hitter, Childs led the league with 136 runs scored and a .443 OBP in 1892. He scored at least 100 runs in seven seasons and produced a .400 OBP six times and .300 average six times. In 1896 he drove in 106 runs while hitting just one home run. An above-average defensive player who led NL second basemen in putouts and assists twice, Childs stole 269 bases during his 13-year career. Playing in the 1892 Championship Series for the Cleveland Spiders, Childs batted .409 in a losing effort.

Another notable second baseman from Maryland is Buck Herzog, who played nearly as many games at short and third. Herzog played 490 at second, 473 at third and 459 at short during a career that lasted from 1908–20. A lifetime .259 hitter, he stole 320 bases (most in Maryland history) with a high of 48. Herzog was player-manager of the Reds for three years (1914–16) but never finished higher than seventh place. An excellent defensive player, he led NL third basemen in putouts and assists in 1912, led NL shortstops in putouts

Frank "Home Run" Baker led the American League in homers four straight years during the Deadball Era. He picked up his nickname after blasting two memorable home runs off future Hall of Famers Christy Mathewson and Rube Marquard during the 1911 World Series (Library of Congress, Prints & Photographs Division, LC-DIG-hec-04682).

in 1915 and led NL second basemen in range factor in 1918.

Team Maryland's third baseman is Frank "Home Run" Baker, an all-around player who led the American League in home runs four consecutive years and finished in the top 10 nine of his 13 seasons, although it was the Deadball Era so his career total of 96 home runs is not impressive. He led the league in triples with 19 in his first full season with the Philadelphia A's and also finished first in RBI two consecutive years (1912–13).

Baker batted .409 to help the A's win the 1910 World Series and then emerged as the hero of the 1911 Series. His two-run homer proved to be the decisive runs in the A's 3–1 win over the Giants in Game 2, then he came back and homered off Christy Mathewson in the ninth inning of Game 3 to tie the score and send it into extra innings. Baker singled and scored the winning run in the 11th inning, finishing the Series with a .375 average. He would win a third ring after batting .450 in the 1913 World Series, winning three additional pennants in later years but falling short.

He didn't look like much of an athlete, but he sure made plays other third basemen couldn't. Baker led AL third basemen in putouts seven times and finished first or second in assists seven times. The lefty swinger batted over .300 four straight years before sitting out the entire 1915 season in a contract dispute with A's owner Connie Mack. He would later miss the 1920 season to care for his sick wife, meaning he lost two full seasons from his career. Baker retired for good after the 1922 season, winding up with a .307 lifetime average and OPS+ of 135 (same as George Brett). He was elected to the Hall of Fame in 1955. Bill James ranks him as the fifth-best third baseman of all-time and expresses the belief Baker might have wound up first if not for the two missed seasons during his prime.

William "Judy" Johnson was widely regarded as one of the best third basemen to ever play in the Negro Leagues, but that's still not enough for him to surpass Baker. Johnson was a capable line-drive hitter but not much of a slugger. He was incomparably poised and agile in the field with a strong arm, teaming up with Josh Gibson to pick runners off third on a regular basis from a combination of sign stealing and smarts. "Judy Johnson was the smartest third baseman I ever came across. A scientific ballplayer, did everything with grace and poise," remarked Pittsburgh Crawfords teammate Ted Page in John Holway's book, *Blackball Stars*.

Johnson used to try any angle to gain a competitive edge such as puffing out the sleeves of his shirt to make it easier to get hit by a pitch. In the rough and tumble game that defined Negro Leagues competition, with infielders finding it necessary to wear shin guards, the man they called "Judy" stood out for his gentlemanly qualities. Johnson helped the Philadelphia Hilldales win three straights pennants in 1923–1925, leading the team to the 1925 Negro Leagues championship over Satchel Paige and the Kansas City Monarchs. He served as player-manager of the Homestead Grays for one year, then came back to Philadelphia as player-manager and later was a key contributor and captain on the powerhouse Pittsburgh Crawfords teams of the 1930s.

The slender Johnson, who liked to hit with a monstrous 40-ounce bat, averaged .293 for his career and in 1975 became the first Negro Leagues third baseman inducted into the Hall of Fame in Cooperstown.

Another third baseman worth mentioning is Bill Werber, who was the last living teammate of Babe Ruth until he died at the age of 100 on January 22, 2009. He also had the distinction of being the first batter when the first televised baseball game took place on August 26, 1939. Werber hit .321 with 200 hits and led the league with 40 stolen bases for the Red Sox in 1934. He led the AL in stolen bases three times and batted .370 to help the Reds win the 1940 World Series.

Werber only played seven games with the Yankees, so his time with Ruth was fleeting. However, he remembers how the Babe welcomed him to the team. Werber was showering after the game when he felt an odd sensation. As he recalled in his 2001 autobiography, *Memories of a Ballplayer*, "All of a sudden I became aware of a warmer stream of water in the middle of my back. I turned to find Ruth using me as a temporary latrine, roaring with laughter."

The All-Time-Maryland team doesn't have to worry about the shortstop being ready to play, as Cal Ripken, Jr., epitomized what it means to show up and do your job day after day. Since the McGwire-Sosa home run race later proved to be a fraud and the Barry Bonds home run record also lacked credibility, it can be asserted that the game in which Cal broke Gehrig's record on September 6, 1995 was the biggest moment in baseball over the past quarter-century. All of America embraced the Iron Man, whose grace and dedication to the game brought back fans who had been disillusioned by the strike of 1994–95. What an uplifting moment it was to watch him walk around the stadium high-fiving fans, a huge weight lifted off his shoulders.

The record seemed especially meaningful to Ripken and to Oriole fans because he was born in Maryland and got to play his whole career there. As he said during his speech the night he broke the record, "As I grew up here, I not only had dreams of being a big league ballplayer, but also of being a Baltimore Oriole. For all of your support over the years, I want to thank you, the fans of Baltimore, from the bottom of my heart. This is the greatest place to play."

It's interesting to note that Ripken's streak encompassed 17 seasons, 1982-1998, yet he only led the league in games played in nine of those seasons. With the Orioles missing a game here or there because of rainouts, this fact is just an odd circumstance.

"The Streak," as it became known, had its roots in Ripken's determination to not ever give another player the chance to take his spot. In other words, let someone else play the role of Wally Pipp. When he joined the club in 1981, Ripken came up with a simple plan to break into the lineup: play well and play every day.

Ripken helped redefine the position with his power bat and power arm, paving the way for slugging shortstops like Alex Rodriquez, Miguel Tejeda and Hanley Ramirez to follow. His 345 home runs while playing short (out of 431 for career) are 68 more than the next best shortstop, Ernie Banks.

Ripken was an old-school player, a fundamentally sound player uninterested in making Sportscenter highlight reels but concerned only with playing the game the right way, the way he and brother Billy had been taught their whole lives by Cal Sr.

"Cal is a bridge, maybe the last bridge, back to the way the game was played," Joe Torre said. "Hitting home runs and all that other good stuff is not enough. It's how you handle yourself in all the good times and bad times that matters. That's what Cal showed us. Being a star is not enough. He showed us how to be more."

Despite his 6-foot-4 frame, Ripken was fluid in the field, not stiff. He led AL shortstops in assists seven times, putouts six times and fielding percentage four times before moving to third base for his last five seasons. The awards and recognition piled up along with the games played: Rookie of the Year, two-time MVP, 19 All-Star teams, eight Silver Sluggers and two Gold Gloves. To Ripken, the most important would be 1983 World Series champion, overshadowing the fact that he only made the playoffs three times in 21 seasons.

It's hard to believe that eight sportswriters decided not to vote for Cal in his first year of eligibility for the Hall of Fame, but he took his rightful place in the plaque gallery of Cooperstown in 2007, delighting the 80,000-plus fans who ventured to upstate New York to watch his induction — the largest crowd ever for an Induction Ceremony.

Ripken was a legendary player, but even he has to take a back seat to the game's most fascinating figure. More words have been written about Babe Ruth than any other baseball player, which is altogether appropriate since he was larger than life on and off the field. He brought the "roar" to the Roaring Twenties. Ruth was the closest thing we have had to American royalty, if you define royalty by a perverse sense of fascination with every aspect of a person's life. The Bambino redefined greatness and helped change the game from hit-and-run "small ball" to a power game that fans have embraced. Chicks dig the long ball, and so do guys and kids and folks of all ages. They have the Babe to thank.

In 1919, his last year with the Red Sox and first as a full-time outfielder on days he didn't pitch, Ruth slugged 29 homers to set a new single-season record. Three players tied for runner-up with 10 homers, so the Babe hit nearly three times as many. The next season, his first with the Yankees, Ruth raised the bar even higher by hitting 54 homers, outdistancing the next best player by 35 homers. Michael Jordan would have had to average 75 points a game to outdistance his peers like Ruth did for most of his career.

Here are just a few stats on the Bambino: 75 years after he played his last game he remains first in Wins Above Replacement (190), slugging (.690), OPS (1.164) and OPS+ (207) and ranks second in RBI (2,213) and at bats per home run (11.8), trailing only Mark McGwire in the latter category. His .342 average is tied for ninth all-time, but of the players ahead of him only Ted Williams (and maybe Rogers Hornsby) can be considered sluggers. Sportswriter Bob Broeg has the proper perspective on Ruthian feats: "To try to capture Ruth with cold statistics would be like trying to keep up with him on a night out."

Appearing in 10 World Series, Ruth won seven championships, three with the Red Sox. He batted only 1-for-11 in Series action for the Sox, although he did go 3-0 with a 0.87 ERA. In 1916 he pitched a 14-inning masterpiece that remains the longest complete-game win in Series history. With the Yankees, the Babe batted .347 with 15 home runs in 36 Series games.

In the 1926 World Series Ruth did something no player had done before or since. And it's not the three home runs he hit in Game 4, since Ruth would do that again two years later and Reggie Jackson would also match that record. No, the Babe remains the only player thrown out stealing to end a World Series. With the Yanks down 3-2 to the Cardinals with two outs in the bottom of the ninth, Ruth kept hope alive by drawing a walk. Catching for the Cardinals was Bob O'Farrell, who threw out 50 percent of base stealers that season. Ruth, who only succeeded on 51 percent of his career stolen base attempts, decided to take off for second and was gunned down to end the game and the Series.

No matter, the Sultan of Swat would bounce back by hitting 60 home runs the next season as the 1927 Yankees (often called the greatest team of all-time) won 110 games and swept the Pirates in the World Series. Ruth stole one base in that Series and didn't get caught once.

The Babe loved kids, perhaps a result of a childhood spent largely in an orphanage because his parents were

On and off the field, Babe Ruth found himself the center of attention. Here he is shown after being knocked unconscious after he ran into a concrete wall at Griffith Stadium in Washington, D.C., during a game in 1924 (Library of Congress, Prints & Photographs Division, LC-DIG-npcc-11744).

unwilling or unable to control him. Baseball became his ticket out, although he didn't view it that way at the time. "If it wasn't for baseball, I'd be in either the penitentiary or the cemetery. I have the same violent temper my father and older brother had. Both died of injuries from street fights in Baltimore, fights begun by flare-ups of their tempers," he was quoted by Fred Lieb in *Baseball As I Have Known It*. The Babe never turned down an autograph request from a kid and refused to endorse alcohol or tobacco products because it set a bad example for kids.

Werber recalls the time the superstitious Ruth grabbed hold of reserve infielder Jimmie Reese and hung him up by his uniform shirt on hooks in the back of his locker. The Babe got a couple of hits that day, so he decided to give Reese the same treatment the next day, much to Reese's howling dismay.

Perhaps only the Babe could get away with the line he said to President Calvin Coolidge, after being introduced to him on a hot day at the ballpark in Washington. "Hot as Hell, ain't it, Prez?" he quipped.

One of the most insightful quotes about Ruth comes from Waite Hoyt, a teammate on the Red Sox and Yankees, who told Ruth biographer Robert Creamer, "All the lies about Ruth are true."

Another all-time great right fielder from Maryland flew considerably more under the radar than Ruth. Al Kaline made his debut with the Tigers at the age of 18, skipping the minors entirely, but he didn't take long to prove he belonged. Two years later he became the youngest batting champion ever, hitting .340 at the ripe old age of 20 while also leading the league with 200 hits and 321 total bases. He hit 27 homers, drove in 102 runs and came in second in slugging at .546 in that 1955 season, finishing second in the MVP vote.

He was no one-year wonder either, remaining productive to the very end of a brilliant 22-year career. Kaline's best attribute was his strong and accurate throwing arm, but he was a terrific all-around right fielder. He led in fielding percentage seven years and assists twice on the way to winning 10 Gold Gloves. Said Kaline in an interview with Rich Westcott, "I feel that I helped more people by being a good defensive player. I was a good offensive player — let's face it. But I never had any slumps in the outfield. I had slumps as a batter, but not as a fielder."

Kaline was no slouch with the bat either, batting over .300 nine times and accumulating 3,007 hits. He does have the distinction of being the first member of the 3,000-hit club who failed to bat .300 for his career, but he was darn close at .297 and finished in the top 10 in batting average 11 times. More importantly, he was a gamer who showed up to play every day, appearing in 2,834 games — seventeenth on the all-time list.

Although it took him 16 years to make it to the postseason, Kaline took advantage of the opportunity. He batted .379 with two home runs and eight RBI as the Tigers overcame a 3–1 deficit to beat the Cardinals in the 1968 World Series. "Getting a chance to play on the only pennant-winner I ever played on was one of the top thrills of my career," says Kaline, who was humbled by his election to the Hall of Fame in his first year of eligibility (1980).

It was a close call for the third outfield spot between Charlie "King Kong" Keller and Bill Nicholson. Nicholson has the edge in hits (1,484–1,085), home runs (235–189) and RBI (948–760), but Keller has the advantage in average (.286–.268), OBP (.410–.365), slugging (.518–.465), OPS (.928–.830) and OPS+ (152–132).

Keller batted .334 as a rookie for the 1939 Yankees squad that won 106 games, making an impact with a memorable play in Game 4 of the World Series. He ran over Reds catcher Ernie Lombardi to score a run in the 10th inning, knocking Lombardi unconscious long enough for the batter, Joe DiMaggio, to circle the bases with an insurance run. In Game 4 of the 1941 World Series, Keller hit a two-run double in the ninth inning that drove in what proved to be the tying and winning runs.

His final stats were impacted by a bad back that limited his playing time for a number of years. When healthy, Keller teamed with Joe DiMaggio and Tommy Henrich to form a powerhouse outfield for the Yankees, who won four pennants and three championships in a five-year period. With the baseball world paying attention to DiMaggio's hitting streak in 1941, Keller's great season was overlooked. He came in second with 33 homers, finished third with 122 RBI, had 102 walks and posted a .416 OBP (fourth in AL), which resulted in him coming in fifth in MVP voting.

Nicholson basically posted five straight good seasons for the Cubs during the war years and didn't make a major impact beyond that. He was especially good in 1943 and 1944, leading the league in homers and RBI both seasons. In 1943 he hit .309 with 29 homers, 128 RBI and a league-leading 116 runs scored, resulting in a third-place finish for MVP. The next year his line was .287-33-122 with a league-leading 317 total bases and a second-place finish in balloting for the MVP Award.

Another notable outfielder from Maryland is Ripken's teammate and close friend, Brady Anderson. Anderson had a solid career as a leadoff hitter, recording 210 homers and 315 stolen bases, but is best known for clubbing 50 home runs in 1996 to beat his previous career high by 29. He played six more seasons and never hit more than 24 dingers.

The All-Time Maryland team features a player who can be considered one of the greatest designated hitters in history. Harold Baines appeared in 1,644 games as DH, topping the 1,061 games he played in the outfield. Baines was a six-time All-Star who slugged 384 home runs in a 22-year career. A .289 lifetime hitter with 1,628 RBI, Baines tended to put the ball in play without striking out much. He led the league by slugging .541 in 1984 and later had one of his best seasons at the age of 40 in 1999, batting .312 with 25 homers and 103 RBI.

Baines spent his whole career in the American League, primarily with the White Sox (14 years) and Orioles (seven years). On May 9, 1984, he made history after hitting a walk-off home run off Chuck Porter in the 25th inning to end the longest night game ever — it took eight hours and six minutes to complete. Joe Posnanski of *Sports Illustrated* points out Baines hit between .290 and .310 10 times — more than anyone — and hit between 15 and 25 homers a record 15 times. With 2,866 career hits, Baines ranks 41st and all the eligible players ahead of him are in the Hall of Fame.

The All-Time Maryland right-handed starter is not the pitcher with the most wins — that would be Bobby Mathews with 297. And it's not the pitcher with the best winning percentage — that would be Dave Foutz at .690. Nor is it Eddie Rommel, who went 171–119 pitching from 1920–32. Hall of Famer Vic Willis stands out despite his short career and the fact he lost 205 games to go with 249 wins. He completed a remarkable 388 of 471 starts, setting a modern-day record with 45 complete games in 1902 that has only been topped by Jack Chesbro's 48 complete games in 1904.

Willis relied on a deceptive delivery to win 20 or more games in eight seasons (four with the Boston Beaneaters and four with the Pittsburgh Pirates), leading the league in shutouts, complete games and ERA+ two times and ERA and strikeouts once. His best year was probably 1899, when he went 27–8 with a league-best 2.50 ERA and five shutouts. He teamed up with Honus Wagner and Fred Clarke to lead the Pirates to the 1909 pennant and they defeated the Tigers in the World Series that year even though Willis didn't pitch up to his usual standards.

Mathews, it should be noted, was reportedly the first pitcher to throw a spitball and also dabbled with a curveball, at least according to some accounts. He has the most wins of any eligible pitcher not in the Hall of Fame, as 300 wins seems to be the promised land for Cooperstown and Mathews fell three wins short. At 5-foot-5, Mathews was three inches shorter than the two shortest pitchers currently in the Hall: Pud Galvin and Mickey Welch.

Rommel led the AL with 27 wins and 51 games (including 18 relief appearances) for the Philadelphia Athletics in 1922, which led to a second-place finish for the MVP Award. He posted a league-high 21 wins in 1925 and won a World Series ring with the A's in 1929 after going 12–2 with a career-low 2.85 ERA that year.

By the time Lefty Grove hung up his spikes in 1941 he had certainly made a case as baseball's best left-handed starter. With a record of 300–141, his .680 winning percentage ranks eighth among all pitchers. Grove won 20 games in seven straight years and led the league in strikeouts his first seven seasons, dominating batters during the Lively Ball Era. He also finished first in ERA and ERA+ nine times and SO/BB ratio eight times.

Grove, who was a notorious hothead who couldn't stand losing, just fired back and threw his fastball as fast as the situation warranted, and Lord help the teammate who made an error to prevent Grove from winning a game. "He was a moody guy, a tantrum thrower like me," says Ted Williams, whose first three seasons on the Red Sox coincided with Grove's last three years. "But when he punched a locker or something else, he always did it with his right hand. He was a careful tantrum thrower."

Grove helped lead the Philadelphia A's to three straight AL pennants, winning championships in 1929 and 1930. He pitched a complete game to win Game 1 of the 1930 Series and then pitched another complete game while losing Game 4 by a 3–1 score. He came back the next day and got the victory after hurling two innings of no-run relief. Grove was often called on to close out games, as he made 159 relief appearances during a career in which he averaged only 27 starts a year.

In his book *Lefty Grove: American Original*, author Jim Kaplan makes a case for Grove as the best pitcher in baseball history. As Kaplan points out, Lefty was the only 300-game winner to pitch the majority of his games during the Lively Ball Era. Furthermore, Grove's ERA was 46 percent better than the league average during his playing days and his ERA+ of 148 is topped only by Pedro Martinez's 154 today, although Martinez pitched 1,112 fewer innings.

Traded to Boston in 1934 mainly for a cash infusion for the A's, Grove was forced to reinvent himself as a soft tosser after struggling to overcome arm injuries. His strikeout totals dropped sharply but he managed to remain a successful pitcher for eight more seasons, hanging on just long enough to win his 300th game on July 25, 1941. If only he had started his major league career a little sooner — he was stuck in the minors playing five seasons for the Baltimore Orioles in the International League, going 108–36 and winning at least 25 games three times before debuting in the majors at age 25.

The year Grove was taking his pitching brilliance to Boston another Maryland lefty was making a name for himself. Slim Jones, all of 21 years old, relied on an overpowering fastball and knee-buckling curveball to go 32-4 for the Philadelphia Stars in the Negro Leagues. He led the Stars to the Negro Leagues championship that 1934 season but less than four years later he was dead of pneumonia, a promising career snuffed out too soon.

Baltimore-born Southpaw Tommy Byrne was one of the wildest pitchers in baseball history. He once walked seven batters in one inning and another time walked 16 in an extra-inning game. He led the AL in walks three times, walked 36 in 21 innings for the Yankees in 1951 and averaged 6.9 BB/9IP for his career.

We went back and forth on the All-Time Relief Pitcher for Maryland, debating between Steve Farr and Jeff Nelson. Nelson and Farr had the exact same won-loss record but that's where the similarities end. Farr had a slight edge in ERA, innings pitched and Career Win Shares and a big advantage in saves, 132 to 33. Nelson was a righty specialist who pitched in 798 games in relief compared to 481 for Farr, who operated as his team's closer about half his career. Nelson's ERA+ was 133 compared to 128 for Farr. Nelson averaged 9.5 strikeouts and 7.3 hits per 9 innings compared to 7.3 strikeouts and 8.2 hits per 9 innings for Farr. Nelson was such a dominant set-up reliever that he made one All-Star team, which has not happened very often, while Farr never made an All-Star team.

Another huge advantage for Nelson is his playoff experience. He played a vital role as a bridge to Mariano Rivera, helping the Yanks make it to five World Series and win four championships in his six years with the team. Nelson appeared in 55 playoff games over 20 playoff series, while Farr appeared in two games in just one playoff series. Nelson made three scoreless appearances in the each of the 1996, 1998 and 2003 World Series plus four scoreless appearances in the 1999 World Series. In the 2000 Series he made two scoreless appearances, getting the win for the Yankees in Game 4 and then gave up three runs in one contest for his only blemish. So in 16 career World Series games Nelson was unscored on in 15, leaving him with a 1.69 ERA. It's that type of impact that gives Nelson the final selection.

Thirteen Maryland natives have managed in the majors but only four have winning records (two managed just one game), and five of them managed fewer than 30 games. Cal Ermer gets the spot, as he took over an underachieving 1967 Twins squad from Sam Mele and nearly led them to the pennant. The Twins went 66–46 down the stretch for Ermer but lost their last two games to the Red Sox, finishing one game behind the Sox. He was not retained after guiding the team to a 79–83 record the next year.

Ermer played only one game in the majors, going 0-for-3 but handling seven chances flawlessly in the field for the Washington Senators in 1947. He overcame that disappointment to serve more than 60 years in professional baseball, largely for the Senators/Twins franchise. He was *Sporting News'* Minor League Manager of the Year in 1958 and finished with a managerial record of 1,906–1,728 over 26 seasons in the minors. He was the consummate baseball man in the tradition of Cal Ripken, Sr., who won 964 games managing in the minors but had a short, unsuccessful stint as Orioles manager.

MASSACHUSETTS

*Names in **bold** represent Major League selections by position, followed by honorable mentions. Negro Leagues players are in **bold italics**, followed by honorable mentions in italics. City of birth is in parentheses.*

Catcher — **Mickey Cochrane (Bridgewater)**. Also: Duke Farrell (Oakdale); Jim Hegan (Lynn); Wilbert Robinson (Bolton); Shanty Hogan (Somerville); Rich Gedman (Worcester); Cy Perkins (Gloucester)

First Base — **Jeff Bagwell (Boston)**. Also: Fred Tenney (Georgetown); Elbie Fletcher (Milton); Stuffy McInnis (Gloucester); Tommy Tucker (Holyoke); John Morrill (Boston); Eddie Waitkus (Cambridge); Dick Siebert (Fall River); Kitty Bransfield (Worcester); Paul Sorrento (Somerville)

Second Base — ***Frank Grant* (Pittsfield)**. Also: Jerry Remy (Fall River); Eddie Mayo (Holyoke)

Third Base — **Pie Traynor (Framingham)**. Also: Richie Hebner (Boston); Mike Pagliarulo (Medford); Hick Carpenter (Grafton); Doc Casey (Lawrence); Eddie Grant (Franklin)

Shortstop — **Rabbit Maranville (Springfield)**. Also: Mark Belanger (Pittsfield); Greg Gagne (Fall River); Leo Durocher (West Springfield); Gary DiSarcina (Malden); Frank Fennelly (Fall River)

Outfield — Joe Kelley (Cambridge)
Outfield — Jimmy Ryan (Clinton)
Outfield — Tommy McCarthy (Boston). Also: Jimmy Barrett (Athol); Tony Conigliaro (Revere); Shano Collins (Charlestown); Paul Radford (Roxbury); Jack Manning (Braintree); Tommy Dowd (Holyoke); Whitey Witt (Orange); Jack McCarthy (Hardwick)
Designated Hitter — Steve Balboni (Brockton). Also: Glenn Adams (Northbridge)
Right Handed Starter — John Clarkson (Cambridge). Also: Tim Keefe (Cambridge); Jack Chesbro (North Adams); Charlie Buffinton (Fall River); Candy Cummings (Ware); Bill Donovan (Lawrence); Vic Raschi (West Springfield); Frank Dwyer (Lee); Adonis Terry (Westfield); Dick Donovan (Boston); Bill Monbouquette (Medford); Bump Hadley (Lynn); Jack Sanford (Wellesley Hills); Joe Coleman (Boston)
Left Handed Starter — Tom Glavine (Concord). Also: Wilbur Wood (Cambridge)
Relief Pitcher — Jeff Reardon (Dalton). Also: Steve Bedrosian (Methuen); Stu Miller (Northampton); Mark Wohlers (Holyoke); Turk Wendell (Pittsfield); Wayne Granger (Springfield); Turk Farrell (Boston); Skip Lockwood (Boston)
Manager — Connie Mack (East Brookfield). Also: Leo Durocher (West Springfield); Wilbert Robinson (Bolton); Pat Moran (Fitchburg); Jim Mutrie (Chelsea)

The Names

Best Nickname: Richie "The Gravedigger" Hebner
Other Nicknames: Harry "The Golden Greek" Agganis; Stan "Polo" Andrews; Steve "Bye Bye" Balboni; Jimmy "Foxy Grandpa" Bannon; "Whispering Bill" Barrett; Steve "Bedrock" Bedrosian; Mark "The Blade" Belanger; Frank "Dodo" Bird; Hugh "Corns" Bradley; William "Kitty" Bransfield; Jack "Slug" Burns; John "Happy Jack" Chesbro; Mickey "Black Mike" Cochrane; Frank "Runt" Cox; Pat "Whoops" Creeden; William "Candy" Cummings; Patrick "Cozy" Dolan; Tim "Bridget" Donahue; "Wild Bill" Donovan; "Buttermilk Tommy" Dowd; Leo "The Lip" Durocher; Charles "Duke" Farrell; Mark "The Bird" Fidrych; Ed "Sleepy" Flanagan; Frank "Black Dunlap" Grant; Irving "Bump" Hadley; Al "Beartracks" Javery; "Sir Timothy" Keefe; Connie "The Tall Tactician" Mack; Walter "Rabbit" Maranville; Eddie "Hotshot" Mayo; James "Chippy" McGarr; John "Stuffy" McInnis; George "Prunes" Moolic; Hugh "Losing Pitcher" Mulcahy; Connie "Stone Face" Murphy; Vic "Springfield Rifle" Raschi; Jeff "The Terminator" Reardon; Jimmy "Pony" Ryan; Wilfred "Rosy" Ryan; Charles "Pussy" Tebeau; William "Adonis" Terry; Harold "Pie" Traynor; Tommy "Foghorn" Tucker; "Vinegar" Tom Vickery; Joe "Tweet" Walsh
Most Unusual Name: Casper Asbjornson; Malachi Jeddidah Kittridge

All-Time Leaders

Games: Rabbit Maranville, 2670
Hits: Rabit Maranville, 2605
Batting Average: Pie Traynor and Mickey Cochrane, .320
Home Runs: Jeff Bagwell, 449
RBI: Jeff Bagwell, 1529
Stolen Bases: Tommy McCarthy, 468
Wins: Tim Keefe, 342
Strikeouts: Tom Glavine, 2607
Saves: Jeff Reardon, 367
Future Star: Matt Antonelli (Peabody)
Best Player: Mickey Cochrane

Historic Baseball Places

Fenway Park in Boston — The oldest major league ballpark, which opened in 1912, was named after the area of Beantown in which it's located. Fenway is one of the few ballparks to use a hand-operated scoreboard, which was added in 1934, and it still features the original wood seats in the grandstand section. The 37-foot-high Green Monster, which has confounded pitchers and left fielders for a century, was originally blue and was not painted green until 1947.
Worcester Baseball Monument in Worcester — Located on grounds of Becker College, it marks the scene of the first perfect game pitched in the National League by J. Lee Richmond on June 12, 1880.
The Story of Westfield Mural in Westfield — Pitcher and Westfield native Adonis Terry is prominently featured in the 44-foot long mural created by muralist David Fichter that hangs in the Westfield Athenaeum. Terry was a nineteenth century player who won 197 games.
Casey at the Bat in Holliston — Statue and plaque dedicated to Ernest Thayer's famous poem is located in Mudville Village, a neighborhood in Holliston. The town claims to be the inspiration for Mudville, since Thayer grew up in nearby Worcester, but the poet denied he based Mudville on any specific location.
Fuller Field in Clinton — Features a sign that says "World's Oldest Baseball Field," as baseball has been played continuously there since 1878. Hall of Famers Tim Keefe and Billy Hamilton reportedly played on the field.
Wahconah Park in Pittsfield — This historic park dates back to 1919 and is one of the few that still features a wooden grandstand. Through the years many batters have undoubtedly been annoyed that the park oddly faces west into the setting sun, but then again ballpark architecture has advanced some in the last century.
Fraser Field in Lynn — Originally built in 1940, this stadium features an unusual cantilevered roof. Fraser Field made history when it held its first minor league game in 1946, as the Lynn Red Sox faced off against the Nashua Dodgers, the first racially integrated team to play in the United States in the twentieth century.

Top: Wahconah Park in Pittsfield, which dates to 1919, is one of the few ballparks remaining that features a wooden grandstand. Al Rosen, Sparky Lyle, Carlton Fisk and Greg Maddux are among the future stars who played minor league ball for Pittsfield at Wahconah Park (courtesy BallparkReviews.com). *Bottom:* Fraser Field in Lynn, Massachusetts, which was constructed in 1940 as a Works Progress Administration project, features an unusual cantilevered roof. The first game was an exhibition featuring the Pittsburgh Pirates. Fraser Field made history when it held its first minor league game in 1946, as the Lynn Red Sox faced off against the Nashua Dodgers. Roy Campanella and Don Newcombe played for the Dodgers, making them the first racially integrated team to play in the United States in the twentieth century (courtesy Digitalballparks.com).

Notable Achievements

Tony Conigliaro became the youngest American League player to reach 100 home runs when he hit his 100th at 22 years of age in 1967. Mel Ott beat him by 65 days as the youngest ever to reach 100.

Greg Gagne was the last player to hit two inside-the-park home runs in one game when he did it for the Twins on October 4, 1986.

Chuck Essegian (Boston) hit two pinch-hit home runs for the Dodgers during the 1959 World Series.

On July 4, 1883, **Tim Keefe** won both games of a doubleheader, holding Columbus to one hit in the opener and two hits in the nightcap.

Wilbert Robinson set a record by going 7-for-7 during a nine-inning game on June 10, 1892. It was later matched by Rennie Stennett in 1975.

Tommy Dowd was the first player to bat in the history of the Boston Red Sox franchise when he stepped up to the plate on April 26, 1901. The team was known as the Boston Americans then.

Robert Keating (Springfield) didn't have much of a career, pitching a complete game in his only appearance in 1887 while surrendering 16 hits and 11 earned runs. However, he made a lasting impact on the game by inventing the rubber home plate.

On July 16, 1904, pitcher **Jack Chesbro** of the New York Highlanders stole home in the 10th inning to make himself the winning pitcher.

Finding the Stories Behind Massachusetts Player Nicknames

It must be something in the chowder. Looking at the roster of major league players from Massachusetts, it seems quite a few possess a colorful nickname. Some are funny, some are mean-spirited and some are a little dated by today's conventions, but all are interesting.

It's safe to say today's ballplayers don't need to moonlight in the offseason, but Richie Hebner was nicknamed "The Gravedigger" because he used to work for his family's grave-digging business in the offseason. Mark Fidrych was nicknamed "The Bird" because he resembled the Big Bird character on Sesame Street.

Leo Durocher was called "Lippy Leo" (later evolved to "The Lip") by a New York sportswriter after he joined the Yankees as a brash, loudmouth rookie in 1928. Durocher had company with that type of designation. "Whispering Bill" Barrett is a sarcastic reference to the fact Barrett had a tendency to be loud and talkative, while Tommy Tucker's Baltimore teammates called him "Foghorn" because he had a booming voice.

Some nicknames were particularly unflattering. Pat Creeden batted 0 for 8 with two errors during his five-game career with Boston in 1931, which is how you end up with the nickname "Whoops." After leading the league in losses twice and sporting a 45–89 career record, it's not surprising that Hugh Mulcahy picked up the nickname "Losing Pitcher." On the plus side, Mulcahy served his country as the first major league player drafted for World War II.

As for "Wild Bill" Donovan, that nickname seemed to aptly sum up his abilities and personality. He walked 69 batters in 88 innings in his rookie year, 1898, then led the league with 152 walks in 1901. When he wasn't walking batters, Donovan was getting thrown out of games for his frequent temperamental outbursts. Donovan, who was Babe Ruth's manager during his short stint with the Providence Grays in the minors, died tragically in a train accident in 1923.

Mark Belanger was called "The Blade" because with his tall, lanky frame he looked like a blade of grass. Then we have Jimmy "Pony" Ryan and Stan "Polo" Andrews, which sure seems like a good match.

Pie Traynor picked up his nickname because pie was his favorite childhood food, which is perhaps how George "Prunes" Moolic and "Buttermilk Tommy" Dowd got their monikers. Candy Cummings, on the other hand, has nothing to do with him having a sweet tooth. "Candy" was a superlative used in the 1860s to describe something that was top-notch, which is how Cummings' pitching dominance as a New York amateur was viewed.

Harry Agganis was called "The Golden Greek" because he was fiercely proud of his Greek heritage and his athletic feats were noteworthy. An All-American quarterback at Boston University who was later inducted into the College Football Hall of Fame, Agganis was also named MVP of the National Baseball Congress tournament in Wichita, Kansas. He chose baseball over football and showed great promise after debuting with the Red Sox in 1954, quickly becoming the Sox starting first baseman. He was batting .313 when he was hospitalized in May 1955 — six weeks later he was dead at age 26 of a pulmonary embolism. The Golden Greek's legacy lives on with Agganis Arena named after him at Boston University.

Two players named Michael Jordan have played professional baseball. The one known as "His Airness" ranks as one of the greatest players in the history of the National Basketball Association. The other, a native of Lawrence, played his baseball more than a century before the NBA star gave the game a try. Nicknamed "Mitty," the outfielder batted .096 with a .104 slugging percentage for the 1890 Pittsburgh Alleghenys, who went 23–113 that year.

Boston Is Steeped in Baseball History

Boston was a founding member of the American League in 1901 with a team called the Americans, which won its first World Series in 1903. Renamed the Red Sox in 1908, the franchise won four World Series between 1912 and 1918 before enduring a championship drought that lasted until 2004.

The city also fielded a team as a founding member of the National League in 1876, which started as the Red Stockings and was later changed to Beaneaters, Doves, Rustlers, Bees and Braves. That franchise enjoyed even less success than the Red Sox over its 77 years in Beantown, appearing in only two World Series with its lone championship coming in 1914.

Built in 1912, Fenway Park is the oldest major league ballpark. The brick façade in front is the only original part of construction that remains, but the ballpark is still steeped in history from the curse of the Bambino to the suspense of Pudge's home run. From the Green Monster and the Fisk Pole in left field to the Pesky Pole and Ted Williams Seat in right (Section 42, Row 37, Seat 21), there is a story behind every nook and cranny in the old park. Scenes from the movie "Field of Dreams" were filmed at Fenway in 1989. "Fenway Park is a religious shrine. People go there to worship," remarked Red Sox pitcher Bill "Spaceman" Lee.

Boston's baseball fans are noted for their long-suffering loyalty, which helps explain the creation of the world's first sports bar — McGreevey's 3rd Base Saloon. Located just 1,200 stumbling steps from Fenway Park, the traditional Irish pub's original version dates back to 1894. The light fixtures are fashioned out of bats donated by Red Sox players and even the Babe himself used to stop in and down a few cold ones. Another popular watering hole is Jerry Remy's Sports Bar and Grill, which is located across the street from Fenway Park. You can order a RemDawg in honor of the namesake, a Fall River native who played seven years for the Sox and has been a broadcaster for more than 20 years.

You can find a statue of Cy Young on the campus of Northeastern University at the former site of Huntington Avenue Grounds. The statue marks the spot where Young and the Boston Americans competed in the first World Series against the Pittsburgh Pirates. If you can't get enough Red Sox history, then visit the Sports Museum of New England. Located in the TD Garden, it highlights the history of the Sox and features a life-size sculpture of Ted Williams.

The neighborhoods of Boston have turned out quite a number of great ballplayers. Boston natives include Jeff Bagwell, Tommy McCarthy, George Wood, Richie Hebner and John Morrill. Hall of Famers John Clarkson and Tim Keefe along with Wilbur Wood and Joe Kelley came from Cambridge. Somerville produced Shanty Hogan and Elbie Fletcher, while Revere is the birthplace of Tony Conigliaro. Bill Monbouquette hails from Medford and Tom Glavine was born in Concord.

All-Time Massachusetts Selections

Let's move on to the selections for the All-Time Massachusetts team, which is filled with Hall of Famers at seven of the 12 positions (plus the manager) with the strong possibility that two more will eventually join the select group.

Hall of Famer Mickey Cochrane is the easy choice at catcher, as his strong bat was a driving force behind five pennant winners. Cochrane hit the ground running with the bat, averaging .331 as a rookie in 1925. He batted over .300 in nine of his 13 seasons, retiring with a .320 average that tails only Joe Mauer among catchers all-time. What stood out most was Cochrane's fiery competitive streak and excellent leadership skills, which is how he ended up managing at age 31.

Cochrane was named MVP with the Philadelphia Athletics in 1928 and with the Tigers in 1934, and those were actually two of his weaker years offensively. He batted .293 in 1928 and was helped by the fact previous MVP winners such as Babe Ruth and Lou Gehrig were ineligible for the award (a stipulation that was changed in 1930). The lefty hit .357 in 1930, .349 in 1931, drove in 112 runs in 1932 and posted a league-leading .459 OBP in 1933 while walking 106 times with just 22 strikeouts. His .419 career OBP ranks twentieth all-time and is by far the best mark for a catcher.

Unloaded to the Tigers before the 1934 season because Mack needed the money to keep the A's afloat, Cochrane took over as player-manager and guided the team to 101 wins and the AL pennant his first year. He chipped in by batting .320 and driving in 76 runs. The next year the Tigers not only won the pennant, Cochrane delivered a World Series title. His career ended prematurely after his skull was fractured from a beaning by Lynn, Mass., native Bump Hadley on May 25, 1937.

Other notable catchers include Jim Hegan, Duke Farrell and Wilbert Robinson. Hegan was a five-time All-Star who couldn't hit a lick (career average .228) but had no peer defensively. He threw out 45 percent of base runners during his 17-year career. Farrell was a nineteenth century player who batted .302 and led the American Association with 12 homers and 110 RBI in 1891. He played more than 500 games at other positions during his 18 seasons and averaged .277 lifetime. In 1897 Farrell threw out eight runners attempting to steal, which remains a single-game record, and he was on the 1903 Boston Americans team that won the first World Series.

Robinson had some good years batting after the pitching mound was moved back, averaging .334 in 1893 and .353 in 1894. "Uncle Robbie" caught 1,316 games over 17 seasons. He also won two pennants and 1,399 games as the long-time manager of the Brooklyn franchise, which was renamed the "Robins" after him. Robinson was inducted into the Hall of Fame as a manager in 1945, despite the fact he won only 50 percent of his games as manager and never led any of his 19 teams to a World Series championship.

The Bergen brothers from North Brookfield were both catchers who gained notoriety. Bill Bergen's lifetime average of .170 over 11 seasons is the lowest by a position player with more than 2,500 plate appearances. His other numbers are just as ugly —.194 OBP, .201 slugging, 21 OPS+ and just two home runs in 3,028 at bats. His older brother, Marty, did much better, batting .265 and displaying great defense playing four seasons for the Boston Beaneaters. There were warning signs of erratic and paranoid behavior, however, exacerbated by the death of his son in 1899. Then on January 19, 1900, he went crazy and killed his wife and two young kids with an axe before slitting his own throat with a razor. It was a tragic ending for a talented player who Connie Mack had once tried to sign.

Another Massachusetts catcher endured a tragic ending to his career and life. Mike "Doc" Powers was a 38-year-old veteran catcher and a starter for Mack's Philadelphia Athletics on Opening Day, 1909, which was the first game ever held at Shibe Park. Powers had been complaining of stomach pain throughout the game, and his condition seemed to be aggravated when he crashed into the fence chasing a foul ball. He collapsed after the game and was rushed to the hospital, where he was initially diagnosed with gastritis and later a strangulated intestine. Three surgeries did not correct the problem and he died two weeks later, with no one sure if an on-field injury, a pre-existing condition or a combination led to his death.

The All-Time Massachusetts team's first base spot goes to Boston native Jeff Bagwell, who teamed up with Craig Biggio to serve as the face of the Astros franchise for 15 years. Traded by his hometown Red Sox to the Astros for relief pitcher Larry Anderson in August 1990, Bagwell immediately proved the short-sightedness of the deal by winning Rookie of the Year in 1991. He was named MVP in the strike-shortened 1994 season after hitting .368 with 39 homers in 110 games and leading the league in runs (104), RBI (116), slugging (.750—the highest in 69 years), OPS (1.201), OPS+ (213) and total bases (300). In 1999 he became just the second player to score 140 runs, steal 30 bases and walk 120 times, joining Lenny Dykstra.

Bagwell, who actually grew up in Connecticut, hit at least 30 homers nine times, drove in over 100 runs eight times and posted seven straight seasons with 100 walks, amazing production when you consider he played two-thirds of his career in the cavernous Astrodome. He ranks 34th on the all-time home run list with 449 homers and his OPS of .948 ranks 21st, which is better than Mays or Aaron. His career OPS+ of 149 is ahead of Willie McCovey, Willie Stargell and Mike Schmidt. Bagwell was considered one of the best base runners in the game, because he knew how to take leads, get a good jump and was always hustling. Despite lacking speed he still stole 201 bases and had two seasons with over 30 steals. Defense was another strong suit, as he was nimble on his feet and adept at making the double play.

Bagwell is in a select group of nine players who have recorded 1,500 RBI, scored 1,500 runs and stolen 200 bases — the other eight are in the Hall of Fame. Baggy's number 5 jersey was retired by the Astros in 2007, and he should eventually gain entry into Cooperstown. Some voters may be troubled by the fact Bagwell was an acknowledged andro user who went from a skinny kid hitting six homers in 731 minor league at-bats to a guy with Popeye forearms hitting 449 homers in the majors during the height of the steroids era. While it may be impossible to determine if Bagwell used performance-enhancing drugs, he still stands head and shoulders above the other candidates for Team Massachusetts' first base spot.

Stuffy McInnis and Fred Tenney were both singles hitters and excellent fielders who were among the first players to stretch out for throws at first. Tenney collected 2,231 hits with a .294 average and led NL first basemen in assists seven straight years. McInnis batted over .300 12 times and averaged .307 over 19 seasons, but he did not hit more than two home runs during any of the eight seasons he played during the Lively Ball Era. He led AL first basemen in fielding percentage six times. Milton native Elbie Fletcher led the NL in OBP three times and walks twice as he had a knack for getting on base and scoring runs. He also led NL first basemen in assists six times and putouts three times.

Another notable first baseman is Eddie Waitkus, a Cambridge native who was the inspiration for Bernard Malamud's novel *The Natural*. A decorated war hero, Waitkus was shot in the stomach by a crazed teen-age fan in 1949 — he had been hitting over .300 at the time and was in the midst of a second straight All-Star season. The obsessed fan, Ruth Ann Steinhagen, had been upset when the Cubs traded her favorite player, Waitkus, to the Phillies after the 1948 season. Waitkus nearly died from the shooting, but he recovered and helped the Philly "Whiz Kids" make the playoffs the next season. The incident seemed to scar him in ways both outward and unforeseen, and his playing career and life were never quite the same. He ended up playing 11 seasons and averaging .285 with only 24 homers.

Frank Grant is not generally considered the greatest Negro Leagues second baseman — Bill James ranks him sixth — but he is the only one in the Hall of Fame. It's difficult to fairly judge his abilities, since he was a nineteenth century player who was forced to play in the integrated minor leagues and with touring black teams in the days before the Negro Leagues were organized. Although just five-foot-seven, the speedy Grant had some pop in his bat, as well as excellent range and quick hands in the field. He batted .336 in three seasons in the International League and then in the 1890s starred on the Cuban Giants, the first black professional baseball team.

Honorable mention at second base goes to Fall River native Jerry Remy, who was able to play seven seasons for the Red Sox and make the All-Star team in his first year with the team, 1978. He only hit seven homers in his career but was a steady player who managed to steal 208 bases with a high of 41 in 1977. Eddie "Hotshot" Mayo had one decent season (1945) and parlayed that into MVP runner-up as he helped lead the Tigers to the World Series title that year.

Pie Traynor is one of those forgotten stars who you don't hear much about anymore, but his numbers are hard to ignore. He had 10 seasons batting over .300 and a lifetime average of .320 — second best by a third baseman behind Wade Boggs. Traynor actually started out as a shortstop, but switched to third when the Pirates picked up fellow Massachusetts native Rabbit Maranville. He spent his entire 17-year career with the Pirates, winning a championship in 1925 and later managing the team for six years with middling results.

Although he led NL third basemen in putouts seven times and assists three times, Traynor's defensive ability has been overrated. He had above-average range but also led in errors five times and grades out at -32 for Runs from Fielding compared to the average third baseman for his era.

Traynor rarely struck out — his high in strikeouts for a season was 28 — and he stole 158 bases and led the league in sacrifice hits twice. He excelled at driving in runs, posting more than 100 RBI seven times despite averaging just 5.8 homers in those seasons. He tends to be devalued because he only hit 58 homers while playing his whole career in the lively ball era. Traynor was merely being smart as a hitter, driving the ball into the expansive outfield gaps of Forbes Field for doubles and triples. He finished in the top 10 in triples 10 times and led the NL with 19 triples in 1923.

Richie Hebner is another notable third baseman from Massachusetts. He hit 203 home runs and posted an adjusted OPS of 119 over 18 years but never made an All-Star team. Hebner was slow and had poor range at third, which is why he moved over to first later in his career. He did help eight teams make the playoffs, winning a ring with the Pirates in 1971.

Eddie Grant was a light-hitting third baseman from Franklin, who stood out because he was a Harvard-educated lawyer who preferred using the grammatically correct "I have it" when calling for pop ups. He hung around for 10 seasons and batted .249 but is remembered for making the ultimate sacrifice for his country. He was killed in the Argonne Forest in France while trying heroically to rescue the "Lost Battalion," becoming the first major leaguer to be killed during World War I. He was honored with a plaque and monument at the Polo Grounds, but the plaque went missing after the Giants' last game there in 1957. A replacement plaque can be found near the Lefty O'Doul entrance to AT&T Park in San Francisco.

There was never a dull moment when Walter "Rabbit" Maranville was around. No one had more fun before, during and after games than Maranville, who still had enough energy left to play shortstop and run the bases at full throttle. If there was a Hall of Fame for practical jokers, then Maranville would be the first inductee. One of the most colorful and popular players ever, Maranville unfortunately never got the satisfaction of knowing what it meant to be a baseball Hall of Famer — he died a few months before his formal induction into the Hall in 1954.

Nicknamed "Rabbit" because he had large ears and was fast, Maranville was known to jump into the arms of teammates on the field, hand a pair of glasses to an umpire or crawl under the legs of the home plate umpire on the way to bat — anything to entertain the fans. His late-night, booze-fueled forays included walking along hotel ledges or having a teammate chase him through Times Square yelling "Stop thief!" After the Miracles Braves stormed back from last place to win the World Series in 1914, Maranville hit the road doing a vaudeville act that was well-received until Rabbit decided to demonstrate his slide into a base — he ended up tumbling into the orchestra pit and breaking his leg.

Here's what Joe McCarthy had to say about Rabbit: "When I first heard about him, about all the stunts he pulled, I said to myself for a fellow to do all those crazy things and still keep his job, he had to be a damned good ball player. When I got into the league, I saw that I was right. He was full of fun, but he could play ball."

With a .258 lifetime average, an OPS+ of 82 and only 28 home runs over 23 seasons, Maranville is one of the least qualified players in the Hall even though he received MVP votes in eight seasons. At five-foot-five Rabbit is not even the shortest Hall of Famer — that distinction goes to five-foot-two Candy Cummings, a fellow Massachusetts native. He did excel as a fielder, leading NL shortstops in putouts six times, in assists and fielding percentage three times and in basket catches every year. Despite the fact he played 513 games at second base, Maranville is still the all-time leader in putouts by a shortstop with 5,139 and ranks fifth in assists with 7,354. By comparison, 11-time Gold Glover Omar Vizquel has played over 500 more games at short but still trails Maranville by more than 1,000 putouts.

Shortly before his death, Rabbit lamented, "Nobody gets a kick out of baseball anymore, because big salaries and the pension fund have made it a more serious business than running a bank." The reality is that baseball became more serious the day Maranville retired.

Mark Belanger was even weaker with the bat than Maranville — hitting just .228 with 20 homers and an abysmal 68 OPS+ — but he was better in the field. With Belanger and his eight Gold Gloves playing alongside Brooks Robinson, the left side of the Orioles defense was impenetrable for a dozen years. Belanger's Runs from Fielding score of 241 is 2 runs better than Ozzie Smith and 111 runs better than Maranville.

Two outfielders from Massachusetts are enshrined in Cooperstown: Joe Kelley and Tommy McCarthy. Clinton native Jimmy Ryan was as good as Kelley and definitely a better player than McCarthy. Ryan earned 317 career Win Shares compared to 303 for Kelley, with McCarthy trailing far behind at 176. The three were nineteenth century contemporaries.

Playing for the Chicago White Stockings, Ryan finished second in batting at .332 and led the National League with 182 hits, 33 doubles, 16 homers and a .515 slugging percentage in 1888. Primarily a center fielder, he batted over .300 in 12 of his 18 seasons, scored at least 100 runs eight times and finished with 2,513 hits, 1,643 runs scored (35th all-time) and a .308 lifetime average. Of the players ahead of him in career runs scored, Rafael Palmeiro is the only eligible player who has not been elected to the Hall of Fame.

Kelley was a leader and key contributor for five pennant winners in the National League between 1891 and 1908. The left fielder posted five straight seasons with more than 100 RBI and ranks ninth all-time in triples with 194. His best season was 1894, when he batted .393 and slugged .602 with 165 runs, 199 hits, 48 doubles, 111 RBI and .502 OBP. Kelley was a nifty base runner who had 443 career stolen bases with a high of 87 in 1896. He went 9-for-9 on September 3, 1894, making him one of nine players to share the record for most hits in a doubleheader. Kelley is the only one whose hits were consecutive.

McCarthy started out with the Boston Reds in the short-lived Union Association but first established himself with the St. Louis Browns in the American Association. He later teamed up with Hugh Duffy to form Boston's Heavenly Twins, riding along on Duffy's coattails to immortal glory. A regular for only eight seasons in a 13-year career, McCarthy posted an adjusted OPS above 100 just five times. He led the league with 83 stolen bases in 1890 while batting .350 that year, but he never led in any hitting categories.

With lifetime marks of 1,493 hits, .292 average, 102 OPS+ and 44 home runs, McCarthy seems to fall short as an all-time great. In fact, his hitting stats were further helped by playing in hitter-friendly parks most of his career, although he did have 468 stolen bases. His neutralized batting stats (adjusted for park and league) show him with a .245 average — not exactly the mark of a Hall of Famer. Nevertheless, he was elected by the Old Timers Committee in 1946, 24 years after he died. Fittingly, the Heavenly Twins are buried in the same cemetery (Old Cavalry) outside Boston.

As Kelley and Ryan's careers were winding down, another Massachusetts outfielder was getting started. Jimmy Barrett was a speedy, lefty-swinging center fielder who broke in with the Cincinnati Reds in 1899. He batted .316, scored 114 runs and stole 44 bases the next year and then jumped over to the Tigers, where he teamed up with Sam Crawford in the outfield. Barrett batted .315 and led the AL in walks and OBP in 1903 and in walks in 1904. In addition to being a good bunter, he had a powerful throwing arm, leading the league in outfield assists three of his four full years with the Tigers. An untimely knee injury in 1905 coincided with the arrival of Ty Cobb, and Barrett was out of a job, and soon out of the league.

Tony Conigliaro was a superstar in the making, a North Shore boy with movie-star looks who made it to the majors with the Red Sox. An instant fan favorite when he slugged a home run in his first at-bat at Fenway, Conigliaro went on to hit .290 with 24 home runs as a 19-year-old-rookie in 1964. He became the youngest player to lead the American League in home runs when he hit 32 the next season at 20. The home runs kept coming, with 28 in 1966, then becoming the youngest AL player to reach 100 career home runs midway through the 1967 season.

Then his fortunes changed with one pitch — a fastball thrown by the Angels' Jack Hamilton on August 18, 1967, that connected with Conigliaro's face right below the eye. Teammate Rico Petrocelli rushed over from the on-deck circle and was taken aback at what he saw, as he recounts in his 2007 book *Rico Petrocelli's Tales From the Impossible Dream Red Sox:* "Tony's face was swelling up like there was somebody inside his skull blowing up a balloon. The first thing I thought was he was going to lose his left eye. Blood was pouring out

Tony Conigliaro seemed destined for stardom playing for his hometown Red Sox. At the age of 20 he became the youngest player to lead the AL in home runs. Everything changed when a ball struck him below his eye during a game in 1967, shattering his cheekbone and damaging his eyesight. He made a comeback two years later but was out of baseball for good at age 30 (National Baseball Hall of Fame Library, Cooperstown, New York).

of his nose. I didn't know what else to do, so I knelt down beside him, loosened his belt a little so he could breathe easier, and whispered into his ear that everything was going to be all right."

The pitch had shattered his cheekbone and nearly caused him to go blind. Conigliaro would miss the rest of the season and all of the next year, but rebounded to hit 20 homers in 1969 and then finish fourth in the AL with 36 homers in 1970. The comeback was short-lived, as Conigliaro was traded to the Angels, where he hit just four home runs in limited action. A later comeback with the Red Sox in 1975 lasted just 21 games, and Conigliaro was out of baseball, his 166 home runs just a tease to the promise his career once held.

The tragedy of Conigliaro's life was just beginning, however. He suffered a massive heart attack in 1982 at age 36 and lived out the rest of his years in a nursing home before passing away in 1990. He was only 45. Left unanswered is whether his later health problems were somehow related to his beaning or just another unlucky break for a gifted player who seemed destined to join Kelley and McCarthy as Boston boys in Cooperstown.

The All-Time Massachusetts team has two good options at designated hitter: Steve Balboni and Glenn Adams. Balboni picked up the nickname "Bye Bye" due to his home-run hitting ability, which is what earns him the selection. He had five straight years with at least 20 homers and finished with 181 in 11 seasons. His high was 36 in 1985, when he also led the league with 166 strikeouts. Balboni appeared in 281 games at DH, while Adams made 373 appearances as DH. However, Adams only hit 34 home runs during his career and never had more than 100 hits in a season due to his part-time role.

Candy Cummings won only 21 games in the National League and 145 games total if you include his four seasons in the National Association. Yet he is in the Hall of Fame as a pioneer, believed to be the inventor of the curveball or at least the first to use it in a professional game. He claimed to have spent several years of his youth perfecting the curve after first gaining inspiration while tossing clam shells into the water. Cummings won 33, 28, 28 and 35 games his first four years while pitching almost all the innings for a series of teams in the National Association, baffling batters who had no idea how to hit a curveball. Many other pitchers have claimed to be the first to throw a curveball, but Cummings' account was upheld at the right time — he was an early inductee into the Hall of Fame in 1939.

When pitchers were allowed to throw overhand beginning in the late 1880s, Charlie Buffinton was one of the first to employ a "drop ball" that behaved similar to a curveball. Buffinton used it to good effect, winning 20 or more games seven times and finishing with a record of 233–152 and 2.96 ERA.

Three other right-handed starters achieved enough success that they were elected to the Hall of Fame: Jack Chesbro, Tim Keefe and John Clarkson. The latter two were nineteenth century pitchers who compiled most of their incredible stats before the pitching mound was moved back.

"Happy Jack" Chesbro was a spitballer supreme who crammed astonishing productivity into what was essentially a 10-year career. His 1904 season for the New York Highlanders will be hard to duplicate. He led the league with 41 wins, .774 winning percentage, 51 games started, 48 complete games and 454 innings pitched while finishing second in strikeouts (239) and WHIP (0.937). The 41 wins are the most by a pitcher in the twentieth century and that year he also became the first pitcher to have led the American and National Leagues in won-lost percentage. With the pennant on the line in the next-to-last game of the 1904 season, Chesbro threw a wild pitch that let the winning run score and clinched the pennant for the Boston Americans.

In 1903 Chesbro pitched the first game in franchise history for the Highlanders, who were later renamed the Yankees. With the Pirates in 1902 he led the National League with 28 wins, .824 winning percentage and eight shutouts. He won two pennants with the Pirates and retired with a 198–132 record and 2.68 ERA. He was elected to the Hall of Fame in 1946.

Keefe won at least 32 games in six straight years, refining a changeup to go with an effective curve and finishing with 342 victories, 10th all-time. "Sir Timothy" also ranks third in complete games with 554, twelfth in innings pitched with 5,049 and 27th in strikeouts with 2,564. During the 1888 season he won 19 straight games, a feat later matched by Rube Marquard, and he went on to win the pitcher's Triple Crown with 35 wins, 1.74 ERA and 335 strikeouts.

The all-time best righty from Massachusetts is Clarkson, a contemporary of Keefe who dominated National League batters from 1882–94. Clarkson won the NL Triple Crown a year after Keefe, with 49 wins, .721 winning percentage and 2.73 ERA. He was even better in 1885 for the Chicago White Stockings, leading the league with 53 wins (second most ever), 308 strikeouts, 70 games started, 68 complete games, 10 shutouts and 623 innings pitched. When he retired his 328 career wins were the most in National League history — he ranks twelfth on the all-time list today. He posted eight straight seasons with at least 25 wins and helped his cause by hitting 24 career home runs.

Quite a few good pitchers have been born in Massachusetts, but only two of them were lefties: Tom Glavine and Wilbur Wood. Wood's career takes a back seat to that of Glavine, who appears to be a first-ballot lock when eligible for the Hall of Fame in 2014. A two-time Cy Young winner, he finished second and third in the Cy Young voting two times each and made 10 All-Star teams over his brilliant 22-year career, teaming up with Greg Maddux and John Smoltz in the 1990s to form arguably the best rotation in the history of baseball. He won 20 games five times, leading the league each year.

Glavine, who was born in Concord but grew up in Billerica as a die-hard Red Sox fan, retired after the 2008 season with a career record of 305–203. He made 35 postseason starts, earning World Series MVP honors in 1995 after winning Game 2 and then shutting out the Indians on one hit through eight innings in the Game 6 finale.

Glavine's ranking as number 21 on the all-time wins list is amazing when you consider he didn't have dominant stuff and never once posted more than 200 strikeouts in a season (his high was 192). The smart and strong-willed lefty relied on spotting his fastball with surgical precision and pounding batters with changeups away until they got impatient and got themselves out. Glavine explained his stubborn and unconventional approach to pitching in John Feinstein's 2008 book *Living on the Black*: "Sometimes I'll walk a guy, even if it means putting someone in scoring position, rather than give in and throw him a pitch he might hit for extra bases or out of the park."

It's safe to say we probably won't see another pitcher post five straight years with over 40 starts like Wood had with the White Sox from 1971–75. Wood's 49 starts in 1972 were the most since Chesbro recorded 51 in 1904. The knuckleballer was moved to the rotation after a three-year stretch in which he set a major league record with 88 appearances in 1968 and then led the league with 76 and 77 games out of the bullpen the next two years.

Wood is the last pitcher to have started both games of a doubleheader. He took the loss in both games against the Yankees on July 20, 1973. Wood's success was surprising when you consider that his record after his first six seasons with Boston and Pittsburgh was 1–8. Wood won at least 20 games four straight years with the White Sox and retired with a 164–156 record and 3.24 ERA.

The ninth inning is in the hands of Jeff "The Terminator" Reardon, who is Massachusetts' all-time leader in saves with 367. He posted 11 straight years with 20 or more saves, finishing first in the majors with 41 for the Expos in 1985, also earning the Rolaids Relief Award. While pitching for the Red Sox in 1992 Reardon passed Rollie Fingers to become the all-time saves leader in major league history with 342. He was quickly passed by Lee Smith and now ranks seventh. Reardon made four All-Star teams pitching for seven teams in 16 seasons, retiring in 1994. His life took a bizarre turn when he was arrested in 2005 for robbing a jewelry store, which was later blamed on medication he was taking for depression over his son's drug overdose death the previous year.

Other notable relievers from the state include Steve Bedrosian and Stu Miller. Bedrosian, nicknamed "Bedrock," accumulated 184 saves and earned the Cy Young Award after saving 40 games for the Phillies in 1987. He was not especially dominant that year, but he finished with 57 vote points to barely edge Rick Sutcliffe (55) and Rick Reuschel (54).

Miller had the best change-up of his era, throwing it masterfully at different speeds to become one of the most effective relief pitchers of the 1960s. He led the NL with 17 saves in 1961 and then led the AL with 27 saves and 71 appearances in 1963. Pitching 182 innings in 1958 while splitting time between the rotation and the bullpen, Miller led the league with a 2.47 ERA. During his career he started 93 games while appearing in 611 in relief, finishing with 105 wins and 154 saves.

We won't see the likes of Connie Mack again in baseball, remaining as manager of the same team for 50 straight seasons. Mack won a record 3,731 games, guiding the Philadelphia Athletics to nine American League pennants and five World Series titles. He also lost more games than he won — 3,948, which is 1,655 more than any other manager — and hung around for 19 years after his last pennant.

Cornelius McGillicuddy, Sr. (thankfully shortened to Connie Mack) wasn't much of a player, batting .244 in 11 seasons as a catcher, but he found quick success after becoming manager and part-owner of the Philadelphia Athletics in 1901. He won his first pennant the next season and went on to build two dynasties of players. His first group — anchored by his ideal player, Eddie Collins, along with Eddie Plank, Home Run Baker and Chief Bender — won four pennants and three World Series between 1910 and 1914. The second group — led by Jimmie Foxx, Mickey Cochrane, Al Simmons and Lefty Grove — won three straight pennants and two World Series between 1929 and 1931 while finishing second four other years.

Mack was instrumental in getting the American League established as an alternative to the National League with the Philadelphia franchise serving as one of the founding teams in 1901. It was the beginning of an influence that extended far and wide over the game for the next half-century.

Known as "The Tall Tactician" for his intelligent and thoughtful approach to managing, Mack looked for smart, disciplined, enthusiastic players who could execute the fundamentals and were self-motivated to improve. Attired like a gentleman in a business suit, tie and hat in the dugout (which meant he could not go onto the field to argue a call), the dignified Mack developed many baseball strategies that continue to be deployed today such as paying attention to opponents' pitching and batting tendencies and positioning players on defense based on who was batting.

He was adept at using his wide contacts in baseball to secure talented young players, shying away from those who couldn't control themselves on and off the field. He often advised his players, "You're born with two strikes against you, so don't take a third one on your own."

In stark contrast to Mack's gentle and calm demeanor was the brash, win-at-all-costs style of another Hall of Fame manager from Massachusetts — the controversial Durocher. Whereas Mack refrained from drinking and shied away from ballplayers who liked the night life, the abrasive Durocher once said, "If any of my players don't take a drink now and then they'll be gone. You don't play this game on gingersnaps." Durocher further summarized his crude approach to the game in his autobiography *Nice Guys Finish Last*: "Give me some scratching, diving, hungry ballplayers who come to kill you."

He took over as player-manager of the Brooklyn Dodgers at age 33 in 1939, as his 17-year playing career was winding down. Leo the Lip would go on to win 2,008 games as a manager over 24 seasons including three pennants and one championship with the New York Giants. He was suspended from baseball for the 1947 season for associating with gamblers, the beginning of the end for him in Brooklyn, but he re-emerged as skipper of the rival Giants.

In 1954 he became one of the first managers to identify and deploy two relievers as a tandem out of the bullpen. He rode the reliable relief pitching of knuckleballer Hoyt Wilhelm and journeyman Marv Grissom, combined with the all-around brilliance of Willie Mays, to deliver the first World Series title for the Giants since 1933.

Durocher never met an umpire he didn't disagree with and used intimidation as a weapon in his relationships with umpires, opponents, players and sportswriters. He was constantly looking for an edge and acting on hunches in an almost pathological quest to win, but he was neither an innovative thinker nor a patient skipper. Mack's players revered and admired him, hoping not to disappoint him, while Durocher's players viewed him with a mixture of fear and loathing.

The ruthless Durocher once famously said, "What are we at the park for except to win? I'd trip my mother. I'd help her up, brush her off, tell her I'm sorry. But mother don't make it to third." Neither Durocher nor his mother was alive to see him inducted into the Hall of Fame in 1994.

MICHIGAN

*Names in **bold** represent Major League selections by position, followed by honorable mentions. Negro Leagues players are in **bold italics**, followed by honorable mentions in italics. City of birth is in parentheses.*

Catcher — Ted Simmons (Highland Park). Also: Bill Freehan (Detroit); Jason Varitek (Rochester); Ernie Whitt (Detroit); Stan Lopata (Delray); Mike Pagliaroni (Dearborn)

First Base — Jack Fournier (AuSable). Also: John Mayberry (Detroit); Kevin Young (Alpena); Vic Saier (Lansing)

Second Base — Charlie Gehringer (Fowlerville). Also: Bobby Grich (Muskegon); Cass Michaels (Detroit)

Third Base — Chris Sabo (Detroit). Also: Bill Stein (Battle Creek)

Shortstop — Mike Bordick (Marquette). Also: Doc Lavan (Grand Rapids)

Outfield — Kiki Cuyler (Harrisville)

Outfield — Kirk Gibson (Pontiac)

Outfield — *Neil Robinson* **(Grand Rapids).** Also: Ron LeFlore (Detroit); Tom Tresh (Detroit); Jim Northrup (Breckenridge); *Harry Moore* (Detroit); Charlie Maxwell (Lawton); Bill Virdon (Hazel Park); Mickey Stanley (Grand Rapids); Ira Flagstead (Montague); Charlie Hemphill (Greenville)

Designated Hitter — Jay Gibbons (Rochester)

Right Handed Starter — John Smoltz (Warren). Also: Bob Welch (Detroit); Milt Pappas (Detroit); Eddie Cicotte (Springwells); Ed Reulbach (Detroit); *Walter Ball* (Detroit); Pat Hentgen (Detroit); Derek Lowe (Dearborn); Rick Wise (Jackson); Bob Buhl (Saginaw); Scott Sanderson (Dearborn)

Left Handed Starter — Hal Newhouser (Detroit). Also: Jim Kaat (Zeeland); Billy Pierce (Detroit); Frank Tanana (Detroit); Jim Abbott (Flint)

Relief Pitcher — Mike Marshall (Adrian). Also: Bill Campbell (Highland Park); Phil Regan (Otsego); Dick Radatz (Detroit); Fred Gladding (Flat Rock); Jim Kern (Gladwin); Paul Assenmacher (Detroit); Steve Howe (Pontiac); J.J. Putz (Trenton)

Manager — Joe Altobelli (Detroit). Also: Bill Virdon (Hazel Park); Clint Hurdle (Big Rapids)

The Names

Best Nickname: Phil "The Vulture" Regan

Other Nicknames: Walter "The Georgia Rabbit" Ball; Anthony "Bunny" Brief; Bob "Bluecheese" Bruce; Charles "Count" Campau; Eddie "Knuckles" Cicotte; Hazen "Kiki" Cuyler; Aloysius "Wish" Egan; Herrick "Spoke" Emery; Albert "Bunny" Fabrique; Charlie "The Mechanical Man" Gehringer; Ray "Dad" Hale; Luke "Hot Potato" Hamlin; Charlie "Eagle Eye" Hemphill; "Coldwater Jim" Hughey; Jim "Kitty" Kaat; "Reindeer Bill" Killefer; Ed "Kickapoo" Kippert; Ron "Jailbird" LeFlore; Bertram "Dutch" Lerchen; Edmund "Stubby" Magner; Charlie "Paw Paw" Maxwell; "Prince" Hal Newhouser; Frank "Flossie" Oberlin; Frank "Stubby" Overmire; Frank "Yip" Owen; Tom "Wimpy" Paciorek; Vernon "Slicker" Parks; Leroy "Tarzan" Parmelee; Clarke "Pinky" Pittinger; Dick "The Monster" Radatz; Frank "Ribs" Raney; Steve "Rainbow" Trout; Maurice "Bomber" Van Robays; Bill "Mr. Milkshake" Virdon; Clyde "Buzzy" Wares; George "Tex" Wisterzil

Most Unusual Name: Casimir Kwietniewski; Bryan Clutterbuck

All-Time Leaders

Games: Ted Simmons, 2456
Hits: Charlie Gehringer, 2839
Batting Average: Kiki Cuyler, .321
Home Runs: Kirk Gibson and John Mayberry (tied at 255)
RBI: Charlie Gehringer, 1427
Stolen Bases: Ron Leflore, 455
Wins: Jim Kaat, 283
Strikeouts: John Smoltz, 3084
Saves: Mike Marshall, 188
Future Star: Daryl Jones (Royal Oak)
Best Player: Charlie Gehringer

Historic Baseball Places

Comerica Park in Detroit — Opened in 2000 as the new home of the Tigers. Check out the decade-by-decade museum with artifacts from each era spread around the concourse. Beyond the brick wall in left center are statues of six Tigers stars: Ty Cobb, Al Kaline, Charlie Gehringer, Hal Newhouser, Willie Horton and Hank Greenberg. A statue of legendary broadcaster Ernie Harwell can be found outside the park.

Wuerfel Park in Traverse City — Designed with a façade that resembles a resort hotel, it opened in 2006 as the home of the independent league Traverse City Beach Bums.

Charlie Maxwell Ball Diamond in Paw Paw — Local ball field was renamed in 2010 to honor "Ol' Paw Paw," one of the most popular players in Tigers history. Also features a monument honoring the accomplishments of Maxwell and another one honoring Bill and Red Killefer, two other locals who made it to the majors.

House of David Museum in Benton Harbor — Tells the story of "The Best Barnstorming Team in America," all members of the House of David religious commune, who were celibate vegetarians forbidden

Wuerfel Park in Traverse City has one of the most unusual appearances for a ballpark. The façade was designed to resemble the summer resort hotels that line the shores of Lake Michigan (courtesy BallparkReviews.com).

from cutting their hair or beards. The House of David not only barnstormed with Negro Leagues teams such as the Kansas City Monarchs, they often insisted the Negro Leagues players be accepted as equals wherever they played, helping pave the way to integration in baseball. The museum showcases photos and artifacts from the baseball team's history, with greats such as Babe Ruth and Satchel Paige playing exhibitions for the House of David.

Notable Achievements

Neal Ball (Grand Haven) executed baseball's first unassisted triple play while playing for the Cleveland Indians on July 19, 1909.

Mike Marshall holds the American League and National League record for appearances in a season. He appeared in 104 games with the Dodgers in 1974 and 90 games for the Twins in 1979.

John Vander Wal (Grand Rapids) set a record with 28 pinch hits in 1995.

Rick Wise hit two home runs while pitching a no-hitter on June 23, 1971.

Ron LeFlore was the first player to lead both leagues in stolen bases. He led the AL with 68 for the Tigers in 1978 and NL with 97 for the Expos in 1980.

Jerry Lynch (Bay City) once held the major league record for career pinch-hit home runs with 18.

Frank Tanana started the first games at the Kingdome (April 6, 1977) and at the new Comiskey Park (April 18, 1991)—pitching shutouts in both games—and also pitched the last game at Memorial Stadium in Baltimore (October 6, 1991).

Bill Campbell won 17 games out of the bullpen for the Twins in 1976, which is the second-most wins by a reliever in a single season behind Roy Face's 18 in 1959.

Count Campau (Detroit) set a major league record that still stands with 15 straight multi-hit games in July 1890.

Motor City Keeps Producing the Stars

Michigan's major leaguers include 118 who were born in Detroit. The Motor City alumni include Bill Freehan, John Mayberry, Cass Michaels, Chris Sabo, Ron LeFlore, Tom Tresh, Milt Pappas, Bob Welch, Ed Reulbach, Pat Hentgen, John Smoltz, Hal Newhouser, Billy Pierce, Frank Tanana, Dick Radatz and Negro Leaguers Harry Moore and Walter Ball.

The Detroit Stars were founded in 1919 and then became charter members of the Negro National League the next year. Playing games at hitter-friendly Mack Park, the Stars fielded a team packed with stars such as Pete Hill, Bruce Petway, John Donaldson, Jimmie Lyons and Ed Wesley. Slugging sensation Turkey Stearnes arrived in 1923 and proceeded to lead the league in homers six times over the next nine seasons. When the baseball season wrapped up, Stearnes would work in the auto plants over the winter.

Clothing retailer John Roesink built Mack Park in 1910, which was located in a white neighborhood and attracted integrated crowds. In 1925 he bought the Stars, becoming just the second white man to own a Negro Leagues franchise. He built Roesink Stadium in

Hamtranck and had Ty Cobb throw out the first pitch when the stadium opened in 1930. Today, Roesink Stadium is abandoned and in threat of demolition.

The Detroit Wolverines were original members of the National League and operated from 1881–1888. They set a record that still stands by allowing 18 runs in one inning during a game in 1883. Frederick Kimball Stearns bought the team two years later and did something that would make George Steinbrenner envious — he bought the entire Buffalo Bisons franchise so he could raid the best players. Dan Brouthers, Jack Rowe, Deacon White and Hardy Richardson — known as "The Big Four" — helped the Wolverines go 87–36 in 1886 and then win the National League pennant the next season while also defeating the American Association champions in an early version of the World Series.

The Detroit Tigers are the only major league team still in existence that has retained the same name throughout its history dating back to the formation of the American and National Leagues. They have stayed the Detroit Tigers since 1901. The Chicago White Sox come close, but they were originally known as the White Stockings.

After losing three straight World Series (1907–09) in the early years of Ty Cobb's career, the Tigers finally broke through with their first championship in 1935 behind the play of Fowlerville native Charlie Gehringer.

Detroit has also brought us the Paciorek brothers. Tom Paciorek bounced around six teams in 18 seasons but was mostly a platoon player. He batted .326 for Seattle and made the All-Star team in 1981, one of the few seasons he played regularly. Brother John Paciorek has the highest batting average in major league history — 1.000! He went 3-for-3 for the Houston Colt 45's in 1963 and no other batters with a 1.000 average have more than two hits. A third Paciorek brother, Jim, played one season for the Brewers. The Paciorek brothers combined for 1,188 major league hits, 1,162 of them by Tom.

Thank goodness Detroit native Casimir Kwietniewski changed his name after one season, giving sportswriters a sigh of relief. He went straight from Hamtramck High School to the White Sox at the age of 18, playing the 1943 season under the name Cass Kwietniewski before shortening it to Cass Michaels.

Before he embarked on his Hall of Fame basketball career, Detroit-born Dave DeBusschere pitched part of two seasons for the White Sox (1962–63). He pitched a six-hit shutout against the Indians on August 13, 1963, and finished with a 3–4 record, 2.90 ERA and ERA+ of 124.

Baseball fans in Michigan, perhaps more than any other state, have been able to watch their native sons play major league ball close to home. The 416 Michigan-born players include enough Tigers alumni to easily fill an All-Star team. Before we get to the All-Time Michigan team, let's have some fun and throw together an All-Tigers team of players from Michigan.

The All-Tigers team would feature Bill Freehan at catcher, Mickey Stanley at first (an outfielder by trade, he played 94 games at first), Hall of Famer Charlie Gehringer at second, Steve Boros at third and Frank Scheibeck at short. The outfield is cluttered with possibilities: Kirk Gibson, Ron Leflore, Tom Tresh, Jim Northrup, Charlie Maxwell, Leon Roberts and Ira Flagstead, just to name the most accomplished. Starting pitchers include Hal Newhouser, John Smoltz (he was traded to the Braves before appearing in a game for the Tigers), Frank Tanana, Eddie Cicotte, Billy Pierce, Frank Kitson, Steve Gromek, Big Bill James, Vern Ruhle and Steve Avery. The bullpen is manned by Mike Marshall, Phil Regan, Dick Radatz, Fred Gladding and Jason Grilli. Not a bad squad.

All-Time Michigan Selections

Three Michigan-born players have made it to the Hall of Fame — Gehringer and Newhouser along with Kiki Cuyler — but many think they should have more company in Cooperstown. Smoltz is not yet eligible for the Hall, but at least four other Michigan natives should have received more consideration than they have to date: Freehan, Ted Simmons, Bobby Grich and Jim Kaat.

It's hard to figure out why Simmons is not in the Hall of Fame. An eight-time All-Star who first played in the majors at 19 (after being the number 10 overall pick a year earlier), Simmons hit over .300 seven times and finished in the top 10 in batting six times — quite a feat for a catcher. He was a dependable, feared slugger who hit for average and was durable — averaging 135 games caught between 1971 and 1980. By the end of his rookie year with the Cardinals, he had already pushed perennial All-Star Joe Torre to third base.

"As far as I'm concerned, there is no greater pleasure in the world than walking up to the plate with men on base and knowing that you are feared," Simmons was quoted in Roger Angell's *Late Innings*.

Looking at Career Win Shares for the decade of the 1970s, Simmons places second among catchers behind Johnny Bench. Next, let's take the career stats of the 13 non-Negro Leagues catchers in the Hall of Fame and see how Simmons compares. We discover he has more hits (2,472) and doubles (483) than any of the Hall of Famers. By comparison, Roy Campanella hit 178 doubles and Ray Schalk had 199. Furthermore, Simmons ranks second with 1,389 RBI (behind only Yogi Berra); fifth in homers with 248 (behind only Bench, Carlton Fisk, Berra and Gary Carter); and fifth in games caught with 1,771 (behind Fisk, Carter, Rick Ferrell and Hartnett). Simmons even ranks sixth in fielding percentage, ahead of acknowledged defensive stalwarts such as Hartnett, Buck Ewing and Schalk.

Quite a few of the best players from Michigan played in the modern Deadball Era (roughly 1963–1976 and then to a lesser extent up to 1992). That's where the beauty of Neutralized Batting comes in. It eliminates the distortions created by ballpark, playing era and length of season. It converts all seasons to 162 games and assumes average team scoring of 4.42 runs/game.

If we look at Simmons' Neutralized Batting stats we see he's up to 2,580 hits, 261 homers, 1,543 RBI and a .288 average. Now we see even more justification for Bill James listing Simmons as the 10th-best catcher in baseball history, just two spots ahead of Freehan.

Since Simmons' numbers demonstrate he belongs with the game's great catchers, it is hard to fathom why he received just 3.7 percent of the vote in his first year of eligibility (1994), causing him to drop off the ballot. Probably the biggest factor working against him was the fact that he was not Johnny Bench. All catchers of the 1970s paled in comparison to the guy generally considered the greatest all-around catcher in history. Although unfairly knocked for his defensive shortcomings, Simmons did possess a weak arm and had a lot of passed balls.

Voters also probably remembered the last five years of Simmons' career when he was hanging around as a DH and first baseman — he only caught in 72 percent of his career games — and stopped hitting. Take 1984, for example, when he posted an OPS+ of 61, which is one of the lowest scores for a position player in the twentieth century. Finally, he spent his first 13 seasons with the St. Louis Cardinals but didn't make it to the playoffs until he joined the Brewers in 1981.

The outspoken Simmons gained notoriety in 1972 for starting the season without a contract (he finally relented and signed in August) and he was later run out of St. Louis because new manager Whitey Herzog didn't want any strong leaders diminishing his authority. Still, his long and distinguished career merited a closer and longer look by Hall voters.

Equally deserving of enshrinement but in different ways, Freehan was even more overlooked by Hall voters. He received just two votes in his first year of eligibility (1982), dropping off the ballot for good.

You had to watch Freehan play every day to appreciate his skill and value. He was a good hitter with power who had a knack for getting hit by pitches, as well as a terrific defensive catcher with a powerful arm. Freehan won five consecutive Gold Gloves, leading the league in fielding percentage three times and finishing second six times. He was a regular catcher during 11 seasons, making the All-Star team every one of those years and playing his entire career with the Tigers.

In 1968 Freehan was MVP runner-up after hitting 25 homers, driving in 84 runs and leading the league with 24 HBP — he had finished third in the MVP voting the previous year. He retired with 200 homers, 1,591 hits, 1,581 games caught and a respectable .262 average (same as Gary Carter). Freehan posted 263 Career Win Shares, which trails Simmons but still places him ahead of five Hall of Fame catchers.

Keep in mind that pitchers dominated play throughout Freehan's career. The American League average during his 15 seasons ranged from .230 to a high of .259. He hit .282 in 1967 (finishing ninth) when the league average was .236 and in 1971 he was 30 points above the league average of .247. When Freehan batted .300 in 1964 (sixth in the AL) it was no small feat considering AL batters hit an anemic .247 that year.

Freehan's Neutralized Batting stats show him with 1,742 hits, 218 homers, 848 RBI and a respectable .279 average with .360 OBP. That's more homers than 10 Hall of Fame catchers produced and a better average than five — all from a catcher known more for his defense. He is certainly a player who deserved way more than two votes for the Hall of Fame.

The reality is that neither Simmons nor Freehan is in the Hall and one of them also has to take a seat on the bench for the All-Time Michigan team. Simmons' hitting credentials outshine Freehan's all-around contributions and he outscores him 317–263 in Career Win Shares, so the spot goes to the pride of Highland Park.

Let's move on to first base, where we have two viable candidates. Jack Fournier's career bridged the Deadball and Live Ball Eras, which is evidenced by the fact that he hit 18 home runs in his first eight seasons and 118 over the last seven years of his career. Fournier, who was subpar defensively, led the NL with 27 homers in 1924, also driving in 116 runs and batting .334 that year. He batted over .300 eight times and finished his career with an outstanding .313/.392/.483 line with a 142 OPS+ (same as Cap Anson). Fournier languished in the minors for three years during his prime because the White Sox acquired Chick Gandil to play first before the 1917 season, which is why Fournier's career stats fall a little short.

Another fine first baseman from Michigan is John Mayberry, a Detroit native who had his best seasons with the Royals. Called up to the majors at age 19 in 1968, Mayberry batted 0-for-9 in his late-season tryout and then proceeded to go 0-for-4 in just five games of action the next season. Undaunted by the slow start to his major league career, Mayberry went on to smack 255 homers and drive in 100 runs three times, making two All-Star teams.

Mayberry had excellent plate discipline for a slugger, leading the AL in walks twice and ending his career with more bases on balls than strikeouts. His best season was 1975 when he was MVP runner-up after hitting .291–34–106, posting a .416 OBP and leading the league with 119 walks and 168 OPS+. His lifetime 123 OPS+ is the same as Jeff Kent, Roy Campanella and Enos Slaughter.

Second base belongs to Gehringer, who earns extra consideration for playing his entire 19-year career for the Detroit Tigers. His manager when he was first called up to the team in 1924, Ty Cobb, certainly knew a good hitter when he saw one and he put Gehringer in the lineup and left him there. He was nicknamed "The Mechanical Man" because he seemed almost robotic in the way he quietly went out there and produced. He built a Hall of Fame career by compiling 2,839 hits, scoring 1,774 runs (nineteenth all-time) and hitting 574 doubles (twentieth-best in history).

Gehringer, who batted over .300 13 times, was named AL MVP in 1937 when he scored 133 runs, led the league with a .371 mark and had a .458 OBP (2nd best) and .978 OPS. He retired in 1942 with a .320 lifetime average and .404 OBP. One of his best seasons was 1929, when he led the league in runs, hits, doubles, triples and stolen bases while driving in 106 runs and batting .339. Unbelievably, he received no MVP votes that year primarily because the Tigers finished sixth. The team did win three pennants during Gehringer's tenure, and he hit .375 as the Tigers won the World Series in 1935.

Gehringer also excelled in the field, leading the AL in fielding percentage six times, assists seven times and putouts three times. If one takes a look at his Neutralized Batting stats, we see how he benefitted from playing in the Lively Ball Era. Gehringer's average drops 23 points to .297, his OBP goes from .404 to .378 and his hits from 2,839 to 2,682.

Grich was given strong consideration, since he is one of the most underrated players in baseball history. Acknowledged as an outstanding fielder with good range, strong arm and soft hands, Grich was also a solid hitter who belted 224 home runs. He earned six All-Star selections and four Gold Gloves, joining teammates Mark Belanger and Brooks Robinson to give the Orioles three Gold Glove infielders in 1972 and 1973. Grich led AL second basemen in putouts and range factor four times, assists three times and fielding percentage twice.

Before players like Jeff Kent and Alfonso Soriano came along, second basemen generally didn't offer much power. Grich, however, tied for the home run crown with 22 during the strike-shortened 1981 season while also leading the league in slugging and OPS+ that year. Not only that, he walked a lot, finishing in the top eight in bases on balls six times.

The argument for Grich's Hall candidacy becomes more compelling after checking out his Neutralized Batting stats. The hits go from 1,833 to 2,106; homers from 224 to 258; RBIs from 864 to 1,006; and most importantly, his average jumps from .266 to .288 while his new OBP is .396. In other words, he was a darn good hitter who played in the wrong era and the wrong parks. That alone doesn't make him Hall-worthy, but when you consider he was an all-time great fielder, then he becomes a viable candidate for Cooperstown.

Unfortunately, Grich suffered the same fate as his fellow Michigan players Simmons and Freehan — he dropped off the ballot after receiving just 2.6 percent of the votes his first year. He had the misfortune to enter the ballot in 1992, the same year as Tony Perez and Tom Seaver (whose 98.8 vote percentage remains the highest ever). It also marked the first year Pete Rose could have been elected to the Hall if he had not been placed on the ineligible list, and writers were undoubtedly preoccupied with debating that subject.

Chris Sabo mans the All-Michigan team at third base, goggles and all. When he was called up by the Reds to replace the injured Buddy Bell in 1988, Sabo played with a reckless abandon that quickly won over Cincinnati fans. His hustling, hard-nosed style of play was reminiscent of another Reds player, Pete Rose, who happened to be his manager. Sabo made the All-Star team that year and went on to be voted Rookie of the Year after batting .271 with 146 hits including 40 doubles while also stealing 46 bases. He hit 25 home runs and was again an All-Star in 1990 as he helped lead the Reds to a World Series title. A .301 average with 26 homers followed in 1991, along with another All-Star selection, but Sabo's production began to decline after that due to injuries.

Mike Bordick emerged as the best shortstop. After attending high school and college in Maine, where games were as likely to be snowed out as rained out, Bordick put together a productive 15-year career. After the Orioles acquired him from the A's before the 1997 season, Bordick had the unenviable task of replacing Cal Ripken, Jr., at shortstop. He didn't hit much for the O's first year but only committed 13 errors and became known for his smart play. He went on to make the All-Star team in 2000 after hitting .285 with 20 homers and 85 RBI.

Bordick was a more than adequate hitter but an outstanding fielder who led the league in putouts and fielding percentage twice and assists three times. Omar Vizquel won the AL Glove Glove at shortstop in 1999 but it should have gone to Bordick, who committed six fewer errors and flashed more range that year. He retired in 2003 with exactly 1,500 hits and still holds the record for most consecutive errorless games (110) and chances (543) by a shortstop.

Doc Lavan basically produced one good statistic in his entire 12-year career — 82 RBI in 1921 — and no Cardinals shortstop has topped it since, not even Marty Marion. Lavan didn't hit for power or average or get on base with walks, and he came from the matador school of defense as evidenced by him leading league shortstops in errors four times. He's best known for joining up with Del Pratt in 1917 to sue St. Louis Browns owner Phil Ball for slander for suggesting the team was losing games on purpose due to their grievances with manager Fielder Jones. Anyone who watched Doc play knew his incompetence was the real deal and not an act.

Anchoring the outfield we have Kiki Cuyler, who fashioned a Hall of Fame career with clutch hitting and deft base running. Cuyler hit .354 with 32 stolen bases his first full year (1924) with the Pirates, but he was just getting started. The next year he batted .357 and led the league with 144 runs and 26 triples while hitting 18 homers, driving in 102 runs and stealing 41 bases. Cuyler not only led the Pirates to the pennant that year, he carried them to a World Series title. He belted a game-winning home run in Game 2, then it was his two-run double off the great Walter Johnson in the eighth inning of Game 6 that ultimately clinched the Series. He would finish second in the MVP voting that year.

Cuyler would be joined by Paul Waner the next year in the Pirates outfield, forming an explosive combination. Cuyler led the NL with 113 runs and 35 steals that year and batted .321, while Waner led the league with 22 triples and batted .336. The team was on the cusp of even greater things in 1927 when Waner's brother, Lloyd, joined the outfield. Paul ("Big Poison") would hit .380 that year with 237 hits while Lloyd ("Little Poison") would bat .355 with 223 hits as a rookie.

However, the Dream Team of outfields was not to be for the Pirates, as Kiki clashed with manager Donie Bush over where he batted in the lineup. Owner Barney Dreyfuss sided with the manager over his star player and Cuyler missed the last two months of the season as well as the World Series, where the Pirates were swept by the Yankees. They would not win another pennant or World Series until 1960.

After the season, the Pirates traded Cuyler to the Cubs, where he led them to pennants in 1929 and 1932. Kiki would go on to bat over .300 10 times with a career average of .321 and led the league in steals four times with a career total of 328.

Cuyler is joined in the outfield by Kirk Gibson, who won the National League Most Valuable Player Award in 1988 despite not leading the league in any hitting categories that season. In fact, he never led the league in any hitting categories and also never made an All-Star roster during his 17-season career (mainly because he declined the chance to play in the 1985 and 1988 games).

Gibson hit one of the most dramatic home runs in World Series history, and most baseball fans have seen the replay dozens of times. He was not expected to play at all in the 1988 Series against the heavily favored A's, because he was nursing bad injuries to his left hamstring and right knee. But behind 4–3 with two outs in the bottom of the ninth of Game 1, Dodgers manager Tommy Lasorda called on Gibson to pinch-hit with one runner on base. He worked the count full against A's closer Dennis Eckersley and then blasted the next pitch into the right field seats, pumping his fist as he limped along the bases. It would be Gibson's only at-bat in the Series, and the deflated A's would not regain the momentum and bowed down to defeat in five games. Here's how legendary announcer Vin Scully famously described Gibson's shot: "In a year that has been so improbable, the impossible has happened!"

Gibson, who was an All-American wide receiver at Michigan State, spent his first nine seasons toiling for his hometown Tigers, where he drew comparisons to Mickey Mantle for his combination of speed and power. It was his three-run homer off Goose Gossage in Game 5 that won the 1984 World Series for the Tigers. Gibson would be declared a free agent in 1988 after an arbitrator ruled the owners were in collusion, and he left his hometown team to sign with the Dodgers. His World Series heroics that year were only possible because he had single-handedly led his team past the Mets in the NLCS, with an unbelievable diving catch in Game 3, an extra-innings homer in Game 4 and a decisive three-run home run in Game 5.

It was a little harder to decide on the third outfielder, with as many as nine candidates given consideration. Four players ultimately emerged as the most accomplished: Tigers speedster Ron LeFlore, Yankees slugger Tom Tresh, Negro Leagues star Neil Robinson and another Tigers player, Jim Northrup.

Robinson was a free-swinging slugger during a Negro Leagues career that lasted from 1934 to 1952. He appeared in eight East-West All-Star games while playing for the Memphis Red Sox, batting .476 in those games including an inside-the-park homer that won the 1938 All-Star game. He reportedly hit 59 home runs during the 1939 season if all games are included. Robinson, who was usually among the league leaders in home runs and stolen bases, is credited with a .303 lifetime average. Birmingham Barons manager Winfield Welch called Robinson, "the kind of player you build a team around."

Signed out of prison by Billy Martin for the Tigers, LeFlore quickly demonstrated he had a singular talent for stealing bases. He became an All-Star in 1976, just his third season, after stealing 58 bases and hitting .316. The next year he produced 212 hits, with 16 homers, 39 steals and a .325 average. In 1978 he led the league with 126 runs and 68 steals while batting .297 with 198 hits. He wasn't done improving, as 1979 brought 78 steals and a .300 average. Traded to Montreal in 1980, his average dropped to .257 but he swiped 97 bases — the ninth-highest total in the modern era. The outspoken LeFlore ended up playing only nine years in the majors but retired with 455 stolen bases and a .288 average.

A switch-hitter with power who could also field, throw and run the bases well, Tresh offered lots of intangibles. Tresh was an All-Star at shortstop and Rookie of the Year for the Yankees' 1962 championship team after batting .286 with 20 homers and 93 RBI. He moved to center field the next year to replace a hobbled Mickey Mantle, unfortunately drawing comparisons with the legendary Mick. He didn't disappoint with 25 homers and another All-Star appearance but the Yanks fell in the Series. His production dipped in 1964 as he moved to left and the Yankees again made it to the Series and fell short. His stellar defensive work was rewarded with a Gold Glove in 1965, but it was his last strong year with the bat.

Northrup was a solid contributor who never led the league in anything. He did go a little crazy with grand slams in 1968, bashing four during the season (including two in the same game on June 24), then hit another in Game 6 of the World Series. Northrup accumulated 1,254 hits over 12 seasons, mainly with the Tigers, and he trails only Cuyler and Gibson among Michigan outfielders with 162 Career Win Shares and 116 OPS+.

LeFlore's career average was 43 points higher than Tresh and he was one of the game's greatest base stealers, but he was also a poor fielder who struck out a lot. Tresh batted .219, .195 and .211 his last three years, while Northrup never made a single All-Star team, mitigating factors that exclude them from the top spot. In the end, it was hard to overlook Robinson's track record of slugging in the Negro Leagues and he got the third outfield spot.

Another Michigan outfielder, Charlie Maxwell, hardly played in nine of his 14 major league seasons but deserves mention here. Maxwell was a popular Tigers player who had the uncanny ability to hit home runs on Sundays — 40 of his 148 homers came on Sunday, hence the nickname "Sunday Charlie." He set a record by once hitting four straight homers over a doubleheader on Sunday. Maxwell also holds the record for most extra-inning home runs in a season with five in 1960.

Another noteworthy outfielder is Harry Moore, who was a star outfielder in the early days of black baseball. Moore, whose career lasted from 1894–1913, stood out for his outstanding range in the outfield but he was an accomplished hitter who consistently hit over .300. He played largely for Chicago-based teams such as the Chicago Unions, Leland Giants and Chicago Giants.

The options were slim for designated hitter, so the spot goes to Jay Gibbons. Gibbons had hit 127 home runs through 2011, with three seasons of 20 or more homers. He has played primarily in the outfield but has appeared at DH in 174 games.

Three right-handed starters from Michigan have won the Cy Young Award: John Smoltz (1996), Bob Welch (1990) and Pat Hentgen (1996). Smoltz is the clear choice as best righty starter, even though he had a pretty impressive run as a relief pitcher, saving 154 games in his 3½ years as a closer for the Braves. He made his mark as a starter, with 481 starts over his brilliant 21-year career. Smoltz's 15 postseason wins ranks second all-time behind Andy Pettitte's 19. He is the only pitcher to record more than 200 wins and 150 saves, with his career coming to an end after the 2009 season with a 213–155 record, 3.33 ERA and 3,084 strikeouts.

Smoltz locked up with the Twins' Jack Morris in one of the greatest postseason duels in baseball history — Game 7 of the 1991 World Series. Neither team scored a run in the first nine innings, although Smoltz had been replaced after getting one out in the seventh. Morris came back out and held the Braves scoreless in the 10th, and the Braves bullpen gave up the winning run in the bottom of the inning. An eight-time All-Star who was an outstanding overall athlete, Smoltz appeared in five World Series with the Braves but won only one title — in 1995. He won the Cy Young Award in 1996 after going 24–8 and leading the league with 276 strikeouts.

Welch won the Cy Young Award with the A's in 1990 after going 27–6 with a 2.95 ERA — no pitcher has won more games since. Welch won two fewer games over his career than Smoltz but lost nine fewer games and posted a similar career ERA. Yet Welch dropped off the Hall of Fame ballot after receiving just one vote in 2000, his first year of eligibility, while Smoltz has an excellent chance of gaining induction. Welch first gained notoriety as a 21-year-old rookie when he struck out Reggie Jackson to close out Game 2 of the 1978 World Series.

Milt Pappas was a steady if unspectacular righty, compiling a 209–164 record over 17 seasons with a 3.40 ERA. Thirteen times he won between 12 and 17 games. In 1972 he became the first pitcher to win 200 games without a 20-win season. He had the misfortune to be traded by the Orioles with two other players for Frank Robinson in December 1965 in one of the most lopsided trades ever. All Robinson did the next season was win the Triple Crown and MVP and lead the Orioles to a World Championship. Pappas nearly pitched a perfect game on September 2, 1972, walking a batter with two outs in the ninth before completing the no-hitter. He didn't hit for a high average but Pappas did slug 20 home runs in the majors.

Ed Reulbach, was a key pitcher on the Cubs teams that reached the World Series in 1906–1908 and 1910. He became the only pitcher to record shutout victories in both games of a doubleheader when he performed the feat on September 26, 1908. Reulbach won 182 games over his career, winning 20 games twice and leading the NL in winning percentage three straight years. He finished with a sparkling 2.28 ERA playing in the Deadball Era, which is tied with Babe Ruth for eighteenth all-time.

Our final righty of note, Eddie Cicotte, appeared headed to the Hall of Fame after leading the White Sox to pennants in 1917 and 1919 and compiling over 200 wins. Known as "Knuckles" for his mastery of the knuckleball, part of his assortment of trick pitches, he led the AL with 28 wins, 1.53 ERA and 0.912 WHIP in 1971 and went 29–7 with 1.82 ERA and 30 complete games during the 1919 campaign. Cicotte proved to be a central figure in the Black Sox Scandal, admitting to a grand jury that he took $10,000 to fix the 1919 World Series against the Reds. "I did it for the wife and kiddies," he was quoted saying afterwards. He was banned for life from baseball as a result.

The two left-handed pitchers with the most losses in American League history hail from Michigan — Frank Tanana tops the list with 221 followed by Jim Kaat with 191. Both received strong consideration for left-handed starter on Team Michigan, but Hal Newhouser is the logical choice since he is in the Hall of Fame. Prince Hal is the only pitcher to win consecutive MVP Awards, which he accomplished in 1944 and 1945. His first five and last five seasons were mediocre, but the middle seven were spectacular enough to gain him entry to Cooperstown.

Newhouser went 29–9 with 2.22 ERA and league-leading 187 strikeouts in 1944, but he was just getting started. He led the league in 11 pitching categories in 1945 including wins (25), ERA (1.81), complete games (29), shutouts (8), strikeouts (212) and ERA+ (195). Granted, those numbers were posted while many of the best players were away for the war. Newhouser showed it was no fluke, by going 26–9 record in 1946 with 1.94 ERA, and leading the league with 21 wins in 1948. Playing most of his career with the Tigers, Newhouser only played on two pennant winners in 17 seasons: the 1945 World Series champion Tigers and the 1954 Cleveland Indians squad that won 111 games but fell short in the Series.

Kaat was a fine pitcher who had no business winning 16 consecutive Gold Gloves, as his only discernible skill was a good pickoff move. He led league pitchers in errors in 1965 and 1969, yet won Gold Gloves both years. He committed eight errors with only four double plays in 1969, while generating an abysmal fielding percentage of .826 — and you guessed it, won another Gold Glove.

Let's compare Kaat's fielding stats to Greg Maddux, since Mad Dog won 18 Gold Gloves as a pitcher. Maddux compiled 1,194 assists with 94 double plays compared to 744 and 65 for Kaat. Maddux committed just 53 errors in 5,008 innings pitched for a .970 fielding percentage, while Kaat committed 56 errors in 4,530 innings pitched for a .947 fielding percentage. Obviously, only one of the two was deserving of the fielding awards. SABR member John Knox did some advanced statistical comparisons to rank the fielding abilities of pitchers, and he has Kaat ranked 272nd out of the 287 qualifying pitchers. In other words, Kaat was actually a pretty bad fielder for a pitcher. Maddux, by the way, ranked second.

Kaat managed to win 283 games by hanging around for 25 years. He went 10–24 in his first three seasons and 36–36 in his last seven seasons, which adds up to a 46–60 slate for 10 years of pitching. Furthermore, he posted 11 seasons with a .500 record or worse, lost 237 games and gave up 9.2 hits per 9 innings over his career.

Still, he was a crafty, smart pitcher who worked fast and used deception more than pure stuff to get results. Kaat won 25 games in 1966 for the Twins and later won 20 games twice for the White Sox. A three-time All-Star, he only received Cy Young votes in one year — 1975.

In 15 years on the baseball writers' ballot for the Hall of Fame, Kaat consistently received 20–25 percent of the vote. He has received greater support from the Veterans Committee, but not enough to get him over the hump. Kaat has a clear understanding of his place in history, as he was quoted saying, "I'll never be considered one of the all-time greats, maybe not even one of the all-time goods. But I'm one of the all-time survivors."

Lefty Billy Pierce was a true ace who anchored the White Sox staff for 13 years, winning 20 games twice and winning 20 games six times while pitching for the Sox across three decades (1949–61). Billy the Kid, who won 211 games with a 3.27 ERA, led the league in complete games three times as well as strikeouts in 1953 (186) and ERA in 1955 (1.97). A seven-time All-Star, Pierce had his number 19 retired by the White Sox.

Tanana managed to win 240 games to go with those 236 losses over 21 seasons. A flamethrower at the beginning of his career, he led the league with 269 strikeouts in 1975 at the age of 21 and then finished second the next year with 261 K's. Pitching 1,293 innings in the majors between the ages of 20 and 24 seemed to do him in, and he battled arm problems the rest of his career. He hung around long enough to retire with the most losses of any left-handed pitcher in American League history — 221. Tanana is one of only two pitchers to surrender home runs to Hank Aaron and Barry Bonds.

Jim Abbott, who was born without a right hand, has served as an inspiration for disabled persons both during and after his playing career. It took tremendous dedication, but a determined Abbott learned how to pitch, field and bat one-handed as a young boy, refusing to let his handicap serve as an obstacle. He carried the flag for the U.S. team in the Opening Ceremonies of the 1988 Olympics and pitched a complete game victory in the Gold Medal game. In 1987 he became the first baseball player to win the Sullivan Award as the top amateur athlete of the year.

After getting drafted by the Angels as the eighth overall pick in 1988, Abbott bypassed the minors and went straight to the rotation, winning 12 games his rookie season. He finished third in the Cy Young Award voting in 1991 after winning 18 games and recording a 2.83 ERA. Another career highlight was pitching a no-hitter for the Yankees at Yankee Stadium on September 4, 1993. Abbott, who won 87 games over 10 seasons, is a member of the Michigan Sports Hall of Fame and College Baseball Hall of Fame.

The bullpen is led by Mike Marshall, actually Dr. Mike Marshall — he has a Ph.D. in kinesiology. Marshall marched to a different drummer during his playing days and he continues to go against conventional thinking with his ongoing work as a pitching consultant, claiming that he has discovered a pitching motion that eliminates injury. Marshall certainly figured out how to pitch effectively, and often, during his 14-year career. He signed as a shortstop with the Phillies out of high school in 1960 but later switched to pitching after an injury. He led the league in games pitched three straight years (four overall), appearing in an astounding 198 games out of the bullpen in 1973–74. He set records for most appearances (106), most closing innings (208), most games finished (84) and most consecutive appearances (13).

It's hard to imagine a manager allowing his closer to pitch 208 innings in 106 games like Marshall did in 1974 — that's pitching two innings in two-thirds of the Dodgers' games that year. That followed 1973, when Marshall pitched 179 innings making 92 relief appearances. Marshall had one more outrageous year, 1979, when he finished a career-high 84 games in 90 appearances covering 142 innings.

Most of Marshall's managers didn't know what to do with the eccentric righty, which is why he ended up pitching for nine different teams. Still, he ended up leading the NL in saves in 1973, 1974 and 1979, winning the Cy Young Award and finishing third in the MVP race for his herculean effort in 1974. He was in on an amazing 27 decisions that year (also a record for a reliever), going 15–12 with a 2.42 ERA. He retired after appearing in 723 games, winning 97 games and registering 188 saves.

Other Michigan relievers of note include Bill Campbell, Phil Regan and Dick Radatz. Perhaps emboldened by Marshall's heavy-duty workload, Campbell pitched 167 innings out of the bullpen for the Twins in 1976, going 17–5 with 20 saves. The next year he was an All-Star for the Red Sox after pitching 140 innings in 69 relief appearances and leading the league with 31 saves. He also led the NL with 82 appearances for the Cubs in 1983 and finished his 15-year career with 126 saves.

Regan switched from starting to relieving after being traded from the Tigers to the Dodgers and he broke out with a 14–1 record, 1.62 ERA and league-leading 48 games finished as an All-Star in 1966. That year his teammate Sandy Koufax dubbed him "The Vulture," after he watched Regan capitalize on extra-inning hit support to pad his win total at the expense of Koufax's hard-earned work to keep the games close. Regan seemed to enjoy his reputation as someone who swooped in to devour the prey someone else had killed. He would win 12 games out of the bullpen in both 1968 and 1969, snatching victory out of the hands of starters on the Dodgers and the Cubs.

Radatz was an intimidating presence on the mound at 6-foot-6 with a 96 mph fastball and shaky control. He led the league with 62 appearances as a rookie in 1962, then made the All-Star team after recording a 1.97 ERA in 66 appearances the next year. Radatz averaged 11.02 K/9IP in 1963 and then set a record with 181 strikeouts out of the bullpen in 1964.

The best choice for the All-Time Michigan manager is Joe Altobelli, who had followed Earl Weaver as the Orioles manager in 1983. All he did was lead the team to 98 wins and a World Series championship that year. That was his only trip to the playoffs in seven seasons of managing in the majors, but he also skippered three league champs in the minor leagues.

Also worth mentioning is Bill Virdon, who is the all-time winningest manager in Michigan history with 995 wins against 921 losses. He led the Pirates to a division title in his first season (1972) and later guided the Astros to the division crown in 1980, but Virdon's teams never advanced to the Series. Clint Hurdle managed the Colorado Rockies for eight seasons, highlighted by a wild-card berth in 2007 that turned into a World Series trip (but no ring). Hurdle, who took over the Pirates beginning in 2011, still has a losing record overall as manager.

MINNESOTA

*Names in **bold** represent major league selections by position, followed by honorable mentions. City of birth is in parentheses.*

Catcher—**Joe Mauer (St. Paul)**. Also: Terry Steinbach (New Ulm); Wes Westrum (Clearbrook); Greg Olson (Marshall)

First Base—**Kent Hrbek (Minneapolis)**. Also: Chick Gandil (St. Paul)

Second Base—**Gene DeMontreville (St. Paul)**. Also: Jack Crooks (St. Paul); Jerry Kindall (St. Paul)

Third Base—**Paul Molitor (St. Paul)**. Also: Joe Werrick (St. Paul)

Shortstop—**Jerry Terrell (Waseca)**

Outfield—**Dave Winfield (St. Paul)**

Outfield—**Roger Maris (Hibbing)**

Outfield—**Jim Eisenreich (St. Cloud)**. Also: Rip Repulski (Sauk Rapids); Walt Moryn (St. Paul); Mike Kingery (St. James)

Designated Hitter—**Paul Molitor (St. Paul)**

Right Handed Starter—**Chief Bender (Brainerd)**. Also: Jack Morris (St. Paul); Joe Bush (Brainerd); Bill Gullickson (Marshall); Aaron Sele (Golden Valley); Dave Goltz (Pelican Rapids)

Left Handed Starter—**Jerry Koosman (Appleton)**. Also: Rube Walberg (Pine City)

Relief Pitcher—**Tom Burgmeier (St. Paul)**. Also: Tom Niedenfuer (St. Louis Park); Chris Reitsma (Minneapolis); Steve Foucalt (Duluth); Michael Wuertz (Austin)

Manager—**Tom Kelly (Graceville)**

The Names

Best Nickname: George "Pea Soup" Dumont
Other Nicknames: Charles "Chief" Bender; Garland "Gob" Buckeye; Leslie "Bullet Joe" Bush; Roger "Peaceful Valley" Denzer; Sylvester "Blix" Donnelly; Arnold "Chick" Gandil; Jerry "Slim" Kindall; Merton "Moxie" Meixell; Eldon "Rip" Repulski; Howie "Stretch" Schultz; Dick "Nimrod Nifty" Stigman; George "Rube" Walberg; Julie "Flop Ears" Wera
Most Unusual Name: Jerry Ujdur

All-Time Leaders

Games: Dave Winfield, 2973
Hits: Paul Molitor, 3319
Batting Average: Joe Mauer, .323 (still active)
Home Runs: Dave Winfield, 465
RBI: Dave Winfield, 1833
Stolen Bases: Paul Molitor, 504
Wins: Jack Morris, 254
Strikeouts: Jerry Koosman, 2556
Saves: Tom Burgmeier and Tom Niedenfuer, 97
Future Star: Ike Davis (Edina)
Best Player: Paul Molitor

Historic Baseball Places

The Original Baseball Hall of Fame Museum of Minnesota in Minneapolis—It's more of a shop than a museum, but admission is free and you can check out the world's largest Twins bobblehead standing 7-feet tall. The museum features artifacts from the collection of proprietor Ray Crump, who was a batboy for the Washington Senators and served as the first equipment manager for the Twins.

Target Field in Minneapolis — Opened as the Twins' new outdoor ballpark in 2010. The gates are numbered after the retired uniform numbers of Twins players Kirby Puckett, Harmon Killebrew, Rod Carew, Kent Hrbek and Tony Oliva. The flag pole is recycled from Met Stadium. Local food choices abound, including walleye, Kramarczak's sausages and wild rice soup. You can take a behind-the-scenes tour to gain insights into the history of baseball in Minnesota.

Midway Stadium in St. Paul — Home of the St. Paul Saints, an independent team in the American Association that is among the most creative with promotions. Acting on the wacky inspiration of part owner Mike Veeck, the team has sponsored Randy Moss Hood Ornament Night and given out Bud Selig neckties. Minnie Miñoso appeared in games in 1993 (at the age of 67) and in 2003 as a publicity stunt. Jack Morris and Darryl Strawberry are among the stars who have played for the home team.

Toni Stone Stadium in St. Paul — Named after the first woman to play in the Negro Leagues. Stone was signed by the Indianapolis Clowns in 1953 to play second base. She batted an estimated .243 and reportedly got a hit off Satchel Paige. She has been inducted into the Women's Sports Hall of Fame and been featured in "Women in Baseball" exhibits at the National Baseball Hall of Fame and Museum in Cooperstown.

Notable Achievements

Joe Mauer became the first catcher to win a batting title in the American League in 2006.

George Thomas played at least one game in every position in the field except pitcher.

Paul Molitor was the first DH to steal more than 20 bases — he had 23 in 1987. He is also the only player to get 200 hits in the same year he reached 3,000 career hits and the only player to hit a triple for his 3,000th hit.

Baseball in the Twin Cities Thrived in Nineteenth Century

Many people think professional baseball in the North Star State dates back to late 1960, when Calvin Griffith moved the Washington Senators to Minnesota and renamed them the Twins. Actually, Minnesota baseball has a much lengthier past.

Minnesota's first baseball club was started in Nininger in 1857, according to Stew Thornley, author of *Baseball in Minnesota: A Definitive History*. The next seminal moment came in 1884, when the St. Paul Saints played nine games as a mid-season replacement in the short-lived Union Association. Experts disagree on whether the Union Association counts as one of the major leagues. Two players from that Saints team went on to more distinguished play in the majors: first baseman Billy O'Brien was the National League home run champion in 1887, while catcher Charlie Ganzel played 14 years and won championships with the Detroit Wolverines (1887) and Boston Beaneaters (1892).

As Thornley points out, professional baseball was thriving in Minnesota as the nineteenth century drew to a close. The Minneapolis Millers had a long, successful run beginning in 1884, learning how to capitalize on the short right-field fence of intimate Nicollet Park, the team's home from 1896–1955. A number of Hall of Famers played for the Millers including Roger Bresnahan (1898–99), Jimmy Collins (1909), Rube Waddell (1911–13), Ted Williams (1938), Ray Dandridge (1949–52), Willie Mays (1951), Orlando Cepeda (1957) and Carl Yastrzemski (1959–60).

The Saints reappeared in St. Paul in 1895 after Charlie Comiskey moved a team there from Iowa. Five years later, Comiskey decided to move the team to Chicago and rename them the White Stockings, becoming a charter franchise of the American League.

The St. Paul Saints were revived as a successful minor league team in the American Association from 1902 until the Twins were formed in 1960. Lefty Gomez, Roy Campanella and Leo Durocher were among the players who appeared in games for the St. Paul franchise during those years. The team's latest reincarnation came in 1993, under the inspired ownership of Mike Veeck, Marvin Goldklang and comedian Bill Murray, who on a few occasions has been found in the coach's box at first or third.

The Twins spent their first two decades playing in the old Met Stadium, which had replaced Nicollet Park as home of the Millers. The Met was a hitter's park perfect for Twins sluggers such as Harmon Killebrew and Bobby Allison. Next came The Hubert Humphrey Metrodome, which is where Minnesota native Dave Winfield got his 3,000th hit on September 16, 1993. The Metrodome offered a nice home-field advantage as the Twins won World Series titles in 1987 and 1991, but its sterile atmosphere did not make for an enjoyable fan experience. After many years of political and legal wrangling, the Twins finally unveiled a new open-air ballpark, Target Field, for the 2010 season.

A number of Minnesota-born players have interesting backgrounds beyond baseball. Roger Maris still holds the national high school record for most kickoff return touchdowns in a game with four, which he accomplished for Shanley High in Fargo, N.D., in 1951. Dave Winfield was drafted by four professional leagues: MLB (San Diego Padres), NFL (Minnesota Vikings), NBA (Atlanta Hawks) and ABA (Utah Stars).

Charlie Walters appeared in six games for the Minnesota Twins in 1969 and then went on to become a distinguished sports columnist. Howie Schultz of St. Paul played six years in the majors and then played three seasons in the National Basketball Association. He won two championships with the Minneapolis Lakers and his teammates included future Hall of Famers George Mikan, Vern Mikkelsen, Slater Martin and Jim Pollard. The 6-foot-6 Schultz was twice rejected for military service during World War II because he was too tall.

The multi-sport accomplishments of Winfield, Maris and Schultz are nice, but they pale in comparison to that of Ernie Nevers. The Willow River native — who spent most of his high school in Wisconsin and his senior year in California — is the only person to play professional baseball, football and basketball in the same season, an incredible feat he pulled off in 1926. That year he pitched in 11 games for the St. Louis Browns, briefly played for George Halas' Chicago Bruins in the American Basketball League and appeared in nearly every minute of the 14 games and 15 exhibitions played by the Duluth Eskimos in the National Football League.

Nevers went on to surrender two of Babe Ruth's 60 home runs during his historic 1927 season. The Babe was so impressed by Nevers' velocity that he expressed a desire that the righty focus on football so he wouldn't have to keep facing him. Nevers once pitched 37 consecutive scoreless innings while at Stanford, where he lettered in four sports and played football under Pop Warner. He outgained the legendary "Four Horsemen" of Notre Dame by himself in the 1925 Rose Bowl despite playing on two injured ankles.

His career record of 6–12 in the majors illustrates the fact that football was Nevers' best sport. He still holds the record for most points in an NFL game, a mark set when he scored all 40 of his team's points (six touchdowns and four extra points) during a game on November 28, 1929 — it's the longest held record in the NFL record book. Named an All-Pro each of the five seasons he played professional football, Nevers was inducted into the College Football Hall of Fame in 1951, the inaugural class of the Pro Football Hall of Fame in 1963 and was named the best college football player of all-time by *Sports Illustrated* in 1962.

All-Time Minnesota Selections

Let's move on to the position selections for the All-Time-Minnesota team, starting with catcher. By the time he is done playing, Joe Mauer may end up with a legacy similar to Cal Ripken, Jr., in Baltimore, an iconic star who stayed with his hometown team his whole career. It's a much different and more satisfying legacy than if he had decided to spurn his hometown Twins and chase the free agent bucks in a bigger market, but he signed a long-term deal in 2010 that ensures he will remain in Minnesota throughout his prime.

If he stays healthy, Mauer has a chance to become the best catcher in baseball history, but his body seemed to break down in 2011. Still, he has already blazed a trail by winning three batting titles by the age of 26. His .323 lifetime batting average through eight seasons is the highest ever by a catcher (minimum 500 games). And to think the Twins were criticized for taking the local boy as the number one overall pick in the 2001 amateur draft over can't miss players like Mark Prior or Gavin Floyd.

Mauer keeps things simple with his compact left-handed swing. Whatever he's doing has been working. During his MVP season in 2009 his .365/.444/.587 line generated a 1.031 OPS and 170 OPS+ (leading the AL in all those categories) and for the first time he showcased his power with 28 homers and 96 RBI. The small-market Twins feel they have a chance to win every year just because he's on their team, and with the opening of Target Field they now have a larger revenue stream to help them stay competitive with the big-market teams.

At 6-foot-5 Mauer is tall for a catcher and he's already struggled with health issues, so there is a good chance he moves to a less demanding position at some point in his career. For now, he's an above-average receiver who already has won three Gold Gloves to go with four All-Star appearances.

Another good Minnesota catcher is Terry Steinbach, who got to finish out his career by playing three seasons for the Twins. Steinbach was a three-time All-Star who finished his 14-year career with 162 homers. He had a breakout season with the A's in 1996, belting 35 homers with 100 RBI while slugging .529. His next highest home run total was 16 in his rookie season. Steinbach was named to the All-Star team in 1988 despite a .216 average at the break and ended up MVP of the game after hitting a home run off Doc Gooden and adding a run-scoring sacrifice fly. He appeared in three straight World Series with the A's, winning a ring in 1989.

First base on the All-Minnesota team is manned by another popular ex-Twin, Kent Hrbek, who played his whole career (1981–94) for the hometown team. Hrbek got the fans on his side early by blasting a game-winning home run in the twelfth inning to win his debut game ... at Yankee Stadium of all places. The next spring he would hit the first home run in the new Metrodome, although it was in an exhibition game.

Hrbek was overshadowed throughout his career by other AL first basemen such as Don Mattingly, Rod Carew and Eddie Murray. As a result, he only made one All-Star team — in his rookie year of 1982, when he hit .301 with 23 homers and 92 RBI.

Hrbek had plenty of great seasons such as 1984, when he batted .311, drove in 111 with 27 homers and slugged .522. He was MVP runner-up that year. In 1987 he helped lead the Twins to their first World Series title in Minnesota by belting a career-high 34 homers (third-best in the AL) and posting a .285 average, .389 OBP and .545 slugging percentage. A second title came in 1991, despite the fact that Hrbek batted just .154 in 24 career playoff games.

Although not Mattingly's equal with the glove, Hrbek wasn't far behind. He led AL first basemen in fielding in 1988 and 1990, flashed above-average range and finished with a .994 fielding percentage.

Chick Gandil received consideration at first, even though he was banned for life from baseball for his role in the infamous Black Sox Scandal. Gandil was reportedly the instigator of the fix who made contact with the gamblers before the regular season was over and then later convinced key teammates to go along with the fix. He was neither surprised nor bothered by his banishment in 1920, since he had already retired after nine seasons. A lifetime .277 hitter, he batted over .300 two times and won a legitimate World Series title with the Sox in 1917.

All the options at second base are from St. Paul. Gene DeMontreville played 379 games at short, making him the most accomplished shortstop from Minnesota, but he made more of a mark from his 510 games at second. DeMontreville accumulated 1,096 hits and posted an excellent .303 average, batting over .300 four times. He averaged .343 in his first full year, 1896, followed by years of .341 and .328. He played for the Baltimore Orioles in 1899 in John McGraw's first year as a manager.

Another second baseman worth mentioning is nineteenth-century player Jack Crooks, who exhibited a talent for drawing walks. He led the league with 136 walks in 1892 and 121 the next year, finishing with a .386 career OBP despite batting just .241. Crooks started with the Columbus Salons in the American Association and then moved on to play with the St. Louis Browns, Washington Senators and Louisville Colonels over his eight-year career. He stole 57 bases in 1890 and 50 the next year, winding up with 220 steals for his career.

Hall of Famer Paul Molitor gets to hold down two positions: third base and designated hitter, not to mention designation as Minnesota's All-Time Best Player. He played more games at DH (1,174) than in the field, so that justified putting him there. And his 791 games at third make him by far the most accomplished third baseman. Heck, he even played 400 games at second over his remarkable 21-year career.

Molitor was an excellent base runner and a versatile fielder, but it was when he stepped up to the plate that his greatness could be seen. He quite simply was one of the most skilled right-handed batters in baseball history. A lifetime .306 hitter, Molitor's 3,319 hits rank ninth all-time and his 605 doubles place him in 11th place. He batted over .300 12 times with a high of .353 in 1987. The seven-time All-Star was MVP runner-up in 1993 when he batted .332 with 22 homers and 111 RBI.

Somewhat injury prone early in his career, Molitor also overcame a drug addiction to end up appearing in 2,683 games with 10,835 at-bats — good for thirteenth all-time. He ranks eighteenth in runs scored (1,782) and led the league in runs and hits three times each. His power-speed # of 319.6 is the thirteenth-best in history thanks to 234 homers to go with 504 stolen bases, but he had extra-base power more than home run power. He is one of four players (with Ty Cobb, Eddie Collins and Honus Wagner) to post 3,000 hits, 500 stolen bases and .300 average — if you add in 200 homers then he's the only one!

Setting aside all his outstanding career marks for a moment, three amazing feats stand out. First, he stole home 10 times, which is the third-best mark in the modern era. Second, he posted a 39-game hitting streak in 1987, which is the seventh best in history and second-longest streak since DiMaggio set the record in 1941. That's not surprising, since Ted Williams once remarked that Molitor's swing and stance reminded him of DiMaggio. Finally, he collected five hits in his first World Series game for the Brewers in 1982 on the way to a .355 Series average, then came back 11 years later and was named World Series MVP after batting 12-for-24 with eight RBI as the Blue Jays won the title. It's no wonder Molitor was a first-ballot electee to the Hall of Fame in 2004.

Jerry Terrell is another Minnesota boy who got to fulfill a dream by playing for the Twins. The Waseca native played his first five seasons with the Twins, getting the most action as a shortstop in his rookie year of 1973 and also 1975, when he batted .286. The utility man collected 412 hits in 656 games with the Twins and Royals.

One of the most famous baseball players in Minnesota history is usually associated with a different state. Roger Maris moved to North Dakota when he was five years old — there's even a museum in his name back in that state — but he was born in Hibbing, Minn. His real last name is Maras, which Roger changed when he entered professional ball because he was tired of kids using a profane pronunciation of his name.

Many baseball fans, and some experts, still think of Maris as the legitimate single-season home run leader. After all, the three players who have surpassed his magical number of 61 homers in 1961 have since been tainted by steroids.

As the magical season wound down, pursuing the Babe took an enormous physical and mental toll on Maris, who couldn't help but be bothered by the fact fans preferred teammate Mickey Mantle be the one to break the Babe's famous record. After the season was finally over he admitted, "As a ballplayer, I would be delighted to do it again. As an individual, I doubt if I could possibly go through it again."

Maris played 12 years in the majors and never hit more than 39 homers in any other season. He retired with a modest total of 275 home runs, or 17 fewer than Sammy Sosa hit between 1998 and 2002. Maris did make four All-Star teams and win one Gold Glove along with MVP awards in 1960 and 1961. In addition to the 61 dingers, Maris led the AL with 141 RBI and 132 runs in 1961 and led the league by slugging .581 in 1960. Although just a .260 lifetime hitter, Maris didn't strike out much and was a smart base runner and excellent fielder with a strong arm.

Still, he never got over the bitterness. "Now they talk on the radio about the records set by Ruth, and DiMaggio and Henry Aaron, but they rarely mention mine. Do you know what I have to show for the 61 home runs? Nothing, exactly nothing," Maris said. He did earn the respect and admiration of his teammate, Mickey Mantle, who said, "I think Roger hitting 61 homers in 1961 was the greatest thing I've ever seen in sports."

Maris holds down one of the outfield spots on the All-Time Minnesota team, alongside another controversial Yankee star. Dave Winfield signed with the Yankees for a record 10 years and $23 million in 1980, but he failed to deliver a championship despite posting impressive numbers. Oddly enough, it was that record contract, as much as anything, that caused Yankees owner George Steinbrenner to later turn against his star player. Originally designed as a $16 million contract, Winfield's contract contained a cost-of-living escalator each year that ended up costing the Boss an extra $7 million. When a New York sportswriter pointed out the inclusion of the escalators in the contract it made Steinbrenner look foolish, which in turn caused him to seek vengeance against Winfield.

Winfield spent eight full seasons with the Bronx Bombers, making the All-Star team every one of those years, along with five of his seven Gold Gloves. But it wasn't enough to satisfy New York's fans and certainly not Steinbrenner, who gave Winfield the moniker "Mr. May" after he went 1-for-22 in the 1981 World Series — the only postseason appearance for the Yankees during Winfield's tenure. The Boss would eventually be suspended from baseball for his dealings with Howie Spira, a shady character and convicted gambler who was enlisted to dig up dirt on Winfield.

Winfield's unfortunate dealings with Steinbrenner overshadowed the otherwise remarkable career the five-tool player had. He hit 465 home runs, drove in 1,833 runs (sixteenth all-time), scored 1,669 runs, collected 3,110 hits (nineteenth all-time) and accumulated 5,221 total bases (thirteenth all-time). He had eight seasons with more than 100 RBI. Two years after leaving the Yankees, Winfield would earn a World Series ring with the Blue Jays in 1992. He was inducted into the Hall of Fame in 2001.

The third outfielder on the All-Minnesota team was never a star like Maris or Winfield, but Jim Eisenreich proved himself a capable hitter over a 15-season career that nearly ended before it got going. Eisenreich's behavior was considered odd, odd enough that he felt compelled to retire in 1984 after three partial seasons with the Twins. Later diagnosed with Tourette's Syndrome, Eisenreich was able to get his symptoms under control enough to continue his career with the Royals in 1987. He was a starter in Kansas City during three seasons, batting .293, .280 and .301 those years, and then he turned up his production during a four-year run in Philadelphia. Eisenreich batted .318, .300, .316 and .361 with the Phillies before moving on to the Marlins, where he won a championship in 1997, batting 4-for-8 with a home run in the World Series.

It was extremely tough selecting the all-time right-handed starter between Jack Morris and Charley "Chief" Bender. Bender is in the Hall of Fame, while many believe Morris belongs in Cooperstown as well. Here's how some of their numbers compare:

	GS	W-L	Pct.	ERA	CG	SHO	SO	ERA+	WHIP	SO/BB
Bender	334	212–127	.625	2.46	255	40	1711	112	1.113	2.40
Morris	527	254–186	.577	3.90	175	28	2478	105	1.296	1.78

We see that Morris started and won more games and had more strikeouts while Bender had a better winning percentage, lower ERA, more shutouts and complete games, lower WHIP and higher ERA+ and SO/BB ratio. Taking it a step further, Morris edges Bender in RAR (Runs Above Replacement) 384–350 and WAR (Wins Above Replacement) 39.3–38.5, while Bender outscores Morris 226.8–221.8 in Career Win Shares.

Morris' advocates like to point out his big-game pitching ability as evidenced by his 7–4 postseason record and three World Series titles. Bender, on the other hand, appeared in five World Series and also won three rings, with a 6–4 postseason record. His ERA in the playoffs outshines Morris, 2.44 to 3.80. Ultimately, it's difficult to compare and contrast their stats fairly because Bender pitched in the Deadball Era from 1903–1917 (not counting the one inning he pitched in 1925), while Morris pitched in the modern era from 1977–94.

Let's back up and examine Bender's path to the Hall, since that seems to be a factor weighed in his favor. Bender received just 0.9 percent of the votes in his first year of eligibility (1936), received little support the next seven years and then mysteriously shot up to 44.7 percent of the vote in 1947. Just as strangely, he was back down to 4.1 percent, 1.3 percent and 3.6 percent the next three years. In 1953 Bender was named on 39.4 percent of the writer's ballots but ended up getting voted in by the veteran's committee that same year — strange indeed! Keep in mind that 83 players received votes that year including Nick Altrock, who was 83–75 for his career. Furthermore, 41 of the players on the ballot that year are now in the Hall of Fame — a virtual cavalcade of mediocrity.

By comparison, Morris received 22 percent of the vote in his first year of eligibility, 2000, and has started to climb in recent years with a high of 53.5 percent in 2011. He just might get in someday. If Morris gets in he would have the highest ERA of any pitcher enshrined in Cooperstown — Red Ruffing's 3.80 is currently the highest.

Morris won 20 games three times, leading the league in wins twice and complete games, strikeouts and shutouts once. The five-time All-Star was durable, pitching at least 235 innings 11 times in 13 seasons. He was a feisty pit bull on the mound who loved to intimidate batters. Morris solidified his big-game reputation by tossing a 10-inning shutout to win Game 7 of the 1991 World Series, outdueling the Braves' John Smoltz, who matched zeroes with Morris into the eighth inning. It was the only year Morris pitched for the Twins. Seven years earlier he went 2–0 in the Series as the Tigers won the championship.

It's not hard to find the negatives in Morris' career, in addition to the high ERA. His 105 ERA+ is barely above-average, which places him tied for 479th all-time with the likes of A.J. Burnett and Steve Busby. He led the league in wild pitches six times and in walks and earned runs once. Finally, Morris' reputation as a big-game pitcher in the postseason is spotty at best. Pitching for Detroit in the 1987 ALCS he gave up six runs in his only start.

Chief Bender's Native American heritage was a source of pride and pain throughout his career, as he endured repeated harassment and racial taunts on and off the field. No one could deny his skill on the mound, as the crafty righty won 212 games over a 16-year career that culminated with election to the Hall of Fame (Library of Congress, Prints & Photographs Division, LC-USZ62-97857).

Then in 1992 he went 0–1 with a 6.57 for the Blue Jays in the ALCS and followed up with a 0–2 mark and 8.44 ERA in the 1992 World Series.

Bender was a smart, crafty pitcher who carved up batters with great skill. He threw what he called a fast curve and might have been one of the first to throw a slider. Bender combined with Eddie Plank and Jack Coombs (and earlier Rube Waddell) to form an intimidating rotation for Connie Mack and the Philadelphia A's, who won the World Series in 1910, 1911 and 1913. Baseball historian Tom Swift, in his award-winning biography *Chief Bender's Burden*, called him the greatest American Indian player in baseball history.

The final deciding factor was to consider the context of Bender's career, playing as a Native American in a time of great prejudice. Bender got the nickname "Chief" because that's what all Native Americans were nicknamed back then ... and he was called much worse names before, during and after games. Bender was a ground-breaking figure in the game, perhaps not on the level of Jackie Robinson, but keep in mind his career started 44 years before Robinson broke the color barrier. With Morris and Bender's career records a virtual toss-up, it was Bender's trail-blazing significance that settled the position on the All-Time Minnesota team.

Let's move on to the left-handed starter. It was a good thing Jerry Koosman could pitch, because he sure couldn't hit. In his rookie season, 1968, he whiffed 62 times while batting, which set a single-season National League record for most strikeouts by a pitcher. Koosman batted just .077 that year, although one of his seven hits was a home run. He batted .048 the next year and finished his 19-year career with a .119 average and -17 OPS+. "I used to be so bad my bat would close its eyes when I came up," he once quipped to sportswriter Maury Allen.

The lefty hurler was much more comfortable on the mound, as his seven shutouts as a rookie tied the existing major league mark (topped later by Fernando Valenzuela with eight). Koosman went 19–12 with a 2.08 ERA and 178 strikeouts that season, making the All-Star team and finishing runner-up to Johnny Bench for Rookie of the Year. He again made the All-Star team the next year after going 17–9 with a 2.28 ERA, then won two World Series games as the Miracle Mets took the title. Koosman held the Orioles without a hit until the seventh inning in Game 2, then pitched a complete game victory to close out the decisive Game 5.

Koosman would go 21–10 with a 2.69 ERA and 200 K's in 1976 and another good year came in 1979 for the Twins — 20–13 with 3.38 ERA. He retired in 1985 after winning 222 games with a 3.36 ERA and posting 2,556 career strikeouts. He finished in the top 10 in strikeouts eight times and ERA six times and surrendered Pete Rose's 4,000th hit on April 13, 1984. Inducted into the Mets Hall of Fame in 1989, Koosman served jail time in 2009 after admitting he failed to pay federal income tax for 2002–2004.

Another notable lefty starter is Rube Walberg, who pitched from 1923–37. He won a total of 155 games, helping the Philadelphia A's win three straight pennants from 1929 to 1931. Walberg recorded a 1.93 ERA pitching in five Series games those years as the A's won the title in 1929 and 1930. His best season was 1931 when he won 20 games.

To close out the game Team Minnesota can turn to Tom Burgmeier, who collected 97 career saves (his five saves in 1968 are unofficial). Burgmeier pitched for five teams including the Twins, all in the American League, appearing in 745 games. His best season was with the Red Sox in 1980, when he saved 24 games with a 2.00 ERA. He retired in 1984 with a 79–55 record and a 3.23 ERA. Another option out of the bullpen is Tom Niedenfuer, who matched Burgmeier with 97 saves and had six straight seasons with double-digit saves.

It's only fitting that the manager for the All-Time Minnesota team made his mark managing the Twins. Tom Kelly skippered the Twins to World Series titles in 1987 and 1991, the only two years he led the team to the division title. He ended up winning 1,140 games over 16 seasons, with a .478 winning percentage. He was AL Manager of the Year in 1991. Kelly's major league career consisted of 49 games in 1975 playing for ... you guessed it — the Twins!

MISSISSIPPI

*Names in **bold** represent Major League selections by position, followed by honorable mentions. Negro Leagues players are in **bold italics**, followed by honorable mentions in italics. City of birth is in parentheses.*

Catcher — ***Sammy Hairston*** **(Crawford).** Also: Jerry Moses (Yazoo City); Jake Gibbs (Grenada)
First Base — **George Scott (Greenville).** Also: *Luke Easter* (Jonestown); *Bob Boyd* (Potts Camp); Sam Leslie (Moss Point)
Second Base — **Buddy Myer (Ellisville).** Also: Frank White (Greenville); Hughie Critz (Starkville); Don Blasingame (Corinth)
Third Base — ***Howard Easterling*** **(Mt. Olive).** Also: Bill Melton (Gulfport); *Herb Souell* (West Monroe); Charlie Hayes (Hattiesburg); Bill Hall (Nettleton); Bubba Phillips (West Point)
Shortstop — **Eric McNair (Meridian).** Also: Skeeter Webb (Meridian)
Outfield — ***Cool Papa Bell*** **(Starkville)**
Outfield — **Dave Parker (Calhoun)**
Outfield — **Ellis Burks (Vicksburg).** Also: Chet Lemon (Jackson); Gee Walker (Gulfport); *Bubba Hyde* (Pontotoc); Larry Herndon (Sunflower); Harry Walker (Pascagoula); *Buddy Armour* (Jackson); Matt Lawton (Gulfport); *Emmett Wilson* (Yazoo City)
Designated Hitter — **Dmitri Young (Vicksburg)**
Right Handed Starter — **Roy Oswalt (Weir).** Also: Guy Bush (Aberdeen); Claude Passeau (Waynesboro); Oil Can Boyd (Meridian); Atley Donald (Morton); Dave Ferriss (Shaw); *Dave Hoskins* (Greenwood); *Rufus Lewis* (Hattiesburg)
Left Handed Starter — **Reb Russell (Jackson).** Also: Vinegar Bend Mizell (Leakesville); Willie Mitchell (Pleasant Grove); *Bill Harvey* (Clarksdale)
Relief Pitcher — **Chad Bradford (Jackson).** Also: Jay Powell (Meridian); Joe Gibbon (Hickory); Marshall Bridges (Jackson)
Manager — **Harry Walker (Pascagoula).** Also: Harry Craft (Ellisville)

The Names

Best Nickname: James "Cool Papa" Bell
Other Nicknames: Don "Corinth Comet" Blasingame; Bob "The Rope" Boyd; Dennis "Oil Can" Boyd; Guy "The Mississippi Mudcat" Bush; Harry "Wildfire" Craft; Atley "Swampy" Donald; Dave "Boo" Ferriss; Ernie "Schoolboy" Johnson; Hal "Sheriff" Lee; Chet "The Jet" Lemon; Exavier "Nook" Logan; Edward "Slim" Love; Lewis "Sport" McAllister; Eric "Boob" McNair; Wilmer "Vinegar Bend" Mizell; Dave "Cobra" Parker; John "Bubba" Phillips; Cohen "Laddie" Renfroe; Gee "The Madman From Mississippi" Walker; Harry "the Hat" Walker; Harvey "Hub" Walker; James "Skeeter" Webb; Fred "Papa" Williams; Dmitri "Meat Hook" Young
Most Unusual Name: Josh Booty

All-Time Leaders

Games: Dave Parker, 2466
Hits: Dave Parker, 2712
Batting Average: Sam Leslie, .304
Home Runs: Ellis Burks, 352
RBI: Dave Parker, 1493
Stolen Bases: Gee Walker, 223
Wins: Guy Bush, 176
Strikeouts: Roy Oswalt, 1759 (still active)
Saves: Joe Gibbon, 27
Future Stars: Wendell Fairley (Lucedale); Donnie Veal (Jackson); Zak Cozart (University)
Best Player: Cool Papa Bell

Historic Baseball Places

Dave "Boo" Ferriss Museum in Cleveland — Located at Delta State University, where the field is also named after the college's longtime coach. The museum chronicles the baseball career of Ferriss, who pitched two outstanding seasons for the Red Sox in 1945 and 1946 before an arm injury curtailed his career.
Trustmark Park in Pearl — Opened in 2005 as the home of the Mississippi Braves. Interestingly, the concession stands are given clever names such as "Hot Corner Slice" (where pizza is served), "The Wheel Haus" and "The Mendoza Line," which seems to glorify mediocrity.
Dizzy Dean Gravesite at Bond Cemetery in Bond — His grave marker features a Cardinals logo and the following inscription: "A friend to many. One of baseball's greatest. Inducted into Baseball Hall of Fame 1953."
Mississippi Sports Hall of Fame and Museum in Jackson — Includes the Dizzy Dean Museum collection, which brings the Gashouse Gang to life. See Dizzy's Hall of Fame and 1934 World Series rings and watch vintage newsreel clips of Dizzy in action. The road leading into the Mississippi Sports Hall of Fame and Museum is named after one of the inductees — Cool Papa Bell Drive.
Homeplate Fish & Steakhouse in Weir — Roy Oswalt opened this restaurant in his hometown in 2009 so locals would have a decent place to eat. The baseball memorabilia on the walls is pretty modest, just like the owner, but patrons might want to try the 44 oz. steak that is a tribute to Oswalt's uniform number.

Notable Achievements

Fred Lewis (Hattiesburg) was the fastest to hit for the cycle, accomplishing the feat in his sixteenth game on May 13, 2007.

Harry "The Hat" Walker was the first player to win the National League batting title while playing for more than one team in the league. He hit a combined .363 for the Cardinals and Phillies in 1947.

Ellis Burks increased his runs scored total more than 100 from 1995 to 1996. He scored 41 runs in 1995 and then led the National League with 142 runs scored in 1996, which is the 10th highest runs total in the majors since 1940.

Sammy Hairston became the first African American player to also have a son play in the majors when Johnny Hairston appeared in a game in 1969.

Vinegar Bend Mizell served three terms in Congress as a representative for North Carolina and later served in government positions in the Ford, Reagan and George H.W. Bush administrations.

Walter Young (Hattiesburg) is reported to be the heaviest player in major league history — he weighed 322 pounds when he made his debut for the Orioles in 2005.

Home to a Cool Papa, an Oil Can and a Madman

It all started with Doug Crothers, who became the first Mississippi native to make it to the majors in 1884. The Natchez-born pitcher won eight games in two seasons before scuffling around the minors the rest of his career. Sport McAllister was the only other nineteenth-century player from the state.

A total of 190 Mississippi-born players have appeared in the majors to date including 16 players who were active in 2011. Jackson has sent the most players (16), followed by Hattiesburg and Meridian (12), Gulfport and Tupelo (7) and Biloxi (6).

A quick glance at the roster from Mississippi reveals players who went by the names of Jamie, Laurin, Jackie, Pat, Kim and Dolly. That looks like the beginnings of a great softball team, but not the sort of intimidating sluggers you'd like to see on an all-time baseball team.

As long as those girlie players don't hook up with the likes of Josh Booty, Nook Logan, Boob McNair, Fred Valentine and most especially, Slim Love. Love was a 6-foot-7 string-bean pitcher who ironically was born in Love, Miss. He was Walter Johnson's teammate on the Washington Senators in 1913, was Babe Ruth's teammate on the Red Sox for one month between the 1918 and 1919 seasons and then played with Ty Cobb on the Tigers in 1919–20. He won only 28 games in six seasons, generating little love but mostly indifference from fans.

Mississippi is home to two of the greatest nicknames of all-time — "Cool Papa" Bell and "Oil Can" Boyd — which both should reside in the Hall of Fame of Nicknames. Cool Papa earned the colorful moniker from Bill Gatewood, who was amazed at the rookie's composure as a pitcher after he struck out slugger Oscar Charleston.

"Oil" is the slang word for beer in Boyd's hometown of Meridian, so "Oil Can" refers to a youthful activity Boyd indulged in that is generally frowned on as a training regimen. Then again, Oil Can didn't behave like the typical baseball player. He was a moody, temperamental, trash-talking, cocky, junk-throwing perfectionist, whose off-balance behavior sometimes clashed with his skill at keeping batters off-balance. Nolan Ryan described Boyd as having a temper that was too big for his body, but he admired his limber build and elastic arm. Oil Can once famously said after a game in Cleveland was called due to fog, "That's what you get for building a ballpark on the ocean."

Boyd had a few shining moments during a 10-year career, serving as the number two starter (behind Roger Clemens) on the 1986 Red Sox team that lost to the Mets in the World Series. He got shelled in his only start in that Series and was heartbroken to have the Game 7 start taken away from him first by a rainout and then by a manager's decision. Boyd won a career-high 16 games that year, but also got suspended and sent to the psychiatric ward of the hospital after flipping out over an All-Star snub.

Despite a career record of 78–77, there was nothing about Oil Can that could be considered average. His hero was Satchel Paige, who had come through Meridian on his barnstorming tours, and Oil Can tried to emulate him by attempting a comeback at age 49 — there were no takers. He once pleaded, "They can take my money, they can take my car, but please don't mess with my family or take the ball out of my hand."

Outfielder Gee Walker had an intriguing nickname — "The Madman from Mississippi." Walker liked to clown around and he tended to take ill-advised liberties on the bases that drove his managers nuts. For example, there was the time he was picked off first base during a World Series game because he was busy arguing with the opposing bench, or the time he tried to steal a base while the batter was being intentionally walked.

All-Time Mississippi Selections

The best baseball players in Mississippi have not always been able to showcase their talents in the major leagues, which is reflected in the fact that eight Negro Leagues players are listed on the All-Time Mississippi team — three are starters.

Behind the plate we have Sammy Hairston, who became the first African American player on the White Sox when he joined them in 1951. He batted .400 but his major league career consisted of just four games. Hairston made his mark playing seven seasons with the Birmingham Black Barons and Indianapolis Clowns. He played in the East-West All-Star Game in 1948 and won the Negro American League's Triple Crown in 1950 with 17 homers, 71 RBI and a .424 average.

Hairston was followed into the big leagues by two sons (John and Jerry) and two grandsons — Jerry Jr. and Scott were still active in 2011— while another son played one year in the minors. The five Hairstons from three generations tops the four members of the Bell and

Boone families that have played across three generations. Sammy would go on to spend 48 years as a scout and coach with the White Sox.

Earning honorable mention at catcher was Jerry Moses, who made the AL All-Star team with the Red Sox in 1970 but was never a full-time starter for the seven teams he played for over nine seasons. He finished with just 269 hits. Also, Jake Gibbs spent 10 years backing up first Elston Howard and later Thurman Munson on the Yankees, serving as the team's starting catcher in 1967–68.

First base goes to George Scott, an eight-time Gold Glover and three-time All-Star from Greenville. Nicknamed "Boomer" for the towering shots he hit, the affable Scott was a fan favorite who pre-dated John Olerud in wearing a batter's helmet while playing in the field.

After winning the Eastern League Triple Crown playing for the Pittsfield Red Sox in 1965, Scott hit 27 homers as a rookie with the Red Sox in 1966, then batted .303 to help the Sox reach the World Series the next year. Then his production plummeted, as he batted just .171 with three homers, 25 RBI and an unsightly OPS+ of 39 in 350 at-bats in 1968. Considering the fact that he played his home games in hitter-friendly Fenway Park, Scott's 1968 season may be the worst by a first baseman in the modern era. He bounced back to have three solid years for the Sox before getting traded to the Brewers as part of a 10-player trade after the 1971 season.

Scott went on to lead the AL with 36 homers (tied with Reggie Jackson) and 109 RBI in 1975. He retired after hitting 271 home runs, which he referred to as "taters." Scott was once quoted as saying, "When you're hitting the ball, it comes at you looking like a grapefruit. When you're not, it looks like a black-eyed pea."

Scott never forgot his roots, which helped him cope with a premature end to his major league career at the age of 35 after playing for three teams in 1979 and failing to attract any interest the next year. "I was born poor, I was born black, and I was born in Mississippi. When you've been through that, you can deal with anything," he said.

Two Negro Leagues first basemen were also considered. Bob Boyd was an accomplished hitter who didn't get a chance to demonstrate his skill in the big leagues until late in his career. After batting over .300 in five straight seasons in the Negro Leagues, Boyd was signed by the White Sox, who let him languish in the minors. Nicknamed "Rope" for the way he roped line drives to the outfield, Boyd batted .373, .342, .320 (with 205 hits), .321 and .310 (with 197 hits) in the minors, with the Sox giving him limited exposure in the bigs.

Picked up by the Orioles in the Rule 5 Draft, Boyd finally got his big chance in 1956 at the age of 36 and batted .311. He finished fourth in the American League the next year with a .318 average and 154 hits, followed by .309 in 1958. He would finally stop playing in the minors at age 44, having collected 1,120 hits in the minors with a .320 average along with 567 hits in the majors with a .293 average. Boyd never flashed much power, hitting only 19 homers in the majors and 53 in the minors, but he knew how to get base hits and seldom struck out. During a doubleheader in 1957 he collected seven straight hits.

Boyd never became a household name despite his skill, but everyone knew about Luke Easter, he of the prodigious blasts to distant reaches of ballparks all around the Negro National League, the International League and the American League. At 6–4 and 250 pounds, Easter was built for power, not speed. "I just hit 'em and forget 'em," he was quoted saying in the 1984 *Baseball Research Journal*.

No one knows for sure what Easter was doing before he turned 32, but he evidently wasn't playing in an organized baseball league that kept stats. What we do know is that Easter hit 385 home runs in professional baseball after he joined the Homestead Grays in the Negro National League for the 1947 season. By comparison, Hank Aaron hit 440 homers and Babe Ruth 358 homers after the age of 32.

Easter hit 23 home runs playing about 100 games for the Grays over two years. Historian Pat Doyle reports that Easter, while playing for the Grays, became the first player in any league to hit a home run into the center field seats in New York's Polo Grounds, a blast that had to approach 500 feet.

Signing with the Cleveland Indians in 1949, Easter's teammates included Satchel Paige and Larry Doby. He played regularly from 1950 to 1952, hitting 28, 27 and 31 homers (second-best in the AL in 1952) for the Tribe while slugging .487, .481 and .513. On June 27, 1950, he hit the longest home run in the history of Cleveland's Municipal Stadium, a 477-foot shot to right field. By 1954, he was 39 years old and relegated to the minors, where he would continue to launch mammoth blasts for 11 more years. Easter became a fan favorite playing for Buffalo and Rochester in the International League, slugging 238 more homers until he finally hung up his spikes at age 49. Tragically, he was shot and killed during a robbery in 1979.

Two highly accomplished second basemen hailed from Mississippi—Buddy Myer and Frank White—and it was tough deciding between the two. Myer, who started out as a shortstop, played most of his 17-year career with the Washington Senators, helping them win the 1933 pennant. He batted over .300 nine times, including .349 to lead the AL in 1935. Driving in 100 runs that year despite hitting just five homers, Myer also collected 215 hits, scored 115 runs and had 96 walks for a .440 OBP. He led the league with 30 steals in 1928. At 34 years of age in 1938, his last year as a regular, Myer batted .336. He would retire with 2,131 hits and a .303 average, numbers that outshine those of White.

White was an all-time great defensive second baseman. He was a five-time All-Star who earned eight Gold Gloves for his defense, which was equal parts steady and spectacular. White was a product of the short-lived baseball academy the Kansas City Royals introduced to turn promising athletes into polished players. He contributed with the bat, hitting 160 homers, and was a threat on the base paths, with 178 stolen bases. However, it was White's quick hands, quick feet and unbelievable range at second that made him a fixture with the Royals for 18 seasons. He played so deep he almost was more of a roving fielder than a second baseman.

White batted .298 in 1982 but otherwise never batted higher than .275. His .255 career average was made worse by the fact he walked just 412 times in 8,467 plate appearances, generating a weak .293 OBP. He did manage to win a Silver Slugger Award in 1986 after batting .272 with career highs of 22 homers and 84 RBI. White was named MVP of the 1980 ALCS after batting .545 against the Yankees, and he won a World Series ring with the Royals in 1985. He remains one of the most popular players in Royals history. Bill James ranks Myer as the #24 second baseman and has White at #31, and Myer also has the edge in Career Win Shares, 257–208. In the end, Myer's offense contributions outweighed White's defensive contributions.

Another notable second baseman is Hughie Critz, who set a number of fielding records during his 12-season career. He led the league in fielding percentage five times, assists four times and putouts twice. Critz also holds the record for most home games played in a regular season with 88, which became possible when he got traded in 1930.

The best option for the All-Time Mississippi team at third base is Negro Leagues star Howard Easterling, one of the best all-around third basemen to ever play the game. Easterling was a five-tool player, a switch-hitter with speed who hit for average and could really pick it at the hot corner. He was selected to play in the East-West All-Star Game in five seasons — 1937, 1940, 1943, 1946 and 1949 — exactly once every three years during the heart of his career. Easterling helped the Homestead Grays win four straight pennants between 1940 and 1943, batting .313 in 1940 and .339 in 1943 (fifth-best in the Negro National League). He also hit .360 for the Cincinnati Tigers in 1937 and .344 for the Grays in 1946.

Easterling almost got a chance to show what he could do at the next level. In 1943 he and two other Negro Leagues players were invited to try out for the Los Angeles Angels, a top minor league team. Unfortunately, the invitation was withdrawn and it would be three more years before Jackie Robinson broke the color barrier. As for Easterling, he would later bat .300 in a series of exhibition games against white stars such as Bob Feller and Bob Lemon, the closest he would get to the big leagues.

Bill Melton had a nice career with the White Sox as a third baseman with good power but weak defense. He finished sixth in the American League with 33 homers in 1970 and then led the league with the same total the next year, becoming the first Sox player to lead the league in homers and also making his only All-Star team. His home run figures — 20 or more in six seasons — were not helped by playing in the cavernous Comiskey Park. When he retired in 1977 Melton was the White Sox all-time home run leader.

At shortstop we have Eric "Boob" McNair, who played 669 games at short along with 288 at second and 220 at third over a 14-year career. The Philadelphia A's reached the World Series in his first three seasons, winning two, but McNair would not return to the postseason after that. His first year as a regular was 1932, when he led the AL with 47 doubles and posted career highs with 18 homers and 95 RBI. He retired with a .274 batting average but a weak 80 OPS+. McNair died of a heart attack suffered a month shy of his 40th birthday.

Moving on to the outfield, let's start with Cool Papa Bell. After moving to center field and flashing his blazing speed on the base paths, Cool Papa seemed an altogether fitting name. The switch-hitter didn't take long to acclimate himself to the game, batting .417 in his rookie year of 1922.

Bell, who played in seven East-West All-Star games, is often called the fastest man in the history of professional baseball, and it's hard to argue with the anecdotal evidence. It is said that Cool Papa could score from first on a bunt, steal two bases at a time and beat out virtually any ball hit to the infield. Teammate Double Duty Radcliffe said, "If he bunts and it bounces twice, put it in your pocket."

Cool Papa's speed was more intimidating and demoralizing to opponents than the power of any slugger, which is why he earns the honor of Mississippi's All-

Cool Papa Bell was considered the fastest player to ever play in the Negro Leagues, and perhaps the fastest in all of baseball history. He regularly stole two bases at a time, scored from second on grounders and advanced two bases on bunts (National Baseball Hall of Fame Library, Cooperstown, New York).

Time Best Player over slugger Dave Parker. Bell played an impossibly shallow center field, because he never doubted he could catch up to any ball hit over his head. He was once described as the only player who could steal first base, with reports claiming he was timed running the bases in 12 seconds flat.

He was one of six future Hall of Famers who played on the powerful 1936 Pittsburgh Crawfords — along with Satchel Paige, Josh Gibson, Oscar Charleston, Judy Johnson and Buck Leonard — but Bell also played on dominant championship teams with the St. Louis Stars and Homestead Grays. His lifetime average was .316, according to the Hall of Fame.

In his last season, 1946, Bell batted an amazing .429 for the Grays, although he would make occasional appearances over the next four years as a player-manager. Inducted into the Hall of Fame in 1974, Bell said that was not the greatest moment in his life but rather seeing Jackie Robinson break the color barrier.

A fair number of people believe Parker should join Cool Papa in Cooperstown. After all, he won the Most Valuable Player Award in the National League in 1978 and was a seven-time All-Star who won three Gold Gloves and three Silver Sluggers. A two-time batting champion, he batted over .300 six times and intimidated pitchers with his 6-foot-6 frame and menacing scowl. In addition, he had good speed and possessed one of the most powerful throwing arms in baseball history.

Parker finished in the top five of MVP voting five different years, which demonstrates a certain level of dominance. Here are some other Hall of Fame outfielders and how many top five MVP finishes they had in their careers: Tony Gwynn (1), Duke Snider (3), Kirby Puckett (3), Richie Ashburn (0), Enos Slaughter (3), Carl Yastrzemski (2), Dave Winfield (3), Lou Brock (1), Rickey Henderson (2), Ralph Kiner (2), Billy Williams (2) and Joe Medwick (3).

Wait, there's more. Parker had more hits (2,712) than 36 Hall of Fame outfielders including Mickey Mantle, Stargell and Jim Rice. He hit more home runs (339) than Roberto Clemente, Chuck Klein or Al Simmons. His 1,493 RBI were more than Williams, Rice, Snider, Clemente or Slaughter. He helped the Pirates win the World Series in 1979 and did the same for the A's a decade later as a DH. Bill James ranks him as the fourteenth-best right fielder in history, and his 325 Career Win Shares ranks ahead of Hall of Fame right fielders Kiki Cuyler, Chuck Klein, Harry Hooper and Ross Youngs.

Yet Parker has never received more than 24 percent of the vote for the Hall in his 15 years on the ballot. He had a surly personality during his playing days and was also caught up in a drug scandal related to his time with the Pirates in the early 1980s, with both factors negatively affecting his appeal to Hall voters.

Parker believes he belongs in the Hall of Fame, as did his manager on the Pirates, Chuck Tanner. "There were a couple of years where my numbers probably weren't what they should have been," Parker said. "But for the majority of those 10 years, from 1975 to '80, I was probably the best player in the game ... I should be in the Hall of Fame. Ain't no doubt about it."

Joining Cool Papa and Cobra in the outfield is Ellis Burks, who evidently didn't do enough to earn a cool nickname. Burks posted deceptively strong career numbers, benefiting from playing five years in the launching pad that was Coors Field in the 1990s. He belted 57 of his 352 career homers at Coors Field, homering once every 15.4 at-bats there. Away from Coors, he hit 295 homers, averaging one every 21.5 at-bats — still respectable numbers. Burks batted .334 in 248 games at Coors and .285 in other ballparks over his 18 seasons.

Burks' best season was 1996 with the Rockies, when he led the league in runs (142), slugging (.639) and total bases (392), finished second in batting (.344) and hits (211), third in OPS (1.047) and fifth in homers (40) and RBI (128). His numbers were especially gaudy that year at Coors Field, where Burks hit .390 with 23 homers, drove in 79 runs and slugged .728. He also stole 32 bases that season and finished third in the MVP vote. Burks made his second and final All-Star team that year.

He was also named an All-Star and won a Gold Glove in 1990 with the Red Sox.

He later hit 31 homers for the Giants in 1999, batted .344 for them the next year and hit .301 with 32 homers for the Indians in 2002. Burks retired with 2,107 hits, 352 home runs, a .363 OBP and 1,206 RBI.

Among the outfielders earning honorable mention were Chet Lemon, Gee Walker and Bubba Hyde. Lemon, nicknamed "The Jet," played seven seasons with the White Sox and then nine more with the Tigers, earning three All-Star selections. He led the AL with 44 doubles in 1979, batted over .300 three times and retired with 215 home runs. Although Lemon didn't win any Gold Gloves, he was an outstanding center fielder with great range. He led the AL in times hit by a pitch four times in five years. Walker played from 1931–45, collecting 1,991 hits and averaging .294. He batted over .300 six times and stole 223 bases, He hit .353 for the Tigers in 1936 and followed up with .335 average, 213 hits and 113 RBI the next season.

Hyde wasn't as fast as Cool Papa Bell, but he was a pretty speedy leadoff batter. Hyde saw his first Negro Leagues action in 1924 and kept playing until 1951. He spent the majority of his career with the Memphis Red Sox, playing in the East-West All-Star game in 1943 and 1946.

Our designated hitter is Dmitri Young, who endured an up-and-down career. Over an eight-day period in 1997, Young was traded to Cincinnati, picked by Tampa Bay in the expansion draft and then traded back to the Reds. He batted over .300 all four years in Cincinnati, but was then on the move again in a trade to the Tigers. In 2005 he became just the third player to hit three homers on Opening Day — it's also the only time a player has homered three times in a game in the short life of pitcher-friendly Comerica Park. Young was an All-Star for the Tigers in 2003 after batting .297 with 29 homers and 85 RBIs.

The 300-pound Young, who was nicknamed "Da Meat Hook," battled substance abuse and alcoholism while in Detroit, and was eventually released before the end of the 2006 season. Later that year he was hospitalized with complications from diabetes. In 2007 he rebounded and made the NL All-Star team representing the Washington Nationals, batting .320 for the year and being named Comeback Player of the Year. He would be out of baseball less than a year later.

Several candidates were considered for the All-Time right-handed starter from Mississippi, but Roy Oswalt emerged out of the pack. Oswalt was the ace of the Astros staff for a decade until he forced a trade and was sent to the Phillies during the 2010 season. The most amazing stat about Oswalt was his 23-1 record against the Reds through the 2009 season — he finally ended up losing twice to the Reds in 2010.

Oswalt has the same lean build as Ron Guidry and has produced remarkably similar career numbers: 159-93 record, .631 winning percentage, 3.21 ERA, 1759 Ks and a 3.52 SO/BB ratio. He led the NL in winning percentage in 2001, wins with 20 in 2004, ERA (2.98) in 2006 and WHIP (1.025) in 2010. The Astros made it to the World Series in 2005, as Oswalt won 20 games for the second time. To demonstrate his dominance, Oswalt finished in the top five for the Cy Young Award five of his first six years in the majors. By comparison, Sandy Koufax, Randy Johnson and Bob Gibson are among the legendary pitchers who failed to place in the top five in the Cy Young race in any of their first six seasons; Roger Clemens and Greg Maddux recorded just two such seasons.

Claude Passeau posted double-figure wins in 10 straight years (1936-45) and was named to five All-Star teams (including the 1946 game that was called off). Passeau hurled a one-hit shutout for the Cubs in Game 3 of the 1945 World Series and finished with a 162-150 record and 3.32 ERA.

Another righty who performed well for the Cubs was Guy Bush. Nicknamed "The Mississippi Mudcat," Bush engaged in a record-setting pitchers' duel with the Braves' Charlie Robertson on May 14, 1927. Both starters were still pitching in the 2-2 game as it entered the eighteenth inning. Robertson finally tired, surrendering to a reliever as the Cubs pushed across five runs in the top half, then Bush closed out the victory in the bottom half of the eighteenth as the Cubs won 7-2. He ended up facing 71 batters and allowing 11 hits. It's unlikely that any manager is going to let his starter go 18 innings again. Pitching 17 seasons in the majors, Bush retired with a 176-136 record, winning 20 games in 1933. He surrendered the last two home runs of Babe Ruth's career on May 25, 1935.

Our lefty starter is Reb Russell, who fashioned a sparkling record of 80-59 with a 2.33 ERA pitching for the White Sox from 1913-18. He won 22 games his rookie year, leading the AL in games pitched with 52, but later threw out his arm. Russell made a comeback as an outfielder, batting .368 with 81 hits in 1922, followed by .289 the next year, but that would be it for his major league career. He played seven more seasons in the minors as an outfielder/first baseman, batting over .300 each year.

Also considered was Vinegar Bend Mizell, who is often mistakenly called an Alabama native because Vinegar Bend is a small town in Alabama. He was actually born in nearby Leakesville, Miss., but Vinegar Bend Mizell sounds a lot better than Leakesville Mizell. He was an All-Star with the Cardinals in 1959 despite posting a pedestrian 13-10 record. Mizell was traded to the Pirates during the next season, going 13-5 with a 3.12 ERA down the stretch as the team went on to win the World Series. He finished out his career pitching for Casey Stengel and the Amazin' Mets in 1962.

The All-Time Mississippi team does not really feature a closer. Joe Gibbon is actually the all-time leader in official saves with 27, but he didn't make much of an impact. Chad Bradford is the most accomplished of the other contenders, as he was a dependable reliever for 12 seasons. Bradford was never a closer, but he did make 561 relief appearances and record a 3.26 ERA with an ERA+ of 138.

Bradford's submarine delivery motion certainly made him stand out, as did the fact he was prominently featured as the ultimate undervalued pitcher by author Michael Lewis in his book, *Moneyball*. Lewis pointed out that Bradford picked up the submarine style from playing toss and catch as a little boy with his father, who had had a stroke and couldn't raise his arm over his shoulder so instead threw the ball underhanded.

What intrigued the A's about Bradford was the fact that he didn't give up many home runs or walks but had a knack for getting batters to ground out. For his career, Bradford's extra-base hit average was 4.7 percent compared to 8.0 percent for the MLB average; his ground ball to fly ball ratio was 1.79 percent compared to 0.78 percent for the MLB average; and his home run percentage of 1.3 percent was less than half the MLB average of 2.8 percent. He wasn't undervalued for long once he started producing those numbers at the major league level.

Only one manager deserved consideration: Harry "The Hat" Walker. He got the nickname from his tendency to nervously adjust his cap in between every pitch of an at-bat. Walker's father, Dixie, pitched for the Washington Senators, and his brother, also known as Dixie, was a five-time All-Star and National League batting champion in 1944.

Harry the Hat played 11 seasons in the majors as an outfielder, leading the NL with a .363 average and 16 triples in 1947. He was a player-manager for the Cardinals in 1955 and then got his first real chance with the Pirates in 1965. He won at a .549 clip in Pittsburgh but couldn't get his teams into the playoffs so he was let go after three seasons. He would skipper the Houston Astros the next five seasons, finishing his managerial career with a 630-604 record.

MISSOURI

*Names in **bold** represent Major League selections by position, followed by honorable mentions. Negro Leagues players are in italics. City of birth is in parentheses.*

C — **Yogi Berra (St. Louis).** Also: Elston Howard (St. Louis); Darrell Porter (Joplin); Walker Cooper (Atherton); Johnny Kling (Kansas City); Muddy Ruel (St. Louis); *Frank Duncan* (Kansas City); Jack O'Connor (St. Louis); Heinie Peitz (St. Louis); Mickey Owen (Nixa)

First Base — **Jake Beckley (Hannibal).** Also: Roy Sievers (St. Louis); Ryan Howard (St. Louis); Norm Siebern (St. Louis); Charlie Grimm (St. Louis); Donn Clendenon (Neosho); Nate Colbert (St. Louis); George Stovall (Leeds); Patsy Tebeau (St. Louis); Walter Holke (St. Louis); Dale Long (Springfield)

Second Base — **Lonny Frey (St. Louis).** Also: Jimmy Williams (St. Louis); Ron Hunt (St. Louis); Jerry Lumpe (Lincoln); Bill Cissell (Perryville)

Third Base — **Ken Boyer (Liberty).** Also: Harry Steinfeldt (St. Louis); Clete Boyer (Cassville); Bill Joyce (St. Louis); Bill Mueller (Maryland Heights); *Dangerfield Talbert* (Platte City); Bobby Byrne (St. Louis)

SS — **Glenn Wright (Archie).** Also: Charlie Hollocher (St. Louis); Bill Gleason (St. Louis); Ivy Olson (Kansas City)

OF — **Zach Wheat (Hamilton)**
OF — **George Van Haltren (St. Louis)**
OF — **Bob Allison (Raytown).** Also: Pete Reiser (St. Louis); Al Smith (Kirkwood); Jack Tobin (St. Louis); *Jimmie Crutchfield* (Ardmore); Hoot Evers (St. Louis); Bernard Gilkey (St. Louis); Bake McBride (Fulton); Ival Goodman (Northview); Casey Stengel (Kansas City); Bug Holliday (St. Louis); Solly Hofman (St. Louis)

Designated Hitter — **Lee Stevens (Kansas City)**

Right Handed Starter — **Pud Galvin (St. Louis).** Also: David Cone (Kansas City); Smoky Joe Wood (Kansas City); Clark Griffith (Clear Creek); Silver King (St. Louis); Mort Cooper (Atherton); Steve Rogers (Jefferson City); Mel Stottlemyre (Hazleton); Curt Davis (Greenfield); Al Orth (Sedalia); Rick Sutcliffe (Independence); Ted Breitenstein (St. Louis); Jeff Tesreau (Ironton); *Bill Drake* (Sedalia); Murry Dickson (Tracy); *Dick Whitworth* (St. Louis); *Reuben Currie* (Kansas City); Sonny Siebert (St. Marys); *Theolic Smith* (St. Louis)

Left Handed Starter — **Carl Hubbell (Carthage).** Also: *John Donaldson* (Glasgow); Jerry Reuss (St. Louis); *Leroy Matlock* (Moberly); Mark Buehrle (St. Charles); Ken Holtzman (St. Louis); *Jim LaMarque* (Potosi)

Relief Pitcher — **Tom Henke (Kansas City).** Also: Mike Henneman (St. Charles); Darold Knowles (Brunswick); Ken Sanders (St. Louis); Mark Littell (Cape Girardeau); Dick Hall (St. Louis); Bob Miller (St. Louis); Steve Mingori (Kansas City); Joe Boever (Kirkwood); Darren Oliver (Kansas City)

Manager — **Casey Stengel (Kansas City).** Also: Earl Weaver (St. Louis); Dick Williams (St. Louis); Charlie Grimm (St. Louis); Clark Griffith (Clear Creek); Mayo Smith (New London)

The Names

Best Nickname: Pearce "What's the Use" Chiles

Other Nicknames: Fletcher "Sled" Allen; Maurice "Flash" Archdeacon; Hank "Bow Wow" Arft; Frank "The Bean" Baumann; Jake "Eagle Eye" Beckley; Lawrence "Yogi" Berra; Marv "Baby Face" Breuer; "Sunset Jimmy" Burke; Elmer "Snake Eyes" Carter; Harvey "Hooks" Cotter; Martin "Toots" Coyne; Frank "Creepy" Crespi; Jimmie "The Black Honus Wagner" Crutchfield; Nick "Tomato Face" Cullop; Reuben "Black Snake" and "King" Currie; Curt "Coonskin" Davis; Clyde "Pea Ridge" Day; Bill "Plunk" Drake; James "Jumbo" Elliott; Walter "Hoot" Evers; Fred "Moonlight Ace" Fussell; James "Pud" Galvin; Clark "The Old Fox" Griffith; Charlie "Jolly Cholly" Grimm; Tom "The Terminator" Henke; Ernie "Tex" Herbert; Arthur "Circus Solly" Hofman; Fred "Bootnose" Hofmann; Walter "Union Man" Holke; Al "Boots" Hollingsworth; James "Bug" Holliday; Carl "The Meal Ticket" Hubbell; Frank "Cactus" Keck; Charles "Silver" King; John "Chicken Hearted" Kirby; Mark "Country" Littell; Arnold "Bake" McBride; John "Trick" McSorley; Frank "Dad" Meek; Heinie "The Count of Luxemburg" Meine; Benny "Earache" Meyer; Don "Mandrake the Magician" Mueller; Dave "Mr. Clean" Nicholson; Jack "Peach Pie" O'Connor; Al "The Curveless Wonder" Orth; Danny "Ozzie" Osborn; Barney "The Yiddish Curver" Peltry; Hubert "Shucks" Pruett; "Pistol Pete" Reiser; Jack "Bunny" Roser; Herold "Muddy" Ruel; Ken "Daffy" Sanders; "Muskrat Bill" Shipke; Norm "Smiley" Siebern; Roy "Squirrel" Sievers; Al "Fuzzy" Smith; Bob "Riverboat" Smith; Samuel "Skyrocket" Smith; Theolic "Fireball" Smith; Bob "Spook" Speake; Casey "The Old Perfessor" Stengel; George "Firebrand" Stovall; Rick "Red Baron" Sutcliffe; Dangerfield "Old Reliable" Talbert; George "White Wings" Tebeau; Oliver "Patsy" Tebeau; Phil "Hook" Todt; George "Rip" Van Haltren; Zach "Buck" Wheat; Albert "Fuzz" White; Jimmy "Button" Williams; "Smoky Joe" Wood; Glenn "Buckshot" Wright; George "Yats" Wuestling; Edward "Dutch" Zwilling

Most Unusual Name: Jewel Winklemeyer Ens; Elam Vangilder

All-Time Leaders

Games: Zach Wheat, 2410
Wins: Pud Galvin, 364
Hits: Jake Beckley, 2930
Batting Average: Zach Wheat, .317
Home Runs: Yogi Berra, 358
Stolen Bases: George Van Haltren, 583
RBI: Jake Beckley, 1575
Strikeouts: David Cone, 2668
Saves: Tom Henke, 311
Future Stars: Ross Detwiler (St. Louis); Jake Arrieta (Farmington); Jacob Turner (St. Charles)
Best Player: Yogi Berra

Historic Baseball Places

Negro Leagues Baseball Museum in Kansas City — A statue of Buck O'Neil greets visitors as they enter the museum, as it was his passion for telling the story of the Negro Leagues players that went a long way toward making the Negro Leagues Baseball Museum a reality. The Negro Leagues were organized in Kansas City in 1920, which is the primary reason why the museum is located in this city, plus the fact the Kansas City Monarchs were one of the all-time great teams. The museum is filled with photos, artifacts, film exhibits and multi-media computer stations that tell the story of Negro Leagues baseball.

Busch Stadium in St. Louis — Check out the statue of Enos Slaughter outside the stadium, which depicts his mad dash to home in Game 7 of the 1946 World Series against the Red Sox. The St. Louis Cardinals Hall of Fame features models of Sportsman's Park and the old Busch Stadium plus exhibits outlining the history of the St. Louis Browns and the Negro Leagues teams that played in St. Louis.

Royals Hall of Fame at Kauffman Stadium in Kansas City — In Dugout Theater you can watch a documentary on the history of baseball in Kansas City dating back to 1884. Hands-on exhibit illustrates the history of the bat, ball and glove, while "The Kansas City Connection" showcases all the Hall of Fame members with ties to the city such as Whitey Herzog, George Brett and Casey Stengel.

Ozzie's Restaurant and Sports Bar — The Wizard of Oz operates a fun sports bar about a mile from Busch Stadium that features a series of photo murals that show the step-by-step progression of Ozzie doing his back flip on the field. Sit in stadium seats and watch highlight clips with a display case showing his 13 Gold Glove Awards in the background.

Mike Shannon's Steaks and Seafood — Shannon won two World Series with the Cardinals and has been the team's radio announcer since 1972. His restaurant is a block north of the Stadium, and he typically broadcasts a post-game show on Saturdays. Inside it's hard to miss the Tower of Baseballs — the 452 autographed balls of Cardinals players that decorate columns in the middle of the restaurant.

Pujols 5 Westport Grill — Opened in 2006 with some great sports photography on the walls that is ever-changing. Deidre Pujols' Dominican recipes can be found on the menu, including Albert's favorite: Arrozo Con Pollo "Homerun Style." (Is now closed.)

Chappell's Restaurant & Sports Museum in Kansas City — Owner Jim Chappell loves sharing stories about his extensive collection of sports memorabilia, which includes an authentic World Series trophy and balls autographed by Dizzy Dean and Babe Ruth.

Notable Achievements

Ted Breitenstein pitched a no-hitter in his first game in the majors, which happened to be the last day of the St. Louis Browns' 1891 season, October 4.

Mickey Owen was the first player to pinch-hit a home run in the All-Star Game, which he did in 1942.

Mort Cooper set a record for most consecutive strikeouts to start a World Series game with five in Game 5 of the 1943 Series, a mark later matched by Sandy Koufax. Cooper recorded only one more strikeout in the game and took the loss.

Nate Colbert became the first player to record 13 RBI in a doubleheader on August 1, 1972.

Max Scherzer (St. Louis) set the record for most consecutive batters retired by a pitcher making his MLB debut as a reliever when he retired all 13 Astros batters he faced pitching for the Diamondbacks on April 29, 2008.

Dale Long set a record by hitting eight home runs in eight games in 1956. He was also one of the last left-handed catchers in the game when he caught two games in 1958.

Mark Buehrle pitched the eighteenth perfect game in MLB history on July 23, 2009, against the Rays. He went on to set a major league record for most consecutive batters retired over two games with 45.

On July 29, 2003, switch-hitter **Bill Mueller** became the first MLB player to hit two grand slams in one game from both sides of the plate.

On August 22, 1917, Pirates reliever **Elmer Jacobs** (Salem) set a record by pitching 16⅔ innings of relief in a game that lasted 22 innings.

Glenn Wright turned the fifth unassisted triple play in baseball history on May 7, 1925.

Casey Stengel is the only person to wear the uniform of all four major league teams that have played in New York City in the twentieth century. Stengel played with the New York Giants, managed and played with the Brooklyn Dodgers, managed the New York Yankees and managed the New York Mets.

The Show-Me State Offers Scoundrels, Counts and Folk Heroes

No offense to the guy in the Dos Equis commercials, but Pearce "What's the Use" Chiles has to be in contention for the most interesting man in baseball history, mainly because he's more mysterious than Mysterious

Walker. After all, no one has any idea when, where or how he died or what he did with his life after he escaped from prison in 1902.

Chiles, a native of Deepwater, Missouri, was by all accounts a charming and rambunctious con man who ran with an unsavory crowd. If a movie about his life were made, it would be called "Dirty Rotten Scoundrels."

He batted .320 with 76 RBI for the Phillies as a 33-year-old rookie in 1899 and then hit .216 in 33 games the next year. Chiles picked up his memorable nickname from his habit of shouting out "What's the use?" to batters who hit pop-ups to him. He gained further notoriety for his clever system of passing on the catcher's signs to the batter by way of an electric buzzer buried under the coach's box.

During the winter of 1901 he got caught conning money off a man on a train and was sentenced to two years in prison. He had fled Missouri in 1896 to beat a rape charge, but this time the authorities had their man. After pleading guilty and serving 16 months of his sentence, Chiles managed to escape from jail. He played for several teams in the minors under assumed names, got booted from a team in Portland after punching a woman in the face and was last seen playing for a semi-pro team in northern California in late 1903. No one has any idea what happened to him after that, but Chiles was finished playing in the majors.

The other 574 major league players from Missouri definitely led less exciting lives than Chiles, but some of them turned out to be pretty good ballplayers. There are famous names like Ozzie Osborn, who went undefeated (3–0) during his career and probably made all the rats run for cover. Then there are hilarious names like Heinie Meine, who managed to overcome his unfortunate name to lead the league with 19 wins for the Pirates in 1931. At least he had a cool nickname — "The Count of Luxemburg." It was a reference to his off-season home in Luxemburg, Missouri, not evidence he was baseball royalty.

If you like furs and pelts, Missouri can offer Squirrel Sievers, Coonskin Davis, Muskrat Bill Shipke and Clark "The Old Fox" Griffith, who should stay away from Buckshot Wright.

A number of Missouri players produced noteworthy feats. Clarence "Hooks" Iott, a native of Mountain Grove, once struck out 25 batters in a nine-inning game in 1941 and a month later struck out 30 in a 16-inning game, both in the minors. Iott would strike out 2,561 batters and win 175 games in the minor leagues, but he won just three games in the major leagues.

Hub "Shucks" Pruett of Malden posted a mediocre 29–48 career record, but he sure had Babe Ruth's number. Pruett struck out the Babe 13 times in 16 at-bats in 1922.

Edward "Dutch" Zwilling, who was born in St. Louis, is one of only two players to play for all three Chicago franchises: the Cubs, the White Sox and the Chicago Whales in the Federal League. Zwilling also has the distinction of having the last name in the alphabetical listing of all major league players in history.

When 3-foot-7 Eddie Gaedel stepped up to the plate on August 19, 1951, he was pinch-hitting for Frank Saucier, an outfielder from the tiny town of Leslie. Saucier only got one hit in 14 at-bats for his career, but he did lead the minors in batting with a .443 average in 1949.

One of the best pitchers from Missouri never made an impact in the majors. Joplin native Frank Shellenback was a right-handed spitballer who won nine games for the Chicago White Sox in 1918 and then went 1–3 with a 5.14 ERA the next year without appearing for the team in the controversial 1919 World Series. He was in the minors at the time, which prevented him from getting caught up in the Black Sox scandal but also proved to be his undoing in the big leagues. The spitball was outlawed before the 1920 season and Shellenback's use of the pitch was not grandfathered in because he was in the minors.

Instead of learning a new way to pitch Shellenback hung around the minors for 22 seasons, winning 20 games five times and compiling a minor league record of 316–191. Pud Galvin is the only Missouri-born pitcher to top Shellenback's 326 wins in pro baseball. Ted Williams' first manager in professional baseball was Shellenback, who skippered the 1936 San Diego Padres in the Pacific Coast League, a team with Vince DiMaggio and Bobby Doerr.

Kansas City Gives Birth to the Negro Leagues

Baseball in Kansas City got off to a slow start, with the Kansas City Cowboys finishing in last place with a 16–63 record in the Union Association's first and last season, 1884. Switching to the National League in 1886, the Cowboys went 30–91 in 1886 and moved up to seventh place. Another move, this time to the American Association, did not produce any better results. The Cowboys went 43–89 and 55–82 in 1888–89 despite having Billy Hamilton in the lineup.

That was the end of major league baseball in Kansas City until the Packers formed a team in the Federal League for 1914 and 1915. The Kansas City Athletics played in the American League from 1955–67 but finished in the bottom of the division every year and seemed to operate mainly as a feeder team for the New York Yankees. That franchise moved to Oakland, but baseball soon returned to Kansas City with an expansion team called the Royals in 1969. The Royals won their only World Series in 1985, which is also the last time they won their division.

Historic actions took root in Kansas City that would forever change black baseball. Rube Foster gathered the top owners of Negro teams in the Midwest for a meeting at the YMCA in Kansas City on February 13, 1920. What resulted was the creation of the Negro National League, the first successful effort to organize leagues for African American players.

J.L. Wilkinson's Kansas City Monarchs set the pace for the new league with a powerful team led by ace pitcher Bullet Joe Rogan and sluggers Dobie Moore, Heavy Johnson and Tank Carr. The Monarchs won 13 league titles and two Negro World Series championships while sending more players to the major leagues than any other franchise, a list of players that includes Jackie Robinson, Satchel Paige, Elston Howard and Ernie Banks. Historians such as Lawrence Hogan have noted that the Monarchs served as a social unifying force for African Americans in Kansas City, giving them something to cheer and rally around despite the hardships they faced in their everyday lives.

It seems fitting that the Negro Leagues Museum would be located in Kansas City, right where it all began. The Museum was founded in 1990, with a permanent exhibit facility opening in the historic eighteenth & Vine Jazz District in 1997. The Museum's mission is to share the story of Negro Leagues baseball and all of its players and teams, rather than just serve as a Hall of Fame for the best African American players.

Through the years Kansas City has sent 44 players to the major leagues including Smoky Joe Wood, David Cone, Tom Henke, legendary manager Casey Stengel and Negro Leagues stars such as Frank Duncan and Reuben Currie.

Stars Are Born in St. Louis

On the other side of the state in St. Louis, pro baseball got off to a promising start. The St. Louis Brown Stockings were a founding member of the American Association in 1882, and the team won four straight pennants from 1885–88 with Charlie Comiskey serving as player-manager. The franchise joined the National League in 1892 and changed its name to the Cardinals in 1900, but the team faced a long dry spell until breaking through to win the World Series in 1926.

A second team had arrived in St. Louis in 1902 when the Browns became an American League franchise. The Browns would win just one pennant in their 52 years in the city, with a World Series appearance in 1944 the only highlight before the team moved to Baltimore and became the Orioles.

The Cardinals were transformed into the so-called Gashouse Gang in the early 1930s, with a motley collection of talented and hard-nosed eccentrics captivating crowds at Sportsman's Park. The Gashouse Gang took the league by storm in 1934, with Dizzy, Daffy and Dazzy running roughshod over the league, literally. OK, so Dazzy Vance was near the end of the line and only won one game that year, but the Dean brothers combined for 49 regular season wins. A cloud of dust seemed to follow infielders Frankie Frisch, Leo Durocher and Pepper Martin wherever they went, and it was tough to tell which was dirtier — their uniforms or their play.

St. Louis could be called the "City of Stars," since a steady procession of iconic stars has guided the Cardinals to greatness over the years. Starting with Dizzy Dean and Joe Medwick in the 1930s, the parade of stars includes Stan Musial and Marty Marion, followed in turn by Bob Gibson, Ozzie Smith and now Albert Pujols.

Speaking of stars, the St. Louis Stars were one of the dominant Negro Leagues teams during the franchise's short history from 1922–31. Playing their games at Stars Park, which was one of the first ballparks built solely for black baseball, the Stars were blessed with terrific players such as Cool Papa Bell, Willie Wells and Mule Suttles. They won the second half pennant in 1925 but lost the league pennant to the Kansas City Monarchs, then won league pennants in 1928 and 1930. The Stars were declared the 1931 pennant winner after the Negro National League (and the team) folded during the season.

St. Louis has sent 282 players to the major leagues, with the first being Dan Collins with the Chicago White Stockings in 1874. The city has given birth to folk heroes (Yogi Berra and Pete Reiser), Hall of Fame managers (Earl Weaver and Dick Williams), nineteenth-century stars (Pud Galvin, Silver King and George Van Haltren), sluggers (Ryan Howard, Roy Sievers and Bob Allison) and Negro Leagues hurlers (Dick Whitworth and Theolic Smith).

All-Time Missouri Selections

Let's move on to the All-Time Missouri team selections. St. Louis has produced a number of great catchers, but there's only one Yogi Berra. He is the easy selection as the All-Time-Missouri catcher, since he is considered one of the top three catchers in baseball history. No player has more World Series rings than Yogi's 10, not to mention he's a cultural icon and folk hero whose Yogi-isms have amazed and amused fans for decades.

Berra grew up in an Italian neighborhood of St. Louis with Joe Garagiola as one of his close friends. Yogi dropped out of school after eighth grade and later signed with the Yankees at age 18, a year after Garagiola signed with the Cardinals. At the age of 20, Garagiola had four hits in Game 4 of the 1946 World Series to help the Cards beat the Red Sox, but he was never more than a journeyman catcher.

Berra, on the other hand, became an instant starter and leader for the Yankees, winning three MVP Awards and getting named to 15 straight All-Star teams. He finished in the top four in MVP voting a remarkable seven straight years. Yogi liked to keep things simple and was fond of saying, "Ninety percent of the game is half mental." Berra quickly learned how to deal with the pressure of playing in the postseason, coming through again and again to help the Yankees win 14 pennants and 10 championships in his 19 seasons.

Berra's greatest thrill as a ballplayer was catching Don Larsen's perfect game in the 1956 World Series, and Larsen has always said Yogi deserves a lot of the credit for his masterpiece. Few remember that Yogi hit three home runs off Don Newcombe during the '56 Series (the most ever by one batter against the same pitcher in a Series) including two in the decisive Game 7, and he batted .360 with 10 RBI for the Series. As Berra put it, "The biggest lesson I learned about World Series pressure was simple: You can't be afraid of making a mistake. There's always the next inning, or the next day. Life goes on."

A good all-around hitter, Yogi finished in the top 10 in homers, RBI and slugging nine times each and retired with 358 home runs and 1,430 RBI. Berra was equally skilled on defense, leading the league in games caught eight straight years and leading in assists three times and putouts eight times. He threw out an outstanding 47.3 percent of base stealers during his career and later won pennants while managing the Yankees and the Mets.

It's a strong lineup of catchers earning honorable mention status, led by Elston Howard, who spent three years as an outfielder in the Negro Leagues before switching to catcher in the minors. Blocked by Berra on the Yankees, Howard mainly played outfield his first six years with the team before becoming the Yanks' full-time catcher at age 32 in 1961. He batted .348 that year and then was named MVP in 1963 after batting .287 with 28 homers and 85 RBI.

In 1964, Howard set an American League record with 939 putouts, hitting .313 and earning a second straight Gold Glove that year while finishing third in the MVP race. Named to nine straight All-Star teams during his 13 years with the Yankees, Howard led the team to nine pennants and four World Series, later playing on another pennant winner with the Red Sox in 1967. In addition to being the first African American player on the Yankees, Howard was the first African American coach in the American League and is also credited with inventing the batting donut.

Darrell Porter was an underrated catcher during his 17-year career, making four All-Star teams and hitting 188 career home runs. In 1979 he became just the second catcher (along with Mickey Cochrane) to have 100 runs, 100 RBI and 100 walks in a season — he led the AL with 121 walks that year. A quiet but intense player, he was the MVP of the 1982 NLCS (batting .556) and the 1982 World Series, batting .286 with one home run to lead the Cardinals to the championship. After battling substance abuse during his career, Porter tragically died from a cocaine-induced heart attack at age 50.

Muddy Ruel was a standout defensive catcher who is credited with coining the phrase "tools of ignorance" to describe the catcher's equipment. He scored the most important run in the history of the Washington Senators, scoring the winning run in Game 7 of the 1924 World Series to deliver the Senators' only championship. Ruel has to be the only former major league player who was sanctioned to argue a case before the U.S. Supreme Court.

Another notable Missouri catcher, Walker Cooper, batted 6-for-6 with three homers and 10 RBI on July 6, 1949. An eight-time All-Star, Cooper was MVP runner-up after batting .318 for the Cardinals in 1943.

Johnny Kling was one of the best defensive catchers of the Deadball Era, relying on a strong and accurate arm to control the running game of opponents. He won World Series with the Cubs in 1907 and 1908, shutting down Ty Cobb and the Tigers running game. Frank Duncan won eight pennants and two championships in the Negro Leagues, playing mainly for the Kansas City Monarchs. An outstanding defensive catcher with a strong throwing arm but mediocre as a hitter, Duncan later served as Jackie Robinson's first manager in 1945.

Selecting Team Missouri's first baseman involved comparing players from distinctly different eras. Hall of Famer Jake Beckley played from 1888–1907 while Roy Sievers' career lasted from 1949–65. Beckley has a huge edge in hits (2,930 to 1,703) and average (.308 to .267), while Sievers produced significantly more home runs (318 to 86) playing in the Lively Ball Era.

Nicknamed "Eagle Eye" for his sharp batting eye, Beckley was one of the best sluggers of his era, finishing among league leaders in homers, RBI, triples and slugging nearly every year. He batted over .300 13 times and is still fourth in career triples with 244. An agile defender, Beckley remains the all-time leader in putouts by a first baseman by a comfortable margin. He was also a skilled base runner who stole 315 bases, providing the final evidence necessary to secure the top spot over Sievers. Beckley was elected to the Hall of Fame by the Veterans Committee in 1971.

Sievers, who played almost as many games in the outfield as at first, was a four-time All-Star who was named the American League's first Rookie of the Year in 1949 playing for his hometown St. Louis Browns. He batted .301 and led the league with 42 homers, 114 RBI and 331 total bases in 1957, despite the fact he played in pitcher-friendly Griffith Stadium. He is the all-time home run leader for the Washington Senators with 180. In 1957 he tied an American League record by homering in six straight games, but falling short of the mark set by fellow Missouri first baseman Dale Long, who had homered in eight consecutive games for the Pirates the previous year. In 1963 he became just the second player (after Jimmie Foxx) to pinch hit grand slams in both leagues.

Sievers was playing for the Browns when owner Bill Veeck sent in three-foot-seven "little person" Eddie Gaedel to pinch hit. As Sievers recalled, "We were having trouble getting men on base and we weren't winning that much anyway, so all of us players figured we might as well go along with it."

Ryan Howard will undoubtedly end his career as one of baseball's all-time great sluggers, but he does not yet have the career longevity. What he has done so far is mash home runs at a Ruthian pace, starting with 22 in 88 games as a rookie in 2005. That type of production led him to receive the Rookie of the Year Award. Howard was named MVP after his first full season, 2006, when he led the league with 58 home runs and 149 RBI. He should surpass 300 career homers during the 2012 season.

Two other notable first basemen from Missouri are Charlie Grimm and Norm Siebern. Siebern was a steady but unspectacular player who won a Gold Glove as an outfielder and then got shifted to first base. He made the first of three straight All-Star teams after batting .308 with 25 homers and 117 RBI for the Kansas City A's in 1962 and ended his career with a 117 OPS+.

Grimm compiled 2,299 hits and 1,077 RBI over a 20-year career, spending his last five years as player-manager for the Cubs. He led the Cubs to two pennants while still playing and a third one later on in 1945, but each time fell short. He hit just 79 homers while playing in the Lively Ball Era, producing a 94 OPS+. One of the better-fielding first basemen of his era, Grimm led the league in fielding percentage six times.

At second base we selected Lonny Frey, who started off as a shortstop for the Dodgers but was switched to second after landing with the Reds in 1938. He developed into an outstanding defensive player at second and made three All-Star teams during his seven years with the Reds. He led the NL in sacrifice hits in 1939; stolen bases, putouts and assists in 1940; and fielding percentage in 1943. He went 0-for-17 as the Reds lost the 1939 World Series and then went 0-for-3 in brief Series appearances for two championship teams: the 1940 Reds and 1947 Yankees. He died in 2009 at the age of 99.

Jimmy Williams had one of the best rookie seasons of any nineteenth-century player in 1899. He set a record for most triples in a season by a rookie with 27 and finished second in the league in runs created and at-bats; third in slugging (.530), hits (220), total bases (329), home runs (9) and RBI (116); fourth in OPS (.946) and extra-base hits (64); fifth in average (.354) and runs (126); and sixth in doubles (28). He attracted attention by being one of the star players who jumped to the American League for the 1901 season, joining the Baltimore Orioles. He led the league in triples and batted over .300 during his two years in Baltimore but failed to match his rookie year production. Still, Williams finished his 11-year career with a 115 OPS+.

Ron Hunt was good at getting hit by a pitch — leading the NL seven straight years in that category and in 1971 became the first player to get hit 50 times by pitches in one season — and that's about it for his accomplishments. He had no power, little speed and was average defensively with a weak arm. He did become the first New York Mets player to start in the All-Star Game in 1964, a year in which he hit .303. Despite his proclivity for taking one for the team, Hunt was not well-liked by teammates.

Jerry Lumpe started his career with the Yankees, winning a World Series ring as a reserve in 1958, but he didn't get a chance for playing time until traded to Kansas City in 1959. He had five productive years for the A's, batting between .270 and .300 each year, and then made his only All-Star team in 1964 with the Tigers. He was above average defensively and finished with 1,314 hits and a .268 average.

While at Fort Riley, Kansas, in 1922, Chalmer "Bill" Cissell showed off his horsemanship by winning 18 silver cups and 53 medals atop "Chance," a horse he named after former Cubs first baseman and manager Frank Chance. Cissell would later be signed by the Chicago White Sox in a deal that netted the Portland Beavers $123,000 in cash and players, a record at the time. Playing slightly more games at second base than shortstop over nine seasons, Cissell batted .315 in 1932 and ended up with 990 career hits.

The all-time third baseman from Missouri is Ken Boyer, who was the best of the seven Boyer brothers who played professional baseball (three made it to the majors). Boyer had a borderline Hall of Fame career as a defensive whiz and a more than capable batter with power. He made seven All-Star teams, earned five Gold Gloves and was 1964 NL MVP for the World Champion St. Louis Cardinals. Boyer batted .295 with 24 homers and a league-leading 119 RBI while scoring 100 runs during his MVP year. It should be noted that the league average was .254 that season, so Boyer was considerably above average with his batting. When he batted .329 in 1961, the league average was .262.

Boyer was joined in the starting lineup for the 1963 All-Star Game by fellow St. Louis infielders Bill White, Julian Javier and Dick Groat. Boyer knocked in 111 runs that year after five straight seasons of driving in 90 or more runs. He ranked among the fielding leaders at third base each year and retired with 282 homers, 2,143 hits and a .287 average. Although he never received more than 25 percent of the vote for the Hall of Fame, a close look at his stats and achievements reveals he is probably more deserving of enshrinement than Pie Traynor, George Kell and Fred Lindstrom.

Younger brother Clete Boyer was an even better defensive third baseman but not nearly as good a batter. Playing his first 11 years in the American League he was overshadowed by the brilliance of Brooks Robinson, but Boyer was nearly Brooks' equal in the field. He is equally or more deserving of the AL Gold Glove in 1961, 1962, 1963 and 1966. Boyer was a master at diving for balls and throwing runners out from his knees, leading AL third basemen in range factor/game six straight years. He won his only Gold Glove in the National League with the Braves in 1969, as his career was winding down. His best year with the bat was 1967, when he slugged 26 homers and drove in 96 runs for the Braves. Boyer played in five straight World Series with the Yankees, winning titles in 1961 and 1962.

The Chicago Cubs steamrolled the competition to win 116 games in 1906 with the famous double-play combination of Tinker to Evers to Chance. Third baseman Harry Steinfeldt was the only member of that star-studded infield not to reach the Hall of Fame, but he was the best position player on the team that year. He led the league with 176 hits and 83 RBI while finishing second in batting at .327. He also stole 29 bases and led NL third basemen in fielding percentage. It was by far the best season of Steinfeldt's 14-year career. He batted .471 in the 1907 World Series to help the Cubs sweep the Tigers. The St. Louis native's major league career ended with a 19-game stint with the Boston Rustlers in 1911 and he died three years later of a cerebral hemorrhage.

Another noteworthy third baseman is Bill Joyce, a nineteenth-century player who ranks seventh on the all-time list for OBP at .435. He led the league in homers once, walks twice and on May 18, 1897, Joyce became the second player to hit four triples in a single game. He is often credited with being responsible (along with Art Sunday) for the origins of the word "Texas Leaguer," but that cannot be verified. Finally, Bill Mueller won a batting title after averaging .326 for the Red Sox in 2003 and then batted .429 for the Sox as they won the Series the next year. Mueller averaged .291 lifetime with 1,229 hits.

Moving on to shortstop, the selection comes down to Glenn Wright or Charlie Hollocher. Wright was such a gifted shortstop with outstanding range that he pushed Rabbit Maranville to second base when he joined the Pirates in 1924. He also had some pretty good years with the bat, knocking in 111 runs in 1924 and 105 in 1927, batting .308 in 1925 and .310 in 1928. He hit .308 with 18 homers and 121 RBI for the Pirates' 1925 championship team, finishing fourth in MVP voting that year, and later averaged .321 with 22 homers and 126 RBI for Brooklyn in 1930. Nicknamed "Buckshot" due to his sometimes errant throws, he saw his production curtailed because of injuries.

Wright was dropped as manager of the Spokane Indians at the beginning of the 1946 season due to a drinking problem and replaced by utility player Mel Cole. On June 24, 1946, the bus carrying the team plunged into a ravine and burst into flames, killing nine players including Cole and seriously injuring three others. Wright was asked back to manage the team, which was cobbled together with retreads, and he guided the Indians to a 22–52 record the rest of the way.

Wright's career outshines that of Hollocher, who played just seven seasons before retiring with undiagnosed intestinal problems. As a rookie in 1918, Hollocher batted .318 and led the NL with 161 hits and 202 total bases. He averaged .340 with 201 hits in 1922 while also setting a modern-day National League record with just five strikeouts in 592 at-bats. Hollocher played only one other full season and finished with a .304 lifetime average. He committed suicide in 1940 at the age of 44.

The outfield is led by Hall of Famer Zach Wheat, who was one of the best left-handed hitters in the National League during a career that bridged the Deadball and Lively Ball Eras. Wheat batted over .300 in 14 of his 19 seasons, leading the league with a .335 average in 1918 and ending with a career mark of .317. A solid and steady contributor, he was the face of the Brooklyn franchise during some lean years and a fixture in left field. He finished in the top 10 in most hitting categories every year and in the years 1923–25 he batted .375, .375 and .359. Wheat was an outstanding defensive outfielder who also stole 205 bases. Retiring with 2,884 hits, he was elected to the Hall of Fame by the Veterans Committee in 1959.

Flanking Wheat in the outfield is center fielder George Van Haltren, a speedy leadoff hitter who excelled at getting on base and scoring runs. He scored 100 or more runs 11 times in 12 seasons and scored 1,642 runs for his career, which ranks 36th on the all-time list. Van Haltren scored one less run than Jimmy Ryan and it should be pointed out that no eligible players above them on the career runs list have not been elected to the Hall of Fame. Van Haltren also stole 583 bases (twentieth all-time) and his 161 triples rank 38th. Van Haltren spent significant time as a pitcher early in his career, winning 40 games.

The third outfielder is the muscular Bob Allison, who played the most in right field. Allison clubbed 30 homers while also leading the league with nine triples to win the Rookie of the Year Award with the Washington Senators in 1959. He formed a powerful combination with Harmon Killebrew in Washington and after the franchise moved to Minnesota, with Allison hitting 256 homers and Killebrew 476 between 1958 and 1970. During a game in 1962 Allison and Killebrew became the first teammates to hit grand slam home runs in the same inning. In 1963 Allison hit a career-high 35 home runs and led the AL with 99 runs, a .911 OPS and 151 OPS+. A three-time All-Star, he was a decent fielder with a strong arm. His career average of .255 was about what the league averaged during his playing days.

Pete Reiser led the Dodgers to the pennant in his first full season, 1941, becoming the first rookie to win the NL batting crown. He seemed destined for greatness, except for the fact that he was determined to catch the ball no matter what it did to his body. One violent collision in 1947 knocked Reiser unconscious, and a priest was summoned to give him last rites (National Baseball Hall of Fame Library, Cooperstown, New York).

Continuing with the honorable mention outfielders, we lead with Pete Reiser. "Pistol Pete" quickly captured the hearts of Brooklyn fans when he debuted in the middle of the 1940 season, demonstrating an unbeatable combination of breath-taking five-tool talent and unrestrained hustle. A speedy switch-hitter with some power and a strong arm, Reiser led the Dodgers to the pennant in his first full season, 1941, becoming the first rookie to win the NL batting crown. That year he also led the National League in runs, doubles, triples, slugging, OPS, OPS+ and total bases, making the All-Star team and finishing second in MVP voting. The next year he led the NL in stolen bases while batting .310. He missed three years for war service but returned to again lead the league in steals in 1946, stealing home a record seven times.

Reiser was determined to catch the ball no matter what the cost to his body, and so he launched himself into the unpadded concrete walls of every park in the National League. He was the ultimate professional in that regard, and he played the same reckless way on the bases. He officially holds the record for most times being carted off the field on a stretcher—11—and his list of maladies includes seven concussions, five skull fractures, dislocated shoulders, torn muscles and more. When he broke his right arm he simply learned to throw lefty. One violent collision in 1947 not only knocked Reiser unconscious, a priest was summoned to give him last rites. Reiser's only concern then was whether he hung onto the ball—he did. He played an average of 86 games a season for his 10-year career until baseball's ultimate crash-test dummy called it quits at the age of 33 in 1952.

Other notable outfielders from Missouri include Al Smith, Jack Tobin and Jimmie Crutchfield. Smith started out in the Negro Leagues and then spent six years in the minors before finally getting called up by the Indians in 1953. He batted .306 and led the league with 123 runs scored in 1955, coming in third in the MVP race that year. The diminutive Tobin was adept at finding the holes to get hits, posting four straight seasons with over 200 hits. In 1921 he batted .352, led the league with 18 triples and finished second in hits (236) and runs (136). Tobin batted over .300 seven times and had a lifetime .309 average. Crutchfield was the same size as Tobin but was faster and more skilled. He played on the Pittsburgh Crawfords in the 1930s, teaming up with Cool Papa Bell and Sam Bankhead to form arguably the fastest outfield in baseball history. Crutchfield made a bare-handed catch in the 1935 East-West All-Star Game that defied description.

Missouri has produced a strong group of right-handed starters over the years, making the final decision a tough one. Pud Galvin and Clark Griffith are in the Hall of Famer, while Smoky Joe Wood was as dominant as any pitcher in baseball for a brief period. David Cone was the ultimate big-game pitcher and gun for hire who won five World Series rings. Al Orth won more than 200 games as did Silver King, who is recognized as the first sidearm pitcher and the first to pitch a no-hit game and lose. Then you have Mort Cooper, who was named NL MVP for his spectacular pitching in 1942, as well as Steve Rogers and Mel Stottlemyre, who were each named to five All-Star teams.

In the end we couldn't overlook the fact that Galvin won 365 games, which ranks fifth all-time and is more than three times the total of Wood and nearly twice Cone's total. Galvin did lose 310 games, which trails only Cy Young, and he pitched his entire career from a short mound distance. It was a different game back in those days, with teams generally relying on only two or three pitchers. For example, Galvin started 75 of the 97 games played by the Buffalo Bisons in 1883. Frequent contract disputes led him to switch teams, and leagues, regularly. He pitched for Pittsburgh teams in three different leagues.

Galvin never led the league in wins or strikeouts despite posting 10 seasons with 20 or more wins and recording as many as 369 strikeouts in a season, but he was the dominant pitcher of his time. He won 46 games two seasons in a row and became the first pitcher to win 300 games, retiring as the all-time leader in wins, complete games, shutouts, games started and innings pitched. He remains second in career complete games with 646 and innings pitched with 6,003.

The gritty and determined Cone pitched roughly twice as many innings as Wood—2,898 to 1,434—but less than half as many innings as Galvin. Cone won 194 games pitching for five teams over a 17-year career and was a five-time All-Star, finishing in the top four in Cy Young balloting four times. He won 20 games twice—a decade apart. The first time was when he went 20–3 for the Mets in 1988, followed by a 20–7 mark for the Yankees in 1998, a year in which he suffered from an aching shoulder all season. Cone also led the NL in strikeouts in 1990 and 1991, striking out 19 Phillies in a game in 1991.

Cone often found his services in demand as the trade deadline neared. In 1992 the Mets traded him to Toronto for Jeff Kent, and Cone helped pitch the Blue Jays to a World Series title. In the off-season he signed a free-agent contract with the Royals, winning the Cy Young Award in his second year with the team. Traded back to the Blue Jays at the beginning of the 1995 season, he was shipped to the Yankees at the trade deadline and went 9–2 down the stretch to help the Bronx Bombers make the playoffs. When healthy he was the staff ace and team leader for the Yankees as they won four World Series titles over the next five seasons. In Game 3 of the 1998 World Series against the Padres, Cone no-hit the Padres for five innings despite needing a cortisone shot to ease the pain in his shoulder.

With Don Larsen in attendance at Yankee Stadium on July 18, 1999, Cone pitched a perfect game against the Expos. Blessed with a powerful arm early in his career, Cone evolved into a crafty pitcher as time went on. He was a tenacious and competitive gamer, always up for the challenge of a big game and willing to experiment with pitches and arm slots to get results. After developing a serious arm aneurysm in 1996 that forced him to miss a significant portion of the season, Cone returned and pitched seven no-hit innings in his first start. Here is how Buster Olney eloquently described Cone in *The Last Night of the Yankee Dynasty:* "His games often played out like action movies, with Cone in the starring role, scraping through one crisis or another, improvising and usually succeeding."

Smoky Joe Wood was probably the most talented righty from Missouri, but his career and reign of dominance was too short. He essentially had a seven-year pitching career, pitching more than 160 innings only three times. Here are his ERA marks for those seven seasons: 2.18, 1.69, 2.02, 1.91, 2.29, 2.62 and 1.49. In 1911 he pitched a no-hitter against the Browns and struck out 15 batters in another game.

At the age of 22 in 1912, Smoky Joe had one of the best seasons by a pitcher in the twentieth century, going 34–5 with a 1.91 ERA for the Red Sox. He led the AL in wins, won-loss percentage (.872), complete games (35) and shutouts (10), and he finished second in ERA, strikeouts (251), ERA+ (179), WHIP (1.015), H/9IP (6.986) and SO/BB (3.146). That year he tied Walter Johnson's record by winning 16 straight games. He also won three games in the 1912 World Series, becoming the first player to record double-digits strikeouts in a World Series game with his 11 K's in Game 1, remarking afterwards, "I threw so hard I thought my arm would fly right off my body."

Wood possessed a blazing fastball that was virtually unhittable, but he suffered first a thumb injury and then an arm injury and later sat out the 1916 season in a contract dispute. He would pitch seven more games across three seasons without winning another game. Switching to outfield, he played 697 games in the outfield, collecting 553 hits and averaging .283. He hit .297 and drove in 92 runs in his last season, 1922. Smoky Joe won just 117 games as a pitcher but ranks fifth all-time in ERA (2.03), 10th in won-loss percentage (.672) and thirteenth in WHIP (1.087) and H/9IP (7.141).

Griffith was elected to the Hall more for his work as a pioneering executive. He posted a splendid 237–146 record and won 20 games seven times in a career that spanned 1891–1914. Serving as player-manager, he led the White Sox to the first American League pennant in 1901 and then managed 19 more years for four teams without winning another pennant. As long-time owner of the Washington Senators, Griffith was instrumental in popularizing night baseball, establishing farm teams for big-league franchises and signing players from Latin America.

One final noteworthy righty is Rick Sutcliffe, who won 171 games over 18 seasons. He was named Rookie of the Year after winning 17 games for the Dodgers in 1979 and then produced a magical season in 1984. After starting the season 4–5 with a 5.15 ERA for Cleveland, Sutcliffe was traded in June to the Cubs. He posted a 16–1 record the rest of the way to lead the Cubs to the playoffs.

The All-Time Missouri lefty is Carl Hubbell, who dominated National League batters during the 1930s, winning MVP Awards in 1933 and 1936. He won 20 games five straight years and led the league in WHIP six times; SO/BB ratio five times; ERA, ERA+ and wins three times; won-lost percentage twice; and complete games, shutouts and strikeouts once. In 1934 "King Carl" won 21 games and gained notoriety for striking out Babe Ruth, Lou Gehrig, Jimmie Foxx, Al Simmons and Joe Cronin in succession during the All-Star Game. However, his most amazing accomplishment was winning 24 straight games over the 1936 and 1937 seasons.

Relying on a devastating screwball, unmatched poise and pinpoint control, Hubbell posted double-figure wins his first 15 seasons and ended up with 253 wins and a 2.98 ERA. As Hubbell put it, "The screwball's an unnatural pitch. Nature never intended a man to turn his hand like that throwing rocks at a bear."

A nine-time All-Star who was also nicknamed "Meal Ticket," Hubbell went 2–0 in the 1933 World Series and didn't surrender an earned run in 20 innings to lead the Giants to the championship. He spent his entire 16-year career with the New York Giants, later serving as farm director and scout for the franchise in an association that lasted for 60 years. He was elected to the Hall of Fame in 1947.

John Donaldson may have been the greatest left-handed pitcher in Negro Leagues history. Possessing excellent control and a sharp-breaking curveball, Donaldson dominated batters throughout his career, which lasted from 1913–34. His stats are often discounted because he spent much of his time barnstorming the country and playing inferior competition, but he demonstrated his ability against top players and teams, too. John Henry Lloyd called him the toughest pitcher he ever faced, while John McGraw said he was the greatest pitcher he ever saw.

Pitching for the All Nations traveling all-star team from 1913–17, Donaldson averaged nearly 20 strikeouts a game and once recorded 240 strikeouts over a 12-game period. He pitched three straight no-hitters while getting noticed for his top-notch batting and speedy base-running. Donaldson batted over .300 over his career, often playing in the outfield when not pitching. Researchers to date have been able to document 235 wins (and possibly as many as 360), 11 no-hitters and a perfect game for Donaldson. In 1949 he became the first African American scout in the majors when he started working for the White Sox. Inexplicably, he was overlooked when the Hall of Fame inducted a special class from the Negro Leagues in 2006.

Other lefties worth mentioning include Jerry Reuss, who won 220 games over 22 seasons, and Mark Buehrle, a four-time All-Star and two-time Gold Glove winner who pitched a no-hitter in 2007 and followed up by pitching a perfect game on July 23, 2009 against the Rays.

Tom Henke is the logical choice for all-time best relief pitcher, as his 311 career saves outdistances runner-up Mike Henneman by quite a bit. Nicknamed "The Terminator," Henke led the AL with 34 saves in 1987 while recording an amazing 12.3 SO/9IP ratio.

His career mark was 9.8 SO/9IP. In 1992 he saved three games in the ALCS and two more in the World Series to help the Blue Jays win the championship. He had six years with more than 30 saves yet only made one All-Star team. He appeared in 642 games, all in relief, and posted a 2.67 ERA.

Henneman threw a forkball and slider like Henke as well as a devastating sinking fastball. He had seven years with at least 20 saves, capped by a career-high 31 in his final season, 1996. Henneman finished with 193 saves for his 10-year career, making the 1989 All-Star team despite posting just eight saves that year.

Darold Knowles remains the only player to pitch in all seven games of a World Series, which he did with the A's in 1973. Knowles served as an effective set-up man for Rollie Fingers, recording a 1.37 ERA in 1972 and retiring with 112 official saves in 757 relief appearances.

Another notable reliever was Bob Miller, who debuted at age 18 in 1957 and hung around to play 17 years for 10 teams. The folks who sew names on the back of uniforms were grateful that Miller changed his name from his birth name, which was Robert Gemeinweiser. His best year was 1971, when he went 8–5 with 10 saves, a 1.64 ERA and 209 ERA+ pitching for three different teams. He appeared in 694 games, including a league-high 74 games in 1964.

Six managers from Missouri are in the Hall of Fame, although only three were elected for their managerial accomplishments: Casey Stengel, Earl Weaver and Dick Williams. Other notable managers from the state include Charlie Grimm, who rode superior pitching to guide the Cubs to three pennants, and Mayo Smith, who skippered the Detroit Tigers to 103 wins and a World Series title in 1968.

Williams and Weaver were great managers, but "The Old Perfessor" resides in a class by himself. Stengel started his managerial career with three unsuccessful seasons with Brooklyn followed by six unsuccessful years with Boston, and he ended with four brutal, last-place finishes with the expansion Mets. In between, he was equal parts brilliant and lucky in guiding the New York Yankees to 10 pennants and seven World Series titles in 12 years, delighted to finally have talented players on his side.

He is the only manager to win five straight pennants let alone five straight world championships, and he did it in his first five years with the Yanks. The first year he missed the playoffs with the Yankees was 1954, when he won a career-high 103 games but finished eight games behind the torrid Indians. That minor setback was followed by four more pennants in succession.

Stengel was a fan favorite for his folksy and bewildering double-talk, known as "Stengelese," but he was always able to get his point across to his players, as he saved the obfuscation for the beat writers to keep them entertained and off-balance. His real gift was in developing talent and putting the right player in the right position at the right time. He second-guessed himself for years about whether he should have kept Mickey Mantle at shortstop, but most of his hunches proved correct. He believed in platooning players and riding the hot hand. A flaky, hotheaded buffoon as a player, Stengel evolved into a wise old sage as a manager because he absorbed many lessons from his mentor, John McGraw, who was his manager on the Giants.

Despite the public perception, Stengel was nobody's fool. Many of his best quotes were generated during his tenure as Mets manager, when he did his best to deflect attention from the putrid play of his team. Like the time he said, "You look there into the Cincinnati dugout and what do you see? All mahogany. Then you look at our bench and all you see is driftwood." The Ol' Perfessor sure was an original.

Williams was elected to the Hall in 2008 after winning 1,571 games over 21 seasons for six teams. In 1967 he took over a Red Sox team that had finished ninth the year before and in his first year as manager guided them to their first pennant in 21 years. He overcame the meddling of Oakland A's owner Charlie Finley to win three straight division crowns and back-to-back World Series in 1972 and 1973. His last turnaround project involved taking the Padres to the playoffs for the first time in their 16-year history in 1984.

Williams, who overcame a hardscrabble childhood with an abusive father, was a stubborn disciplinarian who held players to a high standard and expected things done his way. He excelled at managing the game and evaluating players but was criticized for his poor communication style. Goose Gossage, who was Williams' closer with the Padres, had this to say about him: "He's one of the best managers of all-time, in my opinion, and he's the best manager I ever played for. And that's taking in some great managers."

Whereas Williams generally only lasted about three seasons with a team, Weaver spent his entire 17-year career managing the Baltimore Orioles. He won 100 or more games five times (and won at least 90 games six other times) and guided the Birds to four pennants and the 1970 World Series championship. With an overall record of 1,480–1,060, his .583 winning percentage ranks ninth all-time among managers. And while Williams was aloof and distant from players, Weaver was a personable curmudgeon who relied on humor to diffuse tense situations. Like the time he visited a struggling Ross Grimsley on the mound and said, "If you know how to cheat, start now."

Weaver was a second baseman who spent 14 years toiling in the low minors without ever making it to the majors, a disappointment that helped shape him as a manager. As a skipper, he was feisty and combative but also a brilliant strategist. He was an early proponent of managing based on statistical match-ups and relied on a strong defense and solid pitching to finish above .500 every year except his last season. As Weaver put it, "Baseball is pitching, 3-run homers and fundamentals."

"The Earl of Baltimore" became known for his colorful antics in arguing with umpires, and he had a long-running acrimonious battle with star pitcher Jim Palmer. As he once lamented, "I have more fights with Jim Palmer than with my wife.... Every time Palmer reads about a new ailment, he seems to get it."

MONTANA

*Names in **bold** represent Major League selections by position, followed by honorable mentions. City of birth is in parentheses.*

Catcher — **Rob Johnson (Anaconda)**. Also: John Gibbons (Great Falls)
First Base — **Ed Bouchee (Livingston)**
Second Base — **Jeff Doyle (Havre)**
Third Base — **Dave Meier (Helena)**
Shortstop — **Herb Plews (Helena)**
Outfield — **John Lowenstein (Wolf Point)**
Outfield — **Rob Ryan (Havre)**
Outfield — **Jim Tyack (Florence)**
Right Handed Starter — **Johnny Couch (Vaughn)**. Also: Joe McIntosh (Billings)
Left Handed Starter — **Dave McNally (Billings)**. Also: Jeff Ballard (Billings)
Relief Pitcher — **Taylor Tankersley (Missoula)**. Also: Gary Neibauer (Billings); Kameron Mickolio (Wolf Point); Jim Otten (Lewistown); Steamboat Williams (Cascade)
Manager — **John Gibbons (Great Falls)**. Also: Vedie Himsl (Plevna)

The Names

Best Nickname: Rees "Steamboat" Williams
Other Nicknames: John "Steiner" Lowenstein
Most Unusual Name: Kameron Mickolio; Avitus Himsl

All-Time Leaders

Games: John Lowenstein, 1368
Hits: John Lowenstein, 881
Batting Average: Ed Bouchee, .265
Home Runs: John Lowenstein, 116
RBI: John Lowenstein, 441
Stolen Bases: John Lowenstein, 128
Wins: Dave McNally, 184
Strikeouts: Dave McNally, 1512
Saves: Taylor Tankersley, 4 (still active)
Future Star: Tyler Graham (Great Falls); Mason Tobin (Glendive)
Best Player: Dave McNally

Historic Baseball Places

Dehler Park in Billings — Opened in 2008 to replace Cobb Field, which had hosted minor league games for 75 years. The new park incorporated some of the bench seating from the old stadium and also features a sculpture of Orioles pitcher and Montana native Dave McNally in full pitching motion.

Ogren Park at Allegiance Field in Missoula — Opened in 2004 to host the Missoula Osprey in the Pioneer League, it features a breath-taking view of the Rocky Mountain range in the distance.

Centene Stadium in Great Falls — The ballpark formerly known as Legion Field, which opened in 1940, did a nice job of blending old with the new when a major renovation was done in 2005. Tucked into the ballpark is the Great Falls Baseball Museum and team Hall of Fame, and the artifacts on display include a 2005 White Sox World Series ring.

Notable Achievements

Dave McNally made history in the 1970 World Series, when he belted a grand slam home run in Game 3, becoming the only winning pitcher to hit a Series slam.

John Lowenstein is tied with Rex Hudler for the most positions played while homering with nine (including DH and PH).

Montana's McNally Helped Usher in Free Agent Era

Billings native Dave McNally, who won 20 games four straight years for the Orioles, is the only Montana native to make the All-Star team. McNally, who was selected as an All-Star in 1969, 1970 and 1972, was recognized by *Sports Illustrated* as Montana's Athlete of the Century in 1999.

By far the best season of his career was 1968 — now known as the "Year of the Pitcher" — when McNally posted an incredible 0.842 WHIP while going 22–10 with a 1.95 ERA. He allowed just 175 hits and 55 walks in 273 innings that season, taking advantage of the spectacular defense played behind him by Brooks Robinson, Mark Belanger and Paul Blair.

McNally's mark that year is the fourteenth-best single-season WHIP in baseball history and it beats the best WHIP figures ever posted by Sandy Koufax, Bob Gibson, Juan Marichal, Cy Young, Roger Clemens or Nolan Ryan. It's hard to believe, but McNally did not get a single Cy Young Award vote that season. That's because Denny McLain went 31–6 for the Tigers with 280 strikeouts on the way to winning the Cy Young Award unanimously along with the MVP Award.

McNally finished fourth in MVP Award voting in 1968, just ahead of Luis Tiant, who went 21–9 with 1.60 ERA and 0.871 WHIP. With pitchers dominating the action, it's not surprising that baseball decided to lower the pitching mound in 1969. That didn't slow down McNally, who extended his streak of consecutive victories to 17 by winning his first 15 decisions in the 1969 season.

McNally appeared in four World Series with the Orioles, pitching a shutout in Game 4 of the 1966 World

Centene Stadium in Great Falls, formerly known as Legion Field, first opened in 1940. The ballpark has been able to retain its old-time character despite several major renovations through the years. Eighteen-year-old Pedro Martinez made his professional debut in Great Falls in 1990, going 8–3 and leading the Great Falls Dodgers to their third straight Pioneer League title (courtesy BallparkReviews.com).

Series and blasting a home run off the Mets' Jerry Koosman in the 1969 Series.

He surrendered Al Kaline's 3,000th hit on September 28, 1974. In his last major league start on June 8, 1975, McNally faced off against fellow Billings native Joe McIntosh. McIntosh and the Padres won the game 5–2.

McNally's biggest accomplishment in baseball might have come after he retired from the game in 1975. Although he had no intention of playing again, and thus did not have much to lose, McNally joined Andy Messersmith in fighting baseball's reserve clause. The two had played the previous season without signing contracts, which held them to their current team under the one-year reserve clause. McNally was persuaded by the players' union to join Messersmith in asserting that they should be declared free agents since they had played out their option year.

The Expos tried to forestall the challenge by offering McNally a contract and signing bonus, but he turned those overtures down so that Messersmith would not face undue pressure as an active player. When arbitrator Peter Seitz ruled in favor of the players it opened up the floodgates to free agency, which has had a dramatic effect on the game.

All-Time Montana Selections

In Montana, the average square mile of land contains 1.4 elk, 1.4 pronghorn antelope, 3.3 deer and 0.0001 baseball players. This frontier state has sent only 22 players to the major leagues since Steamboat Williams of Cascade was called up to pitch for the Cardinals in 1914.

Despite the rarity of a Montana-bred major leaguer, three were active in 2011: catcher Rob Johnson and relievers Kameron Mickolio and Mason Tobin.

Our catcher is Johnson, who has played sparingly since debuting for the Mariners in 2007. With a lifetime average hovering around .200, he will have to become more productive with the bat to stick around. Johnson played for Team USA in the 2005 Baseball World Cup held in the Netherlands.

Ed Bouchee's career got off to a promising start, as the first baseman batted .293 with 17 home runs and 76 RBI for the Phillies in 1957. He finished second in Rookie of the Year voting and twelfth in the MVP Award balloting that year. Then he was arrested for exposing himself to young girls in the off-season, leading to three years of probation and a short stint in a psychiatric institution. Bouchee was reinstated to the league in 1958, with few repercussions it seems. He posted good stats in just one more season, 1959, and was out of baseball by 1962. His .265 lifetime average is the best in Montana history (minimum 100 at-bats).

At second base we have Jeff Doyle, who played 12 games in 1983 and produced a respectable .297 batting average. The third base spot goes to Dave Meier, who only played two games at the position and was otherwise an outfielder during his four-year stint with three teams.

Herb Plews of Helena was mainly a second baseman during his four-season career, but he's the only Montana-born player to play shortstop so that's where we placed him. Plews was the player sent to the minors when the Boston Red Sox called up Pumpsie Green in July 1959, becoming the last team in the majors to integrate. He would not appear in the majors again, although he hung around to play six more seasons in the minors.

John Lowenstein holds most of the career batting records for the state. He was mainly a bench player over his 16-year career but was perhaps deserving of a larger role. The only season he got more than 350 at-bats was 1974, when he stole a career-high 36 bases for the Indians. The versatile lefty batter played every position on the field except catcher and pitcher but was primarily a left fielder. His best season was 1982 when he hit .320 with 24 homers and 66 RBI in 322 at-bats.

Even though he hit several big home runs in the playoffs, the most remembered highlight of Lowenstein's career came in 1980 when he was hit by a thrown ball while running the bases. The crowd got concerned as the motionless player was carted off the field on a stretcher. Then just as the stretcher got near the dugout, Lowenstein sat up, raised his fists in the air and screamed, which thrilled the crowd. I guess when you're a .253 lifetime hitter you don't get a lot of chances to wow people.

Joining Lowenstein in the outfield are Rob Ryan, who batted .234 in three partial seasons, and Jim Tyack, who batted .258 in his only season for the Philadelphia Athletics.

McNally, who finished his career with a 184–119 record and 3.24 ERA, is the obvious choice as Montana's left-handed starter. Another notable Montana southpaw also pitched for the Orioles pitcher: Jeff Ballard. Ballard basically had six bad seasons offset by one good season—1989, when he went 18–8 for the Orioles and came in sixth in Cy Young Award voting. His career stats otherwise were a pedestrian 23–45 with a 5.21 ERA. With a career mark of 2.8 strikeouts per 9 innings, Ballard was obviously not a power pitcher.

Johnny Couch is the right-handed starter for Team Montana, although he pitched slightly more games in relief. Couch compiled a 16–9 mark for the Reds in 1922 but then was hit hard the next three seasons and out of baseball by 1925.

The best choice for relief pitcher is Tankersley, who was a first round draft pick of the Marlins in 2004. He appeared in 49 games as a rookie in 2006, posting a 2.85 ERA, and then went 6–1 while making 67 appearances the next year. He has seen sporadic action since then, with poor results, and spent 2011 in the minors. He is the all-time leader in official saves by a Montana pitcher with a grand total of four.

Team Montana is managed by John Gibbons of Great Falls, who managed the Blue Jays from 2004–2008 and wound up with an even .500 winning percentage. Although he never guided the Blue Jays to the playoffs during his tenure, Gibbons did finish ahead of the Red Sox in 2006, no small accomplishment in a division ruled by the big spenders in baseball.

A second Montana-born person actually managed in the major leagues. Vedie Himsl was part of the ill-conceived "College of Coaches" rotational system deployed by the Chicago Cubs in 1961 at the suggestion of backup catcher and coach El Tappe. Actually, it was Tappe's idea to rotate coaches through the minor league system—it was owner Philip Wrigley's idea to try it at the major league level, which Tappe justifiably thought was nuts. Wrigley won out and declared that the team's eight coaches would rotate in and out as manager, with the idea that each had something uniquely positive to contribute and players wouldn't start tuning out the same voice.

Himsl was one of four coaches who managed games for the Cubs that year, guiding the team to a 10–21 record during a season in which they placed seventh and were the laughingstock of the league. The "College of Coaches" system was abandoned early in the 1962 season.

Nebraska

Names in bold represent Major League selections by position, followed by honorable mentions. City of birth is in parentheses.

Catcher — Ted Easterly (Lincoln). Also: Otto Miller (Minden); Les Nunamaker (Malcolm); Todd Pratt (Bellevue)
First Base — Johnny Hopp (Hastings)
Second Base — Bob Johnson (Omaha)
Third Base — Wade Boggs (Omaha)
Shortstop — Ron Hansen (Oxford)
Outfield — Richie Ashburn (Tilden)
Outfield — Sam Crawford (Wahoo)
Outfield — Billy Southworth (Harvard). Also: Les

Mann (Lincoln); Jackie Brandt (Omaha); Bob Cerv (Lincoln); Russ Snyder (Oak); Eddie Brown (Milligan)
Right Handed Starter — Pete Alexander (Elba). Also: Bob Gibson (Omaha); Mel Harder (Beemer); Tom Seaton (Blair); Sloppy Thurston (Fremont)
Left Handed Starter — Clarence Mitchell (Franklin)
Relief Pitcher — Gregg Olson (Scribner). Also: Tim Burke (Omaha); Jason Christensen (Omaha)
Manager — Billy Southworth (Harvard). Also: Darrell Johnson (Horace)

The Names

Best Nickname: Frederick "Mysterious" Walker
Other Nicknames: Grover "Old Pete" Alexander; Richie "Whitey" and "Putt-Putt" Ashburn; Justin "Pug" Bennett; Wade "Chickenman" Boggs; "Glass Arm" Eddie Brown; "Wahoo Sam" Crawford; Bob "Hoot" Gibson; Ron "The Beak" Hansen; Mel "Chief" Harder; Johnny "Cotney" Hopp; Dale "Nubbs" Jones; Sheldon "Available" Jones; Doyle "Porky" Lade; Les "Major" Mann; Cliff "Tiger" Mapes; Otto "Moonie" Miller; Todd "Tank" Pratt; Everett "Pid" Purdy; Hollis "Sloppy" Thurston; August "Gloomy Gus" Williams
Most Unusual Name: Kimera Bartee; Robert Waskgis

All-Time Leaders

Games: Sam Crawford, 2517
Hits: Wade Boggs, 3010
Batting Average: Wade Boggs, .328
Home Runs: Wade Boggs, 118
RBI: Sam Crawford, 1525
Stolen Bases: Sam Crawford, 366
Wins: Grover Alexander, 373
Strikeouts: Bob Gibson, 3117
Saves: Gregg Olson, 217
Future Stars: Alex Gordon (Lincoln)
Best Player: Grover Alexander

Historic Baseball Places

TD Ameritrade Park in Omaha — Replaced Rosenblatt Stadium as the new home of the College World Series beginning in 2011, with a capacity of 24,500.
Museum of Nebraska Major League Baseball in St. Paul — Pays tribute to the more than 140 major league players with ties to the state.

Notable Achievements

Wade Boggs was the first player whose 3,000th hit was a home run. Derek Jeter became the second in 2011.
Cliff Lee (Lexington) was the first player to hit a home run to left field and completely out of the stadium at the Baker Bowl in Philadelphia when he went deep against Art Nehf on May 30, 1922. He hit two homers off Nehf in the game.
Sloppy Thurston is the only pitcher to strike out the side on nine pitches in extra innings, which he did on August 22, 1923.
Sam Crawford is the only player to lead both leagues in home runs and triples. He led the NL in home runs in 1901 and in triples in 1902, then led the AL in home runs with seven in 1908. He led the AL in triples five times.
Todd Pratt is one of eight players to hit a walk-off home run to end a postseason series. He homered for the Mets in the bottom of the 10th inning to end the 1999 NLDS.
Billy Southworth was the first to win a World Series as a player and manager. He won in 1926 as a player and 1942 and 1944 as a manager.
Ron Hansen turned an unassisted triple play on June 30, 1968.

The Road to Championship Goes Through Omaha

Baseball comes alive each summer in Nebraska, as the College World Series has been taking place in Omaha since 1950. Omaha Mayor Johnny Rosenblatt, who was a huge baseball fan, was instrumental in retaining the College World Series as well as bringing minor league baseball to town.

Games originally took place at Omaha Municipal Stadium, which was later renamed Johnny Rosenblatt Stadium and boasted the largest capacity (23,145) of any minor league ballpark. After 60 years of tradition, the College World Series is now held at the newly constructed TD Ameritrade Park.

Some of the highlights of the College World Series through the years include Jim Ehler's no-hitter for Texas in 1950 and Dave Winfield nearly pitching the University of Minnesota to an upset over defending champion USC in the 1973 CWS. Winfield was named Most Outstanding Player (MOP), despite his team losing in the semi-finals, after he batted .467 and struck out 29 batters in 17 innings. It would be the last time he pitched and a week later Winfield made his major league debut with the Padres.

Thirty major league players have been born in Omaha including Hall of Famers Bob Gibson and Wade Boggs. Gibson attended Omaha Technical High School and then received a basketball scholarship to attend Creighton University in his hometown. After his playing career ended he returned to Omaha and operated Bob Gibson's Spirits and Sustenance Bar for a time in the 1980s.

It is fitting that Charlie Abbey's name can be found first in an alphabetical listing of Nebraska-born players, because in 1893 he became the first person from the Cornhusker state to play in the majors. A total of 108 Nebraska-born players have made it to the major leagues and five players from Nebraska have been enshrined in the Hall of Fame, joined by manager Billy Southworth in 2008.

The All-Time Nebraska team has its share of immortal players, but some of the state's lesser-known players don't lack for storylines. Take Lee Riley, for example. He had one son, Lee Jr., who played in the NFL while another son, Pat, played in the NBA and has distinguished himself as one of the greatest basketball coaches of all-time.

Lee Riley's baseball career is interesting. He appeared in four games with the Phillies in 1944, and only made it to the majors because there was a player shortage during the war. He managed just one hit in 12 major league at-bats. However, he played for 22 different teams in 22 minor league seasons, appearing in 2,267 games and collecting 2,418 hits with 248 homers and a .314 average. Riley also managed 12 seasons for eight minor league teams, many of them as player-manager. He led the Nebraska State League in batting while serving as player-manager of the Beatrice Blues in 1937 and 1938. He would certainly make the All-Travelers team.

Then we have the curious case of Frederick "Mysterious" Walker, who has one of the more unusual nicknames. He reportedly got the moniker because he had unexpected success arriving in professional baseball at age 26 in 1910, but frankly much of his background seems shrouded in, you guessed it — mystery! What we do know is that he went from the National League to the American League, back to the National League and then on to the Federal League, all in the span of five years. The result of all this moving around was a career record of 7–23, as evidently batters did not find anything mysterious about his pitches.

Winfield "Win" Noyes was not aptly named, as he collected just 11 wins in his three-season career. Perhaps he should have been called "Few Wins" Noyes. Sheldon Jones picked up the nickname "Available Jones" from a character in the Lil Abner comic strip, but it related to the fact that he was available to start or relieve as necessary. He won 44 games for the Giants between 1948 and 1950 while starting 76 games and coming out of the bullpen 61 times.

Hollis "Sloppy" Thurston from Fremont was not sloppy at all but rather a meticulously groomed man. However, sloppy was a good description of his pitching effort on August 13, 1932, when he tied a modern-era record by allowing six home runs to the Giants — all to future Hall of Famers. He surrendered three to Bill Terry, two to Mel Ott and one to Fred Lindstrom. Believe it or not, he ended up winning the game by nine runs as the Dodgers scored 18 runs.

Other Nebraska players had memorable nicknames bestowed on them such as Wade Boggs, who was called "Chickenman" because he insisted on eating chicken before every game. Sam Crawford was born in Wahoo, so the Hall of Famer became known as "Wahoo Sam" Crawford. "Glass Arm Eddie" Brown refers to the fact that Brown had a weak throwing arm, a major reason he languished in the minors until he was 32. Brown collected 2,171 hits with a .322 average across 15 minor league seasons and hit .303 when given a chance in the majors.

Ad Liska, a righty hurler from Dwight, won 248 games over 21 minor league seasons but won only 17 games in the majors.

Outfielder Cliff Mapes, a native of Sutherland, wore number 3 for the Yankees after Babe Ruth and number 7 for the Yankees before Mickey Mantle. Both numbers were later retired by the club. He also wore number 13 for the team, which will probably be retired after Alex Rodriquez retires. Mapes batted .245 in four seasons for the Yankees.

All-Time Nebraska Selections

Let's get to the All-Time Nebraska team selections. At catcher we have Ted Easterly, who posted a .300 average over seven years. His best year was 1914 when he batted .335 with 146 hits. Todd Pratt managed to carve out a nice 14-year career as a journeyman catcher.

Les Nunamaker also deserves mention for his skill at throwing out base runners. Nunamaker batted .268 over 12 seasons but threw out 44 percent of the base runners who attempted to steal on him. On August 3, 1914, while catching for the Yankees, Nunamaker threw out three Tigers trying to steal second to account for all three outs in one inning, marking the only time a catcher achieved the feat in the twentieth century.

Johnny Hopp gets the selection as Nebraska's first baseman even though he played more career games in the outfield. He did play more games at first base in 1946, the one year he was named to the All-Star team. Hopp appeared in five World Series, winning twice with the Yankees and twice with the Cardinals. He didn't flash much power — just 46 home runs — but finished in the top 10 in stolen bases eight times in the 1940s. A lifetime .296 batter, his best year was 1944, when he batted .336 with 11 homers and 72 RBI.

Another position shift was necessary to fill the second base position. Bob Johnson played all the infield spots during his 11 years but played the most (201 games) at short. His 167 games at second are still better than other candidates such as Pug Bennett and Chad Meyers. Johnson ended up with 628 hits and a .272 average but was really only a starter in 1962.

Some players are quick to credit their success to hard work and discipline, or the helpful tutelage of a talented coach. Then there's Nebraska's third baseman, Wade Boggs, who largely credits his success to the fact he ate chicken every day. If only it were that simple, then Colonel Sanders would be in the Hall of Fame.

Boggs knew early on that he was going to be a professional baseball player, reportedly telling one interviewer he was six years old when he knew he would play in the major leagues. He didn't just make it to the majors, he became one of the greatest hitters of all-time as well as one of the most superstitious. Boggs had to take the same number of grounders each day, exactly 150, and take batting practice at the same time, just two of his many OCD traits.

Boggs hit .349 as a rookie and then proceeded to compile over 200 hits the next seven seasons, making him the only player to accomplish that feat in the twentieth century. He won five batting titles and batted over

.300 in 15 of his 18 seasons, hanging around long enough to collect 3,000 hits (3,010 to be exact).

A 12-time All-Star and eight-time Silver Slugger, Boggs also turned himself into a fine defensive third baseman, earning two Gold Gloves. He led the AL in on-base percentage six times, finishing his career at .415. He was such an accomplished hitter that he also led the league in intentional walks six straight seasons despite not being a home run threat.

Although he played most of his career with the Red Sox, Boggs won a World Series with the Yankees in 1996, leading to the memorable picture of him taking a celebratory ride around Yankee Stadium on a horse. He played a pivotal role in leading the Yanks to the championship, drawing a bases loaded walk in the 10th inning of Game 4 to force in the winning run.

Boggs also made history by playing in the longest professional baseball game in history — a 33-inning grinder in 1981 between the Pawtucket Red Sox and the Rochester Red Wings at McCoy Stadium in Pawtucket. Boggs went 4-for-12 for the victorious Sox.

At shortstop for Team Nebraska we have Ron Hansen, who played for five American League teams between 1958 and 1972. He had some pop in his bat, with 106 homers, but ended his career with a .234 average to go with 1,007 hits. Hansen was named Rookie of the Year and an All-Star for the Orioles in 1960 after hitting 22 homers with 86 RBI. His most noteworthy feat was turning an unassisted triple play for the Senators on July 30, 1968, the first one in 41 years.

The Nebraska outfield is filled by Hall of Famers, although one was elected for his managerial feats. Sam Crawford is the all-time leader in triples with 309. That is roughly three times the number of triples compiled by the active leader, another Crawford (Carl). His 26 triples in 1914 tied the American League record Joe Jackson had just set two years earlier. Teaming up with Ty Cobb, Crawford led the Tigers to the American League pennant three straight years, 1907–1909, although they lost each time in the World Series.

Nicknamed "Wahoo Sam" in honor of his birthplace, Crawford led the league in triples six times, homers twice, RBI three times, and runs and doubles once. He fell just short of 3,000 hits — with 2,961— and finished with a .309 average, with 11 seasons over .300. Like many players from that era, Crawford extended his baseball career by playing four more seasons in the minors. He compiled 781 hits for the Los Angeles Angels in the Pacific Coast League.

Playing in the Deadball Era, Crawford's numbers don't reflect the fact that he possessed above-average power. In 1901 he led the NL with 16 homers but that far surpassed the 11 hit by runner-up Jimmy Sheckard. He would lead the AL in 1908 with just seven dingers. It is believed that he holds the record for inside-the-park home runs with 51. Crawford was elected to the Hall of Fame in 1957.

Despite the fame and glory he achieved, Richie Ashburn always remained a Nebraska boy at heart, which was part of his appeal. He quickly became a fan favorite in Philadelphia as a rookie in 1948, a love affair that extended into his 34-year broadcast career with the Phillies. Ashburn teamed up with the legendary Harry Kalas on Phillies broadcasts for 27 years until his death in 1997.

"Wahoo Sam" Crawford teamed up with Ty Cobb in the outfield, helping the Detroit Tigers capture three straight pennants from 1907 to 1909. Crawford used his speed to steal 367 bases and leg out a record 309 triples. He was elected to the Hall of Fame in 1957 (Library of Congress, Prints & Photographs Division, LC-DIG-hec-02748).

Ashburn played 12 of his 15 seasons with Philadelphia (A's and Phillies), serving as a sparkplug while batting .303 for the 1950 Whiz Kids squad that surprisingly made it all the way to the World Series. He led the league in OBP four times, hits three times, triples and batting average twice. Ashburn is also one of only six players to lead the league in hits and walks in the same season, a feat he accomplished in 1958.

As a rookie he led the NL with 32 steals and finished second to Stan Musial in batting with a remarkable .333 average. He ended up with a .308 career average and 2,574 hits, although his slugging numbers were weak for a Hall of Famer — just 29 home runs and 586 RBI.

Ashburn was an accomplished batter but he really excelled as a center fielder. He ranged all over Shibe Park, where it was 457 feet to center, chasing down line drives and using his cannon arm to cut down runners. He didn't make as many spectacular plays as Willie Mays and wasn't as effortlessly graceful as the "Say Hey Kid," but he was as good as or better than Mays in the field. Ashburn recorded 2.89 putouts per game he played in the outfield (6,089 PO in 2104G) compared to 2.49 for Mays (7095 PO in 2842G). A five-time All-Star, Ashburn spent his last season (1962) as one of the original Mets, batting .306 that year as one of the lone bright spots. He was elected to the Hall of Fame in 1995.

The third outfield spot came down to Les Mann and Billy Southworth. Mann averaged .282 over 16 seasons, batting over .300 six times (but just once as a regular player). Mann has the edge in Career Win Shares — 156.7 to 140.6 — but Southworth has the advantage in average, OBP, slugging, OPS and OPS+ so he gets selected. Southworth was an underrated player whose career OPS+ matches that of Ashburn —111.

A lifetime .297 hitter for 12 seasons, Southworth batted over .300 six times and led the league in triples with 14 in 1919. He batted .345 with 10 hits to help lead the Cardinals over the Yankees for the 1926 World Series title. It was his three-run homer in Game 2 that proved the difference and made a winner out of fellow Nebraska native Grover Pete Alexander. Southworth batted .320 and set career highs with 16 homers, 99 RBI and 99 runs scored that season.

Turning to the rotation, the All-Time Nebraska Team is blessed with two of the greatest pitchers in history: Pete Alexander and Bob Gibson. Unfortunately they are both right handers, which creates a major dilemma. Someone has to take a seat on the bench. It's tempting to select Alexander as the best reliever, since he did make 96 relief appearances. However, that would not be giving him his due as a starter or be fair to Gregg Olson, who deserves the role as closer.

Comparing dominant pitchers from different eras is not easy, but Alexander is always in the conversation when deciding on the greatest pitcher ever while Gibson resides in the hallowed ground one level below. Bill James ranks Alexander number three and Gibson number eight in his all-time pitcher rankings. Looking at Career Win Shares, Alexander ranks second with 476 while Gibson's 317 Win Shares places him in the vicinity of mere mortals like Ferguson Jenkins, Jim Palmer and Eppa Rixey.

Alexander ranks third in wins with 373 (tied with Christy Mathewson) and second in shutouts with 90. A 20-game winner nine times, he finished with 437 complete games, a 2.56 ERA and a .642 winning percentage. Ol' Pete led the league in shutouts and innings pitched seven times, wins, strikeouts and complete games six times and ERA four times. He led the NL with 28 wins in his rookie season, 1911, and won 30 games three straight seasons, 1915–1917. His 16 shutouts in 1916 are a record that may never be broken. Alexander believed in working fast so the batter, in his words, "didn't stand up there and think on my time."

After a career filled with personal accomplishment but little team success, Alexander got some redemption during the 1926 World Series. Pitching against the Yankees, he came on in relief in Game 7 with the bases loaded and two outs and the Cardinals clinging to a one-run lead in the seventh inning. Facing off against Tony Lazzeri, Alexander almost served up a disastrous home run, but the ball landed foul. He struck out Lazzeri on the next pitch and went on to shut out the Yankees the rest of the way, preserving the victory. As he pointed out, "Less than a foot made the difference between a hero and a bum."

It is difficult to determine how much his well-documented alcoholism detracted from his ability to perform on the diamond, and Alexander also suffered from epilepsy. He was elected to the Hall of Fame in 1938, the year he finally stopped pitching professionally (he prolonged his career pitching for the House of David). Grover Cleveland Alexander was not only named after a president, he was portrayed by a future president, Ronald Reagan, in the 1952 movie *The Winning Team*.

A native of Omaha, Gibson was one of the most intimidating pitchers in baseball history. He sneered at batters as though they had no right to come up to bat against him, then knocked them on their butt with a high and tight fastball. Once he had established that he was the boss, it was time to get to work. As he described it, "My pitching philosophy is simple. I believe in getting the ball over the plate and not walking a lot of men."

Gibson was so dominant in 1968 — 22–9 with 13 shutouts and a microscopic 1.12 ERA — that the pitching mound was lowered for the next season. That 1.12 ERA is the fourth-lowest in history and by far the lowest in the Lively Ball Era. Gibson won the Cy Young Award and MVP Award that season and added another Cy Young Award in 1970. A five-time 20-game winner, he led the league in wins, ERA, complete games and strikeouts once and shutouts four times. Before starting his baseball career, Gibson played with the Harlem Globetrotters for a year under the nickname "Bullet."

His 56 shutouts rank thirteenth all-time and his 3,117 strikeouts are fourteenth-best. Gibson was named to eight All-Star teams and won nine consecutive Gold

Gloves, ending his career with 251 victories. An outstanding athlete who played basketball at Creighton University, Gibson hit 24 homers during his 17 seasons. He really shined in the postseason, collecting seven consecutive World Series wins and being named World Series MVP in 1964 and 1967. He set a record by striking out 17 batters while hurling a five-hit shutout in Game 1 of the 1968 World Series. Eight of his nine World Series starts resulted in complete games.

Another notable right-handed starter is Mel "Chief" Harder, who won 223 games and made four All-Star teams playing his entire 20-year career with the Indians. Harder won 20 games twice and led the AL in ERA and shutouts once.

Nebraska's lefty starter is Clarence Mitchell, who won 125 games between 1911 and 1932, although he posted a losing record overall. He won a career high 13 games in 1931 at the age of 40, operating as one of the last legal spitball pitchers in the league. A decent batter with a career average of .252, Mitchell played 98 games in the field, mainly at first base. Perhaps his most noteworthy accomplishment was hitting into the only triple play in World Series history in 1920, which was turned unassisted by Bill Wambsganss.

The ninth inning is in good hands with Gregg Olson, who was named Rookie of the Year in 1989 after saving 27 games for the Orioles. He made the All-Star team the next year on the way to posting a career-high 37 games. He had four 30-save seasons, the last for Arizona in 1998. Olson, who bounced around to nine teams over 14 seasons, finished with 217 career saves.

Joba Chamberlain was a revelation when he was called up by the Yankees for the 2007 stretch drive. It looked like he might rewrite the definition of dominance out of the bullpen after allowing only one earned run in 19 appearances. He used a blazing fastball to strike out 34 batters in 24 innings, posting a 0.38 ERA and an eye-popping ERA+ of 1221. His fairy tale season came to a strange ending during the postseason when he was overcome by a swarm of midges on the mound in Cleveland. Since then, Chamberlain has bounced between starting and relieving and has not been able to recapture the magic he had in 2007.

Southworth was a pretty good player, but he made the Hall of Fame as a manager. His teams never finished lower than fourth in 13 seasons, with four first-place finishes. He won three pennants and two World Series with the Cardinals and one pennant with the Boston Braves. He ranks fifth all-time with a career winning percentage of .597.

"He was one of the first managers who changed pitchers in the middle of the inning in the eighth or ninth innings," recalls fellow Hall of Famer Red Schoendienst, whose rookie season coincided with Southworth's last year of skippering the Cardinals.

Southworth is the only manager in history to guide his team to at least 105 wins in three straight seasons, which he did with the Stan Musial and the Cardinals from 1942–1944. The '42 team would go on to defeat the Yankees in the World Series, while the '44 team knocked off the cross-town rival Browns in the "Streetcar Series."

Here is what Southworth said to his players to loosen them up before Game 3 of the 1944 Series: "Gentlemen, swinging the bat is a great exercise. It strengthens the diaphragm and loosens pent-up emotions in the chest. Besides, you may hit the ball."

NEVADA

*Names in **bold** represent Major League selections by position, followed by honorable mentions. City of birth is in parentheses.*

Catcher — Tyler Houston (Las Vegas)
First Base — Efren Navarro (Las Vegas)
Second Base — Brian Dallimore (Las Vegas)
Third Base — Justin Leone (Las Vegas)
Shortstop — Steve Rodriquez (Las Vegas)
Outfield — Marty Cordova (Las Vegas)
Outfield — Nate Schierholtz (Reno)
Outfield — Rob Richie (Reno). Also: Greg Martinez (Las Vegas)
Right Handed Starter — Jim Nash (Hawthorne). Also: Shawn Boskie (Hawthorne); Wheezer Dell (Tuscarora); Gordon Rhodes (Winnemucca)
Left Handed Starter — Barry Zito (Las Vegas)
Relief Pitcher — Mike MacDougal (Las Vegas). Also: Rocky Biddle (Las Vegas); Brad Thompson (Las Vegas); Ted Davidson (Las Vegas); Randy Messenger (Reno)
Manager — None

The Names

Best Nickname: Barry "Planet" Zito
Other Nicknames: Lee "Rocky" Biddle; William "Wheezer" Dell; Jim "Cotton" Nash; Gordon "Dusty" Rhodes
Most Unusual Name: Nathan Schierholtz

All-Time Leaders

Games: Marty Cordova, 952
Hits: Marty Cordova, 938
Batting Average: Marty Cordova, .274
Home Runs: Marty Cordova, 122
RBI: Marty Cordova, 540
Stolen Bases: Marty Cordova, 57
Wins: Barry Zito, 145 (still active)

Strikeouts: Barry Zito, 1683 (still active)
Saves: Mike MacDougal, 71 (still active)
Future Star: Bryce Harper (Las Vegas)
Best Player: Barry Zito

Historic Baseball Places

Aces Ballpark in Reno — New home of the Reno Aces opened in 2009. Make sure you try the Triple Play BBQ Sandwich, which is a triple stack of thick bread filled with everything from BBQ meatball, pulled pork and smoked brisket to pickles, cherry peppers and coleslaw.

Big League Dreams Sports Park in Las Vegas — Features replica fields of Yankee Stadium, Fenway Park, Wrigley Field, Crosley Field, Dodger Stadium and Angels Stadium for youth baseball.

Notable Achievements

Tyler Houston hit three home runs on July 9, 2000.
Marty Cordova won the AL Rookie of the Year Award while playing for the Twins in 1995.
Barry Zito and **Mike MacDougal** are the only Nevada-born players to be an All-Star.

Baseball's Future King Hails from Nevada

We have seen the future of baseball and he comes from Nevada. Bryce Harper made the cover of *Sports Illustrated* and was called "Baseball's Chosen One," all at the age of 16. Harper, who was born in Las Vegas, left high school two years early because he was not challenged enough by high school pitchers. He got his GED diploma and enrolled in junior college, which put him on track to be the number one draft pick of the Washington Nationals in the 2010 MLB amateur draft.

Harper, who says he models his game after Mickey Mantle and Pete Rose, is the best hitting prospect to come into the game since Ken Griffey, Jr. The left-handed slugger blends incomparable bat speed and prodigious power with the ability to hit for average. Harper also possesses above-average speed and a cannon for an arm. He was moved to the outfield to speed up his path to the majors, and he was called up for good early on the 2012 season.

The Nationals' minor league coordinator, Tony Tarasco, made an ill-fated comparison to Jackie Robinson when describing the scrutiny Harper faces, but it is safe to say the "can't miss hitting sensation" is under the microscope more than any other player his age.

It's a little unsettling to see so much hype about someone so young, but by all accounts Harper has the work ethic to keep getting better. He balances Ty Cobb's will to win with Derek Jeter's team-first professionalism. By now, everyone has heard about the 502-foot home run he hit as a high school sophomore during the International Power Showcase — the longest ball ever hit at Tropicana Field — and the 570-foot bomb he hit during a high school game in Las Vegas while just 15. All the publicity he has received, coupled with Harper's cocky attitude, has placed a big target on his back and turned him into a lightning rod for criticism.

Splitting his first season between Single-A and Double-A, Harper batted .297 with 17 home runs and 26 stolen bases in 2011. However, he was ejected for throwing a tantrum when called out in strikes in one game, and created a stink when he blew a kiss at the pitcher after hitting a home run in another game. Sounds like a typical 18-year-old who will hopefully mature into a real professional.

If we wanted to further the hype, we could anoint Harper as Nevada's all-time best player, even though he has just started his major league career. For now, let's just call him one of Nevada's future stars.

All-Time Nevada Selections

Nevada is starting to become more of a baseball state. A total of 28 players from Nevada have played in the major leagues, with 22 of them appearing in the last two decades. Seven were active during the 2011 season.

Tyler Houston played every position except pitcher during his stint in the big leagues from 1996 to 2003. He played the most at third base, with 291 games at the hot corner, but serves as the catcher for the All-Time Nevada team. Houston was primarily a catcher in the minors and he caught 173 games in the majors. The Atlanta Braves made him the second overall pick in the 1989 amateur draft behind Ben McDonald. Houston belted a career-high 18 homers in 2000 and finished with 63 in his career.

The infielders for Team Nevada are lacking in achievement. First baseman Efren Navarro was a late-season call-up for the Angels in 2011, appearing in eight games. Second baseman Brian Dallimore played 11 of his 18 games in the majors at that position, posting a .260 average with 13 career hits for the Giants. At third base is Justin Leone, who got in 28 games for the Mariners in 2004 and hit .216 with six homers. Steve Rodriquez gets the nod at shortstop after playing five games there in 1995 along with 13 games at second base. He finished with a .179 career average.

Slugging third baseman Matt Williams was known as the "Carson Crusher," since he played his high school ball in Carson, Nev., and later at the University of Nevada, Las Vegas. However, Williams was born in California.

Marty Cordova is about the only position player from Nevada to see extensive playing action in the big leagues. Cordova was an outfielder who also appeared in 177 games as a designated hitter. He was named American League Rookie of the Year in 1995 after hitting .277 with 24 home runs and 84 RBI for the Twins. Cordova followed that up by batting .309 with 111 RBI and 46 doubles the next season, but saw his performance tail off the next three years as he was bothered by back problems. His last good season was 2001, when he hit .301 with 20 homers for the Indians.

Cordova is a contender for the most bizarre injury. He once fell asleep in a tanning bed and burned his face to such an extent that he had to miss several games. Not a good way to endear yourself to your manager.

Nate Schierholtz has been a valuable outfield reserve for the Giants, appearing in 426 games since debuting in 2007. He batted over .300 his first two years in limited action and then set career highs in most batting stats in 2011.

Our third outfielder is Rob Richie, who batted .265 with 13 hits for the Tigers in 1989. Earning honorable mention status as an outfielder is Greg Martinez, who was mainly a pinch runner during his brief stint with the Brewers in 1998, batting 0-for-3 in 13 games.

Our left-handed starter is Barry Zito, who has taken a lot of heat for signing a seven-year, $126 million contract for the San Francisco Giants before the 2007 season and then going 43–61 with a 4.55 ERA over the next five years. Although he was left off the Giants' 2010 postseason roster, Zito joined Schierholtz in winning a World Series ring with the team. He missed much of the 2011 season with a mysterious lingering foot injury.

Zito beat out Pedro Martinez to win the 2002 AL Cy Young Award after going 23–5 with a 2.75 ERA, and was named an All-Star in 2002, 2003 and 2006 for the A's. Although never blessed with much of a fastball, Zito keeps hitters off-balance with a big, sweeping curveball that was once viewed as the best in baseball.

Zito is known as one of the quirkiest players in the game, who is more apt to rely on mystical principles than advance scouting reports. Although he no longer dyes his hair blue, he meditates and does yoga on the field, strums a guitar in the clubhouse and definitely marches to his own drummer.

The Las Vegas native once claimed he spent four days during the 2001 season with his father intensely studying the message behind Ernest Holmes' 1919 book *Creative Mind*, and the power of positive thinking he picked up from the book led him to win 11 of his next 12 games. Perhaps he should have dusted off the book while leading the National League in losses in 2008.

Ted Davidson, who started one game for the Reds in 1965, is the only Nevada-born southpaw other than Zito to start a game. He holds down a spot in the bullpen.

Jim Nash is the right-handed starter on the All-Time Nevada team. Nash finished second to Tommie Agee in the AL Rookie of the Year voting for 1966 after going 12–1 with a 2.06 ERA. His 2.28 ERA in 1968 was seventh-best in the league, while his six shutouts that year was tied for second place. Nash ended his seven-season career with a 68–64 won-loss record.

When Wheezer Dell was called up by the St. Louis Cardinals in 1912, he became the first Nevada-born player to make it to the major leagues. The tall righty was born in Tuscarora in 1876, when the silver mines were still booming. He appeared in three games for the Cards and was picked up by the Brooklyn Robins in the Rule 5 Draft. His manager on the Robins, Wilbert Robinson, declared that Dell was destined to be one of the best pitchers in the National League.

Dell pitched well during his short stint in the majors, pitching four shutouts in 1915 and recording an ERA of 2.26 in 1916. However, he ended up languishing in the minors. He won 20 games seven times in 14 minor league seasons, finishing with a career minor league mark of 231–164. Many of those years were spent pitching for the Vernon Tigers in the Pacific Coast League. Dell was elected to the Pacific Coast League Hall of Fame, where he joins the ranks of Joe DiMaggio and Paul Waner. Another claim to fame is that Dell appeared in the Buster Keaton film "My Wife's Relations" in 1922. He earns honorable mention status as a right-handed starter for Team Nevada.

Team Nevada's closer is Mike MacDougal, who has saved 71 games over 11 seasons and is still active. He made the All-Star team 2003 on the way to saving 27 games for the Royals and saved 20 games for the last-place Nationals in 2009. A first-round draft pick of the White Sox in 1997, Rocky Biddle saved 34 games for the Expos in 2003 despite walking 40 batters in 71 innings. Fans started calling him "The Rocky Horror Show" the next season as his ERA ballooned to 6.92, and Biddle was released at the end of the season.

NEW HAMPSHIRE

*Names in **bold** represent Major League selections by position, followed by honorable mentions. City of birth is in parentheses.*

Catcher — Harry Bemis (Farmington). Also: Tom Padden (Manchester)
First Base — Art Nichols (Manchester)
Second Base — Tim Shinnick (Exeter)
Third Base — Red Rolfe (Penacook). Also: Arlie Latham (West Lebanon)
Shortstop — Bernie Friberg (Manchester)
Outfield — Phil Plantier (Manchester)
Outfield — Joe Lefebvre (Concord)
Outfield — Kevin Romine (Exeter). Also: Bill Hawes (Nashua); Sam Fuld (Durham)
Right Handed Starter — Chris Carpenter (Exeter). Also: Bob Tewksbury (Concord); George Haddock (Portsmouth); Rich Gale (Littleton)

New Hampshire

Left Handed Starter — Mike Flanagan (Manchester). Also: Lefty Tyler (Derry)
Relief Pitcher — Brian Wilson (Londonderry). Also: Stan Williams (Enfield)
Manager — Frank Selee (Amherst). Also: Red Rolfe (Penacook)

The Names

Best Nickname: Arlie "The Freshest Man on Earth" Latham
Other Nicknames: "Gentleman George" Haddock; Tim "Good Eye" and "Dandy" Shinnick; Harry "Doc" Tonkin; Fred "Clancy" Tyler; George "Lefty" Tyler; Lawrence "Dike" Varney; Stan "Big Daddy" Williams; Brian "B-Weez" Wilson
Most Unusual Name: Libeus Washburn

All-Time Leaders

Games: Arlie Latham, 1627
Hits: Arlie Latham, 1833
Batting Average: Red Rolfe, .289
Home Runs: Phil Plantier, 91
RBI: Arlie Latham, 563
Stolen Bases: Arlie Latham, 739
Wins: Mike Flanagan, 167
Strikeouts: Mike Flanagan, 1491
Saves: Brian Wilson, 170 (still active)
Future Star: Michael Bisceglia (Goffstown); Jordan Cote (Sanbornton)
Best Player: Chris Carpenter

Historic Baseball Places

Don Zimmer Field in Windham — Youth baseball/softball field was dedicated in honor of Don Zimmer at Griffin Park. It includes a monument plaque of Zimmer shown wearing a Yankees cap.
Northeast Delta Dental Stadium in Manchester — This ballpark is a lot more inspiring than its name, especially since it was built to replace venerable Gill Stadium. It opened in 2005 as the home of the New Hampshire Fisher Cats. The satellite Ted Williams Hitters Hall of Fame showcases some of baseball's best hitters while also featuring memorabilia from New Hampshire's major league players.
Gill Stadium in Manchester — Only a couple of existing concrete-and-steel stadiums are older than Gill Stadium, which was named Textile Field when opened in 1913.

Only a couple of existing concrete-and-steel stadiums are older than Gill Stadium in Manchester, which was named Textile Field when built in 1913. Gill Stadium features some of the widest foul territories of any ballpark, which enables it to host football games in addition to amateur baseball (courtesy DigitalBallparks.com).

Notable Achievements

Doc Tonkin (Concord) got hits in his only two career at-bats in 1907. More than a century later another Concord native, **Matt Tupman**, got a hit in his only major league at-bat in 2008.

Fred Brown (Ossipee), who went to Dartmouth College, served as governor from 1923–1925 and later served one term in the United States Senate. His big league career consisted of nine games with the Boston Beaneaters in 1901–02.

Arlie Latham was the oldest player to steal a base at the age of 49 in 1909.

Does the Real "Father of Baseball" Hail from New Hampshire?

Everyone has heard about Abner Doubleday and Alexander Cartwright, but is it possible the real "Father of Baseball" hails from New Hampshire? Esteemed baseball historian John Thorn made the case for Daniel "Doc" Adams first in *Total Baseball* and then later in his book, *Baseball in the Garden of Eden*.

Adams, who was born in the New Hampshire town of Mt. Vernon, began playing baseball in New York City around 1839, organizing a New York Base Ball Club before Cartwright. He joined the Knickerbocker Baseball Club shortly after it was formed in 1845 and played in the famous first game at Elysian Fields in Hoboken, N.J., the next year. Adams also chaired a committee to revise and formalize the rules in 1848 (with Cartwright serving under him) and personally developed the position of short-fielder or shortstop somewhere around 1849 or 1850. Thorn concludes, "For his role in making baseball the success it is, Doc Adams may be counted as first among the Fathers of Baseball."

It was Adams, not Cartwright, who decided there should be nine players on a team, nine innings in a game and 90 feet between the bases, although Cartwright is credited with those innovations on his plaque in Cooperstown.

New Hampshire has another tie to baseball history. Roy Campanella and Don Newcombe played for the Nashua Pride in 1946, joining fellow Dodgers farmhands Jackie Robinson, Roy Partlow and John Wright as the first African American players to appear in organized baseball in the twentieth century.

In 1879 Bill Hawes of Nashua became the first New Hampshire native to make it to the majors. Fred Tyler, a native of Derry, caught the last six games of the 1914 regular season for the Boston Braves, which came in three successive doubleheaders. It must have worn him out, because that would be the extent of his major league career.

All-Time New Hampshire Selections

Leading off the All-Time-New Hampshire team at catcher is Harry Bemis, who is number four in hits among New Hampshire natives with 569. Always a key player but never a full-time starter, Bemis batted .312 with 99 hits his rookie year in 1902 but wound up with a .255 average over nine seasons.

Another catcher of note is Tom Padden, who played seven seasons mainly for the Pirates in the 1930s. He batted .321 with a .399 OBP in 1934 but was never a regular starter.

At first base is Art Nichols of Manchester, who collected just 194 hits in a brief career around the turn of the twentieth century. Second base goes to Tim "Dandy" Shinnick, who played two seasons for the Louisville Colonels in the American Association and finished his career with 224 hits. He was fifth in stolen bases and RBI during his rookie season in 1890, helping the Louisville team win its only pennant. The team fell apart the next year and finished eighth and Shinnick was done in the majors after batting .221 that season.

Long before Ozzie Smith was performing back flips on the field there was New Hampshire's own Arlie Latham, who once did a somersault over Cap Anson to elude a tag. Latham was nicknamed "The Freshest Man on Earth" because of his boisterous personality, but that doesn't do justice to his antics. Latham, who was hired by John McGraw as the first full-time coach in baseball history, was a first-class irritant on the diamond. He used to run up and down the third base line yelling and taunting the pitcher. That is why we now have coaching boxes. Sometimes he even did cartwheels as he waved the runner home. Then there's the time he set off a firecracker at third base to get back at Manager Charles Comiskey, who had scolded him for falling asleep during games.

Arlie Latham was nicknamed "The Freshest Man on Earth" because of his boisterous personality. He was the first clown prince of baseball, literally, as evidenced by his habit of putting on a clown nose to mock St. Louis Browns owner Chris von der Ahe. Latham helped the Browns win four consecutive pennants in the American Association from 1885 to 1888 (Library of Congress, Prints & Photographs Division, LC-DIG-ggbain-03271).

As a player, Latham was a speedy leadoff hitter. He stole 307 bases from 1887 to 1889, with a high of 129 the first year. Keep in mind that 1887 was the first year stolen bases were counted and that advancing an extra base on a hit was considered a stolen base. Modern rules for stolen bases came about in 1898. Latham held the career record for steals from 1887 to 1896 and today ranks eighth-best with 739 stolen bases. The third baseman led the league with 152 runs scored in 1886 and followed it up by scoring 163 runs the next season.

The fun-loving lad from West Lebanon always gave fans their money's worth. Later, he ingratiated himself with the Royal Family, spending 16 years in England teaching the game of baseball to King George V and the Prince of Wales.

Latham was an indifferent fielder at third, to put it mildly. In fact, third basemen who made little or no effort to field hot grounders were said "to do a Latham." He holds the record for most errors by a third baseman with 822, including a high of 88 in 1886.

Despite all those accomplishments, we have a better choice at third for the All-Time New Hampshire team — Red Rolfe. Rolfe was an Ivy League graduate from Dartmouth who was overshadowed on the Yankees by more famous teammates such as Gehrig, Dickey, DiMaggio and Lazzeri. Still, he was a key contributor as the Bronx Bombers won five out of six World Series between 1936 and 1941. A four-time All-Star, he led the American League in runs, hits and doubles in 1939 while batting .329, yet finished a distant 27th in voting for the MVP Award, trailing five teammates as DiMaggio finished first.

The lefty-swinging Rolfe didn't hit a lot of home runs, with a high of 14 and a career total of 69, but he was a dependable contact hitter with speed who was sure-handed in the field. Bill James ranks him as the 44th-best third baseman of all-time (Latham is ranked 54th), noting that Rolfe was Yankees manager Joe McCarthy's favorite player in the late 1930s.

Rolfe had some success as a manager for the Tigers, leading them to 95 wins and a second-place finish behind the Yankees in his second season, 1950. Things went downhill after that and he was let go halfway through the 1952 season.

Shortstop is manned by Bernie Friberg, a versatile infielder who played 14 seasons primarily for the Cubs and Phillies. Friberg finished eighteenth in the voting for the NL MVP Award in 1929 after batting .301 with 137 hits in a utility role. Blocked at his primary positions of second and third that year by Fresco Thompson (.324 with 202 hits) and Pinky Whitney (.327 with 200 hits), Friberg wound up playing 73 games at short and 40 games in the outfield.

Friberg finished ahead of Thompson and Whitney in the 1929 MVP voting, although he trailed teammates Lefty O'Doul (second) and Chuck Klein (11th). The Phillies finished fifth that year despite having four starters with 200 or more hits and eight players over .300 in batting average. Although he only played 123 games at short during his career, Friberg was a shortstop during his best season (1929) and is the most logical choice among New Hampshire natives.

The outfield is filled with players accustomed to coming off the bench: Phil Plantier, Joe Lefebvre and Kevin Romine. Plantier burst onto the scene in 1991 by slugging 11 home runs in just 148 at-bats for the Red Sox with a .331 average, coming in eighth in Rookie of the Year balloting. He struggled the next season and then was traded to the Padres, where he hit 34 homers and drove in 100 runs in 1993. He bounced around for four more seasons but had limited success in part-time roles. Lefebvre played six seasons for the Yankees, Padres and Phillies in the 1980s but was never a regular. Romine collected 158 hits in parts of seven seasons for the Red Sox.

Our right-handed starter is Chris Carpenter, who came close to winning a second Cy Young Award in 2009 after leading the NL with a 2.24 ERA. He previously won the Cy Young Award in 2005 after going 21–5 with a 2.83 ERA, four shutouts, a league-high seven complete games and 213 strikeouts (second-best in the NL). His masterful three-hit shutout on the road against Roy Halladay and the Phillies in Game 5 of the 2011 NLDS has to be considered one of the greatest pitching performances in postseason history.

Carpenter has been brilliant when healthy but has had trouble staying off the disabled list in his career as evidenced by the fact that he's been named the Comeback Player of the Year twice. He has great command of five pitches, including a plus curveball and a mid–90s fastball, which allows him to keep batters off-balance.

The Exeter native, who still maintains a home in New Hampshire, has a career record of 144–92 through 2011, with three All-Star appearances. Finishing in the top three in the Cy Young Award voting three times earns Carpenter the nod as the state's All-Time Best Player.

Carpenter won 75 of his first 100 decisions with the Cardinals, matching the record of Cy Young in his first 100 decisions with Boston and trailing only Pedro Martinez (78–22 with the Red Sox) as the best 100-game mark in the modern era. Such success was in stark contrast to Carpenter's performance in his first six seasons with the Blue Jays, where his record was 49–50 with a 4.83 ERA.

Another notable right-handed starter is Bob Tewksbury, who won 110 games over 13 seasons. He gave up a lot of hits (10.2/9IP) and didn't strike out many batters (4.0/9IP), but he didn't walk many batters either. He led the league in SO/BB and BB/9IP twice each, in addition to finishing first in winning percentage in 1992. That year Tewksbury went 16–5 with a 2.16 ERA (2nd-best), made his only All-Star team and finished third in the Cy Young balloting.

Also worth mentioning is "Gentleman George" Haddock, whose performance fluctuated greatly as he bounced from league to league. In 1890 he stumbled to a 9–26 record with 5.76 ERA while pitching for Buffalo in the Players League. The next year he turned things around, going 34–11 with a 2.49 ERA for the Boston Reds in the American Association. Then in 1892 he jumped to the Brooklyn Grooms in the National

League, where he produced a 29–13 mark with a 3.14 ERA. His career record was 95–87.

Our lefty starter is another former Cy Young Award winner, Mike Flanagan, who won the honor after going 23–9 with a 3.08 ERA in 1979. His only All-Star selection came in 1978, a year he won 19 games. He shared a no-hitter while pitching in relief for the Orioles with three other pitchers in 1991.

Flanagan was a good all-around athlete who was a basketball teammate of Julius Erving at the University of Massachusetts. The Manchester native retired after the 1992 season with 167 wins against 143 losses. Flanagan went on to work as a pitching coach, broadcaster and front-office executive with the Orioles, before tragically committing suicide in 2011.

Earning honorable mention status as a southpaw is Lefty Tyler, who was one of the rotation stalwarts for the "Miracle Braves" of 1914. The team lost 18 of its first 22 games to fall into last place, but then got hot and shocked the baseball world by winning 94 games and the pennant. Tyler helped lead the charge with a string of 23 consecutive scoreless innings. Even more shocking was the fact the Braves swept the heavily favored Philadelphia Athletics in the World Series. Amazingly, Tyler's 127 career wins included 30 shutouts. Among the other pitchers with 30 shutouts are Amos Rusie (246 career wins), Dennis Martinez (245 wins), Charlie Buffinton (233 wins) and Rube Marquard (201 wins).

New Hampshire's closer is Brian Wilson, who became an All-Star in his first full year of being the closer for the Giants in 2008. He finished with 41 saves that year despite a high ERA and WHIP. Although he failed to make the All-Star team in 2009, Wilson had a better year overall, striking out 83 in 72 innings and posting 38 saves with a 2.74 ERA.

Nicknamed "The Beard" for his extremely thick and black beard, the eccentric reliever was again an All-Star in 2010 as he led the majors with 48 saves and averaged 11.2 SO/9IP, helping the Giants win the World Series. "Fear the Beard" became a popular slogan for Giants fans during the playoffs, as Wilson and his beard gained increased notoriety. A third All-Star selection followed in 2011 for the Londonderry native, who has 170 career saves through 2011.

Our manager is Frank Selee, who led the Boston Beaneaters to five pennants in the 1890s. He finished with a splendid .598 winning percentage (fourth best in history), with 1,284 wins over 16 seasons. Selee became the first manager to win 100 games in a season when he won 102 games in 1898, although he was aided by the season expanding from 132 to 152 games.

Although he never played the game professionally, Selee showed a knack for evaluating talent and figuring out how to get the most out of his players. It was his skillful maneuvering that created the famous Tinker to Evers to Chance infield combination, since he moved all three of the players from other positions. In addition to those three iconic infielders, nine of his other players would get inducted into the Hall of Fame including Mordecai Brown, Kid Nichols, Jimmy Collins, King Kelly and Billy Hamilton. Selee joined them in the Hall after being elected by the Veteran's Committee in 1999.

NEW JERSEY

*Names in **bold** represent Major League selections by position, followed by honorable mentions. Negro Leagues players are in italics. City of birth is in parentheses.*

Catcher — Frankie Hayes (Jamesburg). Also: Johnny Romano (Hoboken); Rick Cerone (Newark); Earl Williams (Newark); Ron Karkovice (Union)

First Base — Sean Casey (Willingboro). Also: Eric Karros (Hackensack); Joe Cunningham (Paterson); Dots Miller (Kearny); *Eggie Dallard* (Winslow)

Second Base — Hardy Richardson (Clarksboro). Also: Kid Gleason (Camden); Eric Young (New Brunswick); Danny O'Connell (Paterson); Jack Farrell (Newark); *Dick Seay* (West New York)

Third Base — Billy Shindle (Gloucester). Also: Joe Stripp (Harrison); Billy Johnson (Montclair); Mark DeRosa (Passaic)

Shortstop — Derek Jeter (Pequannock). Also: Eddie Kasko (Linden)

Outfield — Goose Goslin (Salem)

Outfield — Joe Medwick (Carteret)

Outfield — Billy Hamilton (Newark). Also: Mike Tiernan (Trenton); Doc Cramer (Beach Haven); Charlie Jamieson (Paterson); George Case (Trenton); Mule Haas (Montclair); Johnny Briggs (Paterson); Danny Green (Burlington)

Designated hitter — Jack Cust (Flemington)

Right Handed Starter — Don Newcombe (Madison). Also: Andy Messersmith (Toms River); Kid Gleason (Camden); Hank Borowy (Bloomfield); John Montefusco (Long Beach); Bill Hands (Hackensack)

Left Handed Starter — Al Leiter (Toms River). Also: Johnny Vander Meer (Prospect Park); Al Downing (Trenton); Duke Esper (Salem)

Relief Pitcher — Ron Perranoski (Paterson). Also: Joe Borowski (Bayonne); Ray Narleski (Camden); Rawley Eastwick (Camden); Dan Micelli (Newark); Jerry DiPoto (Jersey City); Ron Villone (Englewood); *Joe Black* (Plainfield); Barney Schultz (Beverly)

Manager — Jack McKeon (South Amboy). Also: Jeff Torborg (Montclair); Kid Gleason (Camden)

The Names

Best Nickname: John "The Count" Montefusco
Other Nicknames: Tom "Shoulders" Acker; Edward "Jersey" Bakley; Jim "Bulldog" Bouton; Carroll "Boardwalk" Brown; Archie "Iron Man" Campbell; Sean "The Mayor" Casey; Doc "Flit" Cramer; Arthur "Cookie" Cuccurullo; William "Eggie" Dallard; Al "Giggi" Downing; Joseph "Double" Dwyer; Jack "Moose" Farrell; William "Kid" Gleason; Leon "Goose" Goslin; "Sliding Billy" Hamilton; Gil "Colonel" Hatfield; Frankie "Blimp" Hayes; Charlie "Cuckoo" Jamieson; Derek "Mr. November" and "Captain Clutch" Jeter; Billy "Bull" Johnson; "Officer" Ron Karkovice; Joe "Ducky" Medwick; "Wild Bill" Pierson; Alex "Spunk" Pitko; William "Blondie" Purcell; Othello "Chappy" Renfroe; Hardy "Old True Blue" Richardson; John "Honey" Romano; Ernie "Kansas City Kid" Smith; Emanuel "Redleg" Snyder; Morris "Farmer" Steelman; "Jersey Joe" Stripp; Ralph "Sailor" Stroud; Sleeper "Old Iron Hands" Sullivan; "Silent Mike" Tiernan; Russ "Sheriff" Van Atta; Johnny "The Dutch Master" Vander Meer; Huyler "Mamma's Baby Boy" Westervelt
Most Unusual Name: Creighton Gubanich, Mark Lemongello, Will Pennyfeather; Huyler Westervelt

All-Time Leaders

Games: Derek Jeter, 2426 (still active)
Hits: Derek Jeter, 3088 (still active)
Batting Average: Billy Hamilton, .344
Home Runs: Eric Karros, 284
RBI: Goose Goslin, 1609
Stolen Bases: Billy Hamilton, 912
Wins: Al Leiter, 162
Strikeouts: Al Leiter, 1974
Saves: Joe Borowski, 131
Future Stars: Mike Trout (Millville); Zach Braddock (Mount Holly); Todd Frazier (Point Pleasant); Trevor Reckling (Newark); Anthony Ranaudo (Jackson)
Best Player: Derek Jeter

Historic Baseball Places

Yogi Berra Museum at Montclair State in Little Falls — When you win more World Series rings as a player than anyone else in baseball history, you tend to collect some neat artifacts along the way. The museum, which opened in 1998, recently underwent extensive renovations to expand the exhibit area, add new exhibits and refurbish the theater. Now on display are the uniform Yogi wore and the glove he used while catching Don Larsen's perfect game in the 1956 World Series.

Yogi Berra Stadium in Little Falls — This intimate park is also located on the campus of Montclair State, with Yogi's museum situated beyond the seats along the first base line.

Hinchcliffe Stadium in Paterson — The venerable home to many great Negro Leagues games is on the list of America's Most Endangered Historic Places,

The Yogi Berra Museum in Little Falls chronicles the career of the legendary player, who won more World Series rings than any other player. The museum displays the uniform Yogi wore and the glove he used while catching Don Larsen's perfect game in the 1956 World Series (courtesy Yogi Berra Museum).

Yogi Berra Stadium in Little Falls is located on the campus of Montclair State, with the Yogi Berra Museum situated beyond the seats along the first base line (courtesy BallparkReviews.com).

although a preservation and restoration effort is underway. The New York Black Yankees and the New York Cubans played games in the 1930s and 1940s in the ballpark, which opened in 1932.

Elysian Fields in Hoboken—The ballfield that was the site of the first organized game of baseball is no longer there, but you can find an historical marker at the intersection of 11th Street and Washington.

Joe Black Field in Plainfield — Hub Stine Field was renamed in 2010 in honor of the Plainfield native, who was the first African American pitcher to win a World Series game. It's the same field where Black was once told by a major league scout that he'd never play in the big leagues due to the color of his skin.

Delahanty's Tavern on the Square in Phillipsburg — Named in memory of the Hall of Fame outfielder for the Phillies who died in a tragic fall off a bridge into Niagara Falls in 1903, the sports bar features photographs and memorabilia that recap Big Ed's career.

Notable Achievements

When **Al Leiter** beat the Arizona Diamondbacks on April 30, 2002, he became the first pitcher in baseball history to beat all 30 major league teams.

Joe Black of the Brooklyn Dodgers became the first African American pitcher to win a World Series game when he beat the Yankees in Game 1 of the 1952 Series.

Hank Borowy was the first pitcher to win 20 games with at least 10 wins coming from each league. He started the 1945 season 10–5 with the Yankees and then was picked up by the Cubs, where he went 11–2 the rest of the season.

Joe Medwick was the first player to get four hits in the All-Star Game when he went 4-for-5 with two doubles in 1937.

Ron Villone has pitched for 12 different teams over his career, tying Mike Morgan for the most ever.

Sean Casey recorded the first hit at Miller Park in Milwaukee on April 6, 2001, and the first hit at PNC Park in Pittsburgh three days later.

Joe Borden (Jacobstown) won the first game in National League history while pitching for the Boston Red Caps in 1876. Borden also pitched what is recognized as the first professional no-hitter on July 28, 1875, while playing for Philadelphia Whites.

Eddie Smith (Mansfield) of the White Sox gave up the first hit to Joe DiMaggio when he started his 56-game hitting streak on May 15, 1941.

Derek Jeter is the all-time postseason leader in games played, at-bats, plate appearances, runs, hits, total bases, doubles and singles.

New Jersey Is Where It All Began

A seminal moment in baseball history can be traced back directly to New Jersey. The first organized baseball game between two clubs reportedly took place on Elysian Fields in Hoboken on June 19, 1846. The

Knickerbocker Club of New York City, under the direction of Alexander Cartwright and Doc Adams, had been practicing there regularly since the previous year.

That's not all. The first organized game between African American players also reportedly took place at Elysian Fields around 1860. That would seem to give Hoboken a stronger claim to being the birthplace of baseball than Cooperstown. Baseball activity quickly shifted to Brooklyn and other parts, and baseball was last played at Elysian Fields in 1873.

Minor league teams can be traced back to 1883 in Trenton and Camden, with clubs soon following in Jersey City and Atlantic City in 1885. The Newark Stars competed in the Eastern Colored League in 1926, and beginning in 1934 Newark fielded a team called the Dodgers in the Negro National League.

Two years later, the Dodgers joined forced with the Brooklyn Eagles and played through 1948 as the Newark Eagles. The Eagles gained notoriety for being the first professional team owned by a woman, Effa Manley, whose pioneering work led to her election to the Hall of Fame. Two of the Eagles' standout players, Larry Doby and Monte Irvin, would later join the major leagues and produce at a level that gained them entry to Cooperstown. The Eagles won the 1946 Negro World Series.

Newark was also home to a team in the Federal League. The Newark Pepper, who finished in fifth place in their only season, 1915, were led by future Hall of Famers Edd Roush and Bill McKechnie and pitcher Ed Reulbach.

By the end of the 2011 season a total of 409 New Jersey natives had played in the major leagues, from A (Tom Acker) to Z (Eddie Zimmerman). There was a Rambo and a Savage, not to mention Edward "Jersey" Bakley. Bakley played for eight teams in four different leagues, losing 110 games in the four seasons he played between 1884 and 1890.

New Jersey players have been given tough nicknames such as Bulldog, Moose and Bull. Then there's Huyler Westervelt, who was nicknamed "Mamma's Baby Boy" because Huyler was his mother's maiden name. It's not hard to figure out where "Wild Bill" Pierson got his nickname. He issued 31 walks in 32 career innings. Of course, it might also be related to the time he was shot in Atlantic City in 1927 ... or the fact he was convicted of grand larceny in 1929 after going on a store-robbing spree.

In addition to having one of the all-time great names, Mark Lemongello had his own run-in with the law. Growing up on the Jersey Shore, the eccentric pitcher would have been perfect for a Reality TV show if such things existed back then. Four years pitching for Houston and Toronto produced a 22–38 record, along with lots of colorful anecdotes. Lemongello used to literally beat himself up after pitching poorly, and his out-of-control outbursts quickened his departure from baseball. However, he wasn't done making headlines. Along with former major leaguer Manuel Seoane, Lemongello was arrested and charged with kidnapping and robbing his two cousins, Mike and Peter Lemongello, in 1982. Peter Lemongello had brief fame as a singer while Mike Lemongello was a professional bowler. Mark pled no contest and was sentenced to 10 years on probation.

Jim Bouton was one of the best pitchers in baseball in 1963–64, relying on a dominant fastball to win 39 games those years and living up to his nickname "Bulldog." Arm trouble derailed his career, so he turned to the knuckleball. His controversial and entertaining account of baseball life, as chronicled in his 1970 book *Ball Four*, became an immediate best-seller and paved the way for a whole new category of sports books to follow—the behind-the-scenes season diary. As he wrote in the book, "There's pettiness in baseball, and meanness and stupidity beyond belief, and everything else bad that you'll find outside of baseball."

Fans were accustomed to reading sanitized versions of baseball life, and *Ball Four* was one of the first books to tell it like it really was, from the locker room pranks

Shuffled off to the expansion Seattle Pilots in 1969 and then traded to the Houston Astros for the stretch drive, Jim Bouton decided to chronicle the season in a ground-breaking book titled *Ball Four*. Sharing intimate details of clubhouse conversations and activity (such as the rampant use of amphetamines and the way former Yankees teammate Whitey Ford doctored the ball) did not endear him to the baseball community, which felt he had invaded his teammates' privacy and portrayed the game in an unflattering light (National Baseball Hall of Fame Library, Cooperstown, New York).

and head-scratching behavior of coaches and executives to the recurring self-doubt that plagued many players including Bouton.

His writing success led to his demise as a pitcher, as Bouton was summarily blackballed from the majors. He resurfaced for a comeback with a team of misfits aptly named the Portland Mavericks in the mid–1970s and appeared in five games for the Atlanta Braves in 1978. Gone but not forgotten, that's for sure.

All-Time New Jersey Selections

Many people believe Derek Jeter is a Michigan native, since he went to high school in Kalamazoo. But the great Yankee shortstop was born in Pequannock, N.J., and lived in West Milford, N.J., until his family moved to Kalamazoo, Mich., when he was four. He continued to visit his grandparents in New Jersey until his teenage years, by which time he was already obsessed with becoming the starting shortstop for the Yankees. Talk about a dream coming true.

Derek Jeter is not yet finished with his career, but he has already accomplished enough to earn the honor of New Jersey's All-Time Best Player. He was named Rookie of the Year in 1996 and has been selected to 12 All-Star teams. He's won five Gold Gloves and four Silver Sluggers. In 2009 he passed Lou Gehrig for most hits in Yankees franchise history, and he's got more hits than any other shortstop in baseball history. In the final homestand of the 2008 season, Jeter broke Gehrig's record for most hits at the old Yankee Stadium. In 2011 he became the first player to reach 3,000 hits with the Yankees, a mark he reached with a home run as part of a 5-for-5 day. Later in the year he passed Mickey Mantle for most games played in Yankees history.

Jeter has batted over .300 in 11 different seasons, scored over 100 runs 13 times and posted seven 200-hit seasons. His flip toss to nail the A's Jeremy Giambi at home in Game 3 of the 2001 American League Division Series has to be considered one of the most heads-up and crucial defensive plays in playoff history. With playoff appearances in 16 of his 17 seasons and a record number of hits in the postseason, Jeter has earned the nicknames "Mr. November" and "Captain Clutch." A case can be made that he's already the second-best shortstop in history behind Honus Wagner.

Moving on to the mere mortals, at catcher it was a close call between Johnny Romano and Frankie Hayes. Nicknamed "Blimp," Hayes should instead have been called "Iron Man." He caught in 312 straight games between 1943 and 1946, which was a record at the time. Hayes was also the first American League player to catch every game of the season once the schedule was expanded to 154 games. He ended up catching all 155 games for the Philadelphia A's in 1944. Ray Mueller matched the feat that season in the National League for the Reds.

Hayes, who debuted in the majors a month shy of his nineteenth birthday, was selected to six All-Star teams (although the 1945 game was not held) and batted .259 lifetime with 119 home runs. His best years were 1939, when he batted .283-20-83, and 1940, when his line was .308-16-70. Traded four times between 1942 and 1946, he seemed to only play well (and regularly) during his two stints with the Philadelphia Athletics.

Romano made two All-Star teams and batted .255 with 129 homers. He only caught over 100 games in four seasons, but managed to produce double-figure home run totals in seven straight seasons. His best years were his All-Star years of 1961 (.299–21–80) and 1962 (.261–25–81). Romano, who was nicknamed "Honey" but was actually fatter than Hayes, was part of several big trades during his 10-year career. In 1958 he was traded along with Norm Cash to the Indians for Minnie Miñoso and three other players. Then in 1965 he was part of a three-team, seven-player trade that sent Rocky Colavito to the Indians, and Romano, Tommy John and Tommie Agee to the White Sox.

The numbers show that Romano has the edge in OPS+, WAR (Wins Above Replacement) and RAR (Runs Above Replacement). Hayes made significant contributions in five seasons and Romano in just two, and he also has an edge in hits (1,164–706), so "Blimp" Hayes gets selected.

The battle for first base came down to two players whose careers started in the 1990s: Sean Casey and Eric Karros. Casey was not known for his power, but he did hit 130 homers with a high of 25 for the Reds in 1999. Called "The Mayor" for his friendly demeanor, Casey was a skilled, professional hitter who knew how to work the count, get on base and hit with runners on scoring position without striking out a lot. He finished in the top seven in batting average on three occasions and posted a career OPS+ of 109. Despite being painfully slow, he had three years in which he had more than 40 doubles. A three-time All-Star, Casey batted over .300 six times and averaged .529 in a losing effort for the Tigers in the 2006 World Series.

Karros was a slugger who blasted 284 home runs (most in New Jersey history) in 14 seasons, with five seasons in which he had over 30 homers and 100 RBI. He was named Rookie of the Year for the Dodgers in 1992 after hitting 20 homers and driving in 88 runs. In 1999 he set career highs with .304 average, 34 homers, 112 RBI and .912 OPS. Karros finished fifth in MVP voting and won a Silver Slugger in 1995, but he was never named to an All-Star team. Casey was a better overall hitter and much better fielder than Karros, so he gets the selection at first.

Second base featured three candidates who rose to the top: Hardy Richardson, Kid Gleason and Eric Young. We went with Richardson, a nineteenth-century player who played nearly as many games in the outfield as at second. He was an outstanding fielder and excellent base runner. He batted .299 and had 1,688 hits over 14 seasons, leading the National League in hits (189) and homers (11) in 1886 as well as RBI (146) in 1890. He batted over .300 seven times (with a high of .351) and had four seasons with more than 100 runs scored.

Richardson was part of "The Big Four" with Dan Brouthers, Deacon White and Jack Rowe, who played together on the Buffalo Bisons and then were sold as a group to the Detroit Wolverines, turning them into a pennant winner in 1887. Ranked the 39th-best second baseman by Bill James, Richardson posted a career OPS+ of 130, which outshines that of Young (92) and Gleason (78).

Gleason won 138 games playing almost exclusively as a pitcher his first seven seasons. He won 38, 24, 21 and 20 games in consecutive years, pitching between 380 and 506 innings. In 1895 he took over for an injured player at second base and ended up playing that position regularly for the next 12 seasons, finally winding down his career in 1912. He only hit 15 homers in 22 seasons, didn't walk much and averaged just .261 lifetime with a .311 OBP. Gleason did manage to drive in 106 runs in 1897 despite hitting only one homer that year.

Young, who collected the first hit in Colorado Rockies history, was a speed demon who stole 465 bases and collected 1,731 hits playing from 1992–2006. He led the league with 53 steals in 1996 and had three seasons with more than 50 stolen bases. He made his only All-Star team and won a Silver Slugger award in 1996 after batting .324 with 74 RBI.

Another nineteenth-century player gets the nod at third base. Billy Shindle collected 1,561 hits playing from 1886 to 1898. He averaged .269 and stole 318 bases. Shindle played with Richardson and the Big Four on the 1886 and 1887 Detroit Wolverines, but he was just starting his career and didn't make much of an impact. He led the Players League with 282 total bases in 1890, batting .324 with 127 runs and 90 RBI that year.

Joe Stripp didn't walk or strike out much and he only hit 24 homers in 11 seasons, but the third baseman had a .294 lifetime average and collected 1,238 hits. Stripp batted over .300 six times, with a high of .324 in 1931. An excellent fielder, he led NL third basemen in fielding percentage three times.

Two other third basemen from New Jersey deserve mention, mainly because their stats are virtually identical. Check out the career numbers for Mark DeRosa (still active) and Billy Johnson through the 2011 season.

	PA	AB	H	HR	RBI	AVE	OBP	SLG	OPS	OPS+
DeRosa	3734	3325	905	93	449	.272	.341	.417	.758	96
Johnson	3659	3253	882	61	487	.271	.346	.391	.737	102

The All-Time New Jersey team features an outfield filled with Hall of Famers — Joe Medwick, Goose Goslin and Billy Hamilton — and they are the only Hall of Famers from the state to date.

Goslin is the only player to have two walk-off World Series hits — a single in the bottom of the twelfth inning of Game 2 to beat the Cardinals in 1934 and a single in the bottom of the ninth inning to drive in the Series-clinching run against the Cubs in Game 6 in 1935. He is also the only player to play in all 19 of the Washington Senators' World Series games.

Goose hit for average, batting over .300 his first seven seasons (and 11 overall), but he was no singles hitter. He hit 248 home runs, led the league in triples twice and knocked in over 100 runs 11 times. He finished in the top 10 in slugging eight times and top 10 in total bases nine times. He retired with 1,438 runs, 2,735 hits, 173 triples (22nd all-time), 1,609 RBI (30th all-time) and a .316 average.

Goslin's best season was 1928 when he led the league with a .379 average while knocking in 102 runs and posting a slash line of .442/.614/1.056. He had a strong throwing arm early in his career before hurting it, finishing first or second in outfield assists six times and compiling 221 lifetime assists. However, his nickname came from the awkward way he tracked fly balls — it was said he looked like a bird flapping his wings.

Medwick was the last National League player to hit for the Triple Crown when he led the NL with 31 home runs, 154 RBI and .374 average in 1937. He was named MVP that year, as he also led the league in games, at-bats, runs, hits, doubles, slugging, OPS, OPS+ and total bases. A 10-time All-Star, Medwick batted over .300 his first 11 seasons and 14 out of 17 overall. His 64 doubles in 1936 are tied for the second-most in history and remain the National League record.

Fans called him "Ducky" or "Ducky-Wucky," but he preferred the moniker of "Muscles" that his teammates used on occasion. During a World War II visit to the Vatican, Medwick attracted attention by telling the Pope, "Your Holiness, I'm Joseph Medwick. I, too, used to be a Cardinal."

Medwick sparked controversy when he bowled over Tigers third baseman Marv Owen in Game 7 the 1934 World Series. Owen reacted by attempting to punch Medwick, who retaliated by slugging him back. Fans were throwing so many items at Medwick when he took his spot in the outfield that Commissioner Kenesaw Mountain Landis ordered him removed from the game for his own safety. The Gashouse Gang won the game and the Series anyway and Medwick batted .379.

Medwick retired with 205 homers, 1,383 RBI, 2,471 hits and a .324 average, and he was inducted into the Hall of Fame in 1968, 20 years after he played his last game.

Hamilton was the nineteenth century's answer to Rickey Henderson — the first great leadoff hitter in the game. "Sliding Billy" started off by batting .301 with a league-best 111 stolen bases and 144 runs scored in his first full season, 1889. The next year he again led the league with 102 stolen bases while scoring 133 runs and batting .325 with a .430 OBP. He did even better in 1891, leading the league with 141 runs, 179 hits, 111 stolen bases, a .340 average and .453 OBP.

In 1893 Hamilton again led the NL in average (.380) and OBP (.490). He continued to get better each year, scoring 198 runs in 1894 while stealing 100 bases, batting .403 and posting a .521 OBP. No one has come close to Hamilton's record of 198 runs scored, and what's even more amazing is the fact that he did it in just 132 games.

Altogether Hamilton led the league in stolen bases, OBP and walks five times, runs four times and average twice. He retired with 914 stolen bases (third all-time), a .344 average (seventh all-time), .455 OBP (fourth-best) and 1,697 runs (26th-best). He held the record for stolen bases from 1897 until Lou Brock passed him in 1978. Granted, the rules were different back in Hamilton's day, as going from first to third on a single counted as a stolen base. But the most important statistic in the game is scoring runs, and no one did that better and more consistently than Hamilton.

You won't find any other Hall of Famers who averaged more than one run per game for their career like Hamilton did. With 1,697 runs in 1,594 games he averaged 1.06 runs per game — the highest mark in history. By comparison, it took Henderson 3,081 games to score his all-time best 2,295 runs, an average of 0.74 runs per game. Despite his unbelievable stats, Hamilton didn't get elected to the Hall of Fame until 1961, 60 years after he played his last game and 21 years after he died.

Other notable outfielders from New Jersey include Mike Tiernan, Doc Cramer, Charlie Jamieson and George Case. Playing under the same rules as Hamilton, Tiernan stole 428 bases, scored 1,316 runs, collected 1,838 hits and averaged .311. He led the league with 147 runs in 1889 and twice led in homers and OPS. His best average was .369 in 1896. Cramer was a five-time All-Star who accumulated 2,705 hits during a playing career that lasted from 1929–48. He averaged .296, batted over .300 eight times and is the only player to bat 6-for-6 twice in a nine-inning game.

Playing mainly in the Deadball Era, Jamieson spent his entire career with the Indians, batting .303 with 1,990 hits. He batted .345 and led the league with 222 hits in 1923 and then finished second in batting with a .359 average the next year (finishing third in MVP balloting). Case was an All-Star during three seasons and averaged .282 with 349 career stolen bases. He led the AL in steals five straight years and six times altogether.

Our designated hitter is Jack Cust, an active player whose hit-or-miss at-bats are reminiscent of Dave Kingman and Rob Deer. Cust has hit 105 home runs (largely in three seasons) but has also struck out 819 times in 670 games. He does walk a lot, leading the league with 111 walks in 2008, so his OBP is pretty good. Cust is in the company of such sluggers as Babe Ruth, Mickey Mantle and Mike Schmidt, who have all led the league in walks and strikeouts in the same season. Cust hit 205 home runs over 13 minor league seasons as he waited for a team to give him a shot.

Moving on to the pitching staff, our right-handed starter is Don Newcombe, who was a dependable ace for the Brooklyn and Los Angeles Dodgers from 1949–58. Newcombe played two years for the Newark Eagles in the Negro Leagues before signing with the Dodgers shortly after Jackie Robinson. Newcombe stayed three years in the minors before getting called up by the Dodgers, but he made a name for himself as one of the first African American star pitchers.

Newcombe was named Rookie of the Year in 1949 after winning 17 games, pacing the NL with five shutouts and leading the Dodgers to the pennant. He came back the next year and made his second All-Star team on the way to winning 19 games. In 1951 he won 20 games and led the league in strikeouts, making his third consecutive All-Star team. Newcombe went 20–5 in 1955, leading the NL in winning percentage, WHIP, BB/9IP and SO/BB as the Dodgers won the World Series.

He was even better the next year, winning the MVP Award and Cy Young Award after going 27–7 and posting a 0.989 WHIP. It would be his last good season, as he ended his career with a 149–90 record and 3.56 ERA. Not only was Newcombe the first pitcher to win the Cy Young Award and the first to win the Cy Young and MVP in the same year, he is the only pitcher to win the Cy Young, MVP and Rookie of the Year awards.

Newcombe, who battled alcoholism for much of his career, was an excellent batter who averaged .271 with 15 homers. He gained a reputation for coming up short in big games, going 0–4 with an 8.59 ERA in World Series action. Despite the promising start to his career, his lack of longevity hurt his chances to make the Hall of Fame.

Several other right-handed pitchers deserve mention. Andy Messersmith was a four-time All-Star who won 20 games twice and earned two Gold Gloves. Arm trouble derailed his career, but he wound up 130–99 with a 2.86 ERA and ranks fifth all-time with 6.9 hits allowed per 9 innings. Messersmith gained notoriety by challenging the reserve clause in 1975, along with Dave McNally, a landmark event that led to the free agency era for players.

John "The Count" Montefusco picked up the colorful nickname because his last name sounded like Monte Cristo. He is one of the few pitchers to hit a home run and then win his debut game in the majors, a feat he accomplished on September 3, 1974.

Joe Black was a workhorse starter for the Baltimore Elite Giants in the Negro Leagues in the late 1940s who possessed a good fastball and excellent control. He was signed by the Dodgers and burst onto the scene as a 28-year-old rookie in 1952 to help them win the pennant that season. Appearing in 56 games (with only two starts), Black went 15–4 with a 2.15 ERA, allowed just 102 hits in 142 innings. Not only did he win Rookie of the Year, he finished third in the MVP race that year.

The All-Time left-handed starter for New Jersey is Toms River native Al Leiter, who hung around for 19 seasons in the majors and won 162 games (most in New Jersey history). Leiter pitched 10 seasons in the American League and 10 seasons in the National League, yet won 88 more games in the National League. He pitched the first no-hitter in Florida Marlins history in 1996.

After eight seasons with the Yankees and Blue Jays, Leiter had a 23–23 record. However, beginning in 1995 he reeled off 10 straight seasons with double-figure wins, with a high of 17 in 1998. He made the NL All-Star team in 1996 and 2000, striking out exactly 200 batters those years. He finished in the top 10 in ERA six times and won World Series rings with the Blue Jays in 1993 and the Marlins in 1997.

Two other lefties had good careers but are largely known for specific feats. Johnny Vander Meer won 119 games, made four All-Star teams and led the league in strikeouts three times, feasting on the weakened lineups of the National League during World War II. He also produced one of the singular great accomplishments in baseball history — pitching back-to-back no-hitters on June 11 and June 15, 1938.

The first no-hitter came before a sparse crowd of 5,214 at Crosley Field, but the second one took place in front of 38,748 fans who were eager to see the first night game ever held at Ebbets Field. Vander Meer made things interesting in that game, issuing eight walks including walking the bases loaded in the ninth inning. He would pitch into the fourth inning of his next game before allowing a hit.

The other notable lefty is Al Downing, who won 123 games over 17 seasons and made one All-Star team. He led the AL in strikeouts with 217 in 1964 and finished third in Cy Young Award voting in 1972 after winning 20 games and leading the NL in shutouts. Then on April 8, 1974, he became a footnote to history by surrendering Hank Aaron's 715th home run.

The three best relievers from New Jersey are all of Polish heritage: Ron Perranoski, Joe Borowksi and Ray Narleski. Perranoski led the American League with 31 saves in 1969, the first year the save was adopted as an official stat. He came back and led the league again with 34 saves the next year, totaling 79 official saves by the time his career ended in 1973. In 1963 he went 16-3 with a 1.67 ERA, leading the league in appearances (69) and winning percentage (.842), while finishing fourth in the MVP race. The left-handed Perranoski was definitely one of the most dominant relief pitchers of the 1960s, earning him the top spot for Team New Jersey.

Borowski recorded 131 saves (most in New Jersey history) in a career that lasted from 1995 to 2008, but the majority came in three seasons — 33 for the Cubs in 2003, 36 for the Marlins in 2006 and a league-leading 45 for the Indians in 2007. Narleski helped the Indians win the pennant in his rookie year, 1954, posting a 2.22 ERA. He went 9-1 the next year and led the league with 60 appearances. In 1956 he had a 1.52 ERA and made the All-Star team but pitched just 59 innings due to injury. His career lasted only three more years, with many of his appearances as a starter.

The bullpen for Team New Jersey is loaded with productive set-up men including Ron Villone, Dan Micelli and Jerry DiPoto. Rawley Eastwick led the National League in saves his first two seasons but had trouble staying healthy after that and bounced around to six teams in eight years.

The most accomplished manager from New Jersey is Jack McKeon, who managed five teams over 16 seasons spread out between 1973 and 2011. Known as Trader Jack for his propensity to trade players while serving as general manager of the Padres, McKeon became the oldest manager to win a World Series when he led the Marlins to an upset of the Yankees at the age of 72 in 2003. He was named NL Manager of the Year twice (1999 and 2003) and came back to manage the Marlins at the age of 80, making him the second-oldest manager in history behind Connie Mack.

McKeon never won a division title but did guide six teams to second place, finishing with 1,051 career wins. As he once said, "Let's face it, baseball is show business. Some of us take it too seriously, especially the umpires. People come out to enjoy the game, but they want a little pepper in their soup. Arguments with umpires are part of the tradition."

Kid Gleason led the White Sox to the pennant in his first year as manager, but it was 1919 and a number of his players would eventually be banned for life for conspiring to fix the Series. Gleason survived the Black Sox scandal with his reputation relatively unscathed, but he managed the next four years without producing a pennant.

Another noteworthy manager from New Jersey is Jeff Torborg, who produced a 634–718 record managing five different teams over 11 seasons. He was named AL Manager of the Year in 1990 after leading the White Sox to a 25-win improvement. He directed the Sox to back-to-back second-place finishes in 1990–91 but was never able to guide a team into the playoffs.

One of the all-time nicest guys in baseball, Torborg batted just .214 across 10 seasons as a catcher for the Dodgers and Angels. He caught 559 games and three of them were no-hitters, which is tied for the second-most behind Jason Varitek's four. Torborg caught Sandy Koufax's perfect game on September 9, 1965, was behind the plate for Bill Singer's no-hitter on July 20, 1970, and caught the first of Nolan Ryan's seven no-hitters on May 15, 1973. He is on a short list of players who have caught no-hitters in both leagues, joining Ron Hassey and Gus Triandos.

NEW MEXICO

Names in **bold** *represent Major League selections by position, followed by honorable mentions. City of birth is in parentheses.*

Catcher — Al Montgomery (Loving)
First Base — Chuck Stevens (Van Houten)

Second Base — Al Clancy (Santa Fe)
Third Base — Fred Haney (Albuquerque)

Shortstop — Vern Stephens (McAlister)
Outfield — Ralph Kiner (Santa Rita)
Outfield — Cody Ross (Portales)
Outfield — Billy McMillon (Otero)
 Other: Mark Corey (Tucumcari)
Right Handed Starter — Steve Ontiveros (Tularosa)
 Other: Willie Adams (Gallup)
Left Handed Starter — Wade Blasingame (Deming)
Relief Pitcher — Duane Ward (Park View). Also: Scott Terry (Hobbs); Michael Dunn (Farmington)
Manager — Fred Haney (Albuquerque)

The Names

Best Nickname: Steve "Spin Doctor" Ontiveros
Other Nicknames: Fred "Pudge" Haney; Ralph "Mr. Home Run" Kiner; Vern "Buster" and "Junior" Stephens
Most Unusual Name: Wade Blasingame

All-Time Leaders

Games: Vern Stephens, 1720
Hits: Vern Stephens, 1859
Batting Average: Vern Stephens, .286
Home Runs: Ralph Kiner, 369
RBI: Vern Stephens, 1174
Stolen Bases: Fred Haney, 51

Wins: Wade Blasingame, 46
Strikeouts: Duane Ward, 679
Saves: Duane Ward, 121
Future Stars: Jordan Pacheco (Albuquerque); Kyle Weiland (Albuquerque)
Best Player: Ralph Kiner

Historic Baseball Place

Isotopes Park in Albuquerque — Opened in 2003 as the home of the Albuquerque Isotopes and ranks among the leaders in minor league attendance.

Notable Achievements

In 1949 New Mexico natives led both leagues in runs batted in. **Ralph Kiner** led the NL with 127 and **Vern Stephens** led the AL with 159.

Ralph Kiner is the only player to hit home runs in three consecutive All-Star games — 1949, 1950 and 1951.

New Baseball Traditions Are Born in Albuquerque

Professional baseball in New Mexico has a long history dating back to at least 1880, when a team known as the Browns was loosely organized in Albuquerque.

Affectionately known as "The Lab," Isotopes Park in Albuquerque features a slight incline in center field like Minute Maid Park, as well as art sculptures scattered around the ballpark (courtesy DigitalBallparks.com).

The Albuquerque Dons won the Arizona-Texas League championship in their only year of existence, 1932.

Professional baseball returned to Albuquerque in 1937 as an affiliate of the St. Louis Cardinals, playing games in a new ballpark that would be renamed Tingley Field. The franchise changed hands and name (to the Dukes), before finally hitting the big time in 1963 when the Dodgers bought the team and turned it into a Triple-A operation. When the team moved to a new stadium, Albuquerque Sports Stadium, in 1969, Willie Mays was on hand to play in the first game.

The Sports Stadium had a unique feature, as reported by Eric and Wendy Pastore on digitalballparks.com. Cars could drive past the gate and up to the outfield fence and park, so fans could sit there and watch the game like a drive-in movie.

Tommy Lasorda guided the Dukes to the Pacific Coast League (PCL) championship in 1972, finishing with a 92–56 record with a team that featured future MLB stars Ron Cey, Davey Lopes and Charlie Hough. Outfielder Tom Paciorek was named Minor League Player of the Year and the PCL's MVP that year. Lasorda was inducted into the Albuquerque Baseball Hall of Fame in 2007.

Del Crandall led the Dukes to four PCL titles, with the 1981 team going 94–38 and being named the 11th best minor league team in history. First baseman Mike Marshall won the Triple Crown that season with a line of .373/34/137, while second baseman Jack Perconte batted .346 with 45 stolen bases. Perconte played four seasons for the Dukes and was inducted into the Albuquerque Baseball Hall of Fame in 2010.

The city would lose professional baseball, but only for two years. The Dukes were sold to a new owner who moved the team to Portland, Ore., in 2001. New owners stepped in and acquired a team from Calgary and moved it to Albuquerque, but only after the city agreed to underwrite a $28 million renovation of Albuquerque Sports Stadium. Very little was retained, so the current stadium is almost all new. The Isotopes began play in 2003, with the ballpark renamed Isotopes Park.

The team's name originates from an episode of "The Simpsons" in which Homer saved the local baseball team (The Springfield Isotopes) from being moved to Albuquerque. To play up that history, fiberglass statues of Homer and Marge Simpson can be found along the concourse. The irony is probably lost on the folks in Calgary.

Six Albuquerque-born players have gone on to appear in the major leagues, with Fred Haney the most notable. Haney, who actually grew up in Los Angeles, was a third baseman who played seven seasons in the 1920s.

All-Time New Mexico Selections

New Mexico can claim one Hall of Fame player, Ralph Kiner, who was voted in with one vote to spare in his last year of regular eligibility, 1975. However, Kiner should be joined in the Hall by another New Mexico native, Vern Stephens, who was one of the best-hitting shortstops in baseball history.

In the 10-year period between 1942 and 1951, Stephens slugged 224 home runs and drove in 1,046 runs — unheard of production by a shortstop in those days. People say Cal Ripken redefined shortstop as a position for sluggers, but it was really Stephens. His 159 RBI in 1949 are the most ever by a shortstop — ahead of Miguel Tejeda's 150 in 2004 — and Stephens' 144 RBI in 1950 are the third-best mark. If that's not enough, Stephens had 137 RBI in 1948, which is the sixth-best figure for a shortstop. His 440 RBI from 1948–1950 are the most in a three-year period by a shortstop by a comfortable margin — A-Rod is next best with 409 from 2000–2002.

Stephens was named to eight All-Star teams, finished in the top 10 in MVP voting six times and ended his career with 247 homers, 1,174 RBI and a .286 batting average. Ernie Banks and Cal Ripken are the only shortstops in the Hall of Fame with more home runs (Robin Yount hit 251 for his career, but many came as an outfielder).

Playing his prime years in Fenway Park skewed his numbers a little, but Stephens made a similar impact during his six seasons with the St. Louis Browns. He led the league with 109 RBI in 1944, leading the Browns to their only pennant and finishing third in MVP voting. The next year he led the league in home runs and fielding average. Three times he finished in the top 10 in batting average while with the Browns. Stephens was a more than adequate fielder with a strong arm who led league shortstops in assists three times.

As Bill James points out in his book, *The Politics of Glory,* Stephens and Stan Musial both joined the major leagues in September 1941, playing in Sportsman's Park for different St. Louis teams. During the 10-year period from 1941–1950, Stephens compiled 207 homers and 968 RBI compared to 174 and 815 for Musial. And yet only one player is considered an all-time great today. Of course Musial maintained a high level of production for another dozen years, while Stephens was pretty well finished as a regular. James has Stephens ranked as the 22nd-best shortstop in baseball history, ahead of seven other players who are in the Hall of Fame.

Another interesting comparison to Stephens is the career production of Joe Gordon, who was elected to the Hall of Fame in 2009. Their careers came at about the same time and both were standouts at their positions, especially in terms of power. Stephens has better peak value and career stats, outpacing Gordon in hits, RBI and average. Their numbers are nearly identical in home runs, OBP, slugging, OPS and OPS+. Gordon did win five World Series while Stephens lost in his only appearance in the Series. Although Gordon won one MVP Award, Stephens finished in the top 10 in voting for the MVP Award more times.

If Gordon is worthy of Cooperstown, then it appears Stephens also belongs. A review of his statistics leads one to believe he must have come close to being elected to the Hall, but unfortunately that is not the case. Stephens was a heavy drinker who was not well-liked or appreciated by sportswriters while he played, and he didn't receive a single vote when he became eligible in 1962. He was one of 10 pre–1943 players given another chance by a special Veterans Committee that voted in December 2008. Stephens, who died in 1968, came in last place in the voting with just three votes — perhaps his last chance to make it into the Hall.

Hall of Fame voters gave Kiner just enough support to get into Cooperstown, but his injury-wracked career made him anything but a sure thing. Kiner led the National League in home runs his first seven seasons — the only player to do that — and his .946 OPS ranks 24th all-time. He ranks ahead of Willie Mays, Hank Aaron, Ted Williams, Frank Robinson and Mike Schmidt on that list.

Kiner was literally a one-man batting attack for the Pirates, which is why he also led the NL in walks three times. His 54 home runs in 1949 were two more than the rest of the Pirates' starters and that year he became the first National League player to hit more than 50 homers twice. In 1951, he led the league in runs, homers, walks, on-base percentage, slugging percentage and OPS. The six-time All-Star's career on-base percentage was nearly .400 (.398).

He finished with 369 homers and his career average of one home run every 14.1 at bats places him eighth all-time, ahead of Alex Rodriquez, Harmon Killebrew and Mickey Mantle. Four of the players ahead of him on that list are still active, so their home run ratio could drop as they age.

Forced to retire at age 32 because of recurring back and leg injuries, Kiner ended up playing 10 seasons — the minimum requirement to be considered for enshrinement in the Hall of Fame. His next career was longer-lasting, as he started a broadcast career in 1961 that continues to this day.

As a broadcaster, Kiner was known for his head-scratching comments. Like the time he remarked: "The Mets have got their leadoff batter on only once this inning." Then there was this on-air comment: "All of his saves have come in relief appearances." Finally, there was this Yogi-type insight: "There's a lot of heredity in that family."

Stephens and Kiner have to carry Team New Mexico, as the rest of the lineup is not strong. Catcher Al Montgomery had 10 hits during a 30-game career back in 1941. First baseman Chuck Stevens finished with 184 hits in 211 games between 1941 and 1948.

Fred Haney is the only New Mexico-born player to play second base in the majors, but his primary position was third base, where he played 450 games compared to 72 at second. Haney had a good year for the Tigers in 1923, hitting .282 with 142 hits, and then he followed up with a .309 average the next year.

Our second baseman is Al Clancy, who was only noteworthy because he was the first New Mexico native to play in the majors. Clancy played two games at third base for the St. Louis Browns in 1911 and went 0-for-5. However, he did mainly play second base in the minors, so that qualifies him for the spot on the All-New Mexico team.

Joining Kiner in the outfield is Cody Ross, who has already played for five teams in eight seasons. Ross had a breakout year in 2008 with the Marlins, belting 22 home runs and then followed it up by batting .270 with 24 homers and 90 RBIs in 2009. His power numbers dipped in 2010 and he was traded at the deadline to the Giants.

Ross ended up the undisputed star of the 2010 playoffs, driving in the winning run in two games in the Division Series against the Braves and breaking up Derek Lowe's no-hitter with a game-tying home run in the sixth inning of Game 4. He was named MVP of the NLCS after belting two homers against Roy Halladay in the opener and then adding a third homer in Game 2, which broke up Roy Oswalt's no-hitter in the fifth inning. Ross' home run in Game 3 of the World Series was his fifth home run of the 2010 postseason.

The other outfielder is Billy McMillon, who played for four teams in six seasons between 1996 and 2004. McMillon ended his career with 149 hits and a .248 batting average.

McMillon has appeared in more games as a designated hitter (42) than anyone else in New Mexico history, but his main position was outfield so that's where we placed him. Instead, we gave consideration to Chris Cron, whose career consisted of 10 games with one game as a DH.

The right-handed starter is Steve Ontiveros, who was nicknamed "Spin Doctor" because he had pinpoint control throwing six different pitches. He wound up 34–31 with a 3.67 ERA over a 10-season career cut short by arm problems. Ontiveros led the AL in ERA and WHIP in 1994 and then was named to the All-Star team in 1995, going 9–6 that year for the A's.

The lefty starter is Wade Blasingame, who pitched half his games in relief. His best season was 1965, when he went 16–10 for the Milwaukee Braves, but he never had another winning record. Blasingame started 128 games in 10 seasons, retiring with a 46–51 record.

The ninth inning is in the capable hands of Duane Ward, who compiled 121 saves over nine seasons with the Blue Jays. He was an All-Star in 1993, leading the league with 45 saves and registering 97 strikeouts while allowing just 49 hits in 71 innings pitched.

The All-Time New Mexico team is managed by Haney, who guided the Milwaukee Braves to their first and only World Series championship in 1957, riding the bats of Hank Aaron and Eddie Mathews and the pitching arms of Warren Spahn and Lew Burdette. Haney won the pennant again the next season but lost 4–3 in the Series to the Yankees. He stumbled to a second-place finish in 1959 despite having a team with superior talent, and that was the end of his managing days.

Earlier stints managing the Browns and Pirates were also not successful. Haney later became the first general manager of the expansion team the Los Angeles Angels in 1961.

NEW YORK

*Names in **bold** represent Major League selections by position, followed by honorable mentions. Negro Leagues players are in italics. City of birth is in parentheses.*

Catcher — **Joe Torre (Brooklyn)**. Also: Wally Schang (S. Wales); A.J. Pierzynski (Bridgehampton); Doggie Miller (Brooklyn); Paul Lo Duca (Brooklyn); Boileryard Clarke (New York); Buddy Rosar (Buffalo)

First Base — **Lou Gehrig (New York)**. Also: Hank Greenberg (New York); Dan Brouthers (Sylvan Lake); Joe Judge (Brooklyn); Frank McCormick (New York); Dave Orr (New York); Joe Pepitone (Brooklyn); Joe Start (New York); Buddy Hassett (New York)

Second Base — **Eddie Collins (Millerton)**. Also: Craig Biggio (Smithtown); Frankie Frisch (Bronx); Lou Whitaker (Brooklyn); Bid McPhee (Massena); Johnny Evers (Troy); Dave Cash (Utica); Tony Cuccinello (Long Island City); Bucky Harris (Port Jervis); Ross Barnes (Mt. Morris); Snuffy Stirnweiss (New York)

Third Base — **Jimmy Collins (Buffalo)**. Also: Heinie Groh (Rochester); John McGraw (Truxton); Eddie Yost (Brooklyn); Deacon White (Caton); Bobby Bonilla (Bronx); Heinie Zimmerman (New York); Frank Malzone (Bronx); Ezra Sutton (Seneca Falls); Jerry Denny (New York); Bob Ferguson (Brooklyn)

Shortstop — **Alex Rodriquez (New York)**. Also: George Davis (Cohoes); Bill Dahlen (Nelliston); Phil Rizzuto (Brooklyn); Rico Petrocelli (Brooklyn); Johnny Logan (Endicott); George Wright (New York); Dickey Pearce (Brooklyn); Rich Aurilia (Brooklyn); Shawon Dunston (Brooklyn); Billy Jurges (Bronx); Davy Force (New York); Walt Weiss (Tuxedo)

Outfield — **Carl Yastrzemski (Southampton)**

Outfield — **Willie Keeler (Brooklyn)**

Outfield — **King Kelly (Troy)**. Also: Ken Singleton (New York); Rocky Colavito (New York); George Burns (Utica); Tommy Leach (French Creek); Babe Herman (Buffalo); Mike Griffin (Utica); Andy Van Slyke (Utica); *Fats Jenkins* (New York); Cy Seymour (Albany); Sid Gordon (Brooklyn); Tommy Holmes (Brooklyn); Frank Schulte (Cohocton); Lip Pike (New York); Tommy Davis (Brooklyn); Richie Zisk (Brooklyn); B.J. Surhoff (Bronx); Raul Ibanez (New York); Patsy Dougherty (Andover)

Designated Hitter — **Edgar Martinez (New York)**. Also: Tommy Davis (Brooklyn); Richie Zisk (Brooklyn)

Right Handed Starter — **Jim Palmer (New York)**. Also: Charley Radbourn (Rochester); Waite Hoyt (Brooklyn); Orel Hershiser (Buffalo); Mickey Welch (Brooklyn); Will White (Caton); Larry Corcoran (Brooklyn); Jim Whitney (Conklin); Hal Schumacher (Hinckley); Sal Maglie (Niagara Falls); Bill Dinneen (Syracuse); Ice Box Chamberlain (Buffalo); Dennis Leonard (Brooklyn); Howard Ehmke (Silver Creek); *Merven Ryan* (Brooklyn)

Left Handed Starter — **Warren Spahn (Buffalo)**. Also: Sandy Koufax (Brooklyn); Whitey Ford (New York); Frank Viola (Hempstead); Ed Lopat (New York); John Candelaria (New York); Johnny Antonelli (Rochester); Johnny Podres (Witherbee); Hooks Wiltse (Hamilton); Ed Morris (Brooklyn); *Edsall Walker* (Catskill)

Relief Pitcher — **John Franco (Brooklyn)**. Also: Roy Face (Stephentown); Don McMahon (Brooklyn); Johnny Murphy (New York); Jim Konstanty (Strykersville); Billy Koch (Rockville Centre); Joe Sambito (Brooklyn); Tom Ferrick (New York); Dave Giusti (Seneca Falls); Heathcliff Slocumb (Jamaica); Mike Remlinger (Middletown); Pete Richert (Floral Park); Ted Wilks (Fulton); Mark Guthrie (Buffalo)

Manager — **John McGraw (Truxton)**. Also: Joe Torre (Brooklyn); Bucky Harris (Port Jervis); Frankie Frisch (Bronx)

The Names

Best Nickname: Charlie "The Old Woman in the Red Cap" Pabor

Other Nicknames: Bob "The Magnet" Addy; Charles "Lady" Baldwin; John "Honey" Barnes; Edwin "Bazooka" and "Fiddler" Basinski; Curt "Clank" Blefary; Herbert "Buttons" Briggs; Prentice "Pidge" Browne; "Black Jack" Burdock; "Silent George" Burns; John "Candy Man" Candelaria; Elton "Ice Box" Chamberlain; William "Boileryard" Clarke; Eddie "Cocky" Collins; "Peekskill Pete" Cregan; Bob "Crooked Arm" Cremins; "Frosty Bill" Duggleby; Shawon "Thunderpup" Dunston; Elmer "Moose" Eggert; Thomas "Dude" Esterbrook; Johnny "Crab" Evers; Bill "Clinkers" Fagan; Bob "Death to Flying Things" Ferguson; Whitey "Chairman of the Board" Ford; Frank "The Fordham Flash" Frisch; Lou "The Iron Horse" and "Biscuit Pants" Gehrig; Orel "Bulldog" Hershiser; Joe "Ubbo U-bbo" Hornung; Pete "Monkey" Hotaling; Waite "Schoolboy" Hoyt; Frank "The Bald Eagle" Isbell; Clarence "Fats" Jenkins; Alfred "Queens" Jutze; "Wee Willie" Keeler; Mike "King" Kelly; "Harlem Joe" Kiefer; Sandy "The Left Arm of God" Koufax; Gene "Rubber Arm" Krapp; Johnny "Yatcha" Logan; "Steady" Eddie Lopat; Sal "The Barber" Maglie; Jim "Baby Huey" Maler; John "Little Napoleon" and "Mugsy" McGraw; George "Doggie" and "Foghorn" Miller; Albert "Hiker" Moran; Ed "Cannonball" Morris; "Honest Eddie" Murphy; Johnny "Fireman" Murphy; "Subway Sam" Nahem; John "Cinders" O'Brien; Jim "Cakes" Palmer; Mark "Humpty Dumpty" Polhemus; Phil "Grandmother" and "Leather Fist" Powers; Charley "Old Hoss" Radbourn; Phil "Scooter" Rizzuto; Dick "Baldy" Rudolph; Merven "Red" Ryan; Joe "Horse Belly" Sargent; Frank "Dreamy" Scanlan; Frank "Wildfire" Schulte; "Prince Hal" Schumacher; Mose "The Rabbi of Swat" Solomon; Joe "Old Reliable" Start; George "Snuffy" Stirnweiss; George "Specs" Toporcer; Frank "Sweet Music" Viola; Edsall "The Catskill Wild Man" Walker; "Smiling Mickey" Welch; "Sweet" Lou Whitaker; "Will "Whoop-La" White; "Grasshopper Jim" Whitney; George "Hooks" Wiltse; Lewis "Snake" Wiltse; Eddie "Walking Man" Yost; George "The Charmer" Zettlein

Most Unusual Name: Meldon Wolfgang; Bill Goodenough; Heathcliff Slocumb

All-Time Leaders

Games: Carl Yastrzemski, 3308
Hits: Carl Yastrzemski, 3419
Batting Average: Ross Barnes, .360
Home Runs: Alex Rodriquez, 629 (still active)
RBI: Lou Gehrig, 1995
Stolen Bases: Eddie Collins, 744
Wins: Warren Spahn, 363
Strikeouts: Warren Spahn, 2583
Saves: John Franco, 424
Future Stars: Pedro Alvarez (New York City); Dellin Betances (Brooklyn)
Best Player: Lou Gehrig

Historic Baseball Places

National Baseball Hall of Fame and Museum in Cooperstown — The national pastime's rich history comes alive in three floors of exhibits. The Hall of Fame Plaque Gallery showcases the achievements of all the inductees. Babe Ruth has his own room and you can view an overview of baseball history in the Grandstand Theater. Just a small fraction of the museum's artifacts and memorabilia are on display at any given time, but you can find World Series programs from every year, the bat Babe Ruth used to hit three home runs in Game 4 of the 1926 Series, the cap worn by Jackie Robinson in the 1955 Series, Lou Gehrig's locker and the famous Honus Wagner T206 card.

Doubleday Field in Cooperstown — Fans can no longer see the Hall of Fame Game at Doubleday, but the Hall of Fame Classic game features retired stars including Hall of Famers like Goose Gossage and Ozzie Smith. Bob Feller made one of his last public appearances at the 2010 Classic game. You can catch a game (many of them free) just about any day during baseball season.

Yankee Stadium in the Bronx — The House That Jeter Built opened in 2009, replacing the historic House that Ruth built across the street. Come early before a game so there's enough time to see the New York Yankees Museum and all the legends on display in Monument Park.

Babe Ruth's gravesite at Gate of Heaven Cemetery in Hawthorne — Baseball fans continue to pay their respects to the larger-than-life star, turning his gravesite into a shrine with flags, balls, weird trinkets and notes. Billy Martin is also buried in the cemetery, with a number "1" carved into both ends of the stone.

Jackie Robinson gravesite at Cypress Hills Cemetery in Brooklyn — A monument beside his grave contains the following inscription under Jackie's signature:

Baseball may not have been invented in Cooperstown, but the presence of the National Baseball Hall of Fame and Museum solidifies Cooperstown's place as the rightful Home of Baseball. "Pride and Passion: The African American Experience" is a permanent exhibit that outlines the history of African Americans in baseball. The newest exhibits in the Hall of Fame pay tribute to Hank Aaron's life on and off the field as well as baseball records and the stories behind them (photograph by the author).

Doubleday Field in Cooperstown is named after Abner Doubleday, the mythical founder of baseball. The old-fashioned ballpark, which first opened in 1920 and is located two blocks from the Baseball Hall of Fame, does not have lights or any advertising on the fences. For many years it hosted big-league teams every summer in an exhibition called the Hall of Fame Game. That tradition has been replaced by the Hall of Fame Classic, which features Hall of Famers and recently retired players (photograph by the author).

"A life is not important except in the impact it has on other lives."

Lou Gehrig gravesite at Kensico Cemetery in Valhalla — The great Yankee captain's final resting place is beside his devoted wife Eleanor in an unpretentious grave. Gehrig's birth date is erroneously listed as 1905 instead of 1903. He is joined in the same section of the cemetery by Ed Barrow and Jacob Ruppert, Jr., the two men most responsible for getting the Yankees dynasty started.

Jackie Robinson and Pee Wee Reese monument at KeySpan Park in Brooklyn — Unveiled in 2005, the monument features two eight-foot tall bronze statues that commemorate the special bond that developed between the two teammates.

Citi Field in Flushing — New home of the Mets opened in 2009. Features exterior facade and main entry rotunda inspired by Ebbets Field in Brooklyn.

Dan Brouthers Monument in Wappinger Falls — Tribute to the Hall of Fame player stands behind a youth baseball field named after him in his hometown.

Green-Wood Cemetery in Brooklyn — A number of baseball pioneers are among the greats buried in this cemetery including Dodgers owner Charles Ebbets, Hall of Famer Henry Chadwick and James Creighton, Jr., baseball's first great pitching star, whose massive grave monument features crossed bats, a scorebook, cap and base along with a reference to the Brooklyn Excelsiors ball club.

Notable Achievements

Elton "Ice Box" Chamberlin was an ambidextrous pitcher who alternated arms while pitching during at least two games, once in 1884 and again in 1888. Another New York pitcher, **Larry Corcoran**, pitched with both arms during a game in 1889.

Al Cuccinello (Long Island City) of the New York Giants and **Tony Cuccinello** of the Brooklyn Dodgers were the first brothers on opposing teams to homer in the same game, which they did on July 5, 1935.

Ezra Sutton hit the first home run in professional baseball on May 8, 1871, while playing for the Cleveland Forest Citys in the National Association. He also hit the second home run in that same game.

Danny McDevitt (New York) won the final game at Ebbets Field. The rookie pitched a 2–0 shutout for the Dodgers on September 24, 1957.

Ross Barnes hit the first-ever home run in the National League on May 2, 1876.

Deacon White collected the first hit in major league history — a double off Bobby Mathews on May 4, 1871.

Bill Duggleby (Utica) was not only the first player to hit a home run in his first major league at-bat (in

1898), the pitcher is one of just four players to accomplish it with a grand slam.

Will White, who pitched from 1877–86, is believed to be the first player to wear glasses on the field. Another New Yorker, **George "Specs" Toporcer**, became the first position player to wear glasses in 1921.

Tommy Leach collected the first hit and scored the first run in World Series history in 1903.

Charlie Pabor (Brooklyn) was a nineteenth century outfielder and pitcher who holds the record for most career innings pitched without recording a strikeout — 51⅓. He also played and managed in the first all-professional game for the Cleveland Forest Citys in 1871.

Lady Baldwin's 42 wins in 1886 remain the most ever by a left-handed pitcher in the major leagues (not counting Matt Kilroy's 46 in the American Association in 1887).

Red Hoff (Ossining) lived longer than any other major league player — he was 107 years old when he passed away on Sept. 17, 1998. Hoff pitched for the Yankees from 1911–13, winning just two career games while playing for Hal Chase and Frank Chance.

Carl Yastrzemski is the only player to lead the American League in hits and walks in the same season — he led with 183 hits and 95 walks in 1963. **Ross Barnes** is one of five players to accomplish the feat in the National League. He led with 138 hits and 20 walks in 1876 — the exact same totals he had to lead the National Association in 1873.

Warren Spahn has the most career wins while also having the same number of hits as wins. He had 363 wins and 363 hits — a record unlikely to be broken — and also collected four postseason hits to go with his four postseason wins.

Benny Distefano is the last left-handed catcher to play in the majors — he caught three games for Pittsburgh in 1989.

Baseball's Early Days Trace Back to New York

No state can claim a bigger share of baseball history than New York, starting with the belief that the Knickerbocker Base Ball Club of New York was the first organized baseball team. Fittingly, a player named Austin Knickerbocker (born in Bangall, New York) made it to the majors, although he played just 21 games.

Alexander Cartwright, considered the "Father of Modern Baseball," was born in New York City. However, if Major League Baseball's official historian, John Thorn, is to be believed, Cartwright did very little of what he is credited with doing, and most assuredly is not the man most responsible for developing organized baseball in New York City, Hawaii or anywhere else.

The first organized Negro teams squared off in Bedford, New York, in 1862, according to John Holway's *The Complete Book of Baseball's Negro Leagues.* New York is also the native state of Bud Fowler, who is believed to be the first African American professional baseball player. Fowler, whose given name was John Jackson, Jr., appeared in a game with the Lynn Live Oaks of the International Association on May 17, 1878. Fowler, who ironically grew up in Cooperstown, was also the first player to use shin guards, developing a wooden set to protect himself against rough sliders at second base in the late 1880s.

By that time more history was made in New York as the first team of salaried African American players was organized out of the Argyle Hotel in Babylon in 1885. The original purpose was to entertain the hotel guests, but the team soon took to the road as the Cuban Giants, reports James Riley in *The Biographical Encyclopedia of the Negro Baseball Leagues.*

Then you have the various Yankees dynasties adding up to 27 championships, 86 historic years at the old Yankee Stadium, the great Subway Series between the Brooklyn Dodgers and the Yankees in the 1950s, the Miracle Mets of 1969, not to mention that the National Baseball Hall of Fame and Museum is located in upstate New York, even if everyone admits the game was not really invented by Abner Doubleday in Cooperstown.

The Empire State has unleashed some pretty impressive players through the years, as the All-Time New York team is loaded with Hall of Famers at nearly every position. To date 19 players, two managers and four executives from New York have been enshrined in Cooperstown, with Joe Torre and Craig Biggio expected to join that list eventually.

Since the game first became popular in the greater New York City area, it's not surprising to discover that many of the nineteenth century players hailed from the region. A total of 329 native New Yorkers at least started their major league career in the nineteenth century.

Some of the best players from that era did not compile stats that hold up against players from the modern era, yet quite a few found their way onto the All-Time New York team as honorable mentions. Separating those players, we find the makings of a pretty good team, including five Hall of Famers.

C—Doggie Miller; John Clapp; Pop Schriver
First Base—Joe Start; Dave Orr; Harry Taylor
Second Base—Bid McPhee; Danny Richardson; Ross Barnes; Jack Burdock
Third Base—Deacon White; Ezra Sutton; Jerry Denny; Bob Ferguson
SS—George Wright; Dickey Pearce; Davy Force
OF—King Kelly; Mike Griffin; Lip Pike; Pete Hotaling; Joe Hornung
RHP—Charley Radbourn; Mickey Welch; Will White; Larry Corcoran; Jim Whitney; Ice Box Chamberlin; Jack Lynch; George Zettlein; Terry Larkin
LHP—Ed Morris
MGR—Harry Wright

New York has had more than its fair share of players with wild and wacky names, including such first names as Bock, Rivington, Waddy, Phonney, Wickey, Rinty, Bots, Kewpie, Fraley, Overton and Favel.

You could even put together an all-time team of New Yorkers with girlish names. That team would feature Val Picinich, Honey Barnes and Chick Starr at catcher, Babe Herman at first (he played 236 games there), Gracie Pierce at second, Pat Callaghan at third and She Donahue at short. In the outfield you would find Patsy Dougherty, Alta Cohen and Sandy Piez. Southpaw hurlers Sandy Koufax and Lady Baldwin are joined by righties Chick Robitaille and Babe Birrer. The bullpen is manned by Bunny Hearn while Sandy Griffin is the manager.

Baldwin picked up the nickname "Lady" because he did not smoke, drink, curse or carouse, behavior that stood out in the crowd of ruffians he played with in the 1880s. On the subject of great feminine nicknames, Charles Pabor takes the prize with "The Old Woman in the Red Cap." The story behind Pabor's nickname remains elusive — perhaps he was a charter member of the Red Hat Society.

The New York roster is littered with great first-name monikers including Scrappy, Shorty, Sibby, Snuffy, Snake, Spider and Sun. Boileryard Clarke picked up his nickname from having a loud voice that could be heard all around the ballyard. Elton Chamberlin was nicknamed "Ice Box" because he was cool under pressure, a trait that was undoubtedly tested on May 30, 1894, when he became the first pitcher to surrender four home runs to the same batter (Bobby Lowe) in a game.

Lip Pike is not only considered to be the first Jewish major leaguer but is often credited as the first professionally paid player. Pike led the National Association in home runs the first three years of the league's brief existence and held the career home run record from 1872–79 and the single-season record from 1872–75.

Dude Esterbrook was not a surfer from Southern California but rather a talented and troubled nineteenth century player from Staten Island. A .261 hitter as a third baseman over 11 seasons, Dude was on his way to a mental hospital when he leaped off a train to his death in 1901.

In a perfect world, Pi Schwert would be a pitcher with a 3.14 ERA, but instead he was a catcher whose closest stat to Pi is a .316 OBP he posted one year. Mose Solomon was known as "The Rabbi of Swat," after hitting 49 homers one year in the minors. He did little swatting in the majors as his big-league career consisted of three hits and zero home runs.

At least Solomon got a cup of coffee in the majors — Nick Testa had the cup yanked away from him before he could take a sip. The Bronx native made his debut with the San Francisco Giants at the age of 29 on April 23, 1958, entering the game as a pinch runner in the eighth inning and then staying in the game to catch. He dropped a foul ball in the ninth and then was standing on deck in the bottom of the ninth when Daryl Spencer hit a walk-off two-run homer. Shortly after that Testa became the Giants' bullpen coach and ended his career with a .000 fielding average and no batting record. Testa played 1,358 games over 16 minor league seasons.

Going down the roster of the 1,141 players from New York who have made it to the majors through the 2011 season, we find a Monk and a Cardinal, a Sherry and a Wine, not to mention Rip Vowinkel, who pitched six games in 1905 and then evidently took a 20-year nap and awoke to find the game had passed him by. There are two New York players named Bill Kelly — both ended up with 15 career hits. Bill Goodenough made his debut in 1893, lasting 10 games until the St. Louis Browns decided his .161 average was not good enough.

Chuck Connors ground into a double play in his only at-bat for his hometown Brooklyn Dodgers but did go on to collect 48 career hits for the Cubs. He also played 53 games for the Boston Celtics, becoming the first player to shatter a backboard with a shot, and was drafted by the Chicago Bears in the NFL. However, his real claim to fame was as an actor, with the lead role in "The Rifleman" TV series as well as dozens of other roles through the years. Looking back on his baseball career, Connors said, "I was a bum of a hitter just not cut out for the majors." He got that right.

Moe Berg achieved more notoriety for his post-baseball career, which happened to be as a spy for the United States' Office of Strategic Service during World War II. Berg collected 441 hits with a .243 average over 15 seasons as a part-time player, making the unusual switch from shortstop to catcher and confounding teammates with his brilliant and odd intellect. Since he was a graduate of Princeton University and Columbia Law School who spoke multiple languages, Berg always had a mysterious air about him, which proved handy in his work as a spy.

Of course we should not overlook New York's most colorful character — Bo Belinsky, who put the vivant in bon vivant. Belinsky never met a good time he couldn't prolong. Long before Derek Jeter came on the scene, the fun-loving Bo set the standard for dating Hollywood starlets including Mamie Van Doren, Connie Stevens, Tina Louise and Ann-Margret. Not only did he marry a Playboy bunny, Jo Collins, he briefly left the Astros and was suspended because he wanted to spend more time with Collins. Another time he was two weeks late arriving at Angels camp because he was in a pool tournament in New Jersey.

Belinsky was born in New York City but grew up as a pool hustler in gritty Trenton, N.J. Pitching for the expansion Los Angeles Angels in their second year, Belinsky used an overpowering fastball and effective screwball to pitch a no-hitter in his fourth start as a rookie in 1962, boasting afterward that he'd been up until 4 A.M. the night before entertaining a lady friend. It was the first no-hitter in the major leagues pitched on the West Coast, the first in the Angels' brief history and the first in Dodger Stadium history. Bo would win his first five decisions that year, but soon had more lady friends than wins. "Girls tend to make me forget everything," said Belinsky, who soon had lots of reasons to be forgetful.

The no-hitter would be his one and only career highlight, as he went 28–51 pitching for four teams over eight seasons while only making headlines for his social life. Bo roomed with Bob Uecker after getting traded to the Phillies in 1965, but Uecker was usually left to tell one-liners to an empty room. Later in life, after he had given up drinking and become a born-again Christian, Belinsky disputed the notion that he squandered his talent with hard partying, remarking, "I figure I used all I had. I just didn't have as much as people thought."

All-Time New York Selections

Moving on to the team selections, we start out with future Hall of Fame manager Joe Torre, who rightfully belongs in the Hall as a catcher. Or perhaps we should say he belongs in the Hall as a player, and he played more games at catcher than any other position. Bill James ranks Torre as the 11th-best catcher, noting that Torre was known for his bat and not his glove work behind the plate. The nine-time All-Star played 903 games at catcher — along with 787 at first base and 515 at third base — and managed to throw out a respectable 41 percent of base runners during the 10 seasons he caught.

Comparing Torre's career stats to the catchers currently in the Hall, his 2,342 hits trail Carlton Fisk by 14 but rank ahead of all the other catchers in the Hall. He's fifth in homers with 252 and average at .297 and sixth in RBI (1,185). His 128 OPS+ is the same as Mickey Cochrane and behind only Buck Ewing (who's at 129). Torre was a third baseman during his 1971 MVP season with the Cardinals, leading the NL in hits, RBI and average (.363) that year. But his second-best season with the bat was 1966, when he batted .315 with 36 homers and 101 RBI while catching 114 games for the Braves.

Torre's excellence as a hitter wins out over the well-rounded game of runner-up Wally Schang. Schang was a good catcher for a long time, playing on seven pennant-winning teams over a 19-year career. A .284 lifetime hitter, he excelled at drawing walks, posting eight seasons with an OBP over .400. As a rookie Schang batted .357 with seven RBI for the Philadelphia Athletics as they emerged victorious in the 1913 World Series. The switch-hitter batted over .300 for the Red Sox in 1919–20 and then again for the Yankees in 1921–22.

Three Hall of Fame first basemen hail from New York, but Hank Greenberg and Dan Brouthers take a back seat to the greatest first sacker ever — Lou Gehrig. Gehrig was a starter alongside Babe Ruth for 10 seasons on the Yankees — 1925–1934 — and the Iron Horse drove in more runs than the Babe in seven of those (and tied one more); he also had a better batting average in seven out of the 10 seasons. Perpetually overshadowed by Ruth's oversized personality, Gehrig was content to let his bat do his talking for him. As he put it, "I'm not a headline guy. I know that as long as I was following (Ruth) to the plate I could have stood on my head and no one would have known the difference."

Gehrig's Yankee teammates gave him the unflattering nickname "Biscuit Pants" as they observed his thick legs and big butt covered up by the baggy pants of the day. Ironically, he had been called the "Babe Ruth of the schoolyards" while first attracting attention as a high school hitting sensation in Yonkers. Few remember that after Ruth's famous "called shot" against Charlie Root in the 1932 World Series, Gehrig stepped up to the plate as the next batter and walloped the ball over the fence for his second home run of the game.

Shy and unrefined as a player and a person when he first joined the Yankees, Gehrig gradually came of age to become the team's most dedicated and disciplined player, traits that became apparent as "The Streak" grew over the years. Teammate George Selkirk said, "Lou Gehrig was a guy who could really hit the ball, was dependable and seemed so durable that many of us thought he could have played forever."

Gehrig ranks third all-time in slugging (.632) and OPS (1.080) and fifth in OBP (.447) and RBI (1,995). He owns three of the top six RBI seasons in history — 184 in 1931 (second-best); 175 in 1927 and 174 in 1930 — and went over 100 RBI in 13 straight seasons. He is the only player to drive in more than 500 runs in a three-year period — he drove in 509 between 1930 and 1932. He still holds the all-time record for grand slams with 23, although Alex Rodriquez is now tied with him.

The Babe may have hit 60 home runs in 1927, but it was Gehrig who was named AL MVP that season due to a quirk in the voting procedures back then. Ruth had won the award in 1923 and at the time winners were not eligible to win again. Ruth did not regain eligibility for the award until his career was winding down, but Gehrig did receive a second MVP in 1936. Gehrig won batting's Triple Crown in 1934, yet finished fifth in MVP voting that year. Mickey Cochrane was the 1934 MVP despite hitting 47 fewer homers and knocking in 91 fewer runs than Larrupin' Lou.

Gehrig was the first sports figure to have his uniform number retired by a team, starting a tradition followed now by all teams in professional sports. He served as captain of the Yankees from April 1935 until his death in 1941, and would not be replaced in that role until another tragic Yankee hero, Thurman Munson, assumed the mantle of leadership 35 years later. Revered for his determination, perseverance and humility while his amazing consecutive games streak was alive, Gehrig is now admired for his remarkable grace and courage.

Overshadowed by Gehrig's greatness as his career got underway, Greenberg managed to win two MVP awards himself. He was known as "Hammerin' Hank" long before Hank Aaron came along and picked up the moniker. His final numbers are misleading because he missed about four and a half seasons of his prime while serving during World War II — his 45 months of service are the most of any major league player. It's quite possible he would have ended up with more home runs than Gehrig if he had not missed those years.

Greenberg's hitting prowess led the Tigers to four pennants and two World Series titles. His 58 homers in 1938 remain tied with Jimmie Foxx for the most by a right-handed batter in American League history. He led the AL in homers and RBI four times each, collected over 200 hits three times and ranks seventh in OPS (1.017) and slugging (.605). His 63 doubles in 1934 are the fourth most in history. He has two of the top eight seasons for RBI with 183 in 1937 (third best) and 170 in 1935 (tied for eighth place).

As a star Jewish athlete, Greenberg was forced to overcome harassment and prejudice throughout his career, catching hell from fans, and praise from the Jewish community, for refusing to play on Yom Kippur while the Tigers were engaged in a pennant race in 1934. Greenberg increasingly embraced his role as a great Jewish ballplayer, and he became the first Jewish player elected to the Hall of Fame in 1956. In his autobiography, *The Story of My Life*, Greenberg takes credit for revolutionizing the shape of first basemen's gloves and for working out a pension plan between the owners and players.

Brouthers was a powerful slugger who was one of the premier hitters of the nineteenth century. He played for nine teams in three leagues between 1879 and 1896, and then joined his 10th team (John McGraw's Giants) for an abbreviated comeback in 1904. The lefty-swinging slugger won five batting titles for four different teams. His .342 average is the highest for a first baseman and tied with Babe Ruth for the ninth best in baseball history. "Big Dan" led the NL in slugging six straight years and batted over .300 16 straight seasons. Brouthers' .423 OBP ranks sixteenth and his adjusted OPS of 170 is the highest of any nineteenth century player and tied with Shoeless Joe Jackson for eighth all-time.

Gehrig, Greenberg and Brouthers were all tall, powerfully built men, while Brooklyn native Joe Judge was just 5-foot-8 and 155 pounds. An adept fielder who led AL first basemen in fielding percentage seven times, Judge played 18 of his 20 seasons with the Washington Senators, putting together a solid career. A lifetime .298 batter with 2,352 hits and 1,034 RBI, he hit just 71 homers despite playing much of his career during the Lively Ball Era.

Another notable first baseman is nineteenth century hitting sensation Dave Orr, whose career was shortened to eight seasons by a stroke. He never finished below fifth in the league in batting, batted over .300 every year and winding up with a .342 average, good for 11th all-time. Orr's 31 triples in 1881 remain the record for a right-handed batter and tied for second-most in history, and he ranks fourteenth with a career adjusted OPS of 162.

A strong case could be made that Eddie Collins is the greatest second baseman in baseball history. He was a smart, aggressive and skilled player who did everything well except slug home runs, which was not a necessity in his years of play during the Deadball Era. Nicknamed "Cocky" for the confident air of superiority he projected, Collins batted over .300 in 17 of the 20 seasons in which he had at least 200 at-bats, finishing with a lifetime average of .333 and ranking 10th with 3,315 hits.

He finished in the top 10 in batting 15 times, yet never won a batting title in a period dominated by Ty Cobb. He was one of the first players to study pitchers' moves, a primary reason he led the league in stolen bases four times and wound up with 741 for his career (eighth all-time) despite lacking blazing speed. He is the official career leader in sacrifice hits with 512, although researchers have pointed out that many of those were sacrifice flies that have been improperly categorized.

Collins teamed up with first baseman Stuffy McInnis, third baseman Frank Baker and shortstop Jack Barry to form Connie Mack's "$100,000 infield" on the Philadelphia Athletics. He won three championships with the A's between 1910 and 1913, another with the White Sox in 1917 and then two more with the A's in 1929–30 (although he didn't play in those last two Series and barely played during the regular season). Collins was clutch in the postseason, batting .429 in the 1910 World Series, .421 in the 1913 Series and .409 in the 1917 Series.

He played more seasons, 25, than any other player in American League history and still holds major league records for assists (7,630) and defensive games at second base (2,650) while ranking second in putouts (16 behind fellow New Yorker Bid McPhee). Named AL MVP in 1914, Collins knocked in 85 runs, led the AL with 122 runs and finished second in stolen bases (58), OBP (.452) and OPS (.903) that year.

Collins and the A's fell flat in the World Series that year, and he was sold to the White Sox, where his high salary caused dissension among teammates. The Ivy League graduate (Columbia University) had little in common with the other Sox star, the illiterate and unrefined Shoeless Joe Jackson. Collins was not one of the eight Sox players who were accused of fixing the 1919 Series, but he did bounce back the next season to establish career highs in hits, doubles and average. At the age of 36 in 1923, Collins batted .360 (fourth in the AL) and led the league with 48 steals. He came back the next year and did it again, finishing fourth with a .349 average and first with 42 steals.

Collins was one of the 25 original inductees to the Hall of Fame in 1939, yet faced with the chance to really make baseball history he took a pass. He spent the last 18 years of his life as an executive with the Red Sox, and under his direction the Sox were the first major league team to give Jackie Robinson a tryout in April 1945. However, it was a farce designed to silence the team's critics and Robinson actually found himself subjected to racial taunts during the tryout. The Red Sox would be the last team to integrate, in 1959, eight years after Collins died.

Craig Biggio gained notoriety for his singular ability to get hit by pitches, something he did more than any other player in the modern era. Overlooked is his consistency and durability, as well as the fact that he excelled at collecting walks and doubles, getting on base, stealing bases and fielding while also possessing underrated power. A seven-time All-Star and four-time Gold Glover, Biggio retired in 2007 with 3,060 hits including 291 home runs, 1,844 runs and 414 stolen bases. He led NL second basemen in assists six times and putouts five times.

Biggio probably would have been considered a major star if he played in a huge media market like New York, but he was just one of the "Killer B's" in Houston. He made the NL All-Star team as a catcher in 1991 and as a second baseman the next year. His 668 doubles are the most of any right-handed batter. In 1998 he became just the second player to collect 50 doubles and 50 stolen bases in a season, 86 years after Tris Speaker first accomplished the feat. The Smithtown native is considered a lock for the Hall of Fame when he becomes eligible in 2013.

Frankie Frisch was a hard-nosed switch-hitter who played on eight pennant winners with the Giants and Cardinals. The "Fordham Flash" collected 2,880 hits, 419 stolen bases, 1,532 runs and a .316 average over a career that lasted from 1919–37. Frisch exploded onto the scene by batting .341 in 1921 with 211 hits, 100 RBI and a league-leading 49 steals for John McGraw's Giants, who would win the first of back-to-back World Series titles that year. He had a sometimes contentious relationship with the legendary manager, which caused McGraw to trade him to the Cardinals for Rogers Hornsby after the 1926 season.

Frisch was named NL MVP for the Cards in 1931 after batting .311, knocking in 82 runs and leading the league with 28 steals. It was his all-around fiery play that won Frisch the award, as he posted a 101 OPS+ that season. When he became player-manager of the team in 1933 it was the evolutionary beginnings of the Gashouse Gang that would deliver the 1934 championship. That was his last success as a player or manager, as he would go on to endure four more controversial years at the helm of the Cardinals, followed by unproductive stints at the helm of the Pirates and Cubs. Frisch was elected to the Hall of Fame in 1947.

Lou Whitaker also belongs in the Hall for his steady play with the Tigers for 19 seasons. "Sweet Lou" scored more runs than Nellie Fox or Ryne Sandberg, had more hits than Billy Herman or Bid McPhee and drove in more runs than Rod Carew or Sandberg. Rogers Hornsby, Ryne Sandberg, Joe Morgan and Joe Gordon are the only Hall of Fame second basemen to top his 244 home runs. Named Rookie of the Year in 1978, Whitaker went on to make five All-Star teams. He drew a lot of walks (1,197), leading to a respectable .363 OBP, and finished with 2,369 hits, 1,386 runs and 1,084 RBI. Whitaker, who won a championship with the Tigers in 1984, was a superb fielder but won just three Gold Gloves because he played in the American League the same time as Frank White. Inexplicably, he failed to attract enough votes and dropped off the Hall of Fame ballot after one year.

Whitaker was a whiz with the glove, which is not as impressive as being a whiz with your bare hands, which can be said about nineteenth century star Bid McPhee. McPhee spent his entire 18-year career entrenched at second base for the Cincinnati Red Stockings/Reds, and he didn't use a glove until very late in his career. He was the definition of sure-handed, leading the league in putouts eight times, assists six times and fielding percentage nine times. His 529 putouts in 1886 remain the major league record and as noted earlier, McPhee is the all-time leader in putouts with 6,552. Generally among the league leaders in steals each season, McPhee scored over 100 runs 10 times and led the league in homers in 1886 and in triples the next year. He retired with 2,258 hits and 1,684 runs, gaining election to the Hall of Fame in 2000—more than a century after his playing career ended.

Tinker to Evers to Chance had such a nice ring to it that three undeserving players found themselves in the Hall of Fame, immortalized together. Johnny Evers was a fine second baseman, as long as you didn't have to play beside him and listen to him jabber incessantly. It's pretty unlikely that another player will make it to the majors weighing 125 pounds, which is what Evers carried around the diamond for 18 years. Evers walked a lot and rarely struck out, and yes, he was adept at turning the double play. He managed to win the 1914 MVP Award in the National League while posting a .279 average with one home run and 40 RBI. He did demonstrate his worth by batting .438 in that year's World Series to lead the Boston Braves to the championship. He also won titles with the Cubs in 1907 and 1908, recording nearly identical batting stats in those Series. Evers was elected to the Hall of Fame in 1946, a year before he died.

Ross Barnes posted some ridiculous numbers in the 1870s, batting over .400 his first three seasons in the National Association and then winning the National League's first batting crown with a .429 average in 1876. He led his league in runs and hits four times, and finished first in average, slugging and doubles three times. His career average of .360 would rank second all-time if the stats from his five seasons in the National Association counted (they don't officially). Barnes was one of the players who became adept at fair-foul hits, bunting the ball so that it landed in fair territory before rolling foul (until the rule was later changed). Slowed by illness in 1877, Barnes never regained his form and was out of the game for good at age 31 in 1881. Barnes wins the prize as the best second baseman of the 1870s.

Moving on to third base, we find an accomplished quintet of nineteenth century players, two Hall of Famers whose careers bridged the nineteenth and twentieth centuries, two Deadball Era stars named Heinie, a player unfairly denied the Rookie of the Year Award, a converted outfielder who was the highest-paid player in baseball for a few years and a Brooklyn boy who was perhaps the best ever at drawing walks.

Jimmy Collins is the only New York third baseman in the Hall as a player. The agile Collins revolutionized the way third base is played, refining a method of charging bunts and making bare-handed throws to first that is still in use today. He also gave the upstart American League credibility after jumping to the Boston Americans in 1901 and serving as player-manager for six largely successful seasons.

Although he used his glove like a weapon, the classy and respected Collins was also a productive clutch hitter who batted .346 with 132 RBI in 1897 and then led the NL with 15 home runs the next season as the Boston Beaneaters won back-to-back pennants. He averaged .332 and .322 his first two years with the Americans, leading the team to a championship in the first World Series in 1903. The next year, Collins guided the team to a first-place finish with a 95–59 record while using only five pitchers on a staff led by Cy Young. He finished with 1,999 hits and was elected to the Hall of Fame in 1945 — two years after his death.

John McGraw was a contemporary of Collins who also jumped to the American League in 1901 before returning to the National League and starting a dynasty with the New York Giants. Lauded for his innovative and demanding approach as a manager, McGraw possessed a ruthless competitiveness that carried over from his playing days. Always looking for an edge, "Little Napoleon" is credited with developing the hit-and-run, the Baltimore Chop and the squeeze play, as well as perfecting the art of on-field retaliation and dirty play.

In the seven seasons in which he had over 300 at-bats McGraw recorded on-base percentages of .454, .451, .459, .471, .475, .547 and .505. His .466 career OBP ranks third all-time and his .334 average ranks 25th. McGraw collected 124 walks and scored an amazing 140 runs while batting .391 in just 117 games in 1899.

Heinie Groh was one of the top third basemen in baseball as the Deadball Era came to a close, posting an OPS+ over 120 every year from 1914 to 1921. Using a bottle bat (which looked like an elongated milk bottle with a thin handle) to great effect, Groh was a contact hitter whose numbers were suppressed by playing in a pitcher's park. In 1917 he led the league in hits, doubles and OBP; in 1918 he led in doubles, runs and OBP. He batted .474 during the 1922 World Series to help the Giants win the championship and also played on the Reds team that won the infamous 1919 Series over the White Sox. Groh was a terrific fielder who set records in 1924 that have not been matched in the National League since — a .983 fielding percentage and just seven errors.

Eddie Yost was known as "The Walking Man" due to his remarkable ability to draw walks. The Brooklyn native ranks 11th all-time with 1,614 walks, but most of the players ahead of him were frequently pitched around because they were sluggers (except Joe Morgan and Rickey Henderson). Yost led the league in walks six times, recording eight seasons with over 100 walks. He drew a walk once every 5.68 plate appearances and in 1956 came close to having more walks than games played — 151 walks in 152 games. He finished with a .394 OBP despite a .254 batting average. Although he led the league in putouts eight times, defensive metrics show Yost was a below-average fielder.

Deacon White, Ezra Sutton, Jerry Denny and Bob Ferguson were all nineteenth century standouts at third, with White the most accomplished. White was one of the first true superstars of the game, winning two batting titles and leading the league in RBI three times over a 20-year career that ended with 2,067 hits, a .312 average and 127 OPS+. White played primarily at catcher his first eight seasons — catching bare-handed — and didn't become a third baseman until age 34, quickly accumulating more games at that position as the seasons grew longer. He was reportedly the first catcher to move up close to the batter and is generally considered the greatest catcher of the nineteenth century.

A lifetime .294 batter, Sutton led the NL in hits in 1884 while batting .346. He led the league in fielding percentage three times. Denny was like McPhee in that he resisted using a glove yet still led NL second sackers in putouts three times and fielding percentage twice. He batted .324 in 1887 and knocked in 112 runs with 18 homers in 1889. Ferguson picked up one of the all-time cool nicknames — "Death to Flying Things" — for his skill at securing high pop-ups. Ferguson, who is believed to be the first switch-hitter, batted .351 and led the NL in OBP in 1878. He played 397 games at third and 353 at second over 14 seasons.

In 1912 Heinie Zimmerman led the NL in average (.372), hits (207), doubles (41), homers (14), slugging (.571), OPS (.989), OPS+ (169) and total bases (318) — he was three RBI short of winning the Triple Crown, although at the time it was believed he finished first in that category, too. He later led the league in RBI twice and was a career .295 hitter. The "Great Zim" was dim-witted, erratic and impressionable, but his biggest mistake was hanging around with incorrigible cheater Hal Chase. Zimmerman was ridiculed for batting .120 with three errors as the Giants lost the 1917 World Series and then got booted off the team in 1919 after cheating allegations surfaced. He reportedly had a hand in fixing the 1919 Series but was already banned from baseball by then and nothing was ever proven.

Frank Malzone batted .292 with 15 homers, 103 RBI and 185 hits in 634 at bats for the Red Sox as a 27-year-old rookie in 1957. Tony Kubek of the Yankees was also in his rookie season, and he batted .297 with three homers, 39 RBI and 128 hits in 431 at-bats. Kubek received 23 of the 24 first-place votes and was named AL Rookie of the Year. The writers thumbed their noses at Malzone because he had played 33 games with 136 at-bats in the majors the two previous years, but the end result was that standards for at-bats and innings pitched were put into place for the first time. Malzone was a solid all-around player who went on to make six All-Star teams and win three Gold Gloves.

Bobby Bonilla was a six-time All-Star who played slightly more games at third than in the outfield. He accumulated 2,010 hits, 287 homers and 1,173 RBI with a 124 OPS+. Bonilla posted four seasons with over 100 RBI and finished second in MVP voting after clubbing 32 homers and driving in 120 runs in 1990. He signed a lucrative free-agent contract with the Mets in 1992 that made him the highest-paid player in baseball for a short time. Bobby-Bo is one of the few players to hit a home run into the upper deck at Three Rivers Stadium.

Sometime in the near future, most likely during the 2013 season, Alex Rodriquez will play his 1,273rd game at third base. At that point, he will switch from being the All-Time New York shortstop to the All-Time New York third baseman. Maybe he should be honored with both spots — after all, no shortstop has hit more than his 57 homers in 2002 and no third baseman can top his 52 homers in 2007. He was the first Yankees right-handed batter to hit 50 homers.

For now, the slugger known as A-Rod is a better choice than George Davis, Phil Rizzuto or Bill Dahlen at shortstop. Davis and Rizzuto are enshrined in Cooperstown already and Dahlen probably should be, while A-Rod may find himself shut out of the Hall unless prevailing opinions about steroids change. Enough voters may decide his numbers still look impressive even if you chop off an arbitrary 20–25 percent for his "performance-enhancing" misdeeds.

Through the 2010 season Rodriquez had a remarkable streak going of 13 straight seasons with at least 30 homers and 100 RBI, a streak that ended after an injury-plagued 2011. No one else can match that, although Jimmie Foxx posted 13 straight years with 100 RBI along with over 30 homers the first 12 years before falling short with 19 homers. It took clutch hitting for A-Rod to keep the streak going in 2009 and 2010. He needed two homers and seven RBI in the last game of the season in 2009, so that's exactly what he delivered. In 2010 he hit his 30th homer in game number 159. He also put together a string of 13 consecutive seasons with at least 100 runs scored, which was snapped in 2009.

The three-time MVP wasn't the first shortstop to exhibit power and speed, but he is the only infielder to join the exclusive 40–40 club (along with Jose Canseco, Barry Bonds and Alfonso Soriano). Cal Ripken revolutionized the shortstop position as a spot for power, but his career high was 34 homers. If A-Rod manages to keep playing to the end of his contract in 2017, even with a marked decline in production it's possible he will retire as the all-time leader in runs, homers and RBI. Of course, he has also signed the two largest contracts in baseball history and will probably hold the record for career earnings for a while.

George Davis started off as a center fielder and then moved to third base, not becoming a regular shortstop until his eighth season in 1897. That year he finished first with 135 RBI and second with 10 homers. After the mound was moved back in 1893, his average jumped from .241 to .355, the first of nine consecutive seasons over .300. He hit 73 homers over a 20-year career that lasted from 1890 to 1909, which is pretty good for a shortstop from that era. He was a smart and speedy switch-hitter who was adept at hitting for average, stealing bases and fielding the position. Davis led AL shortstops in fielding percentage four times. He ended up with 2,665 hits, 1,440 RBI and 619 stolen bases. Davis was elected to the Hall of Fame in 1998.

If you are looking for the player most similar to George Davis, it would be Bill Dahlen, who joined the majors one year after Davis and played one season longer. Dahlen scored 45 more runs and hit nine more homers than Davis but trails by wider margins in hits, RBI, average and OPS+. He finished with 2,461 hits, 548 stolen bases and a .272 average. John McGraw had tried to bring Davis over to be his shortstop on the Giants in 1903 and when that wasn't allowed, the Giants traded for Dahlen, who led the NL with 80 RBI his first season.

Nicknamed "Bad Bill" because he was prone to outbursts of anger, Dahlen set a record with a 42-game hitting streak in 1894, which was surpassed by Willie Keeler in 1897 and ranks fourth-best in history today. Considered to be one of the best defensive shortstops ever for his combination of range, hands and arm, Dahlen ranks second in putouts and fourth in assists. His 84 home runs trailed only Herman Long among shortstops when he retired in 1911. When Casey Stengel broke into the majors in 1912 with the Brooklyn Dodgers, Dahlen was his manager — the team finished 58–95 that year and Dahlen would last just one more season as manager.

Phil Rizzuto will always be one of the most controversial selections to the Hall of Fame. Bill James devotes considerable attention to Rizzuto's Hall qualifications in his book *The Politics of Glory*. "Scooter" was the sparkplug for nine pennant winners and seven World Series champions for the Yankees, making five All-Star teams while missing three full seasons to the war. He had great range to compensate for a weak arm, and he was an expert bunter and a speedy base runner. Rizzuto was named AL MVP in 1950 after hitting .324 with 200 hits and 125 runs and leading the league with 19 sacrifice hits. He had been MVP runner-up the year before with fairly pedestrian numbers. Scooter ended up with an OPS+ of 93 and posted just three seasons with an OPS+ over 100.

"I'll take any way to get into the Hall of Fame. If they want a batboy, I'll go in as a batboy," said Rizzuto, who was released by the Yankees on Old Timer's Day in 1956. Thanks in no small part to George Steinbrenner lobbying on his behalf, combined with Rizzuto's popularity as a broadcaster, Scooter was finally elected to the Hall of Fame in 1994.

George Wright, Davy Force and Dickey Pearce were all accomplished shortstops in baseball's early days. Wright was a world-class cricket player who took up baseball in 1863 and became a two-way star on the 1869 Cincinnati Red Stockings, baseball's first all-professional team. His ability to field, bat and run at a high level really showed others how the game could be played. The Boston Beaneaters won four straight National Association pennants from 1872–75 with Wright at short and his brother Harry as manager and center fielder, Deacon White at catcher and Ross Barnes at second. Wright batted .301 over 12 seasons in the National Association and National League and was elected to the Hall of Fame in 1937 as a pioneer/executive. Brother

Harry, who was born in England, joined him in the Hall in 1953.

Force, all of 5-foot-4 and 130 pounds, was considered the best shortstop of the 1870s after Wright. He jumped from team to team in the National Association before settling down with the Buffalo Bisons in the National League. He played for 10 teams in 15 seasons and it was a dispute over his contracts with two teams that directly led to the end of the National Association and the formation of the National League. Force batted .335 during his five seasons in the National Association and .211 over 10 National League seasons, which gives credence to the belief the National Association was not good enough to be considered a major league. Force played short and second on the talented Buffalo teams of the 1880s that included the Big Four — Dan Brouthers, Deacon White, Hardy Richardson and Jack Rowe — along with Pud Galvin and Jim O'Rourke.

Dickey Pearce was playing baseball long before the professional leagues started up in 1871, so his career stats don't truly reflect his accomplishments on the diamond. Although he is often credited as the inventor of the bunt, it is believed that Tom Barlow developed the fair-foul hit and that his teammate Pearce then perfected it. Pearce is also credited with revolutionizing where the shortstop played on the field, setting up on the infield rather than as a roving shallow outfielder.

The outfield for the All-Time New York team is filled by Hall of Famers: Carl Yastrzemski, Willie Keeler and King Kelly. A half-dozen other players such as Ken Singleton, George Burns, Rocky Colavito and Tommy Leach also received strong consideration, while the list of honorable mentions is filled with additional names from every era.

Yaz didn't have it easy replacing a legend (Ted Williams) as Boston's left fielder. Despite six years of stellar play that included three All-Star selections, two Gold Gloves and a batting title, Yaz wasn't exactly feeling the love from the Fenway Faithful. That changed once he single-handedly led the team to the World Series while winning the Triple Crown in 1967, and those same fans began worshiping the ground he walked on and naming their first-born children after him.

As that magical 1967 season wound down, it was Yaz who kept delivering in the clutch. He hit safely in each of the last 10 games, batting .541 with four homers and 14 RBI as the Red Sox won the pennant by one game over the Tigers and Twins. He went 7-for-8 with six RBI in the final two decisive games against the Twins. Not only did he become the last American League player to win the Triple Crown that year, he also led the league in hits, runs, OBP, slugging, OPS, OPS+ and total bases while winning the MVP Award and his third Gold Glove. Although the Sox fell short in the 1967 World Series, Yaz batted .400.

In addition to becoming the first American League player to get 3,000 hits and 400 home runs, Yaz remains the AL leader in games played with 3,308 (second all-time to Pete Rose). He ranks sixth in walks and eighth in doubles, total bases and hits. During his Hall of Fame acceptance speech in 1989, Yaz said, "And if there is any message I can leave on the great day of tradition and honor, let it be this: That the race doesn't always belong to the swift nor the battle to the strong. It belongs rather to those who run the race, who stay the course and who fight the good fight."

It's hard to overlook the numbers produced by "Wee Willie" Keeler, who learned to execute McGraw's "Baltimore Chop" to perfection. The 5-foot-4 Keeler was a pesky leadoff batter who topped 200 hits and 100 runs in eight straight seasons. He batted over .300 his first 15 seasons and finished with a .341 average, which ranks fourteenth on the all-time list. Keeler is the only player in major league history to compile eight hitting streaks of 20 or more games, which stands in contrast to Yaz, who was constantly tinkering with his batting stance and never had a hit streak go past 15 games. After a 19-year career of "hitting them where they ain't," Keeler was elected to the Hall of Fame in 1939.

It's too bad that Twitter didn't exist back when Mike

Mike "King" Kelly is widely acknowledged as baseball's first superstar — in fact, one of America's first celebrities — a great showman on and off the field who helped turn the game into America's national pastime with his unmatched popularity in the 1880s. His skillful base running led to one of America's first pop songs titled "Slide, Kelly, Slide," and his popularity is said to have created the whole craze of hounding players for autographs (Library of Congress, Prints & Photographs Division, LC-DIG-bbc-0554f).

"King" Kelly was tearing up the league, because no one would have had more followers. Kelly is widely acknowledged as baseball's first superstar — in fact, one of America's first celebrities — a great showman on and off the field who helped turn the game into America's national pastime. He was given his start in professional baseball in 1877 by "The Old Woman in the Red Cap," Charlie Pabor, who managed him briefly on the Columbus Buckeyes. Kelly certainly deserves his spot in the Hall of Fame, since he was the first player to achieve "fame" in the game. The "King of Baseball" died of pneumonia at 36 in 1894, a month after he had ended his final year of professional baseball with the Allentown Kelly's Killers in the Pennsylvania State League.

King Kelly's teams won eight pennants during his 16 years in the majors, with Kelly winning two batting titles and leading the league in runs three times. He excelled at base running and defense and spent more than a token amount of time at all nine positions during his career, throwing out 46 percent of base stealers while catching 583 games. He finished with a .308 average and a 138 OPS+ and was elected to the Hall of Fame in 1945. As Marty Appel details in his 1996 biography of the player (*Slide, Kelly, Slide*), Kelly was the first baseball player to sign autographs, the first to write an autobiography and the first to be popularized in song. He made a lot of money and spent even more, leaving an indelible mark on the game.

Bill James ranks Ken Singleton as the eighteenth-best right fielder while ranking King Kelly in the number 32 spot. Singleton was productive and consistent, the type of player every good team could use, but he falls short when stacked up against the contributions King Kelly made to the game. Singleton had a good arm but was a below-average fielder and slow with modest power. The switch-hitter was good at drawing walks and getting on base but made just three All-Star teams in 15 seasons.

Kelly was a deserving inductee to the Hall of Fame, while Singleton failed to garner a single vote in his only year on the ballot. Few players attracted more attention during their careers than Kelly, while Singleton was at the opposite end of the spectrum — you could say he was boring. He was MVP runner-up in 1979 after batting .295 with 35 homers and 111 RBI, but he had matinee-idol looks while King Kelly had a matinee-idol following.

Kelly beats Singleton in the Black-Ink Test 23–1 and in the Gray-Ink Test 221–69, as he was among the league leaders in key batting statistics much more frequently.

Rocky Colavito was one of baseball's top sluggers from the mid 1950s to the mid–1960s. A six-time All-Star, Colavito finished with 374 home runs, 1,159 RBI and a 132 OPS+. Here's how his production from 1956–66 stacks up against five peers who are all in the Hall of Fame:

	HR	RBI		HR	RBI
Aaron	402	1481	F. Robinson	373	1131
Mays	426	1261	Colavito	358	1085
Mantle	375	955	Kaline	247	970

Obviously, the biggest difference is that those players had lots of production beyond those years while that was about it for Colavito. His best season was 1958, when he hit 41 homers, drove in 113 runs, batted .303 and led the league by slugging .620 — he finished third in MVP voting. The next year the popular Indians star led the AL with 42 homers and then found himself traded to Detroit, which greatly upset fans in Cleveland. Colavito finished in the top 10 in home runs nine times and in the top 10 in RBI nine straight years. Although his career average was just .266, Rocky walked a lot without striking out much and he possessed a powerful throwing arm in right field. While playing all 162 games in 1965 he became the first American League outfielder to record a perfect 1.000 fielding percentage.

George Burns played from 1911–25, mainly with the New York Giants. He averaged .287 while accumulating 2,077 hits and 383 stolen bases. He led the NL in runs a record five times (later matched by Rogers Hornsby, Stan Musial and Albert Pujols) and also finished first in walks five times and stolen bases twice. Batting leadoff for three pennant winners with the Giants, "Silent George" helped deliver a championship by batting .333 in the 1921 Series. The speedy 5-foot-7 righty drew attention by taking his cuts with a massive 52-oz. bat. His 334 stolen bases with the Giants were a franchise record for more than 50 years until Willie Mays surpassed him by two steals.

Tommy Leach is often labeled as a third baseman, but he played 1,079 games in the outfield compared to 955 at third. A fan favorite during his 14 years with the Pirates, Leach played his entire career in the Deadball Era, collecting 2,143 hits and scoring 1,355 runs but batting just .269. He led the league in triples and homers in 1902 and twice led in runs scored.

Babe Herman was entertaining to watch, whether he was stumbling over bases or having fly balls bounce off his head. Here was his reply to why he reported late to spring training: "I don't do it for the money. The longer I stay away from training camp, the less chance I have of being hit by a fly ball."

Herman's batting was another story. He redefined spectacular in 1930, when he managed to finish in the top three in just about every offensive category without finishing first in anything. He finished second in average (.393), OBP (.455), OPS (1.132), OPS+ (170) and stolen bases (18), ranked third in hits (241), doubles (48), slugging (.678) and total bases (416) and fifth in homers (35) and runs (143). That was the year Hack Wilson hit 56 homers with a record 191 RBI and Bill Terry batted .401. In 1929 Herman batted .381 with 21 homers, 113 RBI and 217 hits.

Herman's career adjusted OPS of 141 and lifetime average of .324 demonstrate the type of talent he possessed. He also ended up playing 13 seasons in the minors, hitting over .300 each year and finishing with 1,545 hits and a .333 average in the minors. Herman ended up compiling 3,363 hits in professional baseball — just 99 less than Willie Mays.

Deciding on the designated hitter for the All-Time

New York team is a no-brainer—who else but Edgar Martinez? He was a clutch hitting machine, who ended up playing roughly two-thirds of his games at DH. It was easy to overlook his greatness, because he spent his entire 18-year career in Seattle and never made it to the World Series. Let's explore whether he belongs in the Hall of Fame.

His career slash line —.312/.418/.515 — is rarified air. Only 20 players have exceeded the .300/.400/.500 mark in average, OBP and slugging, and Mantle, Mays and Aaron are not on the list. Martinez was a key reason the Mariners won a record 116 games in 2001, posting a .306/.423/.543 line with a 160 OPS+ at the age of 38. His career OPS+ of 147 is better than a host of all-time greats such as Harmon Killebrew, Reggie Jackson and former teammate, Ken Griffey, Jr.

Martinez was a better hitter than Paul Molitor, the only DH in the Hall, who produced a far inferior OPS+ of 122 but wins points for longevity (he reached 3,000 hits). Martinez was a seven-time All-Star who posted an OPS+ of 150 or better in eight seasons — that's three times more than Griffey. Edgar was outstanding at collecting doubles and walks and driving in runs. His .418 career OBP ranks 22nd all-time. During his career he ranked in the top 10 in OBP 11 times, OPS+ nine times, walks and OPS eight times, batting average seven times, slugging six times and doubles five times. He was among the most feared batters of his generation and other players greatly respected his hitting abilities.

Hall voters seem skeptical because his counting stats don't overwhelm — 2,247 hits, 1,261 RBI and 1,219 runs — and they probably hold his DH duties against him. He's hurt by the fact he didn't become a regular until he was 27, but that should be mitigated by the fact he was still putting up great numbers in his late 30s. The reality is that it's not hard to build a case that Martinez is one of the greatest right-handed hitters of all-time, and he belongs in Cooperstown.

Picking the starting pitchers for the All-Time New York team was no easy task, since four righties and three southpaws from the state are enshrined in Cooperstown. Eight New Yorkers have won 200 games including three who surpassed 300 wins.

Let's look at righty starters first. Charley Radbourn, Mickey Welch and Will White (brother of Deacon White) all pitched in the nineteenth century and their careers ended before the mound was moved back in 1893, so their career numbers have to be considered in that context.

There's no disputing "Old Hoss" Radbourn put together one of the most amazing seasons ever in 1884. It was the first year pitchers were allowed to pitch overhand and he took full advantage of the change. Radbourn won 59 games for the Providence Grays that year, which is a record unlikely to be broken. At one point he started 35 out of 37 games, winning 20 in a row and winding up with a 1.38 ERA and 441 strikeouts. He started 73 games (fourth-best all-time), completing all of them while tossing 678⅔ innings — the latter two figures are the second-best marks in history.

To top things off, he went 3–0 as the Grays won the 1884 World Series. Radbourn finished with 309 career wins despite pitching only 11 seasons.

Will White's 1879 season was not only on par with what Radbourn produced five years later, it was actually better in several areas. White registered 75 starts (tied with Pud Galvin for most ever) and completed all 75, which remains the record for complete games. His 680 innings pitched barely edges Radbourn for most ever. White ended up with 229 victories, won 40 games three times and recorded a 2.28 career ERA, which ranks sixteenth.

Welch completed 525 of 549 career starts, posting a 307–210 record for a .594 winning percentage. In 1890 he became the third player to win 300 games — a year later Radbourn became the fourth. Nicknamed "Smiling Mickey" because he had a sunny disposition, Welch was a good hitter who played some in the outfield.

Two other contenders are Waite Hoyt and Orel Hershiser. However, both posted ERAs a little on the high side — Hoyt at 3.59 and Hershiser at 3.48 — and both recorded a career ERA+ of 112, which is good but not great. Hershiser won the NL Cy Young Award in 1988 after going 23–8 with a 2.26 ERA, leading the league in wins, complete games, shutouts and innings. He did not allow a run in his last 59 innings in 1988, which remains the record for consecutive scoreless innings. His remarkable pitching continued in the postseason that year as he pitched shutouts in the NLCS and World Series, going 3–0 and being named World Series MVP as the Dodgers beat the A's for the championship. Of the last 101⅔ innings Hershiser pitched that season, 96 of them were scoreless.

Hoyt had a streak of his own — he pitched 27 innings for the Yankees in the 1921 World Series without giving up an earned run. It ranks as one of the most amazing playoff performances in baseball history, since Hoyt shut down a powerful New York Giants lineup featuring Frankie Frisch, High Pockets Kelly, Dave Bancroft and Ross Youngs. However, he did give up an unearned run in Game 8 and ended up losing that game 1–0. Hoyt was a mainstay on Yankee teams that won six pennants and three championships in the 1920s, winning 22 games for the powerhouse '27 squad. He ended up pitching for seven teams during his 21-year career — no small feat considering there were only 16 teams in baseball then — but his 9.7 H/9IP ratio is quite high for a Hall of Famer.

That leaves Jim Palmer, who was the best pitcher in baseball during the 1970s, leading all pitchers that decade in wins (186), shutouts (44) and ERA (2.58). He won 20 games eight times between 1970 and 1978 — only Walter Johnson (with nine) has recorded more 20-win seasons in the American League. Palmer won three Cy Young Awards and finished in the top five in voting five other seasons. He retired with a 268–152 record, which translates to a .638 winning percentage. His 53 career shutouts rank sixteenth and he ended up with a splendid 2.86 ERA and ERA+ of 126. Palmer could be arrogant, condescending and self-absorbed, and he annoyed the crap out of his manager, Earl Weaver. He was also an outstanding pitcher and is a deserving choice for New York's all-time righty.

Deciding on the lefty starter is a little more challenging, since the candidates include Warren Spahn, Sandy Koufax and Whitey Ford.

The Brooklyn-born Koufax, who got to pitch his first three seasons for the hometown Dodgers before they moved to LA, pitched just 12 seasons and his record after six seasons was 36–40 with a 4.10 ERA. His reputation as an all-time great pitcher really comes from the six seasons between 1961 and 1966. He led the league in strikeouts in 1961 but also posted a 3.52 ERA while setting a career high with 18 wins — it was a good but not great year. Then the Dodgers moved into a new stadium and Koufax evolved from a good pitcher into a brilliant pitcher. He led the league in ERA the next five seasons, winning three Cy Young Awards and an MVP Award along the way. "I became a good pitcher when I stopped trying to make them miss the ball and started trying to make them hit it," he explained.

Living up to his nickname, "The Left Arm of God," Koufax threw four no-hitters including a perfect game against the Cubs in 1965. His 382 strikeouts in 1965 remain the modern era record for the National League. Working on two days' rest, he shut out the Minnesota Twins on three hits in Game 7 of the 1965 Series, making up for refusing to pitch Game 1 because it fell on Yom Kippur. In four trips to the World Series, Koufax recorded an ERA of 0.95, which is the best in history (minimum 35 innings). In 1965 he posted 5.8 H/9IP and 10.2 K/9IP to go with a 0.855 WHIP. Bothered by arthritis in his elbow, Koufax walked away from the game at age 30. In his last season he won the Cy Young Award with a 27–9 record, 1.73 ERA, 190 ERA+ and 317 strikeouts. At age 36 in 1972 he joined Gehrig as the youngest players elected to the Hall of Fame.

It's tempting to dismiss Ford as a pitcher not in the same class as Spahn and Koufax, but a closer look at his record reveals it's not cut and dry. Ford won 71 more games than Koufax and recorded a better winning percentage, lower ERA and higher ERA+ than Koufax or Spahn.

Whitey gained a reputation as a big-game pitcher by appearing in 11 World Series and winning six rings. He pitched shutouts in his two appearances in the 1960 Series and then was named MVP of the 1961 Series after going 2–0 without allowing any runs. He had a record streak of 33 consecutive scoreless innings in Series play and still holds the record for most games started (22), innings pitched (146), strikeouts (94) and wins (10) in World Series history.

Ford won the 1961 Cy Young Award after going 25–4. His .690 career winning percentage ranks fourth all-time and his adjusted ERA of 133 is better than all the other top New York pitchers. After going 9–1 as a rookie in 1950, Ford missed the next two seasons while serving in the Korean War. "The Chairman of the Board" led the AL in wins and won-loss percentage three times, and in ERA, shutouts and innings twice. The highest ERA he recorded in his 16 seasons with the Yankees was 3.24 in 1965 and he never had a losing record until his final two seasons as a part-time pitcher. As his career went on, the crafty Ford became adept at doctoring the ball, using various methods to throw a spitball, mudball and scuff ball.

Koufax was great for a short period and Ford was pretty good for a long period, but Spahn was outstanding for an incredibly long period despite not getting his first win until the age of 25. He missed what would have been his first three seasons while serving his country in World War II yet still managed to win 363 games, the most of any southpaw pitcher ever. It seems probable that he would have won more than 400 games if not for the missed time. He was fond of saying, "Hitting is timing. Pitching is upsetting timing."

Spahn proved to be very good at upsetting batters' timing, winning 20 games 13 times, which is tied with Christy Mathewson for second-most in history. He led the league in wins eight times, complete games nine times, and in shutouts, innings, WHIP and strikeouts four times each while pitching almost his entire career with the Boston/Milwaukee Braves. His 63 shutouts are tied with Eddie Plank for the most all-time by a lefty (if Plank's six shutouts in the Federal League are not counted).

Spahn's only subpar seasons came at the ages of 43 and 44 — he won 23 games at age 42. He pitched his first no-hitter at age 39 and came back and hurled another one the next year. Not only did he win the 1957 Cy Young Award, he finished in the top three in Cy Young voting five times in six years. The Buffalo native was a pretty good hitter, too, and was frequently used as a pinch hitter, batting just .194 but compiling 35 career home runs.

A number of other New York-born pitchers played pivotal roles in the postseason for New York teams including Johnny Podres, Johnny Antonelli, Sal Maglie, Eddie Lopat and Ralph Branca.

Podres spent 13 years with the Dodgers (four in Brooklyn), winning three World Series titles and recording a 2.11 ERA in Series play. He pitched a shutout to win Game 7 of the 1955 World Series, ending up 2–0 and being named the first Series MVP. Antonelli won 21 games for the New York Giants in 1954, also finishing first in shutouts, ERA and winning percentage that year while leading the Giants to the championship. Joining Antonelli in the 1954 rotation was Maglie, who pitched seven seasons for the Giants and two each with the Yankees and Brooklyn Dodgers. Nicknamed "The Barber," Maglie led the NL in ERA, shutouts, ERA+ and winning percentage in 1950 and in wins and ERA+ in 1951. He is perhaps best remembered as the losing pitcher when Don Larsen tossed a perfect game in the 1956 World Series — Maglie gave up just five hits and two runs that game.

"Steady Eddie" Lopat pitched eight of his 12 seasons with the Yankees, producing a 166–112 career record with a 3.21 ERA. He won five straight championships with the Bronx Bombers between 1949 and 1953, posting his only 20-win season in 1951. Branca gained ever-lasting fame after serving up Bobby Thomson's "Shot Heard 'Round the World" to lose the pennant for the Dodgers in 1951. Branca debuted with the Dodgers at 18, joined the rotation at 19 and made the first of three straight All-Star teams after winning 21 games at age 21.

Team New York's bullpen is in the capable hands of Brooklyn boy John Franco, who spent 14 of his 21 seasons toiling in New York for the Mets. He was durable, consistent and dependable more than dominant. He was able to stay in the game until he was almost 45, retiring with 426 saves, which ranks fourth in baseball history and first among lefties. Franco also ranks third with 1,119 appearances and fourth with 774 games finished. He led the league in saves three times and posted eight seasons with at least 30 saves. A four-time All-Star, Franco won the NL Rolaids Relief Award in 1988 and 1990. He was quoted as saying, "Closing games in the big leagues is a lot like landing airplanes. A successful effort rarely warrants notice and a failure is considered a full-scale disaster."

Roy Face was one of the premier relievers in baseball from the mid–1950s to the late 1960s. Using a devastating forkball to baffle batters, he led the NL in saves and games finished three times and in appearances twice. He set a major league record for winning percentage (minimum 15 wins) by going 18–1 in 1959, making the first of three straight NL All-Star teams. Adding in victories he garnered to close out 1958, Face put together a streak of 22 straight wins. He finished with 193 career saves.

Face may have been unbeatable in 1959, but it was Don McMahon who led the NL in saves that season with 15. McMahon, who pitched for seven teams over 18 seasons, had seven seasons with double-digit figures in saves and retired in 1974 with 153 career saves and a 2.96 ERA. He won the World Series in his rookie year, 1957, with the Milwaukee Braves and then made his only All-Star team the next year. He won a second championship with the Tigers in 1968.

The term "Fireman" in reference to relief pitchers can be traced back to Johnny Murphy, who picked up the nickname "Fireman" during a relief career that lasted from 1932 to 1947. Murphy led the league in relief wins six times. He appeared in six World Series for the Yankees, winning all six times while recording a 1.10 ERA. He closed out the clinching game of the 1936 World Series.

If you are making a list of one-season wonders, then Jim Konstanty would have to make the list. Everything he touched turned to gold in 1950, as he went 16–7 with a 2.66 ERA out of the bullpen for Philadelphia's "Whiz Kids." Konstanty led the NL with 22 saves, set major league records with 74 appearances and 62 games finished while allowing just 108 hits in 152 innings. He was named league MVP and an All-Star, although the "Whiz Kids" lost in the World Series to the Yankees. He posted 11 saves for the Yankees in 1955, his only other season with double-figure saves.

No New York–born manager can trump the achievements of John McGraw, who wielded an incredible amount of influence over teams, players and leagues across four decades. The intensely competitive McGraw was always in control and his keen eye for talent and innovative style of managing kept the New York Giants in contention throughout his 31 years as the team's skipper. It could be argued that no single person had a greater impact on the game during its first half-century than McGraw.

McGraw posted a .586 winning percentage and his 2,763 victories trail only Connie Mack. He won 10 pennants and three World Series titles and finished second 11 times, which must have really bugged him. Nicknamed "Little Napoleon" for his commanding presence and autocratic style, McGraw was easily enraged when things didn't go his way, which is how he wound up being ejected 131 times including 13 times in 1905. "In playing or managing, the game of ball is only fun for me when I'm out in front and winning. I don't give a hill of beans for the rest of the game," he once said.

McGraw was constantly on the lookout for players who could play his aggressive style of play, and he used whatever means he could to acquire those players. He was a key figure behind the battle for players and power between the more established National League and the upstart American League, clashing repeatedly with American League President Ban Johnson. His stubborn dislike of Johnson caused him to refuse to let the Giants play in the second official World Series in 1904.

His 1905 Giants team was probably his best, featuring three 20-game winners in Christy Mathewson, Joe McGinnity and Red Ames. The offense was a juggernaut, leading the league in runs scored, homers and stolen bases. McGraw won 105 regular-season games that year and then captured his first championship over the Philadelphia Athletics. It would be 16 years before he won a second title in 1921, which was quickly followed with a third the next season. As Mathewson described his former manager: "I have seen McGraw go onto ball fields where he is as welcome as a man with the black smallpox. I have seen him take all sorts of personal chances. He doesn't know what fear is."

Joe Torre's managerial career didn't get off to a good start. In 15 years managing the Mets, Braves and Cardinals, he won just one division title and compiled a record of 894–1003, a .471 winning percentage. "Clueless Joe" is what the New York tabloids dubbed Torre when George Steinbrenner made him the surprising choice as Yankees manager in 1996. At the end of that season Torre and the Yankees were taking a trip down the Canyon of Heroes as World Series champions for the first time since 1978. He would go on to win three straight titles from 1998 to 2000 and guide the Bronx Bombers to the playoffs in all 12 of his seasons before being unceremoniously pushed aside after the 2007 season.

Torre landed on his feet in Los Angeles and led the Dodgers to the playoffs his first two years with the team. Torre won six pennants, four World Series and 13 division titles (including nine straight with the Yankees) and his 2,326 wins as a manager rank fifth all-time.

Another notable manager from New York, Bucky Harris, had the misfortune to spend 29 years managing teams that were for the most part short on talent. Still, he guided the Washington Senators to their first two pennants as well as their only World Series title while serving as a 27-year-old player-manager in 1924. He would win a second championship while skippering the Yankees in 1947. Harris won pennants in his first two years as a manager and won only one more pennant — 22 years later. His teams never finished second and only came in third place twice. Harris was elected to the Hall of Fame as a manager in 1975 despite having a losing record — his record was 2,158–2,219, good for seventh on the all-time win list. He died on his 81st birthday in 1977.

NORTH CAROLINA

*Names in **bold** represent Major League selections by position, followed by honorable mentions. Negro Leagues players are in **bold italics**, followed by honorable mentions in italics. City of birth is in parentheses.*

Catcher — Rick Ferrell (Durham). Also: Smoky Burgess (Caroleen); Mike LaValliere (Charlotte); Jake Early (King's Mountain)

First Base — *Buck Leonard* (Rocky Mount). Also: Mark Grace (Winston-Salem); Whitey Lockman (Lowell); Buck Jordan (Cooleemee)

Second Base — Ray Durham (Charlotte). Also: Johnny Temple (Lexington); Billy Goodman (Concord); Brian Roberts (Durham); Tommy Helms (Charlotte); Jimmy Brown (Jamesville); Brandon Phillips (Raleigh); Burgess Whitehead (Tarboro)

Third Base — Buddy Lewis (Gastonia). Also: Jim Ray Hart (Hookerton); Ryan Zimmerman (Washington); Lew Riggs (Mebane); *Johnny Pugh* (Lewiston)

Shortstop — Luke Appling (High Point). Also: Hal Lanier (Denton)

Outfield — Enos Slaughter (Roxboro)

Outfield — *Charley Jones* (Alamance County)

Outfield — Taffy Wright (Tabor City). Also: Otis Nixon (Columbus County); Chuck Hinton (Rocky Mount); Trot Nixon (Durham); Wes Covington (Laurinburg); Possum Whitted (Durham); Jimmie Hall (Mount Holly); Josh Hamilton (Raleigh)

Right Handed Starter — Gaylord Perry (Williamston). Also: Catfish Hunter (Hertford); Wes Ferrell (Greensboro); Jim Perry (Williamston); *Gentry Jessup* (Mount Airy); *Dave Barnhill* (Greenville); *Laymon Yokely* (Winston-Salem); Lee Meadows (Oxford); Johnny Allen (Lenoir); Alvin Crowder (Winston-Salem); Kevin Millwood (Gastonia); *Chippy Britt* (Kings Mountain); *Lennie Hooker* (Sanford)

Left Handed Starter — Tom Zachary (Graham). Also: Max Lanier (Denton); Rube Benton (Clinton); Mike Caldwell (Tarboro); Cliff Melton (Brevard)

Relief Pitcher — Hoyt Wilhelm (Huntersville). Also: Ted Abernathy (Stanley); Darren Holmes (Asheville); Tom Hall (Thomasville); Sammy Stewart (Asheville)

Manager — Johnny Oates (Sylva). Also: Roger Craig (Durham)

The Names

Best Nickname: Jim "Catfish" Hunter
Other Nicknames: Luke "Old Aches and Pains" Appling; Dave "Impo" and "Skinny Green" Barnhill; Bill "Ding Dong" Bell; George "Chippy" Britt; Forrest "Smoky" Burgess; Alvin "General" Crowder; Alfred "Chubby" Dean; Charles "Whammy" Douglas; Ray "The Sugarman" Durham; Archibald "Moonlight" Graham; Burnalle "Bun" Hayes; Charles "Bunny" Hearn; Frederick "Snake" Henry; Lenial "Elbow" Hooker; Robert "Ham" Hyatt; Gentry "Jeep" Jessup; Charley "Baby" Jones; Mike "Spanky" LaValliere; Ralph "Razor" Ledbetter; Walter "Buck" Leonard; Lee "Specs" Meadow; Cliff "Mountain Music" Melton; Christopher "Trot" Nixon; Gaylord "The Ancient Mariner" Perry; Johnny "Punch" Pugh; Anthony "Razor" Shines; Ernest "Mule" Shirley; Enos "Country" Slaughter; Franklin "Cadillac" Stubbs; James "Shag" Thompson; Herman "Coaker" Triplett; R.T. "Dixie" Upright; Gene "Satchel" Verble; George "Possum" Whitted; William "Mutt" Wilson; Laymon "The Mysterious Shadow" and "Corner Pocket" Yokely; Lemuel "Pep" Young; Henry "Ducky" Yount

Most Unusual Name: Terrmel Sledge; Clyde Kluttz; Herman Fink; Mark Funderburk; Harvey Grubb; Thomas Umphlett

All-Time Leaders

Games: Luke Appling, 2422
Hits: Luke Appling, 2749
Batting Average: Taffy Wright, .311
Home Runs: Ray Durham, 192
RBI: Enos Slaughter, 1304
Stolen Bases: Otis Nixon, 620
Wins: Gaylord Perry, 314
Strikeouts: Gaylord Perry, 3534
Saves: Hoyt Wilhelm, 227
Future Stars: Madison Bumgarner (Hickory); Lonnie Chisenhall (Morehead City); Wil Myers (Thomasville); Jerry Sands (Clayton)
Best Player: Buck Leonard

Historic Baseball Places

Bath Ruth plaque in Fayetteville — Marks the spot of the Babe's first home run as a professional, which took place during an exhibition.

Durham Bulls Athletic Park in Durham gained fame as the main site for the movie *Bull Durham*. The Blue Monster in left field is patterned after Fenway Park's Green Monster, and looming over the wall is a sign of a snorting bull modeled after the one in the movie (courtesy DigitalBallparks.com).

Durham Bulls Athletic Park in Durham — The stadium gained fame as the main site for the movie *Bull Durham*. The Blue Monster in left field is patterned after Fenway Park's Green Monster, and looming over the wall is a huge Bull patterned after the one in the movie, which can be found hanging in the concourse.

McCormick Field in Asheville — Dates back to 1924 but has undergone two extensive renovations. Parts of *Bull Durham* were also filmed at McCormick. The Asheville Blues competed here in the Negro Southern League in the 1940s.

Catfish Hunter gravesite at Cedarwood Cemetery in Hertford — Hunter's monument features a baseball with his signature and the Yankees and A's logos.

Hicks Field in Edenton — Listed on the National Register of Historic Places, Hicks Field dates back to 1930. Bob Feller is among the all-stars who played on the field, which now plays host to a team in the Coastal Plain League.

War Memorial Stadium in Greensboro — Replaced by a new downtown ballpark in 2005, this venerable old park remains in use for college and amateur games. The triple arches of the entrance were briefly featured in the movie *Bull Durham*.

North Carolina Sports Hall of Fame in Raleigh — Dozens of the state's native baseball stars have been inducted including Catfish Hunter, Gaylord Perry and Buck Leonard. The Hall, which is located in the North Carolina Museum of History, opened in 1994.

Notable Achievements

In 1931, pitcher **Wes Ferrell** hit as many home runs (nine) as he gave up that year in 276 innings pitched. In one game that year he hit a home run while pitching a no-hitter. His career total of 38 homers is still a record for players who pitched their entire career.

Pitcher **Hoyt Wilhelm** showed similar promise when he homered in his first game on April 23, 1952. He would never homer again despite pitching in 1,070 games — the fifth-most all-time.

Billy Goodman became the only twentieth century player to lead the league in batting as a utility player. Goodman hit .354 for the Red Sox in 1950 while playing 45 games in the outfield, 27 at third base, 21 at first base, five at second base and one at shortstop. King Kelley accomplished the feat in 1884 and 1886.

Buck Leonard played in 11 All-Star Games in the Negro Leagues, which is tied for the most ever.

Buddy Lewis set an American League record with 15 hits in four consecutive games in July 1937.

Tony Cloninger (Lincoln County) was the first National League player to hit two grand slams in the same game, which he did while pitching for the Atlanta Braves on July 3, 1966. He would hit five home runs that season.

Clive Dudley (Graham) was the first player to hit a home run on the first pitch he saw in the major leagues on April 27, 1929.

Don Cardwell (Winston-Salem) became the first player to pitch a no-hitter in his first game after being traded. He pitched a no-hitter on May 15, 1960 after being traded from the Phillies to the Cubs.

Johnny Allen went 15–1 in 1937 and his .938 winning percentage is the second-highest in baseball history behind Elroy Face (.947 in 1959).

Lee Meadows was the first player in the modern era to wear glasses on the field, beginning in 1915.

Ernie Shore (East Bend) pitched a memorable game for the Boston Red Sox on June 23, 1917. After starter Babe Ruth walked the first batter and was ejected for arguing with the umpire, Shore came on in relief and picked off the runner. He then retired the next 26 batters in order, which goes in the books as a combined no-hitter and not a perfect game.

Luke Appling's .388 average in 1936 is the highest by a shortstop in the twentieth century.

Jim Bibby (Franklinton) no-hit the Oakland A's on July 30, 1973, his first full season in the majors.

The Babe's Legend First Takes Root in North Carolina

He didn't look like much of a ballplayer and he didn't yet have all the nicknames that would always fall short of describing his larger-than-life persona, but even legends have to start somewhere. For 19-year-old George Herman Ruth, the grand adventure began with an invitation to Fayetteville, North Carolina, the spring training home of the Baltimore Orioles (then a minor league team) in 1914.

A plaque in Fayetteville marks the spot where Ruth blasted his first professional home run that spring during an intrasquad game — well beyond the outfield post and into a cornfield 426 feet from home plate. It would be the first of many gargantuan shots that would amaze a generation of fans. Ruth would also pick up his first baseball nickname in Fayetteville — Babe — a commonly used reference to his youthful appearance.

Quite a number of minor league teams have conducted spring training in various North Carolina locations, but even the big league teams occasionally ventured into the state. The Brooklyn Superbas trained in Charlotte in 1901, while the Phillies came to Washington (1902), Southern Pines (1913), Wilmington (1914) and Charlotte (1919). The Philadelphia Athletics held spring workouts in Charlotte in 1902, and the Baltimore Terrapins in the Federal League came to Southern Pines (1914) and Fayetteville (1915).

When the big league teams started migrating to Florida for spring training, it became a common practice for them to stop in the Carolinas on their way back north and play a series of exhibition games. That would be it for major league baseball in North Carolina, although teams such as the Twins and Marlins have explored the possibility of moving to Charlotte within the last two decades.

A North Carolina native helped shape the direction of the Negro Leagues. Gus Greenlee overcame humble roots being born in a log cabin in Marion to become one of the most influential figures in black baseball history. Greenlee bought the Pittsburgh Crawfords in 1931 and quickly set about building a dynasty by acquiring star players such as Josh Gibson, Cool Papa Bell, Oscar Charleston and Satchel Paige. The Crawfords' 1935 championship club is generally regarded as the greatest Negro Leagues team ever. He constructed Greenlee Field, the first black-owned ballpark in the East, was a driving force behind the formation of the new Negro National League in 1933 as well as the popular East-West All-Star game. Greenlee's ongoing involvement in a numbers racket and bootlegging is probably what has kept him out of the Hall of Fame, since he was an unquestioned pioneer.

North Carolina has more wacky baseball player names per capita than any other state. There are so many unfortunate names — Terrmel Sledge, Clyde Kluttz, Herman Fink, Mark Funderburk, Harvey Grubb and Thomas Umphlett rose to the top — that it's necessary to come up with an extensive list of honorable mention candidates. So we bring you Herman Holshouser, Gair Allie, Calvin Koonce, Garland Lawing, Morris Aderholt, Stuart Flythe, Julius Mallonee, Quinton McCracken, Doyt Morris, Dickie Noles, Bronswell Patrick, Thomas Stallcup, Dick Such, John Tsitouris, R T Upright, Kemp Wicker and Lemuel Young.

Even non-baseball fans know the name and can recount the story of Moonlight Graham, the Fayetteville native who was popularized in W.P. Kinsella's Novel *Shoeless Joe* and then Kevin Costner's move *Field of Dreams*. Graham played one game for the New York Giants in 1905, playing in the outfield but never getting to bat. He went on to "go the distance" in the medical field, serving as a small-town doctor in Minnesota for more than 40 years. Ultimately, Graham saw his dream come true, it just happened to be in the medical field and not the baseball field. Back in those days, even being a doctor in a small town was more stable and better paying than being a professional baseball player, so we should salute Moonlight Graham.

Then there's Luke Stuart, who at least got to take one bow. In 1921 Stuart became the first American League player to hit a home run in his first at-bat. His major league career lasted just three games and he never got another hit.

Gastonia native Skipper Friday also didn't have much of a career — he went 0–1 with a 6.90 ERA in seven games — but he did possess a memorable name (His real first name was Grier). Too bad Abbot and Costello didn't find a way to incorporate his name into their famous "Who's On First" routine, because it would have fit on several levels.

A decade or so before Joe Frazier was earning fame and fortune in the boxing ring, another Joe Frazier from Liberty was roaming the outfield for three teams in 1956 alone. North Carolina must be the home of boxers on the diamond, because Mike Tyson also hails from the state—the second baseman for the Cardinals, not the ear-chomping former heavyweight champion. Then we have Brick Smith—yes, Brick is his actual first name and he had the good sense to not become a basketball player.

California has the Boone family and several states can claim the Bell family, but North Carolina can proudly point to the Narron clan. It started with Sam Narron of Middlesex, who caught six games for the Cardinals between 1935 and 1943 but played mainly in the minors. His brother, Milton Narron, played six years in the minors and his nephew, John Narron, also played in the minors. That's not all—another nephew, Jerry Narron, was a catcher in the majors from 1979–1987 and later managed the Rangers and Reds. Finally, Sam Narron's grandson, a Goldsboro native also named Sam Narron, pitched one game for the Rangers in 2004.

All-Time North Carolina Selections

North Carolina can proudly point to the fact that seven of its native sons have been enshrined in Cooperstown: Luke Appling, Gaylord Perry, Buck Leonard, Hoyt Wilhelm, Enos Slaughter, Catfish Hunter and Rick Ferrell.

Let's start with Ferrell, who retired in 1947 having caught the most games in American League history—1,806. He was a pretty good receiver with a strong arm, but if Rufus and Alice Ferrell produced a Hall of Fame player it was more likely Rick's younger brother, Wes.

Rick Ferrell was a contact hitter who walked a lot and didn't strike out much. His best years were 1934–36 with the Red Sox when he batted .297, .301 and .312. His career average was .281 with a respectable .378 OBP.

Just about any statistical analysis of Hall of Fame inductees has Ferrell holding fort at or near the bottom, as evidenced by his pedestrian 206 Career Win Shares. Ferrell's talents can best be described as combining the glove of Brad Ausmus with the bat of Jason Kendall, and that's not a combination that should place one in the rarified air with Bench, Berra and Cochrane.

Actually, it's pretty much a toss-up between Ferrell and Smoky Burgess for North Carolina's top catcher. Both were above-average catchers with good batting averages. As you can see from the comparison below, Burgess has a definite advantage in slugging numbers, while Ferrell scores points for longevity.

	G	H	R	HR	RBI	BA	OBP	SLG	OPS	OPS+
Burgess	1139	1318	485	126	673	.295	.362	.446	.807	116
Ferrell	1806	1692	687	28	734	.281	.378	.363	.741	95

Ferrell was named to eight All-Star teams, although he did not play in the 1944 contest and the 1945 selection was not official due to the war. Burgess was named to six All-Star teams and in 1964 became the only player ever selected an All-Star due to his pinch-hitting prowess. Burgess led the league in fielding three times and has the edge in career fielding percentage, .988 to .984, but Ferrell had to endure two seasons (1944–45) handling knuckleball pitchers nearly every game.

Burgess hit .333 for the Pirates as they won the 1960 World Series, while Ferrell never appeared in the postseason. Burgess was also the catcher for Harvey Haddix when he took a perfect game into the thirteenth inning in 1959. Perhaps the final mitigating factor is that Burgess is perhaps most known for his pinch-hitting abilities—he held the record with 145 career pinch hits when he retired. With the two players nearly equal in abilities, one must look at the body of work and Ferrell wins that examination—10 seasons catching 100 or more games compared to four for Burgess and 667 more games caught in his career. That final point justifies the selection of Ferrell as the starter, with Burgess available for pinch-hitting duties.

First base is in good hands with Hall of Famer Buck Leonard, who got his baseball career started playing at the age of 14 for his hometown Rocky Mount Elks. He went on to play 17 seasons with the Homestead Grays—the most by a Negro League player with one team—winning nine straight titles (1937–45) while teaming up with Josh Gibson to form the most feared lineup tandem in the Negro Leagues. Monte Irvin said, "Buck Leonard was the equal of any first baseman who ever lived. If he'd gotten the chance to play in the Major

Buck Leonard is widely regarded as the best first baseman in Negro Leagues history. He formed a powerful one-two punch with Josh Gibson that propelled the Homestead Grays to nine straight Negro National League championships from 1937 to 1945 (National Baseball Hall of Fame Library, Cooperstown, New York).

Leagues, they might have called Lou Gehrig 'The White Buck Leonard.'"

Not only was he a superb defensive player, Leonard was a clutch, run-producing slugger who crushed fastballs and walked a lot. In 1948, at the age of 40, Leonard led the Negro National League with a .395 average. He batted .343 in league play with 95 home runs. Leonard was even better in action against major leaguers, compiling a .382 average in exhibitions. "You could put a fastball in a shotgun and you couldn't shoot it by him," said Dave Barnhill. Leonard's credentials are strong enough to earn him designation as North Carolina's All-Time Best Player.

During his Induction speech at Cooperstown, Leonard said, "Sometimes we baseball players think our greatest thrill comes from something that we do on the baseball field, but my greatest thrill did not come from a home run that I hit nor a catch that I made or stealing a base. I ought not to have said that maybe, but anyway my greatest thrill came from what somebody did for me, and that was select me for the Baseball Hall of Fame."

Mark Grace falls short of Hall of Fame criteria, but he was an outstanding first baseman. He led the majors in doubles (364) and hits (1,754) during the 1990s, and no other player who led in hits over a decade in the twentieth century has not been inducted into the Hall (besides Pete Rose). Grace made three All-Star teams and won four Gold Gloves but was generally judged as a notch below the superstars such as Mark McGwire and Jeff Bagwell.

Grace did win a World Series with the Diamondbacks in 2001, but his career high was 17 home runs and he never exceeded 100 RBI. First base is supposed to be a power position, and Grace falls short in that regard. Still, he accumulated 2,445 hits, batted over .300 nine times and finished with a .303 average and .383 OBP.

A likable, quotable player throughout his career, Grace offered the following quip after serving up a home run to rookie David Moss while pitching mop-up duty in a blowout loss in 2002: "I didn't have a scouting report on him. Obviously he can hit 65 mph fastballs."

Dick Burrus looked like the second coming of Bill Terry when the first baseman from Hatteras batted .340 with 200 hits and led the league in fielding in his first full season in 1925. Unfortunately, it was a quick downhill slide for Burrus, who never recovered from a hernia and saw his major league career end in 1928 with just 513 hits.

At second base it was a close call between Johnny Temple and Ray Durham. Durham was a capable lead-off hitter who posted 2,054 hits over 14 seasons. He had pretty good power for a little guy (5-foot-8) with 192 home runs, but was even more of a threat because of his speed. Durham stole 273 bases, finishing in the top 10 in steals six times. He made two All-Star teams and had six straight years with more than 100 runs scored. Temple was also a feisty leadoff hitter who batted .284, led the NL in putouts three times and made four All-Star teams. He excelled at the little things, leading the league in walks once and sacrifice hits twice. Durham's power and speed combination edges out Temple.

Three other second basemen from North Carolina deserve to be mentioned. Billy Goodman almost won the MVP award in 1950 while serving as a utility player for the Red Sox. He only played 110 total games that year but led the league in batting (.354) and was fifth in OBP (.427). Goodman made two All-Star teams and finished with 1,691 hits and a .300 career average. Current Orioles player Brian Roberts is a two-time All-Star who has led the league in doubles twice and steals once, stealing 274 bases in his first 11 seasons. His 56 doubles in 2009 set a major league record for a switch-hitter. Tommy Helms won Rookie of the Year in 1966 and was a two-time All-Star and Gold Glove honoree.

Buddy Lewis gets the nod at third base, although Ryan Zimmerman may bypass him in the coming years as he continues to develop as a star. Lewis, who was called up to the majors by the Senators at age 19, was a disciplined line-drive hitter who knew how to get on base. He compiled the second-most career hits in history for a 24-year-old (behind Ty Cobb), but he would lose three years of his prime due to the war. The lefty-swinging Lewis batted over .300 four times, led the league in triples in 1939, made two All-Star teams and retired with a .297 average.

Another third baseman of note is Jim Ray Hart, who burst onto the scene in 1962, clubbing 31 homers for the Giants and finishing second in Rookie of the Year voting. He would hit 139 home runs and average 89 RBI in his first five seasons, making the All-Star team in 1966, but was not a regular after the 1968 season.

Luke Appling was an all-time great at shortstop, one of the few players who seemed to get better as he got older. His career high of eight homers came at age 40 and he played 141 games at shortstop at age 42, batting .301 that year. Appling was a master at fighting off pitches until he could get a pitch to hit, which helped him bat over .300 16 times in 20 seasons.

"Old Aches and Pains" became the first shortstop to lead the league in batting in 1936, with his .388 average the highest posted by a shortstop in the twentieth century. He won another batting title in 1943 and retired with a .310 average and 2,749 hits. Appling didn't strike out much and walked a lot, leading to a .399 OBP.

His defense developed as he matured as a player, and Appling would eventually lead the AL in assists seven consecutive seasons. He retired as the major league leader for games played and double plays by a shortstop, and was first in putouts and assists by an American League shortstop. Appling had the misfortune to spend his career playing for mediocre White Sox teams, never making the postseason. He ranks second all-time in most games played (2,422) without reaching the postseason. The annual postseason drought didn't affect his attitude toward playing. Asked his opinion about competing against the Yankees, he said, "You can't let any team awe you. If you do, you'll wind up a horseshit player."

The All-Time North Carolina outfield is anchored

by Enos "Country" Slaughter, who made the All-Star team 10 consecutive seasons for the Cardinals (not counting the three years he missed for the war). He led the league in triples twice and hits, doubles, total bases and RBI once, finishing with a .300 career average.

An earlier but slightly less frenetic version of Pete Rose's "Charlie Hustle" persona, Slaughter was good at drawing walks, getting on base and finding any way possible to beat the opponent. As he explained, "I never walked on a baseball field from 1938 until I retired. I always left the top step of the dugout running on the field. I played them all to win."

If Slaughter had not missed three prime years during World War II he might have reached 3,000 hits. He was largely a reserve player his last six seasons, during which he picked up two more World Series titles with the Yankees to go with the two he won with St. Louis. He was elected to the Hall of Fame by the Veterans Committee in 1985, a defensible selection.

Flanking Slaughter in the outfield is Charley Jones, a nineteenth-century player who held the career home run record for a handful of years. He led the National League with nine home runs, 62 RBI and 85 runs in 1879 and finished first in the American Association in RBI in 1883. During a game in 1880 he became the first player to hit two home runs in one inning, accounting for 40 percent of his home runs for the season. Jones lost two years of his prime because he was blackballed from the league after a salary dispute, but he managed to collect 1,114 hits with a .298 average for his career.

The third outfield spot came down to two players: Otis Nixon and Taffy Wright. Wright led the AL with a .350 average as a rookie in 1938 but was not recognized as the official batting champion since he only had 263 at-bats. Wright also led the league with 13 pinch hits that season. He batted over .300 his first five seasons and retired with a .311 average. He rarely struck out but had little power or speed. His career lasted just nine seasons because he debuted at 26 and missed three years to the war. Interestingly, Wright started his pro career with five seasons in the minors and ended it with seven more seasons in the minors. He played until he was 45 and wound up with 1,604 hits in the minors.

Nixon was one of the best base stealers in baseball history — he currently ranks sixteenth all-time — but he was strictly a singles hitter. In fact, 87 percent of his career hits were singles, which is tied for the fourth-highest percentage ever, according to Bill James. One can overlook his lack of power (11 home runs), but someone with his speed should have collected significantly more doubles and triples. He collected only 27 triples and 142 doubles in 1,709 games.

He did not become a regular until he was 32 years old, which resulted in another amazing statistic — 83 percent (515) of Nixon's stolen bases came after the age of 30. Rickey Henderson and Lou Brock both stole more bases after 30, but none of baseball's top base stealers can come close to Nixon's percentage of steals after 30. Nixon stole more bases in the 1990s than any other player including Rickey Henderson, and he tied a modern-day record (after 1900) with six stolen bases on June 16, 1991.

Nixon battled drug addiction for much of his career, and missed the 1991 World Series while on drug suspension. Despite Nixon's speed advantage, Wright beats him in the runs created/game metric by 5.7 to 4.2. Wright also holds the edge in slugging (.423 to .314) and a huge advantage in OPS+ (115 to 77). Since Nixon was a one-trick pony who was not able to take advantage of his speed to create many runs for his team, Wright earns the last outfield spot.

When it comes to overcoming obstacles, few have climbed as many hurdles in their career as Josh Hamilton, the former number one pick who nearly threw his life and career away due to drug addiction. He was able to rebound and make a successful comeback with the Reds in 2007, followed by a trade to the Rangers that led to even more success.

Hamilton led the AL in RBI in 2008 while slugging 32 homers, making his first All-Star team in the process. During the All-Star Game festivities, Hamilton put on an awe-inspiring slugging display that delivered a fairy-tale ending to his story, as he clubbed a record 28 home runs in the first round of the Home Run Derby. An even better year followed in 2010 when he won the AL batting crown with a .359 average and won the AL MVP Award. When healthy, Hamilton has positioned himself as one of baseball's biggest threats with the bat.

Another noteworthy North Carolina outfielder with the last name of Nixon is Trot Nixon, whose father, William, served as Catfish Hunter's catcher in high school. Nixon was a dependable right fielder for the Red Sox from 1996–2006, who batted .357 in the 2004 Series.

Speaking of Catfish, he is one of two North Carolina righties who has been enshrined in Cooperstown with the other being Gaylord Perry. Let's start with Perry, whose career numbers are not in dispute but some might object to how he arrived at them. He was an admitted cheater, but evidently folks don't get hot and bothered over pitchers who scuff up balls or put foreign substances on them. It's not like Perry was the only pitcher who ever tried to get an edge through unsanctioned tricks. As Perry wrote in his book, *Me and the Spitter*, "I'd always have (grease) in at least two places, in case the umpires would ask me to wipe off one. I never wanted to be caught out there without anything. It wouldn't be professional."

Just like it is difficult to determine how many extra home runs Mark McGwire hit due to steroids, it is also impossible to gauge how many wins Perry would have had if he kept it clean. Thanks to Perry's shenanigans, a rule was passed that states pitchers cannot go to their mouth while on the mound. At least he didn't take himself too seriously. After announcing his retirement, Perry joked, "The league will be a little drier now, folks."

Perry was a masterful pitcher who used the greaseball as a psychological weapon to keep batters guessing. He won 314 games over 22 seasons and ranks sixth all-time with 5,350 innings pitched. His 3,534 strikeouts are number eight, just ahead of Walter Johnson. He won 20 or more games five times, led the league in innings pitched and complete games twice and made five All-Star teams. Perry won the Cy Young Award in both leagues, winning with the Indians in 1972 and with the Padres in 1978. His Career Win Shares total is 369, which ranks eighth among twentieth-century pitchers who are in the Hall of Fame.

Those numbers, tainted or not, give Perry an advantage over the career marks of Hunter, who was given the nickname "Catfish" because A's owner Charlie Finley wanted his star pitcher to have a country bumpkin appeal. Hunter was an agreeable chap, so he never objected.

Catfish's career highlights were still pretty good: five straight seasons with 20 or more wins, eight All-Star teams, pitched a perfect game, led AL in ERA and won the Cy Young Award in 1974. He also appeared in six World Series, winning five rings. By all accounts, he was one of the nicest guys you could ever meet. Catfish came straight to the majors at the age of 19 without any minor league seasoning, and he was an All-Star by his second season. He made history by capitalizing on a contract breach to become the first free agent of the modern era, agreeing in 1975 to become George Steinbrenner's first big signing with the Yankees.

Here are some of the pitchers who have won more game than Hunter: David Wells, Dennis Martinez, George Mullin and Frank Tanana. No one seems to be clamoring for their induction into the Hall. A total of 203 pitchers rank ahead of him in winning percentage. Hunter is just ahead of Andy Benes and Kevin Appier in the career strikeouts list and his career ERA+ of 104 means Catfish was barely above league average in that important category. The rule of thumb is that pitchers generally need 300 Career Win Shares to be Hall-worthy, and Hunter accumulated 206. Guess it sure helps to have a cool nickname. During his Hall of Fame Induction speech, Catfish thanked his brothers and sisters for teaching him to throw strikes, so he could give up 379 home runs in the big leagues.

Two brothers and two Negro Leagues pitchers also deserve mention as right-handed starters from North Carolina. Gaylord's older brother, Jim, was a pretty accomplished pitcher in his own right. He won 215 games and actually beat his brother to the Cy Young Award, winning the award in 1970 after going 24–12 for the Twins. Rick Ferrell's brother, Wes, is arguable the best-hitting pitcher in history. He batted .280 and hit 10 more home runs than his brother despite 4,852 fewer at-bats. Although he had a relatively high ERA (4.04) and gave up a lot of hits, Wes won 20 or more games six times, retiring with a 193–128 record.

Dave Barnhill was not an intimidating presence on the mound, but he knew how to keep batters off-balance, reportedly by cutting the ball. He got started with a semi-pro team in his hometown of Greenville and then was signed by the Indianapolis Clowns. He was a three-time Negro League All-Star, defeated Satchel Paige in the 1942 All-Star game and led the league in wins with a 15–3 record in 1943. Gentry Jessup was a star pitcher for the Chicago American Giants, appearing in the Negro League All-Star game five straight years, 1944–48 and leading the league in wins and strikeouts in 1945. He was an overpowering pitcher who struggled with his control at times.

As many as five pitchers can stake a claim as the best left-handed starter from North Carolina. Tom Zachary won out literally, as he compiled the most wins, ending up with 186 victories over 19 seasons. He had 11 seasons with double-digit wins and set a record in 1929 that still stands — most wins in a season with no losses, 12. He appeared in three World Series, winning rings with the Washington Senators in 1924 and New York Yankees in 1928.

Zachary had to spend the last 42 years of his life being asked what it felt like to surrender Babe Ruth's 60th home run, which he gave up in 1927. He typically responded by saying, "If you really want to know the truth, I'd rather have thrown at his big, fat head."

Among the southpaw candidates, Max Lanier posted the lowest ERA, best ERA+, best winning percentage and lowest batting average against. The two-time All-Star lost the 1945 year to war service as well as two seasons (1947–48) while under suspension for jumping to the Mexican League. Although Lanier was more dominant during his short career, it's hard to overlook the fact that Zachary won 78 more games so his longevity wins out.

Mike Caldwell and Cliff Melton were the only 20-game winners among the southpaw contenders, and Caldwell also finished second in the 1978 Cy Young Award voting after winning 22 games with a 2.36 ERA for the Brewers. Melton, who was nicknamed "Mickey Mouse" due to his big ears, set a NL rookie record with 13 strikeouts in his debut game in 1937. Rube Benton won 150 games, recording five seasons with at least 15 wins. In 1912, his first full year, he pitched 302 innings for the Cincinnati Reds and won 18 games while leading the league with 50 games and 39 games started.

Considering he didn't make it to the majors until he was nearly 30, Hoyt Wilhelm carved out a pretty remarkable career. We may never again see a great knuckleball reliever, because most managers would not entrust the game's outcome to such an unpredictable pitch.

Wilhelm bounced around the minors for a decade before showing up in the majors in 1952 with low expectations. Considering he had been wounded in the Battle of the Bulge during World War II, for which he received a Purple Heart, Wilhelm was just glad to be alive and playing baseball. All he did his rookie year was go 15–3 and lead the league in winning percentage, appearances and ERA (2.43). He was an All-Star his second season and then went 12–4 in 1954 before seeming to lose momentum.

He got his first taste of starting in 1958, with mixed results except for September 20, when he no-hit the Yankees. Everything seemed to click for Wilhelm in 1959 as he won 15 games, again led the league in ERA (2.19) and pitched a career-high 226 innings. Who knew he was just getting started and would pitch 13 more seasons for a total of nine teams?

As Peter Baida writes in *Cult Baseball Players:* "Hoyt threw the knuckler on perhaps forty-eight out of every fifty pitches. It was a beautiful knuckler: it might dive, soar, flutter, float, skid, speed up, slow down — sometimes it even seemed to stop and head back toward Hoyt, then resume its sixty-foot journey toward home plate. No one, *no one*, knew what the ball would do once Hoyt let it go."

Wilhelm only accumulated 31 official saves and never led the league in that category (even if you go back and artificially count them up in the years before 1969), but then again he wasn't the prototypical closer. By the time "Old Sarge" finally hung up his spikes two weeks before his 50th birthday, he had set records for most games pitched (1,070), most relief appearances (1,018), most relief innings (1,870) and most relief wins (124). He ranks eighth all-time in hits per 9 innings (7.01). In 1985 he became the first relief pitcher inducted into the Hall of Fame, which is pretty good for a player with 31 saves. Even more noteworthy is the fact that he has the lowest career ERA (2.52) of any pitcher since the end of World War II. That was enough to earn Wilhelm strong consideration for North Carolina's All-Time Best Player, but not quite enough to beat out Buck Leonard.

Another relief pitcher worth noting is Ted Abernathy, the one born in Stanley and not to be confused with the relief pitcher named Ted Abernathy who was born in Bynum, N.C., and only pitched in seven games. The noteworthy Abernathy pitched for seven teams over 14 seasons but never appeared in the postseason. He developed a submarine pitching style after an arm injury, going on to lead the National League in games three times and games finished twice. In 1965 with the Cubs he appeared in a league-high 84 games totaling 136 innings and recorded a 2.57 ERA, then came back with the Reds and in 1967 posted a 1.27 ERA in 70 games, allowing just 63 hits in 106 innings. Abernathy was a two-time winner of *The Sporting News'* "Reliever of the Year."

It was another close call to select the manager for Team North Carolina. Roger Craig gained notoriety as a pitching coach who taught his pupils the split-fingered fastball, but he also spent 10 years as a manager with the Padres and Giants. He was essentially a .500 skipper at 738–737, although he guided the Giants to the NL pennant in 1989, before getting swept by the A's in the World Series.

Johnny Oates has a slight edge over Craig at manager. Oates won three division titles with the Rangers and was named AL Manager of the Year in 1996. Although he never won the pennant, his 797–746 record is slightly better than Craig's mark so he gets selected. Craig would make a wonderful pitching coach for the All-Time North Carolina team.

NORTH DAKOTA

*Names in **bold** represent Major League selections by position, followed by honorable mentions. City of birth is in parentheses.*

Catcher — Chris Coste (Fargo). Also: Truck Hannah (Larimore)
First Base — Travis Hafner (Jamestown)
Second Base — Tim Johnson (Grand Forks)
Third Base — Tim Olson (Grand Forks)
Shortstop — Tim Johnson (Grand Forks)
Outfield — Darin Erstad (Jamestown)
Outfield — Ken Hunt (Grand Forks)
Outfield — Lynn Nelson (Sheldon)
Designated Hitter — Travis Hafner (Jamestown)
Right Handed Starter — Rick Helling (Devils Lake). Also: Gary Serum (Fargo)
Left Handed Starter-None
Relief Pitcher — Mark Lee (Williston). Also: Lynn Nelson (Sheldon); Floyd Stromme (Cooperstown); Sid Peterson (Havelock); Frank Brosseau (Drayton); Red Hardy (Marmarth)
Manager — Tim Johnson (Grand Forks)

The Names

Best Nickname: Travis "Pronk" Hafner
Other Nicknames: James "Truck" Hannah; Francis "Red" Hardy; Lynn "Line Drive" Nelson; Floyd "Rock" Stromme
Most Unusual Name: Darin Erstad

All-Time Leaders

Games: Darin Erstad, 1654
Hits: Darin Erstad, 1697
Batting Average: Darin Erstad, .282
Home Runs: Travis Hafner, 189 (still active)
RBI: Darin Erstad, 699
Stolen Bases: Darin Erstad, 179
Wins: Rick Helling, 93
Strikeouts: Rick Helling, 1058
Saves: Mark Lee, 2
Future Star: Kyle Carr (Linton)
Best Player: Darin Erstad

Historic Baseball Places

Roger Maris Museum in Fargo — Opened in 1984 in the West Acres Shopping Center, the museum is free to the public. You can see Maris' 1960 Gold Glove

Award and several of the balls he hit during his record-breaking 1961 season, with pennants hanging down that detail each of the 61 home runs he hit that year. Highlights of his career play in a film loop.

Maury Wills Museum at Newman Outdoor Field in Fargo — Come see the Fargo-Moorhead Redhawks play and you can check out the museum for free. Wills never played in Fargo but did serve as a coach and instructor for two years followed by an ongoing stint as the Redhawks radio analyst. The museum opened in 2001. Roger Maris' number 8 has been retired, since he started his professional baseball career playing for the Fargo-Moorhead Twins in 1953.

Notable Achievements

Rick Helling struck out the side on nine pitches on June 20, 2006 against the Tigers.

Darin Erstad was the punter on Nebraska's 1994 football team that won the National Championship.

Travis Hafner hit six grand slams in 2006 — tying Don Mattingly's all-time mark — with five coming before the All-Star break.

North Dakota Lays Claim to Dream Team and Home Run King

Years before Jackie Robinson broke the color barrier in the major leagues, a semi-pro team in North Dakota proved that not only could white players play alongside black players without incident, they could combine to field a pretty unbeatable team.

Kyle McNary, an expert on North Dakota baseball history, argues that the greatest team in baseball history was the 1935 Bismarck Churchills, which was fully integrated with white players playing alongside stars imported from the Negro Leagues.

Bismarck's pitching staff included five of the greatest pitchers in Negro Leagues history: Satchel Paige, Double Duty Radcliffe, Hilton Smith, Chet Brewer and Barney Morris. Negro Leagues slugger Quincy Trouppe was joined in the lineup by talented white players like Joe Desiderato and Moose Johnson, who hit 25 home runs that season in 192 at-bats.

But it was the "Dream Team" of pitching staffs that had fans packing the stands for every game. Satchel finished 30–2, Radcliffe and Brewer went undefeated and Smith lost just once for Bismarck as it steamrolled all challengers on the way to winning the National Baseball Congress in Wichita. Paige called it the greatest team he ever played on, which is saying something.

North Dakota's role in major league history is a little less grandiose. Truck Hannah was the first North Dakota-born player to make the majors in 1918. He was actually born in the Dakota Territory, five months before North Dakota became a state.

Roger Maris grew up in Grand Forks and Fargo, but he was not born in North Dakota, so he belongs to Minnesota for the purposes of this book. However, Maris is buried in Holy Cross Cemetery in Fargo, with the number 61 carved twice into his gravestone as an eternal reminder of the record 61 home runs he hit in 1961.

Maris' legacy lives on in a museum in Fargo. Opened in 1984 and redone in 2003, the Roger Maris Museum features a replica of Maris' Yankee Stadium monument and his locker from 1961. You can sit in an authentic seat from the old Yankee Stadium and watch video highlights of his career. For the baseball purists who believe Maris is still the rightful holder of the home run record, the museum is a fitting and lasting tribute.

All-Time North Dakota Selections

North Dakota has sent just 15 players to the major leagues and only one was active in 2011: Travis Hafner.

The All-Time North Dakota team's catcher is Coste, and everyone loves the story of the hard-working guy who never gives up on his dream. As he explains, "When I was in the minors, I'd sometimes dream that I was in the big leagues and hitting off Roger Clemens, and it seemed so real that I'd be telling myself that it's not a dream, but then I'd wake up and be back in my bed at Triple-A."

Not only did Coste make it to the majors after toiling for 11 seasons in the minors, he got to play in a World Series game and win a championship with the Phillies in 2008. He has published two books about his baseball experiences: "Hey ... I'm Just a Catcher" and "The 33-Year-Old Rookie."

Coste demonstrated the ability to hit when given a chance, hitting 23 home runs with a .272 average in four seasons of part-time duty for the Phillies and Astros. He compiled 1,153 hits and 98 home runs during his 13-year minor league career, with many coming during four seasons he spent playing for his hometown Fargo-Moorhead RedHawks in an independent league.

Hafner, who played seven seasons in the minors before finally catching on with the Indians for good in 2004, has primarily been a designated hitter during his career since he is not a nimble fielder. We've selected him as the first baseman and the DH for Team North Dakota.

The player known as "Pronk" batted over .300 with more than 100 RBI each season from 2004 to 2006, with his home run total rising from 28 to 42. He even has a candy bar named after him in Cleveland — the Pronk Bar.

Hafner knocked in 100 runs again in 2007 but then missed most of 2008 with injuries. Slowed by a shoulder problem, he played just 94 games in 2009, batting .272 with 16 home runs. His stats were similar in 2010 despite playing 24 more games. His 189 home runs through the 2011 season are the most by a North Dakota player.

Our second baseman is also our shortstop, Tim Johnson, who was a weak-hitting utility player during the 1970s. At third base we have Tim Olson of Grand Forks, who saw limited action for the Diamondbacks in 2004.

Highlighting the outfield is Darin Erstad, who is the all-time North Dakota leader in just about every hitting statistic. Erstad's long and productive career has justified the Angels' decision to select him number one overall in MLB's 1995 amateur draft. He is arguably the most outstanding athlete in North Dakota history, as he also excelled in football, hockey and track while at Jamestown High School.

He is the only North Dakota native to be named an All-Star, making the AL team in 1998 and 2000 while playing for the Angels. He had a season for the ages in 2000, setting career highs with 25 home runs, 100 RBI and a .355 batting average — second-best in the AL. It was the first time a leadoff hitter collected 100 RBI. He also stole 28 bases and led the league with 240 hits, which is tied for the thirteenth-best mark in major league history.

In addition to winning a Silver Slugger that season, Erstad won a Gold Glove for his exceptional defense in left field. It's hard to believe he only placed eighth in the MVP voting that year, but sluggers such as Jason Giambi, Frank Thomas, Alex Rodriquez and Carlos Delgado garnered more attention with their high home run totals.

Erstad won two more Gold Gloves — as a center fielder in 2002 and as a first baseman in 2004. His hard-nosed playing style endeared him to fans but led to a rash of injuries that hampered his playing time. He's an easy choice for North Dakota's All-Time Best Player.

Joining Erstad in the outfield is Ken Hunt, who had 25 home runs and 84 RBI for the Angels in 1961 in his only season as a regular. The third outfielder is a bit of a stretch — Lynn Nelson was a pitcher who played six games in the outfield for the 1937 Philadelphia A's. He was a pretty good batter and adept pinch-hitter — hence the nickname "Line Drive"— and he hit four home runs that season with a .354 average. Nelson was not particularly effective pitching as a starter or out of the bullpen, with a 5.25 ERA in 166 appearances.

Rick Helling is the undisputed ace of the staff. Helling, who graduated from the same high school in Fargo as Roger Maris, played collegiately at Stanford and was a first-round draft pick of the Rangers in 1992. He won a league-best 20 games for a 1998 Rangers that won the AL West Division.

Helling won 61 games for the Rangers between 1998 and 2001, but he always gave up a lot of home runs and had a high ERA. Released by the Orioles in 2003, he hooked on with the right team — the Florida Marlins, who would go on to win the World Series that year. He retired after the 2006 season with a lifetime record of 93–81.

Mark Lee is the only left-handed pitcher in North Dakota history, but his 116 appearances were all in relief so he is the first man in the bullpen. He only pitched in the majors four seasons between 1988 and 1995 but did post an ERA+ of 111. Also, Lee is officially the all-time saves leader for North Dakota with two. Nelson's career ERA+ of 87 demonstrates he was not as effective as Lee.

Floyd Stromme is the answer to a fun trivia question, since he is the only major league player born in Cooperstown ... Cooperstown, North Dakota, that is. Stromme pitched five games in relief for the Indians in 1939.

Tim Johnson is the only manager from North Dakota. He led the Blue Jays to an 88–74 record in 1998, good for third place in the AL East, but was fired during spring training the next year after admitting he fabricated stories about seeing action in the Vietnam War. He continued to manage teams after that in the Mexican League and independent leagues.

OHIO

*Names in **bold** represent Major League selections by position, followed by honorable mentions. Negro Leagues players are in italics. City of birth is in parentheses.*

Catcher — Thurman Munson (Akron). Also: Roger Bresnahan (Toledo); Buck Ewing (Hoaglands); John Roseboro (Ashland); Deacon McGuire (Youngstown); *Chappie Johnson* (Bellaire); Terry Kennedy (Euclid); Johnny Edwards (Columbus); Chief Zimmer (Marietta); Rollie Hemsley (Syracuse); Del Rice (Portsmouth); Mike Matheny (Columbus); Ed McFarland (Cleveland).

First Base — George Sisler (Manchester). Also: Joe Kuhel (Cleveland); Chris Chambliss (Dayton); *Lenny Pearson* (Akron); George Burns (Niles); *Ed Rile* (Columbus); Kevin Youkilis (Cincinnati); John Reilly (Cincinnati); Leon Durham (Cincinnati); *Jelly Taylor* (London).

Second Base — Miller Huggins (Cincinnati). Also: Bill Doran (Cincinnati); *Charlie Grant* (Cincinnati); Jim Delahanty (Cleveland); *Sol White* (Bellaire); Ron Oester (Cincinnati); Frank LaPorte (Uhrichsville); Bill Wambsganss (Cleveland); Johnny Hodapp (Cincinnati); *Nate Harris* (Middleport)

Third Base — Mike Schmidt (Dayton). Also: Sal Bando (Cleveland); Denny Lyons (Cincinnati); Bill Bradley (Cleveland); David Bell (Cincinnati)

Shortstop — Barry Larkin (Cincinnati). Also: *Grant Johnson* (Findlay); Roger Peckinpaugh (Wooster); Woody English (Fredonia); Ed McKean (Grafton); Kid Elberfield (Pomeroy); Sam Wise (Akron); Al Bridwell (Friendship); Ed Brinkman (Cincinnati); Wally Gerber (Columbus)

Outfield — Pete Rose (Cincinnati)

Outfield — Ed Delahanty (Cleveland)
Outfield — Jimmy Wynn (Hamilton). Also: Al Oliver (Portsmouth); Elmer Flick (Bedford); Frank Howard (Columbus); Tommy Henrich (Massillon); Paul O'Neill (Columbus); Dummy Hoy (Houcktown); Topsy Hartsel (Polk): Garry Maddox (Cincinnati); Gene Woodling (Akron); David Justice (Cincinnati); Dode Paskert (Cleveland); Kip Selbach (Columbus); Elmer Smith (Sandusky); Joe Vosmik (Cleveland); Curt Welch (E. Liverpool); Jake Stenzel (Cincinnati); Socks Seybold (Washingtonville); Bennie Kauff (Pomeroy); Larry Hisle (Portsmouth); Shannon Stewart (Cincinnati); Lance Johnson (Cincinnati); Bob Nieman (Cincinnati)

Designated Hitter — Mike Easler (Cleveland). Also: Aubrey Huff (Marion): Pat Tabler (Hamilton)

Right Handed Starter — Cy Young (Gilmore). Also: Roger Clemens (Dayton); Phil Niekro (Blaine); *Ray Brown* (Alger); Urban Shocker (Cleveland); Jesse Haines (Clayton); George Uhle (Cleveland); Sam Jones (Woodsfield); Joe Niekro (Martins Ferry); Sam Leever (Goshen); Charley Root (Middletown); Brickyard Kennedy (Bellaire); Red Ames (Warren); Dean Chance (Plain Township); Jack Taylor (New Straitsville); George Mullin (Toledo); Bob Ewing (New Hampshire); Earl Moore (Pickerington); Sam Jones (Stewartsville); *Porter Moss* (Cincinnati)

Left Handed Starter — Slim Sallee (Higginsport). Also: Rube Marquard (Cleveland); Dutch Leonard (Birmingham); Harvey Haddix (Medway); Joe Nuxhall (Hamilton); Bob Knepper (Akron)

Relief Pitcher — Rollie Fingers (Steubenville). Also: Jeff Montgomery (Wellston); Jeff Shaw (Washington Court House); Jeff Russell (Cincinnati); Kent Tekulve (Cincinnati); Don Elston (Campbellstown); Roger McDowell (Cincinnati); Tom Hume (Cincinnati); Kent Mercker (Dublin); Doug Bair (Defiance); Jack Baldschun (Greenville); Grant Jackson (Fostoria); Jim Brosnan (Cincinnati): Tom Murphy (Cleveland); Dick Drago (Toledo)

Manager — Walter Alston (Venice). Also: Miller Huggins (Cincinnati); Jim Leyland (Perrysburg); *Sol White* (Bellaire); Don Zimmer (Cincinnati); Jim Tracy (Hamilton); Burt Shotton (Brownhelm)

The Names

Best Nickname: Jimmy "Toy Cannon" Wynn
Other Nicknames: Walter "Smokey" Alston; Edward "Goat" Anderson; Earl "One Punch" Averill; Jim "Sarge" Bagby, Jr.; William "Skeeter" Barnes; Amos "Darling" Booth; Roger "The Duke of Tralee" Bresnahan; William "Gates" Brown; "Tioga George" Burns; Dain "Ding-a-Ling" and "Sniffy" Clay; Chester "Squawk" Crist; Roger "The Rocket" Clemens; William "Pickles" Dillhoefer; Edward "Moxie" Divis; Richard "Hummer" Drott; Leon "Bull" Durham; Don "Duffy" Dyer; Mike "Hit Man" Easler; Norman "The Tabasco Kid" Elberfeld; William "Buck" Ewing; Elmer "The Demon of the Stick" Flick; Frank "Inch" Gleich; Charles "Chief Tokahoma" Grant; Don "Buckeye" Grate; Ed "Battleship" Gremminger; Harvey "Kitten" Haddix; George "Old Wax Figger" Hemming; Tommy "Old Reliable" Henrich; Elmer "Herky Jerky" Horton; Frank "Hondo" and "The Capital Punisher" Howard; Miller "The Mighty Mite" Huggins; Roy "Jeep" and "Sage" Hughes; George "Chappie" Johnson; Grant "Home Run" Johnson; Lance "One Dog" Johnson; "Sad Sam" Jones; Sam "Toothpick" Jones; Uriah "Angel Sleeves" Jones; William "Brickyard" Kennedy; Ray "Jockey" Kolp; Sam "The Goshen Schoolmaster" Leever; Johnny "Skids" Lipon; Garry "Secretary of Defense" Maddox; Richard "Rube" Marquard; Jimmy "The Loafer" McAleer; Gene "Stick" Michael; Earl "Crossfire," "Big Ebbie" and "Steam Engine in Boots" Moore; Porter "Ankleball" and "Submarine" Moss; "Wabash George" Mullin; Thurman "Tugboat" Munson; John "Tacks" Neuer; Phil "Knucksie" Niekro; Al "Scoop" Oliver; Paul "Ace" O'Neill; Lenny "Hoss" Pearson; Jack "The Giant Killer" Pfiester; Wally "Cochise" Post; Julius "Icicle" Reeder; Karl "Tuffy" Rhodes; Bob "Buck" Rodgers; "Rawmeat Bill" Rodgers, Charley "Chinski" Root; Pete "Charlie Hustle" Rose; Harry "Slim," "Scatter" and "Scissors" Sallee; Frank "Skeeter" Scalzi; George "Admiral" Schlei; Bill "Blab" Schwartz; Albert "Cheese" Schweitzer; Ralph "Socks" Seybold; Jim "Little Nemo" Stephens; Olan "Jelly" Taylor; Kent "The Book End" Tekulve; George "The Bull" Uhle; John "Podge" Weihe; Ed "Satchelfoot" Wells; Kevin "The Greek God of Walks" Youkilis; Denton "Cy" Young; Charles "Chief" Zimmer; Don "Popeye" Zimmer

Most Unusual Name: Doug Mientkiewicz; Bill Wambsganss

All-Time Leaders

Games: Pete Rose, 3562
Hits: Pete Rose, 4256
Batting Average: Ed Delahanty, .346
Home Runs: Mike Schmidt, 548
RBI: Mike Schmidt, 1595
Stolen Bases: Dummy Hoy, 594
Wins: Cy Young, 511
Strikeouts: Roger Clemens, 4672
Saves: Rollie Fingers, 341
Future Stars: Stetson Allie (Olmsted Falls)
Best Player: Cy Young

Historic Baseball Places

Great American Ball Park in Cincinnati — Opened in 2003 on the banks of the Ohio River. Adjacent to the ballpark is the Cincinnati Reds Hall of Fame and Museum, which includes wonderful interactive features letting fans announce a game or see how fast they can throw a pitch. The exhibits include the Reds Hall of Fame gallery of plaques, life-size bronze figures of the Big Red Machine players, the "Ultimate

The Reds Hall of Fame & Museum highlights the accomplishments of Pete Rose and other members of the Reds franchise, which is the oldest professional team, dating back to the Red Stockings in 1869. You can step in the cage with a radar gun timing how fast your pitches are or try your hand at announcing the play-by-play for a game (photograph by the author).

Reds Room" filled with assorted Reds memorabilia and a tribute to Crosley Field.

Green Diamond Gallery in Montgomery — You must be a member to view the terrific private collection of baseball artifacts and memorabilia dating back to the nineteenth century. The Green Diamond Gallery features game-used bats and jerseys, old stadium seats, historic photos, rare autographs and vintage books and magazines.

Baseball Heritage Museum in Cleveland — Stories, photos, uniforms and memorabilia that tell the story of baseball from the Latin/Caribbean leagues, Women's and Negro Leagues that helped shape the game today. Located in downtown's historic Colonial Marketplace.

Progressive Field in Cleveland — Formerly known as Jacobs Field, the Indians new ballpark opened in 1994 in the middle of downtown. The Indians Hall of Fame is showcased in Heritage Park in center field along with exhibit areas honoring memorable moments in team history and the Top 100 Indians Roster. Outside the park a statue of Bob Feller depicts the fireballer in his windup.

Ray Chapman gravesite at Lakeview Cemetery in Cleveland — The only player to be killed during a major league game has a large headstone that makes no reference to his baseball background. People still drop off balls, bats and other trinkets in his memory.

Thurman Munson gravesite in Canton — The large mausoleum at Sunset Hills Burial Park depicts an image of the Yankees captain with a bat in his hand. A big number 15 is etched in the back of the stone.

Munson's Home Plate Sports Pub in Canton — Thurman Munson's son, Michael, opened up this sports bar in 2008, which serves as a tribute to the famous father who died when he was four. The walls are filled with action shots of Munson.

Notable Achievements

Ned Garver (Ney) is the only pitcher to win 20 games for a team that lost over 100 games. He went 20–12 for the 1951 St. Louis Browns, who finished 52–102.

Mark Lewis (Hamilton) hit the first pinch-hit grand slam in the playoffs on October 6, 1995.

Doug Dascenzo (Cleveland) set a National League record for most errorless games at the start of a career with 242. The outfielder finally committed an error on August 25, 1991.

Karl "Tuffy" Rhodes (Cincinnati) went deep off Dwight Gooden three times on April 4, 1994, becoming the first NL player to homer three times on Opening Day. He finished his career with just 13 home runs.

Tommy Henrich hit the first walk-off home run in World Series history when he homered off Don Newcombe in the bottom of the ninth inning in Game 1 of the 1949 World Series.

David Bell hit for the cycle on June 28, 2004, a feat also accomplished by his grandfather, Gus Bell. That makes them the only grandfather-grandson duo to hit for the cycle.

Rich Reese (Leipsic) is tied for the career lead in pinch-hit grand slam home runs with three.

Earl Moore set a record in 1908 that still stands — most innings pitched in a season without allowing an earned run, with 26.

Charles "Bumpus" Jones (Cedarville) pitched a no-hitter in his first and only game his rookie season, 1892, a year before the pitcher's mound was moved back to 60 feet, 6 inches. Jones ended his career a year later with a record of 2–4.

Ryan Minor (Canton) replaced Cal Ripken, Jr., in the Orioles lineup when his consecutive games streak ended at 2,632 games on September 20, 1998. Minor ended up playing in 2,859 fewer games than Ripken.

Sock Seybold's 16 home runs in 1902 were the American League record until Babe Ruth slugged 29 in 1919.

Bill Wambsganss turned the only unassisted triple play in World Series history in 1920.

On May 16, 1902, baseball history was made when **Dummy Hoy** of the Reds stepped in to bat against pitcher Luther Taylor of the Giants. It marked the only time a deaf pitcher faced a deaf batter. Hoy also hit the first grand slam in American League history on May 1, 1901.

George Strief (Cincinnati) collected four triples on June 25, 1885, pretty good for a lifetime .207 hitter who had 14 career triples. Bill Joyce (in 1897) is the only other player to equal his feat.

Ray Grimes (Bergholz) still holds the record with an RBI in 17 straight games in 1922.

Ohio and Noteworthy and Controversial Figures

Ohio is the birthplace of Pete Rose, Roger Clemens and Kenesaw Mountain Landis, not to mention Dutch Leonard, Ed Delahanty, Bennie Kauff, Slim Sallee and Lee Magee, so there's no shortage of controversial figures. If you want controversy, try to get consensus on whether Roger Clemens or Cy Young deserves selection as the best right-handed starter from the state. Now there's a debate for the ages, but we'll get to that later.

Four giants of the game — all enshrined in Cooperstown — hail from Ohio: Branch Rickey, Ban Johnson, Sol White and Kenesaw Mountain Landis. Rickey made history by signing Jackie Robinson to break the color barrier and was a pioneer in establishing the system of farm teams. He's certainly not in the Hall of Fame for his playing accomplishments. Rickey, whose playing career consisted of 120 games over four seasons, set an American League record for catchers by allowing the opposing team to steal 13 bases on June 28, 1907.

The autocratic Johnson was the founder and first president of the American League, who helped turn a former minor league into a credible force able to compete with the National League. Johnson took advantage of the fact that the National League had instituted a cap on player salaries. Since his American League teams did not have to operate under the constraints of a cap, they were successful in raiding the more established league for some of the top players. As a result, the upstart league was competitive from the beginning. Johnson also made baseball more fan-friendly for women and children by supporting umpires' efforts to enforce rules of conduct and reduce profanity.

White was a pioneering player, manager, league organizer and unofficial historian of the Negro Leagues in the early twentieth century with the 1907 publication of his book *Sol White's History of Colored Base Ball*. In Jerry Malloy's 1995 introduction to a revised edition of that book, he notes that White's first baseball action came in a game against a white team that included Ban Johnson. During his playing career, which lasted from 1887–1912, White played on some of the top independent black teams as well as on teams in integrated minor leagues. He teamed up with two sportswriters (one white and one black) to found the Philadelphia Giants in 1902, turning the club into a powerhouse while serving as player-manager.

Landis served as baseball's first commissioner from 1920 until his death in 1944. He meted out lifetime bans to the eight players involved in the Black Sox scandal, despite the fact that all were acquitted, and his tough stance in that case helped reassure fans that baseball was free of influence from gamblers. Landis' appointment as commissioner had been opposed by Johnson, who saw his power and influence as American League president diminish as a result. While Landis was clearly not a proponent of integration in baseball, there is no conclusive proof that he was a virulent racist either. History merely judges that he lacked the courage or conviction to champion the cause of integration during his quarter-century as commissioner.

Another noteworthy pioneer in the game was Moses "Fleet" Walker of Mount Pleasant, who is often credited as the first African American player to appear in a major league game. He played for the Toledo Blue Stockings of the American Association on May 1, 1884. Actually, William White beat him by five years. Walker did not have a formal contract but appeared in 42 games and his brother, Welday, appeared in five games for Toledo before the team bowed to pressure and dropped them from the roster.

Players from Ohio went by odd names such as Zinn, Delos, Effie, Dode, Lerton, Podge and Welcome, with two latching on to Chappie. There are famous names of not-so-famous players such as Ethan Allen, Bill Bradley and Albert Schweitzer. One finds an Urban (Shocker) and a Sprowl (Bobby).

Two Kennedys are on the Ohio rolls, both with colorful nicknames — Brickyard and Snapper. Brickyard was an accomplished nineteenth century pitcher who won 20 games four times and had 187 lifetime wins, while Snapper played one game in 1902 and went 0-for-5. Bruno Betzel of Chattanooga, whose given name was Christian Frederick Albert John Henry David Betzel, is tied with Alan (and his five middle names) Gallagher for the most names in baseball history.

Two pitchers called Cy were born in the Buckeye State: Cy Young and Cy Swaim. They combined to win 523 games — 511 of them by Cy Young. Then we have the color brigade: Bert Blue, Red Bluhm, Gates Brown, Bob Black, Bill White, Tyler Green and the most colorful of all — Reddy Grey.

Two players were nicknamed Tacks — Tacks Latimer and Tacks Neuer. Latimer's playing career was uneventful, but he later spent time in prison on a murder rap. Neuer's post-career life was uneventful, although he managed to shine during his brief time with the New York Highlanders in 1907. He completed six of his seven starts with three shutouts, winding up with a 4–2 career record and a 2.17 ERA.

Pickles Dillhoefer is one of the all-time great nicknames, but his story is a tragic one. He died of typhoid fever at age 28 in 1922, shortly after he got married. And yes, his nickname relates to dill pickles.

Even more tragic is the case of Cleveland native Elmer Gedeon, an outfielder who played five games for the Washington Senators in 1939. Gedeon was a bomber pilot whose plane was shot down in France in 1944 — he was one of two major league players to die in World War II.

Perhaps Icicle Reeder's nickname was a statement on his hitting ability, or lack thereof — he batted .154 in his six-game stint in 1884. Same goes for Goat Johnson — his lifetime average of .206 with a .225 slugging percentage denotes a career with few high points. Then there's Russ Nixon, who holds the dubious mark of most plate appearances (2,714) without a stolen base. He was 0-for-7 in steal attempts during his 12-year career.

Team Ohio could turn to Nick Altrock to entertain the crowd. Altrock, one of baseball's first and best clown/comedians, is joined by Minnie Miñoso as the only five-decade players. In reality, Altrock's career was over when he got injured in 1909, and he was just making appearances for publicity purposes after that. He did get hits in his only at-bats in 1924 and 1929, making his final appearance at age 57 in 1933. Altrock had three good years as a pitcher, winning 19 games in 1904 and 23 games with a 1.88 ERA in 1905. Then in 1906 he went 20–13 with a 2.06 ERA and helped the White Sox win a World Series title.

All-Time Ohio Selections

Nearly 1,000 (996 to be exact) Ohio-born players have made it to the major leagues through the 2011 season, with 27 of them active in 2011. Sixty-two have been named to at least one All-Star team including Don Zimmer — who knew Popeye had game? Twelve players and two managers from the Buckeye State have been elected to the Hall of Fame to date.

Moving on to the team selections, we find the catcher position to be a close call between Thurman Munson, Roger Bresnahan and Buck Ewing. The latter two are in the Hall of Fame, while some think Munson should get in with a sympathy vote. Despite having a shorter career, Munson actually distinguished himself more than his two counterparts.

Bresnahan's career lasted 17 seasons but he only played 974 games at catcher. "The Duke of Tralee" caught over 100 games just once — 139 in 1908. The most at-bats he had in a season was 449 — Munson had more at-bats in every one of his nine full seasons. Ewing had only one season with 500 at-bats, with exactly 500 in 1893. He played more games at other positions than at catcher, catching just 636 games in 18 seasons. The most games he caught in one season was 97. Munson gets the nod because he was out there day in and day out, catching full-time for the better part of a decade.

Munson, the revered and gritty Yankees captain, earned Rookie of the Year honors in 1970 and led the Yanks to three straight pennants between 1976 and 1978. He was tough and gruff, proud and stubborn and unquestionably the straw that stirred the drink for the Yankees. Munson was named AL MVP in 1976, a year in which he batted .529 in a losing effort in the World Series. His clutch hitting led the team to the title the next two years.

With bad knees hampering his ability to remain at catcher, Munson was at a crossroads in his career when he crashed his Cessna Citation jet on August 2, 1979. Munson's locker was left untouched in the Yankee clubhouse until the new Yankee Stadium was built, where it now resides in the Yankees Museum.

Ewing and Bresnahan probably belong in the Hall of Fame for their overall career accomplishments as much as their catching prowess. Ewing led the league in triples with 20 in 1884, posting 11 seasons with double-figure totals in triples and finishing with 178 career triples. He hit over .300 nine straight seasons and 11 times overall, averaging .303 lifetime with a 129 OPS+. Bresnahan is generally credited with being the first catcher to wear shin guards, a padded face mask and a batting helmet. Another Ohio-born catcher, Chappie Johnson, became the first catcher to wear shin guards in the Negro Leagues around 1910.

Ewing and Bresnahan both set records for stolen bases by a catcher, although under different sets of rules. Ewing's 354 career steals are the most by any catcher in baseball history and he is the only catcher to steal three bases in a game. He posted four of the five highest stolen base totals by a catcher in the nineteenth century. Bresnahan held the modern record for most stolen bases in a season with 34 in 1903 until John Wathan recorded 36 in 1982. Bresnahan's 212 career steals are the most by any catcher since modern steal rules were instituted in 1898.

Deacon McGuire certainly deserves to be mentioned, as he played 26 seasons in the majors, catching games in 25 of them. He held the record for most major league seasons until passed by Nolan Ryan. McGuire batted over .300 four straight seasons for the Washington Nationals in the 1890s, and he briefly held the record for most career games caught with 1,612. He remains the all-time leader in assists by a catcher with 1,859 and managed to play for 11 different teams in an era when there were few teams around.

Columbus native Mike Matheny set a number of fielding records for catchers. His streak of 252 consecutive games without an error was surpassed by Mike Redmond in 2010, but Matheny still holds the record for most consecutive games without an error in one season — 138 in 2003. The player nicknamed "The Toughest Man Alive" also set a record with 1,565 consecutive chances without an error from August 2, 2002 to August 1, 2004.

First base goes to Hall of Famer George Sisler without much need for debate. Sisler was a two-time batting champ, batting over .400 both times and ending up with a .340 lifetime average, which ranks sixteenth all-time. "Gorgeous George" posted six seasons with over 200 hits including an incredible 257 in 1920 that stood as the single-season record until Ichiro broke it with 262 hits in 2004. In his MVP season of 1922, Sisler led the league with 134 runs, 246 hits, 18 triples, 51 stolen bases and a .420 average. His 41-game hitting streak that year was the American League standard until Joe DiMaggio came along. Sisler then missed the entire 1923 seasons due to sinusitis, a contributing factor to him falling short of 3,000 hits. He was viewed as a superb fielder but was overrated in that area — he never led the league in fielding percentage but did lead six times in errors by a first baseman.

Chris Chambliss was a dependable but unspectacular first baseman for the Yankees, Braves and Indians whose claim to fame came in the playoffs — specifically, the 1976 ALCS for the Yankees against the Royals. First, Chambliss hit a two-run homer to help the Yanks win Game 3, and then he stepped up to the plate to lead off the bottom of the ninth inning in the decisive Game 5. Batting against Mark Littell, he drove the first pitch over the right-center fence to send the Yankees to the World Series for the first time since 1964. Who can forget the sight of Chambliss plowing over fans as he attempted to make it around the bases? He batted a record .524 in that ALCS.

Lennie "Hoss" Pearson, who spent most of his career with the Newark Eagles, played in six East-West All-Star Games in the Negro Leagues. He led the Negro National League with a .396 average in 1940 and was often among the home run leaders. He led the Baltimore Elite Giants to the 1949 championship as a player-manager. Another notable Negro Leaguer is Ed "Huck" Rile, who was an intimidating presence at the plate at 6-foot-6 and 230 pounds. Rile had a short but productive career as a switch-hitting slugger with the Detroit Stars and also won 49 games as a pitcher.

At second base the spot goes to Miller Huggins, who didn't post big numbers but who did all the little things that helped his team win games. "Mighty Mite" led the league in walks four times, OBP once and stole 324 bases. Although he never made it to the postseason as a player, Huggins turned into a Hall of Fame manager with the Yankees. He helped build the first dynasty with the Bronx Bombers by winning six pennants and three World Series titles while managing stars such as Babe Ruth and Lou Gehrig.

Cincinnati native Bill Doran got to play a couple of seasons for his hometown team, but the bulk of his career came with the Astros. A lifetime .266 hitter over 12 seasons, Doran stole 209 bases with a high of 42 in 1986. Another noteworthy second baseman is Charlie Grant, who was a slick-fielding standout for black baseball teams from 1896–1916. John McGraw tried to sign the light-skinned Grant to play for him on the Orioles, calling him an Indian named "Chief Tokahoma," but his plan was foiled.

No offense to Sal Bando, but we decided to go with Mike Schmidt as Team Ohio's third baseman, seeing as how he is generally regarded as the greatest third basemen ever. Think how baseball history would have been rewritten if the teams picking ahead of the Phillies in the 1971 amateur draft had selected a different shortstop, which was Schmidt's position at the time. Eight shortstops were picked in the first round and only Craig Reynolds proved to be worth a darn. Schmidt lasted until the 30th overall pick in the second round, one spot after the Royals went for a promising shortstop named George Brett. The Reds were one of the teams who whiffed on a shortstop that year — with the last pick of the first round they drafted Mike Miley, he of the .176 lifetime average in 84 games. Just imagine the Big Red Machine of the '70s with Perez at first, Morgan at second, Schmidt at third and Concepcion at short, along with Bench at catcher and Rose in the outfield. Now that would have been a dynasty for the ages.

Actually, Schmidt looked like he was headed for a short career when he debuted for the Phillies in 1973. He batted just .196 and struck out almost twice as often as he got a hit (136 to 72). Schmidt quickly figured out how to be a successful major league hitter, and he would lead the league in homers the next three seasons, a feat he would accomplish eight times overall on the way to slugging 548 home runs.

In his 2006 book, *Clearing the Bases,* Schmidt reveals that Brett was not the only third baseman suffering from hemorrhoids during the 1980 World Series. The affliction didn't seem to bother the stars as Brett batted .375 in that Series in a losing effort and Schmidt batted .381 with two home runs. Maybe if Schmidt had been similarly afflicted in the 1983 World Series he wouldn't have batted .050.

Bando gets overshadowed by Schmidt's greatness, but he was one of the core players who won three straight championships with the A's (1972–74). Bando hit 242 homers in 16 seasons and blasted some clutch shots in the playoffs. His home run off Jim Palmer was the only run of the game as Vida Blue beat the Orioles in Game 3 of the 1974 ALCS, and Bando also hit two home runs in Game 2 of the 1973 ALCS.

Denny Lyons was a nineteenth century third baseman who came in second in the American Association with a .354 average in 1890 while also leading the league in OBP (.461), slugging (.531) and OPS (.992). He finished with a lifetime average of .310 and a .407 OBP.

Also worth mentioning is Cleveland native Bill Bradley, not the basketball player turned politician but rather one of the top third basemen during the formative years of the American League. He set a record with 60 sacrifice hits in 1908 and had three straight seasons batting over .300. Bradley shone in the field, leading AL third basemen in fielding percentage six times (compared to just twice for noted gloveman and contemporary Jimmy Collins). In 1902 Bradley became the first player to homer in four consecutive games, no small feat during the Deadball Era. Between 1901 and 1904 Bradley batted .312 and recorded an OPS+ of 136 playing for his hometown team.

Barry Larkin got to play his entire 19-year career for his hometown Reds, retiring in 2004 as one of the best all-around shortstops in baseball history. Surprisingly, he attracted just 50 percent of the vote in his first year on the Hall of Fame ballot, which means that quite a few Hall voters were not paying attention in the 1990s. Larkin could do it all, and he did regularly, earning MVP honors in 1995 because he found ways with his five-tool talent to help his team win every day. He didn't lead the National League in a single offensive category that year but did steal 51 bases while getting thrown out just five times. He batted .319 with a .394 OBP, struck out just 49 times and won a Gold Glove after committing just 11 errors. More importantly, he was clutch in 1995, batting .345 with runners in scoring position.

Don Zimmer lauded Larkin as one of the players who played the game the way it should be played. "From my standpoint, I never saw a right-handed hitter any better at hitting with a man on second base," he wrote in his book *The Zen of Zim*.

Larkin was a terrific base runner who stole 379 bases, succeeding on 83 percent of his attempts. He hit 198 home runs and earned nine Silver Sluggers and three Gold Gloves. With 33 home runs and 36 steals in 1996 he became the first 30–30 shortstop, two years ahead of Alex Rodriquez. His .371 OBP far outpaces Cal Ripken (.340) and Ozzie Smith (.337), while Larkin also edges his Hall of Fame contemporaries in OPS (.815 to .788 for Ripken and .666 for Smith) and OPS+ (116 to 112 for Ripken and a weak 87 for Ozzie). His career fielding percentage of .975 is just a tick behind the two.

Larkin drew walks and didn't strike out much while ranking among the fielding leaders each year at shortstop. He gracefully made hard plays look easy while projecting the quiet confidence of a leader. Injuries curtailed his production somewhat — he only played 150 games four times — which is one of the few negative things that can be said about him. He didn't do backflips like Ozzie or date starlets like Derek Jeter or do anything else to draw attention to his excellence, but Larkin is clearly an all-time great who deserves to be enshrined in Cooperstown.

It's a big drop to the next level of shortstops from Ohio such as Roger Peckinpaugh and Woody English, although Grant "Home Run" Johnson made a name for himself in the Negro Leagues. English finished fourth in the NL MVP voting in 1931 after batting .319 with 202 hits. Peckinpaugh played 17 years and collected 1,876 hits but is best known for being named MVP at the age of 34 in 1925, his last year as a regular.

That season he batted .294 for the Washington Senators with just 24 extra-base hits while posting an OPS+ of 90. He was a steady player and terrific fielder, and his all-around contributions were evidently noticed as there were easily a dozen players more deserving of MVP that year. The newly honored MVP's play was especially noticed in the 1925 World Series as Peckinpaugh's record eight errors almost single-handedly kept the Senators from repeating as champions. His two errors in Game 7 directly led to four runs in a game they would lose by a score of 9–7.

Home Run Johnson was one of the top sluggers in the Negro Leagues during the Deadball Era, playing for a succession of teams that often emerged as champions including the Cuban X-Giants and Philadelphia Giants. He played with Pop Lloyd, Cannonball Redding, Spot Poles and Louis Santop on the New York Lincoln Giants teams that won three straight eastern championships. Johnson occasionally filled in as a pitcher and ended up playing professional baseball until he was in his late 50s.

The All-Time-Ohio team features a pretty good leadoff hitter and right fielder, since baseball's lifetime bans don't apply to these selections. To understand the magnitude of Pete Rose's baseball accomplishments, all you have to do is visit the Reds Hall of Fame and Museum next to the Great American Ballpark. There lined up neatly on a wall is a 50-foot-high display of balls — one for each of the 4,256 hits Rose accumulated during his 24-year career, 19 spent with his hometown team. It's an amazing sight to see, but not as awe-inspiring as seeing "Charlie Hustle" launch his body head-first into third base after legging out a triple.

Here's what Hank Aaron had to say about Rose while both were accumulating annual All-Star Game selections: "Does Pete (Rose) hustle? Before the All-Star game he came into the clubhouse and took off his shoes and they ran another mile without him."

Rose is the all-time leader in times on base and outs made, in addition to games, at-bats and hits. Despite his status as the Hit-King, Pete claims to be even more proud of another all-time mark — being on the winning team in 1,972 games. His 1,314 RBI are the most ever for a player without a 100 RBI season. He's also the unofficial leader in head-first slides, dives, hustle plays and dirt stains. Pete is the rare player who would think of bowling over the catcher in an All-Star Game, much to Ray Fosse's regret. After all, this is the same player who once said, "I'd walk through hell in a gasoline suit to play baseball."

Hell is where Rose finds himself now, or at least baseball's equivalent purgatory. Banned for life from the sport he loves and excluded from taking his rightful place along the all-time greats in Cooperstown, baseball's hit king has had to live with his mistakes. As he wrote in his 2004 confessional book, *My Prison Without Bars*, "There hasn't been a day in my life where I didn't regret making those bets. I wish I could take it all back. But I can't. What's done is done."

It seems possible that Rose will someday wind up in

the Hall of Fame, but probably not while he's alive and definitely not while Bud Selig is commissioner. He came close to getting reinstated in 2002 when he confessed to betting on baseball to Selig, but evidently Pete failed to express remorse for his actions and so his misery continues.

Joining Rose in the All-Time Ohio outfield is another legendary player who paid the ultimate price for his addictions (in his case, gambling and alcohol) with no shot at redemption. When a drunk and disorderly Ed Delahanty was kicked off a train and soon plunged to his death in Niagara Falls in 1903, he lost a chance to finish out a career that was unsurpassed to that point. Yes, he's in the Hall of Fame and his .346 lifetime average still ranks fifth all-time, but at the time of his death the 35-year-old Delahanty had shown few signs of slowing down on the field despite his typical self-destructive activity off the field. Five or six more years of decent production and he would have totaled more than 2,000 runs, 2,000 RBI and approached 3,500 hits. His name would have been mentioned in the same breath with Cobb, Speaker and Wagner.

Delahanty, who had four brothers join him in the big leagues, was a fearsome slugger who led the league in slugging and doubles five times, homers twice and RBI three times. He just missed a Triple Crown in 1893 and became the first player to bat over .400 three times. He also was a terror on the bases, stealing 455 bases. On July 13, 1896, he became the second player to hit four home runs in a game (all were of the inside-the-park variety) and in 1899 collected a hit in 10 consecutive at-bats. In some circles he is credited as the only player to win batting titles in the American League and National League, although his 1902 title is in dispute and not officially recognized. Big Ed was elected to the Hall of Fame in 1945.

Selecting the third outfielder was difficult, as strong cases could be made for Jimmy Wynn, Al Oliver, Elmer Flick and Frank Howard. The 6-foot-7 Howard was named Rookie of the Year with the Dodgers in 1960 and went on to blast 382 home runs over 16 seasons. Although he played many of his home games in a pitchers' park, RFK Stadium in Washington, Howard led the league with 44 homers in 1968—the "Year of the Pitcher"—and collected 172 homers between 1967 and 1970. Three of his tape-measure shots in the upper deck at RFK were marked with white seats.

Flick burst onto the scene with the Phillies in 1898, spending his first four seasons matching teammate Delahanty hit for hit while taking advantage of the Baker Bowl's friendly confines. Flick hit .302, .342, .367 and .333 those three years and led the NL with 110 RBI in 1900. He drove in 377 runs in that stretch to go with Big Ed's 446 RBI. He went on to spend nine years teaming up with Nap Lajoie on the Cleveland Naps, winning a batting title in 1905. The lefty-swinging Flick was a gifted natural hitter whose slugging ability belied his small stature. He finished with a .313 lifetime average and used his speed to record 330 stolen bases and post double-figure totals in triples his first 10 seasons. He was elected to the Hall of Fame by the Veterans Committee in 1963.

Oliver was a seven-time All-Star who collected 2,743 hits, seemingly all of them hard-hit line drives. The Portsmouth native was a high school teammate of Larry Hisle, another honorable mention outfielder for Team Ohio. Oliver made his first All-Star team while hitting .312 with the Pirates in 1972 and in 1976 he began a string of nine straight seasons batting over .300. Pirates teammate Willie Stargell said, "Al was the perfect number three hitter because you knew he was going to make contact. You knew he was going to get on base."

Nicknamed "Scoop," Oliver finished with a lifetime average of .303, 529 doubles and 219 home runs. His best year was 1982 with the Expos, when he won a batting title with a .331 average and also led the NL in hits, doubles, RBI and total bases while finishing fourth in OBP, OPS and slugging. Oliver came in third in MVP voting that year, one of 10 seasons he received MVP votes. During the years he played, only Pete Rose and Rod Carew recorded more hits and only Rose had more doubles. His 1,326 RBI during his career were only topped by Reggie Jackson, Tony Perez and Johnny Bench.

Oliver's career accomplishments are even more impressive placed in the context of the challenges he faced at the outset. His mother died when he was 11 and then on what should have been the happiest day of his life—September 14, 1968, when he was called up to the majors—Oliver learned his father had passed away. The 21-year-old player should have been concentrating on learning how to hit major league pitchers but was instead focused on raising his younger sister and brother. He passed both challenges with flying colors and today spreads his wisdom as a youth mentor and motivational speaker.

Oliver, Flick and Howard are all worthy players, but the overall talent of Jimmy "Toy Cannon" Wynn prevailed in the end. In addition to having one of the all-time great nicknames, a reference to the power he packed in his 5-foot-10 frame, Wynn possessed five-tool talent. He hit 291 home runs, stole 225 bases and worked pitchers for 1,224 walks over his 15-year career. Playing in a pitchers' park (the Astrodome) during a pitcher's era greatly suppressed Wynn's numbers. His neutralized batting stats adjusted for ballpark and league context show his career numbers increase sharply. His .250 average jumps to .274, his home runs go from 291 to 331, his runs from 1,105 to 1,268 and his .366 OBP increases to .395.

Oliver has a big edge over Wynn in hits, doubles, triples, RBI and average and he struck out half as many times, but the Toy Cannon comes out ahead in OBP, OPS, OPS+, homers, steals and walks. They posted essentially the same mark for Career Win Shares (305 and 304), but Wynn's overall value as a ballplayer shone through when one compares the two by Runs Above Replacement (RAR) and Wins Above Replacement (WAR). Wynn recorded 59.8 WAR and 549 RAR, while Oliver's scores were 38.8 and 365. Bill James ranks Wynn as the 10th best center fielder of all-time (and notes how similar his game was to that of teammate Joe Morgan) with Oliver at number 31 and Flick at number 23 for right fielders.

Among the players earning honorable mention in Ohio's All-Time outfield are Paul O'Neill, Tommy Henrich, Gene Woodling and David Justice, who won 16 pennants and 14 World Series titles playing a combined 28 seasons with the Yankees. Other notable outfielders include Dummy Hoy, Topsy Hartsel, Garry Maddox and Bennie Kauff.

O'Neill made his major league debut with the Reds on September 3, 1985. Eight days later the awe-struck rookie watched his manager, Pete Rose, break Ty Cobb's all-time hits record. Seventeen years later he would retire from the game having collected almost exactly half as many hits as Rose — 2,105. O'Neill was a fiercely competitive perfectionist who helped the Yankees win four championships between 1996 and 2000. He was a .259 hitter over eight seasons in Cincinnati, but he stepped it up in the bright lights of New York, averaging .303 over nine seasons in the Bronx. A line-drive hitter who was selected to five All-Star teams, O'Neill won the 1994 batting title with a .359 average and finished with 281 homers.

Woodling helped the Yankees win five straight titles from 1949 to 1953, hitting .318 in World Series play. He led the AL with a .429 OBP in 1953 and posted a .386 career OBP. Henrich was known as "Old Reliable" for his clutch play. He spent his entire 11-year career with the Bronx Bombers, missing three years in his prime for World War II. Combining with Joe DiMaggio and King Kong Keller to form one of the best outfields in baseball history, Henrich won four rings in four trips to the World Series. During his career he struck out just 383 times compared to 712 walks and walloped 183 home runs. His best year was 1948, when he led the AL with 138 runs and 14 triples while also recording 42 doubles, 25 homers, 100 RBI and a slash line of .308/.391/.554.

Justice was named NL Rookie of the Year in 1990 after hitting 28 home runs for the Braves. His best overall season was 1993, when he finished third in MVP voting after hitting 40 homers and driving in 120 runs. His home run for the Braves was the only run scored in the decisive Game 6 of the 1995 World Series. Justice helped the Indians reach the 1997 World Series, batting .329 with 33 homers that season. Traded to the Yankees in July 2000, he got hot and carried the team to the playoffs, hitting 20 homers and driving in 60 runs in 78 games. He won his second World Series ring that year and finished his career with 305 homers, 1,017 RBI and a .500 slugging percentage.

Maddox was known as the "Secretary of Defense," earning eight Gold Gloves for his exceptional play in center field. Ralph Kiner famously said, "Two-thirds of the earth is covered by water, the other third by Garry Maddox." He was no slouch with the bat either, batting .285 and stealing 248 bases over 15 seasons.

Hoy was the first deaf player to have a long career in the majors and one of the few to play in four leagues: American League, National League, Players League and American Association. He once threw out three runners at home plate in a game and is given varying levels of credit for starting the practice of the batter receiving signals from the third base coach, since that is how he learned the umpire's calls on balls and strikes. Hoy compiled 2,048 hits over 14 seasons with a .288 average and 596 stolen bases.

All of 5-foot-5, Hartsel was a skilled leadoff hitter in the first decade of the twentieth century. Bill James' research shows Topsy to be the third-best leadoff hitter in baseball history behind Rickey Henderson and Tim Raines. He led the league in walks five times, OBP twice and steals and runs one time each. Hartsel recorded five seasons with an OBP over .400 and he held the American League record with 121 walks (later shattered by Babe Ruth with 150 in 1920).

Flashy-dressing, brash Bennie Kauff was the Federal League batting champion both years the upstart league existed: 1914 and 1915. The first year he led the league with a .370 average and 75 steals and also finished first in runs, doubles, hits, OBP and OPS. The "Ty Cobb of the Federal League" was signed by John McGraw for the Giants, and he was a productive center fielder for the next five years before getting caught up with his half-brother and Giants teammate Jesse Barnes in a stolen car ring. Kauff found himself kicked out of baseball at the conclusion of the 1920 season and although he was later acquitted of the charges, Commissioner Kenesaw Landis refused to reinstate him to baseball, mainly because there were allegations he was involved in the 1919 Black Sox Scandal.

Before Kauff got himself run out of the league, another Ohio-born outfielder, Lee Magee, did likewise. In 1920, a few months before the Black Sox trial swung into high gear, Magee confessed to betting on baseball and attempting to throw a game while playing for the Reds in 1918. He was banned from baseball, ending his career with 1,031 hits and tied for one record — most assists in a game by an outfielder with four.

Honorable mention outfielder Ethan Allen, a native of Cincinnati, averaged .300 over 13 big-league seasons. After retiring he went on to serve as the baseball coach at Yale University for 23 years. One of his players was a first baseman named George H.W. Bush, who credited Allen with teaching him a lot about baseball and life.

Mike "Hit Man" Easler gets selected as the designated hitter, a role he played in 433 games because he was slow afoot and a poor fielder. Traded to the Red Sox before the 1984 season, Easler finally got a chance to be a full-time starter and produced a .313 average with 27 homers and 91 RBI. He batted .302 for the Yankees in 1986 and retired with a .293 average.

Now for the main event — deciding between Cy Young and Roger Clemens as the best right-handed starter from Ohio. Should we go with the pitcher with the most Cy Young Awards (seven) or the pitcher for whom the award was named? Many baseball fans think

Clemens is a Texas native since he's always presented himself as a Texan, but the "Rocket" was born and raised in the Dayton area and moved to Texas at age 15.

We actually went back and forth on this selection—numerous times—while this book was in the works over a period dating back to 2007. We had finally decided to go with Clemens over Young, mainly because we felt Young's stats showed longevity and durability more than dominance, while Clemens had built a career based on a combination of dominance and competitive intensity that was unmatched in the modern era. We felt we could make a strong argument for the Rocket.

Then the Mitchell Report came out, with Clemens' name mentioned prominently. The Rocket also couldn't resist going before Congress in 2008 to profess his innocence, a move that backfired badly when he was indicted in August 2010 on charges of making false statements, perjury and obstruction of Congress. The whole sordid affair has shed a new light on Clemens' career accomplishments and severely jeopardized his chances of even making the Hall of Fame. It also turned a difficult decision into an easy one, with Young earning the coveted spot on the All-Time-Ohio team.

So was Red Sox GM Dan Duquette right when he said Clemens was on the downside of his career in 1996? After all, the Rocket had averaged just 10 wins his last four seasons for the Red Sox, so clearly he was not the same dominant pitcher. Then all of a sudden he recaptured his past brilliance and stayed at that high level for the majority of the next 11 years. That type of pitching rebirth does not pass the smell test, yet so many people wanted to believe it was due to Roger's rigorous year-round workouts, as though he had been a couch potato his last few years in Boston. Now we are led to believe much of that performance can be traced to performance-enhancing drugs, which puts a whole new perspective on his career accomplishments.

It is impossible and fruitless to guess how much Clemens' career was aided by his alleged use of steroids and what his numbers would have looked like otherwise. He won the pitcher's Triple Crown both years he was with the Blue Jays, something he never accomplished in 13 years in Boston. He probably would not have won 300 games, but would he have won 250? Keep in mind that he nearly doubled his strikeout total his last year with the Sox, so he could have been juicing even earlier and it just took him a little while to figure out the right regimen. Ultimately, all the speculation is irrelevant — Cy Young's record of achievement is unblemished, even though he played in an era where thuggish, dirty play was the rule and not the exception and when far too many players got caught up in gambling and drinking.

Young pitched in an era with no pitch counts and when a staff ace typically started one-third of his team's games and was expected to finish what he started. Young did just that, completing 91.9 percent of his starts over a 22-year career that bridged the nineteenth century and the Deadball Era.

When you look at baseball's career records that have no chance to be broken, Cy Young's 511 wins should be at or near the top of the list. Derek Jeter could potentially challenge Pete Rose's record for hits. Alex Rodriquez and Albert Pujols could challenge Barry Bonds' home run record. Nolan Ryan's strikeout mark and Rickey Henderson's stolen base mark are really up there, but it's not inconceivable that someone could come along. In an era in which it's increasingly difficult to win 20 games, a pitcher could average 25 wins a year for 20 years and still fall a little short of Young's mark. It's difficult to imagine a pitcher reaching 400 wins let alone exceeding 500. Young won 439 games after the pitcher's mound was moved back in 1893, so it's not like he capitalized much on the old-time rules.

Young is the all-time leader in games started, complete games, wins, innings pitched and batters faced, as well as losses, hits and earned runs. Interestingly, Young is number one in WAR (Wins Above Replacement) for pitchers at 146 — number two is Clemens at 128. Young led the league in BB/9IP 14 times, SO/BB 11 times and WHIP seven times. He pitched three no-hitters including the first perfect game in American League history. With an even-keel temperament that had him admired as the "Grand Old Man of Baseball," Young embodied the old-fashioned American virtues of hard work, integrity, loyalty, durability and dependability.

Young faced 29,565 batters during his career, 4,150 more than runner-up Pud Galvin and 9,325 more than Clemens. His 749 complete games are 103 more than runner-up Galvin and 195 more than Tim Keefe, who ranks third. He won 94 more games than Walter Johnson in second place. Nolan Ryan stayed remarkably healthy and pitched for 27 years — he still recorded 42 fewer starts than Young. Finally, Young's 2,014 assists as a pitcher are 511 more than runner-up Christy Mathewson and nearly double the total of Greg Maddux.

The game of baseball changed dramatically from when Young made his debut in 1890 to when he threw his last pitch in 1911. Back in the early days of baseball, it used to be the job of pitchers to put the ball in play and they did so without benefit of a glove on their hand. With the pitcher's box (there was no mound yet) just 55½ feet from the plate, it was more akin to "chuck and duck," as line drives went whizzing by pitchers' heads. Then the pitching area got moved back to 60 feet, 6 inches, which gave batters more time to see pitches and effectively slowed the speed of the ball. Next, a 15-inch pitching mound was unveiled, which tilted power back in the hands of the pitcher. However, pitchers during Young's career also benefited from a generous strike zone, spacious ballparks with deep fences and the nearly limitless manner in which they could doctor the ball.

What's remarkable about Young's career is that he adapted to these major rule changes and simply learned how to make it work in his favor. In 1892 — the last year before the pitching distance was moved back — Young won 36 games and posted a 1.93 ERA with nine shutouts and 168 strikeouts. The next year, with the mound moved back, he saw his ERA rise to 3.36, his shutouts drop to one and his strikeouts fall to 102 — yet he still won 34 games. He just kept on winning. His amazing record of success is enough to earn him the additional honor of Ohio's All-Time Best Player, beating out Schmidt and Rose.

Young was elected to the Hall of Fame in 1937, the second year of voting. In 1956, a year after Young's death, Commissioner Ford Frick decided baseball should honor the best pitcher in the majors each year with an award named after Cy Young. As Reed Browning details in his 2000 biography of the pitcher, *Cy Young: A Baseball Life*, Young was selected for that honor not because he was viewed as the best pitcher ever but due to the fact that only one award was given out in the beginning and Young was the only one of the great pitchers under consideration (along with Mathewson, Johnson and Alexander) to enjoy success in both leagues.

The star power of Young and Clemens overshadows that of the other outstanding righties from Ohio, including three Hall of Famers. Just as Mariano Rivera has made a career out of throwing one pitch, Phil Niekro did the same thing and lasted 24 years throwing mainly the knuckleball. He didn't always know where it was going, but neither did batters. "Knucksie" would compile 318 wins (sixteenth all-time) with a 3.35 ERA and record 3,342 strikeouts, good for 11th on the all-time list. Bobby Murcer once said, "Trying to hit Phil Niekro is like trying to eat Jell-O with chopsticks."

Niekro produced some strange stats during the course of his career, leading the NL in losses four straight years including two years with 20 losses. In 1979 he led the league in wins with 21 and losses with 20. That year he led the league in starts (44), complete games (23) and innings (342) but also hits (311), homers (41) and walks (113). His younger brother, Joe, was Cy Young runner-up that season after winning 21 games for the Astros. The two brothers combined to win 539 games, the most ever by brothers and just 10 more than Gaylord and Jim Perry.

Ray Brown was the ace of the Homestead Grays powerhouse teams in the late 1930s and early 1940s, helping the Grays win the Negro National League championship in every one of his nine seasons with the team. He had 28-game and 27-game winning streaks for the Grays, if you include non-league games. Monte Irvin called Brown "almost unbeatable," while Double Duty Radcliffe named him to his all-time all-star team. Brown is credited by the Baseball Hall of Fame with a career record of 105–44 and 3.20 ERA. Brown didn't garner nearly as much publicity as Satchel Paige, but he was just as dominant a pitcher over his 19-year career. He could blow his fastball by batters, tease them with his wicked curveball or use whatever pitch was necessary to get the job done.

Urban Shocker turned 26 during his rookie year of 1916 and he ended up dying suddenly at the age of 38. In between he was a pretty effective pitcher, winning 20 games four straight years for St. Louis Browns teams that finished out of the money. He won 18 games for the powerhouse Yankees team of 1927 and ended up with a lifetime record of 187–117, 3.17 ERA and 124 ERA+, a similar career mark to that of Eddie Rommel and Jesse Tannehill. Shocker led the AL in wins in 1921 and strikeouts and SO/BB ratio in 1922.

Jesse Haines pitched for five pennant winners, but he wasn't the ace of any of those teams. He produced a pretty flimsy record for a Hall of Famer. In fact, Ted Lyons and Red Ruffing are the only Hall of Famers with a higher ERA than Haines' 3.64. Haines won 20 games three times and didn't really have any other standout years. He frequently pitched out of the bullpen his last six seasons to mixed results. Except for one game with the Reds in 1918, he pitched for the Cardinals his entire career.

Nicknamed "Pop," Haines made history by becoming the first pitcher to hit a home run while tossing a shutout in the World Series, which he accomplished in Game 3 of the 1926 Series against the Yankees. He pitched until he was 44, finishing with a career record of 210–158 and never receiving more than 8 percent of the writer's vote before getting elected to the Hall of Fame by the Veterans Committee in 1970.

Bill James leaves Haines off his list of top 100 pitchers while ranking fellow Buckeye George Uhle in the number 91 spot. "The Bull" won 20 games for his hometown Indians three times but posted high ERAs in two of those seasons. He went 22–16 in 1922 but posted an ERA+ of 99 that year. Uhle won 26 games the next season but also led the AL in hits and earned runs. His best season was 1926, when he won a league-high 27 games with a 2.83 ERA and led the league in complete games, innings, games started and won-loss percentage. However, he also finished first in hits, walks, hit batters and wild pitches. He finished with a career mark of 200–166, a 3.99 ERA and an ERA+ of 106. Uhle was frequently called on to pinch-hit, as he was one of the best-hitting pitchers in baseball history. He recorded 393 lifetime hits with a .289 average, including 52 hits with a .361 average in 1923.

Folks sometimes get Sad Sam Jones confused with Sam "Toothpick" Jones, as both were born in Ohio and the latter was often called "Sad Sam." While playing together with the Indians in 1952, "Toothpick" Jones combined with catcher Quincy Trouppe to form the first all African American battery in the American League. In 1955 he became the first African American to throw a no-hitter in the majors and ended his career with a 102–101 record, standing out for his excellent curveball.

The white Sad Sam Jones won 229 games pitching from 1914–35. He won 23 games and led the AL with five shutouts while pitching for the Red Sox in 1921. In 1923 he pitched a no-hitter and won 21 games for the Yankees, who won their first World Series title that year. He pitched two innings of shutout relief to save the decisive Game 6. Sad Sam still holds the AL record for most consecutive seasons pitched — 22. What's even more amazing is that there were only eight teams in the American League during his career and he pitched for six of them.

The bullpen could take the day off when Jack Taylor was on the mound. Taylor set a record by completing 187 consecutive starts between 1901 and 1906, going 1,727 innings without being relieved. He also appeared in 15 games in relief those years but always stayed in until the end. Taylor completed 279 of 287 starts during his career, including a 19-inning complete game win over the Pirates on June 22, 1902. He led the league with a 1.29 ERA and eight shutouts in 1902, won 20 games four times and finished with 152 career wins.

Jim Bagby, Jr., was an average pitcher, as evidenced by his 97–96 career record, but he managed to make baseball history a number of times. On July 17, 1941, he got Joe DiMaggio to ground into a double play in the eighth inning to end his 56-game hitting streak. On September 26, 1940 he became the first pitcher to record three putouts in an inning—11 more pitchers (including Roger Clemens) have accomplished this feat since. Lastly, he and his father, Jim Bagby, are the first father-son duo to pitch in the World Series. The elder Bagby pitched for the Indians in the 1920 Series, while the younger Bagby pitched for the Red Sox in the 1946 Series.

It makes sense to go with Rube Marquard as the all-time lefty, because he's the only Buckeye southpaw in the Hall of Fame. However, his lifetime ERA+ of 103 is pedestrian, to say the least. Marquard had three great seasons for the Giants when he won at least 23 games (1911–13) and later had two good years with the Brooklyn Robins but was otherwise the picture of mediocrity. He won 105 games in those five seasons and went 98–116 the other 13 seasons he pitched. He posted an ERA+ below 100 seven times. Marquard struck out 563 batters in those three stellar seasons with the Giants, which accounted for 35 percent of his career strikeouts.

Slim Sallee, who joined the majors the same season as Marquard in 1908, finished with a lifetime ERA of 2.56 and bested Marquard with an ERA+ of 113. He was one of three aces on the 1919 Reds team that won the World Series and also pitched in the 1917 Series for the Giants. His most impressive season was probably 1913, when he won 19 games with a 2.71 ERA and came out of the bullpen to finish 15 games for a last-place Cardinals team that won only 51 games. A recalcitrant complainer who was perpetually out of favor with his team, Sallee succeeded despite the fact he battled laziness and a drinking problem. After forcing a trade to the Giants during the 1916 season, Sallee posted a 1.37 ERA down the stretch.

Sallee's 2.67 ERA from his nine years with the Cardinals is tied with Dave Foutz for the best in franchise history (minimum 1,000 innings pitched), although Foutz compiled his numbers in the nineteenth century before the mound was moved back. Slim, who was also called "Scatter" and "Scissors," pitched to contact and stayed out of big innings by mesmerizing batters with his unusually slow and awkward motion. On the way to winning 21 games for the Reds in 1919, not only did Sallee record fewer walks than wins, he almost recorded fewer strikeouts. He had 20 walks and 24 strikeouts for the season. Sallee's 174 career wins are 27 fewer than Marquard, but he was a better pitcher and is more deserving of the selection as All-Time Lefty.

One of Sallee's teammates on the 1916 Giants was Ferdie Schupp, whose 0.90 ERA that year was considered to be the record for decades. It was later ruled that Ohio southpaw Dutch Leonard is the rightful record-holder for the 0.96 ERA he posted in 1914 since Schupp only pitched 140 innings with eight complete games. In 1917, the National League began requiring pitchers complete 10 games to qualify for records, while a much later stipulation required one inning pitched for each game a team played. Since there were no such standards in place at the time, Schupp has a right to feel slighted. Tim Keefe's 0.86 ERA in 1880 is discounted because it also came before the mound was moved back and he only appeared in 12 games.

Sallee's obstinacy paled in comparison to that of Leonard, who ended up sitting out nearly three years after refusing to report to the Tigers and signing with an independent team instead. He had been shipped to the Tigers because he refused to report to the Yankees after a 1919 trade unless they deposited his entire salary into his bank account. If only he played in the modern era with a strong players' union and free agency, then he could have concentrated on throwing his blazing fastball and knee-buckling curve. He later relied more heavily on a spitball, which he was able to throw legally to the end of his career.

Leonard went 19–5 for the Red Sox during his wondrous 1914 season, allowing just 139 hits in 224 innings and recording a 0.886 WHIP. His 5.6 H/9IP that year remains the record for a left-handed pitcher. Although he pitched well his next four seasons in Boston, the self-absorbed and universally disliked Leonard never approached his numbers from 1914. He clashed with Tigers player-manager Ty Cobb, who did his best to wear out his star hurler and later succeeded in running him out of the league. Leonard finished at age 33 with a 139–113 record and 2.76 ERA, and he later tried to exact revenge by claiming he had conspired with Cobb and Tris Speaker to throw games. When Leonard refused to travel from California to Chicago to attend a hearing on the matter, it gave Commissioner Kenesaw Landis a valid excuse to let the two stars off the hook.

Another Ohio-born lefty ended up with a nearly identical record to Leonard. Harvey Haddix was 136–113 over 14 seasons, winning three All-Star Game nods and three Gold Gloves. He is best known for pitching one of the best games ever—a perfect game through 12 innings on May 26, 1959, against a Milwaukee Braves lineup featuring Hank Aaron and Eddie Mathews. Unfortunately, Haddix didn't get any run support and surrendered a three-run homer (that went in the books as a run-scoring double due to a base-running gaffe) in the thirteenth inning, and he lost the perfect game, the shutout and the game.

Joe Nuxhall was facing Stan Musial before he was old enough to drive a car. The southpaw made his major league debut with his hometown Reds on June 10, 1944 — he was 15 years, 10 months and 11 days old. He is believed to be the youngest player ever and is without doubt the youngest player in the twentieth century. After his inauspicious debut, Nuxhall had to work his way back up from the minors, which took eight years. He went on to win 135 games (all but five for the Reds) and made two All-Star teams.

Rollie Fingers was the logical choice as the all-time relief pitcher for Team Ohio, but the selection was not a slam dunk. A seven-time All-Star who pitched 907 games in relief, Fingers' success as a reliever was instrumental in helping the position evolve into a valuable specialist's role. He gained notoriety for his elaborate handlebar mustache but was feared for his wicked slider. Fingers was the first reliever to pass 300 career saves and now ranks 10th all-time with 341 saves. He was a four-time winner of the Rolaids Relief Award and led the league in saves three times.

Fingers won the Cy Young Award and MVP Award with the Brewers in the strike-shortened 1981 season after leading the league with 28 saves and posting a microscopic 1.04 ERA with 333 ERA+. Steve McCatty was probably more deserving of the Cy Young Award that year, while Rickey Henderson, Dwight Evans and Eddie Murray were more deserving of the MVP Award than a player who pitched 78 innings over 47 games.

Fingers appeared in 16 World Series games for the A's from 1972 to 1974, recording a 1.35 ERA as the team won three straight championships. It caused his manager, Alvin Dark to say, "A fellow has to have faith in God above and Rollie Fingers in the bullpen."

A number of other great relievers were born in Ohio, many of them named "Jeff." The list includes Jeff Montgomery, Jeff Shaw, Jeff Russell, Kent Tekulve and Don Elston. Shaw equaled Fingers' ERA+ for his career while both Montgomery (135) and Tekulve (132) surpassed him. Fingers wins extra consideration for awards and championships won in addition to his pioneering role in the bullpen, giving him enough gravitas to earn the selection.

Montgomery posted 304 saves with a 3.24 ERA and made three All-Star teams with the Royals. He won the AL Rolaids Relief Award in 1993, a year in which he led the AL with 45 saves. Shaw was only a closer the last five seasons of his career, but he recorded 194 of his 203 saves in those years. He led the NL with 42 saves for the Reds in 1997, when he won the NL Rolaids Relief Award.

Russell started his career as a starter for his hometown Reds, but led the NL with 18 losses in 1984 and was traded to Texas, where he made the 1988 All-Star team pitching primarily as a starter. Converted to closer the next year, he led the AL with 38 saves and made the All-Star team again. He finished in the top 10 in saves six times and retired with 186 saves.

Tekulve was a workhorse with a submarine style, recording three seasons with 90 or more games and leading the NL in appearances four times. His 1,050 games played are a record for pitchers without a start and he ranked eighth on the all-time list in total appearances at the end of the 2010 season, just ahead of Trevor Hoffman. The "Rubber Band Man" had a career high of 31 saves in 1978 and 1979 with the Pirates and finished with 184 saves and a 2.85 ERA.

Don Elston was a bullpen pioneer, forming an effective righty-lefty combination with southpaw Bill Henry on the Cubs in the late 1950s. Elston led the NL with 69 appearances in 1958 and 65 in 1959, earning him the nickname "Everyday Elston."

It came down to Walter Alston or Miller Huggins for the all-time manager for Team Ohio. Alston was above .500 in 19 of his 23 seasons and won seven pennants and four World Series titles with the Dodgers. He was named NL Manager of the Year six times, despite never having more than a one-year contract. Huggins was above .500 in 12 of his 17 seasons. "Hug" started the Yankees first dynasty by skippering the team to six pennants and three World Series titles between 1921 and 1928, a domination that started once Babe Ruth joined the team in 1920.

Huggins had less success as player-manager with the Cardinals, winning at a .455 clip over five seasons and never finishing higher than third. Alston also guided the Dodgers to eight second-place finishes, wielding a steady hand as the franchise moved from Brooklyn to Los Angeles. Alston's 2,040 career victories (ninth on the all-time list) outshines the 1,413 won by Huggins, which is the final deciding factor.

Jim Leyland led the Florida Marlins to the 1997 World Series championship in only their fifth season as a franchise, He returned to the Series in 2006 with the Tigers, a team three years removed from losing 119 games. Leyland also won three straight division titles with the Pirates in the early 1990s in the days when Barry Bonds was content to hit 30 homers. Leyland had won 1,493 games through the 2010 season.

Sol White was a calm and skilled tactician who served as player-manager for the Philadelphia Giants from 1902–09, winning five eastern championships in six seasons by acquiring star players such as Pete Hill, Frank Grant, Bill Monroe, Rube Foster, Pop Lloyd, Home Run Johnson and Bruce Petway. He authored two books, "History of Colored Baseball" and "Sol White's Official Base Ball Guide," which served to chronicle the formative years of African American baseball history. White played in white and integrated leagues and was instrumental in forming three leagues for African American players over the course of his 40-year career.

Don Zimmer's managerial record may not match that of Hall of Famers like Alston or Huggins, but his baseball knowledge and experiences match up with anyone despite his .235 career batting average as a scrappy infielder. The man was a gamer and has a plate in his head to prove it. He was teammates with Jackie Robinson, Sandy Koufax and Ernie Banks, and played for Casey Stengel, Chuck Dressen and Gil Hodges. He played on the inaugural Mets team in 1962, contributing a .077 average (4-for-52), but he also won World Series titles with the Dodgers in Brooklyn and Los Angeles. Since he made his debut in the minors in 1949, Zimmer played for five major league teams, managed five and coached for eight franchises. He marked his eighth decade in baseball while serving as a senior adviser with the Rays in 2010.

The lovable Zim is like everyone's favorite screwball uncle, whether he was yukking it up on Letterman, scuffling with Pedro Martinez, wearing an army helmet in the dugout or telling the world what he really thought about the "Boss" of the Yankees. It's easy to remember "Popeye" joined at the hip with Joe Torre, but Zim won 885 games over 13 seasons managing the Padres, Red Sox, Rangers and Cubs (plus another 21 he won serving as interim manager of the Yankees in 1999). He won 90 or more games three straight years with the Red Sox and was named NL Manager of the Year after guiding the Cubs to a division title in 1989. His place as one of baseball's all-time great characters is secure.

OKLAHOMA

*Names in **bold** represent Major League selections by position, followed by honorable mentions. Negro Leagues players are in **bold italics**, followed by honorable mentions in italics. City of birth is in parentheses.*

Catcher—Johnny Bench (Oklahoma City). Also: Mickey Tettleton (Oklahoma City); Dave Rader (Claremore)

First Base—Willie Stargell (Earlsboro). Also: Gail Hopkins (Tulsa)

Second Base—Johnny Ray (Chouteau). Also: Jerry Adair (Sand Springs); Dave Nelson (Fort Sill)

Third Base—Harlond Clift (El Reno). Also: *Hank Thompson* (Oklahoma City)

Shortstop—Alvin Dark (Comanche). Also: *Jake Dunn* (Luther); UL Washington (Stringtown)

Outfield—Mickey Mantle (Spavinaw)

Outfield—Paul Waner (Harrah)

Outfield—Bobby Murcer (Oklahoma City). Also: Joe Carter (Oklahoma City); Bob Johnson (Pryor); Lloyd Waner (Harrah); Matt Holliday (Stillwater); Johnny Callison (Qualls); Paul Blair (Cushing); Pepper Martin (Temple); Dale Mitchell (Colony); Roy Johnson (Pryor); *Frog Redus* (Muskogee); Rip Radcliff (Kiowa); *Bob Thurman* (Kellyville); Don Demeter (Oklahoma City); *Norm Robinson* (Oklahoma City)

Designated Hitter—Mickey Tettleton (Oklahoma City)

Right Handed Starter—*Bullet Joe Rogan* (Oklahoma City). Also: Allie Reynolds (Bethany); Joe Dobson (Durant); Jesse Barnes (Perkins); Ralph Terry (Big Cabin); Jeff Suppan (Oklahoma City); *Roosevelt Davis* (Bartlesville); Brad Penny (Blackwell); Willis Hudlin (Wagnoner); Gene Conley (Muskogee); Mike Moore (Eakly); *George Jefferson* (Boley)

Left Handed Starter—Harry Breechen (Broken Bow). Also: Al Brazle (Loyal)

Relief Pitcher—Lindy McDaniel (Hollis). Also: Frank Linzy (Fort Gibson); Al Benton (Noble); Braden Looper (Weatherford); Ted Power (Guthrie); Bob Shirley (Cushing); George Frazier (Oklahoma City)

Manager—Bobby Cox (Tulsa). Also: *Bullet Joe Rogan* (Oklahoma City); Alvin Dark (Comanche)

The Names

Best Nickname: Pepper "The Wild Horse of the Osage" Martin

Other Nicknames: Jesse "Nubby" Barnes; Clarence "Footsie" Blair; Paul "Motormouth" Blair; Al "Cotton" and "Old Boots and Saddles" Brazle; Harry "the Cat" Breechen; Alvin "The Swamp Fox" Dark; Joe "Burrhead" Dobson; "Indian Bob" Johnson; Matt "Bison" Kemp; Mickey "The Commerce Comet" Mantle; Allie "Superchief" Reynolds; "Bullet" Joe Rogan; Roy "Linus" Staiger; Willie "Pops" Stargell; Mickey "Fruit Loops" Tettleton; Bob "Big Swish" Thurman; Ben "Millionaire Indian" Tincup; Paul "Big Poison" Waner; Lloyd "Little Poison" Waner; Henry "Flick" Williams; Moses "Chief" Yellow Horse

Most Unusual Name: Moses Yellow Horse

All-Time Leaders

Games: Paul Waner, 2549
Hits: Paul Waner, 3152
Batting Average: Paul Waner, .333
Home Runs: Mickey Mantle, 536
RBI: Willie Stargell, 1540
Stolen Bases: Joe Carter, 231
Wins: Allie Reynolds, 182
Strikeouts: Mike Moore, 1667
Saves: Braden Looper, 103
Future Star: Tommy Hanson (Tulsa)
Best Player: Mickey Mantle

Historic Baseball Places

AT&T Bricktown Ballpark in Oklahoma City—Features huge statues of Johnny Bench, Mickey Mantle and Warren Spahn at the entrances outside the stadium. In 2007 came the addition of bronze busts of Allie Reynolds, Bullet Joe Rogan, Paul and Lloyd

AT&T Bricktown Ballpark opened in 1998 as the centerpiece of a revitalized Bricktown neighborhood in Oklahoma City. Huge statues of Hall of Famers Johnny Bench, Mickey Mantle and Warren Spahn guard each of the three entrances into the stadium, which features streetlights designed to resemble baseballs (courtesy DigitalBallparks.com).

Waner, Pepper Martin, Bobby Murcer and Carl Hubbell atop marble bases that outline each player's accomplishments.

Mickey Mantle Monument Park at Mickey Mantle Field in Commerce — Dedicated in 2000, the field features a nine-foot tall bronze statue of the Mick swinging a bat with the inscription "A Great Teammate."

Mickey Mantle boyhood home in Commerce — After driving into town on Mickey Mantle Boulevard, you can find the tiny home at 319 South Quincy Street where the "Commerce Comet" first learned to play baseball. You can walk around the yard and see where the Mick's father and grandfather used to pitch to him every day, beside the leaning tin barn where he banged balls off the side.

Notable Achievements

Paul and Lloyd Waner hold the record for most times brothers have hit home runs in the same game. They did it three times: Sept. 4, 1927; June 9, 1929; and Sept. 15, 1938.

On July 20, 1947, **Hank Thompson** and **Willard Brown** became the first African American players to appear in a game together. Thompson was in the lineup at second base and Brown at center field for the St. Louis Browns.

Ted Cox (Oklahoma City) set the record for most consecutive hits to start a career with six in 1977.

Al Benton is the only pitcher to face both Babe Ruth and Mickey Mantle. He also pitched to Lou Gehrig and Joe DiMaggio during a career that lasted from 1934 to 1952.

Willie Stargell became the first player to hit a home run out of Dodger Stadium when he belted a 506-foot shot off Alan Foster on August 5, 1969. He did it again on May 8, 1973, off Andy Messersmith.

In 1974 **Alvin Dark** became the third manager (after Joe McCarthy and Yogi Berra) to win a pennant in the National and American Leagues.

Joe Carter not only scored the first run in a World Series played outside of the United States (Game 3 of the 1992 World Series in Toronto), he has the distinction of being the last player to score a run in a World Series played outside the United States (Game 6 of the 1993 World Series in Toronto). Carter also holds the record for most sacrifice flies in the World Series with four. He had one in the 1992 World Series and three in the 1993 World Series.

Bob Johnson is one of only three players in history (George Kelly and Mike Greenwell are the others) to drive in all his team's runs in a game in which they scored at least eight runs. He did it against the St. Louis Browns on June 12, 1938 by hitting three home runs (one a grand slam) along with a single.

Matt Kemp (Midwest City) became the first player in major league history to homer in the last five games of the season, which he did in 2010.

Jerry Walker (Ada) has the distinction of being the youngest starting pitcher in an All-Star Game. He was 20 years old when he started the 1959 game for the American League. Walker pitched three innings and got the win.

Oklahoma Roster Filled with Native American Heritage

Native American heritage can be found up and down the roster of Oklahoma players. Of the 50 full-blooded Native American Indians who have played in the majors, 22 were born in Oklahoma — more than any other state. Two of Oklahoma's greatest players, Johnny Bench and Willie Stargell, also had a little Indian blood in them.

This Indian heritage was reflected in player nicknames, so you'll find Allie "Superchief" Reynolds, "Indian Bob" Johnson, Ben "Millionaire Indian" Tincup, Moses "Chief" Yellow Horse and Pepper "The Wild Horse of the Osage" Martin.

Tincup, a full-blooded Cherokee, only won eight games in the majors, all in 1914 and three of them by shutout. However, he collected 251 wins over a 24-year career in the minors. He was called "Millionaire Indian" because people mistakingly thought he owned valuable oil fields in Oklahoma. Actually, there wasn't any oil on his property. As a 70-year-old coach of the Yankees in 1960, Tincup reportedly put on a blindfold and threw nine out of 10 pitches for a strike. Maybe that's just an old Indian tale, but Tincup sure knew how to pitch.

Chief Yellow Horse was a member of the Pawnee tribe who first learned to pitch at the Chilocco Indian School. After gaining some seasoning with the Arkansas Travelers, where he impressed with his great fastball, he signed with the Pittsburgh Pirates. He pitched in 38 games for the Pirates in 1921–22 but soon developed arm trouble that cut short his career.

Chief Yellow Horse also developed a serious drinking problem, mainly because he made the mistake of hanging out with the hard-partying Rabbit Maranville. It took him the better part of two decades to curb his drinking problem, but Chief Yellow Horse eventually got his life back on track and was accepted back into his tribe to serve as an elder.

Jim Smith hated his common name so much he changed his last name to Bluejacket, which honored his half-Cherokee roots. In 1914 he became the first pitcher to win a game without throwing a single pitch. He entered the game in the ninth inning and quickly picked off a runner for the third out. This unusual feat didn't happen again until B.J. Ryan pulled it off in a game for the Orioles in 2003.

Cal McLish thankfully did not go by his full name — Calvin Coolidge Julius Caesar Tuskahoma McLish. Coolidge was U.S. president at the time of his birth, while Tuskahoma means "Great Warrior" in his native Choctaw language. As for the Roman emperor connection, it must have made sense at the time. McLish was a switch-hitting pitcher who threw right handed. He played for seven teams in 15 years, finally coming into his own with 16 wins for Cleveland at the age of 32. He won 19 games the next season, making his only All-Star team.

Jim Thorpe didn't accomplish much in the majors, collecting 176 hits with a .252 average over six seasons. However, the Sac and Fox tribe member did enough in other sports to be named the "best male athlete of the first half of the twentieth century." He set records in winning the pentathlon and decathlon at the 1912 Olympics, which caused King Gustav V of Sweden to exclaim to him on the medal stand, "Sir, you are the greatest athlete in the world." Thorpe later had those medals stripped because it was revealed he had earned money playing semi-pro baseball, an injustice that bothered him for the rest of his life. The medals were restored to him — 30 years after his death.

In 1913 John McGraw signed Thorpe for the New York Giants solely for the purpose of selling tickets. He didn't see much action with the team during his two stints lasting nearly six seasons. In fact, McGraw even pinch-hit for him in the first inning of Game 5 of the 1917 World Series. So technically, Thorpe did and didn't play in that Series.

Although Thorpe gave baseball a shot, he gave increasing attention to football, a sport that was easier for him to master with his wondrous all-around athleticism. He did hit .327 in his last year playing for the Boston Braves, but then found himself stuck in the minors where he batted .360, .358 and .335. Thorpe was a founding president of the American Professional Football Association, later becoming an original enshrinee in the Pro Football Hall of Fame.

A town in Pennsylvania changed its name to Jim Thorpe after his widow negotiated to have him buried there. Some family members are leading a push to have his remains moved back to Oklahoma for a proper American Indian burial among his ancestors, while other family members are equally adamant that his spirit should not be stirred by moving his remains. America's greatest athlete, who seemingly could do it all on a playing field, remains a pawn of exploitation even after his death.

Other Oklahoma-born players with American Indian heritage include Paddy Mayes, Mike Balenti, Virgil Cheeves, Jesse Petty, Ike Kahdot, Emmett Bowles, Pryor McBee, Art Daney, Roy Johnson (Bob's brother), Euel Moore, Vallie Eaves, Bob Neighbors, Jess Pike and Jim Gladd.

The first organized game in the Indian Territory

(what is now Oklahoma) took place among coal miners on July 4, 1882 in Krebs, according to the Oklahoma Historical Society. Future Hall of Famer Joe McGinnity later helped popularize the game in the Indian Territory while pitching for the Krebs team. The game grew increasingly popular with Native Americans and white settlers who had started out playing stickball or Indian ball.

By 1923 the state was home to 23 minor league teams and the state-wide sandlot tournaments were attracting huge crowds. Major league scouts came in droves to watch the sandlot championships at Duncan and Enid in the late 1930s and early 1940s. Teams from Oklahoma won seven championships at the National Baseball Congress in Wichita and the Denver Post Tournament between 1936 and 1941.

Quite a number of major leaguers got their first taste of competitive baseball playing for semi-pro teams on sandlot fields scattered around dusty Oklahoma towns. Carl Hubbell pitched his first "pro" game on a sandlot field in Sparks, while Roy "Peaches" Davis and Dizzy Dean were Oklahoma sandlot stars. Allie Reynolds played sandlot ball in Stillwater and Seminole, while Mickey Mantle reportedly walked three miles to play his games in Mayes County.

All-Time Oklahoma Selections

A quick glance at the roster for the All-Time Oklahoma team might cause one to believe it's a Yankees reunion. Mickey Mantle, Bobby Murcer, Paul Blair and Bobby Callison in the outfield, Allie Reynolds and Ralph Terry as starters, Lindy McDaniel in the bullpen and Bobby Cox available to man third base.

If Cox is your third baseman, then you're in trouble. Cox broke into the majors with the Yankees in 1968, which was Mantle's last year. Cox didn't exactly pick up where the Mick left off, as he managed just two homers and a .225 batting average in his two seasons with the Bronx Bombers. Within two years he had wisely turned to managing and he spent seven years managing and coaching in the Yankees organization before being hired by the Braves in 1978.

Let's move on to the All-Time-Oklahoma team selections, starting with catcher. Johnny Bench grew up in the tiny town of Binger watching Mantle play with great admiration and thinking, "That's what I want to be." Bench decided to be a catcher because his father suggested that was the quickest path to the majors, and he would go on to be widely regarded as the greatest all-around catcher in baseball history.

In his autobiography, *Catch You Later*, Bench recounts how he and his boyhood pals used to play a variation of baseball by hitting metal milk cans. He still has the scars from trying to catch the cans with the jagged edges, but admits that is how he picked up the skill to hit breaking balls.

Cocky and self-confident from the beginning of his career, Bench quickly proved he had the whole package of agility behind the plate, a powerful throwing arm and great power with the bat. He was NL Rookie of the Year in 1968 — the first catcher to win that award — then earned his first MVP in his third season after clubbing 45 homers and driving in 148 runs to lead the league in both categories. In 1972 he was intentionally walked 23 times while again leading the league with 40 homers and 125 RBI, earning him his second MVP trophy.

He was named Series MVP after batting .533 in the 1976 World Series as the Big Red Machine won their second straight title. Sparky Anderson, his manager on the Reds, once said, "I don't want to embarrass any other catcher by comparing him with Johnny Bench."

Bench earned Gold Gloves in his first 10 seasons and set a record by catching more than 100 games in 13 straight seasons. He would finish in the top five in caught stealing percentage for catchers 11 times. An All-Star his first 13 seasons (14 overall), Bench retired with 389 home runs including a record 327 as a catcher, a mark since passed by Carlton Fisk and Mike Piazza. "A catcher and his body are like the outlaw and his horse. He's got to ride that nag till it drops," said Bench, who closed out his career by playing more than 400 games at first, third and the outfield. Inducted into the Hall of Fame in 1989 with 96.4 percent of the vote, Bench was named to the All-Century Team.

All other catchers born in Oklahoma are destined to be an afterthought with Bench casting such a big shadow. Mickey Tettleton was a slugging catcher who played 14 years for four teams in the American League. He hit 30 or more homers three straight years for the Tigers (1991–93) and compiled 245 homers for his career. He picked up the nickname "Fruit Loops" because he believed the cereal gave him his power. Tettleton was adept at drawing walks, averaging 105 walks between 1990 and 1996 and leading the league with 122 in 1992. A two-time All-Star and three-time winner of the Silver Slugger Award for catchers, Tettleton was below average defensively. He made 361 appearances as a designated hitter, so he makes the All-Time Oklahoma team at DH.

The list of noteworthy outfielders from Oklahoma should include Willie Stargell, who played more games in left field than at first base over his career. However, Stargell did play 848 games at first and was a first baseman in 1979, a year in which he was named co-MVP and led the Pirates to a championship. Considering the lack of accomplished Oklahoma-born first basemen — Randy Bass, Phil Stephenson and Jim Beauchamp don't meet the standard — it didn't seem fair to award Stargell an outfield spot on the All-Time Oklahoma team and relegate a worthy player like Murcer to the bench.

Although Mantle took great pride in being considered "a great teammate," no player was more admired and appreciated by his teammates than Stargell. He picked up the nickname "Pops" for the fatherly way he looked out for teammates during the latter stages of his career. He was instrumental in sparking the Pirates' "We Are Family" spirit on the 1979 title team by handing out gold stars to players who made great plays in each game.

No one made bigger plays than Pops that year, as Stargell hit 32 homers during the regular season, then batted .455 with two homers to earn NLCS MVP honors. He was even more clutch in the Series, batting .400 overall with three home runs and going 4-for-5 with a homer and two doubles in Game 7, earning him his third MVP award of the year. It was a fitting way to end a decade in which he hit 296 regular season home runs — the most of any player in the 1970s.

Being a kind and gracious teammate is all well and good, but what Stargell excelled at was crushing the ball harder than anyone who has ever played the game. A good number of his 475 career homers were monstrous shots. He was the first player to hit a ball out of Dodger Stadium — he did it a second time for good measure — and Stargell accounted for seven of the 18 balls hit out of Forbes Field over its 61-year history. The lefty-swinging slugger hit the longest home run at Olympic Stadium in Montreal. Then there's the ball he walloped off Mudcat Grant during the 1965 All-Star game that hasn't been seen since. As Sparky Anderson remarked, "He's got power enough to hit home runs in any park, including Yellowstone."

Another accomplished slugging first baseman from Oklahoma never made it to the majors. Joe Bauman, who was born in Welch, hit 337 home runs in nine minor league seasons including an amazing 72 in 138 games in 1954. Only Barry Bonds with 73 homers in 2001 can top Bauman's mark in professional baseball. Bauman hit 50 homers in 1952 and 53 in 1953.

Second base is in the capable hands of Johnny Ray, a switch-hitter who finished second for the Rookie of the Year Award in 1982. He won a Silver Slugger with the Pirates the next year after batting .283 and leading the NL with 38 doubles. Ray led the league in doubles again in 1984 while raising his average to .312. He was overshadowed by Ryne Sandberg during his seven National League years, but moved over to the Angels and made his only All-Star team in 1988 after batting .306 with a career-high 88 RBI.

Jerry Adair hung around for 13 seasons largely because of his glove, as his career OPS+ was 80. In 1964 Adair set major league records for a second baseman with just five errors and .994 fielding percentage and he led the AL in fielding again the next year. During those years he also set a record for consecutive errorless games by a second baseman (89) and consecutive chances handled without an error with 458.

Our third baseman, Harlond Clift, was underrated because he was stuck playing for mediocre St. Louis Browns teams for most of his career and never made the postseason. He batted .306 with 29 homers and 118 RBI in 1937, making his only All-Star team, and then followed that up with a .290 average, 34 home runs and 118 RBI the next year. Clift led the AL in putouts three times, assists and fielding percentage twice and retired in 1945 with 178 home runs.

A strong case could also be made for Hank Thompson, who started off in the Negro Leagues before joining the majors just three months after Jackie Robinson broke the color barrier. When he got his first chance to play regularly he produced, batting .289 with 20 homers, 91 RBI and a .391 OBP for the New York Giants in 1950. Another strong year was 1953, when he belted 24 homers, drove in 74 runs and batted .302.

Thompson, who played his last game in the majors at age 30, finished with 129 homers in nine major league seasons. His career OPS+ of 118 is higher than that of Hall of Fame third basemen Brook Robinson, Pie Traynor and George Kell. Thompson had a series of run-ins with the law, killing a man in self-defense in 1948 and serving time for robbery after his playing days. He died of a seizure in 1969 at age 43.

Alvin Dark is an easy choice at shortstop. It was his competitive drive and steady play that willed his teams to three pennants, and he accumulated 2,089 hits and scored 1,064 runs over 14 seasons. He was especially skilled at executing the hit-and-run play. Dark was named Rookie of the Year and finished third in MVP voting in 1948 after batting .322 and leading the Boston Braves to the pennant.

Dark and his double-play partner, Eddie Stanky, were traded to the New York Giants before the 1950 season for Sid Gordon and Willard Marshall, a move that backfired for the Braves. By their second year together Dark and Stanky had helped turn the Giants into winners, capped by Bobby Thomson's historic pennant-winning home run. Dark made his first All-Star team during that miracle 1951 season, a year in which he hit .303 with 196 hits and led the league in doubles. The Giants would lose to the Yankees in the World Series, although Dark batted .417 in the six games.

In 1953 he set career highs with 126 runs (third in the NL), 23 homers and 88 RBI while batting .300 for the last time. Dark was an All-Star for the third time in 1954 as he had one of his best overall years, finishing fifth in the MVP race while again leading the Giants to the pennant. They swept the Indians in the World Series as Dark batted .412. Over his career he led NL shortstops in putouts three times and assists once despite having average range. He was the first winner of the Lou Gehrig Memorial Award in 1955, which honors players for character and integrity.

The stable of outfielders from Oklahoma is loaded with talent but the star power comes from Mantle, who has to be considered the most iconic player of his generation. Worshiped by men and women, young and old, Mantle not only possessed five-tool skills, each of his tools seemed far superior to any other player. He could run like a deer, throw like a cannon, slug homers like the Babe. He was without question the greatest switch-hitter of all-time.

In 1956, at the age of 24, Mantle won the Triple Crown by batting .353, hitting 52 homers and driving in 130 runs. He also led the league with 132 runs scored and posted an eye-popping .464/.705/1.169 line, along with an OPS+ of 210. The sky seemed the limit for the growing legend known as "the Commerce Comet."

Mantle knew that many fans came to the ballpark hoping to see him hit a home run, and he tried not to disappoint. "If I had played my career hitting singles like Pete (Rose), I'd wear a dress," he said in his autobiography, *The Mick*. His 565-foot home run in Griffith Stadium in 1953 is believed to be the first monstrous shot officially measured with a tape rule, which led to the coining of the phrase "tape-measure home run."

A 16-time All-Star and three-time MVP (he was runner-up three times), Mantle led the AL in home runs and slugging four times. His 536 homers currently rank sixteenth, but Mantle was number three on the list behind only Babe Ruth and Willie Mays when he retired after the 1968 season. He was an icon of a generation, which was enough to earn him the selection as Oklahoma's All-Time Best Player.

The Yankees appeared in 12 World Series in Mantle's 18 years, winning seven championships. Hobbled by injuries in the latter stages of his career, Mantle compiled most of his career stats between the ages of 20 and 32, later lamenting the fact that he hadn't taken better care of his body but had instead spent too many late nights drinking and carousing with buddies Whitey Ford and Billy Martin. "I figure I got all the breaks in spite of my legs. Otherwise, I'd have been in the mines," Mantle once said.

Above all, he wanted to be known as "a great teammate," which is how it describes him on his plaque at Monument Park in Yankee Stadium. "If you had a bad day, Mickey would wait for you in the clubhouse, and he'd tap you on the shoulder and invite you out to dinner," recalls Johnny Blanchard, who was Mantle's teammate for a decade. "That's all you needed. The next day you'd go out and get four hits."

Mantle, who was named after Hall of Famer Mickey Cochrane (his dad's favorite player), was elected to the Hall of Fame in his first year of eligibility, 1974, getting inducted with his best friend, Whitey Ford. *The Sporting News* ranked Mantle seventeenth on its 1999 list of "The 100 Greatest Baseball Players" and he also made MLB's All-Century Team.

Broadcaster Bob Costas, who has been carrying a 1958 Mantle baseball card around in his wallet since he was a teenager, delivered the eulogy at Mantle's funeral in 1995. As Costas so eloquently put it, for many kids who grew up in the 1950s and 1960s, Mickey Mantle was baseball. "And more than that, he was a presence in our lives — a fragile hero to whom we had an emotional attachment so strong and lasting that it defied logic," Costas said.

Fans seemed to believe that Mantle could simply pass on his Oklahoma-grown greatness to Murcer who had to suffer his whole career with the unfair comparisons to the Mick. It didn't help that both players were discovered by the same scout, Tom Greenwade, and that Murcer grew up idolizing Mantle.

Murcer turned out to be a pretty terrific ballplayer just the same, and he mans one of the outfield spots on the All-Time-Oklahoma team. He didn't really possess the speed or range to play center field in Yankee Stadium, but he was more than adequate in the field and a talented offensive player. His best overall season was 1971, when he led the league in OBP (.427), OPS (.969) and OPS+ (181) while hitting 25 homers and finishing second in batting at .331. The next year he led the AL in total bases and runs and belted 33 homers — the only season he hit over 30 — and finished fifth in MVP voting. A five-time All-Star, he never drove in 100 runs in a season but could generally be counted on for 85 to 90 RBI.

Murcer was a proud man who loved playing for the Yankees, so it stung when the Yankees traded him to the Giants for Bobby Bonds after the 1974 season. He played like a lost soul during his five years in the National League and although he would return to the Bronx Bombers in 1979 he had missed their magical run of World Series titles. The team fell short in the playoffs in 1980 and 1981, and Murcer retired in 1983 after accumulating 252 homers and 1,043 RBI. Fans loved him for his quiet dignity, and he remained with the team as a broadcaster up until his death from cancer in 2008.

Few remember that Paul Waner finished up his career with the Yankees in 1944–45 — he had one hit in seven at-bats for them. His legacy was forged from 15 spectacular years with the Pirates, starting off with .336 mark his rookie year. A three-time batting champion, Waner batted over .300 13 times for the Pirates, with a career high of .380 during his MVP season of 1927. The lefty swinger finished in the top 10 in on-base percentage 13 times, ending up at .404, and he had eight seasons with over 200 hits.

Waner retired with 3,152 hits, good for sixteenth place on the all-time list, and he ranks 10th in triples with 191 and 11th in doubles with 605. His .333 batting average is pretty incredible when you consider he was a heavy drinker who played many games with a hangover. "I saw a lot of good hitters, but I never saw a better one than Paul Waner," said Hall of Fame hurler Burleigh Grimes. "I once threw a side-arm spitter right into his belly and he hit it into the upper deck. I may have got Waner out, but I never fooled him."

It sure seems like there are more good Oklahoma-born outfielders per capita than any other state. No less than 12 deserving outfielders earned honorable mention on the All-Time Oklahoma team, ready to take over for Mantle, Murcer and Waner.

We have a World Series hero (Joe Carter), a Negro Leagues star (Frog Redus), two Johnson brothers with lifetime .296 averages (Bob and Roy), an eight-time Gold Glover (Blair), a player who hit a game-winning homer in the All-Star game (Callison), one of the all-time great contact hitters (Dale Mitchell), one of the leaders of the Gashouse Gang (Pepper Martin) who hit .500 in the 1931 World Series, a .311 lifetime hitter (Rip Radcliff), an active player who's a four-time All-Star (Matt Holliday) and another Oklahoma-born center fielder who had to replace a legend in New York — Don Demeter, who took over for Duke Snider in center for the Brooklyn Dodgers.

Then we have Lloyd Waner. He may be in the Hall

of Fame with his brother, but that wasn't enough to earn him an outfield position on Team Oklahoma. Waner's lifetime OPS+ of 99 means his batting productivity was just a tick below average for his time — not exactly the mark of an all-time great. Waner didn't hit home runs or doubles, walk or steal bases, and his performance peaked at age 26. He was a singles hitter who batted .316 during a Lively Ball Era. In three prime years of his career — starting when he was 27 in 1933 — Waner posted OPS+ marks of 80, 80 and 95. He was a productive leadoff hitter, but it looks like Little Poison's legacy was helped immensely by the presence of Big Poison.

Carter almost deserves a spot just for his heroics in hitting the three-run walk-off homer off Mitch Williams to win the 1993 World Series for the Blue Jays. As Blue Jays radio announcer Tom Cheek famously said at the time, "Touch 'em all, Joe. You'll never hit a bigger home run in your life!" No one else has either, for that matter. Carter blasted 396 homers and collected 1,445 RBI over his 16-year career, driving in over 100 runs in 10 different seasons. A five-time All-Star, he added 231 stolen bases, resulting in him ranking 27th all-time in power-speed number.

"Indian Bob" Johnson hit 20 or more home runs in each of his first nine seasons and also compiled a string of nine straight seasons with over 100 RBI. He had a strong arm, leading AL outfielders in assists twice. The only time Johnson led in any hitting categories was 1944, when he finished first in OBP (.431), OPS (.959) and OPS+ (174), but he ranked among the leaders in key categories virtually every year of his career. His career OPS+ of 138 ranks ahead of Joe Medwick, Al Kaline, George Brett and Billy Williams.

Johnson's score of 161 on the Gray Ink scale denotes his qualification for Cooperstown, although his career exhibited steady goodness more than spectacular greatness. He was hurt by the fact that he was 27 when he debuted in the majors. Still, he received just one vote for the Hall in 1948 — the same number of votes received that year by Hugh Mulcahy, who earned the nickname "Losing Pitcher" due to his 45–89 career record. Given another crack at the Hall in 1956, Johnson again garnered only one vote and dropped off the ballot.

Johnson's older brother, Roy, had a pretty nice career, but was far inferior as a player. Roy batted .314 with 201 hits, scored 128 runs and led the league in doubles with 45 during his rookie year of 1929. He later batted over .300 in three straight years for the Red Sox but didn't have the power of longevity of his brother.

Harry "The Cat" Breechen, whose tenure with the Cardinals lasted from 1940–52, earns the selection as the All-Time lefty starter. His record was superior to that of long-time teammate and fellow southpaw Al Brazle. Breechen, who won 132 games and appeared in two All-Star games, picked up his nickname for the cat-like reflexes he displayed in going after bunts.

Breechen's best season was 1948, when he went 20–7 and led the league in ERA (2.24), shutouts (7), strikeouts (149), SO/BB (3.04) and ERA+ (182). The Broken Bow native topped NL pitchers with five shutouts in 1946 and then almost single-handedly led the Cards to the championship that year by going 3–0 with a 0.45 ERA in the Series.

Brazle was mainly a starter early in his career before shifting to the bullpen. He relieved in 324 games (versus 117 starts) and finished 178 games over 10 seasons with the Cardinals. He retired in 1954 with a 97–64 record, a .602 winning percentage. Brazle appeared in two World Series with the Cardinals during his years with the team (1943–54), coming out of the pen to lose Game 5 but still earning a ring in 1946.

Several other candidates rose to the top when examining the top right-handed starters for the All-Time-Oklahoma team. Allie Reynolds was the most accomplished pitcher among the many major league candidates, but "Bullet" Joe Rogan was better ... by a lot. Chet Brewer, who was a teammate of Rogan and Satchel Paige on the Kansas City Monarchs, said Rogan was the best pitcher he ever saw in his life and credited him as the inventor of the palm ball.

Bullet Joe Rogan could beat you with his arm or his bat, as he was a dangerous two-way threat with the Kansas City Monarchs. The Oklahoma City native frequently played the outfield and batted cleanup when not pitching. Blessed with a powerful fastball, wicked curve and an assortment of other pitches, Rogan demonstrated he was one of the Negro Leagues' greatest pitchers (National Baseball Hall of Fame Library, Cooperstown, New York).

Rogan put together a pretty impressive career in the Negro Leagues, considering he was 30 when he joined the Kansas City Monarchs in 1920. Rogan went 119–50 with a 2.88 ERA in Negro Leagues competition, according to the Hall of Fame. He only pitched about 20 innings after 1928, as he concentrated on managing the Monarchs for the next decade.

In addition to having great stuff, Bullet was a smart, resourceful pitcher. Short and a little pudgy in build, he was one of the first to pitch without a windup. Bill James names Rogan the best pitcher in 1922, 1924 and 1925, calls him the best-hitting pitcher and writes that he had the best curveball of any Negro Leagues pitcher in the 1920s. In 1922 Rogan had a 14–8 record with 2.83 ERA and did even better with the bat, averaging .369 with 15 homers, 55 RBI and 16 stolen bases, according to the Seamheads.com Negro Leagues Database.

A lifetime .338 hitter with 45 homers and 104 stolen bases in Negro Leagues action (according to Hall of Fame study), Rogan often played in the field and batted cleanup when he was not pitching. "If you had to choose between Rogan and Paige, you'd pick Rogan, because he could hit," notes Frank Duncan, who caught both the legendary pitchers. Bullet Joe was finally elected to the Hall of Fame in 1998, 31 years after he died and 60 years after he threw his last knee-buckling curveball.

"Superchief," as Reynolds was known, had a borderline Hall of Fame career, finishing with a 182–107 record and a 3.30 ERA. "I always felt the pitcher had the advantage. It's like serving in tennis," he once said.

A five-time All-Star, Reynolds posted double-figure totals in wins every year of his career (excluding his two-game debut in 1942). Blessed with an overpowering fastball, he was usually among the league leaders in strikeouts. Reynolds started out with Cleveland, leading the AL in strikeouts as a rookie in 1943 and allowing just 140 hits in 198 innings. After the 1946 season he was traded to the Yankees for Joe Gordon, a trade that benefited both teams.

Reynolds won 19 games and a World Series title in his first year with the Yankees and then helped the team win five straight championships between 1949 and 1953. He went 7–2 with a 2.79 ERA in World Series action, winning at least one game every Series. He even batted .308 in 28 World Series at bats. In 1952 he won 20 games and led the league in ERA (2.06), shutouts (6), ERA+ (162) and strikeouts (160), stats that earned him second place in MVP balloting.

He was probably even more valuable in 1951, when he won 17 games (including two no-hitters), led the league in shutouts with seven and also relieved in 14 games. For his first no-hitter that year, Reynolds outdueled Bob Feller and the Indians 1–0 on July 12. His second no-hitter came against the Red Sox on Sept. 28 — Reynolds ended the game by getting Ted Williams to pop up to the catcher — and it clinched the pennant for the Yanks. He came in third for the MVP Award that year.

Ralph Terry was Reynolds' teammate and a key pitcher for the Yankees during a stretch of five consecutive pennants (1960–64). He went 16–3 for the 1961 championship team, then followed up with his best season in 1962 — a 23–12 record, a league-leading 298 innings, his only All-Star berth and two wins in the World Series as the Yankees repeated as champions. Terry was named MVP of that Series, which makes up for the fact that he surrendered the walk-off home run to Bill Mazeroski that ended the 1960 Series. In 1963 Terry won 17 games and led the AL in complete games with 18, but bounced around to three teams after that.

Righty Gene Conley won three NBA titles as a player while also winning 91 games over 11 seasons in the major leagues, making three All-Star teams. Mike Moore, Willis Hudlin and Jesse Barnes all won more than 150 games, but were essentially .500 pitchers. Joe Dobson pitched a four-hit shutout in Game 5 of the 1946 World Series and didn't give up a run in two other relief appearances for the Red Sox, who fell short in the Series. He went 18–8 with a 2.95 ERA for the Sox in 1947 and then made the All-Star team the next year while winning 16 games — those were the high points of his 14-year career.

Moving on to the bullpen, Team Oklahoma can turn to one of the most reliable and productive relievers of the 1960s — Lindy McDaniel. He finished in the top 10 in games pitched nine times, finished 577 games over 21 seasons and was named NL Reliever of the Year twice. When he retired he had pitched in the second-most games in history — 987, trailing only Hall of Famer Hoyt Wilhelm in that category. McDaniel's 141–119 record is very similar to the 143–122 mark posted by Wilhelm. We're not trying to make the case that McDaniel belongs in the Hall of Fame with Wilhelm — he doesn't — but he certainly belongs in the conversation of baseball's greatest relief pitchers. McDaniel only recorded 50 official saves, because he was 15 years into his career before the save was adopted.

Al Benton deserves mention, as his accomplishments outweigh his somewhat pedestrian stats. He was a swingman in the days before the rise of bullpen specialization dictated by matchups. Benton set a record with 39 consecutive scoreless relief innings in 1949, since matched by Brad Ziegler in 2008. A two-time All-Star, he came in second in the AL with 35 games finished in 1940 and went 15–6 with a 2.97 ERA the next year. Benton posted a 2.02 ERA in 1945 as the Tigers went on to win the World Series, then recorded a 2.12 ERA for the Indians in 1949.

Another notable Oklahoma reliever, Frank Linzy, pitched in 57 games with a 1.43 ERA as a rookie for the Giants in 1965. He relieved in 514 games and recorded a 2.85 ERA during a career that spanned 1963–74, posting 45 official saves.

Bobby Cox wasn't much of third baseman, but he sure proved to be a terrific manager. Although he managed a lot more years and won a lot more games and division titles than Alvin Dark, the two Oklahoma managers earned the same number of World Series titles — one. Cox guided the Braves to the division title 11 straight years and 14 out of 15 years, but fell short in the postseason every year but 1995.

Cox won over 100 games six times with the Braves and holds the record for most ejections in baseball history. A four-time Manager of the Year, Cox's 2,504 wins ranks fourth all-time and he is destined to gain induction into the Hall of Fame, the type of accolades that earn him the selection as manager of the All-Time Oklahoma team.

Dark made a quick transition from playing to managing, as the San Francisco Giants traded for him after the 1960 season so he could become their manager. Success and controversy followed him around during his years as a manager, which is how he wound up managing five teams in 13 seasons despite winning three division titles, two pennants and a World Series with the Oakland A's in 1974.

His increasingly strident religious beliefs caused friction with his bosses and players. While managing the Giants in 1964 Dark was quoted saying the team's black and latino players lacked the mental alertness to succeed, a major reason why he was let go at the end of that year. Dark was fired by the A's in 1975 despite guiding them to a second straight division title after saying Owner Charlie Finley was going to hell if he didn't accept Jesus Christ as his personal savior. He turned down a chance to manage the Cardinals because he thought it was immoral to work for a team owned by a beer company. His last managing job was in 1977 with the Padres, where he quickly lost the support of his players after banning them from drinking beer. Dark's final managerial record was 994–954.

OREGON

Names in **bold** *represent Major League selections by position, followed by honorable mentions. City of birth is in parentheses.*

Catcher — **Scott Hatteberg (Salem)**. Also: Mark Parent (Ashland)
First Base — **Richie Sexson (Portland)**. Also: John Jaha (Portland); Greg Brock (McMinnville)
Second Base — **Harold Reynolds (Eugene)**. Also: Wally Backman (Hillsboro); Dick Egan (Portland)
Third Base — **Scott Brosius (Hillsboro)**. Also: Dave Roberts (Lebanon)
Shortstop — **Johnny Pesky (Portland)**
Outfield — **Dale Murphy (Portland)**
Outfield — **Ken Williams (Grants Pass)**
Outfield — **Aaron Rowand (Portland)**. Also: Carson Bigbee (Waterloo); Jacoby Ellsbury (Madras); Brian Hunter (Portland); Brady Clark (Portland); Matt Diaz (Portland)
Designated Hitter — **Dave Kingman (Pendleton)**
Right Handed Starter — **Larry Jansen (Verboort)**. Also: Syl Johnson (Portland); Jack Wilson (Portland)
Left Handed Starter — **Mickey Lolich (Portland)**. Also: Jim Rooker (Lakeview)
Relief Pitcher — **Larry Andersen (Portland)**. Also: Alan Embree (The Dalles); Kevin Gregg (Corvallis)
Manager — **Del Baker (Sherwood)**

The Names

Best Nickname: Dave "Kong" Kingman
Other Nicknames: Carson "Skeeter" Bigbee; Dale "All American Boy" Murphy; Walter "Jiggs" Parrott; Johnny "The Needle" Pesky; Henry "Happy" Smith; Harvey "Suds" Sutherland; "Black Jack" Wilson
Most Unusual Name: Oswald Orwoll

All-Time Leaders

Games: Dale Murphy, 2180
Hits: Dale Murphy, 2111
Batting Average: Ken Williams, .319
Home Runs: Dave Kingman, 442
RBI: Dale Murphy, 1266
Stolen Bases: Brian Hunter, 260
Wins: Mickey Lolich, 217
Strikeouts: Mickey Lolich, 2832
Saves: Kevin Gregg, 144 (still active)
Future Star: Trevor Crowe (Portland)
Best Player: Dale Murphy

Historic Baseball Places

PK Park in Eugene — Opened in 2009 as the home of the Oregon Ducks and the Eugene Emeralds, a Padres affiliate in the Northwest League. It is the only professional baseball park without any dirt in the infield — only dirt is on the mound and at home plate. What looks like dirt is actually synthetic material designed to be easier to slide on and to drain without puddling, which means they can continue playing during a rainstorm. That's a handy feature for a ballpark in Oregon.

Civic Stadium in Eugene — The Emeralds played here from 1969 until PK Park opened up. The ballpark dates back to 1938, which made it one of the 10-oldest minor league stadiums while it had a minor league team. Now this historic park is in danger of being demolished, although a preservation effort is underway. Civic Stadium was placed on the National

Register of Historic Places in 2008, since it is Oregon's only remaining Depression-era ballpark.

Notable Achievements

Larry Jansen was the last player to win 30 games in the minor leagues. He went 30–6 for the San Francisco Seals in 1946.

Dave Kingman became the first to play for teams in four divisions in the same year when he played for the Mets, Padres, Angels and Yankees in 1977.

Scott Hatteberg was the first player to hit a grand slam and hit into a triple play in the same game, which he did on consecutive at-bats for the Red Sox on August 6, 2001.

Jacoby Ellsbury tied the record for most outfield putouts in a nine-inning game with 12 on May 20, 2009.

Carson Bigbee tied a record with 11 at-bats during a 22-inning game on August 22, 1917.

Portland's All-American Boy Next Door

The year was 1987 and it looked like Oregon would finally see one of its favored sons reach baseball immortality. Dale Murphy had just completed a six-year stretch in which he won back-to-back MVP awards, was named to six All-Star teams, won five Gold Glove and four Silver Slugger awards and ran his career home run total to 310. He was first in home runs, second in runs and third in RBI during that period and was in the conversation as the best player in the game.

Murphy did it all, from stealing bases and robbing hits with his glove to signing autographs with a smile and living the clean life of a true role model. He was the youngest player ever to win consecutive MVP awards, and the best was undoubtedly yet to come, because he was just 31 years old. He seemed like a sure-fire Hall of Famer.

Then a funny thing happened on the way to Cooperstown — Murphy stopped hitting and stopped winning awards, and his play seemed to fall in step with the rest of his lackluster teammates on the Braves. Four disappointing seasons were followed by two seasons as a bit player, and then Murphy was finished with a knee injury, out of the game at age 37. A promising career had turned sour too early.

Perhaps it was the accumulated strain of playing 740 straight games between 1981 and 1986 or the fact the Braves kept finishing near last place. Maybe he placed too much pressure on himself to keep up with his chemically-enhanced peers as baseball entered the darkness of the steroids era. In retrospect, what's commendable is the fact that Murphy refused to point fingers, make excuses or demand to be traded to a contender. It is unlikely he will get much consideration from the Hall of Fame's Veteran's Committee, because 398 home runs and a .265 average is just not good enough to join Mantle, Mays and DiMaggio in Cooperstown. Still, Murphy is richly deserving of the designation as Oregon's All-Time Best Player.

Murphy, who played at Wilson High School in Portland, is the most prominent of the 56 Portland-born players in the major leagues, along with Johnny Pesky and Mickey Lolich. Portland first hosted professional baseball in 1890, and the city has had a long history in the minor leagues primarily as the Beavers in the Pacific Coast League (PCL).

Walter McCredie was the star player on the 1904 Portland Browns, and he (and an uncle) actually purchased the team after the season. McCredie soon took over as manager while continuing to play, guiding the team (later renamed the Beavers) to PCL pennants in 1906, 1910, 1911, 1913 and 1914. The ace of the 1910 staff was Vean Gregg, who showed he was ready for the big time by winning 32 games (including a no-hitter), tossing 14 shutouts and striking out 376 batters. McCredie was instrumental into developing Gregg and a long list of other players into future major leaguers including Hall of Famers Harry Heilmann, Stan Coveleski and Dave Bancroft, reports Brian Campf in *Rain Check: Baseball in the Pacific Northwest*.

The Portland Mavericks commanded attention during their short run in the Northwest League from 1973–77. Owned by "Bonanza" actor Bing Russell, the team was comprised of baseball misfits who raised hell on and off the field, highlighted by *Ball Four* author Jim Bouton and the owner's son, future actor Kurt Russell. Bouton, in an article he wrote for *Rain Check: Baseball in the Pacific Northwest*, notes that Rob Nelson, who pitched for the Mavericks from 1975–77, came up with the idea for Big League Chew bubble gum while killing time in the Mavericks bullpen.

All-Time Oregon Selections

The best choice for catcher is Scott Hatteberg, who played 663 games at first compared to just 369 at catcher. Hatteberg received notoriety when he was prominently featured in Michael Lewis' best-seller, *Moneyball*. Oakland A's General Manager Billy Beane had become enamored with the value of on-base percentage, and he scoured the diamonds for low-cost players who excelled in that area. Hatteberg stood out among all the available players, and he became Beane's pet project after signing with the A's in 2002.

Hatteberg knew how to work the count, foul off tough pitches and either take a walk or put the ball in play. His first year with the A's he led the league in taking the first pitch and finished third in pitches per plate appearance. The A's had modest success following Hatteberg's lead at the plate, losing in the first round of the playoffs in 2002 and 2003, but it could be said that Beane's Hatteberg experiment ultimately failed because he couldn't find eight more players like "Hatty." Hatteberg managed to hang around the majors for 14 seasons and compile 1,153 hits with a .361 OBP.

The first baseman on the All-Time-Oregon team, Richie Sexson, was tall and lanky like Kingman and produced similar results on the diamond. If you add up his home runs (306) and strikeouts (1,313), they accounted for 32.8 percent of his at-bats, almost the same ratio as Kingman. Sexson, a two-time All-Star, was not an adept fielder but nowhere near as bad as Kingman.

Sexson became part of history on Sept. 25, 2001, when he and Jeromy Burnitz became the first teammates to each hit three home runs in the same game. He posted a career high with 45 home runs in both 2001 and 2003 with the Brewers (tying a club record) and drove in at least 100 runs six times.

Moving on to second base, Harold Reynolds earns the selection for his flashy glove work and good speed. He won three Gold Gloves and was named to two All-Star teams in 12 seasons, mainly with the Mariners. He led AL second basemen in assists five straight years and in putouts three times but also led in errors four straight years. Reynolds didn't hit many homers (21 for his career) or knock in a lot of runs, but he stole 250 career bases (despite a high caught-stealing rate) and was a capable batter. He led the AL with 11 triples in 1988 and was the only player besides Rickey Henderson to lead the American League in stolen bases during the 1980s, leading the AL with 60 stolen bases in 1987.

Wally Backman was given consideration at second, but he really only operated as a full-time starter for three seasons during a 14-year career. In one of those seasons, 1986, he hit .320 in the regular season and then .333 in the World Series as the Mets won the championship. Backman hit .275 and led NL second basemen in fielding percentage twice.

At third base we find the surprise hero of the 1998 World Series. On a Yankee team filled with superstars, it was unheralded Scott Brosius who hit two home runs in Game 3 and finished the Series with a .471 batting average as the Yankees swept the Padres. Brosius was named MVP of that Series. However, the lifetime .257 hitter was not done delivering in the clutch. He batted .375 and .308 the next two years in the World Series to help the Yankees win three straight titles. An All-Star in 1998 when he hit .300 with 19 homers and 98 RBI, Brosius followed that up by winning a Gold Glove the next year. He retired with 1,001 hits and 141 home runs.

Looking back at a career that led to him being labeled Mr. Red Sox, you would never guess that Johnny Pesky was not born in New England. His career with the Red Sox started off with a bang in 1942, as the shortstop led the AL in hits with 205 while batting .331. After serving three years in the Navy during World War II, he picked up where he left off and again led the league in hits the next two seasons with over 200 hits and had averages of .335 and .324.

Pesky was overshadowed at shortstop by fellow American League stars Luke Appling, Lou Boudreau and Phil Rizzuto. After the Red Sox traded for Vern Stephens, Pesky switched to third base for the 1948–50 seasons, and was overshadowed by George Kell and Ken Keltner. The only year he made the All-Star team was 1946, the year his Red Sox fell short in the World Series. Pesky's production waned as his career went on, but he retired with a .307 average.

Dom DiMaggio called Pesky one of the outstanding contact hitters in baseball, which was evident on the day he hit five singles in five consecutive innings while playing in a doubleheader. Other notable feats: becoming just the third player to post 11 consecutive hits, tying a major league record by scoring six runs in one game and pulling off the hidden-ball trick three times.

Pesky went on to serve as a manager, coach, broadcaster and instructor for the Red Sox and has been associated with the team for most of his 70 years in baseball. The team retired his number in 2008.

Most baseball fans have never heard of Ken Williams, yet he was one of the best players in the American League during the 1920s. Williams became the first player to hit 30 home runs and steal 30 bases in a season in 1922. It wasn't viewed as remarkable at the time, but no one else did it until Willie Mays in 1956. Tommy Harper was the next American League player to post a 30–30 season in 1970.

Williams had a monster year for the St. Louis Browns in 1922, batting .332 and leading the league with 39 homers (breaking a four-year streak by Babe Ruth) and 155 RBI while also stealing 37 bases (second in the AL) and producing a 1.040 OPS. He finished in the top four in home runs seven straight seasons. His career statistics were diminished by the fact that he didn't become a full-time starter until he was 30, but Williams batted over .300 10 times, had a career OBP of .393 and retired with 196 home runs.

A case could be made for either Aaron Rowand or Carson Bigbee as the third outfielder. Bigbee batted .323 with 204 hits in 1921, then followed up by batting .350 with 215 hits the next season, driving in 99 runs despite hitting just five homers. But his production tailed off quickly due to health problems and he was out of the game at 31.

Rowand, on the other hand, has earned one All-Star team selection as well as one Gold Glove for his stellar defense. That's not a fair comparison, since those honors weren't available in Bigbee's day, but Rowand does have better batting numbers and is still active. If you compare Win Shares they are almost dead even — 120.7 for Bigbee and 122.9 for Rowand. Rowand had 136 home runs through 2011 compared to 17 by Bigbee, whose career bridged the Deadball and Lively Ball eras. It's enough of a gap to provide the final rationale for selecting Rowand as Oregon's third outfielder.

Dave Kingman was one of the greatest home run hitters in baseball history, with his 442 home runs ranking 38th all-time. Thankfully he wound down his career in the American League so he could play his best position — designated hitter — his spot on the All-Time Oregon team.

In 1982 Kingman posted the lowest batting average (.204) ever for a home-run champion. Many of his homers were tape-measure shots of Ruthian dimensions, but he was also the ultimate hit-or-miss player, striking out 1,816 times during his 16 seasons. Kingman either struck out or homered in 33.8 percent of his career at-bats. Kingman was a dreadful fielder, whether it was at third or first base or the outfield. In 1973 he committed 18 errors at third base in just 60 games, while in 1982 with the Mets he was charged with 13 errors at first in just 56 games.

On the hill for Team Oregon is righty Larry Jansen, who went 21–5 with a 3.16 ERA as a rookie for the New York Giants in 1947. He didn't win Rookie of the Year, though, because Jackie Robinson also burst onto the scene that season. Jansen made his first All-Star team after winning 19 games and leading the NL in shutouts in 1950. His stats were almost identical the next season as he won 23 games.

Jansen was not a strikeout pitcher but possessed great control and pitching acumen. Many remember he was the winning pitcher in Bobby Thomson's "Shot Heard Round the World" game in 1951. In addition to winning 122 games in the majors, he won 122 more in the minors.

Also given strong consideration was Syl Johnson, who was a starter and reliever in a career that spanned 19 years over three decades. He won 112 games (with 117 losses) and won two World Series rings with the Cardinals, although he didn't appear in the 1926 Series.

The All-Time lefty for Oregon is Mickey Lolich, who often said he gave fat men hope all across America. Lolich may not have been a prime physical specimen, but the man knew how to pitch. He won 217 games over 16 years, the first 13 with the Tigers, and was a true workhorse. He pitched a league-high 376 innings in an amazing 45 starts in 1971, also leading the AL in strikeouts (308), complete games (29) and wins (25) but losing out to Vida Blue for the Cy Young Award. Lolich, who averaged 41 starts between 1970 and 1974, also won 22 games in 1972. He ranks eighteenth on the all-time list with 2,832 strikeouts and is number one in AL history in strikeouts by a left-handed pitcher.

Lolich's career highlight came in the 1968 World Series. He won MVP honors after outpitching Cardinals ace Bob Gibson to win Game 7 and becoming the only lefty to record three complete game victories in one Series.

Oregon is one of the states where it was necessary to select the best relief pitcher, as opposed to the best closer. The best, most reliable relief pitcher is Larry Andersen, who hung around as a dependable right-handed bullpen option for 17 seasons. He only fashioned 49 saves but finished with a 3.15 ERA and an ERA+ of 121. Andersen holds one record — most innings pitched without a decision, which he earned with 79⅔ innings pitched with the Mariners in 1982. He also has the distinction of being the player traded by the Astros in 1990 to acquire future Hall of Famer Jeff Bagwell. The Red Sox got zero wins and one save from Andersen, who did pitch to a 1.23 ERA in his 15 appearances for them.

Kevin Gregg has accumulated 144 career saves through 2011, all but one coming in the last five seasons. However, there is a reason he is pitching for his fifth team in six years in 2011— he walks a lot of batters and is a blown save waiting to happen. He did post a career-high 37 saves for Toronto in 2010.

A third reliever under consideration was Alan Embree, who carved out a long career as a lefty specialist. Pitching for 10 teams over 16 seasons, Embree accumulated 878 relief appearances. Seventeen of his 25 career saves came for the A's in 2007, when he pitched a career-high 68 innings. His teams appeared in the postseason seven times and he won a World Series championship with the Red Sox in 2004.

Our manager is Del Baker, who gained a coaching reputation as a talented sign stealer. He guided the Tigers to the pennant in 1940 by defeating Bob Feller and the Indians to break a tie on the final day of the season. The Tigers would go on to lose the World Series to the Reds that year, and Baker would eventually be dismissed after his teams floundered the next two seasons. Baker won 419 games in four full and five partial seasons of managing.

PENNSYLVANIA

*Names in **bold** represent major league selections by position, followed by honorable mentions. Negro Leagues players are in **bold italics**. City of birth is in parentheses.*

Catcher — Roy Campanella (Phil.). Also: Mike Piazza (Norristown); Lance Parrish (Clairton); Gene Tenace (Russellton); Charlie Bennett (New Castle); Mike Scioscia (Upper Darby); *Clarence Williams* (Harrisburg); Johnny Bassler (Mechanics Grove); Steve O'Neill (Minooka); Jack Clements (Phil.); Jimmie Wilson (Phil.); Butch Wynegar (York); Osee Schrecongost (New Bethlehem)

First Base — Dick Allen (Wampum). Also: Mickey Vernon (Marcus Hook); Jake Daubert (Shamokin); Harry Davis (Phil.); Henry Larkin (Reading); Charlie Hickman (Taylortown); Ripper Collins (Altoona); Joe Harris (Coulters); Jim Spencer (Hanover)

Second Base — Nellie Fox (St. Thomas). Also: Eddie Stanky (Phil.); Tommie Herr (Lancaster); Max Bishop (Waynesboro); Danny Murphy (Phil.); Bobby Lowe (Pitt.); Tom Daly (Phil.); Claude Ritchey (Emlenton); Glenn Beckert (Pitt.); Fred Dunlap (Phil.); Sparky Adams (Zerbe); Lou Bierbauer (Erie); Bill Hallman (Pitt.); Mickey Morandini (Kittanning); Ed Abbaticchio (Latrobe)

Third Base — Buddy Bell (Pitt.). Also: Jimmy Dykes

(Phil.); Ned Williamson (Phil.); Whitey Kurowski (Reading); Don Hoak (Roulette); Joe Dugan (Mahanoy City); *Harry Williams* (Pitt.); Brook Jacoby (Phil.); Tom Burns (Honesdale)

Shortstop — Honus Wagner (Chartiers). Also: Hughie Jennings (Pittston); Bobby Wallace (Pitt.); Dick Groat (Wilkinsburg); Monte Ward (Bellefonte); Buck Weaver (Pottstown); *Jake Stephens* (York); Mickey Doolan (Ashland); *Bill Yancey* (Phil.); *Frank Forbes* (Phil.)

Outfield — Stan Musial (Donora)

Outfield — Ken Griffey, Jr. (Donora)

Outfield — Reggie Jackson (Abington). Also: Hack Wilson (Ellwood City); Sherry Magee (Clarendon); Jimmy Sheckard (Upper Chanceford); Harry Stovey (Phil.); Roy Thomas (Norristown); Ken Griffey, Sr. (Donora); Fielder Jones (Shinglehouse); Del Ennis (Phil.); Carl Furillo (Stony Creek Mills); Hank Sauer (Pitt.); Vic Wertz (York); Buck Freeman (Catasauqua); Barney McCosky (Coal Run); Elmer Smith (Pitt.); John Titus (St. Clair); Oyster Burns (Phil.); Tito Francona (Aliquippa); Frank Thomas (Pitt.); Amos Strunk (Phil.); *Gene Benson* (Pitt.); Jimmy Slagle (Worthville); Red Murray (Arnot); Bobby Higginson (Phil.); Rube Bressler (Coder); *Judy Gans* (Washington)

Designated Hitter — Jack Clark (New Brighton)

Right Handed Starter — Christy Mathewson (Factoryville). Also: Ed Walsh (Plains); Mike Mussina (Williamsport); Stan Coveleski (Shamokin); Bucky Walters (Phil.); Jack Stivetts (Ashland); John Ward (Bellefonte); Bob Shawkey (Sigel); Guy Hecker (Youngsville); Bill Doak (Pitt.); Pete Vukovich (Johnstown); Pat Malone (Altoona); John Burkett (New Brighton); Bob Purkey (Pitt.); Dick McBride (Phil.); Harry Gumbert (Elizabeth); George Bradley (Reading); Frank Smith (Pitt.)

Left Handed Starter — Eddie Plank (Gettysburg). Also: Rube Waddell (Bradford); Herb Pennock (Kennett Square); Jamie Moyer (Sellersville); Curt Simmons (Egypt); Sam McDowell (Pitt.); Jon Matlack (West Chester); Frank Killen (Pitt.); Bill Sherdel (McSherrystown); Matt Kilroy (Phil.); *George Stovey* (Williamsport); Gary Peters (Grove City)

Relief Pitcher — Bruce Sutter (Lancaster). Also: Sparky Lyle (DuBois); Gene Garber (Lancaster); Joe Page (Cherry Valley); Bobby Shantz (Pottstown); Gary Lavelle (Scranton); Ron Kline (Callery); Steve Kline (Sunbury); Stan Belinda (Huntingdon); Curt Leskanic (Homestead); Ed Roebuck (East Millsboro)

Manager — Joe McCarthy (Phil.). Also: *Cum Posey* (Homestead); Tommy Lasorda (Norristown); Bill McKechnie (Wilkinsburg); Danny Murtaugh (Chester); Mike Scioscia (Upper Darby); Hughie Jennings (Pittston); Steve O'Neill (Minooka); Chuck Tanner (New Castle)

The Names

Best Nickname: Frank "Piano Mover" Smith
Other Nicknames: Ed "Batty" Abbaticchio; Dick "Crash" Allen; Mark "Fido" Baldwin; George "Deerfoot" Barclay; Clyde "Pooch" Barnhart; Glenn "Bruno" Beckert; Joseph "Fireman" Beggs; Max "Camera Eye" Bishop; Lena "Slats" Blackburne; "Handsome Henry" Boyle; George "Grin" Bradley; George "Scoops" Carey; "Jack the Ripper" Clark; James "Ripper" Collins; James "Snipe" Conley; "Dashing Dan" Costello; "Scranton Bill" Coughlin; William "Birdie" Cree; Harold "Sour Mash Jack" Daniels; Harry "Jasper" Davis; Bill "Bullfrog" Dietrich; "Spitting Bill" Doak; "Jumping Joe" Dugan; Fred "Sure Shot" Dunlap; Billy "The Little Globetrotter" Earle; "Piccolo Pete" Elko; Roy "Slippery" Ellam; William "Bones" Ely; James "Steamer" Flanagan; Tom "Sleuth" Fleming; Frank "Silver" Flint; Frank "Strangler" Forbes; Jacob "Nellie" Fox; Carl "The Reading Rifle" Furillo; Ken "Kid" Griffey, Jr.; Harry "Gunboat" Gumbert; Joe "Moon" Harris; Cliff "Rubberhead" Heathcote; Hugh "Bunny" High; Don "Tiger" Hoak; Gene "Twinkles" Host; Reggie "Mr. October" Jackson; Hughie "Ee-Yah" Jennings; Matt "Matches" Kilroy; Charles "King" Lear; Jeffrey "Old Penitentiary Face" Leonard; Chris "The Crab" Lindsay; Bristol "The Human Eyeball" Lord; Bobby "Link" Lowe; Eddie "Mongoose" Lukon; Albert "Sparky" Lyle; Samuel "Leech" Maskrey; Christy "Big Six" Mathewson; James "Swat" McCabe; Charles "Sparrow" McCaffrey; "Sudden Sam" McDowell; "Super Joe" McEwing; Bill "Deacon" McKechnie; "Minooka Mike" McNally; "Long Levi" Meyerle; Rudy "Potato Head" Minarcin; Mickey "Dandy Little Glove Man" Morandini; Stan "The Man" and "The Donora Greyhound" Musial; Ron "The Roundman" Northey; Joe "Gay Reliever" Page; Lance "Big Wheel" Parrish; Herb "The Knight of Kennett Square" Pennock; "Whoa Bill" Phillips; "Gettysburg Eddie" Plank; Thomas "Money Bags" Qualters; Claude "Little All Right" Ritchey; Lew "Old Dog" Ritter; Wilbur "Roxey" Roach; William "Yank" Robinson; Ralph "Human Ripcord" Savidge; Harry "Silk Stockings" Schafer; John "Count" Sensenderfer; William "Spike" Shannon; "Grunting Jim" Shaw; Bill "Wee Willie" Sherdel; Wallace "Toots" Shultz; Jimmy "The Human Mosquito," "Rabbit" and "Shorty" Slagle; John "Phenomenal" Smith; Eddie "The Brat" Stanky; Paul "Country Jake" Stephens; Alan "Inky" Strange; George "Good Kid" Susce; Myles "Duck Eye" Thomas; "Silent John" Titus; Terry "Cotton Top" Turner; Mike "Slugs" Ulicny; Jake "Guesses" Virtue; George "Rube" Waddell; Albert "Butts" Wagner; Honus "The Flying Dutchman" Wagner; John "Rock" Wehner; Harry "Bud" Weiser; Jimmy "Seabiscuit" Wilkes; Howard "Highball" Wilson; Lewis "Hack" Wilson; George "Sassafrass" Winter

Most Unusual Name: Osee Schrecongost; Jack Daniels; John Lush; Charlie Manlove

All-Time Leaders

Games: Stan Musial, 3026
Hits: Stan Musial, 3630

Batting Average: Stan Musial, .331
Home Runs: Ken Griffey, 630
RBI: Stan Musial, 1951
Stolen Bases: Honus Wagner, 722
Wins: Christy Mathewson, 373
Strikeouts: Mike Mussina, 2813
Saves: Bruce Sutter, 300
Future Star: Cory Spangenberg (Clarks Summit); Devin Mesoraco (Du Bois)
Best Player: Honus Wagner

Historic Baseball Places

Peter J. McGovern Little League Baseball Museum in Williamsport — Hall of Excellence pays tribute to famous Little League alumni. Also in Williamsport is **Lamade Stadium,** home to the annual Little League World Series; **Eric Stotz Field,** which was named in honor of the founder of Little League Baseball and hosted the first 12 Little League World Series from 1947–58; and **Bowman Field,** which once featured grandstand seats from Detroit's Briggs Stadium and lights from the Polo Grounds. Oscar Charleston hit the first home run at the new ballpark when it opened as Memorial Field on April 27, 1926.

Philadelphia Athletics Historical Society and Museum in Hatboro — On display are am extensive collection of clippings, photos, uniforms and artifacts from the team's 54-year history. Check out the timeline of A's uniforms, an original 1909 turnstile from Shibe Park, the Wall of Fame plaques from Veterans Stadium and early A's scorecards.

Citizens Bank Park in Philadelphia — The outfield concourse is named Ashburn Alley and you can find statues of Robin Roberts, Mike Schmidt and Steve Carlton by the entrances to the park.

PNC Park in Pittsburgh — A classic-style ballpark with intimate seating and a view of downtown Pittsburgh. Statues of Pirates heroes Roberto Clemente, Honus Wagner and Willie Stargell line the entrances to the park, which ironically opened on the day Stargell died in 2001. A statue of Bill Mazeroski was unveiled in 2010 that depicts him leaping for joy as he rounds the bases after his historic home run to win the 1960 World Series.

The Clemente Museum in Pittsburgh — Clemente fan Duane Rieder restored an old fire house to honor the memory of his idol. Pictures, artifacts and memorabilia highlight Clemente's legacy of achievement as a player and a humanitarian. On display are two of his Gold Glove trophies, his 1961 Silver Bat, cleats and the home plate from the 1971 World Series.

Mickey Vernon Sports History Museum in Chadds Ford — Chronicles the first baseman's career and military service. See video of Vernon in action during the 1940s and 1950s.

Western Pennsylvania Sports Museum in Pittsburgh — Inside the Senator John Heinz History Center you can learn the story behind the Pirates' five world championships and view a two-story mural of Forbes Field as it looked in 1960.

African American Museum in Philadelphia — Features documents, scorebooks and photos of the Philadelphia Stars and the Hilldale Athletic Club/Daisies from the Negro Leagues.

Hilldale Kitchen in Darby — Restaurant's baseball theme is centered on the Hilldale Daisies, featuring photographs of the powerhouse Negro Leagues team from the 1920s.

Notable Achievements

Mickey Vernon ranks first all-time in double plays by first baseman with 2,044.

Jim Russell (Fayette City) was the first switch-hitter to twice hit a home run from each side of plate in same game, which he did on June 7, 1948 and July 26, 1950.

Chuck Tanner was the first player to hit a pinch-hit home run on the first pitch he saw in the big leagues, which he did on Opening Day (April 12) in 1955.

Ernie Padgett (Philadelphia) completed an unassisted triple play in his fourth game in the majors on October 6, 1923.

Carl Scheib (Gratz) is the youngest player in American League history. He was 16 years, 8 months and 5 days old when he debuted on September 6, 1943.

Levi Meyerle (Phil.) is credited with hitting the first double (April 22, 1876) and the first triple (April 24, 1876) in major-league history.

Gene Tenace is one of only two players to homer in their first two World Series at-bats. Tenace did it in 1972 and Andruw Jones of the Braves duplicated the feat in 1996.

Bobby Lowe was the first player to hit four home runs in a game when he accomplished it in consecutive at-bats on May 30, 1894.

Clyde Barnhart (Buck Valley) is the only player to get hits in three games in one day. He got hits in each game of a triple-header played on October 2, 1920.

Curt Simmons gave up the 400th home run to both Ernie Banks and Willie Mays.

Hughie Jennings has the most RBI in a season with no home runs —121 in 1896.

Tom McCreery (Beaver) is the only player to hit three inside-the-park home runs in one game. He did it against Philadelphia's Jack Taylor on July 12, 1897.

Reggie Jackson hit his first home run on September 17, 1967, in Anaheim Stadium and hit his 500th home run in Anaheim Stadium on the same day 17 years later.

Steve O'Neill holds the single-season record for most double plays by a catcher with 36 in 1916.

Frank Forbes batted 7-for-7 for the Lincoln Stars on May 31, 1914.

Pennsylvania natives **Ned Williamson** and **Tom Burns,** along with teammate Fred Pfeffer, all collected three hits in one inning on September 6, 1883. It would be 70 years before another single player accomplished that feat.

Uncovering the Stories Behind Pennsylvania's Unheralded Players

Pennsylvania has been home to 1,359 major league players through the 2011 season, many of them with a unique story behind them. Although most fans know the background of iconic players such as Stan Musial, Christy Mathewson, Honus Wagner and Roy Campanella, few know what's unique about Doug Allison, Lena Blackburne, Paul Foytack, George Bradley and Harry O'Neill.

Doug Allison was a catcher and outfielder who played on the 1869 Cincinnati Red Stockings, baseball's first all-professional team. Allison is believed to be the first player to use a glove in a game in 1870. He caught with a pair of buckskin mittens to protect his injured hand. He also played in the National Association in its first season (1871), the National League in its first season (1876) and the American Association in its second season (1883). Allison ended up playing 10 seasons and batting .271.

Blackburne was a shortstop with a .214 average from eight seasons between 1910 and 1929. In the 1950s he discovered a special mud from the Delaware River that is still being used to rub down major league baseballs.

Foytack became the first pitcher to give up home runs to four straight batters in the same inning when he surrendered consecutive two-out shots to Woodie Held, pitcher Pedro Ramos (his second of the game), Tito Francona and Larry Brown of the Indians on July 31, 1963. Foytack had this feat of futility to himself until Chase Wright of the Yankees served up four straight gopher balls in 2007 to the Red Sox (managed by Francona's son, Terry).

George Bradley seemingly had an up-and-down career that had little to do with his pitching ability. He won 33 games in the last year of the National Association and then went 45–19 for the St. Louis Brown Stockings in the first year of the National League (1876), leading the league with a 1.23 ERA. He pitched the first no-hitter in the National League when he held the Hartford Dark Blues without a hit on July 15, 1876. Then in 1879 he was saddled with a 13–40 record despite a 2.85 ERA, because he was playing for a Troy Trojans team that won only 19 games all season.

O'Neill was a catcher who played one game with his hometown Philadelphia Athletics in 1939. He didn't get up to bat or handle any chances in the field, so his career stats are filled with zeroes. He was decidedly not a zero in life but a real-life hero. He served in the Marines as a lieutenant in World War II and was killed by a sniper at Iwo Jima, one of only two MLB players to die in that war.

One of the most noteworthy Pennsylvania players, Youngsville native Guy Hecker, has also gone largely unrecognized despite his amazing list of accomplishments. He is the only pitcher to lead a league in batting. Hecker led the American Association with a .341 average in 1886 while also winning 26 games and pitching 420 innings. His 52 wins in 1884 are the third-most in baseball history. In his rookie season of 1882 he pitched the second no-hitter in American Association history on September 19 and then finished the year with a 0.77 WHIP, which remained the major league record until Pedro Martinez topped it 118 years later. Hecker won the pitching Triple Crown in 1884 and on September 15, 1886, he became the only player to score seven runs in a game.

Hecker is considered the best hitter/pitcher combination of the nineteenth century, appearing in 336 games as a pitcher, 322 as a first baseman and 75 as an outfielder. He posted a 175–146 lifetime record as a pitcher with a 2.93 ERA and ERA+ of 114. As a batter, Hecker recorded 812 hits with a lifetime average of .282 and 117 OPS+.

Rube Bressler started out as a pitcher and then converted to the field, joining the ranks of Babe Ruth, Smoky Joe Wood, Johnny Cooney, Reb Russell and Rick Ankiel as twentieth century players who successfully made the switch. Bressler was 10–4 with a 1.77 ERA during his rookie season of 1914, but dropped to 4–17 with 5.20 ERA the next year. Injuries and ineffectiveness led to fewer opportunities on the mound and more chances in the outfield and at first base, where he demonstrated sound ability. Bressler spent four years as a pitcher, three years bouncing between pitching and the field and then 12 years as a position player (mainly in the outfield). He batted .347, .348 and .357 from 1924–26 and led NL outfielders in fielding percentage in 1930. Bressler ended up 26–32 with a 3.40 ERA and batted .301 lifetime with 1,170 hits and 110 OPS+.

The roster of players from Pennsylvania offers promise of a spirited time, with players such as Jack Daniels, Bud Weiser, Johnny Lush and Highball Wilson. They are counterbalanced by Jake Virtue, who was a rare left-handed shortstop.

King Lear, who was constantly muttering about his ungrateful daughters and those tiresome French invaders, came from Princeton and had a less than regal career as a pitcher, going 7–12 from 1914–15. Another recognizable name is Bull Durham, who went 2–0 as a pitcher between 1904 and 1909 but did not have a movie made about him.

Poor Allan Travers was among a group of warm bodies from St. Joseph's College who were used to fill in for the regular members of the Detroit Tigers when they went on strike to protest Ty Cobb's suspension in 1912. Travers, who had no pitching experience, was forced to face the stacked lineup of the champion Philadelphia Athletics for the May 18 game. The future priest hung in there to pitch a complete game but surrendered 26 hits and 24 runs (14 earned), leaving him with a career ERA of 15.75. Another Philadelphia native, Ed Irwin, collected the only two hits for the Tigers that day, leaving him with a career average of .667.

There must be something in the water in Donora, as the tiny town (population 5,653) is the birthplace of Ken Griffey, Sr., Ken Griffey, Jr., and Stan Musial. That trio combined for 1,257 home runs, 8,554 hits and 40 All-Star selections. Craig Griffey, Junior's brother, was also born in Donora and played seven years in the minors. Junior Griffey and Musial even share the same birthday, November 21.

Musial started playing semi-pro baseball for the Donora Zincs at the age of 15, where his standout play earned him the nickname "The Donora Greyhound." He played only one season for the Donora High School team, where one of his teammates was Joseph "Buddy" Griffey — father of Ken Sr. and grandfather of Ken Jr. Musial now has a baseball field named after him in Donora. Ken Griffey, Jr., lived in Donora until the age of six, when his father moved the family to Cincinnati.

Ken Griffey and Ken Griffey, Jr., are one of two fathers and sons to play together in the same game (along with Tim Raines and Tim Raines, Jr.). The Griffeys played together on the Mariners in 1990 and 1991 and homered back-to-back off Kirk McCaskill in the first inning on September 14, 1990 — the only time a father and son have homered in the same game.

Brothers Christy and Henry Mathewson combined for 373 career wins, all 373 contributed by Christy. Henry ended his three-game career with 14 walks in 11 innings. By comparison, Christy pitched 306 innings in 1913 and only walked 21 batters all season.

Dick Allen likewise had quite a bit more success than his brothers, Hank and Ron. Dick blasted 351 home runs, made seven All-Star teams and won the Rookie of the Year Award and MVP Award. Hank batted .241 with six career home runs while Ron batted 1-for-11 in his brief stint in the majors.

Shamokin native Stan Coveleski put together a Hall of Fame career by winning 20 games four straight years with the Indians. He led the Indians to the championship in 1920 by pitching three complete game victories in the World Series. Coveleski later helped the Washington Nationals win the pennant by going 20–5 in 1925 and leading the league with a 2.84 ERA. He retired with a 215–142 record and 2.89 ERA, getting elected to the Hall of Fame in 1969. His older brother, Harry, was an excellent pitcher as well, going 81–55 with a career ERA of 2.39. Harry was known as "The Giant Killer" after he beat the Giants three times down the stretch in 1908 to keep the Giants from winning the pennant. Harry later won 20 games three straight years with the Tigers until arm injuries cut short his career. The two Coveleski brothers refused to pitch against each other, although 1916 was the only year the two saw extensive action in the same league.

Lew Krausse and George Susce both saw sons of the same name follow in their footsteps to the majors and have more productive careers. The Keystone State has also produced two players named Charlie Householder along with two Pat Kellys and two Bob Gibsons. Both Gibsons were pitchers, but they were not to be confused with the Hall of Fame hurler. Duncansville native Robert Gibson went 1–3 with a 9.86 ERA, while Philly native Bob Gibson went 12–18 pitching from 1983–87.

Al Gionfriddo, who hailed from Dysart, ended his career on a high note with some defensive piracy. The 5-foot-6 outfielder robbed Joe DiMaggio of a three-run homer in Game 6 of the 1947 World Series, preserving a Dodger victory and forcing a Game 7. The Yankee Clipper kicked the dirt in frustration after he saw Gionfriddo snag his sixth-inning blast in deep left-center near the bullpen. Gionfriddo didn't play in the decisive Game 7, which was won by the Yankees, then got cut by the Dodgers before the 1948 season and never again played in the majors.

Pete Gray made history when he played 77 games for the St. Louis Browns in 1945, a time when rosters were depleted by war-time service. Born Peter Wyshner in Nanticoke, Gray had his right arm amputated at the age of six, but he learned to bat and field one-handed. He batted just .218 in the majors as he struggled to hit breaking pitches, and when the regular players started returning from the war Gray's career came to an end.

Buck Weaver was an outstanding shortstop who led the White Sox to the 1917 championship, batting .333 in the Series. He finished seventh in the league in batting the next year at .300 and then set career highs in most offensive categories in 1919 to help the Sox win the pennant again in 1919. Then came the Black Sox scandal, where it was determined that Weaver had participated in meetings where throwing games was discussed. Although Weaver batted .324 in that Series and professed his innocence, he was one of the eight players banned.

Weaver is not the only player from the state to get banned from baseball. Jim Devlin was a star pitcher who won 30 games in 1876 and 35 games in 1877, leading the league in starts, complete games and innings pitched both years. Incredibly, Devlin pitched all 559 innings for the Louisville Grays in 1877 after pitching 622 of the team's 643 innings the previous year. It's safe to say no pitcher will come close to that accomplishment. His career ERA+ of 151 ranks third in baseball history behind Mariano Rivera and Pedro Martinez. However, Devlin got caught up in a gambling scandal in 1877 and was kicked off the team and banned from the league for life by National League President William Hulbert.

Then we have the strange case of Phenomenal Smith, whose birth name was John Francis Gammon. He picked up his unusual moniker after a dominant performance in the minors when he reportedly struck out 16 batters without allowing a ball to be hit past the infield. He wasn't so phenomenal when he was losing 50 games in 1887–88, but Smith was later credited with discovering Christy Mathewson.

The state's all-time best nickname belongs to another Smith — Frank — who was called "Piano Mover" because he worked for a furniture-moving company in the off-season and frequently bragged about his ability to carry pianos up multiple flights of stairs.

Some of the memorable player nicknames relate to a hometown such as Stan "The Donora Greyhound" Musial, Herb "The Knight of Kennett Square" Pennock and Carl "The Reading Rifle" Furillo.

We find nicknames for dog lovers — Mark "Fido"

Baldwin and Clyde "Pooch" Barnhart — and nicknames for horse lovers — Samuel "Pony" Sager and "Whoa Bill" Phillips. Jimmy Slagle was lucky enough to earn three nicknames: Rabbit, Shorty and The Human Mosquito. We're guessing he preferred "Rabbit."

Joe Page, who in 1949 became the first relief pitcher to be named World Series MVP, picked up the nickname "The Gay Reliever" when gay had a politically correct meaning. There doesn't seem to be anything politically correct or remotely nice about calling Jeffrey Leonard "Old Penitentiary Face." It evidently stemmed from his tendency to look like an unhappy inmate getting a mug shot, although picking up a nickname like that probably makes a person even more of a sourpuss.

Max Bishop earned the nickname "Camera Eye" for his exceptional eye at the plate. The second baseman posted eight straight years with over 100 walks — including five seasons in which he had more walks than hits — and totaled 1,156 walks in 5,779 plate appearances. His .423 career OBP ranks seventeenth all-time. Then we have Bris "The Human Eyeball" Lord, who didn't walk or get on base at a high rate but had the distinction of being traded in 1910 to the Philadelphia Athletics for Morrie Rath and a player to be named later. That player turned out to be a 21-year-old outfielder named Shoeless Joe Jackson.

Charlie Metro wins the prize for having the most unusual birthplace: Nanty Glo, Pa. Metro was a baseball lifer who claims to have invented the batting tee. He played for Connie Mack and Casey Stengel, managed Jim Bunning, Brooks Robinson, Lou Brock, Steve Carlton and Ernie Banks and was one of the Cubs' rotating managers during their idiotic 1962 "College of Coaches" experiment.

Philadelphia and Pittsburgh Key Cities in Black Baseball History

Pennsylvania played a crucial role in the history of the Negro Leagues through the development of top teams in Philadelphia and Pittsburgh. The Pythian Base Ball Club was formed in Philadelphia in 1867 and the Pythians helped establish baseball's long history of segregation after being denied membership in the National Association of Base Ball Players solely because of race.

Sol White joined forces with white sportswriter H. Walter Schlichter and black sportswriter Harry Smith to form the Philadelphia Giants in 1902. The Giants quickly became a dominant force in early black baseball, winning five championships between 1904 and 1909.

The Hilldale Athletic Club, organized as an amateur team by Ed Bolden in 1910, played in Darby outside Philadelphia. The Hilldales, as the team became known, evolved into a powerhouse that won the first three Eastern Colored League championships behind stars Judy Johnson and Biz Mackey. Bolden was the driving force pushing the Eastern Colored League to compete with Rube Foster's Negro National League, and he was one of the most influential pioneers in the history of the Negro Leagues. Bolden later organized the Philadelphia Stars, who won the Negro National League in 1934 behind ace pitcher Slim Jones and third baseman Jud Wilson.

Philadelphia native Effa Manley, co-owner of the Newark Eagles with her husband, Abe, became the first woman elected to the Baseball Hall of Fame in 2006. She broke down racial and gender barriers while taking charge of the business and marketing activities of the team, negotiating fair contracts and improving playing conditions. It was unusual for a woman to be so involved in business affairs in the 1930s and 1940s, and especially one who was thought to be black. That was actually a mistake — Manley's biological parents were both white but she had a black step-father and later married a black man (Manley), which caused people to assume she too was black. While it might be considered unusual for a white person in that time period to prefer to be viewed as black, it sheds a different perspective on Manley's ground-breaking work as a civil rights activist.

Manley was involved in every aspect of the team's operation, even calling plays from her seat in the stands. The Eagles won the 1946 Negro World Series with stars Monte Irvin and Larry Doby, and she later sold Irvin's contract to the New York Giants in a precedent-setting move. Manley was rumored to be carrying on affairs with players such as Terris "Speed" McDuffie, but such gossip could also stem from the fact that she was very close to her "boys" on the team.

Cum Posey hailed from Homestead, just outside Pittsburgh, and in 1912 he organized the Homestead Grays, who would become one of the most successful and longest-lasting franchises in the Negro Leagues. His 1926 team won 43 straight games and barnstormed its way to a 140–13 overall record. Posey was player-manager until 1929, when he concentrated on his managerial and executive duties. He initiated night baseball before anyone in the major leagues and later served as executive secretary of the Negro National League and founded the East-West League. Under Posey's skillful direction, the Grays won nine straight Negro National League pennants and three championships between 1937 and 1945. He was elected to the Hall of Fame in 2006.

The Pittsburgh area was a hotbed of black baseball as the Pittsburgh Crawfords won Negro National League titles in 1935 and 1936 as owner Gus Greenlee was able to raid Posey's Homestead Grays to steal top players such as Oscar Charleston and Josh Gibson. Posey would return the favor a few years later, setting in motion his next dynasty with the Grays.

Gene Benson and Harry Williams are the best Negro Leagues players to come from Pittsburgh, while shortstop Bill Yancey is the best from Philadelphia. Benson was an outfielder who spent the better part of a decade with the Philadelphia Stars. Williams was an infielder (mainly at third) who began playing in the sandlots of Pittsburgh before advancing to pro baseball with the Crawfords and then the Grays. Yancey launched his career with the Philadelphia Giants and later starred for the Hilldale Daisies, Philadelphia Quaker City Giants and Philadelphia Tigers before ending his career with the Philadelphia Stars in 1936.

SABR member Joseph Pisano from Drums, Pa., points out that Pittsburgh's major league team picked up the nickname "Pirates" because of the actions of two Pennsylvania stars. Erie native Louis Bierbauer was a star second baseman for the Philadelphia Athletics of the American Association when he jumped his contract and joined the Players League in 1890. The Players League was established by a group of disgruntled players with the advice of ex-major leaguer turned attorney (and Bellefonte native) John Montgomery Ward. When the Players League folded after just one season, Bierbauer found himself a member of Pittsburgh's team in the National League, then known as the Alleghenys. The Philadelphia Athletics claimed ownership of Bierbauer's contract, but arbitration awarded him to Pittsburgh. For this action the team from Pittsburgh was accused of an act of piracy, hence the name "Pirates."

Pittsburgh features a number of historic baseball sites to see. The Pirates' stadium, PNC Park, features an indoor movie theatre presenting the legacy of the Negro Leagues on many interactive levels. Highmark Legacy Square pays tribute to great players from the Homestead Grays and Pittsburgh Crawfords such as Cool Papa Bell, Oscar Charleston, Josh Gibson and Satchel Paige. The Clemente Museum, which was organized in a restored firehouse, includes more than 300 photos depicting the Hall of Famer's life on and off the diamond. At the Western Pennsylvania Sports Museum you can listen to play-by-play broadcasts from Bob Prince and watch Maz's World Series winning home run on the big screen.

Baseball history is also on display in Philadelphia. The African American Museum showcases artifacts from the Philadelphia Stars and the Hilldale Athletic Club/Daisies from the Negro Leagues. The Hilldale Kitchen restaurant in Darby has a baseball theme centered on the Darby-based Hilldales. The Philadelphia Athletics Historical Society in Hatboro features a museum with autographs from Connie Mack and Chief Bender, authentic seats and a classic turnstile from Shibe Park, replica jerseys through the years, World Series programs and a letter from Jimmy Foxx to a fan.

All-Time Pennsylvania Selections

With that background behind us, let's move on to the selections for the All-Time Pennsylvania team. The catcher position brings up a tough choice between Roy Campanella and Mike Piazza. At first glance, it seems like Piazza's accomplishments with the bat swing the tide in his favor.

Piazza has hit more home runs (396) than any other catcher and he is generally regarded as the best-hitting catcher in baseball history. He is one of only nine players to hit 400 homers, average over .300 and never strike out 100 times in a season. His 35 homers in 1993 are the most by a rookie catcher and his .362 average in 1997 is the National League record for catchers. Piazza is the only catcher (min. 100 games caught) to have more than 200 hits in a season — he had 201 in 1997. In 2000, he drove in a run in 15 straight games, which is the second-best streak. He had at least 30 homers in eight straight seasons and ended up with 427 homers, a .308 average and 142 OPS+. He won a record 10 straight Silver Sluggers, made 12 All-Star teams and was MVP runner-up in 1996 and 1997.

Those are pretty impressive numbers, especially for a catcher. If only we could believe it was all legitimate. It always seemed like Piazza's production came out of nowhere, and not just because he was a 62nd-round draft choice who didn't impress in his first two minor league seasons. Piazza largely managed to escape suspicion during his career despite a pesky case of back acne, but rumors of steroid use have dogged him since he retired in 2008. He was listed in the Mitchell Report and further allegations were raised in Jeff Pearlman's 2009 book about Roger Clemens, *The Rocket That Fell to Earth*. Although the rumors are so far unsubstantiated, it does put Piazza's career in a different light.

Piazza was weak defensively and he threw out only 23 percent of base stealers during his career. He was also one of the worst at tipping pitch location. With Piazza's batting production somewhat tainted and his defense below average, it becomes easier to decide that Campanella deserves the All-Time catcher spot since he was an outstanding two-way player and three-time MVP.

"Campy" dropped out of high school at 15 to join the Baltimore Elite Giants in the Negro Leagues, where he was tutored by future Hall of Famer Biz Mackey. It took him several years to get acclimated before he busted out in 1941, making the East-West All-Star Game and ranking among the league leaders in batting. After eight seasons in the Negro Leagues he was signed by the Dodgers in 1946, shortly after the team had secured the services of Jackie Robinson. Campanella and Don Newcombe were the first African American players in the New England League. In 1948, Campy integrated the American Association, batting .325 for St. Paul before joining the Dodgers for good.

Campanella made eight straight All-Star teams, becoming the first three-time MVP honoree in the National League by winning in the odd-numbered years of 1951, 1953 and 1955. His 142 RBI in 1953 remain a NL record for catchers and a mark that even Piazza couldn't surpass. His 41 homers that season were later topped by Javy Lopez while his 242 career homers were a record for catchers when he retired. Campy is credited with throwing out 51 percent of base stealers over his 10-season career, which ranks as the third-best percentage of all-time. He led the Dodgers to five pennants and one World Series title.

"You have to have a lot of the little boy in you to play baseball for a living," Campanella was quoted saying in 1957 in *Baseball: The Early Years* by Harold Seymour. Shortly after that, he was seriously injured in a car accident that left him a paraplegic and ended his baseball career at age 35. He was elected to the Hall of Fame in his fifth year on the ballot in 1969.

Lance Parrish was also a talented two-way catcher who earned eight All-Star selections, three Gold Gloves and six Silver Sluggers while hitting 324 home runs. Gene Tenace was an underrated catcher who had good power and excelled at drawing walks. He led the league in walks twice and posted six seasons with over 100 bases on balls. His 201 career homers included five seasons with at least 20 homers. Tenace won three straight championships with the A's and later won a fourth ring with the Cardinals.

Charlie Bennett was one of the best catchers of the nineteenth century, finishing among the top 10 in home runs five times and leading the league in fielding percentage seven times. Bennett batted over .300 three straight years for the Detroit Wolverines, helping the team win the 1887 National League pennant and World Series, which was then an exhibition. He later won three straight National League pennants with the Boston Beaneaters (1891–93), along with the 1892 Championship Series, before losing his legs in a train accident. The Detroit Tigers named their park, Bennett Park, after him.

Jack Clements is the greatest left-handed catcher in baseball history, which isn't really much of an accomplishment considering the lack of competition. Clements was a powerful batter who batted .315 with 74 RBI in 1890, finished second with 17 homers in 1893 and averaged .394 in 1895. He compiled 1,231 hits over 17 seasons with a 117 OPS+. Clements was above average defensively, leading league catchers in putouts three times and fielding percentage once.

Osee Schrecongost deserves mention as the personal catcher and road roommate of pitching great Rube Waddell while the two played on the Philadelphia Athletics from 1902 to 1907. The eccentric Waddell was able to harness his immense talent while throwing to Schrecongost, winning 131 games over six seasons on the A's while leading the league in strikeouts each season. With Waddell and Eddie Plank combining for 497 strikeouts while pitching to him, Schrecongost set a record in 1905 with 790 putouts. That mark was later surpassed by Campanella with 807 in 1953; Johnny Edwards now holds the record with 1,135 while Piazza ranks third with 1,055.

Osee (also known as Ossee and Ossie as well as Schreck and Schreckengost) holds the record for most innings caught in one day — 29 innings over a doubleheader on July 4, 1905. A lifetime .271 batter, his OBP was .297 because he rarely walked — 102 bases on balls in 3,216 plate appearances including just three walks in 429 plate appearances in 1905. He certainly ended his career in a dramatic way. In his last game in the majors he was on the losing end of a perfect game thrown by Addie Joss on October 2, 1908. Not only that, it was Osee's passed ball that allowed the game's only run to score.

Although he played almost as much at third base, Dick Allen earns the selection at first base. He seems destined to take over from Ron Santo for the honor of "best player not in the Hall of Fame." Allen hit 351 home runs, which is 20 more than Hank Greenberg and more than eight other first basemen who are in the Hall. Allen's .534 slugging percentage ranks 44th all-time and ahead of such sluggers as Ott, Schmidt, Stargell, McCovey and Killebrew. He finished in the top 10 in OPS 10 times and his .912 career OPS is better than Ken Griffey, Jr., Eddie Mathews, Billy Williams and a host of other Hall of Famers.

Allen had an amazing rookie year in 1964, batting .318 and collecting 201 hits including 29 homers while leading the NL in runs and triples. Not surprisingly, he was named Rookie of the Year. His 1972 season was even more incredible. He led the AL with 37 homers and 113 RBI, batted .308 and finished first in OBP, slugging, OPS and OPS, and after the season was named MVP in a landslide.

Some might be surprised to learn his career OPS+ of 156 is tied for nineteenth all-time with Frank Thomas and just ahead of Aaron, DiMaggio and Mays. He finished in the top eight in OPS+ in 10 different seasons. Despite his accomplishments as one of the greatest hitters of the modern era, Allen never received more than 19 percent of the vote during his 15 years on the Hall ballot. A player who was named Rookie of the Year and AL MVP, led the league in homers twice and made seven All-Star teams cannot get into Cooperstown without buying a ticket.

Not to be overlooked is the fact that Allen was surly, belligerent and filled with anger against managers, teammates, opponents, umpires, fans and especially the media. He suffered through racism in the 1960s and in response lashed out at the world with an unrepentant fury that caused him to be all but blackballed from the majors.

The plaque gallery in Cooperstown is filled with players with huge character flaws, but in Allen's case, "character" seems to be the only criterion by which he has been judged. While playing for the Phillies in 1975 he said, "I wish they'd shut the gates, and let us play ball with no press and no fans." And that's just sad.

If you are looking for a choir boy for first base who also happened to be a good player, then Mickey Vernon is your guy. Another seven-time All-Star, Vernon won two batting titles and led the league in doubles three times while playing in four decades (1939–60). He ranks third all-time in most games played (2,409) without playing in the postseason. The Pirates made the World Series in his last season, but Vernon played just nine games all year and didn't make the Series roster. He retired with 2,495 hits but only 172 homers. His 1953 batting crown was marred by controversy over the actions of his teammates, since their duplicity deprived Al Rosen of the Triple Crown by one point.

Harry Davis is often overlooked but was among the best first basemen of the Deadball Era. He won four straight home run crowns for Connie Mack's Philadelphia Athletics from 1904–1907 and finished the period from 1901–1909 with 67 roundtrippers, 16 more than runner-up Socks Seybold. Davis owns three of the top four WAR marks of the decade among American League first sackers and was easily the top AL first baseman of the decade.

"Jasper" could also serve as the third base coach on the All-Time Pennsylvania team because of his propensity for stealing signs. In the 1911 World Series, Davis was stealing signs, prompting Giants catcher Chief Meyers to tell his pitchers to throw whatever they wanted, "I'll catch you without signals." But Davis knew when John McGraw's hurlers were going to throw their fastballs anyway and signaled the A's hitters. "He knew something," Meyers said later. "I never did find out how he did it."

A final noteworthy first baseman is Jake Daubert, who won consecutive batting crowns in 1913 and 1914 along with the MVP Award in 1913. A .303 lifetime batter and outstanding fielder, Daubert was on the Reds team that won the scandal-plagued 1919 World Series.

Second base is in the capable hands of Hall of Famer Nellie Fox, a St. Thomas native who was named to 15 All-Star teams in his 19-year career. Nellie answered the bell every day, leading the league in games and at-bats five times while setting a major league record for consecutive games played at second with 798. A three-time Gold Glover, he still holds the American League record for double plays by a second baseman with 1,619. The lefty wielded a thick-handled bat with incredible control, striking out only 216 times in 9,232 at-bats, which puts him in third place for lowest career strikeout percentage. His career high for strikeouts was 18 and he also finished in the top 10 in sacrifice hits an incredible 15 times.

Nellie was the catalyst for the White Sox from 1950–63, becoming the first White Sox player to win the AL MVP in 1959 (Dick Allen was the second). That year Fox finished fourth in batting (.306) and second in hits (191) and doubles (34). His number 2 was retired by the White Sox, and he was elected to the Hall of Fame in 1997.

It took Eddie Stanky eight years to make it to the majors, but he quickly proved he belonged. The "Brat" didn't hit for power or average but he knew how to walk and get on base. He topped the league in walks three times and recorded six seasons with more than 100 walks. In 1945 he led the NL with 148 walks and 128 runs scored for Brooklyn. The next season he finished seventh in MVP voting while leading the league in OBP (.436) and walks (137). In 1950 with the Giants he topped the NL with a .460 OBP and 144 walks. His career OBP of .410 ranks 34th. As he liked to say, "The ants get on base and the bulls knock 'em in."

Lancaster native Tommie Herr ranks 10th in career fielding percentage for second basemen (.989), although six of the players ahead of him are still active. Oddly enough, he never led the league in fielding but did finish second or third a total of six times. Herr played in three World Series with the Cardinals, winning the championship in 1982.

The All-Time Pennsylvania team has to make do without a Hall of Famer at third base, but Buddy Bell is a solid option. The Pittsburgh native displayed modest power with 201 home runs while compiling 2,514 hits over 18 seasons. He made five All-Star teams and earned six Gold Gloves for his stellar defense. Bell led the league in assists, putouts and fielding percentage three times each. Bell followed his father, Gus, into the majors and saw two sons, David and Mike, follow in his footsteps. He ranks right behind Vernon in an undesirable category: most games played without playing in the postseason with 2,405.

Other third basemen deserving mention are Jimmy Dykes, Whitey Kurowski and Ned (also known as Ed) Williamson. Dykes played about 1,000 games in other infield positions (mainly second) in addition to 1,257 games at third over a 22-year career with the Philadelphia Athletics and White Sox. He had his best season in 1929, hitting .327 with 13 homers and 79 RBI as the powerhouse A's won the first of three straight pennants. Dykes made two All-Star teams and retired with 2,256 hits and 1,071 RBI.

Kurowski essentially had a seven-year career but made four All-Star teams and posted a 125 OPS+. He played on four pennant winners and won three championships with the Cardinals between 1942 and 1946. Kurowski finished fifth in MVP voting in 1945 after batting .323 with 21 homers and 102 RBI.

Williamson produced several memorable stats in his career and they can be largely attributed to the ballpark factor. The Chicago White Stockings played their games at Lake Front Park, where the right field fence was 196 feet from home. In 1883, balls hit over the fence were considered ground-rule doubles, and Williamson led the league with 49 doubles — 44 percent of his hits were doubles that year. The rule changed the next season with balls over the fence considered home runs, and Williamson ended up with a league-high 27 homers. That stood as the single-season record until Babe Ruth hit 29 in 1919. That season Williamson also became the first player to hit three home runs in a game, which he did on May 30, 1884.

In 1885 the White Stockings moved to the more spacious West Side Park, where it was 560 feet to center and 316 feet to right. Williamson's slugging dropped 230 points and he recorded just 16 doubles and three homers in his first year in the new park.

Our shortstop, Honus Wagner, wins the prize for having the most valuable baseball card — one of his 1909 T206 tobacco cards in near-mint condition sold for $2.8 million in 2007 and a group of nuns auctioned off a dog-eared T206 for $262,000 in 2010.

The son of German immigrants, "The Flying Dutchman" dropped out of school at age 12 to work first in the coal mines and a steel mill, two tough jobs that were a quintessential work experience for many Pennsylvanians in the Industrial Age. The hardscrabble experience helped forge the work ethic that enabled Wagner to keep performing at a high level into his 40s, a humble Everyman that the masses could embrace. He blended exceptional batting and above-average defensive ability with expert base running and smart play. As Wagner put it, "There ain't much to being a ballplayer, if you're a ballplayer."

Wagner played all over the diamond throughout his career and did not play 100 games in a season at shortstop until his seventh year in the majors. This versatility stemmed from his boyhood, when he learned to fill in wherever needed if he wanted to tag along and play with older brothers Al and Luke. Over his 21-year career in the majors he wound up playing 373 games in the outfield, 248 at first base, 210 at third and 57 at second. He even pitched twice, tossing 8⅓ scoreless innings while striking out six batters. There's little doubt Wagner would have been a Hall of Famer no matter what position he played.

Wagner ranks seventh in hits (3,420), ninth in doubles (643), third in triples (252) and 10th in stolen bases (723). He was not viewed as a slugger, particularly since he played in the Deadball Era, yet he still ranks 21st in RBI with 1,733. He had nine seasons with over 100 RBI and led the league five times. Wagner's eight batting crowns are tied with Tony Gwynn for most in National League history. The only time he didn't bat over .300 in his first 17 seasons was during his second season, 1898, when he batted .299. He was one of the five players who gained election to the Hall of Fame in the first year of voting, tying Babe Ruth for the second-most votes (behind Ty Cobb).

Other shortstops from Pennsylvania suffer from any comparison to Wagner, but five others deserve to be mentioned: Hughie Jennings, Dick Groat, Bobby Wallace, John "Monte" Ward and Jake Stephens. Jennings, Wallace and Ward join Wagner as enshrinees in Cooperstown.

Like Wagner, Jennings dropped out of school at 12 to work in the coal mines and the two players' careers overlapped the nineteenth and twentieth centuries. Jennings helped the Baltimore Orioles win three straight National League pennants from 1894–96, batting .335, .386 and .401 those seasons. His 159 runs scored were third in the NL in 1895 while his 125 RBI were fourth best that year. He led the league in fielding percentage three times and putouts four times but the only offensive categories he finished first in were sacrifice hits (once) and times hit by pitch (five times). He remains the all-time leader in the latter category with 287.

Jennings was nicknamed "Ee-Yah" for the ear-splitting scream he used to make from the third base coaching box. He saw his last significant playing time in 1902, making token appearances while serving as manager as late as 1918. Jennings ended up with a .312 lifetime average and was elected to the Hall of Fame in 1945.

Jennings enjoyed early success as a manager, winning pennants in his first three years with the Tigers, 1907–09, while directing stars such as Ty Cobb and Sam Crawford. He won 100 games with the Tigers in 1915 but finished 2½ games behind the Red Sox. Jennings' managerial record was 1,184 wins and 995 losses, good for a .543 winning percentage.

Groat was a top shortstop in the National League from the mid–1950s to mid–'60s. He was named NL MVP for the Pirates during their championship year of 1960, leading the league with a .325 average. Traded to the Cardinals before the 1963 season, he finished third in batting at .319, second in hits with 201 hits and first with 43 doubles, ending up second in MVP voting that year. He won a second World Series title with the Cards in 1964. A five-time All-Star, Groat retired with 2,138 hits but an OPS+ of 89.

Wallace started out as a pitcher when he debuted with the Cleveland Spiders in 1894, but he also played some outfield and then third base for two seasons before finally switching to shortstop in 1899. He quickly demonstrated superior fielding ability, leading AL shortstops in fielding percentage four times and still holds the AL record for total chances in a game with 17. He hung around for 25 seasons, compiling 2,309 hits and 1,121 RBI with a lifetime .268 average. Ward was a jack-of-all-trades on the baseball diamond and later put his law background to good use during a diverse career as player, manager, union organizer, general manager and league executive. He played 826 games at short, 493 at second and 214 in the outfield in addition to making 293 appearances as a pitcher. He was a pretty fair shortstop, batting .275 with a 92 OPS+ and 2,107 hits.

Ward had even greater success in his seven seasons as a pitcher, going 164–103 with a 2.10 ERA. He led the NL with 47 wins and 239 strikeouts as a 19-year-old ace with the Providence Grays in 1879 and followed up by winning 39 games the next season. Ward pitched the second perfect game in National League history on June 17, 1880, just five days after Lee Richmond had thrown the first.

His best year with the bat was 1887 when he scored 114 runs, batted .338 and finished first with 111 stolen bases (under the liberal rules of the day). Ward is the only player to have more than 2,000 hits and 150 pitching wins. He teamed up with Ned Hanlon and a handful of other players to challenge the reserve clause by forming the Brotherhood of Professional Base Ball Players in 1885, the first players union in baseball. That effort led to the short-lived Players League. Ward also served briefly as president of the Boston Braves and went 412–320 as a manager, finishing in second place twice.

"Country Jake" Stephens was a wizard with the leather but he struggled to hit breaking pitches during a 17-year career in the Negro Leagues. He had cat-like quickness and a feisty competitiveness, which he put to use at shortstop and on the base paths. Stephens helped four different franchises win championships, including some of the all-time-best Negro League teams such as the 1931 Homestead Grays, 1932 Pittsburgh Crawfords and 1934 Philadelphia Stars.

Moving on to the outfield, "Stan the Man" has to come first. He was an amazing player but an even better person, one of the happiest and most engaging superstars in any sport. Musial hit over .300 his first 17 seasons and finished with 3,630 hits, which ranks fourth all-time. Not only did he win seven NL batting titles, the Cardinals legend finished in the top five in batting average 10 other times.

Only Babe Ruth and Barry Bonds rank ahead of Musial's 2,562 runs created, while only Hank Aaron has more total bases than his total of 6,134. In addition to winning three MVP Awards, he was runner-up four times. He finished in the top 10 in home runs a dozen times yet still wound up with a lifetime average higher than Honus Wagner. Dodgers pitcher Carl Erskine once commented, "I've had pretty good success with Stan, by throwing him my best pitch and backing up third."

The most fascinating Musial statistic is this: he produced exactly 1,815 hits at home and 1,815 hits on the road. How amazing is that? Want more proof of his consistency? He batted .337 from the number three position and .338 from the clean-up spot. He averaged .323 vs. lefties and .336 vs. righties. His average in his worst month (.323 in May) was not far behind his lifetime average (.331) or his average in his best month (.346 in September/October). Obviously that unorthodox crouch at the plate worked for him. Ted Lyons remarked that "Musial's batting stance looks like a small boy looking around a corner to see if the cops are coming."

In Musial's third MVP season of 1948, he fell a home run short of winning the Triple Crown and becoming the first player to ever lead the league in homers, RBI, average, runs, hits, doubles and triples. He also finished first in OBP, slugging, OPS, OPS+ and total bases that year. The clutch lefty was difficult to strike out, fanning 903 fewer times than he walked during his career and never striking out more than 46 times in a season. He delivered three World Series titles to Cardinals fans and will always be "The Man" in St. Louis.

Moving on to center, we are able to plug in a player who was picked for the Major League Baseball All-Century Team at the age of 29. Perhaps less idolized and admired than Mickey Mantle in his heyday but every bit his equal in ability, Ken Griffey was a once-in-a-generation talent. He was still "The Kid," even when he was a washed-up 40 year old hanging on with a Mariners team that had no use for him. "Junior" still had that smile and he still wore his hat backwards, but by that point his sweet swing resided only in our memories.

Back in his prime, before injuries robbed him of countless at-bats, Griffey showed he could do it all ... effortlessly. He was sublime perfection in a ballplayer throughout his 20s, whether it was crushing mammoth home runs, leaping fences to rob home runs or running the bases like a lithe gazelle. Only he could make over-the-shoulder basket catches look routine. His peers named him "Player of the Decade" for the 1990s. He accumulated 398 home runs before his 30th birthday and seemed on track to easily surpass the Babe and Hammering Hank.

Instead, he slowed down and now his former teammate A-Rod managed to surpass him during the 2011 season for fifth place on the all-time home run list. Just imagine how baseball would have come alive if fans got to witness Griffey — a superstar untainted by the stain of steroids — chase the most important record in baseball. It was not meant to be. Sometimes we denigrate our heroes for their faults without taking time to fully appreciate how much they have given us. Was it Griffey's fault he couldn't stay healthy in his 30s? Was it his fault his teams failed to make it to the World Series during his 22 seasons?

Baseball fans almost never got the chance to see his five-tool talent on display. Seven months after he was picked number one by the Mariners, a depressed Griffey attempted to take his own life by swallowing 277 aspirin. It was a shocking incident that managed to avoid the attention of the press at the time. "It seemed like everyone was yelling at me in baseball, then I came home and everyone was yelling at me there," Griffey told *The Seattle Times* in an interview four years after the incident. "I got depressed. I got angry. I didn't want to live."

A year later Junior made his major league debut, and then the milestone achievements started accumulating. In 1993 he tied Dale Long's record with a home run in eight consecutive games. He became the first Mariners player to start in the All-Star Game. He blasted five home runs against the Yankees in the 1995 ALDS and also raced home from first on a double in the 11th inning to score the winning run in the decisive Game 5. It was a memorable moment that ended up saving baseball in Seattle. A new stadium had been turned down in a previous vote, but with all of Seattle buzzing about the Mariners' march through the playoffs a special session of the legislature was called and funding was approved for a new ballpark. When it opened in 1999 Safeco Field was sometimes referred to as "The House That Griffey Built."

On May 21, 1996, Griffey became the seventh-youngest player to reach 200 career home runs. A year later he became the thirteenth player to be selected MVP unanimously after leading the AL with 56 homers, 147 RBI, 125 runs and a .646 slugging percentage. On April 10, 2000, Junior hit his second home run for the Reds, becoming the youngest player to reach 400 home runs in the process — he was only 30. In 2008 he became the first player to have 400 home runs with one team and 200 with another. Junior retired in June 2010 with 630 home runs and 1,836 RBI and will undoubtedly be a first-ballot Hall of Famer when he becomes eligible.

Musial was the graceful gentleman and Griffey the charismatic kid, which leads us to Reggie Jackson, the outspoken and cocky "look at me" superstar. It was Dizzy Dean who said, "It ain't bragging if you can back it up," but it might as well have been Reggie. He perfected the art of admiring his home runs and led the league in colorful quotes every season. He sold a lot of newspapers during his career; just imagine if he were playing today in the age of the Internet, 24-7 sports talk, Twitter and blogs. "He'd give you the shirt off his back," quipped Catfish Hunter, his teammate on the

A's and Yankees. "Of course, he'd call a press conference to announce it."

When he signed as a free agent with the Yankees Reggie said, "I didn't come to New York to be a star, I brought my star with me." He was pretty good at sparking controversy during his time in the Bronx, clashing with Owner George Steinbrenner, Manager Billy Martin and Captain Thurman Munson. Anyone who played nine years for Charlie Finley and five years for Steinbrenner has some stories to tell, and Reggie doesn't disappoint. He wrote in his autobiography: "There were very few face-to-face confrontations with Steinbrenner; he'd always use intermediaries whenever he could, or leak a story to the press. Charlie only leaked when he went to the men's room."

Reggie has always been proud of his skills as a businessman, which is illustrated by the fact that he patented the nickname "Mr. October." It seems altogether fitting that he should own this moniker, since he seldom failed to come through in the clutch in the postseason. He played on teams that won 11 division titles, six pennants and five World Series. His 18 home runs in the postseason are tied with Mickey Mantle for fourth all-time and Reggie has a .357 average with 10 homers in World Series play. Hitting three home runs in Game 6 of the 1977 Series is arguably the second-greatest feat in World Series history after Don Larsen's perfect game.

His total of 563 home runs is getting passed regularly by players from the steroid generation of sluggers, which annoys Reggie to no end. He's not the least bit bothered that he's the all-time leader in strikeouts with 2,597—finishing in the top seven in strikeouts an incredible 18 straight years—just one of the hazards of the profession when you're a legendary slugger.

Team Pennsylvania's outfield is so deep there isn't even room for all the Hall of Famers. At 5-foot-6, Hack Wilson was an unlikely slugger but in 1930 he produced one of the most amazing seasons a batter has ever had. He drove in 191 runs—a record that hasn't been matched since—and also finished first in home runs (56), slugging (.723), OPS (1.177), OPS+ (177) and walks (105). In addition he batted .356, scored 146 runs and had a .454 OBP. The 56 home runs remained a National League record until Mark McGwire belted 70 in 1998.

Keep in mind that the league batting average was .303 in 1930, one of only two seasons in the National League's 134-year history the league average has exceeded .300 (the other being .309 in 1894). Wilson led the NL in home runs four times while with the Cubs but finished with just 244 for his career along with a lifetime .307 average. He had just six seasons with more than 400 at-bats but rode that one big season all the way to Cooperstown.

Other outfielders of note include Sherry Magee, Jimmy Sheckard, Roy Thomas, Harry Stovey, Carl Furillo and Buck Freeman. Magee was a top slugger with the Philadelphia Phillies during the Deadball Era, which dampens his numbers somewhat. He led the league in RBI four times with totals ranging from 76 to 123. His best season was 1910 when he finished first in batting, RBI, runs, OBP, slugging, OPS and OPS+. He played on the Reds' 1919 championship team and retired with 2,169 hits, 441 stolen bases and a 136 OPS+.

Like Magee, Sheckard was a standout whose numbers don't denote greatness because he played in the Deadball Era. He was an outstanding fielder who led the league three times in outfield assists with totals of 36, 32 and 26—among the highest ever. He ranks eighth all-time with 307 outfield assists. He holds the single-season record for most double plays by an outfielder with 14 in 1899. In 1899 Sheckard led the league with 76 stolen bases. In 1901 he finished first with 19 triples and .534 slugging percentage while posting 104 RBI and a .354 average.

Sheckard briefly jumped to the Orioles in the American League the next year before returning to Brooklyn; he slumped to .265 with 37 RBI. Then he bounced back in 1903 to bat .332 and top the league in homers and stolen bases. Sheckard played on four pennant winners with the Cubs between 1906 and 1910, winning two titles but also enduring an 0-for-21 mark in the 1906 Series. He set a NL record with 147 walks in 1911, which topped his previous career high (set the previous year) by 64.

Thomas was another Deadball Era star who spent most of his 12-year career with the Phillies. The rangy center fielder led the National League in walks seven times in eight seasons and finished with a .413 OBP. Stovey was a nineteenth century star who held the career home run record from 1885 to 1894. He led the league in homers five times, runs and triples four times, slugging three times, stolen bases twice and RBI and doubles once. His stats are sometimes overlooked because he spent seven years in the American Association and one year in the Players League, but he posted a career OPS+ of 143.

Furillo's nickname, "The Reading Rifle," referred to his powerful and accurate throwing arm, which he used to lead the league in outfield assists twice. He was a key contributor for the Dodgers for 15 seasons, batting over .300 five times including a league-best .344 in 1953. Furillo won seven pennants and two World Series with the Dodgers, but was overshadowed by his more famous teammates such as Duke Snider, Pee Wee Reese and Jackie Robinson. He made just one All-Star team despite earning MVP votes in eight seasons. He retired in 1960 with 1,910 hits, 1,058 RBI and a .299 average. "I remember how tough he was, how strong he was, how consistent he was as a player. When he hit a single, it was a bullet. When he hit a homer, it was a rocket," says teammate Carl Erskine.

Buck Freeman was the "first legitimate home run hitter in baseball history," according to baseball researcher Eric Enders. In 1899 Freeman hit 25 of his team's 47 homers and easily led the National League over runner-up Bobby Wallace, who belted 12. In 1901 Freeman jumped to the American League and became the first player to lead both leagues in homers when he belted 13 four-baggers for the 1903 Boston Americans.

From 1899–1904 no one hit more homers than Freeman, who outhomered his competition by 28. He led the AL in RBI in 1902 and 1903 as well as triples in 1904. His career numbers don't stack up to the modern-era players, but there's no doubt Freeman deserves honorable mention on the All-Time Pennsylvania team.

Jack Clark played 1,039 games in the outfield and 580 games at first base, but he's our best candidate to fill the DH spot, where he played 311 games. Known as "Jack the Ripper," Clark was a feared slugger throughout his 18-year career, belting 340 home runs and finishing in the top 10 in homers seven times. His career OPS+ of 137 is better than George Brett, Ken Griffey and Al Kaline. His best year was 1987 with the Cardinals when he led the league in walks, OBP, slugging, OPS and OPS+ while hitting 35 homers and driving in 106 runs. He came in third in that MVP race.

Team Pennsylvania can boast a pretty powerful rotation since six starters from the state have been elected to the Hall of Fame, not counting shortstop/pitcher Monte Ward. Three other pitchers have won at least 200 games and 19 Pennsylvania-born pitchers who were primarily starters have been named to at least one All-Star team.

There is not much point in debating the right-handed starter spot, since Christy Mathewson belongs in any conversation about the best right-handed starter in baseball history. "(Christy) Mathewson was the greatest pitcher who ever lived. He had knowledge, judgment, perfect control and form. It was wonderful to watch him pitch when he wasn't pitching against you," said Connie Mack.

In addition to pinpoint control, Mathewson relied heavily on his "fadeaway" or screwball, although he once commented, "Anybody's best pitch is the one the batters ain't hitting that day." He led the league in strikeouts, ERA and ERA+ five times; wins, shutouts and WHIP four times; BB/9IP ratio seven times; and SO/BB ratio nine times. His 373 wins are tied with Pete Alexander for most in National League history and third-most in major league history. His 79 shutouts rank third, his 1.058 WHIP ranks sixth and his 2.13 ERA ranks ninth. He hurled two no-hitters and won pitching's Triple Crown in 1905 and 1908.

Matty was at his dominant best in the 1905 World Series, shutting out Mack's Philadelphia A's three times in six days as the New York Giants won the championship in five games. In 11 career World Series appearances, Mathewson pitched 10 complete games and generated an ERA of 0.97. He and Stan Coveleski are two of the six pitchers who have pitched three complete game wins in one World Series.

The player known as "Big Six" was involved in two of the most lopsided trades in baseball history. On December 15, 1900, Mathewson was traded by the Reds to the Giants for Amos Rusie, who was at the end of his Hall of Fame career. Reds' owner John Brush knew he was about to wind up controlling the Giants, so he was quite aware the deal was one-sided. Rusie pitched in just three games for the Reds without posting a victory before calling it a career, while Matty emerged as the greatest pitcher in Giants history.

Then with Mathewson's pitching days coming to an end, he was shipped with Edd Roush and Bill McKechnie back to the Reds in the middle of the 1916 season in exchange for Buck Herzog and Red Killefer. Mathewson only pitched in one game for the Reds but assumed control of the team as manager, while Roush went on to forge a Hall of Fame career by winning two batting titles and batting .331 over 12 seasons for the Reds. McKechnie was just a utility infielder but later turned into a Hall of Fame manager. Killefer played in only two games for the Giants before calling it quits, while Herzog made little impact in his short time with the team.

Mathewson was a clean-cut, articulate and thoughtful counterbalance to the ruffians John McGraw carried on the Giants squad in the first decade of the twentieth century, and his broad appeal helped pave the way for more women and families to attend games. "He was an inspiration to everybody and may we have more of his kind. His sense of justice, his integrity, and sportsmanship made him far greater than Christy Mathewson the pitcher," said Commissioner Kenesaw Mountain Landis during the memorial service for the player after he died of tuberculosis during the 1925 World Series.

Righty Ed Walsh was one of baseball's most accomplished spitballers, winning 168 games over a seven-year period for the White Sox. In 1908 Walsh had one of the best seasons ever for a pitcher, leading the league with 40 wins, a .727 winning percentage, 66 games, 49 complete games, 11 shutouts, 269 strikeouts and a twentieth-century record 464 innings. He finished third with a 1.42 ERA. When he wasn't starting games, he was often finishing up for others as he accumulated 103 games finished (leading the league three times). Walsh won 27 games in both 1911 and 1912, finishing runner-up in the MVP voting both years. Although he won only 195 games during his career, Walsh ranks number one all-time with a career ERA of 1.82, number two in WHIP at 1.000 and ninth with an ERA+ of 146. He was elected to the Hall of Fame in 1946.

Mike Mussina was born in Williamsport, home of the Little League World Series, and still lives in nearby Montoursville, so it must have been especially meaningful for him to see his Little League dreams turn into a big league reality. "Moose" was the picture of consistency over an 18-year career with the Orioles and Yankees, setting an American League record by posting double-figure win totals in each of his last 17 seasons — only Greg Maddux with 20 seasons in a row can top that, while Don Sutton (21), Phil Niekro (19) and Walter Johnson (18) are the only other pitchers to post more total seasons with double-digit wins.

A five-time All-Star, Mussina was one of the best-fielding pitchers in baseball history who won seven Gold Gloves. He went out in a blaze of glory in 2008, recording his only 20-win season in his last year, becoming the oldest player to win 20 for the first time.

During the course of his career, the Stanford graduate evolved from a hard thrower to a crafty soft tosser who lived on the edges of the strike zone.

With 270 career wins but a relatively high ERA of 3.68, Mussina is a borderline Hall of Fame candidate. Let's take a closer look at his qualifications. He finished in the top six in Cy Young voting nine times, which is the same number of times as Randy Johnson and Maddux. Furthermore, it's a better showing than Tom Seaver (8), Tom Glavine and Nolan Ryan (6 each) or Bob Gibson (3). Moose finished in the top 10 in SO/BB ratio 15 times and his 3.58 SO/BB ranks thirteenth all-time. He finished in the top 10 in strikeouts 10 times and ranks nineteenth with 2,813 career strikeouts. His .638 winning percentage ranks 39th while his 270 victories rank 33rd on the all-time list.

To make the Hall of Fame threshold, a pitcher must demonstrate excellence and longevity — Mussina seems to meet that qualification. What follows are the number of times he finished in the top 10 in various pitching categories: ERA (11), wins (9), won-lost pct. (9), WHIP (12), BB/9IP (15), S/9IP (10), innings pitched (8), shutouts (11) and ERA+ (11). In other words, he was among the leaders in most pitching categories just about every season of his career. The most similar pitcher to him is Hall of Famer Juan Marichal.

Mussina's ERA+ of 123 reflects the fact that he excelled despite spending his entire career battling the powerful lineups of the American League East. In fact, his ERA+ is better than Bob Feller, Warren Spahn or the pitcher he's often compared to: Glavine. Moose has the exact same winning percentage as Jim Palmer but has two more victories and 601 more strikeouts. Only five pitchers in the twentieth century can top his .638 winning percentage and 270 victories: Pete Alexander, Christy Mathewson, Roger Clemens, Randy Johnson and Lefty Grove. Sure looks like a Hall of Famer to us.

Another notable righty starter is Bucky Walters, who started off as a third baseman and then struggled once he switched to pitching mainly because he was pitching in the hitter-friendly Baker Bowl in Philadelphia. He started demonstrating what he could do once he was traded to Cincinnati during the 1938 season. Walters was named National League MVP in 1939 after winning the Triple Crown with 27 wins, 137 strikeouts and 2.29 ERA; also finishing first in complete games, innings, ERA+, WHIP and H/9IP as the Reds won the pennant. He led the league in wins and ERA the next year and then went 2-0 in the World Series as the Reds won the championship. For the period 1939-46, Walters led the majors in wins, ERA, complete games and innings pitched. The six-time All-Star retired with 198 wins.

It took quite a bit of deliberation to settle on the Pennsylvania's all-time best lefty starter. Hall of Famers Rube Waddell and Eddie Plank were both given strong consideration. Plank was 14 months older but Waddell was already three years into his career by the time "Gettysburg Eddie" joined the majors in the first year of the American League, 1901. The two were teammates on the Philadelphia Athletics from 1902-07.

Plank won 20 games eight times and finished with 326 wins (thirteenth best) and a 2.35 ERA (22nd best). However, he never led in wins, ERA, innings pitched or strikeouts and his ERA+ of 122 is good but not great. Rube edges Plank in ERA and WHIP and has a big advantage in ERA+ with his 135 mark. Waddell wins the Black Ink Test 46-15, while Plank wins the Gray Ink Test 291-158.

It makes sense to compare how the two did during the six seasons they were teammates. In 1902 Rube went 24-7 with a 2.05 ERA and 179 ERA+, far better than Plank's figures of 20-15, 3.30 and 112. Their numbers were fairly similar in 1903 except Waddell set a National League record with 302 strikeouts, which was 115 more than the runner-up and 126 more than Plank in third place. In 1904 Waddell's 165 ERA+ far outpaced Plank's mark of 124 and Rube also established a new AL strikeout record that season with 349. Despite missing the last month of the 1905 season, Waddell still won the pitcher's Triple Crown with 27 wins, 1.48 ERA and 287 strikeouts, so that decides that year. The last two seasons, 1906 and 1907, could be judged a draw. Plank posted a better record while Waddell posted more strikeouts — their other numbers are fairly close.

So we have established that Waddell was the better, more dominant pitcher during their six years together. The problem is that 131 of his 193 career victories came during that stint with the A's, while Plank went 190-112 pitching in 11 additional seasons. Plank had a 10-year stretch from 1903-12 where his ERA never exceeded 2.38.

SABR member Dan O'Brien, who wrote a screenplay about Waddell and operates a website (rubewaddell.net) devoted to all things Rube, offers the following points in his favor. He led the American League in strikeouts in each of his six seasons with the Athletics and still holds the AL single-season record for a lefty (349 in 1904). Only six pitchers have registered back-to-back seasons of 300-plus strikeouts, and Waddell is the only one to do so prior to the 1960s. Waddell racked up his strikeouts in the Deadball Era when hitters were more focused on contact than today.

When Waddell joined the Philadelphia Athletics in late June of 1902, the A's had 87 games remaining and were in fourth place. In that span Waddell won 24 games (including a record 10 in one month) and catapulted the A's to their first AL pennant. He also led the American League with 210 strikeouts, 50 more than runner-up Cy Young, who pitched 109 more innings than Waddell.

On July 1, 1902, in his first home appearance as a Philadelphia Athletic, Rube became the first documented pitcher to strike out the side on only nine pitches, despite the fact that foul balls were not yet strikes in the AL. Rube personally accounted for 7.65 percent of all AL strikeouts in 1902. To do that today, a pitcher would have to strike out more than 1,000 in a season (there are more teams today but Rube missed about 40 percent of the 1902 season). Waddell has the best lifetime ERA by a left-hander and he is the

Rube Waddell was one of the most eccentric flakes in baseball history, which is not surprising when you consider he was born on Friday the 13th and died on April Fool's Day. He won 20 games four times and led the league in strikeouts six straight seasons (Library of Congress, Prints & Photographs Division, LC-DIG-bbc-1729f).

only pitcher prior to World War II to average more than 7 Ks per 9 innings over the course of his career.

Walter Johnson called Rube the best pitcher he ever saw (even though Rube was in decline by the time Johnson broke in). "Waddell had more than any pitcher I ever saw," Johnson said. "He was eccentric. Many times he did not want to pitch. But when he did, he was a wonder." Connie Mack said repeatedly that Rube had the best combination of speed and curves of any pitcher he ever saw.

On several occasions Waddell sent his infielders and outfielders to the sidelines and then struck out the side with no defensive support except for his catcher. However, he did this only during exhibition games and never during the regular season.

Here's what *The Washington Post* had to say about Rube after his passing: "Baseball was more joyous because of him. He was a fun-maker extraordinary. He drove away gloom like the sun dispersing the fog. He made everybody happy. Millions smiled at his antics."

Plank used to annoy the heck out of teammates, opponents, umpires and fans with his weird, ritualistic antics on the mound. With apologies to Mike Hargrove, he was the "Human Rain Delay on the Mound," a chattering nut case long before Mark Fidrych became the poster child for mound soliloquies. However, he won more games than any left-hander in baseball history until surpassed by Warren Spahn in 1962. Plank is the all-time leader in shutouts by a southpaw with 69.

Rube was an original, but Plank gets the nod for his total career production. Plank was a steady winner who was still effective in his late 30s, helping lead his team to the World Series four times in five years. His 1.32 era in the World Series is one of the lowest ever. Waddell, on the other hand, never pitched in the postseason. He scuffled with teammate Andy Coakley toward the end of the 1905 season, injuring his shoulder in the process and making him unavailable as the Athletics bowed to the Giants in the World Series. His selfish attitude and erratic behavior overshadowed his pitching brilliance to the detriment of the teams he was on.

As for the honorable mention southpaws, Herb Pennock is another one of the accidental Hall of Famers who upon closer inspection has no business being enshrined in Cooperstown. He essentially had two careers: he posted good numbers while benefiting from the Yankees' hitting production during their first dynasty and he posted mediocre numbers the rest of his career. He went 162–90 in 11 years with the Yankees and 79–72 in 11 years with the Red Sox and Athletics. His career marks of 3.60 ERA, 106 ERA+ and 9.8 H/9IP are certainly not Hall-worthy, but his candidacy got swept up in a wave of sympathy after his death in 1948 and he got voted in that year.

Pennock won his first game at age 18 and his last game at age 40, one of a handful of players to win games at four age levels. He was a member of six teams that won World Series, although he didn't play in three of those Series. He went 5–0 with a 1.95 ERA in Series action, winning the final game of the 1923 Series for the Yankees and Game 3 of the 1927 Series featuring the famous Murderers' Row squad.

Jamie Moyer has had a remarkable career, and who knows when it will end. The lefty from Sellersville planned to resume pitching in 2012 after recovering from rotator cuff surgery. His 24 seasons in the majors are tied for 10th all-time and he will move up to a tie for fifth if he hangs around at least one more season. Moyer's 140 wins between 2000 and 2009 are the third-most in baseball in that period behind Andy Pettitte and Randy Johnson. Moyer has compiled 267 wins and recorded two 20-win seasons with Seattle but has just one All-Star selection. He has posted double-digit wins in 15 seasons.

During the 2010 season, Moyer passed Robin Roberts for most home runs allowed. Roberts surrendered 505 home runs during his Hall of Fame career while Moyer ended 2010 with 511. With a career ERA of 4.24 and an ERA+ of 104, it's hard to imagine a scenario in which Moyer makes the Hall of Fame, even if he hangs around long enough to win 300 games.

When the game is on the line Team Pennsylvania can turn to two relievers who won the Cy Young Award: Bruce Sutter and Sparky Lyle. Sutter became the fourth relief pitcher elected to the Hall of Fame in 2006 (his thirteenth year on the ballot) and he is the only pitcher in the Hall who never started a major league game (apart from the Negro Leaguers). He is credited with perfecting the split-fingered fastball or splitter, a pitch that saved his career from an early end.

"He's the greatest relief pitcher that I've seen in my 45 years of baseball," said Herman Franks, who was his manager on the Cubs in 1979, the year Sutter won the Cy Young Award. That season he posted a league-high 37 saves with a 2.22 ERA and allowed just 6.0 H/9IP. He finished in the top six in Cy Young voting four other years and placed in the top eight in MVP voting five times.

Sutter led the NL in saves five times in six seasons, ending up with exactly 300 career saves. He was the first NL reliever to reach 200 and 300 saves. He saved two games in the 1982 World Series and was on the mound to record the last out of Game 7 with a strikeout.

Lyle coined the name "Bronx Zoo" in his hilarious tome about the dysfunctional Yankees of the mid-1970s, and he was a dominant reliever throughout that decade. He led the league in saves twice but not during his Cy Young season of 1977. That year he finished second with 26 saves while posting a 13–5 record with a 2.17 ERA and a league-high 72 appearances. In a puzzling move that defined the impetuous behavior of the Yankees under mercurial owner George Steinbrenner, the team signed free agent Goose Gossage to be their closer for 1978. Lyle would eventually be traded to Texas, but he never recovered his past form. He retired with 238 saves and a 2.88 ERA.

Joining Lyle in the honorable mention list of relievers is Gene Garber, who pitched in 919 games over 19 seasons. He recorded 218 saves and had four seasons with at least 20 saves. In addition to setting a record for most losses in relief with 108, Garber's 16 losses in 1979 remain the single-season record for a relief pitcher. A noteworthy feat happened on August 1, 1978, when Garber struck out Pete Rose to end his 44-game hitting streak.

Mussina is not the only great fielding pitcher from the Keystone State. Bobby Shantz, who started 171 games but appeared in 366 games in relief, was the best-fielding pitcher of his era. The 5-foot-6, 139-pound Pottstown native, who was one of the shortest pitchers in MLB history, was honored as the Gold Glove pitcher the first eight years the award was given out (1957–64). Shantz was named AL MVP in 1952 after leading the league in wins (24) and also won-loss percentage, WHIP, BB/9IP and SO/BB. He finished third with a 2.48 ERA.

Few pitchers can top Shantz's performance in his second major league appearance on May 6, 1949. Entering the game in the fourth inning in relief of Carl Scheib, Shantz no-hit the Tigers for the next nine innings. Although he surrendered one hit and two runs in the thirteenth inning, Shantz got the victory — his first in the majors!

Whether Joe McCarthy is the best manager of all-time is open to debate. What's not in dispute is that he is the most successful manager in major league history and the logical choice as skipper for Team Pennsylvania. His .615 career winning percentage ranks first among MLB managers (minimum 320 games). He won 2,125 games (eighth-best) over 24 seasons with only 1,333 losses. His seven World Series championships are tied with Casey Stengel for most ever and his nine pennants are tied with Connie Mack for third-best.

McCarthy came in second seven times, never finished lower than fourth place and never finished below .500 in a season. He won 100 games six times with the Yankees. After winning his first pennant with the Cubs in 1929, "Marse Joe" was hired to replace Bob Shawkey as manager of the Yankees before the 1931 season, inheriting a team with nine future Hall of Famers that had stumbled to a third-place finish in 1930. He guided the Bronx Bombers to a championship in 1932, winning 107 games that year, and then won four straight titles from 1936–39, followed by two more in 1941 and 1943. McCarthy produced a .626 winning percentage during his 16 years with the Yankees.

In 1949 he outlined his "10 Commandments for Success in Baseball," which included principles such as "Nobody can become a ballplayer by walking after a ball" and "An outfielder who throws after a runner is locking the barn door after the house is stolen."

McCarthy toiled in the minors for 15 years as a player without ever making it to the majors. Although short on talent as a player, he certainly had the "right stuff" to manage. In addition to managing Rogers Hornsby on the Cubs and Ruth, Gehrig and DiMaggio with the Yankees, he managed Ted Williams during a final three-year stretch with the Red Sox. DiMaggio remarked, "Never a day went by when you didn't learn something from (Joe) McCarthy."

He has bled Dodger blue in eight decades, but Tommy Lasorda has also been one of baseball's greatest ambassadors. His affiliation with the Dodgers dates back to 1949, when the joined the franchise's Greenville team in the minors. Through more than 60 years of passion and service to the organization he has left an enduring legacy. He once joked, "Say 'Dodgers' and people know you're talking about baseball. Say 'Braves' and they ask, 'What reservation?' Say 'Reds' and they think of communism. Say 'Padres' and they look around for a priest."

Lasorda directed the Dodgers to four pennants and World Series titles in 1981 and 1988, winning 1,599 games over 21 years. He also managed the U.S. Olympic Team to the 2000 Gold Medal and was elected to the Hall of Fame in 1997. "I believe managing is like holding a dove in your hand," he wrote in his book, *Artful Dodger*. "If you hold it too tightly you kill it, but if you hold it too loosely, you lose it."

Bill McKechnie is the only manager to take three different teams to the World Series. He guided the Pirates to a World Series title in 1925 and then led the St. Louis Cardinals to a pennant in 1928. He was hired in 1938 to turn around the Reds and he did in short order, winning back-to-back pennants in 1939 and 1940. His 1940 squad won 100 games, captured the pennant by 12 games and then defeated the Tigers in the World Series.

Nicknamed "Deacon" because he was a devout,

church-going man, McKechnie was a master strategist who excelled at positioning defenders and pulling the right strings with his pitching staff. He won 1,896 games and his .524 career winning percentage is hurt by an eight-year barren stretch with Boston. He was named NL Manager of the Year in 1937 and 1940 and was elected to the Hall of Fame in 1962.

Danny Murtaugh led the Pirates to World Series titles in 1960 and 1971. Murtaugh won 1,115 games during four different stints as skipper of the Pirates, winning five division titles. His 1960 squad was one of the greatest underdog champions in baseball history. The Bucs didn't seem to match up well against a franchise that had won eight pennants and six titles in the 1950s. The Yankees destroyed the Pirates 16–3 in Game 2, 10–0 in Game 3 and 12–0 in Game 6, but the Pirates held tough by holding on for narrow wins in Games 1, 4 and 5.

Despite being outscored 46–17 by the Yankees juggernaut over the first six games, Murtaugh convinced his team they could still prevail. With a little magic from Bill Mazeroski — who hit the first walk-off home run in World Series history — the Pirates became world champions for the first time since McKechnie delivered a title in 1925.

Murtaugh never took himself too seriously as a manager. He could be found after games dispensing self-deprecating humor from his trademark rocking chair. Like the time in 1961 he said, "The night we won the World Series, I was understandably feeling my oats. I asked my wife how many really great managers she thought there were in baseball. Glaring at me, she said, 'I think there's one less than you do.'"

Another notable Pirates manager from Pennsylvania, Chuck Tanner, delivered a World Series title to Pittsburgh in 1979, guiding the "We Are Family" bunch to an improbable comeback. After falling behind 3–1 to the Orioles in the Series, the team rallied behind their grieving manager after his mother passed away before Game 5. They held the Orioles to two runs over the next three games and won the franchise's fifth championship.

Tanner relied on a relentless sense of optimism to survive a tumultuous season managing the Oakland A's in 1976 after the team had traded star Reggie Jackson and lost Catfish Hunter to free agency. While Owner Charlie Finley was trying to sell off his remaining star players like Rollie Fingers and Joe Rudi, Tanner was giving his players the green light to run. The A's stole 341 bases that season, which remains a modern-day and American League record. Eight players stole at least 20 bases including pinch-runner Larry Lintz, who managed to steal 31 bases despite having only one at-bat all season.

After skippering the A's to a second-place finish in 1976, Tanner escaped Finley's circus in a strange way. The A's shipped Tanner and $100,000 to the Pirates in exchange for catcher Manny Sanguillen. Sanguillen was traded back to the Pirates a year later and was still around as a backup to help Tanner bring home the championship in 1979.

RHODE ISLAND

*Names in **bold** represent Major League selections by position, followed by honorable mentions. Negro Leagues players are in italics. City of birth is in parentheses.*

Catcher — Gabby Hartnett (Woonsocket). Also: Morgan Murphy (East Providence); Chris Iannetta (Providence)
First Base — Paul Konerko (Providence)
Second Base — Nap Lajoie (Woonsocket). Also: Davey Lopes (Providence); Charley Bassett (Central Falls)
Third Base — Joe Mulvey (Providence). Also: Fred Corey (Coventry)
Shortstop — Bill Almon (Providence). Also: Jimmy Cooney, Jr. (Cranston); Jimmy Cooney, Sr. (Cranston)
Outfield — Hugh Duffy (Cranston)
Outfield — Johnny Cooney (Cranston)
Outfield — Rocco Baldelli (Woonsocket). Also: Joe Connolly (North Smithfield); Ed Daily (Providence)
Right Handed Starter — Frank Corridon (Newport). Also: *Billy Whyte (Providence — threw unknown)*; Tom Lovett (Providence — threw unknown); Andy Coakley (Providence); Max Surkont (Central Falls); Ed Daily (Providence)
Left Handed Starter — Chet Nichols (Pawtucket). Also: Johnny Cooney (Cranston)
Relief Pitcher — Clem Labine (Lincoln). Also: Dan Wheeler (Providence); Jumbo Brown (Greene); Ken Ryan (Pawtucket)
Manager — Gabby Hartnett (Woonsocket). Also: Nap Lajoie (Woonsocket); Eddie Sawyer (Westerly); Hugh Duffy (Cranston)

The Names

Best Nickname: Rocco "Woonsocket Rocket" Baldelli
Other Nicknames: Walter "Jumbo" Brown; Jimmy "Scoops" Cooney; Frank "Fiddler" Corridon; "Sir Hugh" Duffy; Dennis "Dinty" Gearin; Charles "Gabby" Hartnett; Nap "King Larry" Lajoie; Dan "Link" Sullivan
Most Unusual Name: Napoleon Lajoie

All-Time Leaders

Games: Nap Lajoie, 2480
Hits: Nap Lajoie, 3242

Batting Average: Nap Lajoie, .338
Home Runs: Paul Konerko, 396 (still active)
RBI: Nap Lajoie, 1599
Stolen Bases: Hugh Duffy, 574
Wins: Tom Lovett, 88
Strikeouts: Max Surkont, 571
Saves: Dan Wheeler, 43 (active)
Future Star: Ryan Westmoreland (Newport)
Best Player: Nap Lajoie

Historic Baseball Place

McCoy Stadium in Pawtucket — Opened in 1946, it serves as the home of the Pawtucket Red Sox. Scene of longest game in professional baseball history — 33 innings! Fans can admire wall murals of about 50 former players who played in the major leagues.

Notable Achievements

Davey Lopes set a record for most consecutive steals with 38 in 1975, a mark later topped by Vince Coleman in 1989.

Max Surkont set a record by striking out eight batters in a row on May 25, 1953. The last one came after a 30-minute rain delay.

Phil Paine (Chepacet) became the first former major league player to play professionally in Japan in 1953.

Bill Lefebvre (Natick) was a pitcher for the Red Sox who homered in his first at-bat in 1938. It was the only pitch he faced that season, and he ended the season batting 1.000 with a 1.000 OBP.

Jimmy Cooney carried out the sixth unassisted triple play in baseball history on May 30, 1927, playing for the Cubs. The very next day Johnny Neun had one for the Tigers.

Nap Lajoie was intentionally walked with the bases loaded by White Sox pitcher-manager Clark Griffith on May 23, 1901.

Tom Lovett threw a no-hitter against the Giants on June 22, 1891.

Providence Gets a Taste of the Big Leagues

The fledgling National League got underway with eight teams in 1876 and two years later a team was established in Providence, R.I., playing games at Messer

McCoy Stadium in Pawtucket, which opened in 1946, was the site of the longest professional baseball game ever played — 33 innings — between the Pawtucket Red Sox (featuring Wade Boggs) and the Rochester Red Wings (featuring Cal Ripken, Jr.). The game started on April 18, 1981, and continued until 4 a.m. the next day, with 32 innings in the books. When play resumed on June 23, it ended quickly, with Pawtucket scoring the winning run in the bottom of the thirty-third inning. The game lasted eight hours and 25 minutes (courtesy DigitalBallparks.com).

Street Grounds. Providence native Fred Corey became Rhode Island's first major league player when he debuted for the Providence Grays on May 1, 1878. He was joined a month later by pitcher Tom Healey of Cranston.

The Grays won the National League pennant in their second year of existence, 1879, behind the pitching of Monte Ward (47 wins) and batting of Paul Hines (.357) and Jim O'Rourke (.348). It didn't attract attention at the time, but a major historical achievement evidently took place that year. William Edward White appeared in a game for the Grays on June 21, 1879, becoming the first African American player in the majors.

Still pitching for the Grays in 1880, Ward became the second pitcher to throw a perfect game on June 17. Three more Providence-born players would join the Grays during their run at glory: catcher Charlie Reilley in 1882 and pitcher Edgar Smith and shortstop Joe Mulvey in 1883.

The Grays would win a second NL pennant in 1884 with "Old Hoss" Radbourn leading the way with a major league record 59 wins in 73 starts as the Grays went 84–28. Also that year Grays pitcher Charlie Sweeney struck out 19 batters in a 9-inning game on June 7. Although it was matched a month later by Hugh Daily, the strikeout mark would not be topped until Roger Clemens struck out 20 more than 100 years later in 1986.

Third baseman Jerry Denny hit six of the 21 home runs hit by the 1884 Grays squad. By contrast, the Chicago White Stockings belted 142 home runs that year with four players slugging more than 20 (Ned Williamson, Fred Pfeffer, Abner Dalrymple and Cap Anson). The White Sox finished tied for fourth, 22 games behind the Grays. The Grays went on to defeat the New York Metropolitans of the American Association in a three-game playoff, an early precursor to the World Series.

Providence's franchise lasted eight years in the National League, earning two pennants and finishing in second and third place two times each. The Grays revived as a minor league team playing in the Eastern League from 1891–1929, with Babe Ruth playing for the team for about six weeks in 1914.

Rhode Island no longer has a major league team, but it continues to produce major leaguers — 73 players from the state have appeared in the majors through 2011 including 31 from Providence (plus three more from East Providence).

Three Rhode Island-born players were active in 2011: Paul Konerko, Dan Wheeler and Chris Iannetta. A future star, Ryan Westmoreland, has seen his dreams of glory put on hold. Viewed as one of the Red Sox top prospects, Westmoreland underwent brain surgery in 2010 to address a cavernous malfunction in his brain and it remains to be seen whether he will be able to resume playing.

All-Time Rhode Island Selections

Babe Ruth, Ted Williams, Willie Mays and Ty Cobb were iconic players, but none of these all-time greats had a team named after them. Woonsocket native Napoleon "Nap" Lajoie did. Shortly after Lajoie joined the Cleveland franchise in 1902, the team that had been called the Bluebirds, Blues and Bronchos the previous year changed its name to the Naps to honor their new star player. Now that's some star power.

It was an odd turn of events that delivered Lajoie to Cleveland. He spent his first five years playing for the Philadelphia Phillies in the National League. He batted between .324 and .378 in those years and led the NL in RBI and doubles once. Disappointed with his salary, in 1901 he jumped to the Philadelphia Athletics in the newly formed American League when Connie Mack offered him a big raise. He went on to win the Triple Crown that season, while leading the AL in virtually every hitting category.

The Phillies took Lajoie to court, arguing that he couldn't play for another team in Philadelphia. Lajoie responded by challenging the "reciprocity" issue, which allowed clubs to give a 10-day notice to drop a player without allowing the player to give any kind of notice at all. The Phillies won the case, but not the player. AL President Ban Johnson assigned Lajoie to Cleveland, allowing the league to keep one of its star players away from the National League. Philadelphia's loss was Cleveland's gain.

Lajoie was still in the prime of his career when he came to Cleveland. He would not disappoint the fans with his performance, leading the league in average his first three seasons and batting over .300 in 10 of his 13 seasons with the team.

Known as "Larry" by most of his peers and well-respected around the game, Lajoie was generally considered the best player in baseball until Ty Cobb came along. The Naps could not get over the hump as a team, though, even with Lajoie serving as manager for five years beginning in 1905. He ended up 377–309 as a manager, finishing a half-game back of the Tigers for the 1908 pennant in his best showing.

A steady fielder who liked to control the action as a second baseman, Lajoie was a deadly line-drive hitter who batted over .350 nine times and exceeded 200 hits four times. He was willing to swing at anything, in or out of the strike zone, but managed to post a .380 OBP despite not walking much. He wound up with 3,242 hits, ranking him thirteenth in history. His lifetime average of .338 ranks 21st. He was elected to the Hall of Fame in 1937 as part of the second class of members, and is an easy choice as Rhode Island's second baseman and All-Time Best Player.

Lajoie holds a record that probably won't be surpassed. He has held the record for highest batting average in a season every year the American League has been in existence, since the league officially started in 1901, the year he hit .422. Some sources credit him with a .426 average that season, a discrepancy that arises from the less than precise records that were kept back then — his 1901 average was listed as .405 for a half-century. It was to Lajoie's benefit that foul balls did not count as strikes that year in the American League.

He won two other batting crowns outright and was part of disputed batting races in 1902 and 1910. In 1902, it remains in dispute whether Lajoie had enough plate appearances to win the batting title or whether Ed Delahanty had a higher average. Then in 1910 Lajoie found himself trailing Ty Cobb by four points on the last day of the season, a seemingly insurmountable gap. Cobb was intensely disliked by Lajoie's opponent that day, the St. Louis Browns, and they allowed Lajoie to successfully execute seven straight bunt singles, which gave him the batting crown ... or so it seemed. A recalculation at the time showed Cobb still won, but seven decades later it was discovered that Cobb's stats were in error and Lajoie was ruled the rightful albeit tainted winner.

Let's review the rest of the team. Gabby Hartnett was reportedly given his nickname by a sportswriter who sat next to him on the train that would take him to his first spring training. It was a sarcastic reference, because "Gabby" didn't say one word to the guy, instead heeding his mother's advice to keep quiet until he figured out what this baseball business was all about.

It didn't take Gabby long to figure out the game, as he went on to become one of the best all-around catchers in the first half of the twentieth century. With his confidence in place, Harnett soon lived up to his nickname by becoming a second manager on the field.

Hartnett was baseball's first slugging catcher, becoming the first catcher to reach the 20-homer and 30-homer mark in a season. He finished in the top five in home runs five times, ending his career with 236 home runs. But he also hit for average, batting over .300 six times (including a high of .354) with a career average of .297. His best overall year was 1930 when he batted .339 with 37 homers and 122 RBI, and he was named MVP in 1935 after batting .344 for the pennant-winning Cubs.

Gabby was an accomplished, clutch batter but was even better defensively. He led the National League in assists and fielding average six times and putouts four times. If Gold Gloves were handed out back when he played (1922–1941), he would have won the award more years than not. Recalls Paul Richards, whose baseball career stretched more than 50 years, "The best throwing arm I ever saw on a catcher probably belonged to Gabby Hartnett. And he was accurate."

Hartnett helped lead the Cubs to the World Series four times — coming up short each time — while hitting one of the most famous home runs in Cubs history along the way. Known as the "Homer in the Gloamin', it came just two months after the 37-year-old Hartnett had been asked to take over as manager of a team stuck in third place.

Under Gabby's leadership, the Cubs charged back into the pennant race and found themselves just a half-game back of the Pirates on September 28, 1938, when Hartnett stepped to the plate with a tie score and two outs in the bottom of the ninth inning. He smacked a dramatic walk-off home run off Pirates pitcher Mace Brown in the near darkness — the "Homer in the Gloamin" — sending the Cubs on their way to the pennant.

The Cubs played .620 ball after Hartnett took over the team that year, but they slipped the next two years to fourth-place and fifth-place finishes. Hartnett retired in 1941 with the record for most games caught with 1,793, and a managerial record of 203–176. He was elected to the Hall of Fame in 1955.

At first base is Providence native Paul Konerko. Playing most of his career with the White Sox, he has slugged 365 home runs and posted five years with over 100 RBI. He had his best season in 2010, batting .312 with 39 homers, 111 RBI and career-high marks of .393 OBP, .584 slugging and .977 OPS. Named to four All-Star teams, he was named MVP of the AL Championship Series in 2005 as the White Sox went on to win the World Series. Konerko made history when he hit his 300th home run on April 13, 2009, and was followed by teammate Jermaine Dye hitting his 300th home run as the next batter.

Lajoie's brilliance prevents another great Rhode Island player from making Rhode Island's All-Time team — Davey Lopes. Lopes was a four-time All-Star who won one Gold Glove at second base and had a high of 28 home runs. Where he really excelled was as a base stealer, swiping 557 bases and leading the league twice. Although he is generally acknowledged as one of the greatest base stealers in baseball history, Lopes finished just behind Duffy for most career stolen bases by a Rhode Island player.

Rounding out the infield is third baseman Joe Mulvey, who batted .261 and collected 1,059 hits over a 12-year career in the nineteenth century, and Bill Almon, a utility player who played primarily at shortstop. Almon led the NL with 20 sacrifice hits and was second with 11 triples in 1977, his first season as a starter. He batted .301 for the White Sox in 1981 and finished with 846 hits over 15 seasons.

Rhode Island's third Hall of Famer is Hugh Duffy, who mastered the art of hitting during the early days of baseball. Like Lajoie, Duffy also won the Triple Crown, leading the NL with 18 homers, 145 RBI and an astounding .440 average playing for the Boston Beaneaters in 1894 (some sources list it as .438). It should be pointed out that pitchers were still adjusting to the new mound distance of 60 feet, six inches and the league average was .309 that year.

Still, that means the batting average records for the American League and National League are both held by Rhode Island natives, have been for more than a century and most likely will never be broken. Not bad for the country's smallest state.

Duffy was 5-foot-7 and about 165 pounds soaking wet. He and Tommy McCarthy were known as the Heavenly Twins because they were the same size and blessed with great speed and spectacular fielding ability in the outfield. The duo helped Boston become NL champs in 1892 and 1893, and Duffy was still around as Boston won additional titles in 1897 and 1898.

He wasn't big in stature but Duffy knew how to bring the lumber. He surpassed 100 RBI seven straight seasons and his career total of 106 home runs is one of the highest from that era. He had five hits in a game seven times and also stole 574 bases. Duffy was elected to the Hall of Fame in 1945.

Duffy is joined in the outfield by Baldelli, who looked like a future star until a series of injuries and a mysterious medical condition began to derail his career. The "Woonsocket Rocket" finished third in Rookie of the Year voting after batting .289 with 184 hits and 27 stolen bases in 2003, but was forced to finish his career as a part-time player due to his condition (finally diagnosed as a mitochondrial abnormality).

The third outfielder is Johnny Cooney, who started off as a pitcher for the Boston Braves but played occasionally in the outfield and at first base. After just 34 wins in nine seasons, he went to the minors and refined his batting. Returning to the majors as a 35-year-old, full-time outfielder in 1936, Cooney produced well for six seasons before winding down his career in 1944. He collected 965 hits over 20 seasons with a .286 average. He is also listed on the All-Time Rhode Island team as an honorable mention lefty starter.

Cooney's father and brother, both named Jimmy, played shortstop in the majors. The elder Cooney had 154 hits in his rookie season, 1890, but only lasted three seasons. The younger Cooney, nicknamed "Scoops," batted .295 in 1924 as the double play partner with Rogers Hornsby, who batted .424 that year. He hung around to play seven seasons, highlighted by the unassisted triple play he turned in 1927.

The best pitchers from Rhode Island — Billy Whyte and Tom Lovett — cannot be placed properly on the team because it's not known whether they were righty or lefty. In 1885 Whyte joined the New York Cuban Giants, which made history as the first professional black baseball team. Whyte, who also played a lot of outfield, pitched a perfect game in 1887 and stood out with his distinctive handlebar mustache. Lovett was 88–59 for his career with a 3.94 ERA, including a 30-win season in 1890 and a no-hitter in 1891.

So our right-handed starter is Frank Corridon, who went 70–67 with a 2.80 ERA pitching in the Deadball Era. He pitched 653 innings between 1907 and 1909 without giving up a home run, which is pretty good even for that period. By comparison, Christy Mathewson gave up a total of 13 homers in those seasons despite pitching more innings. "Fiddler" Corridon is one of many pitchers who is credited with inventing or perfecting the spitball, which was legal then.

With Lovett and Whyte a mystery, we're forced to go with Chet Nichols as left-handed starter. Nichols only produced a 34–36 career record but had a respectable 3.64 ERA. His career got off to a promising start, as he led the National League with a 2.88 ERA in 1951, finishing second for Rookie of the Year. His father, Chet Nichols, Sr., was also a Rhode Island native who pitched briefly and poorly in the majors.

Clem Labine is judged to be Rhode Island's best relief pitcher, as he is the all-time leader with 475 relief appearances primarily for the Dodgers. Labine was an integral part of the "Boys of Summer" as they appeared in four World Series in the 1950s, winning two. He won a third ring with the Pirates in 1960.

Labine's greatest pitching performance came as a starter. He only started three games for the Dodgers during the 1956 regular season but was given the Game 6 start the day after Don Larsen threw the perfect game at them. Labine and Bob Turley matched zeroes through nine innings and then Labine hung on to retire the Yankees in order in the top of the 10th. The Dodgers plated a run in the bottom of the inning to give Labine the victory by shutout. The victory was short-lived, as the Yankees decisively won Game 7.

Active player Dan Wheeler has carved out a nice career as a relief pitcher. He had appeared in 577 games through the 2011 season with 43 saves, which is the most in Rhode Island history.

The aptly named Jumbo Brown was one of the first pitchers to be used almost exclusively in relief. He got his nickname due to his large size. At 295 pounds, he was the heaviest player in major league history, a title he held from his debut in 1925 until 320-pound Walter Young came along in 2005. The portly righty appeared in 226 games in relief in a career that lasted from 1925–41. He played on three pennant winners and two teams that won World Series, but Brown didn't see any postseason action.

Beyond Hartnett and Lajoie, another Rhode Island manager worth mentioning is Eddie Sawyer, who managed the Phillies for eight seasons, guiding the 1950 "Whiz Kids" to the National League pennant.

SOUTH CAROLINA

*Names in **bold** represent Major League selections by position, followed by honorable mentions. Negro Leagues players are in **bold italics**, followed by honorable mentions in italics. City of birth is in parentheses.*

Catcher — *George Dixon* (Greenwood). Also: Aaron Robinson (Lancaster); Mickey Livingston (Newberry); Sammy Taylor (Woodruff)

First Base — *Ben Taylor* (Anderson). Also: Dan Driessen (Hilton Head Island); Ken Harrelson (Woodruff); Willie Aikens (Seneca)

Second Base — Willie Randolph (Holly Hill). Also: Del Pratt (Walhalla); Bobby Richardson (Sumter); Orlando Hudson (Darlington); Pokey Reese (Columbia)

Third Base — Al Rosen (Spartanburg). Also: *Candy Jim Taylor* (Anderson); Willie Jones (Dillon); Red Smith (Greenville)

Shortstop — **Marty Marion (Richburg)**. Also: *Willie Williams* (Orangeburg); Chick Galloway (Clinton); *James Clarkson* (Hopkins); Bill Spiers (Orangeburg); Don Buddin (Turbeville)
Outfield — **Shoeless Joe Jackson (Pickens County)**
Outfield — **Larry Doby (Camden)**
Outfield — **Jim Rice (Anderson)**. Also: *Chino Smith* (Greenwood); Reggie Sanders (Florence); *Nat Rogers* (Spartanburg); Mookie Wilson (Bamberg); Gorman Thomas (Charleston); Gene Richards (Monticello); Preston Wilson (Bamberg)
Designated Hitter — **Gorman Thomas (Charleston)**. Also: Matt Lecroy (Belton)
Right Handed Starter — **Bobo Newsom (Hartsville)**. Also: *Steel Arm Johnny Taylor* (Anderson); Van Mungo (Pageland); *Tom Williams* (Charleston); Kirby Higbe (Columbia); La Marr Hoyt (Columbia); Flint Rhem (Rhems)
Left Handed Starter — **Billy O'Dell (Whitmire)**. Also: *Barney Brown* (Hartsville)
Relief Pitcher — **Bill Landrum (Columbia)**. Also: Bobby Bolin (Hickory Grove); Jim Ray (Rock Hill); Art Fowler (Converse)
Manager — **Candy Jim Taylor (Anderson)**. Also: *C.I. Taylor* (Anderson); Willie Randolph (Holly Hill); Marty Marion (Richburg)

The Names

Best Nickname: "Shoeless Joe" Jackson
Other Nicknames: Walter "Dinty" Barbare; James "Bus" Clarkson; George "Tubby" Dixon; Pembroke "Midget Twirler" Finlayson; Clarence "Chick" Galloway; Ken "Hawk" Harrelson; Hernando "Pep" Harris; Bob "Hurricane" Hazle; Orlando "O-Dog" Hudson; Willie "Puddin' Head" Jones; Roy "Popeye" Mahaffey; Marty "The Octopus" Marion; "Spartanburg John" McMakin; Louis "Bobo" Newsom; Jim "Sting" Ray; Calvin "Pokey" Reese; Flint "Shad" Rhem; Johnny "Mutt" Riddle; Al "Hebrew Hammer" and "Flip" Rosen; Charles "Chino" Smith; "Candy Jim" Taylor; "Steel Arm Johnny" Taylor; James "Stormin' Gorman" Thomas; Bill "Ol' Ninety-Six" Voiselle; Willie "Curly" Williams; Charlie "Swamp Baby" Wilson; William "Mookie" Wilson; Horace "Dooley" Womack; Charles "Spades" Wood
Most Unusual Name: Pembroke Finlayson; Van Lingle Mungo; Pelham Ballenger; Delancey Currence

All-Time Leaders

Games: Willie Randolph, 2202
Hits: Jim Rice, 2452
Batting Average: Joe Jackson, .356
Home Runs: Jim Rice, 382
RBI: Jim Rice, 1451
Stolen Bases: Mookie Wilson, 327
Wins: Bobo Newsom, 211
Strikeouts: Bobo Newsom, 2082
Saves: Bill Landrum, 58
Future Stars: Matt Wieters (Goose Creek); Justin Smoak (Goose Creek); Jordan Lyles (Hartsville); Taylor Guerrieri (Columbia)
Best Player: Shoeless Joe Jackson

Historic Baseball Places

Shoeless Joe Jackson Museum and Library in Greenville — Located in the house where Shoeless Joe lived and died, this museum pays homage to his legacy. A life-size bronze statue honoring Shoeless Joe is located in Joe Jackson Plaza in downtown Greenville. His gravesite is nearby at the Woodlawn Memorial Park.
Joseph P. Riley Jr. Ballpark in Charleston — Known as "The Joe," the home of the Charleston RiverDogs opened in 1997. Try the Homewrecker Hot Dog, which is a monstrous half-pound hot dog that can be personally loaded with up to 25 toppings.
Knights Stadium in Fort Mill — Home of the Charlotte Knights opened in 1990. It is probably the only case of a team playing its games in a neighboring state.
Duncan Park in Spartanburg — Dating back to 1926, this old ballpark was home to a team in the South Atlantic League for many years and is now home to a team in the Coastal Plain League. Some of the seats came from Connie Mack Stadium in Philadelphia. Ryne Sandberg played shortstop at Duncan Park for the Spartanburg Phillies in 1979. The historic park, which has not seen pro baseball since 1995, is in need of renovation and a preservation drive is underway.

Notable Achievements

Shoeless Joe Jackson holds the American League record for most triples in a season with 26 in 1912, which was matched two years later by Sam Crawford.
In 1943 **Larry Doby** became the first African American to play in the American Basketball League, an early professional league that pre-dated the NBA. Four years later he would break similar ground in the American League.
Reggie Sanders set a record for runs batted in during a division series with 10 in 2005.
Jim Rice is tied with Ty Cobb for most consecutive seasons leading the league in total bases with three (1977–79).
Dan Driessen was the first designated hitter to hit a home run in the World Series, playing for the Reds in Game 1 of the 1976 Series, which also made him the first DH in the National League.
Pat Luby (Charleston) holds the record for most consecutive games won in a season by a rookie, winning 17 straight games from August 6, 1890 to October 3, 1890.
Willie Aikens hit four home runs for the Royals in a losing effort in the 1980 World Series.
In the first game played at Yankee Stadium between

Shoeless Joe Jackson's home in Greenville was converted into a museum that opened in 2008. It chronicles the baseball achievements and life of the talented but controversial player, who was banned from baseball as a result of the Black Sox Scandal (courtesy Shoeless Joe Jackson Museum).

Duncan Park in Spartanburg, which opened in 1926, features one of the oldest wooden grandstands as well as seats salvaged from Connie Mack Stadium. The 1937 New York Yankees, which featured five future Hall of Famers including Lou Gehrig and Joe DiMaggio, stopped off on the way to spring training and played an exhibition at Duncan Park (courtesy BallparkReviews.com).

two black teams, on July 10, 1930, **Chino Smith** hit two home runs and a triple for the New York Lincoln Giants.

Ken Harrelson is often credited as the first major league player to wear a glove for batting, when he used a golf glove in 1964. He went on to play professional golf and compete in the 1972 British Open.

John Bass (Charleston) played for the Cleveland Forest Citys in the first professional baseball game on May 4, 1871.

Textile Leagues Helped Shape South Carolina Baseball History

When the textile mills started popping up all over South Carolina in the 1880s, baseball activity soon followed as each mill town organized a team of nine. South Carolina's All-Time Best Player, Shoeless Joe Jackson, got his start pitching for his local mill league team.

The year was 1908 and the Greenville Spinners were in their second year of existence in the South Carolina State League. The Spinners' star batter was a promising local boy, Jackson, who batted .346. He also picked up his famous nickname that year during a game in which he took off his spikes because they were hurting his feet and belted a triple without shoes.

The Spinners won the Carolina Baseball Association title in 1910 and Greenville's minor league club would go on to become affiliated with nine different big-league teams between 1939 and 2004. Nolan Ryan went 17-2 with the Greenville Mets in 1966. Other major league players from Greenville include Red Smith, Walter Barbare, active player Jason Hammel and Doug Strange, who closed out his career playing in the minors for the Greenville Braves.

Shoeless Joe may be banned from enshrinement in Cooperstown, but he is still a hero in his native state. All you have to do is visit Greenville, where the Shoeless Joe Jackson Museum and Library opened up in 2008.

You can wander along Joe Jackson Plaza, gaze at a statue of the baseball great and visit the museum to learn more about his fascinating story. The museum is housed in Jackson's former childhood home, which was moved to 356 Field Street (playing off his career average) across from Fluor Field in downtown Greenville. July is celebrated as Shoeless Joe Jackson Month every year in Greenville, and the star, who has been dead for more than 60 years, has several Facebook pages and web sites devoted to preserving his legacy.

Shoeless Joe was illiterate, but that didn't keep him from demonstrating his considerable skill on the diamond. As he put it less than eloquently, "I ain't afraid to tell the world that it don't take school stuff to help a fella play ball."

Jackson batted .382 with a career-high 118 RBI at age 30 in 1920, his last season before being banished from baseball for his involvement in the Black Sox Scandal. Despite the fact he was acquitted in court of fixing the 1919 World Series — he batted .375 over the eight games — Jackson eventually admitted to taking money to throw the Series and received a lifetime ban from Kenesaw Mountain Landis, baseball's first commissioner.

Since his career ended just as the Lively Ball Era was starting up, it is difficult to speculate what sort of numbers Shoeless Joe could have posted with eight or nine more seasons of playing. He might have finished ahead of Ty Cobb's all-time-best average of .366 and most likely would have exceeded 3,000 hits. Not only did Cobb call Jackson the finest natural hitter in the history of the game, Babe Ruth did too and admitted to copying his batting style.

Swinging a massive bat he called "Black Betsy," Jackson batted over .300 11 times, with a high of .408 in 1911, his first full season. Unofficially it's a rookie record that has never been approached, but by the rules of the day it was officially considered his fourth season. He led the league in hits twice, exceeding 200 hits four times, and finished with a career OBP of .423 — eighteenth-best in history. Despite his high career average, Jackson never led the league in batting, although he finished in the top four in eight of his nine full seasons.

Pitcher Ernie Shore said, "Everything he hit was really blessed. He could break bones with his shots. Blindfold me and I could still tell you when Joe hit the ball. It had a special crack."

Lou Brissie, Neil Chrisley and Bill Voiselle are some other textile league players who went on to appear in the majors. Voiselle and his three brothers worked in the cotton mills when they were not playing baseball. He burst onto the scene by winning 21 games as a rookie for the New York Giants in 1944, making the All-Star team after leading the league in games started (41), innings pitched (312⅔) and strikeouts (161). That is the last time a rookie has pitched more than 300 innings in a season.

Four years later he found himself pitching in two World Series games for the Boston Braves. By that time he was wearing uniform number 96 in honor of his hometown, Ninety-Six (he was actually born in Greenwood). That's where Voiselle picked up the nickname "Ol' Ninety-Six." After his playing career wound down in the late 1950s, Voiselle joined brothers Claude and Jim in playing for Ninety-Six's mill team in the Central Carolina Textile League. "I'm a little old cotton mill boy — never had nothing and never been nowhere," Voiselle said in an 1991 story in *Sports Collectors Digest*.

All-Time South Carolina Selections

At catcher for Team South Carolina, the best choice is Greenwood native George "Tubby" Dixon, whose Negro Leagues career lasted from 1917–33. Dixon batted .324 for the Chicago American Giants in 1920, when he helped the team win the first of three straight Negro National League pennants. Dixon had some power and demonstrated good catching skills.

Earning honorable mention at catcher, Aaron Robinson, was mainly a platoon player during his eight-season career. He compiled 478 hits with a .260 average. His best year was 1946, when he hit .297 with 16 homers and 64 RBI for the Yankees. He made the All-Star team the next season but ended up catching only 74 games due to the arrival and development of a young catcher named Yogi Berra. Robinson won a World Series ring with the Yanks in 1947 and then was traded to the White Sox.

The best choice at first base is Ben Taylor, who played from 1908 to 1929 and is considered one of the finest first basemen in Negro Leagues history. Taylor was an outstanding defensive first sacker who is credited by the Hall of Fame with a career average of .322.

Some of Taylor's best seasons came while playing for his older brother, C.I. Taylor, on the Indianapolis ABCs. The Seamheads.com Negro Leagues Database powered by The Baseball Gauge shows Taylor with averages of .321, .393 and .378 for the years 1920–22. Taylor also demonstrated talent on the mound when forced to fill in as a pitcher, and his command of the game earned him managerial positions with seven teams between 1922 and 1938. Two more older brothers played on the ABCs—"Candy Jim" and "Steel Arm Johnny"—and all four Taylor brothers are listed on the All-Time South Carolina team.

Earning honorable mention status is Dan Driessen, a solid player who hit 153 homers and accumulated 1,464 hits over 15 seasons, mainly with the Reds. Driessen wasn't much of a slugger and was merely adequate with the glove, but he did win World Series with the Reds in 1975 and 1976 as well as in his final season, 1987 with the Cardinals.

Another notable first baseman is Ken "Hawk" Harrelson of Woodruff, who also played a lot of right field in a career that ended at age 29. Harrelson came in third in the voting for the 1968 AL MVP after clubbing 35 homers, driving in a league-high 109 runs and finishing ninth with a .275 average. Carl Yastrzemski (at .301) was the only American League player to bat over .300 that season.

Willie Randolph stands out from a crowded field of noteworthy second basemen. Randolph was a steady, dependable, underrated leader on the Yankees for 13 seasons, helping them win World Series titles in 1977 and 1978 (although he missed the '78 Series due to injury). A six-time All-Star, he served as captain of the Yankees from 1986 to 1988. Randolph was an outstanding fielder with excellent hands and good range who had the misfortune to play in the American League at the same time as Bobby Grich, Frank White and Lou Whitaker. Still, he probably should have won Gold Gloves in at least 1976 and 1979.

Randolph hung around for 18 seasons, compiling 2,210 hits (second all-time among South Carolina natives), stealing 271 bases and batting .276 with an excellent .373 OBP. He typically batted in the second spot, since he was adept at bunting, hitting behind the runner and walking. His best overall season was 1980, when he batted .294 with 30 steals, led the AL with 119 walks and finished second with a .427 OBP. He batted a career-high .327 for the Brewers at the age of 37 in 1991, his last year as a regular.

Right behind Randolph is Walhalla native Del Pratt, who fell four hits short of 2,000 for his career. Pratt, who played baseball and football at the University of Alabama before starting his pro career, hit .302 as a rookie in 1912 with 172 hits. He led the American League with 103 RBI in 1916 despite hitting just five homers that year for the St. Louis Browns. In 1921 he drove in 102 runs with five home runs while batting .324 for the Red Sox. A lifetime .292 hitter with 247 stolen bases, Pratt ranks third in Win Shares for the 1912–1924 period, behind Hall of Famers Eddie Collins and Rogers Hornsby. Steve Steinberg's SABR biography of Pratt points out that the term "Murderer's Row" was bestowed on the Yankees by sportswriter Fred Lieb in 1918 after Pratt was acquired from the Browns—two years before Babe Ruth joined the team.

His career stats aren't as impressive as those of Randolph and Pratt but Bobby Richardson managed to make the All-Star team seven years in what was essentially a 10-year career. He led the AL with 209 hits while batting .309 in 1962, winning a Gold Glove and finishing runner-up to Mickey Mantle for MVP that season. A lifetime .266 hitter, Richardson won five Gold Gloves for his fielding and played in seven World Series with the Yankees between 1957 and 1964, winning three titles. He was the MVP of the 1960 World Series, batting .367 with 12 RBI. He didn't hit for power or average and his career OBP was .299, but Richardson was a skilled bunter who rarely struck out. It seemed appropriate that he wore number 1 for the Yankees.

Active player Orlando Hudson has made two All-Star teams while playing for the Blue Jays, Diamondbacks, Dodgers and Twins and now Padres in a career that started in 2002. His career average is .277 and he has demonstrated some pop with 83 homers. He really excels with his stellar glove work at second, demonstrating outstanding range and winning four Gold Gloves.

Third base is in good hands with Al Rosen, who was one of the best players in baseball for his first five seasons, averaging 31 homers, 114 RBI and a .298 average. He had a terrific year in 1962 when he was named American League MVP and narrowly missed a Triple Crown. Rosen led the AL with 43 homers and 145 RBI but was edged out by Mickey Vernon for the batting title, .337 to .336. That season he also led the league in runs scored (115), slugging (.613), OPS (1.034), OPS+ (179) and total bases (367).

Nicknamed the "Hebrew Hammer," Rosen has to be considered one of the greatest Jewish players in baseball history. He got a late start to his career after losing three years to military service and his production waned over his final two seasons, but during his prime his slugging almost single-handedly kept the Indians in the pennant race each year. During his seven seasons as a regular, Rosen led the Tribe to five second-place finishes and a record 111 wins for first place in 1954, when they lost the World Series to the Giants.

Willie Jones, who was nicknamed "Puddin' Head," made two All-Star teams. He had a career .258 average but trails Rosen in OPS .879 to .753. Rosen's 192 homers beat Jones by two despite the fact Jones had 2,101 more at-bats. Jones was an adept fielder, leading the league in putouts seven times and fielding percentage five times. He helped the Whiz Kids win the 1950 NL Pennant by setting career highs in runs (100), hits (163), triples (6), homers (25), RBI (88), total bases (278) and OPS (.828).

Candy Jim Taylor had a distinguished 45-year career in the Negro Leagues as a stellar third baseman and later, a successful manager. He generally batted in the middle of the order and occasionally pitched but his hitting production was sporadic. At age 39 in 1923 he batted .372 and tied for the league lead with 20 home runs while playing for three teams. He batted .340 for the Birmingham Giants in 1907 and .301 for the Indianapolis ABCs in 1916.

Moving on to shortstop, the All-Time South Carolina team is anchored by Marty Marion, who received serious consideration for the Hall of Fame despite posting somewhat pedestrian statistics. A seven-time All-Star, Marion was nicknamed "The Octopus" because at 6-foot-2 he was unusually tall and long-armed for a shortstop. He was named National League MVP in 1944 by one point over Bill Nicholson of the Cubs. Voters obviously noticed that the Cubs came in fourth that year while the Cardinals won 111 games and the NL pennant. Marion's defense, leadership and intangibles evidently carried the vote because his teammate and the reigning MVP, Stan Musial, was a more deserving MVP that year (he finished fourth).

Marion and Musial played together on the Cardinals from 1941–1950, leading the team to four pennants and World Series titles in 1942, 1944 and 1946. Marion retired with just 1,448 hits and a .263 average but was St. Louis' original wizard at short, long before Ozzie Smith was doing back-flips.

Also deserving mention at short is Chick Galloway, who earned MVP votes three straight years for the Philadelphia Athletics (1922–24). Galloway got thrown out stealing 41 times in those years while successfully stealing 33 bases. His best season was 1922, when he batted .324 with 185 hits.

If Jackson had been elected to the Hall of Fame, it would have meant the All-Time South Carolina team was filled with Hall of Famers in the outfield. Larry Doby gained induction in 1998 and Jim Rice joined the exclusive club in 2009.

Doby made seven consecutive All-Star teams as a center fielder for the Indians, but his greatest accomplishment was becoming the first African American player in the American League. Doby debuted with Cleveland on July 5, 1947, less than three months after Jackie Robinson broke the color barrier with the Dodgers.

"I knew being accepted was going to be hard," Doby said, "but I knew I was involved in a situation that was going to bring opportunities to other blacks."

Doby helped lead the Indians to their last World Series title in 1948, batting .301 during the regular season and .318 in the Series. Doby's Game 4 home run was the first by an African American player in World Series history.

He became the first African American to lead the league in home runs when he hit 32 to lead the AL in 1952. Doby would make history again in 1978 when he took over as skipper of the White Sox, becoming the second African American manager in major league history (following Frank Robinson).

His best year was 1954 when he again led the league in home runs with 32 and RBI with 126, finishing second in the MVP race in a close contest with Yogi Berra. Doby actually grew up in Paterson, N.J., which is how he ended up starting his baseball career with the Newark Eagles in 1943. He would play three years as an infielder in the Negro Leagues, with two years off for service in World War II, before being signed to a major league contract by Indians owner Bill Veeck. He would start his career being subjected to the same hatred and bigotry that was directed at Jackie Robinson but without the accompanying plaudits. But while Robinson was determined to ignore insults and not cause waves, Doby demonstrated with his words and actions that he was not going to put up with any nonsense on or off the field.

Rice probably began developing a chip on his shoulder about racial injustice after watching white teammate Fred Lynn trounce him in the Rookie of the Year voting in 1975 despite posting nearly identical numbers. Rice hit 22 homers with 102 RBI and 174 hits while Lynn hit 21 homers with 105 RBI and 175 hits. Lynn did win a Gold Glove that year for his superior defense and also led the league in runs, doubles, slugging and OPS, but his slight statistical edge is not enough to justify the landslide voting—Lynn received 23.5 first-place votes while Rice received 0.5 first-place votes.

Rice was unquestionably one of the most feared sluggers in the American League during his career with the Red Sox from 1974 to 1989. He had an outstanding MVP season in 1978, leading the league in at-bats (677), hits (213), triples (15), home runs (46), RBI (139), slugging (.600), OPS (.970), total bases (406), runs created (147) and OPS+ (157). It was the first time an American League player had topped 400 total bases in a season since Joe DiMaggio in 1937. Rice fell just short of a Triple Crown that year by finishing third with a .315 average.

His career numbers seem less than impressive when compared to the monster numbers put up later by a generation of chemically enhanced sluggers, but Rice could be counted on for 30 homers, 100 RBI and a .300 average every season. He retired with 2,482 hits, 383 homers, 1,451 RBI, .a 502 slugging percentage and a .298 batting average.

Rice compiled eight seasons with more than 100 RBI, batted over .300 seven times and finished in the top five in MVP balloting six times. He was inducted into the Hall of Fame in 2009 in his fifteenth and final year of eligibility on the BBWAA ballot, receiving 76.4 percent of the votes, just enough to get in.

Several other outfielders from South Carolina deserve mention. In 2006 Reggie Sanders became the fifth member of an exclusive club — players with 300 homers and 300 stolen bases. He ended his career the next year with 305 homers and 304 stolen bases, impressive credentials for a player who made only one All-Star team. An underrated fielder, Sanders was a vagabond who played for eight different teams in his last 10 seasons, becoming the only player in MLB history to hit 20 home runs for six different teams. He set a division series record with 10 RBI for the Cardinals in the 2005 NLDS against the Padres.

Chino Smith was as fine a hitter as ever played in the Negro Leagues, according to some who pitched against him such as Satchel Paige and William "Sug" Cornelius. In terms of hitting for average, no one did it better. The lefty-swinging Smith batted .377 in his abbreviated six-year career, which was cut short after he contracted yellow fever and died at age 29 in 1932. Smith, whose nickname stemmed from the fact that he had faint Asian facial features, reportedly posted a combined average against all competition of .388. The right fielder led the East league with a .461 average and 23 homers while playing for the New York Lincoln Giants in 1929 and also batted .439 in 1927 and .468 in 1930, which turned out to be his last season.

Pitchers learned not to mess with the supremely confident and temperamental Chino, because he was skilled enough and crazy enough to hit line drives at their head. Jesse "Mountain" Hubbard, Chino's teammate on the Brooklyn Royal Giants, said woe be the pitcher who decided to sail one by Chino's head. "He could hit those line drives back through the box just like you were throwing a ball over to first. He could shoot a bullet back through there," Hubbard said in John Holway's *Blackball Stars.*

Another skilled Negro Leagues outfielder was William "Nat" Rogers of Spartanburg, a hard-nosed, dangerous line-drive hitter. Although he never got to prove his skill in the major leagues, Rogers considered himself one of the best hitters of all time. "Baseball players are born, not made," he declared on his biographical sheet for the Baseball Hall of Fame. After joining the Chicago American Giants in the middle of the 1927 season he proceeded to hit in 31 straight games, leading the team to the pennant and eventual World Series title. Rogers won the Negro American League batting title in 1939 and was a middle-of-the-order threat for a number of championship teams. If his reported birth date of 1893 is to be believed, he started his Negro Leagues career at age 30 and played until he was 53.

South Carolina has produced two Wilson outfielders of note, who happen to be related to each other. Mookie Wilson is the uncle and stepfather of Preston Wilson, and he taught his nephew/stepson how to play the game. Mookie had 327 career steals but is most famous for hitting the dribbler to first base that got past Bill Buckner to score the winning run in Game 6 of the 1986 World Series. Preston led the NL with 141 RBI in 2003 while hitting 36 home runs that year (his only All-Star selection). He retired in 2007 with 189 home runs, hitting over 20 in a season six times.

Gorman Thomas is another notable outfielder from South Carolina, but he earns the selection as designated hitter. Thomas played 967 games in center field and was a below-average fielder. He knew how to mash the ball, hitting 268 home runs in 13 seasons. He led the AL with 45 in 1979 and 39 in 1982, the year Harvey's Wallbangers made it to the World Series. A .225 career hitter, he also led the league twice in strikeouts.

Bobo Newsom is the logical choice for the right-handed starter, and he would find a spot on anyone's all-eccentric team. He was a colorful character full of bluster who picked up the nickname Bobo because he wasn't good with names and that's what he called everyone. Few ballplayers were tougher — he once completed a game after suffering a broken kneecap and refused to come out of another game after sustaining a broken jaw from an errant throw, primarily because President Franklin Roosevelt was in attendance that day. He ended up with a four-hit shutout that game. "When the President comes to see Ol' Bobo pitch he ain't gonna let him down," Newsom was quoted as saying. Misfortune seemed to follow him around. On the way to spring training in 1932 he drove his car off a cliff — sustaining only a broken leg.

When he wasn't entertaining with quotes, Newsom demonstrated that he could pitch. He won 211 games, 91 more than anyone else from South Carolina. Newsom also lost 222 games, as he played on only two pennant winners pitching for nine teams over 20 seasons (including five separate stints with the Washington Senators). He won 20 games three straight years, 1938–40, and won in double figures for 11 consecutive seasons and 13 altogether.

A four-time All-Star, Newsom led the league in complete games twice and innings pitched and ERA+ once, but also led three times in losses and twice in walks. His best season was 1940 when he went 21–5 with a 2.83 ERA for the Tigers. He pitched a complete game to win Game 1 of the World Series that year, an accomplishment immediately overshadowed by the death of his father the next day. Newsom went out and pitched a three-hit shutout to win Game 5 and pitched another complete game in a losing effort in Game 7.

Newsom's 5.08 ERA in 1938 is the highest ever for a pitcher that won 20 games. If you count his 146 wins in the minors (including 30 for the Los Angeles Angels in the Pacific Coast League in 1933), Newsom had 357 victories in professional baseball.

Earning honorable mention status is Van Mungo, a workhorse for the Brooklyn Dodgers in the 1930s who became known for his temper. He was the youngest player in the majors when he debuted at age 20. Mungo went on to win 90 games for the Dodgers between 1932 and 1937, getting selected to three All-Star teams and leading the NL in SO/BB three times, games started twice and innings, shutouts and strikeouts once. After winning 14 games for the Giants in 1945, Mungo retired with a career record of 120–115. His full name, Van Lingle Mungo, was later immortalized in a popular 1970 song by David Frishberg.

We would be remiss if we failed to mention the accomplishments of "Steel Arm Johnny" Taylor, who was the second-oldest of the four Taylor brothers. The brothers all played together with the Birmingham Giants in 1908 and were united again with the Indianapolis ABCs in 1914, with C.I. as the manager. Blessed with a blazing fastball and deceptive curve, Steel Arm Johnny pitched 17 years in the Negro Leagues. He received his nickname by a white sportswriter who observed him blowing away batters for Biddle University in 1898. Taylor fashioned a 37-6 record pitching for the Birmingham Giants and St. Paul Gophers in 1909 and later served as a manager and coach like his brothers.

Also deserving mention is Charleston native Tom Williams, who went 13–2 with a 1.28 ERA for the Chicago American Giants in 1917. Also not to be overlooked is LaMarr Hoyt, who won the Cy Young Award pitching for the White Sox in 1983. Hoyt went 24–10 that year while leading the AL with a 1.024 WHIP, 1.1 BB/9IP and 4.77 K/BB ratio. The next season his ERA shot up to 4.48 and he led the league with 18 losses. Hoyt won 98 career games in eight seasons.

Another right-handed pitcher wins the prize for most unusual name — Pembroke Finlayson. Nicknamed the "Midget Twirler" due to his diminutive size (5-foot-6, 140 pounds), the Cheraw native debuted for the Brooklyn Superbas in 1908, walking four of the five batters he faced in his only game that year. Finlayson pitched in one more game in 1909 and that would be it for his major league career. His ERA was 11.05. He managed to win 19 games in the minors in 1909 and then 21 the next season, before he was diagnosed with a serious heart condition. Rushing back into a throwing regimen after surgery, Finlayson put too much strain on his heart and died at age 23.

South Carolina's left-handed starter is Billy O'Dell, who made slightly more appearances out of the bullpen. In 1954 he signed as a "Bonus Baby" with the Orioles out of Clemson University and made his major league debut 12 days later without spending any time in the minors. He would miss the 1955 and 1956 seasons while serving in the military. The native of Whitmire won 105 games over 13 seasons and retired with a 3.29 ERA and OPS+ of 109. O'Dell made the All-Star team twice with the Orioles after going 14–11 with a 2.97 ERA in 1958 and 10–12 with a 2.93 ERA in 1959.

O'Dell set career highs with 19 wins, 195 strikeouts and 20 complete games when he concentrated on starting in 1962 with the San Francisco Giants, who won the pennant that year but lost the World Series to the Yankees. Back in the bullpen in 1965, he went 10–6 for the Milwaukee Braves, appearing in 61 games and posting a 1.05 WHIP.

Another southpaw under consideration was Barney Brown, a screwballer who also starred in the Mexican League. Brown played in four East-West All-Star games and was usually among the league leaders in wins.

Bill Landrum has the most career saves among South Carolina pitchers with 58, and he gets selected for the relief spot although he only pitched 361 innings in his career. Landrum saved 26 games (sixth-best in the NL) for the Pirates in 1989 with a 1.67 ERA and then saved 30 games the next two seasons. His father, Joe Landrum, appeared in 16 games for the Brooklyn Dodgers in the 1950s.

Also under consideration was Bobby Bolin, a swingman who made 331 relief appearances and 164 starts over 13 seasons. He saved 15 games for the Red Sox in his last season, 1973, retiring with 29 official saves and a 3.40 ERA. Bolin's best year was 1968, when he went 10–5 for the San Francisco Giants with a 1.99 ERA, allowing just 128 hits in 176 innings with a 0.985 WHIP.

The easy part of settling on the All-Time South Carolina manager is deciding it should be a Taylor — the hard part is figuring out which Taylor since all four managed at one time or another. Managerial records in the Negro Leagues are even sketchier than playing records, but it can be quickly determined that Candy Jim and C.I. were more accomplished managers than their other two brothers.

Candy Jim was acknowledged as a brilliant strategist and motivator. He started managing in 1918 and ended up skippering for a dizzying number of teams right up until his death in 1948. He led the St. Louis Stars to a 68–25 record and the Negro National League pennant in 1928 and then later led the Homestead Grays to Negro World Series titles in 1943 and 1944. According to several sources, Candy Jim managed and won more games in the Negro Leagues than any other manager, which gives him the final nod over his brother. He also managed a team of African American stars, including Satchel Paige, Josh Gibson, Buck Leonard and Cool Papa Bell, that won the prestigious Denver Post Tournament in 1936.

C.I. was a stern taskmaster as a manager who instilled discipline in his teams, a trait that made them stand out among the anything-goes nature of many Negro Leagues teams. He began as a player-manager with the Birmingham Giants in 1904 and in 1914 he started building a dynasty as co-owner of the Indianapolis ABCs, with the help of his brothers. The 1916 team featuring Oscar Charleston, brother Ben and Bingo DeMoss captured the Western championship by knocking off the Chicago American Giants led by Rube Foster. When the Negro National League started up in 1920, Taylor was tapped to serve as vice president, further evidence that his executive accomplishments were nearly as important as his managerial feats. His untimely death at age 47 in 1922 prevented him from carving out an even bigger legacy as a skilled manager.

SOUTH DAKOTA

*Names in **bold** represent Major League selections by position, followed by honorable mentions. City of birth is in parentheses.*

Catcher — **Len Rice (Lead)**
First Base — **Terry Francona (Aberdeen)**
Second Base — **Mark Ellis (Rapid City)**. Also: Marv Olson (Gayville); Sparky Anderson (Bridgewater)
Third Base — **Del Paddock (Volga)**
Shortstop — **Kermit Wahl (Columbia)**
Outfield — **Dave Collins (Rapid City)**
Outfield — **Jason Kubel (Belle Fourche)**
Outfield — **Carroll Hardy (Sturgis)**
Designated Hitter — **Jason Kubel (Belle Fourche)**
Left Handed Starter — **Floyd Bannister (Pierre)**
Right Handed Starter — **Jim Scott (Deadwood)**
Relief Pitcher — **Keith Foulke (Rapid City)**. Also: Terry Forster (Sioux Falls); Kerry Ligtenberg (Rapid City); Justin Duchscherer (Aberdeen)
Manager — **Sparky Anderson (Bridgewater)**. Also: Terry Francona (Aberdeen)

The Names

Best Nickname: "Death Valley Jim" Scott
Other Nicknames: Raleigh "Redskin" Aitchison; Sparky "Captain Hook" Anderson; Allen "Bullet Ben" Benson; Terry "Tito" Francona; John "Pork Chop" Hoffman; Marv "Sparky" Olson; William "Jiggs" Parson; Arnold "Jug" Thesenga
Most Unusual Name: Justin Duchscherer

All-Time Leaders

Games: Dave Collins, 1701
Hits: Dave Collins, 1335
Batting Average: Terry Francona, .274
Home Runs: Jason Kubel, 104 (still active)
RBI: Mark Ellis, 459 (still active)
Stolen Bases: Dave Collins, 395
Wins: Floyd Bannister, 134
Strikeouts: Floyd Bannister, 1723
Saves: Keith Foulke, 191
Future Star: Chris Kessinger (Sioux Falls)
Best Player: Keith Foulke

Historic Baseball Places

Sioux Falls Stadium in Sioux Falls — Known as the Birdcage, it is the home of the Sioux Falls Canaries, an independent team. It first opened in 1941 and from 1966–71 was the Northern League home of the Sioux Falls Packers, who featured future major leaguers such as Ken Griffey, Sr., Ross Grimsley and Don Gullett.

South Dakota Amateur Baseball Hall of Fame in Lake Norden — Depicts the history of amateur baseball in the state and also includes artifacts from many of the major league players who hail from South Dakota.

Memorial Park Stadium in Huron — The bleachers are literally built into the hillside in one of the most unique stadium designs you'll ever see. Greg "The Bull" Luzinski first demonstrated his ability to hit the ball over the fence while starting his baseball career playing for the Huron Phillies in 1968.

Notable Achievements

Mark Ellis was the first South Dakota native to hit for the cycle, which he did on June 4, 2007.

Dave Collins led the American League in triples with 15 in 1984.

Pitcher **Terry Forster** ended his career with a .397 batting average, with 31 hits in 78 at-bats. This earns him the unique honor of the most hits by a player with a higher career batting average than Ty Cobb.

Sturgis Native Was Always in the Right Place at the Right Time

South Dakota-born players have had a number of historic achievements over the years. Most of them are related to Carroll Hardy, who must hold the record for brushes with greatness. He's been aptly compared to Forrest Gump, because he always seemed to be in the right place at the right time when something big happened.

To wit, here are some of the accomplishments of the Sturgis native:

Hit his first home run pinch-hitting for Roger Maris on his 25th birthday.

Only player to pinch-hit for Ted Williams (September 20, 1960).

After Ted Williams homered in the last at-bat of his career, Hardy replaced him in left field for the ninth inning.

Only player to pinch-hit for Carl Yastrzemski, which he did three times.

Only player to hit a walk-off grand slam in the twelfth inning, which he did on April 11, 1962.

Traded for a future Hall of Famer — Dick Williams.

Coached under Billy Martin in the minors.

He earned 10 letters at the University of Colorado in football, baseball and track and was named to the school's Hall of Fame and all-century team in football.

Named MVP of the Hula Bowl.

Drafted by the 49ers in the third round of the 1955

Sturgis native Carroll Hardy was a bit player who had a knack for rising to the occasion. He is the only player to pinch-hit for Ted Williams as well as the only player to pinch-hit for Carl Yastrzemski. His first home run came while pinch-hitting for Roger Maris and his 17 career home runs include a walk-off grand slam in the twelfth inning. Hardy had given professional football a try before turning to baseball, and he would later make a name for himself in the NFL (National Baseball Hall of Fame Library, Cooperstown, New York).

NFL Draft. It's been said that Hardy's indecisiveness that day over whether to play football or baseball was the impetus to the NFL adopting a time limit on teams' draft selections.

Caught four touchdown passes from future Hall of Famer Y.A. Tittle while playing with the 49ers in 1955.

Played in the same backfield as Hall of Famers Joe Perry and Hugh McElhenny.

Spent 20 years as a scout and personnel director for the Denver Broncos, helping build the Orange Crush Defense in the 1970s.

That's a pretty good resume for a guy who batted .225 with 251 hits in his major league career. There are Hall of Fame players who don't have as many career highlights as Hardy. And he didn't exactly take advantage of his opportunity to bat in the Splendid Splinter's place — he lined out to the pitcher. "I wouldn't be anything without Ted," he told an interviewer in 2009. In fact, Hardy only got to pinch-hit for Williams because he fouled a pitch off his foot and had to come out of the game.

Forced to choose between baseball and football coming out of college, Hardy chose football for one year and then switched to baseball, where he made the most of his opportunities. Once his baseball career ran its course, he went back to football and distinguished himself with a long career in the National Football League.

Before he had his brushes with fame in professional sports, Hardy was already a legend for his exploits at Sturgis High School, where he guided the Scoopers to the 1951 state title in basketball and also was the state long jump champion. He was inducted into the South Dakota Sports Hall of Fame.

Hardy's baseball career started with the Reading Indians in 1955, with fellow Dakota boy Roger Maris as his teammate. He played with Maris the next season on the Indianapolis Indians, outhitting Maris .385 to .293 (but in 355 fewer at-bats).

All-Time South Dakota Selections

Although Len Rice's family moved to California when he was a baby, he was born in Lead, South Dakota, which qualifies him to be the all-time catcher for South Dakota. He spent most of his playing career in the minors, batting .354 with 170 hits for Class C Tucson in 1940. Finally making it to the majors in 1944, he managed just 23 hits in 42 games over two seasons.

First base is manned by Terry Francona, now the ex-manager of the Red Sox. Named the Most Outstanding Player while leading the University of Arizona to the 1980 College World Series title, Francona was drafted in the first round by the Expos. A contact hitter with little power, he was largely a bench player throughout his 10-season career.

Rapid City native Mark Ellis played over 1,000 games at second base for the Oakland A's before he was traded to the Rockies in 2011. An outstanding fielder, he's flashed occasional power with a high of 19 homers in 2007.

Del Paddock pitched two no-hitters in the minor leagues for Vancouver, and wound up compiling 1,116 hits over 13 minor league seasons. He appeared in one game for the White Sox in 1912 and then was picked up by the New York Highlanders, for whom he played 46 games that season, mostly at third base. It would be his only season in the big leagues. Paddock is one of five South Dakota players who were actually born in what was known as the Dakota Territory, before South Dakota became a state in 1889. The others are Bob Ingersoll, Jiggs Parson, Raleigh Aitchison and Jim Scott.

Kermit Wahl emerged as the best South-Dakota-born player at shortstop even though he played more games at third. Wahl was a utility infielder who played 58 games at short between 1944 and 1951.

Despite his unimpressive career statistics, Hardy is one of the three best outfielders in South Dakota history. Joining him in the outfield are two more accomplished players: Dave Collins and Jason Kubel. The speedy Collins, who holds most of the all-time South Dakota hitting records, played 16 seasons for eight teams. He batted over .300 three times and stole 395 bases, including a high of 79 in 1980.

Collins signed a lucrative free-agent contract with the New York Yankees for the 1982 season, joining a crowded outfield that included Dave Winfield, Jerry Mumphrey, Ken Griffey, Lou Piniella, Oscar Gamble and Bobby Murcer. After batting .253 in a semi-regular role, Collins was traded after the season along with 19-year-old first baseman Fred McGriff and pitcher Mike Morgan to the Blue Jays for the immortal Tom Dodd and Dale Murray. McGriff would go on to hit 493 home runs and Morgan would pitch 19 more seasons for 10 additional teams, while Dodd never pitched for the Yankees and Murray went 3–6 for the Yankees over three seasons. Collins, on the other hand, bounced back to hit .308 for the Blue Jays in 1984 with 60 stolen bases and a league-leading 15 triples.

At RC Stevens High School in Rapid City, not only was Collins the state's Legion baseball player of the year, he was also named all-state in basketball and football and set a new state record in the 100-yard dash. He joins Hardy as a member of the South Dakota Sports Hall of Fame.

Kubel made his debut for the Twins in 2004 and then was forced to miss the 2005 season with a serious knee injury. He has evolved into a major contributor for the team. Bouncing between the corner outfield spots and designated hitter, Kubel slugged 20 home runs in 2008, followed that up by batting .300 with 28 homers and 103 RBI in 2009 and then added 21 more homers in 2010. He is already South Dakota's all-time leader in home runs with 104 through the 2011 season.

The left-handed starter is Pierre native Floyd Bannister, who won 134 games over 15 seasons. Bannister first attracted attention while pitching for Kennedy High School in Burien, Wash. His senior year he went 15–0 and didn't allow an earned year all season on the way to winning the state championship. The accolades continued at Arizona State, where Bannister was named College Player of the Year as a junior.

Big things were expected of him in the pros, as the Astros made Bannister the first overall selection of the 1976 amateur draft. Bannister led the American League in strikeouts with 209 in 1982, making the All-Star team that season. He had his best years for the White Sox, winning 66 games for the Sox between 1983 and 1987. Armed with a good fastball and above-average breaking ball, Bannister was criticized for an unwillingness to pitch inside during his career. Still, at the end of 2010 he ranked 103rd all-time in strikeouts with 1,723. He was followed to the big leagues by his son, Brian, who has pitched for the Mets and Royals.

South Dakota's right-handed starter is also its first major league player—Jim Scott. Nicknamed "Death Valley Jim," Scott pitched nine seasons for the White Sox beginning in 1909 and was known for his superb pick-off move. The Deadwood native posted the unusual mark of 20–20 in 1913 with a 1.90 ERA and won 24 games in 1915 while leading the league with seven shutouts. He pitched a no-hitter through nine innings on May 14, 1914, but lost the no-hitter and the game in the 10th inning.

Scott was one of the first players to leave baseball and join the war effort in France, leaving the White Sox shortly before they won the 1917 World Series. He declined an offer to return to the White Sox for the 1919 season, which proved to be a fortuitous decision since the team would become infamous because of the Black Sox scandal. One of the eight players banned from baseball in the aftermath of the scandal was Buck Weaver, who was Scott's brother-in-law.

Scott would play nine more seasons, all in the minors, winding up with 175 minor league wins. Combined with his 107 wins in the majors, Scott ended up with 282 victories in professional baseball. Although he pitched during the Deadball Era, his 2.30 ERA ranks eighteenth-best in baseball history. After his playing career he returned to the majors as an umpire for a short time. He was elected to the South Dakota Sports Hall of Fame in 1999.

The closer is Keith Foulke, who made just one All-Star team—with the A's in 2003—but racked up 191 saves over an 11-season career with a terrific ERA+ of 139. Never blessed with a blazing fastball, Foulke instead relied on a devastating circle changeup that was particularly lethal to left-handed batters.

He finished 10th in the Cy Young Award voting in 1999 after striking out 123 in 105 innings with a 2.22 ERA as a set-up man for the White Sox. The closer's job was his after that, and Foulke responded the next two seasons with 34 and 42 saves.

Signed as a free agent by the Red Sox in 2004, he was at his best that year as the Sox marched to their first World Series title since 1918. Foulke appeared in 11 of the 14 games during the 2004 postseason, giving up just seven hits and one run in 14 innings while striking out 19. He was on the mound to close out the decisive Game 4 victory, making him a hero to an entire generation of Red Sox fans. The heavy workload down the stretch might have taken a toll on Foulke, who was stymied by injuries and never the same pitcher after that 2004 season.

It came down to Foulke and Collins as South Dakota's All-Time Best Player. Collins only had one season with over 450 at-bats and was a platoon player for much of his career, while Foulke played an integral role in helping three different teams make the playoffs. Collins didn't make an All-Star team while Foulke did. Foulke's career OPS+ of 140 is better than Goose Gossage, Dennis Eckersley or Rollie Fingers, although he pitched significantly fewer innings. Foulke made more of an impact during the regular season and postseason, so he gets the nod.

Another notable reliever from South Dakota is Terry Forster, who saved 127 games over 16 seasons. He led the AL with 24 saves in 1974, pitching 134 innings in relief that year. Forster didn't give up a run in eight career postseason appearances. Also noteworthy is Justin Duchscherer, who has made two All-Star teams for the A's, as a reliever in 2005 and as a starter in 2008.

Francona has had more success as a manager than player, helping the Red Sox break the "Curse of the Bambino" with World Series championships in 2004 and 2007. The 2004 squad became the first team to overcome a 3–0 deficit in a postseason series by coming back against the hated Yankees. Unfortunately, he's now known for skippering the 2011 Sox team that pulled off the biggest choke job in baseball history as they lost a nine-game lead in the wildcard race to the Rays in September. Francono won 57 percent of his games as Red Sox manager, but left after eight seasons with a mixed bag of memories.

Tito's managerial record falls short of South Dakota's most famous baseball citizen, Hall of Famer Sparky Anderson. Sparky's managerial career far overshadowed his playing career, which consisted of 10 minor league seasons sandwiched around one major league season. Sparky started at second base for the Phillies throughout 1959 but batted just .218.

He was an instant success as a manager, leading the Reds to the NL pennant in his first season, 1970. Another pennant followed in 1972 as the pieces to the Big Red Machine started coming together, and then came back-to-back World Series titles in 1975 and 1976. As Anderson recalled, "They say the first World Series is the one you remember most. No, no, no. I guarantee you don't remember that one because the fantasy world you always dreamed about is suddenly real." Anderson, who frequently stated his belief that players make the manager and not the other way around, was blessed with some all-time great players such as Pete Rose, Johnny Bench and Joe Morgan.

Sparky was once quoted as saying, "If I ever find a pitcher who has heat, a good curve and a slider, I might seriously consider marrying him, or at least proposing." In reality, he viewed pitchers as interchangeable parts and earned the moniker "Captain Hook" for his frequent trips to the mound to take out pitchers.

Cut loose by the Reds in 1978 despite finishing first or second in the division eight of nine seasons, Anderson was hired to inject life into a fifth-place Tigers team. It took seven seasons, but Sparky finally delivered a World Series title to Detroit fans in 1984. It was a well-balanced team that won 104 games behind the strong pitching of Jack Morris, the underrated double-play tandem of Alan Trammell and Lou Whittaker and the slugging of Kirk Gibson and Lance Parrish. Anderson made history, becoming the first manager to win a World Series in each league, the first to win 100 games in each league and the second (after Casey Stengel) to butcher the language in each league.

He was named AL Manager of the Year for the second time in 1987 after guiding the Tigers to 98 wins and a division title, but that would prove to be his last trip to the playoffs. Two years later, the Tigers limped to a 59–103 record, which caused Anderson to comment, "The great thing about baseball is when you're done, you'll only tell your grandchildren the good things. If they ask me about 1989, I'll tell them I had amnesia."

Anderson remains the all-time leader in managerial wins for both the Reds and the Tigers, and his five pennants and three World Series titles were enough to earn him election to the Hall of Fame in 2000. His 2,194 wins as a manager rank sixth in baseball history.

TENNESSEE

*Names in **bold** represent Major League selections by position, followed by honorable mentions. Negro Leagues players are in **bold italics**, followed by honorable mentions in italics. City of birth is in parentheses.*

Catcher — **Tim McCarver (Memphis)**. Also: *Bruce Petway* (Nashville); Ed Bailey (Strawberry Plains); Rick Dempsey (Fayetteville); Joe Oliver (Memphis); Clyde McCullough (Nashville); Johnny Gooch (Smyrna); *Robert Gaston* (Chattanooga)

First Base — **Todd Helton (Knoxville)**. Also: Dale Alexander (Greeneville); Doc Johnston (Cleveland); Harvey Hendrick (Mason); *Art Pennington* (Memphis)

Second Base — **Jim Gilliam (Nashville)**. Also: *Bill Monroe* (Knox County); Phil Garner (Jefferson City); *Bunny Downs* (Chattanooga)

Third Base — **Bill Madlock (Memphis)**. Also: Jimmy Johnston (Cleveland); Sammy Strang (Chattanooga)

Shortstop — ***Joe Hewitt* (Nashville)**. Also: *Morten Clark* (Bristol); Bob Fisher (Nashville); Bobby Reeves (Hill City)

Outfield — ***Turkey Stearnes* (Nashville)**

Outfield — **Vada Pinson (Memphis)**

Outfield — **Steve Finley (Union City)**. Also: Clyde Milan (Linden); Ben Chapman (Nashville); *Wild Bill Wright* (Milan); *Henry Kimbro* (Nashville); Leon Wagner (Chattanooga); John Stone (Mulberry); Tillie Walker (Telford); Roy Cullenbine (Nashville); Jim Hickman (Henning); Earl Webb (White County)

Designated Hitter — **Bubba Trammell (Knoxville)**

Right Handed Starter — **Tommy Bridges (Gordonsville)**. Also: Bob Caruthers (Memphis); Red Lucas (Columbia); *Bob Griffith* (Liberty); Fred Toney (Nashville); Ed Whitson (Johnson City)

Left Handed Starter — **Noodles Hahn (Nashville)**. Also: Claude Osteen (Caney Spring); Lefty Stewart (Sparta); Clyde Wright (Jefferson City); *John Dickey* (Knoxville)

Relief Pitcher — **Bryan Harvey (Soddy-Daisy)**. Also: David Weathers (Lawrenceburg); Rick Honeycutt (Chattanooga); Derrick Turnbow (Union City); Greg McMichael (Knoxville); George Sherrill (Memphis); Clyde Shoun (Mountain City)

Manager — Phil Garner (Jefferson City). Also: *Bruce Petway* (Nashville); *Frank Leland* (Memphis)

The Names

Best Nickname: Hub "The Gallatin Squash" Perdue
Other Nicknames: Dale "Moose" Alexander; "Two Game Johnny" Beazley; Joe "Cupcakes" Blanton; "Parisian Bob" Caruthers; Clydell "Slick" Castleman; Morten "Specs" Clark; John "Steel Arm" Dickey; McKinley "Bunny" Downs; James "Mooney" Ellis; Charles "Slim" Embrey; James "Rags" Faircloth; August "Happy" Foreman; Phil "Scrap Iron" Garner; Robert "Fuzzy" Garrett; Johnny "Patcheye" Gill; Jim "Junior" Gilliam; Dawson "Tiny" Graham; Bob "Schoolboy" Griffith; Frank "Noodles" Hahn; Todd "The Toddfather" Helton; "Still Bill" Hill; Bill "Bird Dog" Hopper; Clarence "Bubber" Jonnard; Henry "Jumbo" Kimbro; Charles "The Nashville Narcissus" Lucas; Bill "Mad Dog" Madlock; Frank "Limb" McKenry; Clyde "Deerfoot" Milan; Bill "Money" Monroe; Claude "Gomer" Osteen; Frank "Wahoo" Pearson; Art "Superman" Pennington; Bruce "Home Run" Petway; Joe "Lumber" Price; Bobby "Gunner" Reeves; Clyde "Hardrock" Shoun; Clarence "Popboy" Smith; Norman "Turkey" Stearnes; John "Stud" Stuart; Sammy "The Dixie Thrush" Strang; Frank "Hoss" Thompson; "Marvelous Marv" Throneberry; Thomas "Bubba" Trammell; "Milkman Jim" Turner; Leon "Daddy Wags" Wagner; Clarence "Tillie" Walker; Roy "Dixie" Walker; Burnis "Wild Bill" Wright
Most Unusual Name: Kevin Mmahat; Carden Gillenwater; Johnny Gooch; Billy Gobble

All-Time Leaders

Games: Steve Finley, 2583
Hits: Vada Pinson, 2757
Batting Average: Dale Alexander, .331
Home Runs: Todd Helton, 347 (still active)
RBI: Todd Helton, 1308 (still active)
Stolen Bases: Clyde Milan, 495
Wins: Bob Caruthers, 218
Strikeouts: Tommy Bridges, 1674
Saves: Bryan Harvey, 177
Future Star: Drew Pomeranz (Collierville)
Best Player: Turkey Stearnes

Historic Baseball Places

AutoZone Park in Memphis — Home of the Memphis Redbirds opened in 2000 in downtown location near historic Beale Street. The team actually has a cheerleader squad, which seems out of place at a baseball game.
Engel Stadium in Chattanooga — If only the bleachers could talk, because there's a lot of history in this stadium, which was built in 1929 to serve as the first minor league affiliate of the Washington Senators. Engel Stadium was placed on the National Register of Historic Places in 2009. It was named after Chattanooga Lookouts owner Joe Engel, who gained notoriety for his creative promotions such as holding ostrich races.

Notable Achievements

Earl Webb (Blue Spring Cove) has held the record for most doubles in a season, 67, since 1931. Webb's next highest doubles total was 30 in 1930.
Dale Alexander posted 83 extra-base hits as a rookie in 1929, second in the American League and more than Babe Ruth, Lou Gehrig or Jimmie Foxx.
The first batter **Tommy Bridges** faced in the majors was Babe Ruth — he got him out, but four years later served up Ruth's 700th home run on July 13, 1934.
Ike Brown (Memphis) was the last player to make the jump from the Negro Leagues to the major leagues when he joined the Detroit Tigers in 1969.
Noodles Hahn was the first pitcher to win 20 games for a last-place team in the twentieth century. He won 22 games for the Cincinnati Reds in 1901.
Ben Chapman was the first player to bat for the American League in an All-Star Game, which he did at Comiskey Park on July 6, 1933.
Bob Montgomery (Nashville) was the last player to bat in the majors without a batting helmet when he batted for the final time in 1979, as he was grandfathered in when Major League Baseball made helmets mandatory in 1971.

Negro Leagues History Comes Alive in Tennessee Cities

They performed their feats of athletic ballet before intimate crowds on historic fields such as Martin Park in Memphis, Engel Field in Chattanooga and Sulphur Dell in Nashville. The players moved around frequently, forced to jump at better-paying opportunities and play year-round to make ends meet. The franchises, too, were often in scramble mode, switching from one league and one city to another in hopes of elusive financial security.

Tennessee's baseball history cannot be recounted without pointing out its ties to the Negro Leagues, with a pantheon of stars represented on teams in Memphis, Nashville, Knoxville and Chattanooga.

History was being made every season, although fans couldn't know it at the time. How were the people who saw Willie Mays play at Engel Stadium in 1945 for the Chattanooga Choo Choos to know he would one day become the best all-around player in the majors? Could anyone foretell Bill Foster was earmarked for the Hall of Fame when watching him play for his first professional team, the Memphis Red Sox, in 1923? Or that Satchel Paige, whose first professional experience came with the Chattanooga Black Lookouts in the Negro Southern League, would evolve into one of the greatest pitchers in baseball history?

Was it a love of baseball or entertainment that brought fans to Brewer's Park in 1920 to watch the Knoxville Black Giants and their one-armed pitcher and outfielder, Forest "One-Wing" Maddox? Who knew the promising pitcher for the 1952 Memphis Red Sox, Charley Pride, would one day develop into a world-famous singer? A fleeting look at Buck O'Neil as he played his first two professional games for the Memphis Red Sox in 1937 gave no clues he was destined to turn into the beloved and admired ambassador for the Negro Leagues, making sure its past stars would not be forgotten.

One could form a formidable All-Star team of Tennessee-born players just from the Negro Leagues, most with colorful nicknames that hinted at their greatness. On the mound you could go with southpaw John "Steel Arm" Dickey or righties Frank "Hoss" Thompson or Bob "Schoolboy" Griffith pitching to rocket-armed catcher Bruce "Home Run" Petway. The outfield would feature "Wild Bill" Wright, Norman "Turkey" Stearnes and Henry "Jumbo" Kimbro, all blessed with terrific speed and power. The infield is anchored by switch-hitting Art "Superman" Pennington at first, with Jim "Junior" Gilliam or McKinley "Bunny" Downs at second, Bill "Money" Monroe able to slide over to third base and Joe Hewitt or Morten "Specs" Clark manning shortstop. Pioneering owner Frank Leland could serve as manager for this talent-laden squad.

Memphis has sent 45 players to the major leagues, more than any other Tennessee city. Vada Pinson, Tim McCarver and Bill Madlock are among the prominent players who were born in Memphis. The first Memphis-based team dates back to 1877, while the Memphis Eurekas and Memphis Eclipse were founding members of the Southern League of Base Ballists in 1886. That was the first formal black baseball league, although it didn't last long. The Memphis Red Sox competed in various Negro Leagues from 1923–50 but were largely unsuccessful on the field. These days the city hosts the Triple-A Memphis Redbirds at AutoZone Park, which was named Minor League Ballpark of the Year by Baseball America in 2009.

All-Time Tennessee Selections

Negro Leaguer Bruce Petway deserves strong consideration for the catcher spot for Team Tennessee, as he was one of the best defensive catchers in Negro Leagues history. Ty Cobb quickly learned not to challenge his arm, as Petway threw him out trying to bunt for a hit and later trying to steal during an exhibition game in Cuba in 1910 (it's often misreported that he threw Cobb out three straight times). Although his nickname was "Home Run," Petway was not a long-ball hitter, instead relying on well-placed hits, bunts and steals to help his team win.

However, our pick for catcher is Tim McCarver, who played 21 seasons across four decades (1959–80). After just 82 games in the minors, he joined the Cardinals at the age of 17, becoming the full-time starter in 1963. He stuck around to catch 1,387 games, making the All-Star team in 1966 and 1967. He was MVP runner-up to teammate Orlando Cepeda in 1967 as he led the Cardinals to the World Series title. His numbers that year were not eye-popping—.295 average with 14 homers and 69 RBI—but on a team filled with stars such as Cepeda, Lou Brock, Curt Flood, Roger Maris, Bob Gibson and Steve Carlton, it was McCarver who was the unquestioned leader.

His career average was a respectable .271 and he amazed the baseball world in 1966 by becoming the first catcher to lead the National League in triples. His 13 triples that year were as many as he had accumulated in his first six seasons in the league. When the pressure was on at World Series time, McCarver demonstrated a knack for the big hit. He batted a team-high .478 with 11 hits during the 1964 World Series, including a tie-breaking home run in the 10th inning of Game 5. His average for three World Series appearances was .311.

McCarver's throwing arm was not in Petway's class, but he was underrated for his defensive abilities. He was an excellent receiver who knew how to call a game, set up batters and get the most out of pitchers. Carlton loved pitching to him so much he all but refused to work with anyone else while both were with the Phillies, leading McCarver to quip, "When Steve and I die, we are going to be buried in the same cemetery, 60' 6" apart."

Two other Tennessee-born catchers deserve mention: Ed Bailey and Rick Dempsey. Bailey was a five-time All-Star who hit 155 home runs but only exceeded 400 at-bats one time. When he saw his first extended action in 1956, he hit .300 with 28 homers. Another career highlight came in the 1962 World Series when Bailey hit a two-run, pinch-hit home run with two outs in the ninth inning of Game 3—his only hit in the Series in 14 at-bats. Dempsey, who was 1983 World Series MVP for the Orioles, hung around for 24 seasons due to his superior defense and strong throwing arm. A lifetime .233 hitter, Dempsey led AL catchers in fielding percentage twice. Between 1976 and 1981 he threw out between 44 percent and 58 percent of base runners each year.

Moving on to first base, the easy selection is Rockies star Todd Helton, who earned five All-Star selections, four Silver Slugger and three Gold Glove Awards between 2000 and 2004. The Knoxville native played quarterback for his hometown University of Tennessee Volunteers and as a junior was ahead of Peyton Manning on the depth chart before getting hurt.

A degenerative back condition has slowed his power numbers the past few seasons and stalled a possible path to the Hall of Fame, but voters will also have trouble overlooking the Coors Field impact on his numbers. In roughly the same number of at-bats through the 2011 season, Helton had batted .354 with 212 homers, 788 RBI and .620 slugging percentage at Coors compared to .291 with 135 homers, 520 RBI and .478 slugging in away games.

Helton's 2000 season was one for the ages. All he did

was lead the league in average (.372), hits (216), RBI (147) and doubles (59) as well as total bases, OBP, OPS and slugging. It was the first time a National League player had at least 200 hits, 40 home runs, 100 RBI, 100 runs, 100 walks and 100 extra-base hits in one season. In addition, he led NL first basemen in assists, putouts and total chances.

When he followed up with another strong campaign in 2001, Helton became the first player in MLB history to have more than 100 extra-base hits in consecutive seasons (103 in 2000 and 105 in 2001). He batted over .300 12 times in his 14 full seasons and has a lifetime .323 average (fourth-best among active players) while his .421 OBP ranks seventeenth all-time. His fluid swing is much admired throughout baseball. "It is such a flat-out sweet swing," said his former manager Clint Hurdle. "I'm reminded of Don Mattingly or George Brett."

Another noteworthy first baseman is Dale "Moose" Alexander, who compiled several outstanding seasons at the beginning of his career before a disabling leg injury in 1933 forced him to spend his last nine years in the minors. During his rookie season, 1929, Alexander batted .343 with 25 homers and 137 RBI while leading the AL in hits with 215. He batted .326 and .325 the next two seasons and then in 1932 his .367 average represented the first time a player led the league in batting while playing for a last-place team. He couldn't continue playing in the majors once the leg injury robbed him of mobility, so instead he went on to compile 2,145 hits with a .334 average in the minors.

The only other Negro Leagues player to earn selection to the All-Time Tennessee team is second baseman Jim Gilliam, who played five years in the Negro National League before advancing to play 14 seasons in the majors. Gilliam was named to the East All-Star team his last three years with the Baltimore Elite Giants, then proceeded to earn Rookie of the Year honors with the Dodgers in 1953. He led the NL in triples with 17 that year, also facing the difficult task of replacing Jackie Robinson at second. He would later make two National League All-Star teams and finish with 1,889 hits.

There wouldn't be much of a drop-off if Negro Leaguer Bill Monroe was the second baseman. Giants manager John McGraw called him the greatest player of all-time and a sure star if allowed to play in the majors. Monroe was an expert fielder at any infield position and delighted in entertaining fans with his on-field antics. He was the biggest star on the powerful 1914 Chicago Giants team, batting .348 that year.

Another good choice at second is Phil Garner, who picked up the nickname "Scrap Iron" due to his scrappy, feisty play. He made three All-Star teams over a 16-year career and posted very similar statistics to Gilliam. Garner has the edge in homers, slugging percentage and OPS+, while Gilliam has a big edge in runs, hits and OBP. Garner batted over .275 just once while Gilliam did it six times. Finally, Gilliam earned MVP votes in four seasons while Garner did not receive a single MVP vote during his career. If you add in Gilliam's years in the Negro Leagues it tips the scales even further.

Our third baseman is Bill Madlock, a four-time National League batting champion who finished second one other year. A three-time All-Star who was named MVP of the 1975 All-Star Game, Madlock finished with 2,008 hits and a .305 average. Traded to the Pirates during the 1979 season, he batted .328 down the stretch for them as they went on to win the championship.

Madlock beats out Jimmy Johnston, who played more games at third than any other position but also played extensively at second, short and the outfield in a career that spanned from 1911 to 1926. Johnston had over 200 hits twice and a .294 career average. His brother, Doc, earns honorable mention at first base with 922 career hits over 11 seasons.

Our shortstop is Nashville native Joe Hewitt, whose Negro Leagues career lasted from 1910–26. A flashy fielder who drew walks and was fast on the base paths, Hewitt served as player-manager for three teams at the tail end of his career and then had middling success managing the Nashville Elite Giants in 1930 and 1932.

Another Negro Leagues shortstop under consideration was Morten "Specs" Clark of Bristol, who batted .287 with 108 hits in 95 games for the Indianapolis ABCs in 1920. It's hard to determine whether Clark or Hewitt was better since statistics are so sketchy. The Seamheads.com Negro Leagues Database powered by The Baseball Gauge shows Clark with 40.1 Win Shares and a .253 batting average for the period 1916–22 compared to 32.2 Win Shares and a .243 average for Hewitt, but Clark was in his prime then while Hewitt's career was winding down.

Heading the outfield is Stearnes, who clearly rises to the top of any list, as his exploits on the diamond were the stuff of legend. He hit for average and power and was a superb center fielder. In John Holway's *Blackball Stars*, Cool Papa Bell was quoted saying, "There's no ball player I know that hit more home runs than Turkey Stearnes. And he was one of the best all-around ball players. Everybody knows he was a great outfielder. He could field, throw, run, hit."

Stearnes wasn't a big man, weighing about 175 pounds, but he could slug with the best of them. Swinging left-handed with an unorthodox batting stance, he led or tied in homers seven times, finishing with 232 — edging Josh Gibson for the most in Negro Leagues history. He batted .430 in 1935 and had a career average of .351 in Negro Leagues action and was even better with a .378 average in exhibitions against white players. He was elected posthumously to the Hall of Fame in 2000, cementing his status as the All-Time Best Player from Tennessee.

Moving on to the outfield, Stearnes is joined by two great all-around center fielders who were underrated during their careers: Vada Pinson and Steve Finley. Check out how similar their career stats are:

	G	R	H	2B	3B	HR	RBI	SB	BA	OBP	OPS
Pinson	2469	1366	2757	485	127	256	1170	305	.286	.327	.769
Finley	2583	1443	2548	449	124	304	1167	320	.271	.332	.775

Pinson and Finley were both lefties who blended speed, power and defensive ability with durability, yet were largely overshadowed by other stars during their playing days. Pinson earned just two All-Star selections and one Gold Glove over 18 seasons, playing in the shadow of Frank Robinson and Pete Rose on the Reds. He didn't even make the All-Star team in 1961 when he batted .343, led the league in hits and finished third in the MVP voting. Pinson had over 200 hits four times, led the NL in doubles and triples twice and ranks 47th all-time in hits with 2,757.

Pinson probably suffered from the fact he was over-hyped at the beginning of his career, which ultimately led to him being underappreciated by the end of his playing days. *The Saturday Evening Post* featured Pinson in a 1960 article titled "Is He the Nearest-Perfect Player?" Reds manager Fred Hutchinson noted that even opposing players would line the top of the dugout to watch Pinson's graceful, compact swings in batting practice. Gushed Gabe Paul, "Imagine a Mantle who doesn't strike out and a Mays who steals sixty bases. That's how good Pinson can be."

Finley became the sixth player to go over 300 stolen bases and 300 home runs (four days after Reggie Sanders), and he retired with 304 homers and 320 steals. He won five Gold Gloves but was named to only two All-Star teams during a 19-season career that ended in 2007. His best season was 1996 with the Padres, when he batted .298 with 30 homers and 126 runs scored. Finley's 2,314 games in center field trail only Willie Mays since 1954, and he ranks third in putouts for a center fielder (since 1954) behind Mays and Richie Ashburn.

While others might rate Clyde Milan or even Ben Chapman ahead of Finley, it's hard to exclude Finley from the position when he posted essentially the same lifetime stats as Pinson. Milan compiled 2,100 hits and stole 495 bases, setting an American League record with 88 steals in 1912 and leading the league with 75 in 1913. He joined the Washington Senators the same year as Walter Johnson, 1907, and would remain the Big Train's teammate and close friend for his entire 16-season career. As Milan recalled, "We bought a car together and roomed together on the road and at home until I was married."

Chapman played with Ruth, Gehrig and Dickey on the powerful Yankees teams of the early 1930s. He patterned his game after Ty Cobb, using speed, aggressive and borderline dirty play to get under the skin of opponents. Chapman led the league in steals four times and retired with 1,958 hits, a .302 average and 287 stolen bases.

Another notable outfielder is Burnis "Wild Bill" Wright, a fearsome switch-hitting slugger in the Negro Leagues. His nickname actually referred to his lack of control as a pitcher early on in his career. Wright, who played his entire career with the Elite Giants franchise in Columbus, Washington and Baltimore, had power from both sides of the plate and was nearly as fast as Cool Papa Bell despite being six-foot-four and 225 pounds. Named to nine East-West All-Star Games, Wright led the Negro National League with a .488 average in 1939 and batted .326 lifetime.

For right-handed starter it's a close call between Tommy Bridges and Bob Caruthers. Bridges pitched his entire career with the Detroit Tigers, from 1930–1946, earning six All-Star selections. He won 20 games three straight seasons, leading the AL in strikeouts two of those years as he relied on an overpowering curveball. In 1932, Bridges fell one out short of throwing a perfect game by surrendering a single to a pinch-hitter. Pitching in a tougher, more competitive era, Bridges' accomplishments outshine those of Caruthers.

Caruthers posted nice career stats — 218–99, 2.83 ERA, 298 complete games, winning 40 games twice. However, his career ended in 1892, the year before the mound was moved back to 60 feet, 6 inches and batters regained the upper hand over pitchers. The diminutive Caruthers — he was 5-foor-7, 140 pounds — was also an outstanding batter, fielder and base runner who played nearly 400 games in the field. He batted .357 in 1887 with 130 hits and 120 runs scored, finishing his career with 29 homers, a .282 average and .391 OBP. He picked up the nickname "Parisian Bob" after traveling to Paris, France, one off-season and engaging in a war of words with St. Louis Browns owner Chris von der Ahe over a salary dispute.

Another righty, Red Lucas, was so good at batting and fielding that he ended up getting 437 at-bats as a pinch hitter and played 18 games in the field. Not only was Lucas the first player to reach 100 pinch hits, his 114 career pinch hits were the major league record for more than three decades. He wasn't bad as a pitcher either, winning 157 games and leading the league in complete games three times and shutouts and WHIP once.

Bob "Schoolboy" Griffith was a spitballer who hung around for 20 years in the Negro Leagues, making three All-Star teams. Also known as "Big Bill" because he was 6-foot-5 and 235 pounds, the right-handed Griffith was nearly unbeatable in the California Winter League and also performed well in the Cuban League.

Johnny Beazley was as talented as any of Tennessee's righties, at least he demonstrated supreme skill in his breakout rookie season of 1942. He went 21–6 with a 2.13 ERA that year and helped the St. Louis Cardinals defeat the Yankees in the World Series with complete-game wins in Game 2 and Game 5. That's where he picked up the nickname "Two Game Johnny." Unfortunately, Beazley threw out his arm while pitching for the army during World War II, bringing a premature end to his career. He finished with a career winning percentage of .721 across six seasons.

"Milkman Jim" Turner toiled in the minors for 14 seasons before finally getting his shot with the Boston Bees in 1937. The 33-year-old rookie shocked the baseball world by winning 20 games and leading the NL in ERA, complete games and shutouts. The Antioch native made the All-Star team in 1938 on the way to winning 14 games and then hung around for seven more years, collecting 69 career wins. If you combine those with his 234 wins over 17 minor league seasons, then Turner can claim 303 wins in pro baseball.

With a career mark of 51–64 Hub Perdue doesn't merit a spot on the All-Time-Tennessee pitching staff, but he takes top honors with his nickname — "The Gallatin Squash." He was given that moniker by the famous sportswriter Grantland Rice in deference to his hometown and a particular type of squash, the hubbard squash. That's not very flattering, since hubbard squash are said to be irregularly shaped, covered in bumpy warts and featuring a bitter after-taste.

When it came time to select the all-time lefty, it came down to a tough decision between two pitchers whose careers took place more than a half-century apart. Noodles Hahn won just 130 games over eight seasons playing from 1899–1906. However, he led the league in strikeouts his first three seasons and also led in complete games, shutouts and innings pitched once. He pitched a no-hitter in 1900 and posted a strong career ERA+ of 132. He set a twentieth century record with 41 complete games in 1901, when he won 22 games for the last-place Cincinnati Reds (accounting for a remarkable 42 percent of their wins). During one game that year he struck out 16 batters, which represented the most strikeouts by a pitcher since the mound was moved to its current distance in 1893. Hahn won his 100th game shortly after turning 24, which makes him the second-youngest pitcher to reach that mark since 1900. However, his heavy workload took a toll on his arm and he was out of baseball at the age of 27. There is a lack of consensus about the origins of his nickname, although it definitely relates somehow to chicken noodle soup.

Claude Osteen won 196 games over 18 seasons, won 20 game twice and was named to three All-Star teams. But he also lost 195 games, never led the league in a positive pitching category and retired with a pedestrian ERA+ of 104. He picked up the nickname "Gomer" from his resemblance to Gomer Pyle on *The Andy Griffith Show*. Osteen wins points for durability and consistency — he recorded 11 straight seasons with over 200 innings pitched — but Hahn was more dominant and had a much cooler nickname.

Team Tennessee's closer is Bryan Harvey, who accumulated 177 saves and made two All-Star teams. He led the league with 46 saves for the Angels in 1991, finishing fifth in the voting for the Cy Young Award that year, and later saved 45 games for the Marlins in 1993. For his career Harvey struck out 10.4 batters per 9 innings.

David Weathers was primarily a set-up man who appeared in 964 games over 19 seasons. He recorded 75 saves, with 33 of them coming as a 37-year-old closer for the Reds in 2007. Rick Honeycutt lasted for 21 seasons and was a starter for the first half of his career, which is when he made his two All-Star appearances. He ended up appearing in 529 games in relief and served as a key contributor out of the bullpen for the Oakland A's 1989 title team.

Garner earned the selection as the manager for Team Tennessee. He only won one pennant in 15 seasons managing the Tigers, Brewers and Astros, but his teams generally reflected his hard-nosed style. He was brought in as Astros manager midway through the 2004 season and he guided them to the wild-card spot by winning at a .649 clip. The next year he led the Astros to the World Series, although they got swept by the White Sox. He won 985 games but experienced only three winning seasons.

TEXAS

*Names in **bold** represent Major League selections by position, followed by honorable mentions. Negro Leagues players are in **bold italics**, followed by honorable mentions in italics. City of birth is in parentheses.*

Catcher — *Biz Mackey* (Eagle Pass). Also: *Louis Santop* (Tyler); Frank Snyder (San Antonio); Gus Mancuso (Galveston); Jerry Grote (San Antonio); *Jim Brown* (San Marcos)

First Base — Ernie Banks (Dallas). Also: Norm Cash (Justiceburg); Cecil Cooper (Brenham); *Ed Wesley* (Waco); Mike Hargrove (Perryton); Ferris Fain (San Antonio); *Robert Hudspeth* (Luling); *Eddie Douglass* (Fort Worth); Eddie Robinson (Paris); Danny Cater (Austin); *Bill Pettus* (Goliath County); Willie Upshaw (Blanco)

Second Base — Joe Morgan (Bonham). Also: Rogers Hornsby (Winters); *Newt Allen* (Austin); Chuck Knoblauch (Houston); Pete Runnels (Lufkin); Randy Velarde (Midland); *Marvin Williams* (Houston); Charlie Neal (Longview); *Jesse Douglas* (Longview)

Third Base — Eddie Mathews (Texarkana). Also: Pinky Higgins (Red Oak); Pinky Whitney (San Antonio); *Dewey Creacy* (Fort Worth); *Marlin Carter* (Haslam); Max Alvis (Jasper); Grady Hatton (Beaumont); Kelly Gruber (Houston)

Shortstop — *Willie Wells* (Austin). Also: Garry Templeton (Lockney); Roy McMillan (Bonham); Freddie Patek (Seguin); Craig Reynolds (Houston); *Jesse Williams* (Henderson); *Jesse Walker* (Austin)

Outfield — Tris Speaker (Hubbard)
Outfield — Frank Robinson (Beaumont)
Outfield — Lance Berkman (Waco). Also: Curt Flood (Houston); Ross Youngs (Shiner); Ron Gant (Victoria); *Hurley McNair* (Marshall); *Chaney White* (Dallas); Carl Crawford (Houston); *Red Parnell* (Austin); Adam Dunn (Houston); Jo-Jo Moore

(Gause); Don Buford (Linden); Sam West (Longview); Bibb Falk (Austin); Gus Zernial (Beaumont); Steve Kemp (San Angelo); Carl Reynolds (LaRue); *Crush Holloway* (Hillsboro); *Henry Milton* (East Texas); Jerry Mumphrey (Tyler); Curt Walker (Beeville); Ruppert Jones (Dallas); Dave Philley (Paris); *Goose Curry* (Mexia)

Designated Hitter — Don Baylor (Austin). Also: Cliff Johnson (San Antonio)

Right Handed Starter — Greg Maddux (San Angelo). Also: *Smokey Joe Williams* (Segui); Nolan Ryan (Refugio); *Hilton Smith* (Giddings); *Rube Foster* (Calvert); *William Bell, Sr.* (Galveston); *Bill Jackman* (Carta); Schoolboy Rowe (Waco); *Jesse Hubbard* (Bering); *Bill Gatewood* (San Antonio); Josh Beckett (Spring); *Sam Crawford* (Dallas); Doug Drabek (Victoria); Burt Hooten (Greenville); Danny Darwin (Bonham); *Henry McHenry* (Houston); Tex Hughson (Buda); Pete Donohue (Athens); John Lackey (Abilene)

Left Handed Starter — *Bill Foster* (Calvert). Also: *Andy Cooper* (Waco); *Dave Brown* (San Marcos); Hippo Vaughn (Weatherford); Fred Norman (San Antonio)

Relief Pitcher — Joe Nathan (Houston). Also: Mike Stanton (Houston); Greg Minton (Lubbock); Mike Jackson (Houston); Mike Timlin (Midland); Firpo Marberry (Streetman); Bill Henry (Alice); Arthur Rhodes (Waco); Kerry Wood (Irving); Donnie Moore (Lubbock); Huston Street (Austin)

Manager — *Rube Foster* (Calvert). Also: Cito Gaston (San Antonio); Mike Hargrove (Perryton); Frank Robinson (Beaumont); *Biz Mackey* (Eagle Pass); *Willie Wells* (Austin); *Andy Cooper* (Waco); Paul Richards (Waxahachie); Rogers Hornsby (Winters); Tris Speaker (Hubbard)

The Names

Best Nickname: Mike "The Human Rain Delay" Hargrove

Other Nicknames: Newt "Colt" Allen; Tom "Rattlesnake" Baker; Ernie "Mr. Cub" Banks; Gary "Ding Dong" Bell; Lance "Big Puma" and "Fat Elvis" Berkman; Larvell "Sugar Bear" Blanks; Joe "Goobers" Bratcher; Lloyd "Gimpy" Brown; Earl "Teach" Caldwell; "Stormin' Norman" Cash; George "Sarge" Connolly; Frank "Dingle" Croucher; Homer "Goose" Curry; George "Storm" Davis; Roy "Peaches" Davis; Walt "Hickory" Dickson; Adam "Big Donkey" Dunn; Roy "Shag" Easterwood; Ferris "Burrhead" Fain; Bibb "Jockey" Falk; Joseph "Boob" Fowler; Ned "Navasota Tarantula" Garvin; Ben "Stomper" Grieve; Doug "Eye Chart" Gwosdz; Clint "Hondo Hurricane" Hartung; Michael "Pinky" Higgins; Burt "Happy" Hooten; Rogers "Rajah" Hornsby; Jesse "Mountain" Hubbard; Robert "Highpockets" Hudspeth; Bill "Cannonball" Jackman; Clayton "Minotaur" Kershaw; Raleigh "Biz" Mackey; Greg "Mad Dog" Maddux; Frederick "Firpo" Marberry; Howard "Polly" McLarry; Henry "Streak" Milton; Greg "Moon Man" Minton; Gene "Rowdy" Moore, Jr.; Joseph "The Gause Ghost" Moore; Joe "The Sweet Pea" Morgan; Fred "Shoemaker" Nicholson; Freddie "The Flea" Patek; Henry "Cotton" Pippen; Mel "Primo" Preibisch; "Broadway" Connie Rector; Emory "Topper" Rigney; Arthur "Tink" Riviere; Frank "The Judge" Robinson; Lynwood "Schoolboy" Rowe; Nolan "The Ryan Express" Ryan; Louis "Big Bertha" Santop; "Suitcase Bob" Seeds; "Art the Great" Shires; Frank "Pancho" Snyder; Tris "The Grey Eagle" Speaker; Monty "Gander" Stratton; James "Hippo" Vaughn; Willie "Devil" Wells; Chaney "Reindeer" White; "Smokey" and "Cyclone" Joe Williams; Walt "No Neck" Williams; Owen "Chief" Wilson; Ross "Pep" Youngs; Gus "Ozark Ike" Zernial

Most Unusual Name: Astyanax Douglass; Fabian Kowalik; Doug Gwosdz; Craig Smajstrla

All-Time Leaders

Games: Frank Robinson, 2808
Hits: Tris Speaker, 3514
Batting Average: Rogers Hornsby, .358
Home Runs: Frank Robinson, 586
RBI: Frank Robinson, 1812
Stolen Bases: Joe Morgan, 689
Wins: Greg Maddux, 355
Strikeouts: Nolan Ryan, 5714
Saves: Joe Nathan, 261 (still active)
Future Stars: Jordan Walden (Fort Worth); Kyle Drabek (Victoria); Jameson Taillon (The Woodlands); Michael Choice (Grand Prairie); Anthony Rendon (Houston); Shelby Miller (Brownwood)
Best Player: Tris Speaker

Historic Baseball Places

Nolan Ryan Exhibit and Center in Alvin — Located on campus of Alvin Community College, the exhibit hall documents the Hall of Famer's illustrious career. Discover what it feels like to catch a Nolan Ryan fastball and see balls from each of his seven no-hitters.

Texas Rangers Baseball Hall of Fame at Rangers Ballpark in Arlington — Located behind right field, the Rangers Hall of Fame honors the top players and individuals in the history of the franchise.

Whataburger Field in Corpus Christi — Opened in 2005 as home of Corpus Christi Hook. The stadium features an 18-foot tall "For the Love of the Game" statue of a young ballplayer that is billed as the largest bronze statue of a baseball player.

Minute Maid Park in Houston — Astros' new stadium opened in 2000 with a distinctive hill in center field. Located at Union Station in downtown Houston, the ballpark features a vintage, full-sized locomotive that runs along a track atop left-field wall.

Dr. Pepper Ballpark in Frisco — Home of the Frisco Roughriders opened in 2003. Neat feature is the fact that the bullpens are built directly into the stands, giving fans an up-close view.

Mickey Mantle gravesite at Hillcrest Mausoleum in Dallas — Hardly a day goes by that someone doesn't stop by and drop off a trinket or a note to the Mick.

Hubbard Museum — Highlights include an exhibit on Tris Speaker, who was born and buried in Hubbard. Speaker was the first Texan to be inducted into the Baseball Hall of Fame and was also inducted in the Texas Sports Hall of Fame.

Notable Achievements

John "Chief" Wilson (Austin) set a record that may not ever be broken — 36 triples in 1912. That is a record in any league, regardless of era. He never hit more than 14 triples in any other season.

Cliff Johnson held the record for most career home runs by a pinch hitter with 20, until passed by Matt Stairs in 2010.

J.J. Trujillo (Corpus Christi) made baseball history when he gave up a walk-off home run to the first batter he ever faced in the majors, Tony Batista, on June 11, 2002.

Kerry Wood not only struck out four hitters in one inning, on September 2, 2002, he became the only player to accomplish that while also hitting a home run in the game. Wood also reached 1,500 strikeouts faster than any pitcher in major league history, requiring just 1,303 innings to reach the mark.

Jo-Jo Moore was the first player to collect more than 200 hits while batting below .300. He batted .295 with 201 hits in 1935.

Joel Youngblood (Houston) was the first player to play for two different teams in different cities on the same day. He played for the Mets during an afternoon game in 1982 against the Cubs, then was traded to the Expos and played for them that night in Philadelphia. He got a hit in each game.

Jason Jennings (Dallas) was the first pitcher in the modern era to hit a home run and throw a shutout in his first game, which took place on August 23, 2001.

Garry Templeton was the first player to collect 100 hits from each side of the plate during one season, which he did for the Cardinals in 1979.

Eddie Mathews was the player featured on the cover of the first issue of *Sports Illustrated* in August 1954.

On May 3, 2009, **Carl Crawford** tied the record for most stolen bases in a game with six.

Tris Speaker is the only player to post three hitting streaks of at least 20 games in one season, a feat he accomplished in 1912.

Lance Berkman hit a home run on the same day, September 21, every year between 2001 and 2007, joining Lou Gehrig as the only players to accomplish this unusual feat.

Don Baylor is the only outfielder with at least 500 games to never have a double play on defense.

Joe Morgan collected six hits as a rookie on July 8, 1965, going 6-for-6 with two home runs and a double.

Everything's Bigger in Texas ... Including Number of All-Time Greats

Deep in the heart of Texas, they sure knew how to grow ballplayers, especially skilled hurlers who could dazzle you with their speed or buckle your knees with a sharp curve. A total of 14 Texas-born players have been inducted into the Hall of Fame (seven from the Negro Leagues) along with one manager.

You could field a pretty good all-star team just with the Negro Leagues players from Texas. You've got Biz Mackey or Louis Santop at catcher; Ed Wesley or Highpockets Hudspeth at first; Newt Allen at second; Dewey Creacy or Marlin Carter at third; Willie Wells at short. The outfield is manned by some combination of Hurley McNair, Chaney White, Red Parnell, Crush Holloway and Henry Milton. The pitching staff includes righties Smokey Joe Williams, Hilton Smith, Rube Foster, Bill Jackman, William Bell, Sr., Jesse Hubbard and Bill Gatewood and lefties Bill Foster and Dave Brown with Andy Cooper available to close out the game. With Hall of Famer Rube Foster running the show and serving as the manager, that would be a pretty imposing team.

On our integrated All-Texas team, three of the Negro Leagues players shoot to the top at their position and it was a close call for several others. A total of 30 Negro Leagues players earned honorable mention status.

In his book *Playing in Shadows: Texas and Negro League Baseball*, Rob Fink points out that the success of Texas' black baseball teams was a source of great pride for African Americans, as was the success of fellow Texans such as Rube Foster, Smokey Joe Williams and Willie Wells. The black press in Texas and around the country paid a lot of attention not just to Foster's accomplishments as a player, but also to his admirable acumen as a businessman and league organizer, Fink notes.

By the end of the 2011 season 812 players from the Lone Star state had played in the majors. They included names such as Wingo, Beveric, Larvell, Odie, Ona, Uel, Debs, Blas, Lemmie and Rontrez. We probably don't want to know how Tink Riviere got his nickname, but he should stay away from Frank "Dingle" Croucher.

Edgar Branom was aptly nicknamed "Dud" — he batted .234 and committed seven errors in 26 games at first base in his only season, 1927. Other unflattering nicknames include Goobers, Gimpy, Boob and Dummy, which are offset by Art Shires' self-proclaimed moniker, "Art the Great." Shires was cocky and rowdy on and off the field, but he did back it up by batting .341 as a rookie in 1928 followed by two more seasons over .300.

Brownsville native Henry Schmidt knew how to go out on top. He went 22–13 in his rookie season for the Brooklyn Superbas, 1903, and then walked away from the game because he didn't like living in the East.

One of Schmidt's teammates on the Superbas was another Texan, Ned Garvin, whose major league days came to a halt a year after Schmidt. Garvin's nickname,

"The Navasota Tarantula," was inspired by his hometown. He pitched for six teams in seven seasons, fashioning an excellent career ERA of 2.72 despite a 58–97 record. He finished second in the NL with a 1.68 ERA in 1904 and his overall ERA of 1.72 that year (including two games with the New York Highlanders) remains the lowest for any pitcher in his last season (minimum 100 innings). Garvin won 20 or more games the next three seasons in the minors and then died of consumption in 1908.

Quite a few of the nicknames for Texas players are related to animals. You have Hippo, Rattlesnake, Grey Eagle, Mad Dog, Big Puma, Sugar Bear and Big Donkey. The best and most creative nickname has to be Mike "The Human Rain Delay" Hargrove, which pokes fun at the exhaustive routine he went through before each pitch of an at-bat, readjusting batting gloves and pulling up his sleeves and so on. Fans didn't mind Hargrove's OCD antics, because they could visit the concession stand or go to the bathroom and not miss any action.

Another great one is Walt "No Neck" Williams, but only because he embraced the nickname. Williams was a good player to have on a team, as he could pinch hit, play good defense and hit for average without striking out. The league was filled with 5-foot-6 middle infielders in the first half of the twentieth century, so you've got to give "No Neck" credit for hanging around for a decade as an outfielder in the more size-conscious 1960s and '70s.

Calvin Murray collected just 146 hits with a .231 average over five seasons, but the Dallas native merits a footnote to history. He was the batter standing at the plate during a spring training game on March 24, 2001, when Randy Johnson threw the pitch that killed a passing dove. Seems like the poor bird should at least have been granted first base.

Houston Goes from Babies and Buffs to Colt .45s

Houston baseball history dates back to 1861, when the first Houston Base Ball Club was formed. In 1867 the city's first organized team was founded — the Houston Stonewalls, named in honor of Confederate General Stonewall Jackson. Houston's first professional team, the Houston Babies, had an inauspicious debut against the powerhouse Cincinnati Red Stockings in 1888, causing such an identity crisis after a 22–3 loss that the team soon changed its name to the Houston Red Stockings. These early findings come from the Larry Dierker Chapter of the Society of American Baseball Research.

The Houston Buffaloes started playing in the Texas Association in 1896, switching later to the South Texas League and in 1907 beginning a long association with the Texas League while playing games at West End Park. When Buffalo Stadium opened as the new home of the Buffs in 1928, baseball's first commissioner, Kenesaw Mountain Landis, was in attendance.

Black baseball in Houston took off with the formation of the Houston Monarchs in 1924, who played their games at East End Park. The team's name changed to the Black Buffs in the 1930s and Arthur Williams remained the club's manager throughout its entire 30-year tenure. The Newark Eagles franchise moved to Houston for the 1949–50 seasons, but it was the beginning of the end for black baseball all over the country as integration slowly created new opportunities for African American players to compete in traditional white leagues.

When the National League expanded by two teams in 1962, Houston was awarded one of the new franchises. The Colt .45s played their games in the hastily constructed, temporary Colt Stadium while the Astrodome was being built. One of the players on the 1962 team was pitcher Al Cicotte, the great-nephew of Eddie Cicotte, who was banned from baseball for the Black Sox Scandal.

The Houston Sports Hall of Fame outlines the history of baseball in Houston featuring artifacts such as Nolan Ryan jerseys and jerseys from the three-year run of the Colt .45s. It has an odd location in the new Finger Furniture store, but admission is free. The store was built on the site of Buff Stadium, home of the minor league Houston Buffaloes, and even incorporates home plate in its original location.

Through the 2011 season Houston has sent 105 players to the majors including relievers Joe Nathan, Mike Stanton and Michael Jackson, second baseman Chuck Knoblauch, outfielders Curt Flood, Adam Dunn and Carl Crawford, shortstop Craig Reynolds and Negro Leaguers Henry McHenry and Marvin Williams.

All-Time Texas Selections

Let's move on to the selections for the All-Time Texas team. The catcher position is a tough call between Mackey and Santop. Bill James ranks Santop as the second-best Negro Leagues catcher after Josh Gibson, with Mackey number three. However, Negro Leagues historian John Holway thinks Mackey was a better all-around catcher than Yogi Berra or Johnny Bench, which is really saying something.

The general consensus is that Mackey was the best defensive catcher in Negro Leagues history, blending an unmatched combination of powerful arm, quick release, smarts and agility behind the plate. Not only was he a master at handling pitchers, Biz was a dangerous switch hitter who had good power from the right side. Fellow Texan Jesse Hubbard called Mackey the greatest player he ever saw, while Cum Posey said Mackey was even better than Josh Gibson.

Mackey made five East-West All-Star teams, led the league in batting with a .413 average in 1923 and is credited with a .329 lifetime average. He spent a number of years as player-manager, taking a promising 16-year-old catcher named Roy Campanella under his wings while managing the Baltimore Elite Giants in 1938. Mackey played until he was 49, batting .307 at age 47 in 1945.

Santop was nearing the end of his career on the Hilldales when Mackey joined the team in 1923. Mackey gradually took playing time from Santop over the next several years, especially after Santop dropped a key foul pop in the first modern black World Series against the Kansas City Monarchs in 1923. Santop's slugging ability is often overlooked because he played in the Deadball Era, but the lefty swinger had few peers when it came to crushing the ball. He picked up the nickname "Big Bertha" due to his slugging prowess and size — 6-foot-4 and 240 pounds.

When he joined the New York Lincoln Giants in 1911, Santop formed a star-studded battery with ace pitchers Smokey Joe Williams and Cannonball Dick Redding. Within a few years, they were joined by John Henry Lloyd and Spot Poles, but it was Santop who led the way with his bat. In 1912 he reportedly walloped a 500-foot home run. Incomplete research credits Santop with a .324 lifetime average, but his average defense tips the scales to Mackey.

Texas is blessed with two Hall of Famers at shortstop but no Hall of Famers at first base. That gets evened out with the selections for the All-Time Texas team. Ernie Banks actually played more games at first than short (1,259 compared to 1,125), so in keeping with the guidelines for this book he gains the selection at first. Banks won two MVP Awards and was named to seven All-Star teams as a shortstop compared to four All-Star nods at first, but it sure beats trying to choose between him and Willie Wells for the shortstop spot.

Signed by Cool Papa Bell for the Kansas City Monarchs in 1950, Banks became the first African American player for the Cubs in 1953. The ever-cheerful Banks was a bright spot in Wrigley Field through 19 years of losing. He was always ready to play two, despite being stuck on bad teams much of his career. The Cubs were 351 games below .500 over the course of Banks' career and the team never finished higher than fifth place in his first 14 seasons. A trip to the postseason just wasn't in the cards, and Banks sits atop the list of most games played without reaching the playoffs — 2,528.

In his second full season, 1955, Banks set records for most grand slams (five) and most home runs by a shortstop (44). He won his first MVP in 1958, when he led the league with 47 homers, 129 RBI and a .614 slugging percentage while batting .313. "Mr. Cub" won the award again the next season after hitting .304 with 45 homers and a league-high 143 RBI. An outstanding fielder at first and short, Banks demonstrated uncommon power for a shortstop and uncommon range for a first baseman. He made 14 All-Star teams over 11 seasons and was elected to the Hall of Fame in his first year on the ballot, 1977.

"His wrists are the secret of Banks' success," noted Bill Furlong in *Baseball Stars of 1959.* "Instead of taking the big Ruthian type swing of the lively ball era, he swings his bat as if it were a buggy whip, striking at the ball with the reflexive swiftness of a serpent's tongue."

If not for Banks, first base would have come down to a two-man contest between Norm Cash and Cecil Cooper. Cash belted 377 home runs, drove in 1,103 runs and made four All-Star teams with the Tigers. He had a season for the ages in 1961, winning the batting title with a .361 average and also leading the league in OBP, OPS and hits while hitting 41 home runs. He hit 39 homers the next season but saw his average plummet to .243 — the largest drop in one season by a batting champion. He was an underrated fielder who led AL first basemen in fielding percentage twice and assists three times. However, Cash also admitted using a corked bat for most of his career.

Cooper had less power but hit better for average, finishing with 241 homers and a .298 average. He posted three seasons with over 200 hits and led the league in doubles and RBI twice each. Cooper did not get much of an opportunity in six seasons with the Red Sox, but he blossomed once he was traded to the Brewers before the 1977 season. He made five All-Star teams and retired with 2,192 hits. He never led the league in fielding percentage but nonetheless won two Gold Gloves. Red Sox fans surely remember his 1-for-19 batting performance for the team in the 1975 World Series.

Ed Wesley was a lefty-swinging slugger in the Negro Leagues in the 1920s who by most accounts ranks in the top 10 for homers. He batted cleanup behind Turkey Stearnes on the Detroit Stars, forming a powerful combination that rivaled Ruth and Gehrig. Wesley led the league with 11 homers in 1920 and then tied Stearnes for the lead with 17 homers in 1923 and 18 in 1925 (also finishing first with a .425 average in the latter year). He batted .344 in 1922, according to the Seamheads.com Negro Leagues Database.

Ferris Fain is another noteworthy first baseman from Texas, since he won back-to-back batting titles with the Philadelphia Athletics with .344 and .327 averages in 1950–51. Fain made five All-Star teams and recorded a .290 lifetime average but hit just 48 homers. A heavy drinker off the field, on the field Fain was a master at getting on base. He had more than 100 walks in five of his nine seasons and his .424 lifetime OBP ranks thirteenth on the all-time list. He also has the top two seasons for double plays by a first baseman: 194 in 1949 and 192 in 1950.

Second base presents a dilemma. When looking at rankings of the top second basemen in baseball history, Joe Morgan and Rogers Hornsby usually reside in the top three. Since a strong case can be made for both of them as the greatest second baseman ever, it's hard to leave one on the bench. Hornsby was a major jerk his whole life, so it would be nice to tell him to ride some pine. Let's see how the two compare:

	R	H	SB	HR	BB	AVE	OBP	SLG	OPS	OPS+
Hornsby	1579	2930	135	301	1038	.358	.434	.577	1.010	175
Morgan	1650	2517	689	268	1865	.271	.392	.427	.819	132

Morgan has a decisive advantage in walks and stolen bases, while Hornsby has a big edge in hits, average and slugging stats. It's hard to overlook the seven batting titles and two Triple Crowns won by Hornsby, who has the second-highest batting average in history and ranks fifth in OPS+. They played in different eras, but Hornsby's lifetime average is 87 points higher as he benefited greatly when the Lively Ball Era began. Both won two MVP awards.

The self-absorbed Hornsby once said, "I don't like to sound egotistical, but every time I stepped up to the plate with a bat in my hands, I couldn't help but feel sorry for the pitcher."

At least he could back it up, batting over .400 three times and collecting over 200 hits seven times. It's unlikely we will see another second basemen have a year like Hornsby did in 1922, when he led the league with 141 runs, 250 hits, 46 doubles, 42 homers, 152 RBI, a .401 average and 207 OPS+. He led the NL in 11 offensive categories the year before and just missed another Triple Crown by two home runs.

Hornsby only won two pennants and one World Series as a player, while Morgan was the offensive sparkplug who led the Big Red Machine to three pennants and back-to-back World Series championships in 1975-76. He was the best player in baseball in the mid-'70s. You've got to give credit to a guy who was 5-foot-7 and 165 pounds but could beat you so many ways, with his feet, bat, glove or brain.

Morgan posted nine seasons with at least 40 steals and was successful on a remarkable 81 percent of stolen base attempts for his career. In 1978 he became the first player to record 200 homers and 500 stolen bases. His back-to-back MVP seasons of 1975 and 1976 were the only years he batted over .300.

He won five straight Gold Gloves but his defense has been a little overrated — his range was slightly below average according to advanced fielding metrics. Still, Morgan led NL second basemen in fielding percentage twice and ranks third all-time in assists, fourth in putouts and second in defensive games at second base, which is pretty good for a player famous for using a tiny glove.

In 1976 he had the best year by a second baseman since Hornsby's 1922 performance. Morgan led the NL in OBP (.453), slugging (.576) and OPS (1.020), batted .320 and finished second in stolen bases (60), walks (114), runs (113) and RBI (111) as well as fifth in home runs (27). He batted .333 in the World Series that year, the only time Morgan batted over .300 in 11 career playoff series — his postseason average was .182.

During a long career as a broadcaster Morgan has been an outspoken critic of sabermetric stats, saying that his experienced eye is a better judge of good performance. That makes it especially tempting to rely solely on sabermetric stats to illustrate why Morgan was a better player than Hornsby. For example, Morgan ranks sixth all-time in Power-Speed # and he edges Hornsby in Career Win Shares 508-493.

Hornsby is arguably the greatest right-handed hitter (not slugger) in baseball history, but Morgan was the better overall player because he could do everything well and served as the irreplaceable catalyst for his teams. Bill James has Morgan #1 and Hornsby #3 and that seems about right. For the All-Time Texas team, Rajah can be on the bench annoying the other players.

Hornsby is buried at Hornsby Bend Cemetery in Hornsby Bend, Texas. The tiny town outside Austin is not named after him, but after Reuben Hornsby, who first settled the community in 1832.

Not to be overlooked at second base is Newt Allen, who was the best second baseman in the Negro Leagues in the 1920s and early '30s. Allen, who spent most of his 23-year career with the Kansas City Monarchs, was without peer as a defensive player and made four East-West All-Star appearances. He was blessed with great quickness, sure hands and a powerful arm, adept at making the pivot and ranging to either side. Allen was skilled with the bat, able to bunt and get on base, where his speed was a weapon. His career average was .287 with 1,017 hits and 126 stolen bases in official Negro League games.

The All-Time Texas team features another all-time great at third base. Eddie Mathews wasted no time demonstrating his ability, blasting a league-best 47 homers at the age of 21 in 1953 while batting .302 with 135 RBI. It was the most home runs ever hit by a third baseman, although the record is now held by Alex Rodriquez. He was MVP runner-up that year and again in 1959 when he led the NL with 46 homers and batted .306. Mathews was good early on and remained a feared lefty slugger for 15 years, which is how one ends up with 512 home runs (exact same number as Banks) and a Hall of Fame plaque hanging in Cooperstown.

Mathews, who became the seventh player to top 500 homers in 1967, posted nine straight seasons with 30 or more homers to set a National League record that has since been surpassed by Barry Bonds (who did it 13 straight years). Teaming up with Hank Aaron in the Braves lineup, the two combined to slug 863 home runs between 1954 and 1966. His rookie season was the last year for the Braves in Boston and his last season with the franchise coincided with the team's first year in Atlanta, so Mathews is the only player to play for the Braves in Boston, Milwaukee and Atlanta. He won a World Series title with the Braves in 1957 and in his last season as a bit player with the Tigers in 1968.

He has his mother to thank for his hitting ability. "My mother used to pitch to me and my father would shag balls. If I hit one up the middle, close to my mother, I'd have some extra chores to do. My mother was instrumental in making me a pull hitter," Mathews said during his Hall of Fame induction in 1978.

Red Oak native Pinky Higgins made three All-Star teams and compiled 1,941 hits playing between 1930 and 1946. He had years where he hit for a high average (.330 in 1934), hit home runs (23 in 1935) and drove in a lot of runs (106 in 1937 and 1938), but generally didn't do it all in one season. Higgins set a record for most consecutive hits with 12 in 1938 (which included two walks). He was not a good fielder, leading AL third basemen in errors four times. Higgins was charged with negligent homicide after killing a highway worker while driving drunk in 1968. He served two months in prison out of a four-year sentence and died of a heart attack within a few days of getting out.

With Banks out of the way at short, Wells gets the well-deserved honor of starting. Nicknamed "El Diablo" (The Devil) in Mexico, where he was a star in the Winter Leagues for nearly 30 years, Wells is generally considered the second-best shortstop in Negro Leagues history behind Pop Lloyd. An outstanding fielder with great range and sure hands, the speedy Wells played in the East-West All-Star Game three times while with the Chicago American Giants and five times while playing for the Newark Eagles. The Hall of Fame study credits him with a .319 average and 98 home runs, but those stats are incomplete. His 27 home runs in 1929 are believed to be a single-season record for the Negro Leagues.

Wells suffered so many beanings he went up to the plate with a construction hat on, becoming one of the first players to regularly wear a batting helmet. He became known as the "Shakespeare of shortstops" while using a glove with a hole in it, which he said aided his fielding. Serving as player-manager for some great Newark teams, Wells helped develop future major league stars such as Don Newcombe and he is credited with teaching Jackie Robinson how to turn the double play.

Among those earning honorable mention at shortstop are Garry Templeton, Roy McMillan and Freddie Patek. Templeton recorded 2,096 hits while making three All-Star teams with the Cardinals and Padres. After leading the NL in hits once and triples three times with the Cards, Templeton was run out of St. Louis for flipping off the crowd. He was traded to the Padres for Ozzie Smith, who was named to the All-Star team and won a Gold Glove each of the next 11 seasons.

McMillan was a weak hitter, posting a lifetime average of .243 with a 72 OPS+, but he won three Gold Gloves for his sterling play at short. He led NL shortstops in fielding percentage five times. At 5-foot-5, Patek was one of the shortest players in his or any other era. Nicknamed "The Flea," he led the AL with 53 stolen bases and finished with 385 steals. Named to three All-Star teams mainly for his glove, he hit just 41 career homers but three came in one game on June 20, 1980.

The All-Time Texas outfield features two Hall of Famers who are superstars among the superstars: Tris Speaker and Frank Robinson. Speaker ranks behind only Willie Mays and Ty Cobb among the best center fielders but then falls into the conversation with Mantle, DiMaggio and Ken Griffey, Jr., at the next level. Robinson was better than all other right fielders in history except the Babe and Hank Aaron. Not too shabby.

Speaker combined with Harry Hooper and Duffy Lewis on the Red Sox from 1910–15 to form one of the greatest defensive outfields in baseball history. No one played a shallower center field than Speaker, who played so close to the infield he could make unassisted double plays, throw batters out at first and field pickoff throws from pitchers. His 449 outfield assists are the most in baseball history as are his 139 double plays, and he holds the American League record for putouts with 6,788. Pretty amazing when you consider he switched to throwing left-handed after breaking his right arm when he fell off a horse as a youth. Teammate Joe Sewell said, "I played with Tris for seven years. I've seen Joe DiMaggio and I've seen Willie Mays ... and all the rest. Tris Speaker is the best center fielder I've seen."

Playing primarily in the Deadball Era, he didn't hit many home runs although he did lead the league with 10 during his MVP year of 1912. That season Speaker batted .383, collected 222 hits, scored 136 runs and led the league with 53 doubles and a .464 OBP. He batted over .300 18 times in a 19-year period—hitting .296 in the one off-year.

His .345 career average ranks sixth all-time while his 3,514 hits are fifth-best. Known as "The Grey Eagle," Speaker had great bat control, never striking out more than 25 times in a season. Speaker led the league in doubles eight times and tops the all-time list with 792. His 222 triples rank sixth, while his 3,514 hits rank fifth. In 1912 he became the first player to record 50 stolen bases and 50 doubles in the same season—Craig Biggio in 1998 is the only other player to accomplish that feat.

He often found himself in acrimonious battles with owners and teammates. After helping the Red Sox win a second championship in 1915, Speaker was traded to the Indians after a salary dispute. The Indians made him the highest-paid player in the game and watched him win a batting title with a .386 average his first year with the team. He led the Indians to their first World Series title as player-manager in 1920. His combination of offensive and defensive brilliance makes him the logical choice as Texas' All-Time Best Player.

Robinson is one of the most overlooked sluggers in history. Often overshadowed by Mantle, Mays and Aaron, he was number four in career home runs with 586 when he retired in 1976—he now ranks ninth. He hit 38 homers as a 20-year-old rookie in 1956 on the way to winning the Rookie of the Year Award. Named NL MVP in 1961 with the Reds, he found himself traded to the Orioles after the 1965 season because the Reds thought his performance would start slipping at age 30. He won the Triple Crown in his first year with the Orioles while becoming the first player to win the MVP Award in both leagues. Robinson finished in the top seven in home runs 15 times and is the only player to hit a ball out of Memorial Stadium.

He played with reckless abandon and fierce intensity all the time, striking fear into middle infielders while on base and earning a reputation as a supreme clutch hitter. In his book *Ball Four*, Jim Bouton recalls being asked how to pitch to Robinson. "Reluctantly" was his reply.

In 1975 he became the first African American manager in the majors, going on to win 1,065 games over 16 years for four franchises but failing to make the playoffs as a skipper. Robinson was elected to the Hall of Fame on his first ballot in 1982. In 2005 he was awarded the Presidential Medal of Freedom by President George W. Bush.

Ross Youngs seemed on track for a Hall of Fame career until he died from Bright's disease at age 30 in 1927. He batted .322 in what was essentially an 8½ year career and was beloved by Giants manager John McGraw for his hard-nosed and spirited play. Youngs never got more than 22 percent of the vote after 16 years on the Hall of Fame ballot but was inexplicably elected by the Veterans Committee in 1972.

Youngs batted over .300 every year but one and scored over 100 runs three straight years, serving as the catalyst for the Giants as they won four consecutive pennants and two World Series in the early 1920s. He ended up with just 1,491 hits but a .399 OBP.

Several Texas outfielders rank ahead of Youngs due to longevity. Lance Berkman mashed the ball with regularity for the Astros from 2000 until being traded to the Yankees at the trade deadline in 2010. He bounced back with a big year for the Cardinals in 2011. He has recorded 358 homers and over 1,100 runs and RBI through the 2011 season along with a .409 OBP. A six-time All-Star, Berkman has played nearly as many games at first and might end up with more games at that position by the time he retires. He has an excellent batting eye, posting nine straight years with at least 90 walks. Berkman's best season was his first full year as a regular, 2001, when he batted .331 with 34 homers, 126 RBI and a league-leading 55 doubles. His career OPS+ of 146 ranks 45th.

A strong case could also be made for Curt Flood, an important figure in baseball history. He was a terrific center fielder who went a record 223 games without committing an error in center between 1965 and 1967. He was no slouch with the bat either, batting over .300 six times and posted two seasons with more than 200 hits. Flood was working on a streak of seven consecutive Gold Gloves when he was traded by the Cardinals to the Phillies in late 1969, starting in motion a chain of events that essentially ended his career.

When Flood refused to accept the trade and decided to challenge baseball's reserve clause he was labeled an ingrate (and worse) who would end up destroying the game of baseball. His argument was that baseball's reserve clause was a form of slavery because it kept players bound to one team for life. In the legal battle, which went all the way to the Supreme Court, Major League Baseball's argument was basically that they had always done business that way and that keeping players with the same team was best for the "Good of the Game." Public sentiment tended to be against Flood, as most people had trouble understanding why a player making $90,000 a year should be complaining about anything. That the player in question was an African American who had just written a book that detailed his daily need for drugs and groupies made him even less of a sympathetic figure. "A well-paid slave is nonetheless a slave," Flood wrote in his 1971 tome, *The Way It Is*.

Although Jackie Robinson testified on Flood's behalf, no active players did. In fact, player sentiment was

Curt Flood's outstanding abilities as a batter and center fielder are overshadowed by his controversial role in fighting baseball's long-established rules that bound players to a team for life. Flood, unhappy about being traded from the Cardinals to the Phillies, challenged the reserve clause when he filed a lawsuit against Major League Baseball in 1970. Although he would lose the case, which went all the way to the Supreme Court, Flood's efforts served as a wake-up call for players, and five years later the reserve clause was nullified and the era of free agency had begun (National Baseball Hall of Fame Library, Cooperstown, New York).

mixed. In ruling against Flood in 1972, the Supreme Court seemed to indicate a fear that taking away baseball's antitrust exemption would lead to the ruination of America's pastime. It was widely criticized as one of the Supreme Court's worst rulings ever from a strictly legal standpoint, but Flood's courageous stand had started to chip away at baseball's long-established system. It opened up other players' eyes about the way they were being treated and brought about a new level of solidarity that would result in the rise of the most powerful union in professional sports. Free agency would follow shortly, after Dave McNally and Andy Messersmith again challenged the reserve clause in 1975, but Flood was bitter about that too since the victory was granted to two white players.

Although an entire generation of wealthy baseball players owes a debt of gratitude to Curt Flood for their good fortune, few of them have ever publicly acknowledged his heroic contribution. Most of today's players probably don't even know who he is. Flood paid the ultimate price for taking on the baseball establishment — after playing 13 games for the Washington Senators in 1971 he retired after being essentially blackballed from the game. "Everybody thinks of baseball as a sacred cow," Flood said. "When you have the nerve to challenge it, people look down their nose at you. There are a lot of things wrong with a lot of industries. Baseball is one of them."

Active players Adam Dunn and Carl Crawford have both demonstrated elite skills in specific areas, but they couldn't be more different in ability. Dunn seemed destined to rank among the all-time leaders in home runs before hitting a major slump in 2011, but he's still on track to pass Reggie Jackson for most strikeouts. Dunn has accumulated 365 homers through the 2011 season, including four straight years when he hit exactly 40 home runs. With seven seasons of more than 100 walks, he has an excellent .374 OBP. Dunn has demonstrated a singular ability to do one of three things when he comes to the plate: walk, strike out or hit a home run — about 60 percent of the time, in fact. At 6-foot-6 and 285 pounds, he is a liability in the field whether in the outfield or at first base.

Crawford is one of the fastest players in the majors, although he was a major free-agent disappointment for the Red Sox in 2011. After 10 seasons, Crawford has 427 stolen bases and he has led the league in steals and triples four times and batted over .300 five times. He uses his exceptional speed to cover enormous ground in left field, a skill that is lost playing in Fenway Park. Crawford won his first Gold Glove in 2010.

Another notable outfielder is Ron Gant, who was Jimmy Wynn without the walks. Gant collected 321 homers and 243 stolen bases playing for eight teams over 16 seasons, but his average was .256. Also worth mentioning is Jo-Jo Moore, who helped the New York Giants reach the World Series three times in the 1930s as their leadoff hitter. The six-time All-Star finished third in the MVP race in 1934 after batting a career-high .331. Known as "The Gause Ghost" in tribute to his hometown, Moore had over 200 hits the next two seasons and retired with a .298 average.

Hurley McNair, Chaney White and Red Parnell are noteworthy Texas outfielders from the Negro Leagues. McNair was a dangerous force batting in the middle of the order for the Kansas City Monarchs from 1920–27. He batted .325, .340 and .374 in the years 1920–22, according to the Seamheads.com Negro Leagues Database powered by The Baseball Gauge. Blending phenomenal speed with a nasty disposition, White was a terror on the base paths — think Ty Cobb but much faster. The righty-swinging leadoff batter averaged .302 over 18 seasons in the Negro Leagues, helping the Bacharach Giants win the Eastern Colored League championship in 1926 and 1927. Parnell started his career with a bang — leading the West with a .415 average as a 21-year-old rookie with the Birmingham Black Barons in 1927. He went on to star for the Philadelphia Stars from 1936–43, finishing with a .326 lifetime average.

The designated hitter position goes to one of the best to ever play that role — Don Baylor. In his MVP year of 1979, he played 65 games at DH for the Angels along with 97 games in the outfield. For his career Baylor appeared in 1,285 games as a DH compared to 822 in the outfield and 148 at first. He was a productive slugger who did not strike out much, finishing with 338 home runs over 19 seasons. Baylor generated eight straight years with at least 20 stolen bases including a personal-best 52 in 1976, and he ended up with 285 steals for his career. He made his only All-Star team in 1979, when he led the league with 139 RBI and 120 runs. Baylor led the league in hit-by-pitch eight times and ranks fourth all-time in that category with 267.

Three Texas-born righties are already in the Hall of Fame but the best Texas righty is not yet enshrined in Cooperstown. Greg Maddux is sure to be a first-ballot inductee when his name lands on the ballot in 2014. All he did was win four straight Cy Young Awards and post five other top-five finishes to go with eight All-Star selections and an unbelievable 18 Gold Gloves. Not all the Gold Gloves were deserved — he led NL pitchers in errors three times and won the Gold Glove each of those years. His success as a fielder often involved him being able to predict precisely where the batter would hit the ball based on his pitch selection.

Perhaps no pitcher ever accomplished more with less when you consider "Mad Dog" did not possess a blazing fastball or knee-buckling curve. He was a pitching genius. Maddux ranks first in putouts by a pitcher with 546, fourth in games started with 740, eighth in wins with 355 and 10th in strikeouts with 3,371. It's hard to imagine too many more pitchers reaching 300 wins let alone reaching the rarified air of 350-plus wins. He only won 20 games twice but posted 17 consecutive seasons with at least 15 wins and 20 straight with at least 13 wins.

Maddux was like a poker player on the mound, offering his own sleight of hand deception. He said his approach to pitching was to make the strikes look like balls, and the balls look like strikes.

"Greg Maddux could probably put a baseball through a lifesaver if you asked him," noted fellow Texan Joe Morgan. In fact, on a lark Maddux once pitched to a catcher who was blindfolded and hit the mitt every time. In addition to being one of the best ever at spotting the fastball, Maddux was always two steps ahead of the batter. If the batter moved an inch closer to the plate, he noticed it and adjusted, sometimes in mid-motion. His catchers often didn't even give him a sign because it was ridiculous to suggest they knew more about what he should do than him. For 23 years, Mad Dog was always in control. Maddux kept hitters off-balance by never throwing them the same-speed pitch in the same spot, combined with the fact that he had the unique ability to sink the ball or cut the ball off both edges of the plate.

Maddux beat out some pretty stiff competition to earn the spot as all-time righty starter from Texas. Strikeout king Nolan Ryan and Negro League stars Smokey Joe Williams, Hilton Smith and Rube Foster would be the ace of just about any other staff.

Ryan was still throwing heat when he finally hung up his cleats at the age of 46 after 27 big-league seasons — more than any other player in baseball history. His record 5,714 strikeouts are 839 more than runner-up Randy Johnson, while his seven no-hitters are three more than any other pitcher. He gave up just 6.55 hits per 9 innings, which is the best ever, and his 9.5 K/9IP ratio is fourth-best. Conservative estimates show Nolan faced 22,575 batters and threw over 65,000 pitches in the majors. Whereas Maddux seemed to figure everything out early in his career, Ryan found the battle between pitcher and hitter to be an eternal struggle. "Pitching is a little like being married; you love it, you fear it, and are often puzzled by it," he wrote in his book *Kings of the Hill*.

Ryan fanned eight father-and-son combinations and 12 sets of brothers while setting a new benchmark for intimidation on the mound. Just ask Robin Ventura, who was pummeled by Ryan when he made the mistake of charging the 46-year-old on the mound a month before he pitched his last game. Ryan had his uniform retired by three teams — Astros, Rangers and Angels — but amazingly pitched in just one World Series game for the New York Mets in 1969. His teams only made the playoffs five times, which is part of the reason he ended up with 292 losses — third-most all-time.

If Maddux was the control artist, then Ryan was the anti-control artist. He led the league in walks eight times and wild pitches six times and ranks number one in walks and number two in wild pitches. His control got better over the course of his career. There's nothing more unsettling to a batter than facing a fast pitcher who isn't entirely sure where the ball is going.

Here's what Reggie Jackson thought about facing the Ryan Express: "Every hitter likes fastballs just like everybody likes ice cream. But you don't like it when someone's stuffing it into you by the gallon. That's how you feel when Ryan's throwing balls by you."

Smokey Joe Williams was not only the dominant pitcher in the Negro Leagues in the early part of the twentieth century, he was voted the greatest pitcher in Negro Leagues history by the *Pittsburgh Courier* in 1952, narrowly topping Satchel Paige. He is generally regarded as the fastest black pitcher, although perhaps not as fast as Walter Johnson. He blended Ryan's speed with Maddux's control.

Williams, who was also nicknamed "Cyclone," was like Ryan in that he was still throwing heat well into his 40s, although he used a deceptive, easy motion. In 1930, a 44-year-old Williams struck out 27 batters for the Homestead Grays while tossing a one-hitter over 12 innings. He may actually rank second to Ryan in no-hitters, as Smokey Joe claimed to have pitched five no-hitters over the course of a career that lasted from 1910–32. Cubs catcher Gabby Hartnett hailed Smokey Joe as the fastest pitcher he'd seen, while Sam Streeter noted that it took two catchers to hold him.

Williams, whose mother was of Indian heritage, was a large man — 6-foot-4 and 200 pounds — and his talent rivaled that of any white pitcher. In fact, he went 22–7–1 when facing teams of white big leaguers. He pitched shutouts in his first three games against white stars and later beat Pete Alexander, Chief Bender, Rube Marquard and Waite Hoyt, among others. Teaming up with Cannonball Dick Redding on the New York Lincoln Giants, the duo was nearly unbeatable, and Williams was still mowing down batters while pitching for the Homestead Grays in the late 1920s. He was elected to the Hall of Fame in 1999.

Smith is one of the least known great pitchers in baseball. He won 20 games in all 12 seasons he pitched for the Kansas City Monarchs (counting all manner of games), combining with Satchel Paige to lead the team to seven pennants. Paige got all the attention, but Smith was just as effective at shutting down the opposition. Smith played in six straight East-West All-Star games from 1937–42. His best season was 1941, when he went 25–1. A study sanctioned by the Hall of Fame shows his career mark as 71–31 in Negro Leagues action with a 1.68 ERA. Smith, who was also a dangerous batter, was elected to the Hall of Fame in 2001.

Rube Foster, who got his nickname by outpitching Rube Waddell in a 1902 exhibition, reportedly won 44 straight games pitching that year. He helped the Cuban X-Giants win black baseball's first World Series in 1903 by winning four games against the Philadelphia Giants. The *Indianapolis Freeman* wrote that Foster "has all the speed of a Rusie, the tricks of a Radbourne, and the heady coolness and deliberation of a Cy Young. What does that make of him? Why, the greatest baseball pitcher in the country," as reported in Robert Charles Cottrell's *The Best Pitcher in Baseball: The Life of Rube Foster, Negro League Giant*.

Bill "Cannonball" Jackman was a star attraction throughout New England while pitching into his 50s. The only reason he's not as widely recognized as Foster and Smith is because he preferred barnstorming around New England with lesser teams to playing in the more established Negro Leagues. Jackman pitched over 1,200 games — going 49–5 in 1929 against all competition — and won a high percentage of his starts, so he probably topped Cy Young's win total. "Jackman is not often mentioned among the select few, but there are men like (Negro Leagues shortstop and Yankees scout) Bill Yawkey who consider him best of all," writes Robert Peterson in *Only the Ball Was White*.

Another notable righty from the Negro Leagues was William Bell, Sr., who posted a career record of 164–122 with a 3.20 ERA. Bell, who possessed excellent control, went 11–2 and 10–4 to help the Kansas City Monarchs win pennants in 1924 and 1925.

The top three candidates for the left-handed starter are all from the Negro Leagues: Bill Foster, Andy Cooper and Dave Brown. The Hall of Fame lists Foster's record as 143–69 with a 3.36 ERA. The half-brother of Negro Leagues pioneer Rube Foster was widely regarded as the greatest left-handed pitcher in Negro Leagues history.

Also known as "Willie," Foster was a durable flame-thrower with a sweeping curve who could seemingly throw the ball wherever he wanted. "He had the best control," noted teammate Nat Rogers, who also had to face him numerous times and considered him the greatest pitcher.

Foster was 25 years younger than Rube and he chafed under his brother's stern directives when forced to pitch for him on the Chicago American Giants. Both were stubborn, but only one was in charge. After Rube's erratic behavior got him committed to an insane asylum in 1926, Bill's pitching seemed to improve greatly overnight. That year he gained notoriety for winning both games of a doubleheader on the last day of the season to clinch the pennant for the Chicago American Giants. Foster was the leading pitcher in the Negro West League in 1927 with an 18–3 record and also started and won the first East-West All-Star Game in 1933. He was elected to the Hall of Fame in 1996.

Cooper spent nine years pitching for the Detroit Stars and 10 years with the Kansas City Monarchs, going from the former team to the latter in a five-player trade. He frequently came on in relief to close out big games. Like Foster, Cooper had a deep arsenal of pitches and pinpoint control but relied less on overpowering speed and more on changing speed to keep batters off balance.

The southpaw pitched 17 innings in a playoff game in 1937, when he was at the beginning of a successful stint as player-manager of the Monarchs. He guided the team to three Negro American League pennants in four years before dying of a heart attack at age 45 in 1941. When Cooper was elected to the Hall of Fame in 2006 he was labeled the second-best Negro Leagues lefty after Foster. Hall records credit him with a career mark of 116–57 and 3.24 ERA.

Brown was just as talented a pitcher as Foster and Cooper, but trouble seemed to follow him starting with a case of highway robbery that dogged him in 1917. After flashing patches of brilliance with Rube Foster's American Giants — helping the team win three straight Negro National League titles by going 29–8 from 1920–22 — Brown again found himself running from the law after allegedly shooting a man to death in a bar fight in New York in 1925. He reportedly continued to pitch under an assumed name, Lefty Wilson, in outlying leagues before eventually dropping out of sight. The San Marcos native had an excellent curveball and was a big-game pitcher, and despite his short career he was named to the second team on the All-Time All-Star team generated by the *Pittsburgh Courier* in 1952.

The bullpen is in good hands with Twins closer Joe Nathan, who has 261 career saves and is the all-time saves leader for Texas. He posted six straight seasons with at least 35 saves before missing the 2010 season with injury. A four-time All-Star, Nathan has allowed just 6.6 hits per 9 innings while striking out 9.4 batters per 9 innings. He's not had as much success in the postseason, with two blown saves, two losses and a 7.88 ERA in eight games.

Five other Texas-born relievers have recorded more than 100 saves: Huston Street (178), Greg Minton (150), Mike Jackson (142), Mike Timlin (141) and Ron Davis (130). Stanton, Jackson and Timlin all appeared in over 1,000 games with Stanton's 1,178 appearances (all but one in relief) over 19 seasons ranking second behind Jesse Orosco. Timlin is seventh on the list while Jackson ranks thirteenth.

Firpo Marberry deserves special mention, since he was a pioneer as the first full-time reliever. He has been credited with 101 saves retroactively, but the save did not exist when he played in the 1920s so that figure is irrelevant. In 1925, his third year in the majors, Marberry became the first pitcher to appear in 50 games without a start. He led the American League in appearances six times and in games finished four times. In 1929 he pitched 250 innings with 26 starts and 23 relief appearances, winning 19 games and leading the AL in WHIP.

Donnie Moore was a quality reliever who saved 89 games over 13 seasons with a high of 31 in 1985, when he made his only All-Star team. With the Angels up 3–1 over the Red Sox in the 1986 League Championship Series, Moore was brought in to protect a 5–4 lead with two outs in the ninth inning of Game 5. One more out and the Angels would be going to their first World Series. With two strikes on the batter, Moore surrendered a two-run homer to Dave Henderson to lose the lead and also gave up what proved to be the winning run in the 11th inning. The Red Sox went on to the Series and Moore was labeled a goat. "Only one pitch away from the World Series. This one is going to follow me around for awhile," Moore said after the game.

That was an understatement. He never recovered from that setback, getting booed relentlessly by fans despite pitching hurt, and two years later he was released by the Angels and then dropped by a minor league team in June 1989. A month later he committed suicide after first shooting his estranged wife in front of their three children. It remains the only suicide in baseball related to on-field action, although a case could be made that ongoing domestic troubles were more to blame.

The larger question remains why Moore was even pitching that night. He was scheduled to undergo cortisone shots for a rib injury, but was forced to pitch nearly three innings by a manager, Gene Mauch, whose final record includes coming within one victory of the World Series three times and falling short each time. Then there's reliever Gary Lucas, who came in and hit Rich Gedman with the pitch that put the tying run on base. Without Moore's clutch pitching that year — 21 saves and a 2.97 ERA — the Angels would not have made the playoffs.

Singer Michael Jackson was at the heart of his popularity when Michael Jackson the baseball player debuted with the Phillies in 1986. He wasn't much of a singer or dancer, but he did lead the NL in appearances with 81 in 1993, and posted 40 saves in 1998 and 39 saves in 1999 for the Indians. Jackson, who wisely went by Mike instead of Michael, ended his career in 2004 with 142 saves.

The All-Time Texas team is filled with Hall of Famers and stars, so it needs a top-notch manager to steer the ship. Cito Gaston seems qualified since he finished first four times and delivered back-to-back World Series titles with the Blue Jays, winning a total of 894 games over 12 seasons.

But there's a much better choice for manager from Texas — Rube Foster — who is the only Negro Leagues manager in the Hall of Fame. (Cum Posey and Sol White also managed but were elected as executives while player-managers such as Willie Wells and Biz Mackey were elected as players). In 1920 Foster founded the first successful Negro league, the Negro National League, which gave African American players a professional showcase for their talents and served as a foundation for their later success once the color barrier was broken. That vision, combined with tremendous determination and business acumen, is why Foster is often called the "Father of the Negro Leagues" or the "Father of Black Baseball."

Jumping to the Leland Giants as player-manager, Foster guided them to a 110–10 record in 1907 in a Chicago semi-pro league dominated by white players. Later taking control of the team as co-owner and changing the name to the Chicago American Giants, Foster established an aggressive style of play that placed a premium on speed and was later copied by other teams throughout the Negro Leagues. The collection of talent he assembled on the American Giants formed what was arguably the greatest team in black baseball history. It featured Pop Lloyd, Home Run Johnson, Pete Booker and Wes Pryor in the infield; Pete Hill, Jap Payne and Frank Duncan in the outfield; Bruce Petway at catcher; and Frank Wickware, Pat Dougherty and Bill Lindsey joining Foster on the pitching staff. They went 123–6 in 1910 and regularly outdrew the White Sox and Cubs.

Foster is credited with inventing the hit-and-run bunt and was adept at seeking any advantage he could get. Once he got the Negro National League up and running, he envisioned the champion playing an annual World Series against the champion white team as a way of preparing black players for eventual integration. Integration took longer than he thought, and Foster wasn't around to see it happen, but African American players were most definitely ready when they were finally allowed into the majors in no small part because of Foster's efforts.

Foster's teams were filled with hustlers who confounded the opposition and wore out pitchers by showing a willingness to bunt in any situation. If the third baseman played back, Foster's batsmen would drop down a bunt; if the third baseman moved in, they would place the ball over his head. They stole regardless of situation and took the extra base at every opportunity. Triple steals were commonplace, as were runners scoring from first on a bunt. Other teams were so nervous guessing what Foster had up his sleeve that they played frazzled. By Rube's reasoning, it took perfect plays to get his players out and he was willing to take his chances with that.

In *Blackball Stars,* Malarcher notes that Rube's teams were so far out in front of the league by July, thanks to his superior baseball knowledge, that they had to break up the season into two halves so there would be interest in the league the second half.

The stress of keeping a league and a team together eventually drove Foster into an insane asylum, where he died in 1930. His casket was viewed by thousands of mourners, black and white, over three days. Despite his early demise, he had created a framework that allowed the Negro Leagues to rebound from the Depression and flourish. His contributions to black baseball dwarf the contributions of any single person to the white game, and successive generations of African American players have Rube Foster to thank as much as Jackie Robinson for their ability to compete in the same league with white players. Foster was elected to the Hall of Fame in 1981.

UTAH

Names in **bold** *represent Major League selections by position, followed by honorable mentions. City of birth is in parentheses.*

Catcher — Duke Sims (Salt Lake City). Also: Herman Franks (Price)
First Base — Chris Shelton (Salt Lake City)
Second Base — Zach Sorensen (Salt Lake City)
Third Base — Spencer Adams (Layton)
Shortstop — Gordon Slade (Salt Lake City)
Outfield — Bobby Mitchell (Salt Lake City)
Outfield — Chad Hermansen (Salt Lake City)
Outfield — George Theodore (Salt Lake City)
Designated Hitter — Doug Howard (Salt Lake City).
Right Handed Starter—Ed Heusser (Salt Lake County). Also: Kelly Downs (Ogden); Fred Sanford (Garfield)
Left Handed Starter — Bruce Hurst (Saint George)
Relief Pitcher — Brandon Lyon (Salt Lake City). Also: Newt Kimball (Logan)
Manager — Herman Franks (Price)

The Names

Best Nickname: Ed "The Wild Elk of the Wasatch" Heusser
Other Nicknames: Newell "Newt" Kimball; Duane "Duke" Sims; Elmer "Smoky" Singleton; Gordon "Oskie" Slade; George "The Stork" Theodore
Most Unusual Name: Chad Hermansen

All-Time Leaders

Games: Duke Sims, 843
Hits: Duke Sims, 580
Batting Average: Chris Shelton, .273
Home Runs: Duke Sims, 100
RBI: Duke Sims, 310
Stolen Bases: Gordon Slade, 12
Wins: Bruce Hurst, 145
Strikeouts: Bruce Hurst, 1689
Saves: Brandon Lyon, 78 (still active)
Future Star: Nate Gold (Bountiful); Jordan Smith (American Fork)
Best Player: Bruce Hurst

Historic Baseball Place

Spring Mobile Ballpark in Salt Lake City — Known as Franklin Covey Field when it opened in 1994 as home to the Salt Lake Bees, the ballpark features a spectacular view of Wasatch Mountains beyond the outfield.

Notable Achievements

Duke Sims hit the last home run in the original Yankee Stadium before it was remodeled in 1973. He had just joined the team a week earlier.

Chad Hermansen was drafted in the first round of the 1995 amateur draft by the Pittsburgh Pirates.

Utah Natives in Middle of Historic Baseball Moments

Sometimes careers are defined less by what a player accomplishes than by what the Gods of Fate have in store for someone else.

Bruce Hurst can identify with that. Utah's All-Time Best Player was moments away from being named the Most Valuable Player of the 1986 World Series after winning two games for the Red Sox. He had done his part — holding the Mets scoreless for eight innings in Game 1 and then giving up just two runs in a complete game victory in Game 5.

Then came Game 6, and Red Sox fans all know what happened there. The Mets came from behind by scoring three runs in the bottom of the 10th inning, aided by Bill Buckner letting a slow bouncer slide off his glove at first. Hurst would get another chance to restore his place in history, since he received the starting nod for the decisive Game 7.

Hurst came close to getting Buckner off the hook. He shut out the Mets for five innings and took a 3–0 lead into the bottom of the sixth. However, he gave up

Spring Mobile Ballpark in Salt Lake City was known as Franklin Covey Field when it opened in 1994 as the new home of the Salt Lake Bees. The best ballpark's feature is a spectacular view of the Wasatch Mountains beyond the outfield (courtesy DigitalBallparks.com).

three runs and left with a tie score, the bullpen would give up five more runs and just like that the Mets were World Champions. Instead of being known the rest of his life as Bruce Hurst, World Series champion and World Series MVP, he's just known as Bruce Hurst, former major league pitcher.

It's been pointed out that if you scramble the letters in Bruce Hurst you can come up with B RUTH CURSE, but that seems like piling on. Hurst did his job during the 1986 season, coming off the disabled list to win 13 games with a 2.99 ERA and winning three games in the playoffs. Buckner didn't do his job and neither did Calvin Schiraldi, who gave up seven hits and seven runs in three relief innings on the way to losing the last two games of the '86 Series.

Hurst would bounce back to make the All-Star team for the Red Sox in 1987 and lead the National League with 10 complete games in 1989 and with four shutouts in 1990. The southpaw ended his 15-year career with a 145–113 record. He was more deceptive than overpowering as a hurler, relying on off-speed pitches and excellent control to outduel batters.

Shortly after the Red Sox broke the so-called curse and won the 2004 World Series, the team inducted Hurst into its Hall of Fame. At least he'll always have that distinction, as well as the honor of being named Utah's All-Time Best Player. Hurst also has a field named after him at Dixie State College in his hometown of St. George.

Herman Franks, a native of Price, was a central figure in one of baseball's biggest and most controversial moments while serving as a coach for the 1951 Giants. Over the last 10 weeks of the season Franks was reportedly stealing signs during home games at the behest of manager Leo Durocher, which helped the Giants erase what seemed like an insurmountable 13½ game lead by the Dodgers in August.

It has been suggested he gave Bobby Thomson the help he needed to hit the "Shot Heard Round the World" to win the pennant for the Giants over the Dodgers. Although Franks may have been stealing signs that year, Thomson swore he didn't get any signal on the pitch from Ralph Branca, who didn't do himself any favors by grooving the pitch letter-high on the inside corner of the plate. For his part, Franks always denied stealing signs.

All-Time Utah Selections

Utah has sent 38 players to the major leagues — the first was southpaw hurler Roy Castleton in 1907. Castleton was born in 1885, 11 years before Utah even became a state but was instead known as the Utah Territory.

Hurst is the only Utah native to make the All-Star team. Three Utah players were active in 2011: Brandon Lyon, Mitch Talbot and Jordan Smith.

The position players on the All-Time Utah team are short on star power. Catcher Duke Sims caught 646 games over an 11-season career playing for five teams. He belted 100 home runs with a high of 23 in 1970 for the Indians.

First base is manned by the versatile Chris Shelton, who has also appeared at catcher, third base, left field, right field and designated hitter in the majors. He demonstrated some power, hitting 18 home runs in 2005 and 16 in 2006 in part-time duty for the Tigers. At second base we have Zach Sorensen, who batted just .143 in 48 games for the Indians and Angels.

Spencer Adams played more career games at second base, but his 32 games at third base qualifies him as Utah's best at the position. Adams played for four teams during a four-year career in the 1920s, playing on teams that lost the World Series in 1925 (Washington Senators) and 1926 (New York Yankees). Our shortstop is Gordon Slade, who put together one good season for the Reds in 1934. He finished fifteenth in MVP voting that year after hitting .285 with 158 hits.

The outfield features the lovable but flawed George Theodore, who certainly left an impression despite playing in only 105 games for the Mets in 1972 and 1974. He probably would have fit in better with the Mets' 1962 team that went 40–120.

Eccentric ex-pitcher Bill Lee described Theodore as the original Napoleon Dynamite in his book *Baseball Eccentrics*: "Theodore was a nerd's nerd.... He had styleproof aviator's glasses that just served to accentuate the 6' 4", 190-pound frame that earned him the nickname 'Stork.' Some pronounced it 'dork.' One writer commented that he 'looks like he swallowed a coat hanger,'" Lee wrote.

Theodore may have been awkward on the diamond and a flake off the field, but you had to feel for the guy when you saw what happened to him during a game in 1973. He collided with teammate Don Hahn in the outfield and had to be carted off on a stretcher after breaking his hip.

Chad Hermansen enjoyed lots of success in the minor leagues, collecting 192 home runs, 1,140 hits and 136 steals over 13 seasons. He slugged 32 homers for Triple-A Nashville in 1999. Producing in the majors proved to be difficult for him as he bounced from the Pirates to the Cubs, Dodgers and Blue Jays between 1999 and 2004. His batting average in the majors was .195.

The right-handed starter is Ed Heusser, who was known as "The Wild Elk of the Wasatch," a reference to the mountain range that cuts through much of Utah. Heusser won 56 games over nine seasons. His best season was 1944, when he went 13–11 and led the NL with a 2.38 ERA for the Cincinnati Reds.

Utah's closer is Brandon Lyon, who had saved 78 games over his first 10 seasons. He saved 26 games for the Diamondbacks in 2008 and then signed with Astros as a free agent after the 2009 season. He saved 20 games in 2010 with a 3.12 ERA.

The All-Time Utah team's manager is Franks, who was a pedestrian catcher in the major leagues. He started his managerial career by guiding the Giants to second place four straight seasons (1965–1968). He won 95, 93 and 91 games in the days before the wild card. The Cubs gave him another shot to manage in 1977, and they played .500 ball for him over three seasons before Franks was let go.

VERMONT

*Names in **bold** represent Major League selections by position, followed by honorable mentions. City of birth is in parentheses.*

Catcher — **Carlton Fisk (Bellows Falls)**. Also: Birdie Tebbetts (Burlington)
First Base — **Pat Putnam (Bethel)**. Also: Daric Barton (Springfield)
Second Base — **Amby McConnell (North Pownall)**
Third Base — **Larry Gardner (Enosburg Falls)**
Shortstop — **Ralph LaPointe (Winooski)**
Outfield — **Fred Mann (Sutton)**
Outfield — **Chris Duffy (Brattleboro)**
Outfield — **Frank Olin (Woodford)**
Designated Hitter — **Pat Putnam (Bethel)**
Right Handed Starter — **Ray Fisher (Middlebury)**. Also: Jean Dubuc (St. Johnsbury); Henry Porter (Vergennes); Lee Viau (Corinth)
Left Handed Starter — **Ray Collins (Colchester)**. Also: Ed Doheny (Northfield)
Relief Pitcher — **Ernie Johnson (Brattleboro)**. Also: Len Whitehouse (Burlington)
Manager — **Birdie Tebbetts (Burlington)**

The Names

Best Nickname: Carlton "Pudge" Fisk
Other Nicknames: Elmer "Big Bow" Bowman; James "Sun" Daly; Jean "Chauncey" Dubuc; Ray "Pick" Fisher; George "Birdie" Tebbetts
Most Unusual Name: Walter Lanfranconi

All-Time Leaders

Games: Carlton Fisk, 2499
Hits: Carlton Fisk, 376
Batting Average: Larry Gardner, .289
Home Runs: Carlton Fisk, 2356
RBI: Carlton Fisk, 1330
Stolen Bases: Larry Gardner, 165
Wins: Ray Fisher, 100
Strikeouts: Ray Fisher, 680
Saves: Len Whitehouse, 4
Future Star: Daric Barton (Springfield)
Best Player: Carlton Fisk

Historic Baseball Places

Recreation Field in Montpelier — Special plaque notes Robin Roberts pitched two seasons and threw a no-hitter on the field, which opened in 1940.
Centennial Field in Burlington — Extensively reno-

Centennial Field in Burlington, which opened in 1922, is believed to feature the oldest complete grandstand structure still in use in the minors (courtesy BallparkReviews.com).

vated with a new grandstand in 1922, today it's the home field of the Vermont Lake Monsters. It is reportedly the oldest complete grandstand structure still in use in the minors.

Notable Achievements

When he retired in 1993 **Carlton Fisk** held the record for most home runs by a catcher with 351 (since passed by Mike Piazza) and most games played at catcher with 2,226 (since passed by Ivan Rodriquez). He is also one of 30 players to play in four different decades.

Larry Gardner drove in the winning run in the 1912 World Series. He hit a sacrifice fly off Christy Mathewson to score Steve Yerkes in the bottom of the 10th inning of the decisive Game 8 as the Red Sox edged the New York Giants.

Ray Collins pitched in three 1–0 games against Walter Johnson in 1913, winning two of them.

Some of Baseball's Biggest Stars Have Played in Vermont

In Burlington, venerable Centennial Field has been entertaining fans for more than a century. Future major leaguer Larry Gardner was the first batter when the ballpark opened in 1906. Tris Speaker played an exhibition game there in 1910, while Connie Mack came to town with his Philadelphia Athletics in 1938. Burlington native Birdie Tebbetts played at Centennial Field with his Red Sox teammates in 1948, while Johnny Podres made his professional baseball debut at Centennial in 1950.

Ken Griffey, Jr., Barry Larkin and Jeff Montgomery all played for Burlington-based minor league teams on the field, while Winooski native Ralph LaPointe could be found playing there for the Burlington A's in 1955, seven years after he last appeared in the majors with the Cardinals.

Vermonters still point proudly to the time the "Home Run King" came to their state. Fresh off leading the American League in home runs for the second straight year, Babe Ruth came to Rutland with the Red Sox and played an exhibition on October 5, 1919. He lived up to his advance billing by blasting the longest home run ever hit over the fence at the fairgrounds. He would be traded to the Yankees less than three months later.

Fred Mann of Sutton was the first Vermont player to make it to the big leagues, debuting in 1882 for the Worcester Ruby Legs in the National League. Mann would finish third in triples and fourth in home runs in 1884, going on to play six seasons for five teams and compiling 597 career hits.

By the end of the 1880s, seven Vermonters had played in the majors. Vergennes native Henry Porter won 33 games for the Brooklyn Grays in 1885 and followed up with 27 wins the next season. In 1888 he led the American Association with 37 losses, which is tied for the sixth most in baseball history. Lee Viau of Corinth won his first eight games as a rookie with the Cincinnati Red Stockings in 1888 on the way to a 22-win season. Viau, who was only 5-foot-4, came back with 22 wins the next season but Dartmouth's first major leaguer would eventually flame out due to problems with alcohol.

Two of Vermont's most talented players accomplished plenty in their athletic careers, just not in the major leagues.

Heinie Stafford was a top-flight collegiate sprinter at Tufts University while also serving as captain and leadoff hitter for the baseball team. A four-year letterman, he led the nation in runs and stolen bases as a senior on a 20–2 team. Stafford's major league career would be exceptionally brief. He was called up near the end of the 1916 season as the New York Giants were in the midst of what would become a record 26-game winning streak. He came in as a pinch-hitter with two outs in the ninth inning of the last game of the season on October 5, 1916. He made an out and would never appear in another major league game again.

Such a fleeting chance at fame would frustrate some people, but evidently not Stafford, since it was his choice to make more money as a research chemist with a textile company. He would go on to invent a chemical process that revolutionized the manufacture of women's hose, reports Tom Simon, and later served in the Vermont legislature. Stafford did play for the company's industrial league team, where he was joined on the Upland team by Chief Bender and Home Run Baker.

Then there's Elmer Bowman, nicknamed "Big Bow" due to his large size. He was a football star in college, starting at fullback for the University of Vermont and once ranking as the third-leading punter in the nation. Bowman also proved capable of belting the ball over the fence at historic Centennial Field. He batted over .300 in eight of his 11 minor league seasons and finished with 1,689 hits, 123 home runs and a .327 average in the minors.

In 1922, Elmer Bowman bested 35-year-old Olympic champion Jim Thorpe for the Eastern League batting title (.365 to .344). It was an Eastern League record for one year, until Bowman topped it by batting .366 the next year (although edged by Wade Lefler's .369) — he regained the record by batting .377 in 1926. Bowman played in just two games in the majors and was hitless in two pinch-hitting appearances in 1920.

All-Time Vermont Selections

Carlton Fisk considers himself a New Hampshire native, since he grew up and went to high school in Charlestown, N.H., and then attended college at the University of New Hampshire. However, Fisk was born in a hospital just across the river in Bellows Falls, Vt., so that technicality makes him a Vermont native for this book. In reality, the whole New England region can claim him as its own, since his career reflected the work ethic, pride and toughness of a true New Englander.

It seems like each decade has a defining moment that takes on a life of its own and stays embedded in fans' memories. In the 1950s it was Bobby Thomson's "Shot Heard 'Round the World," while the 1960s gave us Bill Mazeroski's Series-winning Game 7 home run blast.

The most memorable moment in the 1970s arguably came courtesy of Fisk. We're talking about the home run Fisk hit off Pat Darcy of the Reds in the twelfth inning of Game 6 of the 1975 World Series. What made it so memorable was the fact that it took a few seconds of riveting TV suspense to know he had, at least temporarily, answered the prayers of a long-suffering Red Sox Nation. No player has ever used the power of body language to greater effect, as Pudge seemed to literally will the ball off the foul pole screen and in fair territory. Whether you have seen it replayed 300 times or 3,000 times, the moment always comes to life. It doesn't seem right that the Red Sox lost the World Series in the decisive Game 7, since that relegates Fisk's home run to the realm of cruel tease. The left-field pole at Fenway is now known as the "Fisk Pole."

There's no debate over the All-Time catcher or All-Time Best Player from Vermont — it's Fisk. He caught 2,226 games, including back-to-back seasons where he caught more than 150 games. He hit 72 home runs after the age of 40 (a record since broken by Barry Bonds), and he has more hits and runs scored than any other catcher in the Hall of Fame, which he joined in 2000. Playing 24 seasons is amazing, but playing 24 seasons as a catcher is other-worldly. In fact, Pudge seemed to get better with age, posting career highs in homers, RBI and stolen bases in 1985 at the age of 37.

An 11-time All-Star, Fisk won the Rookie of the Year Award in 1972 after batting .293 with 22 homers and leading the AL with nine triples. Oddly enough, he also won a Gold Glove after a rookie season in which he committed 15 errors and eight passed balls, but never won the award again in 23 more seasons of catching. He has had his number retired by the Red Sox and White Sox.

A somewhat prickly personality who wasn't always embraced by teammates and managers, Fisk was once quoted saying, "If the human body recognized agony and frustration, people would never run marathons, have babies or play baseball."

Unfortunately, Fisk's greatness means we don't have a spot in the lineup for Vermont's third-best player — Birdie Tebbetts, an accomplished catcher in his own right. A four-time All-Star, Tebbetts was a decent hitter (.270 lifetime average) with no power who compiled exactly 1,000 hits over his 14-year career. He missed three seasons of his prime while serving in the Air Force during World War II.

Tebbetts, who picked up his nickname as a kid due to his chirpy, high-pitched voice, was a scrappy player who had a combative, fiery temperament. Like Fisk, he excelled at calling games and working with pitchers. He only made it to one postseason — going hitless in 11 at-bats for the Tigers during the 1940 World Series.

Tebbetts is the only Vermont native to manage in the majors, so he does gain that selection. Although his teams never finished higher than third, he won more than 50 percent of his games for all three teams he managed: Cincinnati and Milwaukee in the National League and Cleveland in the American League. He managed stars such as Hank Aaron, Eddie Mathews, Frank Robinson, Don Newcombe, Warren Spahn, Early Wynn and Luis Tiant, as well as the colorful but talent-challenged Bob Uecker. A true baseball lifer, he later spent 28 years as a scout for several different teams.

Although "Big Bow" Bowman was probably a better player and hitter, we have to go with the Vermont-born first baseman who accomplished the most in the majors — Pat Putnam. Putnam played for Texas, Seattle and Minnesota between 1977 and 1984, collecting 508 hits and 63 home runs. He finished fourth in Rookie of the Year voting.

Our second baseman, Amby McConnell, had a short career but was a starter three of his four seasons. The pickings are slim at shortstop, so Ralph LaPointe gets the honor despite just 115 career hits.

Filling out the infield at third base is Larry Gardner, who had an accomplished 17-year career playing primarily during the Deadball Era. He is sometimes called Vermont's finest player, since folks tend to categorize Fisk as a New Hampshire boy. Gardner batted over .300 five times and finished with 1,931 hits and a .289 average, winning four championships. An outstanding fielder, he led AL third basemen in assists four times. Bill James ranks him as the 29th-best third baseman of all-time.

Gardner had a breakthrough season in 1912, collecting 18 triples (fifth-best in the AL), averaging .315 and driving in 86 runs as the Red Sox won the pennant. He gained a reputation as a clutch hitter and although he batted just .198 in Series action, most of the hits came at the right time. Gardner hit the only home run of the 1912 World Series in Game 7 and matched his regular-season output of homers with two blasts in the 1916 Series. Once the Lively Ball Era started, Gardner drove in 118 runs while batting .310 in 1920 and then hit .319 with 120 RBI and 101 runs scored the next season.

In the outfield, Frank Olin only played two seasons but finished with a .316 batting average. He is flanked by active player Chris Duffy, who has 187 hits through four seasons, and Fred Mann, a nineteenth-century player who accumulated 597 hits over six seasons.

Ray Collins, who was Gardner's teammate at the University of Vermont and later on the Red Sox, stands out as the best southpaw starter from Vermont. He went 84–62 with a sparkling 2.51 ERA. Collins pitched seven scoreless innings in relief in Game 7 of the 1912 Series, winning a ring with Gardner. He went on to win 19 and 20 games the next two seasons before suffering an unexplained loss of effectiveness that ended his career in 1915. Perhaps it was the latent effect of going all the way in both games of a doubleheader the previous September.

Arguments can be made for both Ray Fisher and Jean Dubuc as the right-handed starter. Fisher gets the nod because he won more games (100 to 85), had a lower ERA (2.82 to 3.04) and a better ERA+ (105 to 95). Dubuc's name came up during the Black Sox scandal of 1919 as someone who knew the fix was on, leading to his release by the New York Giants. Although he wasn't banned for life by Commissioner Landis — perhaps because his team wasn't even playing in the Series — Dubuc kept a low profile by playing in Montreal and eventually returned to play four more seasons in the minor leagues.

Ernie Johnson is the best choice for relief pitcher. He appeared in 254 games in relief during the 1950s, finishing 119 games and sporting a 40–23 record. Johnson performed well out of the bullpen for the Milwaukee Braves as they went on to win the 1957 World Series over the Yankees. Johnson appeared in three Series games and allowed just two hits while striking out eight in seven innings.

Len Whitehouse has the distinction of recording the only official saves by a Vermont pitcher (with four), since he is the only player from the state to save a game since the save was officially adopted in 1969.

Virginia

*Names in **bold** represent Major League selections by position, followed by honorable mentions. Negro Leagues players are in **bold italics**, followed by honorable mentions in italics. City of birth is in parentheses.*

Catcher — Randy Hundley (Martinsville). Also: Todd Hundley (Martinsville); *Louis Louden* (West Point); *Buster Haywood* (Whaleysville); *Robert Clarke* (Richmond); *Leon Ruffin* (Portsmouth); Hank Foiles (Richmond)

First Base — George McQuinn (Arlington)

Second Base — Tony Womack (Danville). Also: *Rev Cannady* (Lake City)

Third Base — *Ray Dandridge* (Richmond). Also: *Jud Wilson* (Remington); David Wright (Norfolk); Billy Nash (Richmond); Brandon Inge (Lynchburg)

Shortstop — Granny Hamner (Richmond). Also: Gene Alley (Richmond); *George Wright* (Norfolk)

Outfield — *Pete Hill* (Buena)

Outfield — Paul Hines (Unknown)

Outfield — *Spot Poles* (Winchester). Also: Steve Brodie (Warrenton); Willard Marshall (Richmond); Al Bumbry (Fredericksburg); *Jules Thomas* (Powhatan County); Jim Lemon (Covington); Johnny Grubb (Richmond); George Browne (Richmond); Michael Cuddyer (Norfolk); Cherokee Davis (Ashland); *Jesse Barber* (Charlottesville); *Johnny Davis* (Ashland); *Clarence Winston* (Richmond); *Branch Russell* (South Boston)

Designated Hitter — Willie Horton (Arno)

Right Handed Starter — *Leon Day* (Alexandria). Also: Deacon Phillippe (Rural Retreat); Bobby Witt (Arlington); Ed Willett (Norfolk); *Wilmer Fields* (Manassas); *Rats Henderson* (Richmond); Justin Verlander (Manakin Sabot)

Left Handed Starter — Eppa Rixey (Culpepper). Also: *Dan McClellan* (Norfolk); *Lefty Williams* (Madison County); Brian Anderson (Portsmouth)

Relief Pitcher — Billy Wagner (Tannersville). Also: Mike Williams (Radford); Al Holland (Roanoke)

Manager — *Pete Hill* (Buena). Also: Billy Nash (Richmond); Jim Lemon (Covington); *Buster Haywood* (Whaleysville)

The Names

Best Nickname: Jud "Boojum" Wilson

Other Nicknames: Jesse "Phantom" Barber; John "Sheriff" Blake; Frank "Turkeyfoot" Brower; Clarence "Soup" Campbell; Robert "Eggie" and "Cayuka" Clarke; Jim "Mummy" Coates; Daniel "Davey" Crockett; Ray "Hooks" Dandridge; John "Cherokee" Davis; Albert "Buster" Haywood; Arthur "Rats" Henderson; Cecil "Rebel" Hundley; Charlie "Mule" Peete; Bill "The Virginia Grapevine" Quarles; Eppa "Jephtha" Rixey; Leon "Lassas" Ruffin; Garland "Duck" Shifflett; Edward "Dimples" Tate; Billy "The Kid" Wagner; John "Way Back" Wasdin

Unusual Name: Johnny Grubb; Thomas Toms

All-Time Leaders

Games: Willie Horton, 2028
Hits: Paul Hines, 2134
Batting Average: Steve Brodie, .303
Home Runs: Willie Horton, 325
RBI: Willie Horton, 1163
Stolen Bases: Tony Womack, 363
Wins: Eppa Rixey, 266
Strikeouts: Bobby Witt, 1955
Saves: Billy Wagner, 422
Future Stars: Daniel Hudson (Lynchburg); Mat Latos (Alexandria); Deck McGuire (Richmond)
Best Player: Ray Dandridge

Historic Baseball Places

Virginia Sports Hall of Fame and Museum in Portsmouth — New facility opened in 2005 featuring hands-on, interactive exhibits. Kids can see how fast they throw the ball or call a game like a big-league announcer. More than a dozen baseball players have been inducted including Leon Day, Ray Dandridge, Granny Hamner, Jim Lemon, Al Bumbry and Eppa Rixey.

Harbor Park in Norfolk — Home of the Norfolk Tides, which opened in 1993, sits right by the harbor so fans can watch the boats float by during games.

City Stadium in Lynchburg — Home of the Lynchburg Hillcats, now known as Calvin Falwell Field, opened in 1940. Joe DiMaggio drove in the first two runs in the new stadium during an exhibition between the Yankees and Brooklyn Dodgers.

Notable Achievements

Granny Hamner started an All-Star Game at two different positions: at shortstop in 1952 and at second base in 1954.

Al Bumbry is the last player to hit three triples in a game, which he did on September 22, 1973.

Bob Lacey (Fredericksburg) led the American League in appearances in 1978 with 74.

Paul Hines was reportedly the first player to wear sunglasses in a game in 1882.

Todd Hundley hit a home run for the Mets in the first game of the season every year from 1994 to 1997.

George McQuinn had the longest hitting streak of the 1938 season, hitting in 34 consecutive games.

When the World Series Brought Top Players to Virginia

Baseball has been teasing Virginia for too long. The Boston Beaneaters, featuring star pitchers Kid Nichols and Vic Willis, held spring training in Norfolk in 1901. That same year their American League counterparts the Red Sox were holding camp in Charlottesville, while the Washington Nationals/Senators were conducting their training in Phoebus. That would be the state's first taste of big-league action.

The Philadelphia Phillies came to Richmond for spring training in 1903, while the Nationals/Senators returned to the state a number of years in Hampton, Norfolk and Charlottesville. The Federal League was even represented by two teams in 1914 with the Buffalo Buffeds holding spring workouts in Danville and the Pittsburgh Rebels in Lynchburg.

During World War II, some of the best baseball was being played at the Naval Training Station in Norfolk, where enlisted major leaguers like Bob Feller, Phil Rizzuto, Pee Wee Reese, Fred Hutchinson, Dom DiMaggio and Eddie Robinson were competing for bragging rights and to support the war bond effort. The spirited action between the Bluejackets and the Airmen took place at historic McClure Field.

Reese, then a 25-year-old shortstop, kept coming up with big hits and dazzling plays in the field during the 1943 Navy World Series, a precursor to his later emergence as a star in the majors, but Rizzuto matched him play for play on the other side. The Naval teams more than held their own when playing exhibitions against visiting major league teams, as the Naval teams tended to have more star power.

McClure Field is still standing, representing the second-oldest brick baseball stadium after Wrigley Field. Nineteen Norfolk natives have gone on to play in the majors and the best are all active players: David Wright, Michael Cuddyer and the Upton brothers, B.J. and Justin.

Folks around Virginia got their hopes up when it was reported in 1995 that Drayton McLane, owner of the Houston Astros, was on the verge of selling his team to a group that would move the team to northern Virginia. That never happened, and now the state's baseball fans must wistfully look on as their D.C. neighbors cheer on their own team, the Nationals.

A total of 269 Virginia natives had played in the major leagues by the end of the 2011 season, with 18 active during 2011. Twenty-four Virginia-born players have been named to an All-Star team and five have been elected to the Hall of Fame (four of them veterans of the Negro Leagues).

Terry Bradshaw was not just a Hall of Fame quarterback for the Steelers; he was also an outfielder from Franklin, Va., who played 34 games for the Cardinals in 1995–96, collecting 17 hits. Buck Rogers — the twentieth century edition — was a southpaw pitcher from Spring Garden who pitched like he had been frozen for 500 years. He appeared in two games for the Washington Senators in 1935, allowing 16 hits and six walks in 10 innings.

Davey Crockett, whose real first name was Daniel, proved himself the "King of the Wild Throw. The first baseman from Roanoke was charged with 11 errors in 27 games for the Detroit Tigers in 1901, his only action in the majors. Crockett batted .284 but probably annoyed his teammates by insisting on wearing a coonskin cap in the dugout.

Sometimes fame is fleeting. Michael Neill, a native of Martinsville, had a game-winning hit in the 1999 Pan American Games to clinch an Olympic berth for the U.S. Then in the 2000 Olympics he hit a walk-off home run to help the USA team beat Japan in the first round, followed by a home run and dramatic late-game catch to help the U.S. take the gold medal game. His major league career consisted of four hits in six games for the A's in 1998.

All-Time Virginia Selections

The selections for the All-Time Virginia team might lead to a family squabble. The decision for catcher came down to a father and son — Todd or Randy Hundley. Thank goodness the Upton boys have not accrued enough playing time to be serious contenders for the outfield positions so there's no chance of leaving one brother unhappy. Same thing with the brothers Hamner in the infield since only one had much of a playing career.

Back to the catcher debate. Both Hundleys caught 14 seasons in the majors and their numbers are eerily similar in key categories. Todd has a slight edge in hits (883 to 813) and in games caught (1,096 to 1,026) while Randy edges his son in batting average .236 to .234.

That's where the similarities end. Randy was an excellent receiver who won a Gold Glove with the Cubs in 1967 and led NL catchers in fielding percentage in 1972. He also led the AL by throwing out 50 percent of base runners in 1974. In 1968 Randy caught a record 160 games, playing every inning in 147, according to Baseball-Reference.com. However, after hitting 19 home runs in his first full year in the majors Randy didn't do much with the bat.

By comparison, Todd was a below-average defensive catcher who was in the lineup for his bat. He led NL catchers in errors twice and only threw out 25 percent of base runners for his career. However, he clubbed 202 home runs compared to 82 by his father. Todd holds a big advantage in OBP, slugging, OPS and OPS+. Todd hit 41 homers in 1996, which set a single-season record for catchers, along with 112 RBI. The next season he hit 30 homers with 86 RBI. He was named to two All-Star teams compared to just one selection for his father.

Although Todd would seem to have the edge because of his slugging numbers, the final deciding factor dates to December 2007. That's when the Mitchell Report was released naming Todd Hundley as one of the players who received performance-enhancing drugs from Kirk Radomski. With that mitigating factor in mind, the catcher position goes to Randy.

Four Negro Leagues catchers also received consideration. Louis Louden, who possessed a strong throwing arm and good power, was selected to four East-West All-Star teams. He played for the New York Cubans from 1942–50, helping them win the Negro National League championship in 1947. Albert "Buster" Haywood spent much of his career playing for black semi-pro teams such as the Belleville Grays. A well-rounded player who could field, throw and hit, Haywood finally showed what he could for the Cincinnati and Indianapolis Clowns, making the East-West All-Star team in 1944. As his career began to wind down, Haywood transitioned to a player-manager role with the Clowns and guided them to three straight Negro American League titles.

Robert "Eggie" Clarke of Richmond managed to hang around the Negro Leagues for 24 years, often in a backup role. Clarke was a smart player who was knowledgeable about the game and adept at calling pitches and handling pitchers. Leon Ruffin played 14 seasons in the Negro Leagues and Mexican League, struggling with the bat in some years but demonstrating a strong throwing arm. He played in the East-West All-Star game in 1946, a year in which he hit .391 and helped the Newark Eagles win the pennant.

Only one candidate emerged for Team Virginia at both first base and second base. George McQuinn was named to six All-Star teams as a first baseman, collecting 1,588 hits with 135 home runs during a productive 12-year career. His best season was 1939 when he batted .316 with 20 homers, 94 RBI and 195 hits. McQuinn batted .438 in a losing effort for the St. Louis Browns in the 1944 World Series, followed later by a .130 mark on the 1947 Yankees team that won the championship.

Although he also played quite a bit at short and in the outfield, Tony Womack played the most games at second base — 529 to be exact. An All-Star selection in 1997, Womack led the league in steals three straight years and in triples once. He ended his career with 363 steals but posted a weak .317 OBP, because he was a singles hitter who didn't walk much. He won a World Series while playing for the Diamondbacks in 2001.

Walter "Rev" Cannady didn't stay in one place for long, bouncing between positions on the field as well as changing teams frequently over a 25-year career. His bad temper might have had something to do with that. He started out at shortstop but eventually played more at second base. Cannady hit .328 with the Cleveland Tate Stars in 1921 and later followed with a .399 average and 12 home runs in 1925 and a .321 mark in 1927.

Virginia sure knows how to produce third basemen. The two best Virginia-born third basemen achieved their notoriety in the Negro Leagues: Ray Dandridge and Jud "Boojum" Wilson. Dandridge can best be described as Brooks Robinson's equal as a fielder but much faster and a better overall batter, albeit with less power. He was generally regarded as the best third baseman in Negro Leagues history.

It was difficult if not impossible to hit a ball past the bow-legged Dandridge, who combined cat-like reflexes and sure hands with a quick release and strong arm. Recalls Monte Irvin in Roger Angell's *Season Ticket*, "Ray Dandridge played third base with style and class. He had the quickest hands—I never saw anybody come in and sweep up the swinging bunt the way he could do it." Dave Barnhill called Dandridge the greatest ballplayer ever.

Dandridge batted .315 in the Negro Leagues (according to a Hall of Fame study), .348 in 644 games in the Mexican League and .318 in four seasons for Minneapolis at Triple-A, waiting for a call-up to the majors that never came.

He proved to be a man among boys when he got his first opportunity to play with white players at the age of 35. Dandridge was voted the American Association Rookie of the Year in 1949 and then won the MVP Award the next season, but the Giants couldn't find a spot on their team for the future Hall of Famer. Dandridge would later cuss out Giants owner Horace Stoneham for the slight, bemoaning the fact that he didn't get even a token chance to show he belonged in the majors.

Dandridge got closer to the majors than Jud Wilson, who played in the Negro Leagues from 1922 to 1945. Wilson was just an average fielder at third, known for knocking the ball down by any means with his body, but boy could he hit. He picked up the nickname "Boojum" from the sound made by his hits banging into outfield walls — pronounced with gusto like "Buh-ZHOOM!"

Jud "Boojum" Wilson was one of the most feared hitters in Negro Leagues history. His batting feats seemed to come from a sense of controlled rage. He was a notorious hothead who struck real fear in opponents, and he was once arrested for punching an ump. Chino Smith made the mistake of sliding too hard into third one time. Wilson threatened to break every bone in his body and then proceeded to pick him up and toss him in the air like a bag of garbage (National Baseball Hall of Fame Library, Cooperstown, New York).

"I think he could hit a ball with his fists and knock it out of the park," said fellow Hall of Fame third baseman Judy Johnson. "He could tear you apart, he was so strong."

Wilson, who led four different Negro Leagues teams to championships between 1929 and 1934, was a better hitter than Josh Gibson, according to Double Duty Radcliffe, a teammate of both on the Washington Homestead Grays. Wilson joined the powerhouse Grays in 1940 at the age of 41 and helped them win six straight pennants, playing alongside Gibson, Buck Leonard and Cool Papa Bell. He would join them all in the Hall of Fame in 2006.

Wilson, who was called Jorocon — "the Bull" — in Cuba, is the all-time leader in batting average in the Cuban Winter Leagues at .372, leading that league twice in average. Wilson batted over .300 in each of his first 14 seasons in the Negro Leagues, and his lifetime .351 average is one of the highest in black baseball history. He even batted .330 in exhibitions against white stars such as Dizzy Dean and Lefty Grove.

Other notable third basemen include David Wright, who has already earned five All-Star berths, two Gold Gloves and two Silver Sluggers while emerging as the face of the Mets franchise; and Billy Nash, a steady nineteenth-century player who accumulated 1,606 hits with a .275 average.

Shortstop came down to two qualified candidates. Granny Hamner was a three-time All-Star who compiled 1,529 hits with 104 home runs over 17 seasons. Gene Alley was an adept fielder who made two All-Star teams and earned two Gold Gloves for the Pirates. Alley had the shorter career and his productivity was hampered by a lingering shoulder injury. It's also hard to overlook what a brutal job Alley did batting in four postseason series — 1-for-27 — while Hamner batted .429 for the Whiz Kids during the 1950 World Series. Granny's body of work is larger and demonstrates more productivity, so he gets selected at short.

Paul Hines is either the best outfielder from Virginia or the best outfielder from the District of Columbia, as conflicting information exists on the matter. Evidence seems to point toward a birth somewhere in Virginia, so he belongs to Team Virginia. In any event, he was one of the first great ballplayers.

Hines finished with 2,133 hits, which is even more impressive when you consider he played an average of 83 games for his 20-year career. If you extrapolate his hits to a 162-game schedule, he averaged 208 hits a season. He led the league in batting in 1878 and 1879, batted over .300 11 times and ended his career with a .302 average. His career OPS+ of 131 is the same as Rod Carew and Tony Oliva and better than Hall of Famers Dave Winfield, Carl Yastrzemzki, Eddie Murray and Wade Boggs.

When you are one of the first professional ballplayers you wind up making history a lot, and Hines did that. He was a member of the 1876 Chicago White Stockings, the first team to win the National League championship. He became the first player to accomplish the Triple Crown in batting when he led the National League in 1878 in batting (.358), home runs (four) and runs batted in (50) for Providence. Hines was also part of the first all–.300 outfield in 1878 along with Dick Higham and Tom York. Still in dispute is whether he completed the first unassisted triple play in history, as some say Hines did on May 8, 1878.

Hines made more history by playing in the first "World's Championship Series," a postseason contest held from 1884–1891 between the winners of the National League and the American Association. He became the first National League player to bat, get hit by a pitch and score a run in a World Series game, although those games are now considered exhibitions.

Another overlooked outfielder who was highly regarded by his peers was Spottswood "Spot" Poles, who was often called the "Black Ty Cobb." The lightning-fast lefty batted leadoff and played center field, using his speed to terrorize opponents. Some say he was even faster than Cool Papa Bell. The Winchester native is credited with a lifetime average of .323 but reportedly batted close to .500 in exhibitions against white players.

After starting his professional career with the Philadelphia Giants in 1909, Poles' career took off after he joined the New York Lincoln Giants in 1911. He averaged .440, .398, .414 and .487 with the New York Lincoln Giants from 1911–14 if all manner of games is included, according to James Riley's *Biographical Encyclopedia of the Negro Baseball Leagues*. Bill James ranks him as the best Negro Leagues player from 1914 to 1916, and a case can certainly be made for his inclusion in the Hall of Fame. He won five battle stars and a purple heart while serving as an army infantry sergeant in France during World War I and is buried in Arlington National Cemetery.

The third Virginia outfielder is a late comer, as new research has unearthed the fact that Hall of Famer John "Pete" Hill was born in Virginia and not Pittsburgh, as his original plaque in Cooperstown asserted. Hill was considered the first great African American outfielder, with his playing career in the Negro Leagues lasting from 1899–1926. He was fast but big and powerful, spraying line drives all over the field, terrorizing opposing teams on the bases and possessing a rifle arm in center field. Cum Posey called him "the most consistent hitter of his lifetime" and named him to his All-Time Team. In 1911 Hill reportedly hit in 115 of 116 games counting exhibitions and the Seamheads.com Negro Leagues Database credits him with a .396 average with 16 homers playing for the Detroit Stars in 1919.

Hill won titles with Sol White's Philadelphia Giants in 1905 and 1906, then later played for Rube Foster on the powerhouse Leland Giants and Chicago American Giants. He spent many winters tearing up the Cuban League, leading the league in batting once. Inducted into the Hall of Fame in 2006, Hill for many years was the only Hall of Famer whose burial site was unknown. Dogged research by Dr. Jeremy Krock, coordinator of the Negro Leagues Baseball Grave Marker Project, led to the discovery in late 2010 that Hill was buried in an unmarked grave outside Chicago.

Willie Horton probably belongs in the outfield since he played 1,190 games there, but fielding was not his forte. He played 753 games at designated hitter and would have played even more there if he wasn't a decade into his career when the position came into use. DH was his primary position the last six years of his 18-year career.

Horton was a feared slugger who belted 325 home runs and drove in 1,163 runs primarily for his hometown Tigers. Although he was born in Virginia, Horton was raised in Detroit, which is why he remains an iconic figure in Tigers history. His number was retired by the team in 2000.

A four-time All-Star, Horton's career high was 36 homers in 1968, when he finished fourth in MVP voting. At the age of 36 and in his next to last season, Horton hit 29 homers with a career-best 106 RBI, which led him to be named AL Comeback Player of the Year.

Heading up the honorable mention list of outfielders is Steve Brodie, who currently ranks first in average (.303) and third in career hits (1,728) among Virginia players. A star center fielder on dominant Baltimore Orioles teams of the mid–1890s, Brodie's best season was 1894, when he batted .366 with 210 hits, scored 134 runs and drove in 113 despite just three homers. Brodie came back and batted .348 with 134 RBI the next season.

Richmond native Willard Marshall debuted with the New York Giants in 1942 at the age of 22 and made the All-Star team that year. Although he would lose the next three years to the war effort, he picked up where he left off in 1946, batting .282 with 144 hits. Marshall was a force in 1947, making the All-Star team while batting .291 and finishing third in home runs (36) and total bases (310), fifth in slugging (.528) and RBI (107) and seventh in runs scored (102). The highlight of his season came on July 18, when he achieved the rare feat of homering in three consecutive at-bats in the same game. Marshall would make the All-Star team for a third time in 1949 after batting .307, but he only had the one year with strong slugging stats. He retired after 11 seasons and 130 home runs.

Al Bumbry, who also lost time at the beginning of his career while serving in Vietnam, was a speedy outfielder who played 13 of his 14 seasons with the Orioles. Named Rookie of the Year in 1973 after hitting .337 and leading the league with 11 triples, Bumbry turned into a dependable cog for Manager Earl Weaver. He hit .317 with 42 steals in 1977 and then had his only All-Star year in 1980, batting .318 with 205 hits and 44 steals that season. Bumbry finished his career with 254 stolen bases, winning a World Series in 1983.

Jules Thomas was a dynamic player who played primarily for the New York Lincoln Giants in a career that spanned 1909–25. At 220 pounds, "Jewel" was one of the biggest players in colored baseball during his prime. Thomas hit for power and average and typically batted over .300 each year. Despite his size Thomas was a terrific center fielder with great range who was also a threat on the base paths.

Covington native Jim Lemon strung together five good years with the bat from 1956 to 1960 and finished with 164 career home runs. Like Marshall, Lemon hit three straight homers in a game in 1956 off the great Whitey Ford. In 1959 his 33 homers were third in the American League behind Rocky Colavito and Harmon Killebrew, and the next year he again finished third with 38, one behind Roger Maris and two behind Mickey Mantle. Lemon was an atrocious fielder who struck out a lot, leading the league in strikeouts three straight seasons. Carrying through a familiar theme of the All-Time Virginia outfield, he missed two years while serving in the Korean War. Lemon also managed one season, guiding the Washington Senators to last place in 1968 with a 65–96 record.

Johnny Grubb has one of the all-time great baseball names. The outfielder lasted 16 seasons, batting .278 with 1,153 hits and winning a World Series with the Tigers in 1984.

The rotation boasts Hall of Famers in lefty Eppa Rixey and righty Leon Day, whose stories share an amazing coincidence. They both died shortly after learning they had been elected to the Hall of Fame — Day six days after getting the news and Rixey a month after.

For Day, who was born in Arlington, Va., but grew up in Baltimore, recognition was a long time coming, although his peers knew how good he was. "I didn't see anyone in the major leagues that was better than Leon Day," remarked Larry Doby.

Monte Irvin went one better, calling Day one of the greatest athletes he's ever seen. "People don't know what a great pitcher Leon Day was. He was as good or better than Bob Gibson," he said.

Day blended a powerful fastball, a knee-buckling curveball and a no-windup delivery to dominate Negro Leagues action from 1934–1949. At the age of 20 in 1937 he was literally unbeatable, going 13–0 for the Newark Eagles while also batting .320 with eight home runs. An All-Star in six seasons, Day set a record with 18 strikeouts in a Negro Leagues game in 1942. In 1946, just weeks after being discharged from the army, Day became the only pitcher in Negro Leagues history to throw a no-hitter on Opening Day.

When Rixey learned he had been elected to the Hall of Fame in 1963, he quipped, "They're really scraping the bottom of the barrel, aren't they?"

Actually, it appears that they were. Rixey never received more than 4.1 percent of the votes in his first 12 years on the writer's ballot. His last three years on the ballot he bounced from 12 to 52 to 30 percent of the vote, then a year later 12 guys get together and decide he's in, part of the great stampede by the Veterans Committee to usher 14 borderline players into the Hall in a four-year period.

Rixey's inclusion in the Hall has been controversial due to his career record of 266–251, barely above .500. His ERA+ of 115 ranks 207th in history, which seems pedestrian but happens to be the same as Phil Niekro, Steve Carlton and Fergie Jenkins. Rixey played for bad teams in Philadelphia and Cincinnati for most of his 21 seasons, making the World Series just once. He led the league in losses in 1917 but had a 2.27 ERA that year. His best season was 1916, when he went 22–10 with a 1.85 ERA and career-high 134 strikeouts. Rixey won 20 games four times and retired as the all-time leader in wins by a National League southpaw. He was perhaps the only player who could boast of having a master's degree in chemistry.

Actually, there may be a better southpaw candidate in Negro Leagues hurler Danny McClellan. However, his birthplace of Norfolk has not been fully verified yet so it makes sense to hold off on making him the all-time lefty for Team Virginia. McClellan pitched the first perfect game in black baseball history in 1903 while pitching for the Cuban X-Giants, and he was one of the top pitchers in the early part of the century. He formed a dynamic one-two punch with Rube Foster on the Philadelphia Giants to lead the team to three straight titles from 1904–06. As James Riley notes in *The Biographical Encyclopedia of the Negro Baseball Leagues*, McClellan was a smart pitcher who effectively mixed an assortment of off-speed curves to compensate for the lack of an overpowering fastball. He was a good hitter who often played in the field when not pitching.

Also receiving strong consideration as a right-handed starter was Charles "Deacon" Phillippe, who picked up his nickname for being quiet and staying out of trouble. Known for his impeccable control, Phillippe led the league in fewest walks per 9 innings five times and in strikeout-to-walk ratio four times. He ranks sixteenth in baseball history with 1.25 walks per 9 innings and is 22nd all-time with a 1.105 WHIP. Phillippe pitched from 1899–1911, winning 20 games his first five seasons and finishing 189–109 with a 2.59 ERA. He made his mark pitching for the Pirates in the first modern World Series in 1903, pitching five complete games and accounting for all three of the wins in a losing effort.

For closer, the All-Time Virginia team can call on Tannersville native Billy Wagner, who passed Dennis Eckersley during the 2010 season for fifth on the all-time saves list and also passed Jesse Orosco for most strikeouts by a left-handed reliever. The seven-time All-Star recorded 20 or more saves in 12 seasons and retired after the 2010 season with 422 saves. His career high is 44 saves for Houston in 2003, although Wagner never led the league in saves.

Although not a big guy at 5-foot-10, Wagner relied on a fastball that approached 100 mph combined with a nasty slider to dominate batters, averaging 11.9 strikeouts and just 6.0 hits per 9 innings for his career. His strikeout totals exceeded his innings pitched in every one of his 15 seasons, highlighted by 1999 when he averaged 14.95 K/9IP. Despite his brilliant career as a closer, he is remembered for coming up small in the postseason. In seven postseason series, Wagner had just three saves in 13 appearances with an unsightly 10.32 ERA. Not surprisingly, his teams lost six of those seven series.

During the 2005 season, Wagner blew two games down the stretch to cost the Phillies the wild card spot. In Game 2 of the 2006 NLCS vs. the Cardinals, Wagner entered a tie game in the ninth inning and gave up four hits and three runs to lose the game and return the momentum to the Cards. His failures in key moments will probably hurt Wagner's chances of making the Hall of Fame.

Mike Williams put together a nice career as a reliever. He saved 144 games in 12 seasons, with a high of 46 for the Pirates in 2002. A two-time All-Star, he walked a lot of batters, had a high ERA (4.45) and posted a 32–54 record.

Pete Hill is probably the most accomplished manager from Virginia. His managerial records are sketchy, but he guided the Detroit Stars to the Western championship in 1919 and went 105–88 with the Stars from 1919–21.

Billy Nash only managed one year, guiding the Philadelphia Phillies to an eighth-place finish in 1896 with a 62–68 record. His biggest accomplishment was having a hand in bringing Nap Lajoie to the team that year. Lajoie joined the Phillies for the last 39 games of the season, getting a promising start to his Hall of Fame career.

WASHINGTON

*Names in **bold** represent Major League selections by position, followed by honorable mentions. City of birth is in parentheses.*

Catcher — **Sammy White (Wenatchee)**. Also: Toby Hall (Tacoma); Ryan Doumit (Moses Lake); Mike Redmond (Seattle)
First Base — **John Olerud (Seattle)**. Also: Earl Torgeson (Snohomish); Lyle Overbay (Centralia)
Second Base — **Ryne Sandberg (Spokane)**
Third Base — **Ron Santo (Seattle)**. Also: Ron Cey (Tacoma)
Shortstop — **Kevin Stocker (Spokane)**
Outfield — **Earl Averill (Snohomish)**
Outfield — **Grady Sizemore (Seattle)**
Outfield — **Jeff Conine (Tacoma)**. Also: Geoff Jenkins (Olympia); Billy North (Seattle); Woody Jensen (Bremerton); Ed Kirkpatrick (Spokane)
Designated Hitter — **Ken Phelps (Seattle)**. Also: Champ Summers (Bremerton)
Right Handed Starter — **Tim Lincecum (Bellevue)**. Also: Todd Stottlemyre (Sunnyside); Bruce Kison (Pasco); Fred Hutchinson (Seattle); Larry Christenson (Everett)
Left Handed Starter — **Vean Gregg (Chehalis)**. Also: Jon Lester (Tacoma); Ed Brandt (Spokane)
Relief Pitcher — **Randy Myers (Vancouver)**. Also: Gerry Staley (Brush Prairie); David Riske (Renton); Evan Meek (Bellevue)
Manager — **Fred Hutchinson (Seattle)**

The Names

Best Nickname: Ron "The Penguin" Cey
Other Nicknames: Earl "Rock" and "The Earl of Snohomish" Averill; Bob "The Macaroni Pony" Coluccio; Jeff "the Barbarian" Conine; Fred "Great Stoneface" Hutchinson; Ed "Spanky" Kirkpatrick; Tim "The Freak" Lincecum; Steve "Psycho" Lyons; Clarence "Cuddles" Marshall; Elwood "Speed" Martin; Ford "Moon" Mullen; John "Big Rude" Olerud; Ken "Digger" Phelps; Marv "Twitch" Rickert; Royal "Hunky" Shaw; John "Champ" Summers; Cliff "The Earl of Snohomish" Torgeson; Ray "Deadbody" Washburn
Most Unusual Name: Matt Tuiasosopo; Clarence Podbielan

All-Time Leaders

Games: Ron Santo, 2243
Hits: Ryne Sandberg, 2386
Batting Average: Earl Averill, .318
Home Runs: Ron Santo, 342
RBI: Ron Santo, 1331
Stolen Bases: Billy North, 395
Wins: Todd Stottlemyre, 138
Strikeouts: Todd Stottlemyre, 1587
Saves: Randy Myers, 347
Future Star: Hank Conger (Federal Way)
Best Player: Ryne Sandberg

Historic Baseball Places

SAFECO Field in Seattle — SAFECO features The Baseball Museum of the Pacific Northwest, which pays tribute to professional baseball teams that previously played in the region. Another attraction is the Mariners Hall of Fame, which highlights the accomplishments of four inducted members: Jay Buhner, Alvin Davis, Edgar Martínez and broadcaster Dave Niehaus.
Avista Stadium in Spokane — Open since 1958, this historic stadium has been home to many great players including Duke Snider, Carlos Beltran and Hoyt Wilhelm.
Cheney Stadium in Tacoma — Juan Marichal got the first win for the Tacoma Giants when the ballpark opened in 1960. Alex Rodriguez, Ken Griffey, Jr., Mark McGwire and Gaylord Perry are among the other stars who have played minor league games for Tacoma. Cheney Stadium was extensively remodeled before the 2011 season.
Olympic Stadium in Hoquiam — The stadium, originally built with local timber as a Works Progress Administration (WPA) project in 1937, is one of the last remaining wooden stadiums in America. Although professional baseball has not been played there since the late 1990s, it's a unique sight worth seeing.

Notable Achievements

Ray Washburn (Pasco) followed Gaylord Perry to become the first pitchers to throw back-to-back no-hitters in the same park when they accomplished the feat at Candlestick Park on September 17 and 18, 1968.
John Olerud is one of two players to hit for the cycle in both the National League and the American League. He did it with the Mets on Sept. 11, 1997 and with the Mariners on June 16, 2001. The other player is Bob Watson.
Mike Redmond holds the major league record for most consecutive games without an error at catcher, playing 253 errorless games from July 22, 2004 until May 21, 2010.
Ron Santo is the only third baseman to drive in at least 90 runs in eight consecutive seasons (1963–1970).

It only took three months to build Avista Stadium in Spokane, which opened in 1958, and it's still holding up in its sixth decade. Duke Snider had an unsuccessful stint managing the Spokane Indians in 1965, while Hall of Famers Don Sutton and Hoyt Wilhelm made brief appearances playing for Spokane in 1968 and 1971, respectively (courtesy BallparkReviews.com).

Lumber baron Ben Cheney—who is credited with standardizing the size of a 2 × 4 stud—helped fund the construction of the stadium in Tacoma that bears his name. It opened in 1960 with lights transplanted from Seals Stadium in San Francisco. A statue of Cheney can be found in Row 1 of Section K, depicting the rabid baseball fan smiling and eating peanuts (courtesy DigitalBallparks.com).

Baseball Reigns Supreme in the Pacific Northwest

Professional baseball in Washington state has been a tease, a century-long rain dance that has produced intermittent showers of significance. Dating back to 1890, when the Pacific Northwest League took root with franchises in Portland, Seattle, Tacoma and Spokane, the state has evolved from a baseball afterthought into a hotbed of baseball activity.

Spokane emerged as the champions of that first PNL season and would go on to build a long history of success with different franchises and leagues. The 1946 Spokane Indians made history of another kind when the team's bus crashed down a ravine and caught fire, killing nine players including player-manager Mel Cole. The team managed to finish out the season in a daze and then picked up new support as an affiliate of the Brooklyn Dodgers the next year.

Avista Stadium was constructed in 1958 to host Spokane's Triple-A team for the Los Angeles Dodgers, using batting cages from Ebbets Field. Tommy Lasorda managed the Spokane Indians for three seasons, going 94–52 in 1970.

A winning tradition was restored to Spokane in 1986 when Hall of Famer George Brett and his three brothers purchased the team, which continues to play its games at Avista Stadium. The Indians have won 10 division titles under the Brett family's ownership.

Spokane's most famous ballplayer, Ryne Sandberg, first attracted attention as a Parade All-American quarterback at North Central High School in Spokane. He proved to be pretty good at baseball, too. Ed Brandt attended Lewis & Clark High School in Spokane and then began his pro career with the Seattle Indians of the Pacific Coast League. He would go on to win 121 games over 11 seasons in the majors. Another Spokane native, Kevin Stocker, played high school ball at Central Valley in Spokane and later at the University of Washington before embarking on an eight-year MLB career. Ed Kirkpatrick, who was born in Spokane but later moved to California, picked up the nickname "Spanky" because he looked a lot like Spanky McFarland from the "Little Rascals."

Washington sports historian Jim Price notes that Tacoma has played host to some of baseball's greatest stars, including Gaylord Perry, Willie McCovey, Joe McGinnity, Juan Marichal, Alex Rodriquez, Mark McGwire and Felix Hernandez. Then there's the all-time great who got away. An 18-year-old fireballer named Walter Johnson tried out for the Tacoma Tigers in 1906 — he was sent packing but was in the majors for good a year later.

It's 1938 and all of Seattle is abuzz watching local boy Fred Hutchinson win 25 games for the Seattle Rainiers, who play their games in the newly built Sick's Stadium, which features a breath-taking view of majestic Mount Rainier beyond the right-center fence. The Rainiers would go on to win five Pacific Coast League titles and lead the minor leagues in attendance five times, offering proof the city and the region could support a major league franchise.

The big break finally came in 1969 when Seattle was awarded an expansion franchise, called the Pilots. Playing in Sick's Stadium, which was an inadequate facility for major league play, the Pilots lasted just one season before being bought and moved to Milwaukee by a group led by Bud Selig. The city of Seattle sued the American League for damages as a result of losing their team after one year, a case that dragged on for six years until MLB agreed to award Seattle another franchise.

Since joining the American League in 1977, the Mariners have won just three division titles — 1995, 1997 and 2001 — earned one wild card (2000) and have yet to appear in the World Series. Despite the Mariners' lack of success, the state has been producing professional baseball players at an increasingly higher rate since Jack Bliss became the first Washington-born player to join the majors in 1908.

SABR member Dave Fallen calls attention to the story of Paul Strand from Carbonado. Long before Rick Ankiel made the switch from pitcher to outfielder there was Strand, who made a similar transformation. Strand was a pretty fair left-handed pitcher who went 7–3 with a 2.37 ERA over three seasons for the Boston Braves (1913–1915). He hurt his arm in 1915 and returned to the minors, pitching a perfect game for the Seattle Giants in 1917. He continued in baseball as an outfielder, and in 1923 set a professional baseball record of 325 hits in a single season, a record that has never been broken. That season, he batted .394 in 194 games (825 at-bats) including 66 doubles, 13 triples and 43 home runs. The previous season he had compiled 289 hits with a .384 average.

In 1924 Connie Mack outbid nine other major league teams to obtain Strand, but after one-third of a season, Strand was batting only .228 and Mack sold him back to the minors. Strand went on to complete a fabulous 14-year minor league career, ending up with 1,958 hits, and he was elected to the Pacific Coast League Hall of Fame.

A total of 180 players from Washington have played in the majors to date, with nearly 100 of them playing since 1980. Sixteen were active during the 2011 season including young stars such as Tim Lincecum and Jon Lester.

Jack Bliss of Vancouver was the first Washington-born player to join the major leagues, debuting with the Cardinals on May 10, 1908. Six days later Yakima native Royal "Hunky" Shaw appeared in his only major league game, going hitless in his one career at-bat with the Pirates.

Mel Stottlemyre, Jack Fournier, Jeff Heath, Scott Hatteberg, Roy Johnson and Bob Johnson are among the players born outside Washington who played high school baseball in the state.

Clarence Marshall was given the nickname "Cuddles" by Yankees teammate Joe Page, his roommate on the road, which conjures up some disturbing images. Marshall won only six games with a 5.98 ERA during his three-year stint with the Yankees, so he's lucky Page didn't strangle him in his sleep. As a 21-year-old rookie, Marshall had the distinction of starting the first night game played at Yankee Stadium on May 28, 1946.

You'll win trivia contests if you can name the player who played for the New York Yankees, the New York Giants and the Brooklyn Dodgers, and is in the Hall of Fame. The answer is Morris "Red" Badgro, who played baseball for the St. Louis Browns in 1929 and 1930 with a career batting average of .257. He then switched to football playing for the New York (Football) Yankees, the New York (Football) Giants, and the Brooklyn (football) Dodgers. In 1933 he scored the first touchdown in NFL Football Championship history. In 1981 Badgro was inducted into the Football Hall of Fame in Canton, Ohio.

All-Time Washington Selections

The All-Time-Washington team features Sammy White at catcher. White was an excellent receiver who played 11 seasons, mainly for the Red Sox. He accumulated 916 hits with a .262 average and made the All-Star team in 1953, White is the only player since 1900 to score three runs in an inning, a feat he accomplished on June 18, 1953.

Honorable mention goes to Toby Hall, who batted .265 playing from 2000–2008; active player Ryan Doumit, who batted .318 with 137 hits and 15 homers during his best season in 2008; and Mike Redmond, an excellent defensive catcher and .288 batter over 13 seasons.

Three players received consideration for first base: John Olerud, Earl Torgeson and Lyle Overbay. Olerud possesses the best credentials as the All-Time-Washington first baseman. A slick fielder who earned three Gold Gloves and led AL first basemen in fielding percentage and assists three times, he also stood out by wearing a batting helmet in the field.

Olerud was an underrated batter who hit 255 home runs and batted .295 over 17 seasons. He collected 2,239 hits with an outstanding .398 OBP. Olerud's best year was 1993, when he won a batting title for the Blue Jays with a .363 average and also led the AL in doubles (54) and OBP (.473). In 1998 he hit .354 for the Mets with 197 hits. Olerud drew 1,275 walks for his career, which is 45th-best in history, and hit exactly 500 doubles (ranking 52nd all-time).

Torgeson was known as the "Earl of Snohomish" in tribute to earlier star Earl Averill — the original "Earl of Snohomish." Torgeson led the National League with 120 runs scored in 1950 while hitting 23 homers. He followed that up by hitting 24 homers with 92 RBI the next season. A former player for the Rainiers, Torgeson was good in all phases of the game but not outstanding at anything. He appeared in two World Series — in 1948 with the Boston Braves and 1959 with the White Sox.

Overbay started his career with Arizona in 2001 and is still active. He led the NL with 53 doubles in 2004 and has twice batted over .300. His best season was 2006 with the Blue Jays, when he set career highs in hits, homers, RBI and average. Although not known for his defense, Overbay is an above-average fielder who led AL first basemen in fielding percentage in 2009.

Sandberg is the logical choice as the state's All-Time Best Player. The Spokane native blended power, speed and defensive ability with a commitment to play the game the right way.

Sandberg was named to 10 straight All-Star teams starting in 1984, when he had an MVP season while leading the Cubs to the playoffs for the first time in 39 years. He batted .314 that year with 200 hits and led the league in runs scored and triples. He stole 54 bases the next year on the way to stealing 344 for his career. His best year statistically was 1990, when he hit .300 with 100 RBI while leading the National League with a career-high 40 homers and 116 runs.

He earned nine straight Gold Gloves for his stellar glove work at second along with seven Silver Slugger Awards. Sandberg was not able to deliver a World Series title to the loyal Cubs fans who worshipped him. He retired having hit the most home runs by a second baseman — 277 — a mark since passed by Jeff Kent, and his .989 career fielding percentage currently ranks ninth (six players ahead of him are still active). He was inducted into the Hall of Fame in 2005.

"He was like an old school guy every day of his career," remarked fellow Hall of Famer Billy Williams, who was Sandberg's hitting coach on the Cubs. "All he wanted was to uphold what had happened in the game of baseball."

Sandberg is joined in the infield by another great Cubs player, Ron Santo, who tops many lists of the best players not in the Hall of Fame. To consider Santo's qualifications for the Hall, it's necessary to decide where he stacks among the best third basemen in history. Bill James has been preaching for years about how immensely qualified Santo is for the Hall of Fame, ranking him as the sixth-best third baseman of all-time, one spot ahead of Brooks Robinson. He wrote, "Ron Santo towers far above the real standard of the real Hall of Fame."

There are 11 third basemen in the Hall of Fame (not including Negro Leaguers), and Santo's career statistics place him squarely in the middle of that pack. Let's take a closer look at how those 11 Hall of Famers compare to Santo. Santo has a better average (.277) than Brooks Robinson and Mike Schmidt. Only Schmidt and Eddie Mathews hit more than his 342 home runs. He ranks fifth in RBI, ahead of Wade Boggs, Paul Molitor and Pie Traynor and just 26 behind Robinson despite playing 653 fewer games. He ranks fifth in OPS (.826), ahead of Traynor, Frank Baker, Jimmy Collins and Molitor and way ahead of Robinson, who posted an OPS of .723. One of the best stats for determining a player's value as a batter is OPS+, and Santo ranks sixth in OPS+, ahead of Robinson, Molitor, Kell and Traynor. He played in 2,130 games at third, which is topped by only four Hall of Famers and places him eighth all-time.

Santo led the league in walks four times, OBP twice and in triples once, demonstrating there were many dimensions to his game. He finished in the top 10 in voting for the NL MVP Award four times. He played at least 154 games in 11 straight seasons, so he was durable, and he hit over 30 homers four straight years, so he was consistent. He posted the fourth-best WAR (Wins Above Replacement) in the National League in the 1960s — behind only Mays, Aaron and Clemente. All these facts would seem to demonstrate that Santo had a Hall of Fame worthy career just on the merits of his batting prowess during an era dominated by pitchers, but the nine-time All-Star was also an above-average fielder with good hands and a strong arm. He won five consecutive Gold Gloves and ranks fifth all-time in assists and thirteenth in putouts.

Santo ranks fifth all-time for most games played

without reaching the postseason — 2,243. His critics also point out that he batted .296 with 216 home runs at Wrigley Field compared to .257 with 126 homers away from Wrigley. However, the Hall is littered with players with similar home-away splits. Jim Rice batted .320 at Fenway Park and .277 away from Fenway; Mel Ott hit 323 home runs at the Polo Grounds and 188 in other parks; Kirby Puckett batted .344 at home in the Metrodome compared to .291 in away games.

Santo was the leading vote-getter among the 10 finalists considered by the Veterans Committee in 2008, but he fell short of election by nine votes. He passed away December 2, 2010, resigned to the fact that his talents were not recognized with the sport's highest honor. He finally was elected in 2012, and Santo holds down third base for Team Washington.

We should not overlook another talented third baseman from Washington — Ron Cey. Nicknamed "The Penguin" because he had a squatty build and waddled when he ran, Cey hit 316 home runs and made six straight All-Star teams for the Dodgers. Combining with Steve Garvey, Davey Lopes and Bill Russell to solidify the Dodgers infield for a decade, Cey helped lead the team to four World Series. He was named MVP of the 1981 Series after batting .350. He was a similar player to Santo in that he demonstrated good power, walked a lot and played an excellent third base.

The pickings were slim at shortstop. Mick Kelleher hit just .213 with 230 career hits, while utility player Willie Bloomquist has played more games in the outfield than at short. That leaves Kevin Stocker, who collected 703 hits and batted .254 while playing 838 games at short from 1993 to 2000. Stocker appeared in the World Series as a rookie with the Phillies, hitting .324 that season.

Team Washington's outfield features an all-time great (Earl Averill), an accomplished veteran who recently retired (Jeff Conine) and a promising young star whose productivity has been curtailed by injuries (Grady Sizemore).

Conine was well-respected for his veteran contributions over 17 seasons, helping the Marlins win World Series titles in 1997 and 2003. He fell just shy of 2,000 hits with 1,982 and hit 214 homers with a .285 average. He was an All-Star in 1994 and 1995, batting .319 and .302 those years.

At the age of 23 in 2005, Sizemore hit .289 for the Indians with 111 runs, 185 hits, 22 homers and 22 steals. A star was born, which was desperately needed in Cleveland. He was even better the next year, getting selected to the All-Star team after leading the league with 134 runs scored and 53 doubles while hitting 28 home runs. Two more very good seasons followed, each resulting in All-Star and Gold Glove selection, but Sizemore's production has waned since due to a series of injuries.

Averill also displayed his talents while playing for the Indians in 11 of his 13 seasons. On April 16, 1929, he became the second American League player to hit a home run in his first at-bat in the majors. The six-time All-Star hit .332 with 198 hits his rookie season at the age of 27, the start of a 10-year run of steady production that belied his nickname "The Rock."

Averill batted .339 with 119 RBI the next season and then exploded by batting .333 with 33 homers and 143 RBI in 1931, along with 209 hits and 140 runs scored. He led the league with 232 hits in 1936 while hitting .378 and even batted .330 at the age of 36. Averill's career average was .318 and he ended up with 238 homers. It was his line drive that broke Dizzy Dean's toe during the 1937 All-Star Game.

Averill was a little bitter at having to wait 34 years after retirement to get elected to the Hall of Fame, saying, "What rights does anyone have to ignore cold hard facts in favor of looking for some intangible item to keep a person out of Cooperstown?"

His candidacy was probably hurt by the fact he never made it to the postseason until 1940, when he was a 38-year-old bench player for the Tigers. With 280 Career Win Shares, Averill's stats mark him as a borderline Hall of Fame player. His son, also named Earl Averill, played for five teams in seven major league seasons.

Three other outfielders deserve mention: Geoff Jenkins, Billy North and Woody Jensen. Jenkins played 11 seasons, mainly for the Brewers, and hit 221 career homers. He was an All-Star in 2003 but his best year was 2000, when he hit .303 with 34 homers and 94 RBI. North was a speedster who stole 395 bases, leading the AL with 75 steals in 1976 and 54 in 1974. Jensen hit .324 with 203 hits in 1935 and followed that up with 197 hits the next year, but he didn't do much else in his nine-year career.

The designated hitter is Ken Phelps, who hit 123 home runs, most of them while playing for his hometown Mariners. After languishing in the minors until he was 30, where he hit 151 homers, Phelps started demonstrating his dual ability to hit for power and get on base. A first baseman when playing the field, Phelps recorded 467 games at DH. He finished with a .374 OBP and an outstanding OPS+ of 132 — better than Hall of Famers Sandberg and Averill.

Not many pitchers have had a better start to their careers than Lincecum, the selection as right-handed starter despite his lack of longevity. After a promising rookie campaign in 2007, the wiry Lincecum has relied on his unorthodox pitching motion to dominate NL batters the next four seasons. "The Freak" led the league in winning percentage and strikeouts in 2008 while pitching for a bad team, resulting in him receiving the Cy Young Award. He then added a second Cy Young to his mantle in 2009 after pacing the league in complete games, shutouts and strikeouts. He finished second in ERA both years. Lincecum's performance slipped some in 2010, but he still led the league in strikeouts and SO/BB ratio for the third straight year and won 16 games. He came through with four wins in the postseason to guide the Giants to the championship.

It's a little unconventional to pick a pitcher who has just 69 career wins, but it seemed appropriate to go with a four-time All-Star who has produced four straight dominant years compared to pitchers like Todd Stottlemyre and Bruce Kison, who never made a single All-Star team or ever led the league in a pitching category. Kison's career high in victories was 14, while Stottlemyre's was 15.

Another righty, Fred Hutchinson, made one All-Star team but won just 95 games over 10 seasons. The much-hyped Seattle lad made an inauspicious debut against the Yankees on May 2, 1939, which just happened to be the first game Lou Gehrig missed after playing 2,130 consecutive games. Brought on in relief with the Yankees leading 13-0, Hutchinson gave up five walks, four hits and eight runs in two-thirds of an inning as the Bronx Bombers blasted the Tigers 22-2. Undaunted by such an unpleasant welcome to the big leagues, the gritty and determined hurler would later post seasons with 18 and 17 wins for the Tigers.

Remarked Tigers manager Steve O'Neill, "If I needed one game upon which my whole season was based, if my career depended on that one victory, I'd pick Hutch to pitch it for me."

Hutchinson, or "Hutch" as he was affectionately known, was named player-manager at the age of 32 for the last-place Tigers in 1952. "The one thing he demanded was a 100 percent effort, no alibi-ing at all," says Al Kaline, who joined the team in 1953 as an 18-year-old rookie. "He wanted his teams to be competitive and not embarrass themselves when they play."

Hutchinson later managed the Cardinals and Reds and was named NL Manager of the Year after leading the Cards to second place in 1957. The fiery, competitive skipper guided a young Reds team to the 1961 pennant, leading to another Manager of the Year award for Hutch. His team won 98 games the next year but finished third. He would win 830 games against 827 losses over 12 seasons before succumbing to lung cancer at age 45, a distinguished record that earned him selection as manager for the All-Time-Washington team.

As Hutchinson once said, "The ones who work the hardest are the ones who make it, the ones who win. Sometimes that's the only difference."

Our left-handed starter is Vean Gregg, who went 92–63 and posted 105 complete games with a sparkling 2.70 ERA. Gregg, who not surprisingly did not go by his given name of Sylveanus, won 20 or more games his first three seasons and led the AL with a 1.80 ERA as a rookie in 1911. He was later slowed by arm trouble. Gregg won 32 games with 14 shutouts during the 1910 season for the Portland Beavers of the Pacific Coast League. He also tossed a no-hitter that included eight consecutive strikeouts that season.

Southpaw Jon Lester has not received as much publicity as Lincecum, but through the 2011 season he had pitched in one less game and had seven more wins and seven fewer losses than Lincecum. Another notable lefty is Ed Brandt, who won 121 games (while losing 146) over 11 seasons.

Moving on to the bullpen, Randy Myers is an easy selection as the top reliever. He accumulated 347 saves, which ranks ninth on the career list and is more than Hall of Famers Rollie Fingers, Goose Gossage and Bruce Sutter posted. A two-time NL Reliever of the Year and four-time All-Star, Myers was part of the "Nasty Boys" bullpen for the Reds in 1990 and 1991 with Norm Charlton and Rob Dibble.

Gerry Staley would be a good pitcher to have on the staff, as the versatile righty successfully bounced back and forth between starting and relieving over his 15-year career. He won 134 games and made the All-Star team as both a starter (1952–53) and reliever (1960).

WEST VIRGINIA

*Names in **bold** represent Major League selections by position, followed by honorable mentions. Negro Leagues players are in italics. City of birth is in parentheses.*

Catcher — Andy Seminick (Pierce). Also: Steve Yeager (Huntington); Dick Brown (Shinnston)
First Base — John Kruk (Charleston). Also: Dick Hoblitzel (Waverly)
Second Base — Bill Mazeroski (Wheeling). Also: Dick Padden (Wheeling); Sam Barkley (Wheeling)
Third Base — George Brett (Glen Dale). Also: Toby Harrah (Sissonville); Gene Freese (Wheeling)
Shortstop — Jack Glasscock (Wheeling). Also: Larry Brown (Shinnston)
Outfield — Jesse Burkett (Wheeling)
Outfield — Farmer Weaver (Parkersburg)
Outfield — Greasy Neale (Parkersburg)
Designated Hitter — John Wockenfuss (Welch)
Right Handed Starter — Lew Burdette (Nitro). Also: Rick Reed (Huntington); Win Mercer (Chester); Max Butcher (Holden); Sheriff Blake (Ansted)
Left Handed Starter — Wilbur Cooper (Bearsville). Also: *Barney Brown* (Kimball)
Relief Pitcher — Chuck Stobbs (Wheeling). Also: Seth McClung (Lewisburg)
Manager — Charlie Manuel (Northfork)

The Names

Best Nickname: Ed "The Pitching Poet" Kenna
Other Nicknames: John "Sheriff" Blake; Jesse "The Crab" Burkett; "Pebbly Jack" Glasscock; Ezra "Salt

Rock" Midkiff; Alfred "Greasy" Neale; Dick "Brains" Padden; William "Rabbit" Robinson; Andrew "Skeeter" Shelton; Lewis "Bull" Smith; Jack "Crab" Warhop; William "Farmer" Weaver; Raymond "Corky" Withrow; Wayne "Rasty" Wright

Most Unusual Name: John Wockenfuss; Ezra Midkiff

All-Time Leaders

Games: George Brett, 2707
Hits: George Brett, 3154
Batting Average: Jesse Burkett, .338
Home Runs: George Brett, 317
RBI: George Brett, 1595
Stolen Bases: Jesse Burkett, 389
Wins: Wilbur Cooper, 216
Strikeouts: Wilbur Cooper, 1252
Saves: Seth McClung, 6
Future Star: Jedd Gyorko (Morgantown)
Best Player: George Brett

Historic Baseball Places

Bowen Field in Bluefield — The ballpark, which dates back to 1939, was the setting for the documentary *Minor League*. The box seats were recycled from the old Anaheim Stadium.

Appalachian Power Park in Charleston — Opened in 2005 as the home to the West Virginia Power in the South Atlantic League. The Charleston Baseball Wall of Fame features Dave Parker, who while playing for the Charleston Charlies in 1973 hit a home run that landed in a passing train car carrying coal.

Hack Wilson gravesite at Rosedale Cemetery in Martinsburg — The baseball community pitched in to build an impressive granite memorial to "One of Baseball's Immortals," who died penniless at age 48.

St. Cloud Commons in Huntington — One of the oldest parks around, dating back to 1910, is in need of repair and a team to call it home.

Notable Achievements

Jack Glasscock was the first West Virginia native to play in the majors, making his debut on May 1, 1879, two days ahead of fellow West Virginian John Shoup.

George Brett is the only player to win batting titles in three different decades: 1976, 1980 and 1990.

Jack Warhop (Hinton) surrendered the first two home runs of Babe Ruth's career, on May 6, 1915, and June 2, 1915.

Wilbur Cooper started two triple plays in the same season, 1920, making him the only pitcher to accomplish that feat.

Jesse Burkett has the most inside the park home runs in MLB history with 55.

Bowen Field in Bluefield, which dates back to 1939 but was essentially rebuilt in the 1970s after a fire, features box seats recycled from the old Anaheim Stadium. Two other oddities are the fact that it doesn't sell beer and that the West Virginia–Virginia border literally cuts through the middle of the ballpark (courtesy BallparkReviews.com).

West Virginia Baseball History Starts in Wheeling

Out of the hardscrabble fields of West Virginia's coal country have come some of baseball's greatest stars. The state has sent 118 players to the major leagues so far, and Wheeling leads the way with 15.

Wheeling churned out major league players with regularity in the nineteenth century including one of the greatest shortstops of his time in Jack Glasscock, Hall of Fame outfielder Jesse Burkett, plus second basemen Dick Padden and Sam Barkley.

The Moffet brothers, Joe and Sam, were less accomplished nineteenth-century players, but they also came from Wheeling. Sam was an outfielder and pitcher who batted .169 and posted a 6–29 record on the mound, while Joe was an infielder who batted .201 in his one season with the Toledo Blue Stockings in the American Association.

Bill Mazeroski, generally considered the greatest fielding second baseman in history, was born in Wheeling in 1936. He played his high school ball across the river at Warren Consolidated High School in Tiltonsville, Ohio.

The oddly named Hunkidori Base Ball Club of Wheeling hosted West Virginia's first baseball game in 1865, reports William Akin in his book on West Virginia baseball history.

Folks in Wheeling thought they were seeing some pretty good baseball as local amateur teams such as the Baltics started flexing their muscle. But the Baltics were in for a rude awakening when Harry Wright and the Cincinnati Red Stockings came to town. The Red Stockings won their exhibition handily in 1868, but they were still viewed as an amateur team since not all the players were getting paid. When the Red Stockings returned to Wheeling the next summer, they had made history by becoming the first professional team in baseball history. A large crowd filled the Fair Grounds and watched as the Baltics went down to a resounding 44–0 defeat.

The first organized pro team in Wheeling dates back to 1877, with Glasscock playing on the Wheeling Standard club during their one-year run. After his major league career wound down he returned and helped Wheeling win the Iron & Oil League championship in 1895.

The Wheeling Stogies played in various leagues from 1899–1934. One of the pitchers on the 1901 Stogies team was Ed Kenna, who was born in Charleston. Kenna was known as "The Pitching Poet," because he liked to entertain teammates by composing rhymes. His father, John Kenna, who was the Democratic minority leader in the U. S. Senate, died in 1893 when his son was 16.

There were few highlights for "The Pitching Poet" to muse about, as he appeared in only two major league games for the Philadelphia Athletics in 1902. Kenna was seriously injured in a trolley car incident in 1905, along with some of his teammates on the Louisville Colonels, and although he was able to resume his pitching career he died of heart failure at age 34.

Ezra "Salt Rock" Midkiff picked up his nickname as a tribute to his hometown. Midkiff was a minor league teammate of Babe Ruth during the Bambino's brief stay with the Baltimore Orioles in 1914, and he spent most of his career in the minors while the Babe obviously went on to bigger and better things. Midkiff appeared in 104 games for the Yankees in 1912–13 and his major league career was already finished by the time he joined Ruth on the Orioles.

All-Time West Virginia Selections

At catcher, Andy Seminick could be counted on for excellent production despite less than regular playing time. He managed to post double-figure home runs for eight straight seasons despite averaging just 359 at-bats those years. He never hit much for average but did have a respectable OBP and wound up slugging 164 homers over a 15-season career. Seminick was the first West Virginia player to be named to an All-Star team, representing the Phillies in the 1949 All-Star Game. However, he had his best year in 1950 with 24 homers, 113 hits and a .288 average — good enough for fourteenth place in MVP voting — as he helped Philadelphia's "Whiz Kids" reach the World Series.

Another notable catcher from West Virginia is Huntington's Steve Yeager, who played in four World Series with the Dodgers. A lifetime .228 hitter, Yeager was a skilled receiver with a strong throwing arm. He was named co–MVP of the 1981 World Series after hitting two home runs including a game-winner. After getting hit in the throat with splinters from a shattered bat in 1976, Yeager started wearing a throat protector that dangled below his catcher's mask, a practice that is now the norm.

John Kruk played more than 400 games in the outfield, but eventually settled in as a first baseman. He was named to three consecutive NL All-Star teams as a first baseman, 1991–1993. He literally retired in the middle of a game in 1995, perhaps the only time that has ever happened. It worked out neatly for him, as he ended up with exactly 100 home runs and a .300 average in 1,200 games. Maybe that's why he walked away so suddenly. Earning honorable mention status was Dick Hoblitzel, a steady first baseman in the early part of the twentieth century who compiled 1,310 hits over 11 seasons.

Few second basemen in any era could match the skill of Bill Mazeroski. The eight-time Gold Glove winner was elected to the Hall of Fame mainly due to his fielding prowess but also for hitting the most dramatic, most improbable home run in World Series history. His famous 1960 blast remains the only walk-off Game 7 home run in World Series history. It propelled the underdog Pirates to their first championship since 1925, and it came against the hated Yankees, who had beaten the Bucs 38–3 in their three victories. Mazeroski was a most unlikely batting hero, as he ended his career with a .260 batting average, .299 on-base percentage and 84 OPS+.

Not only is Mazeroski generally considered the best-fielding second baseman of all-time, Bill James believes he might be the best fielder at any position, crediting him with more Win Shares (113) for his defense than any other player in history. Maz led the NL in double plays eight times, assists nine times and fielding percentage three times, ending up with a .983 percentage.

Although George Brett played his high school ball in California, the Hall of Fame third baseman was born in Glen Dale, West Virginia. When one thinks of Brett, a specific, overarching image comes to mind — seeing him sprinting out of the Kansas City dugout like a crazed lunatic to dispute Umpire Tim McClelland's decision to rule him out for having too much pine tar on his bat. It almost overshadows the fact Brett was one of the greatest hitters in baseball history, and is generally considered the second-best overall third baseman behind Mike Schmidt. Bill James ranks him the 30th-best player overall. The competitive juices churned strongly in Brett, who once remarked, "If a tie is like kissing your sister, losing is like kissing your grandmother with her teeth out."

Brett's 3,154 hits rank fifteenth on the all-time list and number one among third basemen (Paul Molitor has more, but many came as a DH). The lefty swinger won three batting titles over a span of 14 years. He led the AL in hits, slugging percentage, OPS and triples three times, doubles twice and batted over .300 11 times, flirting with .400 late in the 1980 season before ending up at .390, which remains the highest average in the American League since Ted Williams posted .406 in 1941. Brett led the Royals to the pennant that magical year of 1980 and was named AL Most Valuable Player, cementing his status as a Royals icon.

Named to 13 All-Star teams, Brett was a steady if not spectacular fielder at third, winning one Gold Glove in 1985. He batted .335 that year with a career-high 30 home runs and 112 RBI to lead the Royals to their first and only World Series. He was also the first to hit three home runs in an ALCS game, accomplishing the feat in Game 3 against the Yankees in 1978.

Toby Harrah had a very productive career as a third baseman and shortstop. He played slightly more games at third (1,099) than he did at short (813), so he gets to back up Brett on Team West Virginia. Harrah, who made four All-Star teams (three as a shortstop), is probably the most accomplished player whose last name is a palindrome. He fell just short of 2,000 hits (with 1,954), and fell just short of 200 home runs (with 195).

By the time Burkett was getting his career started fellow Wheeling native Jack Glasscock was nearing the tail end of an illustrious career. Glasscock was without peer when it came to fielding, leading the league in fielding percentage and assists six times and combining with first baseman Bill Phillips and second baseman Fred Dunlap to form what became known as the "Stonewall infield" on the Cleveland Blues. When he retired in 1895 Glasscock held all the career fielding records for shortstops.

Nicknamed "Pebbly Jack" for his habit of picking out the pebbles from the infield, Glasscock was no slouch with the bat either. He led the NL in hits twice and average once and finished his career with 2,041 hits and a .290 average. He struck out only 196 times in his career in 7033 at-bats, which is amazing considering seven batters have struck out more times in a single season since 2007.

Glasscock probably set a record for switching leagues, as he jumped from the National League to the Union Association, back to the National League, then on to the Players League, which he abandoned before even playing to return once again to the National League. As he succinctly put it, "I have played long enough for glory, now it is a matter of dollars and cents."

Heading up the outfield is the lefty-swinging Burkett, who amassed 2,850 hits during a 16-year career that bridged the nineteenth and twentieth centuries. He ranks eighteenth all-time with a .338 average. His 2,273 singles rank thirteenth, with many coming from expertly placed bunts.

Although he started his career as a pitcher, a 3–10 mark with a 5.57 ERA his first season convinced him to make a full-time switch to the outfield. He batted .405 in 1895 and then followed that up by doing even better the next season, batting .410 with 240 hits and 160 runs scored. The list of players who have hit over .400 in consecutive seasons is a short one: Ty Cobb, Rogers Hornsby, Ed Delahanty and Burkett.

Burkett exceeded 200 hits six times, batted over .400 twice (coming close a third time at .396), stole 389 bases and finished with a .415 OBP. He led the National League in runs twice, hits three times, average three times and was always among the leaders in bases on balls. Eleven times he batted over .300.

Known as "The Crab" for his confrontational demeanor, Burkett was once thrown out of both games of a doubleheader after getting into skirmishes with the other team and umpires. Such behavior didn't exactly endear him to fans, sportswriters and teammates such as Cy Young, who played with him on the Cleveland Spiders for eight seasons.

Joining Burkett in the outfield is Farmer Weaver, a nineteenth-century player whose claim to fame is hitting for the cycle while getting six hits in a nine-inning game. That's only done about once every 119 years. Weaver accomplished the feat in 1890 and it wasn't matched until Ian Kinsler did it against the Orioles in 2009.

The third outfielder is Greasy Neale, who played eight seasons in the majors but earned his fame as a football coach. Long before Deion Sanders was grabbing headlines for his two-sport feats, Neale was making his mark in professional football and baseball. He led the Reds with 10 hits and a .357 average in the 1919 World Series, a feat that was overshadowed by the Black Sox scandal.

John Wockenfuss has one of the all-time great names in baseball. He hung around for 12 seasons as a role player who bounced between catcher, first, outfield and designated hitter. His 146 games at DH earn him that spot.

The All-Time West Virginia team has a reliable ace in righty Lew Burdette. The two-time All-Star twice won 20 games and posted double-figure wins in 10 straight seasons. He pitched in two World Series for the Milwaukee Braves, defeating the Yankees in 1957 in dominating fashion. His three complete game victories included two shutouts, and Burdette was named Series MVP for leading the Milwaukee franchise to its only championship.

Burdette relied on pinpoint control throughout his career — his BB/9IP ratio was 1.8 — and was rumored to throw a spitball, which he used to his advantage. As he explained, "Let them think I throw it. That gives me an edge because it's another pitch they have to worry about."

Often overlooked is the fact that Burdette was the winning pitcher for a historic game in 1959 in which he outdueled Harvey Haddix, who had a perfect game through 12 innings before losing the no-hitter, the shutout and the game in the thirteenth. Burdette would throw a masterpiece of his own the next year, pitching a no-hitter while facing the minimum 27 batters (one batter was hit by pitch and then erased by double play). He was also a dangerous hitter who slugged two home runs in a game three times.

The best left-handed starter is Wilbur Cooper, who won 216 games over 15 seasons, primarily for the Pirates. He averaged over 20 wins a season for a seven-year period (1918–24), leading the National League in wins, innings pitched and shutouts once and complete games twice. In 1924 Cooper became the first NL southpaw to win 200 games, and he remains the Pirates franchise leader in career wins and season ERA (1.87). Like Burdette, Cooper was also adept with the bat, slugging four homers in 1922 and batting .346 another season.

Another southpaw worth mentioning is Barney Brown, who was a good pitcher on some bad Negro Leagues teams between 1931 and 1949. Relying on a screwball and pinpoint control to keep batters at bay, Brown pitched in five East-West All-Star games.

Chuck Stobbs started about half his games, but he's the best of a weak bunch in the bullpen. Stobbs recorded a 4.29 ERA with 221 relief appearances and his ERA+ of 95 is better than Seth McClung's 80. Stobbs' main claim to fame is serving up a 565-foot home run to Mickey Mantle in Griffith Stadium in 1953 that is considered the longest ever hit. The big and burly McClung (6-foot-6 and 280 pounds) pitched in 126 games in relief between 2003 and 2009 while also starting 51 games. His six saves are the most in West Virginia history.

Ridiculed by critics as a country bumpkin who was in over his head, Phillies manager Charlie Manuel had the last laugh by leading the team to a World Series title in 2008, followed by a return visit the next year that came up short against the Yankees. Manuel's teams have finished first or second in every one of his nine full seasons as skipper, including five straight division crowns with the Phillies, making him the best choice as manager for the All-Time West Virginia team.

WISCONSIN

*Names in **bold** represent Major League selections by position, followed by honorable mentions. Negro Leagues players are in italics. City of birth is in parentheses.*

Catcher — **Damian Miller (LaCrosse).** Also: Billy Sullivan (Oakland); Charlie Ganzel (Waterford); Scott Servais (LaCrosse)
First Base — **Ed Konetchy (LaCrosse).** Also: Fred Merkle (Watertown); Fred Luderus Milwaukee); Joe Hauser (Milwaukee)
Second Base — **Mark Grudzielanek (Milwaukee).** Also: Jim Gantner (Fond Du Lac); Duane Kuiper (Racine)
Third Base — **Lave Cross (Milwaukee).** Also: Ken Keltner (Milwaukee); Joe Randa (Milwaukee); Eric Hinske (Manasha)
Shortstop — **Harvey Kuenn (West Allis).** Also: Tony Kubek (Milwaukee); George McBride (Milwaukee)
Outfield — **Al Simmons (Milwaukee)**
Outfield — **Ginger Beaumont (Rochester)**
Outfield — **Andy Pafko (Boyceville).** Also: Abner Dalrymple (Gratiot); *Walter Davis* (Madison); Happy Felsch (Milwaukee); Davy Jones (Cambria); Braggo Roth (Burlington); Walt Wilmot (Plover); Rick Reichardt (Madison); Chet Laabs (Milwaukee)
Designated Hitter — **Craig Kusick (Milwaukee)**
Right Handed Starter — **Kid Nichols (Madison).** Also: Burleigh Grimes (Emerald); Addie Joss (Woodland); Brad Radke (Eau Claire); Pink Hawley (Beaver Dam)
Left Handed Starter — **Ed Killian (Racine).** Also: Jarrod Washburn (LaCrosse); Johnny Schmitz (Wausau); Zane Smith (Madison); Shane Rawley (Racine)
Relief Pitcher — **Bob Wickman (Green Bay).** Also: Ryne Duren (Cazanovia); Billy Hoeft (Oshkosh); Rich Loiselle (Neenah)
Manager — **Pants Rowland (Platteville).** Also: Harvey Kuenn (West Allis)

The Names

Best Nickname: Roy "St. Croix Boy Wonder" Patterson
Other Nicknames: Morrie "Snooker" Arnovich; John "Moose" Baxter; Bob "Butterball" Butz; Walter "Steel Arm" Davis; "Old Pardee" Elliott; Oscar "Happy" Felsch; Jim "Gumby" Gantner; Burleigh

"Ol' Stubblebeard" Grimes; Joey "Unser Choe" Hauser; Emerson "Pink" Hawley; Albert "Beany" Jacobson; Davy "Kangaroo" Jones; Adrian "The Human Hairpin" Joss; Ken "Butch" Keltner; "Twilight Ed" Killian; Ed "The LaCrosse Lulu," "The Big Bohemian," Candy Kid" and "Edward the Mighty" Konetchy; Craig "Mongo" Kusick; Joe "Old Hustler" Mathes; Fred "Bonehead" Merkle; Charles "Kid" Nichols; Braggo "The Globetrotter" Roth; Clarence "Pants" Rowland; Johnny "Bear Tracks" Schmitz; "Bucketfoot Al" Simmons; Bob "Mr. Baseball" Uecker

Most Unusual Name: Mark Grudzielanek; Fabian Gaffke; Rocco Krsnich

All-Time Leaders

Games: Lave Cross, 2275
Hits: Al Simmons, 2927
Batting Average: Al Simmons, .334
Home Runs: Al Simmons, 307
RBI: Al Simmons, 1827
Stolen Bases: Walt Wilmot, 381
Wins: Kid Nichols, 361
Strikeouts: Kid Nichols, 1868
Saves: Bob Wickman, 267
Future Stars: Jordan Zimmerman (Auburndale); Ryan Rohlinger (West Bend)
Best Player: Kid Nichols

Historic Baseball Places

Miller Park in Milwaukee — New stadium for Brewers opened in 2001 with a retractable roof. Autograph Alley features a large number of baseballs autographed by baseball stars and Brewers fans. Outside the park one can find statues honoring Hall of Famers Hank Aaron and Robin Yount as well as Commissioner Bud Selig, a Milwaukee native who was instrumental in bringing baseball back to his hometown in 1970.

Merkle Field in Watertown—Ballfield named in honor of Watertown native Fred Merkle, who is also honored with a memorial monument at the Octagon House-Watertown Historical Society. Memorial monuments to Addie Joss and Pete Kleinow can be found at Washington Park in Watertown, where the two future major leaguers played for Watertown's Sacred Hearts Team. Other Deadball Era players honored with monuments in the state are Bert "Pete" Husting at the Limestone School Museum in Mayville and William Sullivan, Sr., at Jones Park in Fort Atkinson, all thanks to the efforts of SABR member David Stalker.

Fox Cities Stadium in Appleton — Opened in 1995 as the new home of the Wisconsin Timber Rattlers. Baseball in Appleton dates back to 1891. The team operated many years as the Fox City Foxes, with Jack McKeon, Earl Weaver and Cal Ripken, Sr., serving as managers. Players who have played for the franchise include Boog Powell, Goose Gossage, Harold Baines, Dave McNally and Sparky Lyle.

Notable Achievements

Roy Patterson (Stoddard) won the first official American League game on April 24, 1901.

Ed Konetchy hit singles in consecutive games (on Sept. 28 and 30) to deprive New York Giants pitchers Ferdie Schupp and Rube Benton of no-hitters during the Giants' 26-game winning streak in 1916.

In 1908 **Addie Joss** became the second American League player to pitch a perfect game, four years after Cy Young pitched the first.

Kid Nichols is the youngest pitcher to reach 300 wins — he was 30 years old when he reached the mark on Sept. 7, 1900.

Lave Cross is the only major leaguer to play for four different teams (representing different leagues) in the same city. He played for the Philadelphia A's in the American Association, Players League and American League as well as the Philadelphia Phillies in the National League.

Walt Wilmot set a record by walking six times in a game on August 22, 1891, a mark tied by Jimmie Foxx in 1938.

Dave Koslo (Menasha) ended his career by surrendering a walk-off home run to the only batter he faced in 1955 — Bill Virdon.

The Cream City's On-and-Off Romance with Big-League Baseball

Abner Dalrymple became the first Wisconsin native to play in the major leagues when he debuted with the Milwaukee Grays on May 1, 1878. Dalrymple was a pretty good player who led the National League in runs and hits in 1880 and home runs in 1885 — he ended up playing 12 seasons.

The state's baseball history revolves around developments in Milwaukee, which was nicknamed the "Cream City" for the distinctive cream-colored bricks that were produced from the unique clay found in the region. In his book *The Rise of Milwaukee Baseball*, Dennis Pajot reports that organized baseball can be traced back to 1859, followed by the formation of the Milwaukee Base Ball Club in 1860. Baseball's popularity blossomed with the early success of the Cream City Club, which formed in 1865 and began traveling around the region to compete in tournaments. Pajot notes that a crowd of 2,000 watched the Cream City Club get clobbered by Harry Wright's powerhouse Cincinnati Red Stockings at Cream City Park on July 30, 1869 — final score was 85–7.

Milwaukee kept getting a taste of the big time, only to have it taken away. The Milwaukee Grays joined the National League in 1878 but lasted only one year, finishing last with a 15–45 record. The Milwaukee Brewers were a part of the short-lived Union Association in 1884, the first appearance of a name that would keep reappearing. The Brewers began competing in the Northwestern League and then the Western League, which gained strength and eventually evolved into the

American League. The Brewers were founding members of the American League in 1901, but this again lasted just one season as the franchise moved to St. Louis and was renamed the Browns.

The Brewers lived on as a minor league team in the American Association for the next half-century. Bill Veeck explored moving the Browns back to Milwaukee in the early 1950s, but nothing materialized. The city built County Stadium in hopes of attracting another MLB team and it paid off. The Boston Braves had moved their Triple-A affiliate to Milwaukee in 1947, and it was the Braves that surprised the baseball world by announcing a move to the Cream City shortly before the 1953 season.

Bud Selig, baseball's ninth commissioner, grew up watching the minor league Milwaukee Brewers play in his hometown. After the Braves moved to Milwaukee in 1953 the automobile magnet became one of the largest stockholders. When the Braves fled to Atlanta after the 1965 season Selig started looking for a way to get major league baseball back to the Cream City. He had an agreement to buy the White Sox in 1969 with the intent to move the club to Milwaukee, but American League officials nixed that plan. However, in 1970 Selig was able to buy the bankrupt and beleaguered Seattle Pilots and move the franchise to Milwaukee. The Brewers were back in the big leagues.

As commissioner, Selig has been responsible for introducing the wild-card format, realignment into three divisions in each league and interleague play. He has also been widely criticized for failing to act while the steroids era made a mockery of cherished records such as the single-season and career home run marks. Selig eventually commissioned the Mitchell Report and introduced tougher testing, but the damage had been done.

Two Milwaukee natives have been honored by the Hall of Fame for their broadcasting careers: Tony Kubek and "Mr. Baseball" himself, Bob Uecker. Kubek, whose father Tony was an outfielder in the minors with the Milwaukee Brewers, played one year at Bay View High School in Milwaukee before the school dropped baseball. So he turned to the city's sandlot leagues to play the game, where he attracted the attention of scouts from the Yankees. The Yankees signed him as soon as he graduated from high school and within three years he was in the big leagues for good.

Uecker has become synonymous with Milwaukee baseball, and not because of his career as a .200 hitting catcher. He started his broadcasting career with the Brewers in 1970, relying on an upbeat personality and self-deprecating humor to connect with fans. He led the league in "go get 'em next time," and once noted that the best way to catch a knuckleball is to wait until the ball stops rolling and then pick it up. "I set records that will never be equaled. In fact, I hope 90% of them don't even get printed," Uecker said.

Wisconsin has produced 240 major leaguers and 55 were born in Milwaukee. In addition to Uecker and Kubek, other Milwaukee-born players include Hall of Famer Al Simmons, George McBride, Fred Luderus, Ken Keltner, Mark Grudzielanek, Craig Kusick, Lave Cross and Joe Randa.

Another Milwaukee star who is no longer celebrated is Oscar "Happy" Felsch, who was born to German immigrants. Felsch learned the game on the sandlots of Milwaukee's north side before attracting attention for his stellar play for semi-pro teams all over Wisconsin. His professional career started as a shortstop with the Milwaukee Mollys of the Wisconsin-Illinois League in 1913, followed by more seasoning with the Milwaukee Brewers, then a Double-A club. In 1914 Felsch reportedly blasted a home run over 500 feet at Athletic Park while leading the American Association with 19 home runs.

Felsch debuted with the White Sox in 1915, showing great promise by batting .300 his second year and knocking in 102 runs (second in AL) with a .308 average for the world champion Sox in 1917. All of Milwaukee was in a frenzy of excitement over their new hometown star, who had vanquished the Giants with his bat and his glove. However, Felsch was one of the

Oscar "Happy" Felsch learned the game on the sandlots of Milwaukee's north side before joining the White Sox in 1915. He batted .300 his second year and knocked in 102 runs to help the Sox win the title in 1917. However, Felsch was one of the eight players implicated in the Black Sox scandal over the 1919 World Series and banned from baseball for life. He later admitted his guilt and expressed remorse for his actions, recognizing that he short-circuited his career while on the verge of stardom (Library of Congress, Prints & Photographs Division, LC-DIG-ggbain-31142).

eight players implicated in the Black Sox scandal over the 1919 World Series and banned from baseball for life. The uneducated and pliable Felsch later admitted his guilt and expressed remorse for his actions, recognizing that he short-circuited his career while on the verge of stardom. He was batting .338 with 115 RBI in 1920 when his career unceremoniously ended. Felsch would barnstorm around Wisconsin with some of his fellow blackballed teammates and later play semi-pro ball in Montana and Canada, but the player once called Milwaukee's finest was no longer "The Pride of Teutonia Avenue."

If you're paying a visit to Milwaukee and Miller Park, then don't overlook the monument honoring the 1901 Milwaukee Brewers, who played in the inaugural season of the American League. The plaque names the members of the team, which featured five Wisconsin natives: Ed Bruyette, Davy Jones, George McBride, Pink Hawley and Pete Husting.

All-Time Wisconsin Selections

Uecker does not make the All-Time Wisconsin team at catcher — he falls just a little short with his OPS+ of 62 — but his warm embrace of mediocrity seems to have rubbed off on his fellow Wisconsin catchers during the postseason. Uecker won a World Series ring with the St. Louis Cardinals in 1964 but did not see any postseason action, which is not surprising considering his .198 average that year.

Billy Sullivan won a World Series with the White Sox in 1906, although he was not much help as he batted 0-for-21 in the Series. Charlie Ganzel won a World Series with the Detroit Wolverines in 1887 (it was just an exhibition series then), batting .224 over the 14 games. Finally, we have Damian Miller, who was with the Diamondbacks when they won the 2001 World Series over the Yankees despite the fact that he batted .190 and struck out 11 times in 21 at-bats. Can't anybody here play this game?

Despite his weak performance that postseason, Miller gets selected as the All-Time catcher for Team Wisconsin. Miller collected 834 hits playing from 1997–2007, getting to play his last three years for the Brewers. He made the All-Star team for Arizona in 2002, even though his average was just .249 that season. He had some pop in his bat, hitting 87 homers and batting .262 lifetime. He was an above-average fielder, leading NL catchers in putouts and assists in 2001 and in fielding percentage two times.

Sullivan was a weak hitter but a terrific receiver who led the AL in fielding average four times. He was instrumental in turning Ed Walsh into a great pitcher and later served as a mentor to Ray Schalk. Ganzel started out with the St. Paul White Caps in the short-lived Union Association in 1884, going on to play 14 years for four teams. A .259 lifetime batter, he played all the positions on the field except pitcher. Forty-three years after his debut (and 13 years after his death), Ganzel's son, Babe, made his major league debut.

We also gave strong consideration (OK, not really) to Bob Scherbarth, who in 1950 appeared in one game for the Red Sox as a defensive replacement at catcher. He didn't make it up to the plate and didn't handle any chances during his one inning of glory. At least he can say he didn't screw up.

At first base we have "Big Ed" Konetchy, who certainly tops all Wisconsin players by having the most nicknames. He was also known as Edward the Mighty, the LaCrosse Lulu, Koney, the Big Bohemian and Candy Kid. The last one originated from his job working in a candy factory while in his teens. Konetchy accumulated 182 triples — tied for fifteenth on the all-time list — and he is the only player in the top 20 who isn't in the Hall of Fame. He never led the league in triples, but he had at least nine triples in 14 of his 15 seasons, finishing in the top 10 nine times. His best season was probably 1915, when he was playing for the Pittsburgh Rebels in the Federal League — he had career highs with 181 hits, 93 RBI, 18 triples, and a .314 average while also leading the league in total bases.

Konetchy played in the Deadball Era, so he only hit 74 home runs, but he ended up with 2,150 hits. He was an outstanding fielder with phenomenal range, leading NL first basemen in assists and putouts five times and fielding percentage six times. He even stole 255 bases.

Vastly underrated as an overall player, Konetchy had a career filled with interesting accomplishments. He stole home twice in a game on Sept. 30, 1907. He hit two inside-the-park home runs in a game on August 5, 1912. He not only pitched in a game in 1913, he won it after going 4⅔ innings in relief and allowing one hit and no runs. He got 10 consecutive hits from June 21 to July 1, 1919, tying a record that was later broken by Pinky Higgins. He hit a ball completely out of Robison Field in St. Louis. In 1913 he drew a walk off Christy Mathewson to stop his streak of 68 innings without a walk. In 1920 he set a record for most chances by a first baseman in a World Series game with 19 (17 putouts and two assists) during Game 3. Edward the Mighty indeed!

From the player who seemingly could do no wrong to the player most vilified for one mistake. Fred Merkle spent his entire career being called "Bonehead" for a base running gaffe he committed with the Giants in the heat of the pennant race in 1908, failing to touch second as the trail runner while the supposed winning run was scoring. Given new life, the Cubs went on to win the pennant and a second consecutive World Series, although the team hasn't won another title since.

The problem with crucifying Merkle for his youthful exuberance was that touching the base under those circumstances seemed to be an optional thing in those days. Furthermore, it's not like it was the last game of the season — the Giants played 17 more games that year (including the makeup game) and won 11 of them. Still, an intelligent, skilled ballplayer spent the rest of his career getting asked about the cursed play instead of being appreciated for his many accomplishments.

Merkle started his career the same year as Konetchy but was not his equal as a batter or fielder (although he too had excellent range). He helped lead three different teams to five pennants, but lost each time in the Series. Merkle ended up with 1,580 hits, a .273 average and 60 homers, finishing in the top 10 in RBI five times and top 10 in homers four times.

Another contemporary of Konetchy and Merkle was Fred Luderus, who was the starting first baseman for the Phillies from 1911–19. Luderus hit .301 and drove in 99 runs in 1911, but his numbers slipped the next three years. He finished in the top 10 in homers eight times in nine years, mainly because he was adept at going deep in Philadelphia's Baker Bowl. His OPS+ of 150 ranked second in 1915, a year in which he batted .315. The Phillies won the pennant that season, but lost in the World Series to the Red Sox despite Luderus batting .438.

Not to be overlooked is Joe Hauser, "Unser Choe," who hit 80 home runs in six seasons but is best known for his slugging feats in the minors. Hauser hit 63 homers for Baltimore in the International League in 1930 and followed up with 69 for the Minneapolis Millers in 1933, making him the first player to twice hit over 60 home runs in professional baseball. Hauser finished second to Babe Ruth with 27 homers in 1924 while driving in 115 runs, but he shattered his knee the next year and was viewed as damaged goods by major league teams after that. Surely someone could have used a guy who hit 399 home runs in 16 minor league seasons.

Team Wisconsin's second baseman, Mark Grudzielanek, makes a good trivia question subject: which baseball player from Milwaukee appeared on *Saturday Night Live* in 1997? Guess Uecker was unavailable that week. After being unsigned in 2009, Grudzielanek joined his sixth and final team, the Indians, in 2010. Except for his abbreviated rookie season, he never batted below .270 in any of his other 14 seasons. He batted .306 with 201 hits and 33 steals for Montreal in 1996, making the All-Star team that year, then led the league with 54 doubles the next season. A sure-handed fielder who has also played 626 games at short, Grudzielanek won a Gold Glove with the Royals in 2006.

Honorable mention goes to Jim Gantner, who had similar qualities as a player. Steady but not spectacular, Gantner compiled 1,696 hits playing his entire 17-year career for the Brewers. A .274 lifetime batter, he had 137 steals (four more than Grudzielanek), and led the league in assists once and putouts twice. Nicknamed "Gumby," he batted .333 for the Brewers in a losing effort during the 1982 World Series.

Another notable second baseman, Duane Kuiper, inexplicably hit home runs in the minors at a pace 14 times more frequent than he did in the majors. After blasting a home run once every 238 at-bats in the minors, Kuiper mysteriously lost his power and only went yard once every 3,379 at-bats during his 12-year major league career. Must be he got off the juice.

Kuiper holds the major league record for most at-bats with only one career home run—3,379. He also played the most games by a non-pitcher with one or fewer home runs—1,057. That's why it's surprising to learn that such a non-slugger as Kuiper is the last major league player to hit two bases-loaded triples in the same game, which he did on July 27, 1978. Five other players are known to have accomplished this rare feat: Elmer Valo in 1949 and Bill Bruton in 1959 in addition to nineteenth-century players Sam Thompson, Heinie Reitz and Willie Clark. Kuiper didn't have particularly good range but did lead AL second basemen in fielding percentage two times. He was a hustling, scrappy player who got the most out of his talent.

At third base we have two candidates whose qualifications are close. Lafayette "Lave" Cross played from 1887–1907, accumulating 2,651 hits with a .292 average. He batted over .300 five times and his best season was 1894, when he batted .387 with 210 hits, 128 runs and 132 RBI. The next season Cross drove in 101 runs despite hitting just two home runs. He would top that by driving in 108 runs in 1902 without hitting a single home run. He was an above-average fielder by the standards of the day, leading third basemen in fielding percentage four times, which is pretty good for a player who started out at catcher and ended up catching 324 games. Only four third basemen in the Hall of Fame have more hits than Cross: George Brett, Wade Boggs, Brooks Robinson and Paul Molitor (who got many of his hits as a DH).

Cross edges out Ken Keltner, who was one of the best defensive third basemen of his time. He led the AL in fielding percentage twice, assists four times and putouts once. His defensive brilliance was directly responsible for breaking up Joe DiMaggio's 56-game hitting streak on July 17, 1941—Keltner made two spectacular back-handed, diving stops to rob the Yankee Clipper of hits. A seven-time All-Star, "Butch" Keltner received MVP votes in five seasons, retiring with 1,570 hits, 163 home runs and a .276 average. His best season was his last year as a regular, 1948, when he batted .297 and set career highs with 31 homers, 119 RBI, 91 runs scored and a line of .395/.522/.917. Furthermore, it was his three-run homer that led the Indians to victory over the Red Sox in a playoff to decide the pennant that year. The Indians would go on to win the World Series—they haven't won one since.

If you compare the two players by Career Win Shares, then Cross holds a big advantage over Keltner, 279–175, according to The Baseball Gauge. Bill James ranks Cross the 33rd-best third baseman, two spots ahead of Keltner. Finally, Cross scores 85 points on the Gray Ink Test to 71 for Keltner. With the two pretty equal in fielding ability and with Keltner's slight edge in batting ability cancelled out by Cross greater compiling of batting stats, the deciding factor was longevity—Cross played 21 seasons to 13 for Keltner (10 with significant playing time).

Shortstop posed another dilemma. The best candidate seems to be Tony Kubek, who was named to All-Star teams in three years with the Yankees, helping the team win six pennants and three championships during his nine seasons. An outstanding fielder, he was Rookie of the Year in 1957. Interestingly, the Yankees collapsed in Game 7 of the 1960 World Series against the Pirates when Kubek had to leave the game after being struck in the throat by a ground ball. Forced to retire at age 29 due to chronic neck and back pain, Kubek moved on to a successful broadcast career.

We stretched the rules a little, but we came up with a better shortstop — Harvey Kuenn. We had to overlook the fact that he played 826 games in the outfield compared to 748 at short — close enough we say. Kuenn started his career as a shortstop for the Tigers, winning AL Rookie of the Year honors in 1953. He was an All-Star in his first eight seasons, five of them as a shortstop. As a shortstop he led the AL in putouts (twice) and assists, then later led AL outfielders in putouts and AL right fielders in fielding percentage. Kuenn set career highs in hits, runs, homers and RBI while playing short, so he's legitimately qualified to be the shortstop for the All-Time Wisconsin team.

Kuenn led the league in hits four seasons, going over 200 hits his first two years, and he also finished first in doubles three times. He led the AL in batting with a .353 average in 1959 and batted over .300 nine times in 15 seasons. In a strange footnote to history, Kuenn made the last out in two of Sandy Koufax's four no-hitters.

Kuenn was part of a controversial trade in 1960 when he was traded to the Indians for their star slugger, Rocky Colavito. Although he batted .308 in his one year with the Tribe, Kuenn's skill as a singles hitter did not win over fans and he was traded at the end of the season to the Giants. He hit .304 in 1962 as the Giants won the pennant, then played four more years before retiring in 1966 with 2,092 hits and a .303 average.

Placing Kuenn at shortstop leaves room in the outfield for three deserving players: Al Simmons, Ginger Beaumont and Andy Pafko. Simmons got his start playing for the Milwaukee Brewers, who were then a minor league team. He wasted little time demonstrating his abilities after making the Philadelphia Athletics as a 21-year-old rookie in 1924 and quickly became a favorite of manager Connie Mack. He was nicknamed "Bucketfoot Al" because he strode toward third when swinging, which is generally considered a bad technique known as "stepping in the bucket." Simmons possessed top-notch ability in all facets of the game, hitting for power and average, showing good range in left field and having a strong throwing arm.

Simmons teamed up with Mickey Cochrane and Jimmie Foxx to form a powerful lineup that led the A's to three straight pennants (1929–31). He was instrumental in helping the team capture the first of two consecutive championships. Down 8–0 to the Cubs in the seventh inning of Game 4 of the 1929 Series, the A's rallied to bat around and score 10 runs that inning. Simmons providing the spark with a leadoff home run and then singled and scored what proved to be the decisive run later in that pivotal inning.

He drove in more than 100 runs and batted over .300 in each of his first 11 seasons, leading the league with 157 RBI in 1929. Simmons collected over 200 hits five straight seasons and six times overall. His 253 hits in 1925 are the fifth-most in baseball history — he came in second in MVP voting that year after hitting .387. His 165 RBI in 1930 are the thirteenth-best ever, while his .392 average in 1927 ranks 22nd among players in the twentieth century. He won back-to-back batting crowns in 1930 and 1931, with averages of .381 and .390, and finished in the top 10 in home runs, slugging and OPS 10 times. He fell just short of 3,000 hits with 2,927, and retired with a .334 average, which ranks 23rd on the all-time list. Simmons was inducted into the Hall of Fame in 1953.

Clarence "Ginger" Beaumont was a skilled batsman and speedy base runner who played from 1899–1910. You could say he was the king of firsts. He became the first player to bat in a World Series game when he stepped up to the plate on October 1, 1903. During his rookie season he became the first player to get six infield hits in one game. He was also the first player to score six runs in a game. Finally, he became the first player to lead a league in batting average without hitting a home run, when he led the NL with a .357 average in 1902.

Known for using an exceptionally heavy bat, Beaumont led the National League in hits four years, with a high of 209 in 1903. In 1902 he won a batting crown with a .357 average. The next year the center fielder led the NL in hits, runs and total bases as the Pirates won the pennant but lost the Series. He retired with 1,759 hits, a .311 average and 254 stolen bases.

Pafko is often remembered as the poor Dodgers left fielder captured looking up forlornly as Bobby Thomson's "Shot Heard 'Round the World" sailed over his head and into the stands to decide the pennant in 1951. Two years later, he was a fan favorite as the only Wisconsin-born player on the Braves when baseball first arrived in Milwaukee, later earning a World Series ring with the 1957 Milwaukee team. A four-time All-Star, Pafko had his best years with the Cubs. In 1945 he finished fourth in the MVP race after batting .298 with 110 RBI and helping the team reach the World Series — he remains one of the few ties left to the last Cubs team to win a pennant.

Pafko hit 26 homers, drove in 101 runs and hit .312 in 1948, then came back with 36 homers (second-best in the NL) and a .304 average in 1950. Remarkably, he had more homers that season than strikeouts, since he only struck out 32 times. He started the 1951 season with the Cubs, hitting 12 home runs for them before being included in an eight-player trade with the Dodgers in mid-season. Pafko blasted 18 home runs for the Dodgers the rest of the way including one in the first game of the three-game playoff with the Giants, but it was not enough to overcome the Giants magic. He ended up averaging .285 for his career with 213 home runs.

A number of other outfielders deserve mention including Davy Jones, Braggo Roth, Walt Wilmot, Rick Reichardt and Chet Laabs. Jones played on Tigers teams that won three straight pennants (1907–09), teaming up with Sam Crawford and Ty Cobb to form a dynamic outfield the first year before losing his spot to Matty McIntyre. Nicknamed "Kangaroo," Jones stole 207 bases during a 15-year career but was not the person who teamed up with Michael Nesmith, Peter Tork and Micky Dolenz in a 1960s pop rock band.

Roth was shuffled off to six teams in eight years because he was generally disliked, but he had a career OPS+ of 123. He led the AL with seven home runs in 1915 despite being traded for Shoeless Joe Jackson during the season. Wilmot was another old-time ballplayer who led the league in homers (with 13 in 1890). He also led the NL with 19 triples in 1889 and is credited with 383 career stolen bases under the rules of the day. Reichardt hit 116 homers playing from 1964–74, while Laabs hit 27 homers in 1942 and made the All-Star team the next year.

Craig Kusick is the only player from Wisconsin with significant playing time at designated hitter. Eric Hinske seems a natural for the position but has played only 88 games there to date. Kusick appeared in 496 games in his seven seasons, with 209 of them coming as a DH. He started regularly as the DH for the Twins in 1976 and 1977, hitting a combined 23 homers those seasons.

Wisconsin must be a breeding ground for right-handed pitchers, because three Hall of Fame righties hail from the cheese state: Kid Nichols, Burleigh Grimes and Addie Joss. Grimes and Joss were outstanding hurlers, but Nichols has to be considered one of the best pitchers of all time so he earns the spot.

Nichols is frequently overlooked in discussions about all-time great pitchers, largely because he pitched from 1890–1906. Yes, the game was different then, but people weren't paying much attention either. All Nichols did was win 20 or more games each of his first 10 seasons, winning at least 30 games seven of those years. He led the league in wins three straight years, each time with at least 30 victories. In 1898 he started 42 games and went 31–12 with a 2.13 ERA. He finished first in shutouts and WHIP three times each. Nichols pitched more than 400 innings in each of his first five seasons and at age 30 had already won 297 games. By comparison, when Randy Johnson was 30 he had 68 career wins.

Three pitchers must be considered when determining the best pitcher of the 1890s: Kid Nichols, Cy Young and Amos Rusie. Nichols went 297–151 in the decade, which tops the marks of Young (267–151) and Rusie (246–163) and also represents the most wins of any pitcher in any decade. In 1892 Nichols anchored the Boston Beaneaters staff that won the Championship Series over the Cleveland Spiders. He won 35 games that year as did Jack Stivetts, while Harry Staley chipped in 22 wins as the Beaneaters went 102–48. After 12 seasons with Boston, Nichols found himself player-manager of the Cardinals in 1904. He went 21–13 with a 2.02 ERA and career-best 1.003 WHIP, but the Cards limped home in fifth place with a 75–79 record.

Nichols was also a pretty fair hitter, batting .226 for his career with 16 homers among his 472 hits. In 1894 he batted .294 with 34 RBI, while in 1901 he averaged .282 with seven triples and four homers. He occasionally played games in the outfield and at first base, but he clearly made his mark as an ace pitcher despite not having much in his arsenal beyond a fastball. His 361 wins is seventh all-time and he ranks fourth with 532 complete games.

Joss pitched for the Cleveland franchise (mainly the Naps) from 1902–10 and finished with a career record of 160–97 with a 1.89 ERA and ERA+ of 142. He debuted with a one-hitter in 1902, pitched a perfect game against the White Sox with the pennant on the line in 1908 and then no-hit the Sox a second time two years later. Joss produced four straight 20-win seasons and had five seasons with an ERA under 2.00. His 1.16 ERA in 1908 is the sixth-lowest for a single season. He has the second-best career ERA (1.89) in major league history behind Ed Walsh as well as the lowest career WHIP at 0.968.

Who knows what numbers Joss could have posted with a longer career, but he died of tubercular meningitis just after turning 31 in 1911. Joss was so well-liked around the league that a group of players formed an All-Star team and played an exhibition game against the Naps to raise money for his wife and kids.

Joss is the only player in the Hall of Fame with less than 10 years major league experience (excluding Negro Leaguers). He played nine seasons, one short of the Hall's requirement that a player complete 10 years in the majors to be eligible. His son, Norman, lobbied on his behalf for his entire adult life and eventually got several influential sportswriters to take up his father's cause. Joss was finally elected by the Veterans Committee in 1978, 67 years after his death and six months after his son died thinking he had failed in his quest.

Grimes, who was called "Ol' Stubblebeard" for his grumpy demeanor and habit of not shaving on days he pitched, played for seven teams between 1916 and 1934. He won 20 games five times and retired with a 270–212 record but a high 3.53 ERA. His career ERA+ of 108 shows he was not especially dominant, mainly because he had good years and bad years. For example, Grimes led the league in wins twice; strikeouts, won-loss percentage, ERA+ and shutouts once; complete games four times and innings pitched three times. However, he also led the league in losses once, hits twice and earned runs three times. His ERA+ was below 100 in eight of his 19 seasons.

Grimes was the last pitcher in the majors legally allowed to throw a spitball after it was banned in 1920, an edge he took advantage of for most of his career along with a fondness for brushing back batters. Grimes would be particularly disturbed by the current generation of players' tendency to be friendly with the opposition. "Why is it there are so many nice guys interested in baseball?" he once asked. "Not me. I was a real bastard when I played."

When he wasn't dusting batters off the plate, Grimes was helping himself with the bat, averaging .248 for his career and batting .316 in four World Series. He went 2–0 with a 2.04 ERA for the Cardinals in the 1931 Series, coming through with a win in Game 7. Although he got little support from the baseball writers during his 14 years on the ballot, Grimes was elected to the Hall of Fame by the Veterans Committee in 1964.

Another righty deserves mention, even though he falls short of some of Wisconsin's more notable starters. Roy Patterson was born in Stoddard but grew up in St.

Croix Falls, which led to his nickname "St. Croix Boy Wonder." Patterson won the first game in American League history in 1901 and went on to win 20 games that year as a Chicago White Sox rookie.

Five pitchers were considered for the left-handed starter spot on Team Wisconsin: Ed Killian, Jarrod Washburn, Johnny Schmitz, Zane Smith and Shane Rawley. Schmitz had the most All-Star selections (two) and the highest Career Win Shares (116), while Rawley had the most wins (111). Smith led in Wins Above Replacement (24.5), while Washburn tied Killian for the highest ERA+ (109). Rawley actually pitched nine more games in relief and posted 40 saves.

Killian far outpaced the field with his 2.38 career ERA, which was also a function of the period he was pitching in (1903–10). The sinkerball specialist is also the only one of the five to post a winning record — his 102–78 lifetime mark represents a winning percentage of .569. He won 20 games twice with his best season coming in 1907, when he went 25–13 with a 1.78 ERA and 29 complete games. It was evidently too much work, as a sore-armed Killian was only able to provide four innings of relief during the World Series that year as the Tigers were swept by the Cubs. He did pitch 1,001 innings from late 1903 into 1907 without giving up a home run, which is impressive even when you consider it was the Deadball Era.

Nicknamed "Twilight Ed" for his ability to pitch deep in the game even if it went extra innings, Killian once started both games of a doubleheader late in the 1909 season, nearly hurling a no-hitter in the opener and earning complete game wins in both to all but clinch the pennant for the Tigers. Killian never left the bench as the Tigers lost the World Series for the third straight year.

In the bullpen, the All-Time Wisconsin team is led by Bob Wickman, a Green Bay native who played five of his 15 seasons for the Brewers. Wickman posted double figures in saves the last nine years he played, leading the league with 45 for the Indians in 2005 and finishing with 267 career saves. The portly reliever, who was a two-time All-Star, credited his sinking fastball to the fact he lost the tip of his right index finger in a childhood accident.

Another notable relief pitcher is Ryne Duren, who used to scare the bejesus out of batters due to the fact that he had poor vision and threw lightning fast with little or no control. He liked to throw his first warm-up pitch to the backstop to intimidate the batter. Duren also struggled with alcoholism. For his career he struck out 9.6 batters per 9 innings, which was negated by walking 392 batters in 589 innings. Duren managed to make the All-Star team in 1961 despite posting a 6–13 record that year with a 5.19 ERA, 1.615 WHIP and only two saves. He led the league with 20 saves and recorded a 2.02 ERA for the Yankees in 1958, making the first of three All-Star teams and coming in second for Rookie of the Year. In 1960 he recorded 12.3 K/9 but also 9.0 BB/9IP.

The manager for the All-Time Wisconsin team also earns the designation for having the best nickname — Pants Rowland. He evidently picked up that name in his youth playing for a local team while wearing his father's oversized pants, which started to fall off as he rounded the bases. Rowland found himself hired by Charles Comiskey to manage the White Sox in 1915, and he surprised naysayers by leading the Sox to 93 wins and a third-place finish his first year. They went 89–65 the next season but moved up to second place, followed by a 100-win season and a pennant in 1917.

Rowland guided the 1917 team to the World Series title over the Giants 4–2 as he rode the batting of Eddie Collins and Shoeless Joe Jackson and the pitching of Red Faber and Eddie Cicotte. He was relieved as manager after the Sox stumbled to a 57–67 mark and sixth-place finish the next year, a fortuitous event since it saved him from being stigmatized as the skipper of the infamous 1919 Black Sox.

Kuenn also received consideration as the all-time manager. He took over as skipper of the Brewers during the 1982 season and guided them to a 72–43 record down the stretch to win the pennant. Harvey's Wallbangers, as the team became known, featured a lineup packed with sluggers such as Gorman Thomas, Ted Simmons, Cecil Cooper and Ben Oglivie, along with stars Robin Yount and Paul Molitor. They banged out 10 runs and 17 hits to win the first Series game but ended up falling to the Cardinals in seven games. Kuenn managed the Brew Crew one more year but was let go after finishing fifth.

WYOMING

Names in **bold** *represent Major League selections by position, followed by honorable mentions. City of birth is in parentheses.*

Catcher — **John Buck (Kemmerer)**
First Base — **Bucky Jacobsen (Riverton)**
Second Base — **Mike Lansing (Rawlins)**
Third Base — **Mike Lansing (Rawlins)**
Shortstop — **Mike Lansing (Rawlins)**
Outfield — **Mike Devereaux (Casper)**

Outfield — **Rick Sofield (Cheyenne)**
Designated hitter — **Bucky Jacobsen (Riverton)**
Right Handed Starter — **Bob Harris (Gillette)**
Left Handed Starter — **Tom Browning (Casper)**.
  Also: Dick Ellsworth (Lusk)
Relief Pitcher — **Dan Spillner (Casper)**. Also: Bill

Wilkinson (Greybull); Jan Dukes (Cheyenne); Dennis DeBarr (Cheyenne); Jeremy Horst (Cheyenne)
Manager–None

The Names
Best Nickname: John "The King of Scotland" Buck
Other Nicknames: Larry "Bucky" Jacobsen
Most Unusual Name: Mike Devereaux

All-Time Leaders
Games: Mike Lansing, 1,110
Hits: Mike Lansing, 1124
Batting Average: Mike Lansing, .271
Home Runs: John Buck, 106
RBI: Mike Devereaux, 480
Stolen Bases: Mike Lansing, 119
Wins: Tom Browning, 123
Strikeouts: Dick Ellsworth, 1140
Saves: Dan Spillner, 50
Future Stars: Brandon Nimmo (Cheyenne); Jeremy Horst (Cheyenne)
Best Player: Tom Browning

Historic Baseball Place
Mike Lansing Field in Casper — Built in 2002 and named after one of Wyoming's most famous players, it is home to the Casper Ghosts minor league team in the Pioneer League. It seats just 2,500 fans but is the only place to watch professional baseball in Wyoming.

Notable Achievements
Mike Lansing hit for the cycle quicker within a game than any other player. On June 18, 2000, he accomplished the cycle by the fourth inning.

Tom Browning is the most recent pitcher to win 20 games in his rookie season. He went 20–9 for the Reds in 1985, the first time a rookie had won 20 games since Bob Grim in 1954.

Wyoming Can Boast of a Perfect Pitcher

A total of 15 states (plus one foreign country — Nicaragua) can boast that a pitcher born there has thrown a perfect game. It's hard to imagine that one of those states would be Wyoming, which has sent only 13 players to the big leagues and does not even offer high school baseball.

But on September 16, 1988, Tom Browning made history pitching for the Cincinnati Reds, the team he had idolized growing up in Casper. The left-hander, who liked to pitch quickly to establish a rhythm, mowed down the Dodgers on 102 pitches to become the twelfth pitcher in baseball history to throw a perfect game.

Browning did not make the All-Star team that season even though he ended up 18–5 with a 3.41 ERA and allowed just 205 hits in 250 innings pitched. He also wasn't selected to the All-Star team in 1985, his rookie year, despite going 20–9. Instead, he finished runner-up for Rookie of the Year, losing out to Vince Coleman and his 110 stolen bases. Browning's only All-Star selection came in 1991, when his record was 14–14 and he led the league in most earned runs and most home runs allowed.

Browning fashioned a pretty decent career pitching 11 seasons for the Reds plus one final season of two games with the Royals in 1995. His career record of 123–90 is more than respectable, as is his 3.94 ERA. He won Game 3 of the 1990 World Series for the Reds as they swept the A's.

Wyoming has only had two professional teams — the Cheyenne Indians and Casper Rockies. The Indians went 3–0 in 1912 while sharing the team with two cities in Colorado and then the league folded. The Cheyenne Indians remained active but as a semi-pro team, which managed to place high in national tournaments. The Indians returned in 1941 but only played just one season in the Western League, ending Cheyenne's brief run in pro baseball. The Casper Rockies have been competing in the Pioneer League since 2001.

All-Time Wyoming Selections

Only Alaska (with 11) has sent fewer players to the majors than Wyoming. That is not surprising when you consider Wyoming is composed largely of a series of mountain ranges and it's hard to build a baseball field on the side of a mountain. Most of Wyoming's major leaguers went to high school in other states, with the exception of Lansing, Devereaux and Browning. Jim "Death Valley" Scott, who won 20 games twice, grew up in Lander, Wyoming, but was actually born in South Dakota.

Browning's perfect game makes him a lock as the left-handed starter and as Wyoming's All-Time Best Player.

Bob Harris from Gillette became the first Wyoming-born player to appear in a major league game when he made his debut for the Detroit Tigers on September 19, 1938. He bounced around for five seasons, ending his career 30–52, which still qualifies him as the best right-handed starter from the state.

It would take another 20 years until the second Wyoming player, Dick Ellsworth, made it to the majors. He stuck around for 13 seasons and even made the All-Star team in 1964 despite a 14–18 record for the Cubs. He falls in line behind Browning as southpaw starter from Wyoming. Ellsworth's son, Steve (who was born in Chicago) was a 6-foot-8 pitcher and first round draft pick of the Red Sox in 1981 who won one game in the majors.

Since only five position players hail from Wyoming, it's a little difficult to field a full team. Luckily, Mike Lansing played second, third and shortstop in the majors, so he gets selected for all three spots on the All-

Time Wyoming team. Lansing was a productive player throughout his nine-year career, which was spent mostly as a second baseman. His best season was 1997, when he batted .281 with 20 homers and 70 RBI for the Expos. Lansing is the answer to a trivia question: who was the first batter for the Colorado Rockies first home game on April 9, 1993?

Wyoming is proud of its native son as Lansing has his own field named after him in Casper. However, it should be pointed out that Lansing is one of many players listed in the Mitchell Commission Report on performance-enhancing substances through a connection with Mets clubhouse employee Kirk Radomski.

John Buck gives Team Wyoming a capable catcher. Buck spent six seasons with the Royals before signing with the Blue Jays for 2010. He made the AL All-Star team by hitting 20 homers, driving in 66 runs and batting .281, production that led to a free-agent contract with the Marlins for 2011. Buck, who went to high school in Utah, boasts a lifetime on-base percentage of just .301 but is Wyoming's all-time leader in home runs with 106.

That total pushes aside the 105 homers collected by outfielder Mike Devereaux across 12 seasons. The Casper native finished seventh in the MVP balloting in 1992 after batting .276 with 24 HRs and 107 RBI for the Orioles. Another highlight of Devereaux's career was while with the Braves in 1995. He was named NLCS MVP after driving in the winning run in Game 1 and hitting a three-run homer in Game 4. The Braves went on to win the World Series that year over the Indians.

Rick Sofield's career lasted just three seasons, but he did start in the outfield for the Twins most of the 1980 season. Bucky Jacobsen belted 180 home runs over 11 minor league seasons with a high of 31 in 2003. His only season in the majors came in 2004, when he hit nine homers in 42 games for the Mariners. Since he played 21 games at first base and 20 games at designated hitter that year, Jacobsen mans both those positions for the All-Time Wyoming team.

Dan Spillner appeared in 556 games, including 433 in relief, giving him the qualifications as the best relief pitcher in Wyoming history. He finished with 50 saves, with a high of 21 for Cleveland in 1982. Cheyenne native Jan Dukes appeared in 16 career games —13 with the Washington Senators in 1969–70 and three with the Texas Rangers in 1972. Oddly enough, Ted Williams was his manager for all three of those seasons.

Another relief pitcher, Greybull's Bill Wilkinson, pitched three years for the Mariners in the 1980s and collected 10 saves in 1987. Wilkinson is the great-grandson of Jim Bluejacket, who played semi-pro ball in Wyoming, pitched in the majors from 1914–16 and is the only twentieth-century pitcher to win a game without throwing a pitch. Cheyenne native Jeremy Horst is a promising reliever who debuted with the Reds in 2011.

Appendix 1

CANADA

*Names in **bold** represent Major League selections by position, followed by honorable mentions. City and province of birth is in parentheses.*

Catcher — George Gibson (London, Ont.). Also: Russell Martin (East York, Ont.); Larry McLean (Fredericton, N.B.); Nig Clarke (Amherstburg, Ont.)

First base — Justin Morneau (Westminster, B.C.). Also: Bill Phillips (St. John, N.B.); Joey Votto (Toronto, Ont.)

Second base — Pop Smith (Digby, N.S.). Also: Dave McKay (Vancouver, B.C.); John O'Brien (St. John, N.B.)

Third base — Corey Koskie (Anola, Man.). Also: Pete Ward (Montreal, Que.); Frank O'Rourke (Hamilton, Ont.)

Shortstop — Arthur Irwin (Toronto, Ont.)

Outfield — Larry Walker (Maple Ridge, B.C.)

Outfield — Jeff Heath (Ft. Williams, Ont.)

Outfield — Tip O'Neill (Springfield, Ont.). Also: Jason Bay (Trail, B.C.); George Selkirk (Huntsville, Ont.); George Wood (Pownal, PEI); Terry Puhl (Melville, Sask.); Jack Graney (St Thomas, Ont.)

Designated Hitter — Matt Stairs (St. John, N.B.)

Right Handed Starter — Ferguson Jenkins (Chatham, Ont.). Also: Russ Ford (Brandon, Man.); Ryan Dempster (Sachelt, B.C.); Kirk McCaskill (Kapuskasing, Ont.); Rich Harden (Victoria, B.C.)

Left Handed Starter — Erik Bedard (Navan, Ont.). Also: Jeff Francis (Vancouver, B.C.): Oscar Judd (London, Ont.)

Relief Pitcher — Eric Gagne (Montreal, Que.). Also: John Hiller (Toronto, Ont.); Paul Quantrill (London, Ont.); Claude Raymond (St. Jean, Que.); Ron Taylor (Toronto, Ont.); Rheal Cormier (Moncton, N.B.); Reggie Cleveland (Swift Current, Sask.); John Axford (Simcoe, Ont.)

Manager — Bill Watkins (Brantford, Ont.). Also: George Gibson (London, Ont.); Arthur Irwin (Toronto, Ont.)

The Names

Best Nickname: George "Twinkletoes" Selkirk
Other Nicknames: Bob "Magnet" Addy; Richard "Stubby" Clapp; Justin "Nig" Clarke; Charles "Chub" Collins; William "Bunk" Congalton; Maurice "Shorty" Dee; George "Moon" Gibson; Arthur "Sandy" Irwin; Ferguson "Fly" Jenkins; Thomas "Ossie" Judd; "Quiet Joe" Knight; "Medicine Bill" Mountjoy; Edward "The Only Nolan"; John "Chewing Gum" O'Brien; James "Tip" O'Neill; Frank "Yip" Owens; Frank "Cooney" Snyder; John "Tug" Thompson; Harry "Rube" Vickers; George "Dandy" Wood
Most Unusual Name: Camille Van Brabant, Gene Vadaboncoeur; Harvey Shank

All-Time Leaders

Games: Larry Walker, 1988
Hits: Larry Walker, 2160
Batting Average: Tip O'Neill, .326
Home Runs: Larry Walker, 383
RBI: Larry Walker, 1311
Stolen Bases: Larry Walker, 230
Wins: Ferguson Jenkins, 284
Strikeouts: Ferguson Jenkins, 3192
Saves: Eric Gagne, 187
Future Stars: Phillippe Aumont (Hull, Que.), Brett Lawrie (Langley, B.C.)
All-Time Best Player: Ferguson Jenkins

Historic Baseball Places

Canadian Baseball Hall of Fame & Museum in St. Marys, Ontario — Tucked inside a small house is a treasure trove of artifacts related to Canadian baseball history. In addition to highlighting the careers of famous Canadian players such as Larry Walker and Ferguson Jenkins one can find memorabilia related to Babe Ruth (he hit his first professional home run in Canada) and Jackie Robinson (his first professional team was the Montreal Royals). The Canadian Baseball Hall of Fame, which features three ball fields on its 32-acre site, has been inducting members since 1983.

Rogers Centre in Toronto, Ontario — Blue Jays stadium

The Canadian Baseball Hall of Fame & Museum in St. Marys, Ontario, contains photos, documents and artifacts that tell the story of Canadian baseball history. In addition to highlighting the careers of famous Canadian players such as Ferguson Jenkins and Larry Walker, the museum features memorabilia related to Babe Ruth (he hit his first professional home run in Canada) and Jackie Robinson, whose first professional team was the Montreal Royals (courtesy Canadian Baseball Hall of Fame & Museum).

opened in 1989 with the world's first fully retractable roof. Features the largest electric guitar in North America inside the Hard Rock Café, which overlooks right field inside the stadium. You can even get a suite at the adjacent Renaissance Hotel and watch the game from your room.

- **The Saskatchewan Baseball Hall of Fame and Museum** in Battleford, Sask.— Founded in 1983, the museum pays tribute to the players and teams from the region with displays of uniforms, photos, baseball equipment and more. A mural can be found on the outside wall of the museum that depicts the first baseball game played in Saskatchewan.
- **Labatt Park** in London, Ontario — Holds the distinction as the the oldest continuously operated baseball field in the world, with a history dating back to 1877. Ferguson Jenkins pitched for the London Majors in 1984 and 1985 after retiring from the major leagues and Ty Cobb, Satchel Paige and Charlie Gehringer all played on the field in exhibitions. London native Ted Giannoulas (The Famous Chicken) got his start in baseball by operating the manual scoreboard at Labatt Park in the mid–1960s.

Notable Achievements

Jeff Heath was the first American League player to hit 20 home runs, 20 doubles and 20 triples in the same season when he collected 24 homers, 32 doubles and 20 triples in 1941.

Dick Fowler (Toronto) is the only Canadian to throw a nine-inning no-hitter. He beat the St. Louis Browns 1–0 on September 9, 1945, with the only run scoring in the bottom of the ninth. It was Fowler's only victory that season.

Rob Ducey (Toronto) was the only Canadian to hit a home run as both an Expo and a Blue Jay. His first home run came in 1987 as a Blue Jay and his last two (out of a career total of 31) came in 2001 while playing for the Expos.

Jason Bay was the first Canadian to win the Rookie of the Year Award when he won in 2004, also becoming the first member of the Pittsburgh Pirates organization to win the award.

In 2009 **Ryan Dempster** became just the second player to follow three 20-save seasons with two 10-win seasons, joining John Smoltz.

Bob Addy (Port Hope) was the first Canadian to play in the major leagues, playing for the Rockford Forest Citys in the National Association in 1871.

When **Matt Stairs** joined the Padres in 2010 they represented the twelfth different team he has played on during his career, the most ever for a position player. He signed with the Washington Nationals for the 2011 season, but that doesn't technically qualify as a different team since it's the same franchise as the Montreal Expos.

Nig Clarke hit eight home runs in a Texas League game on June 15, 1902, which remains a record for professional baseball.

Canada's Rich Baseball History Continues

Canadian baseball history did not begin when the Expos joined the National League as an expansion team in 1969. The game has a long and storied tradition in Canada with origins that date back to 1838. It was on June 4 of that year, according to the Canadian Baseball Hall of Fame & Museum, when a game resembling baseball was played in Beachville, Ontario. That would be eight years before the Knickerbockers reportedly played the first organized game of baseball at Elysian Fields in New Jersey.

The game seemed to take particular hold in southern Ontario, reports William Humber in *Diamonds of the North*, with organized teams appearing in Hamilton in 1854 and London in 1855. The Canadian Association of Base Ball Players formed in Toronto in 1876.

Some of baseball's biggest names made history in Canada. Jackie Robinson made his professional debut (and played his only minor league season) with the Montreal Royals, the Dodgers top farm team, officially breaking the color barrier on April 18, 1946. He batted .349 with 155 hits that season. Montreal was carefully chosen for Robinson's start in professional baseball, since the city was viewed as having a tolerant attitude toward African Americans.

Actually, African Americans had played sporadically in white baseball up until 1899, when Bill Galloway became the last African American to play in white baseball (until Robinson) while playing a handful of games with Woodstock in the Canadian League.

Babe Ruth hit his first and only minor league home run at Hanlon's Point in Toronto on September 5, 1914, while playing for the Providence Grays. He also pitched a one-hitter that day. Roberto Clemente played his only minor league season for the Montreal Royals in 1954, while Don Drysdale, Duke Snider and Roy Campanella also played for the Royals.

Hall of Fame Manager Sparky Anderson only played one season in the majors but his extensive minor league career included two seasons with the Montreal Royals and four seasons with the Toronto Maple Leafs. Fellow Hall of Fame Manager Tommy Lasorda is the all-time leader in pitching wins for the Montreal Royals. He spent nine seasons with the team, leading the Royals to five International League titles while going 107–57 as a left-handed starter.

Montreal eventually lost its minor league team, the Royals, in 1960. However, the city was awarded an expansion team in 1969, representing the first MLB franchise outside the United States. The Expos played at Jarry Park from 1969–76 before moving to Olympic Stadium, which had been designed as a track-and-field site for the Olympics. The Expos were already under the control of Major League Baseball when the team moved to Washington, D.C., after the 2004 season. Olympic Stadium is still around hosting sporting events, just not baseball. Montreal has sent 15 players to the major leagues including Pete Ward, Sherry Robertson and Eric Gagne.

A surprisingly high number of nineteenth-century players were born in Canada — 60 — which is more than California produced in that time period. The country continues to produce professional players, as 71 Canadians have played in the majors since 1990. Canada's All-Time team features active or recently retired players at nearly every position, either as starters or honorable mention.

A total of 236 major leaguers hail from Canada, with Toronto the most popular birthplace. The 26 Toronto players include an NL MVP in Joey Votto. George Gibson is the most prominent of the 13 London-born players, while active player Jeff Francis is the most accomplished of the 10 players born in Vancouver.

In terms of nicknames for Canadian players, there's a "Yip" Owens and a "Tip" O'Neill (who was not the Speaker of the House), as well as a Stubby, a Shorty and a Chub. It's probably a good thing Harvey Shank decided to be a baseball player instead of a golfer. Shank hurled three scoreless innings for the Angels during his 1970 debut and that was his career.

Edward "The Only Nolan," who actually grew up in New Jersey, was unique in more ways than his nickname. He threw right-handed but batted lefty, and seemed determined to not let baseball interfere with drinking and other nefarious activities. As a rookie he pitched 347 innings for the Indianapolis Blues in the National League in 1878, demonstrating promising ability. He produced a 23–52 record for five teams in four leagues, getting kicked off multiple teams for insubordination and other infractions, which eventually caused him to be blacklisted from the National League in 1885. No definitive explanation has emerged for his unusual nickname, but his managers were certainly glad he was "The Only Nolan."

The pride of Belleville, Ontario, was Johnny Rutherford, not the race car driver but a righty who pitched one year for the Brooklyn Dodgers, 1952. His record was an even 7–7 with 29 walks and 29 strikeouts while allowing a tidy 97 hits in 97 innings. To maintain his consistency, he pitched in one game in the World Series that year, pitching one inning and allowing one hit, one run and one walk while striking out ... you guessed it — one batter.

SABR member David Matchett points out the only time a home run was hit by a Canadian-born batter off a Canadian-born pitcher in a regular season game played in Canada. On August 13, 1999, Matt Stairs of the A's hit the first of his two home runs in the game off Paul Spoljaric of the Jays at the Skydome in Toronto. It was a grand slam on Spoljaric's first pitch after relieving Roy Halladay. Stairs' last at-bat of the game was against another Canadian, Paul Quantrill, but he stuck out.

All-Time Canada Selections

Let's get to the selections for the All-Time Canada team. At catcher, two Deadball Era catchers were considered along with an active player. We went with George Gibson, a native of London, Ontario, who was also the first Canadian manager in the big leagues. Gibson won a World Series with the Pirates in 1909, batting .265 while playing alongside Honus Wagner, Vic Willis and Player-Manager Fred Clarke. Gibson caught 150 out of 152 games that season, part of a three-year stretch where he caught more than 140 games each season. Gibson, who was nicknamed "Moon," only batted .236 for his career but was a dependable receiver who caught 1,194 games over 14 seasons. He was named Canada's baseball player of the half-century and was elected to the Canadian Baseball Hall of Fame in 1987.

Larry McLean played 13 seasons between 1901 and 1915, batting .262 while catching 761 games for five different teams. His greatest accomplishment was throwing out 14 consecutive base runners in 1911 while also picking off two runners during the streak. Russell Martin got his career off to a promising start by making the All-Star team in his second year and winning a Gold Glove in 2007. He had another solid year in 2008, making the All-Star team again, but his productivity has slipped since then. His career has not been long enough to earn the top spot.

The best choice at first is Twins star Justin Morneau, who was the American League MVP in 2006, edging out Derek Jeter by 14 points. Morneau batted .321 with 34 home runs with 130 RBI that season and has developed into a feared slugger who provides protection to Joe Mauer in the Twins lineup. Morneau was named to his fourth straight All-Star team in 2010 as he dramatically increased his batting average, OBP and slugging percentage. Unfortunately, he suffered a concussion that forced him to miss the second half of the season and all of the postseason. Morneau has turned into a solid fielder and all-around hitter whose power numbers don't come at the expense of a lot of strikeouts.

Right on his heels is Joey Votto, who is two years younger and even more talented than Morneau. Votto won the NL MVP Award in 2010 at the age of 26. He finished second in average, third in homers and RBI and led the league in OBP, slugging, OPS and OPS+.

Another noteworthy first baseman is nineteenth-century player Bill Phillips, who is sometimes credited with being the first Canadian to play in the major leagues — he debuted with the Cleveland Blues in the National League in 1879. Actually, Bob Addy was the first, playing for the Rockford Forest Citys of the National Association in 1871 and the Chicago White Stockings in the National League beginning in 1876. Phillips was a good fielder who collected 1,130 hits over 10 seasons.

Our second baseman is nineteenth-century player Charles "Pop" Smith, who bounced around to 10 teams in 12 seasons. He led the American Association with 17 triples in 1883 and ended up with 941 hits but just a .222 average.

At third base Corey Koskie, Pete Ward and Frank O'Rourke all received consideration.

Koskie hit 124 home runs playing nine seasons mostly for the Twins. He batted .300 in 2000 and then had his best season in 2001 with 26 home runs, 103 RBI and 100 runs scored. His career ended in 2006 at the age of 33 after suffering a concussion. Koskie was an integral player on three straight division-winning teams and the Twins haven't adequately replaced him yet at third. He was a better hitter than Ward and O'Rourke and his career stats edge out the other two, so Koskie gets selected to the first team.

Ward, who actually grew up in Oregon, had a father, Jim, who played in the National Hockey League. Ward finished second in voting for the Rookie of the Year Award in 1963 after hitting .295 with 22 homers and 84 RBI. He came in sixth in the MVP balloting the next season after another strong campaign with 23 home runs and 94 RBI but struggled with injuries after that. O'Rourke broke in as a shortstop with the Boston Braves in 1912 but didn't stick in the big leagues until 1921. Before he could get established at shortstop Rabbit Maranville came along to take his job with the Braves. Later switching to second base, he found himself beat out again by future star Charlie Gehringer on the Tigers. He accumulated 1,032 hits but it was mainly his glove that kept him in the game until 1931.

Canada's All-Time shortstop, Arthur Irwin, is credited with being one of the first players to regularly use a glove. After breaking fingers in his hand in 1882, Irwin got a sporting goods company to cobble together a padded half-finger glove he could wear in games. Within a couple of years most players were wearing some kind of glove.

Irwin was born in Canada but grew up in Boston, which is where he first started playing the game. His best season was 1883, when he hit with .286 with 116 hits. As his 13-year playing career was winding down he became a player-manager for the Washington Nationals. In 1891 he took over as player-manager of the Boston Reds and led them to a 93–42 record and the American Association pennant. He would go on to manage eight seasons in the majors and later owned the Toronto Maple Leafs minor league franchise. Irwin died of an apparent suicide in 1921, with details emerging later that he had spent nearly half his life juggling separate families in Boston and New York.

Larry Walker is not only one of the greatest Canadian players of all-time, he got to play his first six seasons for the Montreal Expos before signing with the Rockies as a free agent in 1994. Walker was a multi-talented player who would have starred wherever he played, but there's no question his statistics were artificially inflated playing 10 seasons at Coors Field. He played 30 percent of his games at Coors Field yet hit 40 percent of his home runs there. The park had an even bigger effect on his batting average — Walker batted a hundred points better at Coors Field, .381 compared to .282 at other parks.

Home-field advantage or not, Walker was a productive hitter for 17 seasons. By the time he retired after the 2005 season, Walker held virtually all of Canada's all-time hitting records except batting average and triples. He finished with 2,160 hits, 383 home runs, 1,311 RBI, a .313 average and a .400 OBP. He even stole 230 bases. A five-time All-Star who won three Silver Sluggers, Walker won the National League MVP Award in 1997 after hitting .366 with 49 homers, 130 RBI, 143 runs and 178 OPS+, then won the batting title the next two seasons with averages of .363 and .379. He batted over

.300 nine times, which is pretty good for someone who grew up playing more hockey than baseball.

Walker was also an outstanding fielder who won seven Gold Gloves. There is little debate that he possessed the strongest arm in baseball during his playing days. In 1992 he gained notoriety when he threw out Tony Fernandez at first base after the Padres speedy infielder had singled to right field, but that was not the only time Walker accomplished that amazing feat.

His .565 slugging percentage ranks fourteenth all-time, ahead of Hall of Famers such as Musial, Mays, Aaron, Mantle, Schmidt and Frank Robinson. Does that mean Walker belongs in the Hall? The thin air in Denver certainly inflated his batting stats, but the biggest argument against his election is that his counting stats fall short of established Hall of Fame benchmarks. He probably needed to get to 500 home runs or 3,000 hits to get in, and he falls far short of those marks, mainly because he only got over 500 at-bats in two seasons due to a litany of injuries. He did get inducted into the Canadian Baseball Hall of Fame in 2009, which follows him winning the Tip O'Neill Award nine times as Canada's most outstanding player.

Joining him in the outfield is the guy who the award was named after—James "Tip" O'Neill—a nineteenth-century player who was the first great Canadian player. He reportedly got the nickname from his ability to keep foul tipping pitches until he got one he liked. O'Neill played most of his career in the short-lived American Association, and although some purists don't consider that part of the major leagues its statistics are generally accepted. To exclude O'Neill's numbers would be to pretend one of the greatest seasons with the bat never happened.

In 1887 O'Neill led the American Association with a .435 average, 225 hits and 14 home runs, making him the first and only Triple Crown hitter in the league's short history. At the time he was credited with a .485 average and 275 hits under the rules of the day, which counted walks as hits. Adjusted to the modern standard, O'Neill's .435 average that season still represents the second-highest in baseball history (behind Hugh Duffy's .440). O'Neill led the league in 12 hitting categories that year. It was the only time in baseball history a player has led the league in homers, hits, doubles and triples. He was the first player to get 50 doubles with 52 that year and he also stole 30 bases for the first-place St. Louis Browns.

O'Neill led the league in hits and average again the next year but never came close to duplicating the eye-popping stats he posted in 1887. His 10-year career produced 1,385 hits, a .326 average and 143 OPS+. The "Woodstock Wonder," as he was sometimes called, actually started his career as a pitcher, going 16–16 over two seasons before switching to left field. O'Neill was inducted into the Canadian Baseball Hall of Fame in 1983.

Our third outfielder, Jeff Heath, probably had as much all-around talent as Walker but didn't always apply himself. Heath, who attended high school in Seattle, basically had two outstanding years—1938 and 1941—but otherwise fell short of his potential. In 1938 he led the league with 18 triples, finished second with a .343 average and posted 21 homers, 112 RBI and a .602 slugging pct. He was even better in 1941, making the All-Star team for the first time on the way to hitting .340 with 24 homers, 123 RBI, 199 hits, 162 OPS and again leading the league in triples with 20. He hit 194 career homers with a .293 average over 14 seasons. His career OPS+ of 139 is the same as Reggie Jackson and better than George Brett and Al Kaline.

Three other outfielders from Canada deserve mention: Jason Bay, George Selkirk and George Wood. Bay, a three-time All-Star, passed Heath for third on Canada's all-time home run list in 2011. He handled the pressure of replacing Manny Ramirez by batting .293 after joining the Red Sox in 2008, followed by 36 homers and 119 RBI the next season. He has had four seasons over 30 homers and four seasons over 100 RBI.

Selkirk had the unenviable task of replacing Babe Ruth as the Yankees right fielder, including wearing uniform #3. No pressure there. He responded by batting over .300 his first four years, making the All-Star team in 1936 after driving in 107 runs. He won five World Series with the Yanks and batted .290 over nine seasons but hit 606 fewer home runs in his career than the Bambino. He was nicknamed "Twinkletoes" for the awkward way he ran on the balls of his feet. Wood was a nineteenth-century player who collected 1,467 hits in 13 seasons, leading the National League with seven home runs in 1882.

Fielding was never his forte, so Matt Stairs is right at home manning the designated hitter position. He would be Canada's choice for all-time pinch hitter, too. The New Brunswick native has embodied what it means to be a professional hitter since breaking into the big leagues with the Montreal Expos in 1992. He has collected 105 pinch-hits over 19 seasons and on August 21, 2010, he passed Cliff Johnson when he hit the 21st pinch-hit home run of his career (he now has 23).

Stairs came through with 13 pinch hits in 2009 to help the Phillies make it as far as the World Series. His best years came with the A's in 1998, when he batted .294 and slugged .582 with 26 homers and 106 RBI, and 1999, when he belted 38 homers and drove in 102 runs. Short but powerfully built, Stairs has collected 265 career home runs, number two among Canadian players.

One right-handed Canadian starter stands alone—Hall of Famer Ferguson Jenkins. Fergie won 20 games six straight years pitching for the Cubs in hitter-friendly Wrigley Field and recorded double-figure wins in 14 consecutive seasons. Jenkins had excellent command and control of his pitches, finishing in the top seven in K/BB ratio 13 times and ending his career with an outstanding K/BB ratio of 3.2. He was the National League Cy Young Award winner in 1971 after going 24–13 with a 2.77 ERA and leading the league with 30 complete games. His most impressive stat that season was his 7.1 K/BB ratio—an amazing 263 strikeouts with just 37 walks.

His 3,192 strikeouts ranked sixth all-time when he retired after the 1983 season—he now ranks twelfth. He is one of just four pitchers (along with Greg Maddux, Curt Schilling and Pedro Martinez) to record over 3,000 strikeouts and less than 1,000 walks. Jenkins was pretty good at finishing what he started, too, posting 267 complete games and leading the league in that category four times.

Despite a 284–226 record with a career ERA of 3.34, Jenkins only made three All-Star teams. Looking at his year-end stats (which obviously is not when teams are selected), Jenkins probably deserved to be an All-Star selection in eight seasons. He was runner-up for the Cy Young Award twice and finished third in voting two other years. He does rank third on the all-time list with 484 home runs allowed, but that's about the only negative stat Jenkins produced.

An outstanding athlete who excelled at fielding and hitting, Jenkins hit six of his 13 career homers in 1971 and retired as the all-time leader in putouts by a pitcher with 363 — he now ranks fifth. Fergie had the misfortune to play on teams that were good but not good enough, which is why he is the winningest pitcher to never make the postseason. His teams finished second or third in the division in 13 of his 19 seasons, but unfortunately his career took place in the days before the wild card. He lost five 1–0 games in 1968 alone, yet still won 20 games.

In 1991 Jenkins became the first (and so far only) Canadian elected to the Baseball Hall of Fame in Cooperstown, four years after he was inducted into the Canadian Hall of Fame. Fergie was the first baseball player to win the Lou Marsh Trophy awarded for Canada's top athlete, and he was also made a member of the Order of Canada and inducted into Canada's Walk of Fame. These accolades confirm his selection as Canada's All-Time Best Player.

Another notable righty is Russ Ford, who holds the rookie record for most wins by the New York Yankees franchise with 26 in 1910 (they were called the Highlanders at the time). Ford was also the first Canadian to win 20 games and is credited with perfecting the emery ball, a ball that had been scuffed up by an emery board. He won 99 games in seven seasons, also leading the league in 1914 in winning percentage, ERA+, WHIP, BB/9IP and SO/BB ratio.

Canada has not produced very many left-handed starters but the best two are still active. Eric Bedard has demonstrated occasional flashes of brilliance mixed in with inconsistency, injury and indifference. He won 15 games in 2006 and then finished fifth in the Cy Young Award voting the next season after going 13–5 with 3.16 ERA while allowing just 141 hits in 182 innings with 221 strikeouts (third in the AL). He pitched a two-hit shutout of the Rangers in 2007 while striking out 15, but outings like that have proved to be a tantalizing tease. When healthy and motivated, Bedard has the stuff to be an ace.

Another lefty, Jeff Francis, finished ninth in the Cy Young Award voting after going 17–9 for the Rockies in 2007. The Vancouver native, who attended the University of British Columbia, was drafted ninth overall by the Rockies in 2002 and made it to the big leagues two years later.

A Canadian relief pitcher produced arguably the most dominant season ever by a closer — Eric Gagne in 2003. His selection as the all-time reliever comes with the caveat that Gagne is also one of the players named in the Mitchell Report regarding steroids use. Setting that aside for a moment, Gagne's 2003 season was a thing of beauty. He was as unhittable as a relief pitcher has ever been, cranking out 55 saves without blowing a single save and recording a 1.20 ERA. In 82 innings of work, he gave up just 37 hits while striking out 137 (14.98 K/9IP) with his 100 mph fastball. His 337 ERA+ and 0.692 WHIP in 2003 are not a misprint. Gagne became the ninth relief pitcher to win the Cy Young Award and he finished sixth in MVP voting that season. His blazing fast pitches combined with his goatee and goggles served to intimidate batters.

Gagne was also dominant the year before and the year after, as he converted a record 84 consecutive saves between August 28, 2002 and July 3, 2004. He was hampered by injuries and ineffectiveness his last four seasons and was never able to regain the velocity he had at his peak. He finally retired in April 2010 after failing to make the Dodgers in spring training, finishing his career with 187 saves.

Despite Gagne's success, John Hiller actually is the only Canadian to hold the major league record for most saves in a season. He set the major league mark with 38 in 1973, a number that has been surpassed quite a few times since. Hiller spent his entire 15-year career with the Tigers, recording 125 saves with a 2.83 ERA. He was an All-Star in 1974 after a most unusual year — he went 17–14 while pitching 150 innings without starting a single game. What's remarkable about Hiller is that he was out of baseball in 1971 after suffering a heart attack at age 28. He recovered and ended up playing nine more seasons, getting inducted into the Canadian Baseball Hall of Fame in 1985.

Paul Quantrill appeared in 841 games (777 in relief) over a 14-year career. The London, Ontario, native led the league in appearances four straight years (2001–2004), appearing in over 80 games each season and making the All-Star team as a set-up man in 2001. Quantrill was inducted into the Canadian Baseball Hall of Fame in 2010.

The selection for all-time manager was a tough choice among George Gibson, Bill Watkins and Arthur Irwin. Watkins led the Detroit Wolverines to the 1887 World Series title, as they won what was then an exhibition series 10–5 over the St. Louis Browns. Watkins went 452–444 as a manager in the big leagues, finishing second in 1886 after guiding the Wolverines to 87–36 record. He also won 607 games managing 13 seasons in the minors including guiding the Indianapolis Hoosiers to a 27–4 start in 1885 before the Western League disbanded. As previously mentioned, Irwin won one American Association pennant in the nineteenth century but didn't otherwise distinguish himself as a manager. Gibson has the best winning percentage of the three at .546, but three second-place finishes was the best he did as a manager. Winning a World Series gives Watkins the edge over Gibson and Irwin and his lengthier career as a manager clinches things.

Appendix 2: The 100 Greatest Players of All Time

Now that you have read about the all-time greatest players by state, who wins bragging rights? Isn't it fun to wonder how the All-Time Alabama team's lineup with Willie Mays, Hank Aaron, and Mule Suttles might fare if it faced the deep All-Time Texas pitching staff with Greg Maddux, Smokey Joe Williams, Nolan Ryan and Bill and Rube Foster?

Or how about which state has the best all-time outfield? It might be hard to beat California's trio of Barry Bonds, Ted Williams and Joe DiMaggio, but Pennsylvania's star-studded group of Stan Musial, Ken Griffey, Jr., and Reggie Jackson isn't too shabby either. As for all-time best infield, a strong case can be made for New York (Lou Gehrig, Eddie Collins, Jimmy Collins and Alex Rodriquez) but I say Texas might be better with Ernie Banks, Joe Morgan, Eddie Mathews and Willie Wells.

So which state's all-time team is the best? Ranking all 2,500 players isn't feasible, but we can come up with a top 100 list. That allows you to see how many of the top 100 players came from each state. Only players covered in this book could be included, which means Pete Rose and Shoeless Joe Jackson are eligible, while Roberto Clemente, Mariano Rivera and other international players are not.

To come up with my list, I reviewed top 100 lists from Bill James, SABR, *The Sporting News* and other sources as well as Dr. Michael Hoban's statistical analysis that outlined the top 140 best players of the modern era. I did downgrade some players who are suspected of using performance-enhancing drugs, but you'll still find them in the list that follows.

1. Babe Ruth — MD
2. Willie Mays — AL
3. Honus Wagner — PA
4. Oscar Charleston — IN
5. Ty Cobb — GA
6. Hank Aaron — AL
7. Barry Bonds — CA
8. Ted Williams — CA
9. Mickey Mantle — OK
10. Walter Johnson — KS
11. Stan Musial — PA
12. Tris Speaker — TX
13. Josh Gibson — GA
14. Lou Gehrig — NY
15. Joe DiMaggio — CA
16. Satchel Paige — AL
17. Eddie Collins — NY
18. Lefty Grove — MD
19. Pete Alexander — NE
20. Cy Young — OH
21. Mike Schmidt — OH
22. Joe Morgan — TX
23. Alex Rodriquez — NY
24. Rickey Henderson — IL
25. Rogers Hornsby — TX
26. Jimmie Foxx — MD
27. Frank Robinson — TX
28. Mel Ott — LA
29. Turkey Stearnes — TN
30. Tom Seaver — CA
31. George Brett — WV
32. Christy Mathewson — PA
33. Pop Lloyd — FL
34. Eddie Mathews — TX
35. Arky Vaughan — AR
36. Greg Maddux — TX
37. Warren Spahn — NY
38. Pete Rose — OH
39. Ken Griffey, Jr. — PA
40. Nap Lajoie — RI
41. Johnny Bench — OK
42. Bob Gibson — NE
43. Yogi Berra — MO
44. Cal Ripken, Jr. — MD
45. Carl Yastrzemski — NY
46. Randy Johnson — CA
47. Roger Clemens — OH
48. Frank Thomas — GA
49. Smokey Joe Williams — TX
50. Bob Feller — IA
51. Sandy Koufax — NY
52. Kid Nichols — WI
53. Jackie Robinson — GA
54. Craig Biggio — NY
55. Duke Snider — CA
56. Carl Hubbell — MO
57. Roy Campanella — PA
58. Derek Jeter — NJ
59. Tony Gwynn — CA
60. Eddie Murray — CA
61. Reggie Jackson — PA
62. Robin Yount — IL
63. Charlie Gehringer — MI
64. Johnny Mize — GA
65. Gary Sheffield — FL
66. Ryne Sandberg — WA
67. Mule Suttles — AL
68. Willie McCovey — AL
69. Buck Leonard — NC
70. Steve Carlton — FL
71. Wade Boggs — NE
72. Harmon Killebrew — ID
73. Hank Greenberg — NY
74. Cool Papa Bell — MS
75. Chipper Jones — FL
76. Jim Thome — IL
77. Paul Waner — OK
78. Mark McGwire — CA

79. Al Simmons — WI
80. Mickey Cochrane — MA
81. Ernie Banks — TX
82. Jeff Bagwell — MA
83. Tim Raines — FL
84. Mike Piazza — PA
85. Al Kaline — MD
86. Sam Crawford — NE
87. Shoeless Joe Jackson — SC
88. Willie Stargell — OK
89. Frank "Home Run" Baker — MD
90. Jim Palmer — NY
91. Barry Larkin — OH
92. Willie Wells — TX
93. Paul Molitor — MN
94. Billy Williams — AL
95. Gaylord Perry — NC
96. Brooks Robinson — AR
97. Mordecai "Three Finger" Brown — IN
98. Biz Mackey — TX
99. Ozzie Smith — AL
100. Robin Roberts — IL

Eleven of these players are Negro Leaguers (plus five who played some in the Negro Leagues but more in the majors). The only eligible players who are not in the Hall of Fame are Mark McGwire, Tim Raines and Jeff Bagwell. This may be the first time Mackey is listed in a top 100 list, but everything I've learned about him proves he belongs. Quite a few experts say he was better than Johnny Bench, not to mention he was a switch-hitter. I'll let the rest of these selections stand on their own merit based on what I've outlined in the book.

The only inconsistency with the rest of the book is the fact that I flip-flopped Ted Williams and Joe DiMaggio. Williams is ranked higher on this list, but I judged DiMaggio to be California's All-Time Best Player. The Splendid Splinter's superior hitting statistics place him in everyone's top 10 list, while I've outlined the reasons why DiMaggio deserves to be California's all-time best player (primarily his nine championships and superior fielding/base running). This seems a good way to split the difference.

Texas came out on top with the most players — 10 — as Mackey's inclusion proved decisive. Here is the complete breakdown by state (representing 31 states): TX — 10; CA, NY — 9; AL, PA — 7; MD — 6; FL, GA, OH — 5; IL, NE, OK — 4; AR, IN, MA, MO, NC, WI — 2; IA, ID, KS, LA, MI, MN, MS, NJ, RI, SC, TN, WA, WV — 1.

Source Notes

Sources are listed in the order they were used for each state.

Alabama

1. Barra, Allen. *Rickwood Field: A Century in America's Oldest Ballpark.* New York: W.W. Norton & Company, 2010.
2. Rickwood Field background: rickwood.com and BallparkReviews.com
3. Satchel Paige bio: satchelpaige.com
4. Hirsch, James. *Willie Mays: The Life. The Legend.* New York: Scribner, 2010.
5. Selig quote: Hill, Benjamin. "Hank Aaron Childhood Home Opens with Flare," mlb.com
6. Hank Aaron stadium background: hankaaronstadium.com
7. Player rankings: James, Bill. *The New Bill James Historical Baseball Abstract.* New York: Free Press, 2003.
8. Radcliffe quote: McNary, Kyle. *Ted "Double Duty" Radcliffe.* Minneapolis: Viking Press, 1994.
9. Larry Brown, George Scales and Dan Bankhead bios: Riley, James A. *The Biographical Encyclopedia of the Negro Baseball Leagues.* New York: Carroll & Graf Publishers, 1994.
10. Nat Rogers quote on Larry Brown: Nat Rogers biographical file at National Baseball Hall of Fame Library.
11. Suttles quote: Hogan, Lawrence. *Shades of Glory: The Negro Leagues and the Story of African American Baseball.* Washington: National Geographic Society, 2006.
12. Suttles background: Holway, John. *Blackball Stars: Negro League Pioneers.* Westport, CT: Meckler Books, 1988.
13. Gentile, Derek. *Baseball's Best 1,000.* New York: Black Dog & Leventhal, 2004.
14. Holway, John. *The Complete Book of Baseball's Negro Leagues: The Other Half of Baseball History.* Fern Park, FL: Hastings House, 2001.
15. Showboat Thomas quote: *Denver Post,* 1937, as cited on pitchblackbaseball.com.
16. Honig, Donald. *The Greatest Shortstops of All Time.* Dubuque, IA: Brown & Benchmark, 1992.
17. Mays quote: *Newsweek,* February 5, 1979.
18. Mays HR fact: Gonzalez, Raymond. "Extra Inning Home Runs," SABR Research Journal
19. Dave Anderson on Henry Aaron, *Cult Baseball Players* (Edited by Danny Peary). New York: Simon & Schuster, 1990.
20. McGuire, Mark, and Michael Sean Gormley. *The 100 Greatest Baseball Players of the 20th Century Ranked.* Jefferson, NC: McFarland, 2000.
21. Billy Williams background: O'Connell, Jack. "How Sweet It Is — and Was," National Baseball Hall of Fame Yearbook 2009.
22. Campanella quote on Irvin: Baseball-Reference.com, BR Bullpen
23. Paige, Leroy, as told to Hal Lebovitz. *Pitchin' Man: Satchel Paige's Own Story.* Westport, CT: Meckler Books, 1992.
24. Holway, John. Foreword to *Pitchin' Man: Satchel Paige's Own Story.* Westport, CT: Meckler Books, 1992.
25. Kerrane, Kevin. *The Hurlers.* Alexandria, VA: Redefinition, 1989.

Alaska

1. Freedman, Lew. *Diamonds in the Rough.* Kenmore, WA: Epicenter Press, 2000.
2. goldpanners.com
3. alaskabaseballleague.org
4. Sheehan, Joe. "Schilling Bows Out," *Baseball Prospectus,* March 24, 2009.
5. *Sports Illustrated,* January 26, 2004.
6. baseball-almanac.com

Arizona

1. Warren Ballpark History: friendsofwarrenballpark.com
2. Spring training sites and history: BallparkReviews.com, Cactusleague.com, saltriverfields.com, baseballparks.com/Goodyear and arizonamuseumforyouth.com
3. Vascellaro, Charlie. "History of the Cactus League," cactusleague.com.
4. "Johnson Kills Bird with Pitch," Associated Press, March 25, 2001.
5. Riley, James A. *The Biographical Encyclopedia of the Negro Baseball Leagues.* New York: Carroll & Graf Publishers, 1994.
6. McNeil, William. *Black Baseball Out of Season: Pay for Play Outside of the Negro Leagues.* Jefferson, NC: McFarland, 2007.
7. McKenna, Brian. *Early Exits: Premature Endings of Baseball Careers.* Lanham, MD: Scarecrow Press, 2007.
8. Thorn, John, Pete Palmer, Michael Gershman, ed. *Total Baseball: Seventh Edition.* Kingston, NY: Total Sports Publishing, 2001.
9. Dewey, Donald, and Nicholas Acocella, *The Biographical History of Baseball.* New York: Carroll & Graf, 1995.
10. Kinsler background: Baseball-Reference.com BR Bullpen
11. Lee, Jane. "Perfect in Pink! Mother's Day A+ for Braden," May 9, 2010, mlb.com.

Arkansas

1. James, Bill. *The New Bill James Historical Baseball Abstract.* New York: Free Press, 2003.
2. Teske, Steve. "Major League Baseball Players," *The Encyclopedia of Arkansas History and Culture.* The Central Arkansas Library System.
3. Gregory, Mark. "Historians Working to Tell Full Story of How Spring Baseball Started in Hot Springs," *The Sentinel Record,* May 29, 2011.
4. Duren, Don. *Boiling Out at the Springs.* Dallas: Hodge Printing Co., 2006.

5. *The Sporting News*, March 5, 1892.
6. Leggett, William. "That Black and Orange Magic," *Sports Illustrated*, October 26, 1970.
7. Brooks Robinson official web site, brooksrobinson.com.
8. George Kell biography, National Baseball Hall of Fame web site, baseballhalloffame.org.
9. Elmore Leonard on George Kell, *Cult Baseball Players*. (Edited by Danny Peary) New York: Simon & Schuster, 1990.
10. Dean quote: Thorn, John, Pete Palmer, Michael Gershman, et al. *Total Baseball, Seventh Edition*. Kingston, NY: Total Sports Publishing, 2001.
11. Dizzy Dean official web site, dizzydean.com.
12. Gregory, Robert. *Diz: The Story of Dizzy Dean and Baseball During the Depression*. New York: Viking Penguin, 1992
13. Preacher Roe official web site, preacherroe.com.
14. Verdell Mathis bio, pitchblackbaseball.com.

California

1. Heaphy, Leslie A. *The Negro Leagues, 1869–1960*. Jefferson, NC: McFarland, 2003.
2. Frierson, Lateel. "Chet Brewer Classic Is Big Hit with Youths," *Los Angeles Times*, April 16, 1995.
3. Nelson, Kevin. *The Golden Game: The Story of California Baseball*. Berkeley: Heyday Books, 2004.
4. Thorn, John. *Baseball in the Garden of Eden*. New York: Simon & Schuster, 2011.
5. Blazovich, Phil. *Having Fun with Baseball Nicknames*. Woodbury, MN: MLC Publications, 1996.
6. Greenwald, Dave. "Alumnus Jackie Robinson Honored by Congress," *UCLA Spotlight*, February 1, 2005.
7. Dotinga, Randy. "Ted Williams: A New San Diego Icon," KPBS Radio's Culture Blog, November 1, 2010.
8. Chief Meyers profile by R.J. Lesch in *Deadball Stars of the National League*. Dulles, VA: Brassey's, 2004.
9. Rickey quote about Bordagaray: Dickson, Paul. *Baseball's Greatest Quotations*. New York: HarperCollins Publishers, 2008.
10. Stone, Eric. *The Wrong Side of the Wall: The Life of Blackie Schwamb, the Greatest Prison Baseball Player of All Time*. Guilford, CT: The Lyons Press, 2005.
11. Player rankings: James, Bill. *The New Bill James Historical Baseball Abstract*. New York: Free Press, 2003.
12. Career Win Shares: The Baseball Gauge@Seamheads.com
13. Murray quote by David Ginsburg, Associated Press, January 7, 2003.
14. McGwire quote: *Newsweek*, Dec. 28, 1998.
15. Chase quote: McCabe, Neil, and Constance McCabe. *Baseball's Golden Age: The Photographs of Charles M. Gordon*. New York: Harry N. Abrams, 1993.
16. DiMaggio quote by Musial: thebaseballpage.com
17. Williams quote: Dickson, Paul. *Baseball's Greatest Quotations*. New York: HarperCollins Publishers, 2008.
18. Shantz quote on Williams: baseball-almanac.com
19. Bonds quote: thebaseballpage.com
20. Snider quote: *The New York Times*, January 10, 1980.
21. Seaver quote: *The New York Times*, January 11, 1976.
22. Gomez quote: Dickson, Paul. *Baseball's Greatest Quotations*. New York: HarperCollins Publishers, 2008.
23. Gammons, Peter. "One Eck of a Guy," *Sports Illustrated*, December 12, 1988.
24. Quisenberry quote: *Sports Illustrated*, December 6, 1982.
25. McGraw quote: *Sports Illustrated*, April 1975.
26. Golenbock, Peter. *Wild, High and Tight: The Life and Death of Billy Martin*. New York: St. Martin's Press, 1994.
27. Falkner, David. *The Last Yankee: The Turbulent Life of Billy Martin*. New York: Simon & Schuster, 1992.

28. Martin quote: *The Sporting News*, October 26, 1968.
29. Morris, Peter. *A Game of Inches*. Chicago: Ivan R. Dee, 2006.
30. Frank Chance profile by Gregory Ryhal in *Deadball Stars of the National League*. Dulles, VA: Brassey's, 2004.

Colorado

1. B's Ballpark Museum, ballparkmuseum.com
2. Wong, Stephen. *Smithsonian Baseball*. New York: HarperCollins Publishers, 2005.
3. Noel, Tom. "Denver's Original River Front Park," *Above the Fruited Plain: Baseball in the Rocky Mountain West*. Edited by Thomas Altherr. Cleveland: The Society for American Baseball Research, 2003.
4. Werner, Brian. "Baseball in Colorado Territory," *Above the Fruited Plain: Baseball in the Rocky Mountain West*. Edited by Thomas Altherr. Cleveland: The Society for American Baseball Research, 2003.
5. Atkinson, Chip. "Baseball Nuggets," *Above the Fruited Plain: Baseball in the Rocky Mountain West*. Edited by Thomas Altherr. Cleveland: The Society for American Baseball Research, 2003.
6. Rucker, Mark. "Ghost Town Nines," *Above the Fruited Plain: Baseball in the Rocky Mountain West*. Edited by Thomas Altherr. Cleveland: The Society for American Baseball Research, 2003.
7. Basquez, Anna Maria. "Steeped in Baseball History ... with Sugar," *Above the Fruited Plain: Baseball in the Rocky Mountain West*. Edited by Thomas Altherr. Cleveland: The Society for American Baseball Research, 2003.
8. Seymour, Harold. *Baseball: The People's Game, Volume 3*. Oxford University Press, 1991.
9. Halladay background: Baseball-Reference.com BR Bullpen
10. O'Connell, Jack. "Rise of a Reliever," National Baseball Hall of Fame and Museum 2008 Yearbook.
11. Gossage background: Baseball-Reference.com BR Bullpen and National Baseball Hall of Fame
12. May quote about Gossage: Dickson, Paul. *Baseball's Greatest Quotations*. New York: HarperCollins Publishers, 2008. Originally appeared in *The New York Times*, May 23, 1981.

Connecticut

1. Yale Field facts: yalebulldogs.com and digitalballparks.com
2. Malan, Douglas. *Muzzy Field: Tales From a Forgotten Ballpark*. Bloomington, IN: iUniverse, 2008.
3. Steve Blass Profile by Bob Hurte, SABR Biography Project.
4. Blass quote: Angell, Roger. *Five Seasons: A Baseball Companion*. New York: Warner Books, 1983.
5. Levy, Hal. "Connecticut: Two Games, 40K's for Janinga." Shore Line Newspapers, May 8, 2007.
6. Wright, Sylas. "Digging Up a Wild Tale," *Sierra Sun*, October 21, 2005.
7. Light, Jonathan Fraser. *The Cultural Encyclopedia of Baseball*. Jefferson, NC: McFarland, 1997.
8. Stewart, Wayne. *Baseball Oddities: Bizarre Plays and Other Funny Stuff*. New York: Sterling Publishing, 1998.
9. Piersall background: Westcott, Rich. *Splendor on the Diamond*. Gainesville: University of Florida Press, 2000.
10. Piersall, Jim, and Al Hirshberg. *Fear Strikes Out: The Jim Piersall Story*. Lincoln, NE: University of Nebraska Press 1999.
11. Puma, Mike. "More Info on Jimmy Piersall," November 19, 2003, ESPN.com.
12. Thorn, John. *Baseball in the Garden of Eden*. New York: Simon and Schuster, 2011.

13. Spec Shea: Baseball-Reference.com BR Bullpen.
14. Macht, Norman. *Connie Mack and the Early Years of Baseball*. Lincoln, NE: University of Nebraska Press, 2007.
15. Megdal, Howard. *The Baseball Talmud*. New York: Harper, 2009.
16. James, Bill. *The New Bill James Historical Baseball Abstract*. New York: Free Press, 2003.

Delaware

1. Wilmington Quicksteps: baseball-almanac.com
2. Duffy, John. "Delaware's Baseball History," russpickett.com/history/baseball.htm
3. Gelbert, Doug. *The Great Delaware Sports Book*. Montchanin, DE: Manatee Books, 1995.
4. Hans Lobert Profile by Jonathan Dunkle in *Deadball Stars of the National League*. Written by the Deadball Era Committee of The Society for American Baseball Research, edited by Tom Simon. Dulles, VA: Brassey's, 2004.
5. Ritter, Lawrence. *The Glory of Their Times: The Story of the Early Days of Baseball Told by the Men Who Played It*. New York: Vintage Books, 1985.
6. Riley, James. *The Biographical Encyclopedia of the Negro Baseball Leagues*. New York: Carroll & Graf Publishers, 1994.
7. Career Win Shares: The Baseball Gauge@Seamheads.com
8. Webster McDonald facts: pitchblackbaseball.com

District of Columbia

1. Macht, Norman. "Washington Nicknames," *The National Pastime*, The Society for American Baseball Research, SABR 39, 2009.
2. Rudman, Steve. "Wills No Steal as Manager," *Seattle Post-Intelligencer*, May 12, 1981.
3. Neyer, Rob. *Rob Neyer's Big Book of Baseball's Blunders: A Complete Guide to the Worst Decisions and Stupidest Moments in Baseball History*. New York: Fireside/Simon & Schuster, 2006.
4. Martini, Stephen. *The Chattanooga Lookouts and 100 Seasons of Scenic City Baseball*. Dry Ice Publishing, 2006.
5. Doc White Profile by John Bennett in *Deadball Stars of the American League*. Written by the Deadball Era Committee of The Society for American Baseball Research, edited by David Jones. Dulles, VA: Potomac Books, 2006.
6. McNeil, William. *The California Winter League: America's First Integrated Professional League*. Jefferson, NC: McFarland, 2002.
7. Nip Winters bio: Riley, James A. *The Biographical Encyclopedia of the Negro Baseball Leagues*, New York: Carroll & Graf, 1944.

Florida

1. The Elliott Museum
2. Ballparkreviews.com
3. baseballpilgrimages.com
4. Spring training history: springtrainingonline.com
5. McCarthy, Kevin. *Baseball in Florida*. Sarasota, FL: Pineapple Press, 1996.
6. Marchman, Tim. "Reviewing the Week's Hot Stove," Sports Illustrated.com, December 18, 2009.
7. Street, Jim. "Kotchman's Record Errorless Streak Ends," MLB.com, August 21, 2010.
8. Bitsy Mott: historicbaseball.com
9. Player rankings: James, Bill. *The New Bill James Historical Baseball Abstract*. New York: Free Press, 2003.
10. Career Win Shares: The Baseball Gauge@Seamheads.com
11. Peterson, Robert. *Only the Ball Was White*. New York: Gramercy Books, 1970.
12. Buck O'Neil background: National Baseball Hall of Fame and Museum
13. Pop Lloyd profile: Holway, John. *Blackball Stars*. Westport, CT: Meckler Books, 1988.
14. Dewey, Donald, and Nicholas Acocella. *The Biographical History of Baseball*. New York: Carroll & Graf, 1995.
15. Posnanski, Joe. "Appreciating the Understated Brilliance of Chipper and the Braves," Sports Illustrated.com, Sept. 20, 2009.
16. Riley, James A. *The Biographical Encyclopedia of the Negro Baseball Leagues*, New York: Carroll & Graf, 1994.
17. Dawson bio: National Baseball Hall of Fame and Museum
18. Raines, Gooden background: Baseball-Reference.com BR Bullpen
19. Posnanski, Joe. "Examining the Compelling Cooperstown Case for Tim Raines," Sports Illustrated.com, December 17, 2009.
20. Rivers quotes: mickeyrivers.com
21. Ted Trent bio: Negro League Baseball Players Association, nlbpa.com
22. LaRussa and Lopez managerial records: Baseball-Reference.com

Georgia

1. Ty Cobb Museum, tycobbmuseum.org
2. Robinson, Jackie. *I Never Had it Made*. New York: HarperCollins, 2003.
3. Erskine, Carl. *Tales from the Dodger Dugout*. Champaign, IL: Sports Publishing, 2000.
4. Alexander, Charles C. *Ty Cobb*. New York: Oxford University Press, 1984.
5. Speaker quote on Cobb: baseball-almanac.com
6. Hornsby quote on Cobb: *St. Louis Post Dispatch*, July 18, 1961.
7. Hogan, Lawrence. *Shades of Glory: The Negro Leagues and the Story of African American Baseball*. Washington: National Geographic Society, 2006.
8. The Legend of the Real Crash Davis, Philadelphia Athletics Historical Society.
9. Ross III, William F. "Spring Training in Georgia," *The National Pastime: Baseball in the Peach State*. The Society for American Baseball Research, 2010.
10. Heaphy, Leslie. "The Atlanta Black Crackers," *The National Pastime: Baseball in the Peach State*. The Society for American Baseball Research, 2010.
11. Spatz, Lyle. "Three Georgia-Born Former Dodgers Lead the Crackers to the Pennant," *The National Pastime: Baseball in the Peach State*. The Society for American Baseball Research, 2010.
12. Harwell, Ernie, with Tom Keegan. *Ernie Harwell: My 60 Years in Baseball*. Chicago, IL: Triumph Books, 2002.
13. Gentile, Derek. *Baseball's Best 1,000*. New York: Black Dog & Leventhal Publishers, 2004.
14. Player rankings: James, Bill. *The New Bill James Historical Baseball Abstract*. New York: Free Press, 2003.
15. Career Win Shares: The Baseball Gauge@Seamheads.com
16. Smith, Ron. *The Sporting News Selects Baseball's 100 Greatest Players*. The Sporting News Publishing Co.
17. Guillen quote on Thomas: Cowley, Joe. "Former White Sox Slugger Frank Thomas to Officially Retire," *Chicago Sun-Times*, Feb. 11, 2010.
18. Thorn, John, Pete Palmer, Michael Gershman, ed. *Total Baseball: The Ultimate Encyclopedia* (Eighth Edition). Kingston, NY: Sport Media Publishing, 2004.
19. Brashler, William. *The Story of Negro League Baseball*. New York: Ticknor & Fields, 1994.
20. Dick Redding bio: Holway, John. *Blackball Stars*. Westport, CT: Meckler Books, 1988.

21. Cockrell bio: Riley, James A. *The Biographical Encyclopedia of the Negro Baseball Leagues*, New York: Carroll & Graf, 1994.
22. pitchblackbaseball.com
23. Loverro, Thom. *The Encyclopedia of Negro League Baseball*. New York: Checkmark Books, 2003.
24. Riley, James A. "Red Moore: He Could Pick It," *The National Pastime: Baseball in the Peach State*, The Society for American Baseball Research, SABR 40, 2010.
25. Nap Rucker profile by Eric Enders in *Deadball Stars of the National League*. Written by the Deadball Era Committee of The Society for American Baseball Research, edited by Tom Simon. Dulles, VA: Brassey's, 2004.

Hawaii

1. Hawaiian Historical Society, "The Father of Baseball"
2. Thorn, John. *Baseball in the Garden of Eden*. New York: Simon and Schuster, 2011.
3. Weiss, Bill, and Marshall Wright. "1970 Hawaii Islanders," MiLB.com
4. Hawaii Sports: History, Facts and Statistics by Dan Cisco, 1999, University of Hawaii Press
5. hawaii-baseball.com
6. hawaiiwinterbaseball.com
7. Young, Geoff. "Remembering Wally Yonamine," espn.com, retrieved March 8, 2011.
8. *Sports Illustrated*, March 14, 2011.

Idaho

1. Killebew, Harmon, as told to George Vass. "The Game I'll Never Forget," *Baseball Digest*, February 1972.
2. Berowski, Freddy. "Killer Swing, Generous Heart," National Baseball Hall of Fame website, posted May 17, 2011.
3. Thursby, Keith. "Killebrew dies at 74," *Los Angeles Times*, May 18, 2011.
4. Killebrew bio: Baseball-Reference.com BR Bullpen and Baseball Hall of Fame and Museum 2010 Yearbook
5. Hal Luby bio: Baseball-Reference.com BR Bullpen
6. Andrecheck, Sky. "It's Fun, But When Position Players Pitch, Bad Things Usually Happen," *Sports Illustrated*, April 22, 2010.

Illinois

1. Bottomley-Ruffing-Schalk Baseball Museum.
2. Schwarz, Alan. "For Negro Leagues Players, A Measure of Recognition," *New York Times*, June 30, 2010.
3. Henderson record: Baseball-Almanac.com
4. Jackson, Frank. "Jay Hook: An Original Met," *Elysian Fields Quarterly*, Fall 2007.
5. Milt Stock record: Baseball-Reference BR Bullpen
6. Hershberger, Richard. "Chicago's Early Role in Professional Baseball," *The Baseball Research Journal*, Spring 2011, The Society for American Baseball Research.
7. Rader quote: Gammons, Peter. "He's An Angel Now," *Sports Illustrated*, August 7, 1989.
8. Germany Schaefer profile by Dan Holmes, *Deadball Stars of the American League*. Written by the Deadball Era Committee of The Society for American Baseball Research, edited by David Jones. Dulles, VA: Potomac Books, 2006.
9. Roy Gleason background: roygleason.com
10. Dewey, Donald, and Nicolas Acocella. *The Biographical History of Baseball*. New York: Carroll & Graf, 1995.
11. James, Bill. *The New Bill James Historical Baseball Abstract*. New York: Free Press, 2003.
12. Ray Schalk profile by Brian Stevens, *Deadball Stars of the American League*. Written by the Deadball Era Committee of The Society for American Baseball Research, edited by David Jones. Dulles, VA: Potomac Books, 2006.
13. Schalk quote: John Sheridan, *The Sporting News*, 1923, as referenced in *Deadball Stars of the American League*.
14. Larry Doyle profile by R.J. Lesch, *Deadball Stars of the National League*. Written by the Deadball Era Committee of The Society for American Baseball Research, edited by Tom Simon. Dulles, VA: Brassey's, 2004.
15. Lou Boudreau profile: Westcott, Rich. *Splendor on the Diamond*. Gainesville: University of Florida Press, 2000.
16. National Baseball Hall of Fame 2010 Yearbook
17. Roberts quote: Bechtel, Mark. "The Lives They Lived," *Sports Illustrated*, December 27, 2010.
18. Coffey, Wayne. "On 40th Anniversary of 31-Win Season, Denny McLain Reflects on Life," *New York Daily News*, April 5, 2008.
19. Knox, John A. "The 100 Top-Fielding MLB Pitchers, circa 1900–2008," *The Baseball Research Journal*, The Society For American Baseball Research, Summer 2009.
20. Herzog, Whitey, and Kevin Horrigan. *White Rat: A Life in Baseball*. New York: Harper & Row, 1987.
21. Kahn, Roger. *The Boys of Summer*. New York: Signet, 1973.

Indiana

1. Madden, W.C. *The Hoosiers of Summer*. Indianapolis: Guild Press of Indiana, 1994.
2. Player Rankings: James, Bill. *The New Bill James Historical Baseball Abstract*. New York: Free Press, 2003.
3. Charleston background: Riley, James. *The Biographical Encyclopedia of the Negro Baseball Leagues*. New York: Carroll & Graf, 1994; and Negro Leagues Baseball Players Association, nlbpa.com.
4. Charleston quote: Holway, John. *Blackball Stars: Negro League Pioneers*. Westport, CT: Meckler Books, 1988.
5. Hogan, Lawrence. *Shades of Glory: The Negro Leagues and the Story of African American Baseball*. Washington, DC: National Geographic Society, 2006.
6. Indianapolis ABCs and Indianapolis Clowns history: "Negro League Baseball in Indianapolis," *The Indianapolis Star* library fact file, posted February 1, 2001.
7. Madden, W.C. *Baseball in Indianapolis*. Charleston, SC: Arcadia Publishing, 2003.
8. Donie Bush bio: Baseball-Reference.com BR Bullpen
9. Moyes, Jim. Donie Bush profile in *Deadball Stars of the American League*. Written by the Deadball Era Committee of The Society for American Baseball Research, edited by David Jones. Dulles, VA: Potomac Books, 2006.
10. Bert Shepard background: Tellis, Richard. *Once Around the Bases*. Chicago: Triumph Books, 1998.
11. Goldstein, Richard. "Bart Shepard, 87, an Inspirational Amputee, Dies," *New York Times*, June 20, 2008.
12. Harley Hisner background: Neddenriep, Kyle. "He Found His Own Field of Dreams," *The Indianapolis Star*, July 2, 2011.
13. Spring training: Baseball-Almanac.com
14. Career Win Shares: The Baseball Gauge@Seamheads.com
15. Mattingly bio: Baseball-Reference.com BR Bullpen and Don Mattingly official site, donmattingly23.com.
16. Hodges bio: Baseball-Reference.com BR Bullpen and Gil Hodges official site, gilhodges.com.
17. Hodges background: Dewey, Donald, and Nicholas Acocella. *The Biographical History of Baseball*. New York: Carroll & Graf, 1995.
18. George Crowe background: Marcos Breton, "Man Broke Barriers in Life, Sports," *Sacramento Bee*, January 23, 2011.
19. Crowe tribute: Madden, Bill. "It's a Madd, Madd World," *New York Daily News*, January 22, 2011.
20. Billy Herman background: Westcott, Rich. *Splendor*

on the Diamond. Gainesville, FL: University of Florida Press, 2000.

21. Warfield background: Riley, James A. *The Biographical Encyclopedia of the Negro Baseball Leagues.* New York: Carroll & Graf Publishers, 1994.

22. Edd Roush official site, eddroush.com.

23. Stinson, Mitchell. *Edd Roush: A Biography of the Cincinnati Reds Star.* Jefferson, NC: McFarland, 2010.

24. Carey background: National Baseball Hall of Fame 2011 Yearbook and Baseball-Reference.com BR Bullpen.

25. Carroll, Jeff. *Sam Rice: A Biography of the Washington Senators Hall of Famer.* Jefferson, NC: McFarland, 2007.

26. Thompson background: National Baseball Hall of Fame 2011 Yearbook and Baseball-Reference.com BR Bullpen.

27. Chuck Klein SABR Biography profile by James Lincoln Ray.

28. Broeg, Bob. "Klein and Baker Bowl Made for Each Other," *St. Louis Post-Dispatch,* September 9, 1978.

29. Cy Williams profile by Cappy Gagnon in *Deadball Stars of the National League.* Written by the Deadball Era Committee of The Society for American Baseball Research, edited by Tom Simon. Dulles, VA: Brassey's, 2004.

30. Ted Strong background: Riley, James A. *The Biographical Encyclopedia of the Negro Baseball Leagues.* New York: Carroll & Graf Publishers, 1994.

31. Mordecai "Three Finger" Brown official site, mordecaibrown.com.

32. Amos Rusie SABR Biography profile by Ralph Berger.

33. Babe Adams background: "436 Kisses for Pitcher," *The New York Times,* October 19, 1909, as recounted in *Newsday.*

34. Carl Erskine official site, carlerskine.com

35. Erskine background: Baseball-Reference.com BR Bullpen

36. Erskine, Carl. *Tales from the Dodger Dugout.* Champaign, IL: Sports Publishing, 2000.

37. Larsen, Don, as told to Al Boyle, "The Game I'll Never Forget," *Baseball Digest,* October 2003.

38. Tim Stoddard background: Baseball-Reference.com BR Bullpen.

39. Doc Crandall profile by R.J. Lesch in *Deadball Stars of the National League.* Written by the Deadball Era Committee of The Society for American Baseball Research, edited by Tom Simon. Dulles, VA: Brassey's, 2004.

Iowa

1. Billy Sunday background: Baseball-Reference.com BR Bullpen and billysunday.org

2. J.L. Wilkinson background: Holway, John. *Blackball Stars.* Westport, CT: Meckler Books, 1988.

3. History of Keokuk Baseball, keokuk.net

4. Player rankings: James, Bill. *The New Bill James Historical Baseball Abstract.* New York: Free Press, 2003.

5. Anson background: Baseball-Reference.com BR Bullpen, National Baseball Hall of Fame and Museum and Fangraphs.com

6. Fred Clarke background: Baseball-Reference.com BR Bullpen and National Baseball Hall of Fame 2011 Yearbook.

7. Sickles, John. *Bob Feller: Ace of the Greatest Generation.* Dulles, VA: Brassey's, 2004.

8. Feller, Bob, with Burton Rocks. *Bob Feller's Little Black Book of Baseball Wisdom.* Chicago: Contemporary Books, 2001.

9. Hoynes, Paul. "Blazing Fastball, Mesmerizing Curve: Major-League Peers Remember Bob Feller," *Cleveland Plain-Dealer,* December 16, 2010.

10. Rust Jr., Art, with Michael Marley. *Legends: Conversations with Baseball Greats.* New York: McGraw-Hill, 1989.

11. Joe Hoerner SABR Biography by Brian Cooper.

12. Faber and Vance bios: Baseball-Reference.com BR Bullpen.

13. "Last Iron-Man Recalls Feat" by Pat Harmon, *Baseball Digest,* August 1955.

Kansas

1. Damon achievement: Baseball-almanac.com

2. Kanehl obituary, *The New York Times,* December 31, 2004.

3. Busch, Thomas S. "Sunflower Stars: Big Leaguers from Kansas," *Kansas History,* Summer 1988, vol. 11, no. 2.

4. Cobb quote on Johnson: Cobb, Ty, with Al Stump. *My Life in Baseball—The True Record.* Garden City, New York: Doubleday and Company, 1961.

5. Thomas, Henry W. *Walter Johnson: Baseball's Big Train.* Washington, D.C.: Farragut Publishing, 1995.

6. Walter Johnson background: James, Bill. *The New Bill James Historical Baseball Abstract.* New York: Free Press, 2003.

7. Giles, Mothell, Wickware bios: Riley, James A. *The Biographical Encyclopedia of the Negro Baseball Leagues,* New York: Carroll & Graf, 1994.

8. Tinker background: James, Bill. *The Politics of Glory.* New York: Macmillan Publishing, 1994.

9. Thorn, John, Pete Palmer and Michael Gershman, ed. *Total Baseball: Seventh Edition.* Kingston, NY: Total Sports Publishing, 2001.

10. Holway, John. *Blackball Stars.* Westport, CT: Meckler Books, 1988.

11. Damon, Johnny, with Peter Golenbock. *Idiot: Beating the "Curse" and Enjoying the Game of Life.* New York: Crown Publishers, 2005.

12. "Segui Says He Got Steroids from Ex-Mets Clubhouse Attendant," Associated Press, December 11, 2007.

13. Markusen, Bruce. "Cooperstown Confidential: Ross Grimsley and the Swingin' '70s," *The Hardball Times,* May 21, 2010.

14. Holway, John. *Black Diamonds.* New York: Stadium Books, 1991.

15. Schlossberg, Dan. *The New Baseball Catalog.* Middle Village, NY: Green River Writers/Grex Press, 1998.

16. Chet Brewer bio: pitchblackbaseball.com

17. Clyde background: Spiegler, Marc. "From Hardball to Hardware," *Members* magazine, April 1996.

18. Fimrite, Ron. *Sports Illustrated,* "Bonny Debut for Clyde," July 9, 1973

19. Topkin, Marc. "New Tampa Bay Rays Reliever Kyle Farnsworth Intimidating on Mound, Has Mellowed Off," *St. Petersburg Times,* March 6, 2011.

20. Houk background: Gary Bedingfield, BaseballinWartime.com

21. Mauch quote: Dickson, Paul. *Baseball's Greatest Quotations.* New York: HarperCollins, 2008.

Kentucky

1. Louisville Slugger Museum

2. Pete Browning SABR Biography by Philip Von Borries

3. Ray Chapman SABR Biography by Don Jensen.

4. Sowell, Mike. *The Pitch That Killed.* New York: Macmillan, 1989.

5. Reese quote: Dickson, Paul. *Baseball's Greatest Quotations.* New York: HarperCollins Publishers, 2008. Originally appeared in *The Boys of Summer* by Roger Kahn.

6. Shapiro, Michael. *The Last Good Season.* New York: Doubleday, 2003.

7. The Official Site of Pee Wee Reese, peeweereese.com.

8. Harry Pulliam profile by Bill Lamberty, *Deadball Stars of the National League.* Written by the Deadball Era Com-

mittee of The Society for American Baseball Research, edited by Tom Simon. Dulles, VA: Brassey's, 2004.
9. Conner, Floyd. *Baseball's Most Wanted*. Dulles, VA: Brassey's, 2000.
10. Sammy Hughes and Jim Bunning background: James, Bill. *The New Bill James Historical Baseball Abstract*. New York: Free Press, 2003.
11. Dewey, Donald, and Nicholas Acocella. *The Biographical History of Baseball*. New York: Carroll & Graf, 1995.
12. John Beckwith background: pitchblackbaseball.com
13. John Beckwith and Harry Buckner bios: Riley, James A. *The Biographical Encyclopedia of the Negro Baseball Leagues*, New York: Carroll & Graf, 1994.
14. Pete Browning background: Baseball-Reference.com BR Bullpen
15. Negro League Baseball Players Association, nlbpa.com
16. Levitt, Daniel. "Lowest Season ERA? Ferdie Schupp," *The Baseball Research Journal*, SABR 25, The Society for American Baseball Research, 1996.

Louisiana

1. New Orleans baseball history: Schott-Pelican Chapter New Orleans of SABR; sabrneworleans.com/history.html
2. Career Win Shares: The Baseball Gauge@Seamheads.com
3. Dickey background: Dewey, Donald and Nicholas Acocella. *The Biographical History of Baseball*. New York: Carroll & Graf, 1995.
4. Stein, Fred. *Mel Ott: The Little Giant of Baseball*. Jefferson, NC: McFarland, 1999.
5. Marcelle background and quote: Holway, John. *Blackball Stars* Westport: Meckler Books, 1988.
6. Malarcher quote: pitchblackbaseball.com
7. Bassett, Marcelle, Malarcher and Williard Brown bios: Riley, James A. *The Biographical Encyclopedia of the Negro Baseball Leagues*. New York: Carroll & Graf, 1994.
8. Rusty Staub background: Baseball-Reference.com BR Bullpen
9. Blau, Clifford. "Leg Men," *The Baseball Research Journal*, Summer 2009, Vol. 38, No. 1.
10. Libby, Bill and Vida Blue. *Vida: His Own Story*. Englewood Cliffs, NJ: Prentice-Hall, 1972.
11. Guidry, Pettitte, and Lee Smith background: Baseball Reference.com BR Bullpen
12. Guidry quote: Cimini, Rich. *Baseball Digest*, November 1989.
13. Harper, John. "Pettitte Carves Out Legacy as One of the Yankees' Best Big-Game Pitchers," *New York Daily News*, March 20, 2010.
14. Ted Lyons SABR Biography by Warren Corbett

Maine

1. Stewart, Bill. "Augusta Millionaires Captured Capital City's Attention," *Kennebec Journal*, March 17, 2010.
2. Cummins, Sharon. "Kennebunkport's Bat, Ball and Glove History," Old News From Southern Maine, someoldnews.com, posted September 2, 2010.
3. George Gore SABR Biography by Will Anderson
4. Liberman, Noah. *Glove Affairs*. Chicago: Triumph Books, 2003.
5. Clyde Sukeforth background: Baseball-Reference.com BR Bullpen
6. Louis Sockalexis SABR Biography by David Fleitz
7. Gratwick, Harry. "The Colorful Career of One of the State's Best Players," Island Institute and Working Waterfront, April 2009.
8. Bill Carrigan profile by Mark Armour, *Deadball Stars of the American League*. Written by the Deadball Era Committee of The Society for American Baseball Research, edited by David Jones. Dulles, VA: Potomac Books, 2006.

Maryland

1. baberuthmuseum.com
2. Ivoery, Bill. "Burial Sites of Hall of Famers," SABR *Research Journal*.
3. Justin Maxwell fact: Bill Ladson, MLB.com, September 30, 2009.
4. Monumental Baseball: The National Pastime in the National Capital Region, The Society for American Baseball Research, *National Pastime* SABR 39.
5. Solomon, Burt. *Where They Ain't—The Fabled Life and Untimely Death of the Original Baltimore Orioles, the Team That Gave Birth to Modern Baseball*. New York: Free Press, 1999.
6. Rosenberg, Howard. *Cap Anson 3: Muggsy John McGraw and the Tricksters: Baseball's Fun Age of Rule Bending*. Arlington, VA: Tile Books, 2005.
7. McGraw quote: Dickson, Paul, *Baseball's Greatest Quotations*. New York: HarperCollins Publishers, 2008. As quoted in *The Baseball Card Engagement Book*.
8. Boots Poffenberger background: Conner, Floyd. *Baseball's Most Wanted*. Dulles, VA: Brassey's, 2000.
9. Gisriel, Austin. "Boots Poffenberger: No Taming That Tiger!" Seamheads.com, February 3, 2011.
10. Career Win Shares: The Baseball Gauge@Seamheads.com
11. Millikin, Mark. *Jimmie Foxx: The Pride of Sudlersville*. Lanham, MD: Scarecrow Press, 1998.
12. Foxx quote: Thorn, John, et al. *Total Baseball: Seventh Edition*. Kingston, NY: Total Sports Publishing, 2001.
13. Home Run Baker background: Baseball-Reference.com BR Bullpen
14. Judy Johnson quote: Holway, John. *Blackball Stars*. Westport, CT: Meckler Books, 1988.
15. Ripken, Jr., Cal, and Mike Bryan. *Cal Ripken, Jr. The Only Way I Know*. New York: Viking Penguin, 1997.
16. Dewey, Donald, and Nicholas Accocella. *The Biographical History of Baseball*. New York: Carroll & Graf, 1995.
17. Nelson, Don. "Maryland—Home of Homer Hitters," Monumental Baseball: The National Pastime in the National Capital Region. The Society for American Baseball Research, *National Pastime* SABR 39, 2009.
18. Ruth quote: Safire, William, and Leonard Safir. *Words of Wisdom*. New York: Simon & Schuster, 1989.
19. Werber quote on Ruth: Werber, Bill, and C. Paul Rogers III, *Memories of a Ballplayer*. Cleveland: The Society for American Baseball Research, 2001.
20. Ruth quote: Dickson, Paul, *Baseball's Greatest Quotations*. New York: HarperCollins Publishers, 2008. Originally appeared in Frederick G. Lieb's *Baseball As I Have Known It*. New York: Tempo, 1977.
21. Ruth quote: Creamer, Robert. *Babe: The Legend Comes to Life*. New York: Simon & Schuster, 1974.
22. Ruth quote: Montville, Leigh. *The Big Bam: The Life and Times of Babe Ruth*. New York: Broadway Books, 2006.
23. Kaline profile: Westcott, Rich Westcott. *Splendor on the Diamond*. Gainesville: University Press of Florida, 2000.
24. Kaplan, Jim. *Lefty Grove: American Original*. Cleveland: The Society for American Baseball Research, 2000.
25. SABR Emerald Guide to Baseball 2010
26. Hirsch, James. *Willie Mays: The Life. The Legend*. New York: Scribner, 2010.
27. Thorn, John, and John Holway. *The Pitcher*. New York: Prentice Hall, 1987.

Massachusetts

1. Lee quote: baseball-almanac.com
2. Marty Bergen SABR biography by Brian McKenna

3. Doc Powers background: Baseball-Reference.com BR Bullpen and baseballhistoryblog.com
4. Dewey, Donald, and Nicholas Acocella, *The Biographical History of Baseball*. New York: Carroll & Graf, 1995.
5. Frank Grant background: Riley, James A. *The Biographical Encyclopedia of the Negro Baseball Leagues*. New York: Carroll & Graf, 1994.
6. Player rankings: James, Bill. *The New Bill James Historical Baseball Abstract*. New York: Free Press, 2003.
7. Petrocelli, Rico, and Chaz Scoggins, *Rico Petrocelli's Tales from the Impossible Dream Red Sox*. Champaign, IL: Sports Publishing, 2007.
8. Rabbit Maranville official site, cmgww.com/baseball/maranvil/index.htm
9. Maranville quote: Dickson, Paul. *Baseball Greatest Quotations*. New York: HarperCollins Publishers, 2008. Originally quoted by Stanley Frank in *Sports Illustrated*, August 27, 1962.
10. Career Win Shares: The Baseball Gauge@Seamheads.com
11. Glavine quote: Feinstein, John. *Living on the Black*. New York: Little, Brown and Company, 2008.
12. Durocher, Leo, with Ed Linn. *Nice Guys Finish Last*. New York: Simon & Schuster, 1976.
13. Durocher quote: Dickson, Paul. *Baseball's Greatest Quotations*. New York: HarperCollins Publishers, 2008.
14. Macht, Norman. *Connie Mack and the Early Years of Baseball*. Lincoln, NE: University of Nebraska Press, 2007.
15. Koppett, Leonard. *The Man in the Dugout*. New York: Crown Publishers, 1993.

Michigan

1. Pahigian, Josh. *101 Baseball Places to See Before You Strike Out*. Guilford, CT: Lyons Press, 2008.
2. Holway, John. *Blackball Stars*. Westport, CT: Meckler Books, 1988.
3. Lester, Larry, Sammy Miller and Dick Clark. *Black Baseball in Detroit*. Chicago: Arcadia Publishing, 2000.
4. Angell, Roger. *Late Innings*. New York: Simon and Schuster, 1982.
5. Simmons, Grich, Gibson and Marshall background: Baseball-Reference.com BR Bullpen
6. Freehan, Bill: *Behind the Mask*. New York: World Publishing Co., 1970.
7. Career Win Shares: The Baseball Gauge@Seamheads.com
8. Kiki Cuyler and Billy Pierce background: Dewey, Donald, and Nicholas Acocella. *The Biographical History of Baseball*. New York: Carroll & Graf, 1995.
9. Neil Robinson bio: Riley, James A. *The Biographical Encyclopedia of the Negro Baseball Leagues*. New York: Carroll & Graf, 1994.
10. Cicotte quote: baseballlibrary.com
11. Walter Ball background: NegroLeagueBaseball.com
12. Jim Abbott background: jimabbott.net
13. Knox, John A. "The 100 Top-Fielding MLB Pitchers, Circa 1900–2008," *The Baseball Research Journal*, The Society For American Baseball Research, Summer 2009.
14. John Knox presentation at SABR 40, "Pitchers As Fielders: A Quantitative Analysis or ... Why Kirk Rueter is the best-fielding pitcher of all time"
15. Bisher, Furman. "Vulture of the Year," *Baseball Digest*, April 1967, retrieved May 7, 2011.

Minnesota

1. Thornley, Stew. *Baseball in Minnesota: The Definitive History*. St. Paul, MN: Minnesota Historical Society Press, 2006.
2. Minnesota baseball history, stewthornley.net
3. Barber, Phil. "Who Was Ernie Nevers?" *Press Democrat*, December 24, 2008.
4. Roger Maris Museum, rogermarismuseum.com
5. Career Win Shares: The Baseball Gauge@Seamheads.com
6. Maris quote: Thorn, John, Pete Palmer, Michael Gershman, ed. *Total Baseball, 7th Edition*. Kingston, NY: Total Sports Publishing, 2001.
7. Maris quote: Dickson, Paul. *Baseball's Greatest Quotations*. New York: HarperCollins Publishers, 2008.
8. Mantle quote on Maris: mickeymantle.com
9. Winfield background: Golenbock, Peter. *George*. Hoboken, NJ: John Wiley & Sons, 2009.
10. Swift, Tom. *Chief Bender's Burden: The Silent Struggle of a Baseball Star*. Lincoln: University of Nebraska Press, 2008.
11. Molitor and Morris background: Baseball-Reference.com BR Bullpen
12. Toni Stone profile by Stew Thornley, SABR Baseball Biography Project.

Mississippi

1. Doyle, Pat. "Luke Easter; Myth, Legend, Superstar," *Baseball Almanac*, September 2003.
2. Easter quote: *Baseball Research Journal*, 1984.
3. Career Win Shares: The Baseball Gauge@Seamheads.com
4. George Scott quote: Dickson, Paul. *Baseball's Greatest Quotations*. New York: HarperCollins, 2008. Originally appeared in *Sports Quotes: Grand Slams and Fumbles*. White Plains, N.Y.: Peter Pauper Press, 1989.
5. Nack, William. "George Scott is Alive and Well and Playing in Mexico City," *Sports Illustrated*, August 17, 1981.
6. Frank White background: Baseball-Reference.com BR Bullpen
7. Cool Papa Bell and Dave Parker background: James, Bill. *The New Bill James Historical Baseball Abstract*. New York: Free Press, 2003.
8. Cool Papa Bell bio: Riley, James. *The Biographical Encyclopedia of the Negro Baseball Leagues*. New York: Carroll & Graf, 1994.
9. Holway, John. *The Complete Book of Baseball's Negro Leagues*. Fern Park, FL: Hastings House, 2001.
10. Bradford background: Lewis, Michael. *Moneyball*. New York: W.W. Norton & Company, 2003.
11. Oil Can Boyd background: Ryan, Nolan, with Mickey Herskowitz. *Kings of the Hill*. New York: HarperCollins, 1992.

Missouri

1. Pahigian, Josh. *101 Places to See Before You Strike Out*. Gulford, CT: Lyons Press, 2008.
2. "State v. Pearce 'What's the Use' Chiles," Ron Shuler's Parlour Tricks Blog, May 28, 2006.
3. Negro Leagues Baseball Museum
4. Baldassaro, Lawrence, and Dick Johnson. *The American Game: Baseball and Ethnicity*. Carbondale, IL: SIU Press, 2002.
5. Johnson, Kevin. "The History of a St. Louis Baseball Franchise," Seamheads.com, Dec. 3, 2010.
6. Player rankings: James, Bill. *The New Bill James Historical Baseball Abstract*. New York: Free Press, 2003.
7. Berra, Yogi. *The Yogi Book*. New York: Workman Publishing Company, 1998.
8. Berra, Yogi, with Dave Kaplan. *When You Come to a Fork in the Road Take It!* New York: Hyperion, 2001.
9. John Kling profile by David Anderson, *Deadball Stars of the National League*. Written by the Deadball Era Committee of The Society for American Baseball Research, edited by Tom Simon. Dulles, VA: Brassey's, 2004.

10. Harry Steinfeldt profile by Tom Simon, *Deadball Stars of the National League*. Written by the Deadball Era Committee of The Society for American Baseball Research, edited by Tom Simon. Dulles, VA: Brassey's, 2004.

11. Frank Shellenback, Yogi Berra, Elston Howard, Ryan Howard, Bill Joyce, background: Baseball-Reference.com BR Bullpen.

12. Sievers quote: Westcott, Rich. *Splendor on the Diamond*. Gainesville: University Press of Florida, 2000.

13. Glenn Wright background: *Rain Check: Baseball in the Pacific Northwest*. The Society for American Baseball Research, 2006.

14. Jimmie Crutchfield bio: Riley, James A. *The Biographical Encyclopedia of the Negro Baseball Leagues*. New York: Carroll & Graf, 1994.

15. Reiser background: Boyle, Robert H. "Pete in the Bush," *Sports Illustrated*, September 2, 1957.

16. Pud Galvin and Carl Hubbell bios: National Baseball Hall of Fame and Museum

17. Cone quote: Olney, Buster. *The Last Night of the Yankee Dynasty*. New York: HarperCollins, 2004.

18. Smoky Joe Wood profile: Ritter, Lawrence, and Donald Honig. *The 100 Greatest Baseball Players of All Time*. New York: Crown Publishers, 1986.

19. Smoky Joe Wood profile by Michael Foster, *Deadball Stars of the American League*. Written by the Deadball Era Committee of The Society for American Baseball Research, edited by David Jones. Dulles, VA: Brassey's, 2006.

20. Hubbell quote: Dickson, Paul, *Baseball's Greatest Quotations*. New York: HarperCollins Publishers, 2008.

21. Donaldson bio: Negro Leagues Baseball Players Association and Riley, James A. *The Biographical Encyclopedia of the Negro Baseball Leagues*. New York: Carroll & Graf, 1994.

22. Stengel quote: Dickson, Paul *Baseball's Greatest Quotations*. New York: HarperCollins Publishers, 2008.

23. Weaver quote: Dickson, Paul. *Baseball's Greatest Quotations*. New York: HarperCollins Publishers, 2008. Originally appeared in *How Life Imitates the World Series* by Tom Boswell.

24. Weaver quote on Palmer: Gagnon Torrez, Danielle. *High Inside: Memoirs of a Baseball Wife*. New York: Putnam, 1983.

25. Stengel, Weaver and Williams background: Koppert, Leonard. *The Man in the Dugout*. New York: Crown Publishers, 1993.

26. Bloom, Barry M. "The Impossible Dream: Williams Finds Place Among Elite," National Baseball Hall of Fame and Museum 2008 Yearbook.

Montana

1. Centene Stadium: digitalballparks.com
2. McNally background: Dewey, Donald, and Nicholas Acocella. *The Biographical History of Baseball*. New York: Carroll & Graf, 1995.
3. Abrams, Roger I. "Arbitrator Seitz Sets the Players Free," *Baseball Research Journal*, SABR, Volume 38, Number 2, Fall 2009.
4. Dave McNally obituary by Ed West, *Billings Gazette*, thedeadballera.com.
5. Ed Bouchee background: Fitzpatrick, Frank. "2 Crimes, 2 Consequences," *Philadelphia Inquirer*, August 20, 2009.
6. Lowenstein background: Lee, Bill, and Jim Prime. *Baseball Eccentrics*. Chicago: Triumph Books, 2007.
7. Holtzman, Jerome. "Tappe, Member of Cubs' College of Coaches, Dies," *Chicago Tribune*, October 12, 1998.
8. Chicago Cubs official site: mlb.mlb.com/chc/history/timeline08.jsp

Nebraska

1. Nebraska Baseball Museum, nebraskabaseballmuseum.com
2. College World Series history: cwsomaha.com
3. Borzi, Pat. "C.W.S. Memories: Dave Winfield's final pitch," *New York Times*, June 28, 2010.
4. Sloppy Thurston background: baseballlibrary.com, Retrosheet.org and Baseball-Reference.com BR Bullpen.
5. Career Win Shares: The Baseball Gauge@Seamheads.com
6. Player rankings: James, Bill. *The New Bill James Historical Baseball Abstract*. New York: Free Press, 2003.
7. Caruso, Gary. *The Braves Encyclopedia*. Philadelphia, Temple University Press, 1995.
8. Boggs, Ashburn, Crawford, Alexander and Gibson bios: National Baseball Hall of Fame and Museum and Baseball-Reference.com BR Bullpen.
9. Alexander quote: Dickson, Paul. *Baseball's Greatest Quotations*. New York: HarperCollins Publishers, 2008.
10. Gibson, Bob, with Phil Pepe. *From Ghetto to Glory*. Englewood Cliffs, NJ: Prentice Hall, 1968.
11. Hummel, Rick. "An Unsung Skipper: Southworth Among Game's Most Proven Winners," 2008 Baseball Hall of Fame Yearbook.
12. Southworth quote: *Baseball Digest*, June 1949; also quoted by John P. Carmichael in the *Chicago Daily News* and included in Paul Dickson's *Baseball's Greatest Quotations*. New York: HarperCollins Publishers, 2008.

Nevada

1. Verducci, Tom. "Baseball's Lebron," *Sports Illustrated*, June 8, 2009.
2. Verducci, Tom. "Here He Comes," *Sports Illustrated*, August 1, 2011.
3. Christensen, Joe. "Cordova Gets Burned," *The Baltimore Sun*, Thursday, May 23, 2002.
4. Weiner, Richard. "Pitching the Zen of Zito," *USA Today*, Oct. 3, 2002.
5. Horowitz, Mitch. "Barry's Way," *Science of Mind*, September 2003.
6. "Phils Can't Stop Dodgers; Quakers Shut Out by Wheezer Dell," *The New York Times*, May 11, 1915.

New Hampshire

1. Thorn, John. "The True Father of Baseball," *Total Baseball, 8th Edition*. Kingston, NY: Total Sports Publishing, 2004.
2. Thorn, John. *Baseball in the Garden of Eden*. New York: Simon & Schuster, 2011.
3. Doc Adams SABR Biography Profile by John Thorn
4. Doc Adams background: Williams, Joe, "19th Century Overlooked Base Ball Legends Project — and the 2010 Candidates Are...." Seamheads.com, posted July 18, 2010.
5. Arlie Latham, SABR Biography Project by Ralph Berger.
6. James, Bill. *The New Bill James Historical Baseball Abstract*. New York: Free Press, 2003.
7. Selee background: Dewey, Donald, and Nicholas Accocella. *The Biographical History of Baseball*. New York: Carroll & Graf, 1995.
8. Latham background: Conner, Floyd. *Baseball's Most Wanted*. Washington: Brassey's, 2000.
9. Flanagan quote: Dickson, Paul. *Baseball's Greatest Quotations*. HarperCollins Publishers, 2008. Originally appeared in the *Washington Post*, April 2, 1989.
10. Hill, Benjamin, "Forgotten Members of the Great Experiment," mlb.com, Feb. 14, 2007.
11. Red Rolfe and Chris Carpenter background: Baseball Reference.com BR Bullpen

12. Lefty Tyler profile by Wayne McElreavy in *Deadball Stars of the National League*. Dulles, VA: Brassey's, 2004.

New Jersey

1. Yogi Berra Museum
2. hinchcliffestadium.org
3. "Lemongello Surrenders On Kidnapping Charges," *The New York Times,* January 23, 1982.
4. Jeter, Derek. *The Life You Imagine*. New York: Three Rivers Press, 2000.
5. Romano, Hayes and Richardson background: Baseball-Reference.com and James, Bill. *The New Bill James Historical Baseball Abstract*. New York: Free Press, 2003.
6. Kid Gleason SABR Baseball Biography Project profile by Dan Lindner.
7. Goslin, Medwick and Hamilton background: National Baseball Hall of Fame and Museum and Baseball-Reference.com BR Bullpen.
8. Medwick quote: Dickson, Paul. *Baseball's Greatest Quotations*. New York: HarperCollins Publishers, 2008.
9. Dewey, Donald, and Nicholas Accocella. *The Biographical History of Baseball*. New York: Carroll & Graf, 1995.
10. Bouton, Jim. *Ball Four*. New York: The World Publishing Company, 1971.
11. Bouton, Jim. *I'm Glad You Didn't Take It Personally*. New York: Morrow, 1971.
12. Armour, Mark. "The Revolution Started Here," *Rain Check: Baseball in the Pacific Northwest*. Cleveland: The Society for American Baseball Research, 2006.
13. McKeon managerial record: Baseball-Reference.com
14. Lucas, Ed, and Paul Post, "Jeff Torborg: A Baseball 'Lifer' Still Enamored by the Game," *Baseball Digest*, February 2002.

New Mexico

1. Official site of the Albuquerque Isotopes, http://albuquerque.isotopes.milb.com
2. Albuquerque Historical Society
3. Isotopes Stadium history: digitalballparks.com
4. Kiner background: ralphkiner.com and James, Bill. *The Politics of Glory*. New York: Macmillan Publishing, 1994.
5. Ralph Kiner quotes: baseball-almanac.com
6. Stephens background: Konig, Donald. *The Greatest Shortstops of All Time*. Dubuque, IA: Wm. C. Brown Publishers, 1992.
7. Kiner and Stephens background: Dewey, Donald, and Nicholas Acocella. *The Biographical History of Baseball*. New York: Carroll & Graf, 1995.
8. Haney managerial record: Baseball-Reference.com

New York

1. National Baseball Hall of Fame and Museum
2. *Sports Illustrated's The Baseball Book*. New York: Time Inc., 2006.
3. Notable achievements: Baseball-Almanac.com
4. Nash, Peter. *Baseball's Legends of Brooklyn's Green-Wood Cemetery*. Mount Pleasant, SC: Arcadia Publishing, 2003.
5. Thorn, John. *Baseball in the Garden of Eden*. New York: Simon & Schuster, 2011.
6. Holway, John. *The Complete Book of Baseball's Negro Leagues: The Other Half of Baseball History*. Fern Park, FL: Hastings House, 2001.
7. Bud Fowler SABR Biography by Brian McKenna
8. Riley, James A. *The Biographical Encyclopedia of the Negro Baseball Leagues*. New York: Carroll & Graf, 1994.
9. Dewey, Donald, and Nicholas Acocella. *The Biographical History of Baseball*. New York: Carroll & Graf, 1995.
10. Nemec, David. *The Great Encyclopedia of 19th Century Major League Baseball*. New York: Donald L. Fine Books, 1997.
11. Berg background: "A Look Back ... Moe Berg: Baseball Player, Linguist, Lawyer, Intel Officer," Central Intelligence Agency site
12. Connors quote: *Beckett Monthly*, April 1989.
13. Nahigian, Tom. "Bo and Dean: A Lifetime of Fun and Friendship," *The National Pastime, Endless Seasons: Baseball in Southern California*, SABR 41, 2011.
14. Merchant, Larry. "Oh, Woe is Bo! Another Unhappy Year for the Belinsky Kid," *Baseball Digest*, December 1966.
15. Sorci, Rick. "Baseball Profile: Former Pitcher Bo Belinsky," *Baseball Digest*, August 1994.
16. Vass, George. "Seven Most Improbable No-Hitters: Bo Belinsky's Date With Destiny," *Baseball Digest*, August 2002.
17. Herskowitz, Mickey. "Baseball's Stage Was Too Small for Belinsky," *Houston Chronicle*, Nov. 25, 2001.
18. Player rankings: James, Bill. *The New Bill James Historical Baseball Abstract*. New York: Free Press, 2003.
19. Robinson, Ray. *Iron Horse: Lou Gehrig in His Time*. New York: W.W. Norton & Company, 1990.
20. Greenberg, Hank, with Ira Berkow. *The Story of My Life*. Chicago: Triumph Books, 1989.
21. Eddie Collins profile by Paul Mittermeyer, *Deadball Stars of the American League*. Written by the Deadball Era Committee of The Society for American Baseball Research, edited by David Jones. Dulles, VA: Potomac Books, 2006.
22. Jimmy Collins profile by Stanton Hamlet, *Deadball Stars of the American League*. Written by the Deadball Era Committee of The Society for American Baseball Research, edited by David Jones. Dulles, VA: Potomac Books, 2006.
23. Henry Zimmerman profile by David Jones, *Deadball Stars of the National League*. Written by the Deadball Era Committee of The Society for American Baseball Research, edited by Tom Simon. Dulles, VA: Brassey's, 2004.
24. Rizzuto background: James, Bill. *The Politics of Glory*. New York: Macmillan Publishing, 1994.
25. Rizzuto quote: Dickson, Paul. *Baseball's Greatest Quotations*. New York: HarperCollins Publishers, 2008.
26. Biggio, Frisch, Whitaker, Rodriguez, Singleton, Colavito, Martinez, Hershiser, Franco background: Baseball-Reference.com BR Bullpen
27. Brouthers, Radbourn, Welch, Palmer, Koufax, Spahn bios: National Baseball Hall of Fame and Museum and Baseball-Reference.com BR Bullpen
28. Yastrzemski background: National Baseball Hall of Fame and Museum, Baseball-Reference.com BR Bullpen and official website of Carl Yastrzemski, yaz8.com.
29. Appel, Marty. *Slide, Kelly, Slide*. Lanham, MD: Scarecrow Press, 1996.
30. George Burns profile by R.J. Lesch, *Deadball Stars of the National League*. Written by the Deadball Era Committee of The Society for American Baseball Research, edited by Tom Simon. Dulles, VA: Brassey's, 2004.
31. Herman quote: Michael Gershman's *The Baseball Card Engagement Book*, 1989 edition.
32. Koufax quote: Dickson, Paul. *Baseball's Greatest Quotations*. New York: HarperCollins Publishers, 2008. Originally appeared in Koppett, Leonard. *A Thinking Man's Guide to Baseball*. Toronto, ON: SPORTClassic Books, 2004.
33. Spahn quote: Ryan, Nolan, with Mickey Herskowitz. *Kings of the Hill*. New York: HarperCollins, 1992.
34. Hershiser, Orel, with Jerry Jenkins. *Out of the Blue*. Brentwood, TN: Wolgemuth & Hyatt Publishers, 1989.
35. Franco quote: Thorn, John, Pete Palmer, Michael Gershman, ed. *Total Baseball: The Ultimate Encyclopedia 8th Edition*. Kingston, NY: Sport Media Publishing, 2004.
36. McGraw and Mathewson quotes: Hynd, Noel. *The Giants of the Polo Grounds: The Glorious Times of Baseball's New York's Giants*. New York: Doubleday, 1988.

37. McGraw and Torre managerial record: Baseball-Reference.com.

North Carolina

1. Johnny Allen background: North Carolina Sports Hall of Fame
2. Linthicum, Jesse. "Homer By Ruth Feature of the Game," *The Baltimore Sun*, March 8, 1914.
3. Montville, Leigh. *The Big Bam: The Life and Times of Babe Ruth*. New York: Broadway Books, 2006.
4. *Baseball in the Carolinas: 25 Essays on the States' Hardball Heritage*. Jefferson, NC: McFarland, 2002, edited by Chris Holaday.
5. Career Win Shares: The Baseball Gauge@Seamheads.com
6. Bohn, Michael. *Heroes & Ballyhoo: How the Golden Age of the 1920s Transformed American Sports*. Dulles, VA: Potomac Books, 2009.
7. Rick Ferrell SABR Biography by Kerrie Ferrell.
8. Leonard bio: National Baseball Hall of Fame and Museum and Riley, James A. *The Biographical Encyclopedia of the Negro Baseball Leagues*, New York: Carroll & Graf Publishers, 1994.
9. Leonard induction speech, baseballhall.org
10. Leonard quotes: Buck Leonard obituary by Richard Goldstein, *The New York Times*, Nov. 29, 1997. Grace quote: Associated Press, September 3, 2002.
11. Appling quote: Dickson, Paul. *Baseball's Greatest Quotations*. New York: HarperCollins, 2008. Originally appeared in William B. Mead's *The Official New York Yankees Hater's Handbook*. New York: Putnam, 1983.
12. James, Bill. *The New Bill James Historical Baseball Abstract*. New York: Free Press, 2003.
13. Dewey, Donald, and Nicholas Acocella. *The Biographical History of Baseball*. New York: Carroll & Graf, 1995.
14. Perry, Gaylord, and Bob Sudyk, *Me and the Spitter*. New York: Saturday Review Press, 1974.
15. Perry quote: *Sports Illustrated*, Oct. 3, 1983.
16. Catfish Hunter Hall of Fame Induction speech, National Baseball Hall of Fame and Museum.
17. Zachary quote: *The Sporting News*, Jan. 24, 1969.
18. Baida, Peter. "Hoyt Wilhelm," *Cult Baseball Players*, edited by Danny Peary. New York: Simon & Schuster, 1990.

North Dakota

1. Roger Maris Museum, rogermarismuseum.com
2. McNary, Kyle. "North Dakota Integrated Baseball History," pitchblackbaseball.com
3. ChrisCoste.com
4. Castrovince, Anthony. "Sweet Start for Hafner," April 9, 2006, MLB.com.
5. Hill, Justice B. "Hafner Ties Mattingly for Slams in Season," August 13, 2006, MLB.com.
6. Allen, Maury. *Roger Maris: A Man for All Seasons*. New York: D.I. Fine, 1986.
7. Coleman, Nick. "Heroic Maris Honored a Game Now Debased by Drug Scandal," *Minneapolis Star Tribune*, December 18, 2007.
8. Erstad background: Baseball-Reference.com BR Bullpen
9. Diamos, Jason. "Jays' Manager Is Hounded by War Tales," December 15, 1998, *New York Times*.

Ohio

1. White, Sol, with Jerry Malloy. *Sol White's History of Colored Base Ball*. Lincoln, NE: University of Nebraska Press, 1995.
2. Notable Achievements: Baseball-Almanac.com
3. Ban Johnson profile by Joe Santry and Cindy Thomson, *Deadball Stars of the American League*. Written by the Deadball Era Committee of The Society for American Baseball Research, edited by David Jones. Dulles, VA: Potomac Books, 2006.
4. Appel, Marty. *Munson: The Life and Death of a Yankee Captain*. New York: Random House, 2009.
5. Career Win Shares: The Baseball Gauge@Seamheads.com
6. Sisler, Larkin, Schmidt, Delahanty and Haines background: Baseball-Reference.com BR Bullpen.
7. Schmidt, Mike, with Glen Waggoner. *Clearing the Bases*. New York: HarperCollins, 2006.
8. Rose, Pete. *My Prison Without Bars*. Emmaus, PA: Rodale Press, 2004.
9. Downing, Garrett. "Despite His Past, Pete Rose Wants a Future in Baseball," *Las Vegas Sun*, April 6, 2009.
10. Al Oliver background: al-oliver.com
11. "Tommy Henrichs 1913–2009," *Sports Illustrated*, December 14, 2009.
12. Maddox quote: Ralphkiner.com
13. Wynn background: James, Bill. *The New Bill James Historical Baseball Abstract*, New York: Free Press, 2003.
14. Browning, Reed. *Cy Young: A Baseball Life*. Amherst: University of Massachusetts Press, 2000.
15. Murcer quote on Niekro: Donovan, Dan. "Here Are Some Choice Quotes By, For and About Pitchers," *Baseball Digest*, August 1984.
16. Grant Johnson, Ray Brown and Porter Moss profiles by Kyle McNary, pitchblackbaseball.com
17. Benny Kauff profile by David Jones, *Deadball Stars of the National League*. Written by the Deadball Era Committee of The Society for American Baseball Research, edited by Tom Simon. Dulles, VA: Brassey's, 2004.
18. Slim Sallee profile by Paul and Eric Sallee, *Deadball Stars of the National League*, Written by the Deadball Era Committee of The Society for American Baseball Research, edited by Tom Simon. Dulles, VA: Brassey's, 2004.
19. Dutch Leonard profile by David Jones, *Deadball Stars of the American League*. Written by the Deadball Era Committee of The Society for American Baseball Research, edited by David Jones. Dulles, VA: Potomac Books, 2006.
20. Zimmer, Don, with Bill Madden. *The Zen of Zim*. New York: St. Martin's Press, 2004.
21. Thorn, John, et al. *Total Baseball, 8th Edition*. Kingston, NY: Total Sports Publishing, 2001.

Oklahoma

1. American Indian listing: baseball-almanac.com
2. Parr, Sheila. *Oklahoma: Magazine of the Oklahoma Heritage Association*. Spring/Summer 1999.
3. geneologytrails.com, Mayes County, Oklahoma
4. AT&T Bricktown Ballpark: baseballpilgrimmages.com
5. SABR Biography of Chief Yellow Horse by Ralph Berger
6. Buford, Kate. *Native American Son: The Life and Sporting Legend of Jim Thorpe*. New York: Alfred A. Knopf, 2010.
7. Official Jim Thorpe website, cmgww.com/sports/thorpe/index.html
8. Dewey, Donald, and Nicholas Acocella. *The Biographical History of Baseball*, New York: Carrol & Graf, 1995.
9. Bench, Johnny, and William Brashler. *Catch You Later*. New York: Harper & Row Publishers, 1979.
10. Bench quotes: baseball-almanac.com
11. Anderson quotes on Bench and Stargell: Dickson, Paul. *Baseball's Greatest Quotations*. New York: HarperCollins Publishers, 2008. Originally appeared in 1989 Hall of Fame Yearbook.
12. Justice, Richard. "Orioles' Tettleton Gets Back in Swing." *Washington Post*, March 25, 1990.

13. Bob Costas eulogy at Mantle funeral: theswearingens.com/mick/eulogy.htm
14. Mantle quote: *Great Sports Reporting*, compiled by Allen Kirschner. New York: Dell Publishing, 1973.
15. Mantle, Mickey, with Herb Gluck, *The Mick*. New York: Doubleday, 1985.
16. Mantle, Mickey with Mickey Herskowitz. *All My Octobers*. New York: HarperCollins Publishers, 1994.
17. Burleigh Grimes quote: *The Sporting News,* April 20, 1955.
18. Reynolds quote: Dickson, Paul. *Baseball's Greatest Quotations*. New York: HarperCollins Publishers, 2008.
19. Rogan bio: Riley, James. *The Biographical Encyclopedia of the Negro Baseball Leagues*. New York: Carroll & Graf, 1994.
20. Rogan profile by Holway, John. *Blackball Stars*. Westport, CT: Meckler Books, 1988.
21. Lester, Larry. *Baseball's First Colored World Series: The 1924 Meeting of the Hilldale Giants and Kansas City Monarchs*. Jefferson, NC: McFarland, 2006.
22. Hogan, Lawrence. *Shades of Glory: The Negro Leagues and the Story of African American Baseball*. Washington, D.C.: National Geographic, 2006.
23. Dark background and managerial record: Baseball-Reference.com BR Bullpen

Oregon

1. Civic Stadium: savecivicstadium.org
2. Campf, Brian. "The Man Who Won Big for Portland." *Rain Check: Baseball in the Pacific Northwest*. Cleveland: Society for American Baseball Research, 2006, edited by Mark Armour.
3. Anderson, Paul, and Kip Carlson. "Lucky Beavers Carve Sole Link to PCL's Earliest Days," *Rain Check: Baseball in the Pacific Northwest*. Cleveland: Society for American Baseball Research, 2006, edited by Mark Armour.
4. Bouton, Jim. "Buses, Beer and Emboldended Batboys." *Rain Check: Baseball in the Pacific Northwest*. Cleveland: Society for American Baseball Research, 2006, edited by Mark Armour.
5. Murphy, Kingman and Lolich background: Baseball-Reference.com BR Bullpen and Fangraphs.com
6. Dewey, Donald, and Nicholas Acocella. *The Biographical History of Baseball*. New York: Carroll & Graf, 1995.
7. Lewis, Michael. *Moneyball*. New York: W.W. Norton, 2003.
8. Nowlin, Bill. *Mr. Red Sox*. Cambridge, MA: Rounder Books, 2004.
9. Gentile, Derek. *Baseball's Best 1,000*. New York: Black Dog & Leventhal, 2004.
10. The Baseball Gauge@Seamheads.com

Pennsylvania

1. Hecker background: Baseball-almanac.com
2. Little League Baseball Museum, littleleague.org/museum
3. Philadelphia Athletics Historical Society and Museum, philadelphiaathletics.org
4. The Clemente Museum, clementemuseum.com
5. ballparksofbaseball.com
6. Liberman, Noah. *Glove Affairs*. Chicago: Triumph Books, 2003.
7. James, Bill. *The New Bill James Historical Baseball Abstract*. New York: Free Press, 2003.
8. Phenomenal Smith: New Hampshire Historical Society
9. Metro, Charlie, and Tom Altherr. *Safe by a Mile*. Lincoln, NE: University of Nebraska Press, 2002.
10. Allan Travers SABR Biography by Gary Livacari
11. Pearlman, Jeff. *The Rocket That Fell to Earth*. New York: HarperCollins, 2009.
12. Osee Schrecengost profile by Dan O'Brien in *Deadball Stars of the American League*. Dulles, VA: Potomac Books, 2006.
13. Allen quote: Dickson, Paul. *Baseball's Greatest Quotations*. New York: HarperCollins Publishers, 1991.
14. Stanky quote: Obituary in *Washington Post*, June 8, 1999.
15. Wagner quote: Dickson, Paul. *Baseball's Greatest Quotations*. New York: HarperCollins Publishers, 2008.
16. DeValeria, Dennis, and Jeanne Burke DeValeria. *Honus Wagner: A Biography*. New York: Henry Holt & Company, 1995.
17. Giglio, James. *Musial: From Stash to Stan the Man*. Columbia, MO: University of Missouri Press, 2001.
18. Erskine quote on Musial: baseball-almanac.com
19. Lyons quote on Musial: Dickson, Paul. *Baseball's Greatest Quotations*. New York: HarperCollins Publishers, 2008.
20. Posnanski, Joe. "What Modern Baseball Can Learn from Stan the Man," *Sports Illustrated*, August 2, 2010.
21. Finnigan, Bob. "Young Cry For Help," *The Seattle Times*, March 15, 1992. Retrieved December 27, 2010.
22. Jackson, Reggie. *Reggie: The Autobiography*. New York: Random House, 1984.
23. Reggie Jackson official website, reggiejackson.com
24. Jimmy Sheckard profile by Don Jensen in *Deadball Stars of the National League*. Dulles, VA: Brassey's, 2004.
25. Furillo quote, official Carl Erskine website, carlerskine.com.
26. Mack quote on Mathewson: baseball-almanac.com.
27. Landis quote on Mathewson: *The Sporting News,* August 6, 1948.
28. Osee Schrecongost and Rube Waddell profiles by Dan O'Brien in *Deadball Stars of the American League*. Dulles, VA: Potomac Books, 2006.
29. Waddell quote: *Wisconsin State Journal*, April 11, 1934.
30. Eddie Plank profile by Jan Finkel in *Deadball Stars of the American League*. Written by the Deadball Era Committee of The Society for American Baseball Research, edited by David Jones. Dulles, VA: Potomac Books, 2006.
31. Dulles, VA: Potomac Books, 2006.
32. Posnanski, Joe. "Moose Hunting," joeposnanski.com blog, November 18, 2008.
33. Francis, Bill. "Bruce Sutter Rides Splitter from Gulf Coast League to Cooperstown," National Baseball Hall of Fame and Museum 2006 Yearbook
34. McCarthy 10 rules: *Baseball Digest,* August 1986.
35. Lasorda quote: baseball-almanac.com
36. Lasorda, Tommy, with David Fisher. *Artful Dodger*. New York: Arbor House Publishing Company, 1985.
37. Murtaugh quote: Dickson, Paul. *Baseball's Greatest Quotations*. New York: HarperCollins Publishers, 2008. Originally appeared in *Sport,* May 1961.

Rhode Island

1. Berkow, Ira. "33 Innings, 882 Pitches and One Crazy Game," *New York Times*, June 24, 2006.
2. Holtzman, Jerome. "Free Pass: Players Who Were Intentionally Walked with the Bases Loaded," *Baseball Digest*, May 2000.
3. Cooney record: baseball-almanac.com
4. "Was William Edward White Really First?" Associated Press, January 30, 2004.
5. Nap Lajoie SABR Biography by David Jones and Steve Constantelos.
6. McLaughlin, Dan. "The Path to Cooperstown: The Catchers," *The Hardball Times,* February 10, 2009.
7. Honig, Donald. *The Greatest Catchers of All Time*. Dubuque, IA: Wm. C. Brown Publishers, 1991.

8. Dewey, Donald, and Nicholas Acocella. *The Biographical History of Baseball*. New York: Carroll & Graf, 1995.

South Carolina

1. Shoeless Joe Jackson Museum
2. SABR Biography of Pat Luby by Steve Hatcher
3. Perry, Thomas K. *Textile League Baseball: South Carolina's Mill Teams 1880–1955*. Jefferson, NC: McFarland, 1993.
4. Nester, Bob. *Baseball in Greenville and Spartanburg*. Charleston, SC: Arcadia Publishing, 2003.
5. "Baseball in Greenville," historicbaseball.com
6. Shoeless Joe Jackson background: blackbetsy.com and Baseball-Reference.com BR Bullpen.
7. Jackson quote: Dickson, Paul. *Baseball's Greatest Quotations*. New York: HarperCollins Publishers, 2008.
8. Shore quote on Jackson: shoelessjoejackson.com.
9. Kelley, Brent. "Bill Voiselle Was Key Member of '48 Braves," *Sports Collectors Digest*, July 19, 1991.
10. Bill Voiselle SABR Biography by Saul Wisnia.
11. Nemec, David, and Scott Flatow. *Great Baseball Feats, Facts & Firsts*. New York: Signet Book, 2008.
12. Randolph, Rosen and Marion background: Baseball-Reference.com BR Bullpen
13. Ben Taylor, Doby and Rice bios: National Baseball Hall of Fame and Museum.
14. Chino Smith, Rap Dixon, Ben Taylor, Candy Jim Taylor, Steel Arm Taylor, C.I. Taylor bios: Riley, James A. *The Biographical Encyclopedia of the Negro Baseball Leagues*. New York: Carroll & Graf, 1994.
15. Nat Rogers biographical file, National Baseball Hall of Fame
16. Wilson, Brian. "Too Young to Die: Smith Career Shortened by Injury," mlb.com
17. Chino Smith quote: Holway, John. *Blackball Stars*, Westport, CT: Meckler Books, 1988.
18. SABR Biography of Del Pratt by Steve Steinberg
19. SABR Biography of Bobo Newsom by Ralph Berger

South Dakota

1. Grossfeld, Stan. "His Splendid Moment," *Boston Globe*, December 20, 2009.
2. Crowe, Jerry. "Meet the Only Man to Pinch-Hit for Ted Williams," *Los Angeles Times*, August 31, 2009.
3. South Dakota Sports Hall of Fame
4. SABR member David Trombley, "Major League's South Dakota Born Players," usfamily.net/web/trombleyd/index.html
5. Dewey, Donald, and Nicholas Acocella. *The Biographical History of Baseball*. New York: Carroll & Graf, 1995.
6. Collins and Bannister background: Baseball-Reference.com BR Bullpen
7. Anderson quote: baseball-almanac.com
8. Anderson quote: Dickson, Paul. *Baseball's Greatest Quotations*. New York: HarperCollins Publishers, 2008. Originally appeared in September 1989 *Major League Baseball Newsletter*.
9. Anderson managerial record: Baseball-Reference.com

Tennessee

1. Martini, Stephen. *The Chattanooga Lookouts & 100 Seasons of Scenic City Baseball*. Cleveland, TN: Dry Ice Publishing, 2006.
2. Petway and Monroe bios: Negro Leagues Baseball Museum, and Riley, James A. *The Biographical Encyclopedia of the Negro Baseball Leagues*, New York: Carroll & Graf, 1994.
3. Petway and Monroe bios: Negro Leagues Baseball Museum, nlbm.com

4. McCarver, Madlock and Finley background: Baseball-Reference.com BR Bullpen
5. Turkey Stearnes and Wild Bill Wright bios by Kyle McNary, pitchblackbaseball.com
6. Turkey Stearnes profile: Holway, John. *Blackball Stars*. Westport, CT: Meckler Books, 1988.
7. Earl Webb SABR Biography by Bill Nowlin
8. Berkow, Ira. "The Greatest Player Nobody Knows," *New York Times*, August 15, 2000.
9. Thomas, Henry W. *Walter Johnson: Baseball's Big Train*. Washington, D.C.: Phenom Press, 1995.
10. Cory Gann on Vada Pinson. *Cult Baseball Players*. Edited by Danny Peary. New York: Simon & Schuster, 1990.
11. Red Lucas SABR Biography by Al Quimby
12. Noodles Hahn SABR Biography by Dan Levitt

Texas

1. Fink, Rob. *Playing in Shadows: Texas and Negro League Baseball*. Lubbock: Texas Tech University Press, 2010.
2. Larry Dierker Chapter of The Society for American Baseball Research.
3. Riley, James. *The Biographical Encyclopedia of the Negro Baseball Leagues*. New York: Carroll & Graf, 1994.
4. Holway, John. *The Complete Book of Baseball's Negro Leagues: The Other Half of Baseball History*. Fern Park, FL: Hastings House, 2001.
5. Player rankings: James, Bill. *The New Bill James Historical Baseball Abstract*. New York: Free Press, 2003.
6. Mackey, Santop, Smokey Joe Williams and Rube Foster profiles: Holway, John. *Blackball Stars*. Westport, CT: Meckler Books, 1988.
7. Banks quote: Furlong, Bill. "Baseball Stars of 1959," as cited in baseball-almanac.com
8. Dewey, Donald, and Nicholas Acocella. *The Biographical History of Baseball*. New York: Carroll & Graf, 1995.
9. Seamheads.com Negro Leagues Database powered by The Baseball Gauge
10. Hornsby quote: Dickson, Paul. *Baseball's Greatest Quotations*. New York: HarperCollins Publishers, 2008.
11. Rogers Hornsby profile by Paul Andersen, *Deadball Stars of the National League*. Written by the Deadball Era Committee of The Society for American Baseball Research, edited by Tom Simon. Dulles, VA: Brassey's, 2004.
12. Career Win Shares: The Baseball Gauge@Seamheads.com
13. Mathews quote: National Baseball Hall of Fame and Museum Induction speech.
14. Speaker quote: Cohen, Robert W. *A Team for the Ages: Baseball's All-Time All-Star Team*. Guilford, CT: Globe Pequot Press, 2004.
15. Robinson quote: Bouton, Jim. *Ball Four*. New York: The World Publishing Company, 1971.
16. Flood, Curt. *The Way It Is*. Seattle: Trident Press, 1971.
17. Flood quote: Dickson, Paul. *Baseball's Greatest Quotations*. New York: HarperCollins Publishers, 2008.
18. Maddux quote: baseball-almanac.com
19. Negro Leagues Baseball Museum
20. Negro Leagues Baseball Players Association, nlbpa.com
21. Ryan, Nolan, with Mickey Herskowitz. *Kings of the Hill*. New York: HarperCollins, 1992.
22. Jackson quote on Ryan: baseball-almanac.com
23. Foster quote: Cottrell, Robert Charles. *The Best Pitcher in Baseball: The Life of Rube Foster, Negro League Giant*. New York: NYU Press, 2004.
24. Jackman quote: Peterson, Robert. *Only the Ball Was White*. New York: Gramercy Books, 1970.
25. Keown, Tim. "How Did This Guy Win 347 Games?" *ESPN the Magazine*.
26. Hofstetter, Steve. "Just a Game? The Tragic Story of Donnie Moore." Retrieved on April 28, 2002.

27. "Donnie Moore and the Burdens of Baseball," *The New York Times*, July 30, 1989.

Utah

1. Shaughnessy, Dan. *Reversing the Curse*. New York: Houghton Mifflin, 2005.
2. Dewey, Donald, and Nicholas Acocella. *The Biographical History of Baseball*. New York: Carroll & Graf, 1995.
3. "Loss of a Team," *The Spectrum and Daily News*, December 15, 2009.
4. Theodore quote: Lee, Bill. *Baseball Eccentrics*. Chicago: Triumph Books, 2007.
5. Prager, Josh. *The Echoing Green*. New York: Pantheon, 2006.
6. "The Giants Stole the Pennant," Associated Press, February 2, 2001.
7. Herman Franks obituary by Richard Goldstein, *New York Times*, April 1, 2009.

Vermont

1. History of Centennial Field, The University of Vermont
2. Simon, Tom, ed. *Green Mountain Boys of Summer: Vermonters in the Major Leagues 1882–1993*. Shelburne, VT: New England Press, 2000.
3. Lee Viau SABR Biography by Guy Waterman.
4. Montville, Leigh. *The Big Bam: The Life and Times of Babe Ruth*. New York: Broadway Books, 2006.
5. Elmer Bennett SABR Biography by Bob Bennett
6. Fisk background: Baseball-Reference.com BR Bullpen
7. Fisk quote: *Sports Illustrated*, July 30, 1979.
8. James, Bill. *The New Bill James Historical Baseball Abstract*. New York: Free Press, 2003.
9. Birdie Tebbetts SABR Biography by Tom Simon.
10. Larry Gardner and Ray Collins profiles by Tom Simon, *Deadball Stars of the American League*. Dulles, VA: Potomac Books, 2006.

Virginia

1. Spring training sites: baseball-almanac.com
2. Radford, Rich. "In WWII, Norfolk Hosted Baseball's Best," *The Virginian-Pilot*, July 24, 2011.
3. Smith, Claire. "Baseball: Astros to Virginia? It's All in a Whirl," *The New York Times*, October 27, 1995.
4. Todd and Randy Hundley background: Baseball-Reference.com BR Bullpen
5. The Mitchell Report: Name by Name," *The New York Times*, December 13, 2007.
6. Albert Haywood SABR Biography by Rebecca Alpert.
7. Wilson, Day quotes: Holway, John. *Blackball Stars*. Westport, CT: Meckler Books, 1988.
8. Angell, Roger. *Season Ticket: A Baseball Companion*. Boston: Houghton Mifflin, 1988.
9. Nemec, David. *The Great Encyclopedia of 19th-Century Major League Baseball*. New York: D.I. Fine Books, 1997.
10. Rixey quote: Dickson, Paul. *Baseball's Greatest Quotations*. New York: HarperCollins Publishers, 2008.
11. Poles, Fields bios: Negro League Baseball Players Association, nlbpa.com
12. Dandridge, Wilson, Day: biographical files, National Baseball Hall of Fame and Museum
13. Dandridge, Wilson, Hill, Poles, Day, Fields, McClellan bios: Riley, James. *The Biographical Encyclopedia of the Negro Baseball Leagues*. New York: Carroll & Graf, 1994.
14. Seamheads.com Negro Leagues Database powered by The Baseball Gauge
15. McNeil, William. *The California Winter League: America's first integrated professional league*. Jefferson, NC: McFarland, 2002.

16. Nelson, Zann. "Researcher Discovers Pete Hill's Burial Site," *Star Exponent*, Nov. 10, 2010.

Washington

1. *Rain Check: Baseball in the Pacific Northwest*, Edited by Mark Armour. Cleveland: The Society for American Baseball Research, 2006.
2. Price, Jim. "Stars Leapt to Bigs Through Spokane," *Rain Check: Baseball in the Pacific Northwest*, Edited by Mark Armour. Cleveland: The Society for American Baseball Research, 2006.
3. "Ed 'Spanky' Kirkpatrick" by Bruce Markusen, hardballtimes.com, November 16, 2010.
4. Price, Jim. "You Want Stars, Titles, Nicknames? Tacoma's Got 'Em," *Rain Check: Baseball in the Pacific Northwest*, Edited by Mark Armour. Cleveland: The Society for American Baseball Research, 2006.
5. Price, Jim. "Devastating Crash Reverberates 60 Years Later," *Rain Check: Baseball in the Pacific Northwest*, Edited by Mark Armour. Cleveland: The Society for American Baseball Research, 2006.
6. Lacitis, Eric. "Memories Fade, but Ben Cheney Lives on Through Stadium," *Seattle Times*, April 19, 2005.
7. Dewey, Donald, and Nicolas Acocella. *The Biographical History of Baseball*. New York: Carroll & Graf, 1995.
8. James, Bill. *The New Bill James Historical Baseball Abstract*. New York: Free Press, 2003.
9. Sandberg background: National Baseball Hall of Fame
10. Sandberg quote: Greenberg, Steve. "SN Conversation: Ryne Sandberg," *The Sporting News*, May 24, 2010.
11. Averill quote from Induction speech: National Baseball Hall of Fame and Museum.
12. Career Win Shares: The Baseball Gauge@Seamheads.com
13. Lincecum background: Baseball-Reference.com
14. Fred Hutchinson SABR Biography profile by Clay Eals

West Virginia

1. Akin, William. *West Virginia Baseball: A History, 1865–2000*. Jefferson, NC: McFarland, 2006.
2. Burkett record: baseball-almanac.com
3. Ed Kenna bio: Baseball-Reference.com BR Bullpen
4. Conner, Floyd. *Baseball's Most Wanted*. Dulles, VA: Brassey's, 2000.
5. Brett quote: Thorn, John, Pete Palmer, Michael Gershman, ed. *Total Baseball, 7th Edition*. Kingston, NY: Total Sports Publishing, 2001.
6. Jack Glasscock SABR Biography Project profile by William Akin.
7. Tiemann, Robert L., and Mark Rucker, ed. "John Wesley Glasscock," in *Nineteenth Century Stars*. Cleveland: The Society for American Baseball Research, 1989.
8. Jesse Burkett SABR Bio Project by David Jones.
9. Dewey, Donald, and Nicholas Accocella. *The Biographical History of Baseball*. New York: Carroll & Graf, 1995.
10. James, Bill. *The New Bill James Historical Baseball Abstract*. New York: Free Press, 2003.
11. Burdette quote: Dickson, Paul. *Baseball's Greatest Quotations*. New York: HarperCollins, 2008. Originally appeared in *No-Hitter* by Phil Pepe.

Wisconsin

1. Pajot, Dennis. *The Rise of Milwaukee Baseball*. Jefferson, NC: McFarland, 2009.
2. Uecker quotes: baseball-almanac.com and *Baseball Digest*, June 1972.
3. Lindemer, Adam. "The Power of Cheese: Top Wis-

consin-Born Sports Figures," retrieved on bleacherreport.com, September 8, 2009.

4. Happy Felsch profile by Jim Nitz in *Deadball Stars of the American League*. Written by the Deadball Era Committee of The Society for American Baseball Research, edited by David Jones. Dulles, VA: Potomac Books, 2006.

5. Salin, Tony. *Baseball's Forgotten Heroes*. Chicago: Masters Press, 1999.

6. Ed Konetchy profile by Paul and Eric Sallee in *Deadball Stars of the National League*. Written by the Deadball Era Committee of The Society for American Baseball Research, edited by Tom Simon. Dulles, VA: Brassey's, 2004.

7. Merkle background: Dewey, Donald, and Nicholas Accocella. *The Biographical History of Baseball*. New York: Carroll & Graf, 1995.

8. Gillette, Gary. *Emerald Guide to Baseball 2010*. Cleveland: Society for American Baseball Research, 2010.

9. Kuiper background: Baseball-Reference.com BR Bullpen

10. Cross and Keltner background: James, Bill. *The New Bill James Historical Baseball Abstract*. New York: Free Press, 2003.

11. Career Win Shares: The Baseball Gauge@Seamheads.com

12. Tony Kubek SABR Biography by Joseph Wancho.

13. Simmons and Nichols bios: National Baseball Hall of Fame and Museum

14. Addie Joss profile by Alex Semchuck in *Deadball Stars of the American League*. Written by the Deadball Era Committee of The Society for American Baseball Research, edited by David Jones. Dulles, VA: Potomac Books, 2006.

15. Grimes quote: Dickson, Paul. *Baseball's Greatest Quotations*. New York: HarperCollins Publishers, 2008.

16. Ed Killian Profile by Dan Holmes, *Deadball Stars of the American League*. Dulles, VA: Potomac Books, 2006.

Wyoming

1. Patchen, Mike. "Wyoming's Major Leaguers," *The Baseball Research Journal*, SABR 25, The Society for American Baseball Research, 1996.

2. Browning, Tom, with Dann Stupp. *Tom Browning's Tales from the Reds Dugout*. Champaign, IL: Sports Publishing, 2006.

3. The Mitchell Report: Name by Name," *The New York Times*, December 13, 2007.

4. Browning background: Baseball-Reference.com BR Bullpen

5. Spillner background: Baseball-Reference.com BR Bullpen

Appendix 1

1. Humber, William. *Diamonds of the North: A Concise History of Baseball in Canada*. Don Mills: Oxford University Press, 1995.

2. Canadian Baseball Hall of Fame & Museum

3. Liberman, Noah. *Glove Affairs*. Chicago: Triumph Books, 2003.

4. Dewey, Donald, and Nicolas Acocella. *The Biographical History of Baseball*. New York: Carroll & Graf, 1995.

5. Jordan, David M., Philadelphia Athletics Historical Society, philadelphiaathletics.org

6. "Baseball: Royal Robinson," *Newsweek*, Aug. 26, 1946.

7. "Royals Release Tom Lasorda, Winningest Montreal Pitcher," *The Sporting News*, July 20, 1960.

8. Morneau, Walker, O'Neill and Stairs background: Baseball-Reference.com BR Bullpen

9. Ferguson Jenkins bio: National Baseball Hall of Fame and Museum

10. The Mitchell Report: Name by Name," *The New York Times*, December 13, 2007.

Bibliography

Aleshire, William A. *Sandlot: The Soul of Baseball*. Westminster, MD: Heritage Books, 2005.

Alexander, Charles C. *Ty Cobb*. New York: Oxford University Press, 1984.

Allen, Maury. *Roger Maris: A Man for All Seasons*. New York: Donald I. Fine Inc., 1986.

Angell, Roger. *Five Seasons: A Baseball Companion*. New York: Warner Books, 1983.

_____. *Late Innings*. New York: Simon and Schuster, 1982.

_____. *Season Ticket: A Baseball Companion*. Boston: Houghton Mifflin, 1988.

Appel, Marty. *Munson: The Life and Death of a Yankee Captain*. New York: Random House, 2009

_____. *Slide, Kelly, Slide*. Lanham, MD: Scarecrow Press, 1996.

Baldassaro, Lawrence, and Dick Johnson. *The American Game: Baseball and Ethnicity*. Carbondale, IL: SIU Press, 2002.

Barra, Allen. *Rickwood Field: A Century in America's Oldest Ballpark*. New York: W.W. Norton & Company, 2010.

The Baseball Book, Sports Illustrated. New York: Time Inc., 2006.

The Baseball Research Journal, Spring 2011, Vol. 40, No. 1. Cleveland: The Society for American Baseball Research.

Bench, Johnny, and William Brashler. *Catch You Later*. New York: Harper & Row Publishers, 1979.

Berra, Yogi. *The Yogi Book*. New York: Workman Publishing Company, 1998.

_____, with Dave Kaplan. *When You Come to a Fork in the Road Take It!* New York: Hyperion, 2001.

Blazovich, Phil. *Having Fun with Baseball Nicknames*. Woodbury, MN: MLC Publications, 1996.

Bohn, Michael. *Heroes & Ballyhoo: How the Golden Age of the 1920s Transformed American Sports*. Dulles, VA: Potomac Books, 2009.

Bouton, Jim. *Ball Four*. New York: The World Publishing Company, 1971.

_____. *I'm Glad You Didn't Take It Personally*. New York: Morrow, 1971.

Brashler, William. *Josh Gibson: A Life in the Negro Leagues*. New York: Harper & Row, 1978.

_____. *The Story of Negro League Baseball*. New York: Ticknor & Fields, 1994.

Browning, Reed. *Cy Young: A Baseball Life*. Amherst: University of Massachusetts Press, 2000.

Browning, Tom, with Dann Stupp. *Tom Browning's Tales from the Reds Dugout*. Champaign, IL: Sports Publishing, 2006.

Buford, Kate. *Native American Son: The Life and Sporting Legend of Jim Thorpe*. New York: Alfred A. Knopf, 2010.

Busch, Thomas S. "Sunflower Stars: Big Leaguers from Kansas," *Kansas History*, vol. 11, no 2, Summer 1988.

Carroll, Jeff. *Sam Rice: A Biography of the Washington Senators Hall of Famer*. Jefferson, NC: McFarland Company Inc., Publishers, 2007.

Caruso, Gary. *The Braves Encyclopedia*. Philadelphia: Temple University Press, 1995.

Cava, Pete. *Tales from the Cubs Dugout: A Collection of the Greatest Cubs Stories Ever Told*. Champaign, IL: Sports Publishing, 2000.

Cobb, Ty, with Al Stump. *My Life in Baseball—The True Record*. Garden City, New York: Doubleday and Company, 1961.

Cohen, Robert W. *A Team for the Ages: Baseball's All-Time All-Star Team*. Guilford, CT: Globe Pequot Press, 2004.

Conner, Floyd. *Baseball's Most Wanted*. Dulles, VA: Brassey's, 2000.

Cottrell, Robert Charles. *The Best Pitcher in Baseball: The Life of Rube Foster, Negro League Giant*. New York: NYU Press, 2004.

Creamer, Robert. *Babe: The Legend Comes to Life*. New York: Simon & Schuster, 1974.

Damon, Johnny, with Peter Golenbock. *Idiot: Beating the "Curse" and Enjoying the Game of Life*. New York: Crown Publishers, 2005.

Deadball Stars of the American League. Written by the Deadball Era Committee of The Society for American Baseball Research, edited by David Jones. Dulles, VA: Potomac Books, 2006.

Deadball Stars of the National League. Written by the Deadball Era Committee of The Society for American Baseball Research, edited by Tom Simon. Dulles, VA: Brassey's, 2004.

DeValeria, Dennis, and Jeanne Burke DeValeria. *Honus Wagner: A Biography*. New York: Henry Holt & Company, 1995.

Dewey, Donald, and Nicholas Acocella. *The Biographical History of Baseball*. New York: Carroll & Graf, 1995.

Dickson, Paul. *Baseball's Greatest Quotations*. New York: HarperCollins Publishers, 2008.

Duren, Don. *Boiling Out at the Springs*. Dallas: Hodge Printing Co., 2006.

Durocher, Leo, with Ed Linn. *Nice Guys Finish Last*. New York: Simon & Schuster, 1976.

Erskine, Carl. *Tales from the Dodger Dugout*. Champaign, IL: Sports Publishing, 2000.

_____, with Burton Rocks. *What I Learned from Jackie*

Robinson: *A Teammate's Reflections On and Off the Field*. New York: McGraw-Hill, 2005.

Falkner, David. *The Last Yankee: The Turbulent Life of Billy Martin*. New York: Simon & Schuster, 1992.

Fehler, Gene. *Tales from Baseball's Golden Age*. Champaign, IL: Sports Publishing, 2000.

Feinstein, John. *Living on the Black*. New York: Little, Brown and Company, 2008.

Feller, Bob, with Burton Rocks. *Bob Feller's Little Black Book of Baseball Wisdom*. Chicago: Contemporary Books, 2001.

Fink, Rob. *Playing in Shadows: Texas and Negro League Baseball*. Lubbock, TX: Texas Tech University Press, 2010.

Flood, Curt. *The Way It Is*. Seattle: Trident Press, 1971.

Fox, William Price. *Satchel Paige's America*. Tuscaloosa, AL: The University of Alabama Press, 2005.

Freedman, Lew. *Diamonds in the Rough*. Kenmore, WA: Epicenter Press, 2000.

Freehan, Bill: *Behind the Mask*. New York: World Publishing Co., 1970.

Gagnon Torrez, Danielle. *High Inside: Memoirs of a Baseball Wife*. New York: Putnam, 1983.

Gelbert, Doug. *The Great Delaware Sports Book*. Montchanin, DE: Manatee Books, 1995.

Gentile, Derek. *Baseball's Best 1,000*. New York: Black Dog & Leventhal, 2004.

Gibson, Bob, with Phil Pepe. *From Ghetto to Glory*. Englewood Cliffs, NJ: Prentice Hall, 1968.

Giglio, James. *Musial: From Stash to Stan the Man*. Columbia, MO: University of Missouri Press, 2001.

Gillette, Gary. *Emerald Guide to Baseball 2010*. Cleveland: Society for American Baseball Research, 2010.

Golenbock, Peter. *George: The Poor Little Rich Kid Who Built the Yankee Empire*. Hoboken, NJ: John Wiley & Sons, 2009.

_____. *Wild, High and Tight: The Life and Death of Billy Martin*. New York: St. Martin's Press, 1994.

Greenberg, Hank, with Ira Berkow. *The Story of My Life*. Chicago: Triumph Books, 1989.

Gregory, Robert. *Diz: The Story of Dizzy Dean and Baseball During the Depression*. New York: Viking Penguin, 1992.

Harwell, Ernie, with Tom Keegan. *Ernie Harwell: My 60 Years in Baseball*. Chicago: Triumph Books, 2002.

Heaphy, Leslie A. *The Negro Leagues, 1869–1960*. Jefferson, NC: McFarland, 2003.

Hershiser, Orel, with Jerry Jenkins. *Out of the Blue*. Brentwood, TN: Wolgemuth & Hyatt Publishers Inc., 1989.

Herzog, Whitey, and Kevin Horrigan. *White Rat: A Life in Baseball*. New York: Harper & Row, 1987.

Hirsch, James. *Willie Mays: The Life. The Legend*. New York: Scribner, 2010.

Hogan, Lawrence. *Shades of Glory: The Negro Leagues and the Story of African American Baseball*. Washington: National Geographic Society, 2006.

Holaday, Chris, ed. *Baseball in the Carolinas: 25 Essays on the States' Hardball Heritage*. Jefferson, NC: McFarland, 2002.

Holway, John. *Blackball Stars: Negro League Pioneers*. Westport, CT: Meckler Books, 1988.

_____. *The Complete Book of Baseball's Negro Leagues: The Other Half of Baseball History*. Fern Park, FL: Hastings House, 2001.

Honig, Donald. *The Greatest Catchers of All Time*. Dubuque, IA: Wm. C. Brown Publishers, 1991.

_____. *The Greatest Shortstops of All Time*. Dubuque, IA: Brown & Benchmark, 1992.

Humber, William. *Diamonds of the North: A Concise History of Baseball in Canada*. Don Mills: Oxford University Press, 1995.

Jackson, Reggie. *Reggie: The Autobiography*. New York: Random House, 1984.

James, Bill. *The New Bill James Historical Baseball Abstract*. New York: Free Press, 2003.

_____. *The Politics of Glory*. New York: Macmillan Publishing, 1994.

Jeter, Derek. *The Life You Imagine*. New York: Three Rivers Press, 2000.

Kahn, Roger. *The Boys of Summer*. New York: Signet, 1973.

Kaplan, Jim. *The Fielders*. Alexandria, VA: Redefinition, 1989.

_____. *Lefty Grove: American Original*. Cleveland: The Society for American Baseball Research, 2000.

Kerrane, Kevin. *The Hurlers*. Alexandria, VA: Redefinition, 1989.

Konig, Donald. *The Greatest Shortstops of All Time*. Dubuque, IA: Wm C. Brown Publishers, 1992.

Koppett, Leonard. *The Man in the Dugout*. New York: Crown Publishers, 1993.

Lanctot, Neil. *Negro League Baseball: The Rise and Ruin of a Black Institution*. Philadelphia: University of Pennsylvania Press, 2004.

Lasorda, Tommy, with David Fisher. *Artful Dodger*. New York: Arbor House Publishing Company, 1985.

Lee, Bill, and Jim Prime. *Baseball Eccentrics*. Chicago: Triumph Books, 2007.

Lester, Larry. *Baseball's First Colored World Series: The 1924 Meeting of the Hilldale Giants and Kansas City Monarchs*. Jefferson, NC: McFarland, 2006.

_____, Sammy Miller and Dick Clark. *Black Baseball in Detroit*. Chicago: Arcadia Publishing, 2000.

Lewis, Michael. *Moneyball*. New York: W.W. Norton & Company, 2003.

Libby, Bill, and Vida Blue, *Vida: His Own Story*. Englewood Cliffs, NJ: Prentice-Hall, 1972.

Liberman, Noah. *Glove Affairs*, Chicago: Triumph Books, 2003.

Light, Jonathan Fraser. *The Cultural Encyclopedia of Baseball*. Jefferson, NC: McFarland, 1997.

Loverro, Thom. *The Encyclopedia of Negro League Baseball*. New York: Checkmark Books, 2003

Lyons, Jeffrey, and Douglas B. Lyons. *Out of Left Field*. New York: Times Books, 1998.

Macht, Norman. *Connie Mack and the Early Years of Baseball*. Lincoln: University of Nebraska Press, 2007.

Madden, W.C. *Baseball in Indianapolis*. Charleston, SC: Arcadia Publishing, 2003.

_____. *The Hoosiers of Summer*. Indianapolis: Guild Press of Indiana, 1994.

Malan, Douglas. *Muzzy Field: Tales From a Forgotten Ballpark*. Bloomington, IN: iUniverse, 2008.

Mantle, Mickey, with Herb Gluck, *The Mick*. New York: Doubleday, 1985.

Mantle, Mickey, with Mickey Herskowitz. *All My Octobers*. New York: HarperCollins, 1994.

Martin, Alfred M., and Alfred T. Martin. *The Negro Leagues in New Jersey: A History*. Jefferson, NC: McFarland, 2008.

Martini, Stephen, *The Chattanooga Lookouts & 100 Seasons of Scenic City Baseball*. Cleveland, TN: Dry Ice Publishing, 2006.

McCarthy, Kevin. *Baseball in Florida*. Sarasota: Pineapple Press, 1996.

McGuire, Mark, and Michael Sean Gormley. *The 100 Greatest Baseball Players of the twentieth Century Ranked*. Jefferson, NC: McFarland, 2000.

McKenna, Brian. *Early Exits: Premature Endings of Baseball Careers*. Lanham, MD: Scarecrow Press, 2007.

McNary, Kyle. *Ted "Double Duty" Radcliffe*. Minneapolis: McNary Publishing, 1994.

McNeil, William. *Black Baseball Out of Season: Pay for Play Outside of the Negro Leagues*. Jefferson, NC: McFarland, 2007.

McNeil, William. *The California Winter League: America's First Integrated Professional League*. Jefferson, NC: McFarland, 2002.

Megdal, Howard. *The Baseball Talmud*. New York: Harper, 2009.

Millikin, Mark. *Jimmie Foxx: The Pride of Sudlersville*. Lanham, MD: Scarecrow Press, 1998.

Monteleone, John, ed. *Branch Rickey's Little Blue Book: Wit and Strategy from Baseball's Last Wise Man*. New York: Macmillan USA, 1995.

Montville, Leigh. *The Big Bam: The Life and Times of Babe Ruth*. New York: Broadway Books, 2006.

Morris, Peter. *A Game of Inches*. Chicago: Ivan R. Dee, 2006.

Nash, Peter. *Baseball's Legends of Brooklyn's Green-Wood Cemetery*. Mount Pleasant, SC: Arcadia Publishing, 2003.

The National Pastime, Baseball in the Peach State, SABR 40. Cleveland: The Society for American Baseball Research, 2010.

The National Pastime, Monumental Baseball: The National Pastime in the National Capital Region, SABR 39. Cleveland: The Society for American Baseball Research, 2009.

Nelson, Kevin. *The Golden Game: The Story of California Baseball*. Berkeley, CA: Heyday Books, 2004.

Nemec, David. *The Great Encyclopedia of nineteenth Century Major League Baseball*. New York: Donald L. Fine Books, 1997.

_____, and Scott Flatow. *Great Baseball Feats, Facts & Firsts*. New York: Signet Book, 2008.

Nester, Bob. *Baseball in Greenville and Spartanburg*. Charleston, SC: Arcadia Publishing, 2003.

Neyer, Rob. *Rob Neyer's Big Book of Baseball's Blunders: A Complete Guide to the Worst Decisions and Stupidest Moments in Baseball History*. New York: Fireside/Simon & Schuster, 2006.

Nowlin, Bill. *Mr. Red Sox*. Cambridge, MA: Rounder Books, 2004.

Olney, Buster. *The Last Night of the Yankee Dynasty*. New York: HarperCollins, 2004.

O'Neil, Buck, with Steve Wulf and David Conrads. *I Was Right on Time*. New York: Simon & Schuster, 1996.

Pahigian, Josh. *101 Baseball Places to See Before You Strike Out*. Guilford, CT: Lyons Press, 2008.

Paige, Leroy, as told to Hal Lebovitz. *Pitchin' Man: Satchel Paige's Own Story*. Westport, CT: Meckler Books, 1992.

Pajot, Dennis. *The Rise of Milwaukee Baseball*. Jefferson, NC: McFarland, 2009.

Pearlman, Jeff. *The Rocket That Fell to Earth*. New York: HarperCollins, 2009.

Peary, Danny, editor. *Cult Baseball Players*. New York: Simon & Schuster, 1990.

Perry, Gaylord, and Bob Sudyk, *Me and the Spitter*. New York: Saturday Review Press, 1974.

Perry, Thomas K. *Textile League Baseball: South Carolina's Mill Teams 1880–1955*. Jefferson, NC: McFarland, 1993.

Peterson, Robert. *Only the Ball Was White*. New York: Gramercy Books, 1970.

Petrocelli, Rico, and Chaz Scoggins. *Rico Petrocelli's Tales from the Impossible Dream Red Sox*. Champaign, IL: Sports Publishing, 2007.

Piersall, Jim, and Al Hirshberg. *Fear Strikes Out: The Jim Piersall Story*. Lincoln, NE: University of Nebraska Press 1999.

Prager, Josh. *The Echoing Green*. New York: Pantheon, 2006.

Rain Check: Baseball in the Pacific Northwest. The Society for American Baseball Research, 2006.

Riley, James A. *The Biographical Encyclopedia of the Negro Baseball Leagues*. New York: Carroll & Graf, 1994.

Ripken, Jr., Cal, and Mike Bryan. *Cal Ripken, Jr. The Only Way I Know*. New York: Viking Penguin, 1997.

Ritter, Lawrence. *The Glory of Their Times: The Story of the Early Days of Baseball Told by the Men Who Played It*. New York: Vintage Books, 1985.

_____, and Donald Honig. *The 100 Greatest Baseball Players of All Time*. New York: Crown Publishers, 1986.

Robinson, Jackie. *I Never Had it Made*. New York: HarperCollins, 2003.

Robinson, Ray. *Iron Horse: Lou Gehrig in His Time*. New York: W.W. Norton & Company, 1990.

Rose, Pete. *My Prison Without Bars*. Emmaus, PA: Rodale Press, 2004.

Rosenberg, Howard. *Cap Anson 3: Muggsy John McGraw and the Tricksters: Baseball's Fun Age of Rule Bending*. Arlington, VA: Tile Books, 2005.

Rust, Art, Jr., with Michael Marley. *Legends: Conversations with Baseball Greats*. New York: McGraw-Hill, 1989.

Ryan, Nolan, with Mickey Herskowitz. *Kings of the Hill*. New York: HarperCollins, 1992.

Salin, Tony. *Baseball's Forgotten Heroes*. Chicago: Masters Press, 1999.

Schlossberg, Dan. *The New Baseball Catalog*. Middle Village, NY: Green River Writers/Grex Press, 1998.

Schmidt, Mike, with Glen Waggoner. *Clearing the Bases*. New York: HarperCollins, 2006.

Seymour, Harold. *Baseball: The People's Game, Volume 3*. New York: Oxford University Press, 1991.

Shapiro, Michael. *The Last Good Season*. New York: Doubleday, 2003.

Shaughnessy, Dan. *Reversing the Curse*. New York: Houghton Mifflin, 2005.

Sickles, John. *Bob Feller: Ace of the Greatest Generation*. Dulles, VA: Brassey's, 2004.

Simon, Tom, ed. *Green Mountain Boys of Summer: Vermonters in the Major Leagues 1882–1993*. Shelburne, VT: New England Press, 2000.

Skipper, James K. *Baseball Nicknames: A Dictionary of Origins and Meanings*. Jefferson, NC: McFarland, 1992.

Smith, Ron. *The Sporting News Selects Baseball's 100 Greatest Players*. The Sporting News Publishing Co.

Solomon, Burt. *Where They Ain't: The Fabled Life and Untimely Death of the Original Baltimore Orioles, the Team That Gave Birth to Modern Baseball*. New York: Free Press, 1999.

Sowell, Mike. *The Pitch That Killed*. New York: Macmillan, 1989.

Stein, Fred. *Mel Ott: The Little Giant of Baseball.* Jefferson, NC: McFarland, 1999.
Stewart, Wayne. *Baseball Oddities: Bizarre Plays and Other Funny Stuff.* New York: Sterling Publishing, 1998.
Stinson, Mitchell. *Edd Roush: A Biography of the Cincinnati Reds Star.* Jefferson, NC: McFarland, 2010.
Stone, Eric. *The Wrong Side of the Wall: The Life of Blackie Schwamb, the Greatest Prison Baseball Player of All Time.* Guilford, CT: The Lyons Press, 2005.
Swift, Tom. *Chief Bender's Burden: The Silent Struggle of a Baseball Star.* Lincoln, NE: University of Nebraska Press, 2008.
Tellis, Richard. *Once Around the Bases.* Chicago: Triumph Books, 1998.
Thomas, Henry W. *Walter Johnson: Baseball's Big Train.* Washington, D.C.: Farragut Publishing, 1995.
Thorn, John. *Baseball in the Garden of Eden.* New York: Simon & Schuster, 2011.
_____, and John Holway. *The Pitcher.* New York: Prentice Hall, 1987.
Thorn, John, Pete Palmer, Michael Gershman, ed. *Total Baseball, 7th Edition.* Kingston, NY: Total Sports Publishing, 2001.
_____. *Total Baseball: The Ultimate Encyclopedia, 8th Edition.* Kingston, NY: Sport Media Publishing, 2004.
Thornley, Stew. *Baseball in Minnesota: The Definitive History.* St. Paul, MN: Minnesota Historical Society Press, 2006.
Tiemann, Robert L., and Mark Rucker, ed. *Nineteenth Century Stars.* Cleveland: The Society for American Baseball Research, 1989.
Werber, Bill, and C. Paul Rogers III, *Memories of a Ballplayer.* Cleveland: Society of American Baseball Research, 2001.
Westcott, Rich. *Splendor on the Diamond.* Gainesville: University of Florida Press, 2000.
_____. *Winningest Pitchers: Baseball's 300-Game Winners.* Philadelphia: Temple University Press, 2002.
White, Sol. *History of Colored Base Ball.* Lincoln, NE: University of Nebraska Press, 1995.
Wong, Stephen. *Smithsonian Baseball.* New York: HarperCollins Publishers, 2005.
Wood, Bob. *Dodger Dogs to Fenway Franks: The Ultimate Guide to America's Top Baseball Parks.* New York: McGraw-Hill, 1988.
Wukovits, John. *Life in the Negro Baseball Leagues.* Farmington Hills, MI: Thomson Gale, 2005.
Zimmer, Don, with Bill Madden. *The Zen of Zim.* New York: St. Martin's Press, 2004.
Zminda, Don, with Chuck Miller and Jim Callis, ed. *From Abba-Dabba to Zorro: The World of Baseball Nicknames.* Morton Grove, IL: STATS Publishing, 1999.

Index

Aardsma, David 44, 47
Aaron, Hank "Hammerin' Hank" 5, 7–10, 12–13, 33, 38, 43, 47, 60, 63, 67, 70, 73, 82–83, 85, 88, 92, 142, 154, 158, 163, 197, 200, 206, 212–213, 231, 236, 256, 259, 290, 301 311, 318, 331, 333; Hank Aaron Childhood Home and Museum 8, 10; Hank Aaron Stadium 8–9
Aaron, Tommie 7, 9
Abad, Andy 2, 60–61
Abbaticchio, Ed "Batty" 249, 250
Abbey, Charlie 180
Abbott, Jim 17, 147, 154
Abernathy, Ted 216, 223
Aces Ballpark 185
Accardo, Jeremy 18, 21
Acker, Tom "Shoulders" 191, 193
Adair, Jerry 238, 242
Adams, Babe 89, 99
Adams, Buster 44, 46
Adams, Daniel "Doc" 188, 193
Adams, Earl "Sparky" 249
Adams, Glenn 138, 144
Adams, Joe "Wagon Tongue" 78
Adams, Karl "Rebel" 66
Adams, Spencer 296, 298
Adams, Willie 198
Adcock, Joe 12, 119, 121–122
Addy, Bob "The Magnet" 201, 327–328, 330
Aderholt, Morris 218
Adkins, Grady "Butcher Boy" 21
Affeldt, Jeremy 18
African American Museum 251, 255
Agbayani, Benny "Hawaiian Punch" 73–74
Agee, Tommie 8, 186, 194
Agganis, Harry "The Golden Greek" 127, 138, 140
Aguilera, Rick 28
Aikens, Willie 269–270
Aitchison, Raleigh "Redskin" 277–278
Alabama Sports Hall of Fame 8
Alaska Baseball League 16
Alaska Goldpanners 16
Albuquerque, Al 19
Aldridge, Vic "The Hoosier Schoolmaster" 89, 92
Alexander, Dale "Moose" 280–281, 283
Alexander, Doyle 7
Alexander, Grover Cleveland "Pete" 35, 45, 180, 183, 235, 261–262, 333
Alexander, Matt 119
Allen, Dick "Crash" 11, 249, 250, 253, 256–257; brothers Don and Hank Allen 253
Allen, Ethan 228, 233
Allen, Johnny 124, 216, 218
Allen, Neil 105–106, 110
Allen, Newt "Colt" 91, 285–287, 290
Allenson, Gary "Hard Rock" 28
Alley, Gene 302, 305
Allie, Gair 218
Allie, Stetson 226
Allison, Bob 156, 167, 170, 173
Allison, Doug 252
Almon, Bill 265
Aloha Stadium 74
Alomar, Roberto 123
Alou, Moises 66, 69, 71
Alston, Walter "Smokey" 88, 226, 237
Altobelli, Joe 147, 155
Altrock, Nick 159, 229
Alvarez, Pedro 202
Alvis, Max 285
Ames, Red 215, 226
Anderson, Bob "Hammond Hummer" 89
Anderson, Brady 129–130, 136
Anderson, Brian 302
Anderson, Edward "Goat" 226
Anderson, Garret 27, 38–39
Anderson, Larry 142, 246, 249
Anderson, Sparky "Captain Hook" 43, 241–242, 277, 280, 329
Andrews, "Poison" Ivy 7
Andrews, Stan "Polo" 138, 140
Andres, Ernie "Junie" 89
Ankiel, Rick 55, 252, 310
Anson, Cap 22, 80, 100–103, 150, 188, 267
Antonelli, Johnny 201, 214
Antonelli, Matt 138
Aparicio, Luis 70, 79
Appalachian Power Park 314
Appier, Kevin 28, 222
Appleton, Pete 47
Appling, Luke "Old Aches and Pains" 69, 216, 218–220, 248
Arft, Hank "Bow Wow" 167
Arkansas Travelers 22
Armbrust, Orville 22
Armour, Buddy 161
Arnovich, Morrie "Snooker" 317
Arntzen, Orie "Old Folks" 78
Arrieta, Jake 168
Arroyo, Bronson "Saturn Nuts" 58
Arvest Ballpark 22
Ashburn, Richie "Putt-Putt," "Whitey" 65, 123, 165, 179, 180, 182–183, 251, 284
Ashby, Alan 27
Assenmacher, Paul 147
AT&T Bricktown Ballpark 29, 238–239
Auker, Elden "Submarine" 105, 108
Aumont, Phillippe 327
Aure, Chris 16–17
Aurilia, Rich 201
Ausmus, Brad 47, 49, 219
AutoZone Park 281–282
Averill, Earl "One Punch" 226, 312
Averill, Earl "Rock," "The Earl of Snohomish" 122, 308, 311–312
Avery, Steve 149
Avista Stadium 308–310
Awkard, Russell 130
Axford, John 327

B's Ballpark Museum 3, 44–45
Babbit, Mack "Shooty" 28
Babe, Loren "Bee Bee" 100
Backman, Wally 246, 248
Badenhop, Burke 67, 69
Badgro, Morris "Red" 310
Bagby, Jim, Jr. 236
Bagby, Jim, Sr. "Sarge" 66, 68, 236
Bagwell, Jeff 137–138, 141–142, 220, 249, 334
Bahnsen, Stan 100
Bailey, Abraham "Sweetbread" 78
Bailey, Bob "Beetle" 27–28, 31
Bailey, Ed 280, 282
Bailey, Ola "L'il Catch" 7
Baines, Harold 123, 129–130, 136, 318
Bair, Doug 226
Baker, Del 246, 249
Baker, Dusty 28, 31, 43
Baker, Frank "Home Run" 50, 129, 133, 146, 207, 300, 311, 334
Baker, Gene "Bongo" 100, 103
Baker, Tom "Rattlesnake" 286
Baker Bowl 39–40, 97–98, 180, 232, 262, 321
Bakley, Edward "Jersey" 191, 193

353

Balboni, Steve "Bye Bye" 138, 144–145
Baldelli, Rocco "Woonsocket Rocket" 265, 269
Baldwin, Charles "Lady" 201, 204–205
Baldwin, Mark "Fido" 250, 253–254
Balenti, Mike 240
Ball, Neal 148
Ball, Walter "The Georgia Rabbit" 147–148
Ballard, Jeff 177, 179
Ballenger, Pelham 270
Baltimore Black Sox 95, 118
Baltimore Elite Giants 71–72, 130, 230, 255, 283–284, 288
Bancroft, Dave "Beauty" 100, 102–103, 213, 247
Bando, Sal 27, 225, 230
Bankhead, Dan 7–8, 14–15
Bankhead, Fred 7
Bankhead, Sam 7, 12, 14, 174
Banks, Ernie "Mr. Cub" 64, 80, 103, 108, 134, 170, 199, 237, 251, 254, 285, 286, 289, 333–334
Bannister, Floyd 277, 279
Bannon, Jimmy "Foxy Grandpa" 138
Barajas, Rod 20, 31
Barbare, Walter "Dinty" 270, 272
Barber, Jesse "Phantom" 302
Barber, Steve 129
Barclay, George "Deerfoot" 250
Barfield, Jesse 78
Barker, Len 19, 117
Barkley, Sam 313, 315
Barlow, Tom 211
Barmes, Bruce "Squeaky" 89
Barmes, Clint 89
Barnes, Jesse "Nubby" 238, 245
Barnes, John "Honey" 201, 205
Barnes, William "Skeeter" 226
Barnes, Ross 201–204, 208, 210
Barnhart, Clyde "Pooch" 250–251, 254
Barnhill, Dave "Impo," "Skinny Green" 216, 220, 222, 304
Baron, Red 69
Barrett, Bob "Jumbo" 66
Barrett, Charlie "Red" 29
Barrett, Jimmy 138, 144
Barrett, Michael 66
Barrett, "Whispering Bill" 138, 140
Barrow, Ed 82, 203
Barrows, Roland "Cuke" 126
Barry, Jack 47, 50, 207
Bartee, Kimera 180
Bartell, Dick "Rowdy Richard," "Shortwave" 78, 85
Barton, Daric 299
Baseball Boulevard 59
Baseball Heritage Museum 227
Basinski, Edwin "Bazooka," "Fiddler" 201
Bass, John 272
Bass, Randy 241
Bassett, Charley 265
Bassett, Pepper 119, 121
Bassler, Johnny 249
Battey, Earl 27
Bauer, Hank 78, 86
Bauman, Joe 242

Bay, Jason 327–328, 331
Bayer, Christopher "Burley" 111
Baylor, Don 286–287, 293
Beane, Billy 247
Bearden, Gene "Arkansas Traveler" 21
Beatty, Desmond "Desperate" 129
Beauchamp, Jim 241
Beaumont, Ginger 317, 322
Beazley, "Two Game Johnny" 281, 284
Beck, Clyde "Jersey" 28
Beck, Rod 28
Beck, Walter "Boom-Boom" 78
Becker, Beals 105
Beckert, Glenn "Bruno" 249–250
Beckett, Josh 286
Beckley, Jake "Eagle Eye" 167–168, 171
Beckwith, John 111, 113, 115, 118
Bedard, Erik 327, 332
Bedrosian, Steve "Bedrock" 138, 146
Beecher, Ed "Scrap Iron" 47
Beers, Clarence 110
Beggs, Joseph "Fireman" 250
Bejma, Ollie "Polish Falcon" 89
Belanger, Mark "The Blade" 137, 138, 140, 143, 151, 177
Belardi, Carroll "Footsie" 28
Belinda, Stan 250
Belinsky, Bo 44, 205–206
Bell, Bill "Ding Dong" 216
Bell, Buddy 151, 249, 257
Bell, Cool Papa 69, 161–162, 164–165, 170, 174, 218, 255, 276, 284, 289, 305, 333
Bell, David 225, 227, 255
Bell, Derek 58
Bell, Gary "Ding Dong" 286
Bell, Gus 111, 116, 227, 257
Bell, Heath 31
Bell, Jay 58, 62, 64
Bell, William, Sr. 286, 294
Belle, Albert "Mr. Freeze" 119, 122–123
Beltran, Carlos 308
Bemis, Harry 186, 188
Bench, Johnny 13, 24, 32, 35, 64, 83, 121, 149–150, 219, 230, 232, 238, 240–241, 280, 288, 333–334
Bender, Chief 146, 155, 159–160, 255, 300
Benedict, Bruce 7
Benes, Andy 89, 222
Benjamin, Jerry 7
Bennett, Charlie 249, 256; Bennett Park 256
Bennett, Justin "Pug" 180–181
Benson, Allen "Bullet Ben" 277
Benson, Gene 250, 254
Benton, Al 238–239, 245
Benton, Rube 216, 318
Benton, Stanley "Rabbit" 111
Bentz, Chad 15–17
Benz, Joe "Butcher Boy" 89
Benzinger, Todd "Mercedes" 111
Berg, Moe 205
Bergen, Bill 141
Bergen, Marty 141
Berger, Wally 78, 85
Berkman, Lance "Big Puma," "Fat Elvis" 285, 286, 287, 292
Berra, Yogi 24, 33, 53, 121, 149, 167–168, 170–171, 191, 219, 273–274, 288, 333; Yogi Berra Museum 191–192; Yogi Berra Stadium 191–192
Berry, Claude "Admiral" 89
Berry, "Jittery Joe" 21
Bertaina, Frank "Toys in the Attic" 2, 5, 28
Bessent, Don "The Weasel" 58
Betances, Dellin 202
Betts, Huck 52, 55
Betzel, Bruno 31, 228
Bibbs, Rainey 111
Bibby, Jim 218
Bichette, Dante 58, 64–65
Biddle, Rocky 184
Bierbauer, Lou 249, 255
Big League Dreams Sports Park 185
Bigbee, Carson "Skeeter" 246–248
Biggio, Craig 142, 201, 204, 207–208, 291, 333
Bildilli, Emil "Hillbilly" 89
Billingham, Jack 58
Biot, Charles 10
Birmingham Black Barons 9, 12, 14, 24, 121, 162, 293
Birrer, Babe 205
Bisceglia, Michael 187
Bishop, Max 249; "Camera Eye" 250, 254
Bissonette, Del 126, 128
Black, Joe 190–192, 196; Joe Black Field 192
Black, Bob 229
Black, Bud 31
Black, Don "The Bad Boy of the Diamond" 100
Black Sox scandal 24, 80, 113, 153, 157, 169, 197, 228, 233, 253, 271–272, 279, 302, 316, 319–320, 324
Blackburne, Lena "Slats" 250, 252
Blackmon, Charles 67
Blackwell, Charlie 111, 117
Blackwell, Ewell "The Whip" 28
Blair, Clarence "Footsie" 238
Blair, Paul "Motormouth" 177, 238, 241, 243
Blair Field 29
Blake, Casey 100–101, 103
Blake, John "Sheriff" 302, 313
Blanchard, Johnny 243
Blanks, Larvell "Sugar Bear" 286
Blanton, Joe "Cupcakes" 281
Blasingame, Don "Corinth Comet" 161
Blasingame, Wade 198, 200
Blass, Steve 47–49
Blefary, Curt "Clank" 201
Blethen, Clarence "Climax" 126
Bliss, Jack 310
Blomberg, Ron 66–67
Bloodworth, Jimmy 58
Bloomquist, Willie 312
Blue, Bert 229
Blue, Lu 55, 57
Blue, Vida 119, 123–125, 230, 249
Bluege, Ossie 76, 78, 84
Bluejacket, Jim 240, 326
Bluhm, Red 229
Blyleven, Bert 30, 76, 125
Bobo, Willie 18, 20

Boddicker, Mike 100, 102
Bodie, Frank "Ping" 28
Boesch, Brennan 31
Boever, Joe 167
Boggs, Wade "Chickenman" 48, 64, 93, 142, 179–182, 266, 305, 311, 321, 333
Bolden, Ed 254
Bolin, Bobby 270, 276
Bolling, Frank 7, 11
Bonds, Barry 2, 10, 13, 16–17, 27, 29, 33–34, 37–38, 40, 64, 74, 85, 133, 154, 210, 234, 237, 242, 259, 290, 301, 333
Bonds, Bobby 28, 39–40, 243
Bonds, Bobby, Jr. 74
Bonds, Tommy 17
Bonham, Tiny 28
Bonilla, Bobby 201, 209–210
Bonser, Boof 59
Bonura, Zeke "Banana Nose" 119–120
Booker, Pete 296
Boone, Aaron 32, 71
Boone, Bob 16, 27, 32
Boone, Bret 27, 32
Boone, Ike 14
Boone, Ray 27, 32; "Ike" 28
Booth, Amos "Darling" 226
Booty, Josh 161
Bordagaray, Stanley "Frenchy" 28, 31–32
Borden, Joe 192
Bordick, Mike 147, 151
Boros, Steve 149
Borowski, Joe 190–191, 197
Borowy, Hank 48, 190, 192
Boskie, Shawn 184
Boss, Harley 119
Bosse Field 89–90; *A League of Their Own* 89–90
Bottalico, Ricky 47–48, 51
Bottomley, Jim "Sunny Jim" 78–79, 83; *see also* Bottomley-Ruffing-Schalk Baseball Museum
Bottomley-Ruffing-Schalk Baseball Museum 79, 87
Bouchee, Ed 177–179
Boudreau, Lou "Handsome Lou," "Old Shufflefoot" 78, 80, 84–85, 88, 248; 84
Bouton, Jim "Bulldog" 191, 193–194, 247; *Ball Four* 193–194, 247, 291
Bowa, Larry "Gnat" 27, 28, 37, 57
Bowen Field 314
Bowler, Grant "Moose" 44
Bowles, Emmett 240
Bowman, Elmer "Big Bow" 299–301
Bowman Field 251; *see also* Eric Stotz Field; Peter J. McGovern Little League Baseball Museum; Lamade Stadium
Boyd, Bob "The Rope" 161, 163
Boyd, Dennis "Oil Can" 161–162
Boyer, Clete 172
Boyer, Ken 167, 172
Boyle, "Handsome Henry" 250
Boze, Marshall 18
Braddock, Zach 191
Braden, Dallas 18–19
Bradford, Chad 161, 166
Bradley, Bill 225, 228, 230–231

Bradley, George "Grin" 250, 252
Bradley, Phil 89
Bradshaw, Terry 303
Branca, Ralph 52, 88, 214–215, 298
Brandt, Ed 308, 310, 313
Brandt, Jackie 180
Bransfield, Kitty 137–138
Brantley, Jeff 7–8, 15
Branyan, Russell 66
Bratcher, Joe "Goobers" 286
Braun, Ryan "The Hebrew Hammer" 28, 31
Brazle, Al "Cotton," "Old Bones and Saddles" 238, 244
Breechen, Harry "The Cat" 238, 244
Breitenstein, Ted 167–168
Bremer, Gene 119, 121
Brennan, Don 126–127
Brennan, Thomas "The Gray Flamingo" 78
Bresnahan, Roger "The Duke of Tralee" 32, 156, 225, 226, 229
Bressler, Rube 250, 252
Brett, George 35, 47, 133, 168, 230, 244, 261, 283, 310, 313–314, 316, 321, 331, 333
Brewer, Chet 105, 224, 244
Brewer, Jim 28
Bridges, Marshall 161
Bridges, Tommy 280–281, 284
Bridwell, Al 225
Briggs, Johnny 190
Bright House Field 60
Brinkman, Ed 225
Brissie, Lou 272
Britt, George "Chippy" 216
Brock, Greg 246
Brock, Lou 21–22, 25, 63–64, 85, 123, 165, 196, 221, 254, 282
Brodie, Steve 302, 306
Brooklyn Dodgers 9, 14, 39, 53, 60, 68, 71, 86, 88, 99, 114–115, 132, 146, 168, 174, 203–205, 210, 243, 255, 257, 260, 269, 303, 310, 329
Brooks, Hubie 27
Brosius, Scott 246, 248
Brosnan, Jim 226
Brosseau, Frank 223
Brouthers, Dan 149, 195, 201, 206–207, 211; Dan Brouthers monument 203
Brower, Frank "Turkeyfoot" 302
Brown, Barney 270, 276, 313, 317
Brown, Carroll "Boardwalk" 191
Brown, Charles "Buster" 100
Brown, Charles "Curly" 105
Brown, Charlie 93
Brown, Dave 286–287, 294–295
Brown, Dick 313
Brown, "Downtown" Ollie 7
Brown, Eddie "Glass Arm" 180–181
Brown, Elmer "Shook" 89
Brown, Elmore "Scrappy" 129
Brown, Fred 188
Brown, Ike 281
Brown, Jeremy "The Badger" 7
Brown, Jim 285
Brown, Jimmy 216
Brown, Joe 23
Brown, Kevin 66–67, 71–72
Brown, Larry 252, 313

Brown, Larry "Iron Man" 7, 10
Brown, Lloyd "Gimpy" 286
Brown, Mace 100, 268
Brown, Mordecai "Three Finger" 89, 98, 190, 334
Brown, Ray 226, 235
Brown, Ulysses "Buster" 58
Brown, Walter, "Jumbo" 265, 269
Brown, Willard "Home Run" 119, 121–123, 239
Brown, William "California" 28
Brown, William "Gates" 226, 229
Browne, George 302
Browning, Pete "The Gladiator" 40, 111–114, 116
Browning, Tom 324–326
Broxton, Jonathan 66, 72
Bruce, Bob "Bluecheese" 147
Bruntlett, Eric 91
Bruton, Bill 7, 9, 321
Bryant, Ron 40
Bryson, Robert 52
Buck, John "The King of Scotland" 324–326
Buckeye, Garland "Gob" 155
Buckner, Bill 27, 39, 70, 275, 297
Buckner, Harry "Green River" 111, 117
Buddin, Don 270
Buehrle, Mark 167–168, 175
Buffinton, Charlie 138, 145, 190
Buford, Don 286
Buhl, Bob 147
Buhner, Jay "Bone" 111, 117, 308
Bulkeley, Morgan 49
Bumbry, Al 302–303, 306
Bumgarner, Madison 216
Bumpus, Earl 111
Bunning, Jim "The Lizard" 111–112, 117, 254
Burdette, Lew 200, 313, 317
Burdock, "Black Jack" 201, 204
Burgess, Smoky 216, 219
Burgmeier, Tom 155, 160
Burke, "Sunset Jimmy" 167
Burke, Tim 180
Burkett, Jesse "The Crab" 93, 313–316
Burkett, John 250
Burks, Ellis 39, 161–162, 165
Burleson, Rick "Rooster" 27, 28, 31
Burnett, A.J. 21–22, 124
Burnett, Hercules "Poster Boy" 111
Burnitz, Jeromy 28, 248
Burns, George "Silent George" 201, 212
Burns, George "Tioga George" 225–226
Burns, Jack "Slug" 138
Burns, Oyster 53, 250
Burns, Tom 112, 250–251
Burpo, George 111
Burrell, Pat "Pat the Bat" 21, 26
Burright, Larry "Possum" 78
Burroughs, Jeff 28
Burrus, Dick 220
Busby, Steve 159
Busch Stadium 168
Bush, Donie 88–89, 92, 95–96; Bush Stadium 92; *Eight Men Out* 92

Bush, George H.W. 48, 233
Bush, Guy "The Mississippi Mudcat" 161, 166
Bush, Leslie "Bullet Joe" 155
Bush, Randy 52–54
Buskey, Joe "Jazzbow" 129
Butcher, Max 313
Butler, Brett 28–29, 39
Butler, Cecil "Slewfoot" 66
Butler, Johnny "Trolleyline" 105
Butts, Tom "Pee Wee" 66, 71
Byrd, Bill "Daddy" 66, 71
Byrd, Paul "Frasier" 111
Byrd, Sammy "Babe Ruth's Legs" 66, 68
Byrne, Bobby 167
Byrne, Tommy 137
Byrnes, Eric 28; nicknames "Captain America," "Crash Test Dummy," "Flipper," "Pigpen" 28, 31

Caballero, Ralph "Putsy" 119, 121
Cabell, Enos 105, 108
Cadore, Leon 80
Cahill, Trevor 31
Cain, Lorenzo 67
Cain, Merritt "Sugar" 66
Caldwell, Earl "Teach" 286
Caldwell, Mike 216, 222
California Winter League 14, 20
Callison, Johnny 238, 241, 243
Camelback Ranch 1, 71
Camilli, Dolph 27, 34–35
Camilli, Doug 34
Caminiti, Ken 27, 35–36
Camnitz, Howie "Kentucky Rosebud" 111
Camp, Rick 66
Campanella, Roy 6, 13, 30, 71, 94, 139, 149–150, 156, 188, 249, 252, 255–256, 288, 329, 333
Campau, Charles "Count" 147–148
Campbell, Archie "Iron Man" 191
Campbell, Bill 147–148, 154
Campbell, Bruce 78
Campbell, Clarence "Soup" 302
Campbell, Dave "Chopper" 89
Campbell, Frankie 34
Canadian Baseball Hall of Fame & Museum 327–332
Candelaria, John "Candy Man" 201
Candiotti, Tom 28, 35
Cannady, Rev 302, 304
Cannell, Wirt Virgin "Rip" 126
Canseco, Jose 210
Capilla, Doug 73
Capps, Matt 66
Caray, Harry 80
Cardwell, Don 218
Carew, Rod 64, 156–157, 208, 232, 305
Carey, George "Scoop" 250
Carey, Max "Scoops" 48, 89, 96–97, 123
Carlton, Steve 58–59, 65, 125, 251, 254, 282, 307, 333
Carpenter, Chris 186–187, 189
Carpenter, Hick 137
Carr, Kyle 223
Carr, Tank 66, 69, 170
Carrigan, Bill "Rough" 126, 128

Carroll, Clay 7, 15
Carroll, Cliff 100
Carroll, Jamey 88
Carter, Elmer "Snake Eyes" 167
Carter, Ernest "Spoon" 7
Carter, Gary 2, 27, 32–33, 149–150
Carter, Joe 238–239, 243–244
Carter, Marlin 285, 287
Cartwright, Alexander 30, 74, 188, 193, 204
Caruthers, Bob "Parisian Bob" 280–281, 284
Case, George 190, 196
Casey, Doc 137
Casey, Hugh "Fireman" 66, 69, 72
Casey, Sean "The Mayor" 190, 191, 192, 194
Cash, Bill "Ready" 66
Cash, Dave 201
Cash, Norm "Stormin' Norman" 194, 285, 286, 289
Cassidy, Pete 52
Caster, George "Ug" 28
Castiglione, Pete 47, 50
Castleman, Clydell "Slick" 281
Castleton, Roy 298
Cater, Danny 285
Caudill, Bill "Cuffs" 28
Causey, Wayne 119, 122
Cavarretta, Phil 78, 83
Cecil, Brett 130
Centene Stadium 177–178
Centennial Field 299–300
Cepeda, Orlando 10, 29, 156, 282
Cerone, Rick 190
Cerv, Bob 180
Cey, Ron "The Penguin" 199, 308, 312
Chacon, Shawn 15–17
Chadbourne, Chet "Pop" 126, 128
Chadwick, Henry 203
Chamberlain, Elton "Ice Box" 201, 203–205
Chamberlain, Joba 74, 184
Chambliss, Chris 225, 230
Chance, Dean 77, 108, 226
Chance, Frank "The Peerless Leader" 27–28, 33, 43, 59, 172, 190, 204; see also Tinker to Evers to Chance
Chandler, Happy 104, 114
Chandler, Spud 66, 71–72
Chapman, Ben 280–281, 284
Chapman, Ray 11, 111, 113–114, 116–117; gravesite 227
Chapman, Sam 28
Chappell's Restaurant & Sports Museum 168
Charboneau, Joe 81
Charles, Ed "The Glider" 58
Charleston, Oscar "The Black Ruth," "The Hoosier Comet" 3, 89, 91–92, 96, 117, 122, 165, 218, 251, 254–255, 276, 333
Charlton, Norm "The Sheriff" 119, 125–126, 313
Chase, Hal "Prince Hal" 19, 27, 28, 34, 72–74, 204, 209
Chase Field 18
Chavez, Eric 27, 31
Cheeves, Virgil 240
Cheney, Larry 105

Cheney, Tom 72
Cheney Stadium 308–309; statue of Ben Cheney 309
Chesbro, John "Happy Jack" 136, 138, 140, 145
Chester, Dane "Ding-A-Ling," "Sniffy" 226
Chicago American Giants 11, 15, 26, 64, 108, 117, 122, 125–126, 222, 276, 295–296, 306
Childs, Cupid 129, 132
Chiles, Pearce "What's the Use" 167–169
Chiozza, Lou 119
Chisenhall, Lonnie 216
Choice, Michael 286
Chrisley, Neil 272
Christensen, Jason 180
Christensen, Walter "Cuckoo," "Seacap" 28, 32
Christenson, Larry 308
Cicotte, Eddie "Knuckles" 147, 149, 153, 288, 324
Cihocki, Ed 54
Cincinnati Reds Hall of Fame and Museum 226–227, 231
Cirillo, Jeff 27
Cissell, Bill 167, 172
Citi Field 203
Citizens Bank Park 251
City Stadium (Calvin Falwell Field) 303
Civic Stadium 246–247
Clancy, Al 197, 200
Clapp, John 204
Clapp, Richard "Stubby" 327
Clark, Brady 246
Clark, Earl 55
Clark, Jack "Jack the Ripper" 250, 261
Clark, Tony 105–107
Clark, Morten "Specs" 280–283
Clark, Will "The Thrill" 119–121
Clarke, Fred "Cap" 68, 100–103, 113, 136, 330
Clarke, Justin "Nig" 327–328
Clarke, Robert "Cayuka," "Eggie" 302, 304
Clarke, William "Boileryard" 201, 205
Clarkson, James "Bus" 270
Clarkson, John 138, 141, 145
Clayton, Royce 27
Clemens, Roger "The Rocket" 6, 17, 46, 162, 166, 177, 224, 226, 228, 233–236, 255, 262, 267, 333
Clemente, Roberto 17, 39, 48, 64, 165, 251, 311, 329, 333; The Clemente Museum 251, 255
Clements, Jack 249, 256
Clemons, Verne "Stinger" 100
Clendenon, Donn 167
Cleveland, Reggie 327
Clift, Harlond 238, 242
Cline, John "Monk" 111
Cloninger, Tony 217–218
Clutterbuck, Casimir 147
Clyde, David 88, 110
Coakley, Andy 265
Coates, Jim "Mummy" 302
Cobb, Ty "The Georgia Peach" 1, 9,

23, 34, 38, 40, 66–69, 71, 82, 85, 91, 97, 104, 106, 119, 144, 147, 149, 158, 162, 171, 182, 185, 207, 220, 232–233, 236, 252, 258, 265, 267–268, 270, 272, 277, 282, 284, 305, 316, 322, 328, 333; Ty Cobb Museum 67
Cochrane, Mickey "Black Mike" 13, 121, 137–138, 141, 146, 171, 206, 219, 243, 322, 334
Cockrell, Phil 66, 72
Coffman, Dick 7
Coffman, George "Slick" 7
Cohen, Syd 130
Colavito, Rocky 194, 201, 212, 306, 322
Colbert, Nate 167–168
Cole, A.J. 59
Cole, Gerrit 29
Cole, Leonard "King" 100–101
Coleman, Casey 60
Coleman, Clarence "Captain Cola," "Pops" 111–112, 114
Coleman, Clarence "Choo Choo" 58, 61
Coleman, Gordy 129
Coleman, Joe 60, 138
Coleman, Vince "Van Go" 58, 60, 325
Collard, Earl "Hap" 18
Colliflower, Harry 130
Collins, Dan 170
Collins, Dave 277–279; South Dakota Sports Hall of Fame 279
Collins, Eddie "Cocky" 48, 50, 146, 158, 201–202, 207, 273, 324, 333
Collins, Hub 111
Collins, Jimmy 156, 190, 201, 208–209, 231, 311, 333
Collins, Phil "Fidgety Phil" 78, 81
Collins, Ray 299–301
Collins, James "Ripper" 249–250
Collins, Shano 138
Coluccio, Bob "The Macaroni Pony" 308
Combs, Earle "The Kentucky Colonel" 111, 116
Comerica Park 147, 165
Comiskey, Charlie 78–80, 82, 128, 156, 170, 188, 324
Concepcion, Dave 230
Cone, David 167–168, 170, 174–175
Congalton, William "Bunk" 327
Conger, Hank 308
Conigliaro, Tony 138, 140–141, 144
Conine, Jeff "The Barbarian" 308, 312
Conlan, John "Jocko" 78
Conley, Gene 238, 245
Conley, James "Snipe" 250
Connie Mack Stadium 9
Connolly, "Coaster Joe" 28
Connolly, Joe 265
Connor, Roger 47–50, 97
Conners, Chuck 205
Cooke, Steve 73
Cooley, Duff "Sir Richard" 105, 108
Coombs, Jack "Colby Jack" 100, 160
Cooney, Jimmy, Jr. "Scoops" 265–266, 269
Cooney, Jimmy, Sr. 265, 269

Cooney, Johnny 252, 265, 269
Cooper, Andy 286–287, 294–295
Cooper, Cecil 285, 289, 324
Cooper, Gary 69
Cooper, Mort 167–168, 174
Cooper, Walker 167, 171
Cooper, Wilbur 313–314, 317
Coors Field 44–45, 165, 282, 330
Corbett, Doug 58
Corcoran, Larry 201, 203–204
Corcoran, Tommy 47–48, 50
Cordova, Marty 184–186
Corey, Fred 265, 267
Corey, Mark 198
Cormier, Rheal 327
Cornelius, William "Sug" 275
Correll, Vic 55
Corridon, Frank "Fiddler" 265, 269
Coste, Chris 223–224
Costello, "Dashing Dan" 250
Cote, Jordan 187
Cottier, Chuck 44, 47
Couch, Johnny 177, 179
Coughlin, "Scranton Bill" 250
Counsell, Craig 1, 3, 88, 95
Courtney, Clint "Scrap Iron," "Toy Bulldog" 119
Coveleski, Harry 253
Coveleski, Stan 247, 250, 253, 261
Covington, Wes 216
Cox, Bobby 238, 241, 245–246
Cox, Ted 239
Cox, Zach 111
Coyne, Martin "Toots" 167
Cozart, Zak 161
Craft, Harry "Wildfire" 161
Craig, Roger 216, 223
Cramer, Doc "Flit" 190, 191, 196
Crandall, Del 27, 33, 199
Crandall, Doc 89, 100
Cravath, "Cactus Gavvy" 28, 39–40
Craver, Bill 113
Crawford, Carl 182, 285, 287–288, 293
Crawford, Sam "Wahoo Sam" 144, 179–182, 258, 270, 286, 322, 334
Creacy, Dewey 285, 287
Cree, William "Birdie" 250
Creeden, Pat "Whoops" 138, 140
Cregan, "Peekskill Pete" 201
Creighton, James, Jr. 203
Cremins, Bob "Crooked Arm" 201
Crespi, Frank "Creepy" 167
Criger, Lou 88, 93
Crisp, Coco 28, 31
Crist, Chester "Squawk" 226
Critz, Hughie 50, 161, 164
Crockett, Daniel "Davey" 302–303
Cron, Chris 300
Cronin, Joe 2, 27–28, 36–37, 57, 175
Crooks, Jack 155, 158
Crosby, Casey 79
Crosetti, Frankie "Crow" 27, 31, 35, 131
Crosley Field 45, 185, 197
Cross, Lave 317–319, 321
Crothers, Doug 162
Crouch, Bill "Skip" 52
Croucher, Frank "Dingle" 286–287
Crow, Aaron 106

Crowder, Alvin "General" 216
Crowe, George "Big George" 88, 89, 94–95
Crowe, Trevor 246
Crutchfield, Jimmie "The Black Honus Wagner" 79, 167, 174
Cuccinello, Al 203
Cuccinello, Tony 201, 203
Cuccurullo, Arthur "Cookie" 191
Cuddyer, Michael 302–303
Cuellar, Mike 87
Cullenbine, Roy 280
Cullop, Nick "Tomato Face" 167
Cummings, Candy 138, 140, 143, 145
Cummings, Chance 64
Cunningham, Aaron 15–16
Cunningham, Bert 52, 55
Cunningham, Joe 190
Cuppy, Nig 89, 99
Currence, Delancey 270
Currie, Reuben "Black Snake," "King" 167, 170
Curry, Homer "Goose" 286
Curtis, Chad 89
Cusick, Tony 53
Cust, Jack 190, 196
Cutshaw, George 78
Cuyler, Kiki 48, 86, 96, 147, 149, 151–152, 165

Dahlen, Bill "Bad Bill" 201, 210
Daily, Ed 265
Daily, Hugh 267
Dalkowski, Steve 48–49
Dallard, Eggie 190–191
Dallimore, Brian 184–185
Dalrymple, Abner 267, 317–318
Dalrymple, Clay "Dimples" 28
Daly, James "Sun" 299
Daly, Tom 249
Damon, Johnny "Caveman" 2, 105–106, 108–109
Dandridge, Ray "Hooks" 70, 156, 302–304
Daney, Art 240
Daniels, Harold "Sour Mash Jack" 250, 252
Danning, Harry "The Horse" 27, 28, 31
Dantonio, John "Fats" 119, 121
Dapper, Cliff 69
Darcy, Pat 301
Dark, Alvin "The Swamp Fox" 237–239, 242, 245–246
Darling, Ron 73–75
Darnell, James 29
Darwin, Danny 286
Dascenzo, Doug 227
Daubach, Brian "Belleville Basher" 78
Daubert, Jake 249, 257
Daulton, Darren "Dutch" 105, 107
Dauss, George "Hooks" 89, 99
Davenport, Jim 7
Davenport, Lloyd "Ducky" 119, 121
Davidson, Ted 184, 186
Davis, Alvin 27, 308
Davis, Cherokee 302
Davis, Crash 66, 69
Davis, Curt "Coonskin" 167, 169

Davis, Eric 28
Davis, George "Kiddo" 47
Davis, George 201, 210
Davis, Glenn 58
Davis, Harry "Jasper" 249–250, 256–257
Davis, Harry "Stinky" 119
Davis, Ike 155
Davis, Isaac "Ike" 44, 46
Davis, Jody 66
Davis, Johnny 302
Davis, Lomax "Fence Bustin'" 69
Davis, Lorenzo "Piper" 7
Davis, Mark 41
Davis, Otis "Scat" 21, 23
Davis, Peanuts 119, 121, 125
Davis, Ron 295
Davis, Roosevelt 238
Davis, Roy "Peaches" 241, 286
Davis, Saul "Rareback" 119
Davis, Spud 7, 10
Davis, Tommy 201
Davis, Walter "Steel Arm" 317
Davis, Willie 25–26; "3-Dog" 21, 25
Dawley, Bill 47
Dawson, Andre "The Hawk" 2, 58–60, 64
Day, Leon 302–303, 306–307
Day, Pea Ridge 22, 167
Dayley, Ken 75, 77
Dean, Alfred "Chubby" 216
Dean, Dizzy 8–9, 14, 21–22, 26, 91, 95, 161, 168, 170, 241, 260, 304, 312; gravesite 161
Dean, Paul "Daffy" 21, 22, 26, 170
Deas, Yank 64
DeBarr, Dennis 325
DeBusschere, Dave 149
DeCinces, Doug 27
Decker, Jaff 18
Dehler Park 177
Delahanty, Ed 97, 225, 228, 232, 268, 316; Delahanty's Tavern on the Square 192
Delahanty, Jim 226
Delaware Sports Museum and Hall of Fame 52
Delgado, Carlos 225
Delhi, Lee "Flame" 18–19
Dell, William "Wheezer" 184, 186
Demaestri, Joseph "Oats" 28
Demaree, Frank 28
Demeter, Don 238, 243
DeMontreville, Gene 155, 158
DeMoss, Bingo 91, 105, 108, 276
Dempsey, Rick 280, 282
Dempster, Ryan 327–328
Denny, Jerry 201, 204, 267
Denny, John 18–19, 21, 209
Dent, Bucky 66, 71
Denzer, Roger "Peaceful Valley" 155
DeRosa, Mark 190, 195
Derringer, Paul "Duke" 111, 117
DeSa, Joe 73, 75
DeShields, Delino "Bop" 52–53
Desiderato, Joe 224
Desmond, Ian 59
Detroit Stars 148, 230, 306–307
Detwiler, Ross 168
Devereaux, Mike 324–326

Devlin, Art 55, 57, 128
Devlin, Jim 113, 253
Diaz, Carlos 73
Diaz, Matt 246
Dibble, Rob 47, 51, 125, 313
Dickerson, Lewis "Buttercup" 129
Dickey, Bill 22, 119, 121, 189, 284
Dickey, John "Steel Arm" 280–282
Dickey, Walter "Steel Arm" 66
Dickey, Skeeter 22
Dickey-Stephens Park 22
Dickshot, Johnny "Ugly" 78, 81
Dickson, Murry 167
Dierker, Larry 28
Dietrich, Bill "Bullfrog" 250
Dietz, Dick 88, 93
Dillhoefer, William "Pickles" 226, 229
DiMaggio, Dom "Little Professor" 28, 30, 35, 39, 248, 303
DiMaggio, Joe "Joltin' Joe," "The Yankee Clipper" 2–3, 14, 20, 25, 27, 28–30, 34–35, 37–39, 59, 70, 74, 84–85, 93, 121, 123, 132, 135–136, 158, 186, 189, 192, 230, 233, 236, 239, 247, 253, 256, 264, 271, 274, 303, 321, 333–334; 37
DiMaggio, Vince 30, 35, 39
Dinneen, Bill 201
DiPoto, Jerry 190, 197
DiSarcina, Gary 137
Dismukes, Dizzy 7, 91
Distefano, Benny 204
Divis, Edward "Moxie" 226
Dixon, George "Tubby" 269–270, 272
Dixon, Rap 66, 71
Dlugach, Brent 22
Doak, Bill "Spitting Bill" 250
Dobson, Joe "Burrhead" 238, 245
Dobson, Pat 14
Doby, Larry 163, 193, 254, 264, 274, 307
Dodd, Tom 279
Dodger Stadium 29, 82, 185, 205, 239, 242
Doerr, Bobby 27, 34–36, 169
Doheny, Ed 299
Dolan, Albert "Cozy" 78, 82
Dolan, Patrick "Cozy" 138
Donahue, Red 47, 51
Donahue, She 205
Donahue, Tim "Bridget" 138
Donald, Atley "Swampy" 161
Donaldson, John 79, 148, 167, 175
Donlin, Mike "Turkey Mike" 78–79, 81–82, 86
Donnelly, Brendan 55–56
Donohue, Pete 286
Donovan, Bill 138
Donovan, Dick 138
Donovan, Patsy 53
Donovan, "Wild Bill" 138, 140
Donnelly, Jim 47, 50
Doolan, Mickey 250
Doran, Bill 225, 230
Dorgan, Mike 47
Doubleday, Abner 188, 203–204
Doubleday Field 202–203
Dougherty, Pat 111, 118, 296
Dougherty, Patsy 201, 205

Douglas, Charles "Whammy" 216
Douglas, Jesse 285
Douglas, Phil "Shufflin' Phil" 66, 72
Douglass, Astyanax 286
Douglass, Eddie 285
Doumit, Ryan 308, 311
Douthit, Taylor 21, 23, 26
Dowd, Tommy "Buttermilk Tommy" 138, 140
Downey, Tom 126, 128
Downing, Al "Giggi" 12, 190, 191, 197
Downing, Brian "The Incredible Hulk" 28, 40
Downs, Bunny 280–282
Downs, Kelly 296
Downs, Scott 111, 113, 118
Doyle, Denny 111
Doyle, Jeff 177–178
Doyle, Judd "Slow Joe" 105–106
Doyle, Larry "Laughing Larry" 78, 83–84
Drabek, Doug 286
Drabek, Kyle 286
Drago, Dick 226
Drake, Bill "Plunk" 167
Drake, Sammy 22
Drake, Solly 22
Dressen, Chuck 78, 88, 237
Drew, J.D. 58
Drew, Stephen 66
Dreyfuss, Barney 113, 152
Driessen, Dan 269–270, 273
Dropo, Walt "Moose" 47–48
Drott, Richard "Hummer" 226
Drysdale, Don 2, 28, 40–41, 329
Dubiel, Walter "Monk" 47
Dubuc, Jean "Chauncey" 299, 301–302
Ducey, Rob 328
Duchscherer, Justin 277, 279
Dudley, Clive 218
Duffy, Chris 2, 299, 301
Duffy, Hugh "Sir Hugh" 81, 144, 265–266, 268–269, 331
Dugan, "Jumping Joe" 250
Duggleby, "Frosty Bill" 201, 203–204
Dukes, Jan 325–326
Dumont, George "Pea Soup" 155
Duncan, Chris "Big Dipper" 18
Duncan, Frank 107, 167, 170–171, 245, 296
Duncan Park 270–271
Dunlap, Fred "Sure Shot" 53, 249–250, 316
Dunn, Adam "Big Donkey" 285, 286, 288, 293
Dunn, Jake 238
Dunn, Michael 198
Dunston, Shawon "Thunderpup" 201
Duren, Ryne 44, 317, 324
Durham, Bull 252; *Bull Durham* movie 217
Durham, Leon "Bull" 225, 226
Durham, Ray "The Sugarman" 216, 220
Durham Bulls Athletic Park 217
Durocher, Leo "The Lip" 25, 43, 115, 127, 137–138, 140, 146, 156, 170, 298

Index 359

Dusak, Erv "Four Sack" 78
Dwight, Eddie "Flash" 66–67
Dwyer, Frank 138
Dwyer, Joseph "Double" 191
Dye, Jermaine 28, 268
Dyer, Duffy 226
Dyer, Eddie 119, 126
Dykes, Jimmy 29, 249, 257
Dykstra, Lenny "Nails" 28, 142

Earle, Billy "The Little Globetrotter" 250
Earle, Charles 47
Early, Jake 216
Easler, Mike "Hit Man" 226, 233
Easter, Luke 161, 163
Easterling, Howard 161, 164
Easterly, Ted 179, 181
Easterwood, Roy "Shag" 286
Eastwick, Rawley 190, 197
Eaves, Vallie 240
Ebbets Field 39, 45, 197, 203, 310
Eckersley, Dennis 28, 41–42, 152, 279, 307
Eckstein, David 58
Edmonds, Jim 28, 39
Edwards, Johnny 225
Egan, Dick 246
Egan, Jim "Troy Terrier" 47
Eggert, Elmer "Moose" 201
Ehmke, Howard 201
Ehret, Red 111, 113, 117
Eiland, Dave 60
Eisenreich, Jim 155, 159
Elarton, Scott 44
Elberfeld, Kid "The Tabasco Kid" 225, 226
Elko, "Piccolo Pete" 250
Ellam, Roy "Slippery" 250
Elliott, Bob "Mr. Team" 27, 28, 35–36
Elliott, James "Jumbo" 167
Elliott Museum 59
Ellis, Dock 28
Ellis, James "Mooney" 281
Ellis, John 47
Ellis, Mark 277–278
Ellsbury, Jacoby 16, 127, 246–247
Ellsworth, Dick 324–325
Elston, Don "Everyday Elston" 226, 237
Ely, William "Bones" 250
Elysian Fields 188, 192–193
Embree, Alan 246, 249
Engel, Joe "The Barnum of the Bushes" 55, 57–58, 281; Engel Stadium 281
English, Woody 225, 230
Ennis, Del 250
Ens, Jewel 167
Eric Stotz Field 251; see also Bowman Field; Lamade Stadium; Peter J. McGovern Little League Baseball Museum
Erickson, Paul "L'il Abner" 78
Ermer, Cal 129, 137
Erskine, Carl "Oisk" 68, 89, 99, 259–260
Esper, Duke 190
Erstad, Darin 223–225
Essegian, Chuck 140

Esterbrook, Thomas "Dude" 201, 205
Esterwood, Dude 113
Ethier, Andre 18, 21
Evans, Chin 66, 69, 72
Evans, Darrell "Howdy Doody" 2, 27, 28, 35–36
Evans, Dwight "Dewey" 28, 39–40, 237
Evans, Uriah "Bloody Jake" 129
Everett, Adam 66
Everett, Carl "Jurassic Carl" 58
Everitt, Bill 88
Evers, Hoot 167
Evers, Johnny "Crab" 34, 59, 108, 172, 190, 201, 208; see also Tinker to Evers to Chance
Ewing, Bob 226
Ewing, Buck 23, 149, 206, 225–226, 229
Ewing, John 113

Faber, Urban "Red" 100, 102, 104, 324
Fabrique, Albert "Bunny" 147
Face, Roy 148, 201, 215
Fagan, Bill "Clinkers" 201
Fain, Ferris "Burrhead" 285, 286, 289
Faircloth, James "Rags" 281
Fairley, Wendell 161
Fairly, Ron 66–67
Falk, Bibb "Jockey" 286
Falkenberg, Cy 78
Farmer, Ed 78
Farnsworth, Kyle 105, 110
Farr, Steve 129–130, 137
Farrar, Sid 126, 128
Farrell, Duke 137–138, 141
Farrell, Jack "Moose" 190, 191
Farrell, Turk 138
Fassero, Jeff 78
Faust, Charles "Victory" 105; Charles Faust Memorial 106
Feldman, Scott 73
Feller, Bob "Rapid Robert" 9–10, 14, 18, 22, 41, 54, 100, 102, 104, 131, 164, 202, 217, 227, 245, 249, 262, 303, 333; Bob Feller Museum 101
Felsch, Oscar "Happy" 5, 317, 319–320
Felton, Terry 23–24
Fennelly, Frank 137
Fenway Park 3, 29, 44, 60, 71, 89, 126, 138, 141, 163, 185, 199, 217, 312
Ferguson, Bob "Death to Flying Things" 201, 204, 209
Ferguson, Joe 27
Fernandez, Alex 58
Fernandez, Froilan "Nanny" 28
Fernandez, Sid 73–75
Ferrell, Rick 149, 216, 219, 222
Ferrell, Wes 41, 120, 216–217, 219, 222
Ferrick, Tom 201
Ferriss, Dave "Boo" 161; Dave "Boo" Ferris Museum 161
Fidrych, Mark "The Bird" 138, 140, 263
Field of Dreams 101
Fielder, Cecil "Big Daddy" 27, 28

Fielder, Prince 27, 31
Fields, Wilmer 302
Figgins, Chone 66
Fingers, Rollie 29, 42, 146, 176, 226, 237, 265, 279, 313
Fink, Herman 29, 216, 218
Finlayson, Pembroke "Midget Twirler" 270, 276
Finley, Charlie 113, 124, 176, 222, 245, 260, 265
Finley, Chuck 119, 125
Finley, Steve 280–281, 283–284
Finney, Lou 7
Finnvold, Anders Gar 59
Fisher, Bob 280
Fisher, Brian 73–74
Fisher, Eddie 119, 125
Fisher, "Fat Jack" 129
Fisher, George 53
Fisher, George "Showboat" 100
Fisher, Ray "Pick" 299, 301–302
Fisk, Carlton "Pudge" 1–2, 4, 32, 79, 139, 149, 241, 299–301; Fisk Pole 301
Fitzgerald, Warren 45
Fitzsimmons, Freddie "Fat Freddie" 89, 99
Flagstead, Ira 147, 149
Flair, Al "Broadway" 119
Flanagan, Ed "Sleepy" 138
Flanagan, James "Steamer" 250
Flanagan, Mike 187, 190
Fleming, Tom "Sleuth" 250
Fletcher, Art 78
Fletcher, Darrin 78
Fletcher, Elbie 137, 141–142
Fletcher, Scott 58
Flick, Elmer "The Demon of the Stick" 226, 232–233
Flint, Frank "Silver" 250
Flood, Curt 282, 285, 288, 292–293
Flournoy, Pud 66
Flowers, Tyler 67
Floyd, Cliff 78
Floyd, Gavin 157
Flythe, Stuart 218
Fodge, Gene "Suds" 89
Foiles, Hank 302
Foli, Tim "Crazy Horse" 28
Forbes, Frank "Strangler" 72, 250–251
Forbes Field 9, 45, 143, 242, 251
Force, Davy 201, 204, 210–211
Ford, Hod 47–48, 50
Ford, Russ 327, 332
Ford, Whitey "Chairman of the Board" 124, 193, 201, 214, 243, 306
Fordyce, Brook 47
Foreman, August "Happy" 281
Foreman, Frank "Monkey" 129
Forsch, Bob 28
Forster, Terry 277, 279
Fosse, Ray "Marion Mule" 78, 83
Foster, Bill 281, 286, 294–295, 333
Foster, Eddie 78
Foster, George 7, 13
Foster, Rube 4, 26, 86, 108, 128, 169, 237, 254, 276, 286–287, 293–296, 306–307, 333

360 INDEX

Foucalt, Steve 155
Foulke, Keith 277, 279
Fournier, Jack 147, 150, 310
Foutz, Dave "Scissors" 129, 132, 136, 236
Fowler, Art 270
Fowler, Bud 204
Fowler, Dick 328
Fowler, Joseph "Boob" 286
Fox, Pete 89
Fox, Terry 78
Fox Cities Stadium 318
Foxx, Jimmie "Double X," "The Beast" 36, 70, 103, 129–130, 132, 146, 175, 207, 255, 281, 322, 333
Foxx, Nellie 70, 79, 208, 249–250, 253
Foytack, Paul 252
Francis, Jeff 327, 329, 332
Francisco, Ben 31
Franco, John 201–202, 215
Franco, Julio 50
Francona, Terry "Tito" 128, 252, 277–280
Francona, Tito 250, 252
Franklin, Nick 59
Franklin, Ryan 21–22, 27
Franks, Herman 264, 296, 298
Fraser Field 138–139
Frasor, Jason 78
Frawley Stadium 52
Frazier, Albert "Cool Papa" 58
Frazier, George 238
Frazier, Joe 219
Frazier, Todd 191
Frederick, Johnny 44, 46
Freehan, Bill 147–151
Freeman, Buck 250, 260–261
Freeman, Hersh "Buster" 7
Freeman, Raphael "Choo" 22
Freese, Gene 313
Fregosi, Jim 27–28, 35, 37
French, Larry 28
Frey, Lonny 167, 172
Friberg, Bernie 186, 189
Frick, Ford 235
Friday, Skipper 218
Friedrich, Christian 79
Friend, Bob "Warrior" 89, 99
Frisch, Frankie "The Fordham Flash" 170, 201, 208, 213
Fryman, Travis 111, 115
Fryman, Woodie 111, 118
Fuentes, Brian 28, 31
Fuld, Sam 186
Fuller Field 138
Funderburk, Mark 216, 218
Funk, Frank 55
Furbush, Charlie 127
Furillo, Carl "The Reading Rifle" 250, 253, 260
Fussell, Fred "Moonlight Ace" 167

Gabler, Frank "The Great Gabbo" 28
Gaedel, Eddie 2, 81, 169, 171
Gaetti, Gary "The Rat" 78, 80, 84
Gaffke, Fabian 318
Gagne, Eric 327, 329, 332
Gagne, Greg 137, 140
Gaines, Jonas 119

Galan, Augie 27, 38–39
Gale, Rich 186
Gallagher, Alan, "Dirty Al" 28, 31, 228
Gallaway, Chick 270, 274
Galloway, Bill 329
Galvin, Pud 136, 167–170, 174, 211, 213, 235
Gamble, Oscar 7, 9, 14, 279
Gandil, Chick 19, 150, 155, 157–158
Gans, Judy 250
Gant, Ron 85, 285, 293
Gantner, Jim "Gumby" 317, 321
Ganzel, Charlie 156, 317, 320
Garagiola, Joe 170
Garber, Gene 250, 264
Garcia, Mike "Big Bear" 14, 28, 31, 41
Garciaparra, Nomar "The Whittier Whip" 27, 28, 37
Gardner, Billy 47, 50
Gardner, Jelly 21–22, 26
Gardner, Larry 2, 299–301
Gardner, Ping 55, 58
Garland, Jon 31
Garman, Mike 75, 77
Garner, Phil "Scrap Iron" 280–281, 283, 285
Garr, Ralph "Roadrunner" 119
Garrelts, Scott 78
Garrett, Robert "Fuzzy" 281
Garver, Ned 227
Garvey, Steve 33, 58, 62–63, 312
Garvin, Ned "Navasota Tarantula" 286–288
Garza, Matt 31
Gaston, Cito 10, 286, 296
Gaston, Robert 280
Gatewood, Bill 162, 286
Gearin, Dennis "Dinty" 265
Gedman, Rich 137, 295
Gedeon, Elmer 229
Gehrig, Lou "Biscuit Paints," "The Iron Horse" 17, 22, 42, 49, 58, 62–63, 83, 85, 96, 102–103, 132–133, 141, 175, 189, 194, 201–202, 206–207, 214, 220, 230, 239, 264, 271, 281, 284, 287, 313, 333; gravesite 203
Gehringer, Charlie "The Mechanical Man" 9, 34, 147, 150–151, 328, 330, 333
Gentile, Jim "Diamond Jim" 27, 28
Gentry, Gary 18
George, Charles "Greek" 66
Gerber, Wally 225
Gerhardt, Joe 55
Gharity, Patsy 100
Giambi, Jason 27, 31, 35, 74, 225
Giambi, Jeremy 194
Gibbon, Joe 161, 166
Gibbons, Jay 147, 153
Gibbons, John 177, 179
Gibbs, Jake 161, 163
Gibson, Bob "Hoot" 27, 65, 87, 124, 166, 170, 177, 180, 183–184, 249, 253, 262, 282, 307, 333
Gibson, Derrik 52
Gibson, George "Moon" 327, 329–330, 332
Gibson, Josh 1, 3–4, 10–11, 56, 66,

68–69, 91, 121–122, 133, 165, 218, 254–255, 276, 305, 333
Gibson, Kirk 42, 147, 149, 152, 280
Gilbert, Harold "Tookie" 119
Giles, Brian 28
Giles, George 105, 107–108
Giles, Warren 82
Gilkey, Bernard 167
Gill, Johnny "Patcheye" 281
Gill Stadium 187
Gillenwater, Carden 281
Gilliam, Jim "Junior" 280–283
Gionfriddo, Al 253
Girardi, Joe 78
Giusti, Dave 201
Gladd, Jim 240
Gladding, Fred 147, 149
Glasscock, "Pebbly Jack" 313–316
Glaus, Troy 27
Glavine, Tom 125, 138, 141, 145, 262
Gleason, Bill 167
Gleason, Kid 190–191, 194–195, 197
Gleason, Roy 82
Gleich, Frank "Inch" 226
Gobble, Billy 281
Gold, Nate 297
Goldschmidt, Paul 52–53
Goldsmith, Fred 47–48, 51
Goltz, Dave 155
Gomes, Jonny 31
Gomez, Lefty 28–29, 41, 132, 156
Gonzalez, Adrian 27, 31, 127
Gonzalez, Alex 58
Gonzalez, Luis 58, 62, 64
Gonzo, Mauro "Goose" 47
Gooch, Johnny 280–281
Gooden, Dwight "Doc," "Dr. K" 2, 58, 65, 75, 157, 227
Goodenough, Bill 202, 205
Goodman, Billy 216–217, 220
Goodman, Ival 167
Goodwin, Pep 75, 77
Goodyear Ballpark 18, 20
Gordon, Alex 180
Gordon, Dee 59
Gordon, Joe "Flash" 27, 28, 34–35, 199, 208
Gordon, Sid 201, 242
Gordon, Tom "Flash" 58, 65
Gore, George "Piano Legs" 126–128
Goslin, Goose 13, 57, 86, 190–191, 195
Gossage, Goose 29, 41, 44–47, 152, 176, 202, 262, 279, 313, 318
Gozzo, Mauro 48
Grace, Earl 111, 113
Grace, Mark 121, 216, 220
Graham, Dawson "Tiny" 281
Graham, Kyle "Skinny" 7
Graham, Moonlight 1, 53, 216, 218
Graham, Tyler 177
Grand Ichiro "Iron" Maehara Stadium 73
Graney, Jack 327
Granger, Wayne 138
Grant, Charlie "Chief Tokahoma" 225, 226, 230
Grant, Eddie 137, 143
Grant, Frank "Black Dunlap" 115, 137, 138, 142, 237
Grant, Jim "Mudcat" 58, 60, 242

Grantham, George "Boots" 105–106, 108
Grate, Don "Buckeye" 226
Gray, George "Chummy" 126
Gray, Pete 253
Grba, Eli 78
Great American Ball Pak 226, 231; see also Cincinnati Reds Hall of Fame and Museum
Green, Dallas 52, 55
Green, Danny 190
Green, Dick 100, 103
Green, Pumpsie 179
Green, Shawn 78, 86, 122
Green, Tyler 229
Green Diamond Gallery 227
Greenberg, Hank 89–90, 104, 147, 201, 206–207, 256, 333
Greene, Joe "Pig," "Pea" 66
Greenlee, Gus 218, 254
Greenwell, Mike "Gator" 111–112, 116–117, 240
Gregg, Kevin 246, 249
Gregg, Vean 247, 308, 313
Gregor, Conrad 89
Greinke, Zach 65
Gremminger, Ed "Battleship" 226
Gremp, Buddy 44, 46
Greer, Rusty "The Red Baron" 7
Grey, Reddy 229
Grich, Bobby 147, 149, 151, 273
Grieve, Ben "Stomper" 286
Griffey, Ken, Jr. "Junior," "Kid" 119, 185, 213, 250–253, 256, 259, 261, 300, 308, 333
Griffey, Ken, Sr. 250, 252–253, 277, 279
Griffin, Mike 201, 204
Griffith, Bob "Schoolboy" 280–282, 284
Griffith, Clark "The Old Fox" 76, 107, 156, 167, 169, 174–175, 266
Grilli, Jason 149
Grim, Bob 325
Grim, John 111, 115
Grimes, Burleigh "Ol' Stubblebeard" 9, 104, 131, 243, 317–318, 323
Grimes, Ray 228
Grimm, Charlie "Jolly Cholly" 167, 171–172, 176
Grimsley, Ross 105, 108, 176, 277
Grissom, Marquis "Grip" 66, 69, 71
Groat, Dick 172, 250, 258
Groh, Heinie 201, 209
Gromek, Steve 149
Groom, Bob 79; Bob Groom Monument 79
Grote, Jerry 285
Grove, Lefty 2, 106, 129–131, 136–137, 146, 262, 305, 333
Growden Memorial Park 16
Grubb, Harvey 216, 218
Grubb, Johnny 302, 306
Gruber, Kelly 285
Grudzielanek, Mark 317–319, 321
Gryska, Sigmund 78
Guardado, Eddie "Everyday Eddie" 28
Guerrieri, Taylor 270
Guidry, Ron "Louisiana Lightning" 119, 123–125, 166

Guillen, Ozzie 70
Gullett, Don 111, 118, 277
Gullickson, Bill 155
Gumbert, Harry "Gunboat" 250
Gura, Larry 78, 87
Gustine, Frankie 78
Guthrie, Mark 201
Gutteridge, Don 105, 108
Gwosdz, Doug "Eye Chart" 286
Gwynn, Tony "Mr. Padre" 28–29, 39–40, 123, 165, 258, 333
Gyorko, Jedd 314

Haas, Eddie 111, 118
Haas, Moose 129
Haas, Mule 190
Hach, Irv "Major" 111
Hack, Stan "Smiling Stan" 27, 28, 35
Haddix, Harvey "Kitten" 219, 226, 236, 317
Haddock, "Gentleman George" 186, 189–190
Hadley, Bump 138, 141
Hadley, Kent 75
Hadlock Field 126–127
Hafey, Chick 27–28, 38–39
Hafner, Travis "Pronk" 223–224
Hagadone, Nick 76
Hahn, Don 298
Hahn, Frank "Noodles" 280–281, 285
Hahn, Jesse 48
Haines, Jesse "Pop" 226, 235
Hair, Harold "Buster" 58
Hairston, Jerry 101, 162
Hairston, Jerry, Sr. 162
Hairston, Johnny 162
Hairston, Sammy 161–163
Hairston, Scott 162
Halas, George 82, 157
Hale, Odell "Bad News" 119, 122
Hall, Bill 161
Hall, Blainey 129
Hall, Charley "Sea Lion" 28, 31
Hall, Dick 167
Hall, George 113
Hall, Jimmie 216
Hall, Perry 66, 70
Hall, Toby 308, 311
Hall, Tom 216
Halladay, Roy "Doc" 8, 44–47, 99, 189, 329
Haller, Tom 78, 82
Hallman, Bill 249
Hamels, Cole 31; "Hollywood" 28
Hamilton, Billy "Sliding Billy" 97, 127, 138, 169, 190–191, 195–196
Hamilton, Darryl 119
Hamilton, Josh 216, 221
Hamilton, Steve 111, 118
Hamlin, Luke "Hot Potato" 147
Hammel, Jason 272
Hammond, Chris 67
Hammond Stadium 60
Hamner, Granny 302–303, 305
Hamner, Ralph "Bruz" 119
Hampton, Mike 58, 65
Handley, Lee "Jeep" 100, 103
Hands, Bill 190
Handy, Bill "Duckbreast" 119

Haney, Fred "Pudge" 197–200
Hanlon, Ned 43, 47, 49–51, 55, 69, 130, 258
Hannah, James "Truck" 223–224
Hanrahan, Joel 100–102
Hans L'Orange Park 73
Hansen, Dave 44
Hansen, Ron "The Beak" 179–180, 182
Hansen, Roy "Snipe" 78
Hanson, Tommy 238
Harang, Aaron 31
Harbor Park 303
Harden, Rich 327
Harder, Mel "Chief" 180, 184
Hardy, Carroll 277–278; football career 277–278; South Dakota Sports Hall of Fame 278
Hardy, J.J. 18, 21
Hardy, Red 223
Haren, Dan 31
Hargrave, Eugene "Bubbles" 88–89, 93
Hargrave, William "Pinky" 88–89, 93
Hargrove, Mike "The Human Rain Delay" 285, 286, 288
Harlow, Larry 44
Harper, Brian 27
Harper, Bryce 185
Harper, George 111
Harper, Tommy 119, 248
Harrah, Toby 313, 316
Harrelson, Bud 27
Harrelson, Ken "Hawk" 70, 269–270, 272–273
Harridge, Will 82
Harris, Alonzo "Candy" 7
Harris, Bob 324–325
Harris, Bucky 56, 201, 215–216
Harris, Hernando "Pep" 270
Harris, Joe "Moon" 249–250
Harris, Lenny 60
Harris, Lum 7, 15
Harris, Nate 225
Harris, Vic 58, 64–66
Harris, Willie 18
Hart, Jim Ray 216, 220
Hartnett, Gabby 62, 82, 92, 149, 265, 268–269, 294
Hartsel, Topsy 226
Hartung, Clint "Hondo Hurricane" 286
Hartzell, Roy 44, 46, 233
Harvey, Bill 161
Harvey, Bob 129
Harvey, Bryan 280–281, 285
Harwell, Ernie 69, 147
Hasbrook, Robert "Ziggy" 100
Hassett, Buddy 201
Hassey, Ron 18–20, 197
Hatcher, Billy 18, 21
Hatfield, Gil "Colonel" 191
Hatteberg, Scott 246–247, 310
Hatton, Grady 285
Hauser, Joe "Unser Choe" 317, 318, 321
Hawaii Winter Baseball League 73–74
Hawes, Bill 186, 188
Hawke, Bill 52

Hawkins, LaTroy 89
Hawkins, Lem 66
Hawks, Nelson "Chicken" 28, 31
Hawley, Pink 317–318, 320
Hayes, Bun 216
Hayes, Charlie 161
Hayes, Frankie "Blimp" 190, 191, 194
Haywood, Buster 302, 304
Hazewood, Drungo 8
Hazle, Bob "Hurricane" 270
Headley, Chase 44, 46
Healey, Tom 267
Healy, John "Egyptian" 78, 81
Hearn, Bunny 205, 216
Hearn, Jim 66
Heath, Jeff 310, 327–328, 331
Heath, Mike 58
Heathcote, Cliff "Rubberhead" 250
Hebner, Richie "The Gravedigger" 137, 138, 140, 141, 143
Hecker, Guy 4, 250, 252
Hegan, Jim 24, 137, 141
Heilmann, Harry "Slug" 28, 39–40, 123, 24740
Held, Woodie 252
Hellickson, Jeremy 100
Helling, Rick 223–225
Helms, Tommy 216, 220
Helton, Todd "The Toddfather" 74, 280–283
Hemming, George "Old Wax Finger" 226
Hemphill, Charlie "Eagle Eye" 147
Hemsley, Rollie 225
Hemus, Solly 18, 20
Henderson, Ken 100
Henderson, Arthur "Rats" 66, 302
Henderson, Rickey 10, 25, 78–80, 85–86, 165, 195, 209, 221, 233, 235, 237, 248, 333
Hendrick, George 28
Hendrick, Harvey 280
Hendrix, Claude 105, 108
Henke, Tom "The Terminator" 167–168, 170, 175–176
Henline, Butch 88
Henneman, Mike 167, 175–176
Henrich, Tommy "Old Reliable" 72, 136, 226–227, 233
Henry, Bill 286
Henry, Frederick "Snake" 216
Henry, Leo "Preacher" 58
Hentgen, Pat 147–148, 153
Heredia, Gil 18
Herges, Matt 78
Herman, Babe 71, 201, 205, 212
Herman, Billy 88, 91, 95, 208
Hermansen, Chad 296–298
Hermida, Jeremy 67–68
Hernandez, Felix 310
Hernandez, Keith 27, 33–34, 121
Herndon, Larry 161
Herr, Tommie 249, 257
Hershberger, Willard 30, 33
Hershiser, Orel "Bulldog" 41, 201, 213
Herzog, Buck 96, 129–130, 132–133, 261
Herzog, Whitey "White Rat" 43, 78–79, 88, 150, 168
Heusser, Ed "The Wild Elk of the Wasatch" 296, 298

Heving, Joe 111, 118
Hewitt, Joe 5, 280, 282–283
Hickman, Charlie 249
Hickman, Jim 280
Hicks Field 217
Hi Corbett Field 18, 20
Higbe, Kirby 270
Higgins, Pinky 48, 285, 290–291, 320
Higginson, Bobby 250
High, Andy 78
High, Hugh "Bunny" 250
Hill, Aaron 31
Hill, Jimmy "Squab" 58
Hill, Pete 148, 237, 296, 302, 306–307
Hill, "Still Bill" 281
Hilldale Daisies 57–58, 64, 72, 95, 251, 255
Hillebrand, Homer 81
Hillenbrand, Shea 18, 20
Hiller, John 327, 332
Hilo Walk of Fame 73
Himsl, Vedie 177, 179
Hinchcliffe Stadium 191–192
Hines, Henry "Hunky" 78
Hines, Paul 267, 302–303, 305
Hinske, Eric 317
Hinton, Chuck 216
Hisle, Larry 226, 232
Hisner, Harley 93
Hoak, Don "Tiger" 250
Hoblitzel, Dick 313, 315
Hodapp, Johnny 225
Hodge, Clarence "Shovel" 7
Hodges, Gil "Miracle Worker" 3, 88–89, 93–94, 237
Hoeft, Billy 317
Hoerner, Joe 100, 105
Hoff, Red 204
Hoffer, Bill "Wizard" 100
Hoffman, Danny 47
Hoffman, John "Pork Chop" 277
Hoffman, Trevor 2, 5, 28–29, 41–42, 237
Hofman, Arthur "Circus Solly" 167
Hofmann, Fred "Bootnose" 167
Hogan, Shanty 46, 137, 141
Hogsett, Elon "Chief" 105–106
Hohokam Park 18
Holbert, Bill 130
Holke, Walter "Union Man" 167
Holland, Al 302
Holland, Bill 89
Holland, Will 52, 54
Holliday, James "Bug" 167
Holliday, Matt 238, 243
Hollingsworth, Al "Boots" 167
Hollocher, Charlie 167, 173
Holloman, Bobo 66, 69
Holloway, Crush 286–287
Holmes, Darren 216
Holmes, James "Ducky" 100–101
Holmes, Tommy 201
Holshouser, Herman 218
Holtzman, Ken 167
Homestead Grays 11, 55–56, 65, 68, 91, 133, 163–165, 235, 254–255, 258, 276, 294, 305
Honeycutt, Rick 280, 285
Hook, James "Jay Bird" 78, 80

Hooker, Lennie "Elbow" 216
Hooper, Harry 28, 165, 291
Hooten, Burt "Happy" 286
Hopkins, Gail 238
Hopp, Johnny "Cotney" 179–181
Hopper, Bill "Bird Dog" 281
Horner, Bob 105, 108
Hornsby, Rogers 6, 14, 23, 34, 46, 63, 68, 123, 134, 208, 212, 264, 269, 273, 285–286, 289–290, 316, 333
Hornung, Joe "Ubbo U-bbo" 201, 204
Horsey, Hanson 130–131
Horst, Jeremy 325–326
Horton, Elmer "Herky Jerky" 226
Horton, Willie 147, 302, 306
Hoskins, Dave 5, 161
Hosmer, Eric 59
Host, Gene "Twinkles" 250
Hotaling, Pete "Monkey" 201, 204
Houck, Sargent "Sadie" 55
Hough, Charlie 73–75, 199
Houk, Ralph "Major" 105, 106, 110
House of David 45, 183; House of David Museum 147–148
Householder, Charlie 253
Houston, Tyler 184–185
Hovley, Steve "Orbit," "Tennis Ball Head" 28
Howard, Doug 296
Howard, Elston 163, 167, 170–171
Howard, Frank "Capitol Punisher," "Hondo" 226, 232
Howard, Ryan 167, 170–171
Howe, Steve 147
Howell, Jack 18, 20
Howell, Jay 58, 66
Howell, Millard "Dixie" 111
Howry, Bobby 18, 21
Howser, Dick 42
Hoy, Dummy 110, 226, 228, 233
Hoyt, La Marr 270, 276
Hoyt, Waite "Schoolboy" 135, 201, 213
Hrabosky, Al "The Mad Hungarian" 2, 28, 31
Hrbek, Kent 155–157
Hubbard, Jesse "Mountain" 275, 286, 288
Hubbard Museum 287
Hubbell, Carl "King Carl," "The Meal Ticket" 167, 175, 239, 241, 333
Hudler, Rex 18
Hudlin, Willis 238, 245
Hudson, Daniel 302
Hudson, Orlando "O-Dog" 269, 270, 273
Hudson, Tim 66, 72
Hudspeth, Robert "Highpockets" 285, 286–287
Huff, Aubrey 226
Huff, Mike 73, 75
Huggins, Miller "The Mighty Mite" 43, 225–226, 230, 237
Hughes, Phil 31
Hughes, Roy "Jeep," "Sage" 226
Hughes, "Salida Tom" 44
Hughes, Sammy 111, 113, 115
Hughey, "Coldwater Jim" 147

Hughson, Tex 286
Hume, Tom 226
Hundley, Cecil "Rebel" 302
Hundley, Randy 302, 304
Hundley, Todd 302–304
Hunt, Ken 223, 225
Hunt, Ron 167, 172
Hunter, Brian 246
Hunter, Catfish 216–217, 219, 221–222, 260, 265; gravesite 217
Hunter, Torii "Spider Man" 21, 22, 25
Hurdle, Clint 147, 155, 283
Hurst, Bruce 296–298
Hurst, Don 111, 115
Husting, Bert "Pete" 318, 320
Hutchinson, Bill "Wild Bill" 47–48, 51, 284
Hutchinson, Fred "Great Stone Face" 303, 308, 310, 313
Hyatt, Robert "Ham" 216
Hyde, Bubba 161, 165

Iannetta, Chris 265, 267
Ibanez, Raul 201
Incaviglia, Pete 35
Indiana Baseball Hall of Fame 89
Indianapolis ABCs 91–92, 108, 114, 118, 273, 276, 283
Indianapolis Clowns 12, 24, 60, 92, 156, 162, 222, 304
Inge, Brandon 302
Ingersoll, Bob 278
Iorg, Garth 29
Iott, Clarence "Hooks" 169
Iott, Frederick "Happy" 126
Irelan, Hal "Grump" 89
Irvin, Monte "Mr. Murder" 7–8, 13, 104, 193, 219, 235, 254, 304, 307
Irwin, Arthur 327, 330, 332
Isbell, Frank "The Bald Eagle" 201
Isotopes Park 198–199
Israel, Clarence "Half Pint" 66
Isringhausen, Jason 78–79, 88
Ivie, Mike 60, 68

Jacoby, Brook 250
Jackman, Bill "Cannonball" 286, 294
Jackson, Bo 7, 14
Jackson, Grant 226
Jackson, Jelly 55
Jackson, Larry 75–77
Jackson, Mike 286, 288, 295
Jackson, Randy 21, 23, 25
Jackson, Reggie "Mr. October" 9–10, 27, 75, 77, 86, 123, 153, 163, 213, 232, 250–251, 259–260, 265, 293–294, 331, 333
Jackson, Shoeless Joe 5, 59, 99, 120, 207, 254, 270–272, 274, 323–324, 333–334; Museum and Library 270–272
Jackson, Sonny 55, 57
Jackson, Travis "Stonewall" 21–22, 25, 103
Jacobs, Elmer 168
Jacobs, Robert "Spook" 52–53
Jacobsen, Bucky 324–326
Jacobson, William "Baby Doll" 78
Jaha, John 246
James, "Big Bill" 149
Jamieson, Charlie "Cuckoo" 190, 191, 196
Jansen, Larry 246–247, 249
Javery, Al "Beartracks" 138
Javier, Julian 172
Jay, Joey 47, 51
Jefferies, Gregg 27
Jefferson, George 238
Jeffries, Jim 111, 118
Jenkins, Fats 201
Jenkins, Ferguson "Fly" 40, 183, 307, 327–328, 331–332
Jenkins, Geoff 308, 312
Jenks, Bobby 28, 31
Jennings, Desmond 8
Jennings, Hughie "Ee-Yah" 55, 96, 130, 250–251, 258
Jennings, Jason 287
Jensen, Jackie 28
Jensen, Woody 308, 312
Jessup, Gentry "Jeep" 125, 216, 222
JetBlue Park 60
Jeter, Derek "Captain Clutch," "Mr. November" 25, 37, 70, 94, 111, 124, 180, 185, 190–192, 194, 205, 230, 234, 330, 333
Jethroe, Sam "The Jet" 78, 86
John, Tommy 89, 99, 194
Johnny Mize Baseball Museum 67
Johnson, Alex 21, 26
Johnson, Ban 73, 215, 228, 267
Johnson, Billy "Bull" 190, 191, 195
Johnson, Bob 179, 181, 240, 243–244
Johnson, Chappie 225–226, 229
Johnson, Charles 58, 62
Johnson, Cliff 286–287, 331
Johnson, Connie 66, 72
Johnson, Darrell 180
Johnson, Davey 58, 60, 63, 68
Johnson, Deron 28
Johnson, Don 81
Johnson, Ernie 299, 302
Johnson, Ernie "Schoolboy" 161
Johnson, Goat 229
Johnson, Grant "Home Run" 225–226, 230, 237, 296
Johnson, Howard "HoJo" 58, 63
Johnson, "Indian Bob" 238, 240, 244, 310
Johnson, Judy 52, 122, 129, 133, 165, 254; Judy Johnson Field 52
Johnson, Lance "One Dog" 226
Johnson, Louis "Spitball" 78
Johnson, Mark 44
Johnson, Moose 224
Johnson, Oscar "Heavy" 105–106, 108, 170
Johnson, Peanut 92
Johnson, Randy "The Big Unit" 2, 16–17, 20, 28–29, 41, 49, 92, 124, 166, 262–263, 288, 294, 323, 333
Johnson, Rob 177–178
Johnson, Roy 238, 240, 243–244, 310
Johnson, "Sweet Lou" 111
Johnson, Syl 246, 249
Johnson, Tim 223–225
Johnson, Walter "The Big Train" 30, 33, 42, 56–57, 71, 97, 105–107, 109, 151, 162, 175, 213, 222, 234–235, 261, 263, 284, 294, 310, 333
Johnston, Doc 280
Johnston, Jimmy 280, 283
Johnstone, Jay "Moon Man" 47–50
Joker Marchant Stadium 59–60
Jolley, Smead 22, 26
Jones, Adam 31
Jones, Albert "Cowboy" 44
Jones, Andruw 39, 251
Jones, Charles "Bumpus" 228
Jones, Charley "Baby" 216, 221
Jones, Chipper 58, 60, 63, 67, 333
Jones, Cleon 7–8
Jones, Dale "Nubbs" 180
Jones, Daryl 147
Jones, Davy "Kangaroo" 317, 318, 320, 322
Jones, Doug 28, 42
Jones, Fielder 151, 250
Jones, "Jumping Jack" 47
Jones, "Mack the Knife" 66
Jones, Randy 41
Jones, Ruppert 286
Jones, "Sad Sam" 226, 235–236
Jones, Sam "Toothpick" 226, 235
Jones, Sheldon "Available" 180–181
Jones, Stuart "Slim" 129, 137, 254
Jones, Todd "Rollercoaster" 66–67, 72
Jones, Tom 24
Jones, Uriah "Angel Sleeves" 226
Jones, Willie "Puddin' Head" 1, 269–270, 274
Jonnard, Clarence "Bubber" 281
Joost, Eddie 27
Jordan, Brian 129
Jordan, Buck 216
Jordan, Clarence "Slats" 129
Jordan, Michael "Mitty" 140
Jorgensen, John "Spider" 28, 31
Joseph, Newt 7, 11
Joseph P. Riley, Jr. Ballpark 270
Joss, Addie "The Human Hairpin" 256, 317–318, 323
Joyce, Bill 167, 173, 228
Joyner, Wally 66, 69
Judd, Oscar 327
Judd, Thomas "Ossie" 327
Judge, Joe 201, 207
Jurges, Billy 201
Justice, David 226, 233
Jutze, Alfred "Queens" 201

Ka'aihue, Kila 73
Kaat, Jim "Kitty" 147, 149, 153–154
Kahdot, Ike 240
Kaline, Al 35, 60, 129–131, 135, 147, 178, 212, 244, 261, 313, 331, 334
Kamm, Willie 27
Kanehl, Rod "The Mole" 106
Kansas City Monarchs 9, 11, 45, 54, 63, 70, 72, 95, 98, 102–103, 107–108, 122, 133, 148, 168–170, 171, 244–245, 289–290, 293–295
Karkovice, Ron "Officer" 190, 191
Karros, Eric 190–191, 194
Kasko, Eddie 190
Kauff, Bernie 226, 228, 233
Kauffman Stadium 168; Royals Hall of Fame 168

Keating, Robert 140
Keck, Frank "Cactus" 167
Keefe, Tim "Sir Timothy" 118, 138, 140–141, 145, 234, 236
Keeler, Wee Willie 55, 86, 130–131, 201, 210–211
Keenan, Jim 47
Keister, Bill "Wagon Tongue" 129
Kekich, Mike 81
Kell, Everett "Skeeter" 22
Kell, George 3, 21–22, 24–25, 172, 248, 311
Kelleher, Mick 312
Keller, Charlie "King Kong" 129–130, 135–136, 233
Kelley, Joe 55, 130, 138, 141, 143–144
Kellner, Alex 18, 21
Kelly, George "High Pockets" 27, 28, 34, 213, 240, 242
Kelly, Mike "King," "The King of Baseball" 190, 201, 204, 211–212, 217
Kelly, Pat 253
Kelly, Shawn 111
Kelly, Tom 155, 160
Keltner, Ken "Butch" 248, 317–319, 321
Kemp, Matt "Bison" 238, 240
Kemp, Steve 286
Kendall, Fred 32
Kendall, Jason 27, 32, 49, 219
Kenna, Ed "The Pitching Poet" 313, 315
Kenna, Eddie "Scrap Iron" 28
Kennedy, Adam 27, 31
Kennedy, Ian 31
Kennedy, Snapper 228
Kennedy, Terry 225
Kennedy, William "Brickyard" 226, 228
Kent, Jeff 2, 16, 27, 34, 150–151, 174, 311
Kerins, John 94
Kern, Jim 147
Kershaw, Clayton "Minotaur" 286
Kessinger, Chris 277
Kessinger, Don 21, 25, 27
Key, Jimmy 7, 15
Kiefer, "Harlem Joe" 201
Kiker, Kasey 8
Kile, Darryl 28
Killebrew, Harmon "Killer" 75–76, 92, 123, 156, 173, 200, 213, 256, 306, 333
Killefer, Red 96, 147, 261
Killefer, "Reindeer Bill" 147
Killen, Frank 250
Killian, "Twilight Ed" 317, 324
Kilroy, Matt "Matches" 90, 204, 250
Kimball, Newt 296
Kimbro, Henry "Jumbo" 280–282
Kindall, Jerry "Slim" 155
Kinder, Ellis "Old Folks" 21, 22, 27
Kiner, Ralph "Mr. Home Run" 165, 198–200, 233
King, Jeff 88, 95
King, Silver 167, 170, 174
Kingery, Mike 155
Kingman, Dave "Kong" 16, 246–249

Kinsler, Ian 18, 20, 316
Kinslow, Tom 55
Kinzie, Walt 106
Kipnis, Jason 79
Kippert, Ed "Kickapoo" 147
Kirby, Clay 55, 58
Kirby, John "Chicken Hearted" 167
Kirkpatrick, Ed "Spanky" 308, 310
Kison, Bruce 308, 313
Kitson, Frank 149
Kittle, Ron 89, 98
Klein, Chuck "The Hoosier Hammerer" 89–91, 92, 96–98, 165, 189
Klesko, Ryan 28
Kline, Steve 250
Kling, Johnny 167, 171
Klippstein, Johnny 55, 58
Klobedanz, Fred "Duke" 47, 51
Kluszewski, Ted 78, 83
Kluttz, Clyde 216, 218
Knapp, Gene "Rubber Arm" 201
Knepper, Bob 226
Knight, "Quiet Joe" 327
Knight, Ray 66, 70
Knights Stadium 270
Knoblauch, Chuck 285, 288
Knoop, Bobby 100, 103
Knowles, Darold 167, 176
Koch, Billy 201
Kolb, Dan 78, 88
Kolp, Ray "Jockey" 226
Komine, Shane 75
Konerko, Paul 265–268
Konetchy, Ed 317–318, 320; nicknames: "Big Ed," "The Big Bohemian," "Candy Kid," "Edward the Mighty," "Koney," "The Lacrosse Lulu" 318–320
Konstanty, Jim 201, 215
Koonce, Calvin 218
Koosman, Jerry 155, 160, 178
Kopf, Larry 47
Koskie, Corey 327, 330
Koslo, Dave 318
Kotchman, Casey 60
Kotsay, Mark 31
Koufax, Sandy "The Left Arm of God" 14, 25, 27, 34, 40, 46, 75, 110, 124, 155, 166, 168, 177, 197, 201, 205, 214, 237, 322, 333
Kouzmanoff, Kevin 29, 31
Kowalik, Fabian 286
Krausse, Lew 253
Kreevich, Mike 78
Kremer, Ray "Wiz" 28
Kress, Red 27
Krsnich, Rocco 318
Kruk, John 41, 313, 315
Kubek, Tony 209, 317, 319, 321–322
Kubel, Jason 277–279
Kuenn, Harvey 317, 322, 324
"Harvey's Wallbangers" 324
Kuhel, Joe 225
Kuhn, Bowie 124
Kuiper, Duane 317, 321
Kurowski, Whitey 250, 257
Kusick, Craig "Mongo" 317, 318, 319, 323
Kutcher, Randy 15–16

Laabs, Chet 317, 322–323
Labatt Park 328
Labine, Clem 265, 269
Lacey, Bob 303
LaChance, Candy 47
Lackey, John 286
LaCoss, Mike "Buffy" 28
Ladd, Arthur "Hi" 47
Ladd, Pete 126, 129
Lade, Doyle "Porky" 180
Lafferty, Frank "Flip" 52–53
LaGrow, Lerrin 18, 21
Laird, Gerald 31
Lajoie, Nap "King Larry" 23, 34, 92, 123, 232, 265–269, 307, 333
Lamade Stadium 251; see also Bowman Field; Eric Stotz Field; Peter J. McGovern Little League Baseball Museum
Lamar, Bill "Good Time Bill" 129, 130
Lamar Porter Field 23
LaMarque, Jim 167
Lamont, Gene 83
Landis, Kenesaw Mountain 67, 114, 195, 228, 233, 236, 261, 272, 302
Landrum, Bill 270, 276
Landrum, Joe 276
Lanfranconi, Walter 299
Lange, Bill "Little Eva" 28
Langston, Mark 28, 41
Lanier, Hal 216
Lanier, Lorenzo "Rimp" 7
Lanier, Max 216, 222
Lankford, Ray 28
Lansford, Carney 27
Lansing, Mike 324–326; Mike Lansing Field 325
LaPointe, Ralph 2, 299–301
LaPorte, Frank 225
Larish, Jeff 100
Larkin, Barry 36, 45, 115, 225, 231, 300, 334
Larkin, Henry 249
Larkin, Terry 204
LaRoche, Adam 31
LaRoche, Dave 44, 47
Larsen, Don "Gooney Bird" 29, 33, 89, 99, 170, 174, 191, 214, 260, 269
LaRussa, Tony 42, 58, 66, 85
Lary, Frank "Taters" 7
Lary, Lyn "Broadway" 27, 28
Lasorda, Tommy 43, 49, 99, 152, 199, 250, 264, 310, 329
Latham, Arlie "The Freshest Man on Earth" 102, 186–189
Latham, Chris 75, 77
Latimer, Tacks 229
Latos, Mat 302
Lavagetto, Attilio "Cookie" 28
LaValliere, Mike "Spanky" 216
Lavan, Doc 147, 151
Lavelle, Gary 250
Law, Vance "Long Arm of the Law" 75–77
Law, Vern "Deacon," "Preacher" 75–77
Lawing, Garland 218
Lawrence, Brian 44
Lawrence-Dumont Stadium 106

Lawrie, Brett 327
Lawson, Alfred "Roxie" 100
Lawton, Matt 161
Lazzeri, Tony "Poosh 'Em Up" 1, 2728, 29, 34–35, 183, 189
Leach, Tommy 201, 204, 212
League, Brandon 31
League Stadium 89; *A League of Their Own* 89
Lear, Charles "King" 250, 252
LeBlanc, Wade 119
Lecroy, Matt 270
Ledbetter, Ralph "Razor" 216
Lee, Bill "Spaceman" 28, 141, 298
Lee, Bill 119
Lee, Bob "Moose" 100
Lee, Cliff 21, 26
Lee, Clifford 180
Lee, Derrek 27, 31, 74
Lee, Dud 44, 46
Lee, Hal "Sheriff" 161
Lee, Holsey "Scrip" 55, 58, 122
Lee, Mark 223, 225
Leever, Sam "The Goshen Schoolmaster" 226
Lefebvre, Bill 266
Lefebvre, Joe 186, 189
Leiber, Hank 18, 21
Leibrandt, Charlie 78, 85, 87
Leifield, Lefty 78, 87
Leiter, Al 190–192, 196–197
LeFlore, Ron "Jailbird" 9, 147–149, 152
Leland, Frank 281–282
Leland Giants 109, 118, 296, 306
Lemon, Bob 14, 28–29, 41, 120, 164
Lemon, Chet "The Jet" 161, 165
Lemon, Jim 302–303, 306
Lemongello, Mark 193
Leonard, Buck 165, 216–217, 219–220, 223, 276, 305, 333
Leonard, Dennis 201
Leonard, Dutch 58, 78, 87, 118, 128, 226, 228, 236
Leonard, Jeffrey "Old Penitentiary Face" 250, 254
Leone, Justin 184–185
Les Marakami Stadium 73
Leskanic, Curt 250
Leslie, Sam 161
Lester, Jon 127, 308, 310, 313
Levsen, Emil "Dutch" 100–101
Lewis, Buddy 216–217, 220
Lewis, Colby 31
Lewis, Duffy 28, 291
Lewis, Fred 161
Lewis, Joe "Sleepy" 129–130
Lewis, Mark 227
Lewis, Rufus 5, 161
Leyland, Jim 38, 226, 237
Lidge, Brad 28, 31
Lieber, Jon 100–102
Lieberthal, Mike 27
Ligtenberg, Kerry 277
Lillie, Jim "Grasshopper" 47
Lilly, Ted 31
Lincecum, Tim "The Freak" 308, 310, 312–313
Lincoln Giants 72
Lind, Adam 89, 98
Lindblad, Paul 105, 110

Lindell, Johnny 44, 46
Lindsay, Chris "The Crab" 250
Lindsey, Bill 296
Lindstrom, Chuck 84
Lindstrom, Fred 78–80, 82, 84, 122, 172, 181
Lindstrom, Matt 75–77
Lintz, Larry 265
Linz, Phil "Mr. Laffs" 130
Linzy, Frank 238, 245
Lipon, Johnny "Skids" 226
Liska, Ad 181
Littell, Mark "Country" 167, 230
Livingston, Mickey 269
Lloyd, Pop 58–59, 63–64, 175, 231, 237, 289, 291, 296, 333
Lobert, Frank 54
Lobert, Hans 52–54
Lock, Don 105
Locker, Bob 100, 105
Lockett, Lester 89
Lockman, Whitey 216
Lockwood, Skip 138
Lo Duca, Paul 201
Lofton, Kenny 89, 98
Logan, Johnny "Yatcha" 201
Logan, Xavier "Nook" 161
Lohse, Kyle 31
Loiselle, Rich 317
Lolich, Mickey 246–247, 249
Lollar, Sherm 21–22, 24
Lombardi, Ernie "Schnozz" 27, 28, 30, 32, 35, 135
Lonborg, Jim 28
Long, Dale 93, 103, 167–168, 171, 259
Long, Herman "The Flying Dutchman" 78, 85, 210
Longoria, Evan 31, 35
Looper, Braden 238
Lopat, Ed "Steady Eddie" 201, 214
Lopata, Stan 147
Lopes, Davey 199, 265–266, 268, 312
Lopez, Al 58, 62, 66
Lord, Bristol "The Human Eyeball" 250, 254
Lord, Harry 126, 128
Loretta, Mark 27
Loucks, Scott 15–16
Louden, Louis 302, 304
Louisville Slugger Field 111–112
Louisville Slugger Museum 111–113
Love, Edward "Slim" 161–162
Lovett, Tom 265–266, 269
Lowe, Bobby "Link" 205, 249, 250, 251
Lowe, Derek 147, 200
Lowenstein, John "Steiner" 177, 179
Lowrey, Harry "Peanuts" 28
Luby, Hal 75, 77
Luby, Pat 270
Lucas, Henry 53
Lucas, Red "The Nashville Narcissus" 280, 281, 284
Luderus, Fred 317, 319, 321
Lukon, Eddie "Mongoose" 250
Lum, Mike 73–75
Lumpe, Jerry 167, 172
Lundy, Dick "King Richard" 58, 60, 64, 95

Lush, Billy 48
Lush, Johnny 250, 252
Luther Williams Field 67
Luuloa, Keith 73–75
Luzinski, Greg "The Bull" 78, 86, 277
Lyle, Albert "Sparky" 139, 250, 263–264, 318
Lyles, Jordan 270
Lynch, Jack 204
Lynch, Jerry 95, 148
Lynn, Fred 39, 48, 78, 80, 85–86, 274
Lyon, Brandon 296–298
Lyons, Denny 225, 230
Lyons, Jimmie 78, 86, 148
Lyons, Ted "Sunday Teddy" 48, 119, 121, 125, 235
Lyons, Steve "Psycho" 308

Mabry, John 52–53
MacDougal, Mike 184–186
Mack, Connie "The Tall Tactician" 15, 50, 60, 132–133, 138, 141–142, 146, 160, 197, 207, 215, 254–256, 261, 263–264, 267, 300, 310, 322; Connie Mack Stadium 270–271
Mackey, Biz 254–255, 285–289, 296, 334
Madden, Kid 126–127, 129
Maddox, Forest "One-Wing" 282
Maddox, Garry "Secretary of Defense" 226, 233
Maddux, Greg "Mad Dog" 4, 17, 88, 124, 139, 145, 154, 166, 234, 261–262, 286, 293, 331, 333
Madlock, Bill "Mad Dog" 280–283
Madson, Ryan 31
Magadan, Dave 58
Magee, Lee 228, 233
Magee, Sherry 250, 260
Maglie, Sal "The Barber" 201, 214
Magoon, George "Topsy" 126, 128
Mahaffey, Roy "Popeye" 270
Mahay, Ron 78
Mahtook, Mike 119
Mains, Willard "Grasshopper" 126
Malarcher, Dave 119, 122, 126, 296
Maler, Jim "Baby Huey" 201
Mallonee, Julius 218
Malone, Pat 250
Maloney, Billy 126–128
Maloney, Jim 28, 125
Malzone, Frank 201, 209
Mancuso, Gus 285
Manley, Effa 193, 254
Manlove, Charlie 250
Mann, Fred 2, 299–301
Mann, Les "Major" 72, 179–180, 183
Manning, Jack 138
Manning, Max "Dr. Cyclops" 66, 72
Manning, Rick 42
Mantilla, Felix 60
Mantle, Mickey "The Commerce Comet" 18, 20, 33–35, 37, 39, 44, 59, 93, 110, 111, 123, 152, 158, 165, 176, 181, 185, 194, 196, 200, 212–213, 238–239, 241–243, 247, 259–260, 273, 306, 317, 331, 333; boyhood home 239; gravesite 287;

Mickey Mantle Monument Park at Mickey Mantle Field 239
Manuel, Charlie 313, 317
Manuel, Jerry 66
Manush, Heinie 1, 7, 13
Mapes, Cliff "Tiger" 180–181
Maranville, Rabbit 137–138, 142–143, 173, 240, 330
Marberry, Firpo 286, 295
Marcelle, Ollie "Ghost" 95, 119, 122
Marcum, Johnny "Footsie" 111
Marichal, Juan 29, 177, 262, 310
Marion, Marty "The Octopus" 20, 38–39, 151, 170, 270, 274
Maris, Roger 33, 36, 51, 59, 110, 155–159, 223–225, 277–278, 282, 306; gravesite 224; Roger Maris Museum 223–224
Marquard, Rube 9, 133, 145, 190, 226, 236
Marshall, Charlie 53
Marshall, Clarence "Cuddles" 308, 310
Marshall, Jack 7
Marshall, Mike 147–149, 154
Marshall, Willard 242, 302, 306
Marson, Lou 18
Martin, Billy "Billy the Kid" 28, 35, 42–45, 50, 88, 152, 202, 243, 260, 277
Martin, Elwood "Speed" 308
Martin, Pepper "The Wild Horse of the Osage" 26, 170, 238–240, 243
Martin, Renie 52, 55
Martin, Russell 327, 330
Martinez, Dennis 19, 190, 222
Martinez, Edgar 201, 212, 308
Martinez, Greg 184, 186
Martinez, Pedro 53, 56, 178, 186, 189, 238, 252–253, 331
Martinez, Tino 58, 62–63
Martinez, Tippy 44–45, 47
Martini, Guido "Southern" 7–8
Martyn, Bob 75, 77
Masi, Phil 78
Maskrey, Samuel "Leech" 250
Matheny, Mike 49, 225, 229–230
Mather, Joe 75, 77
Mathes, Joe "Old Hustler" 318
Mathews, Bobby 129–130, 136, 203
Mathews, Eddie 9, 33, 35–36, 63, 69, 88, 122–123, 129, 200, 236, 256, 285, 287, 290, 301, 311, 333
Mathewson, Christy "Big Six" 2, 9, 31, 46, 77, 96, 98, 133, 183, 214–215, 234–235, 250–253, 261–262, 269, 320, 333; brother Henry 253
Mathis, Verdell 21, 27
Matias, John 73–75
Matlack, Jon 250
Matlock, Leroy 167
Matthews, Gary, Sr. "Sarge" 28
Mattingly, Don "Donnie Baseball" 3, 62, 88–90, 93–94, 121, 157, 224, 283
Mauch, Gene 105, 110–111, 295
Mauer, Joe 121, 141, 155–157, 330
Maxwell, Charlie "Paw Paw," "Sunday Charlie" 147, 149, 152–153; Charlie Maxwell Ball Diamond 147

Maxwell, Justin 130
May, Carlos 14
May, Dave 52–54
May, Lee "Boomer from Birmingham," 7, 11
May, Merrill "Pinky" 88–89, 95
May, Milt 88, 93, 95
May, Rudy 47, 105, 108
May, William "Buckshot" 28
Mayberry, John 147–148, 150
Mayer, Erskine 66
Mayes, Paddy 240
Mayo, Eddie "Hotshot" 137, 138, 142
Mays, Carl 111, 113–114, 117; "Sub" 111
Mays, Willie "The Say Hey Kid" 5, 7–10, 12–13, 18, 29, 33, 38–39, 56, 59, 63–64, 70, 91, 96, 121, 130, 142, 146, 156, 183, 199–200, 212–213, 243, 247–248, 251, 256, 259, 265, 271, 284, 311, 331, 333
Mayweather, Eldridge "Chili" 119
Mazeroski, Bill 71, 245, 251, 255, 265, 301, 313, 315–316
McAleer, Jimmy "The Loafer" 226
McAllister, Sport 162
McAndrew, Jim "Moms" 100
McArdle, Dean 100
McAuliffe, Dick "Mugsy" 47, 50
McBee, Pryor 240
McBride, Algie 55, 57
McBride, Bake 167
McBride, Dick 250
McBride, George 317, 319–320
McBride, Tom 93
McCabe, James "Swat" 250
McCaffrey, Charles "Sparrow" 250
McCall, John "Windy" 28
McCann, Brian 66, 68
McCarthy, Brandon 31
McCarthy, Jack 138
McCarthy, Joe 125, 143, 189, 250, 264
McCarthy, Tommy 137, 141, 143–144, 268
McCarver, Tim 280, 282
McCaskill, Kirk 253, 327
McCatty, Steve 237
McClain, Edward "Boots" 111
McClellan, Dan 117, 302, 307
McClung, Seth 313–314, 317
McClure Field 303
McConnell, Amby 2, 299, 301
McCool, Billy 89
McCormick, Barry 111
McCormick, Frank 201
McCormick, Mike 28, 41
McCormick Park 217
McCosky, Barney 250
McCovey, Willie "Stretch" 6–11, 29, 36, 38, 142, 256, 308, 333; McCovey's Restaurant 29
McCoy Stadium 182, 266
McCracken, Quinton 218
McCredie, Walter "Judge" 100
McCreery, Tom 251
McCullough, Clyde 280
McDaniel, Lindy 238, 241, 245
McDaniels, Booker 21
McDevitt, Danny 203
McDonald, Webster "56 Varieties, Submarine" 52, 55

McDougald, Gil 27, 29, 35
McDowell, Jack 28
McDowell, Roger 226
McDowell, Sam "Sudden Sam" 250
McDuffie, Terris "Speed" 7, 10, 254
McElveen, Pryor "Humpty" 66
McEwing, "Super Joe" 250
McFarland, Ed 225
McGann, Dan 111–112, 115
McGee, Willie 28, 33, 88
McGehee, Casey 31
McGinnity, Joe "Iron Man" 78–79, 86–87, 215, 241, 310
McGowan, Bill 53
McGowan, Frank "Beauty" 47
McGraw, John "Little Napoleon," "Mugsy" 31, 72–73, 83, 87, 103, 106, 115, 122, 128, 130–131, 158, 175–176, 188, 201, 207–211, 215, 230, 233, 240, 257, 283, 292
McGraw, Tommy 21, 24
McGraw, Tug 28, 42
McGregor, Scott 28
McGriff, Fred "Crime Dog" 58, 62–63, 279
McGuire, Deacon 225, 229
McGuire, Deck 302
McGwire, Mark 27, 28, 33, 70, 84, 133–134, 220–221, 260, 308, 310, 333–334
McHenry, Henry 286, 288
McInnis, Stuffy 50, 137–138, 142, 207
McIntosh, Joe 177–178
McIntyre, Matty 47, 322
McKay, Dave 327
McKean, Ed 225
McKechnie, Bill "Deacon" 43, 96–97, 193, 250, 261, 264–265; McKechnie Field 60
McKenry, Frank "Limb" 281
McKeon, Jack 190, 197, 318
McKeon, Larry 92
McKinnis, Lefty 7
McLain, Denny 78, 80, 87, 177
McLean, Larry 327, 330
McLish, Cal 240
McMahan, Jack 23
McMahon, Don 201, 215
McMahon, Sadie 52, 55
McMakin, "Spartanburg John" 270
McManus, Marty 78, 84
McMichael, Greg 280
McMillan, Roy 285, 291
McMillon, Billy 198, 200
McMullen, Ken 27
McMullin, Fred 108
McNair, Eric "Boob" 161, 164
McNair, Hurley 285, 287, 293
McNally, Dave 177–179, 196, 292, 318
McNally, "Minooka Mike" 250
McPhee, Bid 201, 204, 207–208
McQuinn, George 302–304
McRae, Hal 58, 65
McReynolds, Kevin 21–23
McSorley, John "Trick" 167
McVey, Cal 100–101, 103
Meadows, Lee "Specs" 216, 218
Meares, Pat 105
Medwick, Joe "Ducky," "Muscles"

123, 165, 170, 190, 191, 192, 195, 244
Meek, Evan 308
Meek, Frank "Dad" 167
Meier, Dave 177, 179
Meine, Heinie "The Count of Luxemburg" 167, 169
Melaleuca Field 76
Melancon, Mark 44
Mele, Sam 137
Melillo, Oscar "Ski," "Spinach" 78
Melton, Bill 161, 164
Melton, Cliff "Mickey Mouse," "Mountain Music" 216, 222
Melvin, Bob 31
Memorial Park Stadium 277
Memphis Red Sox 14–15, 27, 165, 281–282
Mench, Kevin "Shrek" 52, 54
Menke, Denis 100, 103
Mercer, Win 313
Mercker, Kent 226
Merkle, Fred "Bonehead" 31, 114, 317–318, 320–321; Merkle Field 318
Merriman, Lloyd "Citation" 28
Mesoraco, Devin 250
Messenger, Randy 184
Messersmith, Andy 178, 190, 196, 239, 292
Metro, Charlie 254
Metzger, Butch 90
Meusel, Bob 28
Meusel, Irish 28
Meyer, Benny "Earache" 167
Meyer, Joey 73
Meyer, Russ "The Mad Monk" 78, 81
Meyerle, "Long Levi" 250–251
Meyers, John "Chief" 27, 30–31, 257
Meyers, Lou 45
Micelli, Dan 190, 197
Michael, Gene "Stick" 226
Michaels, Cass 147–149
Mickolio, Kameron 177–178
Middleton, "Rifle Jim" 89
Midkiff, Ezra "Salt Rock" 313–315
Midway Stadium 156
Mientkiewicz, Doug 226
Milan, Clyde "Deerfoot" 280–281, 284
Miley, Mike 230
Miller, Bing 100–101, 103–104
Miller, Bob 167, 176
Miller, Damian 317, 320
Miller, Dots 190
Miller, Eddie 38
Miller, George "Doggie," "Foghorn" 201, 204
Miller, Marvin 123
Miller, Otto "Moonie" 179–180
Miller, Ray 129
Miller, Roscoe "Rubberlegs" 89
Miller, Shelby 286
Miller, Stu 138, 146
Miller, Trever 111, 113, 118
Miller, Ward "Grump," "Windy" 78
Miller Park 318
Mills, Brad 18, 31
Millwood, Kevin 216

Milne, Pete 9
Milner, John "The Hammer" 66
Milton, Henry "Streak" 286–287
Milwaukee County Stadium 9
Minarcin, Rudy "Potato Head" 250
Mincher, Don 7
Mingori, Steve 167
Minor, Ryan 228
Minoso, Minnie 79, 156, 194
Minton, Greg "Moon Man" 286, 295
Minute Maid Park 286
Mirabelli, Doug 19
Mississippi Sports Hall of Fame and Museum 161
Mitchell, Bobby 296
Mitchell, Clarence 180, 184
Mitchell, Dale 238, 243
Mitchell, Jackie 58
Mitchell, Kevin "Boogie Bear," "World" 28
Mitchell, Willie 161
Mitchell Commission Report on Steroids 36, 255, 304, 319, 326, 332
Mize, Johnny "The Big Cat" 39, 66–67, 70, 103, 333
Mizell, Wilmer "Vinegar Bend" 161–162, 166
Mmahat, Kevin 281
Mole, Fenton "Muscles" 28
Molesworth, Carlton 130–131
Molina, Bengie 46
Molitor, Paul 60, 108, 155–156, 158, 213, 311, 316, 321, 324, 334
Monbouquette, Bill 138, 141
Monday, Rick 21–22, 26–27
Money, Don 55–57
Moneyball, book by Michael Lewis 166, 247
Monroe, Bill "Money" 237, 280, 281–282, 283
Montefusco, John "The Count" 190–191, 196
Montgomery, Al 197, 200'
Montgomery, Ben 281
Montgomery, Jeff 226, 237, 300
Montgomery Riverwalk Stadium 8
Moolic, George "Prunes" 138, 140
Moon, Wally 21, 24, 26
Moore, Charlie 7
Moore, Dobie "The Black Cat" 66, 67, 69–71, 170
Moore, Donnie 286, 295
Moore, Earl "Big Ebbie," "Crossfire," "Steam Engine in Boots" 226–228
Moore, Eddie 111
Moore, Euel 240
Moore, Gene, Jr. "Rowdy" 286
Moore, Harry 147–148, 153
Moore, Johnny 47, 50
Moore, Joseph "Jo-Jo," "The Gause Ghost" 285, 286, 287, 293
Moore, Matt 59
Moore, Mike 238, 245
Moore, Ray 129
Moore, Red 66–67, 69–70
Moore, Terry 7
Moran, Albert "Hiker" 201
Moran, Pat 138

Morandini, Mickey "Dandy Little Glove Man" 249, 250
Morgan, Connie 92
Morgan, Joe "The Sweet Pea" 6, 30, 34, 39, 208–209, 230, 233, 280, 285, 286, 287, 289–290, 293, 333
Morgan, Mike 29, 117, 192, 279
Morgan, Nyjer "Tony Plush" 28, 31
Morgan, Ray 129
Morneau, Justin 327, 330
Morrill, John 137, 141
Morris, Barney 224
Morris, Doyt 218
Morris, Ed "Cannonball" 201, 204
Morris, Hal 7
Morris, Jack 153, 155–156, 159–160, 280
Morrison, "Jughandle Johnny" 111, 118
Morrissey, Frank "Deacon" 131
Morton, Bubba 55, 57
Morton, Guy, Jr. 7, 15
Morton, Guy, Sr. "Alabama Blossom" 7, 15
Moryn, Walt 155
Moseby, Lloyd "Shaker" 21, 22
Moses, Jerry 161, 163
Moses, Wally "Peepsight" 66, 67, 71
Moss, Porter "Ankleball," "Submarine" 226
Mossi, Don "The Sphinx," "Ears" 28
Mostil, Johnny "Bananas" 78
Mothell, Carroll "Dink" 105–106, 108
Mott, Elisha "Bitsy" 2, 58, 62
Mountjoy, "Medicine Bill" 327
Mouton, James 44
Moyer, Jamie 86, 250, 263
Mueller, Bill 167–168, 173
Mueller, Don "Mandrake the Magician" 167
Mueller, Ray "Iron Man" 105–107, 194
Mulcahy, Hugh "Losing Pitcher" 138, 140, 244
Mulcahy Stadium 16
Mulder, Mark 78, 87
Mulvey, Joe 265, 267
Mullen, Ford "Moon" 308
Mullin, "Wabash George" 222, 226
Mumphrey, Jerry 279, 286
Mungo, Van Lingle 270, 275–276
Municipal Stadium 130
Munns, Leslie "Little Nemo" 28
Munson, Thurman "Tugboat" 163, 206, 225, 226, 229, 260; gravesite 227; Munson's Home Plate Sports Pub 227
Murcer, Bobby 238–239, 241, 243, 279
Murphy, Charles 43
Murphy, Connie "Stone Face" 138
Murphy, Dale "All American Boy" 39, 246–247
Murphy, Danny 249
Murphy, "Honest Eddie" 201
Murphy, Johnny "Fireman" 201, 215
Murphy, Morgan 265
Murphy, Rob 58

Index

Murphy, Tom 226
Murray, Bill "Dasher" 126
Murray, Dale 279
Murray, Eddie 2, 27, 29, 33, 130, 157, 237, 305, 333
Murray, Red 250
Murtaugh, Danny 250, 265
Museum of Nebraska Major League Baseball 180
Musial, Stan "The Donora Greyhound," "Stan the Man" 9, 26, 37, 71, 83, 170, 183–184, 199, 212, 237, 250–253, 258–259, 274, 331, 333
Mussina, Mike "Moose" 250–251, 261–262, 264
Mutrie, Jim 138
Muzzy Field 48
Myatt, Glenn 21, 24
Myatt, George "Foghorn," "Mercury" 44, 46
Myer, Buddy 161, 163–164
Myers, Mike 78, 88
Myers, Randy 125, 308, 313
Myers, Wil 216

Nagy, Charles 47–48, 51
Nahem, "Subway Sam" 201
Napier, Euthumn 67
Narleski, Ray 190, 197
Narron, Jerry 219
Narron, Sam 219
Nash, Billy 302, 305, 307
Nash, Jim 184, 186
Nashville Elite Giants 20, 283
Nathan, Joe 286, 288, 295
National Baseball Congress 16
National Baseball Hall of Fame and Museum 202–204; Hall of Fame election 1, 3, 5, 10, 25–26, 39, 42, 63–65, 68, 82, 97, 117, 133–134, 156, 165, 173, 175, 182–183, 199, 208, 210–211, 214, 216, 221, 229–230, 232, 234–236, 246–247, 254, 256–259, 262–263, 268, 280, 282–283, 294–295, 296, 305–307, 311–312, 315, 320, 323, 332; Hall of Fame Negro Leagues study 122, 245, 304
National Museum of American History: Lou Newman Collection of Baseball Memorabilia 56
Nationals Park 56
Nava, Daniel 29
Navarro, Efren 184–185
Neagle, Denny 129
Neal, Charlie 285
Neale, Alfred "Greasy" 313–314, 316
Negro Leagues Baseball Museum 63, 168, 170
Negro Leagues Grave Marker Project 79, 306
Nehf, Art 89, 99, 180
Neibauer, Gary 177
Neighbors, Bob 240
Neil, Ray 58, 63
Neill, Michael 303
Nelson, Candy 126–128
Nelson, Dave 238
Nelson, Gene 58
Nelson, Jeff 129, 137

Nelson, Lynn "Line Drive" 223, 225
Nen, Robb 28
Nettles, Graig "Puff" 27, 28, 29, 35–36
Neuer, John "Tacks" 226, 229
Neun, Johnny 129, 266
Nevers, Ernie 157
New York Black Yankees 11, 94, 192
New York Lincoln Giants 11, 55, 64, 117, 121, 230, 289, 294, 306
Newark Eagles 13, 54, 72, 193, 254, 288, 291, 307
Newcombe, Don 30, 41, 115, 139, 170, 188, 190, 196, 227, 255, 291, 301
Newhouser, Hal "Prince Hal" 123, 147–149, 153
Newsom, Bobo 270, 275
Newsome, Skeeter 7
Nichols, Al 113
Nichols, Art 186, 188
Nichols, Chet 265, 269
Nichols, Frederick "Tricky" 47–49
Nichols, Kid 190, 303, 317–318, 323, 333
Nicholson, Bill "Swish" 129, 135–136, 274
Nicholson, Dave "Mr. Clean" 167
Nicholson, Fred "Shoemaker" 286
Niedenfuer, Tom 155, 160
Niehoff, Bert 44, 46
Niekro, Joe 226
Niekro, Phil "Knucksie" 74, 125, 226, 235, 261, 307
Nieman, Bob 226
Nimmo, Brandon 325
Nixon, Otis 216, 221
Nixon, Russ 229
Nixon, Trot 216, 221
Nolan, Edward "The Only Nolan" 327, 329
Nolan, Gary 28
Nolasco, Ricky 30–31
Noles, Dickie 218
Norman, Fred 286
Norris, Derek 106
North, Billy 308, 312
North Carolina Sports Hall of Fame 217
Northeast Delta Dental Stadium 187
Northey, Ron "The Roundman" 250
Northrup, Jim 147, 149, 152
Novikoff, Lou "The Mad Russian" 18
Noyes, Win 181
Nunamaker, Les 179, 181
Nuxhall, Joe 226, 237

Oakes, Ennis "Rebel" 119
Oana, Prince 73, 75
Oates, Johnny 216, 223
Oberholtzer, Brett 52
Oberkfell, Ken 78
Oberlin, Frank "Flossie" 147
O'Brien, Frank "Dink" 28
O'Brien, John "Chewing Gum" 327
O'Brien, John "Cinders" 201
O'Connell, Danny 190
O'Connell, Jimmy 82
O'Connor, Jack "Peach Pie" 167
O'Day, Hank "Peep" 78

O'Dell, Billy 270, 276
Odom, John "Blue Moon" 66
O'Doul, Lefty 28–29, 38–39, 74, 143, 189
Oeschger, Joe 80
Oester, Ron 225
O'Farrell, Bob 78, 82–83, 134
Oglivie, Ben 324
Ogren Park at Allegiance Field 177
O'Leary, Charley 80–81
Olerud, John "Big Rude" 30, 163, 308, 311
Olin, Frank 2, 299, 301
Oliva, Tony 156, 305
Oliver, Al "Scoop" 123, 226, 232–233
Oliver, Bob 119
Oliver, Darren 167
Oliver, Joe 280
Olson, Greg 155
Olson, Gregg 180, 183–184
Olson, Ivy 167
Olson, Marv "Sparky" 277
Olson, Tim 223–224
Olympic Stadium 308
O'Malley, Walter 88
O'Neil, Buck 14, 58, 60, 63, 91, 168, 282; Buck O'Neil Baseball Complex 60
O'Neil, Michael "Fancy" 48–49
O'Neill, Harry 4, 252
O'Neill, Paul "Ace" 226, 233
O'Neill, Steve 249–251, 313
O'Neill, Tip 327, 329, 331
Ontiveros, Steve "Spin Doctor" 198, 200
Oquist, Mike 46
Original Baseball Hall of Fame Museum of Minnesota 155
Oriole Park at Camden Yards/Sports Legends Museum 130
Orosco, Jesse 28–29, 42, 295, 307
O'Rourke, Frank 327, 330
O'Rourke, James "Queenie" 48
O'Rourke, Jim "Orator" 47–49, 50, 211, 267; James O'Rourke Statue 48
O'Rourke, "Voiceless Tim" 78
Orr, Dave 201, 204, 207
Ortega, Phil 18
Orth, Al "The Curveless Wonder" 167, 174
Orwoll, Oswald 246
Osborn, Danny "Ozzie" 167
Osborne, Lawrence "Bobo" 67
Osteen, Claude "Gomer" 280, 281, 285
Ostermueller, Fritz 78
Oswalt, Roy 161, 166, 200; Homeplate Fish & Steakhouse 161
Otis, Amos 7, 13
O'Toole, Jim 78
Ott, Mel "Master Melvin" 21, 70, 119, 121–122, 126, 139, 181, 256, 312, 333
Otten, Jim 177
Overall, Orval 28–29, 98
Overbay, Lyle 308, 311
Overmire, Frank "Stubby" 147
Owen, Frank "Yip" 147
Owen, Marv 195

Owen, Mickey 72, 167–168
Owens, Frank "Yip" 327, 329
Owens, Raymond "Smoky" 58
Owens, Will "Gabie" 89

Pabor, Charlie "The Old Woman in the Red Cap" 201, 204–205, 211
Pacheco, Jordan 198
Paciorek, Tom "Wimpy" 147, 149, 199
Packard, Gene 44, 46–47
Padden, Dick "Brains" 313, 314, 315
Padden, Tom 186, 188
Paddock, Del 277–278
Padgett, Ernie 2, 251
Pafko, Andy 317, 322
Page, Joe "Gay Reliever" 250, 254, 310
Page, Ted 64, 91, 111, 117, 133
Pagliaroni, Mike 147
Pagliarulo, Mike 137
Pagnozzi, Tom 18, 20
Paige, Satchel 1, 5, 7–10, 14–16, 27, 45, 63, 72, 104, 125, 133, 148, 156, 162–163, 165, 170, 218, 222, 224, 235, 244, 255, 275, 281, 294, 328, 333
Paine, Phil 266
Pall, Donn "The Pope" 78
Palmeiro, Rafael 20, 33, 70, 143
Palmer, Dean 58
Palmer, Jim "Cakes" 176, 183, 201, 213–214, 230, 262, 334
Palmer, Lowell "Lulu" 28
Papelbon, Jonathan 119, 125, 129
Pappas, Milt 147–148, 153
Parent, Freddy "The Flying Frenchman" 126–128
Parent, Mark 246
Parker, Dave "Cobra" 161, 165, 314
Parker, Francis "Salty" 78
Parker, Jarrod 89
Parkview Field 89–90
Parmelee, Leroy "Tarzan" 147
Parnell, Mel "Dusty" 119, 125
Parnell, Red 285, 287, 293
Parrett, Jeff 89
Parrish, Lance "Big Wheel" 32, 249, 250, 256, 280
Parrish, Larry 58, 63
Parrott, Walter "Jiggs" 246
Parson, William "Jiggs" 277–278
Parsons, Ed "Dixie" 7
Partlow, Roy 32, 188
Paskert, Dode 226
Passeau, Claude 161, 166
Pastorini, Dan 16
Patek, Freddie "The Flea" 285, 286, 291
Patrick, Bronswell 218
Patten, Case 53
Patterson, Pat 78
Patterson, Roy "St. Croix Boy Wonder" 317–318, 323–324
Pattin, Marty "Bulldog" 78
Pavano, Carl 47, 51
Pawelek, Ted "Porky" 78
Payne, Jap 4, 296
Pearce, Dickey 201, 204, 210–211
Pearce, George "Filbert" 78
Pearson, Frank "Wahoo" 281

Pearson, Lenny "Hoss" 225, 226, 230
Pearson, Monte "Hoot" 28
Peavy, Jake 7, 14
Peckinpaugh, Roger 43, 225, 230
Pedroia, Dustin "Laser Show" 20, 27, 28, 31
Peete, Charlie "Mule" 302
Peitz, Heinie 167
Peltry, Barney "The Yiddish Curver" 167
Pendleton, Terry 27
Pennington, Art "Superman" 280–282
Pennock, Herb "The Knight of Kennett Square" 250, 263
Penny, Brad 238
Pepitone, Joe 201
Percival, Troy 28, 42
Perconte, Jack 199
Perdue, Hub "The Gallatin Squash" 281, 285
Perez, Tony 35, 67, 151, 230, 232
Perkins, Bill 66
Perkins, Cy 137
Perranoski, Ron 190, 197
Perry, Gaylord "The Ancient Mariner" 33, 125, 216–217, 219, 221–222, 235, 308, 310, 334
Perry, Jim 216, 222, 235
Pesky, Johnny "Mr. Red Sox," "Needle" 104, 246–248
Petco Park 29
Peter J. McGovern Little League Baseball Museum 251; see also Bowman Field; Eric Stotz Field; Lamade Stadium
Peters, Gary 250
Peters, John 119–120
Peterson, Fritz 78, 81, 87–88
Peterson, Sid 223
Petrocelli, Rico 144, 201
Pettitte, Andy 119–120, 123–124, 263
Pettus, Bill 285
Petty, Jesse 240
Petway, Bruce "Home Run" 148, 237, 280–282, 296
Pezzullo, John "Pretzel" 48
Pfeffer, Fred "Dandelion" 111–113, 115, 251, 267
Pfeffer, Jack 78
Pfiester, Jack "The Giant Killer" 226
Phelps, Babe "Blimp" 129, 130, 131–132
Phelps, Josh 15–16
Phelps, Ken "Digger" 308, 312
Philadelphia Athletics Historical Society and Museum 251, 255
Philley, Dave 286
Phillippe, Deacon 302, 307
Phillips, Bill 316, 327, 330
Phillips, Brandon 216
Phillips, Bubba 161
Phillips, Tony 66, 69–70
Phillips, "Whoa Bill" 250, 254
Phoenix, Steve 19
Phoenix Municipal Stadium 18, 20
Piazza, Mike 6, 121, 123, 241, 249, 255, 300, 334
Pierce, Bill "Bonehead" 89

Pierce, Billy 79, 147–149, 154
Pierre, Juan 7, 9, 14
Piersall, Jimmy "The Waterbury Wizard" 47–49
Pierson, "Wild Bill" 192–193
Pierzynski, A.J. 108, 201
Pike, Jess 240
Pike, Lip 201, 204–205
Pinkney, George 78
Pinson, Vada 123, 280–284
Pillion, Cecil "Squiz" 48
Piniella, Lou "Sweet Lou" 58, 62, 66, 279
Pipp, Wally 78, 83, 134
Pippen, Henry "Cotton" 286
Pitko, Alex "Spunk" 191
Pittsburgh Crawfords 54, 91, 121, 133, 165, 174, 218, 254–255, 258
PK Park 246
Plank, Eddie "Gettysburg Eddie" 146, 160, 214, 250, 262–263
Plantier, Phil 186–187, 189
Plesac, Dan 89, 99
Plews, Herb 177, 179
PNC Park 251, 255
Pocoroba, Biff 29
Podbielan, Clarence 308
Podres, Johnny 201, 214, 300
Poffenberger, Cletus "Boots" 4, 130–131
Poles, Spot "Black Ty Cobb" 231, 289, 302, 305–306
Polhemus, Mark "Humpty Dumpty" 201
Pollet, Howie 119
Pollock, A.J. 48
Polo Grounds 45, 50, 122, 163, 251, 312
Pomeranz, Drew 281
Porter, Andy 21; "Pullman" 22
Porter, Darrell 167, 171
Porter, Dick "Twitches," "Wiggles" 129, 130
Porter, Henry 299–300
Porter, Merle "Fancy Dan" 22
Posada, Jorge 124
Posedel, "Sailor" Bill 28
Posey, Cum 250, 254, 288, 296, 306
Post, Wally "Cochise" 226
Potter, Maryland "Dykes" 111
Potter, Robert "Squire" 111
Powell, Boog 58, 62–63, 318
Powell, Jack 78, 87
Powell, Jay 161
Powell, Ray "Rabbit" 22
Powell, Willie "Piggy" 7
Power, Ted 238
Powers, Mike "Doc" 142
Powers, Phil "Grandmother," "Leather Fist" 201–202
Pratt, Del 151, 269, 273
Pratt, Todd "Tank" 179–181
Presley, Jim 58
Price, Joe "Lumber" 281
Priddy, Jerry 27
Pride, Charley 282
Pride, Curtis 55, 57
Prior, Mark 157
Progressive Field 227; Indians Hall of Fame 227

Providence Grays 68, 213, 258, 267, 329
Pruett, Hubert "Shucks" 167, 169
Pruiett, Charles "Tex" 89
Pryor, Wes 296
Puckett, Kirby 78, 80, 85–86, 156, 165, 312
Pugh, Johnny "Punch" 216
Puhl, Terry 327
Pujols, Albert 170, 212, 234
Purcell, William "Blondie" 191
Purkey, Bob 250
Putnam, Pat 2, 299, 301
Putz, J.J. 147

Qualls, Jimmy 30
Qualters, Thomas "Money Bags" 250
Quantrill, Paul 327, 329, 332
Quarles, Bill "The Virginia Grapevine" 302
Quentin, Carlos 31
Quinn, Wellington "Wimpy" 7
Quisenberry, Dan 28, 41–42

Radatz, Dick "The Monster" 147–149, 154–155
Radbourn, Charley "Old Hoss" 201, 202, 204, 213, 267
Radcliff, Rip 238, 243
Radcliffe, Alex 7, 10–11, 126
Radcliffe, Ted "Double Duty" 7, 10–11, 15, 114–115, 164, 224, 235, 305
Rader, Dave 238
Rader, Doug "The Red Rooster" 78, 81, 84
Radford, Paul 138
Radke, Brad 317
Raines, Tim "Rock" 2, 45, 58–59, 62, 64, 98, 123, 233, 253, 334
Ramirez, Hanley 127, 134
Ramirez, Manny 1, 331
Ramsey, Thomas "Toad" 89–90
Ranaudo, Anthony 191
Rancho Cucamonga Epicenter 29
Randa, Joe 317, 319
Randall, James "Sap" 7
Randolph, Willie 124, 269–270, 273
Raney, Frank "Ribs" 147
Rangers Ballpark 286; Rangers Hall of Fame 286
Rariden, "Bedford Bill" 88–89
Raschi, Vic "Springfield Rifle" 138
Rath, Morrie 254
Rauch, Jon 41, 111, 113, 118
Rawley, Shane 317, 324
Rawlings, Johnny 100, 103
Ray, Jim "Sting" 270
Ray, Johnny 238, 242
Ray Winder Field 22
Raymond, Arthur "Bugs" 78
Raymond, Claude 327
Reames, Leroy 23
Reardon, Jeff "The Terminator" 138, 146
Reberger, Frank "Crane" 75
Reccius, John 113
Reccius, Phil "Donkey" 111, 113
Reckling, Trevor 191
Recreation Field 299

Rector, "Broadway" Connie 286
Redding, Dick "Cannonball" 66–67, 69, 71–72, 231, 289, 294
Redford, Robert: *The Natural* 2, 41, 49
Redmond, Mike 230, 308, 311
Redus, Frog 238, 243
Reed, Jody 58
Reed, Rick 313
Reed, Ron 89, 100
Reeder, Julius "Icicle" 226, 229
Reese, Jimmy 135
Reese, John "Bubbles" 58
Reese, Pee Wee 71, 111–112, 114–116, 260, 303; gravesite 112; monument with Jackie Robinson 203
Reese, Pokey 269
Reese, Rich 227
Reeves, Bobby "Gunner" 280, 281
Regan, Phil "The Vulture" 147, 149, 154–155
Rego, Tony 73
Reichardt, Rick 317, 322–323
Reilley, Charlie 267
Reilly, John 225
Reiser, Pete "Pistol Pete" 167, 170, 173–174
Reitsman, Chris 155
Remlinger, Mike 201
Remy, Jerry 137, 141–142; Jerry Remy's Sports Bar 141
Rendon, Anthony 286
Renfroe, Othello "Chappy" 191
Renko, Steve 105, 109
Repulski, Rip 155
Reulbach, Ed 147–148, 153, 193
Reuschel, Rick "Big Daddy" 78, 80, 87, 146
Reuss, Jerry 167, 175
Revere, Ben 111
Reynolds, Allie "Superchief" 8, 238, 240–241, 244–245
Reynolds, Carl 121, 286
Reynolds, Craig 230, 285, 288
Reynolds, Harold 246, 248
Reynolds, Mark 11, 111, 115
Reynolds, Shane 119
Rhem, Flint "Shad" 270
Rhoden, Rick 58, 60, 65
Rhodes, Arthur 286
Rhodes, Gordon "Dusty" 184
Rhodes, Karl "Tuffy" 226–227
Rhodes, James "Dusty" 7
Rice, Del 225
Rice, Harry 78
Rice, Jim 39–40, 48, 86, 124, 165, 270, 274–275, 312
Rice, Len 277–278
Rice, Sam "Man o' War" 89–90, 96–97
Richard, J.R. 119–120, 125
Richard, Lee "Bee Bee" 119
Richards, Gene 270
Richards, Paul 47, 76, 268, 286
Richardson, Bobby 269, 273
Richardson, Danny 204
Richardson, Hardy "Old True Blue" 149, 190, 191, 194–195, 211
Richbourg, Lance 59
Richert, Pete 201
Richie, Rob 184, 186

Rickert, Marv "Twitch" 308
Rickey, Branch 17, 30, 42, 104, 114, 228
Rickwood Field 8–9, 19, 131
Riddle, Johnny "Mutt" 270
Riddle, Marshall "Jit" 21, 22
Riddlemoser, Dorsey 130–131
Riggins, Bill 78
Riggs, Lew 216
Righetti, Dave 28, 35, 42
Rigney, Bill "The Cricket" 28, 31, 43–44
Rile, Ed 225, 230
Riley, Lee 181
Rios, Alex 7
Ripken, Billy 129, 134
Ripken, Cal, Jr. "Iron Man" 53, 129–130, 133–134, 151, 157, 199, 210, 228, 230, 266, 333; Ripken Stadium 130
Ripken, Cal, Sr. 130, 134, 137, 318
Riske, David 308
Ritchey, Claude "Little All Right" 249, 250
Ritter, Lew "Old Dog" 250
Rivera, Mariano 42, 62, 124, 137, 235, 253, 333
Rivers, Mickey "Mick the Quick" 58, 64
Riverside/Tradewater Park 112
Riviere, Arthur "Tink" 286–287
Rixey, Eppa "Jephtha" 183, 302–303, 306–307
Rizzo, Anthony 59
Rizzuto, Phil "Scooter" 71, 201, 202, 210, 248, 303
Roach, Wilbur "Roxey" 250
Roberge, Bert 126
Roberts, Brian 220
Roberts, Clarence "Skipper" 75–77
Roberts, Dave 246
Roberts, Leon 149
Roberts, Leon "Bip" 28
Roberts, Robin 78–79, 86, 216, 251, 263, 299, 334
Robertson, Bob 129–130
Robertson, Charlie 166
Robertson, David "Houdini" 7
Robertson, Sherry 329
Robinson, Aaron 269, 272–273
Robinson, Bobbie 7
Robinson, Brooks "The Human Vacuum Cleaner" 21–25, 35–36, 57, 122, 130, 143, 151, 172, 177, 242, 254, 304, 311, 321, 334
Robinson, Don "Caveman" 111, 118
Robinson, Eddie 285, 303
Robinson, Floyd 21
Robinson, Frank "The Judge" 30, 112, 153, 200, 212, 274, 284–286, 291–292, 301, 331, 333
Robinson, Henry "Sloe" 7
Robinson, Jackie 9, 11, 22, 26, 30, 32, 39, 54, 59, 60, 66, 68–71, 74, 102, 104, 114, 116, 122, 127, 160, 164, 170–171, 185, 188, 196, 202, 207, 224, 228, 237, 242, 249, 255, 260, 274, 283, 291–292, 296; gravesite 202–203, 327–329, 333; Jackie Robinson Ballpark in Daytona Beach 59–60; Jackie

Robinson Park of Fame 48; monument with Pee Wee Reese 203
Robinson, Neil 147, 152
Robinson, Norm 238
Robinson, Wilbert 43, 130, 137–138, 140–141, 186
Robinson, William "Rabbit" 314
Robinson, William "Yank" 250
Robitaille, Chick 205
Rocker, John 66
Rodgers, Bob "Buck" 226
Rodgers, "Rawmeat Bill" 226
Rodriguez, Alex 37, 64, 76, 132, 134, 181, 199–202, 206, 210, 225, 230, 234, 259, 308, 310, 333
Rodriguez, Francisco 65
Rodriguez, Ivan "Pudge" 32, 49, 300
Rodriquez, Steve 184–185
Roe, Preacher 21–22, 26
Roebuck, Ed 250
Roesink Stadium 148–149
Rogan, "Bullet Joe" 122, 170, 238, 244–245
Rogell, Billy 78
Rogers, Buck 303
Rogers, Emmett 22–23
Rogers, Kenny "The Gambler" 66, 71
Rogers, Mark 126
Rogers, Nat 10, 270, 275, 295
Rogers, Steve 167, 174
Rogers Center 327–328
Rohlinger, Ryan 318
Rolen, Scott 88–89, 95
Rolfe, Red 24, 186–187, 189
Rollins, Jimmy 27, 31, 37
Romano, Johnny "Honey" 190, 191, 194
Romine, Kevin 186, 189
Rommel, Eddie 129–131, 136, 235
Roof, Gene 118
Roof, Phil 111, 115, 118
Rooker, Jim 246
Root, Charley "Chinski" 226
Rosar, Buddy 201
Rose, Pete "Charlie Hustle" 5, 13, 67, 83, 97, 151, 160, 185, 211, 220–221, 225–226, 228, 230–235, 264, 280, 284, 333
Roseboro, John 225
Rosen, Al "Flip," "Hebrew Hammer" 139, 256, 269, 270, 273–274
Rosenblatt Stadium 180
Ross, Cody 198, 200
Roth, Braggo "The Globetrotter" 317, 318, 322–323
Roush, Edd 89, 96–97, 193, 261
Rowand, Aaron 24, 248
Rowe, Jack 149, 195, 211
Rowe, Lynwood "Schoolboy" 286
Rowell, Carvel "Bama" 7
Rowland, Clarence "Pants" 317–318, 324
Rucker, Johnny "Crabapple Comet" 67
Rucker, Nap 66, 72
Rudi, Joe 28, 265
Rudolph, Dick "Baldy" 202
Ruel, Muddy 167, 171
Rueter, Kirk "Woody" 78, 88

Ruether, Dutch 28
Ruffin, Leon "Lassas" 302, 304
Ruffing, Red 78–79, 87, 159, 235; see also Bottomley-Ruffing-Schalk Baseball Museum
Ruhle, Vern 149
Runnells, Tom 44, 47
Runnels, Pete 285
Rupert, Jacob, Jr. 203
Rusie, Amos "The Hoosier Thunderbolt" 89, 92, 98, 190, 261, 323
Russell, Allen "Rubber Arm" 129, 130
Russell, Bill 105, 108, 312
Russell, Branch 302
Russell, Jeff 226, 237
Russell, Jim 251
Russell, John Henry "Pistol" 7
Russell, Kurt 247
Russell, Reb 161, 166, 252
Ruth, Babe "Babe," "The Bambino," "The Sultan of Swat" 4, 8–9, 12–13, 17, 22–23, 29, 33–35, 37–39, 43, 45, 48, 50, 58, 60, 63, 68, 70, 73–74, 82–83, 90–91, 101–102, 112, 120, 128–135, 140–141, 148, 153, 157–158, 162, 163, 166, 168–169, 175, 181, 196, 202, 206–207, 218, 222, 230, 233, 237, 239, 243, 248, 252, 257–259, 264, 267, 272–273, 281, 284, 300, 314–315, 321, 327–329, 331, 333; Babe Ruth Birthplace & Museum 130; first home run plaque in Fayetteville 216, 218; gravesite 202
Rutherford, Johnny 329
Ryan, B.J. 119, 125, 240
Ryan, Buddy 46
Ryan, Connie 119–122
Ryan, Jack "Gulfport" 78
Ryan, Jimmy "Pony" 138, 140, 143–144, 173
Ryan, Ken 265
Ryan, Merven "Red" 201–202
Ryan, Nolan; "The Ryan Express" 4, 8, 14, 36–37, 40–41, 75, 110, 121, 162, 177, 197, 229, 234, 262, 272, 286, 288, 293–294, 333; Nolan Ryan Exhibit and Center 286
Ryan, Rob 177, 179
Rye, Gene "Half-Pint" 78
Rzepczynski, Mark "Scrabble" 2, 28, 29

Sabathia, CC 28, 31, 41, 124
Saberhagen, Bret 27, 78, 87
Sabo, Chris 147–148, 151
Sadecki, Ray 105, 108
Safeco Field 259, 308; Baseball Museum of the Pacific Northwest 308; Mariners Hall of Fame 308
Sager, Samuel "Pony" 254
Saier, Vic 147
Sain, Johnny 21, 26
St. Cloud Commons 314
St. Louis Stars 20, 91, 165, 170, 276
Sakata, Lenn 73, 75
Sale, Chris 59
Salkeld, Bill 75–76
Sallee, Harry "Scatter," "Scissors," "Slim" 226, 228, 236

Salmon, Harry "Beans" 7
Salmon, Tim "Kingfish" 28, 31
Salt River Fields at Talking Stick 18–20
Saltalamacchia, Jarrod 59–60
Saltzgraver, Jack 102
Sambito, Joe 201
Sampson, Tommy "Toots" 7
San Diego Hall of Champions Sports Museum 29
Sanchez, Freddy 31
Sandberg, Ryne 34, 64, 115, 208, 242, 270, 308, 310–312, 333
Sanders, Deion "Prime Time" 58, 60, 100, 316
Sanders, Ken "Daffy" 167
Sanders, Reggie 270, 275, 284
Sanderson, Scott 147
Sands, Jerry 216
Sanford, Fred 296
Sanford, Jack 138
Sanguillen, Manny 48, 265
Santo, Ron 80, 256, 308, 311–312
Santop, Louis "Big Bertha" 231, 285, 287–289
Sardinha, Bronson 75
Sardinha, Dane 73, 75
Sargent, Joe "Horse Belly" 202
Saskatchewan Baseball Hall of Fame 328
Saucier, Frank 2, 169
Sauer, Hank 250
Savidge, Ralph "Human Ripcord" 250
Sawyer, Eddie 265, 269
Sax, Steve 27
Scales, George "Tubby" 7, 11
Scalzi, Frank "Skeeter" 226
Scanlan, Frank "Dreamy" 202
Schaefer, Germany "Liberty" 78, 81
Schafer, Harry "Silk Stockings" 250
Schalk, Ray "Cracker" 78–79, 82, 149, 320; see also Bottomley-Ruffing-Schalk Baseball Museum
Schang, Wally 201
Scheib, Carl 251
Scheibeck, Frank 149
Scherbarth, Bob 320
Scherzer, Max 168
Schierholtz, Nate 184, 186
Schilling, Curt 2, 15–17, 27, 331
Schiraldi, Calvin 298
Schlei, George "Admiral" 226
Schlereth, Daniel 15–17
Schmidt, Charles "Boss" 22, 24
Schmidt, Jason 75–77
Schmidt, Mike 35–36, 142, 196, 200, 225–226, 230, 235, 251, 256, 311, 316, 331, 333
Schmidt, Walter 21
Schmit, Frederick "Crazy" 78, 81
Schmitz, Johnny "Bear Tracks" 317, 318, 324
Schneider, Brian 58
Schoendienst, Red 78, 82–84, 88, 184
Schoeneck, Lewis "Jumbo" 78
Schofield, Dick, Jr. 78
Schrecongost, Osee 249–250, 256
Schriver, Pop 204
Schroeder, Bill 129

Schrom, Ken 75
Schulte, Frank "Wildfire" 201, 202
Schultz, Barney 190
Schultz, Howie "Stretch" 155–157
Schumacher, "Prince Hal" 201–202
Schumacher, Skip 31
Schupp, Ferdie 111, 118, 236, 318
Schwamb, Ralph "Blackie" 28, 32
Schwartz, Bill "Blab" 226
Schweitzer, Albert "Cheese" 226, 228
Schwert, Pi 205
Scioscia, Mike 249–250
Scott, Everett "Deacon" 89, 96
Scott, George "Boomer" 161, 163
Scott, Jim "Death Valley Jim" 277–279, 325; South Dakota Sports Hall of Fame 279
Scott, Mike 28
Scott, Rodney "Cool Breeze" 89
Seale, Johnnie "Durango Kid" 44
Seaton, Tom 180
Seaver, Tom "Tom Terrific" 2, 16, 28–30, 40, 151, 262, 333
Seay, Dick 70, 190
Seeds, "Suitcase Bob" 286
Seitzer, Kevin 78, 84
Selbach, Kip 226
Sele, Aaron 155
Selee, Frank 43, 187, 190
Selig, Bud 10, 127, 156, 232, 310, 318–319
Selkirk, George "Twinkletoes" 206, 327, 331
Selma, Dick "Mortimer Snerd" 28
Seminick, Andy 313, 315
Sensenderfer, John "Count" 250
Sequi, David 105, 108
Serrell, Barney 119
Serum, Gary 223
Servais, Scott 317
Severeid, Hank 100, 102
Sewell, Joe 7, 11, 14, 120, 291
Sewell, Luke 7, 10–11, 14–15
Sewell, Rip 7, 14
Sexson, Richie 246–248
Seybold, Ralph "Socks" 226, 228, 257
Seymour, Cy 201
Shank, Harvey 327, 329
Shanks, Howie "Hawk" 78
Shantz, Bobby 37–38, 250, 264
Shannon, Mike 168; Mike Shannon's Steaks and Seafood 168
Shannon, William "Spike" 250
Shaw, "Grunting Jim" 250
Shaw, Jeff 226, 237
Shaw, Royal "Hunky" 308, 310
Shawkey, Bob 250, 264
Shea, Spec "The Naugatuck Nugget" 47, 49
Sheckard, Jimmy 182, 250, 260
Sheely, Earl 78
Sheets, Ben 119
Sheffield, Gary 2, 58–59, 64–65, 119, 333
Sheldon, Scott 90
Shellenback, Frank 30, 169
Shelton, Andrew "Skeeter" 314
Shelton, Chris 296–298
Shepard, Bert 4, 92–93

Sherdel, Bill "Wee Willie" 250
Sheridan, Mike 56
Sherrill, George 280
Shields, James 31
Shields, Scot 58
Shifflett, Garland "Duck" 302
Shinault, Enoch "Ginger" 22
Shindle, Billy 190, 195
Shines, Razor 216
Shinnick, Tim "Dandy," "Good Eye" 186, 187–188
Shipke, "Muskrat Bill" 167, 169
Shires, Art "Art the Great" 286–287
Shirley, Bob 238
Shirley, Ernest "Mule" 216
Shively, George "Rabbit" 91, 111, 117
Shocker, Urban 226, 228, 235
Shore, Ernie 218, 272
Short, Bob 88, 110
Short, Chris 52, 54
Shotton, Burt 226
Shoun, Clyde "Hardrock" 280, 281
Shoup, John 314
Shultz, Wallace "Toots" 250
Sick's Stadium 16, 310
Siebern, Norm "Smiley" 167, 171–172
Siebert, Dick 137
Siebert, Sonny 167
Siever, Ed 105
Sievers, Roy "Squirrel" 167, 169–171
Simmons, Al "Bucketfoot Al" 146, 165, 175, 317–319, 322, 334
Simmons, Curt 250–251
Simmons, Sy 52, 54–55
Simmons, Ted 147, 149–151, 324
Simpson, Harry "Suitcase" 66, 67
Sims, Duke 296–298
Singer, Bill 197
Singleton, Elmer "Smoky" 296
Singleton, Ken 201, 212
Sioux Falls Stadium 277
Sipin, John 29
Sisler, George "Gorgeous George" 225, 230
Sizemore, Grady 308, 312
Sizemore, Ted 7, 11, 121
Skinner, Elisha "Camp" 67
Skizas, Lou "The Nervous Greek" 78
Skowron, Bill "Moose" 78, 83
Slade, Gordon "Oskie" 296–298
Slagle, Jimmy "The Human Mosquito," "Rabbit," "Shorty" 250, 254
Slapnicka, Cyril 100
Slaught, Don Sluggo" 27, 28
Slaughter, Enos "Country" 26, 150, 165, 168, 216, 219, 221
Sledge, Terrmel 216, 218
Slocumb, Heathcliff 201–202
Smajstrla, Craig 286
Smalley, Roy 27
Smith, Al "Fuzzy" 167, 174
Smith, Andrew 67
Smith, Bob "Riverboat" 167
Smith, Brick 219
Smith, Chino 270–271, 275, 305
Smith, Clarence "Pop-boy" 281
Smith, Dave 28

Smith, Earl "Oil" 21, 22, 24, 97
Smith, Eddie 192
Smith, Edgar 267
Smith, Elmer 226, 250
Smith, Ernie "Kansas City Kid" 191
Smith, Ford "Geronimo" 18
Smith, Frank "Piano Mover" 57, 250, 253
Smith, Hal "Cura" 22, 24
Smith, Henry "Happy" 246
Smith, Hilton 4, 72, 224, 286–287, 293–294
Smith, Jack 78
Smith, John "Phenomenal" 250, 253
Smith, Jordan 297–298
Smith, Lee 119, 125
Smith, Lewis "Bull" 314
Smith, Lonnie "Skates" 78, 80
Smith, Mayo 167, 176
Smith, Ozzie "The Wizard of Oz" 5, 7–11, 36–37, 64, 88, 143, 170, 188, 202, 230, 274, 291, 334; Ozzie's Restaurant and Sports Bar 168
Smith, Pop 327, 330
Smith, Red 269, 272
Smith, Reggie 119, 122–123
Smith, Samuel "Skyrocket" 130, 167
Smith, Sherry 66
Smith, Theolic "Fireball" 167, 170
Smith, Zane 317, 324
Smithsonian Institute: The National Portrait Gallery 56
Smoak, Justin 270
Smoltz, John 85, 124, 145, 147–149, 153, 159, 328
Snead, Esix 60
Snell, Ian 55
Snider, Duke "The Duke of Flatbush" 25, 28, 35, 39, 64, 165, 243, 260, 308–309, 329, 333
Snodgrass, Fred 31
Snow, Felton 7
Snow, J.T. 27
Snyder, Emanuel "Redleg" 191
Snyder, Frank "Cooney" 295, 327
Snyder, Frank "Pancho" 286
Snyder, Pop 55, 57
Snyder, Russ 180
Sockalexis, Louis "Chief" 126–127
Sofield, Rick 324, 326
Solomon, Mose "The Rabbi of Swat" 202, 205
Sommer, Joe 111
Sorensen, Zach 296, 298
Soriano, Alfonso 151, 210
Sorrento, Paul 137
Sosa, Sammy 17, 33, 70, 84, 133, 158
Sothern, Denny 55
Souell, Herb 119, 161
South Dakota Amateur Baseball Hall of Fame 277
Southworth, Billy 43, 179–180, 183–184
Spahn, Warren 26, 40, 88–90, 200–202, 204, 214, 238–239, 262–263, 301, 333
Spalding, Al 22, 71–72, 78, 82, 87
Spangenberg, Cory 251
Sparks, Tully 66
Speake, Bob "Spook" 167

Speaker, Tris "The Grey Eagle" 23, 38, 68, 91, 208, 232, 236, 285–287, 291, 300, 333
Spearman, Clyde "Big Splo" 21, 22
Spearman, Henry "Little Splo" 21, 22
Speier, Chris 27
Spence, Stan 111
Spencer, Daryl 105, 205
Spencer, Jim 249
Spiers, Bill 270
Spillner, Dan 324–326
Splittorf, Paul 89, 99
Spoljaric, Paul 329
Spongberg, Carl 76
Sports Museum of Los Angeles 29
Spring Mobile Ballpark 297
Springer, George 48
Sprowl, Bobby 228
Stafford, Heinie 4, 300
Stafford, James "General" 48
Staggs, Steve 15–16
Stahl, Chick 89
Staiger, Roy "Linus" 238
Stairs, Matt 29, 327–329, 331
Staley, Gerry 308, 313
Staley, Harry 78, 323
Stallcup, Thomas 218
Stallings, George 66, 72–74
Stange, Lee "Stinger" 78
Stanhouse, Don "Full Pack," "Stan the Man Unusual" 78, 81
Stanky, Eddie "The Brat" 242, 250, 257
Stanley, Bob "Stanley Steamer" 126–127, 129
Stanley, Fred "Chicken" 5, 100
Stanley, John "Neck" 129, 130
Stanley, Mickey 147, 149
Stanley, Mike 58
Stanton, Mike 286, 288, 295
Stanton, Mike "Giancarlo" 29, 31
Stargell, Willie "Pops" 30, 34, 123, 142, 165, 232, 238–242, 251, 256, 334
Starling, Bubba 106
Starr, Chick 205
Start, Joe "Old Reliable" 201, 202, 204
Statz, Arnold "Jigger" 78, 82
Staub, Rusty "Le Grand Orange" 119–123
Stauffer, Tim 127
Stearnes, Norman "Turkey" 148, 280–283, 333
Stearns, John "Bad Dude" 44, 46
Steelman, Morris "Farmer" 191
Stein, Bill 147
Steinbach, Terry 155, 157
Steinbrenner, George 43, 59, 65, 149, 159, 210, 215, 260, 264; Steinbrenner Field 60
Steinfeldt, Harry 167, 172
Stengel, Casey "The Old Perfessor" 32, 43, 70, 92, 96, 110, 166–168, 170, 176, 210, 237, 254, 264, 280
Stenhouse, John 46
Stenzel, Jake 226
Stephens, Gene 22
Stephens, Paul "Country Jake" 250, 258
Stephens, Jim "Little Nemo" 226
Stephens, Vern "Buster," "Junior" 198–200, 248
Stephenson, Phil 241
Stephenson, Riggs 7–8
Stevens, Chuck 197, 200
Stevens, Lee 167
Stewart, Dave "Smoke" 28
Stewart, Ian 30
Stewart, Sammy 216
Stewart, Shannon 226
Stewart, Walter "Lefty" 280
Stieb, Dave 28, 41
Stigman, Dick "Nimrod Nifty" 155
Stimmel, Archie "Lumbago" 130
Stirnweiss, George "Snuffy" 201–202
Stivetts, Jack 250, 323
Stobbs, Chuck 313, 317
Stock, Milt 78, 80, 84
Stocker, Kevin 308, 310, 312
Stoddard, Tim 89, 100
Stone, Ed "Ace" 52, 54
Stone, George 100, 104
Stone, John 280
Stone, Toni 92, 156; Toni Stone Stadium 156
Storen, Drew 89
Stottlemyre, Mel 167, 174, 310
Stottlemyre, Todd 308, 313
Stout, Allyn "Fish Hook" 78
Stovall, George "Firebrand" 167
Stovey, George 250
Stovey, Harry 250, 260
Strand, Paul 310
Strang, Sammy "The Dixie Thrush" 280, 281
Strange, Alan "Inky" 250
Strange, Doug 272
Stanky, Eddie 249
Strasburg, Stephen 29, 31
Stratton, Monty 92
Stratton, Scott 112
Strawberry, Darryl 28, 156
Street, Gabby 7, 15
Street, Huston 286, 295
Streeter, Sam 7, 294
Strickland, George 119, 122
Stricklett, Elmer "Spitball" 106
Strief, George 228
Stripp, Joe "Jersey Joe" 190, 191, 194
Stromme, Floyd 223, 225
Strong, Joseph "Baby Face" 111
Strong, Ted 89, 98
Stroud, Ralph "Sailor" 191
Strunk, Amos 250
Struss, Clarence "Steamboat" 78
Stuart, Dick "Dr. Strangeglove" 2, 5, 28, 31
Stuart, John "Stud" 281
Stuart, Luke 218
Stubbs, Franklin "Cadillac" 216
Sturdivant, Tom "Smoke" 105–106
Such, Dick 218
Suck, Tony 78, 80
Suhr, Gus 27
Sukeforth, Clyde 126–128
Sullivan, Billy 317, 320
Sullivan, John 81
Sullivan, Sleeper "Old Iron Hands" 191
Sullivan, Tom 15–16
Sullivan, William, Sr. 318
Summers, Champ 308
Summers, "Kickapoo Ed" 89
Sunday, Billy "The Evangelist," "Preacher" 100–102
Sundberg, Jim 78, 82
Suppan, Jeff 238
Surhoff, B.J. 201
Surkont, Max 265–266
Susce, George "Good Kid" 250, 253
Sutcliffe, Rick "Red Baron" 146, 167, 175
Sutter, Bruce 42, 88, 250–251, 263–264, 313
Suttles, Mule 6–8, 10–11, 170, 333
Sutton, Don "Black & Decker" 7–8, 14, 261, 309
Sutton, Ezra 201, 203–204, 209
Suzuki, Ichiro 74, 86, 230
Suzuki, Kurt 73, 75
Swaim, Cy 228
Sweeney, Bill 111
Sweeney, Charlie 267
Sweeney, Mike 28, 40
Swentor, Augie 48
Swift, Bill 126–129
Swift, Bob 105
Swisher, Nick 120
Swoboda, Ron "Rocky" 130
Sykes, Franklin "Doc" 7
Szotkiewicz, Ken 52, 54

Tabler, Pat 226
Tabor, Jim 7
Taillon, Jameson 286
Talbert, Dangerfield "Old Reliable" 167
Talbot, Fred "Bubby" 55
Talbot, Mitch 298
Tanana, Frank 147–149, 153–154, 222
Tankersley, Taylor 177, 179
Tannehill, Jesse "Powder" 111, 118, 235
Tannehill, Lee 111
Tanner, Chuck 165, 250–251, 265
Tapani, Kevin 101
Target Field 156
Tate, Edward "Dimples" 302
Tatum, Goose 21–22, 24
Taveras, Frank 105
Taylor, Arlas "Foxy" 89
Taylor, Ben 91, 269, 273, 276
Taylor, "Bolicky Bill" 55, 58
Taylor, C.I. 91, 108, 126, 270, 273, 276
Taylor, Candy Jim 79, 91, 269–270, 273–274, 276
Taylor, Edward "Live Oak" 126
Taylor, Harry 204
Taylor, Jack 226, 236
Taylor, Jack "Brewery Jack" 129, 130, 251
Taylor, Johnny "Schoolboy Johnny" 47
Taylor, Luther "Dummy" 105–106, 109–110, 228
Taylor, Olan "Jelly" 225–226
Taylor, Ron 327

Taylor, Sammy 269
Taylor, "Steel Arm Johnny" 91, 270, 273, 276
TD Ameritrade Park 180
Tebbetts, Birdie 2, 299–301
Tebeau, Charles "Pussy" 138
Tebeau, George "White Wings" 167
Tebeau, Oliver "Patsy" 167
Teixeira, Mark 129–130, 132
Tejeda, Miguel 134, 199
Tekulve, Kent "The Book End," "The Rubber Band Man" 226, 237
Tempe Diablo Stadium 18
Temple, Johnny 216, 220
Templeton, Garry 11, 285, 287, 289
Tenace, Gene 249, 251, 256
Tenney, Fred 137, 142
Terrell, Jerry 155, 158
Terry, Adonis "The Story of Westfield Mural" 138
Terry, Bill "Memphis Bill" 66, 67, 69–70, 72–73, 107, 181, 212, 220
Terry, Ralph 238, 241, 245
Terry, Scott 198
Tesreau, Jeff 167
Testa, Nick 205
Tettleton, Mickey "Fruit Loops" 238, 241
Teufel, Tim 47
Tewksbury, Bob 186, 189
Theobald, Ron "Little General" 28
Theodore, George "The Stork" 296, 298
Theriot, Ryan 119
Thesenga, Arnold "Jug" 277
Thevenow, Tommy 89, 96
Thigpen, Bobby 58–59, 65–66
Thomas, Arthur 55
Thomas, Chester "Pinch" 78
Thomas, Clint "Hawk" 111, 117
Thomas, Danny "Sundown Kid" 7
Thomas, Dave "Showboat" 7, 10–11
Thomas, Fay ""Scow" 106
Thomas, Frank "The Big Hurt" 66, 70, 225, 256, 333
Thomas, Frank Joseph 250
Thomas, Gorman "Stormin' Gorman" 270, 275, 324
Thomas, Jules "Jewel" 302, 306
Thomas, Keith "Kite" 106
Thomas, Myles "Duck Eye" 250
Thomas, Roy 250, 260
Thomas, Tommy 129
Thome, Jim 78–79, 83, 86, 333
Thompson, Brad 184
Thompson, Frank "Groundhog" 119
Thompson, Frank "Hoss" 281–282
Thompson, Fresco 189
Thompson, Hank 238–239, 242
Thompson, James "Shag" 216
Thompson, Jason 27
Thompson, John "Tug" 327
Thompson, Lafayette "Fresco" 7
Thompson, Milt 55, 57
Thompson, Robby 58, 63
Thompson, Sam "Big Sam" 89, 96–97, 321
Thomson, Bobby 52, 68, 88, 214, 242, 249, 298, 301, 322
Thon, Dickie 88–89, 96
Thornton, Andre "Thunder" 7, 14

Thorpe, Jim 54, 240, 300
Throneberry, Marv "Marvelous Marv" 45, 281
Thurman, Bob "Big Swish" 238
Thurston, Hollis "Sloppy" 180–181
Tiant, Luis 177, 301
Tidrow, Dick "Dirt" 28
Tiefenthaler, Verle 100
Tiernan, Mike "Silent Mike" 190, 191, 196
Tierney, James "Cotton" 105–106
Tietje, Les "Toots" 100
Timlin, Mike 286, 295
Tincup, Ben "Millionaire Indian" 238, 240
Tingley, Ron 127
Tinker, Joe 34, 45, 59, 60, 105, 108, 172, 190; Tinker Field 60
Tinker to Evers to Chance 34, 108, 172, 190, 208
Titcomb, Ledell "Cannonball" 126
Titus, John "Silent John" 250
Tobin, Jack 167, 174
Tobin, Jim "Abba Dabba" 28, 32
Tobin, Mason 177–178
Todt, Phil "Hook" 167
Tomlin, Dave 111
Toney, Fred 280
Tonkin, Harry "Doc" 187–188
Toporcer, George "Specs" 202, 204
Torborg, Jeff 190, 197
Torgeson, Earl "The Earl of Snohomish" 308, 311
Torre, Joe 121, 149, 201, 204, 206, 215
Torrez, Mike 96, 105, 108
Townsend, John "Happy," "Peach Stone Jack" 52–53
Tracy, Jim 226
Trammell, Alan 27, 36, 280
Trammell, Thomas "Bubba" 280–281
Travers, Allan 252
Travis, Cecil 66, 68, 70
Traynor, Pie 48, 131, 137–138, 140, 142–143, 172, 242, 311
Treanor, Matt 31
Trent, Ted "Big Florida," "Highpockets" 58, 65
Tresh, Tom 147–149, 152
Triandos, Gus 27, 33, 197
Triplett, Herman "Coaker" 216
Trosky, Hal 100–101, 103, 122
Trouppe, Quincy "Big Train," "El Roro" 66, 67, 69, 224, 235
Trout, Mike 191
Trout, Paul "Dizzy" 89, 99
Trout, Steve "Rainbow" 147
Trucks, Virgil "Fire" 7, 8, 14
Trumbo, Mark 31
Trustmark Park 161
Tsitouris, John 218
Tucker, Tommy "Foghorn" 137, 138, 140
Tuiasosopo, Matt 308
Tulowitzki, Troy 31
Tupman, Matt 188
Turbeville, George 29
Turley, Bob 33, 78, 269
Turnbow, Derrick 280
Turner, Henry "Flash" 59
Turner, Jacob 168
Turner, "Milkman Jim" 281, 284–285

Turner, Ted 118
Turner, Terry "Cotton Top" 250
Turner, Tuck 97
Turner Field 67
Tyack, Jim 177, 179
Tyler, Fred "Clancy" 187–188
Tyler, George "Lefty" 187, 190
Tyson, Mike 219

Uecker, Bob "Mr. Baseball" 206, 301, 318, 319–321
Uggla, Dan 111–113
Uhalt, Bernard "Frenchy" 28, 31
Uhle, George "The Bull" 226, 235
Ujdur, Jerry 155
Ulicny, Mike "Slugs" 250
Umphlett, Thomas 216, 218
Underwood, Pat 93
Underwood, Tom 93
Union Association 53, 56, 58, 169, 316, 318, 320
Unser, Al 81
Upright, R.T. "Dixie" 216, 218
Upshaw, Cecil 119
Upshaw, Willie 285
Upton, B.J. 303
Upton, Justin 303
Ury, Lon "Old Sleep" 106
U.S. Cellular Field 79
Utley, Chase 27, 31, 34

Vadaboncoeur, Gene 327
Valentine, Bobby 47–48, 52, 74
Valo, Elmer 321
Van Atta, Russ "Sheriff" 191
Van Brabant, Camille 327
Vance, Dazzy 100, 102, 104, 120, 170
Vander Meer, Johnny "The Dutch Master" 8, 32, 190, 191, 197
Vander Wal, John 148
Vangilder, Elam 167
Van Haltren, George "Rip" 167–168, 170, 173
Van Robays, Maurice "Bomber" 147
Van Slyke 201
Varitek, Jason 147, 197
Varney, Lawrence "Dike" 187
Vaughan, Arky 21–22, 25, 333
Vaughn, Greg 28
Vaughn, Hippo 286
Vaughn, Mo "Hit Dog" 47–48, 50
Veach, Bobby 111, 116
Veach, William "Peek-a-Boo" 89
Veal, Donnie 161
Veale, Bob 7, 15
Veeck, Bill 54, 81–82, 84, 171, 274, 319
Velarde, Randy 285
Ventura, Robin 27, 35–36
Verble, Gene "Satchel" 216
Veres, Dave 7
Verlander, Justin 302
Vernon, Mickey 249, 256–257, 273; Mickey Vernon Sports History Museum 251
Viau, Lee 299–300
Vickers, Harry "Rube" 327
Victorino, Shane "The Flyin' Hawaiian" 73–74
Victory Field 89
Villone, Ron 117, 190, 192, 197

Viola, Frank "Sweet Music" 201, 202
Virdon, Bill "Mr. Milkshake" 43, 147, 155, 318
Virginia Sports Hall of Fame 302–303
Virtue, Jake "Guesses" 250, 252
Vizquel, Omar 11, 143, 151
Voiselle, Bill "Ol' Ninety-Six" 270, 272
Vosmik, Joe 226
Voss, Alex 45
Votto, Joey 327, 329–330
Vowinkel, Rip 205
Vukovich, Pete 19, 250

Waddell, Rube 60, 113, 156, 160, 250, 256, 262–263, 294
Wade, Ed 17
Wadsworth, Louis 49
Wagner, Albert "Butts" 250
Wagner, Billy "The Kid" 5, 302, 307
Wagner, Honus "The Flying Dutchman" 9–10, 25, 38–39, 54, 64, 68, 91, 103, 113, 136, 158, 194, 202, 232, 250–252, 257–259, 329, 333
Wagner, Leon "Daddy Wags" 280, 281
Wahconah Park 138–139
Wahl, Kermit 277–278
Waitt, Charlie 127
Waitkus, Eddie 137, 142
Wakefield, Tim "Melbourne Medicine Man" 58, 59, 65
Walberg, Rube 155, 160
Walden, Jordan 286
Walker, Bill 78
Walker, Clarence "Tillie" 280–281
Walker, Curt 286
Walker, Dixie 166, 281
Walker, Edsall "The Catskill Wild Man" 201, 202
Walker, Fred "Dixie," "The People's Cherce" 66, 67, 69, 71, 166
Walker, Frederick "Mysterious" 180–181
Walker, Gee "The Madman from Mississippi" 161–162, 165
Walker, Harry "The Hat" 161–162, 166
Walker, Harvey "Hub" 161
Walker, Jerry 240
Walker, Jesse 285
Walker, Johnny 81
Walker, Larry 327–328, 330–331
Walker, Moses "Fleet" 228
Wallace, Bobby 250, 258, 260
Wallace, Dick 111
Wallach, Tim 27
Wallis, "Tarzan" Joe 78
Walls, Lee "Captain Midnight" 28
Walsh, Ed 57, 250, 261, 320, 323
Walsh, Ed, Jr. 37
Walters, Bucky 250, 262
Wambsganss, Bill 184, 225–226, 228
Waner, Lloyd "Little Poison" 151–152, 238–239, 243–244
Waner, Paul "Big Poison" 151–152, 186, 238–239, 243, 244, 333
Wanninger, Paul "Pee Wee" 7

War Memorial Stadium 217
Ward, Aaron 21, 24
Ward, Duane 198, 200
Ward, John Montgomery "Monte" 250, 255, 258, 261, 267
Ward, Pete 327, 329–330
Warfield, Frank "The Weasel" 88–89, 95
Warhop, Jack "Crab" 314
Warneke, Lou "The Arkansas Hummingbird" 21–22, 26
Warren, Adam 8
Washburn, Jarrod 317, 324
Washburn, Libeus 187
Washburn, Ray "Deadbody" 308
Warren Ballpark 18–19
Wasdin, John "Way Back" 302
Washington, Claudell 28
Washington, U.L. 238
Washington Senators 56
Waskgis, Robert 180
Wathan, John 100–101, 229
Watkins, Bill 327, 332
Watkins, Maurice "Skeeter" 129, 130
Watkins, Pop 66
Watson, Bob "Bull" 27, 28, 29, 308
Watson, John "Mule" 119
Watt, Eddie 100, 105
Weathers, David 280, 285
Weaver, Art "Six O'Clock" 106
Weaver, Buck 19, 250, 253, 279
Weaver, Earl 155, 167, 170, 176, 214, 306, 318
Weaver, Farmer 20, 313–314, 316
Weaver, Jered 16, 31
Webb, Brandon 111, 117–118
Webb, Earl 280–281
Webb, Skeeter 161
Webster, Mitch 105
Wedge, Eric 89
Wehde, Wilbur "Biggs" 100
Wehner, John "Rock" 250
Weihe, John "Podge" 226
Weiland, Kyle 198
Weimer, "Tornado Jake" 100, 104–105
Weiser, Harry "Bud" 250, 252
Weiss, George 49
Weiss, Walt 201
Welch, Bob 147–148, 153
Welch, Curt 226
Welch, Johnny 55
Welch, Mickey "Smiling Mickey" 136, 201, 202, 204, 213
Wells, David "Boomer" 28, 41, 222
Wells, Ed "Satchelfoot" 226
Wells, Vernon 119
Wells, Willie "Devil" 10, 70, 170, 285–287, 291, 296, 333–334
Welmaker, Roy "Snook" 66, 69
Welsh, Jimmy 44, 46
Wendell, Turk 138
Wera, Julie "Flop Ears" 155
Werber, Bill 129, 133, 135
Werrick, Joe 155
Werth, Jayson "Werewolf" 78
Wertz, Vic 12, 250
Wesley, Charles "Two Sides" 8
Wesley, Ed 148, 285, 287, 289
West, Sam 286
West, "Shifty Jim" 7–8, 10

Western Pennsylvania Sports Museum 251, 255
Westervelt, Huyler "Mamma's Baby Boy" 191, 193
Westmoreland, Ryan 266–267
Westrum, Wes 155
Wetteland, John 28, 42
Weyhing, Gus "Cannonball," "Rubber-Winged Gus" 111–112, 117
Whataburger Field 286
Whatley, David "Hammerman," "Speed" 67
Wheat, Zach "Buck" 167–168, 173
Wheeler, Dan 265–267, 269
Whitaker, Lou "Sweet Lou" 35, 201, 202, 208, 273, 280
White, Albert "Fuzz" 167
White, Bill 58, 62–63, 172
White, Chaney "Reindeer" 285, 286, 287, 293
White, Deacon 149, 195, 201, 203–204, 209–211, 213
White, Frank 161, 163–164, 208, 273
White, Guy "Doc" 55–57
White, Rondell 66
White, Roy 27, 38
White, Sammy 308, 311
White, Sol 64, 225–226, 228, 237, 254, 296, 306; *History of Colored Base Ball* 228, 237; *Sol White's Official Base Ball Guide* 237
White, Will "Whoop-La" 201, 202, 204, 213
White, William Edward 68, 228, 267
Whitehead, Burgess 216
Whitehill, Earl 100, 104–105
Whitehouse, Len 299, 302
Whitney, Jim "Grasshopper Jim" 201, 202, 204
Whitney, Pinky 189, 285
Whitson, Ed 280
Whitson, Karsten 59
Whitt, Ernie 147
Whitted, George "Possum" 216
Whitten, "Hard Hittin'" Mark 59
Whitworth, Dick 167, 170
Whyte, Billy 265, 269
Wicker, Kemp 218
Wickman, Bob 317–318, 324
Wickware, Frank 105–106, 109, 296; nicknames "Big Red," "Rawhide," "Smiley," "Smokey," "The Red Ant" 106, 109
Widger, Chris 52–53
Wieters, Matt 270
Wigginton, Ty 31
Wilcox, Milt 73–75
Wiley, Doc 119, 121
Wilhelm, Charles "Spider" 130
Wilhelm, Hoyt "Old Sarge" 42, 146, 216–217, 219, 222–223, 245, 308–309
Wilhoit, Joe 108
Wilkes, Jimmy "Seabiscuit" 250
Wilkinson, Bill 324–326
Wilkinson, J.L. 102, 169
Wilks, Ted 201
Willett, Ed 302
Willey, Carl 126, 129

Williams, August "Gloomy Gus" 180
Williams, Billy "Sweet Swingin' Billy" 7–10, 13, 80, 123, 165, 244, 256, 311, 334
Williams, Bobby 119, 121
Williams, Clarence 249
Williams, Cy 89, 98
Williams, Dave 15–16
Williams, David "Mutt" 22
Williams, Dick 43, 167, 170, 176, 277
Williams, Earl 190
Williams, Edwin "Dib" 22
Williams, Gerald "Ice" 119
Williams, Harry 250, 254
Williams, Henry "Flick" 238
Williams, Jerome 73
Williams, Jesse 285
Williams, Jimmy "Button" 167, 172
Williams, Johnnie "Honolulu Johnnie" 73
Williams, Johnny "Nature Boy" 119
Williams, Ken 246, 248
Williams, Lefty 302
Williams, Marvin 285, 288
Williams, Matt "Carson Crusher" 27, 28, 35–36, 185
Williams, Mike 302, 307
Williams, Mitch "Wild Thing" 28, 31, 244
Williams, Rees "Steamboat" 177–178
Williams, Smokey Joe "Cyclone" 4, 72, 286–287, 289, 293–294, 333
Williams, Stan "Big Daddy" 187
Williams, Stringbean 4
Williams, Ted 2, 18, 24, 27, 29–30, 34, 36–38, 60, 63, 70, 84–85, 104, 123, 126, 132, 134, 136, 141, 156, 158, 169, 200, 211, 244, 264, 267, 277–278, 316, 326, 333–334; nicknames "Teddy Ballgame," "The Kid," "The Splendid Splinter," "Thumper" 28, 31, 35, 37, 59, 131, 278, 334; Ted Williams Museum and Hitters Hall of Fame 59, 187
Williams, Tom 270, 276
Williams, Walt "No Neck" 286, 288
Williams, Willie "Curly" 270
Williamson, Ned 112, 250–251, 257, 267
Williamson, Scott 119
Willigrod, Julius 100
Willis, Dontrelle "D Train" 28
Willis, Vic 53, 129, 136, 303, 329
Wills, Bump 55–57
Wills, Maury 55–57, 224; Maury Wills Museum 224
Wilmington Quicksteps 53
Wimot, Walt 317–318, 322–323
Wilson, Artie 7, 12
Wilson, "Black Jack" 246
Wilson, Brian "B-Wiz," "The Beard" 187, 190
Wilson, C.J. 31
Wilson, Charlie "Swamp Baby" 270
Wilson, Craig 44
Wilson, Dan 78
Wilson, Don 119, 125
Wilson, Earl 120
Wilson, Emmett 161
Wilson, George "Icehouse" 28

Wilson, Hack 212, 250, 260; gravesite 314
Wilson, Howard "Highball" 250, 252
Wilson, Jack 31
Wilson, Jimmie 249
Wilson, Jud "Boojum" 95, 254, 302, 304–305
Wilson, "Jumping Johnny" 89
Wilson, Mookie 70, 129, 270, 275
Wilson, John "Chief" 286–287
Wilson, Preston 270, 275
Wilson, William "Mutt" 216
Wilson, Willie 7–8, 13
Wiltse, George "Hooks" 201–202
Wiltse, Lewis "Snake" 202
Winfield, Dave 16–17, 29, 93, 155–159, 165, 180, 279, 305
Wingo, Ivey 66
Winkles, Bobby 21, 27
Winston, Clarence 302
Winter, George "Sassafrass" 250
Winters, Jesse "Nip" 55, 57
Wirts, Elwood "Kettle" 28
Wise, Rick 147–148
Wise, Sam 225
Withrow, Raymond "Corky" 314
Witt, Bobby 302
Witt, Mike 30
Witt, Whitey 138
Wockenfuss, John 313–314, 316
Wohlers, Mark 138
Wolf, Jimmy "Chicken" 111, 113, 116
Wolf, Randy 31
Wolfgang, Meldon 202
Womack, Horace "Dooley" 270
Womack, Tony 302, 304
Wong, Kolten 73
Wood, Charles "Spade" 270
Wood, George "Dandy" 141, 327, 331
Wood, Joe 48, 128
Wood, Kerry 286–287
Wood, Smoky Joe 167, 170, 174–175, 252
Wood, Travis 22
Wood, Wilbur 138, 141, 145–146
Woodling, Gene 226, 233
Woods, George "Pinky" 48
Woods, Parnell 7
Worcester Baseball Monument 138
Worley, Vance 31
Worrell, Todd 28
Worthington, Al 7
Wright, Al "A-1" 28
Wright, Clyde 280
Wright, David 302–303, 305
Wright, Glenn "Buckshot" 167–169, 173
Wright, George 201, 204, 210, 302
Wright, Harry 204, 210–211, 315, 318
Wright, John "Needle Nose" 32, 119, 188
Wright, Taffy 216, 221
Wright, Wayne "Rasty" 314
Wright, "Wild Bill" 280–282, 284
Wrigley Field 29, 55, 79–80, 89, 185, 289, 303, 312, 331
Wuerfel Park 147–148
Wuertz, Michael 155
Wuestling, George "Yats" 167

Wyatt, John 78, 88
Wyatt, Whit 66
Wynegar, Butch 249
Wynn, Early 7–8, 14, 41, 301
Wynn, Jimmy "Toy Cannon" 226, 232–233, 293
Wyse, Hank "Hooks" 22

Yale Field 48
Yancey, Bill 250, 254–255
Yankee Stadium 45, 94, 101, 132, 157, 185, 202, 204, 224, 229, 243, 310
Yaryan, Clarence "Yam" 100
Yastrzemski, Carl 156, 165, 201–202, 204, 211, 273, 277–278, 305, 333
Yde, Emil 78
Yeager, Steve 313, 315
Yellow Horse, Moses "Chief" 238, 240
Yokely, Laymon "Corner Pocket," "The Mysterious Shadow" 216
Yonamine, Wally 74
York, Rudy 7, 11
Yost, Eddie "Walking Man" 201, 202, 209
Yost, Ned 31
Youkilis, Kevin "The Greek God of Walks" 127, 225, 226
Young, Bobby 129
Young, Cy 6, 14, 23, 33, 93, 99, 141, 177, 189, 209, 226, 228, 233–235, 262, 294, 316, 323, 333
Young, Dmitri "Meat Hook" 161, 165–166
Young, Eric 190, 194–195
Young, Irv 126
Young, Kevin 147
Young, Lemuel "Pep" 216, 218
Young, Michael 27, 31
Young, T.J. "Shack Pappy" 105, 106, 107
Young, Walter 162, 269
Youngblood, Joel 287
Youngs, Ross "Pep" 165, 213, 285, 286, 292
Yount, Henry "Ducky" 216
Yount, Robin 21, 78–79, 84, 199, 318, 324, 333

Zabel, George "Zip" 106
Zachary, Tom 216, 222
Zahn, Geoff 129
Zeider, Rollie "Bunions" 88–89, 91
Zeile, Todd 27, 29
Zephyr Field 119
Zernial, Gus "Ozark Ike" 286
Zettlein, George "The Charmer" 202, 204
Ziegler, Brad 105–106, 245
Zimmer, Chief 225–226
Zimmer, Don "Popeye" 187, 226, 229–230, 237–238; Don Zimmer Field 187
Zimmerman, Heinie 201, 209
Zimmerman, Jordan 318
Zimmerman, Ryan 216, 220
Zisk, Richie 201
Zito, Barry "Planet" 184–186
Zupo, Frank "Noodles" 28
Zwilling, Edward "Dutch" 167, 169

www.ingramcontent.com/pod-product-compliance
Lightning Source LLC
Chambersburg PA
CBHW081534300426
44116CB00015B/2630